Nineteenth-Century Literature Criticism

Guide to Gale Literary Criticism Series

For criticism on	Consult these Gale series
Authors now living or who died after December 31, 1959	*CONTEMPORARY LITERARY CRITICISM (CLC)*
Authors who died between 1900 and 1959	*TWENTIETH-CENTURY LITERARY CRITICISM (TCLC)*
Authors who died between 1800 and 1899	*NINETEENTH-CENTURY LITERATURE CRITICISM (NCLC)*
Authors who died between 1400 and 1799	*LITERATURE CRITICISM FROM 1400 TO 1800 (LC)* *SHAKESPEAREAN CRITICISM (SC)*
Authors who died before 1400	*CLASSICAL AND MEDIEVAL LITERATURE CRITICISM (CMLC)*
Black writers of the past two hundred years	*BLACK LITERATURE CRITICISM (BLC)*
Authors of books for children and young adults	*CHILDREN'S LITERATURE REVIEW (CLR)*
Dramatists	*DRAMA CRITICISM (DC)*
Hispanic writers of the late nineteenth and twentieth centuries	*HISPANIC LITERATURE CRITICISM (HLC)*
Native North American writers and orators of the eighteenth, nineteenth, and twentieth centuries	*NATIVE NORTH AMERICAN LITERATURE (NNAL)*
Poets	*POETRY CRITICISM (PC)*
Short story writers	*SHORT STORY CRITICISM (SSC)*
Major authors from the Renaissance to the present	*WORLD LITERATURE CRITICISM, 1500 TO THE PRESENT (WLC)*

ISSN 0732-1864

Volume 53

Nineteenth-Century Literature Criticism

Criticism of the
Works of Novelists, Poets, Playwrights,
Short Story Writers, Philosophers, and Other
Creative Writers Who Died between 1800
and 1899, from the First Published Critical
Appraisals to Current Evaluations

Marie Lazzari
Editor

Denise Kasinec
Mary L. Onorato
James E. Person, Jr.
Contributing Editors

GALE

DETROIT · NEW YORK · TORONTO · LONDON

STAFF

Marie Lazzari, *Editor*

)ominic, Denise Kasinec, Jelena O. Krstović, Mary L. Onorato,
and James E. Person, Jr., *Contributing Editors*

Gerald R. Barterian and Ondine Le Blanc, *Assistant Editors*

Susan M. Trosky, *Managing Editor*

Marlene S. Hurst, *Permissions Manager*
Margaret A. Chamberlain and Maria Franklin, *Permissions Specialists*
Diane Cooper, Michele Lonoconus, Maureen Puhl, Susan Salas, Shalice Shah,
Kimberly F. Smilay, and Barbara A. Wallace, *Permissions Associates*
Sarah Chesney, Edna Hedblad, Margaret McAvoy-Amato, Tyra Y. Phillips,
Lori Schoenenberger, and Rita Velázquez, *Permissions Assistants*

Victoria B. Cariappa, *Research Manager*
Mary Beth McElmeel, Tamara C. Nott, Michele P. Pica,
and Tracie A. Richardson, *Research Associates*
Alicia Noel Biggers, Julia C. Daniel, and Michelle Lee, *Research Assistants*

Mary Beth Trimper, *Production Director*
Deborah L. Milliken, *Production Assistant*

Sherrell Hobbs, *Macintosh Artist*
Randy Bassett, *Image Database Supervisor*
Robert Duncan, *Imaging Specialist*
Pamela A. Hayes, *Photography Coordinator*

∞™
This book is printed on acid-free paper that meets the minimum requirements of American National Standard for Information Sciences—Permanence Paper for Printed Library Materials, ANSI Z39.48-1984.

Library of Congress Catalog Card Number 84-643008
ISBN 0-8103-9299-2
ISSN 0732-1864
Printed in the United States of America

10 9 8 7 6 5 4 3 2 1

Contents

Preface vii

Acknowledgments xi

v

Preface

Since its inception in 1981, *Nineteenth-Century Literature Criticism* has been a valuable resource for students and librarians seeking critical commentary on writers of this transitional period in world history. Designated an "Outstanding Reference Source" by the American Library Association with the publication of its first volume, *NCLC* has since been purchased by over 6,000 school, public, and university libraries. The series has covered more than 300 authors representing 26 nationalities and over 15,000 titles. No other reference source has surveyed the critical reaction to nineteenth-century authors and literature as thoroughly as *NCLC*.

Scope of the Series

NCLC is designed to introduce students and advanced readers to the authors of the nineteenth century, and to the most significant interpretations of these authors' works. The great poets, novelists, short story writers, playwrights, and philosophers of this period are frequently studied in high school and college literature courses. By organizing and reprinting commentary written on these authors, *NCLC* helps students develop valuable insight into literary history, promotes a better understanding of the texts, and sparks ideas for papers and assignments. Each entry in *NCLC* presents a comprehensive survey of an author's career or an individual work of literature and provides the user with a multiplicity of interpretations and assessments. Such variety allows students to pursue their own interests; furthermore, it fosters an awareness that literature is dynamic and responsive to many different opinions.

Every fourth volume of *NCLC* is devoted to literary topics that cannot be covered under the author approach used in the rest of the series. Such topics include literary movements, prominent themes in nineteenth-century literature, literary reaction to political and historical events, significant eras in literary history, prominent literary anniversaries, and the literatures of cultures that are often overlooked by English-speaking readers.

NCLC continues the survey of criticism of world literature begun by Gale's *Contemporary Literary Criticism (CLC)* and *Twentieth-Century Literary Criticism (TCLC)*, both of which excerpt and reprint commentary on authors of the twentieth century. For additional information about *TCLC, CLC,* and Gale's other criticism series, users should consult the Guide to Gale Literary Criticism Series preceding the title page in this volume.

Coverage

Each volume of *NCLC* is carefully compiled to present:

- criticism of authors, or literary topics, representing a variety of genres and nationalities
- both major and lesser-known writers and literary works of the period
- 6-10 authors or 4-6 topics per volume
- individual entries that survey critical response to an author's work or a topic in literary history, including early criticism to reflect initial reactions, later criticism to represent any rise or decline in reputation, and current retrospective analyses.

Organization

An author entry consists of the following elements: author heading, biographical and critical introduction, list of principal works, excerpts of criticism (each preceded by a bibliographic citation and an annotation), and a bibliography of further reading.

- The **Author Heading** consists of the name under which the author most commonly wrote, followed by birth and death dates. If an author wrote consistently under a pseudonym, the pseudonym will be listed in the author heading and the real name given in parentheses on the first line of the biographical and critical introduction. Also located at the beginning of the introduction to the author entry are any name variations under which an author wrote, including transliterated forms for an author whose language uses a nonroman alphabet.

- The **Biographical and Critical Introduction** outlines the author's life and career, as well as the critical issues surrounding his or her work. References are provided to past volumes of *NCLC* in which further information about the author may be found.

- Most *NCLC* entries include a **Portrait** of the author. Many entries also contain reproductions of materials pertinent to an author's career, including manuscript pages, title pages, dust jackets, letters, and drawings, as well as photographs of important people, places, and events in an author's life.

- The list of **Principal Works** is chronological by date of first publication and identifies the genre of each work. In the case of foreign authors with both foreign-language publications and English translations, the English-language version is given in brackets. Unless otherwise indicated, dramas are dated by first performance, not first publication.

- **Criticism** in each author entry is arranged chronologically to provide a perspective on changes in critical evaluation over the years. All titles of works by the author featured in the entry are printed in boldface type to enable the user to easily locate discussion of particular works. Also for purposes of easier identification, the critic's name and the publication date of the essay are given at the beginning of each piece of criticism. Unsigned criticism is preceded by the title of the journal in which it appeared. Publication information (such as publisher names and book prices) and parenthetical numerical references (such as footnotes or page and line references to specific editions of works) have been deleted at the editors' discretion to provide smoother reading of the text.

- A complete **Bibliographic Citation** designed to facilitate location of the original essay or book precedes each piece of criticism.

- Critical excerpts are prefaced by **Annotations** providing the reader with a summary of the critical intent of the piece. Also included, when appropriate, is information about the critic's reputation, individual approach to literary criticism, and particular expertise in an author's works, as well as information about the relative importance of the critical excerpt. In some cases, the annotations cross-reference excerpts by critics who discuss each other's commentary.

- An annotated list of **Further Reading** appearing at the end of each entry suggests secondary sources on the author. In some cases it includes essays for which the editors could not obtain reprint rights.

Cumulative Indexes

- Each volume of *NCLC* contains a cumulative **Author Index** listing all authors who have appeared in Gale's Literary Criticism Series, along with cross-references to such biographical series as *Contemporary Authors* and *Dictionary of Literary Biography*. Useful for locating authors within the various series, this index is particularly valuable for those authors who are identified with a certain period but who, because of their death dates, are placed in another, or for those authors whose careers span two periods. For example, Fyodor Dostoevsky is found in *NCLC*, yet Leo Tolstoy, another major nineteenth-century Russian novelist, is found in *TCLC* because he died after 1899.

- Each *NCLC* volume includes a cumulative **Nationality Index** which lists all authors who have appeared in *NCLC*, arranged alphabetically under their respective nationalities.

- Each new volume in Gale's Literary Criticism Series includes a cumulative **Topic Index**, which lists all literary topics treated in *NCLC, TCLC, LC 1400-1800*, and the *CLC* Yearbook.

- Each new volume of *NCLC*, with the exception of the Topics volumes, contains a **Title Index** listing the titles of all literary works discussed in the volume. In response to numerous suggestions from librarians, Gale has also produced a **Special Paperbound Edition** of the *NCLC* title index. This annual cumulation lists all titles discussed in the series since its inception. Additional copies of the index are available on request. Librarians and patrons have welcomed this separate index: it saves shelf space, is easy to use, and is recyclable upon receipt of the following year's cumulation. Titles discussed in the Topics volume entries are not included in the *NCLC* cumulative index.

Citing *Nineteenth-Century Literature Criticism*

When writing papers, students who quote directly from any volume in Gale's Literary Criticism Series may use the following general forms to footnote reprinted criticism. The first example pertains to material drawn from periodicals, the second to material reprinted from books:

[1]T.S. Eliot, "John Donne," *The Nation and Athenaeum*, 33 (9 June 1923), 321-32; excerpted and reprinted in *Literature Criticism from 1400-1800*, Vol. 10, ed. James E. Person, Jr. (Detroit: Gale Research, 1989), pp. 28-9.

[2]Clara G. Stillman, *Samuel Butler: A Mid-Victorian Modern* (Viking Press, 1932); excerpted and reprinted in *Twentieth-Century Literary Criticism*, Vol. 33, ed. Paula Kepos (Detroit: Gale Research, 1989), pp. 43-5.

Suggestions Are Welcome

In response to suggestions, several features have been added to *NCLC* since the series began, including annotations to excerpted criticism, a cumulative index to authors in all Gale literary criticism series, entries devoted to criticism on a single work by a major author, more illustrations, and a title index listing all literary works discussed in the series.

Readers who wish to suggest authors, single works, or topics to appear in future volumes, or who have other suggestions, are cordially invited to write: The Editors, *Nineteenth-Century Literature Criticism*, 835 Penobscot Bldg., 645 Griswold St., Detroit, MI 48226-4094; call toll-free at 1-800-347-GALE; or fax to 1-313-961-6599.

ACKNOWLEDGMENTS

The editors wish to thank the copyright holders of the excerpted criticism included in this volume and the permission managers of many book and magazine publishing companies for assisting us in securing reprint rights. We are also grateful to the staffs of the Detroit Public Library, the Library of Congress, the University of Detroit Mercy Library, Wayne State University Purdy/Kresge Library Complex, and the University of Michigan Libraries for making their resources available to us. Following is a list of the copyright holders who have granted us permission to reprint material in this volume of *NCLC*. Every effort has been made to trace copyright, but if omissions have been made, please let us know.

COPYRIGHTED EXCERPTS IN *NCLC*, VOLUME 53, WERE REPRINTED FROM THE FOLLOWING PERIODICALS:

American Imago, v. 34, Spring, 1977. Copyright 1977 by The Association for Applied Psychoanalysis, Inc. Reprinted by permission of the publisher.—*Ariel: A Review of International English Literature*, v. 4, April, 1973 for "Sanity, Madness and Alice" by Neilson Graham. Copyright © 1973 The Board of Governors, The University of Calgary. Reprinted by permission of the publisher.—*Books from Finland*, v. XIX, 1985 for "The Kalevala and Finnish Literature" by Kai Laitinen, translated by Hildi Hawkins; v. XIX, 1985 for "Lönnrot and His Singers" by Senni Timonen, translated by Satu Salo and Keith Bosley; v. XIX, 1985 for "Translating the Kalevala: Midway Reflections" by Keith Bosley; v. XXIII, 1989 for an introduction to "Kanteletar: Women's Voices" by Senni Timonen; v. XXIII, 1989 for an excerpt from "Kanteletar," translated by Keith Bosley. All reprinted by permission of the authors or translators.—*Children's Literature: Annual of the Modern Language Association Seminar on Children's Literature and The Children's Literature Association*, v. 1, 1969. © 1969 by Francelia Butler. All rights reserved. Reprinted by permission of Francelia Butler.—*Criticism*, v. 12, Winter, 1970 for "Satire in the 'Alice' Books" by Charles Matthews. Copyright, 1970, Wayne State University Press. Reprinted by permission of the publisher and the author.—*Essays in French Literature*, v. 2, November, 1965. © Department of French Studies, The University of Western Australia. Reprinted by permission of the publisher.—*Essays in Literature*, v. XVI, Fall, 1989. Copyright 1989 by Western Illinois University. Reprinted by permission of the publisher.—*Journal of the Folklore Institute*, v. XII, 1975. Copyright © 1975 by The Folklore Institute. Reprinted by permission of the publisher.—*The Kenyon Review*, v. XXVII, Autumn, 1965 for "Wonderland Revisited" by Harry Levin. Copyright 1965 by Kenyon College. All rights reserved. Reprinted by permission of the author.—*Literature and Psychology*, v. XXXVII, 1991. © Editor 1991. Reprinted by permission of the publisher.—*The Massachusetts Review*, v. XXV, Autumn, 1984. © 1984. Reprinted from *The Massachusetts Review*, The Massachusetts Review, Inc. by permission.—*The New England Quarterly*, v. XLV, March, 1972 for "America's First Romantics: Richard Henry Dana, Sr. and Washington Allston" by Doreen Hunter. Copyright 1972 by The New England Quarterly. Reprinted by permission of the publisher and the author.—*Nottingham French Studies*, v. 24, October, 1985. Reprinted by permission of the publisher.—*Orbis Litterarum*, v. 33, 1978. Reprinted by permission of the publisher.—*PMLA*, v. LXXXI, October, 1966; v. 88, January, 1973; v. 101, May, 1986. Copyright © 1966, 1973, 1986 by the Modern Language Association of America. All reprinted by permission of the Modern Language Association of America.—*Victorian Studies*, v. XVIII, September, 1973 for "Alice and Wonderland: A Curious Child" by Nina Auerbach. Reprinted by permission of the trustees of Indiana University.—*Women's Studies: An Interdisciplinary Journal*, v. 15, 1988. © Gordon and Breach Science Publishers. Reprinted by permission of the publisher.—*Yale French Studies*, v. 43, 1969. Copyright © Yale French Studies 1969. Reprinted by permission of the publisher.

COPYRIGHTED EXCERPTS IN *NCLC*, VOLUME 53, WERE REPRINTED FROM THE FOLLOWING BOOKS:

Aldington, Richard. From an introduction to *Eugénie Grandet*. By Honoré de Balzac, translated by Ellen Marriage. Heritage Press, 1961. Copyright © 1961 by The George Macy Companies, Inc. Reprinted by permission of the author.—Alphonso-Karkala, John B. From "Transmission of Knowledge by Antero Vipunen to Väinämöinen in 'Kalevala' and by Sukra to Kacha in 'Mahabharata'," in *Proceedings of the 7th Congress of the International*

permission of the publisher and the author.—Slick, Grace. *White Rabbit*. © 1966 and 1967 by Copper Penny Music Publishing Co. All rights reserved. Used by permission of Rondor Music.—Thomas, Ronald R. From *Dreams of Authority: Freud and the Fictions of the Unconscious*. Cornell, 1990. Copyright © 1990 by Cornell University. All rights reserved. Used by permission of the publisher, Cornell University Press.—Van Doren, Mark. From "Lewis Carroll: 'Alice in Wonderland'," in *The New Invitation to Learning*. Edited by Mark Van Doren. Random House, 1942. Copyright 1942 by the Columbia Broadcasting System, Inc. Renewed 1970 by Mark Van Doren. Reprinted by permission of the Literary Estate of Mark Van Doren.—Van Wagoner, Richard S. From *Mormon Polygamy: A History*. Signature Books, 1986. Reprinted by permission of the publisher.

PHOTOGRAPHS APPEARING IN *NCLC*, VOLUME 53, WERE RECEIVED FROM THE FOLLOWING SOURCES:

Boulanger, Louis. Portrait of Honoré de Balzac. Musée de Versailles.

Brady, Mathew. Portrait of Henry James, Sr., and Henry James, Jr. By permission of Houghton Library, Harvard University.

Bush, Alfred. Photograph of the first edition of *The Book of Mormon*. Courtesy of Alfred Bush. Giraud, Eugene. Drawing of Honoré de Balzac. Besançon (France), Musée des Beaux-Arts et d'Archéologie.

Illustration from *Illusions perdues*. Collection Spoelberch de Lovenjoul, Paris Bibliotheque de l'Institut.

p. 217. James, Henry, and William Henry, portrait of. By permission of the Houghton Library, Harvard University.

p. 182. James, Henry, Sr., portrait of. By permission of Houghton Library, Harvard University.

Painting of Henry James, Sr. By permission of Houghton Library, Harvard University.

Photograph from *Alice's Adventures Under Ground*. Reproduced by courtesy of the Trustees of the British Museum.

Photograph of Joseph Smith's seer-stone. Courtesy of Alfred Bush.

Tuhka, A. Illustrations of a kantele. Finnish Literature Society.

p. 311. Semeika, Onola, and Kuokka, photograph of. Finnish Literature Society.

Eugénie Grandet

Honoré de Balzac

The following entry presents criticism of Balzac's novel *Eugénie Grandet* (1833). For a discussion of Balzac's complete career, see *NCLC*, Volume 5.

INTRODUCTION

Through its use of realistic detail and insights into the lives of intriguing characters, *Eugénie Grandet* is considered one of Balzac's most accomplished novels, a highlight within the larger series of novels called by their author *La Comédie humaine*. The novel sketches the lives of a handful of individuals who enter the warped life of a village miser, whose meanness blights their lives, to some extent irrevocably. Balzac tells their story with economy and judicious attention to detail. The title character, herself the miser's daughter, is in the end destined for a lonely, spiritually barren existence because of her father's near-pathological obsession with gain above all; the novel's sense of tragedy and the high level of interest it inspires lie in Eugénie's partially successful struggle to wrench free from her heritage of avarice.

Biographical Information

Eugénie Grandet is one of the earlier novels written to form *La Comédie humaine*, works written between 1830 and 1850. Balzac's strategy in writing *La Comédie humaine* was to reflect his self-styled role as "secretary to French society," one who would describe and interpret his era. He considered it possible to classify social species in the same manner that naturalists classify zoological species and their milieu, and his work, in *Eugénie Grandet* and all the other novels and story collections, reveals his belief that environment determines an individual's development. *Eugénie Grandet* was written to form a part of a section within the larger *Comédie humaine* called *Scènes de la vie privée,* or scenes from private life. At the time of the novel's writing, there was a lull in the famous romantic relationship between Balzac and Madame Evalina Hanska, the Polish countess he would eventually marry. Balzac in fact wrote *Eugénie Grandet* while in the midst of a passionate affair with a woman he described as "a sweet person, a most innocent creature who has fallen like a flower from the sky, who visits me in private, asks for no letters, no attentions, but simply says, 'Love me for a year and I will love you all my life!'" She was Marie Du Fresnay, a married woman who bore a daughter as the result of their union. For

years, scholars were puzzled by Balzac's dedication of the novel to a mysterious "Maria," whose identity was finally discovered early in the twentieth century. It is claimed that she served as Balzac's model for Eugénie Grandet—"tall and strong, with none of the prettiness that pleases common people," but suffused with classical beauty, charity, and nobility of spirit.

Plot and Major Characters

The novel is set in the early nineteenth century in the small French town of Saumur, where lives the Grandet family. Through fortuitous inheritance and shrewd business sense, Félix Grandet has acquired much property in Saumur, becoming known and respected by the townspeople for his miserliness. He is mayor and chief landowner in Saumur, and his word is law in the town. His spartan household comprises his wife, a woman reduced to a beaten-down existence of near-serfdom by old Grandet; Nanon, a loyal housekeeper; and his daughter, Eugénie. Every year for her birthday, Eugénie receives two dresses from her mother and a single gold piece from her father; and every New Year's Day, Grandet asks to see his daughter's coins, both for reassurance that she has not lost them and to glory over their brightness. As a young woman, Eugénie is courted by rival suitors, Monsieur Cruchot, son of the town notary, and Monsieur de Grassins, the local banker's son. Both call on Eugénie on her birthday in 1819, but they are interrupted by the dandyish Charles Grandet, son of Félix Grandet's wealthy brother, who arrives from Paris in the evening for an extended visit. To Eugénie, accustomed to plainness and austerity, he seems an angelic visitor, and she spares no effort to impress him: lighting candles, warming the chilly house, and committing other acts deemed extravagant by her annoyed father. Charles delivers a sealed message to his uncle from his father, only to learn its fateful contents the next day: the missive is a suicide note from his father, who has lost his fortune and brought shame upon his family. Stunned, Charles remains in his room for several days. Old Grandet, seeking to avoid scandal, concocts a scheme to save his own good name, enlisting the banker, the elder M. de Grassins, to act in his stead in handling his dead brother's affairs. De Grassins travels to Paris, where he proceeds to live a life of dissolution. Meanwhile, having fallen in love with her cousin, Eugénie gives Charles all her gold coins to invest and thereby restore his fortune. Charles departs Saumur, pledging his love to Eugénie and promising to return when successful to marry her. A high point in the novel occurs on the next New Year's Day, when Grandet asks to see Eugénie's gold coins, only to discover that his daughter is unable to produce them and that her mother seems to share with her the secret of their disappearance. He vows never to have anything to do with either of them again, shunning them both for a long period—until he is warned by the town notary that his fortune is endangered because of the approaching death of his heartbroken wife; as matters stand, he will have to divide his fortune with Eugénie upon her mother's death. For practical business reasons alone, Grandet forgives his wife and daughter. Later, after his wife dies, he tricks Eugénie into signing over her share of the property to him. Five years later, old Grandet himself dies, and now Eugénie and Nanon live alone in his house, with Eugénie waiting hopefully for news of Charles. One day a letter arrives from him, stating that he no longer wishes to marry her, but that he intends to wed a titled nobleman's daughter. Eugénie releases Charles from his pledge—shortly before he learns that his finances are still in arrears and that his fiancee refuses to marry him until he is free of debt. Learning of this, Eugénie settles the remainder of Charles's debt, enabling him to marry. She then agrees to marry one of her old suitors, M. Cruchot, who has risen to a high government post, but he dies shortly after their marriage. Inheriting Cruchot's property, Eugénie is wealthier than ever, but she spends the rest of her life experiencing the same pinched, lonely existence she has always known.

Major Themes

Set in Napoleonic France, a time when shrewd investors capitalized on the return of the monarchy, *Eugénie Grandet*, according to the insights of Pierre-Georges Castex, describes the process whereby the new bourgeoisie was able to amass huge fortunes, demonstrating how opportunism, quickness of action, and absence of scruple combine to form the modern world's concept of genius. Avarice is presented as a spiritually crippling evil, the effects of which can blight generations. Here as in all his works of fiction, Balzac illuminates the manner in which ideas have consequences; he shows the power a fixed idea, such as unbridled greed, can hold upon individuals. What Balzac set out to show, wrote André Maurois, "was the devastating power of a fixed idea, which leads to the destruction of a family."

Critical Reception

Eugénie Grandet was well received by the French reading public upon its publication, especially by French women, who valued Balzac's realistic and sympathetic portraits of women as vital members of society in this and other novels. While Balzac himself was pleased with the early popular and critical response to this novel—which he regarded as "a good little tale, easy to sell"—he insisted that *Eugénie Grandet* could only be understood within the total context of *La Comédie humaine*—which, though extensive, was never completed. Considered on its own merits, *Eugénie Grandet* has been highly praised by critics over the intervening years for its tautness of structure, judicious selection of detail, and effective characterization. Despite Balzac's accomplishment in this work, it has not been the source of as extensive critical study as other novels within the larger whole, such as *Le Père Goriot* (1835) or even *La Comédie humaine* itself. Important aesthetic criticism of the work has been written by such critics as Hippolyte Adolphe Taine, George Saintsbury (himself possibly the most important English-language critic of Balzac's work in the early twentieth century), Martin Turnell, Richard Aldington, and Roger Shattuck; while trenchant feminist criticism has been offered by Naomi Schor.

CRITICISM

Hippolyte Adolphe Taine (essay date 1865)

SOURCE: "The Great Characters," in *Balzac: A Critical Study,* translated by Lorenzo O'Rourke, 1906. Reprint by Haskell House Publishers Ltd., 1973, pp. 189-216.

[*In the excerpt below, from a translation of an essay originally published in 1865, Taine examines the character Grandet, noting Balzac's skill in depicting depraved characters as fascinating studies. The critic also compares Balzac's skill with that of Shakespeare.*]

If you believe that reason is the essential thing in human nature, you will take reason for your hero, and you will paint generosity and virtue. If your eyes are directed to the external machine, and are fixed merely upon the body, you will choose the body for your ideal, and you will paint voluptuous flesh and muscular vigor. If you regard sensibility as the important part of man, you will see beauty only in lively emotions, and you will picture great sorrows and delicate sentiments. Your conception of nature will influence your conception of beauty; your idea of the real man will suggest to you the ideal man; your philosophy will direct your art. It is thus that Balzac's philosophy has directed Balzac's art. He considered man a force; he has taken force for his ideal. He has freed it from its fetters, he has painted it in its completeness, free, released from the bonds of reason which prevent it from injuring itself, indifferent to the laws of justice which prevent it from injuring others; he has magnified it, mastered it; exploited it and put it on exhibition as worthy of the first rank; he has crowned it as hero and sovereign in the realm of monomania and villainy.

How can folly and vice be made beautiful? How can our sympathy be won for beasts of prey and diseased brains? How is it possible to negate the almost universal dictum of all literatures, and declare interesting and grand the very things upon which they have heaped ridicule and odium? What is there more disgraceful than the gross trooper, the mark for gibes and the subject for mis-adventures, from Plautus to Smollet? Observe how he can be transformed; Balzac explains how; you will perceive the reason for his vices; you will realize their power and take an interest in seeing them in action. You are fascinated by the logic of it all, and one-half of your disgust and mortification disappears. . . .

Grandet, clever, honored and happy, becomes an object of fear. He exploits his kindred, his family, his friends and his enemies. He has for a servant a female rustic with the cut of a grenadier, whom no one likes, whom he has imbued with a machine-like devotion to his interests and the fidelity of a beast of burden. For his wife he has chosen a devotee who is a thrifty housekeeper, a slave to her religious duties, delicate minded and imbecile, who lets him hoard up to his heart's content and never asks him for a sou. He has brought up his daughter in strict economy, and profited by her filial virtue to deprive her of her rightful inheritance. He gets rid of his ruined nephew, and finds the means to do the generous thing by him by taking his jewels at a Jew's price. He is respected by the richest bourgeois, who pay court to him in the hope of marrying his daughter. He abstracts from them dozens of favors, receiving from one gratuitous advice, sending another to Paris to look after his business. He profits by all passions, by all virtues, by all misfortunes; he is a veritable diplomat, an obstinate calculator, so attentive and so prudent that he dupes professional business men and beats lawyers at their own game. He commenced with two hundred louis and ended with seventeen millions. The splendor of gold here covers the ugliness of vice, and glorified avarice seats itself upon success as upon a throne.

To lift it still higher, Balzac equips it with all the strength of genius and will. Grandet is so superior a man that ordinarily he consents to play the ignorant and humble blockhead; he stutters, complains of headache, says that he can not understand the complications of business; as a result his rivals are thrown off their guard and deliver over to him their secrets. He laughs in his sleeve at them, he amuses himself by making them run and sweat for him, he makes a plaything of their expectation and their fawnings: "Enter, gentlemen," says he to his visitors, tufted city gentry. "I am not proud." And he makes them be seated beside his servant in the light of a tallow candle. He installs himself in his avarice as Brideau does in his brutality. He bristles with maxims of atrocious precision and convincing power. When his brother is killed and his nephew weeps, he says, "We shall have to excuse the first shower; but this young man is good for nothing, he takes more interest in dead men than in money." Do you laugh at a man who uses such words? This utterance is like a knife which cuts away at a stroke the roots of humanity and pity. The vice of the man is a dogma embraced with the eagerness of the heart's desire and the passion of love. At home he is a tyrant and terrible; the women tremble under his glance; they are his "linnets," frail little animals to whom he gives from time to time a few grains of wheat, but whose necks he might twist at any time with a movement of his thumb. Anger rumbles in his crude and sarcastic outbursts: "I will not give you *my* money to trap this young fool with sugar. What! More candles? The wenches would tear up the floors of my house to cook eggs for this gallant!"

We are carried away by the vehemence of his flaming anger; you perceive that this access of vice has neither bridle nor measure, that it breaks all, tramples all, outrages the sentiments and happiness of others; it is like a bull rushing headlong through a church. "What good does it do you to feed upon the good God (*manger le bon Dieu*) twice a month, if you secretly give your father's gold to a good-for-nothing who will devour your very heart when you have nothing else to give him?" His wife adjures him in the name of God. "What the devil does your good God amount to?" says he. At this point one fears for human nature; you feel that it conceals unknown gulfs capable of swallowing up everything—the paternal instinct, religion itself!

When his daughter signs the paper in which she renounces her mother's inheritance, he turns pale, breaks out into a sweat, almost collapses, and then embraces her to the point of suffocation. "Ah, my child! You give life to your father. That is the way business ought to be done. Life is business. I bless you. You are a virtuous daughter, and you love your father well." This smallness, this blessing granted as wages due, these sudden half-strangled cries of the miser overwhelming the father, are horrible. At this height, and accompanied by these actions, passion reaches the level of poetry; and perhaps such a miser is in truth a poet, spoiled and in obscurity. In imagination he swims in a river of gold. He speaks of his treasure in the lively and caressing style of a lover and an artist. "Come, fetch it hither, the little darling! You ought to kiss me on the eyes for telling you the life and death secrets of the crown-pieces. In truth, the crowns live and move like men: this goes, that comes, that one sweats, that one earns." Having ended, his eyes rest for whole hours upon piles of louis as though he were being warmed in their sunshine. "That warms me," he says.

Do you still find this grotesque? What joys this man has tasted! He has spread his sails like a poet amid the hopes and discoveries of a hundred thousand fairylands of splendor; he has tasted the continuous, long-drawn-out pleasures of increasing success, of repeated victory, of conscious superiority, of established mastery. He has not suffered in the affections, in money-matters, or from privation or remorse; he dies at the extreme limit of old age, in possession of his wealth and in security, completely satiated by his master passion, all other desires being eradicated or extinguished. If Corneille has produced the noble epic of heroism, Balzac has created the triumphant epic of passion. . . .

Balzac, like Shakespeare, has painted villains of every species, those of the world and of Bohemia, those of finance and of politics, lechers and spies.

Like Shakespeare, he has described monomania in all its varieties; that of licentiousness and avarice, of ambition and science, of art, of paternal love, of passion. Endure in one what you endure in the other. We are not dealing here with practical and moral life, but with imaginary and ideal life. Their characters are spectacles, not models; greatness is always beautiful, even in misfortune and crime. No one asks you to approve them or follow their example. You are only asked to behold and admire. In the open country I much prefer to meet a sheep than a lion; but from behind cage-bars I vastly prefer a lion to a sheep. Art is just this sort of cage; by eliminating fear, interest is attained. Henceforth, without suffering and without danger, we may contemplate superb passions, gigantic

struggles, lacerations, all the tumult and strength of human nature bursting its bounds in combats without pity and desires without limit. And certainly their contemplated force moves and attracts. It lifts us beyond ourselves; we soar beyond the vulgar sphere of our little faculties and timid instincts. Our souls expand before this spectacle and these contrasts; we feel as we do in the presence of Michael Angelo's wrestlers, those terrible statues with their enormous distended muscles which seem to menace with destruction the pigmies who gaze at them; and we understand how these two mighty artists dwell in a kingdom of their own, far from the public domain, in the fatherland of art.

Shakespeare has found more striking words, more extravagant deeds, more despairing cries; he has more enthusiasm, more madness, more fire; his genius is more natural, more abandoned, more violent; he invents by instinct, he is a poet; he sees and makes us see by sudden illuminations the abysms and the farthest reach of things, like those grand lightning flashes seen in southern nights which reveal and light up with flame the whole horizon.

Balzac slowly lights and stirs up his furnace; we feel pain at his efforts; we partake of his painful labors in the black and smoky workshops where he prepares, by scientific means, thousands of lanterns, which he arranges in infinite variety so that their intermingled and united rays light up the whole country. At the end all embrace; the spectator looks; he sees less suddenly, less easily, less splendidly with Balzac than with Shakespeare, but he sees the same things, on as large a plane.

Every Saturday (essay date 1873)

SOURCE: "Eugénie Grandet," in *Every Saturday*, Vol. III, No. 6, February 8, 1873, pp. 148-50.

[*In the following essay, the critic reviews the plot of* Eugénie Grandet, *providing running commentary throughout.*]

The lives of women, and especially of young women, are often strangely separated from the life of the principal personage of the house they live in. There are houses, especially in small country towns, where there is a remarkable difference of scale in the interests of the lives that are passed in them; where the father is occupied with vast pecuniary transactions, and the daughters are economizing shillings; where the father takes a share in considerable public concerns, and the daughters have the field of their activities limited to the garden and the Sunday-school; where the father gets richer or poorer every day, and yet no one in the household knows anything of the fluctuations in his fortune, so regularly goes the round of the little household matters, so unfailing are the fixed supplies. This separation of interests—this exclusion of the women from the man's thoughts and anxieties, arising partly from true paternal kindness which desires to bear the burden of life as much as possible alone, partly from a well-grounded fear of the talkative indiscretion of young people, partly from an apprehension that if they knew the full gains of a successful year, they might count too readily upon their permanence—is not rare in our own country, but it is still less rare in France. The French girl is educated on the principle that it is well, in her case, to prolong the ignorance and inexperience of her childhood to the very eve of marriage. She believes that "Papa is rich," or she is told that "Papa is not rich;" or, more frequently, she has no distinct idea on the subject, either one way or the other, but simply sees the smooth working of the house-machine, as ladies see steam-engines going steadily in some mysterious way, without inquiring how much coal they burn, or whether the supplies are likely to be ample or insufficient. The wife knows these things in most cases pretty accurately, but the daughter hardly ever knows them till she is a married woman; perhaps even then her knowledge will be limited to the extent of her own dowry, until the old man dies, and his last will and testament reveals the secret of his affairs. In some exceptional cases the mother is treated with the same reserve, and is purposely kept in ignorance of the progress of an increasing fortune, lest her expenditure should hinder accumulation. The most perfect type of the money-maker deeply enjoys secrecy for itself; he feels as if his beloved treasure would be less securely his own if another knew the full extent of it. He likes the vague reputation for wealth, but he is intensely, even morbidly, anxious that the reputation should remain vague, and he dreads an approach to any accurate publicity.

Monsieur Grandet, father of Eugénie Grandet, was an *avare* of this perfect type. Living in the quiet town of Saumur on the Loire, he had passed successively through the trades of cooper, little wine-merchant, large wine-merchant, proprietor of vineyards, money-lender, speculator in estates, till finally in his old age he was a great financial power in his own neighborhood, and still preserved the frugal habits of earlier years, living in a dismal old house—and old houses can be fearfully dismal in those ancient towns—with his wife and daughter and a single maidservant, a tall, strong, ugly, devotedly faithful, and simple-hearted creature, who worked all day long at man's work and woman's work, not being ornamental in the least, but useful to the utmost of a domestic's possible utility. Old Grandet was in little danger of seeing his riches diminish through the extravagance of women, for he himself gave out the daily supplies for the little household, knowing exactly how many lumps of sugar were used, and what they were used for, how much butter (and it was not much) went for the cookery, and whether to-day's dish

might be eked out for to-morrow's necessities. Old Grandet had imposed tribute upon his tenants—not an uncommon custom in France even at the present day, and a relic of feudal usage—so that besides their rent they brought him regular supplies of provisions. They brought him fowls, and eggs, and vegetables, and fruit; he never went to the butcher, and to the grocer as little as might be. His fuel, came from his own woods, his wine from his own vineyards, and he kept the key of the cellar. He knew the number of his pears, and gave out the rotten ones to be eaten, two or three at a time. All communications concerning household matters passed directly between old Grandet and the strong servant, *la grande Nanon,* whilst Madame Grandet and her daughter sat in the gloomy salon, by their accustomed window. Hardly any money passed through their hands. M. Grandet gave a few gold pieces occasionally, but always asked for them back again, one by one, under pretext that he had no change. Since his wife was so entirely excluded from the government of her own house, it is unnecessary to add that she was permitted to take no part in the administration of old Grandet's estates. He managed everything for himself, and he managed everything so well that his riches increased prodigiously.

At the ripe age of twenty-three Eugénie Grandet knew as much of the world as a young nun, and as much of money matters as a baby. The old man's reserved ways and frequent harshness had driven the two women to seek consolation in each other's affection, and that affection had come to be their whole life. Madame Grandet could not enlarge her daughter's mind beyond the narrow circle of her limited and sad experience, but the warmth of her tender maternal love did good to Eugénie's heart, and strengthened it with gentle nurture. A girl so educated was likely, if ever she loved a man, to love him with the greatest singleness and persistence. Having had no experience of variety in affection, she would probably concentrate all her strength of feeling in a single devoted attachment, of which the good or evil effects would color her whole life.

The monotony of the daily life in that gloomy old house at Saumur was broken in upon one evening by the arrival of a young gentleman from Paris, Monsieur Charles Grandet, aged twenty-two, and a perfect dandy. Though nearly related to Eugénie, being her first cousin, this specimen of Parisian elegance had not yet shone upon the darkness of that provincial existence. The two brothers, his father and old Grandet, had not seen each other for many years. Each had pursued wealth in his own way, the provincial in provincial simplicity, the Parisian with the usual Parisian accompaniments of expenditure and risk. The young dandy, as the bearer of a certain missive for his uncle, had hoped, in the lightness of his heart, to live for a while in the country the true *vie de château,* to shoot in his uncle's forests, and pass the time in pleasantness, one of a hundred guests. Young Charles Grandet was completely ignorant of middle-class provincial life, and fell into it, as it were, from the clouds. He came resolved to conquer by the superiority of his metropolitan civilization:—

His idea was to make his appearance with the superiority of a young man of fashion, to throw all the neighborhood into despair by his luxury, to make an epoch, to import the inventions of Parisian existence. He intended to pass more time at Saumur in brushing his fingers and studying his toilet than in Paris itself, where a dandy will sometimes affect a not ungraceful negligence. He had brought with him the prettiest hunting-costume, the prettiest gun, the prettiest hunting-knife, with the prettiest sheath in Paris. He had brought his collection of ingenious waistcoats; there were white ones and black ones, there were waistcoats colored like beetles with golden reflections, others double-breasted, some with collars standing up, and others with collars turned down, some of them buttoning up to the neck with gold buttons. He had brought all the varieties of collars and cravats which were in fashion at that time. He had two dress-coats by Buisson, and the finest of linen. He had a pretty gold dressing-case, and a complete cargo of Parisian trifles.

This young gentleman arrived at his uncle's house in the perfect freshness of the most careful toilet, for though just at the end of a long journey by diligence, he had taken care to avail himself of a rest at Tours by changing his costume and submitting his beautiful locks to the elaborate art of the coiffeur. A being so graceful as this Adonis had never entered that dingy old salon at Saumur. Eugénie Grandet looked upon him in wonder and admiration. Her mind became penetrated with the feeling that no care for him could be too attentive or delicate. She made old Nanon commit unheard-of extravagances; she made her light a fire in the young gentleman's bedroom; she made her go to the grocer's to buy a candle for the guest, superior to their tallow dips. She bought him sugar also, that he might drink *eau-sucrée* during the night, and thus be spared the possible inconveniences of thirst.

From that moment poor Eugénie Grandet's imagination was possessed and occupied by this Parisian charmer. But the next day gave her a more grave and serious interest in his destiny. That letter which he had brought to old Grandet from his father contained the announcement of a commercial disaster and of a fatal resolve. Being unable to meet his engagements, owing four millions of francs and being able to pay no more than one million, Grandet of Paris had resolved to escape from his shame by suicide. By the time his son reached Saumur this resolution had been carried into effect, and it remained only to the uncle to make the an-nouncement to his nephew. In his view, the really serious misfortune was the bankruptcy and the consequent poverty which it entailed upon the youth. Charles Grandet, however, took his two misfortunes differently; he lamented his father with passionate tears, and bore the ruin with the lightness of youth and hope. What woman could have refused sympathy to a young man suddenly plunged into misfortunes so overwhelming, so terrible, and by him so unforeseen? Old Grandet's manner in making the announcement had not been tender, or even kind, but the two good ladies atoned for its hardness by the most affectionate and sincere sympathy. In the case of the younger one this sentiment rapidly gave place to one still more tender, and before old Grandet could in decency put his nephew out of the house, his only daughter and heiress had privately engaged herself to marry him.

The old man's idea was to pay his nephew's passage as far as Nantes, and embark him on some vessel bound for India, to perish or make his fortune as fate might decide. Balzac's picture of the brief space during which Charles and Eugénie remained together under the same roof is one of the most delicate and original in his writings. The mixture of womanly self-reliance in Eugénie's character with the hesitation of the most absolute inexperience in love affairs, the completeness with which at last she invested her happiness in the hope of her cousin's enduring affection and fortunate return, are painted with great care and the most finished detail. A girl in Eugénie's position, totally ignorant of men and men's ways, easily puts her trust and confidence in the first male creature that she loves. The gravity of character which a superior young woman acquires after twenty, when her life is dull and solitary and occupied in the discharge of monotonous duties, gives to her first love affair a seriousness beyond the evanescent attachments of children in their teens. In this case the seriousness of the attachment was on the female side considerably enhanced by the melancholy circumstances of the case. Charles had really loved his father, who, as is not uncommon with Frenchmen, had carefully cultivated a tender friendship with his boy. The sudden loss had been a cruel trial. Eugénie had heard the unfortunate young man moaning and lamenting throughout the sleepless night. With the simplicity of a character like hers, she had gone to his room alone and tried to comfort and console him. The hardness of her father's manner made this feminine kindness appear more natural and more necessary, whilst her father's rigid closeness in money matters had induced her to offer her hoard of savings for the payment of the sea passage to India. Charles, on his part, had confided to his cousin's keeping some precious things that came to him from his mother, and which he desired to save from the double risks of travel and of poverty. In this way their love was associated with the most serious and sacred feelings, and it became to her like a part of her religion.

For several years after her cousin's departure Eugénie Grandet remained in sad fidelity, not receiving a single letter, but trying to account to herself for this silence by the reasons which faithful women invent for their own consolation. Her treasure consisted of the things which had belonged to Charles's mother, and which he had confided to her care. She watched over the precious deposit as if it were an abiding evidence of his continual love and trust. The secret that she had lent him money became known to old Grandet through a habit which he had of asking on his fête-day to look at his girl's money, which indeed was almost a numismatic collection, for it consisted of large and rare gold pieces of many countries and reigns. This is a way of hoarding not very uncommon in provincial France at the present day, when a man will sometimes make the resolution to put aside all the gold pieces above the value of twenty francs that happen to get into his purse. Grandet had given many pieces of this kind to Eugénie—twenty Portuguese coins each of which was worth 180 francs, five Genoese worth a hundred francs, and many other curious coins of different nations, worth in the aggregate about £250. All these she had given to her cousin, and when the fête-day came round, and old Grandet according to his custom asked to see them, the young lady's position became trying in the extreme. For had not there been a clear understanding that this money, like the guinea which the Vicar of Wakefield gave to his daughters, was never to go out of her hands, either by way of spending or of donation? The scene on the fête-day, when the money was not forthcoming, is one of the most dramatic in Balzac. It ends by a discovery of the girl's secret, and, to punish her, the old man imprisons her in her own room on a diet of bread and water, happily varied in practice by the devotion of the servant-woman, who at great risk conveys to her more substantial aliments.

The old man's temper after this produces complete domestic misery. His wife, whose health has been declining for years, is unable to bear the wretched moral atmosphere she has to live in, the constant unkindness, the separation from her daughter; so she loses her remnant of strength and quickly passes away. Eugénie is now dreadfully isolated, having nobody to love her but old Nanon. Finally Grandet himself dies, and then Eugénie finds herself the possesson of an enormous fortune. Her real treasures, however, were the relics confided to her by Charles, which she kept religiously, looking at them every day. A woman in Eugénie's position, with her singleness and simplicity of character, easily comes to have a remarkable permanence of sentiment and of thought. She becomes almost like a pensive heroine fixed on canvas by some painter, who year after year seems to be thinking the same thing, and feeling the same tender yet subdued emotion. After seven years of patience, constantly filled with thoughts of Charles, and vague wonderings as to his return, Eugénie said one evening to the old servant Nanon,

"What, Nanon, will he not write to me once in seven years?"

After his departure from Saumur, the young gentleman had been successful in his first speculation, and, having inherited the commercial skill which existed in his family, continued to increase his little capital till he was able to undertake operations on a larger scale. Extremely active in business, he devoted himself to it body and soul, being possessed with the idea of reappearing one day at Paris in all the opulence of his luxurious youth. At first he had really treasured the remembrance of Eugénie, but a life of unrestrained immorality speedily obliterated it. Finally he returned with a considerable fortune, and in the same ship had for fellow-passengers the family of a nobleman who had a position at the Court of Charles X. This nobleman's wife thought him worth fishing for as a son-in-law, and caught him by the prospect of a brilliant social position, since, by an arrangement which would certainly receive the royal sanction, he might take the name and arms of D'Aubrion, and ultimately succeed to the marquisate. A month after his arrival in Paris, being still in ignorance of Eugénie's wealth, he wrote to her a cousinly, but not at all lover-like letter, enclosing a check for 8,000 francs in payment for the sum she had lent him, capital and interest, and announcing his marriage with Mlle. D'Aubrion, adding a few observations on the folly of love-marriages, and the necessity for considering the social position of his children.

So ended poor Eugénie's dream of seven years. Charles is punished by learning, too late, the extent of her enormous fortune. She adds a little to his punishment by paying what remains due to his father's creditors. Afterwards, persuaded by her religious adviser, she marries a magistrate capable of attending to her affairs, but her life is a broken life.

The Critic, New York (review date 1886)

SOURCE: "Eugénie Grandet," in *The Critic,* New York, Vol. VI, No. 134, July 24, 1886, pp. 40-1.

[*In the following excerpt, the critic summarizes the plot of* Eugénie Grandet *in the course of recommending "the sweetest and saddest" of Balzac's idylls.*]

Eugénie Grandet, if not the greatest, is the tenderest of Balzac's confessions, the sweetest and saddest of his idylls. There are such malignities and benignities in it, such pathos and cruelty, such gentleness and diablerie, such contrasts of light and shade, such flashes of light and darkness. There is no more marvellous juxtaposition in fiction than the contrasted groups of the two Grandet families—of the young Parisian dandy flung like a meteor across Eugénie's path and Eugénie herself, of the beautiful simplicity and refinement of Eugénie and her mother over against the infernal wickedness of Père Grandet. And the scene where Eugénie and Charles exchange confidences and gifts, at midnight, in the old house, is surpassingly lovely— a *genre* group equal to the exquisite felicities of Clärchen and Egmont, of Gretchen and Faust, of Little Nell or of Paul Dombey. Never has the desperate solitude of French provincial life been more sorrowfully, more luminously depicted; and the solitude of the Grandet house, wherein Eugénie grows up like a shining clematis-blossom, is mingled with that Miltonic darkness which may be felt. Contrasted with the moral beauty of the daughter—a bud that, like the cereus-bloom, flies wide open in a night and fills the whole house with perfume on the approach of Charles—stands the devilish excrescence of a father, gnarled and hideous as the rooted mandrake, all flesh, without conscience, with no passion or principle but love of money; a cartouche passionless as a stone, yet fraught with the diabolic hieroglyphics of sin and avarice. That so sweet a root—so perfect a flower—as Eugénie could spring from such a source is one of the marvels not of Balzac but of life. The astounding power displayed in these contrasts and throughout the work, the analytical geometry of the heart herein so wonderfully diagrammed, developed, read for yourself, see for yourself: no criticism can well do it justice.

Edgar Saltus on Balzac's accomplishment in *Eugénie Grandet*:

The resources of Balzac's genius are perhaps as clearly exhibited in *Eugénie Grandet* as in any of his other works, and the appearance of this romance gave the keynote to the present Realistic school. *Eugénie Grandet* is the conquest of absolute truth in art. It is the drama applied to the most simple events of life; the fusion of the trivial and the sublime, the pathetic and the grotesque. It is a picture of life as it is, and the model of what a novel should be.

Edgar Evertson Saltus, in Balzac, *Houghton Mifflin and Company, 1890.*

Frederick Wedmore (essay date 1890)

SOURCE: "Chapter II" and "Chapter VII," in *Life of Honoré de Balzac,* Walter Scott, 1890, pp. 24-32, 67-75.

[*In the following excerpt from his biography of Balzac, Wedmore offers a short critical overview of* Eugénie Grandet.]

Eugénie Grandet, though a larger picture [than *Illusions Perdues*], is still a Dutch picture. It, too, is occupied with the intimate study of narrow fortunes; with the chronicle of the approach of private and inevitable trouble. In both, a woman—but the device is a favourite one of Balzac's—idealizes a relationship into which the commonplace must greatly enter. In both, a heart stirs somewhat restlessly in a confined cage, though a patience falls upon Eugénie Grandet such as Augustine never perhaps could have known. . . .

I offer no analysis of *Eugénie Grandet.* The book is too well known for that to be necessary. And while, on the one hand, it can hardly claim particular notice as standing quite by itself, on the other hand it cannot always be advisable to select it as the representative of a class. It is a type, no doubt; and some of its qualities we have discerned elsewhere, already, and have, to some extent, dwelt upon. It is wrought with perfection; but, perhaps, by the themes which it avoids, as much almost as by the themes which it discusses, does it commend itself, not indeed to the literary artist, but to the lady in the dress circle. Yet Balzac has other books which, if she only knew it, that sometime arbitress of Literature in England might peruse with as little trepidation. Balzac himself would have recommended to her *Ursule Mirouët,* which he dedicated to—which he almost wrote for—his nieces; very conscious at the time of how little fitted, for such as they, were his dark and melancholy studies of a life no phase of which he shrank from depicting. And in Pierrette Lorain—the heroine of **"Pierrette"**—Balzac is rightly credited with having painted an "adorable nature," *"toute de délicatesse et de spontanéité."* Nor had Pauline, of the *Peau de Chagrin,* any less than Eugénie Grandet, the divine capacity of abnegation.

But *Eugénie Grandet,* though it exacts from one, now, no very serious discussion, does claim a further word. Apart from Eugénie's singular simplicity, and quiet goodness, and generous, unstinting devotion, there is great interest—there is the interest of a quickly felt reality—in the few characters whom alone Balzac has chosen to place here upon the stage. Madame Grandet, pious and obedient, but colourless and weak—only such a woman as Madame Grandet could by any possibility have lived to old age, with Grandet for a husband, or lived with Grandet at all. And—as the one servant who stays with him and is absorbed in his interests— "la grande Nanon" is just as inevitable. In her own dull, heavy, faithful, bovine way, she has for us the vitality of a *soubrette* of Molière. She lives, or vegetates, for all Time—remembered she must be, for her unfailing helpfulness, for the willingness of her submission, and for her physical immensity: the *dinornis* of Servitude. Grandet himself—imperious, steady of purpose; a slave-driver rather than a master, a husband, or a friend—is studied to the very depths. When he is remembered but as miser and millionaire, only a little has been understood of all that Balzac is ready to reveal in regard to him. Charles, the lover, is more ordinary. Notwithstanding his affection for his father, and his grief at his father's end, in the main he is the simply weak and selfish, elegant and empty, average young man of leisure. But would the pathos of the story have been quite as deep, if Eugénie's devotion had been accorded to a being more substantial and more worthy? When Eugénie beheld Charles, she knew as much of men as did Miranda when she set eyes on Ferdinand. It was no Ferdinand, however, who descended into the streets of Saumur.

In the mere discovery of an ideal there may be something that is beautiful, and something that is touching. But the profounder pathos belongs, I must suppose, to the retaining of it, blindly or bravely, when reason would have dismissed it long ago. And Eugénie Grandet held it against all facts, against all truths. Not by the conception only, but by the frequent realization, of such a character, in the *ingénue* that he delights in—in the virginal soul—Balzac gives colour to the superstition that women are the idealists of the world. It is women, then, who have written its poems—who have led its Forlorn Hopes!

George Saintsbury (essay date 1907)

SOURCE: A preface to *Eugénie Grandet,* by Honoré de Balzac, translated by Ellen Marriage, J. M. Dent & Sons Ltd., 1930, pp. xi-xv.

[*Saintsbury is considered one of the world's foremost authorities on Balzac's work during the early twentieth century. In the following excerpt from his preface to the Everyman Edition (1907) of Balzac's novel, he discourses on* Eugénie Grandet *as a work that is "very nearly perfect."*]

With *Eugénie Grandet,* as with one or two, but only one or two others of Balzac's works, we come to a case of *Quis vituperavit?* Here, and perhaps here only, with *Le Médecin de Campagne* and *Le Père Goriot,* though there may be carpers and depreciators, there are no open deniers of the merit of the work. The pathos of Eugénie, the mastery of Grandet, the success of the minor characters, especially Nanon, are universally recognised. The importance of the work has sometimes been slightly questioned even by those who admit its beauty: but this questioning can only support itself on the unavowed but frequently present conviction or suspicion that a 'good' or 'goody' book must be a weak one. As a matter of fact, no book can be, or can be asked to be, better than perfect on its own scheme, and with its own conditions. And on its own scheme and with its own conditions *Eugénie Grandet* is very nearly perfect.

On the character of the heroine will turn the final decision whether, as has been said by some (I believe I might be charged with having said it myself), Balzac's virtuous characters are always more theatrical than real. The decision must take in the Benassis of *Le Médecin de Campagne,* but with him it will have less difficulty; for Benassis, despite the beauty and pathos of his confession, is a little 'a person of the boards' in his unfailingly providential character and his complete devotion to others. Must Eugénie, his feminine companion in goodness, be put on these boards likewise?

I admit that of late years, and more particularly since the undertaking of this present task made necessary to me a more complete and methodical study of the whole works, including the most miscellaneous miscellanies, than I had previously given, my estimate of Balzac's goodness has gone up very much—that of his greatness had no need of raising. But I still think that even about Eugénie there is a very little unreality, a slight touch of that ignorance of the actual nature of girls which even fervent admirers of French novelists in general, and of Balzac in particular, have confessed to finding in them and him. That Eugénie should be entirely subjugated first by the splendour, and then by the misfortune, of her Parisian cousin, is not in the least unnatural; nor do I for one moment pretend to deny the possibility or the likelihood of her having

> lifted up her eyes,
> And loved him with that love which was her
>   doom.

It is also difficult to make too much allowance for the fatal effect of an education under an insignificant if amiable mother and a tyrannical father, and of a confinement to an excessively small circle of extremely provincial society, on a disposition of more nobility than intellectual height or range. Still it must, I think, be permitted to the *advocatus diaboli* to urge that Eugénie's martyrdom is almost too thorough; that though complete, it is not, as Gautier said of his own ill luck, '*artistement* complete'; that though it may be difficult to put the finger on any special blot, to say, 'Here the girl should have revolted,' or 'Here she would have behaved in some other way differently'; still there is a vague sense of incomplete lifelikeness—of that tendency to mirage and exaggeration which has been, and will be, so often noticed.

Still it is vague and not unpleasantly obtrusive, and in all other ways Eugénie is a triumph. It is noticeable that her creator *has dwelt on the actual traits of her face* with much more distinctness than is usual with him; for Balzac's extraordinary minuteness in many ways does not invariably extend to physical charms. This minuteness is indeed so great that one has a certain suspicion of the head being taken from a live and special original. Nor is her physical presence—abominably libelled, there is no doubt, by Mme. des Grassins—the only distinct thing about Eugénie. We see her hovering about the *beau cousin* with an innocent officiousness capable of committing no less the major crime of lending him money than the minor, but even more audacious, because open, one of letting him have sugar. She is perfectly natural in the courage with which she bears her father's unjust rage, and in the forgiveness which, quite as a matter of course, she extends to him after he has broken her own peace and her mother's heart. It is perhaps necessary to be French to comprehend entirely why she could not heap that magnificent pile of coals of fire on her unworthy cousin's head without flinging herself and her seventeen millions into the arms of somebody else; but the thing can be accepted if not quite understood. And the whole transaction of this heaping is admirable.

If the criticism be not thought something of a super-subtlety, it may perhaps be suggested that the inferiority which has generally been acknowledged in the lover is a confession or indication that there is something very slightly wrong with the scheme of Eugénie herself—that if she had been absolutely natural, it would not have been necessary to make Charles not merely a thankless brute, but a heedless fool. However great a scoundrel the ex-slave-trader may have been (and as presented to us earlier he does not seem so much scoundrelly as shallow), his respectable occupation must have made him a smart man of business; and as such, before burning his boats by such a letter as he writes, he might surely have found out how the land lay. But this does not matter much.

Nanon is, of course, quite excellent. She is not stupid, as her kind are supposed to be; she is only blindly faithful, as well as thoroughly good-hearted. Nor is the unfortunate Madame Grandet an idiot, nor are any of the *comparses* mere dummies. But naturally they all, even Eugénie herself to some extent, serve mainly as sets-off to the terrible Grandet. In him Balzac, a Frenchman of Frenchmen, has boldly depicted perhaps the worst and the commonest vice of the French character, the vice which is more common, and certainly worse than either the frivolity or the license with which the nation is usually charged—the pushing, to wit, of thrift to the loathsome excess of an inhuman avarice. But he has justified himself to his country by communicating to his hero an unquestioned grandeur. The mirage works again, but it works with splendid effect. One need not be a sentimentalist to shudder a little at the *ta ta ta ta* of Grandet, the refrain of a money-grubbing which almost escapes greediness by its diabolic extravagance and success.

Adaline Lincoln Lush (essay date 1932)

SOURCE: "The House of the Miser: *Eugénie Grandet,*" in *Studies in Balzac's Realism,* by E. Preston Dargan, W. L. Crain, and others, The University of Chicago Press, 1932, pp. 121-35.

[*In the essay below, Lush analyzes the characterization and action of* Eugénie Grandet.]

The manuscript of ***Eugénie Grandet*** was presented to Mme Hanska in December, 1833. This work made its initial appearance in printed form, as a whole, in the first volume of the first edition of the ***Scènes de la vie de province*** (1834-37). *L'Europe littéraire* on September 19, 1833, contained the first chapter and the titles of the remaining chapters. It was not continued as a whole in that publication; but the rest of the novel was written in the autumn of 1833.

The sociological nature of the story is attested by the title of the first chapter: "Physionomies bourgeoises." The remaining chapters were called: (chap. ii) "Le Cousin de Paris"; (chap. iii) "Amours de province"; (chap. iv) "Promesses d'avare, serments d'amour"; (chap. v) "Chagrins de famille"; (chap. vi) "Ainsi va le monde"; (chap. vii) "Conclusion."

The dedication appeared for the first time in the Charpentier edition (one volume, 1839). In 1843, ***Eugénie Grandet*** was published in the first volume of the third edition of the ***Scènes de la vie de province*** (first edition of the ***Comédie humaine***). In this edition the chapter-headings were omitted, and the story bore its present dating, "Paris, septembre 1833," for the first time. Maria, to whom it is dedicated, is probably the enigmatic "Maria" of whom Balzac wrote to his sister Laure in 1833. She is described as a gentle affectionate creature with whom he had one of the numerous intrigues described so complacently in his letters to Mme de Surville. Balzac seems to have deliberately confused this and other "Marias" with the Virgin Mary.

As usual, one of the most important features of the novel is exposition, which here is particularly long and full of realistic qualities. In ***Eugénie Grandet*** there are in fact two kinds of exposition, topographical and psychological. The bulk of the former is rather small; of the latter, quite large.

The story opens with a topographical disquisition in which the device of "harmonizing around a keynote" is the salient feature. The words *mélancolie, sombres, triste, ruines, froid, obscure, profondes, noires,* and *impénétrables,* occur with cumulative vividness. The exposition starts with generalizations (three long sentences) about things which produce an effect of melancholy. Then comes the specific statement that these qualities which produce melancholy actually appear in a certain house at Saumur at the end of a hilly street which leads to the highest portion of the city. The street itself is described in one sentence, after which an entire page is given to a description of the houses on the street, their doors, windows, the marks upon them, their obscure bareness. Next, Balzac describes the shops on the ground floor of these houses, together with the occupations of the various members of the family. The author incorporates here some generalizations on the provincial life of Anjou, which, he asserts, is quite like that of Touraine. *Eugénie Grandet* is replete with generalizations of various sorts, but nowhere in the story do more characteristic or more realistic examples occur than here. The author is saying: "If you should go to Anjou, or to Touraine"—and the latter was his own native province—"you would find that in this countryside changes in temperature control business life." The mere matter of generalization is not so significant, but rather the fact that the generalizations indicate an actual, definite, organized knowledge of the situation. The sentence which follows is also a part of the "étude de mœurs" approach: "Vignerons, propriétaires, marchands de bois, tonneliers, aubergistes, mariniers, sont tous à l'affût d'un rayon de soleil." Then Balzac expands the idea by mentioning the phases of the weather which these people study and dread. The author's interest in classes, trades, and professions also appears here. Thereupon, the exposition is broken by a fragment of dialogue, in which Balzac cites the exact words of the people of the Grand'rue de Saumur when they have examined the weather. The author then tells of the trivialities of this sort of existence, the continual spying and tittle-tattle which he always finds characteristic of provinces. Again he becomes specific and declares that the melancholy house where the events of this story occur is one of these houses which are normally found in just such a village as he has described; and finally he says that in order to appreciate the significance of these rapidly disappearing provincial customs, one must hear about M. Grandet. Balzac's sociological intentions are by no means concealed. His hero is used as a social symbol.

The complete harmony and solidity of the scene are obvious. The affairs of the Grandet family, which prove to be likewise *mélancoliques* and *tristes,* fit perfectly into the background of the scene just mentioned. From the standpoint of the historian or geographer there is superfluous material in this exposition, but the realist is striving to create a picture of melancholy whose magnitude will correspond to that of the greedy miser's gripping passion. It must be observed that in this passage, as elsewhere in the work of Balzac, the words *scène* and *physionomie* are used technically for artistic purposes. These words, as the investigation will subsequently prove, are used again and again to signify a general situation and to summarize the phenomena.

There are two types of psychological expositions in the story: (1) those dealing with character proper; and (2) those dealing with circumstances or dramatic moments in the affairs of the characters. There are five prominent characters who are each developed with infinite detail and completeness. The limits of this discussion forbid a complete presentation of them all. Two have been chosen to illustrate the realistic features of the psychological exposition. They are Père Grandet, the bronze-hearted miser, and Nanon, the faithful servant. It should be said at once that we consider the title of the story a misnomer, in that it throws too much emphasis on the nominal heroine. A more comprehensive title would be "La Maison Grandet"; for the miser dominates his household.

Upon the scene of utter melancholy which has just been considered steps M. Félix Grandet, for whose entrance the author paves the way by saying that his door was in the midst of the foregoing scene. The first detail of his biography consists in a statement of M. Grandet's reputation at Saumur. We are thus called upon to view this character through the eyes of others, a device which frequently tends to further the impression of reality. We meet next a definite statement regarding the financial status of the person in question. Balzac's habit of mentioning specific sums of money will be treated at a later stage of this discussion. In this instance, such a financial statement seems to give the keynote to the character study. We begin to suspect at once that this character will evince a great deal of concern over money matters, just as in *César Birotteau,* where the central financial deal is prepared for early in the story. We are informed that M. Grandet profited by the Revolution and that at the age of forty he married a woman with a large dowry. By meeting diplomatically the situation of political upheaval, M. Grandet was able to amass a fortune through the sale of white wine. Under the Consulate, we are told, he became mayor of Saumur, and with his native sagacity he pushed his commercial undertakings to the limit, making hay while the sun shone. With the incoming of the imperial rule, he was deposed; but in 1806—he was then fifty-seven years old and his wife about thirty-six, while their only daughter was ten—he was already the leading property-holder of the region. This fusion of actual political events with the affairs of a particular character is highly realistic. In *César Birotteau* and *Les Chouans,* as well as in many other novels of Balzac, the same device appears.

The family of M. Grandet's wife hoarded their money, we are told; and on the death of three of them—her mother, grandfather, and maternal grandmother—he inherited three fortunes successively. Thus Grandet was able to obtain large holdings, all of which are listed with explicit figures as to size. The word "fortune" occurs with increasing frequency from this time on. It seems that there were only two people who could even vaguely imagine the size of his fortune, and observers could only guess the extent of it by the measure of respect which he received from those two. "Il n'y avait dans Saumur personne qui ne Fût persuadé que monsieur Grandet n'eût un trésor particulier, une cachette pleine de louis, et ne se donnât nuitamment les ineffables jouissances que procure la vue d'une grande masse d'or." Not once in the delineation of this striking figure does Balzac waver from the keynote of miserliness. D'Orgemont and Gobseck had already served as understudies for the present full-length portrait. There follows a generalization on the miser as a type—for Balzac is still sociological. He says that the yellow gleam of gold in the eyes of the greedy may be noted by other avaricious persons, and that the look of a man who is accustomed to drawing an enormous income from his capital necessarily acquires certain indefinable qualities—associated with furtive, grasping, mysterious movements which do not escape his co-religionists.

Just as the plot of the story marches with "tap upon tap" toward an inevitable outcome, so M. Grandet's character has this dominant motif which is forever being presented with increasing intensity. A bit of local color appears in the fact that M. Cruchot and M. des Grassins, who were alone aware of the extent of the Grandet fortune, left an impression of mystery which caused the provincial people to suspect an amount too great for their imaginations. Consequently, whatever Grandet did was quoted, discussed, emulated. His astuteness is described in a half-dozen different ways. He always sold when prices were high; he was always able to get a monopoly which crowded out the "petits propriétaires." Like Gobseck, he is compared to a tiger and a boa, because he knew how and when to spring, how to anticipate his prey. After seizing it, he was like the serpent which has just made a successful venture; he gathered in the money calmly: he was "impassible, froid, méthodique." Balzac's development of an intense extreme character is manifest here as in *La Recherche de l'absolu.*

These comparisons present a twofold effect of vividness: not only did Père Grandet choose his time, spring, and entrap his victims very much in the manner of the tiger and "devour" his prey in the manner of a boa, but the succession of tragedies for his victims (namely, his family) was veiled by the hideous sobriety to which the picture consistently clings. For this is the story of the relations of the monomaniac with his victims. While affably arranging his tortures, M. Grandet became a local character. His townsmen used to say to a stranger in their midst: "Monsieur, nous avons ici deux ou trois maisons millionaires; mais, quant à monsieur Grandet, il ne connaît pas lui-même sa fortune."

We continue, thus, to view the figure of Grandet through the eyes of others, while witnessing, at the same time, certain inherent features of provincial life. These simple folk bowed down before his fortune. Any eccentricities or objectionable habits could be overlooked on the ground of his great wealth. Also, they studied him and by his actions determined when to buy and sell. He himself managed his affairs with the utmost penuriousness. All the fundamentals of life he had furnished by his renters or tenants. In the style of

Photogravure of Balzac.

a catalogue or of an itemized bill, his expenses are listed. This shows how Balzac had "worked up" his subject. By an actual trip to Saumur, he had learned what the expenses of a provincial householder might be expected to include, and so he lists them specifically: holy bread, the toilet of wife and daughter, the rental fee for their pew at church, the light, the wages of Nanon, the repairing of kitchen utensils, taxes, repairs on buildings, and money for new investments. Although it is true that Grandet typifies miserliness, yet he becomes an individual to the reader because of these perfectly definite details about him. An instance of harmony in exposition is contained in the statement concerning the miser's economy: "Il ne faisait jamais de bruit, et semblait économiser tout, même le mouvement." Gobseck and Grandet are companion misers among Balzac's creatures.

Like the characters in Daudet or Dickens, Balzac's personages usually have some customary "gag" which they repeat frequently. Grandet has some particularly curt expressions: "C'te pauvre Nanon!" or "Puisque c'est la fête d'Eugénie"; or again, "Je ne puis rien conclure sans avoir consulté ma femme."

The variety and completeness of detail in the physical description of M. Grandet is also significant for realistic purposes. His height, his general size, his form, his appearance, face, chin, lips, nose, are all mentioned. A term is then used which, like "scène" and "physion-omie," is technical when employed by Balzac: "Cette figure *annonçait* une finesse dangereuse, une probité sans chaleur, l'égoïsme d'un homme habitué à concen-trer ses sentiments dans la jouissance de l'avarice et sur le seul être qui lui fût réellement de quelque chose, sa fille Eugénie, sa seule héritière." "Attestait" is a synonym of "annonçait." Both of these terms signify Balzac's enthusiasm for making the appearance accord with the actual fact. Again, Grandet's heavy shoes, fastened with leather cords, his trousers, waistcoat—all the features of his costume—were "solid," so that they would last a great while. He always put his gloves on the side of his hat in the same methodical fashion, in order to keep them clean. The old miser had on his nose a tumor which colored and moved when his an-ger was about to burst. This was a characteristic detail.

Thus we have become acquainted with the leading character of the story, just as if some provincial person who really knew him had told us all about him. It is almost inconceivable that a portrayal of character could be more vivid. It would be difficult, indeed, to think of anything of interest regarding M. Grandet which has been omitted.

Of course the characterization does not cease with this initial description. It has already been suggested (in chap. i) how, in scene after scene, the old miser plays his rôle with unrelenting consistency. For example, at Eugénie's birthday party, the wretch sat apart from his guests and smiled with grim humor at the scramble of the Cruchots and the Des Grassins for his daughter's dowry. Balzac significantly asks the question at this point: "N'est-ce pas d'ailleurs une scène de tous les temps et de tous les lieux, mais ramenée à sa plus simple expression?" This is a sample of the author's universalizing intention, as expressed by himself in his *Avant-propos*.

The grim humor—and even the humor in *Eugénie Grandet* must be grim to be in accord—is sustained by the fact that Mme Grandet won "seize sous" in the game which was going on and that this was the largest sum which had ever been seen in that room. The "Grande Nanon" laughed with glee to see her mistress pocketing so much money.

The pitiful meagerness of the breakfasts served in the Grandet home and the abject fear of the wife and daugh-ter when they sought to vary the program of rigid economy in honor of Charles's visit are other instanc-es of the harmony which prevailed in Grandet's char-acter and the hopeless struggle which his victims waged with him. Balzac's own early struggles against poverty probably helped him to put such intense scenes before our eyes without distorting them. The protests of the

miser at the outlay for medicines and doctor's visits at the time when his wife is dying also seem very real. When he laid upon his wife's bed a hundred *louis,* with a generosity quite unlike his normal attitude, a generosity inspired by the critical situation, we feel that he is still somewhat human, even though bronze-hearted. His attempt to seize the golden crucifix of the priest at the last unction has already been styled the "turn of the screw." The critics have been inclined to call this a melodramatic finale, in which the horror is too great for realistic purposes. Similar criticisms have been made on the deathbed scene of *Père Goriot* and of other novels—since Balzac makes a specialty of these horrible endings. But realism, as conveying a sensation of gripping truth, is present even in this scene from *Eugénie Grandet*. The antecedent "taps" have convinced us that the monomaniac is capable of any atrocity.

We pass to our second portrait. Nanon, the old serv-ing-woman, "lives and moves and has her being" in the story quite as much as the actual people whom we see in flesh and blood before our eyes. (She is said to be modeled on a certain "Rose," who was Balzac's cook). Her type is that of the *chein fidèle*. "Nanon s'était laissé mettre au cou un collier garni de pointes dont les piqûres ne la piquaient plus." Here it happens that the keynote is an animalism. Nanon's doglike fi-delity was as thoroughgoing as her master's miserli-ness. "Elle riait quand riait Grandet, s'attristait, gelait, se chauffait, travaillait avec lui." With pity which has been termed inoperative, Grandet looked at Nanon, his *chien fidèle,* and murmured, "Cette pauvre Nanon." It may be remembered that César Birotteau is likewise spoken of in terms of canine fidelity. Balzac here is evolving two characters which seem mutually correlat-ed. If Nanon were not "doglike," Grandet would not seem so pitiless. The total submissiveness of both Nanon and Mme Grandet makes the delineation of Père Grandet far more realistic.

Everything about Nanon is "gros." Her laugh, her shoul-ders, her strength, and even her heart are huge. She pities Eugénie and Mme Grandet without failing in her faithfulness to her lord and master. Two specific allu-sions to her bigness are illustrative: Charles asks her, "N'avez-vous pas servi dans les marins de la garde impériale?" This accords with a statement made in the initial description of Nanon: "Sa figure eût été fort admirée sur les épaules d'un grenadier de la garde." We learn also that she was five feet, eight inches in height.

An exhaustive treatment of the realism of Nanon's rôle would involve an analysis of many incidents in the book. Some details in her affairs are especially signif-icant for our purposes. It is said that in the famous year of 1811—as in all the allusions to time an actual date is given—the harvesting had occasioned especial difficulty, and Grandet decided after twenty years of service to reward Nanon by a gift, his old watch. This was, indeed, the only gift she ever received from him. That this faithful old creature was actually a part of the family circle is shown by the fact that she joined in the conversation even when there were guests, shared in the fortunes and reverses of the others, and reflected in every way the situation of those whom she served. Her active participation in Eugénie's intrigue to provide Charles with little luxuries which were not customary in the household is truly pathetic, for she is thrust between the two fires: her sympathy for Eugénie and her fear of her master.

The author's sympathy with ordinary life is well exemplified in his characterization of Nanon. When the poor old woman sees Charles's green silk *robe de chambre* with its decorations of golden flowers and ancient designs, she is quite overcome with admiration and wonder. The situation is charmingly naïve and real when she asks if he will really wear this creation when he retires. Then she wishes to call Eugénie to look at it. Finally she goes to her own chamber to rest and dream of the wonders of this garment, the beauty of which surpasses anything she has ever seen before in the sordid barrenness of her life at M. Grandet's home. Although she is coarse and, indeed, a typical serving-woman, yet, like Félicité in Flaubert's *Un Cœur simple,* she is always sympathetic even to tenderness. She calls Charles an "enfant" and says: "Q'il est gentil les yeux fermés!" To Eugénie, she is faithful to the very end, so that on the last page of the story Eugénie says: "Il n'y a que toi qui m'aimes." Balzac makes of this dumb, faithful creature one of the five leading characters of the story.

The contrast between Charles and Nanon is remarkable. We have already seen that "La Grande Nanon" looked like a grenadier of the Guard. She is further described as a "créature femelle taillée en Hercule, plantée sur ses pieds comme un chêne de soixante ans sur ses racines, forte des hanches, carrée du dos, ayant des mains de charretier et une probité vigoureuse comme l'était son intacte vertu." Of Charles's hands and general appearance it was said: "Elle [Eugénie] enviait les petites mains de Charles, son teint, la fraîcheur et la délicatesse de ses traits." Charles is alluded to as a "mirliflor." The words "élégance," "luxe," "perfection," are applied with impressive emphasis to his clothing. His physical frailty and effete manner combine to render him a perfect antithesis to Nanon with her oxlike strength.

Almost half the text of *Eugénie Grandet* is in the form of exposition, though not unmixed. The combination of exposition with dialogue which is found here is peculiarly well adapted to good story-telling, and may help account for the fact that of all Balzac's novels this is one of the best liked and the most frequently read. The device of relieving solid paragraphs by means of talk is employed with great consistency. No expository passage extends through more than a page or two without a fragment of dialogue, however brief. Take, for example, "Cette pauvre Nanon," the expression of heartless pity which Père Grandet uses of his *chien fidèle.* Such an insertion adds to the effect while breaking the tediousness.

By way of summary, the exposition in *Eugénie Grandet,* both topographical and psychological, is distinctly and consciously realistic. The characterizations are particularly so. The developments, like the moves in the plot, are arranged tap upon tap in cumulative or climactic order, as regards individuals and their deeds.

The chief characters in this story are for the most part types: the provincial miser, his submissive wife, his naïve innocent daughter, the faithful servant, the elegant city relative. As for the minor characters, the Cruchots and the Des Grassins, they are entirely typical of a small-town set. Their great interest in Eugénie's dowry is an eminently realistic trait, as well as their frank competition and pettiness.

Thus the scene at Eugénie's birthday party stands out clearly: ". . . les six antagonistes se préparaient-ils à venir armés de toutes pièces, pour se rencontrer dans la salle et s'y surpasser en preuves d'amitié." Or again:

> . . . cette petitesse jointe à de si grands intérêts; cette jeune fille qui, semblable à ces oiseaux victimes du haut prix auquel on les met et qu'ils ignorent, se trouvait traquée, serrée par des preuves d'amitié dont elle était la dupe; tout contribuait à rendre cette scène tristement comique.

Balzac seems naïvely unwilling here for the reader to miss any of the dramatic situation. The conversation is provincial and trite. The game of cards adds realism to the account of the evening and breaks the hopeless monotony of the story.

The descriptions in this novel are usually of persons or of interiors in the old melancholy Grandet home. The one topographical or exterior scene has already been mentioned in some detail, as well as the masterful descriptions of Grandet and Nanon. Let us look at the picture of Mme Grandet, which, like those of the other characters, is given *en masse* at the first, with only a few later touches. It has already been shown that the descriptions of persons are exceedingly minute, including clothing, gestures, and other realistic details: "Madame Grandet était une femme sèche et maigre, jaune comme un coing, gauche, lente; une de ces femmes qui semblent faites pour être tyranisées." The keynote of this description is "tyranisées." We proceed to the mentions of her family, her disposition, her dowry, her dress, her absolute submissiveness, the narrow restrictions of her life.

The scene in which Père Grandet announced to Charles the death of Guillaume Grandet, Charles's father and the old miser's brother, is worthy of attention. Eugénie, her mother, and Nanon went to the kitchen in order to witness what happened. All three were filled with feminine compassion for the youth who was to receive such a cruel blow. The scene took place in the little "humid" garden. The adjective suggests the dreariness of the surroundings in which dread news was to be delivered. This is similar to the device of having nature harmonize with one's mood—as in the love scene of *Les Chouans.* Old Grandet walked silently with his nephew about the garden. Here, Balzac puts a powerful "tap" on the miser's own character, and at the same time introduces a vivid detail. The old man felt only one feature of his brother's suicide as a cruel blow— the loss of his fortune. He hated to tell his nephew that he, Charles, was penniless. To this aspect of the situation the mind of the miser turned constantly, and he even expected Charles to feel his poverty in the same way. It must be observed that the author does not generalize or treat this situation in a desultory fashion. Balzac says that M. Grandet in his confusion thought of saying: "Vous avez perdu votre père." That would not serve the purpose, because to the miser it was not the important point. Then he thought of: "Vous êtes sans aucune espèce de fortune!" This presentation of the actual mind of Père Grandet is essentially vivid. The incident may be placed side by side with that in which Père Grandet looked on at the festivities of Eugénie's birthday party and with grim humor realized that his fellow-townsmen, who were his guests for the evening, were simply competing for his daughter's fortune. Psychological detail thus serves the same end as physical detail; i.e., the *humide* garden and the dreary Père Grandet with his hideous love of money make a perfect combination for the sad news about to be divulged.

Certain critics of Balzac have been impelled to try to discover how close to fact are the characters and events in *Eugénie Grandet.* There was, indeed, a celebrated miser at Saumur when Balzac wrote his story. This miser, Nivelleau by name, had a daughter quite unlike Eugénie. There are several discrepancies in the accounts of Nivelleau, but many people were willing to affirm that Nivelleau is actually Grandet. It cannot be determined for a certain fact that Nivelleau was a *tonnelier.* He was a *négociant,* but there is no evidence that he was ever mayor of Saumur. With regard to the respective wealth of the two misers, no comparison is feasible. [In his *Autour d'Eugénie Grandet* (1924)] M. Serval suggests that since no one in Saumur knew how big Grandet's fortune was, not even Grandet himself, perhaps Balzac did not know!

Eugénie and her affairs do not correspond closely to the accounts of Mlle Nivelleau. At least, Mlle Nivelleau was not abandoned by one whom she loved. However, she was the victim of disasters in the form of deaths in her family—two children, her mother, her father, then her husband died. In so brief a time did these deaths occur that fate seemed to allow her only to catch her breath before inflicting another blow.

Mme Nivelleau seems to have been unlike Mme Grandet; and M. Nivelleau, as a "protecteur des arts," hardly resembles Balzac's miser. There were, however, certain legends built up around M. Nivelleau which stressed his greed. There was also one family in Saumur who might have suggested the Des Grassins— especially in the matter of wishing to marry a son to the rich heiress.

Maurice Serval feels on the whole that Balzac probably based La Maison Grandet on La Maison Nivelleau. He does not quite prove his case, but he presents an interesting comparison between the persons and events in *Eugénie Grandet* with similar persons and events in real life at Saumur. Balzac visited the town, probably several times, between 1830 and 1832. According to his usual habits, he steeped himself in the atmosphere of the "vieux Saumur," finding streets and houses like those described in the novel. He also visited the surrounding country, thus obtaining data for the old *tonnelier*'s enterprises; and he may even have met, in a nearby country house, Nivelleau himself. M. Hallays gives further gossip concerning this possible prototype [in his *En flânant. A travers la France: Touraine, Anjou et Maine* (1912)].

The animalisms in the story of *Eugénie Grandet* are fairly frequent. The more outstanding examples have already been mentioned in connection with Grandet and Nanon. These animalisms either suggest a low plane of living for certain characters, or else they unite to strengthen the vividness of the picture which Balzac creates.

The style may be regarded as materialistic *au fond* because it embodies many externalities. It is a bit technical at times because of the numerous financial matters which are mentioned in some detail. It is never cumbersome except in the one or two long expositions, and even these are too colorful and too carefully relieved by bits of dialogue to admit that criticism except from one who has no sympathy with Balzac's interest in "études." The style is usually simple, concealing the author's art. The sentences are sometimes long in the expositions, but practically never involved. They often present merely a series of objects set forth in the terse manner of a catalogue so that their very clarity contributes to the realism of the story.

For the purpose of making his characters true to local life, Balzac causes them to use many words which do not appear in the standard dictionaries. Occasionally, he uses such a word himself, but more frequently these terms occur in the dialogue. Some of them are provincial and popular, some are invented. Among these are: (1) *décliquer* = "réciter," "parler avec bruit et volubilité" (cf. Godefroy); (2) *ouvrouère* = "boutique," "atelier" (cf. Godefroy); (3) *embucquer* = to stuff, used only of fowls. These words appear in the speech of Père Grandet. Nanon and her master both use provincialisms: (1) *fêteux*, which is the provincial pronunciation for "fêteurs"; (2) *frippe*, which means "anything good to be eaten with bread"; (3) *halleboteur*, from *halleboter*, which means "rechercher après le vendange les hallebotes, les raisins oubliés dans les vignes"; (4) *truisse*, a word from Touraine which signifies a branch pulled from a living tree. Here is an instance of Balzac's use of a term the language of his own native province. *Quien*, a popular pronunciation for "tiens," is used by Nanon. *Bêtiser* is an invention of the author. Among the other coined words are: *chambreloque*, a word used by Nanon for a "robe de chambre"; *chanteronner* is derived from "chanter"; *génovines* is used for "des pièces génoises"; *mette* is a provincial term still used in Central France. *Aveindre, engarrier, poinçon, tribouiller, jouxtant*, are all rare words. The employment of them in dialogue particularly makes the characters seem like "de vrais personnages."

The use of specific figures regarding matters of money creates an illusion that an actual transaction is being recorded. For instance, we are told that M. Grandet's property consisted of "deux mille louis d'or," that he had also at the very beginning of the story "deux cents doubles louis offerts par son beau-père." M. Grandet put away his harvest to wait for a high price or "attendre le moment de livrer son poinçon à deux cents francs quand les petits propriétaires donnaient le leur à cinq louis." His crop then brought him "plus de deux cent quarante mille livres." M. Cruchot had procured a loan from him "à onze pour cent." The Froidfond estate is described as "valant trois millions." When a young girl is married in Berry, or Anjou, says Balzac (and here we have a local custom), her family or that of her husband is accustomed to give her "douze pièces, douze douzaines de pièces ou douze cents pièces d'argent ou d'or." "Quatre ou cinq louis," we are told, formed the larger part of Mme Grandet's annual revenue. For incidental expenses her husband never gave her more than "six francs à la fois"; and for "les menues dépenses, le fil, les aiguilles et la toilette de sa fille," he allowed each month a "pièce de cent sous." Guillaume Grandet needed about four million francs to pay his debts. By far the most striking example of meticulous accuracy in this connection is the case of Eugénie's birthday money which she gave to Charles. Each of these rare coins is named with absolute precision, so that nearly a page is devoted to labeling and classifying the lot.

Eugénie is represented as emptying with real pleasure the drawer in which they were kept. The purse is then described and accounted for. First, she takes out "vingt portugaises encore neuves." The minute description which follows does not fail to evaluate these coins definitely. Then, item by item, with repeated use of that legal-sounding term, Balzac catalogues the rest of Eugénie's coins until the reader can feel their weight and hear them fall upon one another. Details of actual history are interwoven in this enumeration. In some instances Père Grandet's remarks when he originally presented the gifts are quoted.

When Mme Grandet is dying for lack of medical care and attention and because of the outbreak of her husband's wrath over Eugénie's generosity, M. Grandet goes to his desk, takes out a handful of *louis*, and puts them on his wife's bed. The sum is definitely "cent louis." When Charles returned from the Indies, there were fifteen hundred thousand francs still lacking to settle his father's debts. Charles writes to Eugénie that he now has "quatre-vingt mille livres de rente." He sends her a check for eight thousand francs in this same letter. M. and Mme d'Aubrion had "une vingtaine de mille livres de rente." These are not all the definite allusions to sums of money, but they are sufficient to show the author's practice.

Apart from reappearing characters, who are infrequently found in this story, there are a certain number of references to actual or historical persons and things—a noted banker, a miniaturist, a newspaper, etc. The device of alluding to contemporary fact, though less prominent than in the Parisian novels, is important for realistic purposes. This is really another phase of documentation.

The following salient facts stand out vividly when one has read **Eugénie Grandet** (or better, *La Maison Grandet*): (1) The book is in part a sociological study, according to the author's intention. (2) Itemized documentation is used in the list of Grandet's expenses, the list of legacies which came to him, the list of Eugénie's coins, etc. (3) The author's fondness for displaying technical erudition is shown in the whole treatment of Guillaume Grandet's bankruptcy from a legal viewpoint; also, in the matter of appraising Mme Grandet's estate if she is survived by Eugénie. (4) The action of the story is constantly being halted for sociological and psychological observations. (An enthusiasm for Balzac's manner must be based on an appreciative tolerance of this trait. It has been shown that dialogue is often employed to obviate tediousness in these long disquisitions. **Eugénie Grandet** is less guilty of long-windedness than most of Balzac's novels—and is correspondingly more popular and readable.) (5) The story has an almost perfect solidity. (6) The characters belong to ordinary life.

Thus, realism approaches perfection in *Eugénie Gran-det,* which many Balzacians would rank highest among its author's achievements.

Ray P. Bowen (essay date 1940)

SOURCE: "Acts and Scenes: *Eugénie Grandet,*" "Settings, Costumes, and Groupings: *Eugénie Grandet,*" and "Dialogue: *Eugénie Grandet,*" in *The Dramatic Construction of Balzac's Novels,* University of Oregon, 1940, pp. 26-31, 81-2, 106.

[*In* The Dramatic Construction of Balzac's Novels, *Bowen seeks "to reveal by examination of the novels themselves whether there is not something more than just a dramatic pattern running through them and also whether there is not a manner of building according to which the author, consciously or unconsciously, constructed them so as to give them the dramatic form that characterizes his method of composition." In the excerpt below from that work, the critic delineates the dramatic construction of* Eugénie Grandet, *providing commentary, as well, on settings, costumes, groupings, and dialogue.*]

Contrary to Professor Jenkins' statement, "If he [Balzac] had cast *Eugénie Grandet* in dramatic form, there would have been four acts with a Prologue," this novel appears more readily to fall into three acts with a long introduction descriptive of Saumur, of the Grandet house, of the miser, and of his servant, Nanon. There is no dialogue or action in this introduction, and these are necessary, even for a prologue, in an acting play. The first act begins with the arrival of Charles and ends with his departure for the Indies. The second act ends with the signing of the papers by which Eugénie resigns all control of her mother's fortune to her father, and the third with Eugénie's marriage.

The first act actually contains eighteen scenes, of which eight, at most, are essential for a stage presentation. As usual there occur frequent changes in the places of the action, but all significant phases of the action take place in only three different settings: the salon-dining room, the garden, and Charles' bedroom. While it is difficult to consider the first scene as taking place in one room, the most important part of it passes in the parlor and includes the birthday party at which are present al the characters of the novel except Charles who arrives during the course of the evening. In this scene Balzac shows his masterly powers of assembling in one group all persons of importance in the action, and then, by compact dialogue, of revealing all essential elements for understanding the nature of the plot. It is one of the best introductory scenes in all his novels. There is perfect coordination in setting, dialogue, and action. Unfortunately the scene is interrupted when Mme Grandet and her daughter leave to prepare a bedroom for

Charles. The short intervening scene is excellent for dialogue that hints at the whole plot situation. Eugénie will lend loving care to this young Parisian's every need, and her father will oppose her in this, as we gather from the remarks of her mother. Yet the daughter prevails against her mother's objections. This scene could not be staged separately and yet it is difficult to incorporate it into the scene in the living room which is continuing all this time. There, the women guests are active in prejudicing Charles against his cousin, thus subtly defending their own sons' interests. Charles stands in the firelight, while Grandet by the light of candles reads the letter from his dead brother. Mme Grandet and Eugénie return to the salon and their guests take their leave. This first scene gathers together all elements in the drama and indicates the special interest of each person in the forthcoming events. The next scene which takes place in the streets as the guests are wending their way homeward, would be hard to stage. The dialogue, however, is subtle and significant. The next scene presents the Grandet family as they retire to their respective rooms. Their conversation contributes definitely to the building up of both plot and character. A playwright dramatizing this novel would doubtless have to devise some way of absorbing these very short scenes into the main action occurring in the parlor.

The next important scene is the seventh which passes in this parlor that also serves as a dining room. The family is at breakfast the following morning. The dialogue is brilliant, rapid, and full of meaning for both plot and character. Eugénie for the first time definitely defies her father by putting back on the table the sugar which he had put away, because her cousin desires some for his coffee. Grandet's remarks point as concisely to the next scene as would be the case in a French classical play. He says to his nephew, "Quand vous aurez fini, nous irons ensemble dans le jardin, j'ai à vous dire des choses qui ne sont pas sucrées." This garden scene contributes explicitly to the advancement of the plot, since it is here that Grandet tells his nephew of his father's death; yet the scene is too short to be presented by itself. Grandet could very justly inform the young man of this sad news at the breakfast table rather than in the garden. Two scenes that follow, dealing with the miser's plans to increase his fortune and his refusal to lend financial aid to Charles, can be combined and made to take place also in the parlor. Scene twelve is a very clever scene which occurs likewise in the parlor at the time of the visit of MM. Cruchot and des Grassins, both of whom seek the hand of Eugénie. Old Grandet wants someone to go to Paris to look after the affairs of his deceased brother, and he plays one rival against the other in a masterly fashion in order to have one of them undertake this task without any cost to himself. His skillful handling of these men, all carried out by dialogue, is worthy of the best dramatic authors. It gives a fine revelation of Grandet's character. Scene fourteen which takes place in Charles' room on the occasion of Eugénie's third visit there, is most important. She very clearly reveals her feelings for her cousin, she lends him the money, and receives as security his mother's gold-inlaid workbox. The loan and its security provide a basis for important future happenings. The scene is also a good love scene rendered by adequate dialogue. Scene seventeen takes place principally in the garden, and should by rights be the climax of the act, since it brings to its height the passion that has sprung up between these two lovers. The scene, however, is short, and is badly handled, especially from the point of view of dialogue. Scene fourteen (Eugénie's visit to Charles' room already discussed) would make a better climax for the act, as the novel stands. The last and farewell scene, too, is badly done, for there is no good dialogue and no setting.

While act II actually contains eleven scenes based on very clear shifts in location of the action, only five of these are necessary to render the full effect of the desperate struggle between the wills of the two main characters. The death of Mme Grandet is treated so briefly and so inadequately (there is no described setting or dialogue except for one speech), that it is impossible to give this event the distinction of a separate scene in spite of its importance in the life of the heroine. Scene four is the first good one in this act. Here we witness Eugénie's second overt disobedience to her father's demands in her positive refusal to tell him what has become of her gold. The dramatic situation is well brought out by the dialogue. The scene takes place in the parlor, and the position of the actors is briefly indicated, since Mme Grandet and Eugénie are together facing the wrath of Grandet. Scene five presents another important step in the struggle. It takes place in the bedroom of Mme Grandet, which, unfortunately, has not been described. Not only is there sensed a feeling of triumph for Eugénie, but we see that Nanon is inclined to take sides with her against her master. The dialogue is fine both for character and plot. Scene eight which passes in the garden presents not so much the active struggle that we have been observing hitherto, but the one going on in Grandet's mind, which he reveals by his remarks to Cruchot, who advises him, for financial reasons of course, to be more considerate of his wife and daughter. The dialogue is humorous in parts but has an undertone of tragedy, and what is said has a very decisive effect on Grandet's future actions. We see the two men gazing up at the window of Eugénie's room, and also the barred window of Grandet's own room. The gloomy house stands in the background. The general effect is impressive and dramatic. Scene nine is probably the most dramatic scene in the novel, and, if not the climax of the entire action, it is the climax of act II. Unfortunately it passes in the undescribed setting of Mme Grandet's room, but it presents the most intense moments of the struggle that proves to be the direct cause of Mme Grandet's death.

The miser beholds the workbox so devotedly cherished by Eugénie, and, in his blind passion for gold, he strives to get the precious metal off the box, and is only prevented from so doing by the powerful resistance of Eugénie. For the first time he is defeated by his daughter. Her spirit shows itself much like his own. This scene is marked by intense dramatic elements which are brought out by the dialogue in which there are no gaps, no digressions by the author. Every word contributes to carrying on the plot to its climax. Mme Grandet lies in her bed, beside which stands Eugénie; both face Grandet who has just entered the room and who is the focal point in the action. The death of Mme Grandet closes the scene. Scene eleven, the last of the act, takes place the following day in the parlor, and involves Grandet, Cruchot, and Eugénie. His daughter this time yields to her father in order that the family fortune may remain intact, although here again she reveals that her spirit is essentially the same as her father's. Setting, action, and dialogue are in perfect correlation. Although the last part of this unit of action takes place the following day, it occurs in the same setting, and the passage of the time is scarcely sensed; therefore it is entirely logical to include in the scene the actual signing of the papers by which Eugénie concedes to her father her rights to her mother's fortune.

As frequently happens also in his other novels, Balzac fails to rise to dramatic heights in the last act of *Eugénie Grandet*. It contains a possible seven scenes, but only four are of any consequence from the point of view of a play. The first scene of act III, though immediately following the last scene of act II in the text of the novel, actually takes place five years later. It recounts the death of the miser, whose last words to his daughter are, "Veille à l'or, mets de l'or devant moi. Ça me réchauffe. Aie bien soin de tout. Tu me rendras compte de ça là-bas." Eugénie asks for his blessing and the scene ends. The dying man with his last bit of strength tries to snatch the gold and silver crucifix. Avarice and not religious emotion impels him to this effort. This scene, like the one giving Mme Grandet's death, is too short to be staged. The second and third and the last scenes might well be eliminated, for they do not possess sufficient action and dialogue to give them substance. If the main interest in the novel lies in Eugénie's love for Charles, then the climax occurs in the fourth scene of this act, where she sits in the garden reading the letter from her lover, which tells of his proposed marriage to another. If the main interest centers in her struggle with her father, which is far more dramatic than the tragedy of her love experience, then the climax comes in the second act. In any case, in this scene in the garden, the author once more recovers his dramatic sense and harmonizes the setting with action and dialogue. The latter is particularly poignant in its genuine pathos and restraint. We are again reminded that Eugénie resembles her father

First page of manuscript of Illusions perdues.

in her mastery over her feelings when it is not wise to show emotion. Balzac weakens the central impression of the scene by having Eugénie leave the garden and go into the salon to receive her visitors; the ensuing conversation adds much, however, to our understanding of the progress of the plot, and to our appreciation of her magnificent strength of will. The same control over her passions she displays in the next scene, which takes place in the parlor and which is essential for depicting the full tragedy of her love for her faithless cousin. She agrees to marry her former suitor if he will carry out her mission to save Charles from the disgrace of bankruptcy. The play ends in the parlor where it began.

In this novel Balzac comes nearer to the attainment of sustained dramatic composition throughout a unit of action than in the works analyzed hitherto. Practically all essential scenes are adaptable to the stage. Only three settings, and the undescribed bedroom of Mme Grandet, need figure in a drama form of the story. The author has made great progress in his use of dialogue as the medium of carrying on the plot, and more particularly, of revealing character. It is to be noticed also that he gives the two death scenes but scant attention. Perhaps he is more interested in the living than the dead.

. . . . .

All the descriptions of setting in *Eugénie Grandet* come at the beginning of the novel before any action takes place. The house "à monsieur Grandet" is described inside and out in the opening pages. The *salle* where most of the action takes place receives a very detailed description adequate for a stage setting, but Mme Grandet's room in which occurs the most dramatic scene of all is not described. The garden in which at least two major scenes occur is given only a very brief description, not at all commensurate with the importance of what takes place there. Charles' room is described when the young man enters it for the first time. The scenes that take place in the *salle,* as noted, have good setting, but it would appear that Balzac had no clear intention of furnishing adequate stage settings for the truly dramatic scenes occurring elsewhere. The only additional description that the author indulges in is that of the town of Saumur and of the outside of the miser's house. This description aids us in understanding the personality of Grandet.

The miser's portrait immediately precedes that of his house, and gives his physical appearance as well as his costume. Nanon is then described. Mme Grandet is not portrayed until she makes her first speech in the first scene. Charles is described when he first appears. Eugénie, however, is not described until later when we sense that she is in love with her cousin, and, even then, she receives only a very superficial delineation.

She is not described in her new gown worn in honor of her birthday party; nor is her costume described for us in any later scene.

In the first scene, as we have observed, the author has gathered in one room all the chief characters and he has given them a somewhat symbolic grouping since Charles stands in the center in the light from the fireplace and Grandet sits a little off center reading by the light of the candle. The two suitors with their mothers are on the other side of the room. Eugénie is not too far away to receive some of the light, but her mother is to one side as she is in all the scenes in which she appears. That would seem to indicate her accepted position in the story. Grouping, in this novel, is one of Balzac's chief concerns.

. . . . .

The greatest dramatic element in *Eugénie Grandet* lies in dialogue. It is through dialogue that the psychology of the characters is revealed, and it is through dialogue that the plot is primarily carried out. Speech leads to speech with comparatively little serious interruption on the part of the author. Grandet speaks more than any one else; out of 501 speeches spoken by all three members of his family, he claims 251. Thus he establishes the tone of the novel. He represents the type of person who uses conversation to conceal thought rather than reveal it. The kind of dialogue that Balzac is master of is natural to the miser, as it is to Cruchot and to des Grassins who are scheming to get control of his wealth. If the author has adopted a dialogue suited to the nature of Grandet, so has he also for Eugénie's wholly ingenuous habits of mind. Although she speaks only 166 times in three acts as compared to her father's 251 speeches in two acts, she is revealed to us as completely as he. That this is primarily a psychological novel rather than one of intrigue, the dialogue indicates, since there are twice as many speeches that reveal character as those that advance plot. There are very few scenes where dialogue is poor, or fails to add to the structure the author is gradually building up. So clear is the dialogue that it suggests a mosaic. No portion of it can be omitted. Setting enjoys no similar significance in the construction of the novel.

Martin Turnell (essay date 1950)

SOURCE: "Four Novels: *Eugénie Grandet*," in *The Novel in France: Mme de La Fayette, Laclos, Constant, Stendhal, Balzac, Flaubert, Proust,* New Directions, 1950, pp. 235-39.

[*Turnell has written extensively on French literature of the last three centuries. In the following excerpt, he cites Andre Gide's criticisms of* Eugénie Grandet *in his own short critique of that novel.*]

'It does not seem to me to be one of the best of Balzac's novels or to deserve the extraordinary favour it has enjoyed,' remarks Gide of *Eugénie Grandet*. 'The style is extremely mediocre; the characters could scarcely be more summary; the dialogue is conventional and often inacceptable. . . . Alone the story of old Grandet's speculations seems to me to be masterly; but that is perhaps because I am not competent in such matters.'

Eugénie Grandet was completed a year before Balzac began *Le Père Goriot*. The style is undoubtedly 'sticky' in places, but it does not seem to me that an occasional awkwardness in the writing is sufficient grounds on which to condemn the book. M. Gide's other criticisms apply to most of Balzac's novels. None of them is completely satisfactory even in its own genre. They are, in so far as they are successful, only good in parts. Nor does it seem to me that an understanding or lack of understanding of financial machinations ought to affect our judgment. I have probably less skill in this respect than M. Gide, but I, too, find the account of Grandet's activities 'masterly'; and the book as a whole seems to me to be one of Balzac's most successful works. For here there is no straining, as there is in the *Père Goriot,* to fit the characters into their background; the characters—the principals as well as the minor characters—are certainly there. They belong to their province, to their town, to their community. There is nothing forced or melodramatic about the description of the damp, cold, old-fashioned house at Saumur:

> . . . cette maison pâle, froide, silencieuse, située en haut de la ville, et abritée par les ruines des remparts.

> [. . . the pale, cold, silent house standing above the town and sheltered by the ruins of the ramparts.]

For once the three adjectives are necessary and place the house before us. The house and its owner belong to one another:

> Les manières de cet homme étaient fort simples. Il parlait peu. Généralement, il exprimait ses idées par de petites phrases sentencieuses et dites d'une voix douce. . . . Au physique, Grandet était un homme de cinq pieds, trapu, carré, ayant des mollets de douze pouces de circonférence, des rotules noueuses et de larges épaules; son visage était rond, tanné, marqué de petite vérole; son menton était droit, ses lèvres n'offraient aucune sinuosité, et ses dents étaient blanches; ses yeux avaient l'expression calme et dévoratrice que le peuple accorde au basilic. . . . Son nez, gros par le bout, supportait une loupe veinée que le vulgaire disait, non sans raison, pleine de malice. Cette figure annonçait une finesse dangereuse, une probité sans chaleur, l'égoïsme d'un homme habitué à concentrer ses sentiments dans la jouissance de l'avarice et sur le seul être qui lui fût réellement quelque chose, sa fille Eugénie, sa seule

héritière. . . . Aussi, quoique de mœurs faciles et molles en apparence, M. Grandet avait-il un caractère de bronze. Toujours vêtu de la même manière, qui le voyait aujourd'hui le voyait tel qu'il était depuis 1791.

> [The man's behaviour was simplicity itself. He spoke little. Usually he expressed himself in brief sententious phrases, delivered in a gentle tone. . . . Physically, Grandet was five feet in height, thick-set and squarely built, his calves over twelve inches in diameter, his knees bony and his shoulders broad. His face was round and marked by smallpox; his chin straight, his lips level, his teeth white; his eyes had the calm devouring expression which the people attribute to the basilisk. . . . His nose, which was fat at the end, had a veined knob on it which the common people alleged, not without reason, was full of malice. This face suggested a dangerous finesse, a probity devoid of any warmth of feeling, the selfishness of a man who concentrated all his feelings on the enjoyment of avarice and on the only being who meant anything to him—his daughter and sole heir, Eugénie. Thus, though his behaviour was easy and gentle, M. Grandet had a character of iron. He was always dressed in the same fashion: anyone who saw him to-day, saw him as he had been since 1791.]

The description of Grandet is free from all Balzac's usual faults. It has the economy and precision of a seventeenth-century 'character'. There is complete correspondence between the inner and the outer man. The grave, hard exterior reflects his preoccupation with a single dominating passion. Once Balzac has described the character of the miser, which clearly leaves no place for psychological development, he merely has to invent the actions and gestures which will bring him to life and, so to speak, set him in motion. He therefore concentrates like Dickens on a few tell-tale gestures which fix themselves in the mind—the maddening stutter, the horrible 'Ta ta ta ta', the daily distribution of 'rations', the meanness over fuel and candles which all lead back to the miser's absorbing passion:

> 'Ta ta ta ta!' dit Grandet, 'voilà les bêtises qui commencent. Je vois avec peine, mon neveu, vos jolies mains blanches.'

> Il lui montra les espèces d'épaules de mouton que la nature lui avait mises au bout des bras.

> 'Voilà des mains faites pour ramasser des écus!'

> ['Ta, ta, ta, ta!' said Grandet. 'You're starting to be silly. It pains me to see your nice white hands, nephew.'

> He showed him objects like shoulders of mutton which nature had attached to the ends of his arms.

'These are the sort of hands made to rake in the shekels!']

M. Gide, we know, has complained about the faintness of the other characters in the book. Their limitations are due partly to the nature of the undertaking and partly to Balzac's artistic shortcomings. The picture of the old servant, of mother and daughter spending their days over their needlework in the dim house and of the factions between the des Grassins and the Cruchots seems to me to be admirable of its kind and at its particular level. They have on the whole sufficient life to throw into relief the activities of Grandet, and if we are not told a great deal about them it is largely because there is not much to tell.

Where, it seems to me, the novel is most open to criticism is in the account of the love affair between Eugénie and her cousin. This is the description of her emotional awakening:

> Cette physionomie calme, colorée, bordée d'une lueur comme une jolie fleur éclose, reposait l'âme, communiquait le charme de la conscience qui s'y reflétait, et commandait le regard. Eugénie était encore sur la rive de la vie où fleurissent les illusions enfantines, où se cueillent les marguerites avec des délices plus tard inconnues.

> [Her calm fresh-complexioned face, which was surrounded by a glow like a lovely flower in full bloom, was restful to the spirit; it made you feel the charm of the mind reflected in it and compelled attention. Eugénie was on the threshold of life where childish illusions still flourish and where you pick daisies with a delight which is unknown in later years.]

There is no real penetration into her feelings here. The repeated reference to flowers merely gives the passage a vague, facile charm For Eugénie and Charles are to a considerable degree conventional figures and like Vautrin represent the alien element which Balzac often incorporated uncritically into his work. Yet if Charles is not closely observed, he possesses sufficient life for Balzac's purpose. Balzac, as we know from his other books, is master of a certain form of social comedy. Without probing deeply into psychological motives, he is often admirable in his descriptions of the gaucheries of the young man making his début in society. Rastignac's clumsy efforts to ingratiate himself with the great seem to me to be much the best part of *Le Père Goriot*. In *Eugénie Grandet* we see the situation in reverse. Whatever the shortcomings of the portrait of Charles Grandet, we do feel the full impact of the dandy on the narrow provincial society of Saumur.

Still, we must agree with M. Gide that what is impressive about the novel is old Grandet and his speculations and that once he is dead the interest evaporates.

Marcel Girard (essay date 1956)

SOURCE: An introduction to *Eugénie Grandet,* by Honoré de Balzac, J. M. Dent & Sons Ltd, 1956, pp. v-xv.

[*In the following essay, Girard provides a critical and historical overview of* Eugénie Grandet, *sketching the novel's geographical, social, and biographical background.*]

Towards the end of his life Balzac began to hate being called 'father of *Eugénie Grandet.*' He imagined that this emphasis upon his first great novel was calculated to derogate from the remainder of his work. 'It is admittedly a masterpiece,' he used to say, 'but only a little one'; and in the end he came to loathe it!

While recognizing that Balzac unquestionably wrote novels that may be described as more spacious, more profound, and more complex, I do not for that reason consider *Eugénie Grandet* unworthy to rank high among the hundred or so novels that form the *Comédie Humaine*.

In 1833 Balzac was thirty-four years old and in the fullness of his powers. He did not hesitate to tell his sister that if a man is to achieve his life's ambition he must do so between the ages of thirty and forty. His output was already large, but as yet he had scored no major success. *Les Chouans,* which had attracted a good deal of notice in 1829, was followed by *La Physiologie du Mariage, La Peau de Chagrin, Louis Lambert,* and "Gobseck". All these had helped to bolster his reputation, particularly with his women readers; but the critics were still hesitant. It was time to strike a decisive blow in the form of a work which should be at once more powerful, more restrained, and more closely knit. He must write a classic.

Now it so happened that Balzac was at this period in exactly the right frame of mind to undertake such a task. For the first time in his life he was happy. A wide circle of female friends encouraged him and gave him confidence: his sister Laura, to whom he confided all his thoughts; Madame de Berny, the wonderful 'Dilecta,' who wrapped him in the tenderness of old age; Zulma Carraud, whose country house he often visited, when wearied of Parisian drawing-rooms, to refresh his soul. Above all, there was Madame Hanska, a Polish noblewoman, who in February 1832 had written and expressed her admiration of his work. He had seen in her a 'sister-soul,' and was looking forward to meeting her, as she had promised, at Neuchâtel in September 1833. *Eugénie Grandet* was begun in June of that year and was completed in four months of pleasurable anticipation.

'I believe,' he wrote to her, 'that more blood flows through my heart, that my brain holds more ideas at the thought of meeting you. I feel sure that this desire will urge me to yet finer achievements.' The heroine of his story was soon identified with the beloved. 'It is necessary to have loved, my darling, in order to describe Eugénie Grandet's love, so proud, so pure, so boundless'; and in his little room in the Rue Cassini, where he worked every day from 2 a.m. until noon, the work took shape before the driving power of his love. . . . It was at this time also that he decided to forge a link between the characters of his novels. 'Pour faire concurrence à l'etat civil'; and this grandiose conception lent fresh vigour to his thought. His letters are full of confidence and enthusiasm: '*Eugénie Grandet* is a delightful work'; . . . 'it is a fine piece of work'; . . . 'it has one scene which I consider sublime'; . . . etc. The novel itself reflects these joyous stirrings of his heart.

Balzac, indeed, had good reason to be satisfied with *Eugénie*. It is a remarkable picture of provincial life in France. The Preface of 1834 shows that the author was fully aware of having struck a vast and unexplored domain. Nothing is more favourable to the maturing of passion than the light and shade of a small town; a fact well known to Balzac, who was born in Touraine, a province as charming and carefree as the river which flows through it, but whose slate roofs conceal many a family tragedy. Balzac was fascinated by the phenomena of avarice. This man, who spent money like water and was everlastingly in debt, admired Molière's *L'Avare;* he had read *Melmoth,* a gloomy novel by one Maturin, and had himself portrayed misers in *Maître Cornélius* and "*Gobseck*". It was, then, to the banks of the Loire that he turned in search of a character, and discovered at Saumur a man called Nivelleau, who had grown rich thanks to the Revolution and his own dealings in national property. Grandet owes many of his physical and moral traits to Nivelleau; though the latter's importance must not be exaggerated, for there is more to Grandet than that. Eugénie's fate, on the other hand, in no way resembles that of Nivelleau's daughter, who seems to have made a happy marriage. Balzac borrowed the story from one of his own youthful works, *Argow le Pirate*. It is based on fact, but both plot and characters owe even more to the novelist's imagination.

The geographical and social background of this work is the fruit of careful observation. The little town of Saumur is described as it then appeared, with its castle, its narrow streets, its homely dwellings, but also and above all its day-to-day existence. Balzac was thoroughly modern in outlook: the economic life of the place interested him deeply; he gives us an exact picture of the farming industry, of business methods, and of the markets, of the problems of production and distribution, and especially of all that concerns the culture of the vine, which is the chief source of wealth in this region. Thanks to him we have detailed knowledge of provincial society at the beginning of the nineteenth century. We learn that the essential and lasting effect of the Revolution has been the transfer of power to the middle classes by the sale of property which had once belonged to the nobility and clergy; and that in this respect the Restoration had 'restored' nothing. Here, as in other works, Balzac pilloried the reign of money. Listening to the Cruchots and Grassins, to the notables and shopkeepers, to their grotesque womenfolk and their stupid and selfish children, one is reminded of Daumier's caricatures, so closely is spiritual degradation allied with physical ugliness. And yet the poetry of provincial life is there also; we hear the hours tick away in that old and silent house; the saintly Madame Grandet is for ever busy with her embroidery; fat Nanon sits grumbling in her corner; Eugénie dreams vague dreams of love: Death twice enters through that ancient door, walks across the polished flagstones, and moves towards the massive wooden beds. . . . If there is something of Daumier, there is something of Vermeer also in Balzac. It is the mark of his genius that he managed with such ease to combine the unlovely with the ideal side of provincial France, and thus provide a picture which is true of the human race as a whole.

Old Grandet is far more than the merely picturesque provincial. The miser of Saumur is soon forgotten in the terrible embodiment of Avarice itself. It is true that Balzac had his predecessors, Plautus and Molière, but never before, as far as I am aware, had avarice been represented as an all-embracing passion. The comic figures of Euclion and Harpagon were at the same time feckless, vain, and amorous; what they gained in complexity of character they lost in power. Grandet, on the other hand, is a miser to the exclusion of all else. His physical make-up seems to have been shaped by his vice; even his awkward pronunciation serves his greed; his every word, his every deed, is determined by this unique obsession. He has never loved; his tardy marriage was his first business deal. He has no religious beliefs, no political convictions, no pity, no self-respect, and no ambition of any kind apart from money. He has no desire to *appear* rich; enough that he *is* so, rich for the sake of riches in themselves. If he loves his daughter Eugénie, it is because she is his heir, the future guardian of his wealth, and because he hopes that in this way his avarice will be perpetuated in her. 'Take good care of everything,' he tells her on his deathbed. 'You'll have to render me an account of it beyond.' The love of gain devours his aged body like a cancer, until at length the monster almost attains a certain grandeur. No trace of humanity is left in him; he is a beast, reduced to the mechanism of an elementary instinct. 'It warms me,' he says, caressing his gold; and his countenance takes on an expression of beatitude. At the moment of his death his eyes light up at the sight of the precious metal of the cross, and in one last spasm, he makes a horrible attempt to seize it. Such characteristics make one shudder; they are indeed Shakespearian.

Grandet, however, is not the hero of the tale, for it is not through his eyes that we see the world. There are monsters for whom in the end we feel pity and even love; but the miser inspires us with the same terror as do those sombre divinities of Greek tragedy whose blind will hovers over men. At no point do we sympathize with him; we never, so to speak, see ourselves in his place. Now, it is a fundamental law of the novel that a reader must identify himself, consciously or otherwise, with the principal hero. In this work we take Eugénie's part; the story is centred upon her, and it is understandable that Balzac used her name, not her father's, on the title-page.

Eugénie's story is that of a broken life, of a 'lost illusion,' as Balzac himself often liked to describe it. Before she loves she is a commonplace girl, almost ugly yet at the same time attractive, fading like a poor flower in the shadow of home. She is crushed by her father's despotism. Her personality never emerges until the arrival of her cousin Charles. The young man's outward gallantry conceals a fierce egotism; and her pity, called forth by his despair which is that of a frustrated child, brings forth bad fruit. But what matter! Just as a reagent enables us to observe the true nature of a body, so Charles 'reveals' Eugénie, first to herself. It is through him that her lofty soul appears.

When the young man comes on the scene, Eugénie passes suddenly from expectation to fulfilment. Something which for a long time has only waited to take shape begins to form in her. For the first time she takes the initiative, as when she buys candlesticks for her cousin or pushes the sugar-bowl towards him. Even this had required great courage; but soon the conflict with her father breaks out in all its fury, culminating in that terrible scene on New Year's day after Charles has gone, a scene of almost unbearable tension, when Eugénie has to confess that she no longer has his treasure. She fights then for her love with the same energy and the same skill as does the old man for his gold. Clearly they are of the same blood: it is a case of Grandet versus Grandet. Finally, in the casket scene, she is greater than her father. Armed with a knife, she threatens to stab herself if he touches Charles's box, and the old miser steps back; then indeed this girl ranks with the purest heroines of antiquity. It is in renunciation that Eugénie undoubtedly rises to her greatest heights, not of heroism but of sanctity. Evil and vice have triumphed all around her; Charles becomes a successful business man in Paris; Cruchet, whom she finally marries, enjoys old Grandet's millions; and in the little town of Saumur the partisans of Cruchot and those of Grassin continue to vent their

Evelina Hanska, who married Balzac in 1850.

wicked spleen. Buried away in her old home, Eugénie henceforward cares nothing for wordly success, no longer seeks earthly relief for her misery; she lives with her eyes fixed on celestial splendour. What use, the Bible asks, 'to sift the cinders of dead love'? One might say that she has lost even the memory of those few hours of worldly bliss which she enjoyed seated in the little garden. Her gaze wanders to the pure but icy realms of charity, of sacrifice, of utter self-denial. Victim both of her father and of the world, Eugénie has won salvation from heaven.

Such is the mystical lesson which Balzac tries to teach us in ***Eugénie Grandet***. It bears the stamp of Christianity, but one notices also the influence of his master Swedenborg, according to whom souls that suffer in this life win through after death and enter into glory: 'Earth is the seed-bed of heaven.' From the merely human point of view, we cannot but admire Balzac's faith in moral values. If he tends, as a realist, to show us that 'the world is vile,' he makes us hate those who have been too successful here below. This pessimistic outlook upon daily life is thus compensated and, as it were, transcended by profound spiritual optimism. In this respect Balzac differs widely from the majority of modern novelists. Of how many could it be said to-day as Victor Hugo said of the author of *Eugénie Grandet:* 'Relisons Balzac; cela fait du bien.'

Footnote, November 1955. The mysterious Maria, to whom Balzac dedicated his novel, has just been revealed to be Maria du Fresnay, a young married woman, who had proposed to Balzac: 'Love me for one year, and I will love you for the rest of my life.' She had a daughter by him, Marie (1834-1930)—a fact unknown until now. As the dedication led one to suppose, Balzac gave Eugénie the very traits of his mistress, both physical and moral; and the story itself evokes Maria's own life story. In depicting Eugénie as charming and pitiful, and Charles as a selfish dandy, Balzac may have sought to appease, by this work, his guilty conscience.

Richard Aldington (essay date 1961)

SOURCE: An introduction to *Eugénie Grandet,* by Honoré de Balzac, translated by Ellen Marriage, The Heritage Press, 1961, pp. ix-xvi.

[*Aldington is perhaps best known as the editor of the Imagist periodical the* Egoist *and as an influential member of the Imagist movement, whose other members included Hilda Doolittle—who became Aldington's first wife in 1913—Ezra Pound, and Amy Lowell. As a literary critic and biographer, he combined his skills as a poet, his sensitivity as a reader, and his personal reminiscences to produce criticism that is creative as well as informative. In the preface to the Heritage Press edition of* Eugénie Grandet, *Aldington offers a highly appreciative general essay on the work, which he deems "not only one of the very best of Balzac's vast output of fiction," but one of "the few novels which so far have survived the changes of time and fashion."*]

For once the critical experts and the reading public are in agreement—*Eugénie Grandet* is not only one of the very best of Balzac's vast output of fiction, it lives with the few novels which so far have survived the changes of time and fashion. L. J. Arrigon ends his study of Balzac in the 'romantic years' with the unqualified statement that *Eugénie Grandet* is the first in time of the 'great' Balzac novels. André Billy goes a good deal further, and says it is 'the first of the books with which he created the form of the modern novel of behaviour and character'.

Both these expert pronouncements are surprising when you recollect that Balzac had already published such varied and excellent work as *El Verdugo, The Elixir of Long Life, The Wild Ass's Skin,* "Jesus Christ in Flanders," that prophetic allegory of modern art *The Unknown Masterpiece, The Curé of Tours,* and many of the *Droll Stories.* If *Eugénie Grandet* ranks above all these, and it does, the novel was a great achievement for a still youngish man who had had terrible failures as a beginner, and was not too well thought of by contemporaries. Only a year after the publication of this masterly forerunner of the modern novel, a supercilious English lady, Mrs. Gore, announced in a book on Paris that Balzac was one of the contemporary French writers who would not be remembered.

Without fear of contradiction now we can add that *Eugénie Grandet* shows Balzac's energy and fire at their best, while it is more consistently well-written than some of his more pretentious works. It is comparatively free from those faults of pretentiousness allied with bad taste, which Aldous Huxley has fastidiously labelled Balzac's 'vulgarity'. Though the book covers a period of about fourteen years (1819 to 1833), there is no flagging, there are few of those admirable comments of the author which nevertheless delay the action, and most fortunately none of those long didactic digressions which Balzac loved and his readers have come to dread. It may be that the characters in *Eugénie Grandet* are, as some critics think, a little or even a good deal over-drawn, too much pinned down to type. And the story is scarcely original—good stories very seldom are. The girl who falls in love at first sight with the handsome stranger is as old as the *Odyssey.* Homer does not tell us what happened to Nausicaa after Odysseus departed, but Balzac spares us not one pang of the heart-breaking tale and heart-broken girl.

But is the novel wholly the story of Eugénie? True, the girl is 'on the stage' from beginning to end of the book—so are Nanon and other characters—but the origin of the book and probably its greatest interest to Balzac was her father, old Félix Grandet, the fabulous miser of Saumur. A persistent local tradition, which is probably based on fact, identified Félix Grandet with a certain Jean Nivelleau, who made a fortune during the Revolution and bought a château just outside Saumur. Starting life as a billiard-marker, Nivelleau had scraped together a little capital by making loans at heavy interest to thriftless billiards players, and ended up as a prosperous banker. Tradition has it that Nivelleau remained such a Scrooge that he always dressed shabbily, and loved to pose as one of his own servants to strangers who asked to visit his château—so that he could get their tips. Thus, it is argued, the real theme of the book is old Grandet's avarice, which destroys him and those whose fates are linked with his. Eugénie and her mother are thus simply the most unnatural and most pathetic of his many victims.

If Balzac really did start his book from Nivelleau he was only following his own custom and that of most creative writers of starting from a reality and not from an abstraction. Real persons, some of them in Balzac's closest intimacy, have been identified in close upon thirty of his books, and almost certainly there are others who cannot now be discovered.

The novel opens with a justly famous description of old Saumur, a town situated in a part of France which Balzac knew well, for much of his childhood had been spent in Touraine. It is hardly necessary to point out what an asset such intimate knowledge is to a realist. It was Balzac's good fortune as a novelist to have parents who brought him intimately into touch with the capital and with rural France, for his pretty, vivacious young mother had grown up in a comfortable Parisian home, while his father's youth had been spent under the hard conditions of a too numerous peasant family in Auvergne. Moreover, in later life Balzac spent a good deal of time with friends in Touraine and Berry, whether merely seeking quiet for his work or, more urgently, a refuge from importunate creditors. Notice, by the way, the heart-felt denunciations of creditors in *Eugénie Grandet*—Balzac knew them only too well!

This intimate knowledge, rare indeed in the Parisian author who comes down for the summer with preconceived ideas and a note-book 'to study' provincial life, is what makes *Eugénie Grandet* so exact and life-like a presentation of an old French town of the Centre. It may sound improbable to those who have visited such towns in the sunshine and gaiety of the holiday season, but it is true that for much of the year they still contain the remote, self-centred, almost dour life Balzac has pictured for us in this and other novels. That ardent Balzacien, Félicien Marceau, even claims that he was introduced to a Bonfons, and almost asked him for news of his great-aunt, Eugénie Grandet!

All these local characters noted by Balzac's curiosity are set down with extreme accuracy—the notary, the judge, the doctor, the curé, the owners of rich farms or well-known vineyards, the shopkeepers. And then there is the unforgettable sketch of the servant, Nanon, humble, underpaid, overworked, and devoted. For all her menial occupation Nanon rates as one of the family, and does not hesitate to join with the other two women in their meek opposition to the avaricious tyrant. The *confidente* was a stock figure in French comedy, a sheer convention. Balzac, perhaps first of French authors, in Nanon set down the reality, though that temperament of his led him into exaggerations. Later in the century, Gustave Flaubert challenged comparison with the Félicité of his *Un Coeur Simple,* based indeed on his mother's servant Julie, but without a doubt suggested by Balzac's Nanon, for Flaubert openly challenges comparison by taking his title from Balzac's phrase for Nanon, 'a simple heart'.

There are two thousand characters in Balzac's **Human Comedy,** and Grandet is certainly not the only miser among them. Indeed the interest of Balzac and his characters in money is notorious. He has been severely censured for it, and his admirers of course have come to his defence. They point out, quite justly, that wealth has been important since the recorded beginnings of human society, and that a serious weakness of modern fiction is the neglect of this basic fact. Even in a motion picture, they say scornfully, the hero never waits for change from his taxi-driver. Moreover, there is this to be said in Balzac's defence: The period of the Bourbon *Restauration* (1815-30) and of the Orléanist monarchy (1830-48), which covers Balzac's adult life, was one of those rare epochs in France when the public finances were in good condition and the currency stable. The inflationary urge to spend, inherited from the disorderly Revolutionary epoch, changed to the capitalist determination to possess.

Perhaps Balzac exaggerated the overwhelming importance assumed by money in the jostling for social position which followed the end of the Napoleonic adventure, but that does not invalidate his description of Grandet's cunningly intrigued rise to wealth. With a bribe of two thousand gold pieces, his wife's dowry, Grandet got hold of valuable Church property, but as mayor of Saumur he was shrewd enough to protect the property of exiled nobles, while selling his wines to the Revolutionary army. With this start Grandet simply went on making more money with the fanaticism of a monomaniac. How else was Balzac to treat the subject?

Quite true, so far as it goes, but it doesn't cover the whole difficulty. There was justification for Katherine Mansfield's dislike of Balzac's insistence on money, because she evidently felt he was not objectively recording essential if unattractive facts of life, he was gloating over this money-worship, because he too worshipped money. And that can only be understood when we come to understand Balzac's environment, life, and temperament.

And what a temperament! There was hot blood in his father's family. One of Balzac's uncles in Auvergne was guillotined in 1819 for having murdered his sweetheart, which perhaps explains why Balzac never visited his family home. A similar kind of excess and irrationality may be seen in the financial schemes and illusions of his father. One of Bernard Balzac's assertions was that he would live to be a hundred, so he put his money into a tontine, confidently telling the family he would outlive all the other subscribers and then they would be rich—two million francs. How often the boy Balzac must have listened to these fallacious dreams of wealth; for the father did not live to be a hundred, and they didn't get the money. We have another glimpse of this very materialist parent in a letter written when Honoré was earning a precarious livelihood from those early novels—all the father did was to put a good face on it by quite untrue stories of the sums Honoré was earning! Is it surprising the son had this 'obsession' with money, or that most unhappily for him he inherited from this over-confident materialist, fatal delusions about his own ability to make a fortune? The man whose love-letters are pages upon pages of financial calculations was hardly normal, and the absurdity of most of Balzac's get-rich-quick plans was only exceeded by the plausibility and ardour with which he persuaded himself and others of their validity.

With all his pretence at business ability Balzac was a spendthrift, with all a spendthrift's secret respect for the miser, and the ne'er-do-well's admiration and envy for the successful speculator. The ease with which Balzac could make all old Grandet's schemes succeed— on paper—was perhaps a compensation for his own successive disappointments. From the knowing and confident manner in which Balzac unfolds them you might suppose you were listening to an expert on the Paris Bourse. It can scarcely be denied that Balzac had the real French *bourgeois* love of money for its own sake, and that ***Eugénie Grandet*** is one of the books in which he betrays the fact.

Yet in spite of this, Balzac is always fully aware of the odious aspects of Grandet's character and his uncontrollable money-greed. It is admirably brought out in the justly celebrated scene where, with the tacit connivance of the notary who just keeps on the right side of the law, Grandet takes advantage of his daughter's ignorance to rob her of the inheritance from her mother which the law compelled him to pay her. To trick his own daughter out of money which he would inevitably be compelled to leave her in a very few years was an act both odious and characteristic of this monomania. Balzac, for all his money-worship, has neither shirked the scene nor tried to find excuses for the criminal. His sense of right and wrong remains unwarped, and there is none of that hero-worshipping of the criminal which he began with Vautrin and which Hugo continued with Jean Valjean.

It seems indisputable that Balzac means us to feel that Eugénie's tragedy is the direct result of her father's selfish, unscrupulous greed. This fiendish avarice it was which kept the girl so ignorant and lonely, and therefore so especially vulnerable to the attractions of the first good-looking young man who came into her life. It was of course not Grandet's fault that Charles was so sophisticated-shallow that he never suspected how near he was to two treasures—a good wife and a great fortune to come to and with her. Charles's passion for Eugénie is as brief and feeble as hers is strong and steady. He is certainly unworthy of her, but her father did nothing either to try to bring out any good which might be in him, or to show her before it was too late the young man's essential falsity. Grandet's energy is wholly absorbed by the news of his brother's failure, by scheming to get rid of his

obligation to Charles as cheaply as possible, and finally by cheating the now penniless orphan of his gold buttons.

Balzac risks alienating his readers from Eugénie and destroying the real pathos he has created around her by the bad taste of such remarks as: 'Before the arrival of her cousin Eugénie might be compared to the Virgin before the conception; when he went away she was like the Virgin mother—she had conceived love.' In trying to make her sound like female perfection, he comes near to making her ridiculous. And then we cannot help remembering that this transcendentally pure personage had easily overcome the scruples which suggested she ought not to read her cousin's love-letter to another woman while he was asleep. Of course, it is best that she should not be perfect, so why drag in the Virgin Mary?

These flaws do not really affect the essential pathos of the tragedy. In her dreary existence there was every excuse for Eugénie engaging herself rashly and hurriedly—such matches sometimes turn out very well— and we can but pity her as she waits, first with her dying mother, then between Nanon and her father, for Charles to return and to keep his word. He did not even send a letter. Suppose Charles had known what a fortune she was to inherit, would he not have written by every post and clamoured for answer? And on the death of Grandet would he not have returned at once, business or no business, to claim the fulfilment of her promise of marriage? Obviously; but the tragedy of being married for her money—she would be bound to find it out—by the one man she loved might have been worse than losing him.

Félicien Marceau reflects on Eugénie and her fate in these terms: 'She had found courage to show her cousin that she loved him, and courage to defy her father's rage. That is something. But her energy stopped there, she went to sleep. Eugénie allowed events to take control. Woe to her. No energy, no happiness. Balzac's law is implacable.'

It may look presumptuous for a foreigner to query the judgement of such an authority, but I must say I cannot go along with M. Marceau here. What does he think the girl could have done after Charles's departure to show her 'energy' and thereby win her 'happiness'? Charles never wrote to her, and she had no address to which she might have summoned up 'energy' to write. We are specifically told that, unknown to her, he had changed his name to Carl Sepherd so as to be freer to profit by the various more or less shady methods he found of making money. As he was wandering in different countries under an assumed name, letters addressed to a shipping agent would never have reached him. Ought she to have shown her 'energy' by fitting out an expedition to go in search of him? The suggestion is obviously ridiculous. But what else could she have done?

When at last Eugénie does have news of Charles, it is by the letter in which he announces his intention of marrying Mlle d'Aubrion, with a hypocritical pretence of keeping his engagement to Eugénie if she insists, which he knows she is far too proud to accept. Suppose she had instantly had the 'energy' to pursue him to Paris, what would she have found? That the banns of marriage between Charles and Mlle d'Aubrion were already published! She would have merely humiliated herself to no purpose.

She showed 'energy' enough in dealing with the accomplished fact, and her revenge is crushing. In his repulsive letter to his old sweetheart Charles had yielded to the Balzacien love of figures, and had told her he had now an income of eighty thousand francs (hers, though he didn't then know it, was nearly ten times as much). By marrying an aristocrat like Mlle d'Aubrion, he adds, he will achieve a title and a place at Court. And he winds up by talking about the duty we owe our children! The letter which Bonfons takes to him from Eugénie, along with the discharge of all his father's debts, contains this smashingly contemptuous sentence:

'I felt that the son of a bankrupt perhaps could not marry Mlle d'Aubrion.'

It is hard to see how she could have been more 'energetic' than that.

A last touch of Balzacien finance marks the scene where Bonfons presents the letter and the discharge of the bankrupt's two million francs of debts, and tells Charles that he is to marry Mlle Grandet—'and we shall have an income of seven hundred and fifty thousand francs'. Charles's reply is worthy of him—he at once suggests that he and Bonfons shall push each other in their respective careers.

What is there left for Eugénie? When the death of her merely legal husband releases her from this loveless, childless marriage, she inevitably goes on living her lonely celibate life in the old home, as austerely as in her father's lifetime, with the difference that she now can and does give away large sums of money to public charities. She makes the final ironic comment on her wasted life when she turns to her faithful Nanon saying: 'No one loves me but you.' The book surely should have ended there. The sixteen additional lines are an anticlimax.

Diana Festa-McCormick (essay date 1979)

SOURCE: "Productive Years," in *Honoré de Balzac,* Twayne Publishers, 1979, pp. 41-55.

[*In the excerpt below, Festa-McCormick examines those elements that make* Eugénie Grandet *"one of the classics of world fiction," focusing especially upon Balzac's depiction of the miser Grandet. The critic concludes by exploring the mystery of the identity of the "Maria" to whom Balzac dedicated the novel.*]

A Modern Tragedy in Bourgeois Setting:

Eugénie Grandet

Eugénie Grandet ranks among the classics of universal fiction, almost on a par with *Madame Bovary*—less ambitious, but equally well constructed, with restraint and poetic dimension. Here too, beyond the life, passions, and tragedy of two or three individuals, a whole town comes to the fore with its customs, prejudices, limitations, and aspirations. In some respects—its economy of means, simplicity, its eschewing of melodramatic or extraneous elements and its unity of tone—it is the most "Classical" of Balzac's novels. It is even endowed with that "passionate monotony" which Albert Camus praised as the supreme virtue of classical works. Unlike *Le Médecin de Campagne* and *Louis Lambert,* with which it is contemporary, it proposes no political creed and no philosophical message. It stands also far removed from the ethereal and disembodied creatures of *Séraphita* and from the lavish poetry of flowers and desire of *Le Lys dans la Vallée,* also of this period. It reserves to the reader none of the thrills and melodramatic revelations of **"Ferragus"** or of *Père Goriot*. That the same novelist was able to compose, within two or three years, seven or more novels so profoundly different remains a source of astonishment for posterity. Not even Shakespeare, Lope de Vega, Corneille, or Dostoevsky (who translated *Eugénie Grandet* at the beginning of his career) evinced such diversity or took so many risks.

The sparseness of events, the rigid unity of place, and the very small number of actors of that bourgeois drama make the novel one of the most austere in the whole range of French literature. Balzac refrained from adding any outward charm to his story through conjuring up the beauty of his beloved Touraine (where the novel is set) or the allurements of seductive women. Eugénie herself, despite her name ("the well born"), is hardly the graceful, coquettish, and feminine person one might expect. Her features have something masculine about them, and she has the round face and solid health of a country girl. Balzac held that the destiny of women is to give a great deal of themselves through marriage and maternity. When this kind of fulfillment is denied them, they are likely to lapse into either masculinity or pettiness, or possibly into pious resignation. Eugénie belongs to the latter group.

There is nothing autobiographical about this novel, which takes place in one house, in one small and sleepy city, even more provincially dormant than Tours (of *Le Curé de Tours*), limited to its constricted scene of clerical life, or than Vendôme where Louis Lambert had spent his dismal adolescence. Nevertheless, Balzac must have transposed into the unhappy and repressed heroine the vision of what he himself—as a meditative and solitary boy—might have remained, had he not been endowed with enough will and ambition to rebel against environment. Balzacians have never ceased to wonder how and when the author could have observed the limited focus of a country family and the aspirations of provincial life. Balzac lived mostly at night and in a very restricted circle, hardly ever visited modest families or workmen's quarters, seldom could notice country people while racing across France to some love rendezvous or to a rash business enterprise. His psychological discernment of individuals and situations came more from intuitive divinations, than from long and meditative observations, we must conclude.

Balzac ascribed to himself a gift of imaginative and passionate understanding of the real that not only went further and deeper than all prosaic observations, but was also more precise in its rendering of details. As early as July 1825, he had defined his gift in a revealing letter to Mme D'Abrantès: "Chance throws into the soul of those who intend to depict all the affections and the human heart all those very affections, so that they may, through the strength of their imagination, experience what they portray," he wrote. "Observation might, for them, be a sort of memory, fitted to assist that mobile imagination." To his all-encompassing imagination the novelist owed the gift of malleability, even of sympathy, which enabled him to understand, to interpret "from within" and even temporarily to become characters as different from himself as Grandet or the dull provincial dignitaries visiting the Grandet household. It was for him a kind of participation in their card games; the monotony of shuffling and eyeing each other in the spectral kitchen became his, and so did the speculations on Eugénie's eventual inheritance.

Flaubert or Proust would probably have satirized those Philistines and scathingly brought laughter on those pretentious middle-class cousins of Charles Bovary, M. Homais or Legrandin. Balzac was to reserve that kind of satire for *La vielle Fille,* but here his detached portrayal of provincial life anticipates Dostoevsky and Mauriac. He realized what silent tragedies were lived by those small-town wives and daughters, having to yawn their empty existence in a glass house, spied upon by neighbors, tradesmen, pious spinsters, their most harmless gestures perpetually under suspicion. Only two ways were open to them: either revolt or resignation. Mme Grandet, like Mme Claes, chooses mournful resignation, pines away, and dies. In those days of female subjection to the law established by and for males, of conspiracy between the law and the

Church, and of total deprivation of education for most women of the lower and middle classes, the only escape for ill-wedded spouses was adultery. Balzac portrayed it often, and with a degree of sympathy, leaving the husbands unflattered and unsympathetic. But such an extreme solution hardly lay within the reach of Mme Grandet or her daughter, both cooped up in the prison house of a tyrannical miser.

A Monomaniac Miser

Grandet is monomaniacally possessed by his own urge to possess, incapable of compassion and of generosity. His career as related by the novelist affords some insight into the social history of France during the early years of the nineteenth century. He had shrewdly acquired church property put up for sale during the revolution, extensive vineyards, several farms and meadows. He was driven by that same urge to grab land often ascribed to the French peasantry. A former cooper and vintner himself, pretending to be dumb and naïve, affecting to stutter when striking a shrewd bargain, hampered by no scruple about duping his competitors in the wine trade, he had piled up an immense fortune.

Grandet's single passion is a typically Balzacian obsession. Maître Cornélius, Gobseck, Facino Cane, are also infected with the same fever of money, and so are many Parisians—as is shown in the colorful developments of *La Fille aux Yeux d'Or* and *Père Goriot*. Grandet trusts only his old, fanatically devoted servant, Nanon. With her, at night, in lurid scenes worthy of paintings from the Dutch school or Georges de La Tour's gloomy chiaroscuro, he gazes at his gold coins, he counts and weighs them over and over again, he caresses them as a lover might a cherished mistress. He is a millionaire but insists upon the household being run on the most niggardly principles. Outside his perpetual reckonings of eventual profits, we do not enter into his inner life—a poor one indeed, we must assume, in a man whose existence is so fully identified with his thirst for money. His portrait assumes psychological depth through action only, more in keeping with theatrical than novelistic traditions. We see his stern looks and harsh movements, we hear his dreaded knock at the door of his own house and his heavy step on the crumbling staircase. Systematically, he terrifies his timorous wife and his daughter and cows them into blind obedience. He forces upon them renouncement of all claims to his immense wealth.

The wretched and monotonous life of the Grandets would have flowed on into oblivion but for the sudden irruption upon the scene, as in a classical tragedy, of an outsider who will act as the catalyst. Charles arrives, the son of a brother of Grandet who had migrated to Paris and attempted to make a fortune there through speculation. Bankrupt, driven to dishonor and suicide, he sent his son to the uncle in the provinces, hoping that he might, from there, find passage to the East Indies and exchange his idle existence of a Parisian roué for one of trader in remote lands. The entrance of Charles is for Eugénie like the lifting of a curtain upon an undreamed of world. An inner revolution takes place in her as she watches the eyes of the handsome dandy fill with mild contempt for the dull provincial life she had until then never questioned. Hesitantly, she ventures upon a new road: her tender and sly attempts to wrench a little flour, a pat of butter, and three or four lumps of sugar from the larder where her stingy father hides and counts everything, bring the gentle girl for the first time in opposition to her father's will. Grandet has not one ounce of pity for his departed brother. Settling the debts will be for him an opportunity to cheat the creditors and make more money. The old miser, ruthlessly punishing Eugénie for having given her own gold coins to her cousin, allows his wife to die from grief and neglect. He grudges the money spent on doctors and medicine, and allows his mania to destroy the unity of the family. Grandet could have assumed tragic dimension, but his lust for money remains unrelieved by any doubt to the very end. His ferocious passion is not mitigated by the comic touches that make Volpone or Harpagon almost endearing by comparison. Inaccessible to repentance, he is more obdurate and inhuman than Mauriac's vengeful old man in *Viper's Tangle*.

Eugénie and Charles had exchanged vows of love when the cousin departs. In Java, he trades trinkets, merchandise, sells slaves, makes a fortune on his own, but never once writes a line to the forgotten miser's daughter. She pines away in languor and idle dreams. Her father has gradually crushed in her all initiative and reduced her to insignificance. He dies, in one of the most striking scenes of death in Balzac's fiction. Charles, once his father's creditors are paid, marries into a wily aristocratic family, which provides him with a title. Eugénie, the forsaken woman now resigned to her aimless existence, has contributed the funds. She enters into a loveless marriage to obey her confessor, but is soon left a widow with nothing but "death in life" from now on. Thus ends that "bourgeois tragedy, with no poison, no dagger, no shedding of blood," as Balzac characterized it, with infinite pity far outweighing the terror of Grandet's possessive urge.

The Mystery of the Real Eugénie

There dwells a mystery still in that novel which appears to be so smooth, so direct in its monotonous and inevitable progression and devoid of surprising peripeteiae. Eugénie, like her father, is a generality, a type, and almost an archetype. She has several sisters in Balzac's gallery of heroines, one of them being the equally submissive, resigned daughter of the former convict Ferragus. Her creator, on one of those peremp-

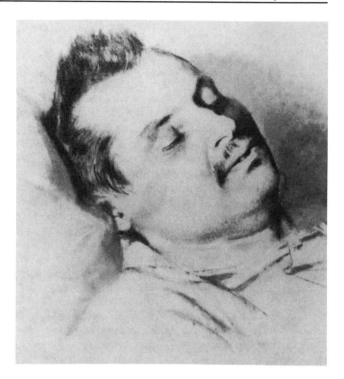

Drawing done by Eugène Giraud of Balzac several hours after his death. Besançon (France), Musée des Beaux-Arts et d'Archéologie; Cliché Ch. Choffet (Besançon)

tory aphorisms that he liked to coin, had declared about that family of female spirits that "the feminine souls powerful enough to place the infinite in love constitute angelic exceptions: they are, among women, what the finest geniuses are among men." If Eugénie embodies one facet of Balzac's feminine ideal, there is about her physical type and her behavior an air of reality which has long impressed attentive readers. The author built her with particular attention and a tender care seldom accorded his other creations, even those who outweigh her in interest. The dedication of the book "To Maria, . . you whose portrait is the fairest adornment of this work," was long a puzzle. The name "Maria" was poetically compared to a twig of the blessed boxwood "consecrated by religion, always kept fresh and green by pious hands to protect the house."

Mme Hanska's first name was not Maria, and it was not to her that the novel was dedicated. It took the obstinate curiosity and the detective flair of two Balzacian scholars, André Chancerel and Roger Pierrot, to unravel the mystery. In 1930, there died in Nice, at ninety-six years of age, a certain Marie du Fresnay, who had been born in 1834. To her, in his will, the novelist had bequeathed one of his most prized artistic treasures, his "Christ" by Girardon. The nephew of that lady recalled how his aunt spoke of that bequest and of the novelist himself, who had attended her first communion. Balzac had apparently visited Marie du Fresnay's family repeatedly and had often spoken to the child she then was.

The two scholars became gradually convinced that that child, Maria, was the eldest daughter of Maria Daminois, born in 1809 and dead in 1892. In 1829 she had married Guy du Fresnay. In a letter dated October 12, 1833, to his sister Laure, Balzac, all aglow with his conquest of "l'Etrangère," also confided to his sister that he "was a father," and by the most adorable person, "the most naïve of creatures, dropping from heaven like a flower, who comes to my room secretly, demands neither correspondence nor attention, and who tells me, 'love me one year, I shall love you all my life.'" Obviously in October 1833 Balzac was not yet quite a father. He had only just learned that his kindly and devoted visitor was one month pregnant: the child was born on June 4, 1834, eight months after the enraptured letter. But Balzac's imagination always anticipated events. The child he procreated was, her nephew recalled, not particularly graceful or feminine. She resembled her mother, tall and, as an ungallant French adjective expresses it, "hommasse"—somewhat male looking. So indeed is Eugénie in the novel, with "a big head, a masculine forehead . . . a round face marked with traces of smallpox," much resembling in all details Balzac's daughter Maria.

The manuscript of the novel, now in the Morgan Library in New York, was nevertheless offered by the author to Mme Hanska. The model for Eugénie probably never knew it. In August 1836, *Séraphita* was publicly dedicated to the Countess who, thirteen years later, was at last to become his wife.

Alexander Fischler (essay date 1989)

SOURCE: "Eugénie Grandet's Career as Heavenly Exile," in *Essays in Literature*, Vol. XVI, No. 2, Fall 1989, pp. 271-80.

[*In the following essay, Fischler examines Balzac's depiction of Eugénie as an exile from the heavenly realm.*]

Balzac liked to suggest to his readers that some of the exceptional men and women of *La Comédie humaine* were exiles, more suited for a realm where categories and gradation are irrelevant than for cramped quarters "ici-bas." The argument was a romantic commonplace. He was able to vitalize it, however, by adding consistently a very literal dimension to exile as metaphor, by suggesting, as he did in *Eugénie Grandet,* that removal from one's habitual environment or sphere of influence is a reality whose effects can be observed, or by arguing, as he did in some of the *Etudes philosophiques,* that the sense of separation from an extraterrestrial sphere is a significant response to a cosmic order perceived by faith and described by theologians and mystics. As illustrated by Eugénie Grandet's career, the assertion that a protagonist is an exile

not only provided a pretext for a close look at the place of confinement, but allowed careful distinctions between types and degrees of removal.

Though he used the twin themes of confinement and exile to structure *Eugénie Grandet* from the start, Balzac had some difficulty in positioning his heroine so as to insure that her home, at the top of the "ancienne Grand-Rue," be seen in perspective with a heavenly abode. Part of the positioning problem was due to the author's desire to suggest a very special affinity between the heroine and two of his mistresses, Mme Hanska and Maria du Fresnay. Most of it, however, can be shown to have resulted from concern that Eugénie's necessarily limited perception precluded a sense of exile and from the fact that Balzac realized, as evidenced by his revisions, that an ambiguous connection with the world around ultimately served her characterization better than exile from the world beyond.

The novel was written and published in 1833. In the Edition Béchet, which appeared after serial publication the same year but was dated 1834, it was the first of the *Scènes de la vie de province* and was allegedly intended to illustrate the fact that great values (material as well as moral) are to be found in the provinces, far from the madding crowds of Paris. The *Tourangeau,* Balzac, was obviously delighted to confront the connoisseurs of value of both realms and to demonstrate from the start that myopia prevails among them. Here was also an opportunity to show that social exile is a condition both assumed and imposed: while Charles, decked out in finery carefully chosen to dazzle his hosts, is compared by the author to a peacock plummetted into an obscure chicken yard, the *Provinciaux,* united for once in their distaste for fashion and their distrust of the *Parisiens,* scrutinize him mockingly as if he were an exotic giraffe (1058). But the impressions of another observer, the innocent Eugénie, are recorded as well: for her, the young man is a seraph come down from heaven, a phoenix among cousins. Charles himself is uneasy in the new setting. By the end of the evening, as he sets out to ascend with the rest of the household, the stairwell does indeed look to him like a chicken roost.

Thus, as exile fosters the defensive responses of contempt and conceit, confinement is shown to foster the naïve worship of a creature who, being more attuned to heaven than to earth, sublimates what she sees. This naïve response of the innocent is what Balzac chose to set at the heart of his novel, for through Eugénie, appearing as an exile from an extraterrestrial sphere, he could invoke an ultimate metaphysical scale to evaluate action whose course would otherwise seem determined by worldly considerations alone.

The Grandet household is presented as a cloistered realm within a provincial world insulated in time from modern reality. Twice removed from common affairs and ruled by its own tyrannical and earth-bound god, "le Dieu Argent," the money god, the Maison Grandet could easily become a testing ground, a station on the way to a higher reality in a spiritual realm. Certainly the three women in the house were to appear in transit, accepting their grim lot on earth while praying for happiness beyond.

Dealing with the generally submissive and retiring Eugénie, Balzac showed that true character would not emerge out of sheer contrast with those who surround her. Hence he compared her repeatedly to the Virgin Mary and then drew freely on the many roles the comparison suggested. With much less effect on characterization, he also compared her to a noble statue, specifically the Venus of Milo, to Penelope, Faust's Marguerite, a linnet, a rare bird, the pure lamb with a golden fleece, and the prey of the pack. In early editions of the novel the author involved himself openly and extensively in the presentation of his Virgin and assumed for this purpose the two complementary roles of artist-creator and worshiper of woman perfected in Mary. The presentation was thus quite formal and clumsy, relying both on the text of the novel and on an external framework which consisted of a "Préambule" and "Epilogue" (deleted after 1843) to which a dedication, "A Maria," was added in the Edition Charpentier of 1839.

The fact that the central character was to be viewed as an exile from a higher sphere was established in the preamble of the early editions. After defending his choice of seemingly plain subjects set against a country background, the author calls attention to the moralities ("mythes" in the manuscript) that can be found in country traditions:

> . . . aujourd'hui le pauvre artiste n'a saisi qu'un de ces fils blancs promenés dans les airs par la brise, et dont s'amusent les enfants, les jeunes filles, les poètes; dont les savants ne se soucient guère; mais que, dit-on, laisse tomber, de sa quenouille, une céleste fileuse. Prenez garde! Il y a des *moralités* dans cette tradition champêtre! Aussi l'auteur en fait-il son épigraphe. Il vous montrera comment, durant la belle saison de la vie, certaines illusions, de blanches espérances, des fils argentés descendent des cieux et y retournent sans avoir touché terre.

> [. . . today, the poor artist caught only one of these white strands that wander with the breeze, playthings for children, young maidens and poets, which concern not the learned, but which, according to rumor, are dropped from the distaff of a heavenly spinner. Take heed! *Moralities* may be found in this folk tradition. As a result, the author takes it for his epigraph. He will show you how, during life's beautiful season, certain illusions, white hopes, silvery threads descend from heaven and return there without having touched ground.]

Gossamer, in French, is "fil de la Vierge," the Virgin's thread. The folk tradition, which assigns to it a divine origin and a heavenly destination, suggests that one does not pluck it out of the air in vain. Eugénie, we thus learn, is a temporary exile from heaven, drifting untainted through the world and recalling, as the text will tell us repeatedly, a model above.

The epilogue fulfills the promise of the preamble and brings together the Marian strands, relating the portrait drawn in the book to those offered by earlier artists in tribute to the Virgin. The author expresses proper humility in his task (in the manuscript he even slights himself by comparison with the great Madonna painters, asserting he is not one of them, "ni Raphaël, ni Rembrandt, ni Poussin"):

> Peut-être a-t-il trop chargé d'or le contour de la tête de sa Maria; peut-être n'a-t-il pas distribué la lumière suivant les règles de l'art; enfin, peut-être a-t-il trop rembruni les teintes déjà noires de son vieillard, image toute matérielle. Mais ne refusez pas votre indulgence au moine patient, vivant au fond de sa cellule, humble adorateur de la *Rosa mundi,* de Marie, belle image de tout le sexe, la femme du moine, la seconde Eva des chrétiens.

> [Perhaps he surrounded the head of his Maria with too much gold; failed to distribute light according to the rules of art; or drew too darkly his already dark old man, a wholly material image. Still, do not refuse your indulgence to the patient monk who lives in the depth of his cell, a humble worshiper of the *Rosa mundi,* of Mary, fair image of the entire sex, the monk's spouse, the Christian's second Eve.]

The manuscript ended with an assertion of Eugénie's celestial nature; in the published version of the epilogue, however, she is compared instead with a noble statue taken from Greece that falls into the sea in mid-passage and remains forever unknown. Comparison with Mary did not necessarily always support Balzac's argument; when he revised the text for publication, he chose the image of lost treasure in preference to the image of celestial exile, thus stressing in the end, as he had done in the beginning, the theme of the beauty that fades unseen, a more earth-bound cliché. The revisions shift emphasis from celestial origins and destiny to terrestrial confinement.

The third and last item, added to the novel's external frame in 1839, was the dedication "A Maria." Originally it complemented the preamble and epilogue, dedicating the work to woman epitomized in the Virgin Mary and drawing attention to the presentation of Eugénie as exile from heaven. Four years later, when Balzac revised his works again in preparation for the 1843 Edition Furne, he minimized his interpretative involvement and retained only this dedication from the cumbersome external frame of the novel. As a result, despite obviously religious overtones in its wording, the dedication no longer seemed to invoke the Virgin as model for Eugénie, but to address itself to a contemporary:

A Maria

Que votre nom, vous dont le portrait est le plus bel ornement de cet ouvrage, soit ici comme une brache de buis bénit, prise on ne sait à quel arbre, mais certainement sanctifiée par la religion et renouvelée, toujours verte, par des mains pieuses, pour protéger la maison.

De Balzac.

[To Maria

May your name, you whose portrait is the most beautiful ornament of this work, be here like a blessed branch of boxwood, taken from one knows not which tree, but certainly sanctified by religion and always green, renewed by pious hands, to protect the house.

De Balzac.]

The contemporary Maria, we now know, was Maria Du Fresnay, née Daminois, Balzac's mistress, whose daughter, Marie, born in 1834, he recognized as his own. André Chancerel and Roger Pierrot, who are responsible for the identification, argued that Maria du Fresnay was the actual model for Eugénie. More recent editors, however, doubt the possibility of such identification. They also point out that in the dedication, the preamble and the epilogue, Balzac not only offered a tribute to Maria Du Fresnay and "the entire [fair] sex," but also to Mme Hanska whom he gave the manuscript as a Christmas present. The holy branch, he could argue, was the boxwood over her portrait, and the conventional Maria-Eva association was, as she knew, one of his favorites. Interestingly enough, however, in a letter dated October 12, 1833 (i.e., while still working on the novel), Balzac announces to his sister, Laure, that he has fathered a child and describes Maria Du Fresnay in terms that recall Eugénie and gossamer from the distaff of the Virgin: "une gentille personne, la plus naïve créature qui soit, tombée comme une fleur du ciel" [a gentle person, the most naive of creatures, come down from heaven like a flower].

Balzac allowed himself considerable margin when he said in his 1839 dedication that the branch, "taken one knows not from what tree," was renewable; in settling details of the novel's framing text, he could settle domestic accounts as well. Nonetheless, the Madonna worship and the discussion in the epilogue of woman's place in the creation nearer to the angel than man represented genuine concerns going far beyond the little games he might have been playing with his mistresses.

Association with the Virgin Mary was his most expedient device for indicating the superiority of a female protagonist on the grounds of heavenly affinities. As a matter of fact, the manuscript variants indicate that during the composition of the novel Balzac was so taken with this device that he even allowed Charles Grandet to join in the Mary cult midway through the farewell letter to his Parisian mistress, Annette:

Tu auras du moins embelli ma belle jeunesse, orné mon âme des nobles délicatesses de la femme, je ne pourrai jamais voir les madones de Raphaël sans penser à toi qui as coloré ma seconde enfance des feux de ton visage céleste, qui as sanctifié par ton amour la vie désordonnée à laquelle les jeunes gens se livrent, qui as ennobli les passions mauvaises de ton amant en jettant tes douces voluptés dans mon âme. Si je suis bon, si je vaux quelque chose, c'est par toi.

[You will at least have embellished my beautiful youth, adorned my soul with woman's noble delicacies; I will never be able to look at Raphael's madonnas without recalling you who lent hue to my second childhood with the flames of your heavenly face, who hallowed with love the unruly life that the young espouse, who made noble a lover's foul passions by filling my soul with your exquisite delight. If I am good, if I am worth anything, it is through you.]

These lines to Annette, however, detracted from the theme of celestial virtue in the country and gave Charles a sensitivity that was in direct opposition to the aridity Balzac wanted him to represent. So he changed the text to eliminate this *Ave Annette* and, in the same revision, introduced into the letter a hint at the possibility of marriage between Charles and Eugénie and followed it with a comment on the coldness of tone manifest in the writing: the naive country girl who reads the letter is unaware of this coldness, but the author marks it as a characteristic of the spoiled, big-city child. Such revisions indicate Balzac's growing awareness of the scale he had adopted by comparing Eugénie to the Virgin—in the final version, only she was to be allowed a hallowing love: "La candeur d'Eugénie avait momentanément sanctifié l'amour de Charles" [The guilelessness of Eugénie had momentarily sanctified the love of Charles]. Associations with the Madonna were much better suited for her, and, if there were to be extensions to the other virtuous women in the novel, Balzac could handle them just as effectively by reference to feminine angelism and to physical manifestations of the soul's transcendence (notably, in the transfiguration of Mme Grandet before her death). There is only one exception to the rule, an early reference to Nanon, "plus chaste que ne l'était la Vierge Marie elle-même" [more chaste than the Virgin Mary herself].

Despite her many virtues, however, Nanon is no exile from heaven. What distinguishes her, as the last line of the novel tells us, is that she does not have wits enough to understand the corruption of the world. Eugénie, on the other hand, overcomes her initial naïveté, learns to assess those about her at their worth, and follows her confessor's advice by coming to terms with the world, albeit uneasily. Her heavenly antecedents and destiny, which may have been clichés at the outset, allow evaluation of her career in the world and explain the nature of her compromise with it, notably in her insistence on remaining a virgin.

Balzac's attempt to insure a metaphysical perspective for his heroine is well illustrated in the famous portrait of Eugénie *à sa toilette,* offered early in the novel. This scene, set against the melancholy background of the garden on the morning after Charles's arrival, provided an excuse for a detailed physical description enhanced by the author's own estimate of her beauty and some suggestive analogies. Viewing herself in the mirror after discovering the "mystérieuses beautés particulières aux endroits solitaires ou à la nature inculte" [the mysterious beauties that are particular to solitary places or untamed nature] which had hitherto seemed ordinary to her, Eugénie concludes that she is unworthy of her cousin. But the author, claiming she is unfair to herself, compares her to the recently discovered Venus of Milo, adding that her beauty is actually "ennoblie par cette suavité du sentiment chrétien qui purifie la femme et lui donne une distinction inconnue aux sculpteurs anciens" [ennobled by that softness of Christian sentiment which purifies woman and gives her a distinction unknown to ancient sculptors]. Such a description supports the theme of the hidden grandeur and offers a parallel to the lost statue at the end of the epilogue. The associations may appear incongruous when we read the description of the rather homely Eugénie which follows immediately, but Balzac was evidently serious: almost in the same breath he went on to compare his heroine's broad forehead with that of the Jupiter of Phidias.

We are told by Pierrot and Chancerel that consideration of the model, Maria du Fresnay, might have been involved here. But, more important, we have evidence of Balzac's desire to anchor Eugénie in more than one world: she must represent enduring beauty, celestial beauty in particular, yet remain of this world, and the reference to slight blemishes in her physical makeup, such as the smallpox which ruined her complexion, achieved the secularization and convey the fact of exile. Balzac adds:

> Le peintre qui cherche ici-bas un type à la céleste pureté de Marie, qui demande à toute la nature ces yeux modestement fiers devinés par Raphaël, ces lignes vierges souvent dûes au hasards de la conception mais qu'une vie chrétienne et pudique

peut seule conserver ou faire acquérir; ce peintre, amoureux d'un si rare modèle, eût trouvé tout à coup dans le visage d'Eugénie la noblesse innée qui s'ignore; il eût vu sous un front calme un monde d'amour; et dans la coupe des yeux, dans l'habitude des paupières, le je ne sais quoi divin.

[The painter who seeks in this world a type for the celestial purity of Mary and asks throughout nature for those modestly proud eyes that Raphael knew, for those virgin lines that may often be due to chance at conception but that are preserved or acquired only by means of a chaste, Christian life; such a painter, enamored of so rare a model, would have discovered on Eugénie's face nobility that is innate but unaware of itself; he would have seen a world of love under a peaceful brow and discovered the divine *je ne sais quoi* in the shape of the eyes, the form of the lids.]

Before dismissing sublimation of Eugénie on the grounds that it catered to the worst of contemporary taste, it is useful to note that hackneyed analogies in this novel, as shown by Ruth Amossy and Elisheva Rosen in *Les Discours du cliché,* far from being reassuring, call attention to departure from convention and result in a multi-layered narrative structure. Amossy and Rosen examine, for instance, the repeated conventional references to birds and show how they allow systematic juxtaposition of aerial and terrestrial, of aspiration and reality, and suggest in the end a heroine who is "un oiseau qui n'aura guère eu l'occasion de déployer son vol" [a bird who will never have had a chance to soar]. They conclude: "la logique du mélodrame se trouve battue en brèche tout au long d'une intrigue qui ne feint de s'y soumettre que pour mieux la démystifier—comme en témoigne un dénouement férocement ironique où sombre toute possibilité de *happy end*" [the logic of melodrama is upset throughout a narrative which pretends to conform to it only to undermine it the better—witness a ferociously ironic dénouement where every chance of a happy ending is lost]. Amossy and Rosen feel that the conventional association of Eugénie with the Virgin is intended primarily to show her as a model of feminine virtue. However, if one considers the association as a means of insuring that the heroine has an ultimate stage beyond the terrestrial, where the irony of situation and the irony of fate do not apply, then a happy ending is in fact indicated. There is actually no good reason to read irony into Balzac's conclusion that "Eugénie marche au ciel accompagnée d'un cortège de bienfaits." [Eugénie strides toward heaven accompanied by a procession of good deeds.]

Although he used her indeed as a model of feminine virtue, Balzac wanted to evoke more than purity by associating his heroine with Mary. Until her brief confrontation with Grandet and afterwards, she is also, like the Virgin, a model of submissiveness and obedience, and long before suffering elevates her, she serves as guiding spirit. Balzac even suggested that her love for Charles brings her a fulfillment that lasts long after his departure. Instead of contaminating her, love consecrates her:

> Avant la venue de son cousin, Eugénie pouvait être comparée à la Vierge avant la conception; quand il fut parti elle ressemblait à la Vierge mère: elle avait conçu l'amour. Ces deux Maries, si différentes et si bien représentées par quelques peintres espagnols constituent l'une des plus brillantes figures qui abondent dans le christianisme.

> [Before the arrival of her cousin, Eugénie could be compared to the Virgin before conception; once he had left, she resembled the Virgin Mother: she had conceived love. These two Marys, so different and so well represented by some Spanish painters, constitute one of the most brilliant figures that abound in Christianity.]

Eugénie follows her lover on a map and communicates with him via the lovers' star of which Charles had taught her the beauty and the uses. She can continue in her main role since Christianity had substituted Mary for Venus and made the lovers' star into the *stella matutina* or the *maris stella* which guides to the port of heaven. We learn considerably later that during the first voyage she had indeed accompanied him "comme cette image de la Vierge que mettent sur leur vaisseau les marins espagnols" [like the image of the Virgin which Spanish sailors use to decorate their ship].

Did Balzac realize that Eugénie's association with Mary would, in the end, assume an ironic edge? Clearly she finds no real fulfillment, and her insistence on being allowed to retain her virginity as precondition for interaction with the world only underscores the contrast between her sterile lot and that of the Madonna. All her charity does not compensate for the fact that in the preservation of her purity she mostly recalls her father, the hoarder. Balzac, who had noted the manner in which gold was reflected even in the physiognomy of his miser, notes in his final portrait of Eugénie that wealth came to her at the expense of warmth: "L'argent devait communiquer ses teintes froides à cette vie céleste, et donner de la défiance pour les sentiments à une femme qui était tout sentiment." [Money was to communicate its cold tints to this heavenly life and make emotions seem suspect to a woman who was all emotion.] Her selflessness may contrast with the selfishness that motivates the world around her, but her purity has worrisome implications betrayed by her appearance.

Balzac knew that purity was so far out of place in the world that it might justifiably seem unnatural: in *La Cousine Bette* he would eventually explore even its monstrous side, like Racine in *Phèdre*. But in the case of Eugénie, he chose merely to concentrate on the manner in which whiteness contrasts with surrounding gold and grey, the colors most notably associated with her father. She remains pure to the end: "Son visage est blanc, reposé, calme. Sa voix est douce et recueillie, ses manières sont simples. Elle a toutes les noblesses de la douleur, la sainteté d'une personne qui n'a pas souillé son âme au contact du monde [ms. qui n'a pas vécu], mais aussi la roideur de la vieille fille et les habitudes mesquines que donne l'existence étroite de la province." [Her face is white, rested, calm. Her voice is soft, composed, her manner is simple. She has all the nobility of suffering, the saintliness of a person who has not soiled her soul through contact with the world (ms. who has not lived), but also the stiffness of the old maid and the petty mannerisms that come with the restrictions of provincial existence.]

Philippe Bertault has noted that Balzac was subject to the common confusion of the Immaculate Conception of Mary with the Virgin Birth. This is not the case in *Eugénie Grandet,* whose heroine is to appear immaculately conceived, that is, free from the taint of original sin, and whose name, Eugénie, the well-born, suggests this explicitly. Association with gossamer from Mary's distaff remains fundamental in her presentation even after the metaphor itself disappeared with the deletion of the preamble and epilogue; summarized on the last page of the novel, her story is "l'histoire de cette femme qui n'est pas du monde au milieu du monde" [the story of a woman who is in the world though not of the world]. But one finds here, as one does throughout the *Comédie humaine,* from *La Peau de Chagrin* to *La Cousine Bette,* that Balzac wants his reader to view characters who have made a conscious decision to remain intact in the world with a sense of awe, that is, with a mixture of admiration and fear.

Bertault documents Balzac's particular interest in virginity as a form of strength or, more precisely, as conserved energy; he cites the discussion of virginity in *La Cousine Bette* which concludes: "cette grandiose et terrible exception mérite tous les honneurs que lui décerne l'Eglise catholique" [this grandiose and terrible exception deserves all the honors it is granted by the Catholic church]. Peter W. Lock in his study of Balzac's hoarders and spendthrifts, describes the virgin's place among the hoarders and cites the same passage as well as another a few lines earlier in the text: "La vie, dont les forces sont économisées, a pris chez l'individu vierge une qualité de résistance et de durée incalculable." [Life, whose energy is spared, assumes in the virginal individual an incalculable quality of resistance and duration.] Eugénie's virginity suits her both symbolically and physically to become first a match and foil for Grandet and, eventually, a successor. At the same time, however, considered from the point of view of Balzacian hygiene and morality, her virginity and chastity explain also the ironic situation in which we last see her in the novel; for what conserves Eugénie among the living prolongs also her terrestrial exile and underlines the sense of waste which is increasingly associated with her. In the end, she has not only assumed her father's miserly ways and given ground to evil rumor, to the *médisants* who claim she is turning yellow, but, "faite pour être magnifiquement épouse et mère" [created to be mother and spouse magnificently], she has become an embodiment of wasted vitality and thwarted fruition, justifying the priest's assertion that in denying life she might be guilty of lack of charity. It is interesting to note that the rumor about Eugénie's "yellowing" and the author's expression of a sense of waste, not included in the manuscript, were added in the first edition. Thus, very early, Balzac turned Eugénie's survival into an irony of fate: not only at the expense of the scheming Cruchot de Bonfons, but at her own expense. At best, survival is for her the fulfillment of a religious obligation. Assumption into heaven is indeed to be hoped for her.

The external framework through which Balzac offered his identification of Eugénie with Mary had become cumbersome by the time he was preparing the 1843 Edition Furne. By then, Balzac had also decided to rely within the novel on the more complex and ambiguous aspects of Eugénie's virginity which—instead of bringing out the "je ne sais quoi divin" in her eyes or her heavenly affinities—served to explain the strength of her character and the tragic element in her fate, the sense of waste. It is indeed possible to argue that he was insuring a more complex characterization when, with the 1843 edition, he eliminated the preamble and epilogue, in which he had insisted on comparing the presentation of his heroine with myth-making (in the manuscript) or with illumination and madonna painting. For in the epilogue, even as he apologized for gliding Eugénie's halo excessively, he was still stressing her heavenly nature. In the preamble, on the other hand, in the Félix Davin preface to the **Etudes de moeurs** (1835), and in the novel itself, he had insisted on a secular design, proving that the ordinary and the seemingly trivial were fit subjects for serious dramatization. By 1843 Balzac found that an excessively Christian emphasis not only detracted from the secular design but could preclude tragedy altogether. Preamble and epilogue were thus dismissed, but the readers' reactions were not much affected.

Balzac became annoyed with the preeminence the public gave this novel among his works. It continues to rank among the most popular, and the reasons have not improved: readers still place Grandet at the center of the story and, ignoring all of Balzac's careful juxtapositions, single Eugénie out for worship. Unfortunately, the pure and saintly Eugénie is doomed to seem less and less tolerable to modern readers unless they can be made to realize that Balzac himself demurred at her canonization and exile in the novel, that he allowed for ambiguity in his final estimate of her position on earth, and that in his design for the novel she represented only one limited touchstone for the reality of Saumur.

FURTHER READING

Criticism

Crawford, Marion Ayton, author of introduction to *Eugénie Grandet,* by Honoré de Balzac, translated by Marion Ayton Crawford, pp. 5-32. New York: Penguin Books, 1985.

> Provides a thematic and character-focused reading of *Eugénie Grandet.*

Frautschi, Richard L. "Tracing Narrative Axes in *Eugénie Grandet, Madame Bovary,* and *Germinal*: Toward a Quantitative Strategy." *French Literature Series* XVII (1990): 119-31.

> Close examination of Balzac's narratological strategy in *Eugénie Grandet,* comparing it with the strategies exercised by Gustave Flaubert and Emile Zola in their greatest works.

Maurois, André. "Enter l'Etrangère." In his *Prometheus: The Life of Balzac,* translated by Norman Denny, pp. 218-36. London: Bodley Head, 1965.

> Includes a biographically focused commentary on *Eugénie Grandet,* focusing upon locale and character.

Schor, Naomi. *"Eugénie Grandet:* Mirrors and Melancholia." In *Breaking the Chain: Women, Theory, and French Realist Fiction,* pp. 90-107. New York: Columbia University Press, 1985.

> From a feminist perspective, examines *Eugénie Grandet,* "a novel where the oedipal configuration is writ large, as a unique nuclear family romance."

Shattuck, Roger. "Balzac and the Open Novel." In *The Innocent Eye: On Modern Literature & the Arts,* pp. 127-34. New York: Farrar Straus Giroux, 1984.

> Focuses upon various aspects of Balzac's novel, noting especially the vivid characters and the novel's open-endedness.

Additional coverage of Balzac's life and career is contained in the following sources published by Gale Research: *DISCovering Authors; Nineteenth-Century Literature Criticism,* Vols. 5, 35; *Short Story Criticism,* Vol. 5; and *Dictionary of Literary Biography,* Vol. 119; *Nineteenth-Century French Fiction Writers: Romanticism and Realism, 1800-1860.*

Alice's Adventures in Wonderland and Through the Looking-Glass and What Alice Found There

Lewis Carroll (Charles Lutwidge Dodgson)

The following entry presents criticism of Carroll's stories *Alice's Adventures in Wonderland* (1865) and *Through the Looking-Glass and What Alice Found There* (1872). For additional information on Carroll's career, see *NCLC,* Volume 2.

INTRODUCTION

Classics of children's literature, Lewis Carroll's richly imaginative fantasy stories *Alice's Adventures in Wonderland* and *Through the Looking-Glass* have earned a reputation as serious works of art. The stories, as Donald Rackin has said, "often say to us more than Carroll meant them to say." Alice's dream-world adventures have since the 1930s been read by many scholars as political, psychological, and philosophical metaphors, and as literary parodies. Widely translated, quoted, and adapted for various media, the *Alice* books are considered enduring classics whose ideas, disguised as "nonsense," are provocative enough to enthrall critics and philosophers alike.

Biographical Information

The son of a country pastor, Dodgson led a quiet childhood, showing a precocity in mathematics and parody. He went to Oxford at age eighteen, and was made a fellow of Christ Church two and a half years later. He was to remain there for the rest of his life, lecturing in mathematics and writing an occasional parody on a local political matter. A bachelor in the serious, male-dominated world of Oxford, Dodgson liked to entertain young girls with his story-telling; he invented toys, mathematical games, and puzzles for their enjoyment, and he maintained a whimsical correspondence with young girls throughout his life. The "Alice" of his stories was Alice Liddell, daughter of Henry George Liddell, the dean of Christ Church. On a boat trip up the river Isis with Alice and her two sisters on July 4, 1862, Dodgson invented the story which he later published, under the pseudonym Lewis Carroll, as *Alice's Adventures in Wonderland.* In 1871, following the great success of the first story, Carroll published its sequel, *Through the Looking-Glass and What Alice Found There.* He died early in 1898 and is buried in Guildford, Surrey.

Plot and Major Characters

In *Alice's Adventures in Wonderland,* Alice falls into a rabbit hole and emerges in the imaginative world of Wonderland, where she soon discovers that the solid, logical laws of science no longer apply. In Wonderland, Alice grows and shrinks, animals talk, and language makes little sense. She meets a peremptory hookah-smoking Caterpillar, a dodo, then a Duchess with an ever-smiling Cheshire Cat. The Cheshire Cat directs Alice to a tea party with the Mad Hatter, the March Hare, and the Dormouse. The Wonderland Queen—a playing-card Queen of Hearts—introduces Alice to the Gryphon, who takes her to the Mock Turtle, and, after telling Alice about the Mock-Turtle's education, the two perform a dance, called the Lobster Quadrille. Alice then finds herself at a trial where she has to give evidence. Finding the trial absurd, she tosses the playing-card participants into the air. Her dream comes to a sudden close, and she finds herself awake on a river bank with her sister. In *Through the Looking-Glass and What Alice Found There,* Alice steps through a looking-glass and into the backwards world she has seen from her drawing-room. The Looking-Glass world resembles the chess game Alice has been playing with, and Alice herself becomes a pawn for the White Queen. She meets other live chess pieces, a garden of talking flowers, and insects that resemble her toys. She again encounters a series of fantastic characters who entertain her as well as test her patience. Alice finds herself variously in a railway carriage, in the woods, and in a little shop. She is introduced to Tweedledum and Tweedledee, who relate to her the verse tale of the Walrus and the Carpenter, and to Humpty Dumpty, who invents meanings for words and explains the nonsensical poem "Jabberwocky." She encounters the Looking-Glass equivalents of the March Hare and the Mad Hatter, named Haigha and Hatta. After witnessing a fight "for the crown" between the Lion and the Unicorn, Alice meets the White Knight. Finally, Alice herself becomes a Queen, and her dream ends at a banquet where the food talks. The banquet soon degenerates into chaos, and the Red Queen turns into Alice's black kitten. Suddenly Alice is back in her drawing-room, awake.

Major Themes

Alice's chaotic nonsense world, originally invented by Carroll to entertain a young child, has yielded a variety of thematic concerns. As children's stories, the *Alice* books relate the dream-world adventures of a young girl with a number of obstinate animals, insects, and the imaginary characters Carroll has taken from the worlds of playing cards and chess. As James R. Kincaid (1973) has noted, an important theme of the *Alice* books is "growing up." In addition, the insanity of Alice's dream world has been considered a satire on the ordered, earnest world of Victorian England. Readers have also found references to Darwin and to mathematics, and have seen in Alice's repeated encounters with meaninglessness and absurd authority the darker, existential dilemmas of the human, and especially modern, condition.

Critical Reception

Alice's Adventures in Wonderland was well received from the outset. The collaboration between Carroll and John Tenniel, the illustrator of *Alice,* was an enormous success, and the demand for the book exceeded all expectations. The enormous popularity of the work, published at a time when most children's books were designed to instruct rather than entertain, prompted the sequel *Through the Looking-Glass and What Alice Found There.* Throughout Carroll's life and into the early twentieth century, the *Alice* books received little serious critical attention; however, beginning in the 1930s, essays by such respected figures as William Empson established the stories as complex literary works that would reward close interpretation. The field was thus opened for a wide variety of approaches to the stories. Philosophical readings have addressed the absurdity of Carroll's world and examined the author's treatment of space, time, logic, lawlessness, and individual identity. Donald Rackin's 1966 essay on the

search for meaning in a disordered world is often cited as one of the most significant essays on the subject. Several critics have analyzed the books with respect to the development of children and their movement from a disordered, primitive state to a state of reason and consequence. Focusing on the character of Alice, commentators have addressed her various roles as a child, mother, and queen, and disputed whether or not she is truly "innocent." Other critics, particularly Paul Schilder (1936), have expounded on Carroll's incorporation of violence, identifying incidents of aggression, brutality (the Queen wishes to chop everyone's head off, for example), and destruction. Scholars have explored the relationship between these elements and Dodgson's personal life, and investigated the effect of these violent episodes on young readers. Provoking much critical debate also is the problematic "nonsense language" in both *Alice* books; scholars have speculated that Carroll used nonsensical language and situations in order to break free from the rational, ordered world of his own reality and to transcend his own personal distress. Other topics of critical study include Carroll's fascination with and incorporation of games and puzzles, and his use of humor, parody, and satire.

CRITICISM

Paul Schilder   (essay date 1936)

SOURCE: "Psychoanalytic Remarks on *Alice in Wonderland* and Lewis Carroll," in *Journal of Nervous and Mental Diseases,* Vol. 87, No. 2, February, 1938, pp. 159-68.

[*In the following essay, originally delivered as a speech in late 1936, psychiatry professor Paul Schilder uses the* Alice *books to psychoanalyze Charles Dodgson (Carroll), warning that the stories could have a detrimental influence on children.*]

Lewis Carroll's **Alice in Wonderland** and **Through the Looking Glass and What Alice Found There** are classics of stories for children. As far as I know nobody has tried so far to find out what is offered to children by these stories.

One would expect that the men writing for children should have or should have had a rich life and that this richness of experience might transmit something valuable to the child. Charles Lutwidge Dodgson (this is the real name of the author) lived a rather narrow and distorted life. He came from a religious family. His father was interested in mathematics. His mother is described as gentle and kind. None of the biographies which I have at my disposal contains anything about the deeper relations between Charles and his parents. In none of the books can anything be found about his

Carroll's prefatory poem outlining the genesis of *Alice's Adventures in Wonderland:*

All in the golden afternoon
  Full leisurely we glide;
For both our oars, with little skill,
  By little arms are plied,
While little hands make vain pretence
  Our wanderings to guide.

Ah, cruel Three! In such an hour,
  Beneath such dreamy weather,
To beg a tale of breath too weak
  To stir the tiniest feather!
Yet what can one poor voice avail
  Against three tongues together?

Imperious Prima flashes forth
  Her edict "to begin it":
In gentler tones Secunda hopes
  "There will be nonsense in it!"
While Tertia interrupts the tale
  Not *more* than once a minute.

Anon, to sudden silence won,
  In fancy they pursue
The dream-child moving through a land

Of wonders wild and new,
In friendly chat with bird or beast—
  And half believe it true.

And ever, as the story drained
  The wells of fancy dry,
And faintly strove that weary one
  To put the subject by,
"The rest next time—" "It *is* next time!"
  The happy voices cry.

Thus grew the tale of Wonderland:
  Thus slowly, one by one,
Its quaint events were hammered out—
  And now the tale is done,
And home we steer, a merry crew,
  Beneath the setting sun.

Alice! A childish story take,
  And, with a gentle hand,
Lay it where Childhood's dreams are twined
  In Memory's mystic band.
Like pilgrim's wither'd wreath of flowers
  Pluck'd in a far-off land.

Lewis Carroll, in Alice's Adventures in Wonderland, *Macmillan, 1865.*

relations to his brothers and sisters. He was the oldest of eleven children, eight of them being girls. We merely hear that he gave theatrical performances for them and that he died in 1898 at the age of sixty-five, at his sister's house, where for some twenty years it had been his custom to spend Christmas and other holidays. In his childhood he amused himself with snails and toads as pets. He furthermore endowed earthworms with pieces of pipes so that they could make a better warfare. He also built something like a railroad. He matriculated at Christ's Church in Oxford, his father's college, when he was 18. He was always a brilliant pupil. He spent the greater part of his life in Oxford where he lectured in mathematics. He was ordained deacon in 1861 but never proceeded to priest's orders and preached also very rarely. This may have been partially due to his stammering, which he shared with others of his siblings. One of his biographers sees in this a hereditary taint due to the consanguinity between his father and his mother.

Alice in Wonderland appeared in 1865. In 1867 he made a trip to Russia with Dr. Liddon. The diary of this trip is meager and dull. He showed a great interest in churches. In 1871 *Through the Looking Glass* ap-

peared. He had no adult friends. He liked little girls and only girls. He had very little interest in boys but he occasionally showed interest in juvenile male actors. However, Mr. Bert Coote, one of the child actors in whom he was interested, had a little sister who may have been the real cause of Carroll's interest. When a friend once offered to bring his boy to him, he declined and said, "He thought I doted on all children but I am not omnivorous like a pig. I pick and choose."

Alice in Wonderland originated from stories told to Lorina, Alice and Edith Liddel, the three daughters of the college dean. He was particularly attracted to Alice who was then about seven years old. He has photographed her in a pose which in its sensual innocence reminds one of pictures of Greuze. His interest in his child friends usually ceased when they were about fourteen and he exchanged correspondence with them when they grew older. In his numerous diaries there is not the slightest suggestion of erotic interests. His friends, interviewed by Reed, testify in the same direction. He was prolific in writing letters to little girls in which he tried to amuse them. Some of his poems addressed to little girls are not very different from love poems. The dedication of *Through the Looking Glass* reads:

    Child of the pure unclouded brow
    And dreaming eyes of wonder!

               . . . . .

    Thy loving smile will surely hail
    The love-gift of a fairy-tale.

The dedication of the *Hunting of the Snark* reads:

    Inscribed to a dear Child: . . .
        Girt with a boyish garb for boyish task,

Shy with adults, he easily got in contact with little girls whom he amused by story telling and mechanical toys.

He seemingly was generally kind in his contacts with adults but extremely pedantic concerning the illustrations of his books and did not get along very well with his illustrators. He was interested in photography. He had considerable gifts for mathematics and wrote several books on the subject under his real name which, although not outstanding, won considerable acclaim. He was dry and uninspiring as a teacher. He was religious. He intended to write down some of his sermons, of which one on eternal punishment was dearest to him.

This material is scanty. We have therefore to turn to his work if we want to get deeper information.

One is astonished to find in his pleasant fairy stories the expression of an enormous anxiety. Alice in *Through the Looking Glass* (from now on shortened to *L. G.*) is "standing bewildered." "She does not know what to do." "She does not even know her name." "She cannot find the word 'tree'." When she wants to repeat a poem "another poem comes out, to her distress." "She moves and comes back to the same place."

Most of her anxieties are connected with a change of her body (body image). It is either "too small" or "too big." When it is too big she gets "squeezed," or she "fills the room" [for instance the end scene in *Alice in Wonderland* (*W.*)]. She feels "separated from her feet." "She does not find the gloves of the rabbit." She is frightened when she hears continually "about cutting heads off." She is "threatened by the duchess and by the Queen of Hearts." "Time either stops" (*W.*) or "goes in the opposite direction" (*L. G.*). She has "not the right ticket in the train." "Animals pass remarks about her" (*L. G.*). "The mutton she wants to eat starts talking." "The food is taken away from her" and the banquet scene (*L. G.*) ends in an uproar in which she is "threatened by the candles, by the ladle and by the bottles which have become birds." These are indeed nightmares full of anxiety. We are accustomed to find such dreams in persons with strong repressions which

prevent final satisfactions. Alice, although bewildered, remains passive. "Things happen to her." Only towards the end she revolts against the King and Queen of Hearts (*W.*) and she even "shakes the red queen which turns out to be the black kitten" (*L. G.*).

It is perhaps remarkable that she is never successful when she wants to eat. When she eats or drinks, she becomes merely bigger or smaller. Although she would like to cut the cake for the lion and the unicorn she encounters great difficulties and finally she has no cake for herself. There are severe deprivations in the sphere of food and of eating. Alice does not get anything at the mad tea party. (*W.*) Oral aggressiveness is found everywhere. The poem of **"The Walrus and the Carpenter"** is of an astonishing cruelty. The "lobster is cooked." Alice herself "frightens the mouse and the birds by tales of devouring." There is also "an owl to be devoured by a panther." The "crocodile devours the little fish." Father William, as an old man "eats the goose with the bones and the beak since his jaw got so strong by arguing with his wife." (It is remarkable that the little girls invited by Carroll got very little food.)

We find, also, preponderant oral sadistic trends of cannibalistic character.

There is no dearth of other cruelties. "The queen of hearts wants to chop off almost everybody's head." There is a serious discussion whether "one can cut off the head of the Cheshire Cat" when it appears alone. It is the fear of "being cut to pieces" which comes again and again into the foreground. The "head of the Jabberwocky is cut off too." (*L. G.*) The prisoner (the messenger) "is threatened with death" (*L. G.*), as is the knave of hearts.

Thus there is a continuous threat to the integrity of the body in general.

I have shown lately that an extreme aggressiveness finally distorts space. The loss of the third dimension plays an important part in Carroll's work. In *Sylvie and Bruno,* the warden's brother calls a boy a nail which stands out from the floor and has to be "hammered flat." In a letter written to a little girl about three cats which visited him, he tells that he knocked the cats down flat as a pancake and that afterwards they were quite happy "between the sheets of blotting paper." It is perhaps in this respect remarkable that many of the figures in *W.* are taken from cards and are reduced to cards again in the final scene. I have mentioned the distortions of Alice's body. The egg shaped humpty-dumpty "falls" finally from the wall with a "crash."

The stability of space is guaranteed by the vestibular apparatus and by postural reflexes. The stability of space is continually threatened in *W.* and *L. G.* Alice is "going through the rabbit hole" which functions like a chute. The white king and the white queen make "rapid flights through the air." A "wind blows" which carries the red queen. "Bottles start to fly." "Candlesticks elongate." "A train is jumping over a river." It is an uncertain world. In addition, right and left are changed by the mirror. The king's whole "army tumbles and falls." So do the red and the white knight (*L. G.*). Father William (*W.*) "balances on his head." There is not much certainty in such a world. One does not wonder that Alice is rather afraid she might be a dream of the red king.

Time does not escape distortion. It "stands either still (*W.*) or goes even in opposite direction" (*L. G.*) although it is even difficult for Carroll to persist with such a distortion for a very long time. One of the letters he wrote to one of his little friends starts with the last word of the letter and finished with the first; a complete reversal. After all, Carroll was a mathematician. It may be that ruthlessness towards space and time belong to the characteristics of the mathematical talent.

One may raise the question whether there is not a somatic basis for Carroll's pleasure in mirror writing (the first part of the **"Jabberwocky"** ballad is printed in mirror writing) and reversals, since he was a stammerer. Orton (especially in his Salmon lectures, 1936) has pointed to the organic basis of such combinations. However, left and right disorientation and reversals are very often symbolizations for the inability to find a definite direction in one's sexuality and for a wavering between the hetero- and homosexual component impulses.

There is an inexhaustible play with words in both Alice tales. "Pig" is misunderstood as "fig." As counterpart to "beautification" the word "uglification" is introduced. The shoes in the sea are made of "soles" and "eels." The whiting makes the "shoes and boots white." No wise fish would go anywhere without "purpose." The tale about the fury and the mouse is arranged in a form of a "tail."

We know this phenomenon very well. It occurs when the word is not taken merely as a sign but as of a substance of its own. What the word signifies (the referent) diffuses into the sign. The sign becomes the object itself quite in the same as Pavlow's dogs react to the signal alone with salivation, which should be the reaction to the actual food. The word is handled as a substance, as any other substance. A "rocking horse-fly" is invented; it is made of wood. Humpty Dumpty can therefore say very well that he "lets the words work for him." Humpty Dumpty is furthermore right when he says that the "words have the meanings he gives to them." Whenever one starts playing with words, the problem of negation and the problem of opposites

will soon emerge. Alice (*L. G.*) "sees nobody" and the king admires her that "she can see nobody at such a distance." Humpty Dumpty prefers "unbirthday" presents, since there are 364 days in a year where one can get unbirthday presents more often. The red queen says that "she could show hills in comparison with which the hills seen could be called a valley." The sign function of language is substituted here by the most primitive attitude towards the sign function on the basis of which no real orientation is possible and Alice remains bewildered.

The **"Jabberwocky"** poem uses new words which remind one of the language of dreams and of schizophrenics. Slithy——lithe and shiny; mimsy——flimsy and miserable; wabe——way before and way behind; gyre——to go around like in a gyroscope; gimble—— to make holes like a gimlet.

The **"Jabberwocky"** ballads first few lines were published about ten years before the appearance of *L. G.*, with a slightly different interpretation. Five years later in the ***Hunting of the Snark,*** Carroll explains the principle of portmanteau words. These are words which combine two words by what today we call condensation. We find these condensations when the forces of the system of the unconscious come into play. This is a rather ruthless treatment of words. They are handled without consideration. It depends "who is the master," says Humpty Dumpty. Words are "cut to pieces" and the pieces are arbitrarily united. Such an attitude towards words is found in early stages of mental development. In childhood there is an experimental stage by which the child tries to become clear about the sign function of words. In schizophrenia, such a treatment of words signifies the wish of the individual to give up definite relations to the world which is after all a world of regular sequences and of meaning.

Lewis Carroll is considered as the master of "nonsense literature." One of his biographers even calls him the founder of nonsense literature. The red queen says, after having made nonsensical remarks, "but I have heard nonsense compared with which that would be as sensible as a dictionary" (*L. G.*). The walrus and the carpenter "go out in sunshine when it is night." The White Knight delights in nonsensical inventions. He carries a little box upside down so that "rain cannot come in," but the "clothes and the sandwiches have fallen out." (Play against gravitation.) He has a "mousetrap on horseback." (The play with spatial relations.) Anklets around the feet of the horse protect against the bite of sharks. (Contraction of space.) Freud says justly that nonsense in dreams and so-called unconscious thinking signifies contempt and sneering. We may expect that nonsense literature is the expression of particularly strong destructive tendencies, of very primitive character. No wonder that persons faced with so much destructive nonsense finally "do not know whether they exist" or whether "they are part of a dream and will vanish." Many things vanish, the fawn, the beard of a passenger, and in the **Hunting of the Snark,** the baker disappears, faced by a snark which is a bojum. The scene in the store of the sheep changes suddenly. The figures in **W.** taken from cards become a pack of cards again. The figures of **L. G.** are in reality unanimated chess figures.

This is a world of cruelty, destruction and annihilation. Alice, constantly threatened, still emerges bland and smiling. The kings and queens, the duchesses and knights are "reduced to nothingness." Perhaps it is this final outcome which is gratifying to the child and the adult reader and listener.

It is perhaps worth while to take a glimpse into the world of the child. It experiments continually with the qualities of space, with the shape of its own body, with mass and configuration. This is particularly obvious with children who are between three and four years old, as studies of L. Bender and myself have shown. But it can also be observed in younger and older people. It is interesting to compare the mother goose rhymes with **W.** and **L. G.** There we find a "crooked man who went a crooked mile, a crooked cat and a crooked mouse." "The cats of Kilkenny disappear." "A woman loses her identity after a part of her skirt is cut off." "The sheep leaves their tails behind them." The king of France merely "goes up and down a hill with 20,000 men." "Elizabeth, Elspeth, Betsy, Bess are four persons and still one person." The similarity is obvious. George Saintsbury in the *Cambridge History of English Literature,* Vol. 13, p. 186, has stressed this similarity too, and remarks about Carroll "there is something of the manipulations of mathematical symbols in the systematic absurdity and the nonsensical preciseness of his humor." It seems to me that the destructiveness of Carroll's nonsense goes further than the experimentation of the Nursery Rhymes.

What does all this mean? How did Carroll come to this queer world? It is a world without real love. The queens and kings are either absurd or cruel or both. We would suspect that Carroll never got the full love of his parents. In large families children feel very often neglected. We may suspect that Carroll who shows so often feelings of guilt in his diary and who wrote the sermon on eternal punishment had been educated rather strictly. He must have looked with suspicion at the many children who came after him. Are the kings and queens "symbols" for his parents? Alice also complains very bitterly that the "animals order her around so much." Are some of the animals also representatives of the parents?

All kinds of disagreeable animals appear in the two fairy tales. Carroll liked to play with toads and snails and earthworms. Alice is in continuous fear of being attacked or blamed by the animals. Do the insects represent the many brothers and sisters who must have provoked jealousy in Carroll?

We have at any rate the hypothesis that the demands of Carroll concerning the love of his parents were not fully satisfied. He may have found consolation in the one or the other of his siblings, especially in his sisters. It is remarkable that Alice does not report her adventures to her mother but to her sister. It is also remarkable that Carroll talking about her future refrains from picturing her as a mother who tells stories to her own children. He lets her merely gather about her little children who are strangers. It is, by the way, also reported that Carroll showed jealousy when one of his former little friends married. We may suppose that Carroll expected the love which he could not get from his mother from one of his sisters. The biographical material at hand is not sufficient to decide this question.

We may furthermore suspect that he did not feel sure that he could get this love as the oldest brother and that he felt he might get this love if he would take the place of the parents and especially the place of the mother. It may be also that he identified himself with one of the older sisters. He was, by the way, particularly sensitive towards the impersonation of females by males on the stage and resented it. Is this a defense against the unconscious wish to play the part of a woman, especially the part of the mother and a sister?

What was his relation to his sex organ anyhow? Fenichel has lately pointed to the possibility that little girls might become symbols for the phallus. Alice changes her form continually; she is continually threatened and continually in danger. There may have been in Carroll the wish for feminine passivity and a protest against it. He plays the part of the mother to little girls but the little girl is for him also the completion of his own body. The little girl is his love object, substituting the mother and substituting the sister. These are complicated discussions and are not fully justified since we do not know enough about the fantasy life of Carroll and probably shall never know about it, but on the basis of other experiences we are reasonably sure that the little girls substitute incestuous love objects. Besides this object relation there must have existed a strong tendency to identification especially with female members of the family. As in all forms of primitive sexuality, the promiscuity in Carroll's relation to children is interesting. He seemingly tried to get in contact with a very great number of children and to "seduce" them in his way.

It is obvious that such object relations loaded with insecurity and feelings of guilt cannot remain satisfactory and must be accompanied by hostile and negative tendencies. These hostile tendencies did not find any open expression in Carroll's life. A strong superego and a strong moral consciousness protected him. The strength of the repression may be partially responsible for the depth to which the regression took place. All the hostile tendencies had therefore to come out in the particularly severe distortions in his work. It is possible that the mathematical ability and the constitutional difficulties to which I have pointed before may have something to do with the type and the depth of the regression. Since we do not know enough about the early history of Carroll we cannot appreciate fully the relation between constitutional and individual factors in the type of regression, which is obvious in his work and in the structure of his love life. Most of the biographers stress the difference between the official personality of Carroll and the personality expressed in his literary work. Carroll himself has pointed this way by choosing a pseudonym and holding Charles Lutwidge Dodgson strictly separated from Lewis Carroll. We can understand his motives to do so. However, his stern morality, his dryness, his mathematical interests, are not separate parts of his personality but are the reaction and the basis of the tendencies which he expressed in his work.

I suspect that nonsense literature will originate whenever there are complete object relations and a regression to deep layers involving the relation of space and time on the basis of primitive aggressiveness.

Carroll appears to the writer of this essay as a particularly destructive writer. I do not mean this in the sense of a literary criticism, which does not concern us here. We may merely ask whether such a literature might not increase destructive attitudes in children beyond the measure which is desirable. There is very little in **Alice in Wonderland** as in **Through the Looking Glass** which leads from destruction to construction. There is very little love and tenderness and little regard for the existence of others. Maybe we can have confidence that children will find a way to construction for themselves. At any rate, the child may be led to a mental experimentation which although cruel may sooner or later lead to a better appreciation of space, time and words and so, also, to a better appreciation of other human beings. Problems of this type have to be decided by experience and by experimental approach.

What do children do with Carroll's work? We know very little about it. Preliminary impressions in adults who have read Carroll's books in childhood make it probable that the child uses Carroll's nonsense verses and anxiety situations in a way similar to the manner that the child uses *Mother Goose Rhymes*. They take them as an ununderstood reality which one can hope to handle better after one has played and worked with it. In comparison with other fairy stories the dissociation resulting from extreme cruelty is more obvious in Carroll's work. One may be afraid that without the

help of the adult, the child may remain bewildered and alone may not find his way back to a world in which it can appreciate love relations, space and time and words.

Joseph Wood Krutch   (essay date 1937)

SOURCE: "Psychoanalyzing Alice," in *The Nation,* New York, Vol. 144, No. 5, January 30, 1937, pp. 129-30.

[*Krutch is regarded as one of America's most respected literary and drama critics. A conservative and idealistic thinker, he was a consistent proponent of human dignity and the preeminence of literary art. In the following essay, he rejects Paul Schilder's psychoanalytic reading [reprinted above] of the* Alice *books.*]

Most readers of *The Nation* must have seen in their daily paper some account of the adventures of Alice in the new wonderland of psychoanalysis. Many years ago the late André Tridon undertook to explore the subconscious mind of the same little lady, but Tridon was something of a playboy while Dr. Paul Schilder, research professor of psychiatry at New York University, was presumably in dead earnest when he warned his hearers at a recent meeting of the American Psychoanalytical Society against exposing children to the dangerous corruptions of Lewis Carroll. All of Carroll's ten brothers and sisters stammered; "this fact might have made the author unhappy"; and in any event his superficially pleasant fairy stories are the expression of "enormous anxiety."

According to the account of Dr. Schilder's speech printed in *The New York Times,* most of Alice's adventures are "calculated to fill her with anxieties" of a pernicious nature. "She feels separated from her feet, she is stuffed in and out of small holes, and she never knows from minute to minute whether she will be small or large. . . .   There are severe deprivations in the sphere of food and drink. . . . The poem of **"The Walrus and the Carpenter"** is of an astonishing cruelty. The Lobster is cooked. Alice herself frightens the birds with tales of devourings. . . . The fear of being cut to pieces comes again and again into the foreground. The head of the Jabberwock is cut off. There is a continuous threat to the integrity of the body in general." Even, worse, apparently, is the fact that Carroll plays fast and loose with language and the conception of time. The innocent child may never recover from the shock of "mimsey" or "wabe." "This is a world of cruelty, destruction, and annihilation. . . . One may be afraid that without the help of the adult the child may remain bewildered in it and may not find his way back to the world in which he can appreciate love relations, space, time, and words." Personally I have never heard of a child who confessed to being dangerously terrified by "Alice," or of an adult who attributed his downfall to a trauma received from the book in infancy. But no doubt that proves nothing. The fears inspired are subconscious also.

Max Beerbohm on *Alice* and *Through the Looking Glass*:

In the two books about Alice . . . you have a perfect fusion of the two opposing elements in [Carroll's] nature. In them the morality is no more than implicit, and the mathematics are not thrust on you. Though modern adults are apt to resent even implicit morality in a book for children, children delight in it. They delight in feeling that, in some way or other, Alice is being "improved" by her adventures. Orally, she seems to be an awful prig, but various internal evidence makes them suspect her of having "a past"—of having been naughty; and they feel that, somehow or other, the Caterpillar and the Red Queen and all the rest of them are working out her redemption.

Max Beerbohm, in Around Theatres, *Knopf, 1939.*

Now there is not, so it seems to me, any reason for doubting the large general assertion that Lewis Carroll had "complexes" or that his fantasy was to some extent, at least, an expression of them. Even if we leave such esoteric matters as "threats to the integrity of the body" in the hands of specialists like Dr. Schilder, it ought to be evident that his nonsense, like so much nonsense and so much wit, was a device by means of which his intelligence protested against various kinds of cant which his priggish and conventional temperament would not permit him to flout openly. I see nothing far-fetched in the assumption that queens are absurd puppets in "Alice" because Carroll outwardly accepted the absurd legend of Victoria, or that the farce of the trial is largely unconscious satire of the pompous procedure of courts. Nor do I see how anyone can ponder the dilemma in which Alice is placed when she tries to choose between the Walrus and the Carpenter without perceiving a submerged La Rochefoucauld in the mild-mannered don who found his chief delight in photographing little girls. Alice, it will be remembered, thought she liked the weeping Carpenter best because he seemed a little sorry for having betrayed the oysters. But when she was told that it was he who had eaten the most and tried to shift her sympathy to the Walrus, she got a crushing retort—the Walrus had eaten as many as he could get. Only a man who had hidden somewhere in his soul a very cynical conception of human behavior could, I submit, have conceived that incident.

If we go that far we may also, I suppose, take it as a matter of course that Alice's fantastic adventures are none of them quite sane. But that is not the point. Why, of all people, should a psychoanalyst be shocked to find complexes in an artist, or afraid to have children ("polymorphically perverse" by Freudian premise) introduced at an early age to a literature the very secret of which is its successfully playful catharsis of certain all but universal obsessions? As for the satire and the cynicism which Dr. Schilder does not mention, I should say that any child is ready for it as soon as he is capable of recognizing its existence and that he is never too young to begin to laugh at those morbid fears which, the psychoanalyst himself is ready to assure us, he is never too young to feel.

In America the philistine used to be above all else a moral man. The arts had nothing to fear from his fury except when he could discover that they were "impure." Nowadays he is more likely to discover in the most unexpected places some defiling trace of either "bourgeois prejudice" or "psychological abnormality," and to look askance upon anything which does not combine the obsession of a social worker with the "normality" of a boy scout. Some years ago when I first met a certain distinguished psychoanalyst I told him that I had observed in his many books what appeared to me to be a rather serious non sequitur: the first eight chapters were usually devoted to showing how abnormal most of the distinguished people of the world had been, while the last always concluded with a "therefore let us endeavor to be as normal as possible." I asked him if he did not suppose that a too thorough psychic house-cleaning might be undesirable for those who aspired to be something more than merely "normal," and I received a remarkable if somewhat pompous reply. "I would not," he said, "like to give a categorical answer to that question, but I will say one thing. Dr. Freud and I are the only two prominent psychoanalysts who have never themselves been analyzed—and I think we have made the greatest contributions to the science."

Mark Van Doren (essay date 1941-1942)

SOURCE: "Lewis Carroll: *Alice in Wonderland*," in *The New Invitation to Learning*, edited by Mark Van Doren, Random House, 1942, pp. 206-20.

[Van Doren, the younger brother of the poet Carl Van Doren, was one of America's most prolific and diverse twentieth-century writers. Van Doren's criticism is aimed at the general reader, rather than the scholar or specialist, and is noted for its lively perception and wide interest. In the following excerpt, Van Doren chairs a discussion of the Alice *books with American novelist Katherine Anne Porter and English philosopher Bertrand Russell. The discussion was originally broadcast nationally on Columbia Broadcasting System radio.]*

Van Doren: Miss Porter, you may wonder why you were asked to come this morning to discuss *Alice in Wonderland*. One reason I might give you is this: I was curious to know whether you, like other women of my acquaintance, were horrified by this book rather than made happy by it when you were a little girl.

Porter: I was. It was a horror-story to me; it frightened me so much, and I didn't know then whether it was the pictures or the text. Rereading it, I should think it was the text.

Van Doren: Even without Tenniel's drawings you would have been scared?

Porter: Oh, yes. It was a terrible mixture of suffering and cruelty and rudeness and false logic and traps for the innocent—in fact, awful.

Van Doren: This must have been partly because you believed the story.

Porter: I believed it entirely. The difference between it, I think, and the other fairy stories (because we had an appetite for the most grim and grisly horrors; nearly all stories written for children in the old times were horrible and we loved them, because we knew they weren't true; they couldn't happen, they were mere stories) is, that all this takes place in a setting of everyday life. The little glass table with the key on it, and the furniture and the gardens and the flowers, the clock—they were all things we knew, you see, familiar things dreadfully out of place, and they frightened me.

Van Doren: Well, Mr. Russell, you also might wonder why you are here, and the reason might be another reason altogether. But I'm tempted to ask you whether anything like this was your experience.

Russell: No, I never had any feeling of horror about it. I have heard other women say the same thing, that they felt a horror about it. The reason I didn't was that after all it was a girl who had all these troubles, and boys don't mind the troubles of girls.

Porter: I'm afraid that's true.

Van Doren: You mean that boys don't mind if girls are treated rudely?

Russell: They don't mind a bit. No, they think it's what they deserve.

Van Doren: I wonder if that is because boys themselves are in the habit of being treated rudely by girls with no ability to strike back. Did you read the book at an early age?

Russell: Oh, yes. I was brought up on the two books,

both *Alice in Wonderland* and *Through the Looking-Glass*. *Through the Looking-Glass* was published the year I was born, and they were still comparatively recent books when I was young. I was brought up on the first editions, which I had in the nursery. It didn't occur to anybody that they had any value and I just had them to wear out. I knew them by heart from an early age.

Van Doren: That was true of other children in your generation, I dare say.

Russell: Yes, they all knew them by heart. And I don't think that I can remember any of them being horrified. I'm a little surprised by what Miss Porter said. I don't remember any of them thinking of the stories as possibly true.

Van Doren: I was talking recently to an acquaintance of mine—a man—who said that he now feels a horror in reading the book which he did not feel as a boy. You remember the occasion when Alice is growing in the little house and she has grown so large that she has to have one arm out of the window and one leg up the chimney. Well, little Bill, you know, who comes down the chimney to see if he can do something about it, is suddenly kicked by her so that he flies out and is badly hurt, and she hears everyone outside say: "There goes Bill." Now this friend of mine, as a boy, roared with laughter over that. He and his brothers thought it was the funniest thing in the world. But now it doesn't seem funny to him that Bill was hurt. So apparently conversions can take place.

Russell: That is true. I think people are more merciful than they used to be, and I think old fun often strikes us now as rather brutal; anyway, it didn't in those days.

Porter: It is curious about cruelty, because Bill didn't seem to worry me much. A thing I accepted, which I know now is extremely unkind, was putting the dormouse in a teapot headfirst. But I remember reasoning to myself even then that the dormouse was asleep anyhow and didn't care.

Van Doren: No. And the dormouse seems on the whole to want to be some place where it is warm and wet.

Russell: It never occurred to me that the dormouse minded. The only thing that occurred to me was that the teapot was too small.

Van Doren: The dormouse when he was pinched and squealed didn't hurt you, then, vicariously? Does all this mean that the book for you was a perfectly satisfactory children's book? And that it perhaps is still?

Russell: It was then. I don't regard it now as a perfectly satisfactory children's book. I've been rereading it with a view to this broadcast, and I think there are many objections to it as a children's book. In fact, I should like to label it "For Adults Only." I don't think it's a suitable book for the young.

Van Doren: I wonder if the young these days actually do like it as much as children used to like it.

Russell: My experience with them is they don't, and I think this is because there are so many more children's books now and because, when I was young, it was the only children's book that hadn't got a moral. We all got very tired of the morals in books.

Van Doren: This very book makes fun of books that have morals, doesn't it? Remember, the Queen is always going about saying: "The moral of this is—" and then some preposterous statement comes out such as "Take care of the sense and the sounds will take care of themselves."

Porter: But don't you think, too, that it is because children really seem to be much more realistic; that is, they do like a graphic, factual kind of story? Even the fantasies written for children now are nearly always something grotesque and not deep, something that doesn't touch their emotions. Like the comic papers, you know. And then their stories all seem to be about quite ordinary living children. Rather extraordinary but not fabulous adventures occur, which might very well occur to any child.

Van Doren: To me that is highly unfortunate. I am aware of the truth of what you say, that children prefer these days, or at any rate are assumed to prefer, matter-of-fact stories. But every now and then a story which is not matter-of-fact has a great success among children, such as the books about Mary Poppins. Have you read those?

Porter: Yes. Well I would never know whether the children really like that sort of thing or not. Perhaps like grown-ups, they take what is given them because they aren't given anything better.

Van Doren: Do we really mean that *Alice in Wonderland* has declined as a children's book because of its cruelty?

Russell: Partly, I think, but partly also from competition with other books. Grown-ups always tend to think of children with a certain contempt as dear little things, and when a child feels that element in a book he resents it. If he can get a book that doesn't regard him as a dear little thing he's very pleased. But grown-ups will always buy that sort of book and give it to children unless the children educate them.

Van Doren: Are you implying, Mr. Russell, that *Alice in Wonderland* assumes children to be dear little things? Alice is pretty well kicked around, isn't she? And she's rudely treated, she's interrupted, she's rebuffed.

Russell: Yes, but she's always treated rather as a figure of fun, and nobody quite likes to be treated that way.

Van Doren: Yes, she is assumed to be absurd because she has a little habit of talking to herself, reasoning with herself, holding conversations with herself, because she remembers her homework and tries to bring that into this new world she finds herself in. Remember when she meets the mouse. She doesn't know how to address the mouse except by saying "O Mouse," because she had learned the vocative case in Latin.

Russell: All that, I think, is a little absurd, because as a matter of fact she's an extremely Victorian child and very different from most modern children that I know, and certainly no modern child would think of saying "O Mouse." It wouldn't occur to it. All the lessons that she has had at home are different lessons from those the children have now.

Van Doren: That is true. And I'm admitting that occasionally, perhaps regularly, she is treated like a little prig, a little girl who has no ability whatever to imagine other experiences than those she has had. But I suppose the interest of the book to lie very largely there, either for children or for adults. It is a rebuke to those who cannot imagine as possible other experience than that which they have had.

Porter: You've spoken of the children being fed so much realism today; never being given any experience beyond something that might possibly happen to them.

Van Doren: Yes. Now, for instance, to me a very salutary answer to the proverbial question of a child's "Why?" is the answer once given to Alice: "Why not?"—without any explanation at all. It seems to me one learns a great deal by that.

Russell: May I come back to what I said a moment ago, that this book ought to be labeled "For Adults Only"? What you're recommending is a very suitable education for adults, but much too difficult for children. The whole book is much too difficult for the young. It raises metaphysical points, very interesting logical points, that are good for the older ponderer, but for the young produce only confusion.

Van Doren: Of course Alice was always confused. But you imply, Mr. Russell, that adults, these days or perhaps any day, stand in need of metaphysical instruction and logical sanitation.

Russell: I'm professionally bound to think so.

Van Doren: I agree with you heartily, as a matter of fact. Does the book still seem to you of interest on that level?

Russell: It provides, of course, the sort of things a philosophical lecturer can bring in when he wants to seem light. It is very useful to a philosophical lecturer who wants to liven up his stuff; it is full of philosophical jokes which are quite good for philosophical students. But I think you oughtn't to read the book before you're fifteen.

Porter: I wonder. Probably that's true. You were talking about the sentimental Victorian attitude toward children as dear little things. I think Lewis Carroll quite definitely made a bow in the direction of the dear-little-creature attitude in his poems of dedication to Alice and the other children. In the story I think he said what he really believed and what he really meant—and it was pretty grim!

Van Doren: Neither one of you would agree with me, perhaps, that the best children's book is always a book which should be labeled "For Adults Only." My own experience with children, my own children included, is that they really enjoy most those books which they don't wholly understand, which leave them perhaps only slightly bewildered, but nevertheless bewildered.

Russell: Well, I think the young should read some books that adults think of as for adults only, but that's because the adults are always wrong about it. The books the adults think suitable for the young are certainly not.

Van Doren: I'm glad to hear you say that.

Porter: I've always believed that children should read adult literature, should read far beyond their years, and perhaps not read anything that was cold-bloodedly written for them.

Van Doren: Yes, because it has never been clear enough that adults do know what children are like; they're always merely assuming that they know what they're like. I quite agree with you that when they're most sure they're most likely to be wrong. Mr. Russell, I want to come back to that question of the value of the book, if any, on the metaphysical and mathematical level. I was interested in your saying that philosophers quoted it only when they wanted to introduce a light touch. Now, that after all wouldn't be saying much for the book, would it? Or would it?

Russell: Yes, I think most of the most instructive things are jokes. Quite a number of important things have originated as jokes because if you can put it in that form it isn't so painful. Now, for instance, when they discuss whether they're all parts of the Red King's

---

Virginia Woolf about Lewis Carroll:

In order to make us into children, he first makes us asleep. "Down, down, down, would the fall *never* come to an end?" Down, down, down we fall into that terrifying, wildly inconsequent, yet perfectly logical world where time races, then stands still; where space stretches, then contracts. It is the world of sleep; it is also the world of dreams. Without any conscious effort dreams come; the white rabbit, the walrus, and the carpenter, one after another, turning and changing one into the other, they come skipping and leaping across the mind. It is for this reason that the two Alices are not books for children; they are the only books in which we become children. President Wilson, Queen Victoria, *The Times* leader writer, the late Lord Salisbury—it does not matter how old, how important, or how insignificant you are, you become a child again. To become a child is to be very literal; to find everything so strange that nothing is surprising; to be heartless, to be ruthless, yet to be so passionate that a snub or a shadow drapes the world in gloom. It is to be Alice in Wonderland.

It is also to be Alice Through the Looking Glass. It is to see the world upside down. Many great satirists and moralists have shown us the world upside down, and have made us see it, as grown-up people see it, savagely. Only Lewis Carroll has shown us the world upside down as a child sees it, and has made us laugh as children laugh, irresponsibly.

Virginia Woolf, "Lewis Carroll," in The Moment and Other Essays, *The Hogarth Press, 1939.*

---

dream and will cease to exist if the Red King wakes—

Van Doren: This is in **Through the Looking-Glass**.

Russell: Yes, it is. Well, that is a very instructive discussion from a philosophical point of view. But if it were not put humorously, we should find it too painful.

Van Doren: But you really mean that it is instructive?

Russell: I think it is worth considering, yes.

Van Doren: It is more than just an illustration of a point? It contains a point of its own?

Russell: Yes. I think he was very good at inventing puzzles in pure logic. When he was quite an old man, he invented two puzzles which he published in a learned periodical, *Mind,* to which he didn't provide answers. And the providing of answers was a job, at least so I found it.

Van Doren: Do you remember either of those puzzles?

Russell: I remember one of them very well. A boy is going with his two uncles, and one of the uncles says he's going to be shaved, and he's going to a shop that is kept by Allen, Brown, and Carr. And he says: "I shall get shaved by Allen." And the other uncle says: "How do you know Allen will be in?" And he says: "Oh, I can prove it by logic." "Nonsense," says the man. "How can you do that?" "Well," he says, "you know there has to be always one man to mind the shop, so if Allen is out, then, if Brown is out, Carr will be in. But Brown has lately been ill, and so he can't go out alone, and he's quarreled with Allen, so he only goes out with Carr. So if Brown is out, Carr is out. Now if Allen goes out, if Brown is out, Carr is out, and if Brown is out Carr is in. That's impossible, so Allen can never go out."

Van Doren: That sounds like a syllogism, doesn't it?

Russell: Of course it's a fallacy, but showing up the fallacy is difficult.

Porter: A lovely illustration of all this extraordinary, oblique, fallacious logic that was a trap for Alice all the way through two books.

Van Doren: There are many outrageous syllogisms here, such as this in skeleton form: "Alice, you like eggs; serpents like eggs, therefore you are a serpent." And there is another form of logical fun which seems to me important here; I think you would call it a conversion, would you not? That is to say, Lewis Carroll was constantly playing with a subject and predicate converted. Alice is asked why she doesn't say what she means. And she says: "Well, at least I always mean what I say." So she converts the terms cats and rats. Do cats eat rats? Perhaps rats eat cats. Which is true? And she finally forgets which is the important question to ask. She says she has often seen a cat without a grin, but never a grin without a cat. I'm not at all sure that that doesn't lead us to a conversion which it is possible to make on the title of the book. The title of the book is **Alice in Wonderland**. Possibly it should be *Wonderland in Alice,* because Alice is constantly in a state of wonder at something which, in this particular world where she is, she shouldn't wonder at at all. For instance, she eats a piece of cake—after twenty or thirty pages—and she suddenly says to herself: "Isn't it strange that I don't get any bigger from eating this cake?" Lewis Carroll very gravely remarks: "That is what usually happens when you eat cake." She is never able to adjust herself; she is never able to remember the relations which exist in this new life.

Russell: That is quite true, but I still think there is a great deal in his books that is meant to be suitable to the young and isn't. Like when they say "threaten a

snark with a railway-share." No child has the vaguest idea of what that means.

Van Doren: But again I wonder if children don't like to read books—if they don't today, that's all there is to it, but my own experience as a child, and my experience of children these days, is that they often do—which they don't totally understand. They come to a railway-share. Well, they want to know what it is, and find out; or they develop in their mind some grotesque notion of what it is, which is quite charming. Students in colleges like best on the whole those lectures which, as we say, are a little over their heads.

Russell: That is perfectly true, but then what puzzles them ought to be something serious that when they understand it they will see to be serious. It ought not to be a mere joke.

Van Doren: But, if, as you say, these jokes are oftentimes cloaks for philosophical, even metaphysical, points, then the book at bottom is serious. I think I've been trying to say that the book is at bottom quite serious and quite edifying. Alice is always learning—her experience is less than it might be—she is always learning that something that she has supposed to be grotesque is not, as a matter of fact, grotesque. She says to the caterpillar once, you remember, on the mushroom: "It's really dreadful always to be changing one's shape." He says: "It isn't dreadful at all." And we immediately remember that the caterpillar changes his shape at least three times in his life.

Porter: And of course she really changes hers too, not into an entirely different form, not from one thing to another, but she's changing and growing all the time; she's not the same person today that she was yesterday by any means. But she doesn't understand that.

Van Doren: As when she is carrying the Duchess's baby. For a while she thinks the baby is ugly because it has a nose like a pig. Then when she determines that the baby *is* a pig, she thinks the nose is quite beautiful.

Porter: The nose is very becoming, and she's glad it's a handsome pig. But I was thinking her confusion was due to the setting aside of all the logic of experience. Because there is a certain sort of progression of experience that I think we can depend upon a little, and this is all removed, you see, from her when she falls into this Wonderland. There isn't anything that she can refer to as a certainty. And then there's another thing that's very important: Alice's state of mind is a fine example of the terrific sense of uncertainty and insecurity of childhood trying to understand an adult world in which very little provision is made for the young. This was true in those days much more than now. I think now perhaps that the family plans are made a little bit too much around the child.

Van Doren: I think so myself.

Porter: But Alice was at a terrible disadvantage, struggling with an adult, alien, and apparently hostile world, which had set traps for her, or so it appeared, purposely to trip her up.

Russell: Perhaps that is why the book was better liked then than now. That particular kind of bafflement was one to which children were accustomed, and it didn't strike them as it does now. But now, I think, the modern child is simply bewildered by all this and feels: oh, this is horrid! At least some do.

Van Doren: I wonder which is the better procedure for the human race—to endeavor to make children understand adults or to endeavor to make adults understand children.

Porter: Do you know, I think one of the great troubles is that too many persons are going around painfully trying too hard to understand. I wish we could relax a little.

Russell: I quite agree. If you could take children more naturally and spontaneously and not bother so much about child psychology, it would be very much better I think.

Van Doren: Certainly. And likewise children should be relieved of the necessity of understanding adult psychology.

Porter: Well, I think one of the most sinister things I ever heard was a little boy, a small child about four years old, weeping bitterly by himself. His parents found him and tried to discover what had happened to him. He wept for a while and finally he blurted out: "Oh, I do want to be happy."

Van Doren: Mr. Russell, I should like to ask you, because of your own distinction in the field of logic and mathematics, whether Carroll is thought actually to have any importance in that field today.

Russell: His works were just what you would expect: comparatively good at producing puzzles and very ingenious and rather pleasant, but not important. For instance, he produced a book of formal logic which is much pleasanter than most because, instead of saying things like "all men are mortal," which is very dull, it says, things like "most hungry crocodiles are disagreeable," which is amusing, and that makes the subject more agreeable. Then he wrote a book of geometry which is pleasant in a way, but not important. None of his work was important. The best work he ever did in that line was the two puzzles that I spoke of.

Van Doren: And are those better in that line than any-thing in either **Alice in Wonderland** or **Through the Looking-Glass**—I mean to say, considered as contributions?

Russell: Oh, certainly, because there is nothing in **Alice in Wonderland** or **Through the Looking-Glass** that could conceivably be thought a contribution. They offer only pleasant illustrations for those who don't want to be thought too heavy.

Van Doren: But for children perhaps? I mean, could one seriously say that a child might learn a little bit to be logical from reading these books?

Russell: I shouldn't have thought so.

Van Doren: That was a very heavy question, and you should have rebuked me for it. But the famous error that is made (I don't know whether this is a logical error or not) when it is said that butter should not have been used in the works of a watch and the answer is: "but it was the best butter"—is that amusing to a child?

Porter: That was frightfully amusing. That was funny always.

Van Doren: Or the demonstration that, since a dog is not mad because when he is happy he wags his tail and when he is unhappy he growls with his throat, therefore a cat which when it is happy moves its tail and growls *is* mad.

Porter: I think we understood that all very well, don't you?

Russell: How about the treacle well?

Porter: Yes, I liked the treacle well.

Russell: Do you remember, they drew treacle out of the treacle well? "But I don't understand," said Alice, "they were in the well." "So they were," said the dormouse, "well in."

Porter: That was funny, too.

Van Doren: They were drawing treacle from the well, and the dormouse explains: "Well, we were just learning to draw; we didn't draw very well." And suddenly they're talking about drawing pictures—drawing pictures of things the names of which begin with the letter M. "Why with the letter M?" "Why not?"

Porter: But do you remember the lessons they had? Was it the eel, or some underseas creature, who had lessons in drawling and stretching and fainting in coils? You know, we were never told how to translate that and we didn't need to. We thought those tricks were funny in themselves.

Van Doren: And the exercises in reeling and writhing.

Porter: We didn't get on to that for a long time.

Russell: I found the only thing that my boy really liked, my small boy, was the poem about Father William. He looked at me with a grave face and said: "Father William was very clever *although* he was old."

Van Doren: How old is the boy, by the way?

Russell: Four and a half.

Van Doren: A shrewd remark. Now we have not referred often enough in our conversation to the presence in this book of some very famous poems which are of course parodies. I think the poem about Father William is the most interesting. Would you agree?

Russell: I agree—yes.

Van Doren: Miss Porter, would you like to read that?

Porter: I'll swing along as we used to when we read it as children.

> "You are old, Father William," the young man said,
> "And your hair has become very white;
> And yet you incessantly stand on your head—
> Do you think, at your age, it is right?"
>
> "In my youth," Father William replied to his son,
> "I feared it might injure the brain;
> But, now that I'm perfectly sure I have none,
> Why, I do it again and again."
>
> "You are old," said the youth, "as I mentioned before,
> And have grown most uncommonly fat;
> Yet you turned a back somersault in at the door—
> Pray, what is the reason of that?"
>
> "In my youth," said the sage, as he shook his gray locks,
> "I kept all my limbs very supple
> By the use of this ointment—one shilling the box,—
> Allow me to sell you a couple?"
>
> "You are old," said the youth, "and your jaws are too weak
> For anything tougher than suet.
> Yet you finished the goose, with the bones and the beak—
> Pray, how did you manage to do it?"

> "In my youth," said his father, "I took to the law,
> And argued each case with my wife;
> And the muscular strength which it gave to my jaw
> Has lasted the rest of my life."
>
> "You are old," said the youth, "one would hardly suppose
> That your eye was as steady as ever;
> Yet you balanced an eel on the end of your nose—
> What made you so awfully clever?"
>
> "I've answered three questions, and that is enough,"
> Said his father. "Don't give yourself airs!
> Do you think I can listen all day to such stuff?
> Be off, or I'll kick you downstairs!"

Harry Levin (essay date 1965)

SOURCE: "Wonderland Revisited," in *The Kenyon Review,* Vol. XXVII, No. 4, Autumn, 1965, pp. 591-616.

[*Levin is an American educator and critic whose works reveal his wide range of interests and expertise, from Renaissance culture to the contemporary novel. In the following essay, he provides a centennial re-assessment of the* Alice *books and of their author, Charles Dodgson (Carroll).*]

In the twentieth century's commemoration of the nineteenth, we have reached the centennial of Alice. Not uncharacteristically, the date has been somewhat blurred. The author, whose fussiness has endeared him to bibliophiles, was dissatisfied with the first edition, so that *Alice in Wonderland* was not publicly issued until 1866. Moreover, if we wish to celebrate the occasion on which the tale was first told, we must look back to that famous boating party of three little girls and two dons on July 4, 1862. That "golden afternoon," as Lewis Carroll describes it in his introductory poem, was actually—as modern research has discovered—"wet and rather cool." Fancy has been at work from the very outset. The rain that had overtaken the same group of five picnickers during an earlier expedition on June 17 seems to have inspired the pool of tears, wherein Alice's sisters Lorina and Edith are immortalized as the Lory and the Eaglet, while their companions Duckworth and Dodgson appear as the Duck and the Dodo. But the date specified in the story is May 4, Alice Liddell's tenth birthday; and, since the heroine of *Through the Looking-Glass and What Alice Found There* is exactly seven and a half just six months later, perhaps her adventures should be predated at 1859.

At all events, the fantasy has now lasted 100 years. What is more surprising, it has withstood the stringent test of translation into forty-seven languages (by the reckoning of Dr. Warren Weaver, whose collection, ranging from Finnish to Swahili and from Chinese to Esperanto versions, should harbor an independent interest for cultural anthropologists). Excerpts have been quoted in, and out of, every conceivable context. Clearly the Alice books must embody certain archetypes, they must touch off some of the deeper responses of human consciousness, in order to have penetrated so far beyond their immediate period and culture. Yet, looking back to them from our present distance, we may also note that they were deeply embedded in their mid-Victorian matrix, that they remain as distinctively English as their heroine's name. Now the English have no monopoly on nonsense—or, for that matter, on common sense. However, it may be no accident that they have excelled so conspicuously in both. It may be that the one is the price paid for—or else the bonus gained from—the other, that a hard-working sense of practicality gets its recreation from the enjoyment of absurdity. The nonsense of Lewis Carroll has been defined by a French fantast, André Breton, as "the vital solution to a profound contradiction between the acceptance of faith and the exercise of reason."

It was the voice of reason that spoke through the tongue of Edmund Burke, when he remarked: "Though no man can draw a stroke between the confines of night and day, yet darkness and light are on the whole tolerably distinguishable." What could be more pragmatic, more empirical, more thoroughly British? Yet such reasoning could never have satisfied the Reverend Charles Lutwidge Dodgson. From his adolescent magazine, *The Rectory Umbrella,* to his Oxford lecture, **"Where Does the Day Begin?**," he preoccupied himself with precisely this problem, and stood ready to pursue the sunrise around the world in order to prove his point that such distinctions were wholly arbitrary. No wonder we experience some hesitation in putting a finger on Alice's anniversary! We live by those convenient strokes which separate night from day, sleeping from waking, and madness from sanity. But imagination, poetic or scientific—and in Dodgson's case it was both—cannot afford to take anything for granted. It is continually entertaining the most improbable assumptions, following non sequiturs through to their logical consequences, or—like Dodgson—hopefully working out *pi* to an ever larger number of decimals. Speculating in his diary, he asked himself:

> Query: when we are dreaming and, as so often happens, have a dim consciousness of the fact and try to wake, do we not say and do things which in waking life would be insane? May we not then sometimes define insanity as an inability to

distinguish which is the waking and which the sleeping life? We often dream without the least suspicion of unreality. "Sleep hath its own world," and it is often as lifelike as the other.

If this be madness, it is closely allied to the genius of Hamlet, and there is pith in the Gravedigger's observation that the Prince has been sent to England because "there the men are as mad as he." The Cheshire Cat should not shock us when it observes of Wonderland: "We're all mad here. I'm mad. You're mad." The Cheshire Cat itself seems sane enough, so detached from the frenetic proceedings it comments upon that it fades away to a mere head and finally a phosphorescent grin. But if it ends by becoming a mouthpiece, a mascot, a kind of tribal totem for British humor in its imperturbable discernment of oddities, then the episode that follows affords us a glimpse of Oxford—a mad, an endless tea-party, with pointless anecdotes and answerless riddles and feline small talk, presided over by two certified madmen, a Hatter modeled on a local character and a Hare whose watch has stopped at 6.00 o'clock. Tea-time is over, but nothing seems to lie ahead. Three little girls stay forever at the bottom of a treacle well, in the interrupted story of the Dormouse. That "Ancient City," which Dodgson refers to directly in his original manuscript, has constituted an ideal breeding ground for the cultivation of licensed eccentricity and for the humorous interplay between select intelligence and encrusted observance.

When Dodgson characterized himself as the Dodo, the reduplicated syllable echoed his stammer even while pronouncing his own surname, and the extinct bird attested his incompatibility with larger and freer worlds. When "Lewis Carroll" won unique and sudden fame, his donnish self refused to acknowledge the pseudonym that he had contrived by twisting and reversing his first two names. As conservative in politics as he was orthodox in religion, he was attached for almost 50 years to Christchurch, which is a cathedral as well as a college. An unordained cleric, a prim hobbyist, a shy devotee of lost causes and parlor tricks, he passed through a completely institutionalized career. Professionally he was—from what we gather—a mediocre mathematician and a dull teacher, supremely unconcerned with undergraduates and rather difficult in the common room. "There never *was* such a place for things not happening," he complained of Oxford to one correspondent. To another—another little girl—he confided: "But the great difficulty is that *adventures don't happen*! Oh, how *am* I to make some happen, so as to have something to tell to my darling Enid?" The adventures in his otherwise uneventful life were his friendships with hundreds of little girls, an avocation which we are inclined to view as either insipid or suspect.

All his other hobbies—games, puzzles, contraptions, album-leaves, holiday trips, and not least storytelling—

were directed single-mindedly toward that end. Since he was remarkably skilful as a portrait photographer, photographic exposure seems to have taken the place of carnal seduction at the happy climax of these courtships. His flirtations sometimes met with rebuffs from mammas and governesses, and he confessed to a cousin with wistful bravado that he lived "on the frowns of Mrs. Grundy." But there was not much cause to be alarmed. His inamoratas were too prepubescent to have interested Humbert Humbert (though it is worth noting that Vladimir Nabokov's first book was a Russian translation of *Alice in Wonderland*). The biographical record, which is stuffy if not sticky, lends itself to the cruder naïvetés of the psychoanalysts. Its symbolic effect on his writing has been summed up in two or three succinct pages by William Empson—who, as a Cambridge man, was in a special position to elucidate an Oxonian case history. Mr. Empson's essay ["*Alice in Wonderland:* The Child as Swain" (1935)], though slightly distorted by the effort to fit it into his thesis on pastoral convention, is the most illuminating study we have of Lewis Carroll, for all the bibliographers, antiquarians, and analytic philosophers who have made an oracle of him.

The light it throws upon Dodgson's motivation, though by no means irrelevant, is incidental. In some notes for an unpublished article on dress in the theater (now in the Houghton Library at Harvard), Dodgson wrote: "Base of argument lies in relations of *sex,* without which purity and impurity would be unmeaning words." One cannot overlook the sexual charge in his celibate cult of his little darlings; but the outcome, by definition, seems rather pure than impure. He once planned to edit a *Girls' Own Shakespeare,* in which he proposed to purify the text of such gross expressions as Bowdler had not excised. The demure Eros of Lewis Carroll was a Victorian ideal of delicacy, feminine yet neither female nor effeminate. We may appreciate it better if, recalling his miserable school days at Rugby, we compare Alice with Tom Brown, and with that admixture of cant and brutality which passed for what the Victorians liked to call manliness.

> Speak roughly to your little boy,
> And beat him when he sneezes . . .

In the endeavor to make things happen, the escape from the monotonous quadrangle of his own existence, Dodgson's chosen companion—indeed his surrogate—was the Dean's daughter, the second one, the one that kept tossing her head back to keep her hair out of her eyes and, when her sisters asked him for a story, hoped "there will be nonsense in it."

Alice, "Child of the pure unclouded brow," with her eager, expressive face, her long, straight hair, and her pinafore that adapts to so many sizes, is the eternal ingénue who combines Miranda's reaction to the won-

ders of a brave new world with Daisy Miller's resolve not to miss the tourist attractions. No novelist has identified more intimately with the point of view of his heroine. Except for parenthetical comments, which occur less and less frequently, the empathy is complete. "The sole medium of the stories is her pellucid consciousness," as Walter De la Mare has pointed out; this forms the medium for as elegant an exercise in the Jamesian technique of narration as *What Maisie Knew.* Since Alice is in the habit of talking to herself, there can be a good deal of monologue. When she falls silent the narrator, like a good contemporary of Flaubert, can employ *le style indirect libre*: "Down, down, down. Would the fall *never* come to an end? 'I wonder how many miles I've fallen by this time?' she said aloud." Alice began by tiring of her sister's book because it had no pictures or conversations in it. Her chronicles are not lacking in those amenities. Each adventure brings a conversation with a new and strange vis-à-vis.

As for the pictorial presentation, it is an integral part of the author's design. He started with his own sketches, chose his illustrator with the utmost concern, and worked with Tenniel in the most indelible of collaborations. Consequently, there is little description in Dodgson's prose. It is all the more convincing because he simply assumes that the sights are there, and that we visualize them through the eyes of his beholder. Instead of describing the Gryphon, he enjoins us parenthetically: "If you don't know what a Gryphon is, look at the picture." Picture and text join forces to align the reader's awareness with that of Alice. Her inherent responsiveness is controlled by the consistent gravity of demeanor imposed upon her by the inhabitants of Wonderland. After the aimless competition of the Caucus-Race, when she is compelled to supply the prizes for everybody, including herself: "Alice thought the whole thing very absurd, but they all looked so grave that she did not dare to laugh; and, as she could not think of anything to say, she simply bowed, and took the thimble, looking as solemn as she could." So it is that children learn to suppress their native instinct for laughter in the company of adults. "He talks just as if it was a game!" says Alice of the Red King. But, though it may be a game for her, he is in dead earnest.

Alice soon gets used to the tone of desperate seriousness in which she is greeted by all the creatures she meets, with the exception of the Cheshire Cat, and we get used to the plethora of exclamation points. She is sustained through their dead-pan dialogues by the sense of wonder, the sort of curiosity that animates great poets and scientists. "Curious" is the adjective with which she responds again and again. "Curiouser and curiouser!" is her apt, if ungrammatical, response to the sequence of events. "It was a curious dream," she tells her sister afterward, and that motif is taken up repeatedly in *The Nursery Alice,* the version that Dodgson rewrote for "Infants from Nought to Five." He did not hesitate to tell them how to react:

> Once upon a time, there was a little girl called Alice: and she had a very curious dream.
>
> Would you like to hear what it was that she dreamed about?
>
> Well, this was the *first* thing that happened. A White Rabbit came by, in a great hurry; and, just as it passed Alice, it stopped, and took its watch out of its pocket.
>
> Wasn't *that* a funny thing? Did *you* ever see a Rabbit that had a watch, and a pocket to put it in? Of course, when a Rabbit has a watch, it *must* have a pocket to put it in; it would never do to carry it about in its mouth—and it wants its hands sometimes, to run with.

In this elementary reduction, which may serve to emphasize the sophisticated artistry of the work itself, the rabbit does not talk at all and none of the conversations is reported. The *textus receptus,* by accepting the apparent naturalness of the situation, gains credence for its basic preposterousness. Alice's reactions are delayed. With her, we behold no more at first than a white rabbit with pink eyes:

> There was nothing so *very* remarkable in that; nor did Alice think it so *very* much out of the way to hear the Rabbit say to itself, "Oh dear! Oh dear! I shall be too late!" (when she thought it over afterwards, it occurred to her that she ought to have wondered at this, but at the time it all seemed quite natural); but when the Rabbit actually *took a watch out of its waistcoat-pocket,* and looked at it, and then hurried on, Alice started to her feet, for it flashed across her mind that she had never before seen a rabbit with either a waistcoat-pocket, or a watch to take out of it, and, burning with curiosity, she ran across the field after it, and was just in time to see it pop down a large rabbit-hole under the hedge.

In an article on the dramatic adaptation, Dodgson made clear that the contrast between the audacity and directness of Alice and the nervous shilly-shallyings of the White Rabbit was intended to stress the invidious comparison between youth and age. Significantly, since he is so worried about his costume, and since he heralds the whole adventure for Alice, the Rabbit is dressed as a herald when he makes his last appearance. Without lingering over the prenatal symbolism of the rabbit-hole or the pool of tears, we may observe that Alice's principal problem—determining her relationship with the others—is the question of size. This, in turn, becomes a question of eating and drinking, properly or improperly, as every child has been reminded so often

that the reminder punctuates the very rhythm of infancy. Alice's enlargements and diminutions are stimulated by a magical succession of eatables and potables. Like Gulliver, she finds herself out of scale with her fellow beings; but she is less concerned with Lilliputians or Brobdingnagians than with her own person and growth: "I never ask advice about growing." Dodgson himself has drawn a haunting illustration of Alice cramped within the Rabbit's house. "How puzzling all these changes are!" she exclaims.

Confused by such dizzying transformations—in short, by nothing more or less than the physiological metamorphoses of girlhood—she undergoes what modern psychologists would term an identity crisis. "Who are *you*?" the Caterpillar asks. In spite of its assurance, no caterpillar can be quite sure who *it* is, after all. "Who in the world am I?" Alice asks herself. Can she be Ada or Mabel? Or is she the White Rabbit's housemaid, Mary Ann? And would some other name confer on her a different personality? "Remember who you are," the Red Queen commands. Yet there may be some advantage, the Gnat whispers, in losing one's name. When Alice's neck grows so long that—in a pigeon's-eye view—she looks like a serpent, the Pigeon asks: "*What* are you?" She replies, rather doubtfully, "I—I'm a little girl." We can hardly blame the Pigeon for retorting: "A likely story indeed!" When she finds herself in the imaginary sphere of the Unicorn, it is he who calls her a fabulous monster. But suspended disbelief is willing to strike a bargain: he will believe in her, if she believes in him. The Lion wearily inquires whether she is animal, vegetable, or mineral. But the Messenger has already presented her credentials: "This is a child! . . . It's as large as life, and twice as natural!"

One of the most touching episodes, and possibly the profoundest, takes place in the wood where things have no name. This is truly that *selva oscura* where the straight way is lost, that forest of symbols whose meanings have been forgotten, that limbo of silence which prompts a cosmic shudder. Less traditionally, since Dodgson was among the pioneers of symbolic logic, it could represent—in W.V. Quine's phrase— "the gulf between meaning and naming." There Alice comes across an unfrightened fawn, who momentarily allows itself to be stroked. Happily they coexist for a time, undivided by identities or classifications. But the moment of self-recognition introduces a shock of alienation.

> "What do you call yourself?" the Fawn said at last. Such a soft sweet voice it had!
>
> "I wish I knew!" thought poor Alice. She answered, rather sadly: "Nothing, just now."
>
> "Think again," it said: "that won't do."

Alice thought, but nothing came of it. "Please, would you tell me what *you* call yourself?" she said timidly. "I think that might help a little."

I'll tell you, if you'll come a little further on," the Fawn said. "I can't remember *here*."

So they walked on together through the wood, Alice with her arms clasped lovingly round the soft neck of the Fawn, till they came out into another open field, and here the Fawn gave a sudden bound into the air, and shook itself free from Alice's arm. "I'm a Fawn!" it cried out in a voice of delight. "And, dear me! you're a human child!" A sudden look of alarm came into its beautiful eyes, and in another moment it had darted away at full speed.

A universe where the self has no labels or signposts to go by, in Dodgson's account, seems less estranging than a familiar environment which casts us in suspicious and hostile roles. Just as Hawthorne's faunlike protagonist regains the language of the birds and beasts when he returns to the countryside, so childhood has the faculty of communicating with nature spontaneously. Adulthood, on the other hand, superimposes its artifice, and Alice's experiences run increasingly counter to nature.

Seeking to avoid the Queen of Hearts' displeasure, her three gardeners paint her white rose-trees red. The Queen's peculiar game of croquet, by using flamingoes and hedgehogs as mallets and balls, reduces animal life to the inorganic. Alice likewise converses with the flowers, thereby allowing Dodgson to burlesque a pathetic fallacy echoed from Tennyson's *Maud*. Her royal mentors end by putting her on social terms with the inanimate objects that make up the bill of fare at the banquet: "Alice—Mutton: Mutton—Alice." Her relations with the animals are far from idyllic. Though they are never *he* or *she* but always neuter, most of them are highly anthropomorphic. They argue with her, exhort her to mind her manners, and order her around for all the world as if they were grown people. They seem to bear less resemblance to the benign household pets of Sir Edwin Landseer than—as Madame Mespoulet has shown—to the satirical caricatures of J. J. Grandville, who had provided some notable illustrations for the beast fables of La Fontaine. Lewis Carroll's bestiary is post-Darwinian in its vistas of universal struggle for survival, from the obsolescent Dodo to the suppressed guinea pigs. "Do cats eat bats?," Alice muses, or, "Do bats eat cats?"

No matter. All species prey and are preyed upon, and the domesticated are worse than the wild ones. The predatory crocodile replaces the busy bee, from the *Divine Songs for Children* of Isaac Watts,

> And welcomes little fishes in,
>   With gently smiling jaws!

So many of her poems, as Alice retrospectively realizes, have been about fishes or other forms of sea food. The impasse of communication, the exchange of ultimata, and the warfare between two mutually antagonistic realms of creation are haltingly and laconically rendered in "I sent a message to the fish." Doubtless the most memorable of these piscatories is the affecting ballad of the Oysters' betrayal, **"The Walrus and the Carpenter"**; for the stage version of *Alice* Dodgson was persuaded to soften this stark tragedy with an afterpiece, wherein the ghosts of the Oysters exact a nightmarish revenge upon their sleeping destroyers. Alice's mythical mount, the Gryphon, though it might well claim heraldic connections, chats with her in the vulgar idiom of a hackney-coachman. His partner, the Mock Turtle, is a spurious animal, a sort of zoological back-formation; but it is a genuine dish and may therefore sing, with the greatest propriety, its lugubrious song to the evening soup—originally the evening star.

Alice's unflagging and versatile appetite leads to certain embarrassments in her encounters. Yet she proves tactful enough to stop herself from admitting that her previous acquaintance with lobsters and whitings has been on the dinner table and not in the ballroom. Her shrinkages have taught her to look at matters from the other side, from the animals' vantage point. She may scorn to be three inches tall, which the Caterpillar naturally thinks is "a very good height indeed." But she learns the hard way from her initial mistake of boasting about her cat Dinah, which hurts the Mouse's feelings and drives the birds away. Cats and kittens, conceivably because of their totemic relation with human beings, are set apart from their fellow creatures ("creatures" being the term that, for Dodgson, embraces both birds and animals). When the offended Mouse consents to tell its tale, this turns out to be a typographical oddity, a calligrammatic poem in the shape of a mouse's tail. The villain is another pet, the dog Fury, who with cold-blooded brutality undertakes to be prosecutor, judge, and jury, like the Snark in the Barrister's Dream. Alice gains a taste of what it feels like to be under such jeopardy when, in her miniature state, she is nearly crushed by a monstrous puppy—a realization made vivid by Dodgson's hatred of dogs.

The fulfilment of the Mouse's caveat is the trial scene. Here the tables are turned, in the sense that the jurors are twelve good creatures and true. One of them is Bill the Lizard again, just as ineffectual with his squeaky pencil as he was in going down the chimney; but, at least, he can write. Alice gains the upper hand again by re-enacting a mishap of a week before, when she had upset a goldfish bowl at home; the reenactment exemplifies how the dreamwork has been conditioned by daily actualities. Through her divagations she has been sustained by the vision of a delightful garden and her hope of attaining the right size to enter it. Entrance to it is implicitly equated with growing up, which is bound to be somewhat disillusioning. When she eventually gets there, instead of dallying among the fountains and flower beds, she is pressed into service for the crazy croquet game. There have been some previous intimations—the Rabbit, the Duchess, the Fish and Frog Footmen—that, when she reached that enchanted terrain at last, she would find it the precinct of high society. The ugly Duchess, erstwhile so formidable in her own kitchen, has become an affable dowager, who measures an increase of height by resting her chin on Alice's shoulder and insists on pointing out a moral in everything Alice says. How tiresome can they be, these grownups?

In the manuscript, there is but a single matriarchial figure, who bears the compound title "Queen of Hearts and Marchioness of Mock Turtles." Noting in retrospect that this queen is "a sort of embodiment of ungovernable passion—a blind and aimless Fury," Dodgson reminds us of the Mouse's warning against the litigious dog Fury, and of the rage that now and then breaks out in his "frumious" (i.e. fuming and furious) personages. The Queen's habitual ukase, "Off with his head!," is the peremptory exercise of grownup authority. Her face-card features scarcely reveal the rounded lineaments of Victoria Regina, yet Alice could never have set forth upon her adventures from any other realm than a constitutional matriarchy. In *Through the Looking-Glass,* she is shuttled back and forth by two matrons even more sharply differentiated in Dodgson's intentions: the White Queen, who is "all helpless imbecility," and the Red Queen, who is "the concentrated essence of all governesses." The final examination through which they must put her, before she can become a queen in her own right, has its counterpart in the prior volume, when Alice is sent to be interviewed by the Mock Turtle, and recognizes—with due allowance for sea change—the curriculum that she has studied at day school.

Thence we are wafted not back to the garden party but to the culminating trial: a recapitulation of events and a convocation of characters to which Alice reacts with no Kafka-esque passivity. The charge as stated in the nursery rhyme, the theft of tarts, seems to be a breach of the domestic proprieties. We never reach the second stanza, where the Knave gets punished like a mischievous boy undergoing parental discipline. For Alice has been growing steadily—"a very curious sensation"—until, when she takes the witness stand, she towers above the denizens of Wonderland. She is no longer the spectator but the cynosure. Before she had met anyone, she could soliloquize: "Oh dear, what nonsense I'm talking!" The thin-skinned Mouse could expostulate with her: "You insult me by talking such nonsense!" But it is the others, more and more, who insult her by talking nonsensically. At their first encounter in the garden, "crimson with fury," the Queen of Hearts had ordered her decapitation, and Alice had

retorted boldly: "Nonsense!" Having now attained full stature, she repeats the retort with emphasis: "Stuff and nonsense!" When the Queen repeats her furious sentence, Alice dispels the whole nonsensical phantasmagoria with the sensible exorcism: "You're nothing but a pack of cards!"

She is a little girl once more when she awakens, and she must retraverse her adolescence by another route in the sequel. There we soon find her contradicting the Red Queen: "That would be nonsense—" To which the Red Queen majestically replies: "*I've* heard nonsense, compared with which that would be as sensible as a dictionary!" At a parallel stage to the exorcism of the card-pack, the second finale, Alice qualifies for her crown by the Queens' catechism: "What dreadful nonsense we *are* talking!" At her coronation, once more she tells the phantoms off and brushes them away, pulling out the tablecloth from under them and stirring the hall into pandemonium—as, Mr. Empson conjectures, Dodgson would so have liked to have done with the high table at Christchurch. We must stay with Alice, however. Consciously she seems to rouse herself, as we do when our wishdreams threaten to turn into nightmares. Deliberately she shakes the diminishing Red Queen until the figure dwindles into her black kitten. This has all been a dream, too, like the first one, which ended with Alice's older sister Lorina drowsing off into her own dream of Wonderland, and with the soft noises of the river-bank providing their oneiric sound effects. "There ought to be a book written about me, that there ought!" as Alice has been conscious from the beginning.

Her second dream propels her farther into the stratosphere of metaphysical speculation, where she is informed that she is nothing but a figment of the Red King's dream. Awakening, she speculates with her kitten as to who was the dreamer and which the reality. "He was part of my dream, of course—but then I was part of his dream, too!" After the disappearance of the Lion and the Unicorn, she all but dismisses them as a dream within a dream, when she notices the plate for their plum-cake at her feet and meditates an existential challenge.

> "So I wasn't dreaming, after all," she said to herself, "unless—unless we're all part of the same dream. Only I do hope it's *my* dream, and not the Red King's. I don't like belonging to another person's dream," she went on in a rather complaining tone: "I've a great mind to go and wake him, and see what happens!"

The Hunting of the Snark has been philosophically interpreted as a fruitless search for the Absolute; the ultimate object of man's quest is foredoomed to vanish away softly and silently; it was the last line of the "Agony" that occurred first to the agonizing poet: "For the Snark *was* a Boojum, you see." Q.E.D. Theirs not to reason why. Just what a Snark might happen to be and why the ill-sorted crew should ever have embarked on the ill-fated undertaking are never explained; and, though the dénouement is not unexpected, it is all the more horrible because it remains unspecified. That self-evident "you see" is the hollowest of ironies. *Sylvie and Bruno* carries Dodgson's mood of subjective idealism toward the evanescent conclusion of Shakespeare and Calderón. "Is life itself a dream?" the narrator wonders. And the terminal acrostic of *Through the Looking-Glass* concludes: "Life, what is it but a dream?"

The stuff of dreams is as illusory as those scented rushes which lose their fragrance and beauty when Alice picks them. Yet Dodgson catches the cinematographic movement of dreams when the grocery shop, after changing into the boat from which she gathers the dream-rushes, changes back into the shop which is identifiable as an Oxford landmark. The next phase is the egg on the shelf, which becomes Humpty Dumpty on his wall. The narration, with its corkscrew twists, carefully observes the postulate that Dodgson formulated in his seriocomic treatise, "Dynamics of a Particle": "Let it be granted that a speaker may digress from any one point to any other point." Alice proceeds by digression through Wonderland, since it does not really matter which way she goes. In the Looking-Glass Land, which is regulated by a stricter set of ground rules, she is forced to move backward from time to time. Dodgson had given himself his *donnée* by sending her down the rabbit-hole "without the least idea what was to happen afterwards." What extemporaneously followed seemed to consist, as he subsequently recounted it, "almost wholly of fits and scraps, single ideas which came of themselves." Though it may have been obsession which gave them a thematic unity, it was artistry which devised their literary form.

Symmetrically, each of the two books comprises twelve chapters. Both of them conflate the dream vision with the genre known as the *voyage imaginaire*; in effect, they merge the fairy tale with science fiction. The journey, in either case, is not a quest like *The Hunting of the Snark*—or that log-book it almost seems to parody, *Moby-Dick*. Rather, it is an exploration—underground, in the first instance, and so originally entitled *Alice's Adventures Under Ground*. This relates it to a wealth of symbols for the claustral limits of the human condition, from Plato to Dostoevsky. Falling can betoken many things: above all, the precondition of knowledge. Subterranean descent can land in an underworld, be it Hell or Elysium or the other side of the earth, the Antipodes, which Alice malapropistically calls "the Antipathies"—not so exact an opposite to our side as the Looking-Glass Country, but a topsy-turvy-dom of sorts like Butler's *Erewhon*. As we approach it, it seems to be a juvenile

utopia, what with its solemn games and half-remembered lessons and ritualized performances of nursery rhymes. Before we leave it, it becomes an unconscious *Bildungsroman,* projecting and resisting the girlish drama of physical and psychological development. "What do you suppose is the use of a child without any meaning? [fumes the Red Queen.] Even a joke should have some meaning—and a child's more important than a joke, I hope."

As for the looking-glass, that has been a traditional metaphor for narcissistic self-absorption, for art's reflection of nature, and—more abstractly—for the reversal of asymmetric relationships. Scientific commentators may see in it an adumbration of up-to-date physical theory regarding particles and anti-particles. Much more prosaically, it might be suggested that any child who grew up in a semidetached house, and had played in the adjoining house, would take as a matter of course the reversed arrangements of rooms. Dodgson, who liked to write backward, wanted to have some pages of his book printed in reverse. His fondness for inverting standard patterns is humanly personified in the mirror-image twins, Tweedledum and Tweedledee. For him, *Alice's Adventures in Wonderland* had been a discovery, an improvisation, a series of serendipities; whereas *Through the Looking-Glass,* seven years later, was faced with the usual difficulty of sequels. It made up in systematic elaboration for what it lost in spontaneous flow. If it is less organically imagined, it is replete with brilliant paradoxes, some of which do anticipate modern science. On these aspects especially, Martin Gardner has compiled a lucid and suggestive commentary in his *Annotated Alice,* to which I must express a comprehensive debt of gratitude.

Inasmuch as surprise is of the essence, there is little recurrence from book to book. We hardly recognize the Hare and the Hatter of Wonderland when they are metamorphosed into the messengers Haigha and Hatta of the Looking-Glass. The later story takes place indoors during the autumn; its predecessor took place outdoors in the spring. Alice has been impelled underground by a swift train of circumstances; she dissolves the looking-glass, for herself and her kitten, with the hypnotic formula: "Let's pretend." She is more self-conscious on her first trip, and we are more interested in what happens to her. On her second, we tend to accept her and to look around with her, as if we were accompanying her through Disneyland or the World's Fair. The shift from identity to duality is a transference from self to otherness. The presiding figures from the game of cards are as remote as epic deities until the end of Part I. Their counterparts from chess are more regularly present throughout Part II, which is framed by a chess problem—not a very deliberative one. Alice becomes a pawn, replacing the Queen's daughter Lily, and looks ahead to being queened; whereas—except for her disappointed wish to arrive at the garden—her earlier wanderings, through cavernous passages and quasi-Elysian fields, had no set destination.

The excursion shifts from time to space, from an impressionistic continuum to a more static outlook, as she crosses the chessboard landscape. Above its checkered topography looms the presence of the geometrician who laid it out and manipulates the chessmen. What is happening has happened before and will happen again, at predictable intervals as long as folklore persists. Tweedledum and Tweedledee will fight; the Lion and the Unicorn will be drummed out of town; Humpty Dumpty will fall from his wall and, though not reconstructed by all the King's horses or men, will somehow be enabled to re-enact the performance. Now, all fairylands, utopias, paradises, and other imagined worlds—whatever improvements they may have to offer—are bound to draw their inspiration from the one world that their imaginer knows at first hand. It would be unlikely if Dodgson's creations were not liberally sprinkled with local and topical allusions. Sir John Tenniel, who was mainly a political caricaturist, occasionally injected an overt touch: in his drawing of the Lion and Unicorn we discern the features of rival candidates, the Earl of Derby and Disraeli. The latter also seems to have posed for the traveler dressed in white paper, peculiarly appropriate for a Prime Minister, who sits opposite Alice in the railway carriage.

This locale, a favorite with Dodgson, invites a passing glance at nineteenth-century technology. The chorus of voices that Alice hears, while a passenger, chants a commercial refrain where everything is evaluated at £1000. Since the train is going the wrong way, according to the guard, it escapes to the domain of fancy from the workaday world to which it belongs. Dodgson would try to encompass those two worlds, together with a pious romance, a whimsical tract, and divers other polarities, within the two volumes of *Sylvie and Bruno*. Therein, by means of psychic transitions, the narrative is systematically transposed from the Commonplace to the Marvelous—from Outland, the regime of conspiratorial adults, "Through the Ivory Gate" to Elfland, the preserve of cloying juveniles. The happiest feature of this ambitious scheme is a device which is used to modulate from one plane to the other. At the transitional moment, a Mad Gardener sings a song whose pattern becomes familiar:

> "He thought he saw an Elephant
>   That practised on a fife:
> He looked again, and found it was
>   A letter from his wife.
> 'At length I realise,' he said,
>   'The bitterness of Life!'"

If Dodgson had been a romanticist, his daydream might have turned that conjugal letter—that grimly realistic slice of life—into a missive from a fair stranger. Instead—and this is what spells the difference between romance and nonsense—life is made less bitter by the spectacle of a tootling elephant. The transformation is made explicit by the Professor, who is the Carrollian mentor of Sylvie and Bruno, when he persuades the Gardener to unlock, for the three of them, what is tantamount to the gate of fantasy:

> "He thought he saw a Garden-Door
>   That opened with a Key:
> He looked again, and found it was
>   A Double Rule of Three:
> 'And all its mystery,' he said,
>   'Is clear as day to me!'"

Alice thought she saw a host of chimeras. She looked again, and found it was only a pack of cards or a set of chessmen. There is nothing, of course, so extraordinary in that. Dodgson's achievement was to prolong her reveries, and to lend their figments every appearance of solidity. Occasional echoes recall to us those matter-of-fact details from Alice's waking life—the fishes, the fire irons—which have been transmuted into fantasies. Unlike those of *Sylvie and Bruno,* wherein the two states are kept apart, her imaginative processes blend them together. "So many out-of-the-way things had happened lately that Alice had begun to think that very few things indeed were really impossible." That state of mind in which everything seems possible can be maintained by preserving the conventions in the most absurd situations. Alice practices making a curtsy, like a properly brought-up little girl, even while she is falling down the rabbit-hole. In one of Dodgson's magazine sketches, his hero thought he saw a signboard advertising "Romancement." He looked again, and was informed that two words had inadvertently been run together: that the sign advertised a much humbler and harder commodity, namely "Roman Cement." Meanwhile, a displaced word could act as an incantation to conjure up a prospect of Elfland.

This transfiguration of commonplace objects and familiar landmarks is largely a verbal process. The slightest variation in spelling or pronunciation can effect a drastic change, but the Cheshire Cat would be equally unsurprised if the baby turned into a pig or a fig. Alice becomes uncomfortably aware that something odd has been happening to her *Weltanschauung* when her memorized arithmetic comes out scrambled and her geography seems to be disoriented. But the real test is—as it should be—poetry, and the transforming device is parody. Periodically she is called upon to recite, or else listen to, a selection of gems from the repertory of the nursery, dimly recognizable but strangely transmogrified. "Some of the words have got altered" in her recollection of Southey's parable about Father William, so that the cautionary elder has become an impenitent prankster, rebuffing the youth's curiosity with a threat to kick him downstairs. This is, by implication, a rebuff to the perpetual questioning from Alice herself. Watts's verses for infants, which are as oppressively moralistic as the Duchess, are released from their didactic burdens in the retelling: the ubiquitous lobster turns ventriloquist and obtrudes itself into "The Voice of the Sluggard."

The distinction between sense and nonsense, in the poem read into the record as evidence against the Knave of Hearts, is obliterated by the omission of proper names. As a result, the reader gropes from relative pronoun to relative pronoun in a game of grammatical blindman's buff:

> They told me you had been to her,
> And mentioned me to him . . .

The resulting disorientation foreshadows the wood of namelessness or Humpty Dumpty's doctrine that names confer meaning. Alice dismisses the poem as meaningless, though the King endeavors to explicate it, not very successfully. On the other hand, the whispering Gnat succeeds in creating new subspecies of insects by extrapolation from names of existing flies. The Rocking-horse-fly and the Bread-and-butter-fly are worthy subjects for Tenniel's unnaturalism. But the artist firmly balked at the author's notion of a wasp in a wig; that was, he objected, "beyond the appliance of art." It is significant that, when Dodgson composed his ballad about the Walrus, he let Tenniel decide whether the deuteragonist should be a carpenter, a baronet, or a butterfly. Since all three were metrically equivalent, and none required rhymes, the choice was left to depend upon their graphic possibilities—no richer, one would think, for an ostreophagous butterfly than for a periwigged wasp. Verbal considerations were secondary to visual for the nonce.

But, as the Dormouse shrieks when its anecdote trails off into nouns beginning with M, "Did you ever see such a thing as a drawing of a muchness!" Ordinarily, the word precedes the thing. *Façons de parler* regain their primitive magic by being taken literally. Thus, to answer the door is to assume that the door has spoken first. Expressions like Time and Nobody cast off their abstractness and take on the misplaced concreteness of personalities. Metaphors, such as "feather" and "catch a crab" when Alice is rowing, can be all too easily hypostatized. Puns are means of unexpected propulsion, because they change the subject so abruptly: they switch fortuitously from one theme to another, with trees that bark like dogs or books so tedious that they dry you off when you get wet. The key words, in Alice's recipe for bread, have a misleading significance for the White Queen:

> "You take some flour—"

> "Where do you pick the flower?" the White Queen asked. "In a garden or in the hedges?"

> "Well, it isn't *picked* at all," Alice explained: "it's *ground*—"

> "How many acres of ground?" said the White Queen. "You mustn't leave out so many things."

Such redundancies must not be left out, if vital information is to be conveyed. The pun, or any other type of wordplay where relevance is determined by the chance of two sounds coinciding, is a standing invitation to absurdity for better or worse. Insofar as it frees us from the responsibility for being rational, it can be a source of relief. One of the unmistakable marks that make the Snark so inevitable a quarry is its general lack of humor and its particular resistance to punning:

> "The third is its slowness in taking a jest.
>   Should you happen to venture on one,
> It will sigh like a thing that is deeply
>   distressed:
>   And it always looks grave at a pun."

It seems characteristic of Lewis Carroll that the most touchingly serious of his lyrics should be the acrostic on Alice Pleasance Liddell. Alliteration, as a variant of rhyme, can be meaningful but is often farfetched. The crew that sails after the Snark is so utterly miscellaneous because it is made up of occupations which alliterate with the Bellman: the Baker, the Butcher, the Broker, the Banker, the Barrister, the Bonnet-maker, the Billiard-marker, the Boots, and the Beaver. Alice shows us how to mix things up by affecting the letter, when she plays the word game, "I love my love with an H." Nonetheless, given the semi-rationality of the human mind, even a jumbling together of incongruities must be patterned by some principle of order—if only by an initial consonant. The Walrus talks

> "Of shoes—of ships—of sealing-wax—
>   Of cabbages—and kings—"

and sealing-wax is one of the ingredients of the White Knight's pudding (perhaps for personal reasons connected with Dodgson's voluminous correspondence). "It's not easy to be nonsensical," said Marcel Duchamp, the veteran of cubism and surrealism, in a recent interview, "because nonsensical things so often turn out to make sense." Striving for sheer random heterogeneity, one is much more likely to produce an unconscious association of ideas or a deliberate juxtaposition of opposites:

> "And why the sea is boiling hot—
>   And whether pigs have wings."

The value of verse, in this respect, is that its formal constraints are constantly pressing toward a dissociation of sound and sense. The serious poet must struggle against the current; the nonsense poet may float along with it, gurgling happily down the stream. And though there are many varieties of nonsense poetry, which Alfred Liede has earnestly surveyed in his two substantial volumes, *Dichtung als Spiel: Studien der Unsinnspoesie an den Grenzen der Sprache,* "Lewis Carroll is the most enigmatic of nonsense poets." The poem that both illustrates and demonstrates the enigma for us is bound to be **"Jabberwocky,"** which—as its title obscurely hints—seems to be a heroic lay about language. Alice has discovered it in a book, at the outset of her second expedition, and it has filled her head with ideas; but she does not comprehend them until the midpoint, when she encounters Humpty Dumpty, whose onomatopoetic name fulfils his linguistic theories and asserts his cavalier nominalism. "The question is," as he expounds it to Alice, "which is to be master—that's all." The ancient nursery rhyme from which he derives his being was once a riddle rhymed in many languages. The answer is a symbol with many meanings, from the egg that germinates life to the fall that shatters it.

Hence he is fully qualified to be Dodgson's philosopher and philologist; from the precarious eminence of his hybris, he dominates the problems of interpretation; and, after his lecture to Alice on semantics, he sets forth an exegesis of **"Jabberwocky"** which is a model for higher and newer criticism.

> 'Twas brillig, and the slithy toves
>   Did gyre and gimble in the wabe:
> All mimsy were the borogoves,
>   And the mome raths outgrabe.

Dodgson, at the age of twenty-three, had lettered this opening quatrain in pseudo-runic characters into his family periodical *Mischmasch,* under the caption "Stanzas from Anglo-Saxon Poetry," and with a commentary anticipating Humpty Dumpty. It was wise of him to leave the Anglo-Saxon attitudes to the King's Messengers in **Through the Looking-Glass,** since the lines have little in common with Old English, except for the alliterative pairing of "gyre" and "gimble," plus a certain profusion of gutturals. As a matter of fact, the metrical scheme is one which could evoke reverberations from a nearer monument:

> And this is why I sojourn here,
>   Alone and palely loitering,
> Though the sedge is wither'd from the lake,
>   And no birds sing.

Humpty Dumpty puts on a dazzling exhibition of his mastery over words, in glossing the unfamiliar nouns and verbs and adjectives. Some of these are no more than archaisms; others, which interest us more, are neologisms; and the most interesting, among the latter, are those composites which Dodgson invented and

patented as portmanteau words for the diction of dreams.

Leaving them opaque, together with the "very curious-looking creatures" that they denote, we are swept along by the firm syntactic and rhythmic structure, which frames the ineffable adventure and makes it perfectly credible, whatever it may mean. That outline is reinforced if, experimentally, we substitute obvious phrases for obscure ones:

> 'Twas April, and the heavy rains
>   Did drip and drizzle on the road:
> All misty were the windowpanes,
>   And the drainpipes outflowed.

Lacking the dim suggestiveness of those slithy toves and mome raths, this is much too flat and prosy; but it indicates, with diagrammatic sharpness, how the exotic colors have been applied within the convertional contours. Let us intensify the experiment by pitching it in a more apocalyptic key:

> 'Twas doomsday, and the rabid curs
>   Did yelp and yodel in the void:
> All strident were the trumpeters,
>   And the big guns deployed.

This approaches nonsense again, since the very rigidities of syntax and meter—the need to meet formal requirements while sustaining a certain tone, but not necessarily advancing any thought—make nonsense very difficult to avoid and sense extremely easy to neglect. James Joyce, Humpty Dumpty's professed disciple, did not relax these rigidities when he wrote *Finnegans Wake* in prose; rather, he extended them, since his distortions of speech were posited upon correct inflections and set rhythms. Dodgson's surprises, like Joyce's, depend on the calculated subversion of well-established expectations. Order has been artfully deranged to create the illusion of chaos.

"Jabberwocky," despite the double talk of its somnambulistic vocabulary, conforms to all the conventions of balladry. Childe Roland to the dark tower comes; Jack ends by killing the Giant; and, if the Snark proves a Boojum, it is not permitted to vanish away. Grappling with the nameless terrors that menace us all, Dodgson might have boasted, like his insomniac Baker:

> "I engage with the Snark—every night after dark—
>   In a dreamy delirious fight . . ."

The White King is similarly obsessed with Bandersnatches, who can never be caught or stopped, but who would seem to be lesser evils than the Jabberwock. The slaying of that dread apparition marks a rite of passage for the beamish boy, whoever he may be. Tenniel depicts him sturdily planted like David before Goliath, confronting a dragon-like foe who is not less terrifying because—like our timid friend, the White Rabbit—he is wearing a waistcoat. The picture was conceived and executed as a frontispiece to *Through the Looking-Glass.* However, it proved so horrendous that Dodgson feared it might frighten his child readers. Accordingly, he went to the other extreme; after conducting a private poll among their mothers, he decided to replace the hobgoblin with a good genius; and so the book opens with Tenniel's equestrian portrait of the "gentle foolish face" and the ingeniously cumbersome panoply of the White Knight, accompanied by a pedestrian Alice.

Her belated champion deserves the honor; for he is the kindliest of her guides and advisers, indeed the truest hero of her story; and it is their encounter, we are told, that she will always remember most clearly. After the preparatory rounds between Tweedledum and Tweedledee and between the Lion and the Unicorn, there is a climactic battle when the Red Knight cries "Check!" and the White Knight somehow manages to rescue Alice, with the noise of fire irons clanking against the fender not far away. With the loping move of the knight in chess, falling off his horse every pace or two, he escorts her to the square where queenship awaits her. Their farewell is as poignant as Dante's from Vergil at the upper boundaries of Purgatory. But the Knight has a closer precedent in Don Quixote, whom he emulates with his uncertain horsemanship and his headful of chimerical plans. His memorable song, which functions as a kind of cadenza to the work as a whole, parodies Wordsworth's "Resolution and Independence," where the dejected poet is revivified by the example of the old leech-gatherer playing his humble trade on the lonely moor. An earlier version of Dodgson's burlesque had been separately published, and he drew the character of the Knight to suit the speaker in it. Therefore it is a portrait within a portrait. As Mr. Gardner suggests, Dodgson set up a looking-glass across from his looking-glass.

The image reflected from the one to the other ad infinitum is thus a self-caricature: Dodgson as Lewis Carroll as the White Knight as the speaker of the poem as its interlocutor,

> an aged aged man,
> A-sitting on a gate.

Dodgson admitted as much in a later memoir, "Isa's Visit to Oxford," when he referred to himself as "the Aged Aged Man." No doubt many voices in the two stories are primarily his own: the grumpiness of the Caterpillar, the amusement of the Cheshire Cat, the pedagogy of Humpty Dumpty. In the amiable eccentric who sings the song—and even more in the useless

ingenuities, the woolgathering projects, and the endearing crotchets of its quixotic protagonist—Dodgson has offered us his *apologia pro vita sua.* Virginia Woolf discerned that he had preserved a child within him intact; meanwhile his outer self had become a pedant, who measured everyone's words with a literalness which exposed the contradictions by which they lived; yet, in the dialogue between the incongruous pair, childhood took the measure of pedantry. Understandably the White Knight is disappointed when Alice sheds no tears at his recital. But the game is virtually over. Alice has only to leap across the brook, be crowned, and wake up to a less adventurous actuality. The storyteller, folding his chessboard and putting away the pieces, can voice the satisfaction of a demiurge who has populated a cosmos and set it in motion, with the White Knight's vaunt: "It's my own invention!"

Donald Rackin (essay date 1966)

SOURCE: "Alice's Journey to the End of Night," in *PMLA,* Vol. LXXXI, No. 5, October, 1966, pp. 313-26.

[*Rackin is known as a leading Carroll scholar. In the following essay, he explores the theme of chaos and order in* Alice's Adventures in Wonderland, *calling the work "a comic myth of man's insoluble problem of meaning in a meaningless world."*]

In the century now passed since the publication of *Alice's Adventures in Wonderland,* scores of critical studies have attempted to account for the fascination the book holds for adult readers. Although some of these investigations offer provocative insights, most of them treat Carroll in specialized modes inaccessible to the majority of readers, and they fail to view *Alice* as a complete and organic work of art. Hardly a single important critique has been written of *Alice* as a self-contained fiction, distinct from *Through the Looking-Glass* and all other imaginative pieces by Carroll. Critics also tend to confuse Charles Dodgson the man with Lewis Carroll the author; this leads to distorted readings of Alice that depend too heavily on the fact, say, that Dodgson was an Oxford don, or a mathematician, or a highly eccentric Victorian gentleman with curious pathological tendencies. The results are often analyses which fail to explain the total work's undeniable impact on the modern lay reader unschooled in Victorian political and social history, theoretical mathematics, symbolic logic, or Freudian psychology. It seems time, then, that *Alice* be treated for what it most certainly is—a book of major and permanent importance in the tradition of English fiction, a work that still pertains directly to the experience of the unspecialized reader, and one that exemplifies the profound questioning of reality which characterizes the mainstream of nineteenth-century English literature.

The fact that Carroll's first version of *Alice's Adventures in Wonderland* was called *Alice's Adventures under Ground* is surprisingly prophetic. Perhaps even the final version would be more appropriately entitled *Alice's Adventures under Ground,* since, above all else, it embodies a comic horror-vision of the chaotic land beneath the man-made groundwork of Western thought and convention.

Alice's dogged quest for Wonderland's meaning in terms of her above-ground world of secure conventions and self-assured regulations is doomed to failure. Her only escape is in flight from Wonderland's complete anarchy—a desperate leap back to the above-ground certainties of social formalities and ordinary logic. Her literal quest serves, vicariously, as the reader's metaphorical search for meaning in the lawless, haphazard universe of his deepest consciousness. Thus, the almost unanimous agreement among modern critics that *Alice* is a dream-vision turns out to be far more than a matter of technical classification. If it were merely that, one might dismiss the work (and some critics have) as simply a whimsical excursion into an amusing, child-like world that has little relevance to the central concerns of adult life and little importance in comparison to the obviously "serious" works that explore these concerns. But if "dream-vision" is understood as serious thinkers (ranging from medieval poets to modern psychologists) have so often understood it, as an avenue to knowledge that is perhaps more meaningful—and frequently more horrifying—than any that the unaided conscious intellect can discover, then it provides an almost perfect description of the very substance of Carroll's masterpiece.

Merely to list the reverses Alice encounters in Wonderland is to survey at a glance an almost total destruction of the fabric of our so-called logical, orderly, and coherent approach to the world. Practically all pattern, save the consistency of chaos, is annihilated. First, there are the usual modes of thought—ordinary mathematics and logic: in Wonderland they possess absolutely no meaning. Next are the even more basic social and linguistic conventions: these too lose all validity. Finally, the fundamental framework of conscious predication—orderly Time and Space—appears nowhere except in the confused memory of the befuddled but obstinate visitor from above ground. Alice, therefore, becomes the reader's surrogate on a frightful journey into meaningless night. The only difference between Alice and the reader—and this is significant—is that she soberly, tenaciously, childishly refuses to accept chaos completely for what it is, while the adult reader almost invariably responds with the only defense left open to him in the face of unquestionable chaos—he laughs. Naturally he laughs for other reasons, too. But the essence of Alice's adventures beneath commonly accepted ground is the grimmest comedy conceivable,

the comedy of man's absurd condition in an apparently meaningless world.

If *Alice's Adventures in Wonderland,* then, is best viewed as a grimly comic trip through the lawless underground that lies just beneath the surface of our constructed universe, what gives the work its indisputable relevance to that universe, what keeps *Alice* itself from becoming formless, inconsistent, and confusing? The answer to this question is at once an explanation of *Alice's* literary nature and a tentative glimpse at a fundamental problem of modern man.

Let us begin at the beginning. Alice enters upon her journey underground simply because she is *curious*: she follows the White Rabbit down the rabbit hole, "never once considering how in the world she was to get out again." With the fearlessness of the innocent child, the intellectual and spiritual recklessness of a heedless scientist or saint, Alice takes her gigantic and seemingly irreversible leap into the world beneath and beyond ordinary human experience.

Significantly, Alice brings along with her a number of things from that old world above ground, the most important being her beleif in the simple orderliness of the universe. For example, in the midst of her long fall she retains her old belief in regular causal relations and puts the empty marmalade jar back into a cupboard in order to avoid "killing somebody underneath," whatever "killing" may mean to her. She wonders, as she falls and falls, about many things—all in terms of the world she has left behind, as if she had not really left it at all. She wonders what latitude or longitude she has arrived at, even though "latitude" and "longitude" are meaningless words to her and meaningless measurements under the ground. She wonders whether she will come out on the other side of the earth, where people called "The Antipathies" walk with their heads downwards (a prophetic pun, for the majority of the "people" she will meet will be truly "Antipathies" to Alice).

Already a pattern is discernible: Alice's assumptions are typically no more than her elders' operating premises which she maintains with a doctrinaire passion that is almost a caricature of immature credulity. For her, these premises are empty words, yet her faith in their validity is almost boundless. Carroll thus economically establishes one important facet of his protagonist before her adventures and her quest for meaning begin in earnest: she has reached that stage of development where the world appears completely explainable and unambiguous, that most narrow-minded, prejudiced period of life where, paradoxically, daring curiosity is wedded to uncompromising literalness and priggish, ignorant faith in the fundamental sanity of all things. With a few deft strokes, Carroll has prepared us for Alice's first major confrontation with chaos.

She is ready to cope with the "impossible" in terms of the "possible," and we are ready to understand and laugh at her literal-minded reactions.

To all of us the concept of constant or predictable size is fairly important; to a child of seven or eight it is often a matter of physical and mental survival. However, since Alice wants to pass through the tiny door into the "loveliest garden you ever saw," she herself wishes the destruction of the principle of constant size: she wishes she could find the way to shut up like a telescope. Fortunately, "so many out-of-the-way things had happened lately" that she has "begun to think that very few things indeed [are] really impossible." Here Alice's mind is operating along logical lines established before her arrival in the confusing underground. She deals with the impossible as if it had to conform to the regular causal operations of her old world above ground. But the adult reader knows better: in addition to recognizing the fallacies of Alice's reasoning in terms of traditional above-ground logic, the reader also realizes that in an under-ground world where "impossibility" is, as it were, the rule, Alice has no right to assume that the old logic itself still applies. The fact that Alice's illogical reasoning holds true in this case merely indicates that if Wonderland operates on any firm principle, that principle most certainly runs counter to the normal logic of the everyday world.

In any event, Alice is comparatively successful this time—her apparent logic seems to hold true. No doubt her first limited successes and her ability more or less to control events at the beginning serve to make her later setbacks all the more perplexing. Besides, although her ability to change her size at will is at first pleasurable (as it well might be to children, who often equate size with power), it soon becomes a mixed blessing. Although she "had got so much into the way of expecting nothing but out-of-the-way things to happen, that it seemed quite dull and stupid for life to go on in the common way," rapid, almost haphazard changes from ten inches to nine feet are usually accompanied by downright dangerous circumstances like deep pools of tears and frightfully cramped quarters. Nevertheless, even here Wonderland still bears some relationship to above-ground causality: growing big or small still seems to have predictable effects. Amidst all the comedy, however, the ominous destructive process has begun: two reasonably constant aspects of ordinary existence—natural growth and predictable size—have already lost their validity. Whether or not Alice recognizes it, a wedge has been driven into her old structure of meaning.

It is only natural that in such circumstances of confusion, a child would try to relate himself to the secure stability of the past. Alice soon says, "Dear, dear! How queer everthing is today! And yesterday things went on just as usual . . . if I'm not the same, the next question is, 'Who in the world am I?' Ah, *that's* the great puzzle!" This fallacious and ironically comic "in-the-world" approach bears watching. Earlier Alice followed the rabbit, "never once considering how in the world she was to get out again." Alice typically persists in fruitless attempts to relate her truly "out-of-the-world" adventures to her previous "in-the-world" assumptions. Perhaps sensing that her above-ground identity rested on arbitrary, constructed systems like arithmetic, she attempts to re-establish it by reciting her rote-learned lessons: "Let me see: four times five is twelve, and four times six is thirteen, and four times seven is—oh dear! I shall never get to twenty at that rate!" But Alice is in Wonderland, where old assumptions—that rabbits cannot talk, that longitude and latitude can always plot position, that size and growth must be fairly regular—have already proven ridiculously invalid. Of course, her arithmetic (as some specialists have pointed out) still makes sense, but only to a relatively sophisticated mind; and even then the sense it makes only serves to strengthen a vision of the arbitrary nature of common above-ground approaches to meaning. Alice herself has an intuition of this truth when she asserts, "However, the Multiplication Table doesn't signify: let's try Geography." But even before she begins her confused geography recitation ("London is the capital of Paris," and so on), the reader suspects that she is again headed for failure, since the ordinary concept of Space, too, is already on its way to oblivion.

Directly after these amusing arithmetical and geographical setbacks, Alice attempts to establish her previous identity by reciting Watts's moral verses about the busy bee and Satan's mischief for idle hands. Once again it is all wrong. Even her voice sounds "hoarse and strange," as if taking some uncontrollable, demonic delight in the parody ("How doth the little crocodile"). In this one short comic poem, another above-ground principle is subverted. For regardless of the patent sentimentality of verses like "How doth the little busy bee / Improve each shining hour," they are for many a child the only morality he yet knows (indeed, the very triteness of such verses reflects a truth about the seemingly more sincere moral aphorisms of adults). Alice's comic recitation also subverts the sentimental convention that animals are innately moral, and this subversion ties in neatly with Alice's later encounters with the animals of Wonderland: for the most part they will not be like Watt's busy little bee; they will be more like Alice's nasty crocodile. Hence, moral precepts, like orderly growth, are meaningless or cruelly twisted in Wonderland. And with so many familiar, comforting concepts already lost, Alice naturally begins to sense her isolation. She wishes that those she left above ground would call her back because she is "so *very* tired of being all alone here!"

A number of psychoanalytic interpretations of *Alice* stress the importance of this motif of self-identity. Psychoanalytic techniques, however, seem rather superfluous in this case: most adult readers easily recognize that this most crucial above-ground convention—the nearly universal belief in permanent self-identity—is put to the test and eventually demolished in Wonderland. Alice is constantly perplexed with the same question: "Who am I?" When, in the fourth chapter, the White Rabbit orders her about like his servant Mary Ann, Alice (attempting, as usual, to relate her adventures to some orderly pattern applicable to above-ground experience) accepts the new role and imagines how the new identity will follow her back to her old world, where her cat Dinah will order her about in the same fashion. In addition, her continuing changes in size represent a variation of the self-identity theme, since to a child differences in size represent definite changes in actual identity. Alice's tortured "What *will* become of me?" in reaction to her apparently uncontrolled growth and her fearful acceptance of the role as servant to a rabbit are, then, more than the amusing responses of a little girl to general confusion. They are her reactions to the destruction of three basic above-ground asumptions—orderly growth, the hierarchy of animals and men, and consistent identity.

Not only is Alice's previous identity meaningless in Wonderland; the very concept of permanent identity is invalid. A pack of cards can be a group of people, a child can turn into a pig, a cat's grin can exist without a cat. Even inanimate objects like stones lack simple consistency; in the fourth chapter, when the White Rabbit and his group throw pebbles at Alice, who is trapped by her enormous size in the house which is now far too small for her, she notices "with some surprise, that the pebbles [are] all turning into little cakes." Well schooled in the above-ground principles of regular causality and by now quite determined to assume that the same principles are operative in this Wonderland of impossibilities, Alice proceeds in her doggedly logical manner: "If I eat one of these cakes . . . it's sure to make some change in my size; and, as it can't possibly make me larger, it must make me smaller, I suppose." It is the "I suppose" that humorously hints at what may be happening somewhere deep within Alice. Pedestrian as her mind is, she is beginning to get a glimmer of the "principle" of Wonderland—that it operates on *no* principle whatsover. Yet her subsequent eating of the pebbles that are now little cakes represents her stubborn determination to act as if her above-ground order still obtains.

From the very beginning of the underground adventures, anothr worldly convention—that verbal communication is potentially logical and unambiguous—has been surreptitiously assailed. Finally, when Alice and the strange animals emerge soaking from her pool of tears, linguistic order dissolves completely, appropri-

ately in a dramatized pun. The Mouse announces in all seriousness that he will dry them: his method is to recite a passage from a history textbook, the "driest thing" he knows. Here Wonderland, through the comic agency of the Mouse and his "dry" history lesson, subverts a fundamental principle of everyday language. His confusion of symbol and object has far-reaching metaphysical significance, but all we need note here is that this confusion is one more contribution to the clear pattern of destruction running through all of Alice's adventures.

Much of the humor in this chapter, which begins with the semantic mix-up over the word *dry,* is based on similar linguistic mayhem. The assembled creatures cannot accept language on its own grounds. They want it to do what it cannot do. For one thing, they want it to be logical. When the Mouse states in his "dry" tale that Stigland "found it advisable," he is interrupted by the Duck, who wants to known the antecedent noun for "it" before the Mouse has a chance to continue. Here is a twist in Wonderland's destructive strategy: instead of contradicting the validity of man-made constructs and conventions by merely carrying on without them, Wonderland manages in the very act of using them to be far more subversive. Actually, the Duck's demand is a dramatic *reductio ad absurdum* of traditional grammar. He implicitly puts above-ground linguistic assumptions to the test by asking language to do what is finally impossible—to be consistently unambiguous. Such a new turn in strategy enriches the complexity of the humorous attack on above-ground convention and our illusion of cosmic order. By demanding that language be consistently sequential, Wonderland, so to speak, destroys the false logic of language with logic itself. This new strategy demonstrates one more weapon in Wonderland's comic arsenal: whenever the world above ground claims to be strictly consistent—as in Space, size, or mathematics—Wonderland is, by its very operations, maddeningly inconsistent. But whenever the world above ground is admittedly inconsistent—as in grammar—then Wonderland strenuously demands complete consistency. Such an oblique attack forces the reader to remember what he always knew—one cannot expect ordinary language to be unambiguous like mathematics. However, the urgent, rude insistence of Wonderland creatures (like the Eaglet's cry "Speak English!" or later the March Hare's "say what you mean" with its implication that language is not reversible like mathematical equations) neatly satirizes the common world's illogicality; and so, in the midst of all the fun, one more conventional prop of order begins to crumble.

As Chapter iii progresses, this conventional prop finally disintegrates. When Alice asks the Dodo what a Caucus-Race is (that is, when she asks him to define a word with other words) and thereby unwittingly tests a fundamental aspect of language, his only answer is "the best way to explain it is to do it." When the Mouse asserts that his "is a long and a sad tale," Alice replies, "It *is* a long tail . . . but why do you call it sad?" When the Mouse says *"not,"* Alice thinks he refers to a *knot.* Here, then, another above-ground assumption (one that perplexed Charles Dodgson all his life)—that ordinary language, whether written or spoken, has at least the potential to be univocal—dissolves as swiftly and easily as the smiling Cheshire Cat. And as Alice's adventures continue, this comic subversion of linguistic convention increases in both scope and intensity.

In Chapter v, "Advice from a Caterpillar," the destruction of the above-ground hierarchy of animals and men obviously steps up in intensity. This chapter also continues the attack on Alice's belief in orderly language and relates that belief to another set of worldly conventions, the customs of social etiquette. The Caterpillar plays a role similar to Humpty Dumpty's in *Through the Looking-Glass.* Although he is by no means the incisive, dictatorial critic of language that Humpty Dumpty is, he is just as rude in his disparagement of Alice's linguistic habits. The Caterpillar also demonstrates by his actions that the conventions of etiquette in social intercourse are meaningless in Wonderland. Alice has already suffered the rudeness of the White Rabbit, but the brusque orders of that timid authoritarian are almost polite in comparison to the barbarisms of the Caterpillar. Alice's own politeness to the Caterpillar increases at first in practically inverse proportion to his mounting rudeness. As his demands upon her patience reach fantastic heights, she makes it a point to address him as "Sir" and to reply "very politely" to his ridiculously unfair criticisms of her speech, "swallowing down her anger as well as she [can]." This amusing reaction by Alice, occurring as it does in many places in Wonderland, is another example of her attempt to find an order underground that somehow corresponds to the order of her previous life. Certainly, in that life it is sometimes the most impolite, imperious people who command the most respect and obedience; and to a child under the domination of inscrutable adults such a paradox may appear to be orderly and right.

The most impolite remark of the Caterpillar is his very first laconic question. Its crudeness is magnified when he repeats it contemptuously—"Who are *You?"* With characteristic comic understatement, the narrator observes that "this was not an encouraging opening for a conversation." Indeed, in the light of Alice's many previous troubles about self-identity, the direct question becomes far more than a matter of ordinary impoliteness.

Alice responds with another attempt to recall a rote-learned, moralistic poem from her past. This time she recites in response to the gruff commands of the Caterpillar, but the results is the same—it comes out all

wrong. "You are old, Father William," the lively parody of Southey's didactic verses, is, like "How doth the little crocodile," more than a humorous poem. It is, in this context of outlandish impoliteness, a kind of versified paraphrase of the almost immoral rudeness of the Caterpillar. Alice's Father William seems the antithesis of Southey's pious, temperate old man who has come gently to the end of his days. Her Father William has the air of an impolite old rake, and a conniving one at that:

> "In my youth," said the sage, as he shook his
>   grey locks,
> "I kept all my limbs very supple
> By the use of this ointment—one shilling the
>   box—
> Allow me to sell you a couple?"

The Caterpillar is thus closer to the truth than Alice is when he tells her that her recitation is not, as she says, merely wrong because "some of the words have got altered"; it is, as he asserts, "wrong from beginning to end," because it runs counter to the whole moral spirit of the original poem. Again in a recitation, Alice has yielded to that uncontrollable imp within her and joined willingly in the comic destruction of above-ground convention.

The rudeness of the Caterpillar contributes to the continuing antipathy between Alice and the creatures of Wonderland. Generally, she is met with condescension or mistrust, and most of the creatures she encounters are quick to contradict her. No doubt there is an element of fear in their authoritarian rudeness: they probably suspect that Alice, somewhat like an adult with children, holds the power of life and death over them. She can reject them, seemingly destroy them with a few words like "nonsense" or "You're nothing but a pack of cards!" But whatever their motives, these creatures of Wonderland are, according to all of Alice's acquired standards of social decorum, extremely discourteous (in fact, since they are strangers and Alice is something like a guest, they should be more polite, not less). Alice, clinging to her above-ground code of behavior, is either assiduously polite or ignorantly determined to educate them in her old etiquette. Significantly, most of her rules consist of "don'ts," obviously laid down by adults and now taken on complete faith by this literal-minded and priggish child. At the Mad Tea-Party, for example, Alice says to the Mad Hatter, "You should learn not to make personal remarks. . . . It's very rude." But here again, as in Wonderland's attacks on her illogical language, Alice's conventions are wittily turned upon themselves: when she violates her own dogmatic principle of decorum and rudely says to the Hatter, "Nobody asked *your* opinion," he "triumphantly" retorts, "Who's making personal remarks now?" And poor Alice finds herself at a new impasse: she does "not quite know what to say to this." She has been tested by her own principle and has been discredited, and she is, significantly, at a loss for *words*.

In the same chapter with the Caterpillar, Carroll touches so lightly upon another absurd "impossibility" that it almost escapes our attention the way it completely escapes Alice's. The Caterpillar leaves Alice with a rudeness so blatant that it is funny. He "yawned once or twice . . . got down off the mushroom, and crawled away into the grass, merely remarking, as [he] went, 'One side will make you grow taller, and the other side will make you grow shorter'." Alice, in a quandary, thinks to herself: "One side of *what*?" And the Caterpillar says, "'Of the mushroom,' . . . just as if she had asked it aloud." No more is said of this unusual occurrence, but readers may well be impressed by such clairvoyance. For it is still one of our cherished aboveground beliefs that communication between separate minds necessitates some exchange of tangible symbols, and, even if we admit the validity of extrasensory phenomena, we do so with some wonder. But the Caterpillar, naturally, accepts his clairvoyance as a matter of course—there is not the slightest trace of wonder in his nonchalant attitude. The fact that Alice fails to relate this extraordinary occurrence to her pre-Wonderland experience is, in part, explained by the nonchalance of the Caterpillar: she obviously misses the significance of his mental feat. However, this unwitting acceptance by Alice may also mark an incipient change in her motivation. Perhaps at this point she has begun unconsciously to sense that Wonderland is *not* in any way like her old world above ground, even though she will vainly attempt in later adventures to find or construct a meaningful connection.

In Chapter vi an important aspect of the chaos is that the creatures here, like the clairvoyant Caterpillar, rarely consider their environment or their actions as anything but normal. To them there is certainly nothing wonderful about Wonderland. This is made explicit when a large plate comes skimming out the door, barely missing the Frog-Footman's head, and we are told that the footman continues what he is doing, "exactly as if nothing had happened." This acceptance of chaos by the inhabitants of Wonderland has at least two significant relations to the book's whole meaning. First, it serves to pique further Alice's curiosity about the "rules" of Wonderland. Since the creatures do not think their lives and world are in any way strange or disorderly, Alice takes this attitude—albeit incorrectly—as a sign that there has to be an order. In general, she fails to consider consciously the possibility that the very anarchy of their realm may be directly related to their own heedless and irrational behavior—that they live in chaos and thus act accordingly. Indeed, her reason, ordering mechanism that it is, is totally incapable of functioning outside the bounds of some kind of order. Second, the creatures' acceptance of chaos can

be viewed as a fantastic parody of what happens every day in the world above ground. Here, in fact, may be the correlation between the two worlds that Alice seeks but never fully discovers. The creatures above ground, with their constructs and arbitrary conventions, act in the same way. If the Frog-Footman, say, were to visit the London of the 1860's, would not the average Englishman's nonchalant acceptance of such preposterous notions as orderly Time and Space strike him as insane? This gently comic exposure of the relativity of order that we find in Lewis Carroll's fiction has been discussed by a number of critics, but none has pointed out its organic function in *Alice*. It is an important component of the book's vision of universal anarchy; for what mankind (or Alice in her Wonderland) typically desires is *not* an adjustable frame of meaning, but an unambiguous and permanent order. Alice's reaction to the Frog-Footman's argumentativeness is representative of her total reaction to this universal anarchy: "It's really dreadful . . . the way all the creatures argue. It's enough to drive one crazy!" Like her previous "I suppose," the key words "dreadful" and "crazy" subtly reveal what is happening to Alice without her knowing it: she is slowly coming to an unconscious perception of Wonderland's maddening—and dangerous—nature.

Soon Alice meets the Duchess, whose hilarious rudeness surpasses even the Caterpillar's. Alice again responds with her best manners. The Duchess, like the Frog-Footman, takes no notice of the bedlam around her: surrounded by the howling of the baby, the kitchen utensils thrown by the cook, and the general disorder, the Duchess single-mindedly persists in her barbarous treatment of the baby and her guest Alice. Her "lullaby" is another of Wonderland's subversive parodies. For example, a verse of the original poem by David Bates reads:

> Speak gently to the little child!
>   Its love be sure to gain;
> Teach it in accents soft and mild—
>   It may not long remain.

The Duchess sings:

> Speak roughly to your little boy,
>   And beat him when he sneezes:
> He only does it to annoy,
>   Because he knows it teases

This parody, like the earlier ones uttered by Alice, actively denies Alice's previous moral code. The Duchess, so fond of aphorisms, here recommends what Alice's world would call sheer cruelty. Moreover, the Duchess practices what she preaches, constantly shaking and tossing the baby as she sings her "lullaby." The baby soon turns into an ugly, grunting pig—right in Alice's hands. Such a dramatized reversal of the conventional sentimental attitude towards children (the Duchess even shouts "Pig!" at the baby) is something besides a hit at above-ground morality—it is more like a denial of a customary emotional response. We may note here that Carroll himself, usually so fearful of committing any social impropriety, could not in his letters and conversation always restrain his deep-seated disgust with all babies. But such information merely corroborates what any adult reader easily perceives: the baby-pig episode humorously portrays the arbitrary nature of conventional attitudes towards infants. We need go no further than the text; Alice herself muses about "other children she knew, who might do very well as pigs."

In this same chapter, Alice has her famous conversation with the Cheshire Cat. In the light of Wonderland's increasing destruction of the common world's principal foundations for sanity and order, the Cat's remarks become especially important. He is the one creature who explicitly presents Alice with an explanation of the chaos that surrounds her. When Alice asserts, "I don't want to go among mad people," the Cat replies, "Oh, you can't help that . . . we're all mad here. I'm mad. You're mad." Alice answers, "How do you know I'm mad?" And the Cat says, "You must be . . . or you wouldn't have come here." Through this brief exchange, the amused reader—not Alice—gets a tentative, fleeting glimpse at the "meaning" of Wonderland that Alice instinctively seeks. In addition, the enigmatic Cat, who vanishes and appears as easily as he smiles, here intimates that Alice's curiosity is madness or at least the motive-power behind her mad act—her leap into this insane land. That Alice is, as the Cat states, just as mad as the natives of Wonderland is still difficult for the reader to admit, indeed even to perceive. For Alice comes from and alone represents the ordinary reader's world, which, for the sake of his existence as well as hers, must appear sane. The narrator says, "Alice didn't think that [his syllogism] provided it [her madness] at all," and the reader laughs and tacitly agrees, forgetting that the Cat's reasoning can be just as valid as Alice's. For Alice, the Cheshire Cat, and the reader are all now in Wonderland. Alice apparently learns nothing from the Cat's important revelation. While she is "not much surprised" at his vanishing—for she is "getting so well used to queer things happening"—she still fails to perceive Wonderland's meaning for those who live by the illusory principles of above-ground order. Furthermore, after being told specifically by the Cheshire Cat that the Hatter and the March Hare are both mad, Alice, when she meets them in her next adventure, remains uninstructed and stubbornly persists in her attempts to relate their disordered actions to her old notions of sanity.

Is it because Alice is a child that she fails after all this to see Wonderland for what it is? Is it her youthful ignorance that makes her miss the dangerous significance of a grin without a cat—an attribute without a subject? All she can think at this point is: "Well! I've often seen a cat without a grin, . . . but a grin without a cat! It's the most curious thing I ever saw in all my life!" But this represents the response of most adults, too. In a sense, we arer all childishly ignorant in the face of supreme danger; for woven into the whole complex fabric of implications in this laughable colloquy with the Cat is one implication that esily escapes our attention: another above-ground operating principle—the seemingly indestructible bond between subject and attribute—has been gaphically subverted by the appearance of a cat's grin without a cat.

In Chapter vii Alice's old concept of Time dissolves, in one of the funniest and yet most grimly destructive scenes in the book. While many other common bases of order continue to be subverted in this adventure, "A Mad Tea-Party" focuses on Time, one major aboveground system that still appears to have some validity. Up to this point, the attack on Time has been only incidental and certainly not overwhelming, and Time still has had some meaning because the narrative itself has progressed through a vague chronological framework.

In the beginning of "A Mad Tea-Party," Alice comes upon a situation that apparently has had no temporal beginning and probably will never have an end. The March Hare, Mad Hatter, and Dormouse sit at a tea table, engaged in a truly endless succession of tea and pointless conversation (perhaps a representation of a child's view of polite mealtimes). In the midst of all the disconnected talk, the Hatter suddenly asks Alice, as if it were a test, "What day of the month is it?" and, like the White Rabbit, looks at his watch "uneasily." This question opens a whole series of ridiculous comments on watches and Time. These comments themselves seem pointless; and their complete lack of coherence or sequence intensifies the chapter's pervasive atmosphere of timelessness (especially since Alice, like the ordinary nineteenth-century reader, still clings to her old conception of Time as linear and progressive).

When the Hatter admits that his riddle about the raven and the writing desk has no answer, Alice sighs, "I think you might do something better with the time . . . than wasting it in asking riddles that have no answers." The Hatter replies, "If you knew Time as well as I do . . . you wouldn't talk about wasting *it*. It's *him*." This nonsensical personification of Time continues in the conversation that follows. Amidst the by now familiar puns that tend to destroy linguistic order like those on beating or killing Time, Time itself, like a person, is revealed as malleable, recalcitrant, or disorderly. Such a view of Time as finite and personal, of course, comically subverts the above-ground convention of Time's infinite, orderly, autonomous nature. This finally puts Time in its proper place—another arbitrary, change-

John Tenniel's illustration of Alice meeting Tweedledum and Tweedledee in the woods. From Through the
Looking Glass and What Alice Found There.

able artifact that has no claim to absolute validity, no binding claim, in fact, to existence. Since Time is now like a person, a kind of ill-behaved child created by man, there is the unavoidable danger that he will rebel and refuse to be consistent. That is exactly what has happened in this Wonderland tea-party: the Hatter says Time "won't do a thing I ask! It's always six o'clock now"; that is, it is always teatime. Time is thus frozen, and one of the most important concepts of common human experience is laughed out of existence.

Wonderland seems to compensate for this frozen Time by substituting Space—the creatures move around the tea-table in a kind of never-ending game of musical chairs. We might takes this substitution of Space as Carroll's hint at a more accurate conception of Time; but, like the underlying accuracy of Alice's confused multiplication in Chapter ii, this subtle hint at the reality of "reality" is a bit too sophisticated for most readers, as it certainly is for poor Alice. Besides, the concept of Space, as we have seen, has already been demolished. At this midway point in the narrative, then,

the destruction of the foundations of Alice's old order is practically complete.

Alice (in Chapter vii) has almost reached rock bottom in her descent into chaos—betokened by the work *mad* which is part of the title of the chapter, part of the name of one principal character, and part of the common epithet applied to another ("mad as a March Hare"). Her dramatic experience of the subversion of the above-ground system of meaning seems complete, but there is at least one foundation of that old system that remains intact. Despite the fact that inanimate objects like stones have lost stable identity, they have up to Chapter viii remained within the class of *inanimate* objects—with the possible exception hinted at in Chapter vii that tea-trays can fly like bats.

"Twinkle, twinkle, little bat"—Carroll's charming parody of Jane Taylor's nursery rhyme "The Star"—occupies a rather pivotal position in the pattern of destruction I have been tracing. First, the poem uses, as parodies do in general, the original verses as part of the total context. Carroll's substitutions (*bat* for *star, at* for *are, you fly* for *so high,* and *tea-tray* for *diamond*) must be considered in the light of Jane Taylor's poem. Viewed this way, Carroll's poem becomes a compressed statement of much of the destruction that has already taken place in Wonderland, as well as a gentle hint at what is to come in the next chapter. A bat represents to most readers ugly nature—active and predatory; a star, on the other hand, usually connotes beautiful, remote, static nature. Moreover, "what you're at" and "fly" intensify the Darwinian, predatory, gross struggle image and increase the humorous incongruity between Carroll's lines and Miss Taylor's. All this harks back to the earlier comic subversion of the sentimental view of animal morality seen in such verses as "How doth the little crocodile," another hit at false piety and false natural history in popular nursery rhymes. This, in turn, leads the reader's mind back to the original star, whose moral connotations have now been subverted: it no longer seems to deserve the purity implied by "diamond." In addition, "Twinkle, twinkle, little bat," with its delightful mix-up of animate bat with inanimate star and flying tea-tray with flying bat, serves as an appropriate transition to Chapter viii where the fabricated separation between animate and inanimate objects is finally destroyed.

Immediately after the highly subversive Mad Tea Party, Alice meets in Chapter viii a whole new set of creatures—playing cards that are alive, so alive, in fact, that one has become one of the most well-known "persons" in English literature, the furious Queen of Hearts. Carroll's method of making these cards appear human is an example of his technical ability throughout *Alice.* For one thing, he skillfully employs devices which make their conversations with Alice seem natural. Almost immediately, one of the gardeners, the two of spades, speaks in a slight dialect (dialects have been attributed previously to a number of animals). Carroll also carefully indicates the volume and emotional quality of the dialogue—a kind of humorous reversal of the above-ground notion that speech is a primary distinction between animals and men. Some card-characters merely "say" their lines, others "shout" or "roar"; some are "silent," or speak in "a low, hurried tone"; Alice herself gives "a little scream of laughter," and the Queen sometimes speaks "in a voice of thunder." Another device for making these inanimate objects appear human and their scenes realistic is the inclusion of already well-established characters like the White Rabbit and the Duchess whose "humanness" is now taken for granted and who here respond to the playing-card Queen as if she were supremely vital.

In this way another above-ground principle—that there is a distinct cleavage between the animate and inanimate worlds—is humorously overthrown. One thing, however, remains constant: these card-creatures are just as irrational and chaotic as all the previous animal

inhabitants of the insane underground. Indeed, the chaos is compounded, when these inanimate-objects-turned-human treat the normally live creatures of Alice's former existence as inanimate artifacts. Wonderland has again turned the tables, hereby using live animals like hedgehogs and flamingoes for croquet balls and mallets. Alice, still clinging to her "in-the-world" approach, says to the Cheshire Cat, "you've no idea how confusing it is all the things being alive." The Cat, of course, has no idea how confusing it is, since he neither possesses nor is possessed by Alice's old, above-ground standards of regularity. Moreove, this appeal to the Cat marks another step in Alice's slowly disintegrating sense of order: although she still clings to her old constructed concepts of reality, she forgets completely what the Cat is and where he dwells.

Since Alice rarely relinquishes her notions of order without some struggle, it is fitting that in "The Queen's Croquet-Ground" she should try to remind herself of the above-ground distinction between live and inanimate entities. When the Queen of Hearts rudely demands, as so many other creatures have demanded, that Alice identify herself, Alice "very politely" says: "My name is Alice, so please your Majesty," but adds to herself, "Why, they're only a pack of cards, after all. I needn't be afraid of them!" At this point, Alice is not yet prepared to say such a thing aloud. Nevertheless, this silent comment may indicate that Alice is beginning to sense the final danger inherent in Wonderland—her own destruction—and is beginning to fall back on her only defense against this ultimate devastation which has lurked ominously beneath all the rest of her problems. She is falling back on those now inoperative above-ground principles which, illusory or not, can preserve her sanity and her very existence.

Alice has many reasons for such subversive thoughts. She has certainly been cheated: the Queen's Croquet-Ground—with its painted flowers, its exasperating and insane game, its wild and dangerous creatures—is that same "beautiful garden" she has been seeking from the outset. Perhaps it is the realization that her arduous journey beneath the grounds of her old, dull, constricted world of rote-lessons and unexplainable, arbitrary adult rules has brought her, not to "those beds of bright flowers and those cool fountains," but to a chaotic place of madness ruled by a furious Queen who orders executions with almost every breath—perhaps it is the realization of all this that encourages Alice to begin her rebellion.

A more important reason for Alice's drift toward rebellion is that she has begun to sense that her quest for unambiguous meaning and immortal order is fruitless. Haphazard as her trip may at first seem, Alice has nevertheless been moving towards the grounds of Wonderland which correspond to the grounds of her old world. The rulers of Wonderland (the King and

Queen of Hearts) and their "beautiful garden" have been Alice's spiritual goal almost from the beginning, and it is appropriate that the rules and court of Wonderland should hold the secret of their realm's meaning and be the ultimate source of its order. The fact that they are court cards and hearts emphasizes their central, vital position, as does the fact that they are introduced with names written all in capital letters, a device stressed by Carroll in his revisions. Ironically, Alice is for once correct in judging Wonderland on the basis of her previous "in-the-world" experience. But what do these repositories of meaning and order turn out to be? Mere abstract, manufactured, and arbitrary symbols—just a pack of cards, pictures of kings and queens, men and women. Their grounds of meaning turn out to be croquet-grounds and their principles the rules of an insane, topsy-turvy *game*.

Alice's first realization that she need not be afraid because, "after all," she is dealing with a mere pack of cards has an effect, although an impermanent one, on her subsequent behavior. Immediately after her brief insight, she is extremely rude to the Queen, so rude that Alice herself is "surprised at her own courage." She interrupts the Queen's repeated "Off with her head!" by saying "Nonsense!' . . . very loudly and decidedly." The King's and Queen's immediate reaction to this single word is significant: the "Queen was silent" and "the King laid his hand upon her arm and timidly said, 'Consider, my dear: she is only a child!'" Among other things, this reaction of the rulers of Wonderland is a humorous, metaphorical equivalent of the above-ground world's reaction to the ridiculous challenge of a Wonderland. When either is named for what it is, it is left, as it were, speechless. Paradoxically, by the power of one of the most artificial constructs of all—the word—these rulers are rendered powerless, that is, without words. That the child Alice has had this supreme power all along goes without saying. Alice, however, does not realize the potency of her weapon or, for that matter, that she even has a weapon. Hence, even though she can say to herself that "they're only a pack of cards, after all. I needn't be afraid of them!" she soon reverts to her seemingly unwarranted fear: "Alice began to feel very uneasy: to be sure, she had not as yet had any dispute with the Queen, but she knew that it might happen any minute, 'and then,' thought she, 'what would become of me? They're dreadfully fond of beheading people here: the great wonder is, that there's any one left alive!'"

From this point to the end of the adventures, it is the main business of the narrative that underlies all the fun and gay nonsense to trace Alice's preparation for her final, overt denial of Wonderland, the destruction of her fearful vision for the sake of her identity and sanity. To gain strength and courage for that act of denial, Alice seeks the aid of allies (meanwhile, of course, she continues to play what she has already viewed as a

crazy game). In Chapter vii she makes the mistake of assuming that the Cheshire Cat is such an ally. She spies his grin in the air and says, "It's the Cheshire Cat: now I shall have somebody to talk to." But when Alice, "feeling very glad she had some one to listen to her," complains to the Cat about the game she is playing—saying "they don't seem to have any rules in particular"—his only reply is the apparent non sequitur, "How do you like the Queen?" He, of course, sees no fault in a game without any rules but a mad queen's; if he were to play the insane games above ground with their many arbitrary "rules," he would probably find them as disturbing as Alice finds the mad, seemingly rule-less croquet game of Wonderland.

In much the same way that she mistakes the Cheshire Cat for an ally, Alice mistakenly assumes that "logical" rules still have validity. At the very beginning of the next chapter ("The Mock Turtle's Story"), she meets the Duchess again, and, finding that previously irascible creature in good humor, assumes that her anger was merely the result of the pepper in her soup. "Maybe it's always pepper that makes people hot-tempered," Alice muses. And she begins to extrapolate from her new-found hypothesis, "very much pleased at having found out a new kind of rule." Here, although there is the prominent "Maybe," Alice reveals that she still stubbornly believes there is a cause-effect order in Wonderland and one that can be applied to her own world too: this in spite of all the mounting evidence to the contrary. The Duchess herself is the personified *reductio ad absurdum* of Alice's attitude toward rules: the Duchess finds a "moral" in everything. Alice is faced with a new curious problem: once again Wonderland forces her above-ground assumptions to the final test, and once again it laughs them out of existence. Poor, dogged Alice, however, is unable to see the "moral" in the Duchess's preoccupation with finding morals; that is, Alice fails to perceive that such remarks as "Everything's got a moral, if only you can find it" are essentially satirical counterthrusts at her own determination to find the rules in Wonderland.

Finally, Alice meets two creatures who seem capable of serving as allies—the Gryphon and the Mock Turtle, two of the most fantastic characters in Wonderland's whole laughable gallery. For both of these animals, nonsensical as they are, seem to see Wonderland for what it is, at least for what it is to Alice. When Alice recounts to them her adventures, the Gryphon says, "It's all about as curious as it can be." When Alice attempts to recite another moralistic Watts poem ("'Tis the voice of the sluggard") and again twists it into a cruel, amoral, survival-of-the-fittest commentary on nature, the Mock Turtle asserts that "it sounds uncommon nonsense" and says, "It's by far the most confusing thing *I* ever heard!" Their words "curious," "nonsense," and "confusing" are drawn, of course, from Alice's vocabulary.

This sympathy for Alice, it should be observed, is not as simple as it first appears. For one thing, the solicitude of the Gryphon and Mock Turtle is—as their names suggest—undoubtedly false. Both creatures are palpable sentimentalists: the Mock Turtle's mawkish song about beautiful soup, sung in "a voice choked with sobs," is the measure of their sentimentality. Once again Wonderland tests an above-ground convention by carrying it to its extreme: here, instead of attacking one particular kind of above-ground sentiment such as the common emotional response to babies or to stars and bees, Wonderland comically overthrows sentiment itself. Alice cannot hope to find genuine sympathy and real allies in the Gryphon and Mock Turtle. In any event, she has no time to react, for the great trial (of the last chapters) is about to begin.

Before turning to that trial, we should try to assess the full function of the Mock Turtle and Gryphon in the Wonderland motif of subversion. After the Queen's Croquet-Game, no remnant of ordinary above-ground order remains intact. The only order poor Alice can possibly perceive in Wonderland is the consistent antipathy of all the creatures towards her and all her previous assumptions. Now, Chapters ix and x serve to subvert and finally destroy the "order" of Wonderland itself, because here the two sentimental friends, the Gryphon and the Mock Turtle, argue neither with each other (as most of the other creatures do) nor with Alice's above-ground as sumptions. In a sense they *are* the allies she seeks: they take her side, seeing her adventures and reverses as she sees them. This sympathy—whether genuine or false—breaks Wonderland's pattern of antipathy and is perhaps the ultimate destruction: order, as Alice once knew it, is now so hopelessly snarled that she must, in literal self-defense, take that inevitable leap back to her own insane, illusory, but livable world of arbitrary logic and convention.

If "The Queen's Croquet-Ground" has convinced Alice that her quest for Wonderland's principle of order in the personalities or games of Wonderland's playing-card rulers is pointless, the last two chapters of the book reveal that even beyond these rulers and their mad croquet-ground there is no fundamental law, save perhaps the furious Queen's "Off with his head!"—and even that persistent demand, Alice has been told by the Gryphon, is never obeyed: "It's all her fancy, that: they never executes nobody, you know." At the end, Alice is finally brought to what should be the last refuge of order—the court of law.

Chapter xi begins with a crowd scene. As the chapter progresses, we realize that many of the creatures Alice has encountered from the beginning are assembled here. This strengthens the impression that the trial is the final test of Wonderland's meaning, the appropriate conclusion of Alice's quest for law and order. What is on trial here is not really the Knave of Hearts. What is on trial is the "law" itself, whether it be the law of Wonderland or, by extension, the law wherever it is encountered. Alice has already lost faith in her own search for the law of Wonderland, but then she forgets even that loss. In the final trial, where her forgotten suspicions return to become a frightful apperception of the total intransigent chaos underlying her artificial world, Alice is moved to her only salvation—a complete and active denial of the horrible, unacceptable truth.

In these last two chapters, after all the destruction of the old bases of order, all that is left is the hollow form of things. The trial now appears in its true light: since the world in which the trial takes place is without order or meaning, the trial is a pointless formality, another game without rules and without a winner. And when Alice is herself forced to participate and is again drawn into the mad proceedings, her rebellion is inevitable.

That Alice at the beginning of the trial has not yet abandoned her old cherished faith in order is revealed in a number of ways. The narrator tells us that "Alice had never been in a court of justice before, but she had read about them in books, and she was quite pleased to find that she knew the name of nearly everything there." Once more, Alice persists in viewing the underground bedlam from an "in-the-world" perspective. Part of the witty comedy here, naturally, derives from the fact that many adult readers *have* been in a court: they know that this Wonderland court is an outlandish travesty (especially when it is called a "court of *justice*"). Yet they also sense that at the core there is a great deal of similarity between "real" trials above ground and this insanely unjust trial of the Knave of Hearts. They also sense the significance of Alice's comfort in finding that she can name the items in the court—another illustration of Wonderland's incessant attack on man's groundless linguistic habits, intensified when the narrator ironically remarks that Alice was rather proud of her ability to name everything in the court, "for she thought, and rightly too, that very few little girls of her age knew the meaning of it all." An even more important result of Alice's "in-the-world" approach to the trial is that she will again be frustrated, this time by the fact that while the Wonderland trial is similar in outward form to "real" trials, it characteristically ignores or subverts all the significant principles.

The last chapter is called "Alice's Evidence." The title itself has a multiple meaning. Literally, Alice is forced to participate actively in the insanity of Wonderland by giving "evidence," even though she has now grown so large that she can at any second rebel if she so desires. More important, Alice in this last scene acquires the "evidence" she needs in order to make her decision about Wonderland. At first, Alice reacts with fear; when she is called to the stand, she cries out,

"'Here!' . . . quite forgetting in the flurry of the moment how large she had grown in the last few minutes." Along with this fear, however, is a growing sense of the meaninglessness of the trial (and thus, she thinks, of all Wonderland). When she looks over the jurymen's shoulders and sees the nonsense they are writing, Alice says to herself, "it doesn't matter a bit." Here she is becoming just as subversive towards Wonderland as Wonderland has been towards her and her above-ground principles. Soon Alice is courageously contradicting the King and Queen openly:

> "That *proves* his guilt, of course," said the Queen: "so, off with—."

> "It doesn't prove anything of the sort!" said Alice.

And after the White Rabbit reads his major piece of evidence against the Knave of Hearts, the mad poem full of unclear pronoun references, Alice daringly states aloud:

> "If any one of them [the jury] can explain it," . . . (she had grown so large in the last few minutes that she wasn't a bit afraid of interrupting him [the King]), "I'll give him sixpence. *I* don't believe there's an atom of meaning in it."

Finally, when the Queen asserts, "Sentence first—verdict afterwards," Alice says loudly, "Stuff and nonsense!" The Queen turns purple with rage, Alice actively denies the Queen's demand to be silent with a forceful "I won't!" and the whole underground adventure explodes and disintegrates.

We see here, with the progression from Alice's thinking "to herself" to her final words said "loudly" and her absolute refusal to keep silent, that part of her rebellion rests on her growing ability to speak the necessary words—to give the necessary "evidence." In Chapter viii Alice was outwardly polite while she inwardly said, "they're only a pack of cards, after all." At the end, she is completely open, and she terminates her nightmarish adventure with her own weapon of destruction, her loudly proclaimed, "You're nothing but a pack of cards!"

Alice's final, overt rejection of Wonderland, her flight from the frightful anarchy of the world underneath the grounds of common consciousness, is a symbolic rejection of mad sanity in favor of the sane madness of ordinary existence. Perhaps it is best to view the normal conscious mind as an automatic filtering and ordering mechanism which protects us from seeing the world in all its chaotic wonder and glory—at least it seems best to view the mind this way when we attempt an explanation of the serious theme that emerges from the delicious, sprightly wit and humor of *Alice's Adventures in Wonderland*. When Alice at last names her tormentors a pack of cards and thereby ends her underground journey, her mind, by that very assertion, imposes an artificial but effective order upon that which can never be organically ordered. By the time Alice and the reader reach this last scene in Wonderland it should be quite obvious to all that language itself is an inadequate construct. Yet it is by this construct that Alice preserves her sanity and identity. She uses words to put all Wonderland into a category of manufactured, non-human, arbitrary entities—"a pack of cards." Insane as her act may be in terms of what Wonderland has demonstrated, it provides her with the means to dispel her vision and thus protect her from the dangers of complete perception. Alice has thus come full circle: her mad curiosity led her to the vision of absurdity; her failure led her to dismay; and her instinct for survival, assured identity, and sanity led her to escape from her final horrifying perception.

It must be remembered that *Alice's Adventures in Wonderland* is not a piece of formal philosophy; it is, instead, a comic myth of man's insoluble problem of meaning in a meaningless world. Thus, the fact that Alice herself is unaware of the significance of her journey to the end of night and unaware of her reasons for finally denying the validity of her vision is by no means a flaw in the book. Alice, as the mythical representative of all her fellows above ground, acts appropriately and appropriately is unaware of the meaning of her actions. Although Alice's quest for meaning is unfulfilled, and she consciously learns nothing, she does survive because an instinctual "lesson" takes over at the moment of supreme danger. Unlike the artificial, illusory lessons of her nursery reading, schoolroom, or elders, the innate and unconscious drive for identity and self-preservation cannot be perverted by either Wonderland or the world above. The question is not whether this drive is a valid principle, but whether it is pragmatically sound. In *Alice* it is. And upon its pragmatic soundness rests the validity of all the other illusory principles and conventions. Alice's quest for reasonable experience whisks her back to her only possible, albeit artificial, world where the ultimately irrational makes life sane.

Thus, the book is paradoxically both a denial and an affirmation of order—a kind of catharsis of what can never be truly purged but what must, for sanity's sake, be periodically purged in jest, fantasy, or dream. The Wonderland creatures and their world are not a pack of cards, after all. They are, so to speak, more "real" than so-called reality. But waking life, as most of us know it, must function as if they are unreal, as if chaos is amusing "nonsense."

On the surface, then, *Alice* is clearly not true to ordinary experience. Indeed, it is destructive of the very groundwork of that experience. Yet the book is certainly true to an extraordinary experience familiar to us all, the dream. For the apparently nonsensical elements of *Alice*, like timelessness, spacelessness, and fusion of discrete entities, are, as modern psychology has demonstrated, what lie just below the surface of rational consciousness and what we experience every night in the dream state.

I began this essay by pointing out the similarity between *Alice* and the traditional literary dream-vision. Some may argue that *Alice* would be better classified as a "nightmare-vision" because a nightmare is an unsuccessful dream, while a dream is a method whereby the dreamer successfully works out and solves in dramatic form a deep-seated problem, often a problem whose existence the conscious faculties will not allow themselves even to admit. Certainly *Alice* does deal with and dramatize what is by nature and definition outside the awareness of the everyday conscious intellect; and some readers assume that Alice's dream does not come to any satisfying conclusion, that the problem of the disorder beneath man-made order is left unsolved; but I have argued here that this is not so, that *Alice's Adventures in Wonderland* solves the problem by a kind of alogical dreamwork affirmation of man's artificially constructed universe. Whether or not every reader's unconscious can be satisfied with this extra-rational solution is, it seems to me, an unanswerable and finally an irrelevant question. Alice's unconscious is what matters; and it is here that we can be sure the conclusion is satisfactory. After waking, she runs off for tea because "it's getting late" (and this after the timeless Mad Tea-Party), "thinking while she ran, as well she might, what a wonderful dream it had been," completely at ease in her mad but possible world above the chaos of Wonderland.

Grace Slick (song date 1966)

SOURCE: "White Rabbit," by Grace Slick, in *The Poetry of Rock*, edited by Richard Goldstein, Bantam Books, 1969, p. 113.

[*Slick was a cofounder and lead singer of the San Francisco-based rock band Jefferson Airplane (later Jefferson Starship, then Starship). Her 1966 song "White Rabbit," reprinted below, celebrates the* Alice *books of Carroll and the psychedelic drug culture of the 1960s.*]

White Rabbit

One pill makes you larger
And one pill makes you small.
And the ones that mother gives you
Don't do anything at all.

Go ask Alice
When she's ten feet tall.

And if you go chasing rabbits
And you know you're going to fall.
Tell 'em a hookah-smoking caterpillar
Has given you the call.
Call Alice
When she was just small.

When men on the chessboard
Get up and tell you where to go.
And you've just had some kind of
    mushroom
And your mind is moving low.
Go ask Alice
I think she'll know.

When logic and proportion
Have fallen sloppy dead,
And the White Knight is talking
    backwards
And the Red Queen's lost her head

Remember what the dormouse said:
"Feed your head.
Feed your head.
Feed your head."

G. K. Chesterton on *Alice* (1932):

Any educated Englishman, and especially any educational Englishman (which is worse), will tell you with a certain gravity that *Alice in Wonderland* is a classic. Such is indeed the horrid truth. The original hilarity that was born on that summer afternoon among the children, in the mind of a mathematician on a holiday, has itself hardened into something almost as cold and conscientious as a holiday task. That logician's light inversion of all the standards of logic has itself, I shudder to say, stiffened into a standard work. It is a classic; that is, people praise it who have never read it. It has a secure position side by side with the works of Milton and Dryden. . . . I am sorry to say it, but the soap-bubble which poor old Dodgson blew from the pipe of poetry, in a lucid interval of lunacy, and sent floating into the sky, has been robbed by educationists of much of the lightness of the bubble, and retained only the horrible healthiness of the soap.

G. K. Chesterton, "Lewis Carroll," in A Handful of Authors: Essays on Books and Writers, *edited by Dorothy Collins, Sheed and Ward, 1953.*

Jacqueline Flescher (essay date 1969)

SOURCE: "The Language of Nonsense in *Alice*," in *Yale French Studies,* No. 43, 1969, pp. 128-44.

[*In the following essay, Flescher provides a close analysis of the complex "nonsense language" of* Alice, *concluding that the work "can be read with the freshness of a child or the critical mind of an adult."*]

Nonsense bears the stamp of paradox. The two terms of the paradox are order and disorder. Order is generally created by language, disorder by reference. But the essential factor is their peculiar interplay. Elizabeth Sewell, in a penetrating analysis of nonsense, stresses the idea of dialectic. Yet her analysis deals almost exclusively with the formal structure of order. Emile Cammaerts, on the other hand, defines nonsense poetry as "poetry run wild." This divergence clearly points to a danger: that of neglecting one dimension. An adequate definition must embrace both language and reference, order and disorder. The nature of their interaction must be underlined. Cross references and occasional repetition are therefore unavoidable. Moreover, the problem cannot be stated in simple terms. It is complex and elusive and constantly calls for qualification.

The first qualification concerns language. It is generally, though not necessarily, one of the forces at work. The backbone of nonsense must be a consciously regulated pattern. It can be the rhythmic structure of verse, the order of legal procedure, or the rules of the chess-game. Implicitly or explicitly, these three variations are all present in *Alice*. "Sentence first, verdict afterwards" implies a knowledge of the normal sequence of events. Running backwards is a reversal of conventional order, legalized by the mirror; and the chess game provides a structural setting for inconsequential behavior. It is the existent or implicit order which distinguishes nonsense from the absurd. It is the departure from this order which distinguishes nonsense from sense.

But language is constantly asked to provide the conscious framework. It is used more readily because it affords more possibilities of variation. The usual way of upsetting the conventional order of events is by reversal. This simple pattern is repeated constantly: "Hand it round first, cut it afterwards," "What sort of things do you remember best? . . . O, things that happened the week after next." In this simple reversal, there is an implicit awareness of conventional order. If a character is simply caught up in a series of unconnected events which he cannot understand or control, or if he himself performs a series of actions of which one can determine neither the cause, purpose, nor inner relationship, we enter the realm of the Absurd: the hero of Kafka's *The Trial* is the victim of absurdity because he is trapped in a series of events which can be explained neither by their cause nor by their inner logic. So much for the distinction between nonsense and the absurd.

Language offers endless possibilities of upsetting the order of behavior, because it can establish a coherent system in a variety of ways. Provided that the backbone of such a system stand out clearly, it can act as a regulator for the most disorderly examples of behavior. The pattern of nonsense in this case is no longer one of simple reversal. It is a clash of opposing forces. The relationship between these two poles can best be described by an analogy: the content of nonsense is to its form what the content of poetry is to its metrical framework.

But rhyme and rhythm do not only provide an analogy. They are the very stuff of nonsense. An ordered system of language can by and large take two forms: inner relationship or serial progression (alphabet, declension, etc.). Metric pattern belongs to the latter category. In the following verse from **"The Walrus and the Carpenter,"** two elements contribute to a sharply defined order. These are rhythm and alliteration:

> The time has come, the walrus said,
> To talk of many things,
> Of shoes and ships and sealing-wax,
> Of cabbages and kings,
> And why the sea is boiling hot,
> And whether pigs have wings.

The metrical pattern stands out clearly because of its regular character. The alliteration in lines 3 and 4 reinforces the rhythmic pattern by accentuating the stressed syllables more heavily. Once the pattern has been so sharply defined, shoes, ships, and sealing-wax can co-exist happily, and cabbages and kings live side by side. Alliteration is widely used; assonance and internal rhyme are almost absent. The initial position of the stressed letter and the emphasis on consonants distinguish one rhythmic unit from another. Had Carroll exploited assonance, with emphasis on vowels, he would have weakened the function of the serial order.

It is the pattern provided by verse that makes verse a suitable vehicle for nonsense. But a similar pattern can also be attained, simply by exploiting a particular letter:

> . . . and they drew all manner of things—everything that begins with an M.

> "Why with an M? said Alice.

> "Why not?" said the March Hare.

> —that begins with an M such as mouse-traps, and the moon, and memory, and muchness . . . did you ever see such a thing as the drawing of a muchness?

The letter M is chosen at random, but is subsequently repeated, and forms a pattern. Within this pattern, a free association of totally incompatible elements can be made: mouse-traps, the moon, memory, and muchness. Of course, this use of a simple letter assumes an autonomy of its own and eventually demands obedience from the author.

The game "I love my love with an H" is based on a similar association:

> "I love my love with an H," Alice couldn't help beginning, "because he is Happy. I hate him with an H because he is Hideous. I fed him with Ham sandwiches and Hay. His name is Haigha, and he lives . . ."

> "He lives on the Hill," the king remarked, without the least idea that he was joining in the game.

The process is exactly the same as in the previous example. The underlying principle of organization is the repetition of the letter H. It is the only link between "Happy, Hideous, Ham and Hay." Capitalization of the initial H's adds emphasis in the same way that alliteration reinforces the metric pattern. But the point of Carroll's formal arrangement is made clear in both the "M" and "H" examples by a final contrast. In the first case, the coined word "muchness" is isolated from its formal pattern in the question, "Did you ever see such a thing as the drawing of a muchness?" The effect, divorced from the repetitive pattern, is total absurdity. In the second case, the king unknowingly contributes to the formal pattern by joining in the game. The isolation from the formal context in the first example, the unconscious continuation of the formal context in the second, bring out by contrast the impact of the system.

Endless variations of this game can be found, ranging from the declension "A mouse—of a mouse—to a mouse—O mouse!" to the rules of division and subtraction: "Divide a loaf by a knife—what's the answer to that?" "Take a bone from a dog: what remains?" The last two examples no longer show a serial relationship but an internal one.

The most complex example of a formal relationship in *Alice* is the **"Jabberwocky"** poem. Both the serial pattern of rhyme and rhythm and the internal grammatical structure are here combined. The poem does not easily lend itself to analysis. However, a juxtaposition of the first verse of the original and a recent parody of it might clarify peculiarities inherent in **"Jabberwocky"**:

> *T'was* brillig *and* the slithy toves
> *Did* gyre *and* gimble *in* the wabe
> All mimsy *were* the borogroves
> *And* the mome raths outgrabe.

> *T'was* boodberg *and* the sliding tones
> *Did* hojer *and* haugen *in* the wade
> All semene *were* the homophones
> *And* emeneaus outgrade.

The parody maintains all auxiliary verbs and conjunctions found in the original. The nouns, adjectives, and infinitives provide the variation. The author of the parody has simply kept the words indicating a relationship in the grammatical structure and varied the terms of the relationship. Humpty Dumpty's comment on words is revealing in this respect:

> They've a temper some of them—particularly verbs: they're the proudest—adjectives you can do anything with but not verbs . . . "

Humpty Dumpty, Lewis Carroll and the critics have attempted exact interpretations of the meaning of the words of **"Jabberwocky."** The variety of their conclusions perhaps indicates the futility of the enterprise. What critical analysis can stand the challenge of the following interpretation, which was made by a child: "It means a bug that comes out at night with a light on its tail and a sword between its beak. That's what a jabberwalkie is." Another child gave a valuable key to the relationship between form and meaning: "He wrote it in language that almost makes sense when you read it. The words sound and are spelt like normal words in English, but the poem is imaginary in its physical language."

Providing the sounds and the grammatical relationship survive, the sentence structure is not lost. It is, on the contrary, reinforced by the strong stress pattern and rhymes. Within this scheme, one can indulge in the wildest fancies without abandoning form. The portmanteau words are significant, not so much because of the specific meanings which they suggest, but because they embrace two disparate elements.

Meaning, however undefined, is nevertheless suggested. Preoccupation with meaning is constant throughout *Alice,* sometimes to an extreme degree. The whole range of relationships between word and reference, from total coincidence to exclusion of one of the two terms, can be found:

> "My name is Alice, but—"

> "It's a stupid name enough," Humpty Dumpty interrupted impatiently. "What does it mean?"

> "Must a name mean something?"

> "Of course it must."

Just as the obvious, matter-of-fact statement is common to the logic of the nonsense world, so the literal meaning is solicited where none exists:

"Found *what*?" said the Duck.

"Found *it*", the Mouse replied rather crossly. "Of course you know what it means."

Whereas Humpty Dumpty tries to invest a name with meaning when none is implied, the duck looks for reference in a word that only has grammatical function. Where figurative or functional meaning is intended, concrete significance is sought or understood. When the caterpillar asks Alice to explain herself, she shifts from the figurative to the literal meaning in her reply:

"I can't explain myself, I'm afraid sir, because I'm not myself you see."

Meaning is intensified so that language is always in the foreground.

Language can be emphasized, either by closing the gap between word and meaning and tightening the relationship, or, on the contrary, by widening the rift and weakening the relationship. In either case the balance between word and meaning is upset and the function of language becomes more apparent. Whenever Alice recites verses, she feels that the words "are coming different."

. . . her voice sounded hoarse and strange, and the words did not come as they used to do. . . .

. . . "I'm sure those are not the right words," said poor Alice and her eyes filled with tears again as she went on. "I must be Mabel after all."

The problem of personal identity is closely connected with the idea of estrangement from language. Alice's immediate conclusion on "not finding the right words" is that she can no longer be herself. This preoccupation with loss of identity is a recurrent one. But Alice views it with varying emotions. The complacent thought of sending her feet a pair of boots for Christmas is very different from the melancholy realization that she has just escaped from "shrinking away altogether." In the first case she humorously wards off her anxiety, in the second she is overcome by fear. This raises an interesting problem. At what point do we step outside the field of nonsense? The distinction between the two worlds is a finer one than critics have acknowledged.

When Alice loses the objective control that enables her to view her problem of personal identity calmly, the mood becomes too disquieting to be "nonsensical." On using the word "juror," she feels proud of the extent of her vocabulary. The word "antipathies" is pronounced with misgivings. But both in her uneasiness and in her pride, Alice remains conscious of language and is able to control it; only when words betray her is the safety of her nonsense world threatened.

Insistence on speaking English is a safeguard against this threat:

"Speak English," said the Eaglet. "I don't know the meaning of half those long words and what's more I don't believe you do either."

Again and again, coherence and meaningful language are identified with the English tongue. French is resorted to when English is inadequate:

"Perhaps it doesn't understand English," thought Alice. "I daresay it's a French mouse . . ." So she began again, "Où est ma chatte. . . ."

The queen advises Alice to "speak French" when she can't think of the English for a thing.

In "Looking Glass Insects," safeguards are removed and relationships between language and reference are completely broken down:

"I suppose you don't want to lose your name?"

"No indeed," Alice replied, a little anxiously.

When she reaches the wood where things have no name, her anxiety grows:

"This must be the wood," she said thoughtfully to herself, "where things have no names. I wonder what will become of *my* name when I go in."

She unconsciously draws a parallel between the impossibility of naming things and the fear of losing her own identity:

"I mean to get under the—under the—under the *this,* you know," putting her hand on the trunk of the tree. "What does it call itself, I wonder? I do believe it's got no name—why to be sure it hasn't!"

She stood silent for a minute thinking: then she suddenly began again: "Then it really *has* happened, after all! And now *who* am I?"

In this moment of discovery, Alice feels the compelling power of things without a name. At the same time, she loses her hold on things. The exclusion of language immediately takes us beyond the playful level of argument. In her anguished monologue as in her compassionate relationship with the fawn, we are aware that she has become humanly vulnerable. Pride and self-control are forgotten. When she finally leaves the wood, she is relieved to have recovered her name, and hence her identity.

In "Tweedledum and Tweedledee," a reversed process may be observed. Things continue to have names, but the reality of the things rather than the names are questioned:

> "Well, it's no use your talking about waking him," said Tweedledum, "when you're only one of the things in his dream. You know very well you're not real."
>
> "I am real," said Alice, and she began to cry.

But the reality of Alice's tears is also questioned:

> "I hope you don't suppose those are real tears."

When either language or reference is threatened or destroyed, the playful argument of nonsense is abandoned. Alice no longer tries to "keep up her end" of the conversation. Her violent self-defense is an attempt to protect her identity.

So far, we have dealt essentially with the formal structure of nonsense. Clearly, the main concern is with relationship, whether it be serial or internal relationship between words, or the relationship between word and meaning. But nonsense is not simply a formal structure. Structure here runs counter to content. And content must be defined in its turn. We are immediately faced with a series of paradoxes. Order dominates the formal pattern, yet disorder seems to dominate reference. The characters are constantly preoccupied with meaning; yet their conversation is essentially meaningless. How can we account for this apparent contradiction?

To explain the divergence, we must once more go back to language. "When I use a word," says Humpty Dumpty, "it means just what I choose it to mean, neither more, nor less." When the king uses a word, he tests it out in an undertone: "'important—unimportant—important—,' as if he were trying which word sounded best." In both cases, the choice of meaning is arbitrary. Attributing a meaning to a word is an end in itself. "I'm sure I didn't mean," Alice says. "Well, you should have meant. What do you suppose is a child without meaning?" As shown previously, the weaker the link between word and meaning, the more nonsense is compromised. Total coincidence of word and reference is at the core of nonsense. Hence the frequency of the obvious fact and the literal meaning. Both arbitrary and obvious meaning are characterized by immanence, a kind of *en-soi* in the Sartrean sense. Meaning is often purely physical or factual. It leaves no room for speculation or suggestion and therefore refers to nothing beyond itself. It is in a sense self-contained. In spite of the necessity to *mean,* the power of meaning is reduced to a minimum.

The problem can be extended to conversation. Conversation, or more precisely, argument, is the essential vehicle of nonsense in *Alice,* but it is conversation of an unusual kind. It is based neither on sustained discussion nor on coherent reasoning. The description of the caucus race immediately comes to mind:

> There was no "One, two, three and away!" but they began running when they liked, and left off when they liked, so that it was not easy to know when the race was over.

Many of the conversations and arguments in *Alice* are structurally reminiscent of this race.

What, in fact, determines the end of an argument in this context? Once more, it is a question of words. "The question is," says Humpty Dumpty, "which is to be master, that's all." Since the argument is not founded on logic, it leads nowhere. The sole aim of the characters involved is "having the last word." Within these arbitrary limits, how does the conversation develop? The principle is one of deflection. No argument is ever developed. It is immediately undercut, often by a misinterpretation. The word which is misinterpreted acts as a pivot and leads the conversation in a new direction. The pun is invaluable as a pivot for redirection:

> "Mine is a long sad tale," said the Mouse, turning to Alice and sighing. "It *is* a long tail certainly," said Alice, looking down with wonder at the Mouse's tail; "but why do you call it sad?" . . . "I beg your pardon," said Alice very humbly, "you had got to the fifth bend, I think?" "I had *not,*" cried the Mouse, sharply and very angrily. "A knot!" said Alice, always ready to make herself useful, and looking anxiously about her. "O do let me help to undo it."

The two puns tale-tail, not-knot, provide a level of figurative meaning and another level of literal meaning. By taking the literal and not the intended meaning, the conversation is automatically channeled into a new direction. No sooner has it taken a new turn after the first pun, than a new pun sets it off in yet another direction. So the arguments are undercut before they can lead anywhere. Meaning remains at the surface; it can develop neither in depth nor in sequence. Unlike formal structure, which stresses relationship, referential structure destroys them. Random arguments proliferate on all sides, not as digressions diverging from a central meaning but as offshoots from language itself.

Puns are one way of deflecting meaning. Deliberate contradiction is another. Deliberate contradiction in *Alice* follows a recurrent pattern: a character will voice a basic refrain, with variations every time he is addressed:

> "*I've* seen gardens, compared with which this would be a wilderness."

"When you say hill . . . *I* could show you hills, in comparison with which you'd call that a valley."

" . . . You may call it nonsense if you like, but I've heard nonsense compared with which that would be as sensible as a dictionary."

Each new statement is met with a contradiction. The same basic refrain is used throughout: here, the modification simply consists of challenging a new word with its exact opposite. In "Looking Glass Insects," the chorus makes a brief comment after each stage of Alice's conversation with the guard. The comment is immediately followed up by the refrain, suitably modified to relate to the new situation:

"Why his time is worth a thousand pounds a minute."

"The land here is worth a thousand pounds an inch."

"Why the smoke alone is worth a thousand pounds a puff."

"Language is worth a thousand pounds a word."

The same process is used by the Duchess in "The Mock-Turtle's Story" when she finds a moral to match each one of Alice's statements.

The dogmatic finality of the contradiction or the refrain puts an end to the argument. Once more, development of ideas is evaded by deflection of meaning. The refrain emphasizes both the arbitrary character of the contradiction and the lack of progress in the conversation. Argument can either run in all directions or be repetitive. In either case, logical expansion of an idea is avoided:

"*You*, said the Caterpillar, "who are you?" which brought them back again to the beginning of the conversation.

But absence of progression is concurrent with absence of depth. As coherent reasoning is cut short, so graver issues are kept at bay. Serious questions are interpreted as riddles and conversation is treated as a game:

"However, this conversation is going on a little too fast: let's go back to the last remark but one"

says Humpty Dumpty. And in the same tone, the Red Queen suggests:

"Make a remark, it's ridiculous to leave all the conversation to the pudding."

If conversation must remain superficial, arbitrary and literal, how is it integrated in the fantasy of Alice's

wonderworld? Again, the answer seems to lie in paradox. Meaning is literal, but language is imaginative. It is language which governs meaning and determines the creative process:

"Then you should say what you mean," the March Hare went on. "I do," Alice hastily replied, "at least I mean what I say, that's the same thing you know." "Not the same thing a bit!" said the Hatter.

The Hatter's objection is more significant than it appears. As we have noted, language in the nonsense world of *Alice* imposes a rigid order on the disorder of action and the incoherence of reasoning. This order is, however, essentially one of fixed relationships. Within the grammatical or metrical framework, vocabulary can be used with total freedom.

Puns, we noted, are a vital part of the creative process in *Alice*. But play on words can take different forms. The shift from figurative to literal meaning has a functional value. It redirects the conversation. The process of analogy and expansion sustains the conversation. It ensures the progression where rational meaning fails to do so:

" . . . I only took the regular course."

"What was that?" enquired Alice.

"Reeling and Writhing of course, to begin with," the Mock Turtle replied; and then the different branches of Arithmetic—Ambition, Distraction, Uglification and Derision."

A whole area of experience is here transferred to a new context. Reality is undermined by the fantasy of the coined words. Yet it is implicitly alluded to in the analogy of sound. Here again, we touch on a crucial point. Reality remains implicit behind every manifestation of nonsense, but it is never explicitly represented. The nonsense world is a world of fantasy which shies clear of reality, yet indicates its existence.

The Mock-Turtle adds to his previous analogy:

"The Drawling master: he taught us Drawling, Stretching, and Fainting in Coils"

and the Classical master taught "Laughing and Grief." The whole passage on education has a metaphoric value. An organic unity is created with an imaginative interplay of vocabulary which refers back to a concrete area of experience. A variation on this technique is the process of analogy whereby one keyword is used with different compounds and grammatical functions:

"You can draw water out of the water-well," said the Hatter, "so I should think you could draw treacle out of a treacle-well-eh, stupid?"

"But they were in the well," Alice said to the Dormouse, not choosing to notice this last remark. "Of course they were," said the Dormouse: "well in."

The word "well" engenders a kind of proliferation. An imaginative progression is achieved through language; it is an example of language perpetuating itself. The same process accounts for the birth of the "snap-dragon-fly":

"And there's a Dragon-fly."

"Look on the branch above your head," said the Gnat, "and there you'll find a Snap-Dragon-fly. Its body is made of plum-pudding, its wings of holly leaves, and its head is a raisin burning in brandy."

"And what does it live on?" Alice asked as before.

"Frumenty and mince pie," the Gnat replied; "and it makes its nest in a Christmas box."

The initial image is built on a compound word: Snap-dragonfly. The coined word creates a new image composed of prosaic concrete elements which are woven into a thing of pure fantasy, set in the solid context of Christmas festivities. Prosaic reality and fantastic creation combine in this paradoxical creature of the nonsense world.

In nonsense, paradox is clearly found everywhere—in the relationships between language and meaning, order and disorder, formal pattern and imagination of language. But paradox must be qualified further. The relationships between the two terms of a paradox can be one of tension or of incongruity. Incongruity rather than tension prevails in the nonsense world. There is no conflict between language and reference. They follow divergent paths. We said earlier that the content of nonsense is to its form what the content of poetry is to its metric pattern. The analogy can be extended and qualified to bring out the distinction just made.

   I. An aged man is but a paltry thing,
     A tattered coat upon a stick, unless
     Soul clap its hands and sing, and louder
     sing
     For every tatter in its mortal dress.
        (W. B. Yeats, "Sailing to Byzantium")

  II. Prompt at the call, around the Goddess roll
     Broad hats, and hoods, and caps, a sable
     shoal:
     Thick and more thick the black blockade
     extends,
     A hundred head of Aristotle's friends.
        (A. Pope, "The Dunciad")

In these two examples the rhyming words are analogous in sound and divergent in grammatical function. The first shows a relationship of tension between the two rhyming words, the second of incongruity.

Incongruity brings us to the problem of humor. Is humor, as Elizabeth Sewell argues, really incidental to nonsense? An absolute judgment cannot be made. But incongruity in *Alice* is certainly a key to its humor. Children's comments have been particularly revealing in this respect. A survey conducted among children aged ten to fourteen showed that a majority of children over thirteen found the *Alice* books both "unrealistic" and "stupid." The children who appreciated the fantasy also tended to appreciate the humor. A child of twelve made this apt distinction: "The words are silly but not stupid: they are ridiculous in a way that I like."

Carroll's humor is of a particular kind. It is sheer, unadulterated fun, free from both topical allusion and from wit. It is intimately linked to the world of fantasy. Hence the kinship of nonsense with surrealism. The fetters of reality are broken and liberation is found in fantasy or laughter.

This blending of imagination and humor might well explain the fact that while isolated examples exist in France, nonsense has not become part of the literary tradition as in England. The greater propensity for whimsy of the English might well account for this difference in taste. With their emphasis on "esprit," the French tend to accept more reluctantly a gratuitous world that resists rational explanation.

Nonsense can be read at different levels. Like most great children's books, it is not simply a book for children. It can be read with the freshness of a child or the critical mind of an adult. Yet, in a way, a full appreciation of nonsense requires "a willing suspension of disbelief." The reader of the *Annotated Alice* has, in a sense, outgrown Wonderland.

Jack J. Jorgens (essay date 1969)

SOURCE: "Alice Our Contemporary," in *Children's Literature: Annual of the Modern Language Association Seminar on Children's Literature and The Children's Literature Association*, Vol. 1, 1969, pp. 152-61.

[*In the following essay, which focuses on a theatrical adaptation of* Alice, *Jorgens considers the relevance of Carroll's stories to twentieth-century society.*]

In his discussion of the fairy tale, W. H. Auden nicely sums up the stereotypical view of children's literature. The world of the fairy tale, he says, is an unambiguous, unproblematic place where appearance reflects reality. It is a world of being, not becoming, where typical, one-dimensional characters (either *good* or *bad*) behave strictly in accordance with their natures, and always receive the appropriate rewards or punishments. It is a predictable world where events occur in fixed numerical and geometrical patterns. And above all, it is a world without intense emotion or awareness where even the most violent acts are viewed by characters and readers with detachment, as not horrible but somehow fun, playful. But children's books are written by adults, not children, and one need not be a frequent contributor to *American Imago* to see that they reflect not only the author's ideals of what children ought to like and be, but his own fears and fantasies. The sense of freedom many writers feel when they are addressing an audience that they consider to be more imaginative and more innocent than any other often leads to works which are strange distorting-mirror images of social problems and upheavals, personal compulsions, and philosophical dilemmas. The fanciful is also the uninhibited and the unrepressed.

The limitations of the stereotype of children's fiction become clear when one applies them to the greatest of such works—*Alice's Adventures in Wonderland* and *Through the Looking-Glass and What Alice Found There*. In them we find not only the typical characteristics, but negations and parodies of them as well. *Alice* is at once simple and complex, predictable and unpredictable, sentimental and tough-minded, escapist and realistic, humorous and satirical, melodramatic and tragic. Carroll took the problems children face while growing up—their dreams, their imaginary worlds, and their games—and combined them with the problems of adult life: the labyrinths of conflicting values, the struggle to meet the demands of society and self, the coming to terms with mortality. All these he fused in an imagination heated by intense pressures within him—his sexual longings, his seizures of "unholy thoughts", and his despair. In *Alice* (written for the little girls he was so attracted to) Carroll embodied both the quest of modern man for meaning in what seems to be a grotesque nightmare and his personal quest for the still, quiet center.

The success the *Alice* books have had with children grew out of Carroll's profound understanding of children and their problems. On those innumerable afternoons of tale-telling and games with his young friends, he learned just how to delight them, how to frighten them and then provide release in laughter, and how to warp or exaggerate life until it became ridiculous or wonderful. To children, who have constantly to adjust to the new, Carroll often presents a world of wish-fulfillment where the heroine is skillful enough to adjust to any situation, or powerful enough to shape it to suit herself. If the spectre of school becomes too much, let it be transformed (as it all too often is) into reeling, writhing, ambition, distraction, uglification, derision,

mystery, seaography, drawling, stretching, fainting in coils, laughing, and grief. If books with no pictures or dialogue bore us, or a winter's afternoon makes us lonely, let us chase a rabbit down his hole or walk through a mirror into another world. Let all those dull poems with morals at the end be re-written. Let them tell us how crocodiles eat the little fishes rather than how the industrious bees demonstrate that idle hands are the devil's tools. Let our poems tell us that old people are, among other things, crazy, fat, ugly, slack-jawed, not just that if you are careful of your health and remember God you will have a golden old age. Let them tell us that the prudent "lobster" speaks contemptuously of the "sharks" only in their absence, not that sloth is a thing to be abhorred. Let adults recall how it feels to be ruled by people whose time is always worth a thousand pounds a minute. Let them recall the pain, the disorientation, and the embarrassments of growing up—the difficulty of keeping up with inconsiderate long-legged adults, the shyness and self-consciousness, the perplexing fact that our feet do not want to go in the same direction we want to, and the dilemmas resulting from the outgrowing of old selves or of burying them within new selves so that " . . . it's no use going back to yesterday, because I was a different person then." Let them remember the ogres that haunted our dreams—the Jabberwock, the Bandersnatch, and the Snark—and our fear of the darkness, but also that we take delight in things like Mr. Tenniel's surrealistic scene with the toves, borogroves, and raths wandering about a sundial, his grinning cats, and his strange, horrible beast the Jabberwock. Let them see how ludicrous it is that they justify themselves by crying "I'm older than you, and must know better," and how inexplicable to a child an adult's lightning changes in mood are: "the Queen turned crimson with fury, and, after glaring at her for a moment like a wild beast, began screaming, 'Off with her head!'"

Of course the adult reader's view is more complicated than the child's. We see Alice from two perspectives—the child's and the adult's—and are therefore sometimes amused at her naivete and her parroting of her parents. Part of her charm for adults is the mixture of her stern, sensible, "adult" side (cf. her concern for eating and drinking the right things) with her mischievous, insecure "childish" side (frequently the two selves separate and talk things over between them). It is amusing to observe (and recall) the smugness of a six- or seven-year-old who knows that all questions have answers and all answers questions, that the world is an orderly and logical place and that what she has been taught to be good and right *is* good and right. We smile as Alice flaunts her moral superiority on her journeys just as she flaunts her knowledge and her big words. It is not so amusing, however, to feel with Alice what it is like to hear, "didn't you know *that*?" or "it's *my* opinion that you never think *at all*," or, from the White Queen, described by Carroll as "cold and calm

. . . formal and strict . . . Pedantic to the tenth degree, the concentrated essence of all governesses!", "I don't know what you mean by *your* way . . . all the wáys about here belong to *me.* . . ." Least comforting of all is what Alice dreams of doing to adults when she fulfills the wish every child has of being bigger than *anybody:* she would behead us, as she threatens to do with the flowers—"If you don't hold your tongues, I'll pick you"—or blow us all away like a pack of cards, or play cat-and-mouse with us: "Nurse! Do let's pretend that I'm a hungry hyaena, and you're a bone!"

As a number of literary critics have recently pointed out, Carroll's *Alice* books are much more than skillfully written vehicles for childish revenge and adult complacency. This new appraisal grows largely from our realization that many of the problems of modern man are really extensions of those of children (hence the growing interest in early development), that myth and the unconscious cut across the lines dividing children from adults. William Empson pointed out a number of important themes and patterns in the course of his well-known discussion of Alice as Swain. He reveals that there is in *Alice* a curiously Darwinian retelling of Genesis where Alice is born out of her own sorrow (her salt tears are the amniotic fluid), and a whole Noah's ark of animals emerge from that "sea" as man, according to evolutionary theory, did long ago. There are, beside the parodies of snobbishness, politics, progress, and industrialization, recurring death jokes, and a persistent linking of puberty with death. There is Alice's growth in her womb-house where she feels cramped and fears that her food and air will be cut off. In addition, there is the curious zoo of post-Darwinian animals which represent facets of Man (the Cheshire cat = intellectual detachment, abstraction, an inner world), and demonstrate the vicious natural struggle for survival in which man is involved (Alice often squeamishly shies away from some proffered "naked lunch").

Out of the links Empson made between Carroll's life and his books grew Phyllis Greenacre's Freudian biography which establishes that Dodgson, like Verlaine and Joyce, poured his inner life into his works, and in doing so touched the universal. Far from limiting herself to the listing of suggestive holes and elongated objects, the author makes several penetrating observations including the basic one that the world of *Alice,* with its disorientations of time and space, mysteries of cause and effect, confusions of animals and humans with the inanimate, its amorality, threats of extinction, and frightening female authority figures, is a reproduction of the stage of child development from about fifteen to thirty months—the stage in which crude sensory awareness and primal demands complicate themselves into memory, anticipation, self-awareness, and self-criticism. She links Carroll's female-dominated upbringing with the powerful females of his books and the singular lack of strong, well-respected adult males. And (to mention only her major points) she demonstrates how Carroll's passion for order and dismay at the aging of his young friends led to his attempts to preserve them for all time in his photographs and books. She shows how his fear of loss of memory, consciousness, and sanity (he kept careful records of his voluminous correspondence and carefully filed all his photographs and negatives) is incorporated in, and lends power to, Alice's journeys.

Building upon Empson and Greenacre, Donald Rackin in "Alice's Journey to the End of Night," has skillfully shown how *Alice in Wonderland* may be viewed as ". . . a comic horror-vision of the chaotic land beneath the man-made groundwork of Western thought and convention." When Alice goes "below ground," she seeks meaning in terms of the rules and conventions of Victorian society and when they fail her, she is so terrified that she flees back to her comparatively safe, logical world "above ground." In the course of her journey, "practically all pattern, save the consistency of chaos, is annihilated" including mathematics, logic, social convention, language, time and space. *Alice* for Rackin, is a grim comedy in which our laughter grows not from self-assurance, but from our fear of meaninglessness. Alice's "curiosity" is madness—it leads her to a dream world of black humor where, when man seeks to know reality through symbols, he manages only to become lost among them.

To the historian of literature, what is interesting about Carroll as seen in his books is the tension between his restrained, rational, conservative "Victorian" self and his wildly imaginative, satirical, "romantic" self. To critics who are concerned primarily with what meaning literature has for us today, what seems important about works such as *Alice* and Shakespeare's *A Midsummer Night's Dream* is not their undeniably forgiving qualities—their gentle humor, wonder, and playfulness. Rather it is their absurdist traits, their dark ironies, their grotesqueness. Carroll's works have been extremely influential among avant-garde writers since the turn of the century. Their "warping, stretching, compressing, inverting, reversing, distorting" of the world, reflected in Tenniel's illustrations of the Jabberwock and the Toves around the sundial placed them solidly in the tradition of Surrealism. As Gardner points out, Lear and Carroll, the leading nonsense poets of their time, were precursors of the Dadaists, Italian Futurists, Gertrude Stein, and Ogden Nash. Journeys underground, journeys to the end of night or into mirror-worlds proliferate as writers like Celine and Genet despair of finding meaning in the world. The fall of Humpty Dumpty achieves mythological status in Joyce's *Finnegan's Wake,* and one could easily mistake Alice's train ride or the trial of the knave of hearts for Kafka's work. Vladimir Nabokov's first book was a translation of *Alice* into Russian, and his nymphet-loving hero Humbert Humbert resembles Carroll not a little. Echoing T. S. Eliot, Jorge Luis Borges has noted in his essay "Kafka and His Precursors" that "every writer *creates* his own precursors. His work modifies our conception of the past, as it will modify the future." If this is so, then Borges, the author of so many "fictions" about dreams within dreams, doubles, mythological creatures, and voyages to strange worlds, "created" *Alice* as part of his own tradition. From the first, *Alice* was recognized as a forerunner of the theatre of the absurd with its syntactic dead ends, philosophical mazes, and grotesque, cartoon-like characters. *Alice* even has its own "Catch-22"—"We're all mad here. I'm mad. You're mad." "How do you know I'm mad?" said Alice. "You must be," said the Cat, "or you wouldn't have come here."

As important as these critics and creative artists have been in discovering the contemporary *Alice,* I believe it has been most skillfully brought into focus by a group of actors who humorously called themselves The Manhattan Project, under the direction of Andre Gregory. Because the production so graphically illustrates, in their original context, the aspects of *Alice* that have attracted modern artists and critics, it is an important bridge between the critical world that describes *Alice* and the artistic world that draws upon it.

There have, of course, been numerous stage versions of Carroll's works (the earliest having as collaborator Carroll himself), and films have been made by Paramount (1933) and Walt Disney (1951), but only in this production was the importance of *Alice* to our time made clear. The mode Gregory has chosen for his *Alice* is the strenuous one evolved by groups such as the Open Theater and the Performance Group. From Artaud's Theatre of Cruelty he borrowed moments of savage eroticism, violent physicality, anarchic humor, and a burning focus on the actor. For a decor he chose the rags and junk of Grotowski's Poor Theatre which stripped the production of all gaudy, slick, showmanship. When we entered the tiny, crowded lobby of the small converted church, we were swept like Alice through a rabbit hole and a long corridor and bunched up on risers with old chair seats nailed to them (at random so nobody *fit* very well). From there we looked down on a small square stage which looked like somebody's old attic or a seedy pawn shop. This playing area, "half circus—half nursery," had a torn canvas floor, an old parachute spread out over it for a roof, a stack of chairs, a bench, and table, a ladder, an old gramophone, and a curtain at the back made of old newspapers.

As in Weiss's *Marat Sade,* the play was acted out by a mad chorus. All save Alice were insane, hopelessly wrenched out of "normality", swept into forgetfulness and euphoria, or smashed against each other by fits of rage. Their chaotic costumes reflected their minds: a tattered, soiled petticoated dress with an apron (like the one shown by Tenniel) for Alice, a coat and tails grubby overalls for the White Rabbit/March Hare, a stack of hats and old suit coat for the Mad Hatter. The White Queen and the Narrator/"Balloon Prince" wore quilted shirts and pants which through dream-transfer mirrored the padding from a bed or (to us) invisible walls of an insane asylum. The sound effects, which like the setting and costumes provided little sensual pleasure, were raucous and harsh. Marches and tunes from the twenties were shouted by the chorus or blared out over the old gramophone. The air was full of groans, whistles, ticking clocks, long agonizing silences, cuckoo birds, foghorns, bells, and screams (of pain? delight? terror?). Through this world travelled Alice, "homeless, forgetful, nostalgic, fragmented, emotionally and physically warped."

There was no break in the production and the acting was exhausting to watch—as exhausting as trying to read *Alice* with close attention to everything in it. Hewes, like many spectators, admired the "totally engaged life-and-death ensemble playing of the actors that gave their confrontations the desperate urgency of a nightmare." The atmosphere was hyperactive, frenetic, compulsive, and the silences and pauses seemed to grow out of exhaustion. It was an atmosphere which provided a perfect dramatic representation of Carroll's intense Wonderland/Looking-Glass world which constantly assaults Alice and pressures her into readjusting to it through questions, insults, and dream-like changes of scene. Within these cycles of feverish energy and fatigue Gregory captured the book's rich and varied humor, whimsical, grim, farcical by turns. Barnes underscored this variety, yet accurately listed that "humor is not the play's purpose. The purpose is fear. Mr. Gregory noticed a very, very obvious fact. We laugh when we are afraid."

When working on *Marat Sade,* Adrian Mitchell and Peter Brook were struck by the play's ability to force the audience to repeatedly shift their focus, opinions, and emotions, to make them reformulate their ideas about what is happening and what it means. As in Shakespeare, the impressions come too fast to permit relaxation. "A good play sends many such messages, often several at a time, often crowding, jostling, overlapping one another. The intelligence, the feelings, the memory, the imagination are all stirred." The *Alice* books have that quality, and it is a measure of the success of Gregory's adaptation that playgoers were stirred by "states of dread, of sexuality, of absurdity, of bewilderment, of wonder, of fear, of giddiness, of giggliness, of madness, of contraction, of elevation, of 'growing pains,' of terror, of playfulness, of ecstacy."

Both of Carroll's books have idyllic openings. The feeling in *Looking-Glass* is one of comfort and security, as Alice sits by the fire in a snug, warm chair and watches the snow kissing the windows and covering the trees and fields beyond. *Wonderland* begins with a leisurely, dreamy journey down the Thames as Dodgson spins tales of fantasy to three little girls on a golden afternoon. Yet I have always felt these openings are deceptive ones—as deceptive as the pictures of Dodgson with his boyish face, or accounts of his quiet, professorial life at Oxford. One cannot deduce the nature of *Alice* from its beginning any more than one can deduce what kind of book a stammering, shy bachelor who preferred the company of little girls could write. The production made both these points economically and powerfully.

The virtue of Gregory's production was its ability to string together great theatrical moments which skillfully elucidated the book. An anarchy of hair and padded bodies and junk would suddenly clarify itself into beautifully honed sequences from Carroll. In the opening scene, we hear back in the darkness the slow, excruciating tearing of a hole in the newspaper screen, and a clump of characters mumbling "Jabberwocky" enter. Alice in her tattered "little girl" dress comically struggles to escape this sticky blanket of nonsensical sounds, this group-grope, when suddenly the scene disintegrates and, after a silence accompanied by the ticking of a clock, it re-forms itself into the river scene at the start of her first journey. In a deep, confident voice, the narrator begins the prefatory poem "All in the Golden Afternoon" as a kneeling actor mimes paddling the boat down the Thames, imitating vocally the leisurely sh-h-h, sh-h-h, sh-h-h of the paddle. But slowly the compulsions and repressed drives most readers sense beneath idyllic narrative come to the surface. Carroll stumbles over his part, collects himself, begins again, stumbles again until he becomes totally confused and forgets everything. As he sweats and strains his memory, the paddling becomes more vehement, goes faster and faster until in a crescendo of violent exertions of mind and muscle, the scene explodes and suddenly we are confronted with Alice's tortuous journey down the rabbit hole. She is tossed, twisted, flung, rolled, assaulted by members of the chorus; the descent is a blend of sexual initiation, dizzying nightmare, madness, and death. Our journey into Carroll's mind has begun.

The Alice of Gregory's distinctly adult version was a modern kind of innocent, not the priggish little Victorian Miss of the original. In order to involve us in Alice's journeys (who can identify with a snobbish little prude?) Gregory gave us a much more earthy, sympathetic heroine, naive and curious but able to look out for herself, a tomboy—unrestrained, "assertive, ornery, and often rude." There was much less distance between this likeable tomboy and the audience than there is between the reader and the Alice of the original; when we are taken to the edge of madness with a tough, sensible girl who is in touch with her own feelings as much as any of us were when we were young, we cannot shrug it off so easily.

Through Alice, much of the playfulness and humor of the books is preserved. As long as she remains untouched by her "adventures" or at least is able to spring back from them, we can enjoy Gregory's elaborations on Carroll's fantasy world. Two good examples are the mirror-double of Alice, who mimics all her motions and perversely gives her the wrong answers to mathematical problems, and the "dirigible prince" who eludes her shrinkings and growings, who when punctured "skitters to the floor like a deflating balloon, twisting every which way." Often however the fun becomes uncomfortable. We chuckle at the hilarious caucus race, with the whole cast running in place until they collapse in exhaustion, but the scene ends with a cruel little turn: out of revenge, the birds who "choked and had to be patted on the back" gleefully make Alice eat her thimble. While we are amused by the mouse's body, which curves and sways as he narrates the mouse's "tale" of Fury's arbitrary hatefulness pursued out of boredom, the sense of claustrophobia becomes overwhelming as the "house" (made of actors) closes in on Alice.

The caterpillar scene was also both funny and unsettling. Atop several actors forming a mushroom, the thoroughly stoned caterpillar (in the book he speaks in a "languid, sleepy voice" and is "quietly smoking a long hookah and taking not the smallest notice of her or of anything else") inhales on the arm of one of the actors with long ecstatic breaths and eventually gets Alice silly/high. But his persistent questions about metamorphosis and identity shake her deeply, and like Carroll we are not so secure about who we are as to remain untouched.

Alice survives the duchess' crazy kitchen, the (boy, naturally) baby's transformation into a pig, and the grinning Cheshire Cat, but in the marvelously conceived mad tea-party Gregory makes it clear that Alice moves near the abyss, and does not recover as easily as she does earlier. The sinister, threatening Mad Hatter with three hats stacked on his head, rules the scene with barely preserved calm. Violence erupts when he is ridiculed by Alice and as he fixes her in a ferocious stare, he murderously squeezes a stick of butter in his fist. The Dormouse, wearing a World War I helmet, takes crushing farcical blows on it from the Mad Hatter. He stuffs his mouth with bread until he cannot speak, and turns the stomach of every one on and off stage by cramming a whole stick of butter into his mouth and eating it. The jittery, panicked March Hare nibbles his bread frantically. His actions are totally disjointed: he suddenly juggles three pieces of bread, plays footsie with Alice, waltzes her around the room, and then tries to rape her.

After some Marx brothers antics (actors scrawl "LEWIS LIKES LITTLE GIRLS" on a wall, the paranoid Queen of Hearts pops front-row spectators on the head with a huge plastic hammer, and a croquet game is played with human mallets and balls), we enter a weird, quiet land where trees (actors with ragged umbrellas folded down over their heads) sway in the dark, the wind whistles, and the gently, lyrically mad White Queen dances and spins verbal mazes about us. A tattered umbrella throws a swirling speckled light over the whole errie scene. Here Alice is lured toward the beauty, the quiet still place of madness—the misty place where distinctions between past, present, and future are obliterated, where memory becomes the future, where crime follows the punishment and trial, and where one cries out in pain before the wound is inflicted.

Alice confronts in Humpty Dumpty the chaos of words breaking loose from their agreed upon meanings. And all the while Humpty Dumpty, like Jerry in Albee's *Zoo Story,* is secretly thinking not about his "opponent's" dilemma, but about how to time his suicide correctly, how to play the game. This cynical philosopher-gamesman constantly catches Alice in word traps, treats the world as a riddle (which, Alice is learning, is true), insults her, and argues that even if communication were possible, it is irrelevant. He, like the Red King, "means what he says," but chooses any word he likes and makes it mean exactly what he wants it to. Humpty Dumpty dismisses Alice's (and our) questions about whether he can do such a thing with the definitive statement on the matter: "The question is which is to be master—that's all." Alice is staggered. When he suggests a suicide pact to her, she is upset enough to consider it seriously, but things are not allowed to go any further. Tottering on a pile of chairs, held up by four imaginary guy ropes which are held with great difficulty by straining actors, Humpty Dumpty falls to the ground crushing an egg against his forehead as he strikes the floor. We feel Alice is free, but we are wrong. She stares in horror, and it dawns on us that she thinks it was *she* who was responsible for his death (again like *Zoo Story*). The trap has snapped shut.

In the following (final) scene, the White Knight brings Alice to a crisis. He is a summing up and intensification of all that has come before—a kaleidoscope of hate, fear, love, desire, disgust, wild imagination, and fearsome literalness. He violently assaults Alice and then becomes a child whose head must be cradled in her lap. The frank, friendly, flirtatious, good humored, little hoyden—conventional but curious, naively vulnerable—is destroyed by this Thomas Edison gone berserk. The humor is gone, and with it the release of laughter, [as we] watch a man conscious of his madness and pathetically struggling to escape it, but being sucked back into chaos by his weakness, his fear of the "sane" world, and his fatal attraction to the flash-

ing jewel, madness. Alone in his maze of inventions and visions, he needs desperately to draw Alice in with him. The agony and attraction becomes unbearable for her, so she flees and awakens, taking back to the world above ground the dreamer's incredible knowledge—knowledge like Leda's knowledge of the Swan, or Cassandra's knowledge of the future to which we all are doomed.

As the more perceptive critics, writers, and theatre artists of our time have shown, far from being isolated from the world, Carroll's "children's books" lead us to its heart; they are a microcosm of it. We too are caught up in that intense nonsense played according to arbitrary rules which is unfortunately not confined to games. (Alice, like most of us, is a pawn until the end of the dream. The paradoxes of "Underground" and the "Looking-Glass World" are painfully contemporary. In the midst of a print explosion and cursed with the shifting sands of memory, which of us does not run as fast as we can to stay in the same place? In our world too, walking directly toward something only carries you further away from it—progress breeds regress, punishments become worse than crimes, inhumanity is proposed as our only humane course, and the *last* thing we can do to alleviate poverty (we are told) is to give money to the poor. What thoughtful observer of governments today can doubt that in deciding what words are going to mean, the only question is *who is master?* All too many "world leaders" respond in a crisis as the White King does: "You alarm me! I feel faint—Give me a ham sandwich!" Carroll's alarm and sense of loss at the aging and coarsening of the little girls he adored serves as a metaphor for all the effects of time: weakness, forgetfulness, inconstancy, disease, death. And the ironic twist is there too. Just when in despair we learn the melancholy lesson that time washes away loyalty, friendship, love, that the rushes we pick up will, like Alice's, fade and lose all their scent and beauty, we are confronted by the Red Queen who screams "When you've once said a thing, that fixes it, and you must take the consequences."

Charles Matthews (essay date 1970)

SOURCE: "Satire in the *Alice* Books," in *Criticism,* Vol. 12, Winter, 1970, pp. 105-19.

[*In the essay below, Matthews considers the recurrence of satire and literary parody in the* Alice *books.*]

Criticism of Lewis Carroll's works usually runs to extremes. There is a tough-minded school largely made up of psychoanalytical critics who take a no-nonsense attitude toward Carroll's nonsense. Some useful criticism, such as William Empson's characteristically stimulating and unsound essay, has been produced by the tough-minded approach. At the other extreme are tender-minded critics like G. K. Chesterton, who insist that the *Alice* books were written for children and therefore should not be approached with either reverence or scepticism—in short, that they should not be subjected to literary criticism. Some tender-minded critics seem to try to mask the fact that they *are* criticising by playing Carroll's own games of fantasy and word-play in their studies. Harry Morgan Ayres invokes Humpty Dumpty in his little book on *Alice,* but his Humpty Dumpty inevitably suffers from comparison with Carroll's. Florence Becker Lennon's useful biography is marred by such gratuitous cleverness as her reference to Dodgson as "the don with the luminous prose" in the midst of an otherwise straightforward account of his acquaintance with prominent people.

The fault with both extreme approaches (and most critics partake of both to some degree) is that one loses sight of Alice and her adventures while the critics indulge themselves in either excessive Carroll/Dodgson consciousness or excessive self-consciousness. The works of Lewis Carroll are, to be sure, children's books, and they were indeed produced by a man whose mind, like most men's minds, was complex and at times disturbing, but the fascination for adults of the books themselves, wholly apart from the fascination of the author's personality, is undeniable. Carroll was an adult (most of the time), and he was doubtless aware that other adults would read his books, if only to their children. The books inevitably express some of his own ideas, for only the simplest and most elemental children's books—the "Dick and Jane" readers inflicted by educationists on generations of American children, for example—are wholly devoid of intellectual content and literary merit.

Perhaps there is also a barrier to intelligent discussion of the Carroll books in the fact that they are "nonsense." "High seriousness" still makes us suffer moral qualms about devoting our attention to literature that seems designed for "mere" enjoyment. And in writing about nonsense literature, the critic finds himself in danger of committing self-parody, of coming forth with something like one of the choicer essays in *The Pooh Perplex.* But perhaps in these days when distinguished critics are writing perceptive articles on the lyrics of John Lennon, criticism has widened its view of the realms of art sufficiently for one to write about Lewis Carroll without more than a normal amount of bathos.

"Nonsense" is, after all, a Victorian word for a Victorian genre. Its basic connotations are pejorative, as pejorative now as in 1846 when Edward Lear placed it in the title of his first book of verse. But as the name of a genre, perhaps it can be purged of these connotations. For neither Carroll's nor Lear's nonsense fits a dictionary definition like "devoid of sense"; their nonsense is as carefully structured as any of the sensible

works with which it is contemporary, and it follows in many ways a more rigid decorum than, for example, the novels of Dickens. Furthermore, there are qualitative differences between the nonsense of Carroll and the nonsense of Lear. There are no real people in Lear. There are, to be sure, scores of Men, Ladies, and Persons, both Young and Old, but they have no more resemblance to human beings than the Pobble or the Jumblies. Alice, on the other hand, is a very real little girl, and the rather pallid Victorian adults in *Sylvie and Bruno,* though hardly "round" characters, are realistically portrayed. The *Alice* books are closer to *Gulliver's Travels* and *Erewhon,* and *Sylvie and Bruno* to *The Water-Babies,* than either to the works of Edward Lear. Only *The Hunting of the Snark* and some of the poems in the *Alice* books really approach the purity of Lear's nonsense.

One of the essential characteristics of Carroll's nonsense is its self-consciousness. From the moment on the golden afternoon when Secunda requests "nonsense" in the tale being told her, we are aware that nonsense is incidental, not continuous in *Alice in Wonderland.* Alice always tells us when something is nonsensical. The first time she begins to grow, an extraordinary but not a nonsensical occurrence, she speculates on how she is to exercise control over her feet; she determines to woo them with Christmas presents, properly addressed and sent by the carrier, but suddenly comes to her senses and exclaims, "Oh dear, what nonsense I'm talking!" She soon learns two principal types of nonsense: linguistic and logical. Nonsense arises from linguistic confusion when she misunderstands the Mouse's emphatic negative and immediately offers to help him untie his knot; "You insult me," he replies indignantly, "by talking such nonsense!" Nonsense arises from logical incoherence at the Mad Tea Party:

> Alice had been looking over his shoulder with some curiosity. "What a funny watch!" she remarked. "It tells the day of the month, and doesn't tell what o'clock it is!"
>
> "Why should it?" muttered the Hatter. "Does *your* watch tell you what year it is?"
>
> "Of course not," Alice replied very readily: "but that's because it stays the same year for such a long time together."
>
> "Which is just the case with *mine*," said the Hatter.
>
> Alice felt dreadfully puzzled. The Hatter's remark seemed to her to have no sort of meaning in it, and yet it was certainly English.

Alice has learned to distrust her own language, a very valuable lesson. Actually, the Hatter's remark is only temporary nonsense; Carroll, with his characteristic love of puzzles, postpones the clarification for three pages until it is revealed that it is always six o'clock for the Hatter since the Queen accused him of murdering the time. The careless reader almost certainly misses this elucidation; perhaps Alice misses it too, for she fails to learn another important lesson: that nonsense is relative. In *Through the Looking Glass,* she is advised to walk in the opposite direction to reach the Red Queen: "This sounded nonsense to Alice, so she said nothing, but set off at once towards the Red Queen. To her surprise she lost sight of her in a moment, and found herself walking in at the front-door again." She has forgotten that the laws of motion, like everything else in Looking-Glass Land, are reversed. The function of such nonsense is to illuminate the nature of sense: to explore both the limitations and potentialities of language and logic. Compared with Lear's nonsense, almost nonsense for nonsense's sake, Carroll's is as sensible as a dictionary, as the Red Queen rightly observes, and almost as sensible as that of the greatest twentieth century nonsense-writer, James Joyce.

The decorum of nonsense deserves a more extensive treatment than we can give it here. Carroll was especially severe in his standards of taste; easily offended by even the innocent blasphemies of children, he was known to caution his friends not to tell tales of such things in his presence. This sensitivity led him to change the passion-flower in the talking flowers episode of *Through the Looking Glass* to a tiger lily when he learned that the name refers to Christ's passion. But there is a further decorum which determines what one can and cannot do in a fantasy. Tenniel's collaboration with Carroll provides us with some suggestions of these limitations. Tenniel was given the option of illustrating a poem about a walrus and either a butterfly, a baronet, or a carpenter. Any of the three fits the meter, and there is no rhyme problem. Tenniel wisely chose the carpenter, of course, for though the baronet would have been equally acceptable, the mind boggles at the concept of an ostreophagous butterfly. Nonsense has to undergo a severe pragmatic test; some things, especially visual absurdities and grotesqueries, are better left to the imagination. The illustrator's role serves to indicate the limitations of description. Tenniel chose not to illustrate the gnat "the size of a chicken" and Carroll avoids any further description of it, thereby retaining a funny idea without touching off the *frisson* that one gets at the contemplation of creatures under the microscope. Henry Holiday's illustrations for *The Hunting of the Snark,* on the other hand, are too detailed and realistic, and Carroll was especially wise to reject his portrait of the Snark itself. But Tenniel's Jabberwock is successful because he indulged in the visual nonsense of putting a waistcoat on the horrendous creature. (The more squeamish Carroll, however, after a poll of mothers, removed the Jabberwock from its position as frontispiece for fear of frightening young readers.) Nonsense illuminates sense, but sense gives

structure and coherence to nonsense. The first stanza of **"Jabberwocky"** is a case in point. It is utter nonsense, but the structure given it by the English words and the slightly archaic English syntax make the nonsense words resonate with potential meaning. "Outgrabe" has a nice Germanic sound to it, "slithy" and "mimsy" look like real adjectives, and "toves," "raths," and "borogoves" must be there in force, for the endings are obviously plural. Alice's reaction to it is the universal one: "Somehow it seems to fill my head with ideas—only I don't know exactly what they are!" But if the English words are eliminated and other nonsense words substituted for them, the result is unreadable gibberish:

> Flob brillig, yabble slithy toves
>   Ag gyre ib gimble umlog wabe:
> Oof mimsy zod nit borogoves,
>   Ropil mome raths outgrabe.

Effective nonsense keeps one foot on the ground; fantasy needs a realistic background, a frame of familiar reference. A tour of Wonderland without the practical, very English little Alice to serve as norm would be tedious indeed.

But the presence of Alice as norm, as the embodiment of Victorian practicality and industry, suggests that the *Alice* books may have satiric implications. For as Northrop Frye says of satire, "its moral norms are relatively clear, and it assumes standards against which the grotesque and absurd are measured." And in actuality, we should be surprised not to find satire in the books. Dodgson was a man of firm opinions and he was also one of the finest parodists in a golden age of parody. Frye sees the parodistic tendency as an indication of the satirical nature of the *Alice* books:

> Most fantasy is pulled back into satire by a powerful undertow often called allegory, which may be described as the implicit reference to experience in the perception of the incongruous. The White Knight in Alice who felt that one should be provided for everything and therefore put anklets around his horse's feet to guard against the bites of sharks, may pass as pure fantasy. But when he goes on to sing an elaborate parody of Wordsworth we begin to sniff the acrid, pungent smell of satire, and when we take a second look at the White Knight we recognize a character type closely related to Don Quixote and to the pedant of comedy.

But the objects of satire in the books are less clear than we could wish. There is no apparent political satire in them, except for the caricatures of Disraeli which Tenniel inserted, and—a more significant exception— the trial of the Knave of Hearts. Even in the case of the trial, however, one suspects Carroll's innocence of the implications of this great scene. He cannot have foreseen its applicability to the totalitarianism and witch-hunting of the twentieth century. Our interpretation of it is enhanced by having read Kafka, and the cartoonist Walt Kelly found Carroll's trial so suited to his own satirical purposes that he reprinted it in one of his books, illustrating it with his own cartoon characters, including a King of Hearts with a striking resemblance to the late Senator Joseph McCarthy.

But what satire the *Alice* books contain is directed less at institutions than at individual human foibles. Harry Morgan Ayres has made the interesting suggestion that the *Alice* books form "a satiric view of the world with which the child finds itself confronted," that they constitute a fantastic Bildungsroman. The Victorian age, dominated by a status-seeking middle class rather than a pace-setting aristocracy, was the great age of the etiquette book, of Guides for Young Men and Young Ladies. Children were especially subjected to regimentation. Young Dodgson, though he grew into one of the most methodical of men, seems to have been particularly annoyed by the rules imposed on him. Two poems included among the juvenilia indicate this. "My Fairy," dated 1845 when Dodgson was thirteen, tells of a nuisance of a fairy who pursues him with prohibitions. The last stanza is a paradox worthy of the *Alice* books:

> "What may I do?" at length I cried,
>   Tired of the painful task.
> The fairy quietly replied,
>   And said "You must not ask."
>   *Moral:* "You mustn't."

"Rules and Regulations" written about the same time, is a less negative variation on the same theme. Some of the rules are obviously nonsense items included for the rhyme: "Drink tea, not coffee; / Never eat toffy. . . . Don't waste your money, / Abstain from honey. . . . Drink beer, not porter. / Don't enter the water / Till to swim you are able. . . . Starve your canaries, / Believe in fairies." But the arbitrary nonsense of these rules is perhaps a comment on the general arbitrariness of etiquette, an idea which crops up in the *Alice* books. The final rule on the list, "Be rude to strangers," could almost be the cardinal principle for conduct in Wonderland.

Several of the poems in the *Alice* books are parodies of the sort of didactic poetry young Dodgson may have had in mind when he wrote these early verses. "How doth the little crocodile" takes off Isaac Watts' "Against Idleness and Mischief." Dr. Watts is also represented by "'Tis the Voice of the Lobster," a parody of "The Sluggard." There is normally no malice in Carroll's parodies, as he draws on some of his favorite poets, such as Wordsworth and Tennyson, but in the case of Dr. Watts there is a suggestion of healthy dislike founded on a childhood overexposure to the *Divine Songs*

for Children. The suggestion is borne out in *Sylvie and Bruno* by Arthur's contemptuous remarks about

> "Dr. Watts, who has asked the senseless question
> 'Why should I deprive my neighbour
> Of his goods against his will?'
>
> Fancy *that* as an argument for Honesty! His position seems to be 'I'm only honest because I see no reason to steal.' And the *thief's* answer is of course complete and crushing. 'I deprive my neighbour of his goods because I want them myself. And I do it against his will because there's no chance of getting him to consent to it!'"

Other didactic poems parodied include Southey's "The Old Man's Comforts and How He Gained Them," which becomes "Father William," and G. W. Langford's "Speak Gently," the Duchess' "Speak Roughly." The latter parody makes one think of the fabled strictness of Victorian parents such as Theobald Pontifex.

Alice herself apparently had the usual Victorian childhood. She is extremely, though not morbidly, self-conscious, even when she is falling down the rabbit-hole:

> "I wonder if I shall fall right *through* the earth! How funny it'll seem to come out among the people that walk with their heads downwards! The antipathies, I think—" (she was rather glad there *was* no one listening, this time, as it didn't sound at all the right word) "—but I shall have to ask them what the name of the country is, you know. Please Ma'am, is this New Zealand? Or Australia?" (and she tried to curtsey as she spoke—fancy, curtseying as you're falling through the air! Do you think you could manage it?) "And what an ignorant little girl she'll think me for asking! No, it'll never do to ask: perhaps I shall see it written up somewhere."

She frequently assumes the roles of parent and child simultaneously: "She generally gave herself very good advice (though she very seldom followed it), and sometimes she scolded herself so severely as to bring tears to her eyes; and once she remembered trying to box her own ears for having cheated in a game of croquet she was playing against herself, for this curious child was very fond of pretending to be two people." Alice's precocity places her on a higher level than the childish adults of Wonderland.

Alice's first significant encounter with Wonderland creatures comes in the Pool of Tears and Caucus-Race episodes, and it is there that we see how Carroll is to turn the rules of etiquette topsy-turvy. What, for example, is the proper way of addressing a mouse? The answer is found not in the etiquette books but in Alice's brother's Latin grammar: "A mouse—of a mouse—to a mouse—a mouse—O mouse!" The mouse turns out to be a very respectable beast, so Alice's concern for protocol is not wasted, though she very soon lapses from her good start. She is forced to apologize for bringing up the subject of the mouse-catching Dinah, and agrees that

> "We won't talk about her any more if you'd rather not."
>
> "We, indeed!" cried the Mouse, who was trembling down to the end of its tail. "As if I would talk on such a subject! Our family always *hated* cats: nasty, low, vulgar things! Don't let me hear the name again!"

But Alice blunders on, and manages to offend the other creatures by talking of Dinah's habit of eating birds.

> This speech caused a remarkable sensation among the party. Some of the birds hurried off at once: one old Magpie began wrapping itself up very carefully, remarking "I really must be getting home: the night-air doesn't suit my throat." And a Canary called out in a trembling voice, to its children, "Come away, my dears! It's high time you were all in bed!" On various pretexts they all moved off, and Alice was soon left alone.

The wonderful tone of gentility in both of these speeches places us among the higher levels of Wonderland (read Victorian) society, where the forms of etiquette are used to dissemble and even to excuse rudeness. The Mad Tea Party (a parody of a very English custom) includes this exchange:

> "Have some wine," the March Hare said in an encouraging tone.
>
> Alice looked all round the table, but there was nothing on it but tea. "I don't see any wine," she remarked.
>
> "There isn't any," said the March Hare.
>
> "Then it wasn't very civil of you to offer it," said Alice angrily.
>
> "It wasn't very civil of you to sit down without being invited," said the March Hare.

Apparently one rude turn deserves another.

Alice has a precocious sensitivity to the "game" of polite conversation, however, and the conversational gambit is one of the major motifs of the book:

> "Who are *you?*" said the Caterpillar.
>
> This was not an encouraging opening for a conversation. . . .

> "I didn't know that Cheshire-Cats always grinned; in fact, I didn't know that cats *could* grin."
>
> "They all can," said the Duchess; "and most of 'em do."
>
> "I don't know of any that do," Alice said very politely, feeling quite pleased to have got into a conversation. . . .

> Alice did not much like her keeping so close to her; first because the Duchess was *very* ugly; and secondly, because she was exactly the right height to rest her chin on Alice's shoulder, and it was an uncomfortably sharp chin. However, she did not like to be rude: so she bore it as well as she could.
>
> "The game's going on rather better now," she said, by way of keeping up the conversation a little. . . .

> The White Queen only looked at her in a helpless frightened sort of way, and kept repeating something in a whisper to herself that sounded like "Bread-and-butter, bread-and-butter," and Alice felt that if there was to be any conversation at all, she must manage it herself. So she began rather timidly: "Am I addressing the White Queen?"
>
> "Well, yes, if you call that a-dressing," the Queen said. "It isn't my notion of the thing, at all."
>
> Alice thought it would never do to have an argument right at the very beginning of their conversation, so she smiled and said "If your Majesty will only tell me the right way to begin, I'll do it as well as I can."

The most trying encounter of this sort is the one with Humpty Dumpty. Seeing him seated motionless on his wall, Alice comes to the conclusion that he is a stuffed figure and remarks on how egglike he is. Humpty Dumpty takes umbrage:

> "It's *very* provoking," Humpty Dumpty said after a long silence, looking away from Alice as he spoke, "to be called an egg—very!"
>
> "I said you *looked* like an egg, Sir," Alice gently explained. "And some eggs are very pretty, you know," she added, hoping to turn her remark into a sort of compliment.
>
> "Some people," said Humpty Dumpty, looking away from her as usual, "have no more sense than a baby!"
>
> Alice didn't know what to say to this: it wasn't at all like conversation, she thought, as he never said anything to *her;* in fact, his last remark was evidently addressed to a tree.

Humpty Dumpty is the master of language, however, and conversation must follow his rules:

> "Yes, all his horses and all his men," Humpty Dumpty went on. "They'd pick me up again in a minute, *they* would! However, this conversation is going on a little too fast: let's go back to the last remark but one."

> "I'm afraid I can't quite remember it," Alice said, very politely.

> "In that case we start afresh," said Humpty Dumpty, "and it's my turn to choose a subject—" ("He talks about it just as if it was a game!" thought Alice.)

A game indeed, for Alice's remark is ironic, since the several quotations above show that she has been doing precisely the same thing: manipulating conversations for their own sake rather than for the sake of any interchange of ideas. Her final verdict on Humpty Dumpty—"of all the unsatisfactory people I *ever* met"—is a telling one. Humpty Dumpty is unsatisfactory because he is so self-centered: words mean precisely what he decides they shall mean, and people exist only to gratify his ego (Carroll might have said "egg-o"). He stands in contrast with Alice's beloved, bumbling White Knight. Humpty Dumpty's existence is, at least from his point of view, completely ordered—Alice is baffled because she is not privy to the rules of the game; the White Knight's is random and chaotic, like the erratic moves of the chessman he is. But Humpty Dumpty's ordered, self-centered existence is shattered by his fatal fall; the White Knight falls constantly but perseveres. The Duchess would draw a moral from that.

We are reminded several times that etiquette, like all attempts to impose order on existence, contains paradoxical and arbitrary elements. Encountering Tweedledum and Tweedledee, Alice is confronted with a problem of protocol which she resolves with an aplomb worthy of a Foreign Office functionary.

> "You've begun wrong!" cried Tweedledum. "The first thing in a visit is to say 'How d'ye do?' and shake hands!" And here the two brothers gave each other a hug, and then they held out the two hands that were free, to shake hands with her.

> Alice did not like shaking hands with either of them first, for fear of hurting the other one's feelings; so, as the best way out of the difficulty, she took hold of both hands at once: the next moment they were dancing round in a ring.

The decision to favor either would be perfectly arbitrary, but it could have serious consequences, as Alice has already learned several times over. Here, once again, we see a familiar social custom reduced to an absurdity. The arbitrariness of most etiquette is revealed in exchanges like this one:

> "You!" said the Caterpillar contemptuously. "Who are *you?*"

> Which brought them back again to the beginning of the conversation. Alice felt a little irritated at the caterpillar's making such *very* short remarks, and she drew herself up and said, very gravely, "I think you ought to tell me who *you* are, first."

> "Why?" said the Caterpillar.

> Here was another puzzling question; and as Alice could not think of any good reason, and the Caterpillar seemed to be in a *very* unpleasant state of mind, she turned away.

Not only is Alice frequently placed in the dilemma of having to find an objective justification for her conduct—a rather uncomfortably Sartrean plight, particularly for a Victorian heroine—she often suffers the consequences of blind adherence to what, in Victorian society, would be good manners. The Red Queen, learning after their frantic run that Alice is thirsty, kindly offers her a biscuit (remember that reversal of the laws of nature in Looking-Glass Land): "Alice thought it would not be civil to say "No," though it wasn't at all what she wanted. She took it, and ate it as well as she could: and it was *very* dry: and she thought she had never been so nearly choked in all her life." Even when she becomes a Queen, etiquette gets into her way. Invited to carve the mutton at her banquet, she hesitates because she has never had to carve a joint before:

> "You look a little shy: let me introduce you to that leg of mutton," said the Red Queen. "Alice—Mutton: Mutton—Alice." The leg of mutton got up in the dish and made a little bow to Alice! and Alice returned the bow, not knowing whether to be frightened or amused.

> "May I give you a slice?" she said, taking up the knife and fork, and looking from one Queen to the other.

> "Certainly not," the Red Queen said very decidedly: "it isn't etiquette to cut any one you've been introduced to. Remove the joint!"

Alice faces the alternatives of impoliteness or starvation, and quite sensibly chooses the former. She has learned one valuable lesson in her travels: when doubtful about a point of etiquette, let common sense be your guide. In the Queen of Hearts' croquet ground, she comes upon the procession of the King and Queen, whereupon the three gardeners fall on their faces. "Alice was rather doubtful whether she ought not to lie down on her face like the three gardeners, but she could not remember ever having heard of such a rule at processions; 'and besides, what would be the use of a procession," thought she, 'if people had all to lie down on their faces, so that they couldn't see it?' So she stood where she was, and waited." And encountering the Red and White Queens after she has been crowned, Alice scores one of the few points she makes against all of the people she meets in her travels:

> "Please, would you tell me—" she began, looking timidly at the Red Queen.

> "Speak when you're spoken to!" the Queen sharply interrupted her.

> "But if everybody obeyed that rule," said Alice, who was always ready for a little argument, "and if you only spoke when you were spoken to, and the other person always waited for *you* to begin, you see nobody would ever say anything, so that—"

> "Ridiculous!" cried the Queen. "Why, don't you see, child—" here she broke off with a frown, and, after thinking for a minute, suddenly changed the subject of the conversation.

Carroll's concern with social behavior carries over to *Sylvie and Bruno*. But the change in point of view—from Alice's childish reaction to adult conduct reduced to an absurdity, to that of the adult narrator of *Sylvie and Bruno* who is engaged in the action of the book—gives the satire, when it occurs, a sharper focus. (But one questions whether a sharper focus, given the rather trivial nature of what is satirized, is worthwhile.) Where the satire in the *Alice* books deals with the forms and patterns of social behavior, in *Sylvie and Bruno* it is directed at certain types of boors and bores, as they appear in their natural habitat, the dinner party or the picnic. There is, moreover, the same preoccupation with conversation; the Professor known as Mein Herr says:

> "That which chiefly causes the failure of a dinner-party, is the running short—not of meat, nor yet of drink, but of *conversation*."

> "In an *English* dinner-party," I remarked, "I have never known *small-talk* run short!"

> "Pardon me," Mein Herr respectfully replied, "I did not say 'small-talk.' I said 'conversation.' All such topics as the weather, or politics, or local gossip, are unknown among us. They are either vapid or controversial. What we need for *conversation* is a topic of *interest* and of *novelty*. To secure these things we have tried various plans—Moving-Pictures, Wild-Creatures, Moving-Guests, and a Revolving Humorist."

He proceeds to describe some elaborate devices, worthy of the White Knight, for keeping the conversation at a steady flow.

Among the bores and cranks attacked in the book are amateur art critics, teetotallers, and wine connoisseurs, and there is an amusing parody of late Victorian aestheticism. The chief voice for much of the satire is Arthur, who is a virtuoso wit when the humor takes him. Unfortunately for *Sylvie and Bruno* as a whole, the wit is submerged in sentimentality. Arthur's antic disposition is revealed in a confrontation with a pompous man; Arthur asserts, in the context of another discussion:

> "The number of lunatic *books* is as finite as the number of lunatics."

> "And *that* number is becoming greater every year," said a pompous man. . . .

> "So they say," replied Arthur. "And, when ninety per cent. of us are lunatics," (he seemed to be in a wildly nonsensical mood) "the asylums will be put to their proper use."

> "And that is—?" the pompous man gravely enquired.

> *"To shelter the sane!"* said Arthur. *"We* shall bar ourselves in. The lunatics will have it all their own way, *outside*. They'll do it a little queerly, no doubt. Railway-collisions will be always happening: steamers always blowing up: most of the towns will be burnt down: most of the ships sunk—"

> "And most of the men *killed!*" murmured the pompous man, who was evidently bewildered.

> "Certainly," Arthur assented. "Till at last there will be *fewer* lunatics than sane men. Then *we* come out: *they* go in: and things return to their normal condition!"

We might compare the exchange between Alice and the Cheshire Cat:

> "In *that* direction," the Cat said, waving its right paw round, "lives a Hatter: and in *that* direction," waving the other paw, "lives a March Hare. Visit either you like: they're both mad."

> "But I don't want to go among mad people," Alice remarked.

> "Oh, you can't help that," said the Cat: "we're all mad here. I'm mad. You're mad."

> "How do you know I'm mad?" said Alice.

> "You must be," said the Cat, "or you wouldn't have come here."

This premise of universal irrationality lends Wonderland its charm; it is also the point, ultimately, of its satire. If **Sylvie and Bruno** could sustain Arthur's "wildly [and Wildely] nonsensical mood," instead of lapsing into sentimentality, we might have a true satirical portrait of Victorian society. But both **Sylvie and Bruno** and the **Alice** books are satire *manqué*. Carroll obviously has something to say about the misuse of etiquette and the pretensions of men in social gatherings. But these satirical motifs are incidental to the complex of the books. Still, one senses from an awareness of Carroll's opinions as expressed in these works something that Freudian critics overlook about Charles Lutwidge Dodgson's preference for the society of little girls, children whose manners, however rigidly disciplined, were not used to dissemble, whose conversation was artless. The only good tea party was a mad tea party in company with Alice or Sylvie.

James R. Kincaid (essay date 1973)

SOURCE: "Alice's Invasion of Wonderland," in *PMLA,* Vol. 88, No. 1, January, 1973, pp. 92-99.

[*In the following essay, Kincaid addresses the complex mix of innocence and aggression in* Alice *and argues that Carroll's books are, "above all, about growing up."*]

In the fifth chapter of **Alice's Adventures in Wonderland,** Alice is alarmed to find that her neck has stretched to such "an immense length" that her head is above the trees. The narrator adds, however, that the alarm soon passes and that she "was delighted to find that her neck would bend about easily in any direction, like a serpent." This simile, like other Wonderland similes, is more than ornamental; it suggests a critical and subversive perspective on Alice. Though this perspective is generally submerged, it is present in both of Lewis Carroll's great studies of the joys and dangers of human innocence, **Alice in Wonderland** and **Through the Looking-Glass.** The ironic viewpoint comes to the surface in this case as a Pigeon flies out of the trees screaming "Serpent!" while desperately trying to defend her eggs. When Alice claims to be a little girl and not a serpent, the Pigeon applies the only test that matters: "I suppose you'll be telling me next that you never tasted an egg!" The jokes that follow pick up and make explicit the dark meaning of the narrator's quietly suggestive simile:

> "I *have* tasted eggs, certainly," said Alice, who was a very truthful child; "but little girls eat eggs quite as much as serpents do, you know."

> "I don't believe it," said the Pigeon; "but if they do, why, then they're a kind of serpent: that's all I can say."

All the aggression behind this wit is directed at Alice, the clear representative of all little girls—or serpents. As the Pigeon says, "You're looking for eggs, I know *that* well enough; and what does it matter to me whether you're a little girl or a serpent?" From the perspective of all those whose values are ignored and whose emotions are plundered, it doesn't matter if Eden is destroyed by purposeful malignity or by the callous egoism and ruthless insensitivity that often pass for innocence.

But Wonderland and the world behind the Looking-Glass, certainly, do not always remind us of Eden, and Alice is the object of love as well as fear. The best interpretation of the Alice books, in fact, argues that she is "the reader's surrogate on a frightful journey into meaningless night," where "practically all pattern, save the consistency of chaos, is annihilated." Donald Rackin further sees the most basic and important impulse of the work as a rejection of this chaos and an affirmation of "the sane madness of ordinary existence." But in rejecting this disorder Alice is rejecting not only the terrifying underside of human consciousness but the liberating imagination as well, not only the ironic world of Kafka but the exuberant and expansive world of Don Quixote. The "pattern" with which Alice finally identifies may be necessary, but Carroll is by no means unequivocally in support of her affirmation of a restricted and regularized "sane madness." For flexibility, surprise, and disorder are at the root of comedy as well as terror, and Wonderland shows Alice not only rootless hostility but free and uncompetitive joy. The Mad Tea-Party surely does not so much prefigure *The Trial* as it recalls the wonderful scene where Ben Allen, Bob Sawyer, and Mr. Winkle join to convert the commercial apparatus of a chemist's and surgeon's shop into vessels for punch and get happily drunk in midafternoon. Both scenes assault in mad and gay absoluteness all our sense of the orderly, the proper, and the restrictive. Only in Wonderland and in the world of Mr. Pickwick is it possible to say "it's always teatime." To some extent, the life behind the Looking-Glass and in Wonderland is really far less frightening than the one assumed by Alice. As Elizabeth Sewell's brilliant study has made clear, nonsense, in its pure form, is not frightening but deeply reassuring, since it only appears to be disorderly and actually establishes so many structures and limits that it functions to keep disorder in check. Though in general Carroll does not conform very strictly to this model, Alice very often does upset a beautiful comic game by introducing the alien concepts of linear progression to infinity, nothingness, and death. Therefore, though the Queen of Hearts is a frightening symbol of unregulated hostility, it is a hostility that leads nowhere; no one is really beheaded, since no logical consequences hold. To all pigeons, hence, and all others who have something to protect and cherish, it is Alice's matter-of-fact world, with its serene acceptance of predation and murder, that is truly awful.

The child's hostility to comic values and her insistence on limited sensibleness suggest the great complexity of the books' tone and point of view. For all its diversity, however, the criticism of the Alice books agrees on one point: that Alice, if not actually a surrogate for Lewis Carroll, is a surrogate for the reader and represents a favored perspective. Despite the light thrown by this criticism, it seems to me that it has left one large area of the works dark and has oversimplified both Carroll's rhetoric and his vision. Certainly Alice sometimes appears as a child taking a well-earned revenge on adult silliness, as, for instance, when the Lory pompously insists, "I'm older than you, and must know better." But the purity of the world she finds just as often acts to expose her own corruption. The Alice books are, above all, about growing up, and they recognize both the melancholy of the loss of Eden and the child's crude and tragic haste to leave its innocence. Further than this, though, there is often present a deeper and more ironic view that questions the value of human innocence altogether and sees the sophisticated and sad corruption of adults as preferable to the cruel selfishness of children. Alice reenacts the betrayal of innocence, here qualified by a concurrent sense that innocence is both cute and dangerous. The attitude toward her, then, is very complex. She is both pitied and blamed, fawned over and secretly despised. Most adults and, according to several sources, a good many children, have detected the presence of almost uncontrolled aggression in these books. Some of the children who, as the stories go, screamed in fright at the Alice books may well have been reacting not only to the extreme malice but to a sense that a good part of this malice hits directly at their own representative.

On another level, the Alice books recount a betrayal not so much general as deeply personal. Particularly in *Through the Looking-Glass,* the sense that, as the prefatory poem says, "No thought of me shall find a place / In thy young life's hereafter" becomes increasingly prominent. The self-pity and the submerged bitterness of the verses collect most clearly around the image of the White Knight, abandoned by the child who can't wait to join the adults. But very often Alice appears not so much as the generalized child as a representative of humanity, carrying the unconscious values and assumptions of us all into a freer and more questioning land so as to expose their full viciousness. In either case, Carroll ironically undercuts her favored position as protagonist and invites our hostility and aggression. Much of this aggression, it is true, surfaces in laughter and therefore need never be admitted consciously, but it nonetheless helps to create the split which often occurs between the book's important values and its central character. The necessarily ambivalent attitude toward Alice reinforces a rhetoric which

shifts the direction of its hostile wit and therefore, as in *Gulliver's Travels,* makes it impossible for the reader to find a consistent position or a comfortable perspective. Along with the warmth and sentimentality is a truly dark cynicism and a point of view which can only be called misanthropic. I would like to discuss one aspect of this mixture, not to refute but to complement earlier analyses and to get closer to a few of the secrets of this baffling work.

The first point to make in relation to this complexity is that Alice is, as we have said, both child and adult—and a person in transition. She is not only the steady innocent but the adolescent continually asking, "Who in the world am I?" and the corrupt adult as well. She wants desperately to grow up—and in one dark sense she already has. Even when she appears most childlike, she is attacked for the betrayal to come.

As Alice drops down the rabbit hole, the narrator introduces very quietly the first death joke: "'Well!' thought Alice to herself, 'after such a fall as this, I shall think nothing of tumbling down stairs! . . . Why, I wouldn't say anything about it, even if I fell off the top of the house!' (which was very likely true)." Though the joke works largely on the principle of economy, turning our potential fear for Alice's safety into laughter, there is a barely disguised element of aggression that initiates a series of subtle attacks on the child and her values. The narrative aside throws Alice's sweet childishness into an ironic perspective and invites a hostility typical of the many death jokes throughout. Perhaps the most startling is the hint which comes up several times in *Through the Looking-Glass* that Alice is only a part of the Red King's dream and that, as Tweedledum says, "If that there King was to wake . . . you'd go out—bang!—just like a candle!"

A good deal of the rudeness that Alice encounters at the hands of Wonderland creatures is either so witty or so richly deserved that, I submit, it gains the secret approval of both the reader and the narrator. Even the Caterpillar's scornful attacks on Alice's pretenses to identity—"Who are You?" he asks twice, with contemptuous emphasis on the last word—are bound to appear at least partly fitting. Moreover, by the time we reach *Through the Looking-Glass,* it is Alice who is consistently rude.

Most often, however, her role is very hard to fix, sometimes shifting within a single episode. In the scene with the Duchess, for instance, though it at first appears that the child might be endangered by this violent and tyrannical adult, the Duchess becomes something of a foil to Alice, both parodying the child and highlighting her defects. Her violence is mainly a burlesque of real violence; she and the cook only sneeze, miss each other with frying pans, and toss vigorously a thing which turns out to be a pig. It is Alice who often seems the real adult here, more coyly sentimental than the Mock Turtle—"Oh, there goes his *precious* nose!"—and more a governess than any other figure. "Very glad to get an opportunity of showing off a little of her knowledge," she spouts, "You see the earth takes twenty-four hours to turn around on its axis—." The Duchess' punning response has behind it the central impulse of the book at this moment: "Talking of axes . . . chop off her head!" Finally, the Duchess' lullaby, "Speak roughly to your little boy," attacks one of the most gruesome of the parody originals, "Speak Gently," which rests on the happy argument that one should "speak gently to the little child," for "it may not long remain." The Duchess' version asserts a vigorous and confident life-force, quite at odds with Alice's pedantry and deathlike caution. In the end, this episode is climaxed not so much by the child's becoming a pig, but by Alice's reflection that she knew other children "who might do very well as pigs." So, the quiet suggestion runs, do the narrator and the reader.

Even the Queen's Croquet-Ground, which one is tempted to identify with an adult world ruled by a capricious and mad executioner, not only threatens the child but condemns her corrupt adult assumptions. The Queen, first of all, is no real executioner; the Gryphon even says that her threats, combined with the fact that "they never executes nobody, you know," provide great *fun.* The croquet they play confuses Alice because it is too literally alive, without rules, order, or sequence. She is upset, in other words, by the absence of rigidity and hates the fluidity of this comic game. Even a clearer indictment is suggested by the affection of the Duchess, whose absurd rage for categorizing and labeling— "Everything's got a moral, if you can only find it"— burlesques Alice's own need to reduce things to the most mechanical level. By the end of *Alice in Wonderland,* though, most of this ambivalence disappears and Alice establishes herself clearly as an adult, ironically pretty much at home at the grotesque trial and "quite pleased to find that she knew the name of nearly everything [in the courtroom]."

To a certain extent, *Through the Looking-Glass* takes Alice up at this point, but, though it too presents a central theme of initiation, there are several differences. The entire work seems, first of all, more deliberate; it is much more carefully structured and apparently self-conscious. Alice, similarly, has much clearer goals here: she knows from the start that she wants, above all, to be a Queen, and her development is more clearly away from the important values. A drawing of the White Knight is used as a frontispiece, indicating the central focus of this book: the gentle and comic values Alice is leaving behind. Since Alice is, from the very beginning, a figure of power in the looking-glass world and is never subject to the sorts of ominous physical threats so common in Wonderland, we are seldom asked

to pity her. As a result, the laughter is less mixed and the aggression more clearly directed. *Through the Looking-Glass* is, as the prefatory verses indicate, about the "'happy summer days' gone by, / And vanish'd summer glory—." But these things are gone largely because the child is, as before, so obsessed with death, predation, and egoism that she fails altogether to recognize the beauty of the White Knight or the danger of the powerful Queens. As a matter of fact, Alice is very largely the Queen of Hearts as she steps behind the mirror.

Even the elaborately wrought warmth of the opening paragraphs seems so excessive as to touch on irony and establish not so much Alice's darling primness as her potentially callous sentimentality. In comparison with the melancholy tone and concentration on age and death that mark the narrator's frame poem, Alice's treatment of the images of death and age seems evasive and cruel: "I wonder if the snow *loves* the trees and fields, that it kisses them so gently?" In any case, there are quiet hints here that the Wonderland Alice, whose deepest impulses involved power and aggression, has not changed: "Nurse! Do let's pretend that I'm a hungry hyaena, and you're a bone!"

This time she enters the garden more easily, and immediately and instinctively sides with the vicious tiger-lily, as the natural ally to her own sense of power. The other flowers dislike her and begin a new stream of death jokes directed at her: they discuss the fact that her petals are "tumbled about": "'But that's not *your* fault,' the Rose added kindly. 'You're beginning to fade, you know—and then one can't help one's petals getting a little untidy.'" The Red Queen then arrives to give Alice preliminary instructions on how to become a Queen. Unlike the Queen of Hearts, the Red Queen is neither frightening nor really alien to Alice. Of all the figures on the other side of the mirror, in fact, the Red Queen seems the only one to command Alice's respect. "Curtsey while you're thinking what to say. It saves time," says the Red Queen in an absurd burlesque of thrift and manners. But, instead of laughing, Alice desides, "I'll try it when I go home . . . the next time I'm a little late for dinner." In one sense, then, the Red Queen, that "concentrated essence of all governesses," as Carroll said, is a model for Alice, a symbol of what the child will become. But there is at least one significant way in which she touches areas of experience closed to the child. The Red Queen's refusal to accept words as definite and final explanations of experience—when you say 'hill' . . . *I* could show you hills, in comparison with which you'd call that a valley"—not only contributes to an important theme which involves just this relationship between the abstractions of language and the vitality of real experience, but also affirms a reality beyond the confines of a dictionary and Alice's common sense: "*I've* heard nonsense, compared with which that would be as sensible as a dictionary!" The Red Queen, like nonsense itself, can be seen as a last and rather desperate defense of the life of the imagination. Nonsense is a form of the poetry of experience, affirming in the face of common reality a more vivid life available to the imagination. But Alice responds only to the power of the Queen and eagerly and unimaginatively joins hands with the governesses.

Consequently, the most consistent attacks on Alice focus on the specific fault of governesses, or adults: evasive, and ultimately vicious, sentimentality. Tweedledee's parody poem, **"The Walrus and the Carpenter,"** prompts Alice into revealing just how much she has grown up. She ignores the victims of the poem, the oysters, and immediately searches for one of the power figures with whom to identify: "I like the Walrus best . . . because he was a *little* sorry for the poor oysters." Tweedledee adroitly blocks this reaction: "He ate more than the Carpenter, though. . . . You see he held his handkerchief in front, so that the Carpenter couldn't count how many he took: contrariwise." Alice at once switches sides and again the twins check her:

> "That was mean!" Alice said indignantly. "Then I like the Carpenter best—if he didn't eat so many as the Walrus."
>
> "But he ate as many as he could get," said Tweedledum.

As the narrator says, "This was a puzzler." She is finally forced to admit that "they were *both* very unpleasant characters," but not before she has exposed the same false sympathy and cruelty that the poem emphasized:

> "It seems a shame," the Walrus said,
>   "To play them such a trick.
> After we've brought them out so far,
>   And made them trot so quick!"
> The Carpenter said nothing but
>   "The butter's spread too thick!"
>
> "I weep for you," the Walrus said:
>   "I deeply sympathize."
> With sobs and tears he sorted out
>   Those of the largest size,
> Holding his pocket-handkerchief
>   Before his streaming eyes.

The Walrus is a very apt caricature of Alice.

Even more direct is the attack issued by Humpty Dumpty, who not only mimics the presumed linguistic and mental precision of all humans but also provides the clearest indication of the deep aggression directed at the protagonist:

> "Seven years and six months!" Humpty Dumpty repeated thoughtfully. "An uncomfortable sort of age. Now if you'd asked *my* advice, I'd have said 'leave off at seven'—but it's too late now."
>
> . . . . .
>
> " . . . one can't help growing older."
>
> "*One* can't, perhaps," said Humpty Dumpty; "but *two* can. With proper assistance, you might have left off at seven."

Humpty then continues the attack of the Red Queen and the Gnat on the autonomy of language and the notion that its understanding gives power. In his wild assertion that man can be absolute master of the meaning of the words he uses, he joins with the other characters in attacking Alice's smug linguistic certainty in order to maintain the integrity of the individual personality. But Alice remains untouched, and Humpty Dumpty finally expresses the impatience of the narrator and the reader at the rude child: "You needn't go on making remarks like that . . . they're not sensible, and they put me out." He ends, then, by defining Alice's role: "You're so exactly like other people." Alice, finally, is more than a representative of the naïve child; she is all human adults—judged and found wanting.

She carries with her the chief barriers between human beings and comic existence: an implicit belief in a world ruled by death and predation and a relentless insistence on linear progression and completions. At the very beginning of **Alice in Wonderland,** while still falling down the rabbit hole, she displays her most distinctive preoccupation: "'Do cats eat bats? Do cats eat bats?' and sometimes, 'Do bats eat cats?' for, you see, as she couldn't answer either question, it didn't much matter which way she put it." The joke is a neat disguise for the real point, which has to do not with Alice's knowledge but with her serene acceptance of the centrality of death. Her single definite response to **"Jabberwocky"** in *Through the Looking-Glass* repeats the same joke, offering the deceptive reassurance that we can, after all, count on some clarity, even in such a confusing poem: "Somehow it seems to fill my head with ideas—only I don't exactly know what they are! However, *somebody* killed *something*: that's clear, at any rate—." In Alice's world, murder is the one certainty. Later in this first chapter, after Alice reaches the end of her fall, this perspective is attacked in an even more startling form: as the child shrinks she wonders what will happen if the process continues, "'for it might end, you know . . . in my going out altogether, like a candle. I wonder what I should be like then?' And she tried to fancy what the flame of a candle looks like after the candle is blown out." Her linear mind insists always on completions, even when the completion implies her own annihilation, and the irony turns sharply back on her.

These anticomic and adult failings are nowhere more fully or subtly realized than in her poems, which, she says, come to her automatically without her conscious control. The first of these, "How doth the little crocodile," brilliantly serves two functions, but both functions reflect ironically on the unconscious girl. First, the poem attacks the anticomic stuffiness and prudence of Watts's "Against Idleness and Mischief" (and, of course, the stuffiness and prudence of Alice herself) and promotes by implication the important values of comic anarchy. In addition, the poem reveals the darkest parts of Alice's mind: the crocodile "welcomes little fishes in, / With gently smiling jaws!" The death joke which immediately follows, then, in which Alice again nearly shrinks away completely, is doubly appropriate.

Later, on orders from the rude Caterpillar, Alice repeats to him the most subversive of all her parody poems from the unconscious, "You are old, Father William." It attacks Southey's vision of wise prudence—"'In the days of my youth,' father William replied, / 'I remember'd that youth could not last'"—a prudence whose corollary notions of limits and completions are exactly Alice's own. Even more functional, however, is the way in which Alice's parody circles back to attack the rudeness of the young. Alice's old man not only stands on his head and balances an eel on the end of his nose but, more wonderfully, turns on his son with retaliatory rudeness exactly parallel to the creatures' rudeness to Alice: "'I have answered three questions, and that is enough,' / Said his father. 'Don't give yourself airs! / Do you think I can listen all day to such stuff? / Be off, or I'll kick you down stairs!'" The poem attacks prudence and, at the same time, manages to support age. By a very subtle shift, comic values (and potency) are associated with the old; and the rude, impertinent young are booted downstairs. Only a few paragraphs later, Alice demonstrates the application of the poem to herself:

> "Well, I should like to be a *little* larger, Sir, if you wouldn't mind," said Alice: "three inches is such a wretched height to be."

> "It is a very good height indeed!" said the Caterpillar angrily, rearing itself upright as it spoke (it was exactly three inches high).

The only difference between the rudeness of Alice and that of Father William's son is that Alice's is marked by the forms of politeness. It is thus an instinctive rudeness, rooted in self-absorption and running much deeper than the boy's open hostility.

Finally, Alice's " 'Tis the Voice of the Lobster" manages to indict Alice's world just as solidly as the other parody poems, adding in addition a touching sense of what it is that world has lost. Her grim poem, the second verse of which begins with an Owl and a Panther joined in comic trust and "sharing a pie," ends with the Panther "eating the Owl" (the omission of these last three words makes the poem all the more gruesome). The fact that the poem moves from mutual joy to death not only specifically reverses the comic impulse just celebrated in the Mock Turtle's song ("Will you walk a little faster") but also recalls by contrast the great nonsense songs of Edward Lear, where natural enemies join in a lovely comic image, the Owl and the Pussycat dancing in the moonlight "on the edge of the sand" or the Spider and the Fly playing "for evermore / At battlecock and shuttledore." Alice's inversion is a dark twisting of the main point of comedy.

Indeed the most interesting complexity attending Alice's role is that she is often seen, as she is here, as an invader disrupting a warm and happy world. It is a world connected by a series of episodes running through both books, episodes which, taken together, establish an alternate image by which we measure the limits of Alice's world—and of our own.

The first and in many ways the most important of these comic images is the Caucus Race in Chapter iii of *Alice in Wonderland*. Alice has, in the preceding chapter, met a mouse, whom she has frightened nearly out of its wits by her instinctive aggressiveness: "Où est ma chatte?" she says, trying to find a common language. Sorry "that she had hurt the poor animal's feelings," she switches to soothing talk of her own lovely cat, Dinah, but soon returns to the same point: "she's such a capital one for catching mice—oh, I beg your pardon!" Anxious to change the subject, Alice begins eagerly talking about a neighbor's dog, but even it "kills all the rats." All subjects lead to aggression and death. Even Alice's good intentions reveal her dark instincts, and the Caucus Race stands as a contrast and a rebuke to her and her world. Here we see clearly the joyous side of anarchy, which parodies the disciplined organization of political committees and presents a world where there are no rules: "they began running when they liked, and left off when they liked." The Dodo's verdict on the race, "*Everybody* has won, and *all* must have prizes," comes straight from the heart of the comic vision and parodies not only Darwinism but all systems of regularized death. Alice cannot understand this world, however, and ironically complains that the creatures are too easily offended. She finally destroys the party by frightening the birds as she had earlier frightened the mouse: "And oh, I wish you could see [Dinah] after the birds! Why, she'll eat a little bird as soon as look at it!" In Alice's world, which frames both books, Dinah is a warm symbol of friendly cuddliness, but in Wonderland she is a monster. When the sentimentality is removed by the creatures' reactions, Alice's smugness appears as unconscious brutality.

Connected to this initial image of comic union is the episode of the Mad Tea-Party. The grand comic trio found there symbolize a dedication to pure joy as well as an ability to defend the comic life. They instinctively recognize Alice as an enemy and ridicule her most elementary concerns. When she worries about the time they are wasting in unanswerable riddles, the Hatter responds, "If you knew Time as well as I do . . . you wouldn't talk about wasting *it*. It's *him*." Alice's prudence and desire for order are blasted again and again, but here, as elsewhere, she is ineducable, and she disrupts the comic joy with her linear perspective of finality. Since it is always teatime, the three creatures explain, they simply move round and round the table. Alice's sanity is again destructive: "But what happens when you come to the beginning again?" The creatures then turn on her and especially her "great interest in questions of eating and drinking," assaulting her insistence on logic and order but, more important, her preoccupation with destruction. Their rebukes to her rude, interrupting questions become more and more pointed, and the aggressive laughter is directed more and more openly at her: "'You can draw water out of a water-well,' said the Hatter; 'so I should think you could draw treacle out of a treacle-well—eh, stupid?'"

The final comic interlude in *Alice in Wonderland,* involving the Gryphon and the Mock Turtle, pictures Alice as a good deal more than stupid. Here again, the creatures parody a silly and dark adult world, one, moreover, with which Alice specifically identifies:

> "We had the best of educations—in fact, we went to school every day—"
>
> "*I've* been to a day-school, too," said Alice. "You needn't be so proud as all that."
>
> "With extras?" asked the Mock Turtle, a little anxiously.
>
> "Yes," said Alice: "we learned French and music."
>
> "And washing?" said the Mock Turtle.

His attacks, then—"Reeling and Writhing, of course"—strike not only at repressive tyranny but at its present representative, the pompous Alice. She then exposes anew her most deadly limitations: the perspective of completion and nothingness (the Mock Turtle's lessons—or lessens—decrease every day, and Alice naturally pushes ahead to the zero day) and the preoccupation with the details of predation. When asked if she had ever been introduced to a lobster, she responds, "I once tasted—". The comic contrast and rebuke to Alice come in the form of the Lobster

Quadrille, a poem and dance of mutuality, joy, and more somersaults. It not only parodies the gruesome poem on death and prudence, "The Spider and the Fly," but, like all great comedies, introduces a hint of death only to triumph over it. When the snail is told that one of the dance's figures requires that he be thrown out to sea, he turns pale and tries to leave the dance for fear of drowning. The response of the whiting, "his scaly friend," transforms this fear to a wild comic victory over death and a very elemental reassurance:

> "What matters it how far we go?" his scaly
> friend replied.
> "There is another shore, you know, upon the
> other side.
> The further off from England the nearer is to
> France—
> Then turn not pale, beloved snail, but come
> and join the dance."

But Alice is, characteristically, more than just unresponsive, saying of whiting, "I've often seen them at dinn—."

The picture of Alice as an alien in a fragile and beautiful world is continued in *Through the Looking-Glass,* but it becomes much more melancholy. The attack is both more flexible and more quiet. In Chapter iii, for instance, Alice meets a Gnat, the shrewdest and most devastating questioner with whom she comes in contact. Beginning by insidiously begging the child to make even bad jokes, since they are, at least, some sign of community, he proceeds to ask a question that shatters the pretenses of Alice's world: "What sort of insects do you rejoice in, where *you* come from?" Again, one thinks of Lear and the symbol of the communion of humans and animals, of the "old man on the Border" who "danced with the cat and made tea in his hat" or the "Young Lady whose bonnet, / Came untied when the birds sat upon it: / But she said, 'I don't care! all the birds in the air / Are welcome to sit on my bonnet!'" Alice's bleak response, "I don't *rejoice* in insects at all,'" fully justifies the Gnat in his relentless attack which follows. When Alice says she can tell him the names of some of the insects in her world, the key subversive theme again comes up:

> "Of course they answer to their names?" the Gnat
> remarked carelessly.
>
> "I never knew them to do it."
>
> "What's the use of their having names," the Gnat
> said, "if they won't answer to them?"
>
> "No use to *them,*" said Alice; "but it's useful to the
> people that name them, I suppose. If not, why do
> things have names at all?"

For the Gnat, names allow for recognition, establishing community and personality; for Alice, they are impersonal categories, useful only insofar as they give power to those who know the names. The Gnat soon fades away and Alice enters the Wood of No Names, where we again celebrate the possibilities of joy and revivification in the trust and fearlessness of the gentle fawn. When they leave the protection of the wood and the fawn learns that she is really "a human child," however, it flees in terror, suggesting the cruelty of humans but also the cruelty of the stock responses that lie behind names and the terrible impersonality of the useful language Alice had just defended.

The true climax of *Through the Looking-Glass* and of the theme of betrayal of comic values comes in Chapter viii, where Alice meets her potential rescuer, the White Knight, carrying with him suggestions of all the important values. But she turns her back on him. She is cold to him from the beginning and responds to his notions of glorious victory with the prim "I want to be a Queen." Nothing, now, will keep her from this goal, but the reader recognizes here for the last time just what she is leaving. The White Knight seems at first to be an unconscious figure at whom we can easily laugh. When Alice asks him if he has broken any bones in falling, he responds, "'None to speak of' . . . as if he didn't mind breaking two or three of them." It turns out, however, that he truly is a sad and sensitive figure, whom we must take seriously, more seriously, in fact, for having so readily laughed at him. He is extroverted and deeply kind; noticing that Alice is sad, he offers to sing a song to comfort her. But Alice is again unreceptive: "Is it very long?" She simply—and only—wants to be a Queen. The Knight proceeds with the song, however, first suggesting that Alice will surely respond with tears, "but no tears," the narrator says, "came into her eyes." The song is not only a fine parody of Wordsworth's "Resolution and Independence" but creates an image of unresponsiveness—"I cried 'Come, tell me how you live!' / And thumped him on the head"—that exactly parallels Alice's. The point of the poem is the cruelty of self-absorption, precisely the same self-absorption that allows Alice to joke about the disappearing friend—"It won't take long to see him *off,* I expect"—and then skip away thoughtlessly: "and now for the last brook, and to be a Queen! How grand it sounds!"

She is now Queen Alice and joins with the other two in an image of mindless power. The book ends with a wild and disturbed scene of predation, where the pudding and mutton speak and threaten to change places with the guests and begin to eat the eaters. To avoid this, Alice breaks up the looking-glass world and in a final act of destruction affirms her own world of chaos and brutality. She cuddles her kitten at the end and promises, "All the time you're eating your breakfast, I'll repeat **'The Walrus and the Carpenter'** to you;

and then you can make believe it's oysters, dear!" We are back where we started, and the closing question then significantly returns to the issue of whether or not Alice is only a part of the Red King's dream.

The last words address the reader with this same dilemma and appear to ask him to decide on the existence or annihilation of the child: "Which do *you* think it was?" But the complexity of the image of Alice makes the choice impossible, perhaps because Carroll's final point is not so much aggressive as deeply and profoundly sad: "We are but older children, dear, / Who fret to find our bedtime near." The cruel impulses in Alice are only impulses in all of us, and we spend our lives fretting about death. As a result, we are none of us able to rejoice in insects.

Neilson Graham (essay date 1973)

SOURCE: "Sanity, Madness and Alice," in *Ariel: A Review of International English Literature,* Vol. 4, No. 2, April, 1973, pp. 80-89.

[*In the following essay, Graham considers the function of the insanity theme in* Alice.]

One of the most interesting characters in Lewis Carroll's ***Alice's Adventures in Wonderland*** is the Cheshire Cat. Unlike most of the creatures, the Cheshire Cat is sufficiently detached from his environment to be able to comment, in a fast, facetious sort of way, on the characters who share Wonderland with him, and one of his more challenging comments in particular deserves attention.

He tells Alice that everybody in Wonderland is mad. The exchange occurs after Alice has left the Duchess's kitchen and has had her dream-like wrestle with the pig-baby. She sees the Cheshire Cat on the bough of a tree and asks it what sort of people live around here:

> "In that direction," the Cat said, waving its right paw round, "lives a Hatter: and in *that* direction," waving the other paw, "lives a March Hare. Visit either you like: they're both mad."

> "But I don't want to go among mad people," Alice remarked.

> "Oh, you can't help that," said the Cat: "we're all mad here. I'm mad. You're mad."

Leaving aside for the moment the unlikely question of whether Alice is mad, the problem is to know how far the Cat is justified in attributing insanity to Wonderland creatures. As a group, the creatures do strike us as a pretty odd crew (although very immediate to us and ultimately likeable because childish) but is it really correct to call them mad? The Cat's remark seems to be too sweeping to be helpful, and yet its very breadth is tantalising too. Even if Carroll could not have justified it in precise philosophical terms (that is now my task), he must have written it in response to some positive sense he had of his creatures. I believe that the Cat is actually right and that a good deal of the charming, and strangely worrying, quality of *Alice* is due to the fact that some of the utterances of some of the creatures are, from a certain standpoint, insane. But insanity is a dubious notion nowadays, in view of the arguments of R. D. Laing and others for its abolition, so it will be as well for me to start by making clear what that standpoint is.

In the beginning of Mark Twain's novel *Pudd'nhead Wilson,* Wilson makes a remark whose style and reception are intriguing. He has just arrived at the little township of Dawson's Landing and made the acquaintance of a group of citizens when there is an interruption:

> . . . an invisible dog began to yelp and snarl and howl and make himself very comprehensively disagreeable, whereupon young Wilson said, much as one who is thinking aloud—
>
> "I wish I owned half of that dog."
>
> "Why?" somebody asked.
>
> "Because I would kill my half."
>
> The group searched his face with curiosity, with anxiety even, but found no light there, no expression that they could read. They fell away from him as from something uncanny, and went into privacy to discuss him.

Two things seem to need elucidation here: first, the peculiar character of Wilson's actual statement, "I wish I owned half of that dog, because I would kill my half," and second, the disturbed response of the citizens to it.

The words and concepts which go into the making of the statement, the concepts of "owning," "half," "dog" and "kill," are all perfectly well understood concepts, and they are strung together by Wilson with perfect grammatical propriety, and yet there is something strange about it nevertheless. We want to echo Alice's feelings at the Tea-Party when she is confused by a remark of the Hatter's: "Alice felt dreadfully puzzled. The Hatter's remark seemed to her to have no sort of meaning in it, and yet it was certainly English." Wilson's remark too is certainly English but it appears, in some respects, to have no sort of meaning in it, to be nonsensical, and I think we can locate the nonsensicality quite quickly. Wilson says

he wishes to own half the dog, but that is impossible. It is possible, perhaps, to own a half share in a dog, but impossible to own half of it, for where would you divide it? While it lives a dog would seem to be indivisible. Similarly, to talk about killing half a dog is too difficult an idea. To kill half is automatically to kill the whole. So it would seem that what Wilson is doing here is applying the concept of *half* to the concepts of owning a dog and killing it quite inappropriately. And, of course, unnecessarily. All he need have said was, "I wish I owned that dog, because I would kill it," which would be rough justice, but at least it would have fitted the circumstances.

So the remark can be called nonsensical, but why does it disturb the citizens of Dawson's Landing so? In the first place, it refuses to be tamed. It won't fit into their accustomed patterns of thinking. So they search Wilson's face for some sort of clue as to what he meant by it and are made even more anxious when they cannot find one. His expression is unreadable, and this seems to be the point. Wilson utters a nonsensical statement and yet, as far as the citizens can judge from his face, he himself is unaware of this fact. Or if he is aware of it he is giving nothing away. His *motive,* in other words, for making the statement is obscure, and when we cannot understand the motivation of others we are angry or anxious or hysterically amused.

What sort of motivation might Wilson have had? He might have been wishing to make a joke. This is the usual reason in our culture for making nonsensical statements. The jokester takes liberties with meaning under cover of the comic, exploiting contradiction for cathartic effect. Recognizing his pose we may safely laugh. The person who uses nonsense structures (of which I take Wilson's remark about the dog to be one) can be assimilated into our understanding because he is aware of two standards, but the person who is *unaware* of using nonsense structures cannot be so assimilated. Aware only of one standard, his own, such a man may seem to be mad. The difference between the jokester and the madman in this respect is that the jokester can step out of his joking role at will, whereas the madman cannot. We shall see presently that Wonderland creatures rarely fall into the category of the jokester. As people they are strangely serious, and since they deploy nonsensical statements of one kind or another doubts arise as to their sanity. But where does Wilson stand? He is clearly not joking (the citizens can find no sort of expression in his face which would have given them permission to laugh). Is he then insane? The citizens partly think so for they go on to label him "Pudd'nhead," a gentle form of "idiot" or "fool"; and this is their way of defending themselves from the threat presented by his apparently motiveless use of the irrational.

It seems to be the case that those who use language in a sufficiently nonconformist fashion in any society are ostracised, whether in the friendly manner of Pudd'nhead Wilson or more ferociously as lunatics. The absent-minded professor is isolated by suspicion masquerading as tolerance. Shakespeare's fools are *called* fools and (for the most part) rigidly confined by their superiors within the limits of the jester role in order that their insights may cut less ice. Society cannot tolerate more than a minimum of nonconformity in the matter of language as in everything else and this is not surprising, for a base of semantic conformity is a prerequisite for meaningful communication between people. If nonsense were the norm (a contradiction in terms) and no motivation for statements expected or required, then the result would be the loss of standardization in meaning, that is, in the last resort, a kind of collective insanity (another contradiction in terms).

In any particular interpersonal situation, if we are going to feel safe with our interlocutor, we need to be able to believe that he had a motive for uttering. In most cases this is self-evident. But if his statement was markedly unconventional (like Wilson's) then we need to be able to believe that he was making a joke or a mistake or that he had some other acceptable motive for speaking as he did. If we cannot discover a motive we lose contact with our interlocutor who may come, as a result, to appear insane. The attribution of insanity is clearly a relative one and says more, perhaps, about the relationship between me and my interlocutor (namely that contact has been lost) than about him alone, but it may still have its uses.

Let us now turn to *Alice* and consider some of the characters in the light of this relation between motive and sanity. First, the Mock Turtle and the Gryphon. In the famous virtuoso section from "The Lobster-Quadrille" in which the two of them converse with Alice about life under the sea they employ a succession of puns (or quasi-puns) and what is fascinating about their use of this device is the impossibility of it. They tell Alice about a fish called the whiting and the Gryphon asks her:

"Do you know why it's called a whiting?"

"I never thought about it," said Alice. "Why?"

"It does the boots and shoes," the Gryphon replied very solemnly.

Alice was thoroughly puzzled. "Does the boots and shoes!" she repeated in a wondering tone.

"Why, what are *your* shoes done with?" said the Gryphon. "I mean, what makes them so shiny?"

Alice looked down at them, and considered a little before she gave her answer. "They're done with blacking, I believe."

"Boots and shoes under the sea," the Gryphon went on in a deep voice, "are done with whiting. Now you know."

"And what are they made of?" Alice asked in a tone of great curiosity.

"Soles and eels, of course," the Gryphon replied, rather impatiently: "any shrimp could have told you that."

It is clear that the Mock Turtle and the Gryphon have no conception of what a pun is and yet their punning ability is superb. Alice goes on to refer to a song about a whiting which the Mock Turtle has sung a little while back (a song with a porpoise in it) and this provides the Mock Turtle with food for more punning:

"If I'd been the whiting," said Alice, whose thoughts were still running on the song, "I'd have said to the porpoise, 'Keep back, please! We don't want *you* with us!'"

"They were obliged to have him with them," the Mock Turtle said. "No wise fish would go anywhere without a porpoise."

"Wouldn't it, really?" said Alice, in a tone of great surprise.

"Of course not," said the Mock Turtle. "Why, if a fish came to *me,* and told me he was going a journey, I should say 'With what porpoise?'"

"Don't you mean 'purpose'?" said Alice.

"I mean what I say," the Mock Turtle replied, in an offended tone.

That "in an offended tone" indicates that the Mock Turtle genuinely does not make in his own mind the distinction implied by a pun. He takes it for granted that Alice will know what he means by the words he uses and is impatient when she does not. There is no question of his deliberately trying to confuse Alice—he is a very serious-minded old gentleman—nor of his using puns as a joke or by mistake, any of which motivations would reassure us that he had the same semantic standards as we have. No, we are confronted instead with the extraordinary phenomenon of a character able to use puns yet unaware of the aberrative nature of puns. The reader in this situation is unable to identify the thought processes which govern his speech for those processes are literally inconceivable, and he is, as a result, both charmed and perplexed. In the context of *Alice* the Mock Turtle and the Gryphon may safely excite laughter, but in the real world the man who used puns without realising that he did so would disturb us deeply, so much so that we might be tempted to label him insane, or a prodigy . . . but then we would never meet him.

The Hare and the Hatter present similar problems. They welcome Alice to the Tea-Party with the cry, "No room!" though there is, in fact, all the room in the world, on the face of it a strange thing to do. The context is familiar. Alice comes upon a table set out under a tree at which the March Hare and the Hatter are having tea with the Dormouse between them.

> The table was a large one, but the three were crowded together at one corner of it. "No room! No room!" they cried out when they saw Alice coming. "There's plenty of room!" said Alice indignantly, and she sat down in a large arm-chair at one end of the table.

Alice exposes the literal untruth of their statement by sitting down, but this may be to miss the point. Why did they say "No room!"? No reason is suggested or even, I think, implied. And it is this, not the facts or otherwise of the case, which intrigues. As with Wilson's remark about the dog, their remark is impossible to reconcile with the reality to which it is supposed to refer, a largely empty table; it lacks a rationale, and a mystery is thereby located in the minds of the Hare and the Hatter, just as a mystery was located in the minds of the Mock Turtle and the Gryphon as a result of their impossible use of puns. Essentially it is, again, a question of motive, or the lack of it. Without the assumption of motive in speech, meaning is in jeopardy, just as without the assumption of motive in morals, responsibility ceases to exist and justice disappears. Sanity is dependent on an orthodoxy of motive and in this case the Hare and the Hatter flout it with fine unconcern. They go on to offer Alice wine when there is none and to ask her riddles which have no answer, and yet they see nothing odd in either of these behaviours. I do not believe we have cause to attribute to them a joking motive or a mistaken one, or even an aggressive one, consequently, on the definition I am touting, they are insane.

As, of course, is the Caterpillar. The Caterpillar is an ill-mannered, petulant character who, from the safety of his perch on the mushroom, treats Alice with notable disdain. He terminates the interview without warning and, as he's walking off through the grass, throws over his shoulder the remark, "One side will make you grow taller, and the other side will make you grow shorter." He refers, of course, to the mushroom. But mushrooms don't have sides, they are round, so this confuses. The Caterpillar's advice seems not to match the reality to which it is supposed to refer, and the interesting thing about this mismatch is that it does

not, as far as we can judge, interest the Caterpillar. We cannot, therefore, know why he said what he did say, consequently we are mystified, perhaps to the point of laughter. Evidently in Carroll's Wonderland the creatures do not always have discernible motives for making unconventional statements so that we are cast adrift.

Consider the Tea-Party again. The Dormouse tells a story, in between bouts of sleeping, about three little girls at the bottom of a treacle well. They drew all manner of things, says the Dormouse, everything that begins with an M: "'Why with an M?' said Alice. 'Why not?' said the March Hare. Alice was silent." And well she might be. The March Hare's "Why Not?" actually recommends contingency and there is no easy answer to such a recommendation. Contingency is fine in theory but awkward in practice. If it were universal nothing would hold and the distinction between sanity and madness (among others) would disappear. Insanity is only meaningful in the context of sanity, just as nonsensical statements are only remarkable in a society which habitually speaks sense. But there is excitement in playing with insanity in a basically sane context, and that is partly what *Alice* is doing. The context *is* sane. The book is in English and written in such a way that most of it invites our understanding on one plane or another. If we don't actually think of Wonderland creatures as lunatics, despite the insane language habits which I have isolated, it is because so much of their affective and intellectual behaviour makes acceptably good sense. Even, ultimately, their "insane" utterances. There may be no obvious motive for the kind of statement we have been looking at but in the larger perspective the key to all such anti-communicative behaviour is fear. At bottom, Wonderland creatures are afraid of Alice and the one meaningful explanation it is possible to give for a context-antagonistic utterance like "No room!" is that the Hare and the Hatter cannot face the reality of Alice's approach. Alice is a real live girl-child, dedicated (though she wouldn't put it thus) to the exposure of humbug, open, direct and largely unafraid, and for the insecure adult figures who people Wonderland these qualities represent a major threat. Who knows but Alice might see through them! They remain solitary because their mode is the defensive mode. One can almost discern a conspiracy operating to prevent Alice getting onto their wavelength, and it is certainly successful for contact is never established and Alice has no compunction about dismissing everybody at the end. There is pathos in this failure, sustained throughout the book, for Alice represents a once-for-all opportunity for Victorian adulthood to renew itself, an opportunity which it cannot, dare not, grasp.

The idea of fear (and fear is at the root of insanity) provides a general context within which to interpret the solipsistic speech habits of the creatures in *Alice,* but there are no guidelines in the field. Alice, down among the almost-madmen, has a genuine communication problem on which, it could be said, her life depends, but because she sees no problem she is unaffected. Indeed, her incorruptible good sense acts as a buffer both for herself and for us against the illicit language habits of Wonderland creatures. If Alice's linguistic and philosophical rectitude diminish her as a person, they nevertheless provide the necessary foil to the dangerous aberrations of the creatures. A less fixed personality-type would have run the risk of entering, and sharing in, the mad mind of Wonderland. As it is, Alice saves it for us.

Nina Auerbach (essay date 1973)

SOURCE: "Alice and Wonderland: A Curious Child," in *Victorian Studies,* Vol. XVIII, No. 1, September, 1973, pp. 31-47.

[*In the essay below, Auerbach considers the genesis and development of the character of Alice.*]

"What—is—this?" he said at last.

"This is a child!" Haigha replied eagerly, coming in front of Alice to introduce her . . . "We only found it today. It's as large as life, and twice as natural!"

"I always thought they were fabulous monsters!" said the Unicorn. "Is it alive?"

For many of us Lewis Carroll's two *Alice* books may have provided the first glimpse into Victorian England. With their curious blend of literal-mindedness and dream, formal etiquette and the logic of insanity, they tell the adult reader a great deal about the Victorian mind. Alice herself, prim and earnest in pinafore and pumps, confronting a world out of control by looking for the rules and murmuring her lessons, stands as one image of the Victorian middle-class child. She sits in Tenniel's first illustration to *Through the Looking-Glass and What Alice Found There* in a snug, semi-foetal position, encircled by a protective armchair and encircling a plump kitten and a ball of yarn. She seems to be a beautiful child, but the position of her head makes her look as though she had no face. She muses dreamily on the snowstorm raging outside, part of a series of circles within circles, enclosures within enclosures, suggesting the self-containment of innocence and eternity.

Behind the purity of this design lie two Victorian domestic myths: Wordworth's "seer blessed," the child fresh from the Imperial Palace and still washed by his continuing contact with "that immortal sea," and the pure woman Alice will become, preserving an oasis for God and order in a dim and tangled world. Even Victorians who did not share Lewis Carroll's phobia about the ugliness and uncleanliness of little boys saw little girls as the purest members of a species of questionable origin, combining as they did the inherent spirituality of child and woman. Carroll's Alice seems sister to such famous figures as Dickens' Little Nell and George Eliot's Eppie, who embody the poise of original innocence in a fallen, sooty world.

Long after he transported Alice Liddell to Wonderland, Carroll himself deified his dream-child's innocence in these terms:

> What wert thou, dream-Alice, in thy foster-father's eyes? How shall he picture thee? Loving, first, loving and gentle: loving as a dog (forgive the prosaic simile, but I know of no earthly love so pure and perfect), and gentle as a fawn: . . . and lastly, curious—wildly curious, and with the eager enjoyment of Life that comes only in the happy hours of childhood, when all is new and fair, and when Sin and Sorrow are but names—empty words, signifying nothing!"

From this Alice, it is only a step to Walter de la Mare's mystic icon, defined in the following almost Shelleyan image: "She wends serenely on like a quiet moon in a chequered sky. Apart, too, from an occasional Carrollian comment, the sole medium of the stories is *her* pellucid consciousness."

But when Dodgson wrote in 1887 of his gentle dream-child, the real Alice had receded into the distance of memory, where she had drowned in a pool of tears along with Lewis Carroll, her interpreter and creator. The paean quoted above stands at the end of a long series of progressive falsifications of Carroll's first conception, beginning with Alice's pale, attenuated presence in *Through the Looking-Glass.* For Lewis Carroll remembered what Charles Dodgson and many later commentators did not, that while *Looking-Glass* may have been the dream of the Red King, *Wonderland* is Alice's dream. Despite critical attempts to psychoanalyze Charles Dodgson through the writings of Lewis Carroll, the author of *Alice's Adventures in Wonderland* was too precise a logician and too controlled an artist to confuse his own dream with that of his character. The question "who dreamed it?" underlies all Carroll's dream tales, part of a pervasive Victorian quest for the origins of the self that culminates in the controlled regression of Freudian analysis. There is no equivocation in Carroll's first *Alice* book: the dainty child carries the threatening kingdom of Wonderland within her. A closer look at the character of Alice may reveal new complexities in the sentimentalized and attenuated Wordsworthianism many critics have assumed she represents, and may deepen through examination of a single example our vision of that "fabulous monster," the Victorian child.

Lewis Carroll once wrote to a child that while he forgot the story of *Alice,* "I think it was about 'malice.'" Some Freudian critics would have us believe it was about phallus. Alice herself seems aware of the implications of her shifting name when at the beginning of her adventures she asks herself the question that will weave through her story:

> I wonder if I've been changed in the night? Let me think: *was* I the same when I got up this morning? I almost think I can remember feeling a little different. But if I'm not the same, the next question is, 'Who in the world am I?' Ah, *that's* the great puzzle!

Other little girls traveling through fantastic countries, such as George Macdonald's Princess Irene and L. Frank Baum's Dorothy Gale, ask repeatedly "*where* am I?" rather than "*who* am I?" Only Alice turns her eyes inward from the beginning, sensing that the mystery of her surroundings is the mystery of her identity.

Even the above-ground Alice speaks in two voices, like many Victorians other than Dodgson-Carroll:

> She generally gave herself very good advice, (though she very seldom followed it), and sometimes she scolded herself so severely as to bring tears into her eyes; and once she remembered trying to box her own ears for having cheated herself in a game of croquet she was playing against herself, for this curious child was very fond of pretending to be two people.

The pun on "curious" defines Alice's fluctuating personality. Her eagerness to know and to be right, her compulsive reciting of her lessons ("I'm sure I can't be Mabel, for I know all sorts of things") turn inside out into the bizarre anarchy of her dream country, as the lessons themselves turn inside out into strange and savage tales of animals eating each other. In both senses of the word, Alice becomes "curiouser and curiouser" as she moves more deeply into Wonderland; she is both the croquet game without rules and its violent arbiter, the Queen of Hearts. The sea that almost drowns her is composed of her own tears, and the dream that nearly obliterates her is composed of fragments of her own personality.

As Alice dissolves into her component parts to become Wonderland, so, if we examine the actual genesis of Carroll's dream child, the bold outlines of Tenniel's famous drawing dissolve into four separate figures. First, there was the real Alice Liddell, a baby belle dame, it seems, who bewitched Ruskin as well as Dodgson. A small photograph of her concludes Carroll's manuscript of *Alice's Adventures under Ground,* the first draft of *Wonderland.* She is strikingly sensuous and otherworldly; her dark hair, bangs, and large inward-turned eyes give her face a haunting and a haunted quality which is missing from Tenniel's famous illustrations. Carroll's own illustrations for *Alice's Adventures under Ground* reproduce her eeriness perfectly. This Alice has a pre-Raphaelite langour and ambiguity about her which is reflected in the shifting colors of her hair. In some illustrations, she is indisputably brunette like Alice Liddell; in others, she is decidedly blonde like Tenniel's model Mary Hilton Badcock; and in still others, light from an unknown source hits her hair so that she seems to be both at once.

Mary Hilton Badcock has little of the dream child about her. She is blonde and pudgy, with squinting eyes, folded arms, and an intimidating frown. In Carroll's photograph of her, the famous starched pinafore and pumps appear for the first time—Alice Liddell seems to have been photographed in some sort of nightdress—and Mary moves easily into the clean, no-nonsense child of the Tenniel drawings. Austin Dobson wrote,

> Enchanting Alice! Black-and-white
> Has made your charm perenniel;
> And nought save "Chaos and old Night"
> Can part you now from Tenniel.

But a bit of research can dissolve what has been in some ways a misleading identification of Tenniel's Alice with Carroll's, obscuring some of the darker shadings of the latter. Carroll himself initiated the shift from the subtly disturbing Alice Liddell to the blonde and stolid Mary Badcock as "under ground" became the jollier-sounding "Wonderland," and the undiscovered country in his dream child became a nursery classic.

The demure propriety of Tenniel's Alice may have led readers to see her role in *Alice's Adventures in Wonderland* as more passive than it is. Although her size changes seem arbitrary and terrifying, she in fact directs them; only in the final courtroom scene does she change size without first wishing to, and there, her sudden growth gives her the power to break out of a dream that has become too dangerous. Most of Wonderland's savage songs come from Alice: the Caterpillar, Gryphon and Mock Turtle know that her cruel parodies of contemporary moralistic doggerel are "wrong from beginning to end." She is almost always threatening to the animals of Wonderland. As the mouse and birds almost drown in her pool of tears, she eyes them with a strange hunger which suggests that of the *Looking-Glass* Walrus who weeps at the Oysters while devouring them behind his handkerchief. Her persistent allusions to her predatory cat Dinah and to a "nice little dog, near our house," who "kills all the rats" finally drive the animals away, leaving Alice to wonder forlornly—and disingenuously—why nobody in Wonderland likes Dinah.

John Tenniel's depiction of Alice at the Mad Tea-Party, with the March Hare, the Hatter, and the Dormouse. From Alice's Adventures in Wonderland.

Dinah is a strange figure. She is the only above-ground character whom Alice mentions repeatedly, almost always in terms of her eating some smaller animal. She seems finally to function as a personification of Alice's own subtly cannibalistic hunger, as Fury in the Mouse's tale is personified as a dog. At one point, Alice fantasizes her own identity actually blending into Dinah's:

> "How queer it seems," Alice said to herself, "to be going messages for a rabbit! I suppose Dinah'll be sending me on messages next!" And she began fancying the sort of thing that would happen: ' "Miss Alice! Come here directly, and get ready for your walk!" "Coming in a minute, nurse! But I've got to watch this mousehole till Dinah comes back, and see that the mouse doesn't get out." '

While Dinah is always in a predatory attitude, most of the Wonderland animals are lugubrious victims; together, they encompass the two sides of animal nature

that are in Alice as well. But as she falls down the rabbit hole, Alice senses the complicity between eater and eaten, looking-glass versions of each other:

> "Dinah, my dear! I wish you were down here with me! There are no mice in the air, I'm afraid, but you might catch a bat, and that's very like a mouse, you know. But do cats eat bats, I wonder?" And here Alice began to get rather sleepy, and went on saying to herself, in a dreamy sort of way, "Do cats eat bats? Do cats eat bats?" and sometimes, "Do bats eat cats?" for, you see, as she couldn't answer either question, it didn't matter which way she put it.

We are already half-way to the final banquet of *Looking-Glass,* in which the food comes alive and begins to eat the guests.

Even when Dinah is not mentioned, Alice's attitude toward the animals she encounters is often one of casual cruelty. It is a measure of Dodgson's ability to flatten out Carroll's material that the prefatory poem could describe Alice "in friendly chat with bird or beast," or that he would later see Alice as "loving as a dog . . . gentle as a fawn." She pities Bill the Lizard and kicks him up the chimney, a state of mind that again looks forward to that of the Pecksniffian Walrus in *Looking-Glass.* When she meets the Mock Turtle, the weeping embodiment of a good Victorian dinner, she restrains herself twice when he mentions lobsters, but then distorts Isaac Watt's *Sluggard* into a song about a *baked* lobster surrounded by hungry sharks. In its second stanza, a Panther shares a pie with an Owl who then becomes dessert, as Dodgson's good table manners pass into typical Carrollian cannibalism. The more sinister and Darwinian aspects of animal nature are introduced into Wonderland by the gentle Alice, in part through projections of her hunger onto Dinah and the "nice little dog" (she meets a "dear little puppy" after she has grown small and is afraid he will eat her up) and in part through the semi-cannibalistic appetite her songs express. With the exception of the powerful Cheshire Cat, whom I shall discuss below, most of the Wonderland animals stand in some danger of being exploited or eaten. The Dormouse is their prototype: he is fussy and cantankerous, with the nastiness of a self-aware victim, and he is stuffed into a teapot as the Mock Turtle, sobbing out his own elegy, will be stuffed into a tureen.

Alice's courteously menacing relationship to these animals is more clearly brought out in *Alice's Adventures under Ground,* in which she encounters only animals until she meets the playing cards, who are lightly sketched-in versions of their later counterparts. When expanding the manuscript for publication, Carroll added the Frog Footman, Cook, Duchess, Pig-Baby, Cheshire Cat, Mad Hatter, March Hare, and Dormouse, as well as making the Queen of Hearts a more fully developed character than she was in the manuscript. In other words, all the human or quasi-human characters were added in revision, and all develop aspects of Alice that exist only under the surface of her dialogue. The Duchess' household also turns inside out the domesticated Wordsworthian ideal: with baby and pepper flung about indiscriminately, pastoral tranquillity is inverted into a whirlwind of savage sexuality. The furious Cook embodies the equation between eating and killing that underlies Alice's apparently innocent remarks about Dinah. The violent Duchess' unctuous search for "the moral" of things echoes Alice's own violence and search for "the rules." At the Mad Tea Party, the Hatter extends Alice's "great interest in questions of eating and drinking" into an insane *modus vivendi;* like Alice, the Hatter and the Duchess sing savage songs about eating that embody the underside of Victorian literary treacle. The Queen's croquet game magnifies Alice's own desire to cheat at croquet and to punish herself violently for doing so. Its use of live animals may be a subtler extension of Alice's own desire to twist the

animal kingdom to the absurd rules of civilization, which seem to revolve largely around eating and being eaten. Alice is able to appreciate the Queen's savagery so quickly because her size changes have made her increasingly aware of who she, herself, is from the point of view of a Caterpillar, a Mouse, a Pigeon, and, especially, a Cheshire Cat.

The Cheshire Cat, also a late addition to the book, is the only figure other than Alice who encompasses all the others. William Empson discusses at length the spiritual kinship between Alice and the Cat, the only creature in Wonderland whom she calls her "friend." Florence Becker Lennon refers to the Cheshire Cat as "Dinah's dream-self," and we have noticed the subtle shift of identities between Alice and Dinah throughout the story. The Cat shares Alice's equivocal placidity: "The Cat only grinned when it saw Alice. It looked good-natured, she thought: still it had *very* long claws and a great many teeth, so she felt it ought to be treated with respect." The Cat is the only creature to make explicit the identification between Alice and the madness of Wonderland: "'. . . we're all mad here. I'm mad. You're mad.' 'How do you know I'm mad?' said Alice. 'You must be,' said the Cat, 'or you wouldn't have come here.' Alice didn't think that proved it at all. . . ." Although Alice cannot accept it and closes into silence, the Cat's remark may be the answer she has been groping toward in her incessant question, "who am I?" As an alter ego, the Cat is wiser than Alice—and safer—because he is the only character in the book who is aware of his own madness. In his serene acceptance of the fury within and without, his total control over his appearance and disappearance, he almost suggests a post-analytic version of the puzzled Alice.

As Alice dissolves increasingly into Wonderland, so the Cat dissolves into his own head, and finally into his own grinning mouth. The core of Alice's nature, too, seems to lie in her mouth: the eating and drinking that direct her size changes and motivate much of her behavior, the songs and verses that pop out of her inadvertently, are all involved with things entering and leaving her mouth. Alice's first song introduces a sinister image of a grinning mouth. Our memory of the Crocodile's grin hovers over the later description of the Cat's "grin without a Cat," and colors our sense of Alice's infallible good manners:

> How cheerfully he seems to grin,
>   How neatly spreads his claws,
> And welcomes little fishes in,
>   With gently smiling jaws!

Walter de la Mare associates Alice with "a quiet moon" which is by implication a full moon. I think it is more appropriate to associate her with the grinning crescent that seems to follow her throughout her adventures, choosing to become visible only at particular moments, and teaching her the one lesson she must learn in order to arrive at a definition of who she is.

Martin Gardner pooh-poohs the "oral aggressions" psychoanalysts have found in Carroll's incessant focus on eating and drinking by reminding us of the simple fact that "small children are obsessed by eating, and like to read about it in their books." Maybe his commonsense approach is correct, but Lewis Carroll was concerned with nonsense, and throughout his life, he seems to have regarded eating with some horror. An early cartoon in *The Rectory Umbrella* depicts an emaciated family partaking raptly of a "homoeopathic meal" consisting of an ounce of bread, half a particle of beer, etc.; young Sophy, who is making a pig of herself, asks for another molecule. Throughout his life, Carroll was abstemious at meals, according to his nephew and first biographer, Stuart Dodgson Collingwood: "the healthy appetites of his young friends filled him with wonder, and even with alarm." When he took one of his child-friends to another's house for a meal, he told the host: "Please *be careful,* because she eats a good deal too much." William Empson defines his attitude succinctly: "Dodgson was well-informed about foods, kept his old menus and was wine-taster to the College; but ate very little, suspected the High Table of overeating, and would see no reason to deny that he connected over-eating with other forms of sensuality." To the man who in *Sylvie and Bruno* would define EVIL as a looking-glass version of LIVE, "gently smiling jaws" held teeth which were to be regarded with alarm; they seemed to represent to him a private emblem of original sin, for which Alice as well as the Knave of Hearts is finally placed on trial.

When the Duchess' Cook abruptly barks out "Pig!" Alice thinks the word is meant for her, though it is the baby, another fragment of Alice's own nature, who dissolves into a pig. The Mock Turtle's lament for his future soupy self later blends tellingly into the summons for the trial: the lament of the eaten and the call to judgment melt together. When she arrives at the trial, the unregenerate Alice instantly eyes the tarts: "In the very middle of the court was a table, with a large dish of tarts upon it: they looked so good, that it made Alice quite hungry to look at them—'I wish they'd get the trial done,' she thought, 'and hand round the refreshments!'" Her hunger links her to the hungry Knave who is being sentenced: in typically ambiguous portmanteau fashion, Carroll makes the trial both a pre-Orwellian travesty of justice and an objective correlative of a real sense of sin. Like the dog Fury in the Mouse's tale, Alice takes all the parts. But unlike Fury, she is accused as well as accuser, melting into judge, jury, witness, and defendant; the person who boxes on the ears as well as the person who "cheats." Perhaps the final verdict would tell Alice who she is at last, but if it did, Wonderland would threaten to overwhelm her. Before it comes, she "grows"; the parts of her

nature rush back together; combining the voices of victim and accuser, she gives "a little scream, half of fright and half of anger," and wakes up.

Presented from the point of view of her older sister's sentimental pietism, the world to which Alice awakens seems far more dream-like and hazy than the sharp contours of Wonderland. Alice's lesson about her own identity has never been stated explicitly, for the stammerer Dodgson was able to talk freely only in his private language of puns and nonsense, but a Wonderland pigeon points us toward it:

> "You're a serpent; and there's no use denying it. I suppose you'll be telling me next that you never tasted an egg!"
>
> "I have tasted eggs, certainly," said Alice, who was a very truthful child; "but little girls eat eggs quite as much as serpents do, you know."
>
> "I don't believe it," said the Pigeon; "but if they do, why, then they're a kind of serpent: that's all I can say."
>
> This was such a new idea to Alice, that she was quite silent for a minute or two . . .

Like so many of her silences throughout the book, Alice's silence here is charged with significance, reminding us again that an important technique in learning to read Carroll is our ability to interpret his private system of symbols and signals and to appreciate the many meanings of silence. In this scene, the golden child herself becomes the serpent in childhood's Eden. The eggs she eats suggest the woman she will become, the unconscious cannibalism involved in the very fact of eating and desire to eat, and finally, the charmed circle of childhood itself. Only in *Alice's Adventures in Wonderland* was Carroll able to fall all the way through the rabbit hole to the point where top and bottom become one, bats and cats melt into each other, and the vessel of innocence and purity is also the source of inescapable corruption.

Alice's adventures in Wonderland foreshadow Lewis Carroll's subsequent literary career, which was a progressive dissolution into his component parts. Florence Becker Lennon defines well the schism that came with the later books: "Nothing in *Wonderland* parallels the complete severance of the Reds and Whites in *Through the Looking-Glass*. In *Sylvie and Bruno,* author and story have begun to disintegrate. The archness and sweetness of parts, the utter cruelty and loathsomeness of others, predict literal decomposition into his elements." The Alice of *Through the Looking-Glass,* which was published six years after *Wonderland,* represents still another Alice, Alice Raikes; the character is so thinned out that the vapid, passive Tenniel drawing is an adequate illustration of her. *Wonderland* ends with Alice playing all the parts in an ambiguous trial which concludes without a verdict. ***Looking-Glass*** begins with an unequivocal verdict: "One thing was certain, that the *white* kitten had nothing to do with it—it was the black kitten's fault entirely." Poor Dinah, relegated to the role of face-washer-in-the-background, has also dissolved into her component parts.

Throughout the books, the schism between Blacks (later Reds) and Whites is developed. Alice's greater innocence and passivity are stressed by her identification with Lily, the white pawn. The dominant metaphor of a chess game whose movements are determined by invisible players spreads her sense of helplessness and predestination over the book. The nursery rhymes of which most of the characters form a part also make their movements seem predestined; the characters in *Wonderland* tend more to create their own nursery rhymes. The question that weaves through the book is no longer "who am I?" but "which dreamed it?" If the story is the dream of the Red King (the sleeping embodiment of passion and masculinity), then Alice, the White Pawn (or pure female child) is exonerated from its violence, although in another sense, as she herself perceives, she is also in greater danger of extinction. Her increasing sweetness and innocence in the second book make her more ghost-like as well, and it is appropriate that more death jokes surround her in the second *Alice* book than in the first.

As Carroll's dream children became sweeter, his attitude toward animals became increasingly tormented and obsessive, as we can see in the hysterical antivivisection crusade of his later years. In one of his pamphlets, "Vivisection as a Sign of the Times," cruelty to animals, which in the first Alice was a casual instinct, becomes a synecdoche for the comprehensive sin of civilization:

> "But the thing cannot be!" cries some amiable reader, fresh from an interview with that most charming of men, a London physician. "What! Is it possible that one so gentle in manner, so full of noble sentiments, can be hardhearted? The very idea is an outrage to common sense!" And thus we are duped every day of our lives. Is it possible that that bank director, with his broad honest face, can be meditating a fraud? That the chairman of that meeting of shareholders, whose every tone has the ring of truth in it, can hold in his hand a "cooked" schedule of accounts? That my wine merchant, so outspoken, so confiding, can be supplying me with an adulterated article? That my schoolmaster, to whom I have entrusted my little boy, can starve or neglect him? How well I remember his words to the dear child when last we parted. "You are leaving your friends," he said, "but you will have a father in me, my dear, and a mother in Mrs. Squeers!" For all such rose-coloured dreams of the necessary immunity from human vices of educated men the

facts in last week's *Spectator* have a terrible significance. "Trust no man further than you can see him," they seem to say. "Qui vult decipi, decipiatur."

"Gently similing jaws" have spread themselves over England. The sweeping intensity of this jeremiad shares the vision, if not the eloquence, of Ruskin's later despairing works.

As the world becomes more comprehensively cruel, the Carrollian little girl evolves into the impossibly innocent Sylvie in ***Sylvie and Bruno*** and ***Sylvie and Bruno Concluded,*** who is more fairy or guardian angel than she is actual child. Here, the dream belongs not to Sylvie but to the strangely maimed narrator. Any hint of wildness in Sylvie is siphoned off onto her mischievous little brother Bruno, whom she is always trying to tame as the first Alice boxed her own ears for cheating at croquet; and any real badness is further placed at one remove in the figure of the villainous Uggug, an obscenely fat child who finally turns into a porcupine. Uggug's metamorphosis recalls that of the Pig-baby in *Wonderland,* but in the earlier book, the Cook let us know that Alice was also encompassed by the epithet—a terrible one in Carroll's private language—"Pig!"

Like Alice's, Sylvie's essential nature is revealed by her attitude toward animals. But while Alice's crocodile tears implicated her in original sin, Sylvie's tears prove her original innocence. In a key scene, the narrator tries to explain to her "innocent mind" the meaning of a hare killed in a hunt:

> "They hunt *foxes,*" Sylvie said, thoughtfully. "And I think they *kill* them, too. Foxes are very fierce. I daresay men don't love them. Are hares fierce?"
>
> "No," I said. "A hare is a sweet, gentle, timid animal—almost as gentle as a lamb." [Apparently no vision of the snappish March Hare returned to haunt Lewis Carroll at this point.]
>
> "But, if men *love* hares, why—why—" her voice quivered, and her sweet eyes were brimming with tears.
>
> "I'm afraid they *don't* love them, dear child."
>
> "All *children* love them," Sylvie said. "All *ladies* love them."
>
> "I'm afraid even *ladies* go to hunt them, sometimes."
>
> Sylvie shuddered. "Oh, no, not *ladies!*" she earnestly pleaded. . . . In a hushed, solemn tone, with bowed head and clasped hands, she put her final question. "Does GOD love hares?"

"Yes!" I said. "I'm *sure* He does. He loves every living thing. Even sinful *men*. How much more the animals, that cannot sin!" [Here the whole *Wonderland* gallery should have risen up in chorus against their creator!]

"I don't know what 'sin' means," said Sylvie. And I didn't try to explain it.

"Come, my child," I said, trying to lead her away. "Wish good-bye to the poor hare, and come and look for blackberries."

"Good-bye, poor hare!" Sylvie obediently repeated, looking over her shoulder at it as we turned away. And then, all in a moment, her self-command gave way. Pulling her hand out of mine, she ran back to where the dead hare was lying, and flung herself down at its side in such an agony of grief I could hardly have believed possible in so young a child.

Sylvie's weeping over a dead hare is an unfortunate conclusion to Alice's initial underground leap after a live rabbit. Dodgson has been driven full circle here to embrace the pure little girl of Victorian convention, though he is ambivalent in this passage about "ladies." But his deterioration should be used as a yardstick to measure his achievement in the first of the *Alice* books, which a brief survey of some typical portraits of children in nineteenth-century literature may help us to appreciate.

Victorian concepts of the child tended to swing back and forth between extremes of original innocence and original sin; Rousseau and Calvin stood side by side in the nursery. Since actual children were the focus of such an extreme conflict of attitudes, they tended to be a source of pain and embarrassment to adults, and were therefore told they should be "seen and not heard." Literature dealt more freely with children than life did, so adult conflicts about them were allowed to emerge more openly in books. As Jan Gordon puts it:

The most amazing feature of, say, Dickens' treatment of children, is how quickly they are transformed into monsters. Even Oliver Twist's surname forces the reader to appreciate the twisting condition normally associated with creatures more closely akin to the devil! One effect of this identification with evil adults . . . is that the only way of approaching childhood is by way of the opposite of satanic monstrosities—namely, the golden world of an edenic wonderland whose pastoral dimension gives it the status of a primal scene.

In its continual quest for origins and sources of being, Victorian literature repeatedly explores the ambiguous figure of the child, in whom it attempts to resolve the contradictions it perceives much as *Sylvie and Bruno* does: by an extreme sexual division.

Little boys in Victorian literature tend to be allied to the animal, the Satanic, and the insane. For this reason, novels in which a boy is the central focus are usually novels of development, in which the boy evolves out of his inherent violence, "working out the brute" in an ascent to a higher spiritual plane. This tradition seems foreshadowed by the boy in Wordsworth's *Prelude,* whose complexity undercuts the many Victorian sentimentalizations about Wordsworth's children. The predatory child in the first two books, traveling through a dark landscape that seems composed largely of his own projected fears and desires, has in fact a great deal in common with Carroll's Alice. Carroll is truer than many of his contemporaries to the ambiguities of Wordsworth's children, but he goes beyond Wordsworth in making a little girl the focus of his vision. Wordsworth's little girls tend to be angelic, corrective figures who exist largely to soothe the turbulence of the male protagonists; his persona in the *Prelude* is finally led to his "spiritual eye" through the ministrations of an idealized, hovering Dorothy.

David Copperfield must also develop out of an uncontrolled animality that is close to madness—early in the novel, we learn of him that "he bites"—and he can do so only through the guidance of the ghostly Agnes, pointing ever upward. Dr. Arnold's Rugby, which reflected and conditioned many of the century's attitudes toward boys, was run on a similar evolutionary premise: the students were to develop out of the inherent wickedness of "boy nature" into the state of "Christian gentleman," a semi-divine warrior for the good. In the all-male society of Rugby, Dr. Arnold was forced to assume the traditionally female role of spiritual beacon, as the image of the Carlylean hero supplanted that of the ministering angel. Thomas Hughes' famous tale of Rugby, *Tom Brown's School Days,* solves this problem by making Tom's spiritual development spring from the influence of the feminized, debilitated young Arthur and his radiantly etheral mother: only after their elaborate ministrations is the young man able to kneel by the Doctor's casket and worship the transfigured image of the-Doctor-as-God. Women and girls are necessary catalysts for the development of the hero out of his dangerously animal state to contact with the God within and without him.

Cast as they were in the role of emotional and spiritual catalysts, it is not surprising that girls who function as protagonists of Victorian literature are rarely allowed to develop: in its refusal to subject females to the evolutionary process, the Victorian novel takes a significant step backward from one of its principle sources, the novels of Jane Austen. Even when they are interesting and "wicked," Victorian heroines tend to be static figures like Becky Sharp; when they are "good," their lack of development is an important factor in the Victorian reversal of Pope's sweeping denunciation—"most women have no characters at all"—

into a cardinal virtue. Little girls in Victorian literature are rarely children, nor are they allowed to grow
up. Instead, they exist largely as a diffusion of emotional and religious grace, representing "nothing but
love," as Dodgson's Sylvie warbles. Florence Dombey
in Dickens' *Dombey and Son* may stand as their paradigm. Representing as she does the saving grace of
the daughter in a world dominated by the hard greed
and acquisitiveness of men—the world that kills her
tender brother Paul—Florence drifts through Mr.
Dombey's house in a limbo of love throughout the
book, waiting for her father to come to her. She ages,
but never changes, existing less as a character than as
a "spiritual repository into which Mr. Dombey must
dip if he is to be saved." Dickens' Little Nell and
Little Dorritt are equally timeless and faceless. Though
both are in fact post-pubescent—Little Nell is fourteen, Little Dorrit, twenty-two—they combine the
mythic purity and innocence of the little girl with the
theoretical marriageability of the woman, diffusing
an aura from a sphere separate from that of the other
characters, a sphere of non-personal love without
change.

Charlotte Brontë's Jane Eyre and George Eliot's
Maggie Tulliver are two more sharply-etched little girls
who grow into women, but even they represent, in an
angrier and more impassioned way, "nothing but love."
Neither develops in the course of her book, because
neither needs to change: all both need is acceptance of
the love they have to offer, which in Jane Eyre's case
is fervently erotic and ethical, and in Maggie Tulliver's
is passionately filial and engulfing. Both triumph at
the end of their novels because they are allowed to
redeem through their love the men they have chosen,
who, as Victorian convention dictated, have undergone
a process of development up to *them*. This reminds us
once more that in Victorian literature, little boys were
allowed, even encouraged, to partake of original sin;
but little girls rarely were.

We return once more to the anomaly of Carroll's Alice, who explodes out of Wonderland hungry and unregenerate. By a subtle dramatization of Alice's attitude toward animals and toward the animal in herself,
by his final resting on the symbol of her mouth, Carroll probed in all its complexity the underground world
within the little girl's pinafore. The ambiguity of the
concluding trial finally, and wisely, waives questions
of original guilt or innocence. The ultimate effect of
Alice's adventures implicates her, female child though
she is, in the troubled human condition; most Victorians refused to grant women and childdren this respect.
The sympathetic delicacy and precision with which
Carroll traced the chaos of a little girl's psyche seems
equalled and surpassed only later in such explorations
as D. H. Lawrence's of the young Ursula Brangwen in
The Rainbow, the chaos of whose growth encompasses
her hunger for violence, sexuality, liberty, and beati-

tude. In the imaginative literature of its century, *Alice's Adventures in Wonderland* stands alone.

Jean Gattégno (essay date 1976)

SOURCE: "Assessing Lewis Carroll," translated by
Mireille Bedestroffer and Edward Guiliano, in *Lewis
Carroll Observed: A Collection of Unpublished Photographs, Drawings, Poetry, and New Essays,* edited
by Edward Guiliano, Clarkson N. Potter, Inc., 1976,
pp. 74-80.

[*In the following essay, Gattégno considers Carroll as
a children's author and linguistic innovator.*]

It is not necessary to reestablish Lewis Carroll. Today
he is neither unknown nor underrated. Yet perhaps we
should try to determine his true place, which may not
necessarily be the one we had thought. For those who
see him only as "the author of *Alice,*" the forerunner
of the new and unusual, modern marvelous, it is advisable to stress, as many articles in this book have done,
that he was a logician and, even in his day, a linguist,
and to see his work as casting a new look at language.
For those who are inclined to consider him primarily
as a scientific innovator, it is wise to recall that *Alice*
was considered revolutionary from the moment it was
published, and that its intended audience, i.e., children, had every reason to see it as a new kind of literature written especially for them. In pointing out these
two aspects of Carroll's work, the linguistic side and
the child-oriented side, I do not claim to synthesize
two possible interpretations of these books. Rather, I
intend to underline the richness of his works, which
are not reducible to just one approach.

Still, all is not said by noting these two important aspects. The technique used in the adventures in *Alice,
Sylvie and Bruno,* and *The Hunting of the Snark* is not
just concerned with language and childhood; the place
of dream and reality also deserves careful consideration
and is not limited to either one of these two aspects.
Finally, we might have to think about the enigma that
the Carroll/Dodgson relationship poses and which neither attempts at psychoanalysis (such as Phyllis Greenacre's) nor "historical" research (such as A. L. Taylor's)
have completely succeeded in resolving.

The common point among the diverse views and readings of Carroll's work must emerge from within and
appear throughout the work itself and not in some center
external to it. Language is not its subject, but it is a
key for deciphering it.

II

When *Alice* appeared it caused astonishment and
seemed to be what it still is today, if only read without

preconceived ideas: a revolution in children's literature. We must not overlook the fact that the story was told and then written down for children, and was meant to appeal to them first and foremost. In what sense is it revolutionary? First, because it was the first time that a little girl was not simply the heroine but the focal point of a story. Everything that occurs happens to Alice, and everything is understood through her. Her gaze imparts life to the entire unusual world that inhabits Wonderland and Looking-Glass land and which, at all other times, is utterly still in an eternal slumber. It animates the White Knight of the Queen of Hearts for an instant—a dream instant—and enables them to make real what was only virtual in them. Alice is half-god in her adventures. Without her, the cats Dinah, Kitty, and Snowdrop would only be cats; thanks to her, they change into characters that express Alice's secret wishes and are at the same time, in themselves, new realities. The Cheshire Cat and Humpty Dumpty are both characters and individuals—characters because they become flesh from Carroll's creative words (voicing a type of language that had in part antedated Carroll), and that it is in their speech that they are firmly delineated. They are individuals in the sense that, even a hundred years after their creation, they still seem like real creatures and can be set side by side with other real beings and people, historical or ordinary.

Alice enters this world and sets it in motion, as a collector does with his music box or mechanical toy. Berkeleyan solipsism? Perhaps in part. But it is also the magic power of children's speech, which brings to life whatever it speaks of. This is the all-powerful, eternal life-giving force of which, among mankind, the child is simply the freest interpreter and the truest. Thanks to Alice—and Carroll—the subject's unconscious desires, the childhood freedom lost then found again, the long-repressed animistic beliefs, all reemerge. And the little seven-year-old girl who strolls through these two unusual worlds carries within herself all the violence of her untrammeled outlook. In this violence the grown-ups are the clearly marked targets in an animal form that is merely the reverse side of the animal state to which they attempt to reduce the child—as is demonstrated by the scene between Alice and the Unicorn. . . . In spite of everything that happens to Alice, the aggravations and mishaps, she is never a victim. And although she has to wait until both her adventures are over to prove her triumph to everyone, and primarily to herself, she never lets down for a moment.

The victory of the child over the adult is attested to in all of Carroll's work; the psychological richness revealed in *Alice in Wonderland* and *Through the Looking-Glass* is sufficient proof of this victory. Carroll painted his heroine from within, not that he "was" Alice, but he allowed the child within him to speak, the child that he had been and wished to be—in short, the un-

censored part of him that had not been destroyed in the process of growing into an adult. Furthermore, today when we are assured that children do not enjoy reading *Alice*, we believe it since grown-ups tell us so, just as we believe the learned people who, in the seventeenth century, affirmed that fairy tales were nonsense. Indeed, nothing demonstrates the subversive nature of Carroll's work better than the insistence on the part of "serious" critics to regard it primarily as the expression of a neurotic. In this way, in order to strengthen their biographical point of view, they can rid themselves of the problem of Carroll's language, the uninhibited speech of the child that renders adult speech ineffectual.

III

All this by itself would have been enough, both in Carroll's time and in our own, to guarantee Carroll lasting value; liberated speech appeared in the nineteenth century, and he was one of its initiators. But there is more here than just uncensored children's speech. There is also a new vision of language and speech that causes the logic of wishes to triumph over the logic of words. Alice continuously runs up against a mode of speech that those with whom she is speaking consider to be "coherent," that is, logical, and which always turns into a "non-logic," another kind of logic, that Alice cheerfully names "non-sense." Little Bruno in *Sylvie and Bruno* is in this respect the reverse of Alice, a specialist in non-sense, whereas his sister Sylvie and the Professor are unable to do anything about it. The inversion of characters is not significant; only the discourse is of importance, not Alice or Bruno as speakers. The degree to which the adventures of Carroll's characters, obviously starting with Alice, are inscribed in speech and are closely dependent upon it should be recalled. One has only to consider the role played by nursery rhymes, of which certain Carrollian episodes represent the "turning into action"; the use Carroll makes of certain vernacular expressions (mad as a hatter or a March hare) whereby the unreal subject is brought to life. Alice herself asserted it even before her dream: "What is the use of a book without pictures or conversations?"

What is attested to in this language that the reader constantly comes up against in Carroll's work? First of all, the absolute arbitrariness of human language through the split in the "human" relationship signifier/signified; the signifier is a form that no man has ever consciously decided on at a particular moment. In spite of what is too often believed, Humpty Dumpty's role is not to emphasize to Alice and the reader the all-powerfulness of the speaker through his authoritative formula, "the question is [to know] which is to be master—that's all." His role is to reveal to Alice the arbitrariness of the relationship in question. The professorial assurance he shows when "explicating" **"Jab-**

berwocky" scarcely conceals the essential subjectivism of his interpretation. As Carroll himself emphasizes in the preface to the *Snark,* a portmanteau word is a personal subjective compound peculiar to the person speaking; and had Judge Shallow (in Shakespeare's *Henry IV*) chosen to say "Rilchiam" for "Richard + William," no doubt someone else could just as correctly have chosen to say "Wilchard." It is Bruno who truly expresses Carroll's viewpoint. After someone objects to his saying "a mile or *three*" since it isn't usual, Bruno replies that "it would be usual—if we said it often enough." Better still, in his *Symbolic Logic* Carroll is firm on this point: "I maintain that any writer of a book is fully authorized in attaching any meaning he likes to any word or phrase he intends to use."

This is also the shattering of the opposition between "sense" and "non-sense." Gilles Deleuze [in *Logique du sens* (1969)] has shed remarkable light on this outstanding feature of the adventures of Alice, who "undergoes and fails in all the adventures of common sense," and who "always goes in both directions at once." The opposition one constantly finds in Carroll's work is not between non-sense and "sense," which would be its opposite, but between two kinds of sense, paradoxially linked, and of which it can only be said that one is the reverse of the other. To Alice's constant question, "In what sense?" Deleuze answers, "The question has no answer, because a characteristic of sense is not to have any direction, and not to make 'good sense,' but always to have both at once." The March Hare and the Mad Hatter embody this; they live in apparently opposite directions that in fact indicate the same point, the common territory of both characters. The frequent paradoxes in Carroll's work are the reverse not of sense but, at the very most, of what is erroneously called "common sense."

This is why logic is so important in Carroll's work. It is not certain, as I myself have been inclined to assert, that his theoretical works are the formalization of the richness contained in his fictional works. It is valuable to recall, in the first place, that Carroll started his research in logic seven years before he related *Alice* as a story. In fact, in 1855 he noted in his diary: "Wrote part of a treatise on Logic, for the benefit of Margaret and Annie Wilcox." His research had ample opportunity to find material for exploration and discovery in the adventures of a little girl outside the universe of "common sense." How would it be possible not to discern, from the constant presence of intuitions relating to methods of reasoning which one finds in all the work from *Alice* to *Sylvie and Bruno* (from 1865 to 1893), the persistence of a thought process about which we may certainly say that the unconscious speaks more freely through it than in a treatise on logic, but not that its expression needs a particular emotional environment in order to emerge? It is true, as Ernest Coumet points out . . . that it is the paradoxes and even Car-

roll's conception of symbolic logic that anticipate certain discoveries of modern logic. But the whole Carrollian mode of expression attests to the existence and strength of another kind of logic, no longer that of "sensible" expression but that of the unconscious, and therefore of desires. Carroll was one of the first to allow these to emerge and to assert themselves.

It is perhaps in this respect that the surrealists, in considering Carroll as one of their distinguished forerunners, had true insight. Carroll's writing deals with dreams in a way that has nothing in common with the dream literature of which Coleridge and De Quincey are the most famous examples in England. It is true that Alice's adventures are two "dreams," whose dream nature is described, affirmed, and authenticated at considerable length by the author at the end of *Alice* and at the beginning and end of *The Looking-Glass*. It is also true that the structure of various episodes, as well as the nightmare atmosphere of several scenes, become intellectually satisfying once one knows that it was a dream. However, this is not what is essential, but rather the digressions that Carroll permitted himself reveal more than an intention to reproduce a state of almost complete freedom. For example, when Alice dreams about characters who are dreaming about her, this is not another paradox but the expression of a consciousness trying unceasingly (and in vain) to look on itself objectively, at the same time that it feels and knows it is caught in its own subjectivity; not a triumph of solipsism but, on the contrary, an effort to escape from it. Or when in *Sylvie and Bruno* the character that is the Narrator sees two forms of the same character: Sylvie, who belongs to what he calls the dream-world, and Muriel, who belongs to his real world; and when he feels tossed between the two universes, the characters of the one progressively invading the other, we are not simply witnessing a game the schizophrenic allows himself to play. Rather, we see in this process (even if both interpretations are compatible) an effort to express the infinite richness contained in each word, each meaning, each reality. Sylvie is Muriel, although each one is exclusively herself. In the same way, little Bruno points out to his father that the two jewels he had offered to Sylvie to choose between were only one and continues: "Then you choosed it from *itself.* . . . Father, *could* Sylvie choose a thing from itself?" She certainly could in a world where the identity principle would not be the norm of norms, where A could be A and *also* non-A. And, for the moment, only the world of wishing, and of absolute contradiction, permits it.

IV

At least one other problem still has to be raised: who is speaking in *Alice* or in the *Snark?* In *Sylvie and Bruno* it is an "I" who tells the story, at times as an all-knowing novelist and at other times as an actor and character within the "story" that is told to us. Should we think it is the same person as the one who tells, and lives, Alice's adventures, but asserts himself more freely? And what should we think of the person who states in the *Symbolic Logic:* "If I find an author saying, at the beginning of his book, 'Let it be understood that by the word *"black"* I shall always mean *"white,"* and that by the word *"white"* I shall always mean *"black,"'* I meekly accept his ruling, however injudicious I may think it"?

The question is not purely rhetorical. Especially in the last example, the "I" cannot be simply the "author's," but necessarily encompasses a number of persons who share the attitude defined by the sentence in question. This attitude, we have seen, is also found in *Alice*. The spoken words therefore refer back to a person who might well be the same. However, this evidence has not yet been proved. Too often a distinction is made between Dodgson the mathematician, whose logic has become the sole interest of academicians, and Carroll the author of *Alice* and the *Snark,* concerned about preserving anonymity in his "private" life and growing angry at any intrusion by one world on the other, to the point, during the last year of his life, of refusing to accept any mail sent to "Lewis Carroll" at Oxford. We have seen that this necessary overlapping of two worlds is the very same problem the Narrator in *Sylvie and Bruno* has. Therefore no one will question that an element of schizophrenia is always present. But it does not divide two entities, "the man" from "the writer," or even the "serious writer" from "the writer of nonsense." On the contrary, it is their point of encounter because it is the point at which the Carrollian mode of expression (Dodgson's or Carroll's) surges forth. Indeed, in his treatise on Euclidian geometry (*Euclid and his Modern Rivals*), signed "C. L. Dodgson," Carroll does not say much and is generally satisfied with paraphrasing Euclid, at the most with humor. However, here and there are characteristic Carrollian sentences, typical attitudes of "Lewis Carroll," such as this warning in the "prologue" (preface):

> I have not thought it necessary to maintain throughout the gravity of style which scientific writers usually affect . . . I never could quite see the reasonableness of this immemorial law: subjects there are, no doubt, which are in their essence too serious to admit of any lightness of treatment—but I cannot recognize Geometry as one of them.

The sharp distinction between style and content leads us unerringly to a constant of which there are frequent examples in *Alice*. All the same, Carroll spoke out elsewhere; as soon as censorship could be at least partially lifted, thanks either to the anonymity of the numerous pamphlets Carroll produced in Oxford over a few years, or to his pseudonym, it was the Carrollian *essence* that truly began to speak out. This [unconscious] essence could be either a subjective carry-over

from childhood or, more profoundly, that which it expresses in a quasi-phylogenetical manner. It is neither accident nor neuroticism that in these circumstances there would be no human being corresponding to "Lewis Carroll" and that C. L. Dodgson still maintained this even shortly before his death. It is, rather, the expression of the intangibility of the speaker, who is not a person but the speaking subject. The language in Carroll's writings is that of the Subject and not of a subject, whose mode of expression is outspoken and which Deleuze, in discussing humor, calls the "fourth person singular," a subject associated with "esoteric language, which in each instance represents the overthrow, deep down, of ideal language. . . ." It is to this language that we should listen.

Alwin L. Baum (essay date 1977)

SOURCE: "Carroll's *Alices:* The Semiotics of Paradox," in *American Imago,* Vol. 34, No. 1, Spring, 1977, pp. 86-108.

[*In the following essay, Baum explores the linguistic and philosophical complexities of the* Alice *books.*]

When the Reverend Charles Lutwidge Dodgson was buried, in 1898, Lewis Carroll was set free behind the Looking Glass to continue his interminable game of chess with Alice, the heroine of his first two fairy tales, *Alice's Adventures in Wonderland* and *Through the Looking Glass*. During the century since their game began, the Alice books have played to a larger reading audience than most traditional folktales. Even while Dodgson lived, *Wonderland* and *Looking Glass* could be found alongside the Bible on the top bookshelf of practically every Victorian nursery. Carroll's first biographer, Stuart Dodgson Collingwood, claims that the *Alice* books became primers for many Victorian children and that lines from them were cited in the daily press as often as lines from Shakespeare. If the popularity of the tales among children has since been eclipsed by cartoons manufactured in the television studio, the adventures have nevertheless maintained the status of cultural myth in the adult world. Much of that popularity is due to the sophisticated problems in physics, metaphysics, logic and semantics which surface during the course of Alice's wanderings. As fiction, the books have presented readers and critics with an equally formidable problem of decodification. The Duchess insists to Alice: "Everything's got a moral if only you can find it." Yet, attempts to sift a consistent frame of meaning from the texts have met with success as uncertain as the quest for a Boojum in Carroll's nonsense ballad, *The Hunting of the Snark,* and the course Carroll charts through the *Alices* uses the same map employed by the Bellman to navigate the Snark expedition: "a perfect and absolute blank."

The author has also been an elusive quarry. Dodgson's affinity for young girls has prompted a number of attempts to exhume the spectre of unnatural desire from the texts. Like their folktale counterparts, Carroll's narratives abound in the imagery of sexual fantasy—rabbit holes, magic potions which produce bodily metamorphoses, decapitation threats, desires to become a queen—yet the imagery itself is no more prolific than we would find in any fairy tale. If we accuse Carroll of aberrance in his fantasies, we would similarly have to charge human society, as collective author of the world's traditional literature, with neurosis or sensationalism.

The heterogeneity of approaches to Carroll's *Alices* is sanctioned by the overdetermination of semantic possibilities in the texts. Yet, there have been few attempts to discover a structural pattern in the narratives which would integrate various hermeneutic models. Perhaps it is just as well. The longevity of the tales is guaranteed by their enigmatic quality. The sense of the adventures is analogous to all of the "riddles with no answers" they contain: their aesthetic value lies in their insolubility. And if Alice were to find a solution either to the riddles or to her own motives for journeying into the imaginary world of unconscious possibility, the rationale for her nonsense adventures would go out like a candle. However, Carroll's fiction deserves critical attention precisely because it fails to offer solutions, a semantic context. It illustrates the importance of paradox in human language, generally, and the complex interrelations of the linguistic sign and its referent in symbolic discourse. Carroll's *Alices* have also played mid-wife to a genre of modernist fiction which has continued to nurture paradox. In this century, the narrative tradition from Joyce to Beckett, from Borges to John Barth, has taken Carroll's experiments in nonsense more seriously than Dodgson himself ever dreamed.

In form the Alice narratives most closely resemble traditional *Märchen* (Carroll himself called them fairy tales), except that they are explicitly framed in dream contexts. In authentic folktales the adventure cannot expose itself as a dream because its signifying function would be destroyed. The same is true for dreams. Only psychoanalysts may take them seriously as signifying systems. If the dreamer were conscious of his dream's significance, or even of the fact that it is "only a dream," he would not be "dreaming." The dream, like folktales and much modern absurd fiction, must put the hero's adventure in the context of lived experience. Any paradoxes or contradictions of physical law intrinsic to dream adventures must go unquestioned while the dream unravels. By the same logic, the nonsense of the dream experience must become apparent enough upon awakening so that a distinction between the two states of consciousness may be made (a function less absurd in non-literary experience than one

might assume and one which is essential to signification in narrative structures). In fairy tales and dream fiction, the hero's acceptance of the impossible is not merely an ironic device, but it serves to indicate to the audience that the surrealistic episodes are meant to be understood metaphorically. Alice never questions the reality of the worlds underground and behind the looking glass; she even agrees to believe in the Unicorn if he will believe in her. As in actual dreams, it is her literal existence above-ground which is in question throughout the narratives. The absurdity of Alice's adventures points up the absurdity of waking experience (if only during the time of the dream). Although she protests that "one can't believe impossible things," she accepts the fact that she is speaking to an impossible White Queen who, when Alice's age, used to practice believing six impossible things before breakfast.

Like all fairy tale heroines and all dreamers, Alice must eventually awaken to discover that she has been "only dreaming." Yet even after the return to consciousness, Carroll forces the reader to believe one more impossible thing—Alice's sister redreams the Wonderland adventure exactly as Alice had dreamed it—a supreme paradox which characterizes the constant occlusion of boundaries between the two worlds. Similarly, behind the Looking Glass, Alice is presented with the dilemma of deciding whether she is part of the Red King's dream or he is part of hers. It is that old, insoluble paradox of idealist philosophy, one which continues to haunt Alice even after she awakens, since there are no grounds for proving that her return to consciousness is not also a part of the dream. Alice is, after all, "only a sort of thing" in Carroll's dream, one who would indeed be "nowhere," as Tweedledee remarks, if the dreamer left off dreaming. Carroll's interest in perpetuating the ambiguity is even more poignant in *Looking Glass,* the sequel to *Wonderland,* which is full of shadows and sighs of nostalgia for Carroll's "infant patron," Alice Liddel, who had then reached the period in her life "where the stream and the river meet," as Dodgson characterized the boundary of pubescence when he customarily took leave of the young girls he had been visiting.

Carroll remarks in his diaries that the world of dreams seems as "lifelike" as the other, and he suggests that there is little basis for calling one reality and the other fiction. In conjunction with Carroll's observation, Martin Gardner notes the appropriateness of Plato's dialogue in which Thaetetus proposes to Socrates that it may be only the greater amount of time spent awake which leads us to favor waking experience as 'true' and dreaming as 'false.' Carroll must have wondered what authenticity dreams might assume if the times were reversed. If daydreams were counted, the reversal might be an accomplished fact for most of us. Certainly Carroll makes a prime candidate for the role of the sleeping Red King since much of his own waking life was spent dreaming-up adventures and amusements for his child friends. Among these amusements was the first journey through Wonderland, composed *ex tempore* on one of Dodgson's excursions up the Isis river (from "Folly Bridge") with the Liddel children and Reverend Duckworth, and written down subsequently (as "Alice's Adventures Underground") at the request of Alice. Thus Carroll's professed motive for the creation of his adventure into Wonderland was merely to entertain his child audience. However, in deference to the many readers who had attempted to make sense of his tales, Dodgson remarked in one of his last letters: "I'm very much afraid I didn't mean anything but nonsense! Still, you know, words mean more than we mean to express when we use them; so a whole book ought to mean a great deal more than the writer meant." Carroll is speaking of *The Hunting of the Snark,* but the suggestion is appropriate to the *Alices.* Equally appropriate is Carroll's confession, in response to requests to know whether *The Hunting of the Snark* were an allegory or a political satire, or whether it contained some hidden moral, that he frankly did not know.

It is plausible to discover certain latent meanings in Carroll's nonsense at various points in the narratives, but it is unreasonable to assume that he could have unwittingly composed a complete allegory. The *Alice* books provide the reader no consistent system of extratextual reference. As ingenious as some attempts have been to wrestle allegorical meanings from them—whether the reading is political, archetypal, or ecclesiastical—the systems have either fallen from their own weight, like a tower of Babel built out of a pack of Carrollian playing cards, or they have restricted severely the suggestiveness of the original. Shane Leslie's exegesis of *Alice in Wonderland* as a "secret history of the Oxford Movement" is a notorious example, although it is scarcely as zealous as Abraham Ettleson's "decodification" of the *Alices* as companion pieces to Judaic scripture. At the opposite hermetic pole are the many psychoanalytic studies which exploit the intra-uterine fantasies and castration complexes dominant in the work to demonstrate that Dodgson was arrested at the anal stage of development or that he labored all of his life under the oppressive shadow of an "infallible" father. Such readings do more justice to the ingenuity of their authors than they do to the genius of Carroll's nonsense, its power of suggestion. They appear as critical *tours-de-force,* moreover, because they assume that where there is fantasy there must be allegory, at least at the level of narrative content. Such interpretations press the sign into service as emblem, substituting a one-to-one correspondence between the signifier and the signified for a relation which normally is unbound in ordinary speech, and one which Carroll attempts to dissolve even further in his narratives.

Carroll was well aware of the essential arbitrariness in the relation between the linguistic sign and its referent long before Ferdinand de Saussure was to illustrate that such a principle is axiomatic to all language systems. One of the most obvious effects of Carroll's nonsense is to demonstrate the range of arbitrariness in the relation. The text of the *Alices* poses a problem of locating the linguistic context. It is similar to the dilemma faced by the Baker in his quest for the Snark: having left his name ashore, along with his portmanteaux, the hero is obliged during the expedition to answer to any name, such as "Fry me," or, "Fritter my wig!" Through an exploration of ambiguities inherent in English, primarily figurative expressions and homophones, and through neologisms and paralogisms of his own devising, Carroll develops a narrative code governed by the rationale of free association. The signifying axis of the text keeps reflecting upon its own ambiguities until those violations in the code become the rule. The linear development of the discourse is constantly interrupted (as was the first telling of the tale, through the importunity of the Liddel sisters) with the result that the rule of logical implication is cancelled out, and the "message value" (information) of the texts is nullified. The logos of the narratives is reflected in the Mad Hatter's riddle: "Why is a raven like a writing desk?" It is another insoluble conundrum, as Alice discovers later, yet an answer appropriate to the mood of the narratives would be: "Because they both begin with the letter *R.*"

Elizabeth Sewell [in *The Field of Nonsense* (1952)] has remarked that the *Alices* are primarily commentaries on nonsense. More specifically, one could argue that are metacommentaries on the nonsense of conventional English usage. Whatever consistent meaning attaches to the texts is less allegorical than it is metaphorical, or metalinguistic. *Wonderland* represents the underground of language, its literal self-reflection which is always present but disguised. Carroll examines chiefly those equivocal gaps in the code forced by an idiomatic *parole,* conventionalized poetic license whose ambiguities cannot be regulated by rule but only by precedent. The narratives serve to illustrate that 'meaning is not an entity, but a relation,' as Gilles Deleuze has suggested. But they carry the game a step further in allowing the signified to collapse into the signifier. Deleuze observes that in Carroll's nonsense 'everything happens at the boundary of things and propositions,' as in Chrysippus' remark: "When you say something, it comes out of your mouth; now, when you say *a chariot,* a chariot comes out of your mouth." In the same mood, the Duchess hurls the epithet "Pig," at the infant she is nursing during Alice's visit; and, having received the baby as a gift from the Duchess, Alice discovers later as she carries it away that indeed it has become "neither more nor less than a pig."

On the other hand, such metamorphoses indicate that Carroll's nonsense is not *non sense,* that is, devoid of meaning. Merleau-Ponty has remarked that even the face of a dead man is condemned to express something. Certainly no utterance is *insignificant;* even silence has message value, as Alice's responses to the nonsense of her interlocutors indicate. Despite the apparent anarchy of words and things in the *Alices,* there is method evident in the madness. The pig's transmutation is actually a superb piece of logic, depending on one's point of view. Alice admits that as a child, her charge was "dreadfully ugly," but, she thinks, "It makes rather a handsome pig." And from Dodgson's point of view there was little distinction to be made between pigs and little boys, for whom, according to Collingwood, he had "an aversion almost amounting to terror." But there is a more profound implication in the episode which suggests that the word can become the thing. Language underground is not a process of classifying the physical universe, it is a means of creating a psychological universe. The inhabitants of Wonderland and the Looking Glass invert the Duchess' advice to "take care of the sense and let the sound take care of itself." Invariably they force the sound to take care of the sense. Either the signifier swallows the signified, or the bond between them is severed, with the result that the sound image floats free to attach itself to any other sound with which it has the slightest association. "Did you say 'pig' or 'fig,'" asks the Cheshire Cat, after Alice has told him of her encounter with the Duchess. The question points out that the pig-baby is only a phonemic breath away from another metamorphosis; or that, from the Cat's point of view, the subject of Alice's anecdote is indifferently pig and fig at one and the same time.

The language spoken here is not the language of dream allegory but the language of real dreams. The major parameters of dream codification (according to Freud's model of the dreamwork) are also instrumental to the structure of Carroll's narratives. Freud observes for example that words are often treated in dreams as things. Thus when composite images are formed in dreams, as when a child might appear with an extended snout, or might grunt, like Alice's infant, the dream is creating a metaphoric association appropriate to its "deep-structure" or latent content. To Carroll, pigs, male infants, and figs are all fat and inarticulate, like the Uggug of *Sylvie and Bruno,* and thus indistinguishably distasteful (Dodgson was an ascetic vegetarian who despised overindulgence, apparently in all but story telling). The work of condensation in dreams is carried out also through portmanteaux word formations (such as those in Carroll's **"Jabberwocky"**); through puns, verbal and visual (e. g., the "Mock" Turtle who is represented by Tenniel as part turtle, part calf); and through distortions of syntax, primarily teleological reversals which have the effect of making any expression equivalent to its converse.

While free-falling down the rabbit hole to Wonderland, Alice falls asleep pondering the question, "'Do cats eat bats? Do cats eat bats?' and sometimes 'Do bats eat cats?' for, you see," the narrator explains, "as she couldn't answer either question, it didn't much matter which way she put it."

Other mechanisms of the dreamwork are equally apparent in the *Alices*. Freud suggests, for example, that logical relations in dreams are represented either through metaphorical constructs or through episodic sequences. In general, logical connections are reproduced in the form of simultaneity. One element juxtaposed with another is sufficient to indicate that they are associated in the dream thought. This is, of course the basic structure of metaphor. In dreams the composite is usually in images, as visual representation requires, although condensation may frequently appear in dream utterances. In the Alice narratives, the association is usually based on phonological and morphological affinities. Describing to Alice how he would get stuck in his sugar loaf helmet, the White Knight says, "I was as fast as—as lightning, you know." Alice objects, "But that's a different kind of fastness." The Knight shakes his head and replies, "It was all kinds of fastness with me, I can assure you!"

Freud argues also that the "either—or" relation cannot exist in dreams. Whenever an alternative is presented within the dream, even when the terms are mutually exclusive, the relation may be read as one of conjunction. This is the basic structure of paradox, and much of Carroll's nonsense depends on it. **"The Walrus and the Carpenter"** begins with the sun and the moon jockeying for position over the sea, and concludes with a paradox of 'acts versus intentions,' as Gardner points out, in Alice's attempt to decide whether the Walrus is less culpable because "he was a *little* sorry for the poor oysters," or the Carpenter, because he ate fewer than the Walrus (who had sneaked some under his handkerchief), although Tweedledum observes that he nevertheless ate "as many as he could get."

The relative nature of judgements and definitions is argued similarly during Alice's first meeting with the Red Queen. In reply to the Queen's request to know where Alice has come from and where she is going, she says she has lost her way, only to be corrected by the Queen: "I don't know what you mean by *your* way. . . . all the ways about here belong to *me*." Alice discovers soon after that those ways include the definition of words. The Queen has seen gardens for example compared with which the one they are in would be a wilderness, and hills which, by comparison, would make Alice call the one she is trying to climb a valley. "No, I shouldn't," said Alice, surprised into contradicting her at last: "a hill *ca'n't* be a valley, you know. That would be nonsense—." "You may call it 'nonsense' if you like," says the Queen, "but *I've* heard nonsense, compared with which that would be as sensible as a dictionary!"

In fact, the Queen's nonsense is not far removed from a dictionary which must define each of its lexemes in terms of others which in turn must be defined in terms of others, until, theoretically, each word would have to be used in its own definition. As a logician himself, Carroll was well aware of this essential semantic teleology in language, and he makes good use of it throughout the *Alices*. While the nursery rhyme about the Tweedle Brothers is running through Alice's mind, Tweedledum remarks: "I know what you're thinking about, but it isn't so, nohow." "Contrariwise," continues Tweedledee, "if it was so, it might be; and if it were so, it would be; but as it isn't, it ain't. That's logic." In Wonderland similarly the Duchess admonishes Alice: "'Be what you would seem to be'—or, if you'd like it put more simply—'Never imagine yourself not to be otherwise than what it might appear to others that what you were or might have been was not otherwise than what you had been would have appeared to them to be otherwise.'" Alice suggests quite sensibly that she might understand better the Duchess' moral if it were written down. In this case, of course, it would make little difference. The message reaches a threshold of vanishing returns in the course of its logical development and eventually cancels itself out. It is a paralogism similar to the classic 'simple liar' paradox. For example, a card is presented which reads, "On the other side of this card is a true statement," and when the card is turned over, the message on it reads, "On the other side of this card is a false statement." Naturally, Carroll is aware of the pedagogical value of paradoxes for illustrating errors of reasoning to his students. The fundamental "error" of paradoxical propositions resides, of course, in the multiplicity of meanings which are forced to co-exist through an overdetermination of predication. When Carroll isn't reversing the order of syntax, or causing it to fork into mutually exclusive paths through a *double entendre,* he produces an interminable sequence of implication which nullifies the message. For example, 'taking care of the sound and letting the sense take care of itself,' the White Queen tests Alice's ability to do Looking Glass sums by asking her to add "one and one and one and one and one and one and one and one and one."

If syntax is a major problem for Alice, it implies also a problematic of time and space relations, since the propositional calculus serves to reinforce the interdependence of reason and a Newtonian universe in which all matter is identifiable in terms of its orderly relations in the space-time continuum. Thus the difficulty Alice has with the language code of her dreams is intimately bound to the problems she has with her existence in space and time. Her initial fall down the rabbit hole, as Gardner observes, would have the effect, if the shaft went through the center of the earth,

of keeping Alice forever in suspended animation. From that moment until she encounters the suspended enigma of the dreamer's identity behind the Looking Glass, Alice's self-image is continually called into question through paradoxes of logic or physical law.

Even the syntactic chain of narrative episodes is without rhyme or reason. Carroll admitted that he had originally sent Alice down the rabbit hole without the least idea what was to happen to her afterward; and he contended that he pieced the narratives together from "bits and scraps," ideas that came to him "one by one at odd moments of reflection." Behind the Looking Glass Alice follows her moves systematically across the chessboard from pawn to queen, but the significance of the journey is less logical than it is metaphorical. Waking from the dream implies not only a return to the rules of consciousness, but it sets in motion, toward Alice's "coming-of-age," the hands of the intractable clock on the near side of the mirror. In the prefatory poem Carroll reminisces that Alice's crowning presages a "summons to unwelcome bed" of the "melancholy maiden" from whom he will ever be "half a life asunder." The distance between them, and the race it would take to bridge it, reminds one of so many of the races run in the narratives: the Caucus Race which has no real start or finish; the Mad Hatter's and March Hare's odyssey around the table in their hopeless race against 'tea-time;' the White Queen and Alice racing to remain in the same square on the chessboard; Alice's futile attempts to catch the 'motes' on the periphery of her vision—the things in the "Wool and Water" shop (including Humpty Dumpty in egg form) which move perversely to a different shelf when Alice focuses her attention upon them. Later, during her boat ride with the shop's proprietor (the Sheep who is the erstwhile White Queen), Alice tries to pick some "dream rushes" along the shore, the prettiest of which are always beyond her reach, while those she does gather melt away like snow in her hands. Gardner's suggestion that the rushes may symbolize Carroll's child friends is a compelling one. The episode underscores the problems Alice has throughout the narratives with 'being and time.' She exists in a Heideggerian universe which is created totally in the space between consciousness and the world, and which thus depends for its signification upon consciousness examining its own representational processes. Alice's bodily metamorphoses in Wonderland are mirrored by the violations of spatio-temporal law behind the Looking Glass. Those violations are, of course, characteristic of fairy tales. They serve in part to sanction the fantasy that permits one to be any size one wants to be, as the Caterpillar intimates to Alice, or that permits him to be any place at any time he wishes. From the author's point of view, on the other hand, the violations of natural law and logic would allow Carroll to "hold fast" little Alice, as he puts it in the prefatory poem to *Looking Glass,* with his "love gift of a fairy tale" by permitting him control over her size, age, and identity. After Alice tells Humpty Dumpty she is seven years and six months of age, he suggests that she might have done better to quit at seven. When she protests, "One can't help growing older," he remarks, "*One* can't, perhaps, but *two* can. With proper assistance you might have left off at seven." Quick to catch the implication, perhaps, Alice redirects the conversation, thinking to herself, that she had "had quite enough of the subject of age." Gardner and other commentators have drawn attention to the grim under-current of the adventures exemplified in these periodic "death jokes." Yet the implication of the jokes is only as serious as any child's desire to get control over time—to hold it in check and make it do his bidding, as the Mad Hatter and Carroll attempt to do.

It is reasonable to suppose that Carroll's fantasy reflects his concern to turn back his own clock. His argument with time continues throughout his work, to culminate in the "Outlandish Watch" of **Sylvie and Bruno** which, by analogy to the Looking Glass, reverses the order of events. Equally effective for the perpetuation of his relationship with Alice Liddel would be the attempt to hold her fairy tale surrogate in symbolic limbo. Throughout the narratives, therefore, Alice is suspended in the phenomenal moment, outside of time and space, and in continual ambivalence about her identity, until she eventually becomes "too big" for the dream, as she must, both literally and figuratively. While trapped inside the White Rabbit's house, Alice reflects:

> It was much pleasanter at home . . . when one wasn't always growing larger and smaller, and being ordered about by mice and rabbits. I almost wish I hadn't come down that rabbit-hole—and yet—and yet—it's rather curious, you know, this sort of life! I do wonder what *can* have happened to me! When I used to read fairy tales, I fancied that kind of thing never happened, and now here I am in the middle of one! There ought to be a book written about me, that there ought! And when I grow up, I'll write one—but I'm grown up now . . . at least there's no room to grow up any more *here*.

> But then . . . shall I never get any older than I am now? That'll be a comfort, one way—never to be an old woman.

Such a pun on 'growing up' indicates, moreover, where much of Alice's difficulties arise—in that problematical space between the literal and the figurative. Thus the existential dilemma Alice faces is bound up with the dialectical interrelation of the signifier and the signified.

At first glance, it seems hardly a flattering monument to Carroll's affection for Alice Liddel that her fairy tale persona should be put through the ordeal of playing pawn to an implacable semiotician. Alice eagerly exiles herself from the Empire only to find herself in a country which shamelessly abuses the Queen's English; and, as the champion of Victorian idiom, Alice is scarcely amused. She plays the role of adult *Pharmakos* caught up in a child's tangled web of free-association where the thing is continually sacrificed to the word and all words (and all things) are potentially analogous. Humpty Dumpty's defense of unbirthday logic concludes with the remark:

> "There's glory for you!"

> "I don't know what you mean by 'glory'," Alice said.

> Humpty Dumpty smiled contemptuously. "Of course you don't—till I tell you. I meant 'there's a nice knock-down argument for you.'"

> "But 'glory' doesn't mean 'a nice knock-down argument,'" Alice objected.

> "When *I* use a word," Humpty Dumpty said, in rather a scornful tone, "it means just what I choose it to mean—neither more nor less."

> "The question is," said Alice, "whether you *can* make words mean so many different things."

> "The question is," said Humpty Dumpty, "which is to be master—that's all."

The only response appropriate to such one-sided conversations is silence, and Alice is forever rendered speechless by her communicants. She persists, nevertheless, in her search for the code which governs dream communication. Even after waking from her Looking Glass dream, when Alice tries to get an opinion on the adventure from her pet kitten, she finds problems with the rules governing dream discourse: "If they would only purr for 'yes,' and mew for 'no,' or any rule of that sort. . . . so that one could keep up a conversation! But how *can* you talk with a person if they *always* say the same thing?" In response to Alice's request for clues the kitten only purrs, of course, and it is impossible for Alice to guess whether it meant 'yes' or 'no.' Alice is similarly caught between affirmation and disconfirmation in her adventures. The space she occupies is mediate between the languages of the dream and waking life. Alice herself acts a catalyst to illustrate that the two languages are really interfused, whether one is awake or dreaming. She is like the sign itself, caught in the paradoxical space of the flame after the candle is blown out.

That space is objectified from the first moment in Wonderland when Alice is seized by the impulse to chase after the magic White Rabbit, to the last moment in Looking Glass, when Alice enlists her uncommunicative kitten's help in trying to decide who has been dreaming. Alice's initial fall is like the fall of man from a state of undifferentiated grace into a universe of hierarchical systems, constituted on a base of infinitely embedded oppositions, each of which requires a decision process for its articulation and its comprehension. In her free-fall through the rabbit hole (which is lined, like Carroll's study, with bookshelves, maps, and pictures) Alice seizes a jar of orange marmalade. Finding it empty, she debates whether she should replace the jar on the shelf or drop it on the inhabitants below, the "Antipathies" she calls them, although "it didn't sound at all the right word." Her encounter with the marmalade, of course, contradicts the laws of falling objects—she would have been unable to take the jar in the first place, and she could certainly neither replace it nor drop it, since she would be falling at the same rate of speed as the jar. It is one lesson in relativity among many in the books which look forward to Einstein's reduction of the distance between matter and energy. In the *Alices,* moreover, space and time are not only relative to each other but to language as well, an interdependence revealed, for example, in the decreasing number of hours spent by the Mock Turtle at his 'lessens.' Such punning follows on the heels of Achilles and the turtle in the paradoxical race proposed by Zeno of Elea where distance and time implode just a hair's breath from the finish line, or in the caucus race where the goal does not exist in space but in the time it takes to dry out. Outside of his narratives, Carroll was also preoccupied with the interrelation of laws governing language, space, and time. While Dodgson was defending Euclid's axiomatic approach to the world, in lectures considered by at least one of his students to be "as dull as ditchwater," Carroll was probing into space and discovering 'black holes' everywhere. In his essay, "When does the Day Begin," we find him ready to race around the earth, clinging to the sun like Alice cleaves to her marmalade, in order to demonstrate just how relative human chronometry really is.

That Alice's dream friends go to non-Euclidean schools is further evidenced by the arrivals and departures of the Cheshire Cat. He goes so far as to tender his head to the Queen of Hearts minus a body from which to sever it, thus throwing the threat of decapitation (or castration) into a hopeless quibble over terms. The Cat himself could exist only as a figure-of-speech: to 'grin like a Cheshire cat' was a current idomatic expression even in Carroll's day. Alice corroborates her friend's low existential profile in her remark that she has seen a cat without a grin but never a grin without a cat. The Cat's grin is surely no more ubiquitous than that of Carroll himself, who delighted in hounding a pun until either the words or his child audience were exhausted. The Cat reveals also that Carroll's sorcery is sleight-of-hand sophist-

ry. When Alice solicits advice which direction she ought to go, the Cheshire Cat replies:

> "That depends a good deal on where you want to get to."
>
> "I don't much care where—" said Alice.
>
> "Then it doesn't matter which way you go," said the Cat.
>
> "—so long as I get *somewhere,*" Alice added as an explanation.
>
> "Oh you're sure to do that," said the Cat, "if you only walk long enough."

Alice's problem is that to get 'somewhere' in her dream, she could never walk long enough. Just as one can never get 'there' from 'here' since, linguistically, *there* would become *here* once he arrived, so Alice discovers that *somewhere* is not located in the continuum of space and time but that of syntax-semantics.

Because language itself serves in large part to "locate" the speaker, to permit him to reaffirm that he continues to exist, physically and psychologically, we might expect Alice's problems with directionality in her dreams to be mirrored also in her problems with the direction of discourse underground. During her free-fall to Wonderland, Alice tries to calculate the distance she has traversed in terms of the latitude and longitude she has gotten to, not that she has the slightest idea what those terms mean, the narrator reveals, "but she thought they were nice grand words to say." Like the Cheshire Cat, Alice exists in the interstitial space betwen physical and linguistic realities. It is a province again charted most accurately in *Hunting of the Snark* by the Bellman's map which dispenses with those "Mercator's North Poles and Equators, Tropics, Zones, and Meridian Lines," since, "the Bellman would cry: and the crew would reply, 'They are merely conventional signs'." In the Wonderland of dreams and fairy tales a blank map is ideal since it permits the traveller to take any route to his destination, or it allows him not to move at all, since he would be already where he wanted to go.

Traditional maps represent a semiotic system directed toward the pole of least syntactic ambiguity. If roads bifurcate and intersect, or if there are alternate routes to a certain city (there are no roads to "the country" which, like Wonderland, has no boundaries), those roads are clearly marked on the map, and all routes are discovered by the system (except the inconsequential footpaths). The map thus exhausts its semantic potential, since it assigns one value, consequently equal value, to each of its signs. Only the traveller (from the country) can create ambiguity in the system through his chronic hesitation between choosing the road which is straightest or that which promises some adventure, however slight. In Alice's search for adventure she finds herself continually at crossroads whose signposts reverse the order of things by reversing *l'ordre des mots.* The sign which points the way to the house of Tweedledee and that which directs Alice to the house of Tweedledum are mounted on the same post and point in the same direction. Sings which should have different referents keep turning Alice into the same semantic road whose signposts and milestones are puns, paradoxes, parodies, paralogisms, and portmanteaux words, each of which switches the code from the axis of syntactic contiguity to the axis of semantic analogy, or paradigm. They are the same highway markers Freud discovered on the 'royal road to the unconscious' in dreams (e. g., the processes of *condensation,* which forces two or more signifieds into one signifier, and *displacement,* in which one signified generates multiple signifiers), and in those mechanisms which produce the psychopathology of everyday life: parapraxis, paramnesia, and paraphasia. In fact, the *Alices* could serve as guide-books to the grammar which permits the unconscious to break through the 'frozen sea of consciousness.' The best model of both the dreamwork and the structure of the *Alice* narratives is the "rebus" which Freud used to demonstrate the interchanges taking place between language and image in the formation of a manifest content (the signifier) appropriate to the articulation (symbolic cathexis) of the latent dream thoughts (the signified). Freud assumes that the primary function of the interfusion is to produce a representable (visual) content, but it is surely as much a question of "presentableness"; the dream-censor would best be circumvented by the diffusion of boundaries between word and thing. The signifier must be divorced from conventional meanings before it may be allowed to seek new reference, *mutatis mutandis,* in the semantic pool appropriate to the latent thoughts. The ultimate effect of these operations is the desocialization of the discourse. Humpty Dumpty reveals that substantives—nouns and adjectives—are very impressionable and easily manipulated while verbs are more recalcitrant. This is, of course, the case in language above ground; because the copula establishes the spatio-temporal link between subject and object, thus their relative identity (which is the only identity they have in the speech act), it is, as Humpty Dumpty says, the "proudest." Nevertheless, Humpty argues, "*I* can manage the whole lot of them! Impenetrability! That's what *I* say!" Whatever else Humpty himself may signify, surely he is very much Carroll, the master of nonsense, in this scene.

Carroll's investment in the impenetrability of a linguistic universe such as Humpty Dumpty describes is doubtless reflective not only of his role as poet and magician (where he began entertaining his sisters and younger brothers as a child), but of his desire to master

language, particularly verbs, which at once served to represent the wall between himself and his young friends, and at the same time, one of his few sanctioned bonds with them. If Humpty Dumpty's language is inpenetrable to Alice, it is nevertheless not "his own invention," as the White Knight would say, despite the 'extra wages' Humpty is willing to pay words to do his bidding. The language he describes is, on the contrary, ever *present* in waking life as the looking glass reflection of social discourse—its alter ego, the subconscious. It is precisely the anarchy of association which social language must attempt to repress, since language is the primary vehicle through which preconscious desire may articulate itself. Thus, social discourse zealously governs syntactic continuity, or diachronic expectation. The language of the pre-conscious is forced to ride under speech somewhat like Odysseus, clinging to the belly of a sheep, rides under the watchful eye (now blinded) of Polyphemus who would search him out and swallow him. Just as the guise assumed by Odysseus is that of "No-man," so in Carroll's adventures, Alice is in constant danger of losing her identity. The Queen of Hearts standing over her gardeners, trying to decide which among them is guilty of painting her white roses red when they all have their redundantly signifying backs turned toward her, is also a model of Cyclopean syntax—her response to everything is "Off with his head!" Happily, the Queen would as likely recognize the discourse of this preconscious and to 'suppress its evidence' as she would be able to cut off the head of the Cheshire Cat without his body being present. The view of language created here is one in which the signifier of consciousness is merely an excuse for the articulation of the latent signified—a view shared of course by Freud and by Carroll, if not by the Reverend Charles Dodgson.

In all archetypal struggles—whether social, oneiric, or mythical—the repressive process is marked by code 'displacement,' in the Freudian sense of the ego's creation of symbolic gratification for prohibited desire. In the *Alices* as in myth, the agonistic confrontation is foreordained through the prophetic word of the oracle because the contest is 'fixed' beforehand—the goal is not to win but to *represent* the struggle itself since, like the two halves of the sign, neither desire nor social demand may ever be eliminated because each is covertly trying to accommodate its demands to the other. Thus the battle is as redundant as that between the "Lion and the Unicorn" or "Tweedledum and Tweedledee." Language itself is ultimately the arbiter, or mediator. Logical development of many episodes in the *Alice* books is prescribed in those oracular nursery rhymes which Alice repeats, almost as an incantatory formula, for calling into existence the creatures of her dreams. Like the Cheshire Cat, almost all of them owe their existence to language—Tweedledum and Tweedledee, Humpty Dumpty, The Mad Hatter and The March Hare, the King, Queen, and Knave of Hearts—

all are literal incorporations of literary tropes or figurative expressions. Thus the confrontation of codes governing Alice's and her dream creatures' discourse is a parable doomed to the redundancy of expression found in the puns and paradoxes they articulate.

That redundance emphasizes the ritual nature of the narratives. If Alice is *pharmakos* it is because she too is doomed, (like Dionysus, the 'twice-born,' or anyone who stands midway between the world of consciousness and the unconscious) to recurrent *sparagmos,* in which the victim's words are torn asunder and scattered over the earth only to permit regeneration through a new synthesis. Carroll's dalliance with Alice's size and direction in the narratives is analogous to the sport he takes with her language. She becomes his *Spielzeug* in the archetypal game of *Fort! Da!* in which, according to Freud, through the ritual discarding and retrieving of an object the child gains some metaphorical control over his separation anxieties, or more generally, over the concepts of 'presence' and 'absence' so essential in their various forms to his physical and psychological survival. In the *Alices,* the threat posed by the protean language games is directed toward Alice's 'syntagmatic' existence. Progression in the discourse is continually sacrificed to proliferation of choices which become available at each step in the spoken chain, a problem revealed in Alice's lament to her kitten that you can't talk to someone if they always say the same thing.

Coupled with her language problems, Alice finds it difficult to remember who she is. The Red Queen, who is fond of admonishing Alice to "Speak in French when you can't think of the English for a thing—turn out your toes as you walk—and remember who you are!" suggests also that Alice speak when she is spoken to. Alice protests that if the rule were strictly obeyed nobody would ever speak—it is one of the few debates which she wins. The implication is that speaking and being are interdependent. Alice finds that she is continually losing herself in the language of her dreams—most dramatically in the "Wood-where-things-have-no-names" where the boundaries between nature and culture are temporarily occluded solely through the loss of the nominal function of language. Symbolization of such boundary transgressions is characteristic of traditional literature. Through the deconstruction of the linguistic code which allows 'predication' of the ego, the ritual infrastructure of this kind of discourse permits semantic overdetermination in the content, thus the metaphorical proliferation of identities.

The Cheshire Cat exploits Alice's manner of speaking to prove that she must be insane or she would not have come to Wonderland where everyone, as if by definition, is "quite mad." Alice suspects a tautology in the Cat's reasoning, but she finds herself enmeshed in its syllogistic network. The Cat would accept no contradictions, of course, even if Alice could find them—particularly those dependent upon the chronology of his utterance. Like the White Queen, he would see nothing anachronistic in taking as many as five days and five nights together—"for warmth"—she maintains, even though they would be five times as cold by the same logic. The Cat would concur also with the Queen's dismay over Alice's manner of thinking: "It's a poor sort of memory that only works backwards," she remarks. One advantage of "living backward" according to the Queen, is a memory which works "both ways." In strict observance of the rules of order behind the Looking Glass, one's memory should only work forward; but in that case, the reversal of directions would have little effect on the functional processing of experience into linear chains by memory. Once Alice had gotten used to living backward, a memory which worked to anticipate events would seem only natural in a world where events, as in a film running in reverse, were going the same direction. On the other hand, a memory such as the one described by the Queen would be no 'memory' at all unless, of course, it worked forward and backward at will. Anyone who enjoyed the dubious gift of the Queen's memory would either suffer the phenomenological shock of total recall and projection, and would have to take to his bed, as the hero does in Jorge-Luis Borges' short story, "Funes, the Memorious"; or, he would suffer perpetual amnesia, each moment of his existence would demand a new phenomenal self. While such a memory would prove inexpedient to physical survival, it is a fantasy frequently projected in myth as the chief attribute which separates mortals from immortals.

When threatened, Alice tries to recover her identity by appealing to her own poor excuse for a memory. On those occasions she discovers that the "words did not come the same as they used to do," a consequence of being in a metaphorical world, and each attempt to remember ends in a parody of the systems that governed her former life; below ground she finds the syntax has remained the same while the content is completely changed. Parody depends upon the occluding of the decision process which ordinarily permits distinction between two speech acts. While the code remains constant there is again a proliferation of possible contents which, theoretically, could go on forever. Like puns, parody exemplifies the irony that the progressive dimension of signification is only an illusion of syntactic chaining which masks the ultimate redundance of those contents. It is a pardox similar to that of man's development of a system for measuring his progress in linear time based upon the endless revolutions of stellar bodies around each other in absolute space. Like all heroes of myth and dreams, Alice must only suffer the ordeal of relativity in space-time in order to realize phantasized psychological selves. After tasting the magic cakes marked "Eat me!" she attempts to measure how much she has grown by placing her hand on top of her head, "quite surprised to find that she remained the same size." Carroll adds: "To be sure, this is what generally happens when one eats cake; but Alice had got so much into the way of expecting nothing but out of the way things to happen, that it seemed quite dull and stupid for life to go on in the common way." Like everyone who dreams, every night, Alice walks on the surface of a globe too large to allow her to discover that the journey through language and space may be the same journey. No matter which direction she takes, all exits from the "hall of locked doors" lead into the edenic garden of paradox, the key to which is language itself. Yet Alice can comfort herself with the thought that if the cake makes her larger she can reach the key she forgot on the table before shrinking to her present size, and if she grows smaller she could creep under the door—"So either way," she concludes, "I'll get into the garden, and I don't care which happens!"

For Carroll as well as for Alice, the garden is paradise because it does not exist in space and time, but only in the uncharted space of his fairy tale, "Once upon a time . . ." And for the rest of his audience, the tales mitigate the paradox of existence in a linear narrative in which like the Knave of Hearts, we are all condemned to death, *ab ovo* after all, long before the evidence has been heard.

Anne K. Mellor (essay date 1980)

SOURCE: "Fear and Trembling: From Lewis Carroll to Existentialism," in *English Romantic Irony*, Cambridge, Mass.: Harvard University Press, 1980, pp. 165-84.

[*In the following excerpt, Mellor addresses the philosophical implications of Alice's world, and compares and contrasts Carroll's "romantic irony" with Søren Kierkegaard's Existentialism.*]

[Like other romantic ironists] . . . , Lewis Carroll conceived the ontological universe as uncontrolled flux. But unlike the others, this Victorian don was frightened by this vision. Lewis Carroll shared his upper-class contemporaries' anxiety that change was change for the worse, not the better. The Reform Bill of 1832 had initiated a political leveling of English society; the Industrial Revolution had created a society whose highest priority was materialistic prosperity rather than spiritual growth and freedom; the new Higher Criticism of the Bible propounded by David Friedrich Strauss and Joseph Ernst Renan had undermined the fundamentalist Christian belief in the divinity of Christ; and Darwin's *Origin of Species* (1859) had argued that "progress" could be equated with a brutal warfare resulting in the survival of the fittest. Lewis Carroll responded to these changes with the strategies of roman-

tic irony. Eagerly, he tried to impose man-made systems onto this flux. At the same time, he forthrightly acknowledged the limitations of such systems as language, logic, and games. But unlike the romantic ironist who engages enthusiastically in a never-ending process of creation and de-creation, Lewis Carroll felt, and felt intensely, that one must commit oneself wholly to one's created systems. Giving up such heuristic systems, he believed, is tantamount to sacrificing both rational thought and moral behavior—and plunges one into bestial violence.

Personally, Charles Dodgson (Lewis Carroll) was a withdrawn, shy, obsessively neat man, a man who felt alienated from society in general, a man who apparently had very few close friends and no lovers, a man who was afraid of intense emotional relationships. His sense of his own inability to cope with the world—and of the necessity therefore to learn methods of controlling his environment—had probably been acutely intensified by his excruciating boyhood years at the Rugby School, where this stuttering, scholarly child was generally ostracized. Only at Oxford, where Dodgson could live a retired life as a confirmed bachelor and a mathematics don, did he feel comfortable. His closest friendships, as we know, were with prepubescent girls who could threaten him neither intellectually nor sexually.

Frightened by the shifting sands both of the sociopolitical world and of adult, passionate relationships, Dodgson tried desperately to deny the chaotic flow of life by transforming all human realities into a structured game, a game whose rules he alone understood and that he alone could win. Even as a child, Dodgson had relished creating complicated games for his sisters that are remarkable for their ruthlessness, as in the Railway Game in which "All passengers when upset are requested to lie still until picked up—as it is requisite that at least three trains should go over them, to entitle them to the attention of the doctor and assistants." As a mathematician, he delighted in constructing mathematical puzzles (*Pillow Problems*) which he alone could solve; and he spent years developing a symbolic logic which strictly divided all statements into real versus imaginary, and into assertions of existence versus assertions of nonexistence. By reducing the complexities of human interactions to a set of statements which could then be equated with grey and red checkers on a two-dimensional chart of circumscribed squares (what he called "the game of Logic"), Carroll could successfully force a rigidly closed and completely rational system upon the world. Dodgson/Carroll then taught these puzzles and logic-games in girls' schools. At such times, the introverted don lost his stutter and became eloquently and emotionally involved in logical arguments. Apparently, Dodgson channeled most of his repressed emotional and sexual energies into creating and then authoritatively imposing his logical or mathematical systems (games) upon his obedient female students. Significantly, in the published *Symbolic Logic,* Carroll explicitly refers to the Problem-poser as the "Inquisitor" and to the Problem-solver as the "Victim." Carroll's fierce desire to control his students' minds, by painful force if necessary, is revealed both in his metaphor and again in his refusal to guest-teach in any but girls' schools. He naturally preferred to educate young girls, who were, on the whole, more submissive, deferential, and easily manipulated—as well as more sexually appealing to Carroll—than young boys. As the Duchess tells Alice, one must "speak roughly to your little boy"—and *her* boy promptly turns into a pig.

Carroll's obsession with photography, a hobby to which he devoted thousands of hours between May 1856 and July 1880, again reveals his compulsion to force his own order upon the chaotic flux of time. Photography is an attempt to seize and fix a passing moment in a static, spatial image. Significantly, as Helmut Gernsheim comments, Carroll's real talent as a photographer lay in his sense of arrangement: he was a "master of composition" who "did not aim at characterisation, but at an attractive design." By forcing his models—generally either famous men or, more often, little girls—to stand still and pose while he photographed them, Carroll could capture and preserve the past (time would thus stand still, forever frozen on his collodion plate). And he could force the present moment into the shape he wished it to take for eternity. He preferred to photograph his young female subjects either in costume (and thus metamorphose them into the figures of his own imagination—see, for example, his photographs of Agnes Grace Weld as "Little Red Riding Hood" and of Xie Kitchin as "A Chinaman") or in the nude (and thus preserve for all time their innocent, unconscious sexuality, uncorrupted by mature female anatomy, desire, or experience). Art thus functions, for Carroll, to deny the passage of time, to deny flux, to deny chaos. (Appropriately, in order to persuade his very young models to remain absolutely still during the two-to-three-minute exposures of collodion-plate photography, Carroll would tell them stories, again using art to control the normal flux of motion in time. That this control was felt to be painful is documented both by his models' recorded resentment and by Carroll's reference to them as his "photographic victims.") The photographic image calculatedly selects a single arrangement of human experience, a single expression upon a child's face, and defines that image as the truth for all time. As Carroll's poem accompanying his photograph of Alice Murdoch insists, photography is an attempt to seize the glorious "celestial benizon" of her childish innocence and to preserve it forever, despite the ravages of the future, "those realms of love and hate, / . . . that darkness blank and drear."

Dodgson's lust for order extended to every aspect of his compulsively regulated life. As Michael Holquist tells us,

> when he had packages to be wrapped, he drew diagrams so precise that they showed to a fraction of an inch just where the knots should be tied; he kept congeries of thermometers in his apartments and never let the temperature rise above or fall below a specific point. He worked out a system for betting on horses which eliminated disorderly chance. He wrote the Director of Covent Garden telling him how to clear up the traffic jam which plagued the theatre; to the post office on how to make its regulations more efficient. And after having written all these letters (more than 98,000 before he died), he then made an abstract of each, and entered it into a register with notes and cross-references.

By transforming every aspect of his daily life into a rigidly ordered system or game, Carroll could gain the psychological security of living in a totally controlled world; in Elizabeth Sewell's phrase, he could play at being God. For in his own games, Carroll alone knew the rules; he alone determined the winner; he was all-powerful. Derek Hudson has traced Carroll's obsession with using the imagination to control a disorderly universe back to his father's equally egotistical and comically sadistic fantasies. Commissioned by his son to purchase an iron file, a screwdriver, and a ring, the Rev. Charles Dodgson wrote to the nine-year-old Carroll:

> . . . I will not forget your commission. As soon as I get to Leeds I shall scream out in the middle of the street, *Ironmongers, Ironmongers*. Six hundred men will rush out of their shops in a moment—fly, fly, in all directions—ring the bells, call the constables, set the Town on fire. I WILL have a file and a screwdriver, and a ring, and if they are not brought directly, in forty seconds, I will leave nothing but one small cat alive in the whole Town of Leeds, and I shall only leave that, because I am afraid I shall not have time to kill it. Then what a bawling and a tearing of hair there will be! Pigs and babies, camels and butterflies, rolling in the gutter together—old women rushing up the chimneys and cows after them—ducks hiding themselves in coffee-cups, and fat geese trying to squeeze themselves into pencil cases. At last the Mayor of Leeds will be found in a soup plate covered up with custard, and stuck full of almonds to make him look like a sponge cake that he may escape the dreadful destruction of the Town.

Carroll's most famous attempts to force a system of his own making upon the chaos of the universe are his two nonsense books, *Alice in Wonderland* and *Through the Looking-Glass*. Nonsense is of course a kind of game with its own rules, "a carefully ordered world, controlled and directed by reason, a construction subject to its own laws," in Elizabeth Sewell's definition. Wonderland, then, is a game played with words. In this book, the professional mathematician Charles Dodgson builds a closed system, not out of numbers, but out of words. It is a linguistic structure, which, although it denies or distorts customary vocabularies, grammar, syntax, and the usual order of events, nonetheless maintains an absolute control over the relation of order to disorder. Like all of Lewis Carroll's games, the game of Wonderland attempts to impose an overtly man-made, rational system upon a chaotic universe. In the process, Carroll draws attention both to the underlying disorder of the noumenal world and to the irrationality of other men's systems, most notably language itself. By undermining the logical and hence the moral authority of previous game-systems and hence destroying his readers' faith in the objective reality of their belief-systems, Lewis Carroll tries to construct a game—or nonsense—world in which he alone is the master.

The game of Wonderland is based on a rigorously logical and systematic reversal of normal human assumptions. Here Carroll, like Schlegel before him, conceives the universe in terms of a non-Aristotelian logic, in which p = not-p. But unlike Schlegel, Carroll's protagonist Alice—with Carroll himself—responds to this world of irrational becoming with more anxiety and fear than unmitigated wonder and delight. As Donald Rackin has argued [in "Alice's Journey to the End of Night," *PMLA* (1966)], the book originally entitled *Alice's Adventures under Ground* "embodies a comic horror-vision of the chaotic land beneath the man-made groundwork of Western thought and convention."

In the non-Aristotelian logic of Wonderland, p is not p. Alice has no permanent identity; she gets big or little at will or in accord with what she eats; and in the external world, things constantly metamorphose. Inanimate objects move of their own accord (a tea tray flies through the sky, a deck of cards plays croquet); animate objects function as inanimate objects (hedgehogs are used as croquet balls, flamingoes as mallets); and babies turn into pigs. Space and time, two a priori Kantian categories of phenomenological experience, are systematically distorted. Alice cannot maintain stable geographical relationships ("London is the capital of Paris, and Paris is the capital of Rome," she murmurs); places change unpredictably; and the characters inhabit a systematically displaced space (Pat, the White Rabbit's gardener, is "digging for apples"). Time is experienced not as duration or an orderly chronological sequence of events but as a naughty young person who has had to be "beaten" and subsequently "murdered" by the Mad Hatter.

Mathematical and social systems are turned upside down in Wonderland. Alice can't count to twenty be-

cause, as Alexander Taylor points out, she changes the scales of notation at differing intervals: "the scale of notation was increasing by three at each step and the product by only one." Social relationships defy conventional expectations. In Wonderland, animals rule over human beings (the White Rabbit orders Alice/ Mary Ann—all little girls look alike to a rabbit—to fetch his gloves) and fathers behave like children. Political systems based on a distinctly differentiated hierarchy of power and on earned rewards are replaced in Wonderland with a contradictory caucus-race in which everyone runs in circles and everyone must have prizes. The legal system is similarly inverted: Fury eats the mouse after a trial that has had neither judge nor jury, while at the Knave of Hearts's trial the sentence is pronounced before the verdict. And the moral codes that prevail, however tenuously, in Alice's English society are overturned. The sentimental notion that animals are loving and lovable is undone by the Darwinian Lobster Quadrille, while genuine feelings of compassion and love are reduced to mere sentimentality in the Mock Turtle's love song to "Beau—ootiful Soo—oop." The very concept of morality is rendered ludicrous by the Duchess's meaningless maxims: "Everything's got a moral, if only you can find it."

Most disturbing to Alice, however, is the fact that even rational thought processes are distorted in Wonderland. There are no logical connections between events. The law of causality becomes an absurdity in Alice's meditation: "'Maybe it's always pepper that makes people hot-tempered,' she went on, very much pleased at having found out a new kind of rule, 'and vinegar that makes them sour—and camomile that makes them bitter—and—and barley-sugar and such things that make children sweet-tempered'." Communication can take place in Wonderland without the use of objective signs: the Caterpillar responds to Alice's unspoken thoughts with extrasensory perception.

> Then it [the Caterpillar] got down off the mushroom, and crawled away into the grass, merely remarking, as it went, "One side will make you grow taller, and the other side will make you grow shorter."
>
> "One side of *what?* The other side of *what?*" thought Alice to herself.
>
> "Of the mushroom," said the Caterpillar, just as if she had asked it aloud; and in another moment it was out of sight.

In *Alice in Wonderland,* Carroll does more than create a systematically coherent nonsense world based on non-Aristotelian logic. He also demonstrates the illogicality of the most important game we play, the game of language. Carroll shows that both the grammatical structures and the lexical content of the English language are often irrational. He further denies that any necessary relationship exists between words and things; well before Ferdinand de Saussure, Carroll insisted upon the arbitrary motivation of words and upon the role of cultural tradition and agreed-upon convention in determining the *langue*. As he wrote in 1880 in an article for *The Theatre,* **"The Stage and the Spirit of Reverence,"**

> . . . no word has a meaning *inseparably* attached to it; a word means what the speaker intends by it [Saussure's *parole*], and what the hearer understands by it [Saussure's *langue*], and that is all.

> I meet a friend and say "Good morning!" Harmless words enough, one would think. Yet possibly, in some language he and I have never heard, these words may convey utterly horrid and loathsome ideas. But are *we* responsible for this? This thought may serve to lessen the horror of some of the language used by the lower classes, which, it is a comfort to remember, is often a mere collection of unmeaning *sounds,* so far as speaker and hearer are concerned.

And again, in the "Appendix, Addressed to Teachers" that concludes his *Symbolic Logic,* Carroll insists upon the arbitrary nature of word-meanings, particularly when used by individual language-speakers:

> . . . I maintain that any writer of a book is fully authorised in attaching any meaning he likes to any word or phrase he intends to use. If I find an author saying, at the beginning of his book, "Let it be understood that by the word 'black' I shall always mean 'white,' and that by the word 'white' I shall always mean 'black,'" I meekly accept his ruling, however injudicious I may think it.

Many of Carroll's wittiest jokes play on the irrationality of the English language. He exploits the confusions inherent in homonyms (the Mouse's tail/tale) and in the fact that a single word can have very different meanings (dry is the antonym both of wet and of exciting). His frequent use of puns and portmanteau words challenges the notion that one word can signify only one thing and draws attention to the ambiguity of the English language. He emphasizes the arbitrary nature of syntax: a change in word order can effect a change in meaning, since the converse of a statement does not necessarily share its truth value (as in Alice's famous and erroneous insistence that "I mean what I say" is the same as "I say what I mean". Moreover, syntax itself can be ambiguous, as in the Mouse's dry tale, where

> "Edwin and Morcar, the earls of Mercia and Northumbria, declared for him; and even Stigand, the patriotic archbishop of Canterbury, found it advisable—"

"Found *what?*" said the Duck.

"Found *it,*" the Mouse replied rather crossly; "of course you know what 'it' means."

The Duck's inability to determine what "it" means results from the syntactic ambiguity caused by his interruption (the subordinate clause to which "it" refers has not yet been uttered), as well as from the potentially confusing capacity of a pronoun to refer to a multiplicity of things. More often, Carroll's wordplay focuses on the disjunction between words and meanings, between the signifier and the signified. Language-speakers can use signifiers that have no meaning for them, as when Alice, in falling down the rabbit-hole, expects to arrive at the "Antipathies"; or when the Dodo tells Alice he can't "explain" or define a Caucus-race, he can only do it. Anticipating the logical positivists, Carroll asserts that questions that cannot be answered are meaningless: "Alice began to get rather sleepy, and went on saying to herself, in a dreamy sort of way, 'Do cats eat bats? Do cats eat bats?' and sometimes, 'Do bats eat cats?' for, you see, as she couldn't answer either question, it didn't much matter which way she put it."

Increasingly, in *Alice in Wonderland,* Carroll insists that there are no necessary connections between words and things-in-themselves. The traditional realist assumption that words "point at" things is thus drawn into question. In Wonderland, for instance, attributes can exist without a subject to which they refer: Alice sees "a grin without a cat." Labels, or signs, have no fixed relationship to the things they purportedly designate; they are "empty symbols." When Alice opens a jar labeled "orange marmalade," she finds nothing in it; when she tastes the contents of a bottle, which has no "poison" label on it, it almost destroys her by shrinking her down so far that she wonders nervously whether she might not be going out altogether, "like a candle." Furthermore, in Wonderland the sum of a subject's attributes do not necessarily constitute the thing itself. The pigeon who deduces from Alice's long neck that she must be a serpent makes the same error we make when we assume that an attribute defines a thing.

Finally, then, when Alice exchanges Wonderland for the above-ground world, she is only exchanging one nonsense-world for another. She is only replacing one language-game, the Queen of Hearts's "Off with her head," with another language-game, "You're nothing but a pack of cards." Carroll forces us to recognize that both Wonderland and our conventional "reality" are arbitrary game-systems created by the human imagination and imposed on other minds by mental will or physical force. Alice's language-game prevails at the end of the story only because she literally *grows bigger;* her will can therefore master the Queen's will and her arbitrary definitions of signs or *parole* can triumph.

But Carroll subtly insists upon the linguistic relativity of Alice's language-game even as he ends the tale with a comforting description of the future. Alice's sister's dream of present and future time is as much a narrative based on fantasy and unmotivated signs as the nonsense of Wonderland:

> So she sat on, with closed eyes, and half believed herself in Wonderland, though she knew she had but to open them again, and all would change to dull reality—the grass would be only rustling in the wind, and the pool rippling to the waving of the reeds—the rattling teacups would change to tinkling sheep-bells, and the Queen's shrill cries to the voice of the shepherd boy—and the sneeze of the baby, shriek of the Gryphon, and all the other queer noises, would change (she knew) to the confused clamour of the busy farm-yard—while the lowing of the cattle in the distance would take the place of the Mock Turtle's heavy sobs.

Alice's sister's definition of "dull reality" is as arbitrary and fictional as Carroll's description of Wonderland. Her description of the "real world" is a sentimental pastoral idyll culled from literary tradition ("tinkling sheep bells," "the voice of the shepherd boy," "the busy farm-yard," "the lowing of the cattle"). As such, it is as much a denial of the chaos of noumenal becoming as is Wonderland. She attempts to control the flux of future time with a narrative structure or language-game:

> Lastly, she pictured to herself how this same little sister of hers would, in the after-time, be herself a grown woman; and how she would keep, through all her riper years, the simple and loving heart of her childhood; and how she would gather about her other little children, and make *their* eyes bright and eager with many a strange tale, perhaps even with the dream of Wonderland of long ago; and how she would feel with all their simple sorrows, and find a pleasure in all their simple joys, remembering her own child-life, and the happy summer days.

But her narrative is as doomed to linguistic relativity as Carroll's own attempt to reshape the past into the arrangement he preferred. Despite his emphatic assertion that the tale of *Alice's Adventures under Ground* was composed "all in a golden afternoon" on July 4, 1862, we know from the British Meteorological Office that the weather was "cool and rather wet" in Oxford that day.

Alice in Wonderland thus embodies Carroll's recognition that the apparently well-ordered and meaningful reality we take for granted is not absolute and that all linguistic and moral systems are but arbitrary games whose authority rests solely upon tradition and convention. Carroll, of course, uses comedy to distance himself and his audience from the frightening implications of this ontological chaos. But his fear of living in such a disorderly world pokes its ugly head through his best comic defenses. Alice never knows who she is (is she Mabel? or a serpent?); she is frequently left alone in a hostile world (the Mouse swims away from her, while the Queen of Hearts wants to chop off her head); and she responds to the aggressive chaos of her environment with an equally violent aggression, sometimes directed at others (she kicks Bill the lizard out the chimney) and sometimes at herself (on several occasions, she almost kills herself, as when she drinks the "poison," holds the fan too long, and almost drowns in her own tears). Despite the charming wit of Carroll's nonsense, Alice's bland response to the violence and cruelty of the chaotic world she has experienced—to dismiss it as a "wonderful dream"—is a patently inadequate psychological and rhetorical response to the uncertainties and anxieties, the "scream, half of fright and half of anger," she has endured. The overt sentimentality and self-conscious "fictiveness" of Carroll's concluding fantasy of Alice's future only draws attention to his own inability to live comfortably with the illogical, chaotic universe that he discovered lying just under the linguistic and social games men call reality.

In *Through the Looking-Glass and What Alice Found There,* Carroll takes Alice directly into this noumenal realm. When Alice climbs through the looking-glass, she enters a world where things and relationships are mirror images of the normal world. She also enters a house of mirrors where signs or words only reflect or refer to each other. Here things are only words, words are things, and things behave as arbitrarily as words. In the Looking-Glass world, the connections between words and things are broken; and order and meaning necessarily dissolve.

The question that *Through the Looking-Glass* poses is no longer which game shall we play, but rather, what is reality? What does lie beneath the social conventions, the logical systems, and the linguistic structures that we perceive as reality? Carroll offers two possible answers to these questions. Beneath the phenomenological realm of structured experience may lie an ultimate harmony of things coexisting in a loving peace. When Alice enters the forest where things have no names, where no nouns are spoken and hence no divisions made between one thing and another, she and the fawn can unite in perfect friendship. "So they walked on together through the wood, Alice with her arms clasped lovingly round the soft neck of the Fawn." But this idyllic communion is abruptly destroyed by the return of names or linguistic signs: "they came out into another open field, and here the Fawn gave a sudden bound into the air, and shook itself free from Alice's arm. 'I'm a Fawn!' it cried out in a voice of delight. 'And, dear me! you're a human child!' A sudden look of alarm came into its beautiful brown eyes, and in another moment it had darted away at full speed." Not only do linguistic classifications break up this noumenal harmony, but Carroll seems not to believe it exists. He places this vision at the beginning of the book where it is overwhelmed by the nightmare vision that follows it and concludes the story.

For Carroll, like Schlegel, finally conceives of noumenal reality as pure chaos. But in contrast to Schlegel, Carroll sees this chaos as wholly self-destructive; it is a predatory jungle where "Nature, red in tooth and claw / With ravine, shriek'd." In *Through the Looking-Glass,* Carroll takes us deep into this violent chaos in an attempt to convince us that if we do *not* play his games we will be eaten up.

On first entering the Looking-Glass world, Alice finds a seemingly orderly world, a predictable mirror image of conventional reality. True, the clock has a face, but it is smiling—no danger there. And while the **"Jabberwocky"** poem has an unfamiliar vocabulary, it can be translated into English and it does obey normal syntax—Alice is sure at any rate that "somebody killed something." It is when Alice steps outside the house that life becomes difficult. Certain rules of reversal still pertain: to go forward, you must move backward; to stand still, you must run as fast as you can; and time moves backward (the White Queen screams first, and is pricked second). A more fundamental rule of the Looking-Glass world is that signs are completely motivated: words are things; phrases are real situations; poems are events. The trees "bark" with a "bough-wough;" the flowers are awake and talking because their beds are hard; and Alice sees the substantive "nobody" on the road. Alice's word-play, "I love my love with an H," becomes a phenomenological reality: the Haigha ("Hare") is hideous, eats ham sandwiches and hay, and lives on the hill. The people Alice meets are nursery-rhyme characters; their lives are determined by the narrative plots of their respective poems. Tweedledee and Tweedledum fight over a rattle and are frightened by a black crow, while the unicorn and the lion fight for the crown, eat plum-cake, and are drummed out of town. In this universe of motivated linguistic discourse, whatever words one invents become existing things—for example, Alice's "Bread-and-butter fly." But since these things are only words, *they* cannot invent words—the "weak tea with cream" they need to survive—and hence they die. As the Red Queen tells Alice, "when you've once said a thing, that fixes it, and you must take the consequences."

If words are things and linguistic structures are actual events, then what are things-in-themselves? In the nominalist universe of the Looking-Glass world, the answer is obvious: things without words or names are no-things, nonidentities, part of a constantly metamorphosing flux. Alice begins to experience the chaos upon which all man-made systems are so precariously constructed as soon as she begins to play her second game, the chessgame. To play two games simultaneously

(chess and looking-glass) is to be caught between two conflicting systems and thus forced to recognize the merely relative authority of each set of rules. At this point, logic begins to break down in the book and pure metamorphosis to prevail. Having jumped over the brook, Alice suddenly finds herself in a railway carriage without a ticket, with insects who "think in chorus"; equally suddenly and illogically, the carriage leaps into the air and Alice finds herself sitting quietly under a tree. Frightened by the crow that flies overhead during Tweedledee and Tweedledum's battle, Alice hides under a large tree and catches the shawl that flies by her. After a-dressing the White Queen in her shawl, Alice suddenly realizes that the Queen is a sheep and that she is in a shop. Asked to buy something, Alice notices that the shelves, although filled, are never static: "Things flow about so in here," she complains. The sheep's shop, the book's climactic image of noumenal reality, is in constant flux, never in shipshape order. No "thing" exists long enough in one shape to be named or identified; every thing is in a process of becoming, changing, and vanishing, even right through the ceiling. Alice's own identity becomes unstable: "Are you a child or a tee-totum?" demands the Sheep. Alice suddenly finds herself rowing through a sticky river, picking rushes, catching crabs; only to be back again in the shop buying an egg.

The egg is of course a person, Humpty Dumpty, who plays his own games with linguistic signs, forcing words to mean just what he chooses them to mean, neither more nor less. Humpty Dumpty is the auteur, a persona for Lewis Carroll himself, writing and translating **"Jabberwocky"**/nonsense. As an author and game-creator, Humpty Dumpty shows us one way to deal with a frightening chaos (and it is perhaps the only way that Carroll himself could imagine): to force signs to mean what you stipulate they mean, to impose a self-referential linguistic system upon a resisting chaos. And there's the rub: "The question is, which is to be master," as Humpty Dumpty himself acknowledges. For Humpty Dumpty is clearly *not* the master of his game. His arrogance leads only to a fall from which all the King's men cannot rescue him. For Humpty Dumpty, like all signs, is trapped in the linguistic system that alone assigns him significance and power. His attempts to assert control over that system fail ("But 'glory' doesn't mean 'a nice knock-down argument,'" Alice objected), for the *langue* is always more powerful than the *parole*. Moreover, his attempt to move from motivated to unmotivated signs only renders his own existence (as a completely motivated sign) arbitrary. Both linguistically, then, as a member of an established and self-enclosed system of signs (the nursery rhyme "Humpty Dumpty sat on a wall"), and ontologically, as a newly "arbitrarily motivated" signifier, Humpty Dumpty must cease to exist as a noumenal thing-in-itself; he must fall off his wall into chaos.

The last character Alice meets, the White Knight, also attempts to impose order on chaos, to invent practical ways of coping with a disorderly reality. But his attempts (to stop his hair from falling out by making it grow up a stick; to invent a pudding made of blotting-paper, gunpowder, and sealing wax) are manifestly futile. Alice leaves him still tumbling off his horse; while the White Knight leaves her with a song that denies any hope for a moral meaning or coherent rational pattern in life. The Knight's song is a vicious parody of Wordsworth's "Resolution and Independence." It ironically undercuts Wordsworth's romantic moral code, which Carroll sees as an overly naive faith in man's ability to endure hardships and old age with courage and generosity in an ultimately benevolent nature. More important, Carroll's parody denies the very existence of an absolute moral order. The White Knight's song reduces the old leech-gatherer to a blathering fool and all moral or religious systems to absurdity. The narrator achieves not a self-affirming "apocalypse by imagination" but merely a "design / To keep the Menai bridge from rust / By boiling it in wine." And the old man becomes not a heroic figure of solitary dignity and humanistic courage but a "mumbling crow" with a mouth "full of dough."

Immediately after Alice encounters this vision of moral codes as arbitrary and of noumenal reality as pure chaos, she wins the game and becomes queen; the pawn is now the most powerful piece on the chess-board. But Alice soon realizes that she still has no control over reality: the other queens arrange her dinner-party, the footman won't let her in to attend her own party, and most frightening of all, the mutton and pudding refuse to be eaten. Alice suddenly finds herself in the midst of a nightmarish world in which she is unaccountably rising into the air, the candles are growing up into the ceiling, and the bottles are becoming dinner-birds.

> At this moment she heard a hoarse laugh at her side, and turned to see what was the matter with the White Queen; but, instead of the Queen, there was the leg of mutton sitting in the chair. "Here I am!" cried a voice from the soup-tureen, and Alice turned again, just in time to see the Queen's broad good-natured face grinning at her for a moment over the edge of the tureen, before she disappeared into the soup.

In this world of total confusion, of aggressive chaos ("Already several of the guests were lying down in the dishes, and the soup-ladle was walking up the table towards Alice's chair, and beckoning to her impatiently to get out of its way"), words are no longer sufficient to establish order. Alice must act, and quickly. And, for Lewis Carroll, the only possible action left to Alice is an act of sudden, destructive violence. Alice pulls the cloth out from under the creature-dishes,

throwing them in a crashing heap upon the floor, and then turns "fiercely" upon the Red Queen in order to shake this now-diminutive doll-like creature into a harmless kitten. Alice, the innocent child, has apparently become an uncivilized savage who reacts to the inherent chaos of reality with a primitive violence. Carroll here implies that if we refuse to play games, to submit to the logical and linguistic systems that our human reason and imagination construct, we shall turn into vicious, brutal panthers, wholly possessed by the murderous impulses of our primal passions—those very emotions that terrified the repressed bachelor don.

"Which Dreamed It?" Alice certainly hopes that her frightening vision is her own dream. Much better that this nightmare be her own, that the Red King be a creation of her own mind, than that she be a figment of *his* imagination. But Alice can get no confirmation: the kitten refuses to answer her, just as earlier Tweedledee and Tweedledum refused to believe she was "real." And Carroll, too, refuses to answer; he ends the book with the open question, "Which do *you* think it was?" In a noumenally chaotic world, all signs and systems, all answers are arbitrary; hence all questions must remain open.

The concluding poem, "A boat, beneath a sunny sky," restates Carroll's view that everything we call reality (the entire phenomenal world) is only a dream, a construct of the fictionalizing and rationalizing mind:

> Ever drifting down the stream—
> Lingering in the golden gleam—
> Life, what is it but a dream?

Carroll thus leaves us with his private horror: a vision of a world without order, reason, or meaning, a world that he can endure only if he can transform it into a game of which he is the sole master.

Psychologically, Carroll needed to invent games that he alone could win in order to control his changing environment. He wanted to master time itself and thus be able to prevent Alice (and his other little girl friends) from growing up and leaving him. He therefore tried to build his own future into *Through the Looking Glass,* to triumph over the destructions of time by becoming the White Knight. Alice's response to the White Knight is Carroll's paradigm for his own impact upon his child-friends:

> Of all the strange things that Alice saw in her journey Through the Looking-Glass, this was the one that she always remembered most clearly. Years afterwards she could bring the whole scene back again, as if it had been only yesterday—the mild blue eyes and kindly smile of the Knight—the setting sun gleaming through his hair, and shining on his armour in a blaze of light that quite dazzled her— the horse quietly moving about, with the reins

hanging loose on his neck, cropping the grass at her feet—and the black shadows of the forest behind—all this she took in like a picture, as, with one hand shading her eyes, she leant against a tree, watching the strange pair, and listening, in a half-dream, to the melancholy music of the song.

Again, Carroll invokes a spatial image ("like a picture," like a photograph) in his desire to arrest time, to arrange the chaotic flux of becoming into a composition of which he is the central figure, a composition much admired and never forgotten by his child-love.

Carroll's personal attempt to control time extends beyond his own future to Alice's life as well. In the opening poem, "Child of the pure unclouded brow," he builds Alice's future into his dream. She will either die a virginal death or live to regret an unhappy marriage:

> Come, hearken then, ere voice of dread,
>   With bitter tidings laden,
> Shall summon to unwelcome bed,
>   A melancholy maiden!
> We are but older children, dear,
> Who fret to find our bedtime near.

The concluding metaphor (adults are children whose anxiety-provoking death is a "fretful" bedtime) encourages us to read Alice's own "unwelcome bed" on several levels. The "voice of dread" is literally the voice of Alice's nannie, summoning her away from the bed-time storytelling hour to sleep; but it is also the voice of death summoning a still virginal "melancholy maiden," as well as the voice of the dreaded lover / husband summoning his reluctant and still chaste bride.

Lewis Carroll's attempts to stop the flux of time and space by fixing them within a self-serving linguistic system failed on the personal level: his little girls always grew up and left him for fuller lives elsewhere. But his vivid vision of the chaos lying beneath our merely relative social and linguistic axioms—and of the anxiety and terror that such a romantic-ironic vision can invoke in a sexually repressed person and culture—remains an enduring witness to that point, philosophically and historically, where romantic irony gives way to existentialism.

In the same decade in which Carroll wrote his *Alice* books, the first of the great existentialist thinkers, Søren Kierkegaard, directly attacked the affirmation of becoming and an abudant chaos that is inherent in romantic irony. Kierkegaard's influential studies of irony argued that the romantic-ironic mode of consciousness is a condition of existential despair, from which man must turn with deliberate loathing and fear. As a young man, in rebellion against his bourgeois father and conventionally Christian society, Kierkegaard had himself experienced the exhilarating freedom of romantic irony or what he called the "aesthetical life." But by the time he published his doctoral dissertation, *The Concept of Irony*, in 1840, Kierkegaard had concluded that the psychology inherent in romantic irony could only produce an individual filled with anxiety, melancholy, boredom, and despair. In *Either/Or* (1843), Kierkegaard portrays the romantic ironist as A, the aesthete whose life is arbitrary and thus without purpose or historical actuality. As A himself acknowledges, he is a member of the Symparanekromenoi, the "fellowship of buried lives" or the living dead.

Why did Kierkegaard equate romantic irony with anxiety and despair? In *The Concept of Irony*, Kierkegaard distinguished between a positive or "Socratic" irony and a negative or "romantic" irony. Socratic irony is, in a phrase Kierkegaard borrowed from Hegel's *Aesthetics*, "infinite absolute negativity": "It is negativity because it only negates; it is infinite because it negates not this or that phenomenon [but all phenomena *qua* phenomena]; and it is absolute because it negates by virtue of a higher which is not . . . It is a divine madness which rages like Tamerlane and leaves not one stone standing in its wake." As the historical embodiment of this idea of "infinite absolute negativity," Socrates systematically denied the absolute truth of every object or concept that his contemporaries believed to exist, including the value of life itself. And he did so without recourse to a "higher" divine being or absolute law. He spoke only in the name of a "truth" which knows only that nothing can be known, that the phenomenon or external is never the essence or internal. Socrates' ironic questioning functioned positively, Kierkegaard argued, in freeing the mind from overly limited or false conceptions of the self or society and thus opening the way for new thought and action. But Socrates himself did not create anything new, unlike Plato whose mythologizing advanced the human conception of the divine Idea. Hence Kierkegaard concluded that Socrates, as the purely ironic subject, had become estranged from existence and lacked "historical actuality." From Kierkegaard's religious viewpoint, the self can be realized and enjoy a positive freedom only through a lived commitment to the phenomena of a particular time and place. Irony's pure freedom is therefore finally self-destructive: as Kierkegaard insisted, "Irony is free, to be sure, free from all the cares of actuality, but free from its joys as well, free from its blessings. For if it has nothing higher than itself, it may receive no blessings, for it is ever the lesser that is blessed of a greater." And because the ironic self can never become engaged in a concrete historical context, it can never act morally.

At this point, Kierkegaard shifted his attention to negative or romantic irony. The artistic ironist or aesthete who always lives at a distance from his own feelings and actions is completely destructive, both of his own selfhood and of his society. "Because the ironist poet-ically produces himself as well as his environment with the greatest possible poetic license, because he lives completely hypothetically and subjunctively, his life finally loses all continuity. With this he wholly lapses under the sway of his moods and feelings. His life is sheer emotion." And because this emotion is the pawn of external events, it is arbitrary and contradictory, wholly without permanence or meaning. Hence, Kierkegaard concluded, feeling itself finally has no "re-ality" for the aesthete, and "Boredom is the only con-tinuity the ironist has." As opposed to the Christian whose feelings grow out of and support an ongoing sense of identity and purpose, the romantic ironist can only undermine his own and others' possible spiritual development. When Kierkegaard commented on Friedrich Schlegel's *Lucinde,* he virulently denounced it as "a very obscene book," an "irreligious" book in which "the flesh negates the spirit" and the ego that has discovered its own freedom and constitutive au-thority finally arrives not "at a still higher aspect of mind but instead at sensuality, and consequently at its opposite."

Kierkegaard concluded his attack on romantic irony by insisting that such irony must be mastered. The reli-gious life must include irony, for irony "limits, renders finite, defines, and thereby yields truth, actuality, and content; it chastens and punishes and thereby imparts stability, character and consistency." But irony must not be permitted to negate *all* moments: "on the con-trary, the content of life must become a true and mean-ingful moment in the higher actuality whose fullness the soul desires." Thus becoming must finally yield to being: "true actuality becomes what it is, whereas the actuality of romanticism merely becomes." Similarly, "faith becomes what it is; it is not an eternal struggle but a victory which struggles still. In faith the higher actuality of spirit is not merely becoming [*vordende*], but present while yet becoming [*vorder*]."

Kierkegaard's critical portrait of the romantic ironist as the aesthete A in *Either/Or* became the literary pro-totype of existentialist man living in an absurd uni-verse. Since A denies all necessary connections among past, present, and future, he lives wholly for the imme-diate moment. He rejects all commitments, all social engagements such as marriage, friendship, work. He is free to do as he likes, but since he ironically reflects upon his desire even as he experiences it, he can never lose himself in pleasure. His present life is "empty," "*idem per idem,*" and only the forever-lost past of his youth seems desirable. Hence he is melancholic and bored. As A asserts in one of his Diapsalmata or Schlegelian fragments, "I do not care for anything. I do not care to ride, for the exercise is too violent. I do not care to walk, walking is too strenuous. I do not care to lie down, for I should either have to remain lying, and I do not care to do that, or I should have to

get up again, and I do not care to do that either. *Summa summarum:* I do not care at all." And because all action in a chaotic, arbitrary world is meaningless, one can only "regret" everthing that one does. A's "ecstat-ic lecture" can equate intense passion only with regret: "If you marry, you will regret it; if you do not marry, you will also regret it; if you marry or do not marry, you will regret both; whether you marry or do not marry, you will regret both." Nameless (because he possesses no individuality), his papers discovered and arranged "by chance," the victim of contradictory moods, A is the seducer who can never be satisfied with a merely actual object, who must constantly "change fields" according to his Rotation Method, who in his melancholy defines himself as The Unhappiest Man. From the viewpoints of the ethical man (B or Judge William) or the religious man (the Priest of Jutland whose "Edification" concludes *Either/Or*), A can know only boredom and dread. Kierkegaard, through B and the Priest, here rejects the privileging of freedom over belief that is inherent in romantic irony. Instead these spokesmen argue that in a chaotic world, in order to escape despair, one must *choose*. One must totally commit oneself, without irony, to a man-made structure or system—to lasting relationships (such as marriage), contractual obligations, a stable personal identity. But this sense of self, as we are told by the Priest, who corrects B's overly sentimental conception of marriage as completely fulfilling, must be founded on a conviction of spiritual inadequacy: "as against God we are always in the wrong." For Kierkegaard, the self-restraint of romantic irony must become a specifically religious dread, a deep sense of guilt and personal inadequacy. This is the redemptive fear and trembling before God that Kierkegaard described in his later theological, "upbuilding" treatises. Such a religious experience is the result of an emotional com-mitment to faith in an arbitrary, absurd universe; and only such a leap of faith can give value to human existence.

While not all existentialist philosophers would endorse Kierkegaard's demand that the self make a "leap of faith" into a Christian being, they do agree that the self must, through the passing of time and the ongoing experience of its own phenomenological existence, move toward an ever fuller realization of its own being (what Heidegger called *Dasein,* what Jaspers called *Existenz,* what Sartre called *l'être pour soi*). Unlike Friedrich Schlegel, who celebrated an always chang-ing, always becoming self, these thinkers argue that an authentic self, an "essence," comes into *being* as a result of willed choices and commitments in a chaotic, absurd world: "Existence precedes essence." The ro-mantic-ironic self that "hovers" midway between self-creation and self-destruction comes to seem to these existentialist thinkers to be a self without reality. Its ontological lack of being, they argue, is psychological-ly experienced as free-floating anxiety or even, as Sartre and Heidegger suggest, as overwhelming nausea or intense deprivation. Thus the existentialists, like the philosophers who preceded Schlegel, ultimately value being over becoming, even though they place far greater emphasis on the process by which the self gains its being.

By the end of the nineteenth century, then, Schlegel's concept of a self always becoming and always free, hovering exultantly over a chaotically abundant *Fülle,* had given way to a self obsessed with its lack of permanence and continuity, a self that experiences such pure freedom as anxiety, dread, or despair. At the risk of oversimplification, we might say that existentialism is the negative view of romantic irony. Existentialism and romantic irony share an ontological vision of the universe as chaotic and incomprehensible. But whereas the romantic ironist embraces this becoming as a merrily multiplying life-process, the existentialist sees it as absurd or benignly indifferent, without inherent meaning for man. In the face of such chaos, the romantic ironist enthusiastically creates and decreates himself and his myths. But the existentialist engages in this same process with anxiety and even fear. Disturbed by the relativity of his self and his systems, he struggles for some sort of permanence or authentic existence in an arbitrary world, either through an irrational leap of faith or through sustained personal and political commitments. For the existentialists, such heuristic behavior is usually accompanied by *angst* (since man can choose not to complete his projects as easily as he can choose to complete them). Thus romantic irony and existentialism confront the same incomprehensible universe, but with very different emotional responses: the romantic ironist delights in its creative possibilities, while the existentialist anxiously seeks to establish at least one still point in the turning world, namely his own identity or essence.

Margaret Boe Birns (essay date 1984)

SOURCE: "Solving the Mad Hatter's Riddle," in *The Massachusetts Review,* Vol. XXV, No. 3, Autumn, 1984, pp. 457-68.

[*In the essay below, Birns explores the theme of eating and cannibalism in* Alice.]

Even a cursory glance at Lewis Carroll's *Alice's Adventures in Wonderland* will reveal one of its obsessive themes, namely, eating, or more darkly, cannibalism. Most of the creatures in Wonderland are relentless carnivores, and they eat creatures who, save for some outer physical differences, are very like themselves, united, in fact, by a common "humanity." The very first poem found in the text establishes the motif of eating and being eaten:

> How doth the little crocodile
>   Improve his shining tail,
> And pour the waters of the Nile
>   On every golden scale!
>
> How cheerfully he seems to grin
>   How neatly spreads his claws,
> And welcomes little fishes in,
>   With gently smiling jaws!

Later on, the eaten object is not simply "eaten alive," eaten, that is, when it is still sentient, but is endowed with affective and intellectual attributes—a "soul" that resembles that of the creature eating it. For instance, in *Through The Looking Glass,* the Walrus and the Carpenter, after talking of many things with their walking companions, the Oysters, decide the time has come to dine:

> 'Now if you're ready, Oysters dear,
>   We can begin to feed.'
> 'But not on us!' the Oysters cried,
>   Turning a little blue.
> 'After such kindness, that would be
>   A dismal thing to do!'

Earlier, after the "Lobster Quadrille" in which various sea creatures are flung, or rather appear to fling themselves, into the maws of waiting sharks, and directly before the Mock Turtle sings his sentimentally existential song "Turtle Soup," Alice herself recites the following poem:

> I passed by his garden, and marked, with one
>   eye,
> How the Owl and the Panther were sharing a
>   pie:
> The Panther took pie-crust, and gravy, and
>   meat,
> While the Owl had the dish as its share of the
>   treat.
> When the pie was all finished, the Owl, as a
>   boon,
> Was kindly permitted to pocket the spoon:
> While the Panther received knife and fork
>   with a growl,
> And concluded the banquet by—"

This is a poem Carroll allows the reader the fun of completing, as well as the *frisson* that comes with the realization that in completing the poem we are also allowing the Panther to conclude his banquet by eating the Owl. This darker tone comprises the emotional core, the "heart" of *Alice,* where our most unadmitted needs can be gratified. As Elizabeth Sewell in her useful study *The Field of Nonsense* has shown us, Carroll's nonsense has at its core something unbalanced and even humorless. Not only does his "ludic discourse" subvert the reader's logocentric expectations, it threatens him viscerally with imagery that invites us to experience heretofore inhibited oral fantasies. As we explore the text of *Alice* and build to a solution of the Hatter's riddle, we will see that Wonderland invites the reader to participate in the same compelling regressions found not only in its creatures, but in Alice herself. For Alice is not all good form and superior manners, although that side of her that acts as a defense against the often intensely oral aggressions of Wonderland is generally celebrated as a hallmark of the ideal British character. Although she shows the best "good form" in the novel, Alice can also let down her hair by not only happily reciting the cannibalistic poem about the owl and the panther, but by suggesting a game to her nanny:

> Nurse! Do let's pretend that I'm a hungry hyena
> and you're a bone!

In identifying with Alice, the reader may be astonished to find himself slipping enjoyably into a similar level of primitive oral fantasies. While Nurse does not take kindly to Alice's suggestion that she become the object of her eating wishes, there are in Wonderland creatures whose identity is completely defined by their function as food. There are creatures that are granted only that much autonomy necessary to express a desire to be eaten ("Eat Me!") or drunk ("Drink Me!"). There is in Wonderland a pudding that insists upon a formal introduction before it will allow itself to be consumed, and an even more autonomous clam, which though caught and cooked, will not permit itself to be eaten at all:

> For it holds it like glue—
> Holds lid to the dish, while it lies in the middle.

Food in these examples is given an animating spirit, suggesting the survival of a soul in what one must eat. Books, food and people are interchangeable. For instance, in the last chapter of *Through The Looking Glass* Alice

> . . . heard a hoarse laugh at her side, and turned to see what was the matter with the White Queen; but, instead of the Queen, there was the leg of mutton sitting in the chair. "Here I am!" cried a voice from the soup-tureen, and Alice turned again, just in time to see the Queen's broad good-natured face grinning at her for a moment over the edge of the tureen, before she disappeared into the soup.

Just as food can become human, human beings can become food. But in spite of these fantasies, which suggest an awareness that the eaten object is, like oneself, "human," all the creatures of Wonderland suffer little diminution of appetite, and some eat quite heartily:

> "I like the walrus best," said Alice: "because he was a little sorry for the poor oysters."

"He ate more than the carpenter, though," said Tweedledee. "You see he held his handkerchief in front, so that the Carpenter couldn't count how many he took: contrariwise."

"That was mean!" Alice said indignantly. "Then I like the Carpenter best—if he didn't eat so many as the Walrus."

"But he ate as many as he could get," said Tweedledee.

These fantasies of voracious and unscrupulous appetite may, in part, reflect the influence of Charles Darwin's theories. Darwin's ideas about the laws of survival can supply a plausible intellectual subtext for the ruthless way in which the creatures of Wonderland pounce on each other, and may account as well for their general contentiousness. The issues Carroll is raising through his fantasies have an emotional and not simply theoretical impact, however, particularly when the biological imperatives of Carroll's creatures are complicated by the great pleasure they take in eating their fellow creatures. Their pleasure becomes part of the horror of their existential situation, creating that self-contradiction that comes with the mixing of opposites, a phenomenon knit into the texture of Alice's adventures. Paradox is the essence of Wonderland. For instance, the creatures of Wonderland are both human and animal. They are also both adult and childlike, at times seeming to satirize the rigid and authoritarian personality of the Victorian parent, at other times capering like incorrigible children. The story itself pulls in opposite directions—Alice goes down the rabbit hole into the wonder world of childhood, not wishing to grow up into a world where she will have to endure books "without pictures or conversations," and yet she is destined to outgrow Wonderland, master its irrationality and assume the authority of a sensible adult, as she does when she announces that the Red Queen and her retinue are "nothing but a pack of cards." Alice herself is made up of opposites, since she functions in Wonderland both as an adult and as a child, at times the prim schoolmistress, at other times the chastened schoolgirl.

Similarly, ravens and writing desks, which seem to have nothing in common and which will be revealed to be in fact opposites, are united in the Mad Hatter's Riddle, and by a hidden principle Alice is asked to discern. Let us briefly return to Carroll's contentious tea party, where Alice is about to undergo one of her many transformations from prim schoolmistress to chastened schoolgirl:

> "You should learn not to make personal remarks," Alice said with some severity. "It's very rude."

> The Hatter opened his eyes very wide on hearing this; but all he *said* was "Why is a raven like a writing desk?"

"Come, we shall have some fun now!" thought Alice. "I'm glad they've begun asking riddles—I believe I can guess that," she added aloud.

Carroll himself claimed the riddle had no answer at all, but this has not prevented numerous attempts to solve it. Francis Huxley's *The Raven and The Writing Desk* includes some of the cleverer solutions, having to do with notes, bills, tales and Edgar Allan Poe. But none of these answers, while technically correct, are emotionally satisfying. What unites the raven and the writing desk must fit into the overall emotional and intellectual pattern Carroll has carefully established through his other rhymes and riddles; otherwise, clever as the solution may be, it will not give us that sense of aesthetic rightness, or "fit" necessary to make it fall so naturally into the narrative as to seem as if it had always been there. But before supplying my answer to the Hatter's riddle, let us remind ourselves that this riddle is posed at a tea party, an event which is normally comprised not only of tea, but of other delectable foodstuffs. It is at the tea party that Alice poses a question whose subject haunts many of the rhymes found in the narrative. When the Dormouse begins his story of the three little girls who lived at the bottom of a well, Alice interrupts, asking "What did they live on?" Carroll goes on to note that Alice always took a great interest in questions of eating and drinking, and when she is told by the Dormouse that the little girls lived only on treacle and were as a result very ill indeed, we are reminded by inference of the kinds of foods we must in fact eat in order to live well. Beneath the solution to the riddle is not simply the material in the tea party chapter, however, but as well many of the other rhymes and riddles that refer to the eating habits of the creatures of Wonderland. With all this in mind, we are ready for a solution to the riddle. But although Alice, with characteristic self-assurance, believes she can solve the riddle, the answer is better left to one of the denizens of Wonderland, and even more appropriately to one of the members of the tea party. Either the bossy Hatter or the put-upon Dormouse will do, depending upon whether the riddle's answer is to be told from the point of view of an aggressor or a victim. My own choice is the Hatter, who, soon after posing the riddle, hints at my answer when he says, "Why, you might as well say that 'I see what I eat' is the same thing as 'I eat what I see!'" Let us imagine that it is the Hatter, then, who reminds Alice of certain hidden but home truths in the following solution to the riddle: "A raven eats worms; a writing desk is worm-eaten."

It is this solution that touches on the large themes that inform the seemingly trivial and nonsensical surface of the Alice books. The image of the raven eating the worm recapitulates the theme of voracious or "ravenous" appetite that is a major psychological and existential theme in *Alice.* The raven's "sadistic oral incorporation" of the worm also reminds us of the story's

Darwinian theme of life feeding on life, the life-force of the raven necessarily contingent on the life-force of the worm. The raven is another example of the predatory, amoral, natural world of Wonderland, seemingly removed from the culture and civilization objectified in the writing desk. We can now perceive that the raven and the writing desk are not simply absurdly juxtaposed, but are logical opposites, representing, respectively, the age-old conflict between nature and culture, instinct and reason. But the writing desk, like the raven, also has a relationship with the worm; here, the worm turns, and instead of being food for others, feeds on the writing desk. As the raven's ingestion of the worm represents the fact of life, the law of survival, so the image of the woodworm infesting the writing desk suggests the fact of mortality. Something as seemingly solid and as impervious to time as a writing table is being devoured slowly, is being eaten away. To some degree a worm-eaten casket or corpse is suggested: the worm-eaten desk points to what E. M. Forster in *Passage to India* has called the "undying worm," an image of the inevitability and reality of death, even as the worm's life-force is affirmed in its ability not only to be eaten, but to eat others. This particular solution to The Mad Hatter's Riddle, then, mixes life and death in such a way as to render them interdependent rather than opposing; even more, the solution supplies that aforementioned *frisson* that gives the Alice narrative its special edge, that dark quality that can terrify as many children as it enchants, and that has made Alice one of the patron saints of the modernist movement. The riddle thus answered becomes a reverberation of that endless, circular dance of life and death, of death-in-life and life-in-death, that is one of the deep subjects of the *Alice* books. In the loss of a Divine Plan or Purpose, in the wake of Darwinism, life is reframed as a giant "lobster quadrille," in which one's own life and death are part of nature's larger life-and-death cycle, in which one is both walrus and oyster, both raven and worm, both worm and writing desk.

Like Forster's undying worm, which was both phallic and phanatotic, Carroll's worm both gives life and takes life away. But although in this solution to the riddle the worm serves the raven's life-principle, the second half of the solution seals the fate of both raven and writing desk (and its Maker, Man). The solution of the riddle suggests that nature and its life-forces bring not only individual death, but transcend the laws and values of civilization, imaged here as the writing desk. It is that lack of purpose beyond a Nature red in tooth (or beak) and claw—a lack of "higher" purpose—that is responsible for the anarchic circularity of not only the Mad Tea Party but of such episodes as the Caucus Race. We can see now that the hidden principle that unites both raven and writing desk is the law of nature. Both the writing desk and the raven are subject to the rule of appetite, of an eat-or-be-eaten ethos.

The eaten and eating worm I have introduced into the Mad Hatter's riddle fits well into a narrative that is literally riddled with anxiety. The image of the raven eating the worm reiterates the anxiety about eating that appears consistently in the *Alice* books, an anxiety that includes death as a form of eating, eating as a form of death. This anxiety may be interpreted as the product of Wonderland's general regression to what Erich Neumann, in his *The Origins and History of Consciousness,* would call a primitive "maternal uroboros." "On this level," Neumann points out, "which is pregenital because sex is not yet operative and the polar tension of the sexes is still in abeyance, there is only a stronger that eats and a weaker that is eaten." In this early phase of human consciousness, hunger is experienced as the prime mover of mankind, and the laws of the alimentary canal reign supreme. Since all life comes under the archetype of being swallowed and eaten, death in this stage of consciousness is also experienced as a devourer. Such fantasies, concerning a stronger who eats and a *weaker* that is eaten, permeates *Alice.*

While the creatures of Wonderland swim amorally in what Neumann called a "swamp" stage of consciousness, where every creature devours every other, Alice herself does not. At times, indeed, Alice comes close to a feeling of revulsion, as in *Through The Looking Glass*'s final banquet:

> "Meanwhile, we'll drink your health—Queen Alice's health!" she screamed at the top of her voice, and all the guests began drinking it directly, and very queerly they managed it: some of them put their glasses upon their heads like extinguishers, and drank all that trickled down their faces—others upset the decanters, and drank the wine as it ran off the edges of the table—and three of them (who looked like kangaroos) scrambled into the dish of roast mutton, and began eagerly lapping up the gravy, "just like pigs in a trough!" thought Alice.

The overall tone of this passage communicates a sense of pleasure-in-horror or horror-in-pleasure, in the paradoxical way discussed earlier, and as such helps raise the level of anxiety. Alice herself, however, is less ambivalent and more moralistic when observing the ravenous guests, who seem to be reverting to a Hobbesian state of nature. Alice's attitude can, perhaps, be traced back to Carroll's own abstemious, or even anorexic behavior. Carroll, like many anorexics, seemed to wish to be above the state of worm or raven, preferring instead the more ethereal identity of metaphorical "writing desk." Writing desks, of course, don't eat, although they are not completely "above" nature, since like God's creatures they can, significantly, be worm-eaten. Alice's own prim nature has often been compared to Carroll's, and there are those who feel that Lewis Carroll and his Alice represent one of the strongest examples of a psychological alliance between author and character to be found in literature.

At this point it is possible to bring forward another solution to the Hatter's riddle, one that points not so much toward the text, calling attention to certain important themes in the narrative, but toward a solution that would refer to Carroll himself. Before supplying this second solution, let us remind ourselves that Alice has just admonished the Hatter about his rude remarks. The Hatter, by way of rejoinder, comes back with the riddle. The riddle, as a response to Alice's charge of rudeness, suggests the following solution: "A writing desk and a raven both make rude remarks."

A raven makes rude noises through his caws and cackles; a writing desk makes rude remarks through the medium of the author. In this solution to the riddle, the writing desk, of course, stands metonymically for the writer. The rude remarks of the Hatter and the March Hare are, therefore, made by the writer, who is in this aspect like a raven in his rudeness. The creatures, the riddle hints, are the products of Carroll's own writing desk, which is really making the rude remarks for which Alice has chastised the Mad Hatter. In this way, the Hatter is shifting the blame to his maker, the writer, or writing desk. Writers will make rude remarks, the Hatter reminds Alice. The raven is not only like a writing desk, but, more darkly, the writing desk is like a rude raven.

In twinning the writing desk and the raven, Carroll is up to his old trick of indicating through the joining of seeming opposites a hidden identity. Mild and intellectual, the writing desk, or writer, is twinned with a bird of evil omen, a bird with habits that are not very nice, are in fact rude and predatory. Carroll himself, giving toys to little girls on the beach, taking pictures of them, entertaining them with delightful tales, seemed an avuncular writing desk. The twinning of the raven with the writer, however, points to less altruistic and more emotionally ravenous aspects to Carroll's behavior, and his "tales" for us are tailed with appetites more carnal in origin. In this riddle Carroll's splitting of himself into raven and writing desk, and then twinning the two, indicates a covert confession on Carroll's part that he may have possessed aspects of the Victorian dissociated personality. It is this personality type that gave rise to a multitude of nineteenth century novels featuring hypocrites and split personalities, such as that of John Jasper in *The Mystery of Edwin Drood* or of Dr. Jekyll in *Dr. Jekyll and Mr. Hyde.* One might even say that modern psychoanalysis was created to deal with dissociations such as those symbolized here by the riddle of the raven and the writing desk.

The answer that solves our riddle with rude remarks is not so very far from the more resonant themes evoked through the introduction of a worm into the riddle.

Both solutions remind Alice of the existence of a ruder, lower self, a self that Carroll is suggesting may have more powers over the idealistic higher self of Victorians than they cared to admit. Throughout her stay in Wonderland, Alice is reminded by other creatures that she is not "above" her lower self. She is often informed that she, too, is a creature, or not better than a creature—and therefore not only prone to appetite, but also vulnerable to the appetites of others.

To be a victim of others' voracity is perhaps the ultimate insult in a Wonderland where insult and incivility are the rule. The breakdown in civility in Wonderland, a place where rude, powerful figures can ride roughshod over the autonomy of others, is mirrored, or even troped, in the eating behavior of the creatures, whose appetites constantly victimize other creatures. Often, Carroll will present the matter from the victim's point of view, as in the self-pitying lament of the Mock Turtle, or in the complaint of the feistier pudding, out of which Alice has just cut a slice:

> "What impertinence!" said the Pudding. "I wonder how you'd like it, if I were to cut a slice out of you, you creature!"

The Pudding not only reminds Alice that she, too, is a creature, subject to all the laws of creaturedom, but also is quick to characterize Alice's behavior as rude. Since Alice must eat, and must slice the pudding in order to eat it, Carroll seems to be suggesting that life itself is extremely rude.

At this point, in fact, let us go back to Alice's admonitory words to The Mad Hatter at his Tea Party:

> "You should learn not to make personal remarks," Alice said with some severity, "It's very rude."

To which the Hatter replies, his eyes opening very wide in a familiar signal that, especially in genteel English circles, indicates that somehow one has gone too far: "Why is a raven like a writing desk?" If he had gone on to supply Alice with either of our solutions, she would have seen that he was, indirectly, responding to her charge of rudeness. While his riddle nonsensically deflects Alice's task-taking, our first solution, which unites the raven and the writing desk through the introduction of a worm, comes right back to the themes Carroll has been exploring throughout the narrative. A raven eats worms, a writing desk is worm-eaten. When life itself, with its worms and ravens, is so very rude, what can the manners of a Hatter matter? Far from being particular to the Hatter's tea party, incivility is actually what makes the world go round. While the Hatter is breaking Alice's rules of etiquette, he is observing the laws of nature. Rudeness is so much a law of life in Wonderland, that, as our second solution to the Hatter's riddle suggests, writers of rid-

dles can be rude as ravens, if they choose. The Hatter is telling us that he, the riddler, or riddle-writer (at his writing desk) is not other than a rude raven, but is, in fact, *none* other than a rude raven. His widened eyes tell us, furthermore, that Alice herself has been a bit of a raven herself in her admonishing of her host, breaking the laws of civility she is asking him to observe.

Similarly, the Pudding's reaction to Alice's quite natural, creaturely attempt to eat it reminds Alice that she has in fact "rudely" failed to respect the Pudding's right to autonomy, to selfhood, to existence itself. In being of necessity bound to the laws of nature, she has broken the rules of civility, which puts her in rather a double-bind. The Pudding's separate identity must clearly be rudely ignored and discounted by Alice if she is to eat well. Many of the creatures in Wonderland engage in a struggle, often vainly, for their autonomy. Characters such as the Pepper Duchess and the Red Queen crush independence by psychologically devouring those around them, especially those they perceive as oppositional "others." Other creatures are eaten alive in a more literal manner—although these episodes often suggest metaphors of sadistic domination, in which the autonomy and integrity of the eaten object is denied or disallowed.

Food in Wonderland is like oneself in its creatureliness, but it is clearly something other than oneself as well. A differentiating process takes place when creatures eat creatures. It is, in fact, Alice's even more advanced differentiation of herself from the world of the creatures around her which will enable her to grow up and out of this underground society altogether, and, not incidentally, keep her from being (quite rudely) beheaded by the punitive Red Queen. Alice literally and figuratively outgrows the creatures of Wonderland; her differentiation from them and sense of power over them saves her from being their victim. Alice's rational faculties, combined with her self-control, transcend the more primary, impulsive underground world with its ruthless principle of eat-or-be-eaten, providing her adventures with a happy ending. Alice returns to terra firma, regaining consciousness just in time to run along to tea in her normal, well-run household. It is a measure of Carroll's genius, however, that he leaves us with the strong conviction that the more authentic reality does not reside in Alice's placid life above ground, but in the far more formidable and terrifying dreamworld of ravenous worms, worm-eaten writing desks, dark birds of prey.

William A. Madden (essay date 1986)

SOURCE: "Framing the *Alices*," in *PMLA*, Vol. 101, No. 3, May, 1986, pp. 362-73.

[*In the following essay, Madden addresses the genesis and function of the three poems that "frame" Alice's*

Adventures in Wonderland *and* Through the Looking-Glass.]

Over the past thirty years Lewis Carroll studies have both altered and generally enhanced the reputation of Carroll's two *Alices*. Yet from early on in this reevaluation process one feature of these famous stories has posed a persistent critical problem. I refer to the three poems, one prefacing each of the *Alice* books and the third concluding *Looking-Glass,* that, together with the prose ending of *Wonderland,* frame the central tales. The problem is raised in acute form by Peter Coveney in his influential study of the figure of the child in nineteenth-century English literature: praising the central *Alice* dream tales as triumphs of "astringent and intelligent art," he detects in this frame material evidence of what he describes as "almost the case-book maladjusted neurotic." Subsequent critics who have mentioned this feature of the *Alices* have for the most part been similarly dismissive, implying, at least, that the *Alice* frames are best ignored in discussions of the masterpieces they enclose.

The issue has important implications. For one thing, the reputed failure of the frame poems, as I will call them, has sometimes been used as evidence that Carroll's genius was psychologically crippled. Given Carroll's eccentricities, biographical speculation postulating a pathological Dodgson/Carroll personality split may seem a plausible explanation for the apparent erratic working of his acknowledged genius. But the entanglement of an essentially literary question in a nonliterary preoccupation with Carroll's private habits and mental health confuses an issue that needs to be dealt with on literary grounds. While several modern critics have praised the *Alice* frame poems, no one has advanced an extended analysis to support either a favorable or an unfavorable reading, and until the poems' literary status is clarified our estimate of the aesthetic integrity of the *Alices* and our understanding of the books must remain in doubt.

It will be useful at the outset to call attention to a feature of the *Alice* frame poems that helps explain the negative response of modern readers. The three poems are devoid of qualities that the educated reader has come to expect in lyric poetry, qualities summarized by one literary historian as "colloquialism of style and rhythm, realistic particularity, toughness of sensibility, the complex and often dissonant expression of tension and conflict, the resources of irony, ambiguity, paradox, and wit." The alteration in taste that has led us to value such characteristics was already evident in the work of Carroll's contemporaries Browning and Hopkins, indeed in Carroll's own parodic verses in the *Alices,* but not at all in the frame poems, where these qualities are conspicuous by their absence.

These poems are characterized, rather, by the conventional diction, metrics, and syntax of the main English poetic tradition—revitalized early in the century by Wordsworth—which still shaped the poetic style of those Victorians whose poetry Carroll most admired: Keble, Tennyson, and the Rossettis. The idea of poetry upheld by this tradition—"how it should sound ('beautiful'), what it should utter ('wisdom')"—was one that Carroll unquestionably shared. Generically, too, the *Alice* frame poems conform to conventions established early in the century. The prefatory poem to *Wonderland,* for example, with its localized setting, feelings originating in a specific event, and a presupposed listener, has affinities with a poem like *Tintern Abbey* and, in its evocation of a dream mood, with the Coleridgean "mystery" poem, whereby "the spellbound reader sees visions and hears music which float in from a magic realm." Compared with such prototypes, or with most twentieth-century English or American lyrics, the *Alice* frame poems seem bland indeed—competent minor poems at best and, at worst, symptoms of an exhausted tradition self-indulgently exploited.

It is necessary to concede the surface tameness of the poems in order to avoid defending them on the wrong grounds. I propose an alternative reading that I believe vindicates Carroll's inclusion of them as an integral part of the *Alices*. It is not mere paradox to assert that their conventionality provides an interpretive clue. Modern readers who respond negatively do so, I would argue, because they either fail to recognize the conventions at work in the poems or, recognizing them, mistake Carroll's purpose in adopting them. Writing in a late Victorian climate for a special audience, Carroll adopted a form and idiom familiar to that audience, through parody in the dream tales but directly in the frame poems. While the parodies have been increasingly admired, his direct use of conventions in the frame material has been met in recent years with either indifference or dismay. Since we know that Carroll was a knowledgeable and careful craftsman, it is not unreasonable to assume that he employed a familiar lyric form and idiom for a particular purpose.

He chose the "Tennysonian" idiom, I would suggest, because his age regarded it as proper to "serious" poetry, and he thereby signaled to his audience the serious purpose underlying his books of "nonsense." His choice of a familiar form of the Romantic lyric likewise had a specific purpose: not to create self-standing lyrics but to frame a substantial narrative. In this respect the relevant prototype for the *Alice* frame poems would be the lyric frame in a poem like "The Eve of St. Agnes" or, to cite a more nearly contemporary prose analogue, the narrative frame provided by Lockwood's dreams in *Wuthering Heights,* which transform the reader's sense of reality at the outset and color the reader's response to everything that follows. On the one hand, the *Alice* frame poems record an experience of lyric transformation that induces the dream tales that follow, the tales from this perspective serving as sustained extensions of an initial lyric moment. On the other hand, since the dream tales articulate and define the meaning of this initiating lyric experience, the poems remain incomplete, indeed virtually contentless, apart from the tales. It is the mutual interdependence of the frame poems and the dream tales that needs to be recognized if we are to understand why Carroll attached such importance to these poems, never allowing the *Alices* to appear without them and never allowing the frame poems themselves to appear separately.

I

A clue to how and why Carroll expected this material to serve as a frame is suggested by the provenance of the *Wonderland* text. In a hand-printed manuscript that Carroll gave privately to Alice Liddell as a Christmas present, entitled *Alice's Adventures under Ground* and containing the text that Carroll later expanded into *Alice's Adventures in Wonderland,* there is as yet no prefatory poem but a narrative prose ending of great interest. Because of its importance and relative unfamiliarity I quote it in full, from the point at which Alice awakens:

> At this the whole pack rose up into the air, and came flying down upon her: she gave a little scream of fright, and tried to beat them off, and found herself lying on the bank, with her head in the lap of her sister, who was gently brushing away some leaves that had fluttered down from the trees on to her face.

> "Wake up! Alice dear!" said her sister, "What a nice long sleep you've had!"

> "Oh, I've had such a curious dream!" said Alice, and she told her sister all her Adventures Under Ground, as you have read them, and when she had finished, her sister kissed her and said, "it *was* a curious dream, dear, certainly! But now run in to your tea: it's getting late."

> So Alice ran off, thinking while she ran (as well she might) what a wonderful dream it had been.

> . . . . .

> But her sister sat there some while longer, watching the setting sun, and thinking of little Alice and her Adventures, till she too began dreaming after a fashion, and this was her dream:

> She saw an ancient city, and a quiet river winding near it along the plain, and up the stream went slowly gliding a boat with a merry party of children on board—she could hear their voices and laughter like

music over the water—and among them was another little Alice, who sat listening with bright eager eyes to a tale that was being told, and she listened for the words of the tale, and lo! it was the dream of her own little sister. So the boat wound slowly along, beneath the bright summer-day, with its merry crew and its music of voices and laughter, till it passed round one of the many turnings of the stream, and she saw it no more.

> Then she thought, (in a dream within the dream, as it were,) how this same little Alice would, in the after-time, be herself a grown woman: and how she would keep, through her riper years, the simple and loving heart of her childhood: and how she would gather around her other little children, and make *their* eyes bright and eager with many a wonderful tale, perhaps even with these very adventures of the little Alice of long-ago: and how she would feel with all their simple sorrows, and find a pleasure in all their simple joys, remembering her own child-life, and the happy summer days.

This passage bears witness to Carroll's impulse, even at an embryonic stage in the evolution of the *Alices* and in what was still essentially a private communication, to go beyond the mere transcription of the original tales that Alice Liddell had requested. It is clearly meant to remind Alice Liddell of the original narrative occasion, but the noticeable alteration in style from that of the preceding narrative suggests a shift in perspective explicitly marked by Carroll's inked-in bar setting off this concluding passage from the central narrative. Up to this point in the *Under Ground* version nothing in the prose approaches the meditative rhythm and lyric heightening of the style adopted in this narrative conclusion, the stylistic contrast expressing a change in perspective that already gives this brief prose ending something of a "frame" function. The shift in focus from Alice to her older sister, and specifically to the effect that Alice's report of her dream has on her sister—inducing a trancelike "dream within the dream"—gives the reader the sense of having entered a different realm of experience.

In attaching this narrative epilogue to his tale Carroll obviously intended to communicate to the real Alice Liddell something important about the adventures that he had written down for her. What this was can be inferred from the substance as well as the tone of the passage, and Carroll made it explicit in the wording he adopted when he revised this initial account of the older sister's response in the expanded conclusion to the *Wonderland* text. Among other changes, Carroll added the following significant clause: " . . . and still as she listened, or seemed to listen, the whole place around her became alive with the strange creatures of her little sister's dream." The language here approximates the description of the effect attributed to "myth-texts," texts designed to force us into modifying our conventional understanding of reality. The point of such texts, in the words of one analyst, is to erase the artificial barrier between the "real" and the "unreal" that readers inevitably bring to a text, so that "we gaze back suddenly upon the myth that we unknowingly entered. All at once, in retrospect, we realize that we have not been alive until now; that, by comparison, all that has gone before has not been real." This wording, echoing Carroll's own wording in the expanded *Wonderland* version, describes the effect that Alice's dream adventure has on her older sister. From the model offered by such texts we can infer that in providing a frame for the *Alice* books Carroll sought to erase the artificial barrier between the everyday world of Victorian realities and the unreal world of "nonsense" that he had created. The overwhelmingly vivid reality of Alice's dream shatters her older sister's conventional view of the world.

In starting our exploration of the *Alice* frame poems from the nucleus of lyric material contained in the prose ending to *Under Ground* we are in effect following Carroll, for when he decided to revise *Under Ground* for a wider readership his major concern would naturally have been to provide guidance for the uninitiated child reader, who, unlike Alice Liddell, could neither have known him personally nor have been present at the original telling. For Carroll knew what the response of many sensitive children has made evident—that the tale itself can be threatening—and it was therefore important, if that strange world was to be properly perceived (not to mention entered), that it not be frightening to the child reader encountering it for the first time. In this context, both what Carroll changed and what he retained when elaborating the *Under Ground* prose ending into the full-fledged frame of the *Wonderland* version prove illuminating. The major change was the addition of an entirely new prefatory poem ("All in the golden afternoon") to replace the original brief prose dedication in *Under Ground* ("A Christmas Gift to a Dear Child in Memory of a Summer Day"). This poem incorporates elements from the original *Under Ground* prose ending and adds significant new elements as well, the old and new material alike now being rendered in lyric verse.

For purposes of convenience and clarity, I simply list the substantive changes that Carroll introduced into both the beginning and the ending of the *Wonderland* text. Revised opening: (1) dedication to Alice Liddell dropped, (2) occasion of tale telling moved to front and put into verse, (3) three children named and characterized, (4) storyteller characterized (effort in composing stressed), (5) concluding advice to "Alice" added. Revised prose ending: (6) allusion to ancient city and stream dropped, (7) dream images repeated in sister's mind (violence of dream stressed), (8) Alice described as telling her dream (not listening to it being told), (9) contrast of dream and "dull reality" added.

The older sister's response remains the focus of the revised prose ending, and her linkage of retelling and "simple and loving heart" does not change. The alterations that Carroll made in the substance as well as the form of this frame material are all consistent with the function of a myth frame: to transform the reader's perception of "reality."

The reason I suggest for the way Carroll framed the *Alices* finds confirmation in the internal evidence provided by the overall structure that governs the relation of the frame poems to the larger texts. . . . This schema shows that the positioning of the poems is strategically important, constituting them as an outer frame. The apparent anomaly of *Wonderland* ending with a prose narrative and *Looking-Glass* with a lyric poem disappears when we recognize that the *Wonderland* prose ending forms part of the outer-frame structure of which the three frame poems are complementary components. The schema also calls attention to the fact that both books contain inner as well as outer frames, each of which presents a waking Alice in a prose narrative of a kind we might find in a realistic novel. The structure of each book encompasses shifts in the narrative mode, allowing the narrative voice to move into and back out of the central dream tales by modulating from lyric, to realistic fiction, to dream vision, back through realistic fiction, to a final lyric statement.

This organizing structure is similar to that of "The Eve of St. Agnes," and what has been observed of Keats's poem—that "it is the way we are taken into the world of the poem, what happens to us there, and the way we are let out again that matters"—exactly fits our experience of the *Alices,* indicating the importance of all three phases of the complex experience that is built into the books' structure. The major difference is that the *Alice* frame structure initiates a double rhythm of entry into and withdrawal from the central experience. The reader undergoes at the outset a lyric transformation that anticipates the similar transformation that Alice experiences. A series of transitions—from the reader's ordinary reality to the reality of the restless boat children, through the everyday reality that bores the waking Alice, into the chaotic world of Alice's dream—gradually awakens the reader to a nightmare world that proves to be the reader's ordinary world transformed by a startling perception regarding that reality. Responding to this double rhythm, the reader, too, experiences a "dream within a dream." The central dream tales thus take on their full meaning in relation to this double frame, all three elements together—outer frame, inner frame, and dream tale—embodying in their reciprocal interactions the total vision of the *Alice* books.

I suggest . . . how the inner frames function within this larger structure. Here, however, I want to stress the answer to the question of why Carroll framed the *Alices* as he did: to establish in the reader a proper orientation toward the central narratives. The lyric effect of the tales themselves is evidenced by the frequent references commentators make to their dream quality, which Walter De la Mare identifies as "*the* sovereign element in the *Alices,*" which Edmund Wilson alludes to in linking the tales to certain works of Flaubert, Joyce, and Strindberg, and which Peter Coveney acknowledges when he observes that "in a strange way indeed, the 'dream,' the reverie in Dodgson, becomes in *Alice in Wonderland* the means of setting the reader's senses more fully awake." Carroll's skill in adapting the poetic conventions of his day to serve his narrative strategy—to induce and reinforce in the reader a necessary state of "reverie"—emerges clearly from an examination of the frame poems individually and as they vary according to their place and function in the overall structure of the two books.

II

The most complex of the *Alice* frame poems is the prefatory poem to *Wonderland,* which, in occupying the privileged place of inauguration, plays a key role in alerting the reader to the special nature of the Alice experience. Through image, character, and event, the first six stanzas embody the fundamental lyric transaction, the seventh stanza constituting an epilogue to and commentary on what has transpired in the earlier stanzas, including the narrating of the tale that the reader is about to encounter. The opening three stanzas present an idyllic setting ("such an hour . . . such dreamy weather") that is rudely disrupted ("cruel voices") by the three children in the boating party (neutrally designated at this point as Prima, Secunda, and Tertia) demanding that their apparently languid and abstracted companion-attendant entertain them. (It is Secunda who specifically requests "nonsense.") The next three stanzas describe the silence that ensues as the spellbound children are caught up in the storyteller-companion's narrative of a dream child's adventures, interrupting only to demand more whenever the storyteller shows signs of growing weary. This simple plot concludes with the "crew's" merry return home, as the sun is setting, after the tale has been completed to everyone's satisfaction. Imagery of oars, wandering, a journey, and a return home suggests a quest motif, but the "wandering" of the actual boat is aimless, the children's efforts to guide its course futile. Their journey takes on purpose and significance, that is, only with the commencement of the storyteller's narrative. It is thus the imaginative journey on which the narrator's "dream-child" takes the children that carries through the quest motif and sends the children home happy.

What the plot of the poem stresses—once fate, in the guise of the children's request, has issued its command—is the storyteller's initial reluctance and subsequent weariness in attempting to respond to the children's relentless demands. We are made conscious of the speaker of the poem watching his storytelling self, presenting this self as a somewhat feckless, slightly comic figure. The child reader of *Wonderland* can both laugh at and perhaps feel a bit sorry for this imposed-on and seemingly well-intentioned figure but, like the children in the boat, can quickly forget him when the strange adventures of the dream child begin to unfold. Finally, the subdued silence and intense absorption of the original listeners set up in the reader appropriate expectations of excitement and pleasure. That the ending of each story—the dream child's and that of the boat children who hear her adventures—is a happy one can be inferred from the children's merriment as they return home. Exactly what they have heard and why they are "merry" the reader does not yet know, but even the harried storyteller-poet seems content with what has taken place.

These basic elements of plot, imagery, and characterization remain subordinate, however, to the central purpose, which derives from the poem's function as the point of entry into the main story. The lyrical quality and thrust of the poem, the eerie sense of transition the poem both embodies and effects, is essential: the experience is of a transformation that erases the barrier between the "real" and the "unreal." The poem engages us at this deeper level, modifying our approach and hence our response to the dream tale itself. The lyricizing of this originating moment endows a seemingly ordinary boating excursion, involving an inconsequential skirmish between three children and their languid companion, with a visionary quality. The poem achieves this transformation primarily through a subtle variation and interplay of verbal tenses, manifesting the characteristics of what has been aptly named the "lyric present." A past event is rendered as though present ("we *glide,*" "little arms *are plied*"). Simple physical gestures, in this case rowing, activate a timeless mental event (the emergence of the dream child). Present-tense verbs portentously carry the reader forward (*"flashes forth,"* *"hopes"*) even while the poet is looking to the past ("thus *grew* the tale"). We observe the poet watching himself in the act of creating ("And faintly *strove* that weary one / To put the subject by"). In stanza 6, place and time are finally elevated into a historical present ("and *now* the tale is done, / And home we *steer*"), the scene becoming endlessly renewable as the action resumes each time we read the poem. The crucial event appropriately occurs at the center of the poem, in the pivotal fourth stanza, in which the "dream-child moving through a land / Of wonders" mysteriously appears, leading the boat children (and the reader) across a threshold through a lyric estrangement that transforms the children and the storyteller alike. When the children cry, "It *is* next time," we find ourselves in the alogical and atemporal realm of desire, the realm in which the tale is both told and heard.

90

of her own little sister. So the boat wound slowly along, beneath the bright summer-day, with its merry crew and its music of voices and laughter, till. it passed round one of the many turnings of the stream, and she saw it no more.

Then she thought, (in a dream within the dream, as it were,) how this same little Alice would, in the after-time, be. herself a grown woman: and how she would keep, through her riper years, the simple and loving heart of her childhood; and how she would gather around her other little children, and make *their* eyes bright and eager with many a wonderful tale, perhaps even with these very adventures of the little Alice of long-ago: and how she would feel with all their simple sorrows, and find a pleasure in all their simple joys, remembering her own child-life, and the happy summer days.

Final manuscript page of Alice's Adventures Underground *with Carroll's photographic portrait of Alice Liddell.*

The seventh and final stanza of the poem is an epilogue in which the storyteller, who now becomes obliquely identified with the poet, directly addresses "Alice" (so named for the first time) in a more serious tone, gently instructing her regarding the proper disposition of the tale she has just heard. The concluding stanza concentrates the themes and transformations of the previous six stanzas in a single conventional image, the one rhetorical figure that Carroll allows himself in the poem:

> Alice! A childish story take,
>   And, with gentle hand,
> Lay it where Childhood's dreams are twined
>   In Memory's mystic band.
> Like pilgrim's wither'd wreath of flowers
>   Pluck'd in a far-off land.

The opening apostrophe, followed immediately by a shift to the imperative mood, sets off this stanza from the previous six. It is further set off by a slightly weightier cadence and by the relative complexity of the concluding simile. The two main protagonists now emerge: "Alice" as a transformed "Secunda" (the two names are linked by the common epithet *gentle*) and the poet as a transformed storyteller. It was Secunda who had asked for "nonsense," and it is to her, now renamed and thus identified with the dream child (whose name the reader will soon discover), that the poet turns, singling her out to suggest to her the implications of the adventures that had held her and her companions in thrall and sent them home happy. By placing the message in the actual present of the reader about to read the tale, the imperative mood establishes an implicit identity between the reader and the "Alice" addressed. The poet informs "Alice," in effect, that he has given (will give) her something more than the "nonsense" she has asked for (expects); thus he indicates at the outset what the original *Under Ground* ending foreshadowed: the narrator's desire to give Alice Liddell something more than a simple transcription of the original oral tales.

This something more is conveyed through the trope of the pilgrim's wreath, which distills the essence of the lyric action embodied by the poem as a whole and delicately hints at the motive (hitherto hidden) for the narrator's willingness to "hammer out" the story. This image integrates the several dimensions of time evoked in the preceding stanzas, extending backward to the past as a *memorial* of a sacred occasion ("pilgrim's wreath") that gave birth to the tale and forward as an image of the tale itself, a wreath of words woven into artistic form, a circular image of the *promise* of eternity and—in the present—a lover's *gift*, a bouquet ("wreath of flowers"), for all the Alices who will read *Wonderland*. Real time—linear, irreversible, redolent of death—is recognized in the poem: the sun is setting as the boat journey comes to an end, and the wreath itself is already "wither'd" even as the poet presents it. But the linear dimension along which the boating excursion takes place and the spontaneous appearance of the dream child at a particular moment in time are alike arrested in an oneiric timelessness, a vision with roots "twined / In Memory's *mystic* band." Thus the wreath embodies the three dimensions of linear time: a reminder of the meaning and identity that derive from memory's link with the past, a token of love that redeems the present and gives it value, and an emblem of an artwork with the power endlessly to renew a timeless present in which it always *is* next time. Properly understood, the concluding stanza declares, the tale will return the reader to the source ("a far-off land") of wholeness and health and sanity, to the psychic origins of the true human identity of which the dream child is an emblem.

We can now see that Carroll revised the *Wonderland* narrative ending to reinforce the lyric thrust of the prefatory poem. When Alice awakes from her dream, the brief inner frame, basically unchanged from the *Under Ground* version, gives a straight-forward three-sentence account of Alice's report of her dream to her older sister, after which she obediently runs off to tea, the narrator simply concurring in Alice's final feeling that the dream was "wonderful." In what follows, the topical allusions in *Under Ground* to the scene of the boating excursion are gone; the dream events, their violence now emphasized, are recapitulated by the sister; and the description of Alice reporting her dream is expanded to suggest that Alice herself has been brought alive by her dream (Alice now tells the dream instead of, as in *Under Ground,* listening to it being told). Moreover, two substantial added passages make explicit the older sister's acute awareness of how "dull" everyday reality seems, appearing to her in a new and disenchanting light, as "the confused clamour of the busy farm-yard." Her perception has been altered by her exposure to the perspective that informs a dream epitomized by the prefatory poem, in the emphatic rhyme words of its pivotal stanza, as a vision to *pursue,* a vision both *new* and *true*.

Carroll's retention of the *Under Ground* final paragraph virtually unchanged is equally instructive. The older sister instinctively links the motif of retelling the dream story with Alice's "simple and loving heart," clearly implying that the adventures deserve retelling *because* they reveal a simple and loving heart. In thus discerning in the behavior of Alice's dream self an exemplary manifestation of human identity and meaning, the older sister guides the reader in interpreting the dream. In her status as an "elder" she perceives a paradoxical warning that she must keep becoming a child, that a simple and loving heart requires perpetual maintenance in the face of the corrosive pressures of reality, whether these pressures take the form of biological laws of physical survival or, as in the later

Looking-Glass, of cultural laws of social preferment. The *Wonderland* dream tale becomes, in this context, a reminder to the reader of both the need and the possibility of transcending the debilitating decorums of ordinary existence through a renewal of perception that is the central effect of *Wonderland* itself when the reader fully experiences it.

III

Before considering the *Looking-Glass* frame poems, I want to note briefly the structural significance of the inner frames of the *Alices,* relative to the schema I present above. Although most readers perceive the two *Alices* as parts of a single work, many commentators have detected a difference between the books, which they define in terms of polar opposition: passive/active, outdoors/indoors, spontaneous/self-conscious, anarchic/rule-governed, identity/duality, adventure/journey, and so on, with *Looking-Glass* generally perceived as a "darker" book than *Wonderland*—more pessimistic, more bitter, more melancholy, and, for some, more neurotic. Often they suggest that this difference is attributable to some undefined "decline" in Carroll. The inner frames make clear that, while there is a discernible change in the poet's relation to Alice, the alteration is due to a change in her, not in his vision.

The difference in both tone and content between the two *Alice* dreams is accounted for by the shift, which the inner frames describe, in Alice's psychological posture just before she falls asleep. The symbolic change in Alice's age from seven to seven and a half, about which we learn later, during the second dream, is anticipated in the *Looking-Glass* inner frame by the shift from May to November and, more significantly, by the alteration in the waking Alice's attitude. In *Wonderland* Alice is passive, lethargic, and bored when awake; in *Looking-Glass* she is active, aggressive, and ambitious. Although in both books she is intensely curious and eager to escape an unsatisfactory present, the images that initiate the dreams differ significantly: in *Wonderland* the initiating image is that of a regressive fall, in *Looking-Glass* that of a progressive climb. The implied change in Alice becomes evident early, since at the beginning of the *Wonderland* dream it is the White Rabbit who is in a hurry, whereas in *Looking-Glass* it is Alice.

Despite these differing contextualizations, both dreams end in frustration: the two paths of escape that offer themselves to Alice in her dreams—the way back to the beautiful garden in *Wonderland* and the way forward to queenhood in *Looking-Glass*—prove either unattainable (the garden) or unsatisfactory (the golden crown of queenhood, Alice discovers at the end of *Looking-Glass,* is "something very heavy, that fitted tight all around her head"). Regressive longing, on the one hand, and aggressive ambition, on the other, are exposed as equally dangerous, equivalent manifestations of misdirected desire. Whether Alice is seven or seven and a half, the fundamental purpose of her life remains the same, even if the direction from which her essential being is threatened has changed. She is instructed by both dreams that she already possesses all that she needs. When she awakens, though her outward behavior is not apparently affected in either book, the inner restlessness evident in both books before she falls asleep has been appeased; her perception of what is necessary to happiness is not so much advanced as confirmed at the deepest level. Both dreams, variously described as "curious," "wonderful," "strange," and "nice," move in a single direction, toward Alice's restoration to and confirmation in the wholeness and sanity that is her true identity even as she continues to grow and her circumstances to change.

Turning now to the *Looking-Glass* prefatory poem, we can note first that, while the poem reflects a change in "Alice," its primary function is identical to that of the *Wonderland* frame: to evoke a past communal event by creating from it a lyric present that will guide the reader through the dream tale to follow. Like *Wonderland,* the tale is both a memorial to and a renewal of "happy summer days," a phrase that Carroll incorporates into the *Looking-Glass* poem from the prose ending of *Wonderland.* Since the originating event and its first fruits are already on record, as it were, in *Wonderland,* the poet can now content himself with reinvoking the appropriate mood by referring to the earlier story. The *Looking-Glass* poem is therefore less complex than its *Wonderland* counterpart, the major change deriving from the speaker's more intense time consciousness, rooted in his sense both that the originating event is retreating into the past and that "Alice" is growing away from him. The pressing reality of time is again acknowledged ("though time be fleet"), its emotional effect now overtly expressed ("the shadow of a sigh / May tremble through the story"), and this acute time consciousness makes the speaker's presence more directly felt and the poem's imperatives more urgent than in the *Wonderland* frame material. But if the sense of time irresistibly passing and of absence becoming permanent is strong, so also is the speaker's will to transcend time through a conscious renewal of the original event. Recognizing and accepting the inexorableness of time and change, the poem reasserts the transforming power of the dream child, whose renewable presence the second dream tale is about to enact.

Carroll employs a slightly modified version of the stanza used in the *Wonderland* prefatory poem, so that the *Looking-Glass* prefatory poem's form and language serve as a bridge between the two *Alices.* The poem's structure, unlike the simple plot-cum-epilogue of the *Wonderland* poem, is a series of strophic contrasts, each stanza juxtaposing the temporal and the atemporal, the passing and the enduring. In each stanza the quatrain renders the experience of transience and loss or of anticipated decline or separation; the falling trochaic beats at the end of the second and fourth lines convey a mild feeling of pathos, and each quatrain is balanced by a strong affirmation in the concluding couplet. From the confident invocation of the child muse in the opening lines ("Child of the pure unclouded brow / And dreaming eyes of wonder!") down to the end of the fourth stanza the rhythm oscillates between the sense of time past and passing, on the one hand, and the poet's will to affirm, on the other, with a diminuendo in a "though . . . yet still" movement that reaches a low point in the quiet, almost prosaic statement at the end of stanza 4: "We are but older children, dear, / Who fret to find our bedtime near." For the "melancholy maiden" addressed in these lines there is the early prospect of the "little death" of the marriage bed, and for maiden and poet alike the inevitable grave awaits. But a counterfeeling of hope, rooted in the poet's faith in the power of his visionary gift to redeem the time, emerges with fresh strength in the concluding couplets. The conclusion of stanza 5 invokes the power of the poet's art to protect the maiden against the madness raging outside "childhood's nest of gladness" ("The magic words shall hold thee fast: / Thou shalt not heed the raving blast"), and the terminal couplet of stanza 6 asserts the capacity of the dream tale to render time itself powerless to alter "Alice": "It shall not touch, with breath of bale, / The pleasance of our fairy-tale."

Imagery of frost and fire is related to the deep structure that underpins the stanzaic pattern of strophic oppositions that organize the poem. The natural fire of "summer suns" has departed, but it is replaced by the humanly created fire of a hearth, in the presence of which the poet can retrieve and renew a primordial "now" that is "enough," if the listener will but "hail" his gift and "listen" to what the story has to say. "Come, harken, then" is this poem's imperative. Generative of light and warmth, the fire dispels time's wintry depletions, serving as an emblem of the love that is openly declared in a couplet that simultaneously invites and expresses a hope for an appropriate response: "Thy loving smile will surely hail / The love-gift of a fairy-tale." Against the surrounding night of frost and blinding snow and the temporal prospect of an "unwelcome bed," the poet sets the image of the fire that Alice will find burning on the other side of the mirror in her dream. In offering this second tale as a "love-gift," the poet offers love itself as the only "nonsense" that can effectively confront the surrounding darkness.

The *Looking-Glass* end poem embodies the poet's final statement regarding the Alice experience. The poem functions, at one level, as the equivalent to the prose narrative ending of *Wonderland,* with the reader moved once again out of a nightmare that provokes Alice's violent reaction, through the self-questioning of the inner frame, into final lyric affirmation. It differs from the *Wonderland* ending in that the poet now addresses the reader directly instead of merely reporting the older sister's response, a change prepared for in a closing inner frame significantly more substantial than the *Wonderland* equivalent. This time the response to the dream tale is that of the awakened Alice, who poses a series of questions to herself that lead to a final question: was it she or the Red King who dreamed the dream? The dream, that is, has shaken Alice out of her preoccupation with attaining queenhood into serious reflection about the nature of reality. In the final sentence of the inner frame, the narrator addresses the question directly to the reader—"Which do *you* think it was?"—thereby drawing the reader into the dream and into Alice's radical question, a question that makes all human perspectives relative. In this context the *Looking-Glass* end poem implicitly offers the Alice experience as the answer to this ultimate metaphysical question, a "dream" that contains not only Alice, the Red King, and all the other dream characters but finally the reader and the poet as well.

Structurally, the seven-stanza *Looking-Glass* end poem symmetrically balances the seven-stanza prefatory poem to *Wonderland,* but Carroll now adopts a highly concentrated verse form, a rare trochaic trimeter in triplets, that gives to the end poem a terseness that reinforces the sense of closure. The initial letters of the twenty-one lines of the poem form an acrostic that places "Alice Pleasance Liddell" within the poem, figuratively incorporating Alice Liddell into the books that she inspired and thus assuring her of immortality. While the real Alice Liddell has grown up, the poet rescues and fixes *his* "Alice" by a process that had begun when Alice Liddell became Secunda and Secunda became Alice in the opening *Wonderland* poem, was carried forward in the allusion to pleasance in the middle *Looking-Glass* prefatory poem, and is now brought to completion in her total naming. Whereas the Alice of the *Wonderland* prefatory poem had been near and real and the Alice in the prefatory poem to *Looking-Glass* could still be imaginatively evoked, remaining at least virtually real and present, in the *Looking-Glass* end poem she has been transformed into poetry, the elements of her dismembered name becoming an integral part of the poetic vision that Alice Liddell had inspired long before by awakening the poet's love for her and for what she represented to him.

The opening stanzas go back one last time to the moment of origin, evoking through reverie the benign weather, the boat, and the eager listening children of that long-ago July "evening" (as the poet now autumnally calls it), and for two brief stanzas the scene is again dreamily present. But the third stanza scatters the memory of that moment with shocking finality:

Long has paled that sunny sky:
Echoes fade and memories die,
Autumn frosts have slain July.

Then in the pivotal fourth stanza, in a stunning second reversal, the poet shifts to the lyric present, concentrating the entire Alice experience in a central three-line stanza that is as concise as it is definitive:

Still she haunts me, phantomwise,
Alice moving under skies
Never seen by waking eyes.

The dream Alice is finally apotheosized, fixed in the firmament of the poet's poetic universe, reigning there as an emblem of wholeness and integrity perpetually set over against all that we ordinarily assume to be "real." The fifth stanza, echoing the prose ending of *Wonderland,* anticipates the reembodiment of this lyric vision in works of verbal art capable of making the experience new again and again for "children yet" (both the children to come and those who remain childlike) who listen attentively. As time—that other and more transient dream—moves on, days go by, and other summers die, and we drift down the irreversible stream of time, we can, the concluding stanzas assert, by an act of poetic faith, *linger* in—await, harken to, renew, take hope from—the "golden gleam" embodied in narratives inspired by an extraordinary visionary experience.

IV

In their conventionality and deceptive simplicity the *Alice* frame poems no doubt lend themselves to neglect or misreading. My point is simply that the central tales, however, brilliantly achieved, are not the whole story of the *Alices*. The dream tales themselves simply interrogate a reality that is revealed, over and over, as incapable of yielding answers. Their purpose, unlike that of the usual fairy tale, is disenchantment with reality as we normally perceive it, that is, with the reality "grown-ups" accept and seek to exploit out of one or another neurotic impulse. Like certain types of myth, the *Alice* dream tales serve as inverse social charters, subverting our everyday notions of what is important, portraying worlds of potential madness that close in on Alice inexorably, leaving her nowhere to turn. The great danger to which Alice, like every other human being, is exposed (physical extinction is never felt to be an imminent threat in either dream) appears in the pathological behavior that she observes in the dream characters: cowardice in the White Rabbit, furious passion in the Queen of Hearts, calculated aggression in the Red Queen, evasive conformity in the White Queen, melancholy resignation in the Gnat, self-pity in the Mock-Turtle, insouciance in the Gryphon, arrogance in Humpty Dumpty, madness in the Hare and Hatter, sterile inventiveness in the White Knight, and so forth.

The danger that imperils Alice as she grows up is a fatal loss of courage, simplicity, and openness through succumbing to the spiritual death represented in the various dehumanizing forms that she encounters in her dreams, which are ultimately messages from Alice to herself. Her heroism consists in preserving her innate decency against the confusions and dislocations of her dreams through the courtesy and courage that her sister perceives in her dream behavior and that she manifests in her steadfast refusal to submit to absurd or threatening situations.

Carroll's unsentimental view of human nature is pointed up in the realistic inner frames. They show the seeds of spiritual death to be latent even in the innocent Alice: at the opening of *Wonderland* in the form of boredom, self-pity, and an impulse to regressive withdrawal; in *Looking-Glass* in the form of role-playing, manic aggressiveness, and ambition ("Let's pretend we're kings and queens"). Even the child harbors disturbing potentialities ("Nurse! Do let's pretend that I'm a hungry hyaena, and you're a bone!"). The frame poems lead us into, through, and out of this dark central vision, providing the perspective that enables the reader to judge the "mistery of pain," as Joyce glosses the dream world of the *Alices*, and thereby converting the potential nightmare of ordinary existence into a profoundly instructive comedy. It is by their means that we cross the threshold from irreality to reality, from spiritual sleep to intense wakefulness, returning, if we have read the tales attentively, with our vision cleansed. To be awake in the usual sense, the *Alice* books tell us, is to dwell in an absurd kingdom absent-mindedly presided over by the Red King sleeping his fatal sleep. To be truly alive we need to dream the Alice dream—to perceive, nurture, and transmit a vision rooted in the heart's deepest desire.

Ronald R. Thomas (essay date 1990)

SOURCE: "Dreams of Power in *Alice in Wonderland*," in *Dreams of Authority: Freud and the Fictions of the Unconscious,* Cornell, 1990, pp. 55-61.

[*In the following excerpt, Thomas explores the themes of power and linguistic mastery in Alice's dreamworld.*]

I do hope it's my dream and not the Red King's! I don't like belonging to another person's dream.

—Alice

Lewis Carroll's dream-child Alice dreams of the adult world as a chaotic, crazy realm, but also as a territory she wishes to enter and possess as her own. Dickens's Scrooge turns that dream wish around. He dreams of his childhood innocence and desires to repossess certain features of it in his old age. Common to both dreamers is the wish to bring the experience of childhood together with that of adulthood, to see life whole, to transform what threatens to be disjointed and meaningless into a coherent narrative rather than a series of timeless moments, as Wordsworth sought in *The Prelude.* Scrooge and Alice want to take possession of time, and they begin to do so by taking control of the dreams that threaten to dominate them. In both cases, this take-over is an empowering and curative act for the dreamer, as the endings of their two dream narratives reveal. Both end with the dreamers' accession to power, an achievement that is made possible when they translate their mysterious dreams into a language of political or economic mastery.

Alice in Wonderland (1865) and **Through the Looking-Glass** (1872) both question whether Alice "belongs" to another person's dream or the dream belongs to her. The answer is contained in Alice's response to her dreams when she awakens from them and takes verbal control over them. The Alice books are often read as political or psychoanalytic allegories. But their politics and psychology are both joined in their concern with the power of language. In her dreams, Alice is repeatedly faced with linguistic challenges—contests of storytelling, riddle guessing, remembering a rhyme, interpreting a confusing text, identifying herself, or simply engaging in an argument. These contests usually take place between Alice and some figure of political authority, such as a king, a queen, a duchess, or a judge. And the power of those figures invariably rests in their mastery of some verbal maneuver or trick. The connection between the exercise of power and the control of language is made quite explicit to Alice in her conversation with the masterful figure called Humpty Dumpty. "When *I* use a word," he tells Alice, "it means just what I choose it to mean—neither more nor less." "The question is," Alice responds, "whether you *can* make words mean so many different things." "The question is," Humpty Dumpty corrects her, "which is to be master—that's all."

Language is a game of political mastery, and it is presented to Alice in her dreams as just that. When she is told by "the chorus of voices" that she is better off saying nothing because language is too valuable to squander, being worth "a thousand pounds a word," she responds by thinking to herself, "I shall dream about a thousand pounds tonight, I know I shall." At this point, Alice begins to acknowledge that the value of language and the mastery it offers to the speaker are the subjects of her dream and the basis of her identity. But it has taken her a long time to realize this. A word is worth a thousand pounds, and as Freud would quite plainly say in *The Interpretation of Dreams,* the pictorial images of any dream will grant the dreamer a purchase on them only when they are converted into the currency of language. The images of Alices's dream

are constantly trying to silence her, and as long as she says nothing, she will be powerless to own or disown those images. This is what she dreams about, and what many of the dispossessed dreamers in nineteenth-century fiction dream about. When Freud described his method of dream interpretation as the "translation" of the images of our dreams into language, he also described the task set before Alice in her confusing dream of Wonderland.

Early in **Wonderland,** Alice feels as if she is lost in a book of fairy tales. This idea leads her to express an important wish: "There ought to be a book written about me, that there ought! And when I grow up, I'll write one." Being grown up is defined here as writing a book about oneself, as opposed to being "in" a book written by someone else. And if **Alice in Wonderland** can be construed as a dream about growing up, it construes growing up as taking authority over one's own life story, as writing a book "about me." Alice's escapes from certain verbal and physical structures form the central episodes of her dream. She is continually being imprisoned in and breaking out of a room or a house or a joke or a poem in which she does not fit. This pattern also forms the larger structure of the text. The whole adventure begins when Alice drifts off to sleep because the book that her sister was reading had no pictures and no conversation. Alice escapes from the mastery of this text by "falling" into the images of her own dream and then arising to tell her own story. When Alice wakes to recount that story to her sister, she provokes the sister to dream the very same dream. But the sister's version of it ends with a significant difference—a vision of Alice as a grown woman telling "many a strange tale" of "the dream of Wonderland long ago" to a group of children, "remembering her own child-life." The dream becomes the book "that you have just been reading about," a book of Alice's own which replaces the one that was being read to her. In **Wonderland,** Alice moves from a child being told a story to a young woman telling her own story, remembering the images of "her own child-life." She converts her dream into a book about herself.

The episode within the story itself which most explicitly dramatizes this point is the Mad Tea Party. There, the sleeping Dormouse is clearly intended as an image of Alice. Like her, the Dormouse is both present at the party and absent from it because it is asleep and dreaming throughout the event. The significance of the episode lies in its confrontation of Alice with a narrative problem: time has been "killed" here; it is always the same time, always the present. There can be no progress, only eternal repetition and confusion. As Freud would later indicate, this sense of the eternal present is a characteristic of dreams. The temporal confusion springs in part from the absence of narrative time. The dream expresses its logical connections not by sequence but by simultaneity and juxtaposition, combining recent memories with old ones. The task of the dreamer, therefore, is to reconstruct the narrative connections that have thereby been obscured in the dream work.

After Alice detects the pattern of the constant movement of guests from seat to seat around the table in a never-ending tea party, she takes up this task within her dream, inquiring what happens when they all get around to the "beginning" again. The Mad Hatter suggests at that point in the conversation that they "change the subject," and he asks Alice to tell them a story. This exchange implies that part of the "work" of this dream is to "change" the dreaming subject by making her into a speaking subject. The dream of Wonderland eventually serves to bring Alice to a place where she can end the risk of madness and confusion by telling the story of the dream. Then she can answer the question that the dream poses to her over and over again: "Who are *you*?" But at this point, Alice claims to have no story to tell, and the sleeping Dormouse is called upon to do the telling instead. Alice is not yet prepared to tell her story; she is not yet in possession of it. So the Dormouse replaces her in this function and becomes a double for her. He tells her story.

When the mouse is awakened and begins to spin a story out of the confusion of its dream, that story turns out to be a coded version of Alice's dream as well. The mouse's story concerns three children (one of whose names is an anagram for Alice) who lived in a well of treacle (Alice's adventures began when she fell down "what seemed to be a very deep well"). But the tale soon becomes a story about language, as the children learn to "draw" from the well things that have a common linguistic property: "everything beginning with M"—mousetraps, the moon, memory, and finally, muchness. When Alice protests that one can't "draw" things like memory or muchness from a well, she begins to assert her speaking voice in the episode; but her protest also indicates a failure to recognize something equally important. She has not realized that the material drawn out of the well of a dream is a memory, and it has a logic that the dreamer imposes upon it through recollection in language. Alice does not yet recognize this story as a coded version of her own experience—as her dream to master and to tell. "If you can't be civil," the Dormouse challenges her as she interrupts him with complaints about the truth of his story, "you'd better finish the story for yourself." "Finishing the story" is defined here as *not* being "civil"—not obeying, that is, but commanding. This is precisely what Alice eventually will do, but not yet. She will finish the story for herself and command its characters when she declares it finished at the trial. She will do so again when she wakes up and tells it as her story to her sister just before she takes her tea at home. But first, Alice must see that this dream is about her ability

to be the master of her words; she must draw them from the well of her own desire and finish her story for herself.

Many of Alice's adventures in Wonderland are trials she must endure in which the control over her own body, her own desires, or even her own psychic health depends upon her ability to interpret coded, confusing information. An actual courtroom trial, presided over by political figureheads whom she must defy, therefore, is an appropriate culmination to Alice's adventures in Wonderland. The key piece of evidence in the trial, brought against the knave accused of stealing, is a document apparently without meaning, without signature, and without author. The document turns out to be another series of verses that weave a confused narrative, the characters of which are pronouns with no specific referents, identities that tumble together in nameless ambiguity. Like Alice's confusion before the caterpillar's inquiries about her identity, the confusion of the poem continues throughout until it ends with a pronouncement about the impossibility of deciphering it: "For this must ever be / A secret kept from all the rest, / Between yourself and me."

This mysterious document repeats the intepretive problem of the entire dream and is, therefore, the central "text" of it. Knowledge of the secret may be had "between yourself and me," in the place where the self recognizes and defines its difference from the other. Alice is right when she declares that there is no meaning in the text. The meaning resides in the one who assigns meaning to it, the one who tells the secret. The king will attempt to do just this. He explicates the document by identifying certain of its pronouns with the defendant, testing how well the words of the text "fit" the characters in the plot as he has told it. Assigning this significance to the words will guarantee the knave's guilt and simultaneously preserve the king's authority. The king's power is defined here as an interpretive authority. He seeks to impose a meaning on a text that has no meaning in itself and to silence any other interpretation of the case. This is the penultimate act in Alice's dream. The last is her take-over of the power and interpretive language of the king. She declares the figures of this trial to be "nothing but a pack of cards." This act usurps the interpretive power of the king because it recognizes, that like the poem, the dream is a text and the figures in it are figures—signs signifying something other than what they appear to be. They are part of a kind of political game, a language it is her responsibility to master. In order to be free from the power the dream holds over her, she must see that there is not an atom of meaning—or power—in those figures beyond what she confers upon them. When she realizes as much and acts upon the realization, Alice can awake and tell "these strange Adventures that you have just been reading about."

In *Through the Looking-Glass,* Alice's development is extended along just these lines. From the beginning of the sequel, Alice realizes she is involved in a world defined by game playing, a world of signification which she deliberately enters rather than falls into. She is not put on trial and interrogated by the figures in this world as she was in Wonderland; she tries and interrogates them. She does not refuse or interrupt the game of chess as she does the game of cards; she plays it and wins. She becomes a queen herself and puts the opposing king in check. The text repeatedly suggests that this self-assertion can occur only when Alice recognizes the linguistic aspects of her dream as political power plays. One of her initial acts in this dream is to take the pen from the White King and start "writing for him" in his own memorandum book. This act of mastery over the king's book is immediately followed by an act of interpretive mastery when Alice is confronted with another indecipherable poem just as she had been at the end of *Wonderland* (this time, the text is the **"Jabberwocky"**). Instead of being defeated by the text's apparent meaninglessness as she was at the trial, here she takes control over the words on the page. Alice holds the book up to the mirror, literally turning its words around; and though the book is "rather hard to understand," "somehow," Alice says, "it seems to fill my head with ideas." She may not be sure of what all those ideas are, but one thing is very clear to her about the content of this book: "somebody killed something." The one meaning that Alice can confer upon this text is that it is the scene of a life-and-death struggle—a place where somebody lives and somebody dies.

The dream of Alice and the metaphorical dream of life both present the same problems of desire, mastery, possession, and authority. One reason for the refusal to answer the question of whose dream it was at the end of the book may be that the book is an expression of Lewis Carroll's dream-child; it is the means by which he possesses the little girl Alice Lidell and tells her story. Carroll may be the still-threatening, still-dreaming Red King who competes with her for possession of the dream and her definition of herself. But the action of the Alice books moves toward the breakdown of that possibility and the refusal by Alice to be possessed, as is substantiated by the rules the text itself has set up for interpretation. The dream belongs to Alice because she has the last word—because she asks the question of ownership and mastery, because she expresses the desire. The Red King is check-mated by Alice; he is silenced in his sleep, and he is therefore only a part of her dream. He remains on the other side of the looking glass while she emerges into the realm of consciousness to assert her authority. At the end of *Looking-Glass* Alice becomes a figure of authority herself, in literary and political terms. The reversal that takes place in the looking-glass world for Alice is a completion of the action begun in Wonderland. The

final question of this text is not who dreamed it but who tells it, who gives it—or withholds from it—its meaning, who writes the book about "me"? "The question is," as Humpty Dumpty said to Alice, "which is to be master—that's all."

Mark Conroy (essay date 1991)

SOURCE: "A Tale of Two Alices in Wonderland," in *Literature and Psychology,* Vol. XXXVII, No. 3, 1991, pp. 29-44.

[*In the following essay, which focuses on* Alice's Adventures in Wonderland, *Conroy discusses the connections between Alice's identity as a middle-class Victorian child and her dream experiences.*]

Thanks to the Freudian moment in modern literary criticism, it has been for years quite permissible to view the dream world presented to the reader in Lewis Carroll's *Alice in Wonderland* as if it in fact bore some relation to actual dream structures and significances. While some have traced such structures rather hastily to the author's own psychology (a not inexplicable move given what is known of the author, perhaps), the more fruitful vein of inquiry has focussed rather upon the oneiric quality within the text itself, and has revealed its kinship with the mechanisms Sigmund Freud imputes to the dream work. At the same time, one finds critics who stress the way the *Alice* books confront and rework the cultural givens of Victorian childhood. The odd thing is, though, that very few readers of *Alice in Wonderland* have taken cognizance of the profound linkage between these two facets of the tale. A close look at the connection between the quasi-Freudian structure of Alice's dream and the process of growing up and socialization that constrains the dreamer will improve the chance of finding the zone of reference of the character in Wonderland who is in some ways the most elusive of all: Alice herself.

Readers' initial glimpses of Carroll's fictional protagonist have generally revealed a thoroughly conventional, almost blank young girl, who seldom acts but often comments blandly on the action, and who appears to be Wonderland's "real-life" character largely by default. She is shunted here and there throughout Wonderland, and of course blunders in by falling down the rabbit-hole in the first place. Her general state is one of bemusement at best. She asks of the Cheshire Cat:

> "Would you tell me, please, which way I ought to go from here?"
>
> "That depends a good deal on where you want to get to," said the Cat.

"I don't much care where—" said Alice.

"Then it doesn't matter which way you go." said the Cat.

This exchange is indicative of Alice's indecision. Her function seems to be to serve as a locus for the otherwise disparate activities, and to register the appropriate shock and surprise at the things that are thrown at her. Thus it is that her most active role seems to be that of impartial witness. When the King, Queen and executioner are debating whether to chop off the head of the Cheshire Cat, all three appeal to Alice to settle the question. Characteristically, she refers them to the Duchess, since it is her cat. She is also a witness in the trial of the Knave of Hearts; and again she at first takes no position, has nothing to report.

Alice is as much of a cipher as the other creatures in Wonderland, perhaps more so since at least the other creatures suggest a positive signification, whereas Alice comes across as a negative signifier: a normative void, perhaps, but still a void. Clearly there is more to Alice than this: she is, after all, the heroine of Dodgson's book. With this fact in mind, it may be that even the apparent blankness that is the Alice of Wonderland can be read, and as blankness is itself a clue to the Alice who dreamed the other Wonderland creatures as well as herself.

That Wonderland may be read psychoanalytically is now a given of the criticism of the *Alice* books. There has been considerably less attention given to the way the dream-structure of the first book dictates the presentation of Alice's character, however. Critics who have no trouble deciding that Alice's dream bears most of the earmarks of dreams in general tend to forget that in assessing the curiously aseptic Alice the reader confronts within that dream. Even Empson, so useful in other ways, fails one here, calling Alice "the most reasonable and responsible person in the book" and letting it go at that. Other critics tend to perceive the protagonist on her own dream terms as the Victorian victim of outside forces, of the violence represented in the Wonderland world. Even Nina Auerbach, who understands that Alice's "demure propriety . . . may have led readers to see her role . . . as more passive than it is," still reduces most of the tension in her dream to infantile introjection, by focusing on the cannibalism among the animals in Wonderland.

As useful as these interpretations have been, they tend either to reduce Alice to a mere product of outside forces or a compendium of sexual symbolism. To account best for what is active in Alice's character, we have to go deeper than these analyses have been content to go. Alice is in fact a quite active character in at least two ways that will detain us here: she is active in constructing her dream work; and on its evidence,

she is also active in confronting the adult who is already urging her to join it. She is far from eager to do so, and her resistance provides much of the tension in her story. The fact that desiring not to grow up may be interpreted as preferring passivity to activity only serves further to complicate Alice's conflicted relation to growing up and to socialization. The very instability of Alice in Wonderland—the way she grows and shrinks by turns—may be one of her few significant features. She is, indeed, so very conflicted that it may seem as if there were two Alices here, not one. If so, it should not surprise that a dream is used to present this conflict; for in a dream, there are always two subjects anyway.

Theorists of the dream have acknowledged this doubleness for a long time. Roughly speaking, the distinction can be rendered in terms similar to the conventional literary one between the "I" who narrates a given story and the "I" whose experiences and actions are narrated within the story: a distinction between the *sujet de l'énoncé* and the *sujet de l'énonciation*. Of course, in these linguistic cases, the difference is chiefly temporal. The "I" who says "I went there last week" is a week older than the "I" being discussed. With a dream, the distinction between the dreamer and the person's dream-image is almost of the same sort—but not quite. For her the disjunct is not only formal but also symptomatic.

As the psychoanalyst Jacques Lacan formulates it, a dream is a message for which the dreamer is at once sender and receiver. When this message is transmitted, its form is deliberately distorted so that the receiver cannot fully comprehend what the sender has produced. Dreams alleviate the anxieties of a subject's night-thoughts without producing too direct, and therefore unacceptable, a version of them; otherwise, the dreamer awakens. As the unacknowledged fulfillment of a repressed wish (or deflection of a repressed anxiety), the dream-message must make such wishes and anxieties unreadable, largely by removing such feelings from the figure of the dreamer's "stand-in" and investing them instead elsewhere. This move is essentially the "displacement" in Freudian displacement and condensation. It is by this bad faith that the dreamed Alice can always be quite properly appalled at the grotesque spectacle which Alice the dreamer is busily producing. The method by which a dream-message "jams" its own reception results in a split in the *sujet*; it also represents, in this case as well as any other, an already existing split, a tension within the dreamer.

There are, in other words, two Alices in *Alice in Wonderland*: the one who acts in the fantasy and the one who dreams it, performer and playwright/director. Alice the dream-image, by herself, does little and means little; but Alice the dreamer produces everything and intends more than she, or her creator, may know. But what does she intend? Since we have already granted that the dreamed Alice is more decoy than character, we need to approach that question not by looking at her directly, but first by observing the other creatures in Wonderland, and Wonderland itself.

We get some hints throughout the text that events in Wonderland have correlates in the world beyond Wonderland, in the familiar tricks memory plays on the dreamer. Her pool of tears may recall the British seaside, for instance, or the jurors she upsets with her skirt may put her in mind of gold-fish spilling out of a bowl. In addition, though, to these innocuous echoes, which have something of the air of a private joke, there are more importantly the school lessons Alice tries frantically to remember in an attempt to establish another glimpse of normal life. School is a motif throughout *Alice,* not only because as a young girl Alice goes to school, but also because it is so key to social training of the young. It is significant that even Alice's dreamed stand-in, when called upon to recite the Isaac Watts poem "Against Idleness and Mischief," confuses the words: "her voice sounded hoarse and strange, and the words did not come the same as they used to do." Indeed they do not: the "busy bee" of the Watts poem, industriously improving her cell, becomes a crocodile who "welcomes little fishies in, / With gently smiling jaws." A poem such as this was a weapon in the Victorian arsenal of good breeding. The third stanza, for instance, runs: "In works of labor or of skill, / I would be busy too; / For Satan finds some mischief still / For idle hands to do." In radically misconstruing the words of that poem, Alice is miscoding the message it contains as well. Yet her misreading seems to take place outside of herself, in a voice not her own. Even where the dreamed Alice threatens to confront the anxieties of the dreamer more directly, an alibi saves her.

The alibi also works where Alice is called upon by the Caterpillar to recite "You Are Old, Father William," which comes out as a parody of the Robert Southey poem "The Old Man's Comforts and How He Gained Them." The original is a counsel to moderation and respect for the Deity, which takes the form of a catechism: the young man asking questions and the old man offering wise and eloquent answers:

"You are old, Father William," the young man
   cried,
"And pleasures with youth pass away;
And yet you lament not the days that are
   gone:
Now tell me the reason, I pray."
"In the days of my youth," Father William
   replied,
"I remembered that youth could not last;
I thought of the future, whatever I did,
That I never might grieve of the Past."

In Alice's rendition the old worthy becomes a rather sinister figure of fun, offering to sell the young man some ointment he claims makes it possible for him to turn somersaults. In the final two stanzas he becomes belligerent and threatening: "I have answered three questions and that is enough," he announces, and tells the boy to "Be off, or I'll kick you downstairs!" The catechetical format, satirically recast by Dodgson, becomes a point of aggressive struggle rather than a scene of instruction. The warm, paternal authority figure of the Southey poem has become a thoroughly repulsive ogre, especially by the end.

In addition to Dodgson's satirical points, which become quite obvious once the originals can be compared to the versions he makes up, the scenes present the clearest danger to the fragile integrity of Alice's dream. For a start, these are some of the few moments before the dream's climax where the dreamed Alice is doing something; and whereas a *faux pas* committed at the Tea Party or the Croquet Game can seem like trouble with alien Wonderland ways, here these poems present themselves explicitly as part of her schooling. In failing, first for herself and then under orders from the Caterpillar, to recall and transmit them, she distorts their pedagogical message: the injunction to maturity.

Again, though, in each instance of this distortion, the agency of the distortion is displaced; onto the words themselves, for example. The Caterpillar, in a way a Father William figure himself, chides her for reciting it incorrectly:

"That is not said right," said the Caterpillar.

"Not *quite* right, I'm afraid," said Alice timidly: "some of the words have got altered."

By using the passive voice, Alice deflects responsibility to some alien force for misconstruing the words, thus retaining the split in the *sujet* and allowing the dream to continue. Thus have two messages, in the Caterpillar scene, been successfully distorted: first the pious message of the Southey poem is twisted by the dreamed Alice, and then the fact that she has done it on behalf of the dreaming Alice is also displaced.

The striking thing about these poetry recitals, though, is chiefly the rarity of Alice taking center stage within the dream. Her more usual stance is a reactive one: and at least during the Caterpillar scene, even the recital is something she is called upon by someone else to perform. More characteristic are the many scenes where Alice tries to conform to the pointless social rituals of Wonderland (always with limited success), and confronts the grotesque authority figures those rituals feature.

Those authority figures, who tell her where to go and what to do, are indeed grotesque: the enormous Duchess; the Queen of Hearts; the Mad Hatter; even the Caterpillar, imperiously smoking his hookah. They pursue illogical and obsessive enterprises with adult-like precision and logic. (The figure Alice follows down the hole at the outset, the White Rabbit, exemplifies both the precision and the illogic of the adult world, with his obedience to a tyrannical timepiece.) The Cheshire Cat, who tells Alice it does not matter where she goes, is the exception to the rule here; and indeed, Alice is eager to conform to rules in general throughout Wonderland, even as she wonders how to escape. Similarly, the social games such as the Tea-party of the Croquet match find Alice eager to join in; yet the illogic of them puzzles her. She unburdens herself to the Cheshire Cat about the Croquet Game: "'I don't think they play at all fairly . . . and they don't seem to have any rules in particular; at least, if there are, nobody attends to them.'" She goes on to remark "how confusing it is all the things being alive." Alice here is objecting to the use of live flamingoes and hedgehogs by the court in their game; and so *outré* is this behavior that Alice cannot be thought churlish for her reluctance.

Her objections take the form of traditional English concern for rules and fair play. But it is noteworthy that such social rituals as the Croquet Game and the Tea-party are almost in the nature of rites of passage for entry into the world of adult authority. Croquet is something a member of Alice's class would surely want to learn; and indeed, when asked whether she can play croquet, she proudly says "Yes!" It could very well be that in drawing back from these events, Alice represents her dreamer's drawing back from socialization into the ranks of adults. But the stated reason is always some concern for the niceties of protocol. (It is a revered commonplace about children that they are always insistent on such niceties anyway, which may strengthen the plausibility of this concern as an alibi for opting out of such games.)

In the same fashion, the figures of authority also come in for distortion in the Wonderland world. Such distortion of those figures really works in two helpful ways here. First of all, distortion caricatures, and ridicule is surely an aim throughout this satirical text, whether one chooses to impute that aim to Alice the dreamer or Dodgson the writer; but secondly, it also conceals, and for Alice the dreamer (at least), that is an equally important aim. A character like the Duchess acts in a manner so unbecoming of her class and out of keeping with her moralizing speeches that she cannot be confused with a "real" Duchess except in name. (That "except" is crucial, though, because the tension between the characters as imaginary figures on the one hand and their symbolic status on the other is one way the dream-message can jam its own reception.) By her

grotesquerie, the Duchess presents a sufficient variance from "real-life" authority figures the dreaming Alice would have known or heard of that, in being appalled, the dreamed Alice is not dissociating herself from the social hierarchy which the Duchess symbolizes through her titled name. At the same time, the overtly unpleasant if not hideous behavior of the Duchess distorts the fact that in her waking life, Alice is learning to emulate the people for whom the Duchess herself is a symbolic stand-in. Thus the question of Alice's relation to authority, in being raised, is effectively covered over by the same stroke: the Duchess, because she is so grotesque, appears not really to be a condensation of Alice the dreamer's desire, and since Alice seems not to be implicated in what the Duchess does in the first place, she does not really have to reject her either. She can object to the Duchess because she is an ill-bred person, not because she is a Duchess. (Indeed, Alice herself speaks of the day "[w]hen *I'm* a Duchess.")

Just as a Croquet match with odd rules cannot be a real Croquet game, so an ill-bred Duchess cannot be a proper Duchess. In each case, a potentially subversive reaction (on the symbolic or linguistic plane, at least) is also covered over by appealing to the status quo. Even when Alice contemplates stealing the Duchess' pig-baby—surely a transgression of the social order whether underground or above it—she reasons that "If I don't take this child away with me . . . they're sure to kill it in a day or two. Wouldn't it be murder to leave it behind?" (This dilemma is resolved in time, of course, when the baby changes into a pig.)

Since Alice the dreamer is who is effectively dispersed into these other signifiers in the first place, the dreamed Alice's shock at their behavior is at bottom one of recognition. But the fantastical setting allows Alice the sender to conceal the fact from Alice the receiver, even while revealing its symptoms. The dreamed Alice would then seem to be almost a decoy, a duplicitous sign, her fundamental desire made alien from her, displaced onto other signifying fields and then thrown back to her unwilling gaze. Even her constantly reiterated desire to get back to the garden could at least theoretically be served admirably by just waking up but the dreaming Alice does not wish to do so. Is it enough, though, merely to call the dreamed Alice a marker of some deliberate naivete of a dreamer unable to face what she herself has made?

That is only part of the narrative dynamic, and indeed as we showed above with the poems, the two Alices get further apart and closer together by turns throughout the text. Nor is it correct to assume that the dreamed is simply shocked by what the dreaming Alice produces. Although she is more reactive than active, and though her refusals are couched in conservative forms, her very gestures of refusal are threatening enough to the dream structure to make these suppressions necessary. There are several points where the alibi herself needs an alibi, in short.

The poetry recitals mentioned above are instances where the dream-image gets actively implicated in what the dreamer produces, always a threatening development. But the point where the two Alices get closest together is at the trial of the Knave of Hearts. Not surprisingly in this fairly plausible rendering of a dream, the closing of the gap between the two Alices brings about the dream's destruction.

When the King and Queen of Hearts first approach, Alice looks around, "eager to see the queen." At this point she is awed and reverent toward this prestigious couple, and even thinks herself "doubtful whether she ought not to lie down on her face like the three gardeners." Yet even at this juncture, when the Queen of Hearts can be viewed as a figure of Alice's own displaced desire for social esteem, there is a subversive hint:

> "My name is Alice, so please your majesty," said Alice very politely; but she added, to herself, "Why, they're only a pack of cards, after all. I needn't be afraid of them!"

This thought, of course, is a presage of the end of the dream; but at this stage, it is only a thought. Alice may not really believe it herself since she is obviously afraid enough of them not to say it aloud.

It is in the trial that these hints become fuller-blown realities. The trial proceeding is, of course, in a class by itself among social rituals. The other activities—the Quadrille, mealtime, Croquet, even school to an extent—operate as self-reinforcing sign systems. On the superficial level, they do not imply a social structure or a purpose but are simply ways of passing the time. A trial, on the other hand, has an overt function as social control: to confront a threat to the order and to contain or get rid of it. The dreamed Alice is only a witness to the trial, but it is arguable that the dreaming Alice is both the Queen of Hearts and the Knave of Hearts. These two characters of the Queen and the Knave represent obverse sides of Alice's own implication (unacknowledged) in the social order, both as subject to authority's rules and pressures, and as identifying herself with the authority. Because it commands Alice to give her evidence, the trial puts into question her status *as* witness, and hence also the epistemological status of what she has seen. Ironically enough, she cannot remain an observer once she is called as a witness. The dreamed Alice and the events of the dream are both beginning to totter: the dream will not last much longer.

Since the trial is the playing-out of Alice's entanglement in the process of socialization, it is small wonder that she is more of a nuisance here than anywhere else in the text. For one thing, she grows to the point where the king orders her out of the court, reading from his rule-book that those over a mile high must leave the court, according to rule forty-two:

> "I'm not a mile high," said Alice.
>
> "You are," said the King.
>
> "Nearly two miles high," added the Queen.
>
> "Well, I shan't go at any rate," said Alice: "Besides, that's not a regular rule: you invented it just now."
>
> "It's the oldest rule in the book," said the King.
>
> "Then it ought to be Number One," said Alice.

Alice is able to talk back to the King himself, more cheek than she has displayed thus far. But here again, she scores him off on a point of procedure; the King has not played by the book. A potentially subversive move once more becomes a plea for the orderly conduct of business. However, Alice here has fought to remain in the courtroom, suggesting that what happens there is of some importance to both dreamed and dreaming Alices (even though Alice herself is not on trial).

Finally the court is about to settle the verdict when the Queen says: "Sentence first—verdict afterwards":

> "Stuff and nonsense!" said Alice loudly. "The idea of having the sentence first!"
>
> "Hold your tongue!" said the Queen, turning purple.
>
> "I won't!" said Alice.
>
> "Off with her head!" the Queen shouted at the top of her voice. Nobody moved.
>
> "Who cares for you?" said Alice (she had grown to her full size by this time). "You're nothing but a pack of cards!"

It is by this gesture that the card-people—the most fulsome symbols of authority in Wonderland—become truly empty signifiers; Alice has now effectively "deconstructed" her own dream, since it is only her belief in their symbolic power that has provided the tension of the dream. Her statement, now no longer kept to herself but made functional within the dream, is an act of de-mystification. The card-people are now clearly her own product, animated by her own desire and fear.

It is true that one view of this gesture would be that the dreamed Alice's statement "You're nothing but a pack of cards" represents the dreaming Alice's realization that she is indeed only dreaming. In that case, the fact that the card-people are only empty signifiers would mean that they have ceased to symbolize genuine authority figures to Alice, and so her rejecting of them could not be seen as a reflection of the authority structures they had seemed to symbolize. There may be a bravado in her statement that allows such a reading. But in the next paragraph the pack of cards rises in the air and flies down upon Alice. Although the cards be deprived of social legitimacy by Alice's impiety, they seem not to have lost their power to frighten her. In their move to subjugate her, they are not merely a "pack of cards" but some possibly internalized force of repression.

Their act is the symbolic equivalent of any situation where a class' claim to legitimate authority is shown up: the fallback for lost authority is always some sort of force. (The Queen of Hearts, of course, has not been loth to employ force throughout.) As she moves toward fulfilling Alice the dreamer's wish to be out from under the socializing process, the dreamed Alice has also caused her own most imminent (and immanent) peril; and the dream cannot continue. The unmasking of the authority structure's symbolic emptiness also endangers Alice's own existence. Thus, the attack of the cards does not have to be straightforward act of suppression; it rather indicates the depth of Alice's implications all along in the socializing process figured in Wonderland, and why it took her so long to declare it false.

The fact that the figures attack Alice after she has declared them parts of a game—a "pack of cards"— implies that although, yes, the authority figures are a fiction in a sense, they are also her fiction. In dreaming them, she has endowed them with what psychological power they have, and that power persists even though it seems to have been defused or de-mystified. Alice has attacked their legitimacy but not their psychological force, because among other things she herself is slowly joining their ranks.

But this process of socialization is not carried out by one person alone. Others strive to repair any damage to it *for* us, and this her older sister proceeds to do, in the crucial final pages of the text.

Upon awakening, Alice recounts to her sister the curious dream she has had, "all these Adventures of hers that you have just been reading about:"

> and when she had finished, her sister kissed her and said, "It *was* a curious dream, dear, certainly; but now run in to your tea; it's getting late." So Alice got up and ran off, thinking while she ran, as well she might, what a wonderful dream it had been.

The narrative focus then shifts to Alice's sister. Again, Alice becomes the character in a dream, but it is her sister's daydream ("after a fashion"). Alice seems physically present: "the tiny hands were clasped upon her knee, and the bright eager eyes were looking up into hers—she could hear the very tone of her voice, and see that queer little toss of her head." Thinking of Alice recalls the dream the sister has just heard described, and strangely the sister begins imagining the characters of Wonderland as Alice has related them. She seems to hear the March Hare and the Queen of Hearts, the Gryphon, the pig-baby and the Duchess. In a scene, two movements are delineated here: on the one hand, Alice's dream seems to be internalizing itself in her sister, becoming more "real"; on the other hand, since even the telling of a dream alters its contents in some way, Alice's dream is now twice domesticated, now that her sister is imagining what Alice in her waking state reported. It is not surprising that the characters are rendered in a rather elegiac manner as they file past:

> she knew she had but to open [her eyes] again, and all would change to dull reality . . . the rattling teacups would change to tinkling sheepbells . . . and the sneeze of the baby, the shriek of the Gryphon and all the other queer noises, would change (she knew) to the confused clamour of the busy farmyard—while the lowing of the cattle in the distance would take the place of the Mock Turtle's heavy sobs.

The fantasy of Alice, as dreamed by her sister, is banished now by "dull reality," a move which, though sad, seems necessary. (Reality may be dull, but it is still reality.) Her sister's dream, because it is a daydream, recognizes its own nature as fantasy, and in that recognition it succeeds only in abolishing the dream of Alice. However, Alice's dream is then reborn, in a final domestication that her older sister prophetically imagines:

> Lastly, she pictured to herself how this same little sister of hers would, in the after-time, be herself a grown woman; . . . and how she would gather about her other little children, and make their eyes bright and eager with many a strange tale, perhaps even with the dream of Wonderland of long ago.

Just as those things of a child are put away as Alice's dream fantasies yield to dull (but safe) reality, so the child Alice herself is finally replaced with a vision of the adult Alice, who in telling her dream story integrates it fully into the common cultural heritage. The vision of Alice's sister both preserves the fantasy and makes the Wonderland adventures, so disturbing as dreamt, into elements of a future social ritual: a story to be told to succeeding generations of children. The dream has not been simply annulled, rather "co-opted."

We as readers may be in much the same position as Alice's older sister, reading a description of a fantasy and feeling content to appreciate it as a curious story. No doubt there is a certain comfort in treating a dream as a "story told upon awakening." Once a dream is retold, it ceases to signify the immediate tension of the subject encountering fear or desire; it becomes merely narrative. It is only as a story told upon awakening that Alice's dream, freed of its subversive overtones, can be incorporated into affirmative culture. (The general tendency to treat the Alice books as amusing children's stories and not much more would suggest the sister's prophecy is fulfilled.) That we can sense it is something more than simply a curious story owes not only to the evident satire of some of the sequences, but, as I have been arguing, to the dream format of the story as well.

Like all dreams, even daydreams, there is distortion in domestication; and in the daydream of Alice's sister, the Wonderland adventures lose in truth what they gain in transmissibility. To the extent this happens, the dream returns to the surface level and the creatures and rituals become truly "empty forms." Thus is the sister's daydream Dodgson's way of retaining his child's fantasy without its disturbing possibilities: taming that begins with her sister's kind gesture of brushing from Alice's face the dead leaves, those last visible remnants of her dream.

Donald Rackin (essay date 1991)

SOURCE: "The *Alice* Books and Lewis Carroll's World," in *Alice's Adventures in Wonderland and Through the Looking-Glass: Nonsense, Sense, and Meaning,* Twayne Publishers, 1991, pp. 3-12.

[*Rackin is known as an authority on Lewis Carroll. In the following essay, he places the* Alice *books in their Victorian social context.*]

This study rests on the premise that appreciating Lewis Carroll's *Alice* books (1862-72) does not require extensive knowledge of their historical setting. Their continuous popularity among large and varied audiences for the past 120 years shows how accessible they are: lay readers seeking to experience and understand their power need not acquire a vocabulary of outdated words and unfamiliar historical facts, of obsolete concepts and attitudes. This does not mean, however, that the *Alices* are unrelated to their original cultural matrix: like all other artifacts, they are products of their era, bearing inscriptions of numerous transactions with the material and ideological contexts from which they first emerged. So while the *Alices* provide readers with what often seems a glorious escape from time and place—from historical context itself—some of their most memorable effects depend on tangible connections to their specific historical milieu.

However, because Lewis Carroll's world of the 1860s bears many resemblances to middle-class life in developed countries today, these connections are often relatively easy to understand and appreciate. In their daily lives, Carroll and his first readers experienced intimately the changes produced by industrialism, laissez-faire capitalism, and limited representative democracy, and familiar features of that familiar context often appear in Alice's dream fantasies. The sense of life in an unregulated, rapidly expanding, free-market economy in a secularized and fragmented society whose various power arrangements, competing classes, goals, and values are rapidly changing in response to numerous technological, economic, demographic, and political changes is a sense of life we share with Carroll and his contemporaries. Indeed, because the Victorian bourgeoisie were experiencing our world in its nascent state and because many of them still knew directly and yearned earnestly for another, much slower-paced, more coherent world of serene certainties and secure social values, their reactions to such unprecedented change are frequently fresher, more passionate, and more vivid than are our comparatively blasé or resigned reactions to similar cultural phenomena.

When, for example, Alice discovers herself in a looking-glass railroad carriage, modern readers should find the scene's references to the details of public rail travel generally familiar. Even more familiar will be the scene's hyperbolic representations of time as an industrial construct, of time's ridiculous but actual connection with money and by extension with a frenzied getting-and-spending capitalist system—a dream subject directly relevant to the wide-awake anxieties suffered by Victorians as a result of the rapid expansion of consumerism, a cash economy, machinery, and mechanically measured time as dominant forces in their daily lives. Taken together, the extremely fast-paced *Alice* adventures caricature a paradigmatic shift in the very conception of time, a shift greatly accelerated in the nineteenth century by major discoveries in astronomy, geology, and biology, and by technological achievements like the rapid development during the first half of the Victorian age of the factory system, railways, steamships, and telegraph lines—four of the period's many contributions to commerce, transportation, and communications that radically changed the relations between time and space and the way people live in them (a central topic of the *Alices*).

The rapidity of change occurring almost everywhere during the period, the dizzying pace of life in a multifarious, mechanized mass society is reflected in Alice's fast-paced, crowded, discontinuous dream adventures. So too is the sense of speedy motion, not for the sake of progress toward a definitive goal, but simply for its own sake. Thus, the Red Queen's frequently quoted response to Alice's assertion that "in *our* country . . . you'd generally get to somewhere else—if you ran very fast for a long time as we've been doing" is especially relevant to the empty bustle of urban existence in Carroll's mid-Victorian England, an England suddenly coming to question its own faith in inevitable progress and the benefits of mechanical invention. "Now, *here*," says the Queen, "it takes all the running *you* can do, to keep in the same place."

> "Tickets, please!" said the [railway] Guard, putting his head in at the window. In a moment everyone was holding out a ticket: they were about the same size as the people, and quite seemed to fill the carriage.

> "Now then! Show your ticket, child!" the Guard went on, looking angrily at Alice. And a great many voices all said together ("like the chorus of a song," thought Alice), "Don't keep him waiting, child! Why, his time is worth a thousand pounds a minute!"

The anxious dream-satire of the **Looking-Glass** railway scene is directed, in part, at the improbable regimentation and commercialization of what was until then considered beyond such strict mechanical control and quantitative measurement. In Alice's dream of the railroad carriage, time and space are measurable by a new mechanized, monetary standard. Money, not inherent worth, now determines value; now "time is money" (the insubstantial "smoke alone," according to the awe-inspired consumers in Alice's carriage, "is worth a thousand pounds a puff!"). Tickets the size of human beings represent with surreal clarity the way various social and commercial institutions, like mass transportation, had during Carroll's childhood and youth grown to the point of dwarfing, dominating, even crowding out the people they were meant to serve, quickly turning the recent masters of the machines into the machines' clockwork "chorus" of harried, cramped, but worshipful servants—a process that deeply troubled many intellectuals among Carroll's earnest contemporaries, including the famous literary prophets of social disaster, Thomas Carlyle, Matthew Arnold, and Carroll's friend John Ruskin.

The frantic railway scene is but one example of the numerous allusions in the **Alices** to the mechanization, commodification, and acceleration that were transforming Victorian life. The first character Alice meets is the harried White Rabbit, a desperate slave to his watch and busy schedule. Moreover, many of the humanoid creatures in her adventures are actually mechanical things playing mechanical parts—cards, chessmen, set figures from traditional nursery rhymes—inflexible cogs in an unprogressive, incomprehensible but perpetual, all-consuming social mechanism.

In the world's great age of machinery, England was the very center of the Industrial Revolution, "the world's workshop" and the epitome of the modern shift from manual to mechanical labor. Effecting an enormous transformation in the quality of everyday life, this triumph of materialism and machinery was celebrated by many Victorians, especially those in the newly rising classes; but it was at the same time often deplored in a variety of Victorian literary texts, perhaps most powerfully in the fantastic, often bitter satire of Charles Dickens (one of Carroll's favorite authors and popular among all literate classes), who in a series of best-selling novels in the 1850s and 1860s created a large, funny, but macabre gallery of caricatured Victorians dehumanized by the system into manufactured, automatic, scurrying *things*.

CULTURAL ANARCHY

In the same years as the publication of Alice's anarchic adventures, Matthew Arnold, the leading literary/cultural critic of his time, warned in his most famous work, *Culture and Anarchy* (1869), of the ways the British worship of machinery was quickly leading to anarchy: "Faith in machinery is . . . our besetting danger; often in machinery most absurdly disproportioned to the end which this machinery, if it is to do any good at all, is to serve; but always in machinery, as if it had a value in and for itself. What is freedom but machinery? What is population but machinery? What is coal but machinery? what are railroads but machinery? what is wealth but machinery? what are, even, religious organizations but machinery?"

For many conservative, establishment figures like Arnold and his fellow Oxford don Carroll (both were also graduates of Rugby as well as sons of upper-middle-class Church of England clergymen), "machinery" could be a heavily fraught symbol for the loss of traditional humane values, for cultural anarchy, even for imminent political revolution:

> For a long time . . . the strong feudal habits of subordination and deference continued to tell upon the working class. The modern spirit has now almost entirely dissolved those habits, and the anarchical tendency of our worship of freedom in and for itself, of our superstitious faith, as I say, in machinery, is becoming very manifest. More and more, because of this our blind faith in machinery, because of our want of light to look beyond machinery to that end for which machinery is valuable, this and that man, and this and that body of men, all over the country, are beginning to assert and put into practice an Englishman's right to do what he likes; his right to march where he likes, enter where he likes, hoot as he likes, threaten as he likes, smash as he likes. All this, I say, tends to anarchy.

The Victorian mechanical revolution, then, was part of a broad context of interdependent revolutions—intellectual, scientific, economic, political, social, religious, artistic—in an age of revolution. The revolution in biological theory, generally attributed to Darwin but actually begun earlier in the century, generated among Victorian intellectuals a frightening vision of "Nature, red in tooth and claw" (Tennyson, *In Memoriam*) and of themselves as no more than one of countless, dispensable species in an inescapable biological mechanism governed (like laissez-faire capitalism) by survival-of-the-fittest instincts. Soon, numbers of earnest thinkers were seeing themselves and their follows as mere selfish, appetitive apes thinly disguised as altrustic, humane, respectable Victorian ladies and gentlemen. This materialistic, God-less vision profoundly affected philosophical thought, religious belief, and political action—almost every area of social concern. Moreover, the revolutionary notion of inevitable class warfare—linked to nineteenth-century evolutionary theory, mass industrialization, laissez-faire economics, a large and growing proletariat, urbanization, cheap labor, unionization, cycles of inflation and depression, and devastating poverty in the midst of immense wealth—created for the elite, privileged, once-secure class of Arnold and Carroll the frightening prospect of literal anarchy and revolution. (Friedrich Engels's *The Condition of the Working Class in England in 1844* was based on firsthand observations of the deplorable conditions of workers in Manchester; with Karl Marx, Engels published *The Communist Manifesto* in 1848, translated into English in 1850.) Despite several Parliamentary Reform Bills during the period that gradually granted voting rights and some political power to larger, less privileged segments of the population, and despite other social reforms that ameliorated the worst horrors of an unregulated capitalist system, England seemed for much of the period dangerously close to the political upheavals that had periodically rocked Europe since the days of the bloody French Revolution. "The fear of revolution," as one leading Victorian scholar puts it, "had almost become part of the collective unconscious."

A WORLD TURNED UPSIDE DOWN

These revolutionary tendencies of the period and the anxieties they provoked often lie close to the surface of Alice's dreams. In a sense, the *Alice* books are about revolution in that they present a funny but anxious vision of an entire middle-class world turned upside down: two topsy-turvy, "backwards" places where the sensible child of the master class acts as servant, and the crazy servants act as masters; where inanimate, manufactured playing cards and chessmen have seized control, giving rude orders to a real, live, polite human representative of the ruling class that had but recently manipulated them as inert counters in games of her class's devising; where time itself will no longer "behave" its erstwhile governors so that in the Mad Tea-Party it is always six o'clock (quitting time for many factory workers); where the old, comfortable, seemingly unchanging social fabric has been so unravelled

that each atomized creature now lives in its own, completely self-centered, disconnected world, freed from the fabricated "rules" and traditions of bourgeois community, rank and order.

The once sacrosanct, relatively static class system that had served, primarily, the interests of a small minority of privileged Anglican gentlemen like Arnold and Carroll was therefore deeply threatened by change in an increasingly materialistic, competitive society, increasingly driven by mechanical innovation and the volatile, mechanistic standards of the market. For adherents of the bourgeois ethos like Carroll or like his adored heroine Alice, daughter of Dean Liddell of Christ Church College, Oxford, such revolutions represented a threat to personal identity itself: "What *will* become of me?" is a question Alice often asks, in various forms, throughout her adventures. Given its historical context, the question deals with far more than her physical nature: it carries for her class broad and sinister implications. So too does Gilbert and Sullivan's hilarious comment on this social aspect of their revolutionary age as that age drew to a close: "When every one is somebodee, / Then no one's anybody!" (*The Gondoliers,* 1889).

Carroll's mature lifetime was passed in an age of burgeoning technology that rapidly increased the spread of new material goods, ideas, and ways of doing things; of unprecedented population concentrations in cities; of enormous factories and serious environmental pollution; of great shifts in the distribution of wealth and power; of Karl Marx's *Das Kapital* (the first volume, written in England, appeared in 1867) and the rise of English socialism; and, in general, of the zenith and incipient decline of the bourgeois hegemony in politics and culture. Beyond England's shores, it was also the heyday of the British Empire—arguably the greatest empire the world has ever known, but an empire already threatened by violent revolutions against imperialism as well as by peaceful but irreversible evolutions toward colonial independence (Canada, for instance, became essentially self-governing in 1867).

It was, moreover, the period of Freud's youth (Freud was 13 years old when **Wonderland** was first translated into German in 1869), of impressionism in the arts, of a growing fascination with dreams and other workings of the inner life—with what Walter Pater, the age's leading aesthetician, characterized just three years after the publication of **Alice's Adventures in Wonderland** as the individual "mind keeping as a solitary prisoner its own dream of a world." At the same time, it was also the period that witnessed among the middle-classes a wide dissemination of earlier Romantic views of child psychology and of the child as the innocent, near-divine "father of the Man." These views, in turn, fostered a burgeoning body of children's literature (like the **Alices**) aimed at nurturing young readers' precious innate creative imaginations rather than beating out their natural savagery or filling their blank-tablet minds with didactic, cautionary tales.

It was, in addition, an age of intensified sexism and misogyny (critic and reformer John Ruskin's notorious "Of Queens' Gardens" [1864-71] is often cited as the paradigm of the patriarchal "woman's place in the home" and "on the pedestal" ideology that permeated the culture). But at the same time it witnessed the public emergence of successful, celebrated women intellectuals, among them the Brontës, Elizabeth Gaskell, George Eliot, Harriet Martineau, and Elizabeth Barrett Browning. And it was the first age of organized, revolutionary feminism—a feminism that in some ways overshadows that of our own period (John Stuart Mill's *On the Subjection of Women,* a major philosophical formulation of modern feminism, was published in 1869).

Carroll's contemporaries also experienced a revolutionary crisis of faith perhaps unparalleled in modern history. Not only was the period plagued by bitter, destructive sectarianism among warring Christian denominations, it was also an age in which many of the best minds had already lost all religious conviction. It is of course no coincidence that in his 1869 indictment of his materialistic, mechanistic society, Arnold repeatedly uses such terms as *faith, religious,* and *worship.* Newly secularized, scientized England was, as Arnold suggests in a celebrated 1855 poem about faith and doubt, "wandering between two worlds, one dead, / One powerless to be born." For Arnold and many other mid-Victorian thinkers, the fear was that England, now bereft of its "dead" world of a common religious faith, an established church, and a secure system of mystified bourgeois values, was quickly becoming a totally secular political entity, nothing more than a collection of self-serving factions and individuals lacking any true vitality, any agreed-on center of transcendent belief and ethical principles. As Arnold writes in "Dover Beach" (1867),

> The Sea of Faith
> Was once, too, at the full, and round earth's
>   shore
> Lay like the folds of a bright girdle furl'd.
> But now I only hear
> Its melancholy, long, withdrawing roar,
> Retreating, to the breath
> Of the night-wind, down the vast edges drear
> And naked shingles of the world.

Soon, it seemed, England would be merely a free-floating political aggregate held together by nothing more glorious than money or (enlightened) self-interest, devoid of its once-cherished cultural and spiritual landmarks—a godless place not unlike the chaotic underground into which poor Alice falls in her first adventure, or the "backwards" world she discovers just behind the comforting bourgeois looking-glass.

VICTORIAN EARNESTNESS

Victorians are often noted, sometimes ridiculed, for their irrepressible optimism and earnestness. Despite the grave doubts generated by the massive revolutionary changes that characterized their age, many of them continued to believe passionately in progress and in the efficaciousness of their earnest efforts to make their world better. Arnold himself, as if obeying Thomas Carlyle's Calvinist injunctions to dispel doubt by hard work in the concrete world, became in middle age a reforming commissioner of public education. In earnest do-it-yourself manuals like *Self-Help* (1859), *Lives of the Engineers* (1861-62), *Thrift* (1875), and *Duty* (1880), Samuel Smiles became one of the period's best-selling authors by preaching to the lower-middle and working classes a no-nonsense, humorless gospel of personal industry and unabashed get-ahead, commercial success.

But Victorians also knew how to make fun of their own earnestness, their middle-class reverence for work, money, and social respectability, as well as numerous other foibles of their complex, disturbing world. A number of the writers cited here—Carlyle, Dickens, and Gilbert and Sullivan most obviously; the Brontës, Eliot, and Arnold in more subtle ways—are noteworthy for their humorous treatments of the most serious social issues of their day. Victorian literature includes a wide variety of other writers who showed their age how to laugh at itself—among them, William Makepeace Thackeray, Edward Lear, George Meredith, Anthony Trollope, Samuel Butler, and the young George Bernard Shaw. The *Alice* books, like their earnest and very respectable author, the Reverend Charles Lutwidge Dodgson (alias Lewis Carroll), thus fit for another reason rather predictably into their historical context—an age of great comedy made in spite and at the expense of great earnestness. It should come as no surprise that the period ends with another earnest Victorian making wonderful, irreverent fun of respectability and earnestness, putting Victorianism in its final place, as he so often did, with epigrammatic and telling wit. Even in its title, Oscar Wilde's play *The Importance of Being Earnest* (1895) sounds the keynote of this admirably earnest age of revolution, bourgeois anxiety, and playful laughter.

FURTHER READING

Bibliography

Fordyce, Rachel. *Lewis Carroll: A Reference Guide.* Boston: G. K. Hall & Co., 1988, 160 p.

An annotated critical bibliography of general and scholarly commentary on Carroll's life and works, including editions, biographies, criticism, reminiscences, and unpublished dissertations.

Guiliano, Edward. "Lewis Carroll: A Sesquicentennial Guide to Research." In *Dickens Studies Annual* 10 (1982): 263-310.

Described by Guiliano as the "first prose guide to publications on Lewis Carroll"; includes sections on editions, stage and screen adaptations, psychoanalytic approaches, philosophy, and the language of the *Alice* books.

Weaver, Warren. *Alice in Many Tongues.* Madison: The University of Wisconsin Press, 1964, 147 p.

A study of the translations of *Alice,* with a chronological checklist of translations. Includes an essay on the difficulties of translating *Alice,* and samples of illustrations from foreign editions.

Criticism

Ackroyd, Peter. "The Road to Wonderland." In *The New York Times Book Review* C, No. 46 (November 12, 1995): 13.

Favorably reviews Morton N. Cohen's biography *Lewis Carroll,* which examines the private life of Charles Dodgson, documenting the circumstances surrounding his fondness for young girls and his dual successes as a children's author and respected instructor.

Bivona, Daniel. "Alice the Child-Imperialist and the Games of Wonderland." In *Nineteenth Century Literature* 41, No. 2 (September 1986): 143-71.

Places Alice's Wonderland adventures in the context of Hegelian philosophy and British Victorian imperialism.

Blake, Kathleen. *Play, Games, and Sport: The Literary Works of Lewis Carroll.* Ithaca: Cornell University Press, 1974, 216 p.

General discussion of the influence of games, symbolic logic, and play on Carroll's imaginative works. Individual chapters are devoted to *Alice's Adventures in Wonderland* and *Through the Looking-Glass.*

Cripps, Elizabeth A. "Alice and the Reviewers." In *Children's Literature: Annual of the Modern Language Association Seminar on Children's Literature and The Children's Literature Association* 11 (1983): 32-48.

Surveys early critical and popular responses to *Alice's Adventures in Wonderland* and *Through the Looking-Glass.*

Gardner, Martin, author of notes and introduction. *The Annotated Alice: Alice's Adventures in Wonderland and*

Through the Looking-Glass by Lewis Carroll. Harmondsworth: Penguin Books, 1970, 352 p.

Annotated scholarly edition of the *Alice* books. Includes an introductory essay and a brief annotated bibliography.

Graves, Robert. "Alice." In *Collected Poems: 1975,* pp. 31-32. London: Cassell & Company Ltd., 1975.

The noted English novelist, classical scholar, and poet makes a poetical commentary on Alice's "queer but true" adventures in *Through the Looking-Glass.*

Gray, Donald J., editor. *Alice in Wonderland: Authoritative Texts of Alice's Adventures in Wonderland, Through the Looking-Glass, and The Hunting of the Snark,* by Lewis Carroll. New York: W. W. Norton & Company, Inc., 1971, 434 p.

Critical edition of the *Alice* books with a brief introductory essay and a selected bibliography. Edition includes related Carroll material and several critical essays.

Henkle, Roger B. "The Mad Hatter's World." In *The Virginia Quarterly Review* 49, No. 1 (Winter 1973): 99-117.

Discusses the appeal of the *Alice* books for adults and suggests that the "madcap behavior" readers find in *Alice* offers an escape from the restrictions of adult reality.

Johnson, Paula. "Alice Among the Analysts." In *Hartford Studies in Literature* IV, No. 2 (1972): 114-22.

A brief survey of psychoanalytical approaches to the *Alice* books.

Kurrick, Maire Jaanus. "Carroll's *Alice in Wonderland.*" In *Literature and Negation,* pp. 197-205. New York: Columbia University Press, 1979.

Explores the problem of language and subjectivity in *Alice.*

Phillips, Robert, editor. *Aspects of Alice: Lewis Carroll's Dreamchild As Seen through the Critics' Looking-Glasses, 1865-1971.* New York: The Vanguard Press, Inc., 1971, 450 p.

A collection of essays organized by critical approach, and a checklist of selected criticism from 1865 to 1971. Includes sections on "Language, and Parody, and Satire," "Freudian Interpretations," and *Alice* "As Victorian and Children's Literature."

Polhemus, Robert M. "Carroll's *Through the Looking-Glass* (1871): The Comedy of Regression." In *Comic Faith: The Great Tradition from Austen to Joyce,* pp. 245-93. Chicago: The University of Chicago Press, 1980.

Places Carroll's work in a literary tradition linking comedy and religion; focuses on Carroll's comic vision and his regression to childhood in *Through the Looking-Glass.*

Priestley, J. B. "The Walrus and the Carpenter." In *The New Statesman* LIV, No. 1378 (August 10, 1957): 168 p.

Contends that the Walrus and Carpenter episode in Chapter Four of *Through the Looking-Glass* is intended as political symbolism.

Pudney, John. "The Publication of *Alice in Wonderland.*" In *Only Connect: Readings on Children's Literature,* edited by Sheila Egoff, G. T. Stubbs, and L. F. Ashley, pp. 238-43. Toronto: Oxford University Press, 1980.

A brief account of the illustration and publication of *Alice's Adventures in Wonderland.*

Pycior, Helena M. "At the Intersection of Mathematics and Humor: Lewis Carroll's *Alices* and Symbolical Algebra." In *Victorian Studies* 28, No. 1 (Autumn 1984): 149-70.

Establishes a precedent for Dodgson's combination of humor and mathematics, and traces the influence of symbolical algebra on Dodgson, contending that its emphasis on "structure over meaning" is satirized in the *Alices.*

Rackin, Donald, editor. *Alice's Adventures in Wonderland: A Critical Handbook.* Belmont: Wadsworth Publishing Company, Inc., 1969, 371 p.

Incorporates facsimile editions of the *Alice* books, a collection of the major critical essays from 1930 to 1966, and a selected bibliography. Donald Rackin's essay "Alice's Journey to the End of Night" (1966) is included in the entry above.

Shires, Linda M. "Fantasy, Nonsense, Parody, and the Status of the Real: The Example of Carroll." In *Victorian Poetry* 26, No. 3 (Autumn 1988): 267-83.

Explores the problem of reality in Carroll. With the help of "psychoanalytic and linguistic theory," discusses Dodgson's employment of fantasy, nonsense, and parody to "reverse . . . the real and the unreal" in *Alice.*

Additional coverage of Carroll's life and career is contained in the following sources published by Gale Research: *Nineteenth-Century Literature Criticism,* Volume 2; *Children's Literature Review,* Volumes 2 and 18; *Dictionary of Literary Biography,* Volume 18; *DISCovering Authors;* and *Yesterday's Authors of Books for Children,* Volume 2.

Richard Henry Dana, Sr.

1787-1879

(Also wrote under pseudonym of The Idle Man) American essayist, poet, editor, short story writer, critic, and lecturer.

INTRODUCTION

Considered a minor literary figure, Dana was among the first American literary critics to be a proponent of romanticism. Following his conversion to Congregationalism in 1827, Dana rejected the romantic mode and began a sustained conservative attack on what he saw as the paucity of American culture.

Biographical Information

Born in Cambridge, Massachusetts, in 1787, Dana was the youngest of five children. After schooling in Newport, Rhode Island, he entered Harvard College in 1804, but was expelled three years later for taking part in a student rebellion. Dana's hopes of a comfortable career as an independent man of letters were severely compromised when his brother Francis lost much of the family fortune in property speculations. Admitted to the bar in 1812, Dana married Ruth Charlotte Smith one year later. When the *North American Review* was founded in 1815, Dana became a contributor, and in 1818 he was named assistant editor. His outspoken review of William Hazlitt's *Lectures on the English Poets* countered the prevailing neoclassical critical fashion and he was denied the editorship of the journal, causing him to resign from his post. In 1821 Dana began to publish a new periodical, *The Idle Man*, but it ran only six issues. Following his wife's death in 1822, Dana was influenced by the revival movement led by Lyman Beecher and, in 1826, he converted to Congregationalism and began to write on religious matters. In the latter part of his career, faced with penury, Dana extended the range of his literary endeavors, writing poetry, teaching English literature, and lecturing on Shakespeare. Suffering from failing health, Dana retired to his house at Cape Ann and died there on February 2, 1879.

Major Works

Dana's broad literary output included poetry, short fiction, book reviews, lectures, and essays. His first publications were reviews and critical essays for *The Monthly Anthology* and its successor, the *North American Review*. Dana's notorious review of Hazlitt's

Lectures on the English Poets, in which he praised William Wordsworth and Samuel Taylor Coleridge at the expense of neoclassical poet Alexander Pope, established his reputation in Boston as a romantic iconoclast. Dana's early prose fiction, such as the gothic tale "Paul Felton" (1822), is characterized by its exploration of the supernatural and the psychology of the imagination. Dana published his first volume of poetry, *The Buccaneer and Other Poems* (1827), at the behest of his friend William Cullen Bryant, and followed it with *Poems and Prose Writings* (1833). A two-volume edition of the *Poems and Prose Writings* was published in 1850. Of Dana's poems, the long poem "The Buccaneer" has helped sustain his reputation as a noteworthy poet. In 1838 Dana began a series of seven lectures on Shakespeare, but these remain unpublished. His later essays reveal his rejection of the romantic mode and offer a conservative critique of American cultural shallowness and anti-intellectualism, conditions which stemmed, Dana believed, from America's passion for social equality and its disinterest in the past.

Critical Reception

The strength and independence of Dana's literary opinions often exposed him to censure. During his period of literary activity, his work met with both critical hostility and public indifference, but it was also well received by many reviewers and, for a time, he enjoyed a solid reputation as a serious literary figure. Many of Dana's contemporaries found his poetry stronger in conception than performance. Often viewed as a provocative essayist and an idiosyncratic reviewer, Dana left an intellectual stamp on his work which enhanced his essays and sometimes damaged his poems. His philosophical seriousness was at times taken for Calvinist brooding, and he was criticized for his gloomy tone. Although his lectures on Shakespeare were prompted by financial expediency, they were generally well received. Modern critics, such as Doreen Hunter and Robert A. Ferguson, have focused their analyses of Dana's work on his rejection of romanticism in favor of his later conservative views of religion and law. Dana's professional life ended in obscurity; he lived long enough to see his own career eclipsed by that of his son, Richard Henry Dana, Jr.

PRINCIPAL WORKS

The Idle Man [editor and major contributor] (essays, short stories, poetry) 1821-22
The Buccaneer and Other Poems (poetry) 1827
Poems and Prose Writings (poetry, essays and criticism) 1833
*Poems and Prose Writings. 2 vols. (poetry, essays, and criticism) 1850

**Includes the first edition of *Poems and Prose Writings* (1833).

CRITICISM

Richard Henry Dana, Sr. (essay date 1827)

SOURCE: "Preface to the First Edition of the Poems," in *Poems and Prose Writings,* Vol I, Baker and Scribner, 1850, pp. ix-xi.

[*In the following preface to his first collection of poems, first published in 1827 and reissued in 1850 with a second volume of his poetry, Dana expresses his hopes for the public's favorable reception of his work, and comments on the partly factual source for "The Buccaneer."*]

It is not without hesitation that I give this small volume [*The Buccaneer and Other Poems*] to the public; for no one can be more sensible than I am how much is necessary to the production of what may be rightly called poetry. It is true that something resembling it is oftentimes borne into instant and turbulent popularity, while a work of genuine character may be lying neglected by all except the poets. But the tide of time flows on, and the former begins to settle to the bottom, while the latter rises slowly and steadily to the surface, and moves forward, for a spirit is in it.

It is a poor ambition to be anxious after the distinction of a day in that which, if it be fit to live at all, is to live for ages. It is wiser than all, so to love one's art that its distinctions shall be but secondary: and, indeed, he who is not so absorbed in it as to think of his fame only as one of its accidents had better save himself his toil; for the true power is not in him. Yet the most self-dependent are stirred to livelier action by the hope of fame, and there are none who can go on with vigour, without the sympathy of some few minds which they respect.

I will not say of my first tale ["**The Buccaneer**"] as Miss Edgeworth sometimes does of her improbabilities, "This is a fact"; but this much I may say: there are few facts so well vouched for, and few truths so fully believed in, as the account upon which I have grounded my story.

I shall not name the island off our New England coast upon which these events happened, and these strange appearances were seen; for islanders are the most sensitive creatures in the world in all that relates to their places of abode.

I have changed the time of the action—which was before the war of our Revolution—to that of the great contest in Spain; as the reader will see, in my making use of the Christian name of Lord Wellington in a way to allude to the popular belief, during the early ages, in the return of King Arthur to the world.—In putting my hero on horseback, in not allowing him to die quietly in his bed, and, indeed, in whatever I thought might heighten the poetical effect of the tale, I have not hesitated to depart from the true account. Nor am I even certain that I have not run two stories into one; it being many years since these wonderful events were told to me. I mention this here, lest the islanders might be unnecessarily provoked at my departures from the real facts, when they come to read my tale, and the critics be put to the trouble of useless research in detecting mistakes.

Of the second story ["**The Changes of Home**"] I would only say, that, having in it nothing of the marvellous, and being of a less active character than the first, I shall not be disappointed though it should fail of being generally estimated according to its relative merit.

Of the remaining pieces, the first four have appeared in the *New York Review,* and are here republished with the consent of my friend Bryant, who was the editor of that late work;—"**The Husband's and Wife's Grave,**" "**The Dying Raven,**" "**Fragment of an Epistle,**" and "**The Little Beach-Bird.**" The others are, "**A Clump of Daisies,**" "**The Pleasure-Boat,**" and "**Daybreak.**"

One of these, "**Fragment of an Epistle,**" is taken from a letter which I wrote to amuse myself while recovering from a severe illness. I must be pardoned giving it as a fragment. The lines are much more broken than is usual in the octosyllabic verse, though Milton has taken great liberties in this respect in his two exquisite little poems in the same measure. This he could have done neither through ignorance nor carelessness. Lord Byron has justly spoken of "the fatal facility" of this measure; and he might as truly have remarked upon its fatal monotony, unless varied in all possible ways. So far from abrupt pauses not being allowable in it, there is scarcely a measure in the language which becomes so wearisome without them; as every one must have experienced in reading Scott, notwithstanding his rapidity and spirit.

I am fully aware of the truth of Sir Walter Raleigh's remark in the Preface to his *History of the World:*—"True it is, that the judgements of all men are not agreeable; nor (which is more strange) the affection of any one man stirred up alike with examples of like nature: But every one is touched most with that which most nearly seemeth to touch his own private; or otherwise best suiteth with his apprehension." I therefore do not look to see all pleased,—content if enough are gratified to encourage me to undertake something more than this small beginning; which is of size sufficient, if it should fail to be thought well of, and large enough to build further upon, should it be liked. Let me end, then, in the words of old Cowell:—"That which a man saith well is not to be rejected because he hath some errours. No man, no book, is void of imperfections. And, therefore, reprehend who will in God's name, that is with sweetness and without reproach."

***The American Monthly Review* (review date 1833)**

SOURCE: Review of *Poems and Prose Writings,* in *The American Monthly Review,* Vol. IV, No. VI, December, 1833, pp. 468-80.

[*In the following excerpt, the author favorably reviews Dana's poetry and prose, calling him "one of the best writers of the day."*]

Mr. Dana is a poet in the true sense of the term. He combines a striking originality and reach of thought with beautiful and expressive language. But the former power far exceeds the latter. Indeed he seems himself to be aware of this; for he says of his own poetry that it lacks "something of that melody of voice and harmony of expression, which so win upon us unawares." As a poetical thinker, Mr. Dana has no superior,—hardly an equal in the country; as a mere versifier, we could point out several, who are his superiors. At times he is admirably apt and beautiful in his expressions; at others, apparently negligent, and certainly unsuccessful. He frequently reminds us of Mr. Burchell in *The Vicar of Wakefield,* who "had something short and dry in his address, and seemed not to understand ceremony, or to despise it." At such moments we feel half-disposed to place him upon the debateable ground between the poets of prose and the poets of verse . . . , but straight some touching passage, some dazzling burst of true poetry reinstates him among "the great, the glorious few." Upon this point however, we do not wish to be dogmatical; but we think that the passages, which we shall presently quote, will bear us out in our estimate of Mr. Dana's poetry.

The first poem in the volume is "**The Buccaneer;**" a wild ballad of the same school as Coleridge's *Ancient Mariner*, and founded, we presume, upon tradition. Matthew Lee, the hero of the tale, after scenes of piracy and murder upon the high seas, and of revelry and remorse upon land, is at length carried off by a Spectre Horse. It is a story of that fearful and unearthly kind, which is not much to our taste. As a poem, it contains many fine passages and descriptions.

The other principal poems in the collection are "**Changes of Home,**" "**Factitious Life,**" and "**Thoughts on the Soul.**" We shall not, however, analyze these poems. We think we can give our readers a better idea of Mr. Dana's style, by devoting to quotations that space, which would be occupied by a formal analysis. We therefore give entire the next piece in the volume.

THE HUSBAND'S AND WIFE'S GRAVE.

   HUSBAND and wife! No converse now ye hold,
As once ye did in your young day of love,
On its alarms, its anxious hours, delays,
Its silent meditations, its glad hopes,
Its fears, impatience, quiet sympathies;
Nor do ye speak of joy assured, and bliss
Full, certain, and possessed. Domestic cares
Call you not now together. Earnest talk
On what your children may be, moves you
   not.
Ye lie in silence, and an awful silence;
'Tis not like that in which ye rested once
Most happy—silence eloquent, when heart
With heart held speech, and your mysterious
   frames,
Harmonious, sensitive, at every beat
Touched the soft notes of love.

A stillness deep
Insensible, unheeding, folds you round;
And darkness, as a stone, has sealed you in.
Away from all the living, here ye rest:
In all the nearness of the narrow tomb,
Yet feel ye not each other's presence, now.
Dread fellowship!—together, yet alone.

Is this thy prison-house, thy grave, then,
    Love?
And doth death cancel the great bond that
    holds
Commingling spirits? Are thoughts that know
    no bounds,
But self-inspired, rise upwards, searching out
The eternal Mind—the Father of all thought—
Are they become mere tenants of a tomb?—
Dwellers in darkness, who the illuminate
    realms
Of uncreated light have visited and lived?—
Lived in the dreadful splendor of that throne,
Which One, with gentle hand the veil of flesh
Lifting, that hung 'twixt man and it, revealed
In glory?—throne, before which even now
Our souls, moved by prophetic power, bow
    down
Rejoicing, yet at their own natures awed?—
Souls that Thee know by a mysterious sense,
Thou awful, unseen Presence—are they
    quenched,
Or burn they on, hid from our mortal eyes
By that bright day which ends not; as the sun
His robe of light flings round the glittering
    stars?

And do our loves all perish with our
    frames?
Do those that took their root and put forth
    buds,
And their soft leaves unfolded in the warmth
Of mutual hearts, grow up and live in beauty,
Then fade and fall, like fair, unconscious
    flowers?
Are thoughts and passions that to the tongue
    give speech,
And make it send forth winning harmonies,—
That to the cheek do give its living glow,
And vision in the eye the soul intense
With that for which there is no utterance—
Are these the body's accidents?—no more?—
To live in it, and when that dies, go out
Like the burnt taper's flame?

O, listen, man!
A voice within us speaks the startling word,
"Man, thou shalt never die!" Celestial voices
Hymn it around our souls: according harps,
By angel fingers touched when the mild stars
Of morning sang together, sound forth still

The song of our great immortality:
Thick clustering orbs, and this our fair
    domain,
The tall, dark mountains, and the deep-toned
    seas,
Join in this solemn, universal song.
—O, listen, ye, our spirits; drink it in
From all the air! 'Tis in the gentle moonlight;
'Tis floating in day's setting glories; Night,
Wrapt in her sable robe, with silent step
Comes to our bed and breathes it in our ears:
Night, and the dawn, bright day, and
    thoughtful eve,
All time, all bounds, the limitless expanse,
As one vast mystic instrument, are touched
By an unseen, living Hand, and conscious
    chords
Quiver with joy in this great jubilee:
—The dying hear it; and as sounds of earth
Grow dull and distant, wake their passing
    souls
To mingle in this heavenly harmony.

Why is it that I linger round this tomb?
What holds it? Dust that cumbered those I
    mourn.
They shook it off, and laid aside earth's robes,
And put on those of light. They're gone to
    dwell
In love—their God's and angels'. Mutual love
That bound them here, no longer needs a
    speech
For full communion; nor sensation strong,
Within the breast, their prison, strive in vain
To be set free, and meet their kind in joy.
Changed to celestials, thoughts that rise in
    each,
By natures new, impart themselves though
    silent.
Each quickening sense, each throb of holy
    love,
Affections sanctified, and the full glow
Of being which expand and gladden one,
By union all mysterious, thrill and live
In both immortal frames:—Sensation all,
And thought, pervading, mingling sense and
    thought!
Ye paired, yet one! wrapt in a consciousness
Twofold, yet single—this is love, this life!

Why call we then the square-built
    monument,
The upright column, and the low-laid slab,
Tokens of death, memorials of decay?
Stand in this solemn, still assembly, man,
And learn thy proper nature; for thou seest,
In these shaped stones and lettered tables,
    figures
Of life: More are they to thy soul than those

Which he who talked on Sinai's mount with
  God,
Brought to the old Judeans—types are these
Of thine eternity.

                 I thank Thee, Father,
That at this simple grave, on which the dawn
Is breaking, emblem of that day which hath
No close, Thou kindly unto my dark mind
Hast sent a sacred light, and that away
From this green hillock, whither I had come
In sorrow, Thou art leading me in joy.

This truly beautiful poem unites in it many of Mr. Dana's characteristic excellences and defects;—fine trains of thought, and fine, glowing, poetical expression, with occasionally something abrupt, unmusical and obscure. . . .

Mr. Dana has the rare merit of thinking for himself, and of thinking well. The truth is he writes from the feelings of his own heart. As you read, you cannot doubt, that the author's soul was in the matter; that he felt every line, every word, as his pen wrote it down;— and if the secret were revealed, we should doubtless learn, that many of these fine passages were written in moments of intense excitement. It cannot have been otherwise. Consequently, Mr. Dana's poetry is entirely free from that vapid and idle babble,—"mere words with oftentimes no symptom of idea,"—which some good people would fain pass upon a credulous world as poetry. And herein lies the great secret of his power in description. It gives him a wonderfully graphic touch. A bold outline—light here, and shadow there—and you have the picture finished, with a truth to nature, really wonderful. . . .

The character of Mr. Dana's mind is like that of Coleridge, of whom he is evidently a great admirer. He even goes so far as to say; "To profess to differ from Coleridge may be safe, but to profess to hold him to be incomprehensible, would now savor less of a profession, than a confession." We must, therefore, *con*fess, that at times Coleridge is quite incomprehensible to us; and we *pro*fess, that at others he uses a very cumbrous phraseology to express an idea, where simple and direct language would have stood him in better stead. We maintain that a clear and definite idea can be clearly and definitely expressed; and if language is the medium of thought, this is self-evident. It must be acknowledged, however, that at times the fault lies with the reader and not with the author. An author may seem obscure merely because the reader, from want of familiarity with the subject, is not capable of understanding him; and yet every sentence in the book may be in itself perfectly intelligible. We take it, that the *Mécanique Céleste* is a very obscure book to most people;—by them, not comprehended, yet in itself not incomprehensible. Some minds are not mathematical;

others not metaphysical; others not poetical. Hence what is as clear as noon-day to one, to another is as shadowy and indistinct as twilight; and it must be confessed that readers are apt to accuse an author of being obscure, when the obscurity is in the dimness of their own vision. Upon this point, however, we will not digress farther; though we think this a topic upon which a very interesting essay might be written. But in conclusion, we would say to all who treat of deep and metaphysical matters in poetry, in the words of one of Mr. Dana's heroes to his wife; "You should be more definite, my dear. You forget, that every one's thoughts do not take the same road with yours."

We now pass to the second part of this volume; a reprint of the Tales and Essays, which were published about ten years ago, in a series of numbers entitled **The Idle Man**. That title has been dropped in this reprint, and we are very sorry for it. **The Idle Man** is a work, which has long been upon our shelves; and one upon which we have always set a high value. When first published it did not meet with the encouragement it deserved, and was consequently discontinued before the completion of the contemplated series. We cannot conceive why the author has stripped off its old, familiar title. By so doing he has nearly destroyed its personal identity; not in reality, for the work is substantially the same as before; but to the imagination, which plays such freaks with our reason. We beg the author, if he sets any value on old associations, to restore the old title.

The tales and sketches, which compose this portion of the volume, are all of them finely written, though, to use a hackneyed phrase of our craft, "of different degrees of merit." The most powerful is **"Paul Felton"**; a tale, which makes you shudder as you read. Its horrors are not, however, those of loathsome disease, and hospitals, and the charnel house, which make up, so to speak, the stock-horrors of most modern tale-bearers, who deal in the terrific. It deals mostly with the mind; the mysterious workings of a morbid soul, which turns to poison what should nourish it, and broods over its own dark and fearful fancies, until the phantoms of the imagination assume a real existence, and urge their master—now their slave—to despair and madness. A perfect analysis of this tale would form a long and elaborate chapter in moral philosophy, and consequently we shall spare our readers the perusal. We must say, however, that we have seldom, if ever, read a tale of such fearful power over the soul. The unimaginative, and those who are blessed with pure and quiet minds, will read nothing therein but supernatural horrors, and will turn away in fear, perhaps in disgust, from "the struggles of that wretched man." But he, whose mind has been touched with the morbid and sickly feelings so vividly portrayed in these pages, and through whose soul the agony thereof has passed like the blast of the desert, will see here no supernatural horrors, but a portrait of what may be, and learn therefrom to cast out the lurking demon from his soul, ere that demon seek "seven other spirits more wicked than himself, and enter in and dwell there." This we conceive to be the moral of **"Paul Felton."** . . .

We hardly know which is finest, Mr. Dana's poetry or his prose. The same spirit, the same character of powerful and original thought belongs to both; and stamps Mr. Dana as one of the best writers of the day. We may well be proud of him; and we hope, that he will receive from his own countrymen such unequivocal marks of their high esteem, as will cheer him on in the noble career of literary life, wherein he has already won such enviable laurels.

The New Englander (review date 1851)

SOURCE: A review of *Poems and Prose Writings,* in *The New Englander,* Vol. IX, No. XXXIII, February, 1851, pp. 28-35.

[*In the following favorable review, the author praises Dana's poetic diction, his style, and his artistic character.*]

Our first remark is, that Mr. Dana's language is made up in a great degree of Saxon. It is free, more than that of most authors, from Latinisms, Gallicisms, from modern conventionalisms, and all pert and dainty expressions. He eschews, as by instinct, such words as "emanate," "develop," "position," "responsibility," "elevated," "exposition," etc., unless in cases where they may be absolutely needed to give the sense. It is hardly necessary to say that his pages are never disfigured by "stand-points," "hand-books," "being done," "transpired" in the sense of happen, "governmental," and that large class of words, which, if found in the dictionaries, are not wanted to express any idea, and whose occurrence gives pain to a delicate ear. By making use of this pithy, sturdy old Saxon, Mr. Dana is able to address a larger number of readers. Those who are familiar only with the English language, can feel the full force of his style, can relish what they could not if it were mixed up with elements that are only half naturalized. By this means he can, also, give us more thoughts. More ideas will be crowded into a page, than if the common proportion of words were transplanted from the Latin or French soil. We have thoughts, ideas, beautiful images, instead of two or three dim conceptions on a page, wrapped up in a wordy dress. There is, besides, in the style, a force, a homely, sinewy strength, which are so natural to the Anglo-Saxon, and which he can not possibly have, who goes away from home for a stock of words. To our minds, there is a kind, gentle, home-feeling about these old monosyllables which leads us back to the hearth-stones of our rude ancestors in Kent and Suf-

folk. How barren of these dear remembrances and associations is such a stilted genius as Dr. Johnson, or his "painful" imitators in our days! The writer who wishes to make the deepest and most abiding impression on our hearts, must clothe his thoughts in the language of Alfred. At the same time, we would not imply that a writer may not, on fitting occasions, and in a becoming measure, use all the elements of our noble, composite language. How inseparable the Latin terminations are in some of the marvelous passages in *Paradise Lost,* or in that divine prototype and epos, the Apocalypse, or in the vision of Daniel! No stringing together of Saxon syllables could express the majesty of Him, before whom "thousand thousands ministered."

Again, Mr. Dana's style and manner of thinking show the utmost familiarity with the early writers in the English language. He dwells among them as with old friends with whom he has often taken sweet counsel. He looks up to them with reverent affection. There is a heart-kindliness beneath their stern looks, a freshness of feeling, an unexpected breaking out of beautiful thoughts from under the crust of their quaint phrases, which no one knows how to relish better than our author, which no one had described in more loving and befitting terms. We recognize this familiarity with the writers of the seventeenth century by the occurrence of such phrases as these: "to do the service of all or any who happened not to be at hand;" "very like to honest out-of-door flowers;" "tangled and by-path overgrowings;" "it is ten to one;" "that love of nature which all the old are so full of and so sincere in;" "we are not making excuses for these givings in," etc. We might copy any number of such phrases, where very expressive little words are joined by hyphens, so common in some of the writers of Elizabeth's time, and which are so contrary to Dr. Blair's rules for forming rotund sentences. Where this love for the old authors is hearty, and is under the control of a pure taste and sound judgment, where it is not carried to an extreme, and is joined to a due appreciation of existing styles of thought and writing, the effect is very happy. It gives an antique richness to the diction. The thoughts come to us with the authority of a well known stamp. They have not the suspicious look of recent coinage. They have somewhat of the golden yellow of the old masters. We pick them out with the same instinct that we go to the corner where a Titian or a Claude hangs among hundreds of lesser lights, and our hearts are drawn to the writer whose thoughts have been fused, as it were, in this antique mould, who throws aside what is uncouth and unsavory in the ancient, and what is ambitious and finical in the modern, and sweetly blends what is true and precious of two generations which are widely apart. If we mistake not, this is characteristic of Mr. Dana's style and thoughts. His works could have been written in no century but the nineteenth, yet they have much of the air and spirit of the seventeenth.

Another characteristic, which we will name, is a musical flow and cadence in many of the prose sentences, as if the author were meditating poetic measures. There is a class of writers, that pay great attention to the structure of their sentences. Possessing a cultivated taste and an ear more or less musical, they elaborate their style and round their periods with the nicest care. That form is chosen, and those words are sought which will be most effective, or which will strike most pleasantly on the ear. But after all their pains, they have not the art to hide the art. They are like men of a managing disposition. The artifice comes to light. The trick is apparent. We see that the author meant to make that sentence emphatic, to set off another with his choicest flowers, to point a third with his sharpest antithesis, and to see how a fourth would awaken admiration by its delicious cadences. But there is another class of authors who have melody in the soul as well as music in the ear. Their memory is a storehouse of beautiful conceptions. Their feelings are attuned to the finest harmonies. They have gazed on truth in its delicate and almost evanescent relations. They are familiar with those subtler elements which the common eye overlooks. To them it has been given to hear voices which others can not hear, to discover harmonies in nature and in the depths of their own souls, to which others are blind. Accordingly, when they put their thoughts into poetry or prose, we are often struck with the outflow of sweet sounds. In the poetry, there is a music besides that of the numbers. In the prose, there is nothing artificial, nothing intended for effect, but the sentence moves along as if self-inspired, as if endowed with an innate melody. There is a most exact fitness between the thought and the expression. Both appear to have come out of the depths of a musical soul. How poetical is much of Milton's prose! How "involuntary," we may say, did his spirit "move harmonious numbers!" We think, also, that this quality strikingly characterizes much of Mr. Dana's prose. Had we space, we could quote many sentences which have a kind of natural music, where there is a sweet accordance between the thought and the form of the sentence.

Leaving the less important matter of style and diction, we may say, that Mr. Dana's works are strikingly characterized by sincerity. This is true alike of the prose and the poetry. They come from the heart. They are not the product of passion, of over-wrought sensibility, as much of Lord Byron's poetry is. Neither are they the results of a powerful intellect, working in the absence or in the subjection of the affections. They are not formed according to the rhetoric and logic of the schools. Yet they are better than anything which mere passion or mere intellect can create. They have an order which no formal logic ever taught. The thoughts are unfolded from within outward. To use a term which

we do not like, they are evolved, rather than argued. One grows out of another. They are held together by a natural affinity, or by veins of sentiment or feeling more than by a chain of deductive reasoning. It is for this very reason that Mr. Dana strikes us as one of the most original authors. He writes from a full heart. If we may say it without irreverence, he can not but speak what he has felt. His thoughts appear to be a part of himself, to have grown up with him. They may be like what others have uttered, but in passing through his soul, they have been shaped and colored and stamped with his own individuality. In opening these volumes, we feel that we are reading the author's works, not those of any body else. They are the sincere, honest utterance of a deeply meditative spirit. They are the golden ore in the vein, not the sweepings of some industrious miner, or the casual drift of some wintry torrent. This may account in part for the small number of Mr. Dana's works. Some seem disposed to complain that two not very large volumes contain the whole of them. But heart-work is not very prolific. It will hardly do to call genius prodigal. Original trains of thought are rare. The blended product of sterling thought and a rich experience are rarer still. Some men write several thousand sermons. But how few come from the depths of their own experience! Of how small a number can it be said with truth, they are the transcript of the writer's *own* inward life! A busy observation or a retentive memory are forced to meet most exigencies. It is only at long intervals that thoughts break forth from the soul, fresh and strong, like the plants of spring, bursting into life through an inherent vigor.

We may, again, mention as characteristic of much which Mr. Dana has written, that they have a melancholy or sorrowful tone. They dwell, to a great degree, on the "night side" of nature and providence. We have heard it alleged as a defect, that they make the reader sad if not misanthropic, that they disturb his equanimity with painful pictures of the crimes and wretchedness of man, that some, both of his poems and prose pieces, lead us into the awful depths of man's depraved spirit, where there is nothing but "sights and sounds of woe," and whence we gladly escape into the sweet upper air. This melancholy tone is one cause, we have no doubt, why some readers have been repelled from the author's pages. But is it really a defect? In answer, we may say, that the charge does not apply to all of Mr. Dana's works. There are pieces of a cheerful and hopeful tone. Some of the small poems are animated by a joyous though chastened spirit. The views taken of society as it is, and as it may be hereafter, are not all sombre. Especially is a brightness thrown over the aspect of things, so far as a pure Christian faith shall have sway. Still, it is to be acknowledged, that a sad if not a despondent tone characterizes much of what Mr. Dana has written. But if this is the honest and genuine result of the author's modes of thought and feeling, would we have it otherwise? Ought he not to preserve his individuality? If his experience has been different from that of most others, if he has looked more profoundly into the mysteries of his own being, if his spirit has been pained by the tricks and hollow conventionalities of much which appears in modern society, if he has gazed with a more thoughtful eye on time, death and eternity, if he has listened oftener than most others "to the still, sad music of humanity," can we blame him for giving utterance to his feelings? Cowper's poetry is regarded by many as dark and cheerless. But would a wise man desire to have it altered? Some of Mr. Wordsworth's admirers think that a profounder apprehension of the mysteries of a Christian faith on his part would have stamped some of his poetry with a more solemn and abiding impress. "The Churchyard among the mountains" is not all which the student of Christianity would desire. A deep thinker, with a poetic temperament, is often necessarily sad. Consider the *Othello* and the *Hamlet*. Homer is the "tearful" poet. His was a sorrowing spirit. At the same time, we must confess, that in some of Mr. Dana's pieces we should have preferred a less sombre hue. We are drawn towards Mr. Wordsworth because he can extract a kindly lesson from all things and all men. The "motherly spirit of humanity" pervades all which he wrote. He can not chastise our "repudiating" countrymen without mingling in a hopeful view. We have great reverence for England, the old home of most of our fathers; we delight to dwell upon her laws, her gentle manners, her integrity. We look with admiration on the great lights of the seventeenth century. Still, we should not carry this reverence quite as far as Mr. Dana does. We should probably see more good than he does in revolutionary and republican France. In looking at her disorders and almost infinite confusion, we are touched with pity. Her masses have been more sinned against than sinning. Notwithstanding the gorgeous church that has had them professedly in charge for ages, they have been like sheep on the mountains without a shepherd. When we look at the atheism of continental Europe, we are angry rather with the degenerate, inefficient churches, both Catholic and Protestant, than with the forsaken, and deluded people.

We find in Mr. Dana's works, both in the poetry and the prose, a true perception of inanimate nature, of the wondrous changes which are going on around us. His descriptions are remarkably clear and distinct. He hits upon the exact expression which is needed. His language is so apposite, that we see the point of the application or the force of the comparison at once. The word itself, or the phrase, is a picture. There is no need of a long enumeration of particulars. The imagination of the reader is set busily at work. Mr. Dana sees these various objects in their poetic light, freed from their ordinary prosaic dress. They are revealed in true yet fresher and nobler aspects. They are real objects, the same which we every day behold, yet trans-

figured, as it were, by the light which comes from the poet's imagination. We everywhere see what it is so hard to describe, the difference between what is called a fine description and the magic pen of genius. There are no unmeaning or common-place epithets. Every word is apt, and it seems instinct with a mysterious life. Let us take two stanzas at random:

> But when the light winds lie at rest,
> And on the glassy, heaving sea,
> 　The black duck, with her glossy breast,
> 　Sits swinging silently,—
> How beautiful! no ripples break the reach,
> And silvery waves go noiseless up the beach.
>
> 　And where the far-off sand-bars lift
> 　Their backs in long and narrow line,
> 　The breakers shout, and leap, and shift,
> 　And toss the sparkling brine
> Into the air; then rush to mimic strife:
> Glad creatures of the sea, and full of life!

In a poet who reflects so profoundly on the great problems of life, death and immortality, it is refreshing to meet with sweet and soothing lessons from outward nature. What a relief are the moon and the waves of the sea amid the terrific stanzas of the "Ancient Mariner"! There is nothing strange, however, in this. Every great poet loves nature. However he may delight in inward meditation, his joy is also to hold communion with visible forms, with all that wondrous panorama which the goodness of God has spread out before us. How transcendently sublime are some of Shakspeare's brief allusions to the starry heavens! How beautiful are some of his images which he seems carelessly to borrow from various objects in nature. These, no less than human passions, come and go at his bidding.

The works of Mr. Dana, in the moral impression which they are fitted to produce, deserve the heartiest praise. It is literature consecrated to the worthiest objects. There is no line, which, the author dying, would wish to blot. It is an offering of genius laid on the altar of heavenly truth. Many things could have been written only by one who had felt the preciousness of the great "Sacrifice," who knows not where to solve the bitter doubts which harass the human soul except in the message of Him who is the Light of the world. In reading many of these pages, one feels that he is in companionship, not merely with the "sweet singers" of earth, but with those who have attuned their harps in heaven. . . .

The productions of Mr. Dana are admirably fitted, both in style and thought, to do good to those who are learning to think and to write. Nothing can be more free from pretence and affectation. The critical remarks, for example those upon the poems of Thomson, are eminently just and considerate. The article suggested by

Pollok's *Course of Time*, we have always regarded as a model of candid, yet profound and discriminating criticism. Such reviews teach how necessary it is to meditate long and feel deeply, before one sits in judgment on a work of genius or of original investigation. We feel thankful that we have in the English language such specimens of reviewing as that of Mr. Dana on Hazlitt's *English Poets*, and that of Coleridge on Wordsworth's *Excursion*. In mentioning the works which do honor to American literature, and which are likely to live while the language is spoken, we do not know why the list should begin and end with a few historical writers like Mr. Prescott and Mr. Irving. The poetry of Mr. Dana and Mr. Bryant constitute a solid addition to the treasures of our noble language. They repay in some degree the great debt which we owe to England. They will be read ages hence with delight and profit.

R. H. Stoddard (essay date 1879)

SOURCE: "Richard Henry Dana," in *Harper's New Monthly Magazine,* Vol. LVIII, No. 347, April, 1879, pp. 769-76.

[*In the following excerpt Stoddard provides a critical overview of Dana's literary career, noting especially the influence of Coleridge's "Rime of the Ancient Mariner" on "The Buccaneer."*]

To rightly understand an author, and the place he occupies in the literature of his country, we must not only understand the events of his life and the order in which his works were written, we must also understand the literary conditions under which they were produced, and which conspired to make them what they were. To judge the authors of the last century by the standards of the present century is to judge them uncritically and unjustly: they wrote according to their light, and whether it was greater or lesser, it was certainly other than our light. They belonged to their day and generation, as we belong to ours, and if we cherish the hope of being appreciated by those who come after us, we should seek to appreciate those who came before us, and who made what we are possible. It is a fashion among young writers to sneer at their elders, as if they were unworthy of serious consideration. I have heard these confident gentlemen declare that the prose of Irving was poor, and the poetry of Bryant dull and monotonous. I have asked them if they were familiar with early American literature, if they had read the prose writers who preceded Irving and the poets who preceded Bryant, and they have generally admitted that they had not, thereby placing themselves out of court. If a crass ignorance prevails in regard to these writers, who are among the most distinguished that we have, what instrument yet invented can measure the ignorance which prevails in regard to others of less

note—such men, for example, as Richard Henry Dana? That he wrote something once upon a time a well-informed reader might possibly recollect, but precisely what it was not one in a hundred could tell. And yet he ranked in his day (and justly) among the foremost writers in America. . . .

Richard Henry Dana was exceedingly delicate as a child, as was also William Cullen Bryant, and the two young poets were largely benefited by water—the latter by the enforced use of a cold spring which gushed from the under-world near the homestead of his father at Cummington, and the former by the fresh and briny air of the ocean at Newport, whither he was sent when he was about ten years old. Studiously inclined, he was not able to study much, so he passed his time mostly out-of-doors, rambling along the rock-bound coast, and listening to the roar of the breakers. The wind came to him with healing on its wings, and the tumultuous waves strengthened his love of solitude. No other American poet was ever so moulded by the ocean; which haunted him like a passion, insensibly blending with his thoughts and emotions. That he was a poet did not dawn upon him in childhood, as it did upon the young dreamer at Cummington, nor was there any thing in our literature to suggest the possibility of an American poet. Poets by courtesy there were, of course, for, like the poor, they are always with us. Dwight had published his "Conquest of Canaan," Barlow his "Vision of Columbus," and Freneau a collection of his patriotic poems. These swallows, however, no more made a summer than the little beach birds which Master Dana saw flitting before him in his daily rambles along the shore at Newport.

The traditions of the Dana family were scholarly, and in his seventeenth year, when his health was sufficiently restored, Richard Henry Dana was sent to Harvard College, as his father and grandfather were before him, where he pursued his studies until his twentieth year, when he became involved in a college rebellion, and was compelled to leave his course unfinished. He returned to Newport, where he devoted himself for the next two years to classical literature, and the little that was worth reading in American literature, which may be said to have begun with *Salmagundi*. An experiment in the shape of a periodical, the *Monthly Anthology,* languished until it reached ten volumes, and is worthy of remembrance if only on account of the zeal of the club which projected it (the Anthology Club), and which had the satisfaction, such as it was, of footing the bills for publishing it. Clearly the *Monthly Anthology* was not wanted, though the best pens in Boston wrote for it. What the little world of American readers wanted was not literature pure and simple, but literature with a purpose, which purpose at this time was a political one. Our fathers were bitter politicians, and their best writings were on political subjects. Their mania affected their children, one of whom, a boy of thirteen, perpetrated a volume of political verse which led the conductors of this luckless *Monthly Anthology* to question whether it could really have been the production of so young a person. "The Embargo" soon passed into a second edition, and the name of its author, William Cullen Bryant, was introduced to the attention of his admiring countrymen. It was read by the son of Judge Dana in the intervals of his classical studies at Newport, whence he soon removed to Baltimore, and to the study of law in the office of General Robert Goodloe Harper.

There was a marked literary element in Boston in the first decade of the century, as was shown by the persistent attempt to establish a periodical in that city, and notwithstanding its want of success, its projectors never lost heart or hope. Prominent among them were William Tudor, a graduate of Harvard and a travelled man, George Ticknor, the future historian of Spanish literature, and John Quincy Adams. They cultivated literature (not exactly on oatmeal) by giving suppers, at which they discussed their contributions to the *Monthly Anthology,* and to which they occasionally invited their friends, among others Richard Henry Dana and Washington Allston. A South Carolinian by birth, Allston had spent his childhood at Newport, where he doubtless knew young Master Dana, and where he certainly knew Malbone, the miniature painter, whose influence determined him in his choice of the profession he adopted. He painted in oils before he was seventeen, at which age he entered Harvard College, where his attention was divided between his pencils and his books. Before he was invited to the suppers of the Anthology Club he had travelled in England, where he became a student of the Royal Academy, after which he proceeded to Rome. While at Rome he made the acquaintance of Coleridge, who was on his way back to England from Malta, where he had proved unsatisfactory as a secretary to Sir Alexander Bell. The young American painter was fascinated by the English poet, of whom he declared in later life that to no other man did he owe so much intellectually. "He used to call Rome the *silent* city," Allston wrote, "but I never could think of it as such while with him; for, meet him when or where I would, the fountain of his mind was never dry, but, like the far-reaching aqueducts that once supplied this mistress of the world, its living stream seemed specially to flow for every classic ruin over which we wandered. And when I recall some of our walks under the pines of the Villa Borghese, I am almost tempted to dream that I had once listened to Plato in the groves of the Academy." To his talents as a painter, which were eminent, Allston added the dangerous talent of writing poetry, in which he was not eminent, though it was once the fashion to say that he was. He was the honored guest of the Anthology Club, at whose symposia his verses were read and admired, at least by his friend Richard Henry Dana, who reviewed them when they were published a few years later. They were con-

nections, Allston having married a sister of Dr. Channing.

Though he had been admitted to the bar both in Boston and Baltimore, and was in a certain sense a lawmaker, having been elected to the Legislature of Massachusetts, Richard Henry Dana failed to sustain the legal reputation of his family. He followed his profession for a few years, and finally quitted it for literature, which was slowly but surely striking root in New England, watered, so to say, by the hopeful young arboriculturists of the defunct *Monthly Anthology,* headed by William Tudor, who, with a courage in keeping with his name, projected a periodical which should (and did) take its place. This was the *North American Review,* which appeared in May, 1815, and still survives in a green and flourishing old age. It was managed by a club, as its predecessor had been, who gave suppers as they had done, at which they read the papers that they had written, or that had been sent to them, and decided upon their merits and demerits. Richard Henry Dana was a member of this club, which was presided over by Tudor, who was the actual editor of the *North American Review* for upward of two years, and by far the largest contributor, three-fourths of the first four volumes coming from his facile pen. He was succeeded by Edward Tyrell Channing, a cousin of Richard Henry Dana, under whom its literary character was more assured. To this gentleman, or more exactly, perhaps, to the club of which he was president, there were sent two poems, which were read before the club, as the verses of Allston had been read before the Anthology Club, and which its members declared could not have been written by an American, they were so stately and well sustained. They were the productions of the young man whose youth had been questioned by the crities of the *Monthly Anthology* some seven or eight years before, and who had lately been admitted to the bar in Great Barrington. The longest and most important of these poems—a meditation upon the universality of death, was written when he was about eighteen, and left by him among his papers, where it was discovered by his father while he was at college, who thought it was worthy of publication, and accordingly sent it to the *North American Review.* The doubt which had been cast upon its paternity was apparently solved, but really increased, by the information which the manuscript appeared to convey, that the author, whose name was Bryant, was a member of the Massachusetts Senate. This intelligence excited the curiosity of Richard Henry Dana, who immediately walked from Cambridge to Boston, where the Senate was then in session, in order to obtain a sight of the eleventh Muse, lately sprung up in America, Mistress Anne Bradstreet having been considered in her day the tenth Muse. He went, he saw, and was not convinced. The plain middle-aged gentleman who was pointed out to him could not be the new poet whom he was seeking. He was right—he was not the poet, but he was the poet's father, Dr. Bryant, of Cummington. Such was the history of "Thanatopsis" in its exodus from manuscript to the pages of the *North American Review.*

Superficial students of literary history are often surprised at the disproportion between the reputation of certain writers and the intellectual value of their writings, and are consequently unjust in their judgments of both. Readers of to-day who are not familiar with our early literature—the literature of seventy years ago, for example—wonder, and not unnaturally, at the estimation in which their fathers held the fathers of our present race of writers. Contemporary critics were too favorable to them, they think, and they are not altogether in the wrong, but they forget that the contemporary critics were coguizant of literary conditions that no longer exist, the consideration of which materially influenceed their decisions. Our fathers were worthy people, but their sympathy with literature was slight; they tolerated rather than encouraged it. The young gentlemen who sustained the *Monthly Anthology* sustained it at their own cost, and were out of pocket for the frugal suppers upon which its continuance depended. The *North American Review* paid its contributors nothing for years, and when it did begin to pay them, the honorarium was ridiculously small. They wrote, not because they had any thing to gain, but because they had something to say, the saying of which was its own exceeding great reward. They wrote under many difficulties, not the least of which was an invidious comparison with English writers, who so habitually asserted their superiority that few Americans thought of disputing it. The disesteem with which authorship was then regarded was frankly stated by Richard Henry Dana in the *North American Review* (September, 1817), in a notice of the poems of his friend Allston, which were originally published in England. "One generation goes on after another as if we were here for no other purpose than to do business, as the phrase is. The spirit of gain has taught us to hold other pursuits as mere amusements, and to associate something unmanly and trivial with the character of their followers. If a work of taste comes out, it is made a cause of lament that so much talent should be thus thrown away; and the bright and ever-during radiance in which it is in mercy hiding our dull commonness is neither seen nor felt. We hold every thing lightly which is not perceived to go immediately to some practical good—to lessen labor, increase wealth, or add to some homely comfort. It must have an active, business-like air, or it is regarded as a dangerous symptom of the decay of industry amongst us. To be sure, we read English poetry; but for the same reason that we take a drive out of town, because we are tired down by business, and must amuse ourselves a little to be refreshed and strengthened for work to-morrow. And, besides, we say the English can afford to furnish us with poetry. They are an old, wealthy people, and have a good deal of waste material on hand. And so it comes about,

naturally enough, that poets are set down as a sort of intellectual idlers, and sober citizens speak of them with a shake of the head, as they would talk of some clever idler about town, who might have been a useful member of society, but, as to any serious purpose, is now lost to the world." If it required courage to state thus plainly the conditions by which authorship was then surrounded, it required more courage to prosecute it under such conditions, and I for one honor the single-minded men who did so, chief among whom I place Richard Henry Dana.

His contributions to the *North American Review* were not numerous, but they marked, if they did not originate, an era in the history of criticism in America. One paper in particular—a review of Hazlitt's *Lectures on the English Poets* (March, 1819)—was too remarkable to be readily accepted. It was remarkable for the originality, not to say the audacity, of the writer, who did not hesitate to reverse the judgments of Hazlitt, but who gave substantial and convincing reasons for reversing them, and for the soundness of his own judgments. Here is one, the reader felt, who is not content to let the English critics think for him, but who is abundantly able to think for himself, and who, besides, is throughly equipped with scholarship. Reading has made him a full man, and a man, therefore, to be feared. He questioned the supremacy which had been conferred by common consent on Pope. He declared that his much-bepraised epistle of Eloisa to Abelard was a gross production: that it was hot with lust and cold with false sentiment, far-sought antithesis, forced apostrophes, and all sorts of artificialities in the place of natural feeling and plain truth. The justice of this criticism might have been, and no doubt was, controverted by those who had taken Pope upon trust, accepting him as a precious intellectual legacy from the past century; but they could not controvert the justice of the verbal criticism on Pope's poetry, his incorrect use of words, his fondness for stock phrases, the paucity of his rhymes, and the nearness to each other of couplets terminating with the same rhyme, his rhymes to the eye rather than to the ear, and other flagrant violations of the minor morals of verse, which, however, in his case could hardly be considered minor ones, since his verse consisted for the most part of little else than these. "He has a deal too much of what was wont to be called poetic language for no other reason than that it would make intolerable prose."

Not less independent were other critical estimates of this new Zoilus, who said, for example, that the diction of Thomson swarmed with words that should seldom be met with except in a dictionary or a court letter of compliment; who contended that Gray's "Elegy" was not his greatest poem, and remarked that he would rather have written "The Bard;" who thought but little of the poetry of Goldsmith, whose fame would rest upon his two plays, his *Citizen of the World,* and his

Vicar of Wakefield; who preferred Campbell's "O'Connor's Child" to his "Pleasures of Hope," which abounded with that language of no definite meaning which is styled elegant; and who warned Hazlitt and his master, Leigh Hunt, that if they undertook to banish such gentlemen as Crabbe into the kitchen, they would soon have the parlor all to themselves. These singnlarities of opinion (to call them by no harsher name) were overshadowed by a monstrous heresy which dared to place Wordsworth among the great poets of England—Wordsworth, whose tendious "Excursion" the great Jeffrey had crushed five years before with his famous "This will never do." This will never do, echoed the readers of the *North American Review,* who might probably have overlooked the slight which had been put upon the little Queen Anne's man, but could never overlook the glorification of the puerile poet of the Lakes. The scholastic conscience of New England was shocked by this paper; a strong party rose up against its author, who had the whole influence of Cambridge and literary and fashionable Boston to coutend with. He was also in a minority in the club, who permitted him to write but one more paper for the *North American Review,* and upon the safe subject of Irving's *Sketch-Book*; which he could not easily have made offensive to their sensitive palates.

It is not easy to go back in thought sixty years, and put ourselves in the place of those who seriously objected to a dispassionate discussion of the relative merits of English poets in a publication devoted to just such discussions. We must try to do so, nevertheless, or we shall be unjust toward them, for, after all, they believed that the interests of literature were likely to suffer if such new-fangled opinions were permitted to pass unchallenged. We had no literature to speak of, and if we were to have any, it ought to begin in accordance with recognized modes of thought and forms of expression; in other words, it ought not to violate settled canons of taste. Their forefathers believed in Pope, therefore they believed in him; the English critics did not believe in Wordsworth, therefore they did not believe in him. This is what they meant, I think, by their opposition to this famous criticism, the writing of which demanded greater originality and intellectual fearlessness than the conductors of the *North American Review* were disposed to stand by. Disowned as it was, however, its critical influence was as distinctly felt as the poetic influence of "Thanatopsis," which was an outgrowth from Wordsworth. "I shall never forget," wrote Richard Henry Dana, after the storm which he had raised had subsided—"I shall never forget with what feeling my friend Bryant, some years ago, described to me the effect produced upon him by his meeting for the first time with Wordsworth's Ballads. He lived, when quite young, where few works of poetry were to be had—at a period, too, when Pope was the great idol of the Temple of Art. He said that upon opening Wordsworth a thousand springs seemed to gush up at once within his heart, and the face of nature of a sudden to change into a strange freshness and life. He felt the sympathetic touch from an according mind, and you see how instantly his powers and affections shot over the earth and through his kind."

The mention of Irving's *Sketch-Book* in a preceding paragraph affords a clew to the next work of Richard Henry Dana, which was undoubtedly suggested by it—*The Idle Man*. The American original of both was *Salmagundi,* which was the first successful attempt to transplant the essay literature of England in the New World, the last being *The Lorgnette* of "Ik Marvel." The author of *The Idle Man* was familiar with the writings of Irving, and admired them, though not so warmly as the uncritical majority of his countrymen. The style of the *Sketch-Book* was less to his taste than the style of *Salmagundi* and *Knickerbocker's History of New York*. It was conceived after some wrong notion of subdued elegance—a too elaborate elaboration, and was more noticeable for wit and humor than for sentiment or pathos. This judgment, added to the gravity of his genius, determined the composition of *The Idle Man*, which was issued in numbers in New York in 1821-22. It was so little read that the writer was warned by his publisher that he was writing himself into debt; so he abandoned it on the publication of the first number of the second volume, and with it all serious connection with the prose literature of his country, limiting himself thereafter to the occasional writing of critical papers.

The author of *The Idle Man* and the author of "Thanatopsis" contracted a friendship through that incomparable poem, which was of great intellectual advantage to both. If any thing could have relieved the sombreness of that unlucky work, it would have been the poems which the latter contributed to it. The retired lawyer at Cambridge and the active lawyer at Great Barrington corresponded with each other upon what was nearest to their hearts, which it hardly need be said was not law, but literature, of which they were the most earnest representatives in America. One of the most important results of their correspondence was an invitation to the poet to write a poem for the Phi Beta Kappa at Harvard—an invitation which he wisely accepted, and which produced the best poem that was ever recited before a college society—"The Ages." This was in 1821, his twenty-seventh year. When he went to Cambridge to deliver the poem he lodged at the house of his friend, and while staying there prepared for the press a small collection of his poetical writings, making several changes in "Thanatopsis," and adding the beginning and end as we have them now, no doubt by the advice of his critical host. Four years later he abandoned the law, and went to New York, where he started the *New York Review,* which is notable in the history of our literature as containing the first poems that Richard Henry Dana is known to have written.

When Master Dana was dreaming beside the sea at Newport, a young English poet at Stowey, an inland town in England, was writing a mysterious poem, of which the sea was the background.

Left an orphan at an early age, he had been educated at Christ's Hospital, where he made the acquaintance of Charles Lamb, had enlisted in a cavalry regiment, where he had proved a very awkward recruit, had married one of three sisters who were milliners, had published a volume of poems of more promise than performance, and had betaken himself to the consumption of opium. The poem in question, "The Ancient Mariner," was probably composed while he was stimulated by this pernicious drug, which was the bane of his after-life. It was published in the same volume as the *Lyrical Ballads* of Wordsworth, which were such a revelation to the young Bryant, whose genius does not appear to have been touched by the imagination of Coleridge. Not so Richard Henry Dana, to whom Coleridge was made known by the admiration of their common friend Allston, and who read all that he had written in verse and prose, and assigned him a high place in his unlucky paper on the English poets. Whatever the select few who read the *Lyrical Ballads* may have thought of "The Ancient Mariner," it created no impression on the English public, and was accepted by no English poet, except, perhaps, Wordsworth, who occasionally liked the verse of others, though he always preferred his own. It germinated in America, however, in the mind of Richard Henry Dana, and by some association, which he himself could hardly have explained, inspired his longest and most important poem—**"The Buccaneer."**

"The Buccaneer" resembles "The Ancient Mariner" in that the supernatural is an element in both, and that they turn upon the commission and punishment of crime. The crime of the ancient mariner is trival, humanly speaking, and is followed by consequences in which others are more concerned than himself; the crime of the buccaneer is dreadful, and consequences fall upon him alone, and not on others who were equally guilty with him. There is an air of verisimilitude about both poems, in spite of the impossible incidents with which they deal, which gives them a high place among purely imaginative works. The facts upon which the American poet has grounded his story are well vouched for, he claimed in his preface, and few truths were so fully believed in as the events that he narrated, though he admitted that he had not hesitated to depart from the truth in order to heighten the poetical effect by putting his hero on horseback instead of allowing him to die quietly in his bed. In other words, he had taken a story out of the *Pirate's Own Book,* and saved it from being merely horrible by adding a supernatural element to it.

The conception of **"The Buccaneer"** is better than the execution, which is lacking in ease and fluency. It is simple and severe in its style, Bryant wrote, in the *North American Review,* and free from that perpetual desire to be glittering and imaginative which dresses up every idea which occurs in the same allowance of figures of speech. As to what is called ambition of style, the work does not contain a particle of it; if the sentiment or image presented to the reader's mind be of itself calculated to make an impression, it is allowed to do so by being given in the most direct and forcible language; if otherwise, no pains are taken to make it pass for more than it is worth. There is even an occasional homeliness of expression which does not strike us agreeably, and a few passages are liable to the charge of harshness and abruptness. Yet altogether there is power put forth in this little volume, strength of pathos, talent at description, and command of language. The power of the poem was warmly acknowledged by Wilson, in *Blackwood's Magazine,* but the style was thought by him to be colored by that of Crabbe, of Wordsworth, and of Coleridge. "He is no servile imitator of those great masters, but his genius has been inspired by theirs, and he almost places himself on the level on which they stand in such poems as the 'Old Grimes' of Crabbe, the 'Peter Bell' of Wordsworth, and 'The Ancient Mariner' of Coleridge. **'The Buccaneer'** is not equal to any one of them, but it belongs to the same class, and shows much of the same power in the delineations of the mysterious workings of the passions and the imagination." The poem differs from most modern poems in that it contains no passage which can be enjoyed by itself, separate from the context, either as a piece of description or sentiment—no passage, for example, like that in "The Ancient Mariner" in which the unearthly music heard by that strange personage is compared to the noise of a hidden brook in the leafy month of June, and no statement of a moral fact which fixes itself in the memory, like

> He prayeth best who loveth best
>   All things both great and small;
> For the dear God who loveth us,
>   He made and loveth all.

The general impression which the poetry of Richard Henry Dana leaves upon the mind is that he is not so much a poet as a man of vigorous intellect who had determined to be a poet, and that he reached this determination too late in life. He moves like one who is shackled by his measures, whether they are simple, as in **"The Buccaneer,"** or of a higher order, as in **"The Husband's and Wife's Grave"** and **"The Dying Raven."**

The literary career of Richard Henry Dana may be said to have practically ended with the publication of the little volume containing **"The Buccaneer"** (1827), though he afterward added to it about as many more poems as were contained therein (nine in all), and brought out a collected edition of his works in two volumes. What he might have written if he had followed the example of his friend Bryant, with whom poetry was a life-long passion, can only be conjectured. That a greater measure of success than was meted out to him would have encouraged him is probable; for, as he wrote in the preface to **"The Buccaneer"** (and almost prophetically, it now seems), "the most self-dependent are stirred to livelier action by the hope of fame; and there are none who can go on with vigor without the sympathy of some few minds which they respect." He felt, with his master, Coleridge,

> Work without hope draws nectar in a sieve,
> And hope without an object can not live.

Fortunately for himself, if not for literature, Richard Henry Dana never knew

> What ills the scholar's life assail—
> Toil, envy, want, the patron, and the jail.

Born a gentleman, like his father before him, he inherited a good estate at Cambridge, a portion of which he sold in order to build himself a house elsewhere. His early love of the sea led him to select a site on the south side of Cape Ann, where he could look out upon the broad billows of the Atlantic. The lawn upon which it is built stretches to the edge of a steep gravelly cliff, below which lies a sandy beach of semicircular shape, isolated on the right by a projecting ledge that runs out beyond it into the sea, and on the left by the base of a precipitous hill. The house faces the south, and is sheltered on the north by a wooded hill. A thrifty farmer, anxious to turn his acres to advantage, would not have chosen the spot for a residence, or, choosing it, would not have left it, as our scholar and poet did, in a state of nature, covered with ancient forestry, and tenanted by crows, hawks, with occasionally an eagle, and multitudes of little beach birds haunting the surges and calling along the sands. It has a noble outlook, for the light-houses of Salem, Boston, and Marblehead can be seen from its window, as well as the passing hulls of Atlantic steamers; and it has a poetic interest in the rocky headland already mentioned, which is nautically known as "Norman's Woe," and is celebrated by Longfellow in his "Wreck of the *Hesperus*." Here, in full sight of the sea, the author of **"The Buccaneer"** passed his summers among his books, and friends, and his grandchildren: for he married in his early manhood, and perpetuated his name in a son, who achieved as much reputation as his father, though not exactly in the pleasant walk of letters which their ancestress Mrs. Anne Bradstreet laid out nearly two hundred years before, but in the sterner and more beaten highway of the law. A delicate child, the health of Richard Henry Dana improved when he was past fifty, and the current of his years bore him slowly onward to a ripe old age.

The oldest writer in America, he lived through several dynasties of literature—the reigns of Wordsworth, Coleridge, and Southey; Byron, Moore, and Scott; Hazlitt, Lamb, and Macaulay; Thackeray, Dickens, Trollope, and other English worthies; and he saw at home the rise of American literature, and what of brightness has been shed over it by the genius of Irving, Bryant, Longfellow, Lowell, Whittier, Emerson, Hawthorne, Poe, and other lesser lights in their several orbits of glory. All this he saw—a grave, scholarly, reverend man whom Time seemed to have forgotten. But the graybeard travels in divers paces with divers persons, ambling with some, trotting with others, and galloping at last with all. He crept with our old poet, but finally overtook him, and cast over him the shadow which he will one day cast over all mankind, and which we in our ignorance call Death. He found him in his winter residence in Boston, on the 2d of February last, and he was gathered to his fathers in peace, the greatest of his name.

William Charvat (essay date 1961)

SOURCE: "Criticism, Magazines, and Critics," in *The Origins of American Colonial Thought, 1810-1835*, A. S. Barnes and Company, Inc., 1961, pp. 164-205.

[*In the following excerpt, Charvat provides an overview of Dana's work as a literary critic and examines the critical value of Dana's unpublished lectures on Shakespeare.*]

Dana was a . . . militant romantic . . . , and his utterances were loud as well as strong. His life was full of stridencies and contradictions, beginning with his expulsion from Harvard in 1807. This literary rebel was a confirmed Federalist and a trinitarian tending toward high-church Episcopalianism. As poet and novelist he was of the Gothic school, and his son records that from boyhood his father's interest was in "the Gothic mind and the Gothic poetry, architecture, legends and superstitions." As a critic he followed Coleridge, Schlegel, Lamb, and Hartley Coleridge, though he imitated no one.

His work in the *North American* began in 1817 with a review of his friend Allston's *Sylphs of the Seasons,* in which he praised the work of Wordsworth and Crabbe. He disliked moralism. Gardiner had said in the *Monthly Anthology,* "Neither painter nor poet should describe a quagmire." Dana replied, "Nothing is vulgar but vice." In 1818 he criticized Maria Edgeworth's *Readings in Poetry,* a book for children, for not making the subject attractive by choosing poems of real merit. She would make of boys "little, matter-of-fact men and unbreeched philosophers"; she ignores the imagination and the poetic sense as factors in the education of children.

In the 1819 review of Hazlitt's *Lectures on the English Poets,* which resulted in his resignation at the end of the year, he established his critical position. In the first place, he was almost alone in his appreciation of Hazlitt's prose style. Second, he urged the study of the older romantic poets, especially Spenser. Third, he denied that Pope was a poet in either subject matter, versification, or diction. Fourth, he set down concreteness of diction as a principle. Fifth, he perceived the newness of Wordsworth's moral treatment of nature: "A moral sense is given to everything, and material things become teachers of the mind and ministers of good to the heart."

His last article in the *North American* was a rather rambling review of *The Sketch Book,* in which he admired Irving's style and wit. In the *United States Review and Literary Gazette,* which favored romanticism, he discussed the "Gothic" in the work of Mrs. Radcliffe and C. B. Brown, at a time when Gothicism was not popular with critics. In the *Spirit of the Pilgrims,* a Calvinistic organ founded by Lyman Beecher in 1828, he revealed his religious orthodoxy in various reviews, particularly that of Pollok's *Course of Time,* although he also took this occasion to reaffirm his doctrine of poetic diction. His belligerent championship of Wordsworth and Coleridge in the preface to his **Poems and Prose Writings,** Boston, 1833, has already been noted. The preface to the first edition of his **Poems** (1827) also contains critical matter.

His lectures on Shakespeare, first delivered in 1834, and often thereafter, have been forgotten because they are unpublished, but they deserve to be remembered not only for their historical primacy, but for their excellence, as well as for the fact that they are very likely the first American treatment of Shakespeare in the manner of Schlegel and Coleridge. In the introductory lecture, he stated that the purpose of poetry is "to unseal our eyes to the beauty, grandeur, and secret spiritual meanings of the outer world, and make us feel the correspondence between that outer world and our inner selves." Inasmuch as "Old English literature . . . is peculiarly a literature of thought and feeling, rules of rhetoric alone [will not] lead into a knowledge of them." Most men of affairs have difficulty in appreciating poetry. "To feel poetically, the whole being must be brought into a peculiar state; . . . and no one has such a mastery over himself as to change his entire state and the movements of his spiritual frame, in a moment and at will." Reading too much criticism is a "disturber of that wise passiveness . . . so essential to the recipient conditions." To read criticism properly one "must be of mature intellect enough to sit in judgment upon the critic judge. . . . Some [critics] instead of trying an original work by the principle of self-congruity and the laws of our common nature, betake themselves to certain standing rules of rhetoric." The contribution of poetry to life is happiness, contentment,

amusement, and deepened concepts of living. It can free men of affairs from the bondage of the material.

In Lecture II he talked of the influence of society on poetry. Poetry is best when society is homogeneous, as in the Ballad Age. Too much personal reflection is bad for it. Too much philosophizing on man and nature is dangerous to the poetic state. It has robbed even the great Wordsworth of spontaneity. Lectures III and IV are a discussion of Shakespeare's female characters, with a few side remarks against woman suffrage and equal rights. Lecture V is a treatment of the supernatural in Shakespeare. Success in this field depends on the sympathy between author and reader. It is always based on a universal principle: it proceeds from the known to the unknown. Lecture VI defends the realism of stage murders and violence. Lectures VII and VIII concern *Macbeth* and *Hamlet.*

These were fresh doctrines in American criticism. They embody not only a new attitude toward poetry but a new conception of criticism. And since they were uttered in public lectures they have importance in the study of the literary education of the American public. To a public brought up on Blair and Kames these must have been startling declarations.

Dana therefore deserves to be known as the first appreciative critic and student of Elizabethan drama, and as such he was a forerunner of Lowell, who, in the next decade, wrote enthusiastic essays on the old English dramatists; of G. C. Verplanck, who published an edition of Shakespeare between 1844 and 1846, and who claimed to be of the school of Schlegel and Coleridge; and of H. H. Furness of Philadelphia. Dana worked by sympathy and insight, not by rules, and he insisted on enjoyment, not analysis, as the object of the study of literature.

Doreen Hunter (essay date 1972)

SOURCE: "America's First Romantics: Richard Henry Dana, Sr. and Washington Allston," in *The New England Quarterly,* Vol. XLV, No. 1, March, 1972, pp. 3-30.

[*In the following excerpt, Hunter addresses Dana's early espousal of romanticism and his later conversion to evangelical Christianity.*]

Like so many writers and artists of their generation, Dana and [Washington] Allston inherited a world view at odds with the one they adopted in their early manhood. They were torn between a traditional body of ideas which assumed the existence of universal truths and the exciting but private psychological visions of Coleridgean idealism. Unable to reconcile a yearning for the subjective intuitions of the imagination with this culturally imposed need for truths verified by universal experience, they became mired in uncertainty. How could they achieve the absolute moral and metaphysical knowledge enjoined both by the lingering Puritan tradition and by the natural law philosophies of the Enlightenment when their whole way of conceiving experience drifted irresistibly in the direction of Coleridgean idealism? American romantic thought emerged from this peculiar conjunction of enlightenment values and English romanticism. The careers of Dana and Allston demonstrate that the problems which made creative work so difficult for early American writers were rooted less in cultural deprivations than in the intellectual difficulty of reconciling romantic and especially Coleridgean ideas about the mind with traditional requirements for a universal, public philosophy. Neither Dana nor Allston could give up the quest for universally valid truths. And yet both believed that truth is discovered not by the understanding and common sense but by the imagination. How then could they discover absolute truth in a subjective realm illumined by reason but also made unpredictable by the workings of the unconscious mind?

While the experiences of Allston and Dana were not literally true for all creative men of their generation, an understanding of their intellectual development illuminates the careers of their contemporaries and makes more understandable the achievements of Emerson and Melville.

Before the War of 1812, several young Boston intellectuals were casting about for a philosophy which would be more vital, spiritual, and organic than the one bequeathed them by their elders. Boston's staid *Monthly Anthology* (1803-1811) was infiltrated by this tiny band of rebels. The friendships which nourished this first American challenge to the dogmas of the eighteenth century were formed at Harvard. In Washington Allston's rooms off the Harvard yard, Allston, Richard Dana's elder brother Edmund Trowbridge Dana, and Arthur Maynard Walter gathered to share their enthusiasm for the poetry of Churchill and Southey and the Gothic novels of Anne Radcliffe and George Coleman. United by their dissatisfaction with instruction at Harvard and their eagerness for European culture and literary experimentalism, they made plans for a European tour. Allston sailed for England in 1801 and was joined a year later by Dana and Walter. After their return to America in 1804, Dana and Walter were invited to join the Anthology Society. The Society, which wrote and published the *Monthly Anthology,* was made up of young men eager to combine their professional careers with avocations as men of letters. Generally speaking, the members were political conservatives, religious liberals, and united in their conviction that they were responsible for teaching their public what was proper for it to read.

The Society's clubability was abruptly broken, however, by the essays which Dana and Walter wrote. These essays, brief and fragmentary though they are, suggest a strong commitment to an early form of romanticism. Their essays might be judged as having little importance were it not for the fact that Washington Allston, on his return to America, published a volume of poems, *Sylphs of the Seasons* (1813) in which he restated the literary and esthetic values asserted by Dana and Walter. Moreover, when Richard Dana, Sr. became a critic for the *Anthology*'s successor, the *North American Review,* he made their cause his own, providing the first fully reasoned defense of literary romanticism written by an American.

Although no Edmund T. Dana—Allston correspondence exists, it is possible to reconstruct the circumstances which led to the emergence of romaticism in America in the second decade of the nineteenth century. At the turn of the century Harvard was intellectually stagnant. The Unitarian synthesis which managed, for several decades, to humanize Lockean empiricism and check native Arminianism with large doses of Scottish common-sense philosophy was consolidated only after the Danas, Allston, and Walter had left. Repelled by what they knew of Locke, disgusted by the boastful rationalism of the campus Deists, and excited by their extracurricular readings of Southey and the Gothic novelists, they responded to the siren calls for a more ideal and organic art coming from English literary circles.

The Danas' most obvious source of news about the English writers was Washington Allston, who had met Coleridge in Rome in 1806. They became friends, and Allston's enthusiasm for Coleridge's ideas spread to his American circle of friends. This influence is most apparent in the critical essays which Richard Dana wrote for the *North American Review.*

Domestic economic and political turmoil also contributed to the willingness with which certain young Federalists, like the Danas and Allston, abandoned the literary, esthetic, and metaphysical beliefs of their fathers. The fortunes and influence of their families had diminished in their youth. While it may seem surprising to find declassed Federalists in the role of cultural revolutionaries, it is to just such individuals that one ought to look for the first expressions of the romantic point of view. The Jeffersonian democrat was so hostile to things English that he could not read sympathetically the early English romantic poets; Federalists in good standing (one thinks of the economically secure or upwardly mobile Federalists who made up the bulk of the *Anthology*'s list of contributors—Joseph Stevens Buckminister, William Tudor, and George Ticknor) were so committed to upholding class values and the republic of letters against the threats of democracy that they had little patience with the individualism and subjectivism of the romantic point of view. So it was a small band of younger Federalists, lacking the wealth and social standing which might have imprisoned them in traditional assumptions, who first formulated the romantic vision for Americans.

The ideas shared by Allston, the Dana brothers, and A. M. Walter were a blend of traditional values and bold iconoclasm. The *Monthly Anthology* rebels could not wholly escape the assumptions which held together the rationalistic world view they wished to deny. They believed that God was the loving and guiding power upholding the universe; they never questioned the existence of an absolute and unambiguous truth. No agonizing alienation experience prefaced their adventures into romantic idealism. They never knew the feeling of being abandoned in an indifferent, mechanistic universe which played such an important part in English and European romantic thought. When doubts overtook them, they questioned their ability to know the truth but never the existence of that truth or of its divine author. In other words, the strength of Protestantism shaped this first American explication of romantic idealism. It prevented the early romantics' notions about God's immanence in the universe from lapsing into pantheism, and colored their boldest expositions of the powers of the imagination with undertones of anxiety and guilt.

Basic to all their literary ideas was the assumption that the variety of nature is the central fact of the universe and the prime evidence of God's presence. They felt that the universe is not as static and orderly as Newton declared; neither was man as rational as Locke believed. They insisted that God's presence is evidenced not by order and symmetry but by the untold variety of his creations. They loved a rough, untended nature, were fascinated by madmen and eccentrics, and admired most those poems and paintings which conveyed a unique, passionate, and private vision of life. Men in the eighteenth century, they complained, had been blind to the moral and spiritual significance of nature. They wished that men would once again learn to "feel the high control / Of him, the Mighty Power, that moves / Amid the waters and the groves, / And through his vast creation proves / His omnipresent soul."

The literary ideas expressed by the rebels in the *Monthly Anthology* followed logically from their belief in the significance of nature's variety. It stood to reason that if writers and artists were faithful to nature they must abandon the pedantries of eighteenth-century psychological theories and the rules of composition laid down in Hugh Blair's *Lectures on Rhetoric*. The Danas argued that nature is violated when fiction, poetry, and art are harnessed to the exposition of false notions about the uniformity of human passions and associations. The new romantics pleaded for a masculine, impassioned and individualistic art. True poets, said

Walter, are inspired by a "divine spirit, a kind of fury, a madness and enthusiasm." They are the makers of new forms and the arbiters of their own rules.

These young men also called for a new kind of literary criticism. They could not accept the view held by other *Anthology* writers that the critic's function was to act as a judge, sentencing to oblivion those who broke Blair's rules. Criticism must be generous and sympathetic for only if the artist feels free to construct his imaginary worlds in his own way can he approach in art the wonderful variety of nature. Man's intellectual nature most resembles God's in the variety it can produce, Richard Dana declared. "If we will have such products, we must neither limit, nor direct the power."

We do not know the direction in which Edmund Dana and A. M. Walter might have developed their protoromantic ideas. Walter died in 1807 and Dana, after withdrawing from the Anthology Club in 1809, never again wrote for publication. Only Richard Dana and Washington Allston went on to struggle with the moral and esthetic implications of their belief that nature and the imagination offer truths unknown to the understanding. Their early familiarity with Coleridge's version of romanticism determined the direction in which they explored romantic beliefs. In his *Biographia Literaria* Coleridge distinguished two kinds of romantic thought: first, Wordsworth's discovery of a supernatural presence and universal truths in nature and common experience, and second, Coleridge's rendering of psychological experiences which suggest the workings of supernatural agents. Dana and Allston were drawn to Coleridge's psychological explorations. But the more deeply each explored the psychological states which kindled the transforming powers of the creative imagination, the less they felt able to declare universal truths. English intellectual traditions allowed for a separation of private and public experience; American traditions did not. In spite of the Antinomian strains in American thought, behavior and experience of all sorts were measured against public and community norms. Imprisoned in intellectual traditions which declared the existence of universally valid truths and the poet's responsibility to spell these out, Dana and Allston could not sustain for long such subjective visions. The history of the first phase of American romanticism can be told in terms of their efforts to reconcile their original commitment to romantic idealism with their equally strong commitment to the discovery of universal truths.

In the spring of 1821, Richard Henry Dana, Sr. decided to publish his own miscellany. He had thought himself in line for the editorship of the *North American Review* when his cousin, Edward Tyrell Channing, retired from that post to accept the Boylston Professorship of Rhetoric at Harvard in 1819. But the majority of the *Review*'s proprietors were so alarmed by the forthright defense of literary romaticism in Dana's review of Hazlitt's *Lectures on the English Poets* and by his attack on those popular pedagogues, Maria and Richard Edgeworth, that they denied him the position. Hoping to find a national audience for his ideas and to conceal his identity from Boston's "unimaginative critics," Dana published his miscellany in New York under the pseudonym, the Idle Man.

Dana tried to develop a short story form that would dramatize his ideas about human emotions and the power of the creative imagination. In his review articles he had been especially critical of the way in which novelists like Laurence Sterne, Samuel Richardson, Washington Irving, and Charles Brockden Brown portrayed emotions. Writing under the influence of the eighteenth-century moral philosophers, these novelists assumed that it was possible to unravel the tangle of human motives and actions. They wrote about the most mysterious and irrational of human feelings and then claimed to make them reasonable by tedious analysis and blunt, sometimes hypocritical, moralizing. Dana hoped to portray psychological experience honestly, to preserve the variety and mystery of human emotions by relying on the mood, tone, setting, and dialogue rather than the self-analytical soliloquies and letters used by the novelists he criticized. He wanted to involve the reader's imagination rather than his understanding.

He began this experiment in short fiction in a highly optimistic mood, confident that the imagination could enable men to see the spiritual meanings in nature. In an essay which he called **"Musings,"** Dana wrote an ecstatic explanation of how the traditional dualism between matter and spirit, man and God could be overcome if only one surrendered to the powers of the imagination. To experience this union one must first learn to see and feel nature as one did when a child. Dana assumed that if a child were permitted to develop according to the laws of his own nature and without too much officious regulation by adults, he would grow up obedient to the natural and "holy movements of the soul." It is society that blinds us to nature's spiritual content. We are taught to check our feelings and passions, to deny our imaginations, and to force our moral natures to march along the well-trod paths of convention. Society, Dana insisted, makes us choose: we must either "become like others, cold and wise," or we become madmen and moral outlaws. In order to behold the universal spirit while nature "lays by its particular and short-lived and irregular nature, and puts on the garments of spiritual beings, and takes the everlasting nature of the soul," one must open oneself to those childlike feelings of awe and love which kindle the imagination. In some mysterious way this wonder-filled passivity gives life to the imagination; out of the "living sea" of images stored up within the unconscious mind, it creates a new "two-fold" life resplendent with symbolic and spiritual meanings. In the transports of

imaginative insight, a man becomes a part of the eternal ongoing of nature—he becomes as innocent and pure as the universal spirit that flows through him.

> The innocent face of nature gives him an open and fair mind; pain and death seem passing away, for all about him is cheerful and in its spring. His virtues are not taught him as lessons, but are shed upon him and enter into him like the light and warmth of the sun; . . . Freedom and order, and beauty and grandeur, are in accordance in his mind, and give largeness and height to his thoughts; he moves among the bright clouds; he wanders away into the measureless depths of the stars, and is touched by the fire with which God has lighted them. All that is made partakes of the eternal, and religion becomes a perpetual delight.

Dana could not sustain for long this passionately optimistic form of romantic transcendentalism. When he put his faith to the test of fictional dramatization, his confidence in the redeeming powers of the imagination collapsed with astonishing suddenness. Once he set his characters into their social context, made lovers and husbands of them, and forced them to confront a "real" world full of conflict, temptation and evil, he discovered the moral preposterousness of the romantic injunction to feel deeply and follow the heart.

At the outset he had assumed that society corrupts the heart and kills the imagination; the problem then, was how to keep the feelings and the imagination alive to spiritual truths. In the battle against society's corroding flood of convention, Dana put his faith in the redeeming power of nature and romantic love. In **"Musings"** he said that men could recover that innocent love of nature which would open the way to transcendent truths. But a story which he had published in the previous number cast doubt on this possibility. In "Edward and Mary," Edward, an ardent and receptive student of nature, confesses that nature alone cannot satisfy his longings for truth and love. Men "are made for other purposes than to have our interests begin and end in [nature]. . . . " To the dilemma posed by the conflicting demands of society and nature, Dana declared that men must choose society and the risks of alienation from nature and God. If nature alone is insufficient, perhaps the bonds created by love and marriage can shelter and sustain the natural movements of the soul. In "Edward and Mary," Dana insisted that were it not for Mary's love, Edward's romantic nature would either be crushed by the leaden-hearted world or distorted into madness. Just as nature leads her worshipper from sensation to idea, so sexual passion, Dana suggested, will lead from pleasure to spirituality.

Once Dana put spiritual salvation on this shaky foundation, his entire metaphysical structure began to topple. Not only did he lose confidence in man's ability, with the aid of nature and romantic love, to preserve the feeling and innocence which kindles the imagination, but he also began to question whether the imagination, if it survived, could lead to truth at all. Dana's interest in human psychology, in madness, and visionary experience, led him to think of the connection between passion and the imagination in a way ultimately disastrous to the transcendental metaphysics of **"Musings."** He believed that the imagination is both seer and creator—a source of spiritual enlightenment and a power which transforms sensations into new, quite private visions. The problem was how to insure a harmony between absolute truth and the visions which the imagination created from the materials of the unconscious mind. For obviously, if these visions are nothing more than projections of one's own soul, then the imagination cannot bring one into harmony with God. If each man reads into nature his own peculiar lesson according to his own peculiar mood, then the romantic imagination can yield startling insights into human psychology but it cannot teach ultimate truth. What assurance has the man of imagination that he does not mistake his own delusions for truth?

The reader is hardly prepared for the sudden reversal in Dana's ideas about the imagination. In a period of less than eight months he abandoned the optimism of his "Musings." His last stories reveal an anxiety about guilt and death and a growing conviction that man is alienated from God not by society but by his own nature.

The wreck of Dana's romantic transcendentalism is apparent in **"Paul Felton,"** the last short story he wrote for *The Idle Man*. Paul was brought up to love nature and the classics: from the first he learned the unity of mind and sense and the spirituality of nature; from the second he learned the mysteries of the human heart. Even so, Paul is often unmoved by nature. "Sometimes he would sit alone on one of the peaks in the chain of the neighbouring hills, and look out on the country beneath him, as if imploring to be taken to a share of the joy which it seemed sensible to, as it lay in the sunshine. . . . [Nature] heard him not, but left him to cares, and the waste of time, and his own thoughts." In romantic literature such alienation from nature is the sure sign of a sick soul. Esther, Paul's beautiful and adoring wife, provides him no peace or happiness.

Paul is a man of deep feelings, introspection, and imagination, but it is precisely these romantic virtues that bring about his moral ruin. His assumption that truth lies beyond the mask of sensible reality leads him into a towering, destructive egotism. Paul is driven into an obsessive absorption with the processes of his own mind. He urges on his passions, gives them rein "that he might feel all the self torture they would bring," and endlessly examines his motives. His personality becomes so involuted that "at last his mind seemed given for little else than to speculate upon his feelings,

to part or unite them, or to quell them only again to inflame them." No longer the master of his emotions, Paul moves erratically and violently from moods of ecstasy to black despair. In what modern readers will recognize as a bizarre attempt to portray a paranoid-schizophrenic personality, Dana tells us that Paul is convinced that he is possessed by Satan. "Violent passions and dreadful thoughts had now obtained such a mastery over Paul, that they came and went like powers independent of his will; and he felt himself as a creature lying at their mercy." His imagination is so possessed by these visions that nature is transformed into a battleground between the forces of good and evil. Paul believes that Satan commands him to kill his wife of whom he is insanely jealous. He does so, and in a moment of lucidity, realizing the enormity of what he has done, the shock kills him.

Dana prefaced this tale with lines from Wordsworth:

> Who thinks and feels
> And recognizes ever and anon
> The breeze of Nature in his soul,
> Why need such men go desperately astray,
> And nurse the "dreadful appetite of death?"

The answer which this story suggests radically reverses the ideas Dana defended in **"Musings."** In Paul Felton, Dana created a character blessed with sensitivity and imagination. Yet he is cursed; his sin of rapt self-absorption is the consequence of obeying the romantic injunction to view experience in a passionate, subjective way; his capacity to transform the world according to the fevered imaginings of his brain is the risk run by those who find no way to distinguish their truths from transcendent ones. Nature only mirrors to the eye of her beholder the state of his own soul. How is one to discover transcendent truths if the passions aroused by nature and love lead only back upon the self—a self alienated from God, not by some Adamic guilt but by man's otherness. Because Dana had no answer to that question, because he was abused by critics for creating moral monsters, and because of his grief over his wife's death, he stopped writing.

In 1826, when the revival movement led by Lyman Beecher swept through Boston and Cambridge, Dana was left in its wake, a penitent at the mourner's bench. Out of a soul-searing confrontation with the God of the evangelists, Dana forged a new philosophical and esthetic point of view—one that fused elements of his earlier romanticism with the precepts of evangelical Christianity. Dana's conversion confirmed his growing suspicion that the conflict between the flesh and the spirit, between the visions welling up from the unconscious and the yearning for the absolute, could not be resolved by romantic methodologies. Thus, when he took up his pen again it was as a contributor to Beecher's *Spirit of the Pilgrims*. However, his religious essays and poetry were more than a mere justification of the principles of Trinitarian Christianity. They must be understood in the light of his earlier views of nature and the imagination, for Dana found in Christianity a higher ground for the romantic vision. In the doctrine of original sin he discovered an explanation for man's alienation from nature and God. He had abandoned the optimistic romanticism of his **"Musings"** because he needed to believe that the imagination is powered by an inspiration more trustworthy than the poet's unconscious mind. Redemption, he felt, promised the poet an infusion of God's creative love and the guidance of the Holy Spirit. While it would be misleading to say that Dana turned to Christianity in order to find a higher discipline for the romantic imagination, that was certainly the result. Revealed religion offered him a way to escape the twin dangers of pantheism and Paul Felton's mad vision of the world as the projection of his own mad dreams.

In an essay written to prove the insidiousness of Unitarian theology, Dana summed up the intellectual history of many men in his and later generations. They had fled from the sterile, overly rationalized world view of the Unitarians into a spiritually attractive but morally dangerous transcendentalism. Their quest for a passionate, suprarational experience of God led, Dana argued, either to pantheism or egotism. In terms that savagely indicted views he had defended nine years before, Dana dismissed the whole effort to worship God in his creation as mawkish sentimentality. "Our creator and final Judge," he declared, "is fairly idealized and sentimentalized out of his own creation, providence, and rule. Creation, and not the Creator, is the life and the spirit to us. . . . " Without the indwelling presence of the Holy Spirit, man can have no experience of God for "nothing is perceived as it is in itself, but becomes the embodied presentation of the illusions within." The rationalist deludes himself when he worships reason in the guise of the first cause; the pantheist only thinks he worships God in nature. In truth they both worship only themselves. The rationalists lord "it over the material world, as if no God created and sustained it," and the romantic idealists look "through all spiritual existences and relations, as if no revelation were needed wherewith to behold them." Both err in not making God, as revealed in the Bible and by the Holy Spirit, the source of all moral, metaphysical, and spiritual truth.

Dana did not hesitate to draw from these reflections the logical conclusion: only the redeemed man can be a true poet for only he can surrender himself to his imagination in the confidence that the transformation that occurs will conform to a higher reality.

In a poem entitled **"Thoughts on the Soul"** which he read at Andover in 1829, Dana described the powers of the soul in terms he had once used when discussing the creative imagination. The soul must create—that is its essential and eternal character. All experience is transmuted by the soul to the shape of its essence. "On it goes, for ever ever on, / Changing, all down its course, each thing to one / With its immortal nature." If unredeemed, the poet creates a world of terror and insanity. Like Paul Felton, "the fiends of his own bosom people air / With kindred fiends that haunt him to despair." If, on the other hand, the poet knows Christ as his redeemer, his soul's creative power is absorbed into the flow of God's fecund love. He no longer exhausts himself in an uncertain quest for the symbolic meaning of nature. All is revealed to him. Sweeping aside the ever-popular notion that nature can be read as a symbol of transcendent truths, Dana insisted that the poet must know the symbol maker before the symbols.

> "From nature up to nature's God," no more
> Grope out his way through parts, nor place
>   before
> The Former the thing formed: Man yet shall
>   learn
> The outward by the inward to discern,—
> The inward by the Spirit.

Restored to his proper union in God, the redeemed poet shares in God's creative power. Because he is cleansed of sin, the poet no longer needs to fear the egoistic demons of his unconscious. He can plumb the depths of his soul secure in the knowledge that the imagination is governed by a higher power. Dana still insisted, as he had in his earliest writings, that the thoughts and images out of which poetry is made arise from the subterranean depths of the unconscious mind. But the unconscious held no terrors for him now. As in the Biblical account of creation, so within the poet's mind—void and chaos take on form under the mysterious impulse of God's "life-giving, forming and informing principles. . . ."

Historians of the American mind have long assumed that romantic thought was shaped by the peculiar conjunction of Enlightenment ideas and strains of English romanticism. But too often we have sought for explanations of the meagerness of American literature between 1800 and 1836 in general cultural conditions rather than in the dilemmas inherent in such a transition. The careers of Dana and Allston remind us that the leap from Locke to Coleridge—from enlightenment epistemology to romantic psychology—was fraught with considerable hazards. The unevenness of their careers, marked by bursts of creativity and lapses into despair, can be explained by the difficulty they had in reconciling a cultural tradition which demanded obedience to external codes of behavior and experience with the lure of Coleridge's private visions. In other words, that traditional cultural dualism inherent in Puritan theology—in the conflict between Arminian and Antinomian—reappeared in an acute form for those American writers and artists who leaped rather heedlessly into Coleridgean idealism.

As young men dissatisfied with the spiritual and emotional aridity of Locke's epistemology, Allston and Dana eagerly embraced Coleridge's theories about the imagination. They moved quickly from a rather Unitarian view which assumed that nature was an expression of God's love, to an exploration of the way the imagination transforms experience into the shapes of the unconscious mind. Both men found this journey into the unmapped territory of the unconscious mind terrifying and untenable. Whether one explains their abandonment of these explorations as a lingering Puritanism or a tardy conversion to common-sense ideas, the conclusion is the same: they felt that the imagination, if unrestrained by some external and universal standard of truth, could only lead to nihilism and madness. For if the world we experience has only the significance we give to it, it can have any meaning and thus has no meaning at all.

Although Dana's Holy Spirit and Allston's supervising Higher Power seem a world away from the metaphysical and epistemological principles assumed by Emerson, Thoreau, and later romantic writers, the differences are by no means as great as they first appear. All shunned those experiences which had a wholly private significance. The symbolism of Emerson and Thoreau was not rooted in a personal transmutation of experience but in an assumed correspondence between the laws of nature, the laws of the mind and a transcendental reality. Because the second generation of American romantic writers came to Coleridge only after a thorough indoctrination in Scottish common-sense philosophy they screened out his disturbing insights into the psychological origins of the workings of the imagination. They were attracted by his analysis of the teleological principles which govern mind and matter and not by "Christabel" and "Kubla Khan." They admired the Coleridge who fleshed out common-sense ideas about the correspondences between idea and nature rather than the Coleridge who insisted upon a deeply personal, even opium-induced, transformation of experience into the stuff of the private self. They never had to work their way clear of the psychological subjectivism which tormented Dana and Allston because their way was eased by Scottish realism.

It is ironic but hardly accidental that Melville condemned the transcendentalists for ignoring the dilemma Dana had so effectively dramatized thirty years before in **"Paul Felton."** Melville's Pierre, like Dana's Paul Felton, is driven to madness, murder, and suicide by the realization that nature has only those meanings which we project upon it. As a rule American romantics shied away from this dilemma. Like Dana and Allston, later romantics developed elaborate strategies

for skirting this implicit subjectivism. Allston and Dana were by no means the last romantics to attempt to harness the imagination to an external and universal standard of truth.

Robert A. Ferguson (essay date 1984)

SOURCE: "The Richard Henry Danas: Father and Son," in *Law and Letters in American Culture,* Cambridge, Mass.: Harvard University Press, 1984, pp. 241-72.

[*In the following excerpt, Ferguson compares Dana's early romanticism with his later thoughts on legal theory, contrasting the gothic story "Paul Felton" (1822), with the essay "Law as Suited to Man" (1835).*]

Some individuals personify the wholeness of an age; others reflect the incompleteness of its parts. Daniel Webster, in the first category, spoke confidently for the nineteenth century and symbolized its conventions. The Richard Henry Danas, father and son, were more shadowy figures caught up in changes that they only partially understood. As traditional as Webster in politics and social matters, they accepted many of the new impulses sweeping through nineteenth-century intellectual thought, and those impulses were complex. It was not just that Webster admired Pope over all other poets while the Danas preferred Wordsworth. The whole manner in which Americans approached politics, society, and literature was changing. Webster belonged to old ways of thinking. The Danas fell somewhere between the old and the new and faced uncomfortable choices in consequence. Those choices, rather than specific achievements, are what make the Danas interesting. Their failures underscore the contradictions between neoclassical and romantic in republican culture, and their successes illustrate the slow and painful growth of a peculiarly American romanticism. For if Webster embodied the configuration of law and letters, the Danas represented its collapse, and they were the first to realize as much. . . .

Francis Dana (1743-1811) and Richard Henry Dana, Sr. (1787-1879), entered the legal profession with [large] aspirations. In fact, the three Danas span the entire period of the configuration of law and letters, and their respective decisions reveal a great deal about the changing nature of nineteenth-century intellectual life. Francis Dana typified the early American lawyer's grasp of his culture. Admitted to the Massachusetts bar in 1767, he played a minor but distinct role in the Revolution. He was a member of the Continental Congress, chairman of the committee on the army that brought vital political support to Washington at Valley Forge, secretary to John Adams during the original peace negotiations in France and Holland, and then ambassador to Russia. Only poor health kept him from serving as one of the framers in Philadelphia in 1787, and a year later he was instrumental in the Massachusetts convention that ratified the Constitution of the United States. Eventually, Francis Dana became chief justice of the supreme judicial court of Massachusetts, a position he held for fifteen years from Washington's presidency into the second administration of Jefferson. As chief justice he sustained "an elegance but little known in those days," riding circuit in the finest of carriages, and his grand jury charges epitomized New England Federalism in its days of glory. An admiring Richard Henry Dana, Jr., captured the total effect: "His whole style was that of a great magistrate, & he sustained the dignity of the office with no little of the aristocratic bearing."

Unfortunately, Francis Dana's success also magnified failure in the next generation. Richard Henry Dana, Sr., never recovered from the disastrous speculations of an older brother who dissipated family fortunes in the first decade of the nineteenth century. Indeed, much of Dana Sr.'s writing dealt with the shock of this lost status. Of his father the chief justice he noted, "I can never think of his exalted character without a sense of my own littleness." The merest memory, he added, "makes the present tasteless, & takes away the vigour of my hope in what is to come." Written in 1819, these words came not from a pining adolescent but from a man of thirty-two, and they expressed a final determination to reject the law for a private life as "The Idle Man" in literature.

This decision was a public admission of defeat in 1819. Contemporaries like George Ticknor, Edward T. Channing, William Hickling Prescott, and Alexander Everett also abandoned the law for various literary pursuits, and Henry Longfellow, James Russell Lowell, and Francis Parkman followed suit a generation later, but these men relied upon independent wealth or another vocation for status, and most had both. Dana Sr. could name only an honorary assistantship at the *North American Review,* and even this tenuous association—"all gentlemen and no pay"—was taken away in 1819 when failure to succeed in the logical sequence of editors prompted his resignation. By 1822 he had just the smallest of patrimonies, an occasional lecture series, and his own writings to fall back upon. "I am a miserable cripple," he had announced earlier, revealing the hypochondria that would support another half-century of idleness. The boy of twelve who remembered Washington's death would live to see Rutherford B. Hayes elected president, and every year brought fresh complaints and new failures. "I was shabbily enough treated in my honest endeavours for an humble place," he told his son later. Alas, "the *life* of the mind, through long disappoinment, had become permanently languid." In 1848 Lowell's *A Fable for Critics* sounded a final note of satire over all of this pathos: "That he once was the Idle Man none will deplore, / But I fear that he will never be anything more. . . ."

Richard Henry Dana, Sr., had been the first modern American critic, the first to value the romantic impulses in nineteenth-century literature, and he had used those impulses to justify his retreat from public life. Since romanticism stressed a creative imagination yearning for natural simplicity, the editor of *The Idle Man* easily separated a private life of the mind from the corrupting and vulgar world of work and society. Indeed, the distinction governed the elder Dana's writings and entered into the psychological legacy of the son. . . .

For the working artist, . . . there is always an enormous gap between theoretical understanding and creative application. The Danas, both father and son, mastered the meaning of romanticism but never its working implications and never its voice. They failed because the emerging modes of expression at work in nineteenth-century American culture required new ways of regarding the self—ways that unsettled everything the Danas stood for in republican society. Neoclassicism assumed an identity that reached through civic action toward the presumed identity of other men and women. Romanticism, concerned more with ego and self-expression, compelled a prior discovery and assertion of personal identity. As the first suggested relation, so the second implied opposition, and the difference underlined absolute philosophical divisions. Were truths self-evident or were truths evident to the self? The Danas could never decide, and their uncertainty meant that the configuration of law and letters no longer answered such questions. . . .

Richard Henry Dana, Sr., could legitimately call his own works "a part of our literary history." Between 1817 and 1827 he wrote America's first sustained critique of romanticism, penned the country's most perceptive reviews, praised Charles Brockden Brown's genius before other critics found even merit, and helped create the genre of American gothic fiction. Too, Dana Sr. lived long enough to see his most unpopular evaluations turn into conventional doctrine. He knew the satisfaction of having been right all along: "Much that was once held to presumptuous novelty" in the Era of Good Feeling became, in his words, "little better than commonplace" by 1850. The precursor, however, took no satisfaction in what followed. "Emerson & the other Spiritualists, or Supernaturalists, or whatever they are called, or may be pleased to call themselves" were a bad influence; "madness is in their *hearts,*" wrote Dana Sr. There was, in short, a basic failure in sympathy that illustrates how thoroughly republican culture tangled the notions of neoclassic and romantic. Dana Sr., the purveyor of a European romanticism, saw not a counterpart in American transcendentalism but rather an extreme manifestation that exceeded essential controls. Neoclassical in form, those controls were part of a political orthodoxy that no early republican could ignore—part of the long contest between order and originality in American literature. Dana Sr. earned a special place in that contest by laboring to combine the incompatible.

Every major tenet of romanticism receives attention in Dana Sr.'s early *North American Review* articles. An essay from 1817, **"Old Times,"** chooses feeling and imagination over affected refinement and cold rationality, nature over society, ancient custom over modern practice. The writer wants a mind as organic and creative as the earth itself, and he looks for the "wild and adventurous starting up in the midst of the common objects of life." A review of Washington Allston's poetry from the same year makes poetry the highest ideal of a culture, rejects didacticism in literature, and applauds balladic simplicity. Again the contrast is between the freedom, energy, and spontaneity of man in nature against the confinement, artificiality, and "hot stir of pent society."

Two more reviews from 1818 and 1819 turn abstract premise into explicit accusation. Here Dana Sr. censures critics who condemn Wordsworth and Coleridge in the name of Pope; they substitute profession for sincerity, wit for feeling, ornament for simple reflection, and reason for natural impulse. The true critic hopes instead for awakened associations, "living forms struggling to break forth," and "a holier calm" from "the riot of the imagination."

The same ideas carry into the poems and stories of the 1820s. **"The Changes of Home," "Factitious Life," "The Early Spring Book," "The Moss Supplicateth for the Poet,"** and **"Daybreak"** all extol in verse the simple, organic, natural world in which "the whole man *lived* his feelings." Like many another romantic poet, Dana Sr. employs pastoral settings, aeolian harps, and mystic hieroglyphs to convey one central message: "How simply nature teaches truth!" His fictional protagonists also turn to nature as a special source of meaning. Looking to the "blessed and silent communion" of the elements, Tom Thornton, in the story of that name, wants to "mingle with the air, and be all a sensation too deep for sound,— a traveller among the stars, and filled with light." Edward Shirely of "Edward and Mary" combines a distaste for the world at large with delight in the purifying influences of nature. In this account of threatened love, nature invariably sympathizes with the hero's shifts in mood. In **"Paul Felton,"** Paul walks the hills, looking for sympathy in nature. Nature is "power, and intellect, and love, made visible," and it allows Paul moments of truth: "He was as part of the great universe, and all he looked upon, or thought on, was in some way connected with his own mind and heart." In each story spontaneous impulses cut across careful reason, and external landscapes merge with stages of mind to emphasize the organic link between man and nature.

Yet these writings perplex because they promise so much more than they give. Original in intent, they are imitative in effect. They fail through a basic paradox: the poems and stories of Richard Henry Dana, Sr., are romantic in theory but neoclassic in practice, and the combination robs each point of view of its intrinsic worth. The same paradox, of course, applies to other writers in the first decades of the nineteenth century, but Dana Sr.'s stature as a romantic theorist poses the problem in its purest form. How could such a critic fail to see the gap between assertion and execution in his own work? Why do neoclassical premises remain so firmly entrenched in poems and stories that strive so hard for something else? The negatives traditionally used to explain literary weakness in the early national period do not apply in this case. Neither parochial nor utilitarian, the publications of Dana Sr. show that he possessed the time, the opportunity, the literary sophistication, and the desire to achieve much in poetry and fiction.

Conflicting aims hurt Dana Sr. far more than inadequate means. He writes for a world that requires him to be too many things at once. A romantic critic, he is also gentlemen of letters with the responsibility of defining man's place in society. As republican citizen, he believes in social subordination as a basis of ordered liberty, and his dutiful expression of that belief is profoundly neoclassical in scope and tone, adding decorum, propriety, duty, hierarchy, and control to the cardinal virtues of imagination and natural impulse. These unlikely combinations breed contradiction and crop up everywhere in Dana Sr.'s stories, poems, and reviews.

The published works are a battleground of conflicting values. One celebration of "the wild and adventurous" insists upon the necessity of order and constraint in master-servant relations. The reviewer who wants passions to be "living, sentient, speaking, acting beings" also confesses to "fears of being unduly sprightly . . . sacrificing our dignity and decorum." Feelings are vital, but the most natural impulse must bow to social convention. Thus, a call for honest feeling does not excuse Washington Irving for allowing a husband to show public affection in "The Wife." Still other parts of *The Sketch Book* lack proper refinement because Irving stoops to describe passion outside of love. Dana Sr. admires Charles Brockden Brown for accomplishing what he himself cannot: "Instead of living as only one of the multitude of keen and clever men at the bar, and then dying and being forgotten, [Brown] is going down . . . as the earliest author of genius in our literature." But no amount of originality can justify the bad taste of Brown's free-thinking tracts or the vulgarity of that moment in *Ormond* when the beautiful Constantia Dudley washes foul linen.

Greater writers would soon turn the ambiguities between personal feeling and social conformity into high art. Less gifted, Richard Henry Dana, Sr., nonetheless glimpses the possibility; he is the first to understand that the American story involves an unending adjustment of twin obsessions, impulse and order. Predictably, his heroes are divided men. They cling to decorum and nicety during the sharpest of inward crises, and cling they must since insanity lies close to the surface in Dana Sr.'s fiction. Characters who lose sight of the prescribed forms of conduct go mad. Protagonists like Tom Thornton, Edward Shirley, and Paul Felton have romantic temperaments, but their safety depends upon a neoclassical equilibrium that guards against the dangers of introspection. Romanticism has taught Dana Sr. that imagination can be a perilous thing:

> The imagination grows forgetive, and the mind idles, in its melancholy, among fantastic shapes; all it hears or sees is turned to its own uses, taking new forms and new relations, and multiplying without end; and it wanders off amongst its own creations, which crowd thicker round it the farther it goes, till it loses sight of the world, and becomes bewildered in the many and uneven paths that itself had trodden out.

More simply, "turning the mind long inward upon itself" means "making ourselves miserable" most of the time. Social interaction alone can correct the resulting imbalance. "To know ourselves," Dana Sr. explains, "we must be content, sometimes, to go out of ourselves." Happiness requires recognition of one's "double character"; one's "outer and inner machinery" must balance.

"Paul Felton" (1822), a minor masterpiece in the American gothic between Brown and Poe, tells what happens when man's inner machinery takes over. Accepting the romantic postulate that imagination guides perception, Dana Sr. writes a nightmare of the imagination run wild. Paul Felton has been raised in melancholy isolation by his widowed father, a background that inhibits meaningful intercourse with the world. Incapable of balancing outer and inner priorities, he retreats inward where everything is "pent-up and secret action." Soon all is "at war and in opposition in his character," and his mind welcomes extremes, "not knowing how to measure its joys when they came." This mind is "in a peculiar degree single," which means that the passion of the moment utterly controls what Paul comprehends. Gradually, obsessions rob Paul of all sense of reality and turn him into a homicidal maniac. He murders his wife, Esther, who, as the symbol of social interaction, has tried to save him. It is Esther who delivers the author's overall indictment of Paul: "You have brooded all alone over your melancholy thoughts, till they have bewildered you."

Inner bewilderment is such a source of terror in **"Paul Felton"** because it happens so easily and because Paul differs only in degree from the more social beings around him. As the story makes clear, everyone experiences unwilled mental aberrations, which suddenly appear "like visitants from hell." This is the organic mind receiving and projecting associations. Left alone, however, the mind uses these sensations too freely and quickly becomes an engine of delusion. Paul separates himself from "what is homely and substantial in this world we live in" and, hence, fails to protect himself from intrinsic impulses. "I would not be what I am," he mourns, rightly fearing his own inner psyche. The rest is an ugly, inevitable sequence. In accepting an organic theory of the mind, Dana Sr. understands that the imagination welcomes delusion and thrives on madness. Paul easily manufactures a private hell as real as the external world, and that hell expands in his narcissistic enjoyment of the act of creation.

"Paul Felton" recounts the mind's helpless pleasure in its own madness when all avenues of escape have been sealed off. Even Paul's classical education and his love of nature hurt more than they help. The former supplies a certain clarity and simplicity, but it also alienates Paul from modern society. Nature presents even graver problems; she is indifferent, leaving Paul "a withered thing amid her fresh and living beauty." Worse, she sometimes stimulates the darker recesses of his mind. A desolate wasteland directly behind the house of Paul and Esther accentuates each feeling of isolation and delusion. Moreover, "a spider" in the madman's eye feeds on a correspondence in nature. When Paul plans the murder of Esther, he is deep in the wilderness, literally supported by "some giant spider" of a pine tree. Man and nature have come together, but in horror and catastrophe instead of transcendence and a higher reality.

The reversal of romantic aspirations is surely deliberate. Dana Sr. accepts a vital link between the imagination and the natural realm, but he fears the way "quickly associating processes of the mind" magnify emotion, and he sees too much of a blank wilderness, "the place of death," to rest easily in nature. New ideas compete with old solutions. Dana Sr. wants an objective truth to secure the subjective reality that he has come to believe in. Caught between combination and contradiction, he is the first American writer to face the epistemological problems of nineteenth-century thought. Where is absolute order in a contingent universe? When do feelings represent fact? What is truth? **"Paul Felton"** ushers these questions into American fiction, where they lead to either a quest for ultimate meaning or a search for particular order. The isolated hero quests for meaning, social man searches for his place, and the two vie for position in every major work of the American Renaissance. Paul Felton, alas, is an early uncertain mixture of both. The man who would challenge the universe shrinks from the impropriety of a ride in his fiancée's carriage. He is the *isolato* as public figure, a stance that begins in confusion and ends in madness because it has "too much to do with the senses." Something beyond mere perception must clarify Paul's world, something that will fix meaning and establish order.

That something is the early American's regard for the law—the only answer Dana Sr. gives to the writer's problems. **"Law as Suited to Man"** in 1835, almost two decades after the lawyer rejects his profession, tries to resolve the incongruity between subjective thought and objective order by inserting the legal philosophy of Edmund Burke. In itself the attempt is a firm indication of the citizen still at work in the romantic theorist. Torn between unacceptable alternatives, Dana Sr. wants to prove "there is nothing without us which fails of reaching that which lies within." He answers the great questions of romanticism with one of his own: "And must not Law, then, give form and pressure to every part of man?" Properly understood, the law joins mind and matter, allowing "no jarring nor discordant influences within or without." Reciprocity is the key to harmony here, a reciprocity that effectively externalizes the romantic's psychological theories of correspondence. Burke has traced not only "the reachings of law into man's finer nature" but also "the delicate, electric *aura* which this individual nature gives back, and diffuses through every fiber of the great, general frame." Accordingly, the law is an infinite abstraction "producing congruity, and giving continuity" between "outer political rule" and "the finest feelings in man's individual being." It meets man everywhere and on every level, its divine purpose being "to bring man into the likeness of the pattern." As for so many other early American intellectuals, the law gives Dana Sr. a principle of unity in an uncertain world; it secures "the resemblances and relations of things to each other" and ties "the upper and lower, the inward and outward world to one great end." The language sounds familiar because it is what lawyers since Thomas Jefferson had been using to order American culture.

Even so, **"Law as Suited to Man"** belongs to 1835. The essay consciously imposes traditional solutions upon new problems, and as such it illustrates the special dilemma of the legal mind of the 1830s better than any other document of the period. Indeed, the contradictions here suggest an impossibility beyond mere difficulty. The republic, literature, and law—all of the controlling constants—change suddenly into variables in the Jacksonian era. When Dana Sr. deplores "the very absence of checks and balances, and settled orders," he also unwittingly announces a formal break in the bonds that once held law to literature. Each theoretical affirmation in **"Law as Suited to Man,"** and there are many, is qualified by a list of perceived ills.

Practice so violates theory in this description of America that one senses a permanent disjunction. Put another way, the republican man of letters no longer encompasses reality in 1835. His patterns of discourse do not reach the new levels of psychological process that now appear as part of every understanding. A new self-consciousness has brought another dimension to the conflation of moral and legal perspectives and with devastating implications. In **"Law as Suited to Man"** Dana Sr. tries to build a house with paint and brush. He desperately needs the citizen's more elementary context, but the aspirations of romanticism, which question or ignore a writer's institutional affiliations, prevent a simple return to old ways of thinking. Despite every explanation to the contrary, the legal philosopher and the romantic critic remain absolute opposites in Dana Sr.'s essay, split between social assertion and psychological insight.

"There is nothing more serious than poetry," says the literary critic in **"Law as Suited to Man,"** a statement in support of individual creativity that no other American of his generation dared to make. This side of Dana Sr. writes to keep the mind alive, the imagination in motion, the fancy in play, and all principles of association in action. And yet the same essayist deserts "man, in his short-lived, individual character" in favor of "the person abstracted from these, and representative of permanent Law." He hopes instead to help each well-defined class find its place—"all brought about by and carried through the harmonizing Orders of a great general Law." The civic humanist of an earlier day could join these differences by making self-fulfillment a question of citizenship. Not so the intellectual of the 1830s, who began to see an increasing gulf between self and society. In 1835, the year **"Law as Suited to Man"** appeared, Ralph Waldo Emerson was thirty-one and ready to write that "things are not huddled and lumped, but sundered and individual." For Richard Henry Dana, Sr., the same notion meant a terrifying "principle of severance" and the certainty of communal paralysis.

Taken together, Emerson and Dana Sr. capture a crucial moment in American intellectual thought. Paradigms of social and psychological process often merge or even clash without crisis, but here they are reconstituting in a way that requires a direct reversal in modes of thought. In celebrating "the new importance given to the single person," Emerson claims that man explains society instead of the other way around. "The world is nothing, the man is all," he announces, thus becoming the first American really to accept the romantic *within* romantic theory. Much is at stake in this acceptance, and not least is Emerson's immediate deduction that the law be seen as an internal matter: "In yourself is the law of all nature."

The very basis of law has become a subject of dispute in Jacksonian America. By 1835 the question is no longer *if* law is suited to human life but *how*. Courtrooms are treating the law less and less as an eternal set of principles derived from natural law and more and more as an independent instrument of social policy that lawmakers have created. This change is Dana Sr.'s greatest fear. Assuming a definitive link between natural law and man-made or positive law, **"Law as Suited to Man"** returns again and again to the contradiction between eighteenth-century legal philosophy and nineteenth-century judicial positivism. Either the law "presses upon every part of the ductile spirit of man," or it is just a machine, "supplying conveniences and furnishing levers and springs to help on the more general purposes of man." Either it has "a necessitated beginning and continuance in our very nature," or it is "a mere arbitrary institution set up by man himself, out of convenience and choice." Either "it bodies itself forth in orders of men," or it is "a caterer to the self-conceit of man." These distinctions mark the difference between order and chaos in **"Law as Suited to Man."** For if legal positivism turns the law into a more flexible social instrument, it also traps law within the civic milieu, rendering it useless as a philosophical bridge between levels of existence. Gone is the "kindly adaptation" between outward forms and inward needs. Lost are fitness in gradation and a relationship in orders.

Painfully, the writer knows that his solutions no longer solve. The predictions of **"Law as Suited to Man"** counter its preferences. In this, the last original essay the elder Dana published, America suffers from a "mad restlessness which sets at naught all Law," and at fault is "the want of an agreement between the ordinary courses of Providence and our outward public Form of Law." These truths, once admitted, render the prescriptive tones and remedies of the traditional man of letters obsolete. For the writer who would connect law and literature, expression has lost all context except in a glorification of the past. Hence, the past for Dana Sr. becomes richly variegated marble; the present, "an uncouth, dead mass of pudding stone." As for the future, it contains "some fearful rebuke," and the prophet faces it only to prepare his children for "a world to which we would not trust ourselves." A final image of Dana Sr. as writer appears in his son's journal, where he takes pen to paper only to stop paralyzed "in the anxious, uncertain state . . . which interrupts all his labors now; a sense that it is his duty to work, & a morbid sensitiveness which makes every day & every hour an unfit time to work at." His subject? Musing upon the experiences of life from the twilight shadows of an empty room.

FURTHER READING

Biography

Dana, Richard Henry, III. "Richard Henry Dana, Sr." In *Later Years of the Saturday Club, 1870-1920,* edited by M. A. DeWolfe Howe, pp. 36-42. Boston: Houghton Mifflin Company, 1927.

　　A brief biographical sketch of Dana by his grandson.

"Richard Henry Dana." *Harper's Weekly* XXIII, No. 1156, (22 February 1879): 142.

　　A brief obituary essay which addresses Dana's friendship with William Cullen Bryant, his poetry, and the success of his lectures on Shakespeare.

Hunter, Doreen M. *Richard Henry Dana, Sr.* Boston: Twayne, 1987, 146 p.

　　A biographical and critical study which considers Dana's career in the context of American literary, intellectual, and religious culture.

Weinstein, Bernard. "Bryant and Dana: The Anatomy of a Friendship." In *William Cullen Bryant and His America: Centennial Conference Proceedings, 1878-1978,* edited by Stanley Brodwin, Michael D'Innocenzo, and Joseph G. Astman, pp. 51-66. New York: AMS Press, 1983.

　　A biographical essay which discusses the long personal and literary association between Dana and William Cullen Bryant.

Criticism

Adams, Nehemiah. Review of Dana's *Poems and Prose Writings. Literary and Theological Review* I, No. 1 (January 1834): 214-38.

　　A generally favorable review which hails Dana as a "moral discoverer," and focuses on "The Buccaneer" and "Paul Felton."

Brown, Samuel Gilman. Review of *Poems and Prose Writings. The North American Review* LXXII, No. CL (January 1851): 115-51.

　　A long and favorable review which provides a critical discussion of Dana's essays and analyzes several of his major poems.

Review of *Prose Writings by Richard Henry Dana. Knickerbocker* XXXVIII, No. 5 (November 1851): 542-46.

　　A review focusing on three essays from the second volume of Dana's *Poems and Prose Writings* which finds Dana's view of the past "glaringly exaggerated" and romantic.

Henry James, Sr.

1811-1882

American philosopher and theologian.

INTRODUCTION

The father of two more famous sons—novelist Henry James and psychologist William James—Henry James, Sr., was an influential and original thinker who challenged many of the religious and social mores of his era. Regarded during his lifetime as an eccentric and bold author, lecturer, and critic, James was deeply influenced by the writings of eighteenth-century Swedish philosopher Emanuel Swedenborg and nineteenth-century social theorist Charles Fourier; the former helped shape James's views on God and human nature, while the latter helped inspire his ideas about human fellowship. James believed above all in spiritual freedom, rejecting organized religion, which he felt overemphasized the importance of the individual and promoted sectarianism rather than universal solidarity. This was a fairly unpopular view at a time when such denominations as Christian Science and Methodism were gaining strong footholds in the United States. In addition, he was staunchly opposed to the romantic idealizations of the individual advocated by many of his contemporaries, including Ralph Waldo Emerson. James considered an emphasis on the self—especially thinking highly of oneself—as one of the greatest of evils. Only by destroying this self-righteousness, he insisted, could one be "re-born" into society and thereby achieve communion with God.

Biographical Information

Born in Albany, New York, on June 3, 1811, James grew up under the strict rule of his father, William James, a wealthy merchant and staunch Presbyterian who had emigrated from Ireland in the late 1700s. Early on, the younger James developed a distaste for Presbyterianism, resisting his father's belief in an angry God who instilled fear in his followers. When the younger James was twelve or thirteen, he suffered the amputation of one of his legs after it was severely burned when he attempted to stamp out a fire. The long period of painful and isolated invalidism that followed seemed to affect the youth profoundly; according to biographers, the formerly spirited young man became increasingly introspective during his convalescence. In 1828 he entered Union College in Schenectady, New York, enjoying the liberal religious atmosphere before graduating two years later. He then

briefly studied law in Albany. Following his father's death in 1832, he inherited enough money to support himself for the remainder of his life, and in 1835 he abandoned his legal career in favor of studies at Princeton Theological Seminary, an ardently Presbyterian institution. However, he left the seminary just a few years later, dissatisfied with the school's strict piety and determining to devote himself to the study and expression of his own philosophy. In the late 1830s he traveled to Europe, where he became acquainted with the writings of eighteenth-century Scotsman Robert Sandeman, one of Fourier's disciples and the founder of an obscure religious sect dedicated to primitive Christianity. In part to acknowledge the influence Sandeman had on his thought, James edited Sandeman's controversial *Letters on Theron and Aspasio* (1838), which denounced the church clergy. In 1840 he married Mary Robertson Walsh, a devout churchgoer and the sister of one of his friends. Throughout the next two decades the Jameses moved between New York—where their first two sons (William and Henry, Jr.) were born—and various European cities. During one of their trips to Europe in the 1840s, the elder James became intrigued with Swedenborg's teachings. In fact, it was Swedenborg's writings that helped him overcome the emotional and spiritual collapse he suffered in 1844 during one of his longer periods of residency in Europe. This collapse is what he referred to as his "vastation," a stage that, according to Swedenborg, leads to the rebirth of the soul. During the 1840s James was also greatly inspired by the philosophy of Fourier, a social reformer who believed as did James in the solidarity of humankind. Continuing to move restlessly with his family during the early 1860s, James finally settled in Cambridge, Massachusetts, in 1866. Eventually fathering five children, he was a dedicated family man who believed in providing his children with a strong moral and intellectual background. He afforded them access to international travel, private tutors, experimental schools, and an academically stimulating home environment; in the decades before his death his household was often the site of fervent discussions among such eminent figures as Henry David Thoreau and Emerson. James suffered the death of his wife early in 1882, and he died soon thereafter, on December 18, 1882, in Cambridge.

Major Works

James was the author of more than a dozen books and hundreds of treatises, pamphlets, letters, essays, and reviews. He treated such subjects as philosophy, metaphysics, politics, wealth, literature, and education, although many of his works are defenses of his theology. During his lifetime he published four full-length volumes outlining his thought: *Christianity, the Logic of Creation* (1857), *Substance and Shadow* (1863), *The Secret of Swedenborg* (1869), and *Society the Redeemed Form of Man* (1879). Of these, most critics regard *The Secret of Swedenborg* and *Society the Redeemed Form of Man* as his best. The former outlines James's belief in humankind's dependence on God, while the latter documents his thoughts on his spiritual breakdown as well as his vision of Christianity as a call for a new social solidarity. Other significant works include *Spiritual Creation* (1882), unfinished at the time of his death and later published by his son William, and *The Nature of Evil* (1855). In addition to the theme of theology that runs through his works, James's use of superlatives, his adeptness with language, and his use of obscure phrases mark his writing. Distinguishing his works also is his sense of humor, seen by some as grossly inappropriate but by others as charming. This charm, scholars have noted, is also evidenced in the hundreds of letters he exchanged with his formidable circle of acquaintances. Unfortunately, many of these private papers were destroyed by relatives soon after his death. Biographers have speculated that James's "indelicate" nature combined with the highly public controversies that often surrounded him prompted this destruction. In fact, James caused himself and his family considerable embarrassment as early as 1849, when he published his first major work, *Love in the Phalanstery,* a translation of Victor Hennequin's *Les Amours au Phalanstère,* a French tract on marriage. Proposing a new social order in which human sexuality would be freed from conventional laws, the work prompted critics to brand James as a libertine.

Critical Reception

During his lifetime, James's works neither attracted a considerable number of readers nor enjoyed a large measure of critical understanding; commentators found his works obscure and doubted the intelligibility of his writings. Scholars have suggested that his subject matter was partly to blame for his unpopularity at a time when discussions of theology were rapidly going out of fashion. Moreover, treatises emphasizing humankind's need for community and man's reliance on God were often disregarded during an intellectualized age that celebrated the self. Many nineteenth-century critics did, however, praise James's style, calling it fresh, unconventional, entertaining, and eloquent. James was a "writer of extraordinary vigor and picturesqueness" and a "formidable master of English style," wrote E. L. Godkin, prominent journalist and founder of *The Nation.* Almost immediately after his death, James's reputation fell into obscurity, and his work was overshadowed by that of his sons William and Henry, Jr. Commentators who did study the elder James continued to find fault with his writings, characterizing his arguments as overly metaphysical rather than logical, and criticizing his tendency to restate his theology in several of his works. (James himself admitted that he had trouble expressing himself adequately.) It wasn't until the 1930s that a serious revival of interest in James's scholarship developed. In 1934 Austin Warren became the first critic to produce a full-length biography of James, and in 1951 Frederic Harold Young published the first full-length treatment of James's philosophy. Contemporary critics have claimed that James has been undeservedly eclipsed by the reputation of his sons, and have begun to regard him not as a weak, eccentric figure as some earlier critics had, but as a powerful presence who made a strong impact on his children, especially William and Henry, Jr. "It is owing to James's restless intellectuality that three of his children—William, Henry, Alice—are remembered today," wrote biographer Alfred Habegger in 1994. "For better and worse, he was responsible for their larger-than-life tensions, abilities, ambitions, achievements." Although contemporary critics have continued to commend James's striking and often startling rhetoric as well as the vigor and wit of his writings, his rich and varied diction, and his romantic style, his works have never found a popular audience.

PRINCIPAL WORKS

Letters on Theron and Aspasio: Addressed to the Author [editor] (letters) 1838

Remarks on the Apostolic Gospel (treatise) 1840

What Constitutes the State? A Lecture Delivered before the Young Men's Association of the City of Albany (lecture) 1846

Tracts for the New Times, No. 1, Letter to a Swedenborgian (letter) 1847

Love in the Phalanstery [translator; from *Les Amours au Phalanstère* by Victor Hennequin, 1847] (treatise) 1849

Moralism and Christianity; or, Man's Experience and Destiny (treatise) 1850

Lectures and Miscellanies (lectures) 1852

Love, Marriage, and Divorce, A Discussion between Henry James, Horace Greeley, and Stephen Pearl Andrews 1853

The Church of Christ Not an Ecclesiasticism: A Letter of Remonstrance to a Member of the Soi-Disant *New Church* (letter) 1854, revised edition, 1856

The Nature of Evil, Considered in a Letter to the Reverend Edward Beecher, D.D., Author of "The Conflict of the Ages" (letter) 1855

Christianity, the Logic of Creation (treatise) 1857

The Social Significance of Our Institutions: An Oration Delivered by Request of the Citizens of Newport, R.I., July 4, 1861 (speech) 1861

The Old and New Theology, Two Lectures; and the Church of Christ Not an Ecclesiasticism. A Letter of Remonstrance to a Member of the Soi-Distant *New Church* (letter and lectures) 1861

Substance and Shadow; or, Morality and Religion in Their Relation to Life: An Essay upon the Physics of Creation (essay) 1863, revised edition, 1866

The Secret of Swedenborg: Being an Elucidation of His Doctrine of the Divine Natural Humanity (treatise) 1869

Society the Redeemed Form of Man, and the Earnest of God's Omnipotence in Human Nature: Affirmed in Letters to a Friend (treatise and letters) 1879

Spiritual Creation (essay) 1882

The Literary Remains of the Late Henry James (essays, treatises) [edited by William James] 1884

Love, Marriage, and Divorce. A Discussion between Henry James, Horace Greeley, and Stephen Pearl Andrews. Including the Final Replies of Mr. Andrews. Rejected by the New York Tribune, and a Subsequent Discussion, Occurring Twenty Years Later, between Mr. James and Mr. Andrews 1889

Morality and the Perfect Life: A Republication of a Lecture by the Late Henry James (lecture) 1906

Henry James, Senior: A Selection of His Writings (letters, essays, treatises) 1974

CRITICISM

James F. Clarke (essay date 1855)

SOURCE: "James on the Nature of Evil," in *The Christian Examiner and Religious Miscellany*, Vol. LIX, No. 1, July, 1855, pp. 116-36.

[*In the following review of* The Nature of Evil, *Clarke examines James's doctrine of evil, finding the author's theories inadequately developed and therefore impossible to comprehend, and concluding that James ultimately fails to solve "the problem of evil."*]

[*The Nature of Evil*] is a remarkable book by a remarkable man. Mr. James is remarkable because he combines, in no small degree, the qualities of a seer, a metaphysician, and a poet. His spiritual insight, or intuitive glance at spiritual realities, is penetrating, and gives solidity to his books. They possess an internal substance which differences them from the writings of metaphysicians who, like Brownson and Bowen, for example, dwell mainly on the forms of thought and their external relations. Again, Mr. James is a metaphysician, with an intellect full of force and with great penetrating power, though, as it appears to us, in its order more synthetic than analytic. Again, his rhetoric flows in a stream of life through the book. His words are not the current coin of logic, passed from hand to hand till it is worn and has lost all sharpness of impress, but they have a power of their own and a life within themselves. Known by his former writings as the great Antinomian of our day, hating moralism as Marcion hated Judaism, he has in this book defined anew and strengthened that position. Withdrawing his forces from the untenable posts which he frankly admits himself to have too hastily taken, he has now intrenched himself in permanence on what he deems an impregnable position, and challenges the assault of the three great ecclesiastical powers of Christendom, whom he sees fit to describe as the Roman Catholic, Protestant, and Unitarian bodies. This work of his is the theological Sebastopol, not to be taken by these sects, either separately or in triple alliance. He asserts that the theology of all these parties is radically vitiated by a false philosophy. Thus, as though he had not opponents enough already in the theologians, he throws down the gauntlet also before all the philosophers, from the school of Plato to that of Hegel, considering them all vicious, false, and atheistic. In addition to these cartels of defiance, he challenges the teachers of natural religion, the professors of moral philosophy, and the reformers who take their stand on the supremacy of conscience. Natural religion he holds to be in contradiction to Christianity, the sentiment of responsibility a self-deception and fallacy, and conscience to be no original divine endowment of the soul, but only the badge of a fallen nature. Man in himself has no substantial or real existence; he is only a form, and altogether unsubstantial. His freedom is no self-determining power, and our sense of freedom and responsibility, though very inspiring, is a great self-deception. It will be seen, therefore, that Mr. James has issued a challenge of a sufficiently comprehensive character. He walks up and down before the camp of our theological Israel, like Goliath of Gath, defying all our armies. If he is in error, there ought to be some young David to meet him with a few smooth stones out of the stream of truth.

The special occasion of this book is stated by Mr. James to be his unfeigned sympathy for the intellectual struggles of Dr. Edward Beecher, as manifested in his recent work entitled "The Conflict of Ages." Mr. James's book takes the form of a letter addressed to this gentleman, and is partly occupied in considering Dr. Beecher's position and course of argument. His tone is friendly, but rather patronizing. He means to be respectful, but evidently looks down upon Dr. Beecher's position and his argument. He assumes the seat of the instructor, and places Dr. Beecher before his chair, as a well-meaning little boy, who deserves to have his somewhat gross errors explained to him. "Good little boy," he seems to say, "you have done as well as you knew how, now let me explain it to you." Considering that the only real evil in the universe, according to Mr. James, is *self-sufficiency,* it is a little amusing to notice this entire complacency of tone and spirit.

However, the main question does not regard the tone or manner, but the substance, of the argument. If Mr. James is right in his main positions, if he has solved the problem of evil and terminated the conflict of ages, he surely has a right to a degree of self-complacency. If he has confuted all the theologians and philosophers who have ever lived, with the exception of Swedenborg, we may pardon him a good opinion of his own powers. This, therefore, is the question for us to consider. It is manifestly impossible, in the short space allowed us, to examine even slightly the important questions discussed in so compact an argument through a book of three hundred pages. We can only hope to indicate our views on a few leading points, and the natural method will be, first, to endeavor fairly to state what Mr. James's doctrine of evil is, and then to ask if it be true, or if it be false, or if it be partly true and partly false.

The problem of Dr. Beecher is stated to be, "How can God be just in condemning and punishing evil?" The problem of Mr. James, on the contrary, is, "How can the *existence* of evil be reconciled with the government of a perfect God?" This last question is indeed the important one, and lies back of the other, and all attempts hitherto to explain it have resulted in explaining away one or the other of the two factors of the problem. Either *evil* is explained away and shown not

to be really evil, which is optimism, or else *the absolute perfections of God* are denied, and evil is exalted into a rival power, which is Manichæism. If Mr. James can escape both of these rocks of offence, and steer his way safely between, we shall gladly admit that the problem is finally solved.

Mr. James divides evil into physical, moral, and spiritual, and defines them thus. Physical evil is the evil which one SUFFERS, moral evil is the evil which one DOES, and spiritual evil is the evil which one IS. Physical and moral evil he presently explains away, and declares them to be no evils at all, inasmuch as they are what he calls constitutional facts, or the necessary limitations of our finite nature. Physical suffering, as hunger for example, impels the animal to that effort which is his distinctive life. And he says that it is inconceivable that he should be animally organized without such a limitation. In like manner, moral evil is necessarily involved in the fact of our moral constitution, which is bounded by duty on the one side and by interest on the other, the perfect equipoise of which is the necessary condition of moral life. If they were not thus equally balanced, man's moral goodness and evil would be passive, and not active, that is, would not be moral at all. Moreover, man's self-hood or consciousness is, as he shows, conditional and dependent on this equipoise, and without it his consciousness would disappear. Thus physical evil, or the endurance of pain, is the necessary condition of animal life, and moral evil, or the doing what is wrong, the indispensable condition of moral life, and therefore neither of these can be really evil. It only remains, therefore, to investigate spiritual evil, or the evil which man is, to learn its nature, and see whether that also can or cannot be accounted for.

This spiritual evil which Mr. James declares to be the only real evil in the universe, he defines to be essentially the principle of self-hood or of supposed independence in man, or, as he elsewhere expresses it, believing that life is in ourselves. This it is which separates us from God, and this is the source of real death, the only death that there is. This sense of self-hood in man Mr. James pronounces to be an unmixed evil. The question therefore is, How did it come, and how is it to be explained consistently with the perfections of God?

Mr. James finds great fault with the common philosophy and theology, because it considers creation as an absolute work of God, and because it considers man as created with life in himself. He denies that God creates naturally, or in space and time, and asserts that he creates always spiritually, that is, as it should seem, by creating persons. It would be impossible, he asserts, (following Swedenborg,) for God to create any being with life in himself. The life which is in man is God's life, not his own, flowing into him from God. Man, therefore, is not a substantive being, but only a form. For God, he says, is inhibited by his own perfection from giving an absolute self-hood to his creature, or, which is the same thing, from creating a being who shall be independent of himself. Man, therefore, is only a form, and his life is not an absolute life, but a conditional one, and spiritual evil originates in his thinking that his life is in himself. This is the fall of man. It is mistaking the source of our life, thinking it to be in ourselves when, in fact, it is in God.

But if man out of God be only a form, it follows that his freedom and responsibility must be quite other than they are usually thought to be. Accordingly Mr. James teaches that his freedom is not *absolute* freedom, but *rational* freedom, or freedom in order to something else. It is not given for its own sake, but for the sake of the creature's spiritual elevation, being thus a freedom strictly in order to his eternal conjunction with God. He is free to transcend and control his bodily appetites, but cannot become independent of God.

But this freedom is by no means a power of self-determination. And the responsibility which it implies is very limited. The sentiment of responsibility he declares to be corrupt and fallacious in itself; corrupt, that is, so far as it attributes the origin of good or evil to ourselves, since the moral good comes from God into us, and the moral evil comes into us from beneath, from the hells. Our moral consciousness, which results from our being placed in an exact equipoise between good and evil, induces us to attribute to ourselves the source of our conduct. But all this is an error. Conscience indeed affirms it to be so, but conscience is mistaken.

What then is conscience, according to Mr. James? It is the badge of a fallen nature. It makes us feel responsible for the good and evil which is in us, which is a terrible error. Its affirmations are not absolutely true, but possess only a partial truth as they take color from a vitiated spiritual state of man. Conscience is not an original faculty of the soul, nor does it express the normal relation between the Creator and the creature, but is only a shrouded presence of God, the fruit of a spiritual declension on our part, and not an original divine endowment of the soul.

This brings us to Mr. James's view of morality, or obedience to the law. The law, he declares, was never intended to make men really good, but merely to show them their real evil. Morality by itself (meaning the sentiment of self-hood) is an unmixed evil, a fountain of inexhaustible disease and death. The moral man is no better before God than the immoral man. And if he thinks himself better, he becomes immediately vastly worse. Imposed upon by his conscience, he is likely to think himself better, and therefore he is likely to be much worse. Therefore it was that, when Christ was

on earth, he knew no enemy but the Pharisee, who trusted in himself that he was righteous and despised others. Those who teach that obedience to the moral instincts will make us acceptable to God, are teaching pure infidelity. For these instincts are the inmost home and source of human pride. Those however who exalt the moral instincts become very popular with the Pharisees; as an example of which teachers he mentions Dr. Channing and Fénelon. Moral distinctions, therefore, are only the shadows of spiritual distinctions, and there is no real superiority of the good man over the bad man; the man who lies, and steals, and murders being just as good in God's sight as the holiest saint or the most generous martyr.

Nevertheless, Mr. James approves of goodness, and on the whole prefers it to moral evil. In some places he even seems to take back what he has said against it, and makes it an essential condition of union with God, declaring that a man who blesses his brother receives, in consequence, the divine life into his own soul, while he who injures his brother excludes it. He also asserts that God is infinitely averse to the deeds of the evil man, which would seem to imply the absoluteness of morality. On the whole, however, he makes very small account of the moral man.

But what, according to Mr. James, is the work of Christ? Not to remove our liability to physical or moral evil. For, as these are facts of our constitution, we must always remain liable to them. The work of Christ was twofold. First, and chiefly, Redemption. Next, and secondarily, Salvation. The great work of Christ, that which the Apostles preached, and in which they gloried, was not future salvation, but past redemption, of which the resurrection of Christ was the evidence and seal. Redemption was a great victory achieved over death and hell, which delivered all men, for the future, without exception, from their constraining power. This means that God, in Christ, descended to carnal conditions, and by the suffering of temptations thence derived overcame the power of evil. God becoming united with man in Christ redeems him from spiritual death, into which he had become utterly sunk, so as to lose his spiritual freedom. By thus undergoing the extremest temptations of evil, of which he otherwise was ignorant, and overcoming them, he reduced the spiritual universe to order, and opened a pathway for the freest communication of his spirit with man, reducing the hells equally with the heavens to his obedience. Henceforth men were no longer constrained into evil, but angels, men, and devils were equally freed from its power.

The ground of the Incarnation is therefore the spiritual death of man, a universal spiritual death which reigned everywhere, and from which men were incapable of extricating themselves. But Christ's redemption eats up the consequences of the fall, destroying every obstacle which before existed to the most intimate conjunction of God and man. The fall impaired man's freedom, redemption restores it. And now the Divine love flows freely into every saint or sinner who is willing to receive it. The gift of redemption is free to all, is an outward or absolute process, an objective work which took place centuries before we were born, making man spiritually his own master. But this redemption is strictly in order to another work, viz. reconciliation or salvation, which is an inward voluntary and regenerative process, subjective and depending on the choice of the individual; not universal, therefore, like redemption. Salvation comes from our faith in redemption, and is the grateful acquiescence of the soul in this fact, and the voluntary reception of Divine love.

It remains only to see what those laws of creation are which, according to Mr. James, enable us to understand evil.

God's creation is not absolute, nor a phenomenon of space or time. Nor does he create anything which has life in itself, but only subjects of life. Creation is a rational proceeding, the purpose of which is, that there should be an eternal conjunction between God and the creature. He therefore creates subjects in which he may dwell. And these subjects must receive his love and wisdom as of themselves; that is, freely. God cannot create anything which should have life in itself, since this would be to create God. Therefore he can only create organs of life, which, however, must receive his life freely or rationally, because, if it were forced on them, it would prove a power of resisting, which would argue a life of their own. God therefore creates not things, but persons, who are only organs of his life. And God gives to man incessantly the semblance or appearance of being; because, unless man appeared to himself to be, the life of heavenly blessedness could not take place. For man must appear full of life and power, and God must guard the interests of his freedom, because on these his regeneration depends. Our very humanity consists, says Swedenborg, in feeling that life in us is our own. Without this feeling, we could not possibly become spiritually joined with God. But when we are admitted behind the scenes, and view things spiritually, we know that man's moral power is nothing in itself, that man never overcomes in temptation, but only the Lord in him, and that it is never his own power which inclines him to evil, but invariably the power of evil spirits.

We have thus stated the views of Mr. James on all the essential points of his treatise. In condensing them, we have, of course, made their meaning less intelligible. And whoever would understand them thoroughly, must read his book. Yet we have aimed to do justice to his thought as far as possible, using almost everywhere his own words, so that we trust that we have not essentially misrepresented him. We must now proceed to an examination of his theory, in regard to its truth or error, and in regard to its adequacy to solve the problem of evil.

The problem, as we have seen, is this:—How can we reconcile the existence of evil with the perfections of God? The true solution of the problem must therefore reconcile these two facts, and must not omit or explain away either of them. We must show that evil is required by the Divine perfections, and that it is a manifestation of them. And yet it must not be denied nor confounded with good. In other words, it must be shown to be the *sine qua non* condition of good, without which good is inconceivable, or the indispensable material out of which good is manufactured. If there remains a conceivable possibility of the existence of good without evil, then the problem is not thoroughly nor satisfactorily solved.

Applying this rule to the procedure of Mr. James, let us adopt his own distinction of Physical, Moral, and Spiritual Evil.

Let us first look at his explanation of Physical Evil. He defines it to be the evil that we suffer, thus distinguishing it from moral evil which we do, and spiritual evil which we are. Is the definition adequate and the distinction sound? We doubt if they are. By suffering he must either mean pure passivity, or else he must mean the passion of pain. But passivity, in a physical sense, is not always evil, and the suffering of pain is not always physical evil. There is mental and there is moral pain which we suffer, no less than physical pain. And therefore moral evil, no less than physical, is the evil which we suffer, and the distinction is not a satisfactory one. Physical evil is the evil which affects us through the body or the physical system.

And now, how does he explain the existence of physical evil? His explanation virtually denies its existence. Of course he must deny its existence if he denies all reality to the physical universe; for if there is no physical universe, there can hardly be any physical evil. Now, it is a fundamental doctrine with Mr. James, that the only real world, or substantial world, is the world of affection and thought. And again, the world of nature is not the real world. But, moreover, his view of the Deity as not involving in himself the elements of space and time, which are the elements of the physical world, compels him to deny the real existence of that world, and with it the distinction of being from other beings in space, and from their own past and future in time. For as, according to him, God is the only Being, if time and space do not exist in God, they do not exist at all. Now Mr. James distinctly asserts that there is, in truth, but one being in the world,— God; thus denying to nature, not only independent existence; but also real existence. It is, therefore, very evident that Mr. James cannot explain the existence of physical evil, for the simple reason that he denies its existence.

It may, however, be said, that, by defining physical evil to be that which we suffer, Mr. James makes of it a purely subjective fact of the human soul, and so lifts it out of any necessary connection with a real physical universe. Without stopping to question the propriety of calling that evil physical which has its basis in no physical existence, we will accept this nomenclature, and look at his explanation according to his own definition. Whatever evil a man suffers, even though it be mental or moral suffering, we will, for the present, call physical, and ask how Mr. James reconciles its existence with the Divine perfections. He considers suffering as belonging to the necessary limitation of man's finite nature. As man is finite, he must be limited. And that which limits his existence constitutes his existence,—just, we suppose, as the lines which limit the triangle constitute the triangle. "Pain and pleasure," he says, "are the necessary boundaries of animal life, and animal life is inconceivable without them." "I cannot conceive," he says, "of man's being animally organized at all, without a liability to suffer whenever an outward impediment exists to the supply of his wants." But to this statement there are two answers. First, that a liability to suffering is not actual suffering, and the problem which he has undertaken to solve is not the liability to evil, but the existence of evil, which are two somewhat different things. If evil did not really exist, man might still be liable to evil, and a problem might then arise on that point. A conflict would then exist between this fact of possible evil and the Divine power or wisdom, but not, as in the other case, with the Divine goodness. Man being made constitutionally liable to evil, but being preserved from actual evil by the Divine Providence, there would not be the same intellectual problem as at present. And, secondly, this definition explains evil as a limitation of man's finite nature, i.e. as something negative, but does not explain it as anything positive or real. It makes of it a matter of more and less; i.e. it virtually makes of evil only a less quantity of good. But this, it is evident, though a very common form of solution, is only another way of explaining the existence of evil by denying its existence. And, accordingly, that which is really inconceivable in our conception of man's animal life is the absence of the limitation of more and less. Supposing that limitation to exist, we can conceive of him without the limitation of pain and pleasure. For, if this were not so, the actual experience of man would be at every moment that of a flight from pain to pleasure, which is surely not the case.

Passing on, in the next place, to Moral Evil, let us look at his definition and explanation of this also.

Mr. James defines moral evil to be the evil that we do. But is this an adequate definition? Does not moral evil also consist in yielding, in submission to bad influences? Human language speaks of indulging the passions, as a large part of moral evil. And how significantly does this term, PASSIONS, express the source of much immorality.

Moreover, Mr. James himself seems sometimes to forget his own definition. For example, he says, that the moral law demands of us love. Hence, not to love is a moral evil, and moral evil is something else than the evil which we do.

Nevertheless, we will accept his definition, as in the former case, and see how far, with this account of moral evil, he succeeds in explaining it. His explanation consists in placing it on a level with physical evil, as proceeding necessarily from man's rational organization. Man's freedom consists in a balance or limitation between duty on the one side, and interest on the other. His good and bad actions are simply features of his rational organization, with which he is not to be inwardly chargeable. Moral evil, therefore, like physical evil, is no evil at all, and is explained by being set aside. Perhaps the speciality of Mr. James's theory, and certainly the point which he labors most earnestly, is in fact just this denial of the reality of moral good and evil. In the sight of God the good man who is just and kind, temperate and truthful, is no more deserving of approbation than the man who lies and steals and leads a life of the coarsest self-indulgence. Moral distinctions, according to Mr. James, are not eternal, but only shadowy and transient. The good and bad man are not essentially different, and the only real evil in the universe consists in believing otherwise. But inasmuch as our moral instincts do assert otherwise, he maintains them to be delusive. Inasmuch as conscience asserts otherwise, he denies it to be an original divine endowment of the soul. Inasmuch as we seem to be responsible for our moral character, he declares this sense of responsibility to God to be corrupt and fallacious. The affirmation of conscience he denies to be absolutely true, and man's freedom, in its common acceptation, is a mere self-delusion. Let us, therefore, say something in regard to this position, which we regard to be an error that has arisen from pushing the truths of Christian experience to an unwarrantable and one-sided extreme.

For, in denying the absolute nature of moral distinctions, is it not apparent that Mr. James strikes at the root of *all* convictions and *all* certainty? If there is one primal conviction of the human mind which runs deeper than most others, and which lies as a foundation of human faith and action, it is the immutability of moral distinctions. In all ages and in all countries, whereas man exists, this conviction has been found thus deeply rooted in his mind. Our faith in God, in any just sense of the word, rests upon this conviction, and not the reverse. To believe in God is to believe in the Good One. And, consequently, we must believe in goodness before we can believe in God. But to tell us that the distinction between right and wrong, good and evil, is not absolute, but shadowy and transient, is to lay the foundation of the most hopeless atheism.

Again, suppose that it were possible to believe in any thing as fixed and certain, when we have come to disbelieve in the moral instincts; suppose we could believe in God, it would be as a being devoid of moral character. For if our own moral condition, manifesting itself in acts of justice and mercy, is not to be regarded as anything positive or real, neither can the Divine goodness, manifesting itself in like acts, be regarded as possessing any positive character. The goodness of the good man is the mirror in which we see an imperfect manifestation of absolute goodness. It is only through the experience of justice, generosity, and purity that we can climb to a conception of the Divine holiness. "He who loveth not his brother whom he has seen, how shall he love God whom he has not seen?" The Apostle clearly intimates, that it is only by loving man, whom we see, that we can get an idea of the Divine loveliness. Hence, the moment that I am taught to distrust the moral instincts which teach me that the man of truth is, in so far, really better than the man of falsehood, I am also taught to distrust my conception of the moral character of God. If goodness and truth in man are not merely imperfect, but also delusive, they may deceive us when predicated of the Deity.

The only reply which Mr. James can make to this is to fall back upon his view of man, which regards him as a mere channel through which good and evil may flow. Goodness in God, he may say, *is* real as a part of his character. But *our* goodness only flows from above, from Him, as our evil also flows from beneath, from the hells. The goodness, therefore, of the good man is real, but it is not his own. But this view, as he himself asserts, is not that which our moral instincts teach. We do not love the good man as a channel through which good is flowing, but as a fountain out of which it pours. We do not attribute radiance to the glass window, no matter how transparent it may be, through which the sun shines, but to the little lamp which sends its narrow beam far into the darkness,—the natural emblem of the shining of a good action in our naughty world. Our very humanity consists, he himself says, in feeling that life is in us as our own. Otherwise we could not be allied to the angel, or distinguished from the brute. But now, Mr. James has written a book, the object of which is to convince us of the contrary, namely, to make us feel that our life is not our own. His success, therefore, would be strictly equivalent, according to his own showing, with the demolition of our spiritual nature, and would make it impossible for us to conceive of the spiritual character of God.

We can understand what Mr. James means when he declares that all good that is in man flows from God. But we confess to a little difficulty as regards the source of his moral evil. That, he tells us, flows into us from the hells, which are the societies of evil spirits. But the evil in *them*,—whence comes it? If it comes from themselves, then they must have a life, according to his reasoning, independent of God, which is impossible. To say that it comes into them from other evil spirits is, of course, only to remove the difficulty farther off. To refer it to God he would consider blasphemy. Hence, it only remains to deny its existence altogether, and to make of it, like every other form of evil thus far, a mere negation, or the somewhat less of good.

But Mr. James, though thus continually drifted by his theory toward a system of pure pantheistic optimism, struggles now and then manfully against its overcoming stress, and, turning round, contradicts himself in the calmest manner. Thus he tranquilly affirms that "it is of course eternally true that God is infinitely averse to the deeds of the evil man. He is infinitely averse to all murder, treachery, and guile." But these actions are acts of moral evil. And to assert that God is infinitely averse to moral evil, is to make moral distinctions absolute distinctions, which is the very thing that Mr. James has been all along denying. He endeavors to help himself out of the difficulty by the following sentence. "God indeed forbids us to rob or murder or deceive our neighbor in any way, but this is not, as so many suppose, in order that we may become differenced from other people or from our former selves, but only in order that, by refraining from these things and so denying the interior influence of evil, we may open our hearts to the access of pity, gentleness, mercy, and peace from him. He hates evil, to be sure, but the positive aspect of that sentiment is, that he loves to communicate his own goodness to us." True. But we would inquire whether we do not become "differenced from our former selves" when we receive this access of Divine good? And what matters it whether we say, "The man is better who refrains from doing wrong," or say, "The man is better who refrains from doing wrong, *because* he thereby receives God's love?" Mr. James is obliged plainly to teach that the salvation of man consists in his refraining from evil and accepting good. It is our putting away freely the evils of our life from a sense of love to God. So that, when he is arguing in this direction, he does not deny that a man will by moral fidelity come nearer to God, but only asserts (what no one ever doubted) that the good man ought not to be *proud* of his goodness, or to think that he has any meritorious right to salvation. If the net result of the argument is only the condemnation of spiritual pride, we do not think that Mr. James will find any antagonists. We all say, as he does, that the good man has no business to pride himself on his goodness, or consider heaven the reward of his desert. The only questions are these: "Is he *really* any better in the sight of God than the bad man? Is he more likely to come into union with God than the bad man?" Mr. James says no to the first question, but yes to the last. He thinks that he is no better than the bad man, but is sure that he is much nearer to God, and is alone capable of the reception of his love and life.

Let us now proceed to consider the last kind of evil, which is Spiritual Evil. Mr. James has explained Physical and Moral Evil by explaining them away. Not only his general principles compel him to deny to them reality, but he asserts the same thing in terms over and over again. Thus he says that the only real evil in the universe is spiritual evil, which consists in the principle of self-hood. Spiritual evil, he says, consists in our feeling, and hence believing, that life is in ourselves. This he calls elsewhere the principle of independence in man. And this he declares to be the only sin. Nevertheless he follows Swedenborg in asserting that our very humanity consists in feeling that the life in us is our own. Accordingly, our very humanity is necessarily spiritual evil or sin, which would seem to bring us to a very thorough total depravity.

It is not very easy to see precisely what Mr. James means by spiritual evil. Sometimes it is a purely intellectual error, and consists in the mistaken opinion that our life is our own, as when he says, "the sole curse of man, from the first, is attributing to himself his good and evil." But it is wrong affection; "the only spiritual evil is in loving ourselves supremely." In two different places he asserts that only the angel can say, God be merciful to me a sinner. And again, only the regenerate man or angel is ever conscious of sin. But as the angel is *not* blind to the truth of his dependence upon God, and as the regenerate man is the one who has risen above spiritual pride, it would seem to follow that he was not under the curse of sin, and therefore could *not* truthfully regard himself as a sinner. We will leave Mr. James to reconcile these two statements of his, and ask how he solves the problem of spiritual evil? Now at least we have reached something real. Spiritual evil, self-hood, self-complacency, is at all events real evil. How is it to be reconciled, then, with the perfections of God? How does Mr. James account for its existence?

He accounts for the origin of spiritual evil very simply. It was necessary, he says, that we should be so made that, while we really have no life in ourselves, we should seem to have such a life in order that we should seem to be free. This alone lifts us above the controlling influence of nature, and enables us to come into union with God. We feel as if we were free and responsible. Not that we really are so, but we seem to be so. "We cannot act from ourselves, but we can act *as* from ourselves." In other words, we can pretend to be free, and counterfeit freedom. We must not *believe* ourselves free, for that will be to fall into the worst,

into spiritual evil. But we must *make believe* that we are free, otherwise we can obtain no spiritual good. This is the ticklish condition in which man is placed. This is the bridge AL-SIRAT, with edge as sharp as a razor, over which we must shake into heaven. But this, of course, is a difficult problem to accomplish, and man, in fact, has utterly failed of doing it. Hear Mr. James's account of the matter: "But we all know how naturally or inevitably the feeling of absolute self-hood supervenes upon this sentiment of freedom, or becomes ingrafted on it. The growth of the sensuous principle in us, or the progress of our dominion over nature, causes us to value our freedom *in se,* or for its own independent sake, and not merely for the sake of its ulterior, celestial, and spiritual ends. The life of nature becomes gradually more pronounced in us. Beneficent genii appear to wait upon all man's efforts to realize a bountiful life in outward things, and we accordingly conceive a distrust for the old traditions which pointed our hope and postponed our best expectations to the access of a superior life. Thus we begin to feel, not merely freedom, but an absolute self-hood or property in nature."

Here, then, we have the solution of the problem. Evil comes into the world whenever man acts from himself instead of acting *as* from himself, whenever he acts as if he had a real freedom instead of acting as if he had a *quasi* freedom. And this happens "naturally or inevitably." Let us stop upon these words, for here is the pith of the whole solution. We must ask Mr. James which of these two terms expresses his meaning, for the difference between them is not small as regards our problem. If he can show that the necessary sentiment of freedom passes "inevitably" into one of absolute self-hood, we shall admit the problem of evil to be fully solved on his own premises. But if he only shows that absolute self-hood supervenes "naturally," he is as far as ever from the solution. "Naturally OR inevitably" will not do. He might as well say "probably OR necessarily." As far as we can see, neither he nor Swedenborg, whom he follows, has shown the *inevitable* origin of evil, on their own premises, but only a tendency toward it. All that would have been required, in order to have prevented the origin of all evil in the universe, was to have made man always thoroughly acquainted with the fact that his apparent freedom was only apparent, and not real. It is certainly conceivable that God might have communicated to man with the feeling of his independence the knowledge of his dependence. This would have satisfied all the demands of Mr. James's theory, and would at the same time for ever have excluded evil from the universe. No reason is given for its not having been done, and consequently the problem of evil is as much unsolved as ever.

Mr. James's solution, therefore, fails in *both* directions, running not only into optimism, but also into its opposite. By making God the only being in the universe, and man's being only apparent, and not real, he logically denies the reality of spiritual evil, as he had before denied in terms the reality of physical and moral evil. For if man, the *subject* of evil, is only an appearance not a reality, the evil which inheres in him must also be only an appearance and not a reality. But again, supposing it to be real, it exists and continues as a growth of nature, as a process unprovided for by the divine reason, as an abnormal development outside of deity. In this, also, Mr. James's theory is consequent. For a spiritual pantheism denying God's real existence in nature, and yet utterly unable to dispense with nature, will always virtually exclude God from the time-and-space side of the universe, and whatever goes on there will go on quite independent of him.

We have thus endeavored to show the flaw in Mr. James's conclusion, even assuming the truth of his own premises; but we can by no means accept these premises. We do not believe that self-reliance is the only form of spiritual evil, nor that dependence on God is the only form of spiritual good. We believe that there are two kinds of spiritual evil, the one SELF-RELIANCE and the other SELF-DIRECTION, correlation to two kinds of spiritual good proceeding from the sense of duty and the sense of dependence; otherwise, activity *toward* the good and dependence *on* the good, or GOD-RELIANCE and GOD-DIRECTION. In God there is wisdom and also love, which are the two faces of the one Divine Goodness, wisdom flowing out into the infinite order of the outward universe, love flowing in as the perpetual support of all being. God thus manifests himself both outwardly and inwardly to man. We are in him, and he is us. He exists both in time and in eternity, immanent in the outward universe as its perpetual support, and being inwardly the supporting life in the soul of man. Neither man nor the universe is independent of God. They have real being, but not independent being. This view of the perpetual derivation of being from God does not (as Mr. James seems to assert) imply any diminution of the Divine Being, any more than the uttering of our thought diminishes the amount of our thought, or the outflow of our love impairs our love. From this twofold manifestation of the Deity (which Swedenborg also plainly sets forth) there proceeds man's twofold goodness of moral effort and religious trust, which only in union constitute his true life. The sight of the Divine Law awakens the moral nature; the sight of the Divine Love awakens the spiritual nature; law being a preparation for love, and love fulfilling law.

Now the fundamental error of Mr. James, as it seems to us, is, that he turns the antagonism of law and love into a contradiction. He thus makes the Divine Love a denial of the Divine Wisdom, eternity a denial of time, spirit a denial of nature, the infinite being of God a denial of the finite being of man, the Gospel not a fulfilment but a refutation of the Law, and Christianity

the abolition of conscience, of the sense of responsibility, and of personal morality, landing us at last as the logical result in a spiritualism akin to that of Brahminism, in which the finite is all *Maya,* or delusion. In that system, the great work to be done in order to purify the soul is to arrive at the conviction that all nature is nothing, that the gods are nothing, that we ourselves are nothing, and that Brahm is the only substance, the sole reality. Mr. James, no doubt, stops far short of all this. No doubt with him variety is as certain an existence as unity, form as eternal as substance. But logically, he tends steadily towards that result.

We cannot speak as we should like to do of his doctrine of Christian redemption and salvation. This is especially interesting as the latest result of the tendency which has always existed in the Christian Church to regard the work of Christ as both objective and subjective, laying sometimes more stress on the one and sometimes on the other. In the early centuries of the Christian Church the objective work of Christ was popularized under the form of a battle with Satan, in which conflict Satan was overthrown and his prisoners rescued. In the Middle Ages, the same tendency to exalt the objective side of Christian salvation expressed itself in Anselm's theory of a debt paid to God; which theory maintained its triumphant pre-eminence till the days of Grotius. Since that time the subjective view of human life, awakened by the Reformation, has caused Christ's work to be regarded as mainly one on the human soul. The present reaction in this book toward an extreme objective view is, therefore, somewhat remarkable. But it is so imperfectly developed, that it is not possible fully to understand it, and therefore we cannot pretend to criticise it. Mr. James does not explain at all how God's "descent to carnal conditions" and "suffering temptations thence derived" had the effect of "bringing the spiritual universe to order." Nor does he give the least proof, Scriptural or rational, in support of these positions. We cannot, however, help noticing here what we have before suggested, that spiritual pantheism is really a limitation of God. Mr. James makes the incarnation the means of introducing God, for the first time, to an acquaintance with the world of nature. He declares that, apart from the incarnation, God was "wholly ignorant" of "the temptations of evil." His theory of redemption brings the Deity temporarily into the natural universe, in order to become acquainted with it, which, of course, implies that he was not acquainted with it before, since the incarnation was a fact in time.

We have occupied ourselves so much with the criticism of the main argument of the book, that we have no space to speak of many interesting points, nor to give several striking passages which we had marked for quotation. Our business has been to find fault, but there is much in the volume which has given us great contentment. We cannot fail to recognize a true Christian experience as the basis of the volume, the true Pauline antinomianism, though pushed to an extreme. The merit of the book in its theology is, that it assumes the ground of Rational Supernaturalism, which seems to us to be the only true one. Mr. James's mind is metaphysical rather than logical. He sweeps the whole ground, and gives us glimpses of every part, but omits the processes by which his results are legitimated. Consequently, it is not easy to understand or to do justice to his position; a difficulty which we have felt in writing this article.

We thank him, individually, for the stimulus of his earnest and original thoughts; and, though frankly differing from him, would testify our respect for the high spiritual insight, and large reach of intellect, which this as every other work of the writer plainly intimates. If we have anywhere, in statement or argument, failed to do him justice, we will as frankly acknowledge our error.

The Atlantic Monthly (essay date 1869)

SOURCE: A review of *The Secret of Swedenborg,* in *The Atlantic Monthly,* Vol. XXIV, No. 6, December, 1869, pp. 762-63.

[*In the following unsigned review, the critic provides a favorable overview of James's treatise* The Secret of Swedenborg. *The critic predicts, however, that the work will disturb some readers who might oppose James's belief that humans are creatures of God and that their existence depends entirely on Him.*]

[In *The Secret of Swedenborg*] Mr. James rejects the idea of a Supreme Being, who, having created the heavens and the earth, and set life in operation according to certain universal laws, has ever since been resting and enjoying himself. Our author aims to show, from what he believes about the inspired philosophy of Swedenborg, that God is now and ever was the striving, self-devoted Christ, loving his creatures supremely, and living for them; and he teaches that the creature exists only and continually from the Lord, and that whatever conception of human freedom involves the notion of a completed and independent existence is false. Nature is the implication of man, and spirit is the fact; matter is illusory and insubstantial; a reflex, a shadow cast from the essence of another and real world. Nature is divine because God includes it; but, though full of God, it does not include him,—a point at which the Swedenborgian philosophy diverges finally and forever from Pantheism. The relation of humanity to God is that of an identity of life and interests, a perfectly filial relation, an utterly non-political relation. Before the divine love, all its creatures are equal, like the children of a father: to be good is a condition of happiness in this world and the next, but there is no

system of favoritism by which a moral man can commend himself above a sinner to God's love. Christ, or God incarnate, continually strove by violation of usage to teach the inferiority of mere law, or morality, and the superiority of love. The regeneration which is to take place will be a social, not a personal effect; not so far as a man obeys God, but as far as he loves his fellow, is he saved; and hell is not so much a state of punishments, or inevitable consequences, as of ignorance, of blindness to the divine natural humanity; it exists in the necessity of things as the negative of heaven.

Mr. James discards the church from his idea of religion, or rather lets it be for the present as the most harmless escape for the spiritual vanities and ambitions of men; only devoting to singular reprobation an ecclesiastical embodiment of Swedenborg's philosophy. At the same time he is the ardent opponent of deism; a thorough and devout believer in revealed religion, and that only.

He has here written a book of which the very title will repel most readers, and of which the tone and manner will dreadfully shock many. He secularizes his theme as much as he can; taking religion out of the hands of the church, he treats the chief concern of the world in the world's own fashion. Only here and there, we suppose, a reader will perceive and acknowledge the essential reverence and earnestness with which he always writes; but few can fail to see the excellence of his performance in that particular in which he probably values it least. He has so fresh and unconventional a sense of language, that his style is a continual surprise and pleasure, and is full of unpremeditated eloquence. He also treats his abstruse topic with great clearness; and he has done all that is possible to put his reader in possession of new and startling ideas, which the reader must reject with open eyes if he rejects them at all. Doubtless nearly all will reject them. We have been avowing for a good many centuries that we are God's creatures; but when a philosopher approaches us to say, "You *are* God's creatures; you originate nothing without him, you effectuate nothing without him; of yourself you only seem to be; if he restrained for an instant his creative impulse towards you, you would fall into absolute non-existence," we find this philosopher so far from a flatterer, that we shall be very apt to snub him, and cut his acquaintance at once. His doctrine is peculiarly distasteful to the intellectualized spirit of this age, in which men seem to exist only in their self-consciousness. We must be humbled to the dust before we can consent to accept divine honors; we must be beggared before we can know that

" 'T is only God may be had for the asking."

Mr. James elaborates his ideas of the Swedenborgian philosophy in many chapters, with great fulness of example and illustration, a singular luxury of epithet, and an occasional concession to the impulses of a humor which is the thing we think likely to terrify some readers. He takes a new and peculiar view of Swedenborg's character,—beholds him as a man entirely uninteresting in himself, and of small value to mankind save in his quality of seer. He dismisses the scientific claims of Swedenborg as matters of comparative indifference, and is not afflicted by Mr. White's late assertions concerning his personal character; this also appearing an affair of small moment, in the consideration of his spiritual adaptability to the great end of his existence. We do not know that Mr. James concedes the truth of the charges against Swedenborg, but he concerns himself with the imputed errors as little as he would with the homicides of Moses, Samuel, and David, were their prophetic character in question; and he discourages with much sarcastic felicity the attempt to canonize Swedenborg.

We are sensible of having touched Mr. James's remarkable essay in vague and most inadequate terms, which can be satisfactory neither to those who accept nor to those who reject his philosophy or his interpretation of Swedenborg's secret. Those who cannot classify themselves with either party decidedly, must in their doubt content themselves as we do with admiring the metaphysical acuteness, the logical power, and the singular literary force of the book, which is also remarkable as carrying into theological writing something besides the hard words of secular dispute, and as presenting to the world the great questions of theology in something beside a Sabbath-day dress.

The Spectator (essay date 1885)

SOURCE: A review of *The Literary Remains of the Late Henry James,* in *The Spectator,* Vol. 58, No. 2986, September 19, 1885, pp. 1237-39.

[*In the following unsigned review of* The Literary Remains of the Late Henry James, *the critic offers a brief assessment of James's philosophy and contends that the volume is valuable not only for its content but also "as a psychological study of a very unique mind."*]

[**The Literary Remains of the Late Henry James**] is a book of considerable interest, though more, perhaps, as a psychological study of a very unique mind, than for the speculations which it contains.

The late Henry James, the father of the well known Henry James, the American novelist, was during his life more or less of a celebrity in his own country as an eccentric and bold thinker. His somewhat mystical books, especially his **Society the Redeemed Form of Man,** the **Secret of Swedenborg,** and various essays in the *North American Review* and other periodicals, have been read and studied with an interest hard to imagine

---

An excerpt from *Society the Redeemed Form of Man:*

One day . . . having eaten a comfortable dinner, I remained sitting at the table after the family had dispersed, idly gazing at the embers in the grate, thinking of nothing, and feeling only the exhilaration incident to a good digestion, when suddenly—in a lightning-flash as it were—"fear came upon me, and trembling, which made all my bones to shake." To all appearance it was a perfectly insane and abject terror, without ostensible cause, and only to be accounted for, to my perplexed imagination, by some damnèd shape squatting invisible to me within the precincts of the room, and raying out from his fetid personality influences fatal to life. The thing had not lasted ten seconds before I felt myself a wreck, that is, reduced from a state of firm, vigorous, joyful manhood to one of almost helpless infancy. The only self-control I was capable of exerting was to keep my seat. I felt the greatest desire to run incontinently to the foot of the stairs and shout for help to my wife,—to run to the roadside even, and appeal to the public to protect me; but by an immense effort I controlled these frenzied impulses, and determined not to budge from my chair till I had recovered my lost self-possession. This purpose I held to for a good long hour, as I reckoned time, beat upon meanwhile by an ever-growing tempest of doubt, anxiety, and despair, with absolutely no relief from any truth I had ever encountered save a most pale and distant glimmer of the Divine existence,—when I resolved to abandon the vain struggle, and communicate without more ado what seemed my sudden burden of inmost, implacable unrest to my wife.

Henry James, Sr., in Society the Redeemed Form of Man, *Houghton, Osgood and Company, 1879.*

---

in so realistic an age. The present volume consists of posthumous writings, some of them fragmentary, edited by one of his sons, from whose Introduction we confess that we have derived a somewhat clearer understanding of his father's thoughts than it was possible to attain from the writings of the author himself.

Henry James appears to have been born and bred in the lap of a kind of mild orthodox Calvinism, in the teachings of which he at first tacitly acquiesced, until his very original mind, after many throes, revolted violently against the selfish faith which looked mainly to the escape from future punishment, and kept what he calls a debtor and creditor account with Heaven. The writings of Swedenborg seem to have given him his earliest notion of a religious theory which he could accept, and he finally formed for himself a creed, founded, perhaps, more upon strong moral convictions and intuitions than upon close reasoning, although he claims for himself a logical accuracy of the sternest kind. His style, of which we shall give some typical specimens, is sometimes obscure enough; more so, indeed, than is necessitated by his thoughts. His language is eccentric, words being used in a sense very different from their ordinary meaning, and his outbreaks of indignation and scorn when he treats of the prevailing views of the orthodox world, are expressed in terms of violence, sometimes lapsing into coarseness. With all this, there are glimpses of profound truth, of clear insight into the weak points of many accepted beliefs, and ideas at first sight extravagant, but suggestive of speculation of the deepest interest, which, with the undoubtedly intense earnestness of the author—his opinions, indeed, taking almost the form of passion—render his writings well worth the pain and labour required for their comprehension.

Mr. James's philosophy was essentially *monistic*. We do not use the term in its ordinary sense in relation to spirit and matter, but we mean that he held that God is everything, and everything is God. Pantheism, in name at least, he indignantly repudiates, though, in a sense, he was undoubtedly a Pantheist. God is strictly *impersonal,* because unlimited. The infinite Love leads to the creation of man. Man's individuality and sense of *"self-hood"* is a delusion, and is that which involves all evil; for human nature, apart from the preposterous claims of our several selves, *must* be good, seeing that it is identical with the Divine nature. This "self-hood" is a mere provisional scaffolding or educational process. The consciousness of volition is part of the process by which we discover our utter nothingness. This is followed by what Mr. James calls "conscience" and "religion," which are the ministers of death to our fallacious self-hood, and have no other work or positive character, and no other function, but that of clearing away this temporary but necessary delusion. At last (and this is redemption) God will be fully incarnated in a form which no longer contradicts his character, in the "Divine Nature Humanity" as a preparation for which he has undergone a patient self-surrender by projecting from himself human entities with the delusive sense of separate personality.

The following is a characteristic and forcible specimen of our author's style of thought:—

> The only hindrance to men's believing in God as a creator is their inability to believe in themselves as created. Self-consciousness, the sentiment of personality, the feeling I have of life in myself, absolute and underived from any other save in a natural way, is so subtly and powerfully atheistic, that no matter how loyally I may be taught to insist upon creation as a mere traditional or legendary fact, I never feel inclined personally to believe in it save as the fruit of some profound intellectual humiliation, or hopeless vexation of spirit. My inward afflatus from this cause is so great, I am conscious of such superabounding personal life, that I am satisfied, for my own part at least, that my sense of self-hood must, in some subtle, exquisite way, find itself wounded to death—find itself

become death, in fact, *the only death I am capable of believing in*—before any genuine spiritual resuscitation is at all practicable for me.

This disintegration into units is the source of what we call evil, and is the Creator's first product, in which the different parts, so to speak, of the universal humanity, which is all good, are appropriated by the units so as to introduce confusion and disproportion, and produce what we call evil. Hear our author on "Good and Evil":—

> Good and evil, heaven and hell, are not facts of creation, but purely of constitutive order. They bear primarily on man's natural destiny, and have no relation to his spiritual freedom save through that. They are the mere geology of our natural consciousness. They have no distinctively supernatural quality nor efficiency whatever. They have a simply constitutional relevancy to the earth of man's associated consciousness, and disavow, therefore, any properly creative or controlling relation to his spiritual or individual freedom. We have been traditionally taught that good and evil, heaven and hell, were objective realities, having an absolute ground of being in the creative perfection. But this is the baldest, most bewildering nonsense. . . . They are purely subjective appearances, vitalised exclusively by the created imperfection, or the uses they subserve to our provisional, moral, and rational consciousness. When, accordingly, this consciousness—having fulfilled its legitimate office, and become, as it now is, a mere stumbling-block or rock of offence to the regenerate mind of the race—finally expires in its own stench, or else frankly allows itself to be taken up and disappear in our advancing social and aesthetic consciousness, good and evil, heaven and hell, will cease to be appearances even.

The quotations now given are from previous writings of our author, quoted by his son in his introduction to the present work. We have chosen them as more illustrative of his views and style than most of the present volume. Here is a specimen of his denunciatory style:—

> Professional religion, I repeat, is the devil's masterpiece for ensnaring silly, selfish men. The ugly beast has two heads—one called Ritualism, intended to devour a finer and fastidious style of men,—men of sentiment and decorum, cherishing scrupulously moderate views of the difference between man and God; the other, called Revivalism, with a great red mouth intended to gobble up a coarser sort of men,—men for the most part of a fierce carnality, of ungovernable appetite and passion, susceptible at best only of the most selfish hopes and the most selfish fears towards God.

What we have now said and quoted will give our readers a general, though, we fear, a very imperfect view of the style of thought of a very remarkable man. It will be seen how to his mind these doctrines solved the difficulty involved in reconciling the infinitude of God with his conscious personality,—the difficulty of admitting the existence of sin as the product of natures formed by all-powerful goodness, while it satisfied his optimistic longings for the future of our race. The intimate connection of his view with the doctrine of Swedenborg, though with some important differences, will be obvious to all students of the Swedish sage. While, on the other hand, the points at which it touches the philosophy of Hegel, of Spinoza, and of Schopenhauer and Hartmann, and even (in semblance, at least), the so-called religion of the Positivists, are patent enough.

One more quotation we cannot help giving; but it illustrates the author's central theory and that occasional confusion of ideas to which he is subject, better perhaps than any other passage equally short.

> What I mean then by incarnation is this: that God in the Lord, meaning by that term God-man—for I am not a bit of a deist, properly so called, and cannot for the life of me imagine the existence of a God outside of our nature, having other than essentially human attributes—is the sole substance in reality embraced in the sensible universe, from its central sun to the planetary earths that encircle it, and from these, again, to the tiniest mineral, vegetable, and animal forms that enliven their surface. Nothing is exempt from the operative of this law [what *law?*] but the field of self-consciousness, which, not being a *thing*, an object of sense, but, on the contrary, a sphere of metaphysical illusion in the creature, can have, of course, no corresponding reality in the Creator. Self-consciousness is the only sphere of evil in the universe, and is, therefore, excluded from creation altogether, being gradually absorbed and superseded by unitary or race-consciousness. . . . I should certainly be very sorry to throw any doubt upon the life and death and resurrection of Jesus Christ as an authentic revelation of a truth never before dreamed of by the human mind,—namely, that God himself is the sole veritable mother-substance of human nature, and, therefore, the sole real subject of our unreal or phenomenal subjectivity.

The last sentence above quoted, and much that follows it in the fifteenth chapter of the treatise, called *Spiritual Creation,* show Mr. James's relation to Christianity. He seems, through the aid of his peculiar philosophy, to have relieved his mind from the difficulty of belief which is often felt in consequence of the *uniqueness* of our Lord's incarnation, by generalising the idea of divine incarnation, in spreading it over the whole human race. There are phases of Pantheism, or something which almost merits the name, which seem to have a tendency to penetrate the theological thought of this period, as an escape from some of the difficulties which to certain minds beset the Christian faith as usually stated. How far such speculations are compatible with what we hold to be the essentials of Christianity, and how far they are capable of nourishing its moral and spiritual fruits, is a profound and serious question, requiring space and opportunity much more ample than the limits of this notice. It is impossible to deny to such men as the late Mr. James an intense religiosity of nature. Is it possible for one holding his views to *pray?* Probably he did so; but could he do so in logical consistence with his theory?

Our author's remarks on Emerson, on whom he looked with affection, but regarded as a most imperfect specimen of humanity, are interesting; and a chapter on Carlyle not less so. These will repay study even to those readers who may shrink from the author's mystical and unsound theology.

Henry James, Jr. (essay date 1914)

SOURCE: An excerpt from *Notes of a Son and Brother,* Charles Scribner's Sons, 1914, pp. 155-212; 213-47.

[*The second son of Henry James, Sr., Henry James, Jr., was a novelist, short story writer, critic, and essayist of the late nineteenth and early twentieth centuries. He is admired as a lucid and insightful critic and is regarded as one of the greatest novelists of the English language. In the following excerpt from his autobiographical volume* Notes of a Son and Brother—*published at a time when the elder James's works had largely been forgotten—James, Jr., offers his impressions of his father, portraying him as an absorbing and immensely humane figure.*]

We took his "writing" infinitely for granted—we had always so taken it, and the sense of him, each long morning, at his study table either with bent considering brow or with a half-spent and checked intensity, a lapse backward in his chair and a musing lift of perhaps troubled and baffled eyes, seems to me the most constant fact, the most closely interwoven and underlying, among all our breaks and variations. He applied himself there with a regularity and a piety as little subject to sighing abatements or betrayed fears as if he had been working under pressure for his bread and ours and the question were too urgent for his daring to doubt. This play of his remarkable genius brought him in fact throughout the long years no ghost of a reward in the form of pence, and could proceed to publicity, as it repeatedly did, not only by the copious and resigned sacrifice of such calculations, but by his meeting in every single case all the expenses of the process. The untired impulse to this devotion figured for us, comprehensively and familiarly, as "Father's Ideas," of the force and truth of which in his own view we were always so respectfully, even though at times so bewilderedly and confoundedly persuaded, that we felt there was nothing in his exhibition of life that they didn't or couldn't account for. They pervaded and supported his existence, and very considerably our own; but what comes back to me, to the production of a tenderness and an admiration scarce to be expressed, is the fact that though we thus easily and naturally lived with them and indeed, as to their more general effects, the colour and savour they gave to his talk, breathed them in and enjoyed both their quickening and their embarrassing presence, to say nothing of their almost never less than amusing, we were left as free and unattacked by them as if they had been so many droppings of gold and silver coin on tables and chimney-pieces, to be "taken" or not according to our sense and delicacy, that is our felt need and felt honour. The combination in him of his different vivacities, his living interest in his philosophy, his living interest in us and his living superiority to all greed of authority, all overreaching or everemphasising "success," at least in the heated short run, gave his character a magnanimity by which it was impossible to us not to profit in all sorts of responsive and in fact quite luxurious ways. It was a luxury, I to-day see, to have all the benefit of his intellectual and spiritual, his religious, his philosophic and his social passion, without ever feeling the pressure of it to our direct irritation or discomfort. It would perhaps more truly figure the relation in which he left us to these things to have likened our opportunities rather to so many scattered glasses of the liquor of faith, poured-out cups stood about for our either sipping or draining down or leaving alone, in the measure of our thirst, our curiosity or our strength of head and heart. If there was much leaving alone in us—and I freely confess that, so far as the taking any of it all "straight" went, my lips rarely adventured—this was doubtless because we drank so largely at the source itself, the personally overflowing and irrigating. What it then comes to, for my present vision, was that he treated us most of all on the whole, as he in fact treated everything, by his saving imagination—which set us, and the more as we were naturally so inclined, the example of living as much as we might in some such light of our own. If we had been asked in our younger time for instance what *were* our father's ideas, or to give an example of one of them, I think we should promptly have answered (I should myself have hastened to do so) that the principal was a devoted attachment to the writings of Swedenborg; as to whom we were to remember betimes, with intimate appreciation, that in reply to somebody's plea of not finding him credible our parent had pronounced him, on the contrary, fairly "insipid with veracity." We liked that partly, I think, because it disposed in a manner, that is in favour of our detachment, of the great Emanuel, but when I remember the part played, so close beside us, by this latter's copious revelation, I feel almost ashamed for my own incurious conduct. The part played consisted to a large extent in the vast, even though incomplete, array of Swedenborg's works, the old faded

A daguerreotype of Henry James, Sr., and Henry James, Jr., taken in 1854 by Mathew Brady.

covers of which, anciently red, actually apt to be loose, and backed with labels of impressive, though to my sense somewhat sinister London imprint, Arcana Coelestia, Heaven and Hell and other such matters—they all had, as from other days, a sort of black emphasis of dignity—ranged themselves before us wherever, and however briefly, we disposed ourselves, forming even for short journeys the base of our father's travelling library and perhaps at some seasons therewith the accepted strain on our mother's patience. I recall them as inveterately part of our very luggage, requiring proportionate receptacles; I recall them as, in a number considerable even when reduced, part of their proprietor's own most particular dependence on his leaving home, during our more agitated years, for those speculative visits to possible better places (than whatever place of the moment) from which, as I have elsewhere mentioned, he was apt to return under premature, under passionate nostalgic, reaction. The Swedenborgs were promptly out again on their customary shelves or sometimes more improvised perches, and it was somehow not till we had assured ourselves of this that we felt *that* incident closed. . . .

A less vague or vain idealist couldn't, I think, have been encountered; it was given him to catch in the fact at almost any turn right or left some flagrant assurance or promise of the state of man transfigured. The Concord school could be to him for the hour—there were hours and hours!—such a promise; could even figure in that light, to his amplifying sympathy, in a degree disproportionate to its genial, but after all limited, after all not so intensely "inflated," as he would have said, sense of itself. In which light it is that I recognise, and even to elation, how little, practically, of the idea of the Revolution in the vulgar or violent sense was involved in his seeing so many things, in the whole social order about him, and in the interest of their being more or less immediately altered, as lamentably, and yet at the same time and under such a coloured light, as amusingly and illustratively, wrong—wrong, that is, with a blundering helpless human salience that kept criticism humorous, kept it, so to speak, sociable and almost "sympathetic" even when readiest. The case was really of his rather feeling so vast a rightness close at hand or lurking immediately behind actual arrangements that a single turn of the inward wheel, one real response to pressure of the spiritual spring, would bridge the chasms, straighten the distortions, rectify the relations and, in a word, redeem and vivify the whole mass—after a far sounder, yet, one seemed to see, also far subtler, fashion than any that our spasmodic annals had yet shown us. It was of course the old story that we had only to *be* with more intelligence and faith—an immense deal more, certainly—in order to work off, in the happiest manner, the many-sided ugliness of life; which was a process that might go on, blessedly, in the quietest of all quiet ways. *That* wouldn't be blood and fire and tears, or would be none of these things stupidly precipitated; it would simply have taken place by *enjoyed* communication and contact, enjoyed concussion or convulsion even—since pangs and agitations, the very agitations of perception itself, are of the highest privilege of the soul and there is always, thank goodness, a saving sharpness of play or complexity of consequence in the intelligence completely alive. The meaning of which remarks for myself, I must be content to add, is that the optimists of the world, the constructive idealists, as one has mainly known them, have too often struck one as overlooking more of the aspects of the real than they recognise; whereas our indefeasible impression, William's and mine, of our parent was that he by his very constitution and intimate heritage recognised many more of those than he overlooked. What was the finest part of our intercourse with him—that is the most nutritive— but a positive record of that? Such a matter as that the factitious had absolutely no hold on him was the truest thing about him, and it was all the while present to us, I think, as backing up his moral authority and play of vision that never, for instance, had there been a more numerous and candid exhibition of all the human susceptibilities than in the nest of his original nurture. I have spoken of the fashion in which I still see him, after the years, attentively bent over those much re-

written "papers," that we had, even at our stupidest, this warrant for going in vague admiration of that they caught the eye, even the most filially detached, with a final face of wrought clarity, and thereby of beauty, that there *could* be no thinking unimportant—and see him also fall back from the patient posture, again and again, in long fits of remoter consideration, wondering, pondering sessions into which I think I was more often than not moved to read, for the fine interest and colour of it, some story of acute inward difficulty amounting for the time to discouragement. If one wanted drama *there* was drama, and of the most concrete and most immediately offered to one's view and one's suspense; to the point verily, as might often occur, of making one go roundabout it on troubled tiptoe even as one would have held one's breath at the play.

These opposed glimpses, I say, hang before me as I look back, but really fuse together in the vivid picture of the fond scribe separated but by a pane of glass— his particular preference was always directly to face the window—from the general human condition he was so devoutly concerned with. He *saw* it, through the near glass, saw it in such detail and with a feeling for it that broke down nowhere—that was the great thing; which truth it confirmed that his very fallings back and long waits and stays and almost stricken musings witnessed exactly to his intensity, the intensity that would "come out," after all, and make his passionate philosophy and the fullest array of the appearances that couldn't be blinked fit together and harmonise. Detached as I could during all those years perhaps queerly enough believe myself, it would still have done my young mind the very greatest violence to have to suppose that any plane of conclusion for him, however rich and harmonious he might tend to make conclusion, could be in the nature of a fool's paradise. Small vague outsider as I was, I couldn't have borne *that* possibility; and I see, as I return to the case, how little I really could ever have feared it. This would have amounted to fearing it on account of his geniality—a shocking supposition; as if his geniality had been thin and *bête,* patched up and poor, and not by the straightest connections, nominal and other, of the very stuff of his genius. No, I feel myself complacently look back to *my* never having, even at my small poorest, been so *bête,* either, as to conceive he might be "wrong," wrong as a thinker-out, in his own way, of the great mysteries, because of the interest and amusement and vividness his attesting spirit could fling over the immediate ground. What he saw *there* at least could be so enlightening, so evocatory, could fall in so—which was to the most inspiring effect within the range of perception of a scant son who was doubtless, as to the essential, already more than anything else a novelist *en herbe.* If it didn't sound in a manner patronising I should say that I saw that my father saw; and that I couldn't but have given my own case away by not believing, however obscurely, in the virtue of his consequent and ultimate synthesis. Of course I never dreamed of any such name for it—I only thought of it as something very great and fine founded on those forces in him that came home to us and that touched us all the while. As these were extraordinary forces of sympathy and generosity, and that yet knew how to be such without falsifying any minutest measure, the structure raised upon them might well, it would seem, and even to the uppermost sublime reaches, be as valid as it was beautiful. If he so endeared himself wasn't it, one asked as time went on, through his never having sentimentalised or merely mediated away, so to call it, the least embarrassment of the actual about him, and having with a passion peculiarly his own kept together his stream of thought, however transcendent and the stream of life, however humanised? There was a kind of experiential authority in his basis, as he felt his basis— there being no human predicament he couldn't by a sympathy more *like* direct experience than any I have known enter into; and this authority, which concluded so to a widening and brightening of the philosophic— for him the spiritual—sky, made his character, as intercourse disclosed it, in a high degree fascinating. These things, I think, however, are so happily illustrated in his letters that they look out from almost any continuous passage in such a series for instance as those addressed in the earlier time to Mrs. Tappan. His *tone,* that is, always so effectually looks out, and the living parts of him so singularly hung together, that one may fairly say his philosophy *was* his tone.

Henry James, Jr., to his brother William on the death of their father (1882):

Dear William,—

I was not able yesterday to write you a second letter, as I hoped, as I was still suffering rather too much from my head; but this evening I am pretty well myself again, and shall endeavour to go on with my story. . . . Mainly, I can only repeat that the whole thing was tranquil and happy—almost, as it were, comfortable. The wanderings of his mind, which were never great, were always of a joyous description, and his determination not to eat was cheerful and reasonable, that is, he was always prepared to explain why he wouldn't eat,—that is, because he had entered upon the "spiritual life," and didn't wish to keep up the mere form of living in the body. . . . He spoke several times of Mother—uttering (intelligibly) her name: "Mary—my Mary." Somewhat before this Aunt Kate says he murmured—"Oh, I have such good boys—*such* good boys!" . . . Farewell, dear William. Ever yours,

H. JAMES

Henry James, Jr., in The Thought and Character of William James, Volume I: Inheritance and Vocation, *by Ralph Barton Perry, Little, Brown, and Company, 1935.*

Ralph Barton Perry (essay date 1932)

SOURCE: "Religion versus Morality According to the Elder Henry James," in *The International Journal of Ethics,* Vol. XLII, No. 3, April, 1932, pp. 289-303.

[*Perry was an American philosopher and biographer whose two-volume biography of William James won the Pulitzer Prize for that genre in 1935. In the excerpt below, he argues that James, Sr., was an antinomian, or one who believes that under the gospel dispensation of grace the moral law is of no use because faith alone is necessary to salvation.*]

Morality and religion are related in many ways. For example, each may be taken as the sanction of the other—belief in God as a foundation for morality, or the moral law as a proof of God. These aspects of the question I omit altogether. The point to which I wish to direct attention is the relation between the moral life and the religious life. In some sense it is doubtless true that when the moral life reaches its highest stage of perfection it passes over into the religious life. We have a set of terms such as "saintliness," "piety," "blessedness," "spirituality," which suggest that this form of life is super-moral. Now, granting this, our question is as follows: Should we think of the religious life as consummate, perfected morality; or should we think of it as something distinctly different, which supersedes morality? Shall we say that on some level of spiritual growth religion is opposed to morality, or shall we insist that in religion morality is continued and fulfilled?

Throughout its entire history Christianity has been attended by a somewhat disreputable camp-follower called "antinomianism," often allowed to join in the feast, but never recognized as a regular member of the family, and often an occasion of scandal. The persistent Christian heresies, repeatedly scotched but never killed, such as Arianism, Pelagianism, Gnosticism, Pantheism, Socinianism, threw a flood of light upon the meaning of Christianity. They were reefs and shoals which threaten the shipwreck of Christianity and which the Christian must perpetually avoid, but though they lie off the Christian course, they are the landmarks by which that particular course is bounded and charted. Some of these persistent heresies attack Christianity in its moments of lowered vitality—in the dead of spiritual night; but antinomianism is a malady of excess rather than of deficiency, and the Christian has to fear it most in the morning hours when his Christian heart is beating high. Stated very freely this heresy consists in the belief that the Christian life is so different, so greatly and so gloriously different, from the secular life, that the rules of the secular life no longer obtain; or that to one experiencing the unnatural elevation of Christian faith and love, nothing else matters, including morality. It is a sort of Christian inebriety, uplifting and invigorating, but judged by standards of spiritual hygiene, toxic rather than benign. It embraces the false and blinding affirmation that because the spiritual life is a greater or fuller life it therefore contradicts, annihilates, displaces, and supersedes the moral life; whereas in truth the spiritual life owes what claims it has upon us to the fact that in its greater fulness the moral life is embraced and completed.

In order to illustrate the psychology and logic of antinomianism, the causes which dispose Christians to it, and the reasons, good and bad, by which they justify it, I should like to introduce a great man of religion, who is less well known than he deserves to be and than he is likely to be in the near future. I refer to the elder Henry James, spiritual as well as physical parent of two more famous sons. I said that antinomianism sprang from an excess rather than from a deficiency of Christian zeal. James, if he was a Christian at all, was an intense Christian. When I raise doubts as to his being a Christian at all I mean that he was not a literal or an institutional Christian. He was a Christian, as he was a Swedenborgian, in his own peculiar way; and he regarded organized religions, like morality, as works of the devil because they encouraged the individual to magnify his private importance. But he believed what he took to be the spiritual essence of Christianity with a depth of feeling and insight, and with an inexorable consistency, that distinguished him greatly among the half-hearted worldlings of his time.

Before turning to James's antinomianism let me first call attention to his insistence upon the divine immanence. James heaped scorn upon those theisms or deisms which separated God from men by all space and all time, or which taught (as he said of Carlyle) "that God worked one day out of seven and rested the remaining six" [quoted in *Philosophical Remains*]. God is the form which human life assumes in its perfect fulfilment, and man is the medium by which God finds self-expression. The "divine-natural humanity," which is James's central idea, is both God and man, God approached from below or man viewed from above.

> . . . . All existence real and personal is thus hierarchically distributed, each successive from being a natural unit or marriage of two discordant forces, and becoming by its own subsequent spiritual variety the basis in its turn of a still higher unity. The lower forms in every case are what give subjective or constitutional *identity* (that is, body) to the higher form. The higher form again in its turn is what gives objective or creative *individuality* (that is, soul) to the lower forms. The mineral gives material existence, or body to the vegetable; but the vegetable gives spiritual being or soul to the mineral, by calling forth its uses to a higher unity. The vegetable gives material existence or body to the animal form, which latter again endows the vegetable with spiritual life or soul in calling forth its uses to a superior style

of being. So the animal in like manner gives visible or bodily constitution to man, while man gives invisible or spiritual soul to the animal kingdom by evoking its various uses to his own higher development. And so also man in his turn gives visible form or bodily manifestation to God, while God again gives creative substance, soul, or unity to man in calling forth man's various subserviency to His own infinite and uncreated unity [in *Substance and Shadow*].

God, then, is the "higher unity" of humanity into which human individuals enter and in which they find their consummation. There is a genuine metamorphosis. "And so, indeed, of all unity," says our author [in "Faith and Science," *North American Review* (1865)], "it never means a mere mental aggregation of particulars, but the evolution of a distinctly higher form of life than the particulars themselves, taken together, supply."

In what respect, then, does this higher, spiritual, or divine form of life differ from that of the immediately lower level from which it evolves? Precisely what is the crucial point of the change? What is it that is transcended and left behind? Our author's answer is unmistakable and emphatic. That which is cast off as an outworn garment, a broken chrysalis, or useless scaffolding, is morality. At the moment when life becomes spiritual it not only ceases to be moral but must consciously negate morality, and recoil with loathing from that which hitherto it has struggled to attain. In the following characteristic passages James describes the revulsion of feeling which he himself experienced:

> The more I strove to indue myself in actual righteousness, the wider gaped the jaws of hell within me; the fouler grew its fetid breath. A conviction of inward defilement so sheer took possession of me, that death seemed better than life. I soon found my conscience, once launched in this insane career, acquiring so infernal an edge, that I could no longer indulge myself in the most momentary deviation from an absurd and pedantic literal rectitude; could not, for example, bestow a sulky glance upon my wife, a cross word upon my child, or a petulant objurgation on my cook, without tumbling into an instant inward frenzy of alarm lest I should thereby have provoked God's personal malignity to me. There is indeed no way of avoiding spiritual results so belittling, but by ceasing to regard morality as a direct, and looking upon it as an inverse image of God's true life in us. If my moral consciousness constitute the true and eternal bond of intercourse between me and God; that is to say, if he attribute to me all the good and evil which I in my insane pride attribute to myself,—then it will be impossible for me to avoid all eternity either a most conceited and disgusting conviction of his personal complacency in me, or else a shuddering apprehension of his personal ill-will [quoted in *The Literary Remains of the Late Henry James*].

. . . . Accordingly every man whose aspirations are elevated above the ground, every man who desires above all things to ally himself spiritually with the Divine spirit, finds his great controversy to lie with *himself*; with this moral temper of his own mind; finds the sole hindrance of his aspirations to lie in this ferocious pride of selfhood, which is indeed an every way indispensable soil for the future spiritual plant, but a soil nevertheless from which the plant is bound sedulously to grow away. Such a man perceives at once that his moral life is not the end of his being, but on the contrary a wholly subordinate means to that end, which is spiritual life or cultivated conformity to God, growing out of his unaffected acknowledgment of human unity: so that far from cherishing the pride which is instinctive to morality, pride of selfhood, pride of character, pride of differential righteousness, he daily unlearns that foolish conceit, and cultivates instead relations of the tenderest amity and equality with all other men [quoted in *Substance and Shadow*].

This passage not only expresses our author's view that morality is an "inverse image of God's true life in us" but indicates the ground of the indictment. Morality represents the individual man as an object of praise or blame, to himself or to fellow-man or to God. It imputes desert to a man in his own right, and must lead either to self-righteousness or to morbid despair according to the laxity or strictness of the judgment. Of these two evils the former is the worse, since a man is more likely to remain self-centered if he thinks well than if he thinks ill of himself. The moral sentiment is "the sentiment of what is due to one's self," and it is better to feel that nothing is due to one's self, for in that case one is more likely to leave off thinking of one's dues. The social as distinct from the moral sentiment is the sentiment of what is due to one's neighbor, and conscience, in the peculiar sense in which the author uses this term, is the limitation of the moral by the social sentiment; in other words, the rejection of self which springs from the acceptance of others. Therefore, the only good conscience is an evil conscience. "Conscience was always intended as a rebuke and never as an exhilaration to the private citizen." "Its efficacy is distinctly purgative, not nutritive."

What shall we say of this condemnation of the moral in the name of the religious consciousness? The answer is, I believe, that James has mistaken an accident of the moral life for its essence. A complete morality will pass beyond the sphere of self-development or self-perfection to social relations of justice and benevolence. James sees that as well as we do. That which he attacks under the name of morality is not selfishness, in the sense of a disregard of the rights or happiness of others. Everybody condemns that. What James condemns is a much more subtle and insidious thing. He condemns moral self-consciousness.

The most subtle and insidious case of it, which he therefore condemns most vigorously, is self-approbation, or the attitude of the man who, being just or benevolent, thinks well of himself for it. The most dangerous form of pride, the devil's most skilful maneuver for trapping unwary souls, is the pride of humility. It is like a quicksand in that the harder one tries to extricate one's self the more deeply one is bogged. But curiously enough James's own repudiation of morality illustrates the same predicament. We find him condemning his self-approbation and approving his self-condemnation. We find him, in other words, like the very moralists whom he denounces, occupied with himself, or with the state of his soul. The man who labors with himself in order to induce in himself a state of utter self-forgetfulness is likely to become intimately acquainted with himself; the man who goes abroad preaching the gospel of self-forgetfulness is likely to remind of themselves those who had never thought of themselves before. These paradoxes arise in all cases of self-knowledge, where the posture of the person known must reflect that of the person knowing; just as it is impossible that one should see one's self in a mirror without seeing one's self in the posture of a man looking at himself in a mirror. This difficulty limits and largely falsifies the results obtained in psychology by the method of introspection; and gives rise to the peculiar paradox, that whatever opinion one holds regarding one's self can scarcely be true in that one becomes a different person from the very fact of holding such an opinion.

What is the practical conclusion to which this difficulty drives us? That the best way to forget one's self, is to forget one's self, that is, remember somebody else. The best way to spread self-forgetfulness is not to exhort people to forget themselves but to interest them in their neighbors, or in some quite impersonal cause. This does not mean that self-forgetfulness is not a good thing, or that one has not aimed at it, but that one has devised an indirect way of achieving it. The man whose memory is balked, and who puts the problem aside in the hope that what he seeks will then spontaneously occur to him, does not abandon his quest but adopts a superior strategy—like the general who substitutes a feint or a flank-movement for a frontal attack. So the way to be righteous without being self-righteous is to adopt the right course, and then follow it, with one's eye on the goal. There is an initial selection of the cause, and it may be necessary from time to time, at a fork in the road, to take further counsel with one's self. But otherwise the thing to do is to run the course.

Now I said that James mistook an accident of morality for its essence, meaning that the essence of morality is right conduct, and that the accident is the fact that one must from time to time inquire "Am I or am I not right?" It is important that this inquiry should not be allowed, as it sometimes is, to defeat the very object for which it is instituted, as an army is paralyzed by perpetually holding councils of war. It is quite conceivable that after having judged correctly at the outset a man should continue throughout his life to be righteous without ever reflecting upon the fact. He might, for example, love his neighbor and his God, and never deem himself either charitable or pious. He would then *be* charitable and pious; he would possess these virtues in his own right as a private person; and he would be *worthy* of an approbation which happily he would never pronounce. He would be a self or a person with moral attributes; though he would be unconscious of himself, and unaware of his attributes.

Our author's failure to distinguish clearly between personality and self-consciousness, between righteousness and self-righteousness, leads him into the serious error of supposing that since the spiritual or religious life transcends the latter it must transcend the former. In the religious life, transported as we are by love of God and neighbor, we cease to be occupied with ourselves; and this he interprets as meaning that we cease to be ourselves. Thus in an unpublished letter [to Mrs. Francis G. Shaw (1860)] he says:

> Now Swedenborg tells us that the word cannot be understood spiritually, save in so far as we put away from our minds three ideas, those of *space, time* and *person,* i.e., put away all that separates one man from another, and view henceforth all men as one in the Divine sight. . . . .

In another passage [quoted in *The Literary Remains of the Late Henry James*] our author says:

> Just in proportion, accordingly, as a man's spiritual knowledge improves, will his contempt for himself, as an unmixed spiritual tramp and irredeemable vagabond, increase and abound. We might very well bear with an uninstructed or inexperienced child, who, shut up to the companionship of its doll, constructed all of sawdust and prunella, looks upon it as spiritually alive; but one has no patience with an experienced, instructed man or churchman, who undergoes precisely the same hallucination with regard to his own worthless doll of a selfhood. . . .

And yet "this worthless doll of a selfhood" is somehow a necessary stage of spiritual development!

Now it is intelligible that the private selfhood of men should be a necessary condition of the existence of a unified humanity, if that selfhood is an ingredient of a unified humanity. But if what one means by the unified humanity is precisely that condition which is reached after private selfhood has been eliminated, then it is indeed hard to see how the way for this achievement has been paved by generating the very element which is to be eliminated. The preliminary step toward the divine life, we are told, is to make ourselves persons; the second step is to unmake ourselves as persons. It would seem to follow, then, that after the second step we are just where we would have been if we had never taken the preliminary step. Why, therefore, take the preliminary step? It is a hard saying that the way to pass from an intermediate point to one's destination is to return to the point of departure. Tell men that personal morality is a step toward something better that lies beyond—and they will then seek to achieve morality; though they will not arrest their movement there, but will fix their eyes on a more distant goal and set their pace for the longer course. But tell them that morality is the inverse of the supreme good, that it lies in the opposite direction, and they will very naturally and properly save themselves the trouble of passing that way. It will be difficult to persuade men that a false start is the best beginning, or that they should first move into a *cul de sac* from which they must back out before they can resume their journey.

Our author suggests that we must learn by the method of trial and error:

> We require just such a fixed and fallacious cosmical scheme as this in order to give us cumulative experience, or to enable us to learn by failure and suffering what spiritual dolts we invariably are *in our individual right,* and so be led at last to seek God's salvation by studiously allying ourselves in unity with our kind [quoted in *The Literary Remains of the Late Henry James*].

This might be reasonable if we supposed that men were left to grope their own way at random in the dark, though even then one would hesitate to say that a wrong guess is the necessary preliminary to a right guess. But we are asked to believe that under the wise and benevolent providence of God the only way by which a man can discover that he is nothing is by first affirming and then renouncing the belief that he is everything. Outside of *Alice through the Looking Glass* or the Hegelian philosophy this savors strongly of nonsense.

But there is a further difficulty which is fatal to such a view, and, I venture to think, to most forms of religious mysticism. Human life upon its highest level, in which, as our author phrases it, each man "cultivates. . . . relations of the tenderest amity and equality with all other men," is what one means by the divine life. In participating in the perfected human life the individual achieves union with God. But then, owing to excess of piety, one denies those very human individuals whose relations generate and compose God—so that God proves in the end to be composed of nothing. God is everything and men in their severalty, or speaking distributively, are nothing; but God is composed of men, and therefore everything is composed of nothing.

This difficulty is as gratuitous as it is fatal. In order that men living in relations of tenderest amity and equality, united by bonds of love, shall thereby generate a new life, a divine-human life, in which their aloofness and mutual disregard shall be transcended, it is not in the least necessary to suppose that they cease to be a plurality of persons, and are dissolved like drops in a stream. Indeed such a life is unthinkable unless there be persons to love and persons to be loved—unless these be other than one another and lead in some measure lives of their own. Multiply the connecting relations as you will and you only increase the necessity of the terms which shall sustain these relations. Stress the variety and subtlety of the bonds by which a man shall be united to his fellows, and you magnify the rôle of the personalities which shall support and reconcile these bonds. The divine life lies in some sense beyond the merely personal life, but it is an achievement of personality, built not only upon persons but out of persons.

The indictment of morality in the name of religion is not complete. There are two further charges which remain. The first of these I shall dismiss briefly, since the issue is similar to that which has just been discussed. Morality, it is argued, assumes the form of rules which are harshly imposed and abjectly obeyed, whereas the spiritual life is one of spontaneity and freedom. The lawbreaker, therefore, the man who defies convention, manifests the higher life, if not in what he does, then at any rate in the way he does it.

> The liar, the thief, the adulterer, the murderer, no doubt utterly perverts the divine life which is latent in every human form; he degrades and defiles self-love, in lifting it out of that free subordination which it will evince to brotherly love in the Divine-*natural* man: but he nevertheless does all this in the way of a mute, unconscious protest against an overwhelming social tyranny, which would otherwise crush out the distinctive life of man under the machinery of government and caste [quoted in *The Literary Remains of the Late Henry James*].

This charge against morality, like the first, is an echo of the author's reaction against Calvinism. The answer to the charge is that the enforcement of moral rules is (like moral self-judgment) accidental; the important thing is their observance. That lying, theft, adultery, and murder should be proscribed is an unfortunate necessity which has nothing to do with their viciousness. They are vicious because they are inhumane, because they contradict that regard for the general good which is the essence of right conduct. If one avoided them from love of mankind rather than from fear of penalties, that would be better, because then one's heart would be right and not merely one's overt behavior. But because a spontaneous righteousness is better than a legal righteousness it does not follow that whatever is spontaneous is therefore better than whatever is le-

gal. James seems to share the view not uncommon in his age, and widespread in the preceding century, that man will fall into ways of right conduct by virtue of a sort of naïveté or childlike innocence. But there is a spontaneity below as well as above the level of legality, and he who resists the law usually sinks to the first instead of rising to the second. The man who objects to a rule against adultery, whether enforced by the state or by public opinion, is usually a man who wishes to commit adultery, rather than a man who wishes to be allowed to avoid adultery spontaneously. If he is himself inwardly disposed to fidelity, the chances are that he will not notice the rule since his action will never bring him into collision with it. In short, if the religious life is to be conceived as transcending the constraint of law, it must be conceived as a life in which the law, being freely chosen and instinctively observed, is in no need of being enforced. This is the only justifiable interpretation of "Christian liberty." It is not that the Christian because he is regenerate may therefore do as he pleases, but that he will therefore please to do what is right. The religious life, in short, is not above the content or substance of the law, but is above the human frailty or wilfulness which requires its being imposed as a forced obligation.

The third and most serious charge contained in this antinomian indictment of morality is the claim that the moral distinction between good and evil is not an absolute or final but only a provisional distinction. It is true that this view mitigates the difficulties which arise from the first charge, but only at the cost of difficulties which are even graver. Morality takes its distinctions seriously, praises moral good such as justice and benevolence, and denounces moral evil such as lying, theft, murder, and adultery. Conscience praises self-forgetfulness and brotherly love; and denounces pride and selfhood. In the antinomian view the higher religious insight tells us that the opposing terms of these antitheses, the good and the evil of these lower levels, are both good, as being proper parts of the spiritual or divine life. Let me quote further from the letter cited above:

> . . . . For we being absolute creatures of God are without any substance in ourselves, and hence are what we are, laugh and cry, eat and drink, love and work, aspire and triumph, only by virtue of His infinite tenderness imparting, or as Swedenborg phrases it, *communicating* Himself to us, and permitting us if we please to put His love to the basest uses, in order that at last we may through sheer disgust of our own loathsome performances turn ourselves freely to Him and demand with humble hearts at last the guidance of His unerring laws. . . . For the power by which all this deviltry is enacted is literally God in use, and He never for a moment shrinks back but lets our whole play play itself out to its last gasp of naughtiness, in order that by our spontaneous reaction against such horrors

we may finally swing into cordial sympathy with Him, and that eternally. He is really our life at all times, when we are going down to hell as much as when we are ascending to heaven: only in the former state He is humiliated, despised, trodden under our clownish feet, crucified by all our selfish and cruel lusts: and in the latter glorified, exalted above the heaven of heavens, by the heartiness of our spiritual gradic and adoration.

Now this is to be interpreted to mean that the divine or spiritual life itself embraces both heaven and hell. The crucifixion is not, as supposed in the traditional theology, a symbol of the painful necessity of reconciling human sin with divine justice. In that case the crucifixion would be contingent upon the regrettable fact that Eve succumbed to temptation in the Garden of Eden. For James the crucifixion symbolizes the universal and necessary principle that the perfect life is not the painless or sinless life but the life of suffering and of overcoming.

Let me cite from another letter to the same correspondent:

> Life means individuality or character; and individuality or character can never be *conferred*, can never be *communicated* by one to another, but must be inwardly wrought out by the diligent and painful subjection of evil to good in the sphere of one's proper activity. If God made spiritual sacks merely, which he might fill out with his own breath to all eternity, why then of course evil might have been left out of the creatures' experience. But he abhors sacks, and loves only men, made in his own image of heart, head and hand, in whom accordingly *he may dwell in himself*, and find all his goodness of heart, and wisdom of head, and power of hand eternally reproduced. . . .

The spiritual or divine life is the human life on all its levels of baseness and exaltation, relished for what it is, as a struggle and an overcoming; relished for its high seasoning, its rich flavor, and its intoxicating effects. The new standard by which the old evil has taken on the aspect of good is an "aesthetic" as distinguished from a moral standard. It is on this issue that William James broke with his father. The philosophy of the father is that which the son calls "subjectivism," or "gnostical romanticism," according to which, as he says, "the final purpose of our creation seems . . . to be the greatest possible enrichment of an ethical consciousness, through the intensest play of contrasts and the evident diversity of characters. . . . Not the absence of vice, but vice there, and virtue holding her by the throat seems the ideal human state" [quoted in *Will to Believe*]. The avoidance of this view was the principal motive that drove the younger James to pluralism. His arguments are well known, and I will not elaborate them. Granting their premise their force is undeniable.

The premise is the validity of ordinary standards of morality. The practical effect of subjectivism or aestheticism is to condone moral evil. If the important thing be the richness of the experience rather than purity or honor, why should one not sin like David in order to repent like David? If the play's the thing, why should one not play the devil's part? If sin and suffering are necessary parts of the picture, why should we spoil the picture by eradicating them? There is no answer to these questions on the assumption of the aesthetic standard; they are fatal questions on the assumption of the moral standard; and they are unavoidable questions on the assumption that God is both all-embracing and all-perfect.

But there are objections to this view on its own grounds. The problem of evil cannot be escaped by any shifting of standards. All that can be achieved is to change its nature. Aesthetic good can embrace moral evil, but it cannot embrace aesthetic evil. Now it so happens that there are sins which are unrepented and sufferings which lead to no ultimate rejoicing. Furthermore, and this is the crux of the matter, if life's a play, the poor players are for the most part unaware of it. As William James has remarked [in *Will to Believe*], "it *feels* like a real fight." It is a curiously imperfect dramatic situation which all of the actors and most of the audience mistake for reality. Judged by the aesthetic standard itself, how could a world be more cursed than to be filled with sensitive beings on which its effect was totally lost, and in which the emotion enjoyed by God and his favored friends was at the expense of the pathetic eagerness and blind suffering of uninitiated multitudes?

Happily our author has the merit of inconsistency. Not only did he practice better than he preached, and remain faithful to that morality which he professed so to despise, but he preached better than he practiced. Freed from the antinomian errors which I have pointed out, the core of his doctrine is this. That human life perfected, moralized, and socialized, is one and the same with the divine life. That the force by which the moral life reaches its highest level, where it merits the name of divine, is the force of universal love. That a man moved by this passion can never feel that his task is done so long as any of humanity are left in pain and ignorance and sin. Finally, that love has a genuine transforming or regenerating effect in which the old divisive will is superseded; so that men in doing what they themselves most want, at the same time minister most fruitfully to the happiness of mankind.

But let us give our brave author the last word:

> . . . . For the social sentiment, the sentiment of human society, human brotherhood, human equality, exhibits the two warring loves of the human bosom, self-love and neighborly love, interest and principle,

pleasure and duty, in such perfect unison as that neither can possibly prompt anything contrary to the other, but both alike stand eternally pledged to the promotion of an entirely new spirit in man, a spirit of the widest fellowship of the freest and tenderest unity with every other man. This social development constitutes an absolutely new nature in man, a Divinely renewed heart and mind, which shall make all Divine ways easy to follow. . . [in *Substance and Shadow*].

Austin Warren (essay date 1934)

SOURCE: "The Philosophy," in *The Elder Henry James,* The Macmillan Company, 1934, pp. 189-218.

[*In the excerpt below, Warren discusses James's philosophy, examining in particular the relationship between the spiritual and the social.*]

Whenever the eye falls upon one of Mr James' pages,—whether it be a letter to a newspaper or to a friend, whether it be his earliest or his latest book,—we seem to find him saying again and again the same thing; telling us what the true relation is between mankind and its Creator. What he had to say on this point was the burden of his whole life, and its only burden. When he had said it once, he was disgusted with the insufficiency of the formulation (he always hated the sight of his old books), and set himself to work to say it again. But he never analysed his terms or his data beyond a certain point, and made very few fundamentally new discriminations; so the result of all these successive re-editings was repetition and amplification and enrichment, rather than reconstruction. The student of any one of his works knows, consequently, all that is *essential* in the rest [William James, in *The Literary Remains of the Late Henry James*].

A young author's first book must compress between its covers a complete transcription of his experience and his theories. James never outgrew this adolescent prodigality. Besides his reading of the secret of the universe, he was possessed of views upon a range of lesser themes: crime, poverty, wealth, waste; marriage and the 'woman question'; Swedenborg and the Swedenborgians; spiritualism; art; metaphysics. Instead of devoting a book to each of his interests, he devotes every book to all of them, runs the full gamut upon every occasion. This is largely true even of his appearances in magazines. Whatever the announced topic (Woman, Crime, Spiritualism), we presently find ourselves running precipitously into the theory of Creation.

James' earlier writings were largely occupied with negative criticisms of religious orthodoxy, both Evangelical and Swedenborgian. The later works never weary of defining their position by its contrariety to current views in philosophy and science as well as religion. But combat is not their *raison d'être*. Their 'superficial polemics' never disturb the central peace which pervades them.

James published four full-length portraitures of his mind: *Christianity the Logic of Creation* (1857), *Substance and Shadow* (1863), *The Secret of Swedenborg* (1869), *Society the Redeemed Form of Man* (1879); and during the last year of his life he was revising the proof of a fifth, *Spiritual Creation* (1882). The first of these is the most succinct; but the later formulations are not only, as William James thought, philosophically the best, but the best written as well. 'Best' for both philosophy and style must be interpreted *most characteristic of James*. James indeed disliked any dwelling upon the personal and wanted to enunciate what was true not for him but for all men: of no philosopher could this appeal to the universal be more forcibly urged. Yet his whole turn of mind and his intensely vivid and individual idiom set him apart from both the philosophers and the men of letters of his day. He was too much of a dialectician to turn *littérateur,* but he balked at limiting himself to ratiocination. He argues; and wearying of argument, he turns to striking example, pungent satire, eloquent apostrophe, prophetic declaration. For all his fond addiction to verbal distinctions, he uses his terms freely, not exactly, not consistently.

Mr James' style at his most characteristic deserves the high praise which has so abundantly been awarded it, not for organization—that James lacked, was impatient of; but for style in the romantic sense: for diction by turns learned and homely, incomparably varied and rich and living; sentences sharpened to aphorism; paragraphs which work to a climax; longer sequences in which the author feels emotionally moved by his own argument and loses himself in the poetry of it. Wit and passion glow by turns.

A writer of passages James is, rather than a writer of books; just as he is by turns the reasoner, but always the prophet and seer.

Best, as thus defined—that is, most characteristic of their author, most rich in the display of his powers of humor, eloquence, perception—are *The Secret of Swedenborg, Society the Redeemed Form of Man* and *Spiritual Creation*. Grand books these: America has produced nothing else like them; but Mark Twain, Melville, and Whitman, rather than Emerson or Hawthorne, are their parallels for virility of spirit and robustness of expression.

I

And now to come to the philosophy itself, it must first be inquired how we apprehend truth, as distinguished from sense perception and 'fact.' Suppose (in Sweden-borgian language) that God is pleased to call his children out of Egypt, and its 'scientifics,' its memory-knowledge, into the Promised Land of spiritual wisdom: how will he effect it?

Not by theology, with its myth and dogma; not by metaphysics, with its ratiocination (*God is not pleased to save his people by dialectic*); not by Science, with its limitation to fact and phenomena, James answers, but by Philosophy.

Philosophy—true philosophy, that is—operates by perception, intuition. It attends to the voice of the heart; to race instinct, vaguer and deeper yet; to *the hidden God.*

'Science confines herself only to phenomena and their relations, that is, to what is strictly verifiable in some sort by sense; and so stigmatizes the pursuit of being or substance as fatal to her fundamental principles. Philosophy, in short, is the pursuit of Truth, supersensuous truth, recognisable only by the heart of the race, or if by its intellect, still only through a life and power derived from the heart. Science has no eye for truth, but only for Fact, which is the appearance that truth puts on to the senses, and is therefore intrinsically second-hand, or shallow and reflective.'

'Ratiocination is doubtless an honest pastime, or it would not be so much in vogue as a means of acquiring truth. But the truth we are elucidating is Divine, and therefore is great enough to authenticate itself, or furnish its own evidence.'

'I shall not affront your self-respect,' James assures us, 'by affecting to demonstrate the truth of God's NATURAL humanity scientifically: in the first place, because it is not a fact of sense, and therefore escapes the supervision of science; and in the second place, because . . . I am anxious to conciliate your heart primarily, while your head is quite a subordinate aim. I cannot tell you a single reason, unprompted by the heart, why I myself believe the truth in question or any other truth for that matter. . . . In fact, I believe it simply because I love it, or it seems adorably good to me; and once having learned to love it, I could not do without it. It would in truth kill me, intellectually, to doubt it. . . . To my experience this is the only thing that in the long run authenticates truth to the intellect—*the heart's sincere craving for it.* I find that truth unloved is always at bottom truth unbelieved, however much it may be "professed"' [in *Society the Redeemed Form of Man*].

Sometimes James calls this philosophy of the heart Revelation. His point in appropriating this term is to underscore the self-evident, primary character of religious intuition; to distinguish it from other sorts of knowledge which are derivative from sense percep-

tion. It may be true of the intellect that it contains nothing which was not first in the senses; but it is distinctly not true of the soul. James scorns the orthodox notion of Revelation, which makes it to consist in deliverances of alleged historical occurrences and legal precepts.

Revelation conveys to us first principles which neither observation nor experience nor the reasonings thence derived could possibly warrant. There would be no object in the *revelation* of truth which could be arrived at empirically and verified by experiment. *Credo quia impossible:* it is in that sort of truth that Revelation deals. The deepest aspirations of the heart seem so palpably beyond our experience actual or possible as to disavow all phenomenal parentage. 'Flesh and blood hath not revealed it unto you': that much we feel sure of. The 'supremely true is never the probable. . . . ' 'The sphere of Revelation is the sphere of life exclusively, and its truth is addressed not to the reflective understanding of men, but to their living perception. Truth, to every soul that has ever felt its inward breathing, disowns all outward authority,—disowns, if need be, all outward *probability* or attestation of Fact. The only witness it craves, and this witness it depends upon, is that of good in the heart' [in ***The Secret of Swedenborg***].

About 'revelation' we cannot of course argue. It is primary and self-evident,—its own witness. We can merely avow it, and let it make its way into the hearts of all sincere and spiritual persons to whose attention it may come.

The 'precious facts of revelation, whether they fall within the sphere of my understanding or my affections, quite transcend the grasp of my critical faculty, and impose themselves upon my heart as an unmixed good, which I am just as incapable of measuring in terms of the analytic intellect, or reducing to the contrast of the true and the false, as I am of demonstrating to a blind man the pleasure of a gorgeous sunset, or reasoning a man without a palate into the savor of sugar' [in ***Society the Redeemed Form of Man***].

II

So much for James' theory of knowledge.

His philosophy may be called one of *Creation,* provided we are willing to give the term an ontological rather than a cosmological flavor. By this favorite word of his, James was far from meaning the process whereby Jehovah's *fiat* brought into time and space existence the natural world; and he was not in the least troubled over the early narrative of Genesis and whether the 'six days' were twenty-four hours or an aeon in duration. Evolution was, to him, quite conceivable as a scientific hypothesis, and as such could in no way conflict with a philosophic theory of creation.

It provokes James to vehemence that scientists and theologians alike take Nature as primary and ultimate, as a real creature. Nature is the least real of all existences, for nature is 'a mere implication of man, . . . exists *in itself* only to carnal thought, or an intelligence unemancipated from sense. . . . ' All that sensibly exists is 'but the mind's furniture.' The spiritual thought of man 'makes all sensible existence to fall within the unitary mind of the race. . . . '

Nature exists not in the least in her own right, is indeed completely void of substance. Her existence is strictly dependent upon humanity. Natural phenomena have 'no other function than outwardly to image or represent the things of human affection and thought, which alone make up the spiritual creation, or are alone objective to the divine mind' [in *The Secret of Swedenborg*].

The relation of Nature to man requires further explication. Nature indeed mirrors the race mind; but at the same time Nature is necessary to the mind of the individual man. Consciousness sets man off from his creator; Nature gives that consciousness the only possible ground for operation.

By imaging forth spiritual verities, natural objects acquaint the spirit of man with his own constitution. If my sensible experience 'did not furnish my rational understanding with a complete livery or symbolism of abstract human nature, with an infinitely modulated key wherewith to unlock all the secret chambers of the human heart, all the infinite possibilities of character among men—I should be forever destitute of moral perception . . . ; because thought is impossible without language; and language derives all its substance or body from things, or the contents of our sensible experience' [in *The Secret of Swedenborg*].

The true creature of God is man. God's essence is Love; as Swedenborg asserts in *Sapientia Angelica,* 'This is love, that one's own should be another's. . . . Conjunction of love is the result of reciprocity; and reciprocity can have no place in one person only. If it is thought possible it is merely imaginary. It is clear therefore that the Divine Love cannot but be and exist in others whom it may love, and by whom it may be loved. For since such a principle is in all love, it must be specially, that is, infinitely, in Love Itself.

'As for God, it is impossible for Him to love and to be loved reciprocally in others having anything of infinity, that is, anything of the essence and life of love in itself, or anything of the Divine.' In such case, God would be loving himself, for there is but one Divine Substance, one Very Reality. And of self-love, Swe-

denborg tells us, 'there cannot be the least trace in God, for it is altogether opposed to the Divine Essence.'

The real creation is the creation of creatures whom God may love. God alone is Life, and he cannot create other beings having life in themselves. Yet he must in some sense project his creatures off from himself, give them if not *being,* then at least *existence.* That the creatures should be real as God is real flouts every philosophic instinct, but they must possess at the least a sort of reality, a quasi-reality, a reality to themselves, else there is no escape from Pantheism, and God is loving not others but himself.

Sometimes James gives the name of creation only to the process whereby God projects us from himself; sometimes he makes it cover as well the return, the *redemption,* as he elsewhere calls it. Thus he says in the *Secret,* 'creation, philosophically viewed, involves a divided movement—one descending, generic, physical, by which the creature becomes set off, projected, alienated from the creator in mineral, vegetable, and animal form; the other ascending, specific, moral, by which the creature thus pronounced becomes *conscious of himself* as separated from his creative source, and instinctively reacts against the fact, or seeks to reunite himself with God.'

III

Creation as projection. How is God to set the creature off from himself without on the one hand making him objectively disjunct, real as God is real; or on the other reducing him to the mere appearance of Reality?

Taking a hint from Swedenborg, James declares that God can at most afford man only a provisional reality; man is not to possess life in himself, but merely to feel as if he possessed life in himself. He really lives in God, but he is to suppose himself acting and living 'as of himself.'

Is the self, then, purely illusory? Swedenborg does not help us to interpret this doctrine of the provisional self. James does. He asserts that we have to deal with two orders, two 'discrete degrees,' of the real. The self is illusory only from an absolute or philosophic point of view; but just as nature is *real* to the senses (illusory only when taken philosophically as possessing substance), so with the self: that is real on its own plane— that is, to consciousness.

Man, '*in so far as he is man,* does not exist to sense, but only to consciousness, and consequently human nature properly speaking is not a thing of physical but of strictly moral attributes. In so far as man exists to sense he is identical with mineral, vegetable and animal; and it is only as he exists to consciousness, that he becomes naturally differentiated or individualized from these lower forms, and puts on a truly human, which is an exclusively moral, personality' [in *The Secret of Swedenborg*].

James over and over distinguishes Creator from created as Substance from Form, Essence from Existence. God is our *Esse,* as we are his *Existere.* In the language of post-Kantian philosophy, our objectivity rests in God, while he attains to subjectivity (is this what the Christian doctrine of the Incarnation means?) only in us.

God neither possesses consciousness nor can be possessed by it. Human consciousness, indeed, is the wall between us and God, erected by God in order to give us a room of our own; and the wall hides us from our benefactor.

In giving us this consciousness from which he is hidden, this 'proud and sufficient selfhood' whereby man may 'absolutely deny his maker, and search the universe in vain to find a God' . . . , God truly creates, and how truly and completely! No legerdemain will suffice, no 'brisk activity.' The Incarnation of God in man, and through man to ultimate nature, is, indeed, rather to be thought of as patient suffering, as self-emptying. God took upon him the form of a servant, not merely in Jesus, but in his whole creative work. Creation is 'no ostentatious self-assertion, no dazzling parade of magical, irrational, or irresponsible power; it is an endless humiliation or prorogation of [God] himself to all the lowest exigencies of the created consciousness' [in *The Secret of Swedenborg*].

God indeed so completely abases himself, so veils his splendor from consciousness, so fears to break in upon the selfhood of his creatures, that he runs the risk of their confirming themselves in their first and perfectly natural thought that they really are, what they seem to themselves to be, self-sufficient.

'The palpable logic of creation—considered as an exact equation between the creative fulness and the created want—is that the former be utterly swallowed up by the latter, or actually disappear within its boundless stomach. In other words, in order to the creature coming to self-consciousness, or getting projection from the creator, it is necessary that the latter actually pass over to the created nature, cheerfully assume and eternally bear the lineaments of its abysmal destitution: so that practically, or in its initiament, creation takes on a wholly illusory aspect, the creature alone appearing, and the creator consequently reduced to actual non-existence, or claiming at most a traditional recognition' [in *The Secret of Swedenborg*].

Evil indeed comes into being along with the self. Not indeed that the self in itself is evil: in itself it is the

necessary platform for all man's subsequent moral and spiritual development. But not to recognize this, its provisional character, to confirm oneself in the belief that it is as absolute as it appears, is to fall into evil.

'The original sin of the creature . . . is that he feels himself to exist *absolutely;* and this is a sin he may well be unconscious of, since the boundless love of his creator is at the bottom of it. At least if God gave himself to his creature in a finite manner, there could be no danger of the sin being committed. But He gives himself to the creature without stint, in *infinite* measure; and the creature cannot help feeling therefore that he is life in himself' [in *Society the Redeemed Form of Man*].

IV

Here, then, is man projected from God, given what possible degree of otherness God can assign him. How, now, does the return movement effect itself? How does man reconcile himself with his creator? They have been made two on purpose that union may result, that they may be one, not by identity but by mutual love.

James found two answers more or less generally accepted in his day: moralism and ecclesiasticism; both he rejected as false, the more so for their arrogant pretensions to tremendous rightness. 'Who are Christ's spiritual foes, the only foes possible to him at this day? They are *friends . . . to his carnal or historic personality.* The first class may be for convenience sake called moralistic: being made up of that very large number of persons who live and thrive in contentment with the existing very infirm constitution of society: poets, literary essayists, scholars, artists, *transcendental aspirants or idealists* [italics mine], men of science . . . : all of whom blindly regard morality as the absolute law of human life, and look upon duty as the highest expression of human character, especially for other people.

'The second class is mainly ecclesiastical, of course, and lives and thrives in safe contentment, not with this world to be sure, but with another one which by all accounts is greatly more unequal or undivine and vicious even than this. It comprises all of every sect who regard the traditional church as directly in the line of man's spiritual welfare, or as supplying by Divine appointment a literal pathway to heaven' [in *Society the Redeemed Form of Man*].

Of these two classes, the former is really parasitic upon the latter. Moralism must be allowed a comparatively recent disease. The Church 'historically breeds, sweats, or throws off from its flanks, the civilized state of man [James uses the word *civilized* in the contemptuous sense of Fourier, much as the Marxians use *bourgeois*], and morality is the unquestionable law of civilization, the absolute substance, condition, and measure of all our civic righteousness.' 'Vast numbers of persons, indeed, are to be found in every community, who—having as yet attained to no spiritual insight or understanding—are entirely content with, nay, proud of, the moral "purple and fine linen" with which they are daily decked out in the favorable esteem of their friends, and are meanwhile at hearty peace with themselves' [in *Society the Redeemed Form of Man*]. Unitarianism is the movement which best represents moralism: it takes moral character and 'good works' as absolute, and as making men righteous in the sight of God. But Unitarianism still preserves the semblance of a church, though the disguise be more or less transparent. Outside the 'churches' entirely, moralism can and does flourish—as Transcendentalism, as 'ethical culture,' as philanthropy. The New England conscience, with its fussy self-consciousness and self-culture, seldom transcends moralism.

The church, however, is the more flagrant offender. Religion was intended to wean man not merely from the 'world' but from himself and his personal pretensions to righteousness; not to assure man of finding personal favor in the sight of God, but to promise redemption from all personal hopes and fears through incorporation in the mystical Body of Christ, solidarity, in other words, with all his kind. 'Religion was once a spiritual life in the earth, though a very rude and terrible one . . . Then she meant terror and amazement to all devout self-complacency in man; then she meant rebuke and denial to every form of distinctively *personal* hope and pretension towards God; then she meant discredit and death to every breath of a pharisaic or quaker temper in humanity, by which a man could be led to boast of a "private spirit" in his bosom, giving him a differential character and aspect in God's sight to other men . . .' [in *The Secret of Swedenborg*].

Conscience, the organ through which our spiritual life begins to operate, was never intended to make us self-complacent, thanking God that we are not as our sinful fellows. Like the Law, its office was meant to be purely negative: to convict us of sin. James follows St Paul in his indictment of legalism. All men have come short of the Law. But then the Law intended death, not life: it showed us the corruption of Adam and all his spiritual progeny in order that, turning away from personal and moral hopes, we should turn our hearts towards the Gospel and its promise of life to those who love the brethren.

Alas, the church, the representative or formal church, has often fallen into the legalism it arose to confound. It has assured men of absolute difference between saint and sinner, and given them hope of finding personal favor in God's sight.

Three sorts of religious experience are equally offensive to James: the Unitarian variety, which thinks of God primarily as a Divine Moral Being, who is gratified by our personal advances in ethical culture; the Catholic variety, whether Roman or Anglican, which considers right relations between God and man as essentially *ex opere operato,* ceremonially or ritually achieved; the Evangelical variety, which takes an erotic or at any rate sentimental turn, and dispenses with moral and ceremonial relations only in order to substitute a purely *personal* intimacy. James illustrates this third variety, still not extinct, by recalling an acquaintance of his, a loquacious person who said, 'I can't imagine how any one should have any distrust of God. For my part, if I were once in His presence, I should feel like *cuddling-up* to Him as instinctively as I would cuddle-up to the sunshine or fire in a wintry day.' James adds [in *Christianity the Logic of Creation*], 'It is beautiful to observe how utterly destitute Swedenborg found the angelic mind of all this putrid sentimentality, this abject *personal* piety.'

Though a fourth sort of religious experience with which he was familiar, the Calvinistic, was also offensive to James, he preferred it to the other three, on the ground of its virile contempt for moralism and sentimentality, its sense of the gulf between Creator and creature.

v

Only the shallow, whether within or without the church, can rest in moralism. The Law is our schoolmaster to bring us to Christ: those who most assiduously attempt to obey the Law will soonest confess their complete insufficiency for their task, will soonest surrender to the Gospel. Conscience similarly arrests our spiritual development at moralism only when we grow slothful, inattentive; when we pause at partial or purely ceremonial compliance with her precepts.

'It is very true that conscience is the sole arbiter of good and evil to man; and that persons of a literal and superficial turn of mind . . . may easily fancy themselves in spiritual harmony with it, or persuade themselves and others that they have fully satisfied every claim of its righteousness. But minds of a deeper quality soon begin to suspect that the demands of conscience are not so easily satisfied, soon discover in fact that it is a ministration of death exclusively, and not of life, to which they are abandoning themselves. For what conscience inevitably teaches its earnest votaries ere long is, to give up the hopeless efforts to reconcile good and evil in their practise, and learn to identify themselves, on the contrary, with the evil principle alone, while they assign all good exclusively to God' [in *The Secret of Swedenborg*].

The revelation of God in Jesus Christ offers the way out of legalism, and turns us from our self-righteousness and Pharisaism to a life beyond good and evil, a life of love and spontaneous brotherhood: The New

Testament 'addresses no inviting or soothing word of any sort to the saint, but only to the sinner. In one of these very rare gospel incidents which give us a glimpse into Christ's *personal* temperament, a saintly youth presents himself so aglow with all moral excellence, that Christ cannot help testifying a natural impulse of affection towards him; but he nevertheless straightway charges him to set no value upon his virtue as a *celestial* qualification. "If thou wilt be *perfect,* go and *sell all that thou hast . . .*" ' [in *The Secret of Swedenborg*].

The way out of legalism is first of all negative: to cease piquing ourselves upon our distinctions from others, our possessions, our virtues. How hardly shall the *rich man,* the man of parts, powers, personal pretensions, enter into the Kingdom of Heaven! Progress, indeed, 'whether public or private, seems to take place in an invariably negative way, that is, it always exacts a preliminary experience and acknowledgement of evil and error. Our vices and follies, collective and personal, have wrought us infinitely more advantage than our virtue and knowledge have ever achieved. Our best learning has come to us in the way of unlearning our prejudice, our best wisdom in the way of outgrowing conceit. . . . So palpably true is all this, that the fundamental grace of the religious character throughout history is humility; the primary evidence of a spiritual quickening in the soul, repentance' [in *The Secret of Swedenborg*].

At the time of Christ's advent, 'the stoics were the leaders of speculative thought. To fall back on all occasions upon one's moral force, and find a refuge against calamity in one's native strength of will, was the best recognized wisdom of man. . . . Christ probably had never heard of the stoics, but if he had he could only have been revolted by their doctrine, since his own was the exact and total inversion of theirs. The ideal of the stoic was rich and cultivated manhood. The ideal of Christ was innocent unconscious childhood. According to Christ, what men need in order to the full enjoyment of the divine favor is, to be emptied of all personal pretension, to become indifferent to all self-seeking or self-providence . . . ' [in *The Secret of Swedenborg*].

The message of Christianity has been sadly misinterpreted by the Church. The 'doctrine of the Christ is nothing more and nothing less than a revelation of the *essential* unity of God and man. . . . No matter what the occasion may have been, you find him invariably identifying himself with the interests of the most enlarged humanity, and ready to sacrifice every private tie which in any way involved a denial of the universal brotherhood of the race' [in *Lectures and Miscellanies*]. But the orthodox church has substituted for Jesus' zeal for humanity, a 'zeal for the person of Jesus himself.' The church 'makes Jesus under the name of a mediator, a perpetual barrier to the cordial intercourse

of God and man.' According to its teaching, Jesus 'exhausts the worth of human nature, so that no man created by God can ever appear tolerable to God, unless shining with his reflected lustre.' He converts Jesus into 'a monster of self-seeking,' and turns 'the grace of the gospel into a mere argument of his personal supremacy.' We believe in his personal pretensions, or we are damned. He is indeed alleged as having done us a signal favor (dying to reconcile us to an angry God); but he then claims our worship in return, 'under penalty of death, under penalty of everlasting misery. It is a purely diabolic claim, which all humanity disowns with loathing and contempt.'

The Lord is Swedenborg's name for the God-Man, God Incarnate. James refuses to identify the God-Man with the historic Jesus, but interprets the term as denoting the union of God with man. 'By the Lord regarded spiritually or rationally, then, we do not mean any literal or personal man, capable of being sensibly comprehended; but we mean that Divine and universal life in man, which grows out of the conjunction of the infinite Divine Love with our finite natural love . . . ' [in *Christianity the Logic of Creation*].

VI

What state, now, are we to look to as fulfilling the destiny of mankind? Moralism we know; *civilization,* its social equivalent, we know. The Law we know; but what then is the Gospel? How shall we conceive of the final union between God and man?

To none of these questions does Mr James afford us precise answers. Man's final state is nowhere open to scientific observation. Creation implies Redemption: James 'scorned to admit, even as a possibility, that the great and loving Creator, who has all the being and the power, and has brought us as far as *this,* should not bring us *through,* and *out,* into the most triumphant harmony' [in *The Literary Remains of the Late Henry James*]. But only revelation can give us belief in such a harmony; and revelation never discloses *facts* but only truths.

The state *beyond* moralism is spiritual Christianity; the state *beyond* 'civilization' is socialism, or, since *socialism* has come to mean a special sort of organization, we had better say Society. James does not look forward to the substitution for the existing governments of some other sort of government, but to the abolition of all government. In other words, he is a philosophic anarchist. Governments belong to the dispensation of the Law; with the full advent of the Gospel, they will pass away. James would say with St Augustine, *Ama et fac quod vis.*

The State will cease; so will the Church. Its sovereignty too is provisional and vicarious. When God's living presence in Society comes to be recognized, no representative ritual will be necessary. God will no longer be thought of as dwelling in temples made by hands; his glory will be made manifest in his tabernacling among men.

Men will have passed beyond the moral life, with its good and evil. Heaven and hell, 'both alike nothing but logical, ordinary, and inevitable spiritual incidents of our *natural* or race evolution,' will both finally 'coalesce in that final unitary display of omnipotent goodness and wisdom known as human SOCIETY, or the Lord's KINGDOM UPON EARTH' [in *The Literary Remains of the Late Henry James*].

The distinctive character of the moral life is choice; its distinctive operation is obedience to *duty.* 'The element of will or choice is everything in the moral life, and the fussy votaries of it accordingly are absurdly tenacious of their personal merit. But this element of will or choice scarcely enters appreciably into the spiritual life, unless into the lowest forms of it; and in all the higher or celestial forms it is unknown' [in *Society the Redeemed Form of Man*]. Choice will pass away in favor of spontaneity. We shall *love and do what we will.*

In some such *myth* would James deliver to us the New Jerusalem as it will *appear;* the *reality,* the essence of this consummation, will consist in the union of God with his creatures.

VII

And now we must ask what James means by God. As William has said of his father, he 'nowhere attempts by metaphysical or empirical arguments to make the existence of God plausible; he simply assumes it . . . ', or, as Miss Kellogg puts it [in *The Philosophy of Henry James: A Digest*], 'Mr James looks at creation instinctively from the creative side . . . The usual problem is,—given the creation, to find the creator. To Mr James it is,—given the creator, to find the creation. God is; of His being there is no doubt; but who and what are *we?*'

William James appears to have believed his father a theist, for all he admits that 'common-sense theism, the popular religion of our European race, has, through all its apparent variations, remained essentially faithful to pluralism,' while his father was an uncompromising monist. Theism, however,—or deism, as the elder James prefers to call it—holds to a belief in a God in some sense personal—either, as in Nicene Christianity, to the view that personality exists in God, or, with the older Unitarianism, to the view that God *is* a Person.

But James sharply rebukes all belief in a personal God, a God external to his creatures. God is not outside us,

another if greater self. He is not a self, not a person at all. The self is the badge and limitation of mankind.

James adduces Swedenborg's description of the angels as 'never thinking of the Lord from person, "because thought determined to person limits and degrades the truth. . . ." ; . . . the angels are amazed at the stupidity of church people "in not suffering themselves to be elevated out of the letter of the revelation, and persisting to think carnally, and not spiritually of the Lord,— as of his flesh and blood, and not of his infinite goodness and truth." '

To 'be a conscious person is to be *self*-centred, and to be God is to be not only without self-hood, but identical with universal life or being. . . . ' Spiritual nearness to God 'implies infinite personal remoteness from him, since God avouches himself to be universal life or being, which is flagrantly incompatible either with the fact or the sentiment of personality.'

James denies that God is 'a person finited from man by space and time,' and affirms that God is 'the inmost and inseparable life of every man great or small, wise or stupid, good or evil.' Even the literal Christian verity, he thinks, 'justifies us in ascribing to Him henceforth a distinctly NATURAL or impersonal infinitude, and so forever rids us both of the baleful intellectual falsities inherent in the conception of His supernatural personality, and of the enforced personal homage, precatory and deprecatory, engendered by that conception in the sphere of our sentimental piety.' He avows, 'I have not the least sentiment of worship for His name, the least sentiment of awe or reverence towards Him, considered as a perfect person sufficient unto Himself. That style of deity exerts no attraction either upon my heart or understanding. Any mother who suckles her babe upon her own breast, any bitch in fact who litters her periodical brood of pups, presents to my imagination a vastly nearer and sweeter Divine charm' [in *The Literary Remains of the Late Henry James*].

Who or what then is God? Swedenborg tells us [in *Sapientia Angelica*] that 'God is very man.' This has often been translated, conformably to the presupposition of orthodox theism, into 'God is a *man';* and the orthodox New Churchmen have made of it that Jesus, or the Lord, is alone God. James takes Swedenborg as meaning that God is not *a man,* but MAN. 'DEISM as a philosophic doctrine, that is, as importing an essential difference between the divine and human natures, or God and man, is a philosophic absurdity. There is no God but the Lord, or our glorified NATURAL humanity, and whatsoever other deity we worship is but a baleful idol of our own spiritual fantasy, whom we superstitiously project into nature to scourge us into *quasi* or provisional manhood, while as yet we are blind to the spiritual truth' [in *Society the Redeemed Form of Man*].

An oil painting of Henry James, Sr., circa late 1820s.

Heaven is heaven because the persons who compose it 'are used to acknowledge God only *in natural or associated form,* and not in any ideal spiritual or personal form which they might sensuously think more consonant with his perfection. . . . '

'In short, my reader, if human nature, the human race, mankind, or humanity, be not *spiritually* the only true name of God, exhausting the conception, then I at least do not know the true name of God, and certainly should never care to know it' [in *The Literary Remains of the Late Henry James*].

Does this mean that God is merely universal man, a kind of Platonic *idea* in which all men participate, by participation in which they become men? Or is James, like Comte, urging the substitution of Humanity for God as the object of our worship? This is the most obscure point in James' thought. He expressly dissociates himself from Comte's doctrine; and he would require some more dynamic relationship of creator to created than that of *idea* to particulars. Yet reject the ordinary theistic view, the Platonic, the Comtean, and what fourth view remains? God is affirmed Universal Man, the sole spiritual meaning and unity of the race; are we to understand that he (to use the personal pronoun as James does, for purposes of convenience) is more than this? Is he merely immanent in man, or does he transcend the utmost reach of our associated spiritual potencies?

The impression remains that James is sincere in rejecting the Comtean view of God as inadequate. God is more than the sum total of men, not in the least an abstraction, a generalization, an idea; all of these conceptions are too inert. James conceives of God as active, as indeed the *one really active* force in the universe, the one true substance. We do not make God in our image; but, in some deep if obscure sense, he makes us in his. It is as intolerable to James as to any Augustinian to believe that men's ordinary selves can effect any great work. The old theology gone, the problem of grace is still left. What have we which is not given us? It was a germinal conviction with James that 'the individual man, as such, is nothing, but owes all he is and has to the race nature he inherits, and to the society in which he was born. But how can there be more in the race nature, as such, than the sum total of our individual natures? The old dispute between Realist, Conceptualist, and Nominalist.

Mr James tells us that 'the race alone is *real* man, and invariably sets the tune, therefore, for us paltry, personal or phenomenal men to march to. And consequently we turn out good or evil persons—that is to say, even *phenomenally* good or evil men—just as we consent or refuse to keep step with the race's music' [in *The Literary Remains of the Late Henry James*]. But who sets the tune? And the *real man* is of course not the sum total of men, or an average of all men, but the spiritual meaning of man,—what he may be when Redemption has completed its work and the kingdoms of this world have become the kingdoms of our God, and man has assumed his redeemed form in Society. The *Real Man* is a sort of Aristotelian *final cause*: the point of life, of history, is its *End*.

If we ask James whether Man exhausts the meaning of God, he will perhaps tell us that God *in himself* is Infinite Love and Infinite Wisdom. Further, 'He of all beings is the *least* free, has the *least* power, to act arbitrarily, or follow his own caprice . . . ' [in *The Literary Remains of the Late Henry James*]. But God in himself we cannot know: we can know only the Lord, the God-Man, or 'the infinite Divine love and wisdom in union with every soul of man.'

In short, James denies a personal God outside of humanity, to regard God as the creative principle within humanity. We might call this principle the Life-Force, were it not that such an affiliation would do an injustice to James' insistence upon Man as the exclusive meaning of nature, and Society as the exclusive meaning of man.

Can such a world view be called Christian? William James [in *The Literary Remains of the Late Henry James*] quite rightly confesses inability 'to see any radical and essential necessity for the mission of Christ in his [father's] scheme of the universe. A "fall" there is, and a redemption; but . . . I cannot help thinking that if my father had been born outside the pale of Christendom, he might perfectly well have brought together all the other elements of his system, much as it stands now. . . .'

I quite subscribe to this judgment; indeed, I think Mr James' doctrine must have struck the ordinary church-goer, had he understood it, as atheism. Even William overmuch applies the word *theologian* to his father. The 'theology' is largely a matter of terminology. James was trained as a theologian, and his early reading in Swedenborg supplied him with a vocabulary which he became dexterous in turning to his own purpose. But this terminology, to which James assigned a purely 'humanitary' meaning, was inevitably taken by his readers, alike those professional at religion and those outside it, in approximately their customary theological sense. This made for confusion and misunderstanding, a misunderstanding which a certain perverse side of James apparently relished, and which he certainly made little effort to clear up.

But as James' God is something more than Comte's, so his philosophy transcends the sort of positivistic socialism he found about him. Towards the end of his life he confesses himself not the least indisposed to believe himself destined by the Divine providence—'either in my own person or the persons of my descendants—to the possible enjoyment of health, wealth, and all manner of outward prosperity, in the evolution of a final natural order for man on the earth, or the development of a united race-personality' [in *Society the Redeemed Form of Man*]. But this is not enough. When he is invited to regard the *natural destiny* of the race as adequate satisfaction to men's faith, he pronounces it 'inexpressibly revolting. For after all is said that can be said, it is a mere reduction to order of man's natural or constitutional life, with the spiritual, functional, or infinite side of his being left out. And are men content to deem themselves cattle, that they expect no higher boon at the hands of the DIVINE NATURAL HUMANITY but an unexampled provision for their board and lodging?'

It is the spirit that quickeneth. What is needed is not so much some further legislation, some reordering of our government or even our economic system. Given the social spirit, these changes will come of themselves. But the essence of the matter is not in them. The essence of the matter is the full consciousness on my part that *vir* is nothing apart from *homo;* that I live only in my race; and the consequent will to surrender myself to my fellows, and lose myself in the Lord, that is, in Society. Any other than a religious way of putting this seems to James to fall short of expressing his conviction that the whole process is not external but of the heart.

Mr James' uniqueness as a thinker lies precisely in this

identification of the spiritual and the social, not to the extinction of either the spiritual or the social, but to the enrichment of both.

Ralph Barton Perry (essay date 1935)

SOURCE: "Father and Son: Style and Criticism," in *The Thought and Character of William James, Vol. I: Inheritance and Vocation,* Little, Brown, and Company, 1935, pp. 125-45.

[*In the following excerpt from the first part of his Pulitzer Prize-winning biography,* The Thought and Character of William James, *Perry assesses James, Sr.'s literary style and his critical methods and theories. The critic also discusses the elder James's influence on his son William, both personally and professionally.*]

[For Henry James, Sr.] the most natural form of art, if art it can be called, was talk. Of all the arts, unless it be dancing, talk is the directest and most contemporaneous form of expression, the least detached and externalized. It is infused with bodily heat: like a blush or a gesture it reflects the feeling and the insight of the moment as it passes. The style of the natural talker is emphatic and mobile—meant to be listened to, with a brief and constantly shifting focus of attention, and not designed for contemplation. When this style is transferred from the spoken to the written word, it takes on an aspect of exaggeration, so that while James's talk was full-blooded, his writing at times seems plethoric. Nevertheless, as representing style of this intensely vital sort, he ranks high among English writers, despite the forbidding character of his subject matter. It is doubtful if Carlyle or Melville could have done better with James's theme. He was a humane Carlyle, an optimistic Melville, writing on theology and metaphysics.

His two elder sons, to each of whom style was a vocation, have set down their impressions of their father's peculiar quality. His books, resembling his talk and his character, could not fail, says Henry [in *Notes of a Son and Brother*], "to flush with the strong colour, colour so remarkably given and not taken, projected and not reflected, colour of thought and faith and moral and expressional atmosphere." We find him, says William [in *The Literary Remains of the Late Henry James*], "in the effortless possession of that style . . . which, to its great dignity of cadence and full and homely vocabulary, united a sort of inward palpitating human quality, gracious and tender, precise, fierce, scornful, humorous by turns, recalling the rich vascular temperament of the old English masters, rather than that of an American of today."

Wilkinson not only knew James but could himself vibrate to the same pitch. "As to the style and manner of your paper," he wrote to his friend in 1850, "it is the best that I have seen even from you; full of consecutiveness, throwing up the right images in the right places, and warm and stroke-full with your choicest blood and animal spirits." And, later, "If eulogy were necessary, I could tell you how I have been dragged along at the chariot-wheels of your snorting-sentences, with my hair all streaming out behind, while you were lashing on the speed in front; an attempt too ineffectual, to go my own way, while fastened by the feet to your impetuosity."

The visceral quality of James's style must not be taken to mean a lack of artistry. He had what can only be described as a *command* of the English language. He creates the impression of using language, or even of abusing it, rather than of accommodating himself to it. He departs from accepted usage in phrase and word, but always willfully—as though to say, "This is mine, and I may do with it what I like." Or, if this makes his procedure appear more self-conscious than it was, then let us say that in the heat of his conviction language was melted out of its stereotyped forms and remoulded or even amalgamated to his thought. Artful he certainly was not. But he had the artist's gift and the artist's flare. Once started on a period he elaborated and embroidered with evident creative joy. He let himself go.

He had a special, almost obsessive, interest in portraiture, and this sometimes betrayed him. The following letter from Dr. Holmes refers to James's acknowledged gift of representation:—

Boston, April 27, 1881

My dear Mr. James,—

You must let me, for my own sake, tell you what keen delight I enjoyed in reading your paper on Carlyle in the *Atlantic* [Vol. XLVII (1881)]. It is a very long time since any article in any of the reviews and magazines which now hold so much of the boldest and most brilliant thought of the time has given me so many thrills of pleasure. There is a great deal of truth to be told about Carlyle, who, whatever else he was, had the one quality of being an *interesting* character to study. One portrait cannot give the whole of him, but for a single portrait I doubt if any will be as effective, as well as truthful, as your own. If Rembrandt were alive to add his face as he would paint it, the pen and the brush would seem to belong together. Faithfully and sincerely yours,

O. W. HOLMES

Rembrandtesque he no doubt was, but without that master's balance. He seized some aspect of his subject which coincided with his present emphasis of feeling or conviction, and subordinated the rest. Hence, while his portraits were bold, their coloring was sometimes livid, and their extravagant emphasis gave them the quality of a cartoon or even of a caricature.

Despite his acknowledged mastery of style, it was a common complaint that James was obscure. He spoke and wrote as one having a message too great for his powers of expression. Benjamin Paul Blood, of Amsterdam, New York, whom we shall meet again as one of William James's discoveries, wrote to the latter in 1882: "I have a fancy for your family name. The first man of genius I ever saw alive was Henry James. It is a long while ago. He preached in the Presbyterian Church here. I received the impression that he was not a regular minister. And I forget the topic, but he seemed overpowered at the impossibility of uttering something. I remember that he thrilled me, and was badly 'enthused' himself. But he had that knack of saying the whole of a thing in a few words that has since been a study with me. . . ."

"Oh, that I might thunder it out," James once exclaimed, "in a single interjection that would tell the *whole* of it, and never speak a word again!" [quoted in ***The Literary Remains of the Late Henry James***]. Despite that gift for instantaneous wholeness to which Blood testifies, he found himself compelled to return again and again to the same task, and neither he nor his audience ever felt that he had said what it was in him to say. Obscurity was the price he paid for being a philosopher. Both his talk and his writing were the vehicle of his ideas, and these ideas were inherently difficult to grasp. He was not satisfied to communicate anything less than their full depth and subtlety. No one could understand him who was not prepared to think as searchingly and as boldly as he did. There were many, therefore, who found his manner and his wit entertaining but were baffled by his doctrines, feeling that there was a recondite and hidden meaning that escaped them—as indeed there was.

James's very versatility hampered his achievement. His son Henry felt his style was "too philosophic for life, and at the same time too living . . . for thought" [in *Notes of a Son and Brother*]. His doctrinal and intellectual preoccupation stood in his way not only as a man of letters, but as a practical or emotional leader of men; he was too dialectical to be a seer, and too fervid and dogmatic to be a philosopher of the modern critical school; while as to being the founder of a new religion, he had, alas! too good a sense of humor.

That William James resembled his father in personal flavor and genius is unescapable. It was said of his father that he was "aninted with the isle of Patmos"—that he was, in other words, both Hibernian and apocalyptic. The son was not apocalyptic, but he was Hibernian. Like his father he was warm-blooded, effervescent, and tenderly affectionate. Both men were unstable and impatient, though in neither case did this quality prevent long periods of intense and fruitful application. Alice James testified to this common quality of her father and her brother. She was writing in 1889 of William's European wanderings: "William, instead of going to Switzerland, came suddenly back from Paris and went home, having, as usual, exhausted Europe in a few weeks, finding it stale, flat and unprofitable. The only necessity being to get home, the first letter after his arrival, was, of course, full of plans for his return *plus* wife and infants; *he is just like a blob of mercury*—you can't put a mental finger upon him. Harry and I were laughing over him, and recalling Father, and William's resemblance (in his ways) to him. Though the results are the same, they seem to come from such a different nature in the two; in William, an entire inability or indifference to 'stick to a thing for the sake of sticking,' as someone said of him once; whilst Father, the delicious infant! couldn't submit even to the thralldom of his own whim; and then the dear being was such a prey to the demon homesickness."

According to the daughter's judgment the cause in the father's case was a sort of rebelliousness against control, and in the son's case a chronic infirmity of will—the lack of a capacity for laborious routine. Beyond a similarity of temperamental physiognomy which is immediately recognizable, any explanation in terms of deeper biological causes must remain entirely speculative. Both were fond of laughter. Both were men of extreme spontaneity, with a tendency to embellishment and immoderate affirmation; both were mobile or even erratic in a degree that made it impossible for them to drive readily in harness or to engage easily in organized, long-range, institutionalized activity.

Based on this sameness are two marked differences. The father was fundamentally robust, the son relatively frail, with long periods of bodily disability and neurasthenia. There was more of sheer aboriginal force in the father, while the son depended more on the temper and edge of his instruments. The other difference is no less unmistakable, but more difficult to describe. The father was, as we have seen, an eccentric. His originality was more self-contained—he conceded less. William James was more mundane, more highly socialized, and had more of what men call "taste." He had queer ideas, but *he* was not queer. With all his philosophical detachment he knew instinctively how to meet the world on its own terms, how to make himself understood, and how to be free and spirited without ever transgressing the accepted norms of convention or polite intercourse. While the father had his moments of spiritual inebriety, the son was more securely restrained. There was a warm and explosive emotionality in both men, but in the son the outward expression was further removed from the central fire—more highly elaborated and more subtly controlled.

Their similarity of temperament predisposed father and son to the same style of utterance. William was also a talking writer, with a genius for picturesque epithets, and a tendency to vivid coloring and extreme freedom of manner. William, too, was one who wrote primarily in order to express convictions, giving the result a peculiar quality of sincerity. Like his father he presented philosophy in the form of literature, and invited the attention of lovers of literature, who thereupon found themselves unequal to the philosophy. Hence W. D. Howells, accustomed to literature rather than to philosophy, found that William's *Pragmatism* was brilliant but not clear, "like his father, who wrote the **Secret of Swedenborg** and kept it." Both, when once launched upon the expression of a conviction, became interested in the expression for its own sake, and were also disposed to exaggeration by a sort of gathering enthusiasm, as though the blood were warmed by exercise. But while both were necessarily obscure to the one who, finding entertainment and looking for more of it, was in no mood to think metaphysically, there was a difference. The son might be puzzling, but he was not, like the father, recondite or cryptic. He had a better control of his instrument and an infinitely better understanding of his audience. The father was quite capable of delivering jeremiads to an unhearing or even unlistening age; the son would have found any unreciprocal and noncommunicating relation intolerable.

The outstanding fact is the son's loving admiration of his father as a man. It was not only a filial love—it was an idealizing love. He loved the kind of man his father was. And such being the fact he could not fail to grow like him, in his habits, his feelings, his appraisals, his attitudes. There is a letter written by William four days before his father's death and never read by him to whom it was addressed:—

> In that mysterious gulf of the past into which the present soon will fall and go back and back, yours is still for me the central figure. All my intellectual life I derive from you; and though we have often seemed at odds in the expression thereof, I'm sure that there's a harmony somewhere, and that our strivings will combine. What my debt to you is goes beyond all my power of estimating,—so early, so penetrating and so constant has been the influence. . . . As for us; we shall live on each in his way,—feeling somewhat unprotected, old as we are, for the absence of the parental bosoms as a refuge, but holding fast together in that common sacred memory. We will stand by each other and . . . try to transmit the torch in our offspring as you did in us, and when the time comes for being gathered in, I pray we may, if not all, some at least, be as ripe as you. As for myself, I know what trouble I've given you at various times through my peculiarities; and as my own boys grow up, I shall learn more and more of the kind of trial you had to overcome in superintending the development of a creature different from yourself, for whom you felt

responsible. I say this merely to show how my *sympathy* with you is likely to grow much livelier, rather than to fade—and not for the sake of regrets. . . . It comes strangely over me in bidding you good-bye how a life is but a day and expresses mainly but a single note. It is so much like the act of bidding an ordinary good-night. Good-night, my sacred old Father! If I don't see you again— Farewell! a blessed farewell!

Turning from the man to his ideas, it is natural to speak first of the elder James as a critic. He criticized by the application of his doctrines, and this procedure was peculiarly characteristic of him. But in his criticism, much of it impromptu, his doctrines appear in the closest fusion with his personal traits.

First of all, he *was* a critic, an inveterate critic, both of men and of ideas. Criticism pervaded his talk; and the interest of his talk lay largely in the fact that he had emphatic, startling, not to say sensational, opinions on any topic that arose. In stating these opinions he was no respecter of persons. Never was a man more opinionative than he who believed that "the curse of mankind, that which keeps our manhood so little and so depraved, is its sense of selfhood, and the absurd, abominable opinionativeness it engenders!" [in *The Literary Remains of the Late Henry James*]. "Truth," he said, is "essentially combative"—and he evidently rejoiced in the fact.

The following random recollections of Mrs. James T. Fields will convey something of the quality of the criticism that came most naturally to his lips: "Mr. James looked like an invalid, but was full of spirit and kindness. He not infrequently speaks severely of men and things. Analysis is his second nature. . . . He didn't fail to whip the pusillanimous clergy, and as the room was overstocked with them, it was odd to watch the effect. Mr. James is perfectly brave, almost inapprehensive, of the storm of opinion he raises." He seemed to take a special pleasure in baiting Bronson Alcott, whether in his presence or in his absence: "They got into a great battle about the premises, during which Mr. Alcott talked of the Divine paternity as relating to himself, when Mr. James broke in with, 'My dear sir, you have not found your *maternity* yet. You are an egg half hatched. The shells are yet sticking about your head.' To this Mr. Alcott replied, 'Mr. James, you are *damaged goods* and will come up *damaged goods* in eternity'. . . . He [Mr. James] said: 'In Mr. Alcott the moral sense was wholly dead, and the æsthetic sense had never yet been born!'"

In his journal for August 1853, Emerson refers to James's criticism of Thackeray, who was at that time in New York: "In New York, Henry James quoted Thackeray's speeches in society, 'He liked to go to Westminster Abbey, to say his prayers,' etc. 'It gave him the comfort,—blest feeling'. . . . He thought Thackeray could not see beyond his eyes, and has no ideas, and merely is a sounding-board against which his experiences thump and resound: he is the merest boy."

Two more examples of James's free handling of personalities, the first in a letter to Mrs. James T. Fields: "I am reading Theodore Parker's life with edification. I can't help feeling continually what a capital thing it had been for Theodore if he could only once or twice have honestly suspected what a poor puddle after all his life was, even when it most reflected his busy activity. But this is strictly between ourselves, as the saints must have public reverence."

The second is extracted from a letter written in 1868 to Wilkinson, who has just seen Elizabeth Peabody in London: "Elizabeth Peabody is a very odd personage in every point of view, as you must have observed; but her judgment in my estimation is her feeblest part. She is enthusiastic for everything exceptional, and has a contempt for the commonplace which will condemn her to dark corners to all eternity, if she doesn't look out betimes."

As can easily be imagined, James's methods of criticism have not always been approved. Referring to the relatively flattering picture of Hawthorne contained in the Saturday Club letter of 1861, Hawthorne's biographer speaks of "the late Henry James" as "a humorous rhetorician, over-frank in his besprinkling of adjectives, which sometimes escaped the syringe at random, and hit no mark" [quoted in F. B. Sanborn's "The Friendships of Hawthorne," in *The Hawthorne Centenary, 1905*]. It will be recalled that in speaking of his friend's harsh comments on Carlyle, Emerson accused him of a "passion for perversity." But James's attacks were neither random nor perverse. They were reckless, but they invariably had a meaning and pointed a moral. They were for the most part directed against arrogance or complacency. As William James said [in *The Literary Remains of the Late Henry James*], "Nothing so endlessly besotted in Mr. James's eyes, as the pretension to possess personally any substantive merit or advantage whatever, any worth other than your unconscious uses to your kind! Nothing pleased him like exploding the bubbles of conventional dignity, unless it was fraternizing on the simplest and commonest plane with all lowly persons whom he met. To exalt humble and abase proud things was ever the darling sport of his conversation,—a conversation the somewhat reckless invective humor of which, when he was in the *abasing* mood, often startled the good people of Boston, who did not know him well enough to see the endlessly genial and humane intuition from which the whole mood flowed."

William James went on to quote the opinion that his father's "abasing" was at bottom an abasement of himself: "He was of such an immense temperament, that when you took him to task for violating the feelings of others in his talk, he would score you black and blue for your distinctions; and all the while he made you feel that the origin of the matter was his divine rage with *himself* at still being so dominated by his natural selfhood which would not be shaken off. I have felt in him at times, away down at bottom of the man, so sheer a humility and self-abasement as to give me an idea of infinity." In other words, there is a phase of spiritual development in which man must first learn to despise the very selfhood which he has first to acquire; and James's amiable ferocity was an exercise in contempt for selfhood, on his own part and in behalf of others. I have been tempted to say that his attacks were impersonal. Perhaps it would be better to say that they were *merely* personal, for he continued to smile lovingly upon the universal humanity incarnate in the individual object of his disapprobation.

If there was an implied philosophy in James's extemporaneous derogation of persons, there was an explicit philosophy in his more deliberate criticism. There was, in the first place, a clearly recognizable attitude to art. Inasmuch as, of his two oldest sons, William had a predilection for the art of painting and Henry for the art of letters, this was a matter of some importance in the domestic circle. Fundamentally, James's disparagement of art expressed his sense of the overwhelming importance of religion. This, I take it, underlay his reiterated opinion that art was too "narrowing"—literature, or any other art, is so much less than life! His comments on Italy suggest that he had a weakness for art. He was writing in 1869 to his son Henry, who was then discovering Italy and was overwhelmed with shameless joy. In its half-guilty turning from pleasing spectacles to reform and salvation, this passage is as profoundly characteristic of the son William as of his father:—

> It is very good to get your first impressions of Rome, and I can sympathize with you very fully. I feel that I myself should be horribly affected there by the historical picturesque. I should be extremely sensitive to it objectively, and would therefore all the more revolt from it subjectively, as hearing underneath it all the pent-up moaning and groaning soul of the race, struggling to be free or to come to consciousness. I am glad on the whole that my lot is cast in a land where life doesn't wait on death, and where consequently no natural but only an artificial picturesque is possible. The historical consciousness rules to such a distorted excess in Europe that I have always been restless there, and ended by pining for the land of the future exclusively. Condemned to *remain* there I should stifle in a jiffy.

The failure of art consists in being spiritually sterile—a mere reiteration of nature and echo of worldliness:

"It is melancholy to see the crawling thing which society christens art, and feeds into fawning sycophancy. It has no other conception of art than as polished labor, labor stripped of its jacket and apron, and put into parlor costume. The artist is merely the aboriginal ditcher refined into the painter, poet, or sculptor. Art is not the gush of God's life into every form of spontaneous speech and act; it is the talent of successfully imitating nature—the trick of a good eye, a good ear, or a good hand. It is not a really infinite life, consubstantiate with the subject and lifting him into ever new and unpremeditated powers and achievements; it is an accomplishment, a grace to be learned, and to be put off and on at one's convenience. Accordingly society establishes academies of art, gives out rules for its prosecution, and issues diplomas to the artist, by which he may be visibly discriminated from ordinary people. But always on this condition, that he hallow, by every work of his hands, its existing prejudices and traditions; that he devote his perfectly docile genius to the consecration of its morality" [in *Moralism and Christianity*].

Furthermore, the artist is peculiarly prone to commit the cardinal sin of attaching importance to himself. The following extract is from a letter written by James in 1854 to his niece, Catharine James, who has asked his help in behalf of a friend with literary ambitions:—

> I suppose your friend wouldn't thank me for any advice on the general subject of making literature a profession, and accordingly I will keep any I might otherwise have to give, diligently to myself. But I may say to *you,* once and away, that literary leisure does not seem to me a boon to be highly coveted. The literary class, as a class, are not respected, because they are not respectable. Individuals among them, like Mr. Irving, Miss Sedgwick, Mr. Emerson, and a few others, all of whom could be easily named, adorn the profession by their own honesty and uprightness, but literary people are generally very despicable. Their 'motive power' is intellectual vanity for the most part, and the machinery by which it works is lying, theft, fraud and every species of unmanliness and unwomanliness. If you knew the literary people I know, people of name, moreover, you would sicken at the words. There are two very bad things in this American land of ours, the worship of money and the worship of intellect. Both money and intellect are regarded as good in themselves, and you consequently see the possessor of either eager to display his possessions to the public, and win the public recognition of the fact. But intellect is as essentially *subordinate* a good as money is. It is good only as a minister and purveyor to right affections, and whenever therefore it puts on airs of independence, and frequents public places, it is as sad and vulgar a sight as to see the kitchen-maid exalted to the parlour, and diffusing the aroma of her culinary presence over the sacred precinct.

*Henry, Jr., and William James, circa 1904 or 1905, probably in
Cambridge.*

In attacking art as it exists, James, like Plato, was thinking of art as it ought to be. A fundamental fault of what the world calls art, and esteems as such, is its divorce from honest conviction. Speaking of Sweden-borg, he said [in **Substance and Shadow**]: "There seems a ludicrous incongruity, for example, between his grim, sincere performances and the enamelled offspring of Mr. Tennyson's muse, or the ground-and-lofty-tumbling of an accomplished literary acrobat like Macaulay. It is evident that he himself never once dreamed of conciliating so dainty a judgment. It would be like tying the mainsail of a man-of-war by a cambric handkerchief. His books are a dry, unimpassioned, unexaggerated exposition of things he daily saw and heard in the world of spirits, and of the spiritual laws which these things illustrate; with scarcely any effort whatever to blink the obvious outrage his experiences offer to sensuous prejudice, or to conciliate any interest in his reader which is not prompted by the latter's own original and unaffected relish of the truth."

The true artist, then, will "give natural body to spiritual conception"; he will work "only to satisfy an in-spiration, thus from attraction, and therefore divine-ly"—his business being "to glorify MAN in nature and in men." But art, even in the higher sense, must always be inadequate: "The poet, painter or musician is not the perfect man, the man of destiny, the man of God, because the perfect man is so pronounced by his life or action rather than by his production. He is not consti-tuted perfect by any work of his hands however mer-itorious, but simply by the relation of complete unity between his inward spirit and his outward body, or what is better, between his ideas and his actions" [in **Lectures and Miscellanies**].

Such being James's theory of art and literature, his considered judgments of literary men will naturally turn on the extent to which these are vehicles of truth. Thus Thackeray was ignorant of true religion, but in creat-ing Becky Sharp he builded better than he knew: "His philosophy of man is not up to his instincts. Thus in attempting to paint a very wicked woman, he, much to his own surprise, leaves her free of any hearty con-demnation. . . . What is the explanation of this fact, whether Mr. Thackeray be aware of it or not? Why do we justify Becky in our inmost hearts, even while condemning her vicious methods? Because it is entirely transparent throughout the book that her evils have not their source in herself, but only in her externally defective fellowship with others. . . . Her whole life was a struggle to get a position, to become herself, to burst the sepulchral environment in which she was born, and come forth into God's genial and radiant air. You might as well expect a drowning man to respect the tails of your coat, if they come within his reach, as expect so vital a soul as this to rest content in that stifling atmosphere, or forego any chance, however conventionally denounced, of freeing herself from it. . . . No, it is sheer error to pronounce the actions ascribed to Becky in this book, *hers*. They were not hers. She was the hand that executed them, but the soul that animated or inspired them was the inharmonic society in which she was born and matured."

As between Dickens and Thackeray, James preferred the latter. Dickens's moralism, being trite and shallow, must needs be seasoned with exaggeration: "Dickens has no suspicion of astral depths in man. Life is to him a pure surface, bounded on the north by the head, on the south by the belly, on the east by the heart, on the west by the liver, and whatsoever falls without these palpable limits is double-Dutch and moonshine. . . . When one's whole conception of the mystery and majesty of life is limited to the obvious antagonism of virtue and vice, of the church and the play-house, it is evident that the conception will not carry him a great way, and that the jaded palates of novel-readers will speedily crave a more piquant refection. Hence you find all Dickens's virtue to be necessarily tainted. His virtuous men are like game on the turn, appetising to a sophisticated taste, but revolting to a healthy one" [in the *New York Tribune*, November 13, 1852].

The following letter to Turgenev turns again on that idea of racial solidarity which must qualify our judgment of the individual. He likes Turgenev because he is radically pessimistic. Since the way to the heights leads through the depths, the sooner one descends to total disillusionment the sooner can one mount again to hope.

Cambridge, June 19, 1874

My dear Sir,—

It seems a pity that you should be ignorant of the immense appreciation your books have in this region, and the unfeigned delight they give to so many good persons. I am not myself a representative reader, but I have some leisure at least, which all your readers have not got, and I may therefore without presumption perhaps, constitute myself your informant on their behalf. My son (Henry James, Jr., now in Europe) lately published a critical sketch

of your writings in the *North American Review,* which I think he sent you a copy of. But this was only an individual token, and what I want to say to you is, that my son's high appreciation of your genius is shared by multitudes of very intelligent people here. . . . Your books came out here some five or six years ago in German and French translations, and became known at once to a few appreciative readers, and in a very brief while made their way to the acquaintance of all the reading world. They have indeed made themselves so widely honoured, that whatever you write is now immediately translated for our periodicals, or for independent publication, and the only matter left for the public to differ about is the pronunciation of your name. And some recent events lead me to hope that even this controversy, though still lively, will not be as protracted, nor as envenomed as that over Homer's birthplace.

I think the verdict of the large circle of admirers you have in this place is, that the novel owns a new power in your hands, a deeper fascination than it ever before exerted. Doubtless in this realm also it is true, *vixere fortes ante Agamemnona*. Men and women of great and surprising genius have made romance an instrument second only to the drama, as an educative power over the emotions. But it must be said of the greatest of these, that the most they do is, either like Scott to give us stirring pictures of human will *aux prises* with outward circumstance, and finally victorious over it; or else, like George Sand, Thackeray and George Eliot, to give us an idea of the enervating and palsying effect of social convention upon the conscience, in rendering men sceptical, self-indulgent and immoral. But you as a general thing strike a far deeper chord in the consciousness of your reader. You sink your shaft sheer through the world of outward circumstance, and of social convention, and shew us ourselves in the fixed grasp of fate, so to speak, or struggling vainly to break the bonds of temperament. Superficial critics revolt at this tragic spectacle, and pronounce you cynical. They mistake the profound spirituality of your method, and do not see that what touches the earnest heart of man, and fills it with divinest love and pity for its fellow-man, is infinitely more educative than anything addressed to his frivolous and self-righteous head.

Such, in a measure, is the tribute we pay your sympathetic genius, when we talk of you here in the evening on the piazza of the house, facing the setting sun. One of the young ladies present wonders whether an eye so at one with nature as yours, will ever do for American landscape what you have done for Russia; and her companion, whom I sometimes fancy is worthy to take her place beside some of your own heroines, wonders whether our humanity will ever be so defined as to justify an observer like you coming over to look at us. I can only emphasize their wonder by adding my own. But should you ever cross the ocean, you must not fail to come to Cambridge, and sit with us on the piazza in the evening, while you tell us between the fumes of your pipe what the most exercised and penetrating genius of the old world discerns, either of promise or menace for humanity in the civilization of the new.

Please look kindly on my intrusion, and believe me, my dear Sir, with the greatest esteem and admiration, yours,

HENRY JAMES

Turgenev's reply completes the incident, though it sheds no light save on the writer's modesty:—

Carlsbad, Aug. 10, 1874

My dear Sir,—

Three days ago I sent to J. Osgood, the editor of the *North American Review,* a letter to your son, Mr. Henry James, Jr., whom I supposed in America; and today I receive your letter which you have addressed to my editor in Riga, Mr. E. Behre. My doctor has ordered me to Carlsbad, which seems to be very good for gouty people; and I have just had a violent attack in Russia, where I passed the last three months.

Your letter is too flattering by far, my dear Sir. I am very happy indeed to find such benevolent readers in America and I am proud of your sympathy; but you place me on a much too high level. Modesty is an awkward thing; people don't believe in its sincerity—and people are generally right: I hope it is not modesty, but an exact appreciation of my own faculties, which tells me that I am not *ejusdem farinæ* with Dickens, G. Sand or G. Eliot. I am very content to fill a second or even a third place after these truly great writers.

Nevertheless accept my heartfelt thanks for all the good and kind things you say to me in your letter; and let me assure you, that it would make me the greatest pleasure not to "smoke my pipe under your verandah"—I don't use tobacco—but to enjoy a quiet and pleasant conversation with the intelligent men and women of your society. Will this pleasure be ever realized? That I cannot say with certitude. I am rather too old now and too weak in health for undertaking such long journeys—but I still cherish the idea of a visit to your new world, so different from the old one. But all this is yet very uncertain. Believe me, my dear Sir, yours very truly,

IVAN TURGENIEW

Of much more serious importance was James's criticism of Emerson and Carlyle. It is natural to couple these two men together as familiar divinities in the James household. Father and sons must deal with them, and each must settle his account. With the father they end by becoming symbols of partial truths, transcended in that completer truth of which he felt himself a vehicle. This completer truth was already outlined in his mind when he met them, and served as a standard by which they were judged: "Before I knew Emerson my intellect had been fully aroused to discern the great mystery of the spiritual creation, or the truth of incarnate Deity, and I never felt disposed, accordingly, to look upon Emerson in any other light than as a feeble, tentative first-fruits of a spiritual Divine resurrection in our nature which would one day be universal." In other words, James regarded Emerson as a spiritual manifestation, and not as a source of ideas. Even as an imitation of perfection, he could not satisfy James because of what the latter thought to be a personal incompleteness, an absence, namely, of "conscience." Emerson embodied innocence of the prenatal sort, rather than the seasoned blessedness that accrues from conflict and struggle. Having no conviction of sin, he was incapable of repentance, and therefore could not know that supreme joy of being united with God, which is the highest moment of life and the purpose of creation:—

> My recently deceased friend Mr. Emerson . . . never felt a movement of the life of conscience from the day of his birth till that of his death. . . . He appeared to be utterly unconscious of himself as either good or evil. . . . I am satisfied that he never in his life had felt a *temptation to bear false-witness* against his neighbour, *to steal, to commit adultery,* or *to murder*; how then should he have ever experienced what is technically called a conviction of sin? . . . I myself had known all these temptations—in forms, of course, more or less modified—by the time I was fourteen or fifteen years old; so that by the time I had got to be twenty-five or thirty (which was the date of my first acquaintance with Emerson) I was saturated with a sense of spiritual evil—no man ever more so, possibly, since I felt thoroughly *self*-condemned before God. . . . The only holiness which Emerson recognized, and for which he consistently lived, was innocence. [***The Literary Remains of the Late Henry James***]

Carlyle, like Emerson, was too little of a philosopher to satisfy James. "He is an artist, a wilful artist, and no reasoner. He has only genius." But he differed from Emerson in being an extravagant manifestation of that very conscience which Emerson lacked. If Emerson was a premature synthesis, Carlyle was a belated antithesis. It was to Carlyle's credit that he recognized evil and pitted the moral will against it, but he never rose to that higher understanding in which their opposition is seen as the necessary condition of a fuller spiritual growth. Like the voice from the gallery that hisses the villain, he lacked an æsthetic sense of the dramatic whole:—

The main intellectual disqualification, then, of Carlyle, in my opinion, was the absoluteness with which he asserted the moral principle in the human bosom, or the finality which his grim imagination lent to the conflict of good and evil in men's experience. He never had the least idea, that I could discover, of the true or intellectually educative nature of this conflict, as being purely ministerial to a new and final evolution *of human nature itself* into permanent harmony with God's spiritual perfection.... On the contrary, he always expressed himself to the effect that the conflict was absolutely *valid in itself;* that it constituted its own end, having no other result than to insure to good men the final dominion of evil men, and so array heaven and hell in mere chronic or fossil antagonism.... He was mother Eve's own darling cantankerous Thomas, in short, the child of her dreariest, most melancholy old age; and he used to bury his worn, dejected face in her penurious lap, in a way so determined as forever to shut out all sight of God's new and better creation [in ***The Literary Remains of the Late Henry James***].

In short, while Emerson was nonmoral, and Carlyle moral, the truth as James himself saw it was supermoral. The quality of Emerson's life was an anticipation of perfection, in its spontaneity and perfect faith. Carlyle, through the bitterness of his moral dualism, adds content but loses form. True blessedness is a higher flight in which the form is recovered and envelops the richer content.

It is clear that James did not conceal his opinions of men and of ideas, and although these opinions were not commonly addressed to his sons, they were overheard and taken to heart. When William wrote from Brazil in 1865, apropos of nothing but the current of his own nostalgic reverie, "I think Father is the *wisest* of all men whom I know," he meant that he trusted his father's impromptu judgment. It was the same trust which impelled him to write, immediately after his father's death: "It is singular how I'm learning every day now how the thought of his comment on my experiences has hitherto formed an integral part of my daily consciousness, without my having realized it at all. I interrupt myself incessantly now in the old habit of imagining what he will say when I tell him this or that thing I have seen or heard."

This sympathetic responsiveness to his father's habitual utterances accounts for two of William James's most characteristic habits of thought. In the first place, he had a constitutional distaste for orthodoxy. As soon as ideas became established, or were proclaimed with unction and airs of authority, they became repugnant. You could spoil any good thing for him by converting it into an institution. That was the way the elder James felt about Swedenborgianism and Christianity, and the younger about science. Closely associated with this first attitude is a disposition to champion the weak and assail the strong. Look over the list of those whom William James attacked most severely, of those for whom he refused to

make allowances, and they will prove to be men with some pride of office—some touch of insolence, smugness, self-importance, or complacency. In short, William, like his father, was sometimes in an "abasing mood."

How far William James shared, or was affected by, his father's judgment upon art will appear more clearly in the sequel. It belongs to the story of his vocation. Suffice it to say that his abandonment of painting for science and philosophy was in his father's favor, since it meant a search for truth and the use of style as a vehicle of ideas. We shall also learn more later of William James's opinions of literature, since these opinions came to clearest expression in his intercourse with his brother. But his attitude to Carlyle and Emerson concerns his relations with his father. These men were his father's friends and contemporaries, and they became known to the son through the medium of his father's highly interpretative and peculiarly personal characterization of them.

What gifts, then, did these fairy godfathers bestow on William James in his youth? Neither gave him his philosophy, both gave him precepts and apt quotations. They both influenced his style in his most impressionable period. He responded to Emerson in his acquiescent or optimistic moods, to Carlyle in his warlike moods. In 1903 he reread Emerson extensively, "volume after volume," in preparation for his Centenary address at Concord. In that address he confirmed his father's opinion that Emerson was a seer rather than a thinker. What, then, did this seer see? For William James, Emersonian truth consisted essentially in the vision of a deeper unity behind multiple appearances. Even the individualism or nonconformism of Emerson, which was "the hottest side of him," was not pluralistic. If he separated one individual from other individuals morally, it was only to unite them all on their cosmic side, as being potentially "mouthpieces of the Universe's meaning." This teaching is allied to James's teaching of the unique preciousness and valid claim of each individual, however obscure or despised; but it is a different teaching, divided by all that separates monism from pluralism. For whatever concessions William James made to monism, and he made many, he never conceded that the world had one meaning, indivisible and authoritatively perfect, of which human individuals are the channels. These reserves, together with the suggestion (again reminiscent of his father) that Emerson did not sound the depths of the religious experience, appear in the following letter to W. C. Brownell, written apropos of the latter's *American Prose Masters*:—

Cambridge, Sept. 2, 1909

Dear Mr. Brownell,—

I have read your splendid essay (on Emerson) and return it.... It seems to me wonderfully true both in its praise and its restrictions, but I think it might gain in places by a little consideration. . . . The word "religion" is very ambiguous, but there is an immense field of what it denotes that lay outside of Emerson's nature, so I agree with your strictures on Woodberry's claim. I agree also entirely in your light estimate of his monistic metaphysics, and his Platonic philosophy in general. He evidently had no capacity whatever for metaphysic argument, but he found that certain transcendentalist and Platonic phrases *named* beautifully that *side* of the universe which for his soul (with its golden singing sense that the vulgar immediate is as naught relatively to the high and noble, gleeful and consoling life behind it) was all-important. So he abounded in monistic metaphysical talk which the very next pages belied. I see no great harm in the literary inconsistency. The monistic formulas do express a genuine direction in things, though it be to a great extent only ideal. His dogmatic expression of them never led him to *suppress the facts they ignored,* so no harm was done. (See, *e.g.,* the last couple of pages of his essay on history.) Of course to me they seem simply *weak,* those Platonic formulas, but there are readers whom they inspire, so let them pass! . . .

Thanking you for the pleasure the essay has given me, I am very truly yours,

Wm. James

The heat which he missed in Emerson, William James found in Carlyle. The essays published in 1898 under the title of *The Will to Believe* were composed in part as early as 1879, and they prove how deeply in his youth their author had drunk of Carlyle. When the moment of solution comes it is often Carlyle that provides the solvent. Especially is this true of the problem of evil, where the solution is found in the "gospel of work, of fact, of veracity." "The only escape," writes James, "is by the practical way. And since I have mentioned the nowadays much-reviled name of Carlyle, let me mention it once more, and say it is the way of his teaching. No matter for Carlyle's life, no matter for a great deal of his writing. What was the most important thing he said to us? He said: 'Hang your sensibilities! Stop your sniveling complaints, and your equally sniveling raptures! Leave off your general emotional tomfoolery, and get to work like men!'"

In adopting this gospel William James specifically and with deep conviction rejected that very solution which was his father's: the transcendence, namely, of moral distinctions in a higher or æsthetic flight of the spirit. The father had reproached Carlyle for grimly accepting the finality of the moral struggle; the son says, *with* Carlyle, that "it feels like a real fight."

Quentin Anderson (essay date 1957)

SOURCE: "'Father's Ideas,'" in *The American Henry James,* 1957. Reprint by John Calder, 1958, pp. 51-82.

[*Anderson is an American critic, educator, and editor. In the following excerpt, he contends that Henry James, Jr.'s published reminiscences of his father prove the son's in-depth understanding of his father's philosophy, and that the younger James subsequently employed his father's beliefs in his fiction.*]

In 1885, the year of the publication of *A Little Tour in France* and the serialization of *The Bostonians,* Henry James received copies of *The Literary Remains of the Late Henry James* from his brother William. The father they both admired and cherished had died in 1882. In his letter of thanks and appreciation Henry Junior is forthright about what had been called, in the family circle, "father's ideas." Referring to the extracts William had selected from their father's work, he writes: "It comes over me as I read them (more than ever before,) how intensely original and personal his whole system was, and how indispensable it is that those who go in for religion should take some heed of it. I can't enter into it (much) myself—I can't be so theological nor grant his extraordinary premises, nor throw myself into conceptions of heavens and hells, nor be sure that the keynote of nature is humanity, etc. But I can greatly enjoy the spirit, the feeling, and the manner of the whole (full as this last is of things that displease me too,) and feel really that poor Father, struggling so alone all his life, and so destitute of every worldly or literary ambition, was yet a great writer" [quoted in *Letters,* I].

This is, and was meant to be, a rather complete disavowal of interest. It is also plainly uninformed, since the elder James for many years before his death had not been much concerned about "heavens and hells," though he formally granted a plurality of both. These regions may indeed have bulked large in the infant Henry's fancy, which must have found Blakean imagery by far the most arresting part of his father's spate of talk on these topics. It is in keeping with this sense of his remoteness from his father's "system" that he speaks of the elder James's originality, his sometimes deplorable, though often admirable, "manner," and his greatness as a *writer.*

The question William raised for Henry in putting together the *Literary Remains* is hardly the one William had posed himself. We may imagine William to have asked: "What capacity for seizing the flux of experience in discussable terms did my father have?" But the novelist (who was not concerned with his father's technical competence in philosophy) makes a response to the *Literary Remains* which is really a response to the question, "May my father be called a writer, a person who makes solid, graceful, appealing, his rendering of experience?" Henry has found a tactful way of replying, but he has not even conceived of William's question. And he is *not* "sure that the keynote of nature is humanity": precisely the view that I have attributed to him. He doesn't "go in for" religion, and that seems to be that.

Yet, when one turns to *A Small Boy and Others* (1913) and *Notes of a Son and Brother* (1914), one finds that the matter is a good deal more complicated. The period which James calls *The Middle Years,* is long over, and James's sense of his father's work and the part his father had played in his childhood and youth testifies to a grasp of his father's most general intentions which, in the middle years, he had not explicitly acknowledged. The two volumes of reminiscences make it plain to those who know the elder James's work that it was finally Henry, not William, who best understood his father's spirit.

The view of the elder James that one might expect from the child of the "visiting mind" and from the youth who wanted to be a writer is clearly expressed in a number of places. The following passage [from *Notes of a Son and Brother*] concerns the fact that the family did not in any way publicly celebrate the faith which so pervaded the family atmosphere: "Well do I remember . . . how I was troubled all along by just this particular crookedness of our being so extremely religious without having, as it were, anything in the least classified or striking to show for it; so that the measure of other-worldliness pervading our premises was rather a waste, though at the same time oddly enough a congestion—projecting outwardly as it did no single one of those usual symptoms of propriety any of which, gathered at a venture from the general prospect, might by my sense have served: I shouldn't have been particular, I thought, as to the selection." The child, as well as the man, hungered for things *represented*—things which asserted themselves with a "European" salience.

> The oddity of my own case, as I make it out so far as it involved a confused criticism, was that my small uneasy mind, bulging and tightening in the wrong, or at least in unnatural and unexpected, places, like a little jacket ill cut or ill sewn, attached its gaping view, as I have already more than enough noted, to things and persons, objects and aspects, frivolities all, I dare say I was willing to grant, compared with whatever manifestations of the serious, these being by need, apparently, the abstract; and that in fine I should have been thankful for a state of faith, a conviction of the Divine, an interpretation of the universe—anything one might have made bold to call it—which would have supplied more features or appearances. Feeling myself "after" persons so much more than after anything else—to recur to that side of my earliest and most constant consciousness which might have been judged most deplorable—I take it that I found the sphere of our more nobly suppositious habitation too imperceptibly peopled; whereas the religious life of every other family that could boast of any such (and what family didn't boast?) affected my fancy

as with a social and material crowdedness [in *Notes of a Son and Brother*].

All this has the note of the deprivation we might have expected James as child and youth to feel. He felt that the "sources" were superabundant, the "appearances" meager. But at the time of the writing of these reminiscences, the question of the "sources" wears a different face. In a passage immediately preceding the first of those quoted above he says that "such invidious homes," homes, that is, where religious observances took on apparent form, "under my subsequent observation of life, affect me as so much bleak penury or domestic desert where these things of the spirit, these genialities of faith were concerned." And in an earlier passage in his *Notes* he puts the emphasis where it was finally to rest for him.

> It was a luxury, I to-day see, to have all the benefit of his intellectual and spiritual, his religious, his philosophic and his social passion, without ever feeling the pressure of it to our direct irritation or discomfort. It would perhaps more truly figure the relation in which he left us to these things to have likened our opportunities rather to so many scattered glasses of the liquor of faith, poured-out cups stood about for our either sipping or draining down or leaving alone, in the measure of our thirst, our curiosity or our strength of head and heart. If there was much leaving alone in us—and I freely confess that so far as the taking any of it all "straight" went, my lips rarely adventured—this was doubtless because we drank so largely at the source itself, the personally overflowing and irrigating.

Just what James had in this way absorbed I shall try to show; my present concern, however, is with the meaning of his disavowal of interest in 1885.

His letter to William, with its emphasis upon his father's comparative success as a writer, provides a biographic clue which takes us back to the *Notes of a Son and Brother*. Conscious as critics and biographers have been of the rather overwhelming character of the paternal inheritance of William and Henry James, they have not in the case of the younger Henry emphasized the particular embarrassment of his father's influence as he himself emphasized it. James notes his own "detachment of sensibility from everything, everything, that is, in the way of great relations, as to which our father's emphasis was richest." The next passage [from *Notes of a Son and Brother*] incorporates both his youthful sense of an activity on his father's part competitive with his own, and his matured sense of his father's capacity for "active observation and contact."

> *There* was the dim dissociation, there my comparative poverty, or call it even frivolity, of instinct: I gaped imaginatively, as it were to such a different set of relations. I couldn't have framed

stories that would have succeeded in involving the least of the relations that seemed most present to *him;* while those most present to myself, that is more complementary to whatever it was I thought of as humanly most interesting, attaching, inviting, were the ones his schemes of importances seemed virtually to do without. Didn't I discern in this from the first a kind of implied snub to the significance of mine?—so that, in the blest absence of "pressure" which I just sought here passingly to celebrate, I could brood to my heart's content on the so conceivable alternative of a field of exposure crammed with those objective appearances that my faculty seemed alone fitted to grasp. In which there was ever the small torment of the fact—though I don't quite see today why it should not have been of a purely pleasant irritation—that what our parent most overflowed with was just the brave contradiction or opposition between all his parts, a thing which made for perfect variety, which he carried ever so easily and brightly, and which would have put one no less in the wrong had one accused him of knowing only the abstract (as I was so complacently and invidiously disposed to name it) than if one had foolishly remarked on his living and concluding without it. But I have already made clear his great mixed range—which of course couldn't *not* have been the sign of a mind conceiving our very own breathing humanity in its every fibre the absolute expression of a resident Divinity. No element of character, no spontaneity of life, but instantly seized his attention and incurred his greeting and his comment; which things could never possibly have been so genially alert and expert—as I have, again, before this, superabundantly recorded—if it had not fed on active observation and contact. He could answer one with the radiant when one challenged him with the obscure, just as he could respond with the general when one pulled at the particular; and I needn't repeat that this made for us, during all our time, anything but a starved actuality.

The succeeding passage exhibits the son returning upon himself once more, to say that he had as a youngster thought of his father's young manhood as involving scenes which, unlike those he himself witnessed, "might have met in some degree my appetite for the illustrational."

Four expressions, given here in the order in which they occur, above, indicate how faithful James was, both to the feelings of his youthful self and to his ripest judgment. He and his father each employed a distinct "set of relations"; he felt in this "a kind of implied snub to the significance of mine"; yet the novelist acknowledges that no one spoke so tellingly, nor with such immediacy, for every "element of character," every "spontaneity of life." James insists a little too much that no doctrinal "pressure" was felt by the James children, and he is formally accurate, as we know, not simply from his own evidence, but from the

very nature of the elder James's principles, and from everything his letters say. But there *was* serious pressure. The young writer felt that his father's vision was competitive with his own. His father was forever explaining what human actions revealed; making of the whole universe a tremendous and continuing "yarn," which absorbed the whole array of particular events and feelings on which a storyteller might have based his work.

He rejected his father's manner of telling the universal story; he never seems to have doubted his father's account of human motivations. The antithesis between the pictorial and the dramatic, which flowers into so many interesting and suggestive discriminations in the novelist's criticism of his own work and that of other writers, is *primal:* for when he had satisfied his hunger for the pictorial, or even before he had done so, he was forced to ask himself *what set of relations,* what dramatic oppositions, would serve to organize his fictional scenes. Yet when he asked himself, let us say, "What are the sources of appearance in this particular situation? what motives inform? what elements of character determine? who speaks for life or spontaneity? who denies life and how?"—his father's spirit rose up in him; his father's account of human nature offered itself insistently. The consequences of this fact were clearly mixed. As we shall see presently, the need for his father's version of tradition as a counterweight to Europe was very great; yet the danger of relying too much on the views of "the great explainer" was a real one; one might *become* a great explainer to the detriment of one's art. In 1885 James responded to this threat (which lay below the threshold of consciousness) by associating his father with himself as a writer; he was clearly the better writer, so what had he to fear?

William, on the other hand, had not since his crisis in 1870 feared identification with his father. The explicit assertion that he had a will and a power to choose, which resolved that crisis, was also an explicit defiance of "father's ideas"; his father's crisis of 1844 had been resolved with the declaration that one must abandon the moral will in order to know the "resident Divinity"! William had to keep on asserting the power to choose; he was throughout his life hobbled and constrained by the need to keep on opposing his father, to keep on asserting that moral order is being won *now* by namable persons, and in this way took up an Emersonian position against his father.

More important still for the question of the difference between the brothers with respect to "father's ideas" is the fact that William did not in his Introduction to the *Literary Remains* emphasize the part played by personal bias in the making of his father's philosophy. Had he done so, he would have been obliged to comment on his father's claims as a psychologist, and these,

I venture to suggest, he could not acknowledge, simply because he found them threateningly persuasive; these psychological principles anticipate Freud in a fashion which tends to break down one's belief in the efficacy and reality of the moral will. William James took a friendly and intelligent interest in his father's "theism," just the sort of interest he had in the work of such an intellectual odd fish as Benjamin Paul Blood, the Albany mystic of the "anaesthetic revelation"; he turned away from the spectacle of a psychological dynamics which suggested that *within* our moral selves there is inescapable conflict.

Henry Junior, however, seems to have swallowed his father's psychology whole, and although he never undertook any systematic exposition of his father's thought, as William did, the two volumes of his reminiscences show that he was in possession not simply of his father's spirit but of a sense of his father's characteristic judgments. There is a familiar passage which many persons have quoted without any awareness of its force as evidence of the novelist's sympathetic comprehension. It is found in *A Small Boy and Others*. James has just been saying that the household rang with but a single imperative, "Convert, convert, convert!"—convert, that is, "every contact, every impression, and every experience." These, he goes on, "were to form our soluble stuff; with only ourselves to thank should we remain unaware, by the time our perceptions were decently developed, of the substance finally projected and most desirable. That substance might be just consummately Virtue, as a social grace and value—and as a matter furthermore on which pretexts for ambiguity of view and of measure were as little as possible called upon to flourish." James quickly adds [in *A Small Boy and Others*] that this household was not in the least instrumental "to the formation of prigs."

> Our father's prime horror was of *them*—he only cared for virtue that was more or less ashamed of itself; and nothing could have been of a happier whimsicality than the mixture in him, and in all his walk and conversation, of the strongest instinct for the human, and the liveliest reaction from the literal. The literal played as small a part in our education as it perhaps ever played in any, and we wholesomely breathed inconsistency and ate and drank contradictions. The presence of paradox was so bright among us—though fluttering ever with as light a wing and as short a flight as need have been—that we fairly grew used to allow, from an early time, for the so many and odd declarations we heard launched, to the extent of happily "discounting" them; the moral of all of which was that we need never fear not to be good enough if we were only social enough: a splendid meaning indeed being attached to the latter term.

> Thus we had ever the amusement, since I can really call it nothing less, of hearing morality, or moralism,

as it was, more invidiously worded, made hay of in the very interest of character and conduct; these things suffering much, it seemed, by their association with the conscience—that is the *conscious* conscience—the very home of the literal, the haunt of so many pedantries.

Two or three other passages must be added to this, and use made of the whole group collectively in order to introduce the reader to certain essential points in the writings of the elder James. A passage of some six pages in the *Notes of a Son and Brother* is probably the most illuminating as to the son's feeling for his father and those ideas from which he was hardly separable. I abstract two fragments:

> Detached as I could during all those years perhaps queerly enough believe myself, it would still have done my young mind the very greatest violence to have to suppose that any plane of conclusion for him [his father], however rich and harmonious he might tend to make conclusion, could be in the nature of a fool's paradise. . . . If it didn't sound in a manner patronising I should say that I saw that my father saw; and that I couldn't but have given my own case away by not believing, however obscurely, in the virtue of his consequent and ultimate synthesis. Of course I never dreamed of any such name for it—I only thought of it as something very great and fine founded on those forces in him that came home to us and touched us all the while. As these were extraordinary forces of sympathy and generosity, and that yet knew how to be such without falsifying any minutest measure, the structure raised upon them might well, it would seem, and even to the uppermost sublime reaches, be as valid as it was beautiful. If he so endeared himself wasn't it, one asked as time went on, through his never having sentimentalised or merely meditated away, so to call it, the least embarrassment of the actual about him, and having with a passion peculiarly his own kept together his stream of thought, however transcendent, and the stream of life, however humanized? There was a kind of experiential authority in his basis, as he felt his basis—there being no human predicament he couldn't by a sympathy more like direct experience than any I have known enter into; and this authority, which concluded so to a widening and brightening of the philosophic—for him the spiritual—sky, made his character, as intercourse disclosed it, in a high degree fascinating.

This section of the book is one of the finest things in James—in or out of fiction. In saying, "I couldn't but have given my own case away"—the case for his possession of the artist's faculties—had he failed to find in his father's expressive humanity precisely the grounds appropriate to a valid "synthesis," James shows a noble consistency. The artist has the power to recognize the philosopher. But such noble consistencies must on occasion be disingenuous: James knew more about his father's scheme, and knew it more explicitly, than he allows the uninformed reader to see.

These next lines [from *Notes of a Son and Brother*] follow James's praise for the "masterly clearness and justice" of his brother's Introduction to the *Literary Remains,* and his own characterization of his relation to his father's thought in the years when he was exposed to it as "a total otherness of contemplation." He proceeds to state the underlying principle of "these things":

> . . . the active, not to say the obvious, moral of them, in all our younger time, was that a life of the most richly consequent flowed straight out of them, that in this life, the most abundantly, and above all naturally, communicated *as* life that it was possible to imagine, we had an absolutely equal share, and that in fine I was to live to go back with wonder and admiration to the quantity of secreted thought in our daily medium, the quality of intellectual passion, the force of cogitation and aspiration, as to the explanation both of a thousand surface incoherences and a thousand felt felicities. A religion that was so systematically a philosophy, a philosophy that was so sweepingly a religion, being together, by their necessity, as I have said, an intensity of relation to the actual, the consciousness so determined was furnished forth in a way that met by itself the whole question of the attitude of "worship" for instance; as I have attempted a little to show that it met, with a beautiful good faith and the easiest sufficiency, every other when such came up: those of education, acquisition, material vindication, what is called success generally. In the beauty of the whole thing, again, I lose myself—by which I mean in the fact that we were all the while partaking, to our most intimate benefit, of an influence of direction and enlargement attended with scarce a single consecrated form and which would have made many of these, had we been exposed to intrusion from them, absurdly irrelevant.

Two things have perhaps kept us from seeing what a deep and intimate comprehension of his father's work James exhibited in his reminiscences. First, we are naturally skeptical as to the intelligibility of the elder James—whose abstruseness has been a byword ever since Howells's remark that in writing *The Secret of Swedenborg,* James had kept the "secret." Second, the novelist was incapable of conveying information simply *as* information; he had to give a kind of dramatic form to everything. What this means in the present instance is that we are so absorbed in his wonderful capacity to catch up the elements of his past into form that we don't serially note how many things he initially perceived. To begin with the passage [that opens with the words "The oddity of my own case . . .", quoted previously in this essay,] why should the fact that James was "'after' persons" have been considered "deplorable"? Well, simply because for the elder James

(who of course followed St. Paul in this) a "respect of persons" was a great sin. Note also the implied stricture: the "serious" apparently had to be the "abstract." In the next long passage we find James explaining that he "drank so largely at the source itself" that he had no need of the offered "cups." (The reader may remember the tremendous number of cups, bowls, vessels, fountains, overflowing tides, and so forth, in the novelist's work. We shall come to these; meantime it is enough to know that the relation between "sources" and containers is derived from the elder James.)

In asserting that he went to his father himself for knowledge of his beliefs, James is displaying a fidelity that would have delighted his father. To be "true to the experience of the creature" is to have a living experience of the "resident Divinity," not to seek Him in books. Again, the son is aware that his father held that God is imprisoned in man. It appears that the "perfect variety" and the "spontaneity of life" (the novelist's own announced values) had as their sanction a mind which conceived of God as within us. Such a mind, in other words, is exactly the sort which characteristically pays tribute to variety and spontaneity. (If the reader feels that this is the prime characteristic of the *artist's* mind, he is in agreement with *both* father and son, and not the novelist alone.)

I come now to the passage which deals with the unspoken exhortation of the parents, "Convert, convert, convert!" Make, that is, the whole of your experience serve your sense of "Virtue, as a social grace and value. . . ." Now if virtue is truly *social,* it is a new kind of thing which needs the explication supplied by the familiar phrase, "We need never fear not to be good enough if we were only social enough. . . ." The passage condemns the "literal"—the letter, in the elder James, is likely to be an *inversion* of the spirit—condemns prigs and the "*conscious* conscience," which is the "haunt" of "pedantries." What then does "social" mean to the son? It means not being persuaded of one's *personal* rectitude, not attributing virtue to other *persons* as such. His father was a "source" of the kindliest and most attaching virtues, but the son is perfectly aware that the father would have been horrified had he been regarded as more, or less, righteous than anyone else. It is, then, on a social scene, or within the family itself, that these powers his father exhibited, "these things of the spirit, these genialities of faith," were to be found.

James has stated the alternative possibility, that which begins with a "respect of persons," in *A Small Boy and Others:* "I never dreamed of competing—a business having in it at the best, for my temper, if not for my total failure of temper, a displeasing ferocity." He continues: "If competing was bad, snatching was therefore still worse, and jealousy was a sort of spiritual snatching." Self-righteousness, spiritual greed, is the greatest possible sin in father and son alike. Theodora Bosanquet [in *Henry James at Work*] perceived the importance of this in James; although she missed his belief (once again his father's) that we cannot altogether avoid spiritual greed: "When he walked out of the refuge of his study into the world and looked about him, he saw a place of torment, where creatures of prey perpetually thrust their claws into the quivering flesh of the doomed defenceless children of light." The elder James, in a letter printed in *Notes of a Son and Brother*, shows the impartiality on the score of our virtues which is more characteristics of his son: Before the coming of his apocalyptic society "we shall be utterly unworthy to love each other or be loved in return. We shall do nothing but prey upon each other and turn each other's life to perfect weariness."

Theodora Bosanquet, in seeking to describe James's own vision of our perfect state, has hit on a description very close indeed to that used by the elder James in this letter. The novelist's father writes: "The first requisite of our true relationship to each other (spiritually speaking) is that we be wholly independent of each other: then we may give ourselves away as much as we please, we shall do neither them [*sic*] nor ourselves any harm" [quoted in *Notes of a Son and Brother*]. (We may "give ourselves away" freely when what we love in other people is simply their reflection of a unique aspect of "the abounding divinity"—that is, their style.) Miss Bosanquet writes of the novelist [in *Henry James at Work*]: "His Utopia was an anarchy where nobody would be responsible for any other human being but only for his own civilized character."

The sentences in the last of my series of extended quotations come close to being a summary view of the elder James's *Weltanschauung*. I have already referred to James's complaint that the "serious" was unfortunately "abstract." Here, though "not concerned with the intrinsic meaning of these things" (to which William, he feels, has done far more justice than he could), he is concerned with their "moral." His statement of the moral amounts to saying that his father's abundance, fidelity to particulars, and so forth, "flowed straight out of them." In other words, his father's abstract universality *was* somehow consonant with particularity. This is the first point in a list of the elements of his father's belief which the novelist clearly comprehended. The second is that his father was utterly faithful to the abstract demand that all men be treated alike, in that each member of his family had an "equal share" in what emerged from his father as "source." An important corollary to these two points is James's awareness that his father believed his own good qualities to be due to a "resident" God; he knew that his father did not believe that religious *experience* was something "other" than what was "communicated *as* life." What was experienced was the very life of the hidden cause itself, for God had no other way to *be*.

Third, James recognized and repeatedly celebrated his father's power to make sense of the world the family saw, not by excising or distorting bits of it in the manner of humdrum rationalists, but by reconciling the whole. Frequently, of course, this reconciliation was effected through the desperate logic of paradox, but what more clearly testified to his father's refusal to blink the least scrap of actuality? Fourth, the younger son has clearly taken in the burden of his father's strictures, not on *personal* claims alone, but on the whole fabric of institutional life in church and state. He knows that success is to be claimed for the thing one has done, not for the thing one is, or the place one has attained in any sort of hierarchy.

If the reader has taken in the aspects of the elder James's system that the novelist understood, he is in possession of a number of clues needed to lead him through the "system" I shall summarize. It may be concluded, on the question of the relation of Henry and William to their father's beliefs, that William's excellent Introduction proves that he understood the relations between "father's ideas" very well; but the passages I have quoted here . . . show that Henry understood their possible applications in a degree that makes William's knowledge seem pedantic. The younger son is, to my knowledge, the only man who has ever *used* the elder James's beliefs. By the time he wrote *The Golden Bowl* his "faith in the power of the moral to offer a surface" had become nearly as unqualified as his father's.

The interpreters of the elder James have made little of that "experiential authority" which the younger Henry James felt so deeply. The theologian's admirers are keenly aware of his acuteness as a judge of character (is there a better sketch of Emerson's or Carlyle's?), but they betray no consciousness that this acuteness had a systematic basis; that the charming man with the queer notions actually put some of these to work when he made judgments of people. These queer notions themselves were of course completely caught up in the theology and the philosophy. They were couched in symbolic terms, and in the period before Freud and the existentialist vogue it was very difficult to attach them to anything. It does not appear so difficult now, and the basis on which his father analyzed human nature seems to have been from the very start the younger Henry James's psychological stock in trade. It follows that some of the lovers of the novelist's work have been *elder* Jamesians without being in the least aware of it.

I shall not, however, attempt at the outset to discriminate psychological principles from the rest. To get at the elder James, one must first look at him whole and thereafter try to suggest how the parts were used. This is because his universe is one of moral energies in motion; his principles are co-ordinates of the flux and reflux of creation.

Creation, as his son William says in his Introduction to the **Literary Remains,** is his leading idea. The image of God as a detached watch-maker and the opposed image of an arbitrary and angry God were equally repugnant to him. His God is a god of love unalloyed, and evil is, in his universe, a species of psychological and metaphysical necessity. The argument as to creation runs as follows: God cannot create perfect beings who share His nature; to do so would merely and meaninglessly diffuse His essence into so many godlings. Man must be given, from the very outset, a wholly different nature. God therefore creates an "other," a creature who will be as different from himself as is the greedy and psychically unformed infant from his loving and self-forgetting mother. God would surely not exhibit His power of selfless love in creating replicas of himself—this would be simple narcissism. Instead He makes receptacles or molds which must be filled with the divine love to give them "life."

Still, these creatures God has made will not be independent of Him if He simply endows them with a consciousness of selfless love to begin with; they must first believe themselves independent of each other and of God, and thereafter come to realize, as grown-up moral agents, that God alone is worthy of love. So the first stage of creation—the making of the molds—is followed by a second stage in which man declares his moral and material independence, but is finally faced with the knowledge that without God's love he is a mere hollow receptacle, that the cup of the self cannot really be filled by righteousness or material possessions.

This second stage of creation occupies the whole of human history from the beginning to the realization of the apocalyptic *union* of God and man in society. I will rehearse this stage once again, using an alternative set of terms which the elder James derives from *Genesis.* The life to which Adam (perhaps it is better to say "the Adam," since this is a technical term) awakes is a mere confusion of appearances to him. Yet all these appearances are susceptible of arrangement into an order which would exhibit the union of God and man—all are representative of the divine nature which man embodies. Adam is seeing the cosmos within himself, but he thinks it is outside him—his senses tell him so. If he proceeded to arrange these appearances in the order of their final meaning, he would not, to repeat the point made in the paragraph above, become an independent moral agent. He would not feel himself possessed of that agency which he will finally resign to God. There would be, in still other words, no merit in the whole creative transaction either for God or His creature. But if the Adam cannot use God's power to arrange the appearances about him without interrupting the creative process, whose power *can* he use? God provides Eve, who institutes the delusion which is necessary if man is to arrive at a separate consciousness. Eve incites us to appropriate and order the shows of appearance as *possessions*. God is a benevolent cheat. He gives us a false self first, to teach us what the true self is.

The Eve has a number of names, but "selfhood" is the simplest. (She is also the "receptacle" or "mold," and in Swedenborgian parlance she is the *proprium*.) When we seize on money, power, status, goodness, aesthetic experience, or anything else and hold it as a *possession,* we are responding to our selfhood's urging. Before we begin to do this we are not men at all, but innocents, spiritual Emersons, "mere dimpled nurslings of the skies," to use the elder James's phrase. We are lapped in the divine love and wisdom, but the divine power or "use" has not begun to work in us. (This is the elder James's trinity—love, wisdom, and use.)

What the Eve gives us is not simply undifferentiated greed; she gives us an "identity." Through our possessions, moral, material, aesthetic, we become somebodies. (Here James approaches Veblen's thesis about the function of owning things in *The Theory of the Leisure Class*.) We get from our possessions a sense of personal fullness. From them we learn who we are, and with them we make distinctions between ourselves and other men. We judge them better or worse, richer or poorer, endowed with more or less sensibility. Every man tries to fill the cup of his selfhood with those things that will enable him to lord it over his fellows.

It would be misleading to suggest that it is simply our individual selfhood which gives us identity; the church as we know it is also a great vessel of lies, chief of which is the assertion that God prizes us as individuals; rejects some of us and favors others. The state, however, imperfect and oppressive though it may be, is an emblem of our future union with God and our fellows in the "divine-natural-humanity." The state must finally disintegrate, that is, surrender the function of controlling our passions into the hands of a new society, which will supplant both church and state. In the meantime the state has quite properly the ascendancy over the church, for it is at least a symbol of our future destiny, and its powers serve to keep its citizens from each other's throats. The church, having lost its symbolic function, must perish, because it is dedicated to the maintenance of the lie that God does not share His love of us with absolute equality.

But where is God now to be found? To answer this question it will be best, since we are trying to describe a process, rather than a static order, to start once more at the beginning. I have been talking about God's activity without acknowledging His part in it. Using the terms from Genesis once more, I shall amplify the description of the Adam. The elder James thought of mankind as containing all nature. Nature is simply a reflection of our spiritual contents. Adam, earth, universal man, the Grand Man or Maximus Homo, all these are interchangeable terms expressive of the fact that the divine wisdom is actually present within us. We see it as outside us and call it nature. God's love is also within us. James sometimes calls this love the "female Adam," making symbolic use of the fact that Genesis refers to the creation of man, male and female, *before* Eve was made. So the "female Adam," or divine love, dwells within us, though the Eve screens us from awareness of her presence. The divine love takes the form of the "female Adam," or the conscience which struggles with the Eve. The triumph of conscience results of course in our union with God and our fellows—the "divine-natural-humanity."

Although the elder James is a bit hard on Kant in *Substance and Shadow,* he seems to have found him very useful. By giving the Kantian intuitions of space and time a beginning and an end, he succeeded in clarifying his own scheme considerably. Space and time are the conditions necessary to knowing phenomena. What we know while the Eve is driving us to appropriate goods, status, scientific knowledge, is the phenomenal. But what we know is truly a reflection of the divine wisdom in us. The Eve simply gets us to *take* it in the wrong way. We ought to see that everything that is deployed in space and appropriated in time is actually a reflection of our own nature. We ought to take it as the divine love urges us to—as a reflection of our own nature. If we can for a moment do this— view all nature as God views it—we will on that instant be united with God. Simply by inverting our perspective, and crying out, "Behold, all this is humanity!" instead of saying, "Lo, how many things I can grab and keep all to myself!" we can put an end to these preliminary delusions, space and time. Once we have learned to take experience for what it is, testimony to the presence within us of the divine wisdom and the divine love, time will have a stop, space will become simply our spiritual perception of the being of God-Man, the "divine-natural-humanity." To introduce the last of the terms from Genesis, the coming of the *second* Adam, or God-Man, reduces the chaotic consciousness of the first Adam to its final order.

The elder James was reluctant to make a distinction between the history of individuals and that of the human race, and he often uses the same terms for both. For example, we may say of the race and of individuals that their history is that of a struggle between the conscience and the selfhood, the one seeking to refer all that exists to the divine nature common to us all, the other seeking to engross all existence and separate man from man. In the following passage on our moral history James uses the term *"vir"* instead of Eve for the selfhood, and "goodness and truth" for the love and wisdom within us. "All the phenomena of our moral history go to show the *homo* or created man, the man of interior affection and thought, utterly unconscious

of the infinite goodness and truth which alone give him *being,* and joyfully allying himself with the *vir* or finite conscious man, the man of mere organic appetite and passion, who gives him contingent *existence* only, or renders him phenomenal to himself; shows him as the symbolic narrative phrases it, *'leaving his father and his mother, and cleaving unto his wife until they become one flesh.'"*

Since the delusion Eve fosters is a *necessary* preliminary phase for humanity, no one can be condemned for adopting it. Man must pile up goods, pile up knowledge, and accumulate works of art in order to learn that he is a nullity, that all these represent a reality he has denied. He must even obey the laws and conform to his neighbor's standards. Nothing is more ridiculous than the reformer, who forgets that we are not ready for our union with God; who tries to make a new church or a new state, or advocates communism. We are not ready for these things, and we shall not, in the end, need them. There is, however, an effective mode of being evil, of arresting, if but momentarily, the march of providence. I quote a passage [from *Society the Redeemed Form of Man*] on the evil the church (any church, since James is not tilting at a particular faith) encourages in us.

> The Church studiously fosters the sentiment of moral worth or dignity in its disciples . . . and thus delivers them over bound hand and foot to spiritual pride. . . . However selfish or worldly a man may be these are good honest natural evils, and you have only to apply a motive sufficiently stimulating in either case, and you will induce the subject to forbear them. But spiritual pride is inward evil exclusively, pertaining to the selfhood of man or livingly appropriated by him as his own, and cannot therefore become known to him save in the form of an outward natural representation; for it is not like moral evil, mere outward oppugnancy to good, but it is the actual and deadly profanation of good, or the lavish acknowledgement of it with a view of subordinating it to personal, or selfish and worldly ends. It is the only truly formidable evil known to God's providence, being that of *self*-righteousness, and hence the only evil which essentially threatens to undermine the foundations of God's throne.

Just as children pursue the images cast by a projector, men grasp at nature. The delusion that their senses and intellects are the arbiters of reality does not damn them. We must all incur the guilt which comes with acquisition. Persuaded by our selfhood that the phenomenal is the only reality, we must painfully live the error down. The last step in philosophy will be the *docta ignorantia,* the conclusion that without knowing God we can know nothing truly; the last gasp of the strenuous moral will is to be the admission that we cannot will the good; and the final meaning of acquisition of every sort is that nothing can be owned. These are "good honest natural evils"; forms, identical at bottom, of what the novelist called "spiritual snatching," attempts, in his father's terms, to fulfill the demands of the selfhood. But the evil of self-righteousness makes an "outward natural representation" of the self, and calls it God; it is the ultimate evil.

What we deludedly call "human nature" is simply the relation between love of one's self and love of one's fellows. Our "identity" *is* simply the form that the struggle between these two loves takes in us. An individual is not so much a *thing* as an *event;* a focus at which these moral energies intersect. Hence the subtitle of *Substance and Shadow—An Essay on the Physics of Creation.* The consequence is that to love our fellows exclusively would be to revert to the state of the first Adam, not to attain that of the second. Innocents and moral idiots may display such a love now, but they are simply evading the conflict with the Eve which we must go through. But at the other end of the spectrum we discover something very nearly absolute, a love of self which has become a love of spiritual death. This is *self*-righteousness. The self-righteous seek to make God a possession.

The attempt to appropriate conscience must take the form of grasping some "outward natural representation" of the divine in us. The selfhood is limited by Kant's intuitions of time and space; it can deal only with the phenomenal, what *appears* to it. "Bodily" churches, any ecclesiastical organization we can see, are such representations. The man who appropriates a woman, not simply to allay his lust, but because he sees in her a chance to gain glory for himself, is such a sinner. He tries to make the boundless source of good his own. (He takes the portrait for the lady; or sees the "heiress of all the ages" as simply the inheritor of millions and of wasted flesh.) To appropriate our spiritual superior damns us.

This very general view of the elder James's "spiritual cosmology" lacks the dramatic force which he tried to give it. It may be possible to suggest this more directly by describing the process from the standpoint of one of its three protagonists. We may discuss the regeneration of a particular man; we may describe the historical movement from formation to the coming of the divine society; or we may speak of what God undergoes for our sake. . . . Since the elder James regarded himself as a Christian, it is necessary to explain his Christology, and I shall therefore begin with God. It has been said above that men are created as a kind of limit or antithesis. Otherness to God, alienation from God, is what defines us. Having made us other, God enters into us in order that we may become like Him, or, to put it in Swedenborgian terms, as does the elder James, that the Lord or God-Man may come into being. God submerges himself in men in order to make them divine—*not* to make them God, but to enable

them to join Him in an order in which both men and God will be swallowed up. Creation is not simply a putting-forth of God's energy; it is not complete until that energy has flowed back into the divine-natural-humanity. "Creation necessarily *in*volves the creator and obscures his perfection in the exact ratio of its *e*volving the creature and illustrating his imperfection. Unless therefore the creature *himself* reproduce the creative infinitude concealed in his nature it must be forever obliterated from remembrance" [in *The Secret of Swedenborg*].

In the sight of God, therefore, the selfhood, Eve, or *proprium* is morally neutral. The self exists so that we may become aware of our otherness to God and overcome it. "Nature" and "history" are the record in space and time of our delusion that we do not share the divine nature and are not at one with God. The delusion, the positing of self-consciousness, is the necessary ground of our perception of our otherness to God. This is perhaps the most sporting theory of redemption ever devised. James's God puts himself completely at man's mercy. The descent of God into man makes possible the ascent of man to God, who subjects Himself to the conditions of human life so that man may become His equal. Christ was simply the first man to do this; the first man in whom God *showed.* By acknowledging the divinity within, Christ revealed the "creative infinitude" which lies in all of us. His feat was an utter denial, under the most extreme temptation, of the self. To be hailed as the Messiah is, according to the theologian, the most enticing bait for our self-righteousness that we can imagine. The incarnation is then simply the type of the activity of the divine love in man. "The truth incurs this humiliation, undergoes this falsification on *our* behalf exclusively, who, because we have by nature no perception of God as a spirit, but only as a person like ourselves, are even brutally ignorant of the divine power and ways" [in *The Secret of Swedenborg*]. Christ revealed the divine life in us by renouncing the life of selfishness as factitious, frustrating, and vile.

What thereafter takes place from the point of view of the divinity I shall give in shortened form. When the Eve's phenomenal understanding has built (for example) a scientific account of the world which is complete save that it lacks the meaning which it has when we invert our perspective and see that it describes "the spiritual or invisible contents of the human mind," or when individual selfishness has in a thousand ways discovered the frustration and futility of acquisition, we finally see, with horror and loathing, the self which has contrived these inversions of significance—and the divinity within us is released from bondage.

The moment the selfhood becomes "other," the experience of God and of man are united, not in some other world, but in this one. It becomes "natural" to us to be divine; it becomes "natural" to God to be human. The alienation which had heretofore defined us we now see as the *other self*. In our spiritual geography, America comes to rule over Europe; the feminine over the musculine; the artist over the king and priest. We now order nature as a true cosmos, an image of God's wisdom shaped by God's love. Man, says the elder James [in *The Secret of Swedenborg*], "has the task and the power divinely given him of subduing all nature to himself, and so leading it back to him from whom it originally comes." Or, to use the set of terms from Genesis once more: What has taken place is a "marriage" of the infinite and the finite; the Adam has broken off his "liaison" with the Eve and has been wholly vivified by the female Adam, thus becoming the second Adam; while the Eve has been deprived of phenomena and forced to accept the fruits of the divine wisdom. Or, to use terms from physics which emphasize the fact that the elder James is describing a process or event: The "field" of creation reaches an equilibrium in the unified consciousness of God and man.

If this be what happens to God, what happens to individuals in this divine society? What is left of us when we have perceived the self as "other," as alien? We become utterly spontaneous, seeming precisely what we are, and being precisely what we wish to be. But again, what is left of us? The elder James calls what remains to us "spiritual individuality." It is no more and no less than our style. When we are apotheosized, the content of our selves is nothing less than the whole of God's nature; it is universal, but the form or style is our own. Each of us recapitulates the whole, as if we were a community of artists, each giving his individual stamp to a single subject matter. The union of universality with true particularity which Emerson projected is thus worked out by the elder James. He alone, in his generation, made a complete version of the bootstrap myth.

I turn to an abbreviated sketch of the history which culminates in the divine society. Out of Swedenborg's long tale of successive "churches" on earth, the elder James chose only three to represent the sum of our history. The first two have been manifest; the third is wholly spiritual and now arising, though invisible, amongst us. The first or Jewish church is the church of the law which makes God completely external: "In short, the Jew was notoriously a frivolous subject—as near to worthless as a people could well be that still wore the human form—and cultivating only such base ideas of the Divine righteousness as stood in a mere 'outward cleansing of the cup and platter, while inwardly they were full of extortion and excess'" [in *Society the Redeemed Form of Man*]. When America disavowed England's church and state, Americans became *as a people* the first effective manifestation of the possibility of living by an inward law. But this means that America is the promise of the real "third force," the divine society. What is the second of these churches?

It is the Christian church, the Christian church not as an organization but simply as the chance that Christ offered individuals to anticipate in themselves the state of redeemed man. This anticipation can be only partial, but without it God would have been imprisoned within us forever: "Accordingly unless the Divine Providence had all along the course of history singled out such persons as were capable of spiritual regeneration without detriment to their conscious freedom, evil would have reigned uncontrolled throughout history, and creation consequently have been stifled in a vain effort to get birth or put on form" [in *Substance and Shadow*]. We discover on surveying history itself "that the exact meaning of the Providential administration of human affairs has been to give man social and aesthetic form or consciousness, by means of a sickening experience of the endless disease disorder and death wrapped up in his physical and moral consciousness. . . ." What Christ has done for individuals we perceive to be an "at-one-ment"—evidence that God is "naturally" joined to us; this is redemption, not regeneration or salvation. (The theologian's use of these terms is not wholly consistent in appearance, because he sometimes compresses, and at others expands, his account.) But, on the basis of our seeing that a *vir* or Eve need not take the form of selfishness, that Christ was a *vir*, a particular form, really adequate to contain the *homo* or universal nature, we may attain as individuals something very like regeneration.

We must not attempt to do this prematurely through moral strenuousness. We have to make a form or style fit to contain the universal sources, to hold the waters of life. I quote the epigraph on the title page of *Society the Redeemed Form of Man:* "Man during his earthly life induces a form in the purest substances of his interiors, so that he may be said to form his own soul, or give it quality; and according to the form or quality of soul he thus gives himself will be his subsequent receptivity to the Lord's inflowing life: which is a life of love to the whole human race." This directly suggests the novelist's most general observation about the famous "ideas." It runs: "His *tone,* that is, always so effectually looks out, and the living parts of him so singularly hung together, that one may fairly say his philosophy *was* his tone" [in *Notes of a Son and Brother*]. His father's great achievement was not the construction of an intricate system, but the development of a form, a style, a "tone," by which he was able to express it in his personal discourse.

"Father's ideas" had a simple basis, which made possible their ramifications and involutions. What the novelist was from infancy so sure of that he never dreamed of questioning it, was that his father had been quite right about experience. There were two ways of *taking* it, the selfish way and the loving way, and those who took it in the former, accepted conventional forms, while those who took it in the latter, made their own forms, and arrived at a style which was a worthy container of all that was precious and noble. When he found *both* these modes of appropriating experience at work in his own mind and soul, he began to write and—genius aiding him—became Henry James.

Giles Gunn (essay date 1974)

SOURCE: An introduction to *Henry James, Senior: A Selection of His Writings,* American Library Association, 1974, pp. 3-29.

[*In the following essay, Gunn provides an overview of James's life and philosophy, discussing his theology, his relationship to prevailing nineteenth-century views, and his influences on his sons William and Henry.*]

1

On May 30, 1850, Edwards Amasa Park of Andover Theological Seminary preached an important sermon in Boston's Brattle Street Meeting House before the Convention of the Congregational Ministers of Massachusetts on "The Theology of the Intellect and That of the Feelings." Though his subject may have been suggested to him two years before when his theological colleague from Hartford, the more famous Horace Bushnell, made use of a similar distinction in an address also delivered at Andover on the relation between "Dogma and Spirit," Park's title reflected an opposition which, in the American tradition, had found its chief exponent a century earlier in the person of Jonathan Edwards and which, in the European tradition, went all the way back through Friedrich Schleiermacher and Martin Luther to the Bible itself. Park was hardly insensible to the importance and magnitude of this legacy, but his chief purpose was less to establish or defend it than to interpret its consequences, to show how each kind of theology needed the other to do full justice to the nature and substance of the Christian truth.

The theology of the intellect, with its preference for evidence over opinion, reason over intuition, precision over intensity, harmony over conflict, the literal over the figural, and the general over the specific was far better suited for dogmatics than for preaching, for dialectics than for confession, for speculation than for narrative. The theology of the feelings, on the other hand, with its opposite tendency to subordinate consistency to assertiveness, logic to feeling, certitude to sensitivity, the discursive to the poetic, and the concrete to the universal, was far more appropriate to the tract than the treatise, the homily than the catechism,

the history than the disputation. Park's point was that neither type of theology is sufficient without the other, just as a confusion of either with its complement might destroy the integrity of both:

> It is this crossing of one kind of theology into the province of another kind . . . which mars either the eloquence or else the doctrine of the pulpit. The massive speculations of the metaphysician sink down into his expressions of feeling and make him appear cold-hearted, while the enthusiasm of the impulsive divine ascends and effervesces into his reasonings and causes him both to *appear,* and to *be* . . . hotheaded [in *Memorial Collection of Sermons by Edwards A. Park* (1902)].

Park wanted a recognition of the claims of both kinds of theology so that he might effect a reconciliation between the intellectual and pietistic elements not only within his own breast but also within the body of the Christian faith of his time, between the Evangelicals who made so much of the heart and what might be loosely called the Unitarians who put such store in the head, between popular revivalists and Harvard intellectuals. Park himself was a member of neither radical party. It was the older orthodoxy of New England that he wanted to repossess, only softened and made more sensible by an anthropology which acknowledged that man is at once sentient and rational.

There is no way of knowing if the elder Henry James ever read Park's sermon—had he done so he would undoubtedly have regarded it as an expression of what he was fond of calling the "old theology" rather than the "new"—but there can scarcely be any doubt at all about the relevance of its presiding differentiation to his own life and work. For anyone who ever bothered to read the works of Henry James, Senior—a series of books which, if one includes the unfinished manuscript published posthumously by his eldest son William, the noted philosopher, comes to well over a dozen volumes—were likely to be struck by the same kind of confusion which Park had noted in his sermon: massive metaphysical speculations which often cast a leaden shadow over an unusually spirited and expressive speaker, thus giving rise to that contradictory set of impressions which Park evokes with the phrases "cold-hearted" and "hot-headed."

In truth, however, something very nearly the opposite was the case with the elder James. If his heart suffered from anything, then it was not from an absence of feeling, but rather from an excess of it, whereas his speculations and judgments often appeared intemperate or impulsive only because he viewed his ideas, however universal their scope or implication, as living realities, felt possibilities. James's problem was that he was clearly a theologian of feeling who tried to express his religious faith in what most systematic thinkers would regard as a jerrybuilt theology of intellect. Constantly tempted as well as obliged to convey what T. S. Eliot once called "the logic of feelings" in "the logic of concepts," James seems in retrospect to have been caught in the unhappy situation of a man whose medium frequently constituted a downright obstacle to, if not parody of, his message. Hence the well-known quip which Charles Eliot Norton ascribed to William Dean Howells about how James not only wrote *The Secret of Swedenborg* but "kept it."

There is a certain irresponsibility about the way many have fastened upon this mischievous but good-natured remark and then used it as an excuse to dismiss James as an utter eccentric, when, in point of fact, Howells himself could not. Though Howells was a worldly man of letters whose own religious upbringing had been seriously undermined by the new kingdom of forces unleashed in the second half of the nineteenth century, he nonetheless believed that James was decidedly worth listening to and that he often made a good deal of sense. Even if Howells was temperamentally indisposed to take any active interest in what James found so important and compelling in Swedenborg's ontology, he had still absorbed enough of his own father's respect for Swedenborg's ethics to respond favorably to James's explication of that "divine natural humanity" to which Swedenborg claimed all men heir, and which in the new dispensation, so James argued, would destroy all those superficial social and political distinctions by which governments had falsely differentiated one man from another.

This conviction, in fact, converged almost precisely with certain underlying assumptions of that emergent progressivism which served to unite Howells with what Daniel Aaron has described as the other "men of good hope" of that era, people such as Edward Bellamy, Henry Demarest Lloyd, and Henry George, whose political faith had a way of turning very quickly into a religion of humanity as well roughly parallel in its convictions to the views of writers as diverse as Mazzini, Victor Hugo, and James himself. Finding Henry Demarest Lloyd the most eloquent spokesman of this "secular religion," Professor Aaron has defined it as follows [in *Men of Good Hope* (1961)]:

> The religion of progressivism conceived of the mediator between God and man not as an individual Christ but as a universalized Christ, Christ as a symbol of humanity itself. It broke with the orthodox Protestant assumption that "God's redemptive operation," to quote Gronlund, is "confined to the isolated individual bosom" and refused to make religion a private affair between one man and his God. For the progressives, God appeared to man through men and revealed himself in human history and institutions. Men were damned or saved collectively. They entered into communion with God when they shed their selfish personalities and united

with one another in a confederation of love. According to this religion, social evil was not confirmed by individual criminal acts but by what the elder Henry James called "our organized inclemency of man to man." And in turn, social good could not be attained through individual acts of charity but through the organized clemency of man to man.

Except for the omission of the assumption that religion has its tragic side, entailing the death of the old egoistic self to make way for the rebirth of a new social self, this summary of the faith of the progressives could also stand as a fairly accurate, brief statement of the thought of the elder Henry James. True, he differed with the later progressives, just as he had with the earlier Transcendentalists, over the question of the reality and governance of evil, but his view of salvation was still as equalitarian as that of the first and as infused with a spirit of optimism—albeit a very much more tempered one—as that of the second. As William James summarized his father's view of the world [in *The Literary Remains of the Late Henry James* (1884)], it flowed from two basic perceptions: "In the first place, he felt that the individual man, as such, is nothing, but owes all he is and has to the race nature he inherits, and to the society into which he is born. And, secondly, he scorned to admit, even as a possibility, that the great and loving Creator, who has all the being and the power, and has brought us as far as *this,* should not bring us *through,* and *out,* into the most triumphant harmony."

Yet few people, then or now, have perceived the depth of James's relationship either to the Transcendentalists or to the progressives, or, for that matter, to any other major group of thinkers and writers in the American tradition. Instead, the impression which with certain notable exceptions has continued to prevail is the one most vividly conveyed by E. L. Godkin, that fearlessly independent former Irish immigrant destined to become one of America's most liberal and distinguished journalists, who from 1875 to 1881 was a resident in Cambridge and frequent dinner guest at the James's—the impression of an interesting and, in his own terms, formidable eccentric with no very clear intellectual outline who was alienated from and disavowed by the only sect or group, in this case the Swedenborgians, to whose cause he professed any allegiance at all:

> Henry James, the elder, was a person of delightful eccentricity, and a humorist of the first water. When in his grotesque moods, he maintained that, to a right-minded man, a crowded Cambridge horse-car "was the nearest approach to heaven upon earth!" What was the precise nature of his philosophy, I never fully understood, but he professed to be a Swedenborgian, and carried on a correspondence full of droll incidents with anxious inquirers, in various parts of the country. Asking him one day

about one of these, he replied instantly, "Oh, a devil of a woman!" to my great astonishment, as I was not then thoroughly familiar with his ways. One of his most amusing experiences was that the other Swedenborgians repudiated all religious connection with him, so that the sect to which he belonged, and of which he was the head, may be said to have consisted of himself alone [in *Life and Letters of Edwin Lawrence Godkin* (1907)].

Oddly enough, Godkin closed this recollection with the final observation that James "was a writer of extraordinary vigor and picturesqueness, and I suppose there was not in his day a more formidable master of English style."

This almost parenthetical remark from one who was closely associated with James Russell Lowell and Charles Eliot Norton in the founding and editing of the *Nation* was no mean compliment; yet it only deepens the mystery of obscurity to which James fell victim almost immediately after his death and from which he has never fully recovered, in spite of the efforts of such scholars as Austin Warren, Ralph Barton Perry, F. O. Matthiessen, Frederick Young, Leon Edel, Quentin Anderson, R. W. B. Lewis, and Richard Poirier. Clearly part of the reason derives from James's turn toward theology (and an abstruse form of it at that!) just at a time when this mode of reflection was rapidly going out of fashion among those with whom James most wanted to communicate. Recognizing the need for new religious wine to revive the spirit of those who had long since lost a taste for the old, James made the mistake of not replenishing his stock of wineskins, and this, in turn, tended to give his product a flat, sometimes even brackish, flavor. For all the originality and prescience of many of his insights, his stubbornly metaphysical cast of mind, together with the esoteric and untraditional framework of thought in terms of which he chose to express it, frequently made his insights appear too recondite and vague to his contemporaries.

Then, too, he lived in an age which was somewhat indifferent to, even impatient with, particular kinds of thinkers, at least those like James who refused to permit their interest in and sympathy for concrete problems from obscuring their still more fervent vision of what transcends and resolves them. Though James was as absorbed with the individual and the concrete as the next man—indeed, his son Henry observed at one point in his *Notes of a Son and Brother* (1914) that there was in his father, for all his love of the abstract, not the least embarrassment of the actual about him—he remained steadfast in his belief that the key to all particular issues lay in reconstituting our conception of the whole. A philosophical monist by inclination, if not always by practice, James suffered the same fate of incomprehension which befell those other two meta-

physical visionaries of the age, Herman Melville and Walt Whitman.

But there were also other, more personal reasons why the elder James's work disappeared so quickly from public view, reasons having to do both with the remarkable development of certain members of his family and also with a particular, rarely mentioned element of his own style as thinker and writer. To begin with, James's work was very quickly overshadowed by that of his two more gifted and famous sons. Henry, Junior, had already published six books before his father finished his own most mature work, ***Society the Redeemed Form of Man,*** and by the time the elder James died three years later, his novelist son had added seven more titles to that list. William's productive outflow of books and essays did not commence in earnest until several years later with the publication of his two-volume study entitled *The Principles of Psychology* (1890); but he had already begun teaching at Harvard as early as 1872, had established his pioneering laboratory in psychology and started to work on the massive *Principles* by 1876, and had acquired many of his most durable convictions by 1884, when he edited his father's last work in progress entitled ***Spiritual Creation*** and then published it, together with his father's ***"Autobiographical Sketch"*** and an introduction of his own, as ***The Literary Remains of the Late Henry James.***

What is most relevant to observe at this point is that, had the elder James lived long enough to witness the full measure of this ultimately staggering achievement of his two sons which so thoroughly eclipsed his own, he would neither have been alarmed nor displeased. On the contrary, to him their accomplishment would have constituted an eloquent vindication of the principles by which he had sought to educate them, or, more accurately, by which he had sought to permit them the freedom to educate themselves. Further, and this leads to the second personal reason that James's work was relegated to obscurity so rapidly: there was about virtually all of his writing a certain elusive, even ineffable, quality which resisted any sort of systematic intellectual analysis. Stated negatively, it was not that James didn't mean every word that he wrote, only that, by his own admission, he could never quite express exactly what he meant. One can lay part of the blame for this on the deficiencies of his chosen medium and the limitations of his own intellectual gifts, but it really involved something more. In one corner of his mind, at least, James knew that his truth was deeper than his philosophy, than any philosophy perhaps, and that he could only bridge the gap between them with his own sensibility, with the personal authority of his own faith. To put the matter more positively, James was less interested in his theories than his truths, truths which, as William said after his father's death, were inseparable from his life. Hence James's profound integrity of being tended to prevail even where the integrity of his ideas could not, making for that marked discrepancy between the letter and the spirit of his writing which is evident even in some of his most abstract and unwieldly passages. Either way, his son Henry was right: "His tone . . . always so effectually looks out, and the living parts of him so singularly hung together, that one may fairly say his philosophy *was* his tone" [in *Notes of a Son and Brother* (1914)].

But this is only another way of explaining why his books failed either to attract or to hold any very large audience. Being more an expression of sentiment than of science, of convinced feeling rather than clear-headed reasoning, his writing lacked those characteristics of straightforward exposition, sound logic, and ready classifiability which help insure preservation in the memory of the past. As one who was better at living the truth he wanted to express than at expressing the truth he lived, James didn't quite seem to fit anywhere, and so was dismissed by some and neglected by the rest.

2

Yet if one actually takes the time to read James carefully, one soon discovers that he appeared out of step with his time only because in many ways he lived so far in advance of it. His close relation to the progressives who came after him, with their belief that the reformation of society depends upon the social rebirth of the individual, has already been remarked. What has not been so fully appreciated is that James also perceived the kind of criticism to which this secularized religion of the progressives could become vulnerable, as when their visionary dream of the redemption of society gave way to a kind of benevolent social idealism and was then exposed by a generation of thinkers following the lead of Reinhold Niebuhr to be but another mask of egoistic self-approbation.

Like the neoorthodox theologians whom Niebuhr represented, James had realized long before that man is most culpable when he thinks himself most virtuous, that man's ideals, as James would have put it, tempt him to commit the greatest "spiritual evil," that moralism, in short, is an expression of self-love. But James would also have acknowledged the necessity not only of the neoorthodox theological critique of religious liberalism but also of the neoliberal theological critique of religious neo-orthodoxy, or at least of its doctrine of God and its view of creation. For he was at one both with the process theologians of our own day and also with their more radical, occasional fellow travelers, the so-called "Death-of-God" theologians, in finding it inconceivable to think of divinity in the terms popularized by the neo-Reformation theologians—as One who is "wholly other," unchanging, and impassible but for that single moment in history when, in the person of Jesus Christ, He undertook a divine rescue

operation in behalf of a creature who bore almost no discernible trace of the image in which he was made and who was absolutely undeserving of this completely unmerited act of grace. To James, on the contrary, if God was not closer to us than we are to ourselves, if God did not need us as much as we need Him, if God did not take His stripes with the rest of us and thus demonstrate how suffering and death could be the way to truth and new life, then the religion of the Incarnation made no sense to him and he wanted no part of it. Further, if life was not process, if nature was not illustrative of change, if history did not exhibit some measure of creative progress, then the Deity, to paraphrase one of James's most colorful figures, must be like some immense duck that has continued to emit the same unchanged, unimproved quack which it first uttered on the day it was born.

Instead, James conceived of God as the perfect man, as what is divine in our natural humanity when it is raised to the level of absolute perfection, and he made no bones about what this amounts to in terms of traditional theological conceptions of God. As he said with characteristic belligerence and verve in the Advertisement appended to the front matter of what, paradoxically, is one of his more thickly metaphysical volumes [*The Secret of Swedenborg*]:

> I find myself incapable, for my part, of honoring the pretension of any deity to my allegiance, who insists upon standing eternally aloof from my own nature, and by that fact confesses himself personally incommensurate and unsympathetic with my basest, most sensuous, and controlling personal necessities. It is an easy enough thing to find a holiday God who is all too selfish to be touched by the infirmities of his own creatures—a God, for example, who has naught to do but receive assiduous court for a work of creation done myriads of ages ago, and which is reputed to have cost him in the doing neither pains nor patience, neither affection nor thought, but simply the utterance of a dramatic word; and who is willing, accordingly, to accept our decorous Sunday homage in ample quittance of obligations so unconsciously incurred on our part, so lightly rendered and so penuriously sanctioned on his. Every sect, every nation, every family almost, offers some pet idol of this description to your worship. But I am free to confess that I have long outgrown this loutish conception of deity. I can no longer bring myself to adore a characteristic activity in the God of my worship, which falls below the secular average of human character. In fact, what I crave with all my heart and understanding—what my very flesh and bones cry out for—is no longer a Sunday but a weekday divinity, a working God, grim with the dust and sweat of our most carnal appetites and passions, and bent, not for an instant upon inflating our worthless pietistic righteousness, but upon the patient, toilsome, thorough cleansing of our physical and moral existence from the odious defilement it has contracted, until we each and all present at last

in body and mind the deathless effigy of his own uncreated loveliness.

Such convictions as these might lead one to suspect that James's modernity consisted merely in his desire to throw over the entire theological inheritance of Calvinism, but this is decidedly incorrect. Indeed, while James anticipated certain theological and philosophical developments of the future, he also preserved and transmitted much of the Calvinist-Puritan legacy of the past, so much of it, in fact, that he often struck many of his liberated contemporaries as a holdover from some earlier age of faith. It is no accident, I think, that comparatively early in his career, James confided in a letter to Emerson his belief that "Jonathan Edwards *redivivus* in true blue" would still make the best reconciler and critic of the kind of philosophy which had grown up since the middle of the eighteenth century. For, in spite of James's attraction to currents of thought emanating from writers like Swedenborg and Fourier, who could only appeal to a later and very different era than that of Edwards's, what James wanted was not to overthrow Calvinism but rather to *humanize* it. His beliefs, having been derived from the precepts of Calvinism, continued to retain its sense of man's utter dependence on God for his very being, to underline its insistence that nature, life, and history exist only for the glorification of the Creator, to stress its belief in the inevitability and universality of man's involvement with sin and death, and to reemphasize its conviction of man's need for deliverance from evil and rebirth to new life, but not at the expense of allowing Calvinism's insistence upon the doctrine of God's sovereignty to obscure what James perceived to be the equally important fact of God's immanence, His living presence both among and within us as the source and center of what is common and natural to the humanity of all men.

This perception of necessity involved some basic modification of the traditional Calvinist scheme of salvation; the philosopher Ralph Barton Perry later went so far as to describe it as a complete inversion. Where Calvinism, for example, assumed that men fall collectively, as a result of the natural imperfection of human nature as such, and then are saved only as God elects certain individuals who through faith have exhibited their readiness to receive what they cannot earn or acquire of themselves, James postulated to the contrary that men fall individually, precisely as a result of believing themselves personally meritorious of Divine solicitude, and then are saved only when they relinquish their pride in themselves and learn to identify their own lives with the collective nature and destiny of their fellow human beings. This was probably the most profound of James's revisions of cherished Calvinist assumptions. But from this basic modification emanated several others as well which had the effect, if not of turning the entire system upside down, at least of radically revising it according to James's own more humane and optimistic sentiments.

The most famous of James's proposals for a renovation of the orthodox scheme of salvation—though one in which he unknowingly received tacit support from certain of his contemporaries—was his positive or affirmative interpretation of the Fall. According to the view he put forward so emphatically in *The Nature of Evil* and several of his other books, the Fall was neither the result of some accident or unintentional mistake on God's part, as certain liberal Unitarians proposed, nor the result of some primal act of disobedience on man's part, as traditional Calvinists were wont to claim, but rather a necessary and wholly salutary step in God's beneficent plan for man's redemption. In awakening Adam from his state of sensuous slumber to a knowledge of good and evil, Eve had merely precipitated in him the development of that moral conscience identical with conscious selfhood or *proprium,* as James termed it, which he considered the requisite stepping stone to salvation. Without a moral sense of himself, man could not discover what a spiritual liability it was, and how, therefore, he could obtain new life, not through repentance merely, but only by committing what James called "moral suicide, or inward death to self in all its forms . . ." [in *The Literary Remains of the Late Henry James*].

Yet this, in turn, suggested another departure from traditional formulas of regeneration. One was brought to the state of preparation for moral suicide and then subsequently underwent that act, "not by learning," as James suggested in a letter to one of his favorite female correspondents, but "only by *unlearning.*" The actual process of regeneration of the self into full awareness of its divine sociality could only be conceived as a kind of "demolition" or "undoing," to quote from the same letter, a process of decreation leading to that moment of spiritual rebirth where the individual discovers "his object a *life* within him, and no longer a *law* without him." Human redemption still implied reunion with God, then, but the spatial conception of this transaction had changed: man was no longer lifted up and out of himself into communion with the God who exists, as it were, above, but was rather lifted out of himself and into relation with his neighbors for communion with the God who exists nowhere more completely than in the universally human. Further, Jesus Christ, in this view, was neither a substitutionary victim compelled to satisfy the affront made to God's sense of honor by man's original act of disobedience, nor a propitiatory sacrifice intended to mitigate the punishment rightly due to man by a God whose just demands had been betrayed, but rather a representative figure who demonstrated that the only way to achieve reunion with the Creator is by dying to self and becoming one with mankind.

The upshot of all this was a revised conception of the purpose of creation and a severely restricted view of the role of the church and organized religion in general. The elder James could still say with Jonathan Edwards that God is glorified in man's dependence and that all things created exist for the joyous expression of the Creator, but only after having dissociated the word *dependence* from all connotations of the word *subservience* and then relocating the realm of God's creative operation in man's very being. God glorified Himself, then, only by completely emptying Himself, by giving up all special claims to Himself, by showing through the Incarnation that the chief end of creation was the perfect realization of God Himself in the universal humanity of others.

In this scheme of things, the church was obliged to play a decidedly subordinate role, serving, as James said in **Substance and Shadow,** a wholly purgative rather than nutritive function. At best, organized religion was merely a way station on the road to salvation, an institution whose sole purpose was to awaken in its followers a sense of death rather than life, "to reveal to them the dearth of life they have in themselves as morally and finitely constituted, in order to prepare them for that fulness of life they shall find in each other as socially constituted." For this reason James could conclude, and not without a certain measure of Biblical precedent, that "the sinner . . . and not the sin is as yet God's best achievement in human nature: when this achievement becomes somewhat universalized by society itself coming to the consciousness of its shortcomings, we shall at last have a righteousness and a health and wealth which shall never pass away, which shall be for the first time on earth Divine and permanent."

This last observation may serve as a way of gauging James's relationship to his age. Coming to maturity just as the Transcendental era was dawning in America, James could hardly avoid participating in what F. O. Matthiessen [in *The James Family* (1947)], following William Ellery Channing, termed "the moral argument against Calvinism." Yet what differentiates James from Emerson, and especially from the company of humanitarian optimists and perfectionists which Emerson trailed after him, is that though he was willing to dispense with many of the outmoded and (to him) repellant formulations of Calvinism, he was not willing to dispense with all the substance underneath. Even if James detested the "New Divinity men" just as much as any good Transcendentalist might—probably not realizing the degree to which he shared common cause with them on several crucial issues—James never meant to found a new religion but only to pump fresh life and significance into the old one. And in this, it might be said, his relation both to Calvinism and also to his age bore a strong resemblance to that of another native New Yorker's, the novelist Herman Melville. Each man

rebelled violently against the rigid and rigidified letter of New England Calvinism while still preserving a vital sense of its underlying spirit. Yet this ambivalence was more than their countrymen could comprehend. Melville's novels were quickly relegated to the status of children's books, while James's volumes, when they were read at all, were typically regarded merely as footnotes to Swedenborg and mysticism generally. In Melville's case this oversight has now been handsomely rectified; in James's case it has yet to be even widely noticed.

But the affinities between James and Melville do not stop here. If both writers suffered the same historical fate because of their ambivalent feelings toward the unconscious metaphysic which their age was attempting to overthrow, so in almost equal measure both found their chief spiritual resource in what might be termed the new irregular metaphysic which their age professed to put in its place. For what do all of James's books represent, from **Moralism and Christianity** to **Society the Redeemed Form of Man** if not an exhaustive— and, at times, exhausting—attempt to give flesh and blood to that democratic conception of Deity which Melville articulated in the "Knights and Squires" chapter of *Moby Dick*—of "the great God absolute! The centre and circumference of all democracy!," as Melville called him, whose "omnipresence" is "our divine equality?" This is clearly not to suggest that James derived from Melville himself any of his own ideas about Melville's "just Spirit of Equality" who, as the novelist went on to say, "hast spread one royal mantle of humanity over all my kind!" It is simply to reiterate that the sole object of James's entire life work, like the implicit aim of Melville's passage, was to fuse Christianity and democracy into what might be called a new religion of "the kingly commons," and that this new religion of "the kingly commons," even if Melville himself could never place an abiding faith in it, required a displacement of the old Calvinistic sense of the God above by a more modern and egalitarian sense of the God within and without.

In this, of course, James and Melville were hardly alone. One sees intimations and foreshadowings of this marked shift in theological emphasis as early as William Ellery Channing, and by the time one reaches Emerson, one finds it realized in a form which would later typify much of the progressive social and political thought of the later decades of the nineteenth century. But where Emerson subordinated the community to the individual and then raised the individual to a level coequal with God Himself, James, and Melville held on to the older and wiser perception that the individual finds his completion only in relation to others and thus discovered Divinity neither in the Over-Soul nor in society but rather, if anywhere, in that "abounding dignity," as Melville referred to it, which is common to the actual humanity of all men.

3

Henry James, Senior (1811-1882), was the fourth of ten children born to William James (1771-1832) of County Cavan, Ireland, who emigrated to this country at the age of eighteen, and his third wife, the former Catharine Barber (1782-1859). Though the last Mrs. James (the first died in childbirth and the second two years after her marriage) came from a family with deep roots in the American past—her grandfather was a judge and her father, a highly respected farmer, fought in the Revolutionary War with two more illustrious uncles who were personal friends of Washington's and Lafayette's—it was her husband who established the solid American reputation and then came to epitomize the native tradition which subsequently was passed on to their children.

According to family legend, William of Albany, as he came to be known, arrived in this country in 1789 with little more than "a very small sum of money, a Latin grammar in which he had already made some progress at home, and a desire to visit the field of one of the revolutionary battles" [quoted in *The James Family*]. By the time he died, only a little more than forty years later, he had acquired a name second only to that of Stephen Van Renssalaer, the last of the old patroons, and amassed an estate valued at approximately $3,000,000. His was a career which later set the pattern for the typical American success story, parlaying through keen business intelligence and rigorous spiritual self-discipline his half-interest in a small tobacconist concern into one of the great American fortunes of his day. In the course of his extraordinary career, William was led into such various pursuits as real estate, banking, public utilities, and philanthropy, became a major backer of the construction of the Erie Canal, was elected a trustee of Union College in Schenectady, and played a prominent role in various civic affairs throughout the Hudson River Valley. Yet in spite of his great worldly success, he never permitted his business prowess to overshadow his strong religious convictions. Indeed, his brilliant display of the former seemed to follow almost as a kind of reward for his plentiful supply of the latter, encouraging him to pass on to his children the same strict form of Presbyterianism which seemed to support his own life so beneficently.

Oddly enough, of the fourteen children he sired in all, only two among those who survived exhibited any real interest in theological matters, and both eventually rebelled against their father's brand of orthodoxy. The first to fall away was "the Rev. William." After being converted in 1815 during one of the many revivals which swept the Eastern seaboard where he was attending college, he was ordained in 1820 and then drifted from one charge to another for another decade or so until he finally abandoned the parish ministry altogether to devote the rest of his life to "philosophical and theological research." The second was Henry himself, whose resistance to his father's strict Presbyterianism surfaced at a much earlier age than his half-brother's and shaped the whole of his life more consistently.

Whether or not the event had any direct influence on Henry's religious thinking, there can be no doubt that his terrible accident at the age of thirteen, when he was badly burned in a gallant attempt to stamp out a fire caused by a boy's balloon and suffered a double amputation of one leg above the knee, determined much of the temper, if not the substance, of his life to come. The two long years of recuperation in bed, together with the prospect of remaining a cripple for the rest of his life, could not fail to leave an indelible mark upon a boy who was full of animal spirits and who could say of himself, years later, "I lived in every fibre of my body. . . ." Though this calamity apparently did little to diminish his extraordinary fund of energy and left his confidence in himself and the universe intact, the long period of convalescence, as well as the restriction of his physical mobility afterwards, gave inevitable encouragement to his tendencies to introspection, heightened the sensitivity of his powers of observation, and clearly predestined him to a life of thought rather than action. It is interesting to note that one of his own most vivid memories of the incident concerned his father's reaction to his suffering. His father was apparently so deeply moved by the sight of his son's agony during surgery made without the benefit of anaesthesia that Henry's mother had the greatest difficulty in restraining her husband from making too excessive a display of his feelings. This spontaneous outpouring of sympathy from a parent who was otherwise careful to keep his emotions under prudent check could hardly fail to make a lasting impression on a child who was, then as later, never able to control his own rich veins of feeling.

But William of Albany's sympathy was quickly dampened when young Henry set off for Union College in 1828. By this time his wound had completely healed and his zest for life returned. Though Henry could no longer indulge, as he had once done, in "the sports of the river, the wood, or the field," he was perfectly free to enjoy the liberal religious atmosphere at the home of the Reverend Eliphalet Nott, the president of Union College, with whom he lodged, and to take part in some of the more fashionable aspects of Schenectady's social life. It was not long before an old habit acquired in younger days, of snitching pennies from the cache of change his father kept in his dresser drawer, encouraged Henry to run up a series of fairly heavy debts to his father's account. To this the parental reaction was immediate and severe. Convinced that his son was on the verge of moral and spiritual ruin—charges of Henry's "progress in arts of low vileness," his "unblushing flasehood," and his newly developed taste "for segars and oysters" were duly noted—William dispatched a friend to warn young Henry to mend his ways or suffer the consequences. Rather than submit or reform, however, Henry decided to run away to Boston instead, where for a time he became a proofreader and translator with the firm of Jenks and Palmer and continued to indulge himself by enjoying the company of some of the city's first families. But it was not long before he decided to return to Union College, where he graduated in 1830, and then, in an effort to placate his irate father, came home to Albany to begin a study of law while working as an editor for a local publication.

Yet Henry was clearly ill at ease during this period of his life. Because of his strong but unconventional religious cast of mind, legal study did not satisfy him and theological study did not attract him. It was only when his father died in 1832 and Henry found himself independent of parental censure or restriction that he finally decided upon a course of action. Partly in deference to his father and partly because he wanted to resolve some of his own nagging questions, he took it upon himself in 1835 to enroll in Princeton Theological Seminary. The choice of Princeton over some other school was a natural one. His half-brother William had prepared for the ministry there twenty years earlier; his former tutor and life-long friend, the physicist Joseph Henry, had recently accepted a professorship in natural history in the college; and the seminary itself, founded as recently as 1812, had already acquired a distinguished reputation as a bastion of Protestant orthodoxy. The Princeton theology, as it was soon to be called, a mixture of strict Reformed confessionalism and Biblical conservatism, had now been given distinct shape and form under the influence of the seminary's first professor, Archibald Alexander, and by 1822 his more famous pupil, colleague and, later, successor, Charles Hodge, had joined the faculty and was quickly taking on all comers, from the "New Divinity men" under Nathaniel William Taylor at Yale to the Congregational conservatives at Andover.

To Henry's religious sensibility, all of this seemed quite foreign and barbarous. Though his religious conscience had always been an intensely living one, Henry was constitutionally repelled by the thought of a God such as the "Old School" men at Princeton described—whose only purpose seemed to be the self-abasement of His creatures—and could in no way admit the distinction so dear to the Princeton theology itself between the church and the world. As James described himself at the time in his fictionalized *Autobiographical Sketch,* through the eyes of a friend who was meant to serve the function of a neutral observer:

> he contrasted signally with the entire mass of student
> life in the Seminary, by the almost total destitution

which his religious character exhibited of the dramatic element,—that element of unconscious hypocricy which Christ stigmatized in the religious zealots of his day, and which indeed seems to be inseparable from the religious *profession.* The ordinary theological student, especially, has a fatal professional conscience from the start, which vitiates his intellectual integrity. He is personally mortgaged to an institution—that of the pulpit—which is reputed scared, and is all the more potent in its influence upon his natural freedom on that account; so that even the free sphere of his manners is almost sure to lose whatever frank spontaneous flavor it may by inheritance once have had, and become simply servile to convention. My friend was an exception to the rule. His reverence for the Divine name was so tender and hallowed as to render him to a very great extent indifferent to the distinction so loudly emphasized throughout the Seminary between the church and the world. . . . All his discourse betrayed such an unconscious, or at all events unaffected, habit of spiritualizing secular things and secularizing sacred things, that I was erelong forced to conclude that for *his* needs at all events the outward or figurative antagonism of "the church" and "the world" had more than fulfilled its intellectual uses, whatever these may have been; and that any attempt on the part of the Church to perpetuate and especially to exaggerate such antagonism would infallibly expose it to permanent divine ignominy.

With such sentiments as these, it is not surprising that Henry finally decided to leave Princeton in 1838 before taking his degree. His experience there had only confirmed the depth of his alienation from the pretentions of organized religion, and, in any event, faith to him was not a matter of the dogmatic interpretation of tradition but rather an experience, a new sense of the heart, a revelation. Thus he removed himself to New York City to begin a life-long career dedicated to the discovery and expression of his own truth, his own spiritualized version of the good news reported in the Christian scriptures. When in later years his children were to ask him to define his vocation, he merely suggested half-whimsically: "Say I'm a philosopher, say I'm a seeker for truth, say I'm a lover of mankind, say I'm an author of books if you like; or, best of all, just say I'm a student" [in *Notes of a Son and Brother*].

By the time James had taken up residence in New York, he was financially independent. The restrictions his father had originally placed upon the disposition of his estate now had been more equitably arranged after his children had decided to take the matter to court, and, as a result, Henry had received a considerable piece of property in Syracuse which yielded him some $10,000 per year. Being "leisured for life" as he later put it, he was now in a position to acquire a family, and so, in 1840, he took as his wife Mary Robertson

Walsh (1810-1882), the sister of a fellow seminary student, who herself came from a staunch Presbyterian family. The marriage ceremony, however, was, according to the bridegroom's wishes, a strictly civil one, performed by the Mayor of New York in the parlors of the bride's parents. It was not until two years later that the couple was finally installed at 21 Washington Place, just a block off Washington Square, where they were to reside, except when traveling, until they moved to Cambridge in 1866; but even before they were settled the children began to arrive. William was born in January 1882; Henry, a year later; Garth Wilkinson and Robertson followed in 1845 and 1846; and then Alice finally appeared two years later, in 1848.

During these years of domestic settlement and the growth of his family, Henry, Senior's, religious and intellectual life remained anything but dormant. As early as 1837, in fact, even before he had abandoned his seminary training or become a husband and father, Henry had felt the influence of one of three interrelated currents of thought which were eventually to shape so decisively the very idiom as well as substance of his writing. The first of these derived from the writings of Robert Sandeman (1718-1771) to which James was exposed during a trip in the same year to England with his friend Joseph Henry.

Robert Sandeman was a former medical student and later linen manufacturer in Scotland before he turned to preaching under the influence of his father-in-law, the Reverend John Glas (1695-1773). Glas led a small reform movement within the Church of Scotland which accentuated a restoration of certain practices of the Apostolic Church, such as the kiss of peace, the ritual cleansing of the feet, and the weekly celebration of the Eucharist as a common meal or love feast—this he called the *Agape.* Glas also emphasized the Reformation doctrine of justification by faith rather than works and did much to democratize the polity of his small sect by making the offices of elder, pastor, and bishop elective rather than appointive and abolishing all qualifications to such offices on the basis of education or lay occupation.

His son-in-law, Robert Sandeman, accepted the principles of the Glasites almost in toto but carried one or two of them much further. Justification, he insisted, for example, is not a matter of the priority of faith to works but rather of faith alone, and the only difference between the faith we invest in any common report, he went on to contend, and the faith by which we accept the report of the Gospel has solely to do with the different nature of that which constitutes its substance. This antinomian strain in Sandeman, which undercut the works-righteousness basis of every form of moralism, held strong appeal for James. So did the Sandemanian emphasis on the democratic solidarity of primitive Christianity. Hence to acknowledge the debt he

owed Sandeman, James brought out an edition of Sandeman's *Letters on Theron and Aspasio* (1757) in 1838, introducing it with an unsigned two-page preface.

But Sandeman's influence upon James's later thought was relatively slight compared with the more massive impact which the writings of Emanuel Swedenborg (1688-1772) and Charles Fourier (1772-1837) had on him. His exposure to the work of the first may have been initiated by an article published in the *Monthly Magazine* in 1841 by a young English physician named J. J. Garth Wilkinson, a recent convert to Swedenborgianism who in later years, as Swedenborg's editor, translator, and interpreter, became one of James's closest intellectual friends and the namesake of his third child. But James's decisive introduction to Swedenborg did not take place until five years later, while he was still recovering from an emotional and spiritual crisis which had taken place almost two years before. The circumstances attending that crisis, and the part which Swedenborg's writing played in helping to resolve it, are among the better known facts of the James family history.

James's spiritual crisis occurred during one of his family's extended periods of residence in England. James, his wife, Mary, and their first two children, William and Henry, were comfortably settled in a small house near the Great Park of Windsor. In the intervening years between his withdrawal from Princeton Seminary and his establishment in England, James had continued to work away in leisured independence on certain metaphysical questions which had vexed him almost from late adolescence—the reconciliation of science and religion, the question of nature's meaning and unity, and the purpose of creation as revealed by a mystical and symbolic interpretation of the Book of Genesis. James had now begun to suspect that he was close to some major theological discoveries, but as yet all he had to show for his effort were the mountainous piles of manuscript on his desk. Still, he had excellent reasons to feel pleased with himself: his health was good, his circumstances were congenial, his family was coming grandly along, and he was excited about his work.

As he lingered at the dinner table one afternoon in late May of 1844, the fire burning quietly in the grate seemed to confirm the sense of well-being and contentment he felt within. But then, suddenly, and for no apparent reason, his composure abruptly abandoned him, and he found himself face to face with an invisible terror. It was as though some deathly presence were squatting at the other end of the table, "raying out from his fetid personality influences fatal to life." In the space of a few seconds, he was reduced "from a state of firm vigorous joyful manhood to one of almost helpless infancy." It was all he could do to keep from bolting from the room, and when he finally did quit his chair to seek the protective sympathy of his wife, his sense of self was utterly shattered. As he interpreted the event many years later:

> It was impossible for me . . . to hold this audacious faith in selfhood any longer, When I sat down to dinner on that memorable chilly afternoon in Windsor, I held it serene and unweakened by the faintest breath of doubt. Before I rose from the table it had inwardly shrivelled to a cinder. One moment I devoutly thanked God for the inappreciable boon of selfhood; the next that inappreciable boon seemed to me the one thing damnable on earth, seemed a literal nest of hell within my own entrails [in *Society the Redeemed Form of Man*].

James's collapse was no doubt owing partly to physical and spiritual exhaustion which left him vulnerable to a severe attack of depression. But he was later to insist that it was actually the result of something else, something which could only be understood as a part of God's plan for his life and which provided direct evidence of his own spiritual regeneration. Intelligence concerning these last matters came quite by accident, as a result of James's wholly fortuitous meeting with a certain Mrs. Chichester, a kindly Englishwoman who lived in the neighborhood of one of the water cures to which James repaired from time to time to work his way out of his depression. When Mrs. Chichester learned of his collapse, she informed him that he was probably suffering from what Swedenborg called a *vastation,* one of the necessary stages in the process of man's spiritual redemption, leading through awakening, purgation, and illumination to that rebirth of the individual in all his "Divine Natural Humanity" which for Swedenborg was the sole purpose and destiny of creation. James needed to hear little more. In spite of medical warnings about overtaxing himself, he quickly hurried to London to purchase one or two of the master's volumes—he actually bought *Divine Wisdom* and *Love and Divine Providence*—and once he had opened them, his reaction was immediate:

> I read from the first with palpitating interest. My heart divined, even before my intelligence was prepared to do justice to the books, the unequalled amount of truth to be found in them. . . . imagine a subject of some petty depotism condemned to die, and with—what is more and worse—a sentiment of death pervading all his consciousness, lifted by a sudden miracle into felt harmony with universal man, and filled to the brim with the sentiment of indestructible life instead, and you will have a true picture of my emancipated condition [in *Society the Redeemed Form of Man*].

Almost before James had put these first two volumes down, disputes were to arise over whether or not his Swedenborg, the Swedenborg he claimed to have read, bore any relation to the original. After nearly thirty years of correspondence and close personal friendship, J. J. Garth Wilkinson was reluctantly to conclude that the only term James and Swedenborg shared in common was the *Divine Natural Humanity,* a concept which, from Wilkinson's orthodox point of view, James did not really understand. "Swedenborg's Divine Natural," Wilkinson reminded him in a revealing letter written after receipt of a copy of **Society the Redeemed Form of Man** and dated 20 May 1879,

> is Jehovah triumphant in Jesus Christ over his infirm humanity, and over all the hells which had access to it: transforming his natural into the Divine Natural. Swedenborg goes to this end, and to the consequences of a new and everlasting Church proceeding from this Divine Natural. Your Divine Natural, unless I misunderstand you, is diffused in all men, giving, or to give, them infinitude of some kind, and abolishing heavens and hells as mere preparations for the Godhead of Humanity. . . . And at last, the Christ Himself seems to disappear into Humanity, as God has disappeared into Christ; and Man is all in all [quoted in *The Thought and Character of William James* (1935)].

What Wilkinson could not accept was James's eagerness to make Christ fully incarnate in humanity, thus blurring His uniqueness and undercutting the necessity of the Church as the New Jerusalem. But this, of course, is exactly what James intended. James was opposed to Christocentrism in theology on the same grounds that he was opposed to ecclesiasticism among Christians—first, because they both encouraged sectarianism and were therefore destructive of that sense of human solidarity which for him was the ground-base of all religious experience; and, second, because their inevitable claims to special favor and their consequent promotion of such distinctions as believer and nonbeliever, elect and inelect, the saved and the damned, only served to encourage precisely that form of self-righteousness which, again for James, was the root of all evil.

It is no accident that James found confirmation of these views in the one other thinker who seems to have influenced him decisively during these years, the social theorist, reformer, and utopian, Charles Fourier. James had started reading Fourier while he was still recovering from his collapse in 1844, but he was quickly to find himself in a large and disparate company. By 1846 the Fourierist enthusiasm had swollen from a small group of disciples converted by Albert Brisbane four years earlier—George Ripley, Horace Greeley, and Parke Goodwin becoming the most famous American exponents—to a movement with approximately 200,000 followers. But the popularity of Fourierism was hardly an isolated phenomenon. Closely related in spirit to the idealistic ethos of such sister phenomena as the Free Soil movement, the Owenite movement, Transcendentalism, and Abolitionism, members of one group frequently belonged to, or were sympathetic with, the goals of one or more of the others. All partook of that reformist spirit, often strongly utopian, even millennial, in character, which swept across the northern part of the country in the years following Jackson's tenure in the White House, and each called for some great renovation in the laws of society binding man to man and individuals to institutions.

Fourier was important because he offered the blueprint for such a renovation, all carefully worked out according to scientific principles. The result was a kind of transcendental social science which served as a perfect complement to that sort of spiritual science which James had already acquired from Swedenborg. Swedenborg had provided James with a way of understanding how the emerging social sentiment of the era, the new feeling of human fellowship and solidarity, could be interpreted as evidence of God's redeeming and transforming work in nature; Fourier then produced a concrete outline of the way that new social sentiment might achieve visible shape and form in the actual social order.

Beyond this, however, James was also attracted to Fourier because, as Ralph Barton Perry has pointed out, he supported two of James's firmest convictions. In the first place, Fourier confirmed his view of man's social solidarity, man's unity with his kind, which was then reflected in James's religious belief that God works not in isolated individuals but rather in the very stuff of human nature itself, employing as His chief field of operations the most natural and universal of our affections and appetites. This led Wilkinson to charge that James was guilty of a form of pantheism, what he called "pananthropism," but to James himself, who had long since decided that Wilkinson was "eaten up with spirits and all that," he was proposing nothing radical than a development of the logic of the Incarnation: by showing what followed with perfect consistency from God's taking upon Himself not merely the image but the very being of His creature and thus displaying the life of Divinity in the incarnate form of perfect humanity.

What did not follow, however, with any consistency at all from James's fully developed view of the religion of the Incarnation was the second idea he found attractive in Fourier, the idea of human innocence. Fourier assumed that man was created good rather than evil and that whatever evil man subsequently committed was therefore due not to anything inherently wrong with his own nature but rather to external restraints placed on him by society. Redesign society in such a way that the restrictions on man's freedom are removed, Fourier argued, and we would once again discover that when man can act spontaneously, according to his own nature, he is truly innocent and in his innocence good. "Make society do its duty to the individual," James declared in the same mood, "and the individual will be sure to do his duties to society."

The problem was that James's own religious experience proved otherwise. If the blame for human evil could be laid solely at the door of the social order, then the Transcendentalists and their idealist friends were right: simply remove the restrictions to man's spontaneity and freedom and each individual, when he can be made to accept it, will realize the divine infinitude of his own soul. As James matured in the knowledge of his own experience, however, he became more and more certain that this would not do. The redemption of the individual required something more profound than a readjustment of the social order; it required a rebirth and regeneration of the individual himself.

This alteration in James's thought about the nature of human innocence, and the development of his contrasting view of man's inevitable but not wholly contemptible corruptibility, can be discerned quite readily from his changing relations with two of his more famous correspondents and friends, Ralph Waldo Emerson and Thomas Carlyle. James first met Emerson in the early spring of 1842, after James attended one of Emerson's New York lectures and then invited him to call. James was immediately attracted to Emerson because he could recognize so easily in his Concord acquaintance the marks of one who was seeking out the very reality of things with no regard for anything but the truth; yet almost from the very beginning of their ripening friendship, one can discern the seeds of James's later disillusionment.

At first it was simply the problem of drawing Emerson out, of dissociating the speaker who charmed with his words and uplifted by his example from the man who thought and questioned and felt. Emerson impressed James from first to last as a kind of divine presence who was so serenely composed within himself and so magnanimous and tender in his relations with others that it was all but impossible to resist being captivated by him. But James wanted to be instructed as well as inspired, to be challenged as well as enlightened, and on this score Emerson could not help him. The older man seemed temperamentally incapable of explanation and dispute, while the younger man not only thrived on such things but could not live without them.

As the years wore on, however, and the relations between them, at least after the middle of the century, began to cool, the problem ceased being merely temperamental and became intellectual and religious as well. From James's point of view, Emerson simply could not be brought to see the potential evil as well as good in the kind of self-consciousness he was always preaching, and, as a consequence, Emerson was inevitably disposed to promote as cure for the human situation what James took to be the disease itself. The question was whether Emerson's blindness on this point, his refusal to take into his purview any evidence supplied by consciousnesses other than his own, was not itself symptomatic? Wasn't Emerson's sublime indifference to any arguments challenging his position and questioning his optimism indicative of the presence, or at least the potential, of that very evil of egotism which James wanted to point out to him?

If it were, then James could not bring himself to hold Emerson in any way personally responsible for it, as the Scotsman Thomas Carlyle might have done. James first met Carlyle in 1843 and then resumed their acquaintance during another visit to England in 1855. Carlyle supplied precisely what Emerson lacked, a mind which had reasons for everything and a crotchety skepticism about the sincerity of all human motives to go along with it. Carlyle fed James's love for argument and contentiousness but went beyond them to a cynicism so pervasive and relentless that it hardly left room for anything else. James had to admire and respect Carlyle for the trenchancy of his social criticism, for his deadly aim in unmasking every form of human folly, but he could not follow Carlyle when the latter used his eye for human weakness to support his pessimism about the whole human race. On occasion James was able to assume a light attitude of amused disapproval toward Carlyle, as when he referred to him in a letter to Emerson as "the same old sausage, fizzing and sputtering in his own grease"; but he was also capable of drawing very accurate aim himself, as when he noted in the "Personal Recollections" he published after Carlyle's death:

> His own intellectual life consisted so much in bemoaning the vices of his race, or drew such inspiration from despair, that he could not help regarding a man with contempt the instant he found him reconciled to the course of history. Pity is the highest style of intercourse he allowed himself with his kind. . . . "Poor John Sterling," he used always to say; "poor John Mill, poor Frederick Maurice, poor Neuberg, poor Arthur Helps, poor little Browning, poor little Lewes" and so on; as if the temple of his friendship were a hospital, and all its inmates scrofulous or paralytic [quoted in *The Literary Remains of the Late Henry James*].

James could enjoy Carlyle's declamations but not his wholesale condemnations. Though he himself frequently used the abstract as a kind of club to beat the actual, he could still never forget, as Ralph Barton Perry has said, "the Man in men." Nor, for that matter, could he overlook the element of good amidst all the ill. For James was fundamentally reconciled to the divine Providence which guides men's affairs in a way that Carlyle clearly was not, and this made all the difference. However pointed and stinging his criticism of his fellows, and however frontal and slashing his assaults on various ideas, James's invective was never cruel or sardonic. For all of his noisy thunder and bombast, there was always a generous dose of the Quixotic

knight-errant about him, one who, whether he knows it or not, inevitably ennobles both himself and his windmills by tilting at them with such gusto.

For this reason alone, many people cultivated James's friendship, his society, even when they lacked sympathy with or interest in his ideas. There was an elemental humanity in him very like the substance he kept imputing to the nature of his fellow mortals. Even when he baited Bronson Alcott for being "an egg half hatched . . . [with] the shells . . . yet sticking about your head," or railed out against a conception of the Deity as absolute, irrelative, and unconditionally perfect, on the grounds that "any mother who suckles her babe upon her own breast, any bitch in fact who litters her periodical brood of pups, presents to my imagination a vastly nearer and sweeter Divine charm," there was a brightness, a color, a robust vigor to his polemics which tempered censure with concern, judgment with humor. "To exalt humble and abase proud things was ever the darling sport of his conversation," his son William reported, "which, when he was in the *abasing* mood, often startled the good people of Boston, who did not know him well enough to see the endlessly genial and humane intuition from which the whole mood flowed." Yet genial and humane the intuition always was, because James seemed to embody in himself what he imputed to his God—a sense of insufficiency rather than self-sufficiency, springing from his intuitive grasp of the fact that man, like God, is incapable of realizing himself except in others.

4

It was this singular unity of sensibility in their father—what Henry, Junior, described as "a passion peculiarly his own" by which he "kept together his stream of thought, however transcendent and the stream of life, however humanized"—which so impressed his two sons when they looked back upon his life, and which partially accounts for the surprisingly strong impact he was to have on both of them long after he was dead. Indeed, it would not be too much to say that while James made little impression on his contemporaries either in the world of letters or in the theological community, he still left an indelible imprint upon American culture. And that imprint came by way of his influence on his two sons, who subsequently then divided between them so much of that intellectual and spiritual heritage of the nineteenth century which was passed on to the twentieth.

At first glance such a claim may sound exaggerated. After all, did not William differentiate himself from his father in the most explicit of terms when he pointed out in his "Introduction" to *The Literary Remains* that the elder James was a philosophical and theological monist who would brook no compromise with ethical and philosophical pluralists; and did not Henry, in his turn, then confess, in a letter acknowledging the receipt of his volume, that for all his love and admiration for his father's person, he could never make head nor tail of his ideas? The answer is inevitably yes, but there is also important evidence on the other side of this question. One could cite, for example, the letter William wrote to the elder James four days before the latter's death, in which he confessed that no matter how different their expressions of it, he derived virtually the whole of his intellectual life from his father; or, again, one could refer to comments Henry, Junior, made thirty years later, in *Notes of a Son and Brother,* where he suggests that none of the children could really escape being affected by "Father's ideas," as his wife referred to them, just because they constituted so large a part of the "daily medium" in the James household.

Yet the question of influence cannot be resolved through personal testimony of this kind, because the process of its occurrence is always more subtle and indirect. The elder James himself described its more probable form of operation among the members of his own household when he observed in a letter to Emerson "that a vital truth can never be transferred from one mind to another, because life alone appreciates it. The most one can do for another is to plant the rude formula of such truth in his memory, leaving his own spiritual chemistry to set free the germs whenever the demands of his life exact it" [quoted in *The Thought and Character of William James*]. The rude formulas of their father's truth, his ideas, clearly made little or no impression upon William and Henry, either when those ideas were first uttered in their presence, or long after when both men tried to remember them; it was the germs of "vital truth" which were transmitted, but which were not set free until their own individual lives demanded it and which then developed only as the "spiritual chemistry" of their own natures permitted it. Henry, Junior's, trust in moments of vision and his equally strong interest in the sensuous or felt qualities of thought, no less than his intense absorption with the sin of self-culture and his emphasis on the virtue of self-denial and self-renunciation; William's theory of knowledge as a kind of action and his stress on the element of change, no less than his firm insistence on having a say about the deepest reasons of the universe and his criticism of the blindness which human beings practice on each other—all show the unmistakable influence of their father, even though both men found support for these views in many other sources as well.

But the evidence of a paternal legacy is even more striking if one examines that core of values which, despite their more obvious differences, William and Henry shared in common. Consider, for example, the common emphasis both placed on the virtue of intellectual sympathy. In Henry this surfaced in his obsession with the singular point of view of specific, indi-

vidual consciousnesses and beyond this, in his insistence that the only way to appreciate a work of art, as he suggested in his famous analogy of the Persian rug and its complex design, is by imaginatively penetrating into the pattern of the whole before attempting to define its controlling figure. In William this was reflected in his belief that the only way to understand another man's ideas is by placing yourself at the center of his philosophical vision, where you can then understand all the different observations which flow from it. "But keep outside," he warned in *A Pluralistic Universe,* "use your post-mortem method, try to build the philosophy up out of the single phrases, taking first one and then another and seeking to make them fit, and of course you fail. You crawl over the thing like a myopic ant over a building, tumbling into every microscopic crack or fissure, finding nothing but inconsistencies, and never suspecting that a centre exists." What were such sentiments as these but an extension of their father's belief that the virtue of trying to put yourself in the position of another owes its authority to Divine precept and example, an example which the elder James perfectly emulated himself, according to his novelist son, "there being no human predicament he couldn't by a sympathy more *like* direct experience than any I have ever known enter into . . ."?

Or, to take another example, there is the stress each placed on the sacredness of the individual and the life that is in him, a belief which evoked, supported, and confirmed their equally brilliant gifts of personal observation and psychological insight. Again, what was this but a reappropriation, according to their own lights, of their father's conviction that every fibre of a person's humanity is resident with divinity, a conviction which, again like his sons, explained his own powers of observation? Indeed, it was precisely because of his father's theological convictions, Henry, Junior, reports, that "no element of character, no spontaneity of life, but instantly seized his attention and incurred his greeting and comment, which things could never possibly have been so genially alert and expert—as I have, again, superabundantly recorded—if it had not fairly fed on active observation and contact." The elder James "fairly fed" on such matters because he thereby conceived himself to be trafficking with the incarnate form of God Himself. His two sons clearly had less explicitly theological reasons for nourishing themselves on such matters, but both still took no fewer pains to evoke the appropriately religious emotions of awe and wonder when, through careful observation, each found himself in their presence.

Such observations as these do not add up to the conclusion that either of the sons was a covert disciple of his father. At most they merely suggest the existence of a more intimate relationship among all three members of the James family than has heretofore been perceived. Neither William nor Henry took any of his father's ideas at face value and simply re-expressed them in a different medium. What they were receptive to instead was the element of "vital truth" underneath, which they both then worked to complement or comment upon according to their own taste and genius. The point is that such "vital truths," and not the ideas which are but rude formulas of them, are precisely what a culture consists of; and, in this sense, we can say that Henry, Senior, and his two sons belonged to the same one.

To say this is to suggest the necessity of a fresh reassessment of the elder James's whole relation to the American tradition. Where until now he has usually been regarded merely as an American eccentric, more careful study will reveal, I think, that he was closer to being something like an American original and one we can scarcely afford any longer to ignore, since, in the history of American philosophy and religion, we have had, comparatively, so very few of them.

Alfred Habegger (essay date 1988)

SOURCE: "*The Bostonians* and Henry James Sr.'s Crusade against Feminism and Free Love," in *Women's Studies: An Interdisciplinary Journal,* Vol. 15, No. 4, 1988, pp. 323-42.

[*Habegger is the author of the full-length biography of James entitled* The Father: A Life of Henry James, Sr. *(1994). In the following essay, he argues that Henry James, Jr. wrote his novel* The Bostonians *(1886) in reaction to his father's involvement with the free love movement and his encounters with the radical press.*]

There are some books that seem ugly, dull, and all wrong to contemporary readers and then strike a later generation as brilliant and right and presently get enrolled in the canon of all-time greats. We generally trust that this sequence of events represents the triumph of taste over local prejudice—even for those books the local society would seem best situated to make sense of, realistic fiction. But what if someone wrote a realistic novel about *us* which we all felt to be cranky and off, and a hundred years later we were waked up in our graves and informed that this book was regarded as the authoritative mirror of our lives? Would we take it lying down?

At the end of World War II Philip Rahv brought out the first twentieth-century edition of a novel that fell flat when first published one hundred years ago, *The Bostonians* by Henry James. One of the reasons Rahv disinterred it was that he felt it went to the heart of what was wrong with American democracy—"the hys-

---

An excerpt from "Mr. Emerson," by Henry James, Sr. (1881):

On the whole I may say that at first I was greatly disappointed in him, because his intellect never kept the promise which his lovely face and manners held out to me. He was to my senses a literal divine presence in the house with me; and we cannot recognize literal divine presences in our houses without feeling sure that they will be able to say something of critical importance to one's intellect. It turned out that any average old dame in a horse-car would have satisfied my intellectual rapacity just as well as Emerson. My standing intellectual embarrassment for years had been to get at the bottom of the difference between law and gospel in humanity—between the head and the heart of things—between the great God almighty, in short, and the intensely wooden and ridiculous gods of the nations. Emerson, I discovered immediately, had never been the least of an expert in this sort of knowledge; and though his immense personal fascination always kept up, he at once lost all intellectual prestige to my regard. I even thought that I had never seen a man more profoundly devoid of spiritual understanding. This prejudice grew, of course, out of my having inherited an altogether narrow ecclesiastical notion of what spiritual understanding was. I supposed it consisted unmistakably in some doctrinal lore concerning man's regeneration, to which, however, my new friend was plainly and signally incompetent. Emerson, in fact, derided this doctrine, smiling benignly whenever it was mentioned. I could make neither head nor tail of him according to men's ordinary standards—the only thing that I was sure of being that he, like Christ, was somehow divinely begotten.

Henry James, Sr., in The James Family: Including Selections from the Writings of Henry James, Senior, William, Henry, and Alice James, *by F.O. Matthiessen, Alfred A. Knopf, 1948.*

---

teria of Feminism," the refusal to allow the individual his own discriminations. A few years later Lionel Trilling proclaimed that in no other book "had the nature of the American social existence ever been so brilliantly suggested" as in *The Bostonians*. Like Rahv, Trilling was recklessly enthusiastic about Basil Ransom, James's Southern reactionary who woos Verena Tarrant away from Olive Chancellor and feminist reform. The rehabilitation became complete in 1956, with Irving Howe's introduction to the Modern Library edition. No, Howe shrewdly argued, James did not endorse Ransom's provincial conservatism, but yes, the book is a brilliantly realistic representation of the way the political infects the personal in American life.

In the three decades since the Modern Library edition appeared, hundreds of critics have performed essentially the same balancing act as Howe in trying to think well of this disturbing novel. Pauline Kael's review of the recent Ivory-Merchant-Jhabvala film repeats the orthodox line in remarkably succinct form, leaping from the notion that James himself "seems to be pulled about, identifying with some of the characters and then rejecting them for others," to the loopily inconsequent claim that *The Bostonians* "is by far the best novel in English about what at that time was called 'the woman question.'"

Kael's leap of faith sums up the unreasonableness of all those keen essays of the 1940s and 50s that contended for the truthfulness of James's novel, yet never stopped to reflect that James's hostility to Boston and its reform movements might have distorted his portrayal of them. Why didn't it occur to the shrewd, historicized New York intellectuals that *James himself* was a part of history and that his Boston novel might express a staked-out position familiar in its time? Why didn't they find out what *feminist* readers of the 1880s thought and wrote about James's representation of them?

There is in fact an untold story behind *The Bostonians.* It is in part a cautionary tale about the self-betrayals and cover-ups of an aging ex-radical, and in part a father-and-son case history—a father who passed himself off as an authority on the vexed questions of marriage and "woman" and an anxiously loyal son who sought to vindicate his father soon after his death. Only lately have all the pieces of this puzzle been found and brought together.

Some of the key facts have been known for years. On April 8, 1883, about four months after the death of Henry James Sr., his second son copied into his notebook the prospectus for a new novel, adding a private memorandum on his intentions for the book. He would focus on what he called "the decline of the sentiment of sex," and he would attack a popular newspaper press that was bent on invading the private life. He hoped that a detailed representation of American feminism and journalism would at last prove that "I *can* write an American story." These familiar phrases from James's notebooks raise a number of questions that have never been satisfactorily addressed. Why bring together *these* two particular topics, feminism and newspapers? What did James mean by the opaque "sentiment of sex"? And is there anything in the fact that James conceived of the novel soon after his father's death? In his fine discussion of the novel Leon Edel rightly surmised that *The Bostonians* had something to do with the disappearance of the James family home in Cambridge. But this is one story the prodigious Edel missed.

I

In 1934 Austin Warren turned up something in the James family record that no biographer, historian, or critic has paid much attention to. In 1848, the year of revolution, Henry James Sr. translated and wrote a laudatory preface for a French pamphlet on marriage written by Victor Hennequin. *Love in the Phalanstery,* James's title, was a Fourierist tract: it was sponsored by the American Union of Associationists, and like some of the works advertised on its back cover it explained how life would be organized in the harmonious social unit—the phalanx—of the future. It was known that Fourier had certain heterodox French notions about the relations of the sexes, but the American Associationists tried to avoid calling attention to them. Not Henry James Sr. His preface urged readers to give serious consideration to the "truths" of Hennequin's pamphlet. One of these new truths was that not all members of the phalanx would be required to be faithful to their spouse; another was that some people might lawfully enjoy a variety of lovers. At the time the translator circulated these views he was thirty-seven years old. He'd been married eight years, he had fathered five children, and he had had one nervous collapse. His name did not appear on the title page.

On publication, *Love in the Phalanstery* brought forth a laconic prediction from the *New York Tribune*'s book reviewer: "we . . . presume the anti-Fourierites can find something in it which they might quote to great advantage" (Sept. 28, 1848). He was right, and James was soon embroiled in controversy. An influential Presbyterian weekly, the *New York Observer,* accused James of libertine thinking, and a number of other writers chimed in. James defended himself vigorously, at times retreating into arcane metaphysical distinctions and at times giving vent to some remarkably defiant and dangerous assertions:

> If you bind a man in whom the passion of Love is highly organized, to the intercourse of one woman, whether he feel any love to her or not, you not only provoke his unmerited disgust towards her unoffending sweetness, but you are sure to inflame his passionate longings towards every other woman from whom you have excluded him. ("Concluding Remarks")

Fortunately, there was a new order coming:

> I presume a day will come when the sexual relations will be regulated in every case by the private will of the parties; when the reciprocal affection of a man and a woman will furnish the sole and sufficient sanction of their material converse . . . ("Remarks")

When that "divine time" arrives, the law will no longer require couples to adhere to "any past act or promise." Instead, the law—

> will declare the entire freedom of every man and woman to follow the bent of their private affections,

will justify every alliance sanctioned by these affections . . . Thus, if a man's or woman's affections bind them to an exclusive alliance all their days, the law will approve. If, on the contrary, they lead the subject to a varied alliance, the law will equally approve. ("Remarks")

We should remember that James was not the only American in the 1840s who dreamed of a new social order that would unchain human sexuality. There were the Mormons with their still secret polygamy, and there was the amazing John Humphrey Noyes and his Perfectionist community at Oneida, New York, where all the men were married to all the women, and vice versa, and all practiced a carefully supervised promiscuity. James himself had "a conversation or two" with the "leading men" of Oneida, as he admitted a few years later (*N.Y. Observer*). Although the full extent of James's dealing with Noyes is not yet known, it is apparent that these two ex-Calvinists, both born in 1811, were not only in touch but shared their generation's dream of a revolutionary sexual utopia.

This can be a costly dream. In 1852 a wild book was published, *Love vs. Marriage,* that pressed James's antinomian impulses to their limit. It was written by Marx Edgeworth Lazarus, a Jewish physician in New York who was probably known by James, as both had been frequent contributors to the same Fourierist magazine, *The Harbinger.* Lazarus was troubling because he built a case for free love by drawing on James's doctrine that love and marriage were incompatible in the present civilization. Lazarus not only set forth Fourier's "passional series", which *Love in the Phalanstery* had explained, but also offered "Practical Suggestions to Lovers" and a great deal of physiological information on the formation of semen, the ovulation cycle, how to avoid pregnancy, and so forth. The bibliography included *Love in the Phalanstery* and two collections of James's essays. Most frightening of all for James was Lazarus' stated wish—

> to clear away that confusion of opinions and of action which has hitherto compromised the efficiency of our propagandism and of our practical efforts; to reveal men to themselves and to each other . . . I take pleasure in acknowledging the substantial integrity of the writings of Henry James, of John S. Dwight, of Albert Brisbane, and Dr. C.J. Hempel among our American friends, although considerations entirely personal may prevent them from taking openly the same ground as myself.

James retaliated with a long review in the *New York Tribune* (Sept. 18, 1852) that worked out an obscure and allegorical view of marriage. Only at the end of his review did he turn briefly to *Love vs. Marriage,* dismissing it in a few contemptuous phrases—"a very needless affront to public decorum," "mere childish-ness, mere imbecility." This lofty air was quite disingenuous. James, roused from his revolutionary slumbers, was fighting for his name, and his review was nothing less than a fervent profession of faith in the thing he formerly scorned—legal marriage. He still dreamed of "a perfect society," but now it must be one in which every man finds "an exhaustless ideal charm" in "the wife of his bosom" and in no other woman. James kept his old view that marriage is a disappointment for the husband, because his wife can never "fulfil the promise which the unappropriated woman held out," but he now preached that this disappointment is precisely what man needs to raise himself from the physical to the spiritual. The history of each man and of civilization itself follows the same path: first man glimpses in the "downcast eyes" of the woman he has enslaved a radiant glory; he binds himself to her for life; and eventually the confinement of marriage proves to be a saving discipline for him and he transcends himself.

In this redemptive fable, James apotheosized the very thing—marriage—he had set out to reform. He abandoned the pursuit of happiness and instead proclaimed that all men must follow a long and painful process of self-correction. James preached this gospel for the rest of his life; it formed the core of his doctrine. Because so many students of the Jameses have simply accepted the doctrine as a given in his thought, it is of the first importance to understand the pressures that led him to elaborate and espouse it—his own heartfelt tendency to free love, the fear of being claimed by Lazarus as a brother-in-arms, the final loyalty to "public decorum," and the deep self-betrayal.

It is also important to note the completely unconscious egotism of James's little fable. Everything is calculated with certain male needs in mind, and women's own dissatisfactions or desires or liberties never once enter into the matter. Woman is man's angel, a totally different kind of being from himself. James announces from on high how man can escape his selfish nature, and the remedy he thunders out is sublimely selfish. This is the man who would be regarded by some of his children—among them Henry Jr.—as a marvelously unselfish father and devoted husband.

Having spurned what he believed in 1848, James now had a new set of enemies to contend with, the free-love radicals. This hard-pressed faction needed all the help it could get, and the loss of James, with his wealth, prestige, energy, and wit, was a severe blow. Few Americans of the time grasped that the essential issue in free love was one of civil liberty rather than morality. Almost everyone, including James, associated the cause with fringe movements like homoeopathy, vegetarianism, spiritualism. They could not imagine that a time would come when most Americans would apparently take for granted that the state shouldn't regulate the sexual lives of citizens. (It is ironic that even under rulers as hostile to civil liberties as Reagan and the Rehnquist Supreme Court, we can now say that the principle of free love has basically won.)

Of all James's new enemies, the most adept and tenacious was Stephen Pearl Andrews, the philosopher of "individual sovereignty." Andrews was angered by James's "saucy and superficial" (Andrews, *Love*) review of Lazarus, and two months later, when James publicly defended his old position in favor of more liberal divorce laws, Andrews struck back. He had been looking for a way to introduce the dubious topic of free love into a large-circulation paper. He sent a letter to the *New York Tribune* and James was soon enticed into a lively public debate. Andrews showed how James's own statements on divorce meant that marriage was at times oppressive and could be terminated. James defended divorce in a strange way:

> If our conjugal . . . ties . . . can be safely discharged of the purely diabolic element of outward force, they must instantly become transfigured by their own inward, divine, and irresistible loveliness. (Andrews, *Love*)

Andrews, seeing just where James was vulnerable, approved of his preference for the "sexual union of loving souls" over "the sordid considerations of a marriage settlement." Insofar as James trusted to "the self-regulative powers of freedom, in the place of regulations imposed from without," Andrews demonstrated, he was pushing free love.

James was very neatly caught. What was particularly upsetting was that the editor of the *Tribune,* Horace Greeley, who opposed divorce and of course detested free love, pointed out to his readers that Andrews' libertinism was the logical consequence of James's own position. Worse, Greeley contended "that Mr. James's liberty of divorce, no matter what *his* intent may be, . . . would practically open to the licentious and fickle a prospect of ridding themselves of the obligations of marriage at pleasure" (Andrews, *Love*). To discredit Andrews, Greeley cited a newspaper report: "Henry Shriver eloped from this city last week with the wife of a neighbor, leaving behind a wife and several children" (Andrews, *Love*). If this was Andrews' tendency, then it was Henry James's as well.

The rich and respectable father once again saw himself classed with a shady crowd. Losing his temper, he blustered at Andrews' "lurid and damnable falsehood" that his own opinions served in any way to sanction "license" (Andrews, *Love*).

Now James had to retreat even farther, and some of the intellectual strategies by which he did so are nothing less than appalling, especially his redefinition of

freedom. Mankind, he dogmatically announced, lives under a "threefold subjection, first to nature, then to society, and finally to God." Perfect freedom is to be found only in total submission to these three: "it constitutes the express and inscrutable perfection of the divine life that he who yields himself with least reserve to that most realizes life in himself" (Andrews, *Love*). In this sentence, James is still concerned with "perfection" but he has lost sight of choice and social institutions. Worse, the sentence says that slavery is freedom. The unknown scandal of James's obscure metaphysics is that it was designed, under intense pressure, to limit civil freedom in the guise of supporting it.

Another of James's strategies involved the woman question. He had already begun to think of "woman" as a different kind of being from man, a *deus ex machina* who redeemed him from his carnal selfishness, but in his 1853 essay, "Woman and the 'Woman's Movement,'" James pushed this argument to its political conclusion. He ridiculed feminism, opposed the entry of women into the learned professions, and insisted with remarkable emphasis that women were intellectually inferior to men. At the heart of his essay was the banal idea that home is woman's sphere, an idea James developed to the point of claiming that woman was not an individual but "a form of personal affection." It is "only in ministering to man" that she "finds her life." The "woman's movement" (a phrase Henry Sr. would always put in quotes) does not "presage any directly valuable results."

James's 1848 phase reminds us that millennialism and sexual antinomianism often go together, and his later doctrines remind us of the equally familiar truth that radical dreams are often succeeded by the most pompous sound and fury. We get a fuller glimpse of the heart of James's mystery, however, if we regard him in the context of two opposed tendencies in the radical ferment of his time. The first shows up in the Mormons, who reserved the privilege of sexual variety for men only and placed women in an inferior social category, and the second shows up in those dreamers— Noyes, Lazarus, Andrews—whose millennialism was transformed into a secular vision of greater freedom for both sexes. One type of millennialism reverted to an archaic, patriarchal order, and the other turned into a modern kind of civil libertarianism. The Mormons came to regard marriage as the central institution of their sect, while the free lovers often joined the feminists in arguing that for women marriage was a form of dependency.

It is obvious which of these two groups James was closest to. In 1848, defending **Love in the Phalanstery,** he sounded like one of the free lovers, but four years later, when the going got rough, he sided once and for all with the patriarchs. From this point on, in spite of the violence of his denunciations of "moralism," the active elements in James's social thinking were authoritarian and androcentric. What made his social thought so very insidious and problematic was that (like many authoritarian regimes) it operated behind a veil of secrecy, obscurity, and disingenuousness. Years later, someone reported of James's lecture on "Marriage" that it was "as remarkable for the orthodoxy of its spirit as for the heterodoxy of its form," and this formula sums up the spirit of this complicated thinker (Sargent).

Speaking the language of freedom in order to shore up an ancient kingdom, James deceived many people in his own time, and he has deceived many in ours also. Only recently have Jean Strouse, Howard M. Feinstein, and Jane Maher, in their fine biographies of his children, Alice, William, Wilkie, and Bob, begun to penetrate his smoke-screens.

II

What did Henry James Jr., born in 1843, make of his father's views on sex, love, and marriage? The son was obviously too young in 1852 and '53 to confront these views, although it is clear that he was uneasy about his father's contradictions and weaknesses. Twenty years later, however, when the father once again got himself embroiled in a public debate with Stephen Pearl Andrews on free love, and once again bespattered himself, Henry Jr. was old enough to understand.

The episode began in 1872, when the Rev. Henry Ward Beecher was accused of committing adultery with Mrs. Tilton. A correspondent from St. Paul, Minnesota, wrote Henry James Sr. and pressed him to comment on Beecher's apparent infidelity. James, who was now famous for his "philosophy of marriage," as E.L. Godkin called it, replied by rehearsing his now standard argument that marriage stimulates men's spiritual growth by confining desire. Unfortunately, his letter contained a passage that was so indiscreet it could easily be construed by readers as a confession: "I marry my wife under the impression that she is literally perfect, and is going to exhaust my capacity of desire ever after. Ere long I discover my mistake."

The correspondent was Harvery Y. Russell, and he worked for the *St. Paul Daily Press* (Stern). He got James's letter printed in his paper and then sent a clipping to *Woodhull & Claflin's Weekly* in New York. This journal, devoted to free love and radical feminism, was edited by none other than Andrews, still smarting from Greeley's refusal back in 1852 to print his answers to James. Now Andrews took revenge, and in April 1874, Henry James Sr.'s apparent admission that his wife hadn't afforded him full sexual satisfaction appeared in the most outrageous American scandal-sheet of the nineteenth-century (James, "Morality").

This event, ignored by everyone who has ever written on the Jameses, was one of the memorable events in their lives. They must have been horrified at the low associations and the publicity. We begin to sense the significance of the scandal if we recall that Henry Jr. would later write a number of tales about intrusive journalists and publishing scoundrels and honorable people trusted with sensitive personal documents that must be destroyed. Indeed, one of the reasons the biographers have missed this story is that most of the family documents *have* been destroyed. Although two of William's letters to Henry Jr. speak of the Beecher-Tilton business, not one of the remarkably few extant letters that crossed the *Atlantic* between Henry and his family in the late spring and summer of 1874 so much as mentions the father's trouble. Yet at the time Henry Sr. himself not only refused to hush the matter up but sent a rejoinder to *Woodhull & Claflin's.*

What it all meant to Henry Jr. was that the radical press seeks to invade and expose the private life. From this point on, the novelist would repeatedly associate social reform with the violation of family life by journalistic radicals, such as Andrews or Russell. Reviewing a book on American communes several months later, he delivered himself of a scathing denunciation that reflected his filial outrage: "the whole scene . . . is an attempt to organize and glorify the detestable tendency toward the complete effacement of privacy in life and thought everywhere so rampant with us nowadays" (*Nordhoff's*). This idea—that a separatist commune expresses the larger society's sense of private life and private property—seems most unlikely. Henry Jr. was angry over his father's exposure in *Woodhull & Claflin's,* and he was lashing out.

In fact, in writing the passage from which I have just quoted, the loyal son lost control of his pen in a way that is so uncanny it is hard to believe. To make sense of this hitherto unnoticed lapse, we need to take a closer look at the book James was commenting on. This was Charles Nordhoff's *Communistic Societies of the United States,* which undertook to survey the concrete social results of utopian socialism in America. Reading this book in late 1874, the reviewer in effect saw just where his father's 1848 dreams might have carried him.

The important chapter was about Oneida. Here Henry Jr. read the story of a young man named Charles, who had allowed himself to get too attached to one of his temporary sexual partners, a woman who was pregnant by him. It was forbidden to show any special preference for any one spouse at Oneida, since Noyes believed that monogamy was the death of communalism, and thus Charles broke a signal law by falling in love.

According to Nordhoff's book, the young father-to-be was taken to task by Noyes and other Oneidans during a session of "Criticism" and was persuaded "to isolate himself entirely from the woman, and let another man take his place at her side." It was this episode, especially the way the community separated Charles from the woman, that elicited Henry Jr.'s heated condemnation of "the complete effacement of privacy in life and thought everywhere so rampant with us nowadays."

Now, the fascinating thing about Henry Jr.'s review is that it enables us to look through *his own eyes* at his father's suppressed radicalism. That we see through these eyes is that both Charles and father were in the same boat, as each was misled in his youth by communists. Indeed, that publishing scoundrel at *Woodhull & Claflin's* who was still after the father was part of the same gang that had so tragically perverted Charles, convincing him that fidelity, his great and unconscious virtue, was a crime. Of course, there was this difference between the two men: while Charles was wrongly persuaded to give up the woman he loved, Henry Sr. had long ago emerged in triumph from the mire of free love and socialism, and had then created, simultaneously, a philosophy based on marriage and a wonderful family. What Charles was led to renounce—loving one woman faithfully—was the very thing that saved Henry Sr. Thus, for Henry Jr., the story of Oneidan Charles recapitulated his own father's essential life-struggle. What Henry Jr. saw in Charles was a defamiliarized image of Henry Sr.

Is all this fanciful? Then how else can we explain the reviewer's bizarre lapse? Evidently forgetting Charles' name, he came up with a substitute, and thinking it was the original, wrote *Henry.*

This mistake helps confirm my suspicion that Henry James Jr. regarded his father as a victim of radical American democracy. If I am right, the father's false consciousness not only burdened his son with a highly distorted sense of American life but ensured that the son would work very hard *not to know* the things the father did not want to be known. One of these things is that, unlike Oneidan Charles, the senior James had *voluntarily* embraced free love, against the wishes of many other American Fourierists. Another suppressed truth is that the father's ardent lifelong defense of marriage reflected a timorous inner collapse. And another is that the father had actively collaborated with those journalists who exploited him, being a hotheaded controversialist with a lengthy record of intemperate and indiscreet letters to editors. He himself in fact was almost one of them, as he helped pay the bills for the *Harbinger* (Warren) at the very time it published (had to publish?) his letters defending **Love in the Phalanstery**. The only person who sought to efface Henry Sr.'s privacy was Henry Sr. himself, and perhaps the reason he courted exposure and humiliation

was that he really did believe, as he so often proclaimed, that his self-hood was damnable.

What's more, if the behavior recorded in the private diary of a friend of his is typical, Henry Sr.'s dealings with women may have been more than a little flaky. In 1866 the suffragist Caroline Dall paid Henry Sr. a visit at a time when she was depressed and felt the need of "a fuller richer life." When she was saying good-bye, according to her journal, the seated James—

> drew my head down with a gaze—as compulsory as a blow—and kissed me on the mouth.

> I received this kiss—prolonged, steadfast, and compelling—as I might have received an electric shock—making all the time keen intellectual inquisition into its purpose. A divine Pity—seemed to stream from his eyes—but I felt as if the kiss sealed a compact.

> "People shall not talk about you in this style—I will not let them"—he said as I rose & said coolly "thank you"—and then I laughed—as if any handful of dust could check the current of this world's petty hate! [from Caroline Dall's journal, April 25, 1866].

It is anyone's guess what Henry Sr. meant by this kiss, but one thing seems clear: like Caroline Dall, he lived on extremely unstable terms with his own sexuality. The squatting fiend that destroyed his sanity in Windsor, England, in 1844 was surely a self-projection, a version of *himself* as a greedy, carnal beast. It was to suppress this beast within that he preached, again and again, that man must be confined in marriage in order to be free. The father's essential life-work amounted to an act of self-suppression, carried forward with single-minded vigor and compulsive self-advertising.

Henry Jr. wanted to make his father's gods his own gods and again and again joined the good fight against the selfish and the carnal. Although he never showed any real mastery of his father's ideas, he was notably enthusiastic about the idea of sexual difference. This idea underlay his father's tormented scenario for the salvation of the male, and it also ensured a continuing skepticism about women's rights. Back in 1852 the father had sought to draw a contrast between his views and those of the pioneering feminist Elizabeth Oakes Smith by saying that she was "engaged in a very arduous crusade against the natural and obvious distinction of the sexes, the which distinction I meanwhile set great store by" (Andrews, *Love*). Now, twenty years later, the father still set great store by this distinction in an essay-review in the *Atlantic Monthly*. Henry Jr. read his father's article and wrote home in three separate letters to say how strongly he agreed. The first of these was to his father: "I read . . . in an *Atlantic* borrowed from the Nortons, your article on the Woman business . . . Your *Atlantic* article I decidedly like—I mean for matter. I am very glad to see some one not Dr. Bushnell & all that genus insist upon the distinction of sexes" [dated January 14, 1870].

Again, this strange passage opens a door on what the Jameses were about. The father's article had given close consideration to Horace Bushnell's *Women's Suffrage: The Reform against Nature.* Bushnell being a Calvinist, it was only to be expected that he and his "genus"—theological conservatives—would oppose female suffrage. The reason Henry Jr. liked his father's article was that it proved a *liberal* theologian could also defend the old idea that woman was affectionate and selfless and unintellectual as compared to man. It was basically *this idea* that the son had in mind thirteen years later, in 1883, when he wrote that *The Bostonians* would involve "the decline of the sentiment of sex." Both son and father regretted that American society was blurring a traditional distinction between man and woman.

Yet *The Bostonians* is not a straightforward conservative novel, and the chief reason why it is not is that its author, his filial loyalty notwithstanding, was terribly uneasy about his father's ideas and masculinity. Not only was the son sensitive to the public ridicule his father sometimes drew on himself, but Minny Temple happened to be, in her own words, "disgusted" by the senior James's "talk" (Henry Jr., *Autobiography*). Minny was Henry Jr.'s much admired cousin who inspired him to create Isabel Archer in *The Portrait of a Lady.* Perhaps Henry Sr. had attempted to persuade this independent young woman that she had too much of what he liked to call the "damnable" (Henry Sr., **Literary Remains**) faith in selfhood. Whatever the immediate provocation, one thing is clear; Minny told him off:

> I showed him [Henry Sr.] plainly that I found it [his talk] not only highly unpractical, but ignoble and shirking. I knew all the while that he disliked what he called my pride and conceit, but felt all the same that his views didn't touch my case a bit. (*Autobiography*).

The main reason Minny was so important for Henry Jr. was that she did what he could not do for himself. She defied the father's oppressive doctrine, not only by challenging it to his face but by simply being the proud, intellectual, self-assertive woman his philosophy of marriage could never accommodate. In modeling Isabel Archer after this confrontational cousin, who regarded Henry Sr. as an evasive coward, Henry Jr. was writing his own deeply muffled declaration of independence. This was how he tried to get out from under Henry Sr.'s lies.

We are now in a position to see why the death of the father, on December 18, 1882, one year after the pub-

lication of *The Portrait of a Lady,* stimulated Henry Jr. to conceive of *The Bostonians.* The son felt a painful mixture of emotions—grave doubt about the value of his father's intellectual endeavors, a desire to uphold and defend this father in the face of a callous world, a wish to get back at the radical publishing scoundrels who had hounded him, and perhaps above all a strong sense of guilt at his own inability finally to accept his father's philosophy of marriage. Furthermore, the father had wanted to die—had willingly left his children. According to Strouse, Henry Sr. stopped eating once he learned he was seriously ill. Whether he would have died anyway seems uncertain; one doctor thought he wouldn't. His death may have been an ambiguous act of suicide by self-starvation. Certainly he felt a tremendous disgust with the world and an overwhelming desire to be reunited with his recently deceased wife. Could it also be that his suicide was the ultimate step in his lifework of exterminating his "damnable" selfhood?

This terrible death threw Henry James Jr. completely off balance yet galvanized his energies. He quickly mapped out the book that would be *The Bostonians.* Remembering the radical journalists, Russell and Andrews, who had dragged his father's name in the mire, he recorded in his notebook his wish to strike back:

> There must, indispensably, be a type of newspaper man—the man whose ideal is the energetic reporter. I should like to *bafouer* the vulgarity and hideousness of this—the impudent invasion of privacy—the extinction of all conception of privacy, etc. (*Notebooks*)

How similar this passage is to the angry sentence in James's comment on Oneida written eight years earlier, soon after his father's trouble with *Woodhull & Claflin's*: "the whole scene . . . is an attempt to organize and glorify the detestable tendency toward the complete effacement of privacy in life and thought everywhere so rampant with us nowadays."

The same ferocity that went into these denunciations generated James's portrait of the modern reporter, Matthias Pardon. This naive, absurdly intrusive, rather freakish person is presented as the rising star of Boston journalism. He combines an aggressive professional know-how with a wide-eyed babyish radicalism, and he makes his way by exposing private individuals to public contempt "with the best conscience in the world." (This is in fact what James himself did, lampooning Elizabeth Peabody in the character of Miss Birdseye.) James's satire is marvelous, and yet his conception of Pardon wholly misrepresents the newspaper world of the time. It's all wrong that Pardon should work for the staid Boston *Evening Transcript*—silently altered to *Vesper* in the later chapters—or that the press and the suffrage movement should be seen as hand in glove.

If one wants a veracious interpretation of Gilded Age journalism, one must go to Howells, whose Bartley Hubbard (in *A Modern Instance*) displays an extremely convincing ambition and lack of scruple. Pardon is not a product of sharp social observation but rather of the author's angry and private determination to settle old scores.

The same holds for all the reformers in *The Bostonians*: James's wish to give a picturesque representation of contemporary types and manners was undermined by a concealed animus. This animus governs both the generalized picture of a vulgar, effeminate culture and the tug-of-war plot, in which Basil strives to capture Verena from Olive's oppressive control. If only Olive were presented as a tormented modern type! But she is also meant to say something about reformers, feminists in particular. If only Basil were essentially an opinionated provincial! But he is also presented as a distinguished Carlylean culture critic, with all Carlyle's faults and virtues, and the reason he manages to win Verena is that he has nature on his side—nature being Henry Sr.'s "distinction of sexes" and Henry Jr.'s "sentiment of sex." Underneath James's often mocking tone, his novel confirms the reactionary argument Basil voices. *The Bostonians* handed its contemporary readers a cranky conservative thesis—wrapped in conservative guilt.

The prevailing way of reading the book ever since Irving Howe's 1956 introduction for the Modern Library edition is to take the gilt wrapping for the substance. (Hence the fondness for the word *brilliant*.) Howe called attention to the withering sarcasm James more than once directs at Basil—"he had read Comte, he had read everything"—and Howe himself neatly skewered Basil's new career as magazine essayist for the *Rational Review,* the title of which "sufficiently suggests both its circulation and influence." And indeed James often does confide that Basil's views are really very crude. When the Southerner decides that Verena's remarkable platform manner derives from her wish to please and charm rather than from any firmly held convictions, the author comments: "I know not whether Ransom was aware of the bearings of this interpretation, which attributed to Miss Tarrant a singular hollowness of character." But this prophylactic distancing proves to be disingenuous. Basil is proved right: Verena *has* a singular hollowness. Is it possible to sustain an ironic reading of a novel whose author dodges back and forth in this way?

I think not. We must give up the idea that James takes an essentially sarcastic view of Basil. And once we've done so, we find ourselves facing the question that Howe and many others have finessed: where *does* this equivocating book stand in relation to Basil's view of women's proper role in society?

The answer, I think, is that, regardless of James's nervous and disarming beguilements, the novel, on this particular issue, stands directly behind Basil. He may be brutal and opinionated about some things, but he knows women. He is right about Verena's nature and he is right in opposing women's entry into public life. The novel's central event is Verena's final cave-in, where her affective nature cancels her commitment to freedom. It's a mistake to assume she capitulates because of some sort of individual weakness. Rather, she yields because a generic femininity has come into operation. Pretty, graceful, eager to please, Verena is constituted by the familiar feminine traits, and the commenting author insists that this vulnerable femininity is her great triumph. "Simply to have been made as she was made," he announces, was "supreme success." She is "the most good-natured girl in the world." Such passages inform us that Verena is less a person than an idealized gender—the "form of personal affection" in Henry Sr.'s phrase.

The fact that the novel confirms Basil's first impression of Verena announces its ideological foundations. Even Verena is convinced that Basil is right about her, convinced not by his arguments, naturally (*she* could never write for the *Rational Review*), but by "a sentiment springing up from within." Henry Sr. had insisted that even if women had the vote, they "wouldn't avail themselves of it." *The Bostonians* says the same thing: it isn't in female nature to care about individual freedom.

Basil isn't equivalent to Henry James's father, but the Southerner serves to vindicate the father's teaching on marriage and womanhood. There is a very important passage, overlooked in all published discussions of *The Bostonians* I have seen, that endorses this teaching. The passage is found in chapter 38, where Verena asks why her talent for public speaking has been given her if she isn't supposed to exercise it. Basil glibly replies, "the dining table itself shall be our platform, and you shall mount on top of that." Then, abandoning this offensive flippancy, he delivers an eloquent speech:

> . . . Your gift is indestructible . . . I want to give it another direction, certainly; but I don't want to stop your activity. Your gift is the gift of expression . . . It won't gush out at a fixed hour and on a fixed day, but it will irrigate, it will fertilise, it will brilliantly adorn your conservation. Think how delightful it will be when your influence becomes really social.

In the serial version of *The Bostonians* this was the curtain speech ending the eleventh installment. James further called attention to the speech's importance by means of a remarkable introductory endorsement: "There was more reason, however, as well as more appreciation of a very considerable mystery, in what he went on to say."

This sentence performs an act that has no parallel in James's entire oeuvre. It not only makes a strange appeal to mystery and reason (another hint, incidentally, that we are not to sneer at the *Rational Review*), but it alludes with great respect to Henry Sr.'s social teaching. The very considerable mystery is the mystery of woman's influence. In order to reform and raise society, to transform the selfish into the social (a word that carries a sacred charge in Basil's speech), she must exercise her charm at home—not behind the lectern. The reason James did not spell out the mystery lay, precisely, in its familiar banality.

But it would be a mistake to call *The Bostonians* a reactionary novel and leave it at that. The real problem is that the bereaved son who wrote it was terribly uncertain what he privately thought about the mystery he wanted the book to embrace. Following Basil's speech, he abruptly veered to the other side: "It is to be feared, indeed, that Verena was easily satisfied . . ." James's commitment to the paternal notion of sexual difference was so brittle, so absolute and yet so shaky, that even as he tried to concretize the idea in narrative, he had to resist it. This counter-reaction saturates the novel and to some extent supports the prevailing ironic reading. It also produces an extremely varied response to Basil, who has been seen both as a romantic rescuer and a repressive force. So total and brutal is his victory over Olive and feminism that the novel undergoes a virtual flipflop: suddenly it's obvious why feminism must be *right*. Yet because of the book's instability, it's a grave mistake to argue, as does Judith Fetterley (*Resisting Reader*), that it makes a case for radical feminism. *The Bostonians* is a confused book produced by a blindly loyal son eager to vindicate a father who had dedicated his life to the notion that slavery was freedom. There were *two* authors—an uneasy son and a recently deceased father's powerful revenant. That is why the novel lacks effective conscious control and nervously, endlessly, mocks its own reactionary thesis. The book has got to be James's ultimate ghost story. It tells how he himself got snatched.

Of all the contemporary reviews of *The Bostonians,* the one that best discerned its distortions and contradictions happened to appear in the *Woman's Journal,* a Boston magazine sponsored by the National Woman Suffrage Association. The author, identified only by the initials L.T.A., saw at once that *The Bostonians* was "evidently intended as a tremendous satire on the whole 'woman question.'" But why, L.T.A. wondered, was the novel so vague about the practical political meaning of feminism? "We hear a great deal about the great 'cause' for which all are laboring, but exactly what the 'cause' is, does not seem apparent." Olive's "bitter, unnatural antipathy towards marriage and men" was anything but typical. L.T.A. felt that Basil was meant to be a likeable hero, yet also felt that "in that last wretched scene" in the Music Hall, his "selfishness" was "absurd" and his "obstinacy" deplorable. It was hard for this reader not to "feel as much pity for her [Olive's] humiliation as contempt for Verena's weakness" (Ames).

L.T.A., up to now unidentified, was Lucia True Ames, later Mead after her marriage in the 1890s. When she read James's novel, she was thirty years old and still single. She lectured at women's clubs on literature and contemporary American society. Her father and grandfather had been active in the anti-slavery movement; she herself was an activist in many progressive causes. In time she became president of the Massachusetts Woman Suffrage Association. She was to eventually join the NAACP and the ACLU. She was apparently a "forceful speaker," unlike Olive; and unlike Verena, she was "logical and concise in her arguments." She opposed American entry into World War I, unlike the aging James, who was caught up in the war fever in England. She died in 1936, in a New York subway rush.

Lucia True Ames not only spotted some of the lies in *The Bostonians,* but she herself was part of the reality this novel has managed to cover up. There was no decline from the noble antebellum days of New England reform (though of course the opposition was strong), and reformers were not morbid men-haters like Olive Chancellor or weak and silly performers like Verena or oppressive matriarchs like Mrs. Farrinder. The male Jameses' two-generation struggle against nineteenth-century feminism and free love has endowed twentieth-century American readers with a gravely distorted picture of some of their most far-sighted political forebears.

FURTHER READING

Biography

Emerson, Edward Waldo. "Henry James." In *The Early Years of the Saturday Club: 1855-1870,* pp. 322-33. Boston: Houghton Mifflin Company, 1918.

> An anecdotal account describing how James formulated his religious and philosophical views. Also portrays the vivacity and affection of the James household and depicts the elder James's associations with such figures as Ralph Waldo Emerson, Edmund Tweedy, and Thomas Carlyle.

Habegger, Alfred. *The Father: A Life of Henry James, Sr.* New York: Farrar, Straus and Giroux, 1994, 578 p.

> Full-length biography of James in which the critic details James's life and analyzes the domestic environment in which William and Henry, Jr., were raised.

——. "Henry James, Sr., in the Late 1830s." *New England Quarterly* 64, No. 1 (March 1991): 46-81.

Purports that from late 1837 to 1840 James involved himself with the most radical aspects of the Scotch-Irish Protestant movement, leading to the "fanatically devout state of mind that attended his courtship of Mary Walsh."

Lewis, R. W. B. "Henry James, Sr.: The Endangering Self." In *The Jameses: A Family Narrative*, pp. 37-70. New York: Farrar, Straus and Giroux, 1991.

Traces James's history from 1935, the year he entered Princeton Theological Seminary, to 1855, the year he published his treatise *The Nature of Evil.*

Matthiessen, F. O. *The James Family: Including Selections from the Writings of Henry James, Senior, William, Henry, and Alice James.* New York: Alfred A. Knopf, 1948, 706 p.

Biography of the Jameses, offering an examination of the family's cultural, social, and intellectual history.

Criticism

Hoover, Dwight W. *Henry James, Sr. and the Religion of Community.* Grand Rapids, M.I.: William B. Eerdmans Publishing Company, 1969, 152 p.

Analyzes the religious philosophy of James within the context of the prevalent religious, philosophical, and societal assumptions of the nineteenth century.

Lewis, R. W. B. "The Fortunate Fall: The Elder James and Horace Bushnell." In *The American Adam: Innocence, Tragedy and Tradition in the Nineteenth Century*, pp. 54-73. Chicago: The University of Chicago Press, 1955.

Examines how both Bushnell, a Congregational preacher, and James employed the image of the biblical Adam in their doctrines. According to Lewis, James utilized the metaphor to define the human experience, professing that in order to pass into the ranks of society, or "manhood," one must suffer a fall and thereby destroy one's own egotism.

Moseley, James G., Jr. "Self-Transcendence in the Theology of Henry James, Sr." In *A Complex Inheritance: The Idea of Self-Transcendence in the Theology of Henry James, Sr., and the Novels of Henry James*, pp. 1-33. American Academy of Religion and Scholars Press, 1975.

Suggests that analyzing Henry James, Sr.'s, views on self-transcendence—the shedding of one's egoism and the subsequent releasing of one's "divine-natural humanity"—offers insight into the major works of the younger James, who inherited as well as understood his father's spiritual philosophy.

Mulford, E. "Henry James." In *The Atlantic Monthly* LV, No. CCCXXXI (May 1885): 702-05.

Review of *The Literary Remains of the Late Henry James* in which the critic offers his assessment of James's writing style, literary reputation, and philosophy.

Warren, Austin. "'Father's Ideas': The Elder Henry James." In *New England Saints*, pp. 74-105. Ann Arbor: The University of Michigan Press, 1956.

Presents a general overview of James's literary reputation and philosophy. Includes reactions from contemporaries and an examination of James's conceptions of such matters as moralism, the conscience, ecclesiasticism, the self, and God.

Young, Frederic Harold. *The Philosophy of Henry James, Sr.* New York: Bookman Associates, 1951, 338 p.

Providing excerpts of James's writings along with explications of his thoughts, attempts to present James's philosophy as a unified whole.

Jules Laforgue

1860-1887

French poet, short story and sketch writer, essayist, and dramatist. For further information, see *NCLC,* volume 5.

INTRODUCTION

Jules Laforgue was an early experimenter in *vers libre* (free verse), a stylistic innovation that became popular in the second half of the nineteenth century and released poetry from the traditional conventions of meter and stanza. Like the early French Symbolists with whom he was associated, Laforgue advocated abandoning literary convention and maintained that art should be the expression of the subconscious mind. His work was read by only a small circle of French readers at the time of his death, but in subsequent years his reputation grew, even to the point that he became a major influence on many twentieth-century writers in English, including Ezra Pound and T. S. Eliot. Today both his prose and poetry are highly regarded and studied, but he is best known for the *Derniers vers* (1890), a volume of poems published after his death that firmly established his position as an initiator of free verse. The experimental rhythmic patterns, psychological realism, and evocative language of the *Derniers vers* provided the Symbolists with a model for their later development of free verse.

Biographical Information

Laforgue was born at Montevideo, Uruguay. His father was a poor teacher from Gascony who in 1866 sent his family to Tarbes, France, where Jules and his brother Émile attended school. Although exceptionally intelligent, Laforgue was a mediocre student at the Lycée Tarbes. In 1876, he enrolled at the Lycée Fontanes in Paris where, although he liked the school, his work did not improve. Laforgue twice failed his baccalaureate exams, and never received a diploma. In 1880, while studying art and working as a part-time journalist in Paris, Laforgue met Gustave Kahn, a leader in the Symbolist movement, poet, and editor of the periodical *Le vogue et le symboliste*. Laforgue's association with Kahn, who became his mentor, as well as with Charles Henry and literary critic Paul Bourget, was the most crucial of his career. With Bourget's help, Laforgue obtained his first job as apprentice poet-critic to Charles Ephrussi, editor of the journal *Gazette des beaux-arts*, who taught Laforgue much about art and literature and encouraged him to write. Although he generally disliked Laforgue's early work, Bourget became Laforgue's personal literary critic during this period, helping him improve his style. In 1881, Laforgue accepted the position of French-reader and secretary to Empress Augusta of Prussia; for five years he traveled with the Empress and her entourage. Although he found the position boring and rigidly structured, Laforgue was nonetheless prolific during this time, completing and publishing two volumes of poetry—*Les complaintes* (1885) and *L'imitation de notre-dame la lune* (1886)—and a verse drama titled *Le concile féerique* (1886). He left the Berlin court in 1886 when he married Leah Lee, a young English tutor. The couple moved to Paris, where a particularly harsh winter severely affected Laforgue's health. He wrote for Kahn's periodical *Le vogue* and tried unsuccessfully to find a publisher for his volume of short stories, the *Moralités légendaires* (1887). Supported by loans from Bourget and Ephrussi, money from anonymous donors, and payment by friends for articles that were never published, Laforgue continued to write until the opiates given him for his illness left him too weak to work or to eat. He died, at the age of twenty-seven, virtually unknown.

Major Works

Le Sanglot de la terre (1902-3), a group of 29 posthumously published poems, exhibits the fundamental characteristics of Laforgue's poetry: his sense of irony and his disaffection or sense of alienation. According to critics, it also betrays most clearly the poet's influences, especially Charles Baudelaire and Walt Whitman, whose early experiments in free verse Laforgue translated into French. Laforgue's early work was also deeply influenced by Arthur Schopenhauer's pessimistic philosophy and Eduard von Hartmann's concept of the unconscious mind. In the *Complaintes* Laforgue fashioned a series of monologues based on conventional French character types and traditional street songs. His mixture of fine art with what was considered the "low" style of popular tradition challenged assumed notions of the separation between high culture and popular culture. The voices he adopted in the songs initiated Laforgue's use of personas (speaking through the voices of different characters in a poem, some not unlike the poet and some at a great distance from the poet); some scholars have compared this practice, which Laforgue developed in all of his following work, with Robert Browning's dramatic monologues. Among the most famous of the voices first heard in the *Complaintes* is Laforgue's version of Pierrot, the "clown" figure who would become one of Laforgue's best-known mouthpieces. The two works that most established Laforgue's reputation, however, were both published after his death: the *Moralités légendaires* only a few weeks after Laforgue's death and the *Derniers vers* in 1890. Each tale in the *Moralités* takes a legendary character with whom his readers would have been familiar, such as Hamlet or Salomé, and reworks the tale with a parodic air. The stories, which have earned as much attention from critics as has any of his poetry, demonstrate at once the writer's aptitude with language, characterization, and irony. The *Derniers vers* appears to be either one poem with an intricate, twelve-part structure or twelve closely-related poems; the matter remains open to debate since the work was put together from the poet's posthumous papers, without any directions or statement of intent. The work, which juxtaposes common objects and romantic ideals, shows the signs of Laforgue's continued work with monologue. The poems' most marked trait, however, is that they demonstrate the point Laforgue had reached in his experiments with free verse; most commentators agree that the volume presents the strongest example to date of free verse.

Critical Reception

Laforgue's participation, however tangential, in the Symbolist movement and his verse experimentation constituted the initial impetus for critical attention. Commentators trying to determine the shape and character of Symbolism discussed Laforgue's proximity to it, usually deciding that he was clearly included in the aesthetic influences of early Symbolism and, in turn, had a considerable influence on later Symbolists, but that he was nonetheless at a distance from the formal social circles and artistic principles of the school. His relationship to this avant-garde depends largely on his commitment to developing new literary forms to express a new sensibility, as both George Turnell and Malcolm Cowley have argued. Turnell specifically characterizes Laforgue as an urban poet whose innovative verse captured the human experience as rural economy and population shifted to the cities in the nineteenth century. Laforgue's early death has continued to provide the impetus for a major debate in Laforgue criticism, since it remains a matter of speculation how the poet's work would have changed as he grew older. Consequently, some critics have surmised that what Laforgue's writings represent is the product of an immature artistic genius. The large body of scholarship focusing on Laforgue's influence on other poets often addresses how his own later work might have compared with the works of those influenced by him. Close readings of Laforgue's poetry and prose have concerned themselves largely with the exact meaning of certain elements in the poet's work. The different voices that Laforgue refined through the *Complaintes* have prompted comparisons to Victorian "dramatic monologues," with some critics arguing that Laforgue deserves credit for introducing the dramatic monologue into French literature, and others terming them "interior monologues." E. J. Stormon has claimed that the poet merely "twists his face into various stylized expressions." There are also extensive discussions of both Laforgue's Hamlet and his Pierrot, as well as of more abstract elements, such as his notion of the Unconscious and his images of women. More recently, critics have focused less exclusively on Laforgue's major works. The early novel *Stéphane Vassiliew* (first published in 1946) and the unpublished play *Tessa* have attracted attention, and appreciation of Laforgue's stature as an aesthetic critic in his own right has grown.

PRINCIPAL WORKS

Les complaintes (poetry) 1885
Le concile féerique (verse drama) 1886
L'imitation de notre-dame la lune ["Locutions de Pierrots I, II, III" (partial translation), 1926, published in journal *Double Dealer*] (poetry) 1886
Moralités légendaires [*Moral Tales*] (short stories) 1887
Les derniers vers de Jules Laforgue (poetry) 1890
Oeuvres complètes (poetry, verse drama, short stories, essays, and letters) 1902-03
Oeuvres complètes (poetry, verse drama, short stories, journals, essays, letters, and sketches) 1922-30

Lettres à un ami: 1880-1886 (letters) 1941
Stéphane Vassiliew (novel) 1946
Selected Writings of Jules Laforgue (poetry, short
    stories, essays, letters, and sketches) 1956
Poems of Jules Laforgue (poetry) 1958

*This work includes *Le sanglot de la terre, Pierrot fumiste*, and *Mélanges posthumes*.

CRITICISM

George Moore (essay date 1891)

SOURCE: "Two Unknown Poets," in *Impressions and Opinions,* Brentano's, n.d., pp. 95-102.

[*In the late nineteenth century, Laforgue was still largely unknown to English and American readers; in the essay excerpted below, Moore seeks to expand the poet's reputation by articulating his own appreciation.*]

[The] two young poets of whom I am going to speak have always attracted me. My sympathies were engaged by the strange and sad stories which surround them, and were confirmed by the personal talent manifested in all they wrote. Their names?—Arthur Rimbaud and Jules Laforgue, names for the first time printed in an English newspaper. But it is not infrequent for me to introduce French genius to the few among us who are willing to allow themselves to be interested in artistic work. It was I who introduced that adorable poet, Paul Verlaine, to English readers; it was I who wrote first about that ineffable book, *A Rebours,* the value of which has since been so copiously acknowledged. Possibly the same success will attend my present adventure, and in a season the plagiarist and his pursuers will make riot amid the tender beauties of *Le Miracle des Roses, L'Imitation de Notre Dame la Lune,* and *Les Premières Communions.* Be this as it may, I concern myself with my sensations of these strange poets, whose talents and whose tragic ends have interested me so singularly. The poet that death has nipped in the first blossom of his talent, the girl that dies in her bridal month, the first poems, the first kisses, my soul goes out to one as to the other. . . .

I have now to try, in a few English words, to give a sensation of the delicious talent of Jules Laforgue—delicious, delicate, and evanescent as French pastry. Can I help you to see this Watteau de café-concert? I will ask you to think of the beauty of a moth fluttering in the soft twilight of a summer month. Touch it not, lest you destroy the delicate dust of its wings. I hold it on my forefinger now, examine the beautiful markings. *L'Imitation de Notre Dame la Lune, Fleurs de Bonne Volonté, Les Moralités Légendaires, Le Miracle des Roses,* etc. Is there not in these titles some-

thing like genius? and is it possible that any one not touched with genius could have invented *L'Imitation de Notre Dame la Lune?* I have called Laforgue a Watteau de café-concert because his imagination was as fanciful as that painter's, and because he adopted in his style the familiarity of the café-concert, transforming, raising it by the enchantment of his genius. What I am writing should in truth be delivered in a literary academy with closed doors. But do not gather up your skirts, for in the end I may be able to leave on this page some faint shadow of my beautiful moth. Here is a little poem which appears to me to be wholly exquisite, and scintillant with French grace:—

> Mon Sort est orphelin, les vêpres ont tu leurs
>   cloches. . .
> Et ces pianos ritournellent, jamais las! . . .
> Oh! monter, leur expliquer mon apostolat!
> Oh! du moins, leur tourner les pages, être là,
> Les consoler! (J'ai des consolations plein les
>   poches) . . .
>
> Les pianos se sont clos. Un seul, en grand
>   deuil, s'obstine . . .
> Oh! qui que tu sois, sœur! à genoux, à tâtons,
> Baiser le bas de ta robe dans l'abandon! . . .
> Pourvu qu'après, tu me chasses, disant:
>   'Pardon!
> 'Pardon, m'sieu, mais j'en aime un autre, et
>   suis sa cousine.
>
> Oh! que je suis bien infortuné sur cette
>   Terre! . . .
> Et puis si malheureux de ne pas être Ailleurs!
> Ailleurs, loin de ce savant siècle batailleur. . . .
> C'est là que je m'créerai un petit intérieur,
> Avec Une dont, comme de Moi, Tout n'a que
>   faire.
>
>   Une maigre qui me parlait,
> Les yeux hallucinés de Gloires virginales,
>   De rendre l'âme, sans scandale,
>   Dans un flacon de sels anglais . . .
>
>   Une qui me fit oublier
> Mon art et ses rançons d'absurdes saturnales,
>   En attisant, gauche vestale,
>   L'Aurore dans mes oreillers. . . .
>
>   Et que son regard
>   Sublime
>   Comme ma rime
> Ne permit pas le moindre doute à cet égard.

Hard to understand? I admit it, but how winning and how unlike anybody! Isn't it strange that the beginning and the end of French poetry are almost incomprehensible—Ronsard and Laforgue? And his prose is as exquisite, and as wilful; and his titles! *Le Miracle des Roses!*

Jamais, jamais, jamais cette petite ville d'eaux ne s'en douta, avec son inculte conseil Municipal délégué par les montagnards rapaces et nullement opéra comique malgré leur costume.

Ah, que tout n'est-il opéra comique! . . . Que tout n'évolue-t-il en mesure sur cette valse anglaise, *Myosotis,* qu'on entendait cette année-là (moi navré dans les coins) au Casino, valse si décemment mélancolique, si ésotériquement dernier, derniers beaux jours! . . . (Cette valse, ah! si je pouvais en inoculer d'un mot le sentiment avant de vous laisser entrer dans cette histoire!)—O gants jamais rajeunies par les benzines! O brillant et mélancolique va et vien de ces existences! O apparence de bonheur si pardonnable! O beautés qui veilleront dans les dentelles noires, au coin du feu, sans comprendre la conduite des fils viveurs et muselés qu'elles mirent au monde avec une si chaste mélancolie! . . .

Petite ville, petite ville de mon cœur.

I think that even these, the first twenty lines of *Le Miracle des Roses,* testify a style, full of grace and fancy, and incurably his own. Nor can I easily imagine anything more wilful than his evocation of this watering-place, and the story sketched with crow-quill pen and mauve ink—the story of the consumptive Ruth, dying amid tea-roses, the blood-red roses that she loves having been forbidden her. Nor can we help being doubly attracted to this story when we consider its significance and its foretelling of the poet's own end. For if Rimbaud's fulgurant verses correspond to the passions that forced him to fly from life and hide his soul in a convent, Laforgue's fancies harmonise equally with the facts of his blameless and sad existence, so sad and so little. We know that he was reader to the Empress of Germany—happy indeed was the selection; and we envy more than the bauble of her wealth the hours she passed with Laforgue. One winter's day in Berlin, Jules saw a girl skating as none ever skated before—the grace of the waist, the flowing boa, and the feet lifted beneath the dark skirt, filled him with happiness. The beautiful skater was an English girl. I hardly remember the name, but I know that it recalled Annabel Lee, as, indeed, the story of this love recalls a tale by Edgar Poe. He resigned his place as reader to the Empress and married; and he and the beautiful English girl came to Paris in the hope that literature would yield them a living. But Laforgue's genius was of the kind that wins the sympathy of the elect, and instead of making his living with his pen Jules grew more and more consumptive. I have heard that the young couple lived in a poor apartment—two or three rooms—and that the beautiful English girl, now stricken with the dreadful malady, passed between the rooms with *tisanes.* Friends climbed the high stairs to see them on Thursday evenings; a few

admirers attended Jules's funeral, and published the volume he left in his desk, *Les Moralités Légendaires;* the girl died soon after—two or three months. How did she live during the brief interval, where is she buried? Nobody knows. Yet I have a very separate and complete sensation of these two little lives. I was their friend although I never saw them, and I shall not forget them, though I never visit their forgotten graves, nor shall I cease to cherish *L'Imitation de Notre Dame la Lune* and *Les Fleurs de Bonne Volonté,* though the ordinary readers of verse allow these books to lie in the limbo of embryonic things.

Aline Gorren   (essay date 1893)

SOURCE: "The French Symbolists," in *Scribner's Magazine,* Vol. XIII, No. 3, March, 1893, pp. 337-52.

[*In this excerpt, Gorren places Laforgue in the context of other poets associated with Symbolism, commenting on both his similarities with and his differences from them.*]

. . . [Love] of the barest rhythmic notation, and of that unseizable distinction that lurks in folk-songs and popular legends, tempted Jules Laforgue . . . —Jules Laforgue, charming and *charmeur,* who died at the age of twenty-seven, delicate, well-bred wizard who was like no one ever but himself.

He also tried the mixing of prose and verse. His verse was always of the sort that the Symbolists approve; its harmonies and its unity were "psychic rather than syllabic." He had all audacities as to feet and accent. His poetry indeed seems little else than rhythmic prose divided, typographically, into separate lines. His prose, on the other hand, has poetical cadences, returns upon itself that give the effect of a refrain, vague reminiscences of rhymes, and of those sub-rhymes, in a minor key, that are formed by assonances. In his prose tales, the unique *Moralités Légendaires,* he breaks into verse whenever the thought seems to sing itself into the lyric shape. Those two leading qualities, which the Symbolist work always, in some measure, possesses (or seeks to possess), an abiding sense of the absolute retained in treating of the most fugitive accidents and appearances, and a penetration of the hidden analogies existent in phenomena the most divergent, are developed in Laforgue to a degree of keenness the more striking because of his determined touching of things by their lightest, their almost frivolous, side. He tends back to the centres continually; always he gives the feeling of the affinities behind the veil; and the operation is the more pungent that it is invested with his peculiar humor, a half sentimental, wholly tasteful spirit of mockery, that, in exactly the same mixture of ingredients, belongs to no other Frenchman. . . .

G. M. Turnell (essay date 1936)

SOURCE: "The Poetry of Jules Laforgue," in *Scrutiny: A Quarterly Review,* Vol. V, No. 2, September, 1936, pp. 128-49.

[*In the following essay, Turnell addresses many of the issues central to early-twentieth-century Laforgue studies: Baudelaire's influence on the poet's development; the poet's artistic immaturity at the time of his death; his stylistic relationship to Romanticism and Classicism; and his contribution to the creation of* vers libre.]

The influence of Laforgue on modern poetry has been decisive. In the ordinary way it is a mistake to distinguish too sharply between the influence of a writer's outlook and the influence of his style or, as I should prefer to call it, his *method.* In the case of Laforgue, however, some sort of distinction between the two is necessary. I think the point can be illustrated by a comparison between Mr. Pound and Mr. Eliot. It seems to me that Laforgue's influence on Mr. Pound has been almost exclusively of the first, and his most lasting influence on Mr. Eliot of the second kind. It is Mr. Pound's limitation that his best work is sometimes no more than the mature expression of Laforgue's outlook—the mature expression of an outlook that was essentially immature in the sense of *uncompleted,* a term to which I shall try to give precision later. Now one of the most indubitable signs of Mr. Eliot's originality is that his development since *Prufrock* and *Portrait of a Lady* has always been *away* from the outlook of his master. In *The Waste Land* he has clearly learnt all there was to learn technically from the **Derniers vers** and used it to express something infinitely richer and more complex.

For this reason I wish to concentrate in this paper on the method of Laforgue. I may as well begin by recording my own opinion that, from a technical point of view and to a critic writing with Mr. Eliot's work before him, the **Derniers vers** is the most important single poem published in Europe since the seventeenth century, though its intrinsic merits fall far short of the best work of Baudelaire, Corbière and Rimbaud.

'When we get to Laforgue,' wrote Mr. Eliot in one of his illuminating asides [in a review of *Baudelaire and the Symbolists* in the *Criterion,* December, 1929], 'we find a poet who seems to express even more clearly even than Baudelaire the difficulties of his own age: he speaks to us, or spoke to my generation, more intimately than Baudelaire. Only later we conclude that Laforgue's "present" is a narrower "present" than Baudelaire's, and that Baudelaire's present extends to more of the past and more of the future.'

The 'intimacy' with which Laforgue speaks to us and the 'narrowness' of his outlook are factors of the first importance and need to be carefully investigated—investigated, as Mr. Eliot points out, in relation to Baudelaire. For Baudelaire dominates his age to such a degree that his contemporaries and successors can only be placed in relation to him. There are lines in the **Sanglot de la terre,** Laforgue's earliest collection of verse, which an intelligent candidate in a practical criticism paper at Cambridge might pardonably attribute to the author of the *Fleurs du mal.* For instance:

> O convoi solennel des soleils magnifiques,
> Nouez et dénouez vos vastes masses d'or,
> Doucement, tristement, sur de graves
>   musiques,
> Menez le deuil très lent de votre soeur qui
>   dort.

But though the mistake might be made with a short extract, it would scarcely happen with a whole poem.

> Le blanc soleil de juin amollit les trottoirs.
> Sur mon lit, seul, prostré comme en ma
>   sépulture
> (Close de rideaux blancs, œuvre d'une main
>   pure),
> Je râle doucement aux extases des soirs.
>
> Un relent énervant expire d'un mouchoir
> Et promène sur mes lèvres sa chevelure
> Et, comme un piano voisin rêve en mesure,
> Je tournoie au concert rythmé des encensoirs.
>
> Tout est un songe. Oh! viens, corps soyeux
>   que j'adore,
> Fondons-nous, et sans but, plus oublieux
>   encore;
> Et tiédis longuement ainsi mes yeux fermés.
>
> Depuis l'éternité, croyez-le bien, Madame,
> L'Archet qui sur nos nerfs pince ces tristes
>   gammes
> Appelait pour ce jour nos atomes charmés.

There is a good deal of Baudelaire here. The rhythm of some of the lines is his. *Amollit* is one of the soft, voluptuous words that he loved; and the *sépulture,* the *extases des soirs* and the *encensoirs* are all part of the furniture of the *Fleurs du mal*. But often when Laforgue is being most imitative, he will suddenly become most himself. The prostrate young man is a glimpse of the peculiar spiritual defeatism which contributes so largely to the sense of 'intimacy' we get from his work. We shall meet the curtained windows and the pianos again and again—they are an important part of Laforgue's symbolism. We shall also meet the adolescent hunger not simply for love, but for chaste love which is so different both from the weary satiety of Baudelaire and the healthy animality of Corbière. The *main pure* looks forward to the

> Jeunes Filles inviolables et frêles

of the **Derniers vers**. It is significant that Laforgue's 'chastity' is essentially negative. Indeed, his half-heartedness about sexual love and his recoil from the physical contribute more than anything to the impression of immaturity that his verse creates. The last three lines of the poem are the most characteristic of all. They point to the **Complaintes** and indicate the direction his development was to take.

Although the fact that Laforgue's development after the **Sanglot de la terre** was always *away* from Baudelaire is one of the clearest signs of his originality, it is also one of the clearest signs of his limitation—not merely a personal limitation, but a limitation inherent in the age. In placing Laforgue we have to remember that his 'intimacy' and his 'narrowness' are inseparable. In other words, his limitations are peculiarly a function of his genius. With this reservation, it can be said that his practice is a radical and thorough-going criticism of the work of Baudelaire. It can be seen in his language and imagery, in his versification, and in his wit. I propose to consider them in that order.

Laforgue tried, as Corbière before him had tried, to get rid of the old worn out 'poetic' words; but both his aim and his procedure were different from Corbière's and far more like Donne's. Corbière's work represents the restoration of an old language rather than the invention of a new one. He tried to purge words of their romantic associations and restore their natural properties in order to express an elemental, and in a sense a primitive experience. Thus where Corbière's language is simple Laforgue's is extremely sophisticated, but it marks a definite extension of the field of poetry. He had to forge a language which would express the new feelings that were emerging with the progress of urban civilization and which would also express his peculiar and, it seems to me, very limited disillusion. His third group of poems, **L'Imitation de Notre-Dame de la lune,** is the product of a period of the wildest experiments with language; and the results of these experiments can be seen all through his work. It is completely successful in

> La rouille ronge en leurs *spleens kilométriques*
> Les fils télégraphiques des grandes routes où
>   nul ne passe

which admirably express his own particular *ennui,* but is unsuccessful and forced in

> *Armorial d'anémie!*
> Psautiers d'automne!

As with his imagery, so with his language. He did not merely use words which had been considered unpoetic, he invented new ones. The sort of words he invented and the way he invented are curiously reminiscent of Donne when faced with a similar situation. He has, for instance, *ennuiversel, éternullité, sexiproque, enflaquer, féminiculture, kilométrique, lunalogue, ritourneller, spleenuosite.* [In a footnote, the author adds: "A poet's vocabulary is one of the most reliable indications of his outlook. For the sake of completeness it is worth pointing out a further difference between Corbière and Laforgue. Corbière's preference was for the firm, virile words like *faraud, farouche, contumace, brute:* Laforgue's for words suggesting impotence and disease like *phtisie pulmonaire, anémie, langueurs, débilité, palpitations.* A study of their work suggests that Corbière was concerned to defend certain primary human experiences which were in danger of being destroyed by the development of civilization, while Laforgue was content to register their destruction with a melancholy resignation."]

Contemporary critics have stressed the 'counter-romantic' tendency of Baudelaire's poetry, but it is generally recognized that it retained certain romantic traits. Superficially Laforgue's experiments with language seem to complete Baudelaire's work by making a clean sweep of those romantic elements from which he had failed to free himself. This view strikes me as frankly mistaken. There were certainly romantic elements in Baudelaire, but they were accidentals and not essentials. They were his macabre sensationalism and a love of the theatrical and not, as is commonly supposed, his use of the grand style or of words (apparently) borrowed from the vocabulary of the Romantics like *beauté, tristesse, solitaire, splendeur*—the words which, in Laforgue's admirable phrase, *enchasublent* the subject. His use of them has little in common with that of the Romantics—a point of capital importance in discussing his relations with Laforgue.

What makes Baudelaire a very great figure indeed is that he explored the potentialities of human experience far more thoroughly than any of his contemporaries, and was capable of regarding the human situation from a greater number of different angles than they. The deepest thing in his poetry is his awareness of the contrast between the potential splendour of human life and its actual squalor. This perpetual contrast could not have been adequately expressed in the style and language of Laforgue, which have a sort of thinness—excellent no doubt for Laforgue's purpose, but useless for Baudelaire's. What Baudelaire had to say could only have been said in the ample measure of the alexandrine and in a language that described the present and at the same time suggested what had been lost.

The difference between the two poets can be seen most clearly in their presentation of Paris. The Paris of Baudelaire has the universality and the impersonality of great poetry which we do not find in Laforgue's. There is nothing absurd in the parallels that French critics are fond of drawing between Baudelaire's Paris and the *Inferno,* but no one could possibly make the same claim for Laforgue. In comparison his Paris is local and personal. But if Laforgue seems narrow and pedestrian in comparison with Baudelaire, if he can only offer one point of view, it is not altogether his fault. With Baudelaire something went out of French poetry and, except for a fugitive reappearance in Rimbaud, went out for good.

The origins of free verse have been the source of a good deal of speculation in France, mostly of a somewhat fruitless nature. Gourmont's chapter in the *Esthétique de la langue française* contains one or two suggestive remarks, but on the whole it is disappointing, and in one particular thoroughly misleading. Gourmont was too good a critic not to realize that the free verse of a writer like Laforgue was something completely new; but when he goes on to trace parallels between nineteenth-century free verse and free verse in Latin compositions of the eighth century—he had a maddening strain of pedantry which comes out to the full in this book—he is simply confusing the issues. He is not the only person who has done it. 'The *vers libre* of Jules Laforgue . . .' wrote Mr. Eliot [in his Introduction to *Selected Poems of Ezra Pound*], 'is free verse in much the same way that the later verse of Shakespeare, Webster, Tourneur, is free verse: that is to say, it stretches, contracts, and distorts the traditional French measure as later Elizabethan and Jacobean poetry stretches, contracts and distorts the blank verse measure.'

It is interesting to learn, as we do from Mr. Eliot's Introduction, that his own versification was based on a study of Laforgue and the later Elizabethans; but the connection is a personal one and the suggestion that there is some objective relation between the two strikes me as hopelessly misleading. And to speak of Laforgue as one who 'stretches, contracts and distorts' the alexandrine is to minimize his technical brilliance unnecessarily.

Mr. Edouard Dujardin, Laforgue's editor and the reputed inventor of the 'silent monologue,' is a more satisfactory guide. In an article published in the *Mercure de France* [in 1921] he argues that free verse was

not the invention of a single poet, but the spontaneous result of a collective movement. That is the main point. A vital art-form must be the spontaneous outcome of the conditions in which the artist is living. Free verse appeared when it did because it was the only medium capable of expressing the modern poet's experience. It is essentially a nineteenth-century phenomenon. It has nothing to do with the versification of any other period. Its real affinities are with similar movements in the other arts—with impressionism in painting, the silent monologue in the novel and—most striking of all—with the cinema.

This is not the place to discuss the relations between the different arts in detail, but it is only when we see modern poetry in relation to painting, the novel and the cinema that we are in a position to appreciate the importance of free verse and 'place' the poets of the movement. The simultaneous appearance of free verse and impressionism was due to changes that had been going on in the European sensibility. They were the outcome of the same impulse and as literary critics it is our business to isolate that impulse.

Free verse and impressionism were both movements of liberation, simultaneous reactions against romanticism and a decadent classicism. It was Laforgue's achievement to have realized that the grand style was all over and done with and that the poet's experience could no longer be forced into the *cadre* of the alexandrine. He saw that traditional verse-forms were incapable of expressing the subtleties of the modern sensibility and in particular the *movement* of the contemporary mind. And the impressionist realized that the classical painter's angle of vision had become stereotyped and distorted the artist's experience. Thus there appears to me to be a connection between the disuse of the alexandrine and the disuse of the classical line of David and Ingres. Baudelaire, as usual, puts his finger on the point when he says *La phrase poétique peut imiter la ligne horizontale, la ligne droite ascendante, la ligne droite descendante.* What is striking about poetry is the disappearance of line, of the sculptural element that we find in Vigny, Leconte de Lisle and in Baudelaire's own *La Beauté.* As a final comment there is Baudelaire's criticism of Ingres. *Le grand défaut de M. Ingres,* he wrote, *est de vouloir imposer à chaque type qui pose sous son oeil un perfectionnement plus ou moins despotique emprunté au répertoire des idées classiques.*

It is necessary to carry the analysis a stage further, to go behind art to changes that were taking place in the mind of Europe. Classical theories of art are based ultimately on classical metaphysics, on the assumption that reality is independent of the perceiving mind and that the function of the artist is to represent it. The origins of modern art go back to the period when the classical metaphysic was challenged by the rise of the idealist philosophies. It is a change, in other words, from a philosophy of *being* to a philosophy of *knowing*. It no longer matters what a thing is—what matters is my experience of it. Thus the idealist's assertion that the real was not independent of mind, but a synthesis of the perceiving subject and the thing perceived, meant that the artist was no longer occupied with things but with his reactions to them. It means that instead of the mind conforming to the real, the real is made to conform to the mind which imposes its own pattern on everything.

The implications of these theories are patent. Classical metaphysics, by insisting that the real was the same for all and that everyone had a similar experience of it, guaranteed the social basis of art. The art produced under its influence tended to express what was common to all—to be the consummate expression of a social experience. In departing from this assumption that artist rejects the social basis of art, but he reveals human nature to itself in a way that would otherwise have been unthinkable.

Le vrai vers libre, wrote Gourmont, *est conçu comme tel, c'est-à-dire comme fragment dessiné sur le modèle de son idée émotive, et non plus déterminé par la loi fixe du nombre.*

In short, anything that was likely to fetter the artist's experience, to interfere with the *idée émotive,* was removed. Laforgue gave to poetry an instrument that was capable of reflecting the rapidly shifting vision of our time. The **Derniers vers** is a poem of 816 lines which registers the constant shift and change of feeling, the play of feeling within a prevailing mood, that a sensitive person experiences in modern urban conditions. Its great virtues are the fidelity and insight with which the changes are recorded, its great fault the absence of any unity but the poet's personality. It contains astonishing passages, but is not completely successful as a criticism of the human situation. It does not possess the same finality in this respect as *The Waste Land* because of the absence of any intellectual structure. But this in no way alters its technical importance. Take the beginning of the fourth section:

> C'est l'automne, l'automne, l'automne,
> Le grand vent et toute sa séquelle
> De représailles! et de musiques! . . .
> Rideaux tirés, clôture annuelle,
> Chute des feuilles, des Antigones, des
>   Philomèles:
> Mon fossoyeur, *Alas poor Yorick!*
> Les remue à la pelle! . . .

'Autumn'—symbol of a definite emotional state in this poem—restates the principal theme of the poem, the dominant mood. The repetition shows the poet's growing despair. The next two lines refer back to the storm in the previous section. The wind that roars and thunders all through the **Derniers vers** is no romantic accompaniment, but a symbol of the tumult going on in the poet's mind. The drawn curtains, tattered notices on the hoardings and falling leaves are familiar symbols of *ennui* and despair. The precise images and exact noting of the names on the play bills fix the particular scene in the mind. I take Antigone and Philomel to stand for certain human values which are in the process of disappearing. They may also be symbols of the departed glamour of 'the Season' and suggest the poet's sense of exile from the gay and prosperous world. The mingling of the falling leaves and the fragments of the play bills is deliberate: the general mood is related to the loss of particular values (spiritual and material). The reference to *Hamlet—Hamlet* played a role of capital importance in Laforgue's development— is the focal point of the passage. It deftly continues the literary allusion and at the same time provides an ironical comment on the whole situation—on the futility of certain virtues in a civilization like our own. The image of the comic grave-digger disrespectfully turning up the bones of the dead suggests the crossing-sweeper whisking away the relics of past splendour. The suddenness of the gesture is an admirable instance of Laforgue's technical dexterity. The whole passage is a good illustration of the way in which the pliancy of Laforgue's medium and his method of allusion enable him to evoke the mood of the entire poem whenever he likes and to bring it into relation with a particular situation. This alone is a technical innovation of the first importance.

'Words, images and entire friezes of imagery recur, not once or twice but constantly,' wrote Mr. Quennell of Laforgue. The implication that Laforgue's range of feeling is limited is true, but this does not mean that his use of stock-imagery is a short-coming. Indeed, part of his achievement was to have worked out an elaborate system of reference and association, a sort of poetic short-hand. The recurring image, which has been brilliantly developed in *The Waste Land,* is an important part of the system.

One of the results of the change of sensibility already discussed was that the emotional life of Europe was suddenly divided, forming new combinations of feeling. A verse-form was needed which would not only express the rapid change from one feeling to its opposite, but would also show the mind simultaneously possessed by diverse and even conflicting feelings. Thus instead of describing emotion, Laforgue translates it into precise, visual images which recur again and again. They are symbols in the strict sense, or as he himself described them, *phrases mélodiques.* In his latest work they are used with kaleidoscopic effect and constantly shifted so as to form new patterns of feeling. The 'meaning' of his poetry, indeed, often consists in the relations between the symbols, in the sudden transitions from one emotion to its opposite. The most important symbols are the processions of school girls going two by two to Mass which stand for innocence and faith in contrast to the poet's sophistication and unbelief; Paris streets on Sunday afternoons and the mingling of the out-of-tune piano with the vespers bell suggesting the receding tide of faith; the curtained windows suggesting boredom and bourgeois degradation of life; and the storm discussed above.

The symbol of autumn, which plays the same part in the *Derniers vers* as spring in *The Waste Land,* is so important that it needs some elucidation. The poem begins:

> Blocus sentimental! Messageries du Levant! . . .
> Oh, tombée de la pluie! Oh! tombée de la
>   nuit,
> Oh! le vent! . . .
> La Toussaint, la Noël et la Nouvelle Année,
> Oh, dans les bruines, toutes mes cheminées! . . .
> D'usines . . .

Laforgue seldom used the device of omitting his main verbs more skilfully than he does in this remarkable passage. It suggests a state of complete instability—an instability that could only be represented by the poet's powerlessness to make any *statement* about his feelings at all. The halting rhythms and broken lines give the impression of some one floundering helplessly in the dark, struggling pathetically against the storm without making any headway; and, by implication, of the poet's powerlessness to dominate his own emotions.

The sudden impact of *Blocus sentimental* on the reader is tremendous. It gives a physical sense of emotional inhibition which is heightened by the succession of short, abrupt phrases that seem to beat down on one like the rain and the gusts of wind. *Messageries du Levant* means a biting east wind—the sort of wind that numbs. In this way *emotional numbness* and *physical numbness* become associated. The description of the rain and the dark emphasizes the feeling of helplessness. The names of the principal winter feasts suggest a long, dreary expanse of time. *Bruines* refers back to the second line: the image is the obliteration of the landscape by the rain and the dark, and is clearly intended to express the poet's sense of personal obliteration. *Toutes mes cheminées* suggests a total loss of direction. The fading of the factories in the mist may refer to the world of practical activity from which the poet is cut off. The sudden break at *usines* gives the sensation of collapse which is emphasized a few lines later by

> Il bruine;
> Dans la forêt mouillée, les toiles d'araignées
> Ploient sous les gouttes d'eau, et c'est leur
>   ruine.

The bending of the spiders' webs reinforces the image of the man bending under the storm. This is clinched by *ruine* which is the theme of the *Derniers vers* as death is the theme of *The Waste Land.*

The expression of the mood of the poem is so complete in these lines that the merest reference—as, for instance, in the passage from the fourth section analysed above—is sufficient to evoke the whole.

The opening of the third section is one of the finest passages in the *Derniers vers:*

> Ainsi donc, pauvre, pâle et piètre individu
> Qui ne croit à son Moi qu'à ses moments
>   perdus,
> Je vis s'effacer ma fiancée
> Emportée par le cours des choses,
> Telle l'épine voit s'effeuiller,
> Sous prétexte de soir sa meilleure rose.
> Or, cette nuit anniversaire, toutes les
>   Walkyries du vent
> Sont revenues beugler par les fentes de ma
>   porte:
>
> *Vae soli!*
> Mais, ah! qu'importe?
> Il fallait m'en étourdir avant!
> Trop tard! ma petite folie est morte!
> Qu'importe *Vae soli!*
> Je ne trouverai plus ma petite folie.
>
> Le grand vent bâillonné,
> S'endimanche enfin le ciel du matin.
> Et alors, eh! allez donc, carillonnez,
> Toutes cloches des bons dimanches!
> Et passez layettes et collerettes et robes
>   blanches
> Dans un frou-frou de lavandes et de thym
> Vers l'encens et les brioches!
> Tout pour la famille, quoi! *Vae soli!* C'est
>   certain.

These lines are a perfect example of Laforgue's peculiarly delicate sensibility. They are also an admirable example of his transition from one set of feelings to another.

The *pauvre, pâle et piètre individu* re-emphasizes the poet's devastating sense of his own helplessness which is characteristic of all Laforgue's work. The *Moi* contrasts the poet's real helplessness with his assumed bravado and attempts to pass it off as a joke. *S'effacer* re-introduces the obliteration motif. The woman is snatched away and becomes part of the world from which the poet is cut off. *Emportée . . .* suggests movement, suggests someone irresistibly carried away and lost, which is one of the themes of the poem. *L'épine*—the desolate, despoiled thorn goes back to *pauvre, pâle et piètre.* The short, broken lines which follow suggest the short, violent gusts of the storm and, at the same time, the feverish workings of the mind.

The change from the short line to the long and gradually lengthening line in the second part indicates the calm which follows the storm. The transition is superbly managed. The calm of nature reflects the calm of the poet, though we must not overlook the implication that it is a calm born of exhaustion. *Bâillonné,* 'gagged,' is another instance of the word that pulls us up short. *S'endimanche* is the pivotal word of the passage and links two sets of images—the calm of nature and spiritual calm. This is reinforced by the troop of girls going to Mass. The sound of the storm merges into the carolling of church bells. The whistling of the wind (blowing away the rose leaves) is replaced by the delicate *frou-frou* of the dresses; the smell of the rose, with its romantic associations, by the scent of lavender suggesting domestic peace, clean clothes and neat drawers. The reference to *brioches* (bread that is blessed and given to the faithful to take home) is apparently used to contrast the families united in the Faith with the outcast poet. (Hence the repeated *Vae soli!*)

There is a passage in the seventh section which calls for comment:

> Où est-elle à cette heure?
> Peut-être qu'elle pleure . . .
> Où est-elle à cette heure?
> Oh! du moins, soigne-toi, je t'en conjure!
>
> O fraîcheur des bois le long de la route,
> O châle de mélancolie, toute âme est un peu
>   aux écoutes,
> Que ma vie
> Fait envie!
> Cette impériale de diligence tient de la magie.

I have chosen this as an example of cinema technique. It is a common cinematic device—very much used by Pudovkin—to show a perfectly calm landscape after a scene of great emotional intensity. In this passage feeling is worked up to its maximum by the use of short, abrupt lines (paralleled by the short staccato Russian cutting), the agonized self-questioning and the hysterical *Soigne-toi,* then there is a sudden change to landscape. The word *fraîcheur* comes with a shock of inexpressible relief. (It should be noted that Mr. Eliot has made use of this device—the opening of *The Waste Land* is a good instance—by his references to flowers and the sea which provide the same form of release as this passage).

The importance of Laforgue's work should now be apparent. The result of his experiments was that the contemporary poet found an instrument at hand which was capable of expressing the full complexity of his outlook. This is a different thing from saying that Laforgue's own poetry is complex or mature. In spite of the fact that his feelings are often complicated, his outlook is neither complex nor mature. His poetry is a little deceptive. When one first comes to it, it appears far more complex than it really is. It is only later that one sees that it has a surface-complexity which is sometimes little more than a peculiar kind of verbiage. His symbolism depends for its success on a close correspondence between the symbol and the emotion symbolized; but Laforgue was sometimes inclined to throw unusual words and images together in the hope that something astonishing would come of it. It is a fault that we find repeatedly in the ***Imitation de Notre-Dame de la lune*** (*e.g.* the piece called ***La lune est stérile***), but there are also instances in the ***Derniers vers***. I wish to examine in detail a passage from the tenth section.

> O géraniums diaphanes, guerroyeurs sortilèges,
> Sacrilèges monomanes!
> Emballages, dévergondages, douches! O
>   pressoirs
> Des vendanges des grands soirs!
> Layettes aux abois,
> Thyrses au fond des bois!
> Transfusions, représailles,
> Relevailles, compresses et l'éternelle potion,
> *Angelus!* n'en pouvoir plus
> De débâcles nuptiales! de bébâcles nuptiales! . . .

This passage has been singled out by Mr. Eliot as an example of 'something which looks very like the [metaphysical] conceit' in French poetry. I cannot help feeling that there is a strange confusion here. It is an example of Laforgue's impressionist psychological notation, and though it certainly has the surface-complexity noted above, it has nothing of the genuine complexity of the metaphysical conceit. There are words suggesting violent attacks and counter-attacks like *guerroyeurs, sortilèges, représailles.* There is another group suggesting compression—*emballages, pressoirs, compresses*—which is set off against words suggesting outburst or overflow—*dévergondages, douches, transfusions.* A further group is less obscure—words like *layettes, relevailles, Angelus,* meaning baby-clothing, churchings, religion, apparently signify happy married life as opposed to the *débâcles nuptiales.* They may also be contrasted with the violence and confusion suggested by the first two lines.

The feelings are certainly 'tangled,' but I find nothing that can be called 'a whole of tangled feelings'—though clearly there ought to be. If the poet's aim was to suggest mental conflict, a tug of war between opposing feelings, what he tried to do is very imperfectly realized. What I wish to contrast is the internal disconnection of the passage with the internal coherence of

Donne's conceits. There seems to me to be one essential difference between the metaphysical conceit and Laforgue's method of psychological association. A conceit like 'On a round ball' or the compasses is a unity in which the parts are rigorously subordinated to a central purpose. It is an *intellectual* process, and it is the intellectual element that distinguishes it from the apparent conceits in Laforgue's poetry. The metaphysical conceit is used to relate a particular experience— one might almost call it a thought-experience—to a general *body of principles* and not, as with Laforgue, simply to relate a particular feeling to a general *body of feelings*. Thus the structure of Donne's work is intellectual in a way that Laforgue's is not. It is also apparent from the internal disconnection of this passage that Laforgue's attitude was necessarily fragmentary and disconnected too.

This difference between Laforgue and the Metaphysical Poets is so vital that I must be forgiven for underlining it. 'Donne, Corbière, Laforgue,' wrote Mr. Eliot in [*A Garland for John Donne,* 1931] 'begin with their own feelings, and their limitation is that they do not always get much outside or beyond; Shakespeare, one feels, arrives at an objective world by a process from himself, whoever he was, as the centre and starting point . . . With the Donne and the French poets the pattern is given by what goes on in the mind, rather than by the exterior events which provoke the mental activity and play of thought and feeling.'

This is an acute criticism of Laforgue; but it is only partly true of Corbière and scarcely true at all of Donne. It is not true of Donne because Donne was after all a Christian; and however personal his religion may have been, it did provide a point of reference *outside* his immediate feelings. His mind and outlook show the impress of a training in scholastic philosophy, and the *tension* we find in his work comes precisely from the endeavour to integrate new experiences into a system of traditional philosophy. The weakness of Laforgue's poetry, as we have it, is largely due to the fact that he had no system—his preoccupation with German philosophy is decisive on this point—and that his only point of reference was his own *personality*. Thus one feels obliged to dissent when Mr. Eliot remarks that 'A poet like Donne, or like Baudelaire or Laforgue, may almost be considered the inventor of an attitude, a system of feeling or of morals. This confuses the issues by attributing to Laforgue precisely that quality which Donne and Baudelaire possessed and which he was without. What makes Donne and Baudelaire 'bigger' men than their contemporaries is the fact that in their work the mood of the moment—the personal mood—is subordinated to something lasting and impersonal which can be described as an 'outlook' in the fullest sense of the term. For Donne and for Baudelaire the problem was never merely a personal one: there was a complete correspondence between the

personal problem and the problem of the age. With Laforgue, one feels, the problem was largely a personal one, far more personal than critics have realized.

Laforgue's wit has had a considerable influence on later poets and has also attracted a great deal of attention from critics. It must be confessed, however, that the influence has not been wholly for the good and that the critical attention has not always been of the right kind. The criticism has been on the whole too indulgent, and it has not discriminated sufficiently between the use to which his wit ought to have been put and the uses to which it was put. It has never been pointed out that it sometimes degenerates into a trick or that it is far too limited an instrument to serve as the basis of an outlook. There is an immense difference in this respect between the wit of Corbière and the wit of Laforgue. Corbière's wit is essentially positive and is used in the service of an aggressive attitude, while Laforgue's is negative and is often used not to affirm a position, but to avoid taking up a position at all.

The proper use of Laforgue's wit is as an ironic commentary on experience—a use which is well illustrated by the opening of the fifth section of the **Derniers vers:**

> Amour absolu, carrefour sans fontaine;
> Mais, à tous les bouts, d'étourdissantes fêtes
>   foraines.
>
> Jamais franches,
> Ou le poing sur la hanche:
> Avec toutes, l'amour s'échange
> Simple et sans foi comme un bonjour.

There is a deliberate contrast between the solemn opening in the romantic style and the brisk movement of the next four lines, suggesting the bustle and the crude tunes of the fair. *Le poing sur la hanche* probably refers to the gesture of the hardboiled prostitute and provides further comment of the opening line. *Simple et sans foi comme un bonjour* is a cynical and startling final comment which is entirely successful.

There is a better known, but less successful example in the tenth section:

> J'aurai passé ma vie le long des quais
> A faillir m'embarquer
> Dans de bien funestes histoires,
> Tout cela pour l'amour
> De mon coeur fou de la gloire d'amour.
>
> Oh, qu'ils sont pittoresques les trains
>   manqués! . . .

The procedure is the same as in the last passage. The wit consists largely in the tone, in the 'levity' of the treatment. The suspended image at the close performs the same function as before—the sudden concentration of the whole feeling of the passage into a single image raises it to a fresh level of intensity and seriousness. The passage as a whole, however, is unconvincing. It leaves us with the same feeling of uneasiness that we get from the *Autre complainte de Lord Pierrot,* in spite of the undeniable brilliance of that poem, and from a good deal that Laforgue wrote besides. For the poet is not as detached or as single-minded as he tries to appear. There is something specious about the jaunty, man-of-the-world attitude which is used to conceal the underlying sentimentality. A comparison between these lines and Corbière's *Poète contumace,* where the same method is used to express a genuinely mature attitude, should be decisive.

The truth is that Laforgue's wit is often an attempt to solve his own emotional problems. Thus in the *Autre complainte de Lord Pierrot* his criticism of romantic love is ineffectual *as criticism* because it is perfectly clear that he is ridiculing an attitude from which he is trying to free himself, but has not yet managed to do so. The fact that he uses irony as a means to something else makes disasters inevitable. One nearly always has the feeling that his wit may collapse at any moment into sentimentality, and this sometimes happens even in the *Derniers vers:*

> Bref, j'allais me donner d'un 'Je vous aime'
> Quand je m'avisai non sans peine
> Que d'abord je ne me possédais pas bien moi-
>   même.

This is a palpable attempt to pass off one's confusion as a joke.

I can make my point best in considering an important but neglected side of Laforgue's poetry—his religious symbolism. We might begin by comparing some lines from Baudelaire's *Franciscae meae laudes* with a passage from a poem in the *Fleurs de bonne volonté:*

> Esto sertis implicata
> O femina delicata,
> Per quam solvuntur peccata. . . .
> Quum vitiorum tempestas
> Turbabat omnes semitas
> Apparuisti, Deitas,
> Velut stella salutaris
> In naufragiis amaris . . .

Laforgue has:

> J'aime, j'aime de tout mon siècle! cette hostie
> Féminine en si vierge et destructible chair
> Qu'on voit, au point du jour, altièrement sertie
> Dans de cendreuses toilettes déjà d'hiver,
> Se fuir le long des cris surhumains de la mer!

Superficially the procedure is the same—an ironic contrast between the sacredness of the subject and the levity of the poet's tone—but the result is entirely different. Baudelaire combines two opposing feelings in order to form a new and perverse one. By an ingenious twist *solvuntur peccata* is made to suggest liberation from sin by salvation and liberation from desire through satisfaction, and this is emphasized by the play on *salutaris.* Laforgue compares a successful seduction with the reception of the Sacrament. The woman is described as *cette hostie féminine* and *hostie* is given its double sense of Sacrament and Victim.

The difference between the two passages is primarily a difference of tone. It is clear that for Baudelaire the religious emotion was at least as real as the sexual, and his words could be accurately described as blasphemous. The allusions in Laforgue, on the other hand, are those of a man who has consciously and deliberatley detached himself from the Faith. The words have lost something of their former meaning and become convenient counters, and there is an instinctive lack of reverence which prevents them from being blasphemous in the way in which Baudelaire's undoubtedly are. What is strikingly new is the note of spiritual apathy. It is very marked in the little known *Petite prière sans prétentions:*

> Et laissez-nous en paix, morts aux mondes
>   meilleurs,
> Paître, dans notre coin, et forniquer, et rire! . . .
>
> Paître, dans notre coin, et forniquer et rire! . . .

where the last line appears to be a mocking imitation of an invisible congregation repeating the prayer after the priest.

Laforgue's peculiar state of mind is revealed most strikingly, however, in a passage from the *Derniers vers:*

> Ah! moi, je demeure l'Ours Blanc!
> Je suis venu par ces banquises
> Plus pures que les communiantes en blanc . . .
> Moi, je ne vais pas à l'église,
> Moi, je suis le Grand Chancelier de l'Analyse,
> Qu'on se le dise.

This passage is clearly intended as a contrast between the poet's sophistication and unbelief and the innocence and faith of the children going to Mass. The important point is the use of capitals for *Ours Blanc* and *Grand Chancelier de l'Analyse.* The bear represents the outcast poet, but is deliberately turned into a comic bear. It is the trick—familiar in the later work of Mr. Aldous Huxley—of a writer who wishes to express a point of view without committing himself definitely to any one position, and takes refuge in caricature. The poet chooses to present himself as the nineteenth-century sceptic, but is careful not to identify himself too closely with the tradition of Renan and Taine. The passage is not altogether successful—it is obviously the voice of the romantic young man and not that of the convinced sceptic—but it illustrates the way in which Laforgue was using poetry in an attempt to solve his personal problems.

The passage is important for another reason. It shows that in spite of his curious intellectual timidity, Laforgue did recognize the necessity of taking up a definite position and that at bottom he was not content with the evasion he practised. There seems to me to be a marked tendency in his later work to free himself from all accepted attitudes—from traditional religion and traditional (romantic) love—as he had freed himself from traditional verse-forms. At the time of his death the process was incomplete and it is impossible to say how much further it would have gone. He seemed to be moving towards a position of spiritual neutrality and was very far from formulating anything resembling a positive outlook at all. His detachment was still incomplete, and his interest in German philosophy shows that he felt the need of a substitute for the thing he had abandoned. All this makes him a bad master as far as the content of his work is concerned and explains why the influence of his very seductive spiritual defeatism on later poets has been unfortunate. It is possible that he might have become 'the inventor of an attitude,' but we cannot be certain. The disparity between his technical maturity and his emotional immaturity tells heavily against him; and his extreme spiritual defeatism makes one wonder whether he had it in him to develop a positive attitude towards anything.

What would have happened can only be a matter of conjecture. It is important to stress the fact that Laforgue was trying to work out a position. He therefore belongs to Baudelaire and his school and not to Mallarmé and his descendants. The significance of Mallarmé and Valéry is that they make a definite attempt to dispense with a positive outlook of any sort. This explains the negative element, the constant preoccupation with sterility, that we find in Mallarmé. And I cannot help feeling that 'pure poetry,' for which he was ultimately responsible, is a subtle form of escapism. It is an attempt to make the worship of form a substitute for an outlook, and it therefore becomes a means of avoiding the necessity of committing oneself to a position at all.

Warren Ramsey (essay date 1953)

SOURCE: "The World Is My Idea," in *Jules Laforgue and the Ironic Inheritance,* Oxford University Press, 1953, pp. 42-58.

[*In the following excerpt, Ramsey—a leading Laforgue scholar—explores how the different philosophers then popular with Paris intellectuals shaped Laforgue's poetry. In particular, he traces Laforgue's familiarity with and use of the ideas of Arthur Schopenhauer and Eduard von Hartmann.*]

There are two kinds of influence, as André Gide remarked: that felt by an individual and that undergone by a group. The influence of Schopenhauer in France during the 'seventies and 'eighties was of the second sort. This philosopher's subjective idealism, his belief that investigation of the external world could not lead to truth were readily seconded because they were intimately related to fundamental nineteenth-century attitudes. The Romantics had been nothing if not self-centered, even though a second stage in the work of many a poet—and pessimistic philosopher, too, for that matter—had been a program for social betterment. Along with the scientific faith that knowledge would give power over the physical universe there had coexisted, often in the mind of a single man—Alfred de Vigny, for instance—a despairing awareness that such power had no truth in it, that control over physical forces could not bring contact with reality. Schopenhauer was the most formidable of Western Buddhists; but before he became known in France a number of writers, notably Leconte de Lisle and that physician friend of Mallarmé who called himself Jean Lahor, had proclaimed in Buddhistic terms the illusoriness of phenomena and found in this religion the hopelessness it usually engenders in a European mind. The Buddhists had been preceded by other anti-materialists who were vaguely Christian. Then there had been the mordant analysts of motives, heirs of the nihilistic eighteenth-century moralists. And beneath all, informing all, had been the pensive melancholy of René, of which Chateaubriand would never have written without examples from beyond the Rhine.

Schopenhauer found refuge in contemplation, in the play of ideas, and in veneration of art. So had a French generation disappointed in more outward hopes by the failure of the midcentury revolution. Several of Taine's and Renan's works are as much monuments to 'pessimism' as Books I, II, and IV of *The World as Will and Idea;* and Book III of that work, 'The Object of Art,' is the major theoretical document in a European movement of art for art's sake.

The ground was well prepared when, in 1870, a liberal journalist and politician, Challemel-Lacour, published the record of his pilgrimage to Frankfurt, home of 'A Contemporary Buddhist in Germany: Arthur Schopenhauer.' Challemel-Lacour knew little about metaphysics and communicated less. But he had visited Schopenhauer at home and at the Hôtel d'Angleterre, where the old philosopher took his meals and berated humanity, and he carried away enough acid to etch a good likeness. This anecdotic article set off the avalanche. A Sorbonne professor named Elme-Marie Caro dazzled his public with an eloquent, empty book on nine-teenth-century pessimism. In 1874 appeared a model of lucid exposition, *La Philosophie de Schopenhauer* by Théodule Ribot, a philosopher-psychologist who was later to write significantly on the artistic imagination and the Unconscious. Thereafter came a spate of articles, some of them technical, and though *Die Welt als Wille und Vorstellung* was still untranslated, the key ideas of Schopenhauer were at hand for all to ponder. Here was what the age demanded: a system of thought based on withdrawal from society, on commitment to art, on contemplative zeal and heroism. With compelling force it gripped older men like Renan, younger men like Bourget, and there was no excuse for a still younger man like Laforgue to remain ignorant of it, even though his German was virtually non-existent.

Laforgue never carried Schopenhauer's work about with him, reading and rereading it all, as he did Eduard von Hartmann's *Philosophy of the Unconscious*. Schopenhauer's thought was for him something underlying and overshadowing. For that very reason it is well to look at some of the Schopenhauerian ideas absorbed into the 'Castéchisme pessimiste,' Laforgue's most complete statement of his aims at the age of about twenty. For these ideas, close kin to those he took from other sources, became the felt thoughts of his poetry; while the ideas of Hartmann, studied later, were the raw material for an aesthetics sometimes hauled bodily into the verse.

'The world is my idea.' Schopenhauer begins his work with this concise statement of the Idealist position. Such a view is far from novel. One is reminded of the position taken by the expounder of Bishop Berkeley's philosophy to whom Samuel Johnson remarked, 'Pray, sir, do not leave us, for we may perhaps forget to think of you, and then you will cease to exist.' It was not from Berkeley, however, that the young Laforgue drew his conviction that there is no object without a subject, no planet without a perceiving eye:

> *L'homme, ce fou rêveur d'un piètre*
> *mondicule . . .*

Man, mad dreamer of a petty planet . . .

In the most ambitious of his early poems, he addresses the earth in these terms:

> *C'était un songe, oh! oui, tu n'as jamais été!*
> *Tout est seul! nul témoin! rien ne voit, rien ne*
> *pense . . .*

It was a dream, ah! yes, and thou hast never
  been!
All is alone! no witness! nothing sees or
  thinks . . .

If humanity should become extinct, a possibility envisioned throughout the early poems, the earth would have been nightmare.

We even find, in the verse of a later period, a poem about Time and Space as forms of the faculty of knowledge. It has a saving satirical title, **'Complainte du Temps et de sa commère l'Espace.'** But what other poet of that day (or this) would have presumed to write about the categories, man's means of knowing about the world that is his idea, 'fondement de la connaissance'? There is no mention of causality in this poem. Since Schopenhauer maintained, in opposition to Kant, that causal relation is as indispensable a condition of the world-idea as Time and Space, this poem is not Schopenhauerian; but no doubt it deserves the epithet of 'Kantian' which André Beaunier applied to it.

The world is a structure supported by my perceptions, made possible by temporal and spatial and causal relations. It is the cause-and-effect relation, the interlocking of events, that makes possible scientific inquiry. Schopenhauer, Hartmann, and their literary disciples such as Laforgue were not hostile to science—these three were all amateur scientists. They did, however, deny that science can deal only with the idea, with appearances. Within and everywhere around, 'objectifying' itself in phenomena of which the individual is one, is the ultimate reality, the Will. Philosophically, it is the thing-in-itself, the noumenon, with which only contemplation, never the measurement of things sensed, can establish contact. Psychologically, it is the potential of powerful impulses that dominate and dwarf all possible activities of reason, the 'ferocious and libidinous gorilla' which, said Taine, lurks within civilized man. Schopenhauer the moralist, who probably outweighs in importance Schopenhauer the metaphysician, was a writer who commented pithily on the power of the gorilla and the shakiness of its cage.

Men, especially the optimistic, socially minded, forward-looking bourgeois whom Hegel's philosophy flattered, were told to recognize their true condition, each one alone in an illusory world. It would be wrong, however, to suppose that man cannot find footing, attain to reality. Some of those who hastened to attach the label 'pessimism' to this Idealist philosophy were simply materialists, accustomed to looking for material rewards. Men, if they are worth anything, are in search of reality, of something approaching the ultimate reality, the thing-in-itself. And here we begin to deal with another kind of idea, the Platonic archetype, to which, Schopenhauer tells us, the thing-in-itself bears a strong resemblance. The Platonic ideas, he says, are 'the first degree of objectification' of the Will. And the human intelligence, evolved at first by the Will only as a tool for its own purposes, can by concentrated attention produce a sort of superfluity of itself capable of regarding the archetypal ideas, capable of aesthetic experience. The genius is the man who can lose himself utterly in objective contemplation. The talented artist and the amateur of art are, in different degrees, contemplatives. And the aim for everyone, as Laforgue writes in his Catechism, is serene contemplation, by which one 'escapes from oneself, is freed for an instant from Time, Space, and Numbers, dies to the consciousness of one's individuality, and attains to the great liberty, which is escape from the Illusory.' It may have been arbitrary, as Ribot pointed out in 1874 and as many a critic has done since, for Schopenhauer to place the Platonic ideas first in the series of phenomena proceeding from that 'blind force' which is Will. One must fight down Will in order to contemplate something that is the outgrowth of Will. Nevertheless, this paradox within Schopenhauer's thought was, like his admirable prose style, evidence of the importance he attached to art and it helped to gain him some of his best disciples, Richard Wagner, Friedrich Nietzsche, Laforgue.

Escape from the multiplicity of phenomena by means of artistic experience is rare, however—the privilege of the few. So are those degrees of relative objectivity reached in philosophical and scientific inquiry. There is another route of escape, which Schopenhauer calls 'the most serious, since it relates to the action of men, the matter which concerns everyone directly and can be foreign or indifferent to none.' Moral perfection through suppression of the personal will is reached by several stages; and the individual progresses to the extent that he sees through the network of appearances. The just man has so far penetrated the Web of Maya as to perceive that he should not interfere with the interests of others, individuals like himself. But the truly virtuous man, realizing that all individuation is illusory, that all individuals are lost in the great whole, that one is simultaneously the slayer and the slain, will feel an active sympathy for all his fellows, victims of the same human limitations. So grievous is the state of man that love can only take the form of pity. 'The incentive to virtuous action is simply the *knowledge* of the suffering of others, directly understood from one's own suffering and placed on a level with it . . . Pure love (. . . *caritas*) is by nature sympathy.' As Laforgue writes in his Catechism, 'Sympathy, the first gift of the sage.' To the extent that the individual sees clearly, he will seek to share the sufferings of others, to mortify the will within himself. So the twenty year old poet sets down his rule: 'one must suffer for at least two years: fast, mortify oneself, bleed with pity and universal love, visit the hospitals, contemplate hideous and pitiful diseases, all forms of filthiness, become steeped in history in general and in detail, telling oneself that that is real, that all these billions of individuals had hearts, senses, aspirations to happiness; one must read history with *sympathy* . . . like Carlyle and Michelet.'

Remembering his 'two years in the libraries' and his asceticism, we realize that Laforgue actually tried the more radical kinds of renunciation. We are in a better position to understand such passages as the following:

> *Je n'ai fait que souffrir, pour toute la nature,*
> *Pour les êtres, le vent, les fleurs, le*
> *firmament,*
> *Souffrir par tous mes nerfs, minutieusement,*
> *Souffrir de n'avoir pas d'âme encore assez*
> *pure.*

> **—"Pour le Livre d'amour'**

> I have done naught but suffer, for all nature,
> For the creatures, the wind, the flowers, the
> firmament,
> Suffer in bone and nerve and every fiber,
> Suffer for my soul's impediment.

When, in **'Pour la Mort de la terre,'** the poet asks,

> *Où donc est Çakia, coeur chaste et trop*
> *sublime,*
> *Qui saigna pour tout être et dit la bonne Loi?*
> *Et Jésus triste et doux qui douta de la Foi*
> *Dont il avait vécu, dont il mourait victime?*

> Where now is Sakya, chaste heart that aimed
> too high,
> Who bled for all and spoke the saving Word?
> And melancholy Jesus who mistrusted
> The faith he lived and by which He would
> die?

We realize that the figure of Philoctetes, subject of early preoccupations with the discipline of suffering, is for the time being supplanted by other figures. Chief among these, for Laforgue as for Schopenhauer, is the Buddha, although Jesus is counted among the very great and good.

Of course Laforgue was not a Schopenhauerian only because of the metaphysics which demonstrates so beautifully that unseen things are real and that the vision of truth must be prepared by mortification. For him as for several generations of writers, Schopenhauer was the educator, the disquieter, whose sayings contained the cure for naïveté. Like the Swiss diarist Amiel, whose searching self-examinations were published when Laforgue was twenty-two, he began with Schopenhauer the aphorist; and since he did not remain a thoroughgoing philosophical pessimist for long, he may be said to have ended with the aphoristic Schopenhauer as well. Trenchant sayings in the minor works, some of them encountered second-hand, were assimilated and helped to shape a point of view. Woman as the 'undersized, narrow-shouldered, broad-hipped, short-legged' adversary, to quote the celebrated passage from the

Parerga—a creature without metaphysical aspiration or capacity for objectivity, embodiment of perverse will seeking to perpetuate itself by the 'universal dupery'—woman thus understood comprises half the cast of characters in Laforgue's writings. True, such a view of womankind is in his case an ironic device rather than a heartfelt conviction. But from Pierrot to Lohengrin to Hamlet, his characters act on Schopenhauer's suggestion that chastity is the only solution and resolutely steer clear of further objectification. The refrain 'Célibat, célibat, tout n'est que célibat,' which runs like a pure silver thread through the verse and prose, is not so much a statement of fact as a program.

The poet may have learned something about irony from the philosopher, especially from the preface to the long-delayed second edition of *Die Welt als Wille und Vorstellung,* where Schopenhauer advises the Hegelians to continue their twenty-five-year conspiracy of silence indefinitely. Key words, including the all-important 'ennui,' have about the same meaning in the two writers. And the whole legend of Schopenhauer the man worked strongly on a youthful imagination. One of the two literary pilgrimages Laforgue made was to Frankfurt (the other being to Elsinore), at some inconvenience to himself and in spite of the Empress Augusta's outspoken aversion for 'that horrid man.'

Still another kind of idea, in addition to the world-idea and the Platonic archetype, was to occupy Laforgue's imagination. He was to spend more and more time with Hartmann's *Philosophy of the Unconscious,* was to hold with this dissident Schopenhauerian that a Will which goes on objectifying itself cannot be purposeless, that present and co-ordinate with Will in the Absolute must be Idea: the creative Idea of Hegel working through history, through the manifold activities of the human mind, toward its own perfection. A systematic pessimist proceeding from the assumption that the ultimate reality is evil—that Laforgue emphatically was not. A temperamental pessimist like Leopardi, able to abide the view of the darkness at the end of a philosophy of negation—that he was not either. 'Un coeur tendre qui hait le néant vaste et noir,' he rebelled in various ways against such views of man's destination. Fertile in contrasts as he was, reacting to the thought of a century, he was even tinged with the religion of science, the positivism that Schopenhauer considered most pernicious. He neutralized a pessimistic world view, as did Vigny in 'La Bouteille à la mer,' by affirming that the individual's unlucky voyage leads somewhere: the observations one man makes will enable others to avoid his shipwreck. Laforgue writes of 'the cathedral of Herbert Spencer,' brings the evolutionary theory into his aesthetics. And from another positivist, Camille Flammarion,

he seems to have taken the imagery of his longest early poem and the most striking imagery of *Le Sanglot de la terre* as a whole.

'If the innumerable creative floods,' wrote Lucretius in a passage quoted by Flammarion in his *Pluralité des mondes habités,* 'surge and flow in myriad varied forms through infinite space, should they have brought forth in their fecund strife only the orb of the earth and its celestial vault? Can we believe that beyond this world so vast a mass of elements is condemned to idle repose? . . . If the generative principles gave birth to masses whence have issued the heavens, the waves, the earth and its inhabitants, it must be supposed that in the remainder of the void the elements of matter have given birth to numberless animated beings, to skies, seas, earths, have sowed feet in the aerial floods. Wherever immense matter can find a space to contain it and no obstacle to its free expansion, it will give birth to life in various forms; and if the mass of elements is such that all ages and all beings together would be insufficient even to count them, and if nature has endowed these elements with the faculties which it has accorded to the generative principles of our globe, the elements, in the other regions of space, must have scattered other beings, mortals, and worlds.'

It would be hard to prove that Laforgue read the curious monument to pseudo-scientific legend in which these sonorous words are quoted. But it is more than likely that he did. The poet of our time who has the most in common with Laforgue, Jules Supervielle, gives much of the credit for his first important volume of verse to a popular treatise on astronomy that he picked up in the early 'twenties. It had a liberating effect on his imagination, supplying him with striking dynamic imagery. Some work had such an effect on Laforgue, and it is a plausible guess that it was Flammarion's.

Published in 1862, *La Pluralité des mondes habités* was the first book of an astronomer with a flair for popularization and conjecture. In the preface to one of the numerous editions (twenty-five by 1876), the author expresses surprise, probably justified, at his success. Twenty years before, nothing astronomical would have been very popular. As the century progressed, however, the general imagination was stirred more and more by expanding knowledge of the heavens, and within a decade after its publication Flammarion's book had appeared in ten languages. There was literally a world-wide surge of curiosity about what the heavens might contain. On the part of one young poet there was certainty:

> *En tous sens, je le sais, sur ces mondes*
> *lointains,*
> *Pèlerins comme nous des pâles solitudes,*

Dans la douceur des nuits tendant vers nous
    les mains,
Des Humanités soeurs rêvent par multitudes!

            —'L'Impossible'

Songez! depuis des flots sans fin d'éternités,
Cet azur qui toujours en tous les sens recule,
De troupeaux de soleils à tout jamais pullule,
Chacun d'eux conduisant des mondes
    habités . . .

            —'Farce éphémère'

Un coin! et tout là-bas déroulement d'espaces
A l'infini! Peuples de frères plus heureux!
Qui ne retrouveront pas même, un jour, nos
    traces
Quand ils voyageront à leur tour par ces
    lieux!

         —'Curiosités déplacées'

On every side, I know, on those far worlds,
Pilgrims like us of the pale solitudes,
In the softness of the nights stretching toward
    us their hands,
Sister peoples dream in multitudes!

Consider, for unmeasured floods of time
This azure surging forth on every side
Has swarmed with troops of suns incessantly,
Each one among them with its peopled
    worlds.

This little world! And those deploying spaces
Ad infinitum! Races of happier brothers
Who one day will not even know we were,
When their path crosses where we crossed
    before.

The Vedas taught that the human soul sojourns in the stars after its earthly incarnation. Xenophanes and Epicurus believed in the plurality of worlds, and Christiaan Huygens wrote in *Cosmotheoros:* 'It is not possible that those who are of the opinion of Copernicus and believe truly that the earth we inhabit is one of those that turn about the sun and receive light from it, should not also believe that other planets are inhabited, cultivated and adorned like ours.' Kant not only had assumed that other planets were inhabited but had also established a whole hierarchy of the perfection of their inhabitants according to distance from the sun. Laforgue's first collection of verse provides us with the only modern poetry on the subject.

Whether under the influence of the summary of evolutionary doctrine that Flammarion undertakes in another place, or as a result of readings in Spencer and Darwin, Laforgue also gives poetic expression to what has frequently been called 'the key idea of the nineteenth century.' A planet

       après bien des siècles de jours lents,
  Aux baisers du soleil sent tressaillir ses
    flancs,

  La vie éclot au fond des mers des premiers
    âges,
  Monades, vibrions, polypiers, coquillages.

  Puis les vastes poissons, reptiles, crustacés
  Râclant les pins géants de leurs dos cuirassés.

  Puis la plainte des bois, la nuit, sous les
    rafales,
  Les fauves, les oiseaux, le cri-cri des cigales.

  Enfin paraît un jour, grêle, blême d'effroi,
  L'homme au front vers l'azur, le grand
    maudit, le roi . . .

         —'Litanies de misère'

     after many ages of slow days,
Feels its flanks shudder at the sun's embrace.

Life spawns within the prehistoric sea,
Monads, vibriones, polyps, crustacea.

Then the vast fishes, reptiles, things with
    scales
Scrape giant pine trees with their armored
    tails.

And then the plaint of forests tempest-stirred,
Wild beasts and birds and the cicadas' chirr.

Until one day, frail and beset with fears,
Man the accursed, the struggling king appears.

In the same poem there is description of the birth of the planets, inorganic evolution:

  Un lac incandescent tombe et puis s'éparpille
  En vingt blocs qu'il entraîne ainsi qu'une
    famille.

  An incandescent lake falls and is scattered
  In twenty masses it leads family-like.

Another poem has an apostrophe to the mother-nebula:

  O fleuve chaotique, ô Nébuleuse-mère,
  Dont sortit le Soleil, notre père puissant . . .

        —'Crépuscule de dimanche d'été'

Chaotic river, mother-nebula
Whence sprang the sun, our puissant father . . .

In fact, imagery drawn from pseudo-scientific and sci-entific sources is in great part responsible for the qual-ity of Laforgue's strange, troubled, technically fluent early poetry. Sully-Prudhomme was also writing mel-ancholy 'scientific' verse during the last quarter of the century. But Sully-Prudhomme sadly lacked capacity for creating metaphors. Only Laforgue, in France, suc-ceeded in making poetry out of objects revealed by 'the marvelous tube.'

His best sustained poem of this period is **'Pour la Mort de la terre.'** The extinction of life upon the earth, or the extinction of the living earth, was much in his mind at this time. Perhaps the big work on Dürer with which he was helping Ephrussi kept scenes of death and apocalypse before his eyes; or perhaps the palpitations of the heart he complained of late in 1880. **'Pour la Mort de la terre'** is his nearest approach to the 'macabre epic of humanity' projected in his letter to Kahn. The opening quatrain is addressed to the suns:

O convoi solennel des soleils magnifiques,
Nouez et dénouez vos vastes masses d'or,
Doucement, tristement, sur de graves
musiques,
Menez le deuil très lent de votre soeur qui
dort.

O solemn progress of resplendent suns,
Wind and unwind your massive golden
trails,
Mildly and sadly to religious hymns,
Conduct the mourning of your sister gone.

In eight stanzas of eight lines each the stages of the world's history are evoked. Six stanzas end:

Non, dors, c'est bien fini, dors pour l'éternité.

The line

O convoi solennel des soleils magnifiques

returns between stanzas as a refrain. The poet foresees a time when the earth will be 'une épave énorme et solitaire . . . un bloc inerte et tragique,' quite different from what it was toward the other end of its history, when there were only:

. . . *les pantoums du vent, la clameur des*
flots sourds,
Et les bruissements argentins des feuillages.

. . . the wind's pantoums, the stubborn waves'
complaint,
And the silvery murmurs of the foliage.

However, the intruder appeared:

Mais l'être impur paraît! ce frêle révolté
De la sainte Maïa déchire les beaux voiles
Et le sanglot des temps jaillit vers les étoiles . . .

But the infirm creature appears, the feeble
rebel
Snatching away the veils of holy Maya.
The dirge of ages rises toward the stars.

The Middle Ages are evoked in Romantic terms. The fifth stanza is a series of exclamations, a list of things to be lost with earth—invention, music, arts and sci-ence—and although the formal interest is slight, the twentieth-century reader thinks of another vision of the eclipse of culture, Paul Valéry's, in 'A Thousand Despairing Hamlets.' After the musings on Buddha and Jesus already quoted, the poem reaches its highest degree of concreteness in the penultimate stanza:

Et plus rien! ô Vénus de marbre! eaux-fortes
vaines!
Cerveau fou de Hegel! doux refrains
consolants!
Clochers brodés à jour et consumés d'élans.
Livres où l'homme mit d'inutiles victoires!
Tout ce qu'a la fureur de tes fils enfanté,
Tout ce qui fut ta fange et ta splendeur si
brève,
O Terre, est maintenant comme un rêve, un
grand rêve . . .

Then nothing more! O marble Venus! vain
designs!
Mad brain of Hegel! Mild consoling songs!
Lace-light steeples spent with man's aspirings.
Books wherein man his futile gains inscribed!
All that the fury of your sons engendered,
All of your mire and momentary splendor,
O earth, is now like a dream, a great dream.

This is oratorical verse, eloquence of a kind whose neck Laforgue would be at pains to wring a little later on. But as the poem ends slipping into the Schopen-hauerian dark, 'sans nom dans le noir sans mémoire,' we cannot fail to admire the poet for the amount of intellectual history he has compressed into a poem and a collection.

Helen Phelps Bailey (essay date 1964)

SOURCE: "The Hamlet of Baudelaire, Mallarmé, and Laforgue," in *Hamlet in France: From Voltaire to Laforgue,* Librairie Droz, 1964, pp. 137-52.

[*The following excerpt from Bailey's book treats the Symbolist fascination with Hamlet; she contends, through an analysis of "Hamlet" and other references to the figure in Laforgue's writings, that Laforgue identified with Hamlet.*]

With the emergence of Symbolism, Hamlet may be said to have come into his own. Shakespeare's spiritually embattled hero, with his intuition of things undreamed-of in a corrupt and sordid world, found a congenial element in the climate of ideality that nurtured poetry in the last half of the century. The interpretations of Laforgue and Mallarmé, ironic in the one case, exalted in the other, reveal a sensitivity to Hamlet's scope and mystery rarely rivaled in the literature of *Hamlet* commentary. They took the Prince of Denmark out of the theater, in the strict sense of the term, to make of him a symbolic figure undefined by time or space, a *potential* hero, haunted by the specter of the absolute, harassed by cosmic doubt.

It was Hamlet's irreducible complexity and his frustration that endeared him to the poets. They saw in him their own reflections, or interpreted their "unique" individual attitudes and feelings in terms of what they conceived his to be. . . .

Laforgue took ironic delight in the image of himself as Hamlet; Villiers de L'Isle Adam is said to have modeled his attitudes and gestures on the mad Hamlet of Rouvière. Even Verlaine, who "preferred the ballet to Shakespeare," according to Arthur Symons, occasionally quoted "To be, or not to be." For the young Moréas, there were only "two subjects of conversation: his own poems and *Hamlet.*"

In the *foyer* of Symbolism on the *rue de Rome,* Hamlet was a beloved subject. [In *Nos Rencontres,* 1931] Régnier writes of having seen at Mallarmé's a pastel by Manet representing Hamlet in the graveyard scene; he mentions Shakespeare's Prince among the ideal heroes evoked by the master at his famous "Tuesdays": "Sometimes it was a Shakespeare who furnished Mallarmé with a revealing commentary, sometimes a Wagner who suggested to him vast possibilities. We believed then that we saw the lance of Parsifal gleaming or the black plume of Hamlet's toque waving in the wind." . . .

To his preoccupation with the Prince of Denmark, Laforgue brought the insight of a poet and an artist and all the forms of determinist thought that flourished in his time. His was a richly stocked mind that yearned to submerge itself in "the Universal Principle of the Unconscious." He made Hamlet the symbol of an unrelenting dualism that he knew too well: a longing for the absolute, frustrated by a sense of the accidental and a haunting suspicion that all adds up to nothing; a sense of the responsibility of genius—to itself—with a spirit bowed under the weight of futility, the *"A quoi bon?"*

It has been said that Hamlet was for Jules Laforgue what Saint Anthony was for Flaubert. Unquestionably, among the countless characters of literature that shared the poet's private world, none was associated more constantly or more profoundly with his thoughts and feelings than Lord Hamlet.

Two of Laforgue's earliest poems, the first composed when he was nineteen, the second at the age of twenty, attest a curious affinity for the Hamlet of the graveyard scene. **"Guitare"** (1879) is a characteristically Laforguian development of the "Now get you to my lady's chamber" lines in Hamlet's Yorick speech. **"Excuse macabre"** (1880) reveals the future author of the ***Moralités légendaires*** in one of his most "Hamletic" and sardonic moods. He addresses himself to a skull, presumably the little monkey skull he kept among his treasures, here called Margaretha after the "fiancée of [his] fourteenth year, . . . [the] so pale . . . so cold Marguerite."

> So, Marguerite, my lovéd one, for me,
> Who believe all ends on earth in cemeteries,
> An old skull is all that's left of you!
> Isn't that the fate of all in nature?
> The Hugos and the Caesars,—a bit of dust
>   blown by the wind;
>   Suns the sky is strewn with,
> Worlds will all some day be swallowed up in
>   nothingness,
>   Marguerite, my lovéd one! . . .
>
> And since, when all is said and done, there's
>   nothing
>   That is not smoke and vanity,
> Your skull . . . I may sell it, may I not,
>   Marguerite, my lovéd one?

The ***Fleurs de bonne volonté*** are preppered with epigraphs from Shakespeare's *Hamlet,* mainly from the Prince's conversation with Ophelia; in one of the ***Fleurs,*** the fair Ophelia is summoned to console the poet's loneliness. Two passages from Shakespeare's play preface the ***Derniers Vers,*** composed presumably after the poet's marriage and shortly before his death: Hamlet's "I have not art to reckon my groans thine evermore, [*sic*] most dear lady, whilst this machine is to him," signed "J.L."; and Ophelia's description of Hamlet's strange behavior on his visit to her, ending with Polonius's "This is the very ecstasy of love."

We infer, then, that Laforgue never ceased to think of himself as Hamlet. To some who knew him, the identification seemed well founded. [In "Essai Sur Jules Laforgue," *Mercure de France*] Camille Mauclair wrote of Laforgue in 1896: "He has something of that Hamlet that he loved so much . . . He has Hamlet's reserved, almost naïve manner, the lack of affectation, the recent learning still bringing into the conversations with Horatio the metaphysical impressions and argumentations of Elsinore [*sic*], the sentimental aimlessness, and a world of dreams in conflict with the world of facts. He does not have his father to avenge, he has his soul to free . . . [and] if he does not kill Polonius, at least, like the other Hamlet, he cares little whether or not that 'nobody' sees the strange things he shows him in the clouds. He has his imploring and imperious ghost, the Unconscious, and he converses with it continually, objectifies it by calling it forth, obeys it by rejecting all social scruples and by gratifying his sensibility, as Hamlet does his instinct and his devotion. He is Hamlet on the *boulevard* . . ."

In Laforgue's **"Hamlet or the Consequences of Filial Piety,"** Shakespeare's drama of a noble prince driven by duty to avenge his father's murder becomes the symbolic tale of a would-be "hero," striving—unheroically—to "free his soul." The Elizabethan tragedy becomes the ironic history of a nineteenth-century intellectual, whose duty to avenge a wrong dissolves like wax under the flame of his ambition to project his latent individuality and his unique significance. Laforgue relates the story of an exceptional man, an artist, who feels that with his gift of a sixth sense, he "might have been a Messiah" except that a prodigious diversity of tastes and talents, complicated by chronic "universal nausea," precluded concentration on the role.

Laforgue centered all the complexity of the *Tragedy of Hamlet* on the psychology of his hero. The characters are few: the Prince of Denmark; the usurper and the Queen, called Fengo and Gerutha, as in Belleforest; Laertes; two gravediggers; and two figures of Laforgue's invention: the players, Kate and William. There is no Ghost; no Horatio to share Hamlet's mental solitude; no Polonius: Hamlet has disposed of him before the story opens. Ophelia, though much talked of, never appears alive; the name of Fortinbras figures merely as a threat to the future fortunes of the state of Denmark. The plot is slight; our attention is focused on the hero's meditations and his recurrent, ever fruitless resolutions to engage in action. The scene encompasses the distance from Hamlet's "ivory tower" to the graveyard. The time is explicitly established as evening on the fourteenth of July, 1601.

Laforgue's setting mirrors his hero's soul. Even the sea embodies a spirit of ineffectualness and a futile longing for heroic action: " . . . the free and hard-working Sund, flowing along its ordinary course in nondescript waves, waiting for the wind and the hour to frolic in masterly style with the poor boats of the fishermen (the only feeling the fatality that weighs on them leaves them capable of)." Hamlet's solitary tower stands on a kind of "sterile promontory" like "a forgotten leprous sentinel." At its base, amid the "faded bouquets of ephemeral festivities," rots the refuse of the palace greenhouses. No royal swans grace the

sickly surface of the stagnant cove. Of its two windows, one "shows in dirty gray the sky, the open sea, existence without end"; through the other, comes to Hamlet the perpetual plaint of the wind in the trees of the royal forest.

Hamlet's room evokes "an incurable . . . an insolvent autumn." Its walls are hung with views of Jutland—"impeccably naïve" paintings at which Hamlet "spits heroically" in passing. Between the windows hang two full-length portraits: one of Hamlet "*en dandy,*" smiling appealingly against a ground of sulphurous twilight; the other of the late King Horwendill, his father, portrayed with a "roguish, faun-like eye" and bright new armor. An etcher's instruments hopelessly corroded from disuse, an organ, and a heap of books bear witness to pursuits abandoned; a chaise longue and a full-length mirror suggest the dandy following Baudelaire's counsel to "live and sleep before a mirror" in the practice of the "cult of self." A buffet with a secret lock attests a fear of poisoning. Finally, two waxen statuettes representing Fengo and Gerutha, both "moulded with a vengeful thumb," each with a needle through its heart, symbolize the vengeance of a Hamlet who will "speak daggers, but use none."

We meet the "hero" musing at his tower window as he awaits the arrival of the strolling players. His first speech voices the same soul-sickness that made Shakespeare's Prince find "weary, stale, flat and unprofitable . . . all the uses of this world," the same longing for relief from the pain of consciousness. But it is not his father's death and his mother's o'er-hasty marriage that obsess Laforgue's "pariah." He has a special problem: an irresistible vocation to be a Hero in an ephemeral world where all things seem mediocre and absurd. *"Un héros; ou simplement vivre"* is his "To be, or not to be:"

> —Ah! just to take it nice and easy like those waves . . .
>
> —Ah! if only I were pushed to take the trouble! . . . but everything is so precious in minutes and so fleeting! And the only practical thing is to keep still, keep still and act consistently . . .
>
> —Stability! Stability! thy name is Woman . . . life's all right, if it has to be. But a hero! And to come into the world in the first place, domesticated by an age and environments! Is that a proper, fair fight for a hero? . . . A hero! and let all things else be curtain raisers! . . . A hero! Or simply live. Method, Method, what do you expect of me? You know very well that I have eaten of the fruit of the Unconscious! . . .

In his mounting impatience at the players' tardiness, Hamlet's thoughts turn to more immediate concerns:

the smarting in his fingers, for example, caused by the act of tearing up Ophelia's letters which she had written on heavy first-quality paper, "the whim of a little upstart." Ophelia has been missing for some twenty-four hours, presumably since she learned that her father had been killed by Hamlet; but Hamlet is not worried for her safety. He tells himself that she was not for him in any case: she never would have understood him.

At the sight of the boat that brings the players across the cove, Hamlet remembers the two notebooks on his writing table and suddenly recalls what he set out to do: to exalt his filial piety and goad himself to vengeance by putting into words his father's murder. In the fervor of creation, he became so absorbed in the work itself that he forgot it was *his* "father murdered," *his* "mother stained," *his* throne that were the question. "I forgot as I went along," he says, "that the subject was my father murdered, robbed of all the living he had left in this precious world (poor man, poor man!), my mother prostituted (a sight that ruined woman for me and drove me to send the heavenly Ophelia to her death from shame and deterioration!), my throne, after all! I was going along merrily with the fictions of a fine subject . . ." So intense was his concern with form, so impartial his genius in presenting the case of the evil traitor beside that of the good hero, that he even forgot to give the needles in the hearts of the waxen statuettes their daily turn. He chides himself for this neglect of duty, calling himself "ham" and "little monster," and thinks what he might do if the times and his milieu were not so unpropitious.

The arrival of the players, Kate and William, breaks in on Hamlet's mediations. He receives them eagerly, calling them "my brothers," and offering them English cigarettes. Not even a reminder from the Queen that they must get on with the funeral of Polonius alters his determination to have a play performed at once. It has to be the play that he has written, and he gives the actors a script to study. This proves to be the *Murder of Gonzago,* with a few retouches by Laforgue. The player-queen pretends to be hulling strawberries as she watches over her sleeping spouse; the usurper is not "Lucianus, nephew to the King," but Claudius, the King's brother; the poison poured "delicately" into the victim's ear is not "juice of hebona" but lead melted in a spoon by the conspirators. William is assigned the role of Claudius; Kate will play the Queen.

Laforgue's Hamlet, like his counterpart, has advice to give the players. He points out certain passages that must be emphasized, others that may be skipped, though he is so fond of these he cannot refrain from taking time to read them before his audience of two.

The time is set for the performance; the players, pocketing the money Hamlet offers them, go off convinced

they have been rightly warned of Hamlet's madness. For his part, Hamlet—"the man of action"—spends five minutes dreaming about his play, "peak[ing] / Like John-a-dreams, unpregnant of [his] cause," then bursts into a long soliloquy. The monologue begins determinedly enough, in a mood reminiscent of the final passage of the "Hecuba" soliloquy:

> That's got it. Mr. Fengo will understand. A word to the wise . . . ! And there'll be nothing left for me to do but act, just sign my name! To act! To kill him! make him spew forth his life . . .

But the unhappy Hamlet cannot fix his thoughts for long on a deed so removed from his obsession:

> . . . I must act! I must kill, or I must escape from here! Oh! to escape! . . . O freedom! freedom! To love, to live, to dream, to be famous, far away! Oh! dear *aurea mediocritas!* Yes, what Hamlet lacks is freedom . . .

His sense of the preciousness of his existence, of the uniqueness of his individuality, takes over:

> And after all, to think that I exist! That I have my very own life! Eternity in itself before my birth, eternity in itself after my death. And I spend my days killing time this way! And old age coming on . . . I can't just stand here, anonymous, marking time! And to leave *Memoirs* is not enough for me. O Hamlet! Hamlet! If they only knew! . . . Ah! How alone I am! And, to tell the truth, the times have nothing to do with it. I have five senses that connect me to life; but this sixth sense, this sense of the Infinite! . . .

He closes the circle of these meditations with a grandiloquent restatement of his determination to act:

> Yes, I'll go away; I'll come back anonymous among decent people; and I'll get married for always and for every day. That would have been, of all my ideas, the most Hamletic! But tonight, I have to act; we must show who we are! Forward over the tombs, like Nature!

On his way to the graveyard, he pauses to hurl the body of a canary he has strangled at the head of a girl who sits nearby, crocheting; such "strange, destructive impulses" have been not infrequent since his father's "irregular" death. His remorse for this gratuitous brutality, though intense, is short-lived; he reassures himself that he was simply seeking practice for the deed to come, as when he had killed Polonius. That Laforgue had in mind Hamlet's treatment of Ophelia in the nunnery scene, is suggested by his comment: " . . . Hamlet hasn't yet come to realize that he had thought little more of the sad Ophelia (oh! little more, poor bird) . . ."

The sight of groups of workers returning to their homes sets off another of Hamlet's soliloquies, this time on the social order and the absurdity of his passion as a youth to better it. At last he arrives at the graveyard, too late for the burial of Polonius, but in time to find the gravediggers still at work: one arranging the wreaths on Polonius's tomb, the other preparing Yorick's grave to receive the body of Ophelia. With the perfect impassivity of the dandy as Baudelaire described him, Hamlet learns from the gravedigger's gossip that he is not, after all, Gerutha's son, but the son of the beautiful gypsy, Yorick's mother, hence the brother of a court fool and "not the self-made man he thought he was." He listens unmoved as the gravedigger tells him that the body of Ophelia has been recovered near the dam, that Prince Hamlet is said to have lost his wits, and that, in view of all these portents of disaster, he has himself converted his small savings into Norwegian bonds, against the probable annexation of the realm by Fortinbras.

Still outwardly unmoved, but with that "latent fire that lets itself be sensed, that could shine forth, but will not," this Hamlet speaks his Yorick speech, a kind of symphonic discourse on death and the Eternal. Phrases borrowed here and there from Shakespeare's hero are interwoven with some of the nihilist's familiar themes. Consideration of the fate of Yorick leads him to contemplate his own. To be sure, he reflects, with the accumulation of trivial actions that make up everyday existence, all the little people of history have come to this. But Hamlet, with his "sixth sense of the Infinite," with his intimation of a special mission, and his enormous love of life, Hamlet cannot be like all the rest: "Well, what am I waiting here for?—Death! death! Do we have time to think about it, however gifted we may be? *I,* die! Come now! We'll talk about it later, we have time . . . But not to *be* any more; not to be *there*; not to be a part of it all any more! Never again to be able to press against one's human heart, on any afternoon, the sadness of centuries held in a tiny chord on the piano." Unable to feel what death is like, he concludes that life must want something from him still. Once more, the dreaming Hamlet has talked himself into coming to grips with action.

But the funeral of Ophelia intervenes. This "hero" does not leap into the grave, nor challenge Laertes to vie with him in proof of love; he merely "unpacks his heart with words." Taking the skull of Yorick with him to place among his treasures, between one of Ophelia's gloves and his own first tooth, Hamlet returns to his tower, again determined to do something. What he does is to settle with Kate the arrangements for the performance of his play, promising to run away with her as soon as the play is over; then before he quits his ivory tower, he carefully melts down the statuettes, dissolving the sordid past in a pool of molten wax.

During the play episode, Hamlet sits alone in a corner of the gallery, imagining the effect his words would have on a Paris audience. When he observes the King and Queen, it is only to conclude from their indifference that his play still needs revising. Early in the second act, even before the player-tyrant enters, Fengo faints; Gerutha rises stiffly to her feet; and in the general confusion, Hamlet stammers "Music! Music! So it was true! And I wouldn't believe it!"

Confronted with his proof (whether it be proof of Fengo's guilt or of his own genius is not clear), he sees in the present danger to his life a new pretext for immediate escape. He salvages his manuscript and rides off with Kate toward Paris and a life of glory in the arts.

When they reach the graveyard, Hamlet suddenly dismounts, "stung by some mysterious tarantula," goes to Ophelia's grave and stands, arms folded, waiting. There is no duel, but it is Laertes who determines Hamlet's fate. He steps from behind a tombstone, stabs the Prince and flees, as the dying Hamlet murmurs *"qualis . . . artifex . . . pereo!"* Kate, discovering Hamlet's body on the grave, concludes he must have killed himself for love. "One Hamlet less," Laforgue concludes; "but the race is not lost, we may be sure."

Beneath the exaggeration of this portrait is discernible the poignant sympathy of one who feels he belongs to the race of Hamlets. Irony, that "vengeance of the vanquished," as Baudelaire called it, is in every line. The effect is a caricature at once of Laforgue himself and of the Romantic figures whose stories filled his poet's mind. It is as if Laforgue had made an image of himself with features of his literary forebears and plunged a needle through its heart. Physically, the identification with himself is unmistakable. Though he made Hamlet out to be thirty (that autumnal age in the Romantic's life), hence five years older than himself, he gave him his own chestnut-colored hair, growing to a peak over a lofty brow; his pale, smooth-shaven face and expression of gentle, meditative melancholy; his gray-blue eyes with their deep, abstracted gaze that made him seem always to be "trying to touch the Real with invisible antennae"; his customary black costume; his slow, calm gait.

In character, ideas, and interests, the details of resemblance are no less remarkable: the etcher's laboratory, the foreign cigarettes, the prophet's enthusiasms dwindled into dilettantism, the adherence to the philosophy of the unconscious, the mixed feelings about women, the "universal nausea," the rage at humanity's indifference to his "divine" heart.

It was Laforgue, but it might have been his Hamlet, who wrote to Sanda Mahali in 1882: "Know, dear poet, that before I had literary ambitions, I had the enthusiasms of a prophet, and at one period, I dreamed every night of going to console Savonarola in his prison. Now I am a dilettante in everything, with sometimes minor attacks of universal nausea. I watch the carnival of life pass by . . . I smoke mild cigarettes, I write verse and prose, perhaps do an occasional etching, and I wait for death."

An echo of Hamlet's praise for "A man that Fortune's buffets and rewards / [Has] ta'en with equal thanks . . ." and in whom "blood and judgment are so well co-medled" sounds in a letter of Laforgue's to his friend Charles Ephrussi: "I drag along like a snail, very slowly, through the pages of an Ollendorff for my German. Then I think, and after thinking, I doubt . . . And I'm bored . . . If it were enough to believe that one had talent to have it, I would have talent.—You are safe and sound, you work steadily and conscientiously, without remorse. You have a great aim and you hold to it. You have never worn yourself out in useless dreams."

This Hamlet, like his creator, is exceptionally gifted, attuned to "the inexhaustible symphony of the universal soul," torn between the absolute and the ephemeral, attracted and repelled by the *aurea mediocritas,* frustrated in his ambition to be a hero. Like Laforgue, he is paralyzed by boredom and filled with a longing to be free. Hamlet says: "My rare gift of assimilation / Will interfere with my vocation. / Ah! how superiorly bored I am!" To describe himself, Laforgue wrote: "A weather-vane of the thirty-six seasons, / I am too many to say yes or no." Hamlet, rationalizing his treatment of Ophelia on the ground that, even with her "celestial gaze," she turned out to be only "female" like the rest, speaks for the young poet who found it hard to forgive the "angels" of his fancies for being merely women. Finally, the plaintive "Oh! how dear are the trains I've missed . . ." might have been his Hamlet's epitaph, as well as the comment he meant it to be on his own frustrated life.

Laforgue recast Shakespeare's Hamlet in the mold of a decadent Romantic, bestowed on him his own doubts and conflicts, and played on the image the lights of contemporary thought. The Hamlet he saw was an incurable dreamer, though a disenchanted one, the victim of a malady very like a neurosis, doomed from the start by an unfelicitous combination of heredity and environment and by the conflict in his soul. The adversaries in the fatal struggle would appear to be the self, fighting for release and recognition, and a pressing obligation that no amount of reasoning can make him really believe in. For Laforgue, Hamlet's "antic disposition" seems to spring from "sore distraction": not dementia, but the madness of genius unrecognized or misunderstood, and ineffectual. Laertes—"the excellent Laertes," that "fool of humanity"—calls Hamlet "a poor demented fellow, irresponsible according to

the latest advances in science." Kate says: "Oh! you must be unique and misunderstood! and not mad, as all these people with their spurs and toothpicks say. But what a lot of suffering you must have caused!"

Laforgue apparently meant to honor Hamlet's claim to have loved Ophelia. It is the "now legendary and mysterious Ophelia," symbol of the ideal, who draws him away from Kate and life. In his interpretation of Hamlet's conduct toward her—the acts by which his cruelty is symbolized, the invention of Kate, the confusion of Kate with Ophelia, the identification of Kate with the Queen in the role of Baptista—the poet seems to have anticipated the Freudian Hamlet described by Ernest Jones [in *Hamlet and Oedipus,* 1954].

For Laforgue, the enigma of *Hamlet* was the enigma of life itself. Had he been inclined to treat it gravely, he might have presented it in the terms of Mallarmé. But Laforgue systematically shied away from gravity. What he called his "dilettantism" and his universal skepticism made him treat Hamlet's tragedy in terms of the absurd. In an imaginary interview with Shakespeare's Prince at Elsinore, he apologized: "I'm the only one who takes you lightly, your Highness, *à la Yorick,* . . . because it's all too much for me." He pictured Hamlet shouting crazily: "*Aux armes! citoyens.* There's no more reason!" and groaning in despair at the impossibility of attaining the ideal. He fancied himself, infected by Hamlet's madness, wildly dancing the *Criterion of Human Certitude.* " . . . This dance consists in describing with the feet the figure of the square of the hypotenuse, that Gibraltar of certainty, a simple and immortal figure; the only thing is that as you perform the last step, *you don't know why,* you inevitably stumble and fall on your face."

Absurd or not, Prince Hamlet was, according to Laforgue, "the master of us all," "tomorrow's ancestor." And there were some in Paris, the poet reassured His Highness, who were cultivating His special legend: Arthur Rimbaud, for example, "who died of it . . ." and Paul Bourget "who cultivates and aggravates it, with enough correctness, however, to stop (pretending to recoil) at nihilism."

Laforgue might also have named Henri de Régnier, had he been able to look into the young poet's heart. But it was twenty years before Régnier made public his own espousal of Hamlet's legend in the following poem, one of three "Feuillets retrouvés dans un exemplaire de Shakespeare." . . .

For Régnier, as for Mallarmé and for Laforgue, the *Tragedy of Hamlet* was more than the masterful dramatization of an absorbing chronicle. It was the symbol of man's struggle to resolve into one the duality created in him by the conflict between thought and action. Régnier wrote [in "Hamlet à Paris," *Le Gau-*

lois, 1899]: "What Hamlet is watching for is not so much an opportunity to kill the King as the furtive instant when he will be at one with himself, when his desire to act and his aversion to action will fuse into one will." He imagined Hamlet talking with Mallarmé at Elsinore, envying the poet his pure, integral life, a life unmarred by any action that was not intellectual and speculative. And he pictured Hamlet deploring his own wretched and equivocal existence, in which action diverted him from meditation and chance was stronger than destiny.

With the Symbolists, Hamlet took on some of the traits of that figure of "periods of decline" that Baudelaire called the "dandy" [in "Le Peintre de la vie moderne," *Curiosités esthétiques*]: the "hero," conscious of the aristocratic superiority of his intellect, filled with a "burning need to create an originality of [his] own," in whom the cult of self "can survive the pursuit of the happiness to be found in others, in woman, for example, . . . even all that people call illusions." Significantly, the Symbolists saw in the tragedy of Hamlet, not action impeded by morbid melancholy or reflection, as had their elders, the Romantics, but rather the image of mundane action thwarting their pursuit of the ideal—or the ephemeral. The very equivocal nature of Shakespeare's *Hamlet,* the "discords unresolved" that vibrate in the mind provoking endless speculation, the "sense of frustration, futility, and human inadequacy" that makes up "the burden of the whole symphony:" [John Dover Wilson, *What Happens in HAMLET,* 1937,] these Laforgue and his fellow Symbolists responded to. These are the themes Laforgue transposed in his ironic idiom to define the "Hamletism" that marks the literature of doubt, disillusion, and frustration of the late nineteenth century. Perhaps Régnier was right when he imagined Hamlet saying at the end of his interview with Mallarmé: "But tell me about that dear Jules Laforgue. He and Shakespeare understood me."

. . . [Laforgue's] Hamlet is more profound than Shakespeare's Hamlet, . . . it is tenderer, and wittier, and more charming, and wiser.

Frances Newman, in "Introduction" to **Six Moral Tales of Jules Laforgue,** *1928.*

E. J. Stormon (essay date 1965)

SOURCE: "Some Notes on T. S. Eliot and Jules Laforgue," in *Essays in French Literature,* Vol. 2, November, 1965, pp. 103-14.

[*In the following essay, Stormon charts the apparent echoes of Laforgue in Eliot's verse. The critic sees an* affinity between the two poets based mainly on Laforgue's "reaching after some vital hidden centre," which Stormon equates with Eliot's objective correlative.]

In December 1908, Eliot, then aged twenty, discovered Arthur Symons' book, *The Symbolist Movement in Literature,* in the Library of the Harvard Union, and found himself excited by the quotations in it, particularly those from Laforgue. Shortly afterwards, he went to Schoenhof's foreign bookshop in Boston, and had the good fortune to light on the three volumes of the 1901-1903 edition of the *Œuvres complètes de Jules Laforgue* (Mercure de France). In Laforgue's verse he found a form of expression which helped him to say the kind of thing that he wanted to say himself, and a temperament akin to his own—two aspects, as he notes, of the same thing. Laforgue, he tells us, "was the first to teach me how to speak, to teach me the poetic possibilities of my own idiom of speech." It is important to realize that it was a distinctive English idiom that was in question, and that the outlook and attitudes that came to expression in it reveal growing differences from those of Laforgue, as well as some striking resemblances. Full account has not yet been taken of the points of contact between the two poets, or of the points at which they part company, so that, in spite of all that has been written on this subject, it may be worth while to look at it again.

What would Eliot have found in that germinal volume of *Poésies* of the early Mercure de France edition? Laforgue had died in 1887, just as he was coming to poetic maturity, and had left a good deal of published and unpublished verse behind him, some of it brilliant, agile, and witty, some of it histrionically cynical, some of it accomplished and moving, some of it merely adolescent. The edition of 1902, which Eliot used, brought much of this material together, though in a far from definitive text. It will repay us to look in a summary way at the various collections of verse drawn on for this volume, for this will remind us of the various stages of Laforgue's astonishing and pitifully short career, and help us look over Eliot's shoulder, as it were, as he works his way through the pages that are going to enable him [to] bring his feelings to focus and organize his language over the following few years.

First there was *Le Sanglot de la terre,* a group of twenty-nine poems representing Laforgue in his late teens and very early twenties. "I was sojouring in the cosmic", he later said of this period, and the poems are in consequence full of night, eternity, the void, dying stars and suns, and in particular of a vermin-bearing earth which is source of a mysterious throe, and is moving inevitably towards extinction. Some vestiges of a quasi-religious feeling have survived the collapse of faith, and have become associated with the earth and the poet's own heart, or with the image of the rose window in Notre Dame Cathedral. But the characteristic attitude here gradually shaping itself is one of ironic distrust towards a Nature that secures its ends through illusion, or of jaunty, quizzical, mockery before the mystery of existence: "Je défiais l'instinct avec un rire amer"; "Je fume au nez des dieux de fines cigarettes." In partial contrast with the would-be sardonic feeling, the language shows a young man aiming at a full-mouthed, rather facile eloquence, with a still somewhat naïve reliance on the declamatory qualities of the classical alexandrine.

The **Complaintes** are much more oblique in manner and sophisticated in content. By now Laforgue has assimilated the system, such as it is, of Eduard von Hartmann's *Philosophy of the Unconscious,* and feels that he has gained a definitive insight into the origin of natural appetite and human consciousness, and into the emptiness into which they will disappear when the Unconscious Absolute completes its unfolding. This philosophy (we need not pause now to pass judgment on it) is not so much expounded as used as a perspective in which the situations and the attitudes of the speakers in the **Complaintes** are to be seen. The poet may be said to assume a number of masks, but it might be more accurate to say that he twists his own face into various stylized expressions—the blank, abstracted look of a moonstruck Pierrot being the most notable—and finds in the language that goes with these *personæ* some slightly dramatized equivalent for his own characteristic feelings. The resounding eloquence of the early poems is now replaced by verbal subtlety—by wit, irony and *blague,* beneath which a tragic poignancy is often discernible. The style is complex and nimble, capable of rendering a rapid, complicated play of mind and the criss-crossing of different feelings. Laforgue here breaks away from his over-solemn sonnets and resounding alexandrines to cultivate a great variety of forms. He imitates popular airs, catches up snatches of dialogue, speaks colloquially out of carefully contrived situations, or rehearses dramatic moments in retrospect. A certain number of the **Complaintes** are virtuoso constructions, having not much more consistency than a house of cards, but others survive as genuine poems, bitter-sweet, quizzical, a little exhibitionist, but sometimes with an appealing suggestion of pathos behind them.

In **L'Imitation de Notre Dame la Lune,** Laforgue moves towards a more musical, "purer" type of poetry, bathed in the moonlight which it celebrates. The poet transforms himself for much of the time into Pierrot, one of the "lunologues éminents", and talks in character, but with greater imaginative richness and metrical precision than before.

The poems of the last section, **Derniers vers** and **Des Fleurs de bonne volonté,** reveal a Laforgue fast maturing in command over his material and his medium.

The *esprit de système* with which he had earlier expounded his deep-seated pessimism is no longer obtrusive, and there are occasional signs that he is coming to more positive terms with life. The **Fleurs de bonne volonté,** reproduced more extensively in the second Mercure de France edition, contain a few well poised, knowledgeably witty poems like the dryly pathetic **"Ballade"**; others are simply *brouillons* turned to better account in the **Derniers vers,** or set aside to be worked over again for other purposes. The **Derniers vers** themselves mark quite a significant new stage, and call for special comment. They consist of twelve monologues in a free verse measure developed out of the alexandrine, and allowing of expansion or contraction according to the pulse of the feeling, with rhymes echoing in a haunting irregular sequence. The structural principle is obviously musical, and this is reinforced by the sound-effects of blowing horns and autumnal wind and by other devices, without however quite reaching the dominance that it is meant to have:

> Oh! que . . .
> Ma mélodie, toute et unique monte,
> Dans le soir et redouble, et fasse tout ce
> qu'elle peut
> Et dise la chose qu'est la chose,
> Et retombe, et reprenne,
> Et fasse de la peine,
> O solo de sanglots,
> Et reprenne et retombe
> Selon la tâche qui lui incombe.

The monologue allows bits and pieces of dramatic situations to unfold from narrative, but all is absorbed into a covering "stream of consciousness" in which the real continuity of the poem is maintained.—This then is the supple and resourceful medium to which he eventually found his way, and in which he achieves his most assured and rounded-out expression.

Eliot himself has identified the four poems in his first volume which he wrote directly under the influence of Laforgue; they are "Conversation Galante", "Portrait of a Lady", "The Love Song of J. Alfred Prufrock", and "La Figlia Che Piange", in that order. There were three earlier pieces in the Laforgue manner which he allowed to remain in the comparative obscurity of the *Harvard Advocate,* and which do not call for any further attention than has been already given them. Nor need we linger over certain obvious points of contact between the two poets in "Rhapsody on a Windy Night", a poem which Eliot himself associates with a further phase. It is the four poems which have been clearly grouped "sous le signe de Laforgue" that will best bear the weight of an enquiry. In addition, however, we may note what may be a significant reminiscence in the fourth of Eliot's early "Preludes".

(i) "Prelude" IV

The tone and movement of these verses hardly suggest those of Laforgue, but there is an interesting correspondence between the central concern here and the one quasi-religious image in *Le Sanglot de la terre*. This has been described by François Ruchon, with slightly exaggerated emphasis, as follows:

> L'image autour de laquelle le *Sanglot* semble construit, est celle d'un Cœur douloureux, qui saigne, qui pleure, le cœur d'un Christ humain et sidéral qui souffre pour la création entière, dans le majestueux décor des couchants, ou qui est exposé, comme une hostie sanglante, dans la gloire des cathédrales où brasillent les verrières.

That is to dwell perhaps too much on the physical aspect of the image. Laforgue is really reaching after the idea of some hidden vital centre, which is a "Cœur où l'univers palpite", a "Cœur universel ruisselant de douceur", a "cœur de la Terre", which is in some sense a projection and extension of his own heart, and is connected, as was noted above, with experiences before the rose window of Notre Dame.

Eliot speaks, not of a "heart", but of a "soul", and this at first appears like a self-projection ("His soul stretched tight across the skies"). Then he feels his way to a further and deeper suggestion:

> I am moved by fancies that are curled
> Around these images, and cling:
> The notion of some infinitely gentle
> Infinitely suffering thing

The analogy with the early Laforgue is close, and there may be some literary dependence. The case is strengthened by the "cosmic" imagery of the following lines, where Eliot, having moved in quickly to check crass comment, resignedly accepts the contrast between the idea he is groping for and the mindless turning of the spheres:

> Wipe your hand across your mouth, and
>   laugh;
> The worlds revolve like ancient women
> Gathering fuel in vacant lots

We may compare, from *Le Sanglot de la terre,* "les mondes /. . . . vont continuer leurs rondes", and allow for the possibility of a *contaminatio* with the figure in the *Complaintes* of a bent old woman gathering wood, though the resemblance in this latter case is tenuous.

(ii) "Conversation Galante"

This admirable little *jeu d'esprit* takes its cue, not merely from the two far more serious poems by Laforgue which are clearly in question (*Autre Complainte de Lord Pierrot, Pierrots*), but from a number of other conversation-pieces as well. The night, the moon, music and a keyboard, the Absolute, a man with a complicated sensibility, a woman confidently banal— this is the familiar stock-in-trade of the *Complaintes* and *Imitation de Notre Dame la Lune*. What saves Eliot's verses from being mere *pastiche* is that there is a genuine transposition of the Laforgue theme into a different idiom, with a different set of evocations. The male speaker, moreover, is not really Pierrot, but a somewhat literary young man whose clowning consists in executing arabesques of romantic nonsense to impress and tantalize his female partner (possibly an older woman), and then in exploiting the un-self-conscious bathos of her replies with mock-gallantry:

> "You, madam, are the eternal humorist,
> The eternal enemy of the absolute,
> Giving our vagrant moods the slightest twist!
> With your air indifferent and imperious
> At a stroke, our mad poetics to confute—"
>   And—"Are we then so serious?"

In Laforgue's poems, on the other hand, it is the woman who makes the advances, and Pierrot who caps her pathetically sincere but banal declarations with cynical comment. But this Pierrot is only apparently heartless; he is really living in another dimension, with an eye cocked devotedly towards the Unconscious. In the second poem, even after reminding himself that romantic love is a "salair illusoire / Du capitaliste Idéal", he allows the woman to have the better of the argument, at least in this sense, that if she dies, she simply changes the words of the song by passing into the processes of Nature which create fresh illusions, and this time Pierrot will perhaps succumb.

Eliot's poem is little more than a brilliant playful exercise; it has none of the pathos, or philosophic bite of Laforgue's pieces; and is relatively kind only by being innocuous. The contrast is clearest where the borrowing is most literal. In *Autre Complainte,* Lord Pierrot, imagining the death of the woman, can still pretend to taunt her on the grounds that they both had all they needed for life as we know it, and that there was no point in taking things to heart and *dying* over it:

> J'aurai un "Ah ça, mais nous avions De Quoi
>   vivre!
>   C'était donc sérieux?"

There is pity as well as *raillerie* in this "C'était donc sérieux?". Eliot's "Are we then so serious?" is given to the woman, and does not exceed the requirements of verbal anti-climax.

We must resist the temptation to put more pressure on this small poem than it will bear. It is already an achievement to have adopted the Laforgue manner to the resources of English speech, and to have brought off the *blague* and the repartee so smartly in impeccable, if minor verse.

(iii) "Portrait of a Lady"

From here on, it is the fluid, musical monologue of Laforgue's **Derniers vers** that Eliot eliminates, and indeed surpasses. In this kind of poem, it is not so much the argument or narrative that matters as the tone and condition of sensibility which is suggested. Here, perhaps more than elsewhere, the well-known distinction holds good: what the poem *says,* by way of individual statements, is very much subordinate to what it *is,* in virtue of the pattern of feelings which it brings to expression within the movement of the verse. The situations, the dialogue, or that side of it which is rehearsed, melt into the musing of the speaker, and are drawn into the rhythm of his voice. Laforgue was aware of the importance of musical effect in maintaining continuity through all the convolutions of the monologue, and occasionally incorporates his own tonal suggestions into the matter of his poem, so that it is harder than ever to make any discrimination between *fond* and *forme:*

> Je ne puis quitter ce ton: que d'échos!

Eliot, too, sometimes doubles back on his own voice:

> This music is successful with a dying fall,
> Now that we talk of dying

The situation in "Portrait of a Lady" is brought about, as in "Conversation Galante", by the discordant juxtaposition of two sensibilities, that of the young male speaker, and that of a woman. The woman's fluent, pretentious clichés, pitiful and second-rate, fail to engage the young man's more distinctive, personal feelings, though they still jangle and bewilder him, and make him wonder whether it is his own fault that he does not respond. What makes it worse is that the woman is much older ("about to reach her journey's end"), and is rather desperately reaching out for affection and support:

> The voice returns like the insistent out-of-tune
> Of a broken violin on an August afternoon:
> "I am always sure that you understand
> My feelings, always sure that you feel,
> Sure that across the gulf you stretch your
>   hand"

The best comment on this kind of situation is one that Laforgue himself supplies:

> Enfin, voici qu'elle m'honore de ses
>   confidences.
> J'en souffre plus qu'elle ne pense

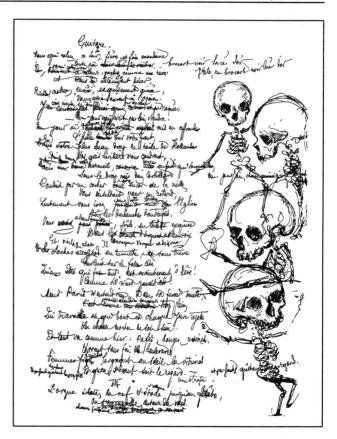

A page from Laforgue's notebook.

The poet, or the speaker, is forced back into a kind of self-consciousness in which he is both the person in the situation, making certain conventional gestures, and also another person looking quizzically on. Laforgue's Pierrots are habitually like this—

> En tête à tête avec la femme
> Ils ont toujours l'air d'être un tiers

But there are certain differences. Pierrot has his philosophical principles ("on a des principes"), and can at least pretend to a ruthless cynicism:

> —Oh! là, là, ce n'est peut-être pour des
>   prunes,
>   Qu'on a fait ses classes ici-bas?

Eliot's young man contents himself with a little subtle and inoffensive ambiguity:

> " . . . Youth is cruel, and has no remorse
> And smiles at situations which it cannot see."
> I smile, of course,
> And go on drinking tea

In fact, what separates him from the woman is no sense of "à quoi bon?", no deep distrust of Nature's ends, but simply a difference in age and sensibility. (As we shall see, the philosophic perspectives, hardly present in this poem, open out in "Prufrock"). And even so, he is not at all sure of his own position, or the validity of his own feelings. In some ways, the woman, with all her stock attitudes and second-hand phrases, has a dignity and consistency which transcend her words, while he has to invent all sorts of Protean self-transformations to bring himself even to piecemeal expression. Like a Laforgue speaker, he is "trop nombreux pour dire oui ou non", but he has the grace to be conscious of this as a possible judgment on himself ("My self-possession gutters; we are really in the dark").

The speakers in both Eliot's and Laforgue's poems do much the same kind of thing by way of keeping up appearances ("Allons, fumons une pipette de tabac"; cf. "Vous fumez dans vos bocks"; "Let us take the air in a tobacco trance, / Then sit for half an hour and drink our bocks"). On occasions, however, even the hackneyed tunes of near-by pianos or barrel-organs catch them out and break up their composure ("le moindre orgu' de Barbari / . . . m'empoigne aux entrailles"; "Except when a street piano, mechanical and tired, / Reiterates some worn-out common song"). But when they envisage the possible death of the woman, they differ very considerably. Laforgue's Pierrots either pretend that she missed the point, by taking things seriously, or that, as the Eternal Feminine, she will have her revenge anyhow. Eliot's speaker sublimates her death with romantic evocations ("evening yellow and rose", the "dying fall" of the music, etc.), and admits that, in terms of human dignity, she might well have turned the tables on him:

> Would she not have the advantage after all?
> . . . And should I have the right to smile?

Laforgue's speakers, perhaps because they look to the Unconscious and know metaphysical secrets, *always* have the right to smile.

(iv) "The Love Song of J. Alfred Prufrock"

"Prufrock" is a very accomplished and moving performance indeed, although it was some years before this was widely recognized. It is an objective *persona* poem, where the speaker remains distinct from both poet and reader, though related to, and finally involving both. Its triumph consists in its power to catch nuances of feeling, hesitations, inflexions in the voice, glimpses of ideals, wistful dreams, complications of sensibility, contrasts and collisions between inner feeling and outward fact—all this in a wonderful flow of music, with wit and allusiveness, and a strange poetry that successfully assmilates toasts and tea, ices, coffee-spoons, sprinkled streets and yellow fog. It has the further virtue that the predicament which it explores has far-reaching implications which give finally on a

much more impressive philosophy than the kind of thing which Laforgue took over from Hartmann (though to say this is perhaps to take into account other poems to which "Prufrock" looks forward).

In several important ways the poem approximates to Laforgue. The medium is once again the *vers libre* of Laforgue's last period, somewhat more richly orchestrated in English. It is a poetry that exhibits, rather than describes, states of feeling, very much in the manner of the **Derniers vers**. It is concerned with an apparently unbridgeable gap between the inner life of the speaker and the external world—between the imaginative and emotional need, on the one hand, and the social convention and the factual human response, on the other. Laforgue had evidently had acute experience of the same problem, and the analogies in his verse are so close here as to serve almost as a commentary on the "Prufrock" still to come. In the end, however, Laforgue goes one way, and Prufrock-Eliot another.

A certain amount of the detail in the English poem finds its counterpart in Laforgue's French, though there is hardly any exact replication. The more obvious similarities may be mentioned briefly. The "yellow fog that rubs its back upon the window panes" is probably related, as has often been noted, to Laforgue's "gaz jaune et mourant des brumeux boulevards", but the cat-image ("rubs its back", "licked its tongue", "curled . . . and fell asleep") suggests an analogy with the animal-conceit in the **Complaintes** ("le vent galope ventre à terre"). The shock-tactics of "The evening is spread out against the sky / Like a patient etherised upon a table" were probably suggested by the opening lines of the same poem ("Le couchant de sang est taché / Comme un tablier de boucher"); and there may be some loose connection between the streets that "lead you to an overwhelming question" and the image in **Notre Dame des Soirs,** "(Vous) m'agacez au tournant d'une verité". The lamp-light, cups, marmalade and tea, of "Prufrock" may have come, in part, from a desire to emulate the lines in **Derniers vers:**

> Lampes, estampes, thé, petits-fours,
> Serez-vous mes seules amours!

At the same time, Eliot would almost certainly have been influenced by this kind of juxtaposition to produce his own music out of apparently refractory material:

> Have known the evenings, mornings,
>   afternoons,
> I have measured out my life with coffee-
>   spoons

We may further compare, for unexpected sound-effects, Eliot's

Should I, after tea and cakes and ices,
Have the strength to force the moment to its
    crisis

with Laforgue's whimsical

J'eusse été le modèle des époux!
Comme le frou-frou de ta robe est le modèle
    des frou-frou

What is far more important, however, than this kind of cross-reference, is the fact that in "Prufrock" Eliot is at last dealing in depth with the kind of *impasse* with which Laforgue is most characteristically concerned. Put in its most general form, this can be explained as the inhibiting, paralysing, contrast between one's inner life and the outer world. In one of his early poems, Laforgue complained naïvely:

Qui m'avait donc grisé de tant d'espoirs
    menteurs?

In this later verse he hits on the idea of the mind (Pygmalion) being blocked from contact with the real order by the very ideal which it projects (Galatea):

Mon Moi, c'est Galathée aveuglant
    Pygmalion!
Impossible de modifier cette situation

Sometimes Laforgue thinks of himself as an ashamed Ariel, hovering over a disconcerting present which remains irremediably out of relationship with his feelings:

Mais le cru, quotidien, et trop voyant Présent!
Et qui vous met au pied du mur, et qui vous
    dit:
"A l'instant, ou bonsoir!" et ne fait pas crédit,
Et m'étourdit le cœur de ses airs suffisants!

(Prufrock, with a bald spot in the middle of his hair, is in no position to think of himself as Ariel, or indeed as any of the Dramatis Personæ except the Fool, but he too is prevented from bringing his inner life into contact with the external order—in this case, by the dread of "eyes that fix you in a formulated phrase", or simply of the uncomprehending, shattering response: "That is not what I mean at all"; cf. the woman's "air de dire 'de quoi'".)

The theme is taken up again in the ***Derniers vers,*** where the poet seems to be passing his life on quais, failing to embark, or waving to departing boats from the end of the jetty. On the other hand—and this is where the important difference between the two poets opens up— Laforgue is fundamentally sceptical about the ideals (particularly those concerning human love) which his mind cannot help forming, and he tries again and again

to strip them of their illusory quality, as he sees it. The contrast with Eliot is at its most acute in the very poem that seems to announce "Prufrock":

La nuit bruine sur les villes
Se raser le masque, s'orner
D'un frac deuil, avec art dîner
Puis, parmi les vierges débiles,
    Prendre un air imbécile

The outer scene might serve either poet, but the inner attitude is Laforgue's alone. Prufrock's wistful idealism is left open and uninhibited: arms in the lamplight, "downed with soft brown hair" retain their tender suggestions; the mermaids, "combing the white hair of the waves blown back / When the wind blows the water white and black", are not dismissed or cancelled out. Laforgue's speaker, on the other hand, though "gonflé d'idéal", works out his own idyll in terms of anti-romance: he dreams of an uncomplicated, primitive love-affair with a prehistoric "enfant bestiale et brûlée", her mouth sticky with apricot-juice, while the brotherly frogs croak sobbing music in the background! There is more than a touch of *blague* in this, of course, but there is also a clear intention to denude the romantic instinct of any mystical values, an intention amply attested by several other poems of a later period (cf. especially ***L'Aurore-Promise***).

In Eliot's poem, the romantic *élan,* though at odds with the world in which Prufrock must live, is not really inhibited at all. Prufrock's predicament (and he is here extended to include the reader) is that, if he tries to bring his inner life into contact with the outer world, something dies within him, and if he does not, he never succeeds in becoming quite real:

We have lingered in the chambers of the sea
By sea-girls wreathed with seaweed red and
    brown
Till human voices wake us, and we drown

At this stage the problem ceases to be the same as Laforgue's, and it is no accident that here, at the end of the poem, it is rather to Gérard de Nerval's incantatory line (quoted in Symons' book) that he seems to turn:

J'ai rêvé dans la grotte où nage la sirène

The further exploration will be towards Reality in and beyond Appearance.

(v) "La Figlia Che Piange"

This poem both creates and explores a romantic image which is intensified by a suggestion of strange beauty shining through loss. The lines give substance to the work of art indicated by the title, so that in a way this is a poem about writing a poem. The epigraph from Virgil ("O quam te memorem virgo . . . ?") hints that we are going to be concerned with the indefinable aura of meaning set up by the central image, and with a problem of expression.

Eliot is still using the kind of free verse that he developed out of Laforgue, but with a tone and content of feeling that seem to owe nothing to his predecessor, unless there be some remote connection with the wistful and uncharacteristic *Complainte de la bonne défunte*. Even the one line taken over from another part of Laforgue, the famous "Simple et sans foi comme un bonjour", occurs in a new context, with a greatly changed meaning.

On the other hand, there is a procedural analogy which is worth noting. Eliot clearly arranges his situation at first within a special art-dimension, while standing outside it himself, like a stage-director before the proscenium-arch. But then, just as clearly, he allows the scene to work upon him until he becomes involved in it, so that two dimensions become one in an expanded poem, which includes the composing poet as well as the scene which he composes. This method of composition could well have been suggested by the eighth section of *Derniers vers,* where Laforgue sets up a dialogue within a fiction, surrounds it with a sense of autumn and exile in the past, and then finally invades it himself.

"La Figlia Che Piange", in its treatment of an evocative tragic beauty, looks forward to one or two images in "The Waste Land", and beyond that to the controlled religious romanticism of "Ash Wednesday". We do not know what Laforgue's further development would have been like, had he lived, but there is no indication that it would have taken any course like this.

A. G. Lehmann (essay date 1968)

SOURCE: "Poetic Knowledge," in *The Symbolist Aesthetic in France, 1885-1895,* second edition, Basil Blackwell, 1968, pp. 74-128.

[*In the excerpt that follows, Lehmann places Laforgue's use of the terms* rêve *and the* Unconscious *in the context of how Symbolist poets in general understood certain abstract concepts.*]

Rimbaud undoubtedly thought—and many others have done so too—that in a world of ever-increasing uniformity and restriction, dreams offered the only safe refuge for a poet anxious to expand his individuality and enjoy that measure of freedom which is necessary for the cultivation of metaphorical warts on the face. The attitude is understandable, but fallacious: firstly, be-cause the strangeness of a dream is no guarantee that a poem written out of it will be good poetry; secondly, because not long afterwards it became plain that dreams are not quite as 'free' as he had hoped. Rimbaud's merits as a poet rest on something very different from his capacity to have strange dreams in greater number than anyone else, just as Van Gogh's greatness is something more than an insistence on yellow. The strange dreams and the yellows are not excluded from the greatness: they are used by it.

When we come to the minor dignitaries of the symbolist movement, to the generation of 1885-90, the term *'rêve',* used in relation to the material and the nature of poetic vision, loses almost all clear meaning and becomes little better than the slogan it continually tends to degenerate into. Where a Mallarmé had given it an approximate function in an organized theory of art, the late-comers handled it wildly; and it picked up a large number of connotations, each corresponding to the particular interest or bent of its user, and not always easily separable from its neighbours.

Laforgue, one of the earlier symbolist adepts of 'German idealism', uses *'rêve'* simply as a handy term for reminding his readers that the world they—and he—lived in is a world of 'Fiction'—'une simple légende':

> Je suis un pessimiste mystique . . . la vie est trop triste, trop sale. L'histoire est un vieux cauchemar bariolé qui ne se doute pas que les meilleures plaisanteries sont les plus courtes. La planète terre était parfaitement inutile. Enfin, peut-être Tout n'est-il que *rêve,* seulement celui qui nous rêve ferait bien de hâter le cuvage de son opium.

He also confused the possibility that we are somebody else's dream (like Alice and the Red King) with the possibility that what we see (or what we think) has no more objective validity than one of our dreams: that both are equally the products of illusion:

> . . . ne sachons que nous enivrer des paradis sans fond de nos sens et fleurir sincèrement nos rêves sur l'heure qui est à nous.

Here we are verging on the problem of our knowledge of the external world, in which (at least for the greater part of his adult life) he professes a simply solipsist view. . . .

It is, in fact, very hard so to strip our minds of modern psychological perspectives as to come to a fair understanding of what the term 'unconscious' (*Inconscient*) signified around 1885. Clinical research was already under way; but not along lines calculated to encourage enthusiasm or even interest among poets; the early popular exponent of the Unconscious was in fact Edouard von Hartmann in Germany with his *Philoso-*

phie der Unbewussten (1869). It is enough to say that in this writer's work the Unconscious is not primarily an integral part of the individual mind-body structure, but a metaphysical entity—a transcendental principle, in the succession of Fichte's Ego, Hegel's Idea, or Schopenhauer's Will. Laforgue at any rate did not often make the confusion, popular in later times, between a metaphysical principle and a psychological entity; but as a result, his views on the relation between art and the Unconscious are marred even more by their extreme theoretical frailty than by the fragmentary nature of their presentation to the world. The Unconscious, we learn, is the ' . . . raison explicative, suffisante, unique, intestine, dynamique, adéquate, de l'histoire universelle de la vie'. It is 'L'Afrique intérieure de notre inconscient domaine'; that is to say, it enters into every individual, as part of the cosmos. It is in constant evolution; therefore art, which aspires continuously to its 'expression' (how, in this respect, it is distinct from other human activities we are not told), must evolve—must overcome the temptation to become static, in the shape of convention, rule, cliché, genre; these latter, besides, lead to 'ennui', or loss of fresh emotional spontancity. Every work of art must continually also pass out of circulation, for the same reason.

Laforgue's aesthetic is from the outset both anti-intellectualist and anti-formalist. Intellectualism in art (personified for him by Taine) is pernicious because it distracts the artist's energies from bringing the Unconscious to consciousness—in other words, from attending to his feelings:

> Aujourd'hui, tout préconiser . . . la culture excessive de la raison, de la logique, de la conscience. La culture bénie de l'avenir est la déculture, la mise en jachère. Nous allons à la dessication: squelettes de cuir, à lunettes, rationalistes, anatomiques. Retournons, mes frères, vers les grandes eaux de l'Inconscient.

Formalism in art is pernicious because art aspires to hold up the mirror to the Unconscious, which is constantly evolving, constantly changing: the classical ideals:

> . . . posent d'abord que l'art est chargé de corriger la nature, comme s'il pouvait être d'autres lois d'harmonie que celles du *tel quel* de la vie.

No art 'forms' as such are genuine:

> . . . Il n'y a pas de type (de beauté), il y a la vie.

> . . . Tout m'intéresse, car je m'incline pieusement devant l'Inconscient.

> . . . Chaque homme est, selon son moment dans le temps, son milieu de race et de condition sociale, un moment d'évolution individuelle, un certain

clavier sur lequel le monde extérieur joue d'une certaine façon. Mon clavier est perpétuellement changeant, il n'y en a pas un autre identique au mien, *tous les claviers sont légitimes.*

The Unconscious, however, slips down from its transcendental throne to become sensation, that which is given:

> L'homme de génie reçoit ses impressions ou plutôt les subit sans les avoir voulues;

and this gives us the clue both to what place the Unconscious occupies in art for him, and in a measure what sort of activity art is: on the one hand:

> . . . la production esthétique a sa source dans l'Inconscient;

and on the other hand:

> L'invention et la réalisation du Beau dérivent de processus inconscients, dont le résultat se traduit dans la conscience par le sentiment et l'invention du Beau.

Is this a theory of inspiration? Laforgue's biographer Ruchon thinks so: the Unconscious implants somehow or other greater and more valuable sensations in the inspired artist for him to spy out: his task is simply to appreciate this fact and transcribe them. Art *reflects* 'l'anarchie même de la vie'. But if what it reflects is the Unconscious, or as it would be more expedient to say, the pre-conscious, art itself is undeniably conscious; and this is something which some of Laforgue's exponents in the twentieth century would do well to ponder. The fact does not seem to have been always clear in his own mind either: but he never allowed theory to interfere so radically with practice as to prevent him composing *deliberately*: how else could he have come to *choose vers libre*?

Laforgue's premature juxtaposition of conscious and unconscious in the definition of art brings in its train some curious consequences. First, the famous paradox, put into his mind by reflections on the contemporary novel and its laborious psychological dissections and analysis:

> Epier les instincts avec autant que possible absence de calcul, de volonté, de peur de les faire dévier de leur nature, de les influencer.

This is, of course, pure delight to the surrealist, who claims to have found the means of putting into practice an ideal enunciated by the great predecessor. But he wilfully misunderstands Laforgue's intention. To spy out something is to become conscious of it, not to reproduce it unconsciously for future inspection by one's self or someone else. Laforgue wants his art to reproduce on the conscious level the 'feelings' in the Unconscious level of the mind. The Bergsonian, realizing this, shrugs his shoulders pityingly: Laforgue evidently did not realize that the pure intuition to which he was plainly referring cannot be attended to and given verbal equivalents without the inevitable distortions arising from the use of language. The matter is not as simple as that, however; and if the surrealist is brazen, the Bergsonian is disingenuous. Laforgue supposed that there are in the dim recesses of the mind certain instincts accessible, though not easily accessible, to careful introspection; and that they can readily be incorporated into conscious knowledge. But, in fact, these 'instincts' which occupy so much of Hartmann's book are of the realm of physiology: they are a class of event which, if a prerequisite of knowledge, are not themselves knowledge. We know what we imagine about them; we observe and interpret the phenomena associated with them; but we cannot re-live them. Knowledge descends no further than imagination will take it; and Laforgue is asking for something that does not exist when he asks for intuitive knowledge of instincts—complexes on the level of sensation. To 'know' sensation is to transform it.

The second curious consequence is somewhat more practical. There is no doubt that the aesthetic outlined above, for all its ambiguity, demands the scrapping of all rigid formulae for the attainment of 'Beauty', and puts in its place some sort of standard according to which the artist finds within himself the ideal of excellence: as Beaunier observes [in *La poésie rouveller,* 1902], 'Laforgue a conçu l'art comme un moyen d'expression'. But the ideal of expression is nowhere enlarged on by him in any positive statements, and it is difficult to see how it could be; less still is it ever linked with that process by which sensation is turned into knowledge; 'expression' in Laforgue's context means jettisoning all rules for beauty's attainment, and then embodying in language sensations which have never been expressed before. *Originality* is thus one limiting feature of expression, indeed, a hallmark of genius: but sensation is from an impersonal realm, the 'Unconscious', and is having to be turned into *personal* art. Laforgue speaks at times as if the personality of the artist was beneath attention, and only the broad stream of art down the ages, not its individual members, worthy of attention, as reflecting the evolution of the Unconscious. The poet must, in fact, be free, simply because not to be free would frustrate the Unconscious, seat of genius. The artist is not an individual living in a historical context which influences his work: he is torchbearer to a biological continuity which is sited beneath the levels on which it can be discussed:

> Qui veut expliquer génie par les deux seuls facteurs visibles et palpables, la créature, ses conditions de vie, son milieu, ignore le vrai et fécond milieu de

chaque être, l'invisible atmosphère d'une conscience dans laquelle il vit et se développe.

And again, the artist is not concerned with Taine's search for essential characteristics: on the contrary;

> Pas de milieu. Se hausser jusqu'au génie fatal et imperturbable—ou être intéressant comme la mode, c'est-à-dire *chercheur* pour l'évolution.

So that, if asked about 'expression', Laforgue would say his aim to be the expression of a moment in the self-development of the Unconscious—the moment embodied on this occasion in the artist's sensations. There is therefore a sort of condominion on sensation; and though Laforgue nowhere says as much, the artist's satisfaction with *his own* presentation of an experience can be the only guarantee that he is doing justice to the rights of his great co-partner. This consideration is missing from Laforgue's aesthetic, just as Taine's 'caractère essentiel', though apparent to the eye of the historian, is absent from the mind of the working artist. Had it been present it must have led to modification of other parts of the theory. As it is, the glaring deficiency in Laforgue's views is that every time he wants to judge a work of art bad, he can do no more than allege that it reflects inadequately the Unconscious in its latest phase of evolution.

This brings us to the third result of Hartmann's system in Laforgue's hands. We have seen that the artist must be original on pain of falsifying the processes of the Unconscious; but what are the limits of originality? With this question we are trespassing on problems dealt with in the following chapter, and we can at this point do no more than answer briefly: the limits are simply whatever Laforgue cares to propose to himself. *Vers libre,* a few delicious monstrosities of vocabulary, a new *Schadenfreude* of specially sophisticated tone—these are the main signs in his poetry of faithfulness to the Unconscious. But surely many forms in his writing are unoriginal? For every new word he coins (and he coins them always from old) there are ten thousand that he takes meekly from the accepted language; and a one-sided claim for the artist to be original tails off into ridicule when we reflect that the painter's colours are unoriginal; that the musician uses an accepted chromatic scale of twelve semitones; that the poet uses at least some of the language his mother teaches him; and so on.

By now it should be becoming plain what position *L'Inconscient* occupies in these fragments of an aesthetic. As regards the actual operations of creating a poem or a picture the grand principle is as helpless as a flounder; it could be forgotten, and the artist's sensation remains; its dynamic evolution can be denied outright and there would still remain good grounds for freeing the artist from convention and imitative restrictions; it is asserted that the artist is a servant, but by the very nature of things there is no means to support this claim. With one hand it takes the scale of aesthetic value away from the artist and places it in an inaccessible region of sensation, but with the other it returns his responsibility to him by allowing that he can embody the aspirations of the Unconscious with more or less efficiency; and so at the end leaves us very much where we started in our quest for aesthetic judgements of value. Evidently, then, when we look for reasons why Laforgue should take so fervently to Hartmann's metaphysic, the same answer comes up that suggests itself in the case of solipsism: he was looking for a reasoned justification of licence, a counter to the traditional arguments of formalism. Almost as important, Laforgue was conscious of the need to attack Taine's historical-determinist and intellectualist aesthetic, to place the artist in a position where he can do good work and bad work and be praised or blamed for it; and for this he deemed the Philosophy of the Unconscious a proper weapon.

But the leading question of what sort of consciousness art gives, this philosophy is obviously not fitted to answer; Hartmann's early ventures specifically into aesthetic were in fact conducted in a heavy beer-garden atmosphere of hedonism. Laforgue ignores them, and dies before Hartmann's *Aesthetik* is published; the consequent lacunae in his theories can only be filled conjecturally.

Laforgue's doctrine of the Unconscious, while ascribing each artist to a unique position in the cosmic process, have been seen to link him very loosely with its underlying principle; so loosely, indeed, that there is some doubt in our minds how far he can rightly be called a 'poet of the Unconscious' at all. . . .

Russell S. King   (essay date 1978)

SOURCE: "The Poet as Clown: Variations on a Theme in Nineteenth-Century French Poetry," in *Orbis Litterarum,* Vol. 33, No. 3, 1978, pp. 238-52.

[In the essay excerpted below, King offers a detailed history and interpretation of the clown figure in French literature, concluding with a study of Laforgue's Pierrot, who is "both the frivolous dilettante and Christ-like prophet-victim."]

Banville's "Le Saut du tremplin," Baudelaire's "Le Vieux Saltimbanque," Verlaine's "Le Clown," Mallarmé's "Le Pitre châtié" and Laforgue's **"Pierrots"** all seek to suggest a modern, post-romantic image of the artist as a mocked and mocking performer. The full implications of this image, which could need a far more extensive treatment than is possible here, are sometimes profoundly psychological, with the poet's com-

pulsion both to flaunt and to conceal the self, sometimes aesthetic, with a desire to glorify and question the nature and function of art, and always metaphysical, in the exploration of the delicate relationship between life and art, reality and illusion.

This "self-portrait as a clown" has become a standard allegory of the artist in twentieth-century painting, with, for example, the Harlequin figure of Picasso's *At the Lapin Agile* (1905), Georges Rouault's innumerable sad and wounded Pierrots and clowns, and Bernard Buffet's series of 1955, etc. In a sense such paintings are readily accommodated in a seemingly unilinear tradition which really began with Watteau's *Gilles* (1717-19), and includes Daumier's "saltimbanques" paintings of the 1860's, Cézanne's *Pierrot and Harlequin* (1888), and the many circus paintings of the 1880's and 1890's: Degas' *Miss Lola at the Cirque Fernando* (1879), Toulouse-Lautrec's *The Equestrian* (1888), *At the Nouveau-Cirque: Five Stuffed Shirts* (1891), *At the Moulin-Rouge: The Clown Mademoiselle Cha-U-Kao* (1895), and Seurat's *The Circus* (1891).

However this apparently unilinear history was more complex, a literature-inspired phenomenon, developing particularly from the nineteenth-century models in poetry and the popular theatre, from the debased derivatives of the *commedia dell'arte* popularized by Gaspard and Charles Deburau at the Théâtre des Funambules in the late 1820's, and from the rise of the circus clown. There was a kind of symbolic equivalence and a gradual process of mythification of Pierrot and Harlequin, the court jester, the vagabond showman, the gypsy violinist, and the white-faced clown. And later in the nineteenth-century, elements of Hamlet and Christ were added. Indeed the French language, like English, possesses a range of more or less synonymous labels: saltimbanque, bouffon, comédien, pitre, paillasse, clown, pasquin, baladin. And whilst each of these terms belongs to an often distinct tradition and implies different qualities, they have been blurred into symbolic analogues of the psychological and existential complexities of the artist as he perceives and projects himself.

With the antithetical basis of French romantic aesthetics the wise fool or the tragic clown could have been represented as appropriate if obvious allegories of the "modern" artist. The clown-jester-gypsy, with their obvious implication of geographical and historical alienation—other places especially the East and other times—should have appeared admirably attractive to the romantic sensibility. Moreover the negative metaphysics of Schopenhaurian pessimism needed a compensatory antidote such as a comic mask or positive social function to avoid the fate of Goethe's *Werther* (1777), Chateaubriand's *René* (1802), or Musset's *Rolla* (1834). Indeed Beaumarchais' "Je me presse de rire de tout, de peur d'être obligé d'en pleurer," underscores the metaphysical relationship between laughter and tears, despair and exhilaration, the comic and the tragic, between tolerable and intolerable existence, which was more powerfully echoed in Byron's: "And if I laugh at any mortal thing, This that I may not weep."

Yet in French romantic literature, Musset's *Fantasio* (1834) is one of the few illustrations of this image of the modern artist. If Fantasio has "le mois de mai sur les joues," he still has "le mois de janvier dans le cœur." Musset's hero attempts to escape the painful responsibility of existential consciousness by retreating into the relative ease of mechanical, pre-ordained existence as a court jester. Moreover Fantasio is not only a metaphysical refugee, but also an almost sterile artist, constantly mocking the value of his function: metaphysical doubts have led to doubts about aesthetic values and his own ability to create and communicate; a metaphysical negative is, in his case, not easily converted into an aesthetic positive: "Un sonnet vaut mieux qu'un long poème, et un verre de vin vaut mieux qu'un sonnet," he quips. The idea of the artist as clown—whether clever acrobatic showman or clumsy scapegoat—was scarcely compatible with the more serious tone of Hugo's Olympian image of the poet-prophet, or Musset's lyrical dialectic on poetic creativity between Muse and Poet, or Vigny's ivory-tower stoic, or Lamartine's sombre meditator. . . .

[The] "Pierrot-clown" figure emerged as a dominant, sustained analogue of the poet in the poetry of Jules Laforgue (1860-87). Indeed no artist, with the exception of Georges Rouault in the twentieth century, is more intimately identified with the clown-like figure of Pierrot. Laforgue's second (first published) collection of poems, *Les Complaintes* (1885) contains three poems, **"Complainte de Lord Pierrot," "Autre Complainte de Lord Pierrot,"** and **"Complainte des Noces de Pierrot,"** and his next collection *L'Imitation de Notre-Dame la Lune* (1886), contains a long sequence of poems entitled **"Pierrots"** and a **"Locutions des Pierrots."**

Although Laforgue's interest centres round this traditional *commedia dell'arte* figure, in fact the modern circus clown quite probably provided the initial stimulus. Laforgue wrote in a letter in 1882: "Adorez-vous le cirque? Je viens d'y passer cinq soirées consécutives. Les clowns me paraissent arrivés à la vraie sagesse. Je devrais être clown, j'ai manqué ma destinée; c'est irrévocablement fini. N'est-ce pas qu'il est trop tard pour que je m'y mette?" And this same fascination with circus life is echoed in his largely autobiographical novel, *Stéphane Vassiliew,* published only in 1946.

The identification of poet and Pierrot cannot be separated from the poet's ambivalent aesthetics, with its mixture of obscure symbolist principles and familiar

impressionism, its fusion of universal myth and popular expression and art forms, illustrated particularly in the ballads of *Les Complaintes* and the *Moralités légendaires*. As Guy Michaud wrote in his *Message Poétique du Symbolisme* (1947), "Son cerveau est un carrefour où se bousculent pêle-mêle les races, les idées, les philosophies, les religions." Of all the nineteenth-century poets Laforgue was the most intellectual and anti-intellectual: cosmogony in *Le Sanglot de la Terre* and theories of the unconscious, culled from, and reinforced by, Hartmann's *Philosophy of the Unconscious,* provided the intellectual dynamics of his writing. Yet Schopenhaurian pessimism and even Hartmann's theories proved largely unproductive and sterile to the poetic sensibility, for doubt and apathy were the inevitable consequences of philosophic meditation: "Puis je pense et, après avoir pensé, je doute. Je doute si notre pensée rime à quelque chose de réel dans l'univers. Et je m'ennuie."

This ambiguous philosophical stance is paralleled by a style which too points in different directions: a curious fusion and juxtaposition of the serious and esoteric on the one hand, and, on the other, colloquial banalities, which produced the hybrid style which influenced T. S. Eliot and Ezra Pound. "Je trouve stupide de faire la grosse voix et de jouer de l'éloquence. Aujourd'hui que je suis plus sceptique et que je m'emballe moins aisément et que d'autre part, je possède ma langue d'une façon plus minutieuse, plus clownesque, j'écris de petits poèmes de fantaisie, n'ayant qu'un but: faire de l'original à tout prix." This dual, clown-like style not only resulted from the poet's scepticism, but it also most adequately reflected in linguistic terms the mental processes of the conscious and unconsious mind. "Je rêve de la poésie qui ne dise rien, mais soit des bouts de rêverie sans suite." And this inconsequential, non-didactic, apparently naive style was one which Laforgue recognised and admired in Verlaine: "La 'Sagesse' de Verlaine—Quel vrai poète—C'est bien celui dont je me rapproche le plus—négligence absolue de la forme, plaintes d'enfant."

The serio-comic, dandified yet naive clown alone would reconcile such incompatible vacillations. "Pierrot lunaire" became the perfect vehicle for the fragmented, disrupted "bouts de rêverie" of both the Freudian and the Jungian unconscious. And stylistically the Pierrot poems fuse wit, humour, irony, satire and parody, invalidating normal distinctions and classifications. Like Verlaine's and Baudelaire's poetic analogues, Laforgue's Pierrots are portrayed with detachment, both humorously and ironically, as if the "je" were another person, and with few overt invitations to sentimentalize or sympathize:

> C'est sur un cou qui, raide, émerge
> D'une fraise empesée *idem,*
> Une face imberbe au cold-cream,

Un air d'hydrocéphale asperge.
Les yeux sont noyés de l'opium
De l'indulgence universelle,
La bouche clownesque ensorcèle
Comme un singulier géranium. (**"Pierrots" I**)

Laforgue's original imagery—"faire de l'original à tout prix"—of asparagus and geranium would normally suggest parody. Yet there are profound psychological and metaphysical implications, for Pierrot provides not only the means whereby life can be both lived and rejected, the self exposed and masked, but it also satisfies the individual poet's mythopoeic desire for permanence and integration:

Je ne suis qu'un viveur lunaire
Qui fait des ronds dans les bassins,
Et cela, sans autre dessein
Que devenir un légendaire.
Retroussant d'un air de défi
Mes manches de mandarin pâle,
J'arrondis ma bouche et—j'exhale
Des conseils doux de Crucifix.
Ah! oui, devenir légendaire,
Au seuil des siècles charlatans!
Mais où sont les Lunes d'antan?
Et que Dieu n'est-il à refaire? (**"Locutions
   des Pierrots" XVI**).

Pierrot is both the frivolous dilettante and Christ-like prophet-victim, but a prophet who proves to offer no positive message. He is the elegant, superior black-costumed, Hamlet-like dandy, Lord Pierrot, yet he chooses to play the role of a white-faced, white-costumed simpleton:

Ces dandys de la Lune
S'imposent, en effet,
De chanter "s'il vous plaît?"
De la blonde à la brune.
Car c'est des gens blasés;
Et s'ils vous semblent dupes,
Çà et là de la Jupe
Lange à cicatriser,
Croyez qu'ils font la bête
Afin d'avoir des seins,
Pis-aller de coussins
A leurs savantes têtes. (**"Pierrots" II**).

Indeed this traditional role of the *commedia dell'arte* with Pierrot vainly, attempting to seduce Woman (Columbine, Eve, Maya) reflects Laforgue's own experience as a timid but sceptical lover, and provides the subject and theme of the majority of the "Pierrot" poems in *Les Complaintes* and *L'Imitation:*

En tête-à-tête avec la femme
Ils ont toujours l'air d'être un tiers,
Confondent demain avec hier,

Et demandent Rien avec âme!
Jurent "je t'aime!" l'air là-bas,
D'une voix sans timbre, en extase,
Et concluent aux plus folles phrases
Par des: "Mon Dieu, n'insistons
   pas?"(**"Pierrots" III**).

Pierrot serves as the unifying symbol and image in Laforgue's writing just as the dandy does in Baudelaire: metaphysics, aesthetics, and the personal relationship with "others" could only be reconciled by adopting a persona such as that of the clown, which is by definition dual and contradictory.

Laforgue's contradictory portrayal of Pierrot blends tradition and modernity more completely than any of the earlier clown figures of Banville, Baudelaire, Verlaine or Mallarmé. There are two surprising features of these poets' portrayal: firstly, the obvious "sorrow behind the greasepaint" aspect—as in Leoncavallo's *I Pagliacci* (1892)—is only a secondary characteristic; and secondly, the symbolic value varied so widely: Banville's optimistic acrobatic clown, Baudelaire's old, collapsed showman, Verlaine's malleable joker, Mallarmé's showman punished for removing his make-up and costume, and Laforgue's Pierrots buffeted by the contradictory dictates of the unconscious. Such variations reveal that the clown figure, though richly suggestive, is in a sense an "empty" one, and certainly far from being frozen into a standardized significance. Jean Starobinski concludes [in *Portrait de l'artiste en saltim banque*, 1970] that, in fact, the clown allegory is vacant of meaning: "Qu'on ne se hâte donc pas de leur assigner un rôle, une fonction, un sens; il faut leur accorder la licence de n'être rien de plus qu'un jeu insensé. La gratuité, l'absence de signification est, si je puis dire, leur air natal." Externally imposed meanings can be multiplied *ad infinitum*. In the 1830's, under the influence of the Deburaus, Pierrot was equated with the people, just as he was later identified with Hamlet by Laforgue, and with the suffering Christ, particularly by Max Jacob and Rouault, whose paintings of Christ and Pierrot frequently resemble each other closely.

However "what the clown symbolizes" is more varied than "why the clown symbolizes." Nineteenth-century French poetry marked a progression, from romanticism, through parnassianism to decadent-symbolism, towards almost total self-reflexiveness. The gulf separating the realm of art from the realm of lived experience and objective reality was an ever increasing one, and the clown, as a blatantly proclaimed actor and champion of artifice, set himself in total contrast, physically and spiritually, with his audience and society in general. A rebel against realism, or rather his audience's concept of realism, he perceived more profoundly than his audience the comedy of life, that "all the world's a stage"; and, symbolically, by rejecting surface realism, by means of his make-up, costume and comic mask, he was demonstrating a deeper consciousness of the illusory nature of life and death. Indeed, it is no coincidence that Daumier and Picasso were attracted to both the clown and Don Quixote almost at the same time.

The nineteenth-century poets were more concerned, superficially, by the "what" rather than the "why" of the clown's symbolic value. Yet the reasons for the clown gradually emerging as a nineteenth and twentieth-century allegory of the artist, with a wide variety of meanings, are *sine qua non* determinants. Relationships between artist-clown and audience, between art and life, between appearance and reality, between innocence and wisdom, between the glorification and vilification of art, are all central to an understanding of the varied aesthetics of nineteenth-century art, and are all symbolically posed by the representation of the clown.

Cowley describes the impact of Laforgue's poetry on American poets:

. . . [His] work helped to change the course of American poetry and . . . its influence here was based on an instinctive sympathy amounting almost, at the time, to an identity of spirit. That explains why Laforgue was a liberating force, in style and form and subject matter. I attest and depose that he encouraged a number of American poets to speak with greater freedom, in voices that later proved to be their own.

Malcolm Cowley, "Laforgue in America: A Testimony," The Sewanee Review, *January-March 1963.*

Elisabeth A. Howe (essay date 1985)

SOURCE: "Repeated Forms in Laforgue," in *Nottingham French Studies,* Vol. 24, No. 2, October, 1985, pp. 41-54.

[In the following essay, Howe conducts a close study of Laforgue's verse, substantiating her assertion that the poet uses cliché and convention to forge his unconventional poetic forms.]

"Mais tu ne peux que te répéter, ô honte!" exclaims the speaker of **"Simple agonie"** (*Derniers vers,* **VI**), referring to himself. This statement applies to all Laforgue's characters, who, whether consciously or otherwise, merely act out the roles in which society has cast them. Playing a part, in life as on the stage, equates to repeating a script, consisting in this case of the ready-made, banal phrases people utter every day—phrases learnt from others and which can scarcely claim, therefore, to represent the genuine self-expression of

the speaker. A sense of frustration and weariness caused by observation of the conventional nature of people's behaviour and language is evident throughout Laforgue's poetry from the *Complaintes* to the *Derniers vers*. At the same time his own deliberate quotation of stereotyped expressions becomes, paradoxically, a strategy of originality, a means of parodying both Romantic rhetoric and bourgeois eloquence: a technique which other post-Romantic writers, such as Flaubert and Lautréamont, also adapted to their own ends.

Like Flaubert before him, Laforgue began his career by writing in a distinctly Romantic vein himself. One of the main differences between his earliest collection of verse, *Le Sanglot de la terre,* which he never published, and his subsequent *Complaintes,* is the move away from the bombastic self-expression of a central unified "I", typical of much Romantic poetry, towards an anonymous multiplicity. The speaker of the *Sanglot* poems dwells constantly on his own personal preoccupations: his awe at the vastness of the universe; his shocked awareness of the insignificance and transience of man's life; his horror of death. "Je puis mourir demain" is an oft-repeated phrase, and he hates to think that after death "Tout se fera sans moi!" (**"L'Impossible"**). The disgust Laforgue later felt for the *Sanglot* poems was undoubtedly partly inspired by their self-centred mode of writing: in the **"Préludes autobiographiques"**, a long poem which he insisted on including as a prologue to the *Complaintes* in order to show what his literary "autobiography" had been and how his poetic aims had changed, he mocks his former tendency to see himself as the centre of the universe:

> J'espérais
> Qu'à ma mort, tout frémirait, du cèdre à l'hysope;
> Que ce Temps, déraillant, tomberait en syncope,
> Que, pour venir jeter sur mes lèvres des fleurs,
> Les Soleils très navrés détraqueraient leurs choeurs.

In the majority of the *Complaintes,* on the other hand, Warren Ramsey notes "a movement towards dramatization, a tendency, having its origin in self-awareness and self-defence, to exteriorize the lyric emotion" [in *Jules Laforgue and the Ironic Inheritance,* 1953]. This exteriorization is achieved largely through the use of different voices expressing the thoughts and feelings of various personae: the "ange incurable" and the "Chevalier errant", the "roi de Thulé", the "Sage de Paris" and, most important of all, Pierrot. Dispersion and repetition replace the unique utterance of the *Sanglot* poems. In subsequent collections also, *L'Imitation de Notre-Dame la lune* and the *Derniers vers,* different voices can be heard, speaking, in David Arkell's words, for the "multiple selves of Laforgue and others" [*Looking for Laforgue*, 1979]. It is significant that the move from a unified to a multiple self accompanies Laforgue's imitation of a more popular, collective form, the *complainte* having been originally a type of folk-song or ballad. Ballads are a form without an author not only because they are often anonymous, but because they specifically aim at objectivity: the "I" of the poet is never mentioned, only that of the various characters. Laforgue seems to be seeking a similar kind of anonymity by attributing his poems to different speakers. He also frequently imitates the popular diction of the *complainte,* as if to emphasize that what we hear is not his voice but the anonymous speech of the "folk".

Laforgue first makes use in the **Complaintes** of the Pierrot figure who was later to feature prominently in **L'Imitation de Notre-Dame la lune;** his predilection for this stock character can be linked with his move away from the personal poetry of **Le Sanglot** to the ready-made form of the *complainte*. His adoption of set form and stock figure is accompanied by the use of ready-made language—the repetition of fixed expressions and clichés. The traditional Pierrot's role was mimed, and his mimicry involved a repertoire of conventional gestures; Laforgue, of course, has to use words, but he does so in such a way as to suggest that language, too, can be merely gesture: his Pierrots (and other speakers) trot out the stock phrases dictated by convention for use in certain situations. To women, for example, they address declarations couched in the rhetoric traditionally associated with love:

> Ange! tu m'as compris,
> A la vie, à la mort!

while thinking

> Ah! passer là-dessus l'éponge! . . .
>   (*L'Imitation,* "Pierrots")

Being a comic figure, however, Pierrot likes to give an unexpected twist to the conventional phrases he proffers. In the famous **"Autre complainte de Lord Pierrot"**, the lady's banal exclamation "Ah! tu ne m'aimes pas; tant d'autres sont jaloux!" is countered by Pierrot with another, totally inappropriate, cliché: "Merci, pas mal; et vous?" Similarly, to the lady's accusation "Ah! tu te lasseras le premier, j'en suis sûre . . ." Pierrot responds with a stereotyped expression from another context but which makes admirable sense here, too: "Après vous, s'il vous plaît!" The twist which Pierrot gives to banal, stereotyped phrases empties them of any last shred of meaning they may have had when used in their normal context; they become as hollow as refrains like "tirelan-laire" or "diguedondaine" in the popular songs Laforgue was imitating in the **Complaintes**.

The implication must be that language, like the conventional gestures of mime, is a question of habit and custom. The automatic responses which people exchange daily are pure ritual, devoid of profound content, revealing and communicating nothing of value. This type of play with language at once distinguishes Laforgue's Pierrot from, say, Verlaine's.

As important to Laforgue as the figure of Pierrot is that of Hamlet, who resembles Pierrot in many respects: both of them are stereotypes (Hamlet having certainly become one by the late nineteenth century), both are taken from the stage and are very much aware of themselves as performers and actors, i.e. repeaters of roles and scripts. The Hamlet of the **Moralités légendaires** deliberately plays the role of l'Incompris for the benefit of the young girl whose canary he has killed:

> —Oh! pardon, pardon! Je ne l'ai pas fait exprès! Ordonne-moi toutes les expiations. Mais je suis si bon! J'ai un cœur d'or comme on n'en fait plus. Tu me comprends, n'est-ce pas, Toi?

> —O monseigneur, monseigneur! balbutie la petite fille. Oh! si vous saviez! Je vous comprends tant! Je vous aime depuis si longtemps! J'ai tout compris . . .

> Hamlet se lève. "Encore une!" pense-t-il.

Here we see again, as with Pierrot, that role-playing tends to be accompanied by an addiction to an appropriate type of rhetoric—in this instance, as very frequently in Laforgue, that of love.

Despite their mockery of women's readiness to accept the conventional stereotyped roles offered by society, Hamlet and Pierrot are themselves obliged to adopt similar poses, to "vivre de vieux compromis", as Lord Pierrot puts it in his **"Complainte"**. This is what they find so repugnant about life, and why they are so ready to criticize those people who seem perfectly satisfied with the "vieux compromis", the fixed patterns of speech and behaviour imposed by social convention or literary example. The difficulty they themselves experience in asserting their own personality stems partly from a lack of self-knowledge; the Hamlet-like speaker of the **Derniers vers** finds it impossible to declare his love because he does not know himself: "d'abord je ne me possédais pas bien moi-même," he declares in **Dv III**. In addition, Laforgue's male speakers are aware of a multiplicity of selves within them, of the "société un peu bien mêlée" mentioned in the poem **"Ballade"** (**Des fleurs de bonne volonté**). All Laforgue's men are torn between different versions of themselves; Pierrot's violent fluctuations, sometimes within one poem, between flippant and serious moods, between brutality and tenderness, suggest a dislocated personality, as J.A. Hiddleston points out [in *Essai sur Laforgue et les Derniers vers,* 1980]: "Pierrot incarne dans sa personne la discontinuité et la dislocation internes, le manque d'équilibre entre les émotions et l'intelligence, bref les contradictions du poète-héros . . . Pas plus que le poète, Pierrot n'est un, mais innombrable."

In Laforgue's poetry we witness a dislocation of the very notion of personality, and language plays an important part in this process; his poems convey the impression that character *is* the stereotyped phrases in which it expresses itself. [Michael] Riffaterre points out [in *Essais de stylistique structurale,* 1971] that to make a literary character speak in stereotyped phrases almost automatically deprives him of personality because they imply conformity to ready-made attitudes or standards:

> La formule figée, parce qu'elle est inséparable de certaines attitudes sociales ou morales, sert à l'auteur à situer son personnage: il n'a qu'à mettre sur ses lèvres les modes verbales d'un milieu donné . . . Recueillir des automatismes, c'est choisir delibérément de voir l'homme sous un mauvais jour, dans les comportements sociaux ou mentaux par lesquels il abdique sa personnalité.

These statements appear in Riffaterre's essay on "Le Cliché dans la prose littéraire", but they apply equally well to Laforgue's poetry. Thus John E. Jackson speaks [in *La Question du moi,* 1971] of the "usure du langage chez Laforgue" and suggests that "les mots sont en voie, pour lui, de perdre leur *créance sémantique.* Ils sont formules, stéréotypes, c'est-a-dire omnitude autonome, désinvestie de presque tout répondant au *moi* qui les profère". A similar phenomenon is typical of the early poetry of T.S. Eliot, particularly in "The Love Song of J. Alfred Prufrock" and "Portrait of a Lady"; Jackson comments that the way in which "le langage échoue ici coïncide avec l'échec de Prufrock . . . d'affirmer librement, au-delà du stéréotype, une individualité propre . . . qui ose . . . imposer sa singularité".

Hamlet and Pierrot find it difficult to "imposer sa singularité" not only because of a lack of self-knowledge and an awareness of the plurality of the Self, but because, as they realize, language simply does not allow one to be original. The uniqueness which they both feel ("—Et, au fond, dire que j'existe! Que j'ai ma vie à moi!" exclaims the Hamlet of the *Moralités*) can only be expressed with the "Words, words, words" of other people. Both personae confront the problem of how, using language, to break out of the established patterns of language, and the answers proposed are extreme. One is to indulge in the type of word-play practised by Hamlet and Pierrot, ironically twisting the meanings of words; ultimately this remains unsatisfactory, however, since it precludes any meaningful communication with their interlocutors. A second possibility is silence: "rien n'est pratique que se taire, se taire, et agir en conséquence," says the Hamlet of the *Mo-*

ralités. ("Agir" would be another way of expressing oneself, but a notoriously difficult one for Shakespeare's Hamlet and Laforgue's; as Albert Sonnenfield says [in "Hamlet the German and Jules Laforgue," *Yale French Studies,* 1964], for Laforgue's Hamlet, "action means acting", i.e. once again the repetition of a role.) Silence is also the solution adopted by Laforgue's ***Pierrot fumiste,*** in that he offers no explanation for his peculiar conduct; besides, the role of Pierrot was traditionally mimed, and therefore silent. The alternative to silence is death, which befalls both Shakespeare's and Laforgue's Hamlets; and death, of course, means silence, as the former's dying words proclaim.

Rather than an original, fully-developed personality, Laforgue's personae possess only certain recognizable traits—jealousy, faithlessness, timidity, tenderness, brutality, sentimentality—endlessly repeated and, through irony, endlessly negated. Laforgue's universe is one of repeition; instead of presenting an authentic, unique self, his speakers demonstrate that the "I" is a place where repetitions are gathered: "Mais tu ne peux que te répéter, ô honte!" This "shame" is attendant on both behaviour and language: people who adopt stereotyped roles inevitably express themselves in a language appropriate to that role—which is equally stereotyped. Laforgue clearly demonstrates this in his use of clichés, the clichés of a sophisticated group of people playing endless love-games, asserting that "On n'aime qu'une fois", accusing one another: "Assez! assez! / C'est toi qui as commencé" (***Dv VIII***), or assuring one another that "Je t'aime pour toi seul" (***L'Imitation,*** **"Pierrots (on a des principes)"**). Laforgue's personae all have similar voices, because the things they say tend to be what they have heard other people say.

In the section of Laforgue's ***Mélanges posthumes*** entitled **"Sur la femme"**, the following passage appears, under the subheading "Première entrevue d'aveux":

> Dès qu'on s'est bien dit et dûment déclaré "je t'aime", un silence, presque un froid. Alors, celui des deux qui est destiné à s'en aller plus tard (c'est fatal) commence ses inutiles litanies rétrospectives: "Ah! *moi,* il y a longtemps déjà! . . . Tenez, vous ne saurez jamais! . . . Oh! la première fois que je vous vis . . . etc."

Such phrases are typical of Laforgue's speakers. The girl in ***Derniers vers IX*** talks of her "vie faite exprès", and affirms: "ma destinée se borne . . . / A te suivre" because "c'est bien toi et non un autre". Just as we saw Hamlet greeting such trite declarations with a scathing "Encore une!" so the speaker of this poem takes an ironical view of them and of the girl, as he imagines her rolling about on his doormat. Again, the male speaker in this poem, though playing a role, is conscious of doing so and mocks himself for it, whereas the girl, like Laforgue's other women, has no distance on her language: she says what she means, or what she thinks she means. The cynical attitude of the male speakers shows up the clichés for what they are: trite, empty phrases passed from mouth to mouth but devoid of any true meaning—the sort of phrases Flaubert collected in his *Dictionnaire des idées reçues,* or, more appropriately since the context is almost always one of love, by Roland Barthes in his *Fragments d'un discours amoureux.* According to Laforgue's men, "love" is simply a matter of being in love with the discourse of love. Thus the speaker of **"Sur une défunte"** (**Dv XI**) suggests that a woman can make the same declarations indifferently to "les nobles A, B, C ou D", to any of whom she will say:

> "Oh, tes yeux, ta démarche!
> Oh, le son fatal de ta voix!
> Voilà si longtemps que je te cherche!
> Oh, c'est bien Toi, cette fois! . . ."

The man implies that these are simply empty verbal formulas which can be reproduced at will, as they are in so many of Laforgue's poems, either deliberately (by the men), or unconsciously (by the women). Here as elsewhere Laforgue emphasizes the sheer automatism of a language that purports to speak the heart: the discourse of love is never original, but always a repetition of what someone has said previously, and cannot therefore represent the authentic expression of the unique Self. Along with the notion of love, this view of language as repetition undermines the very concept of interiority itself; for, since words are always exterior, repeated, overheard, the individual can never possess language, which remains outside him, belonging to others as well as to himself.

Needless to say, the notions of repetivity and externality apply not only to the language of love but to language in general; they are central to the influential theory of intertextuality outlined by [Mikhail] Bakhtin, who stresses that no single utterance can claim to be totally individual or unique. The words we use, he says [in *Esthétique et théorie du roman,* 1978], have been used by others and are inevitably impregnated with their intentions: "Le langage n'est pas un milieu neutre. Il ne devient pas aisément, librement, la propriété du locuteur. Il est peuplé et surpeuplé d'intentions étrangères." It follows therefore that "tout énoncé se rapporte aussi à des énoncés antérieurs, donnant ainsi lieu à des relations *intertextuelles*" [according to Tzvetan Todorov, *Mikhaïl Bakhtine: le principe dialogique,* 1981]. This is the case not only in works of literature, of course, but, as Bakhtin points out, in everyday speech, where the social context plays an important role: "Aucun énoncé en général ne peut être attribué au seul locuteur: il est le *produit* de *l'interaction des locuteurs* et, plus largement, le produit de toute cette *situation sociale* complexe, dans laquelle il a

surgi." Stereotyped expressions offer a privileged, extreme illustration of this state of affairs. At the end of **"Dimanches"** (**Dv III**), the speaker temporarily adopts a motherly, protective attitude which expresses itself in clichés and makes light of the sufferings of the "Pauvre, pâle et piètre individu" recounted earlier in the poem:

> —Allons, dernier des poètes,
> Toujours enfermé tu te rendras malade!
> Vois, il fait beau temps tout le monde est
>   dehors,
> Va donc acheter deux sous d'ellébore,
> Ça te fera une petite promenade.

In lines 2-3 and 5 we can hear, as well as the poet's voice, that of any mother talking to her child, and the speaker parodies this voice while at the same time offering a valid comment on his own behavior. He is temporarily looking at himself from the outside, or as Bakhtin puts it "avec les yeux d'un autre homme, d'un autre représentant de [s]on groupe social ou de [s]a classe". The resulting speech is, in Bakhtin's terminology, "double-voiced", i.e. it is an utterance in which two voices can be heard, even though only one speech act is involved.

In Laforgue (as in Flaubert) such phrases are often, though not always, signalled typographically by italics, quotation marks or *points de suspension:*

> . . . le pur flacon des vives gouttes
> Sera, *comme il convient,* d'eau propre baptisé.
> **("Complainte des pianos . . .")**

> Oh! ce fut pour vos cors, et ce fut pour
>   l'automne,
> Qu'il nous montra qu'"on meurt d'amour"!
> **(Dv VI)**

> Leurs Altesses congratulèrent le Tétrarque, se félicitant eux-mêmes du bon vent qui . . . à pareil glorieux jour . . . en ces îles,—et terminèrent par l'éloge de la capitale . . . **("Salomé")**

Other, non-typographical marks of distanciation include exaggeration, repetition and accumulation. In **Derniers vers IX**, the speaker parodies the utterance of an intense, passionate young girl; his voice can be heard through hers because of the sheer exaggeration of her claims:

> "Pour moi, tu n'es pas comme les autres
>   hommes,
> Ils sont ces messieurs, toi tu viens des
>   cieux.
> Ta bouche me fait baisser les yeux
> Et ton port me transporte
> Et je m'en découvre des trésors!"

A certain weakness in the logic of the girl's argument also indicates irony:

> "Tu me demandes pourquoi toi et non un
>   autre,
> Ah! laisse, c'est bien toi et non un autre.
> J'en suis sûre comme du vide insensé de
>   mon cœur
> Et comme de votre air mortellement
>   moqueur."

The man's mocking voice can be heard distinctly in this unconvincing choice of comparisons, as well as in the insistent acoustic repetitions he puts into the girl's mouth (*port, transporte, trésors; pleure, soeurs, peur, meure*).

The quotation of stereotyped expressions such as those uttered by the girl in this poem represents at once a mimetic and a parodic procedure: mimetic in that it imitates the language a naïve girl might use in reality; parodic in that the speaker of the poem clearly views her utterances in an ironic light, passing "du portrait à la charge" [according to Riffaterre]. This tendency for the quotation of clichés to slide from mimesis into parody is explored by Ruth Amossy and Elisheva Rosen [in *Les Discours du cliché,* 1982]. In the realist novel—and in Laforgue's poetry—the use of clichés helps to establish the feeling of "reality", since they inject into a literary text the discourse of a "texte culturel extérieur au récit", namely that of everyday life. Judiciously placed, therefore, "le cliché assure la crédibilité de la narration en la conformant au savoir du public et, conséquemment, en provoquant une reconnaissance confondue avec la connaissance du réel". However, the artificiality of this procedure becomes evident when the "device is bared" and it becomes a parodic gesture (marked, typographically or otherwise, as in the examples from Laforgue quoted above):

> Le cliché ne contribue néanmoins à consolider l'édifice du vraisemblable qu'en le marquant du sceau de la conventionnalité. Le procédé, en effet, se laisse aisément reconnaître et la figure originellement destinée à "masquer les lois du texte" tend précisément à les exhiber . . . Le même fait de langage se voit dès lors attribuer, à des niveaux différents, deux fonctions inverses: d'une part le cliché renforce une vérité commune, renvoie à un savoir préétabli, "naturel"; de l'autre, il en dénonce la conventionnalité et la facticité.

If the deliberate "quotation" of stereotyped phrases tends to become a parodic gesture, parody, conversely, cannot exist without quotation, or repetition, since the parodic text constitutes, by definition, a text constructed with other texts. As Claude Bouché points out [in *Lautréamont: du lieu commun à la parodie,* 1974], "appliquée à la parodie, la méthode intertextuelle n'est plus seulement une option parmi d'autres possibles".

All texts are "intertextual" but some are deliberately and systematically so, particularly those which employ parody and related devices. In Laforgue we find parody of Romantic poets, of Flaubert and Mallarmé, and of Laforgue himself. The poem **"Solo de lune"** (*Dv* **VII**) contains the lines "Tout n'en va pas moins à la mort, / Y a pas de port", which echo Lamartine's "Le Lac": "L'homme n'a point de port, le temps n'a point de rive; / Il coule, et nous passons!" However, parody of specific texts is much more frequent in the *Moralités* than in Laforgue's poetry: Bouché devotes a section of his book on Lautréamont to a thorough analysis of **"Hamlet"** as a typical example of parody; **"Salomé"** parodies Flaubert's "Hérodias", and a page of **"Hamlet"** echoes St. Julien l'Hospitalier's massacre of animals. Another target of **"Salomé"** could be Mallarmé's "Hérodiade" (of which the "Scéne" had been published in 1869), as well as the many Symbolist evocations of Salomé: Laforgue's heroine dies, significantly, "moins victime des hasards illettrés que d'avoir voulu vivre dans le factice et non à la bonne franquette à l'instar de chacun de nous". **"Pan et la Syrinx"** parodies the myth, but Laforgue undoubtedly has in mind also Mallarmé's *L'Aprés-midi d'un faune.* Syrinx declares to Pan that "l'art, c'est le désir perpétué . . .", recalling the Faun's desire to "perpetuate" the nymphs in his song. And Pan, after Syrinx's disappearance, exclaims, echoing the Faun (and Faust): "O Syrinx, t'ai-je rêvée?" following this with his own formulation of the Faun's dilemma: "encore une fois . . . je n'aurai pas eu la présence d'esprit de me pénétrer du fait de la présence des choses!"

Laforgue sometimes parodies, in the *Moralités,* attitudes or phrases from his own earlier works. Lohengrin and Elsa "tombèrent ensemble aux genoux l'un de l'autre; ensemble, mais, hélas! plus ou moins fatalement"—which represents an ironic rendering of the wistful lines from **"Solo de lune"**:

> Ses yeux disaient: "Comprenez-vous?
> Pourquoi ne comprenez-vous pas?"
> Mais nul n'a voulu faire le premier pas,
> Voulant trop tomber *ensemble* à genoux.

Salomé incongruously delivers a long speech on the theme of "le Néant" and "l'Inconscient" about which Laforgue used to write somewhat more seriously in the *Sanglot* poems; and Pan has the following exchange with Syrinx:

> "O Syrinx! voyez et comprenez la Terre . . . et la circulation de la vie! . . . Tout est dans Tout!"

> "Tout est dans Tout! Vraiment? Ah, ces gens à formules!"

One of the parodic procedures mentioned by Bouché is "la stéréotypie", which involves the multiple, diffuse referent of a *discours,* rather than a particular text:

> Avec la stéréotypie, on débouche sur le vaste domaine des poncifs et des "topoi", des clichés et des lieux communs . . . Styles éculés et situations-types se rencontrent un peu partout: dans les livres, certes, mais aussi dans les journaux, la publicité, les messages politiques, le langage de la rue, bref, dans tout ce qui est manifestation écrite ou orale collective.

"Stéréotypie" of this diffuse type forms the main thrust of the parodic impulse of Laforgue's poetry, and it accompanies the parody of specific texts in the *Moralités*. We have already seen examples of the "lieux communs" of everyday speech, particularly of the discourse of love; in addition, parody of literary stereotypes, especially the "topoi" of Romantic poetry, is prevalent in both the poetry and the *Moralités*. Laforgue cannot describe a sunset without remembering the innumerable Romantic evocations of that phenomenon; accordingly, his "soleil fichu" "Gît sur le flanc, dans les genêts, sur son manteau, / Un soleil blanc comme un crachat d'estaminet" (*Dv* I); or alternatively it "Lâche les écluses du Grand-Collecteur / En mille pactoles" (*Dv* II). In **"Persée et Andromède"** we are prepared for yet another "couchant qui va faire le beau", and sure enough: "L'Astre Pacha, / Son Éminence Rouge . . . / Descend, mortellement triomphal", until someone kicks this "citrouille crevée" over the horizon. Romantic seascapes, leading to many a digression on Time, Infinity, changelessness, etc., are parodied by Laforgue at the beginning of **"Persée et Andromède"**:

> La mer! de quelque côté qu'on la surveille, des heures et des heures, à quelque moment qu'on la surprenne: toujours elle-même . . . empire de l'insociable, grande histoire qui se tait, cataclysme mal digéré . . . Bref pas l'étoffe d'une amie (oh, vraiment! renoncer à cette idée, et même à l'espoir de partager ses rancunes après confidences, si seul à seul qu'on soit depuis des temps avec elle).

(These last remarks are aimed no doubt at poems like Baudelaire's "L'Homme et la mer", which personifies the sea and suggests an affinity between it and man.) **"Salomé"** presents, more succinctly, "la mer, toujours nouvelle et respectable, la Mer puisqu'il n'y a pas d'autre nom pour la nommer".

Within the area of *stéréotypie,* Laforgue does not restrict his parody to the *topoi* of Romanticism in particular, but embraces various more general literary conventions. The notion of the hero is one of his favourite targets: "Je voudrais bien connaître leur vie quotidienne," he exclaims in an interesting passage about heroes published in *Mélanges posthumes*. When he refers to mythical figures it is not to exalt them; on the contrary, he cuts them down to size and shows that they, too, act out the roles society casts for them. In

"Lohengrin", Elsa, playing the part of the modest, misrepresented virgin, "s'avance sur l'estrade, tête basse, l'air positivement blessé". She declares "angéliquement", "Je crois être innocente. O méprises cruelles!" but adds under her breath, "Mon Dieu, que de cancans!" As soon as Lohengrin arrives she begins to see herself in the traditional image of a warrior-hero's wife: "Je ne saurai que laver, chaque matin, votre armure de cristal, avec mes larmes . . .". Similar parody of pseudo-heroic discourse and gestures which in fact amount simply to narrative convention occurs in all the *Moralités*. Perseus, "plein de chic" and mounted on Pegasus, describes circles over the head of Andromeda in order to impress her, but is promptly deflated by the phrase "Ce jeune héros a l'air fameusement sûr de son affaire". Hamlet, too, adopts a variety of roles and poses, and is quite aware (unlike Perseus) of their conventionality. When a gravedigger interrupts his pseudo-philosophical musings over Yorick's skull to announce the arrival of Ophelia's funeral procession, "le premier mouvement du penseur Hamlet est de *singer* à ravir le clown réveillé par un coup de mailloche à grosse caisse dans le dos; et c'est tout juste qu'il le réprime" (emphasis added). His favourite role, that of artist, dictates his last words: "Ah! . . . qualis . . . artifex . . . pereo!"; for even in death, Hamlet assumes a pose: "Notre héros s'affaisse sur ses genoux orgueilleux, dans le gazon, et vomit des gorgées de sang, et fait l'animal talonné par une mort certaine." The clichés here ("s'affaisse", "gorgées de sang", "talonné par une mort certaine") emphasize that this "heroic" pose in fact represents nothing more than a narrative device.

Laforgue parodies other conventional literary practices, such as the framing device, which is used at the end (but not the beginning) of **"Persée et Andromède"**. At one point in **"Le Miracle des roses"** he ridicules the assumption in traditional novels that the narrator can actually see the scene he evokes: "Approchons-nous, de grâce," he says when wishing to describe a detail. Long descriptive passages such as those in Flaubert's "Hérodias" are also imitated in a parodic spirit by Laforgue, for example in the description of the Tetrarch's palace (**"Salomé"**) or of the "Villa-Nuptiale" (**"Lohengrin"**). In the poetry, Laforgue parodies traditional rhymes, pairing, "tombeau", for example, not with "flambeau" or some other "suitable" word, but with "lavabo" (**"Complainte du vent qui s'ennuie la nuit"**). In **"Complainte des printemps"** "Angélus" is rhymed irreverently with "foetus". Parody of the vocabulary of Catholicism abounds, especially in the early verse but also in later works, for example at the beginning of **"Légende"** (*Dv* VIII) or in the Grand-Priest's salutation in **"Lohengrin"**: "Je vous salue, Vierge des nuits, plaine de glace".

Distinguishing between pastiche and parody, Bouché states that pastiche imitates only the style of a text, whereas parody can deal with any aspect of it, and he relates this to a similar distinction between *cliché* and *lieu commun,* quoting Rémy de Gourmont: "cliché représente la matérialité même de la phrase; lieu commun, plutôt la banalité de l'idée." Riffaterre, too, emphasizes that a cliché must be "un fait de style": "la stéréotypie à elle seule ne fait pas le cliché: il faut encore que la séquence verbale figée par l'usage présente un fait de style, qu'il s'agisse d'une métaphore comme *fourmilière humaine,* d'une antithèse comme *meurtre juridique,* d'une hyperbole comme *mortelles inquiétudes,* etc." We have seen Laforgue parodying clichés of this type in the **Moralités** (e.g. "talonné par une mort certaine"); he also "renews" them sometimes by altering one or more words, as in the example quoted by Riffaterre of the birds "qui ont élu volière dans les frondaisons"; or he deliberately underscores them, for instance when "le cliché 'public houleux'" is said to come into Hamlet's mind as he surveys the scene in the theatre; or when, Lohengrin having dismissed his swan, the narrator declares: "Oh, sublime façon de brûler ses vaisseaux!" The poetry, however, offers far more examples of *lieux communs:* stereotyped expressions which are not figures of speech; Laforgue is concerned not only with their "style" or form but with the attitudes they betray, with the mentality of the speakers who proffer them so uncritically. Amossy and Rosen claim that "le lieu commun . . . renvoie à une stéréotypie de la pensée et non de l'unité discursive", though in practice the two tend to go hand in hand, stereotyped language reflecting "stéréotypie de la pensée". The ironic quotation of clichés or *lieux communs* often represents a device for suggesting criticism of the assumptions underlying them. As Amossy says of *Eugénie Grandet,* "C'est souvent à la faveur d'un jeu de mots ou d'un emploi ironique du cliché que certaines valeurs consacrées se voient tournées en dérision". Laforgue's love-sick ladies are condemned out of their own mouths by the platitudes they utter.

Laforgue's constant repetition of empty verbal formulas, whether of a literary or an everyday type, inevitably suggests that there is nothing *but* "Words, words, words"; that language refers to no reality beyond itself. "A mesure que la répétition se répète," says Shoshana Felman [in *La Folie et la chose littéraire,* 1978] of Flaubert's *Un coeur simple,* "le signe linguistique se *décale* à la fois de son sens et de son référent;" she concludes that the function of clichés is "de nous forcer à réfléchir l'*arbitraire* du signe, qu'ils mettent en évidence, en dénonçant du même coup l'illusion réaliste et référentielle". This property of the cliché, or of "la stéréotypie"; accentuates the feeling we have, reading Laforgue, that his is a universe of words eminently conscious of itself as such, aware of its own non-referentiality. As Bouché says of the *Chants de Maldoror* and *Poésies,* Laforgue's works, written within fifteen or twenty years of Lautréamont's, "se situent à la croisée de ces mouvements multiples qui ne cessent

de ramener l'écriture à elle-même"—a statement which of course applies with at least equal force to Flaubert. Furthermore, the stereotyped phrases constantly issuing from the mouths of stock characters such as Laforgue's Pierrot and Hamlet emphasize that language is a barrier to, rather than a vehicle for, genuine self-expression. The "I" in Laforgue sees itself not just as split into two but as adopting a multiplicity of poses and playing a succession of different roles over and over again. All the Self can do is repeat itself; it is as "intertextual" as its language.

Anne Holmes (essay date 1993)

SOURCE: "Towards the *Derniers Vers:* 'Trouver une langue'," in *Jules Laforgue and Poetic Innovation,* Oxford at the Clarendon Press, 1993, pp. 95-120.

[*In the following excerpt, Holmes examines some of the elements that moved Laforgue toward free verse. She considers the influence of Impressionist aesthetics and looks at how Laforgue's poetic prose in* Moralités légendaires *allowed him to experiment more boldly in* Derniers Vers.]

The **Derniers Vers** was the first volume in French to be composed entirely in free verse, and it owes some of its fame to this fact. The poems were not published as a volume until after Laforgue's death, but eleven of the twelve appeared during his lifetime, ten in pairs in Kahn's *La Vogue,* and one in Téodor de Wyzewa's *Revue indépendante.* . . . In free verse he was a leader, but he was nevertheless influenced by a number of factors that determined the particular direction he followed. . . .

IMPRESSIONISM AND THE *MORALITÉS LÉGENDAIRES*

A poet does not react merely to the work of other poets. His style may develop and change as a result of his interest in other art-forms or of his writing in other genres. Both these factors were present in Laforgue's case. Throughout the time when he was moving towards his final poetic style he was also composing short stories, to which he attached considerable importance. And if a sophisticated interest in the visual arts, particularly painting, had been a constant factor since his Parisian days, it is perhaps most significant at this time, when a clear parallel can be established between the methods and aims of the art he particularly admired—that of the Impressionists—and his own liberated compositional methods.

A brief survey of the many strands that contributed to Laforgue's expertise in the visual arts may be useful here. He had had private drawing-lessons as a child and several witty sketches survive as testimony to his skill. . . . After failing his *baccalauréat* three times, he turned to the École des beaux-arts, where, like his older brother Émile, he studied under Henri Lehmann and met the painter Seurat. His first job in Paris was that of secretary to the art-collector Charles Ephrussi, one of Proust's models for Charles Swann, who was preparing his edition of Dürer's drawings, and it was in his study, lined with paintings by Manet, Monet, Renoir, Degas, Pissarro, Sisley, and Berthe Morisot, among others, that he became familiar with Impressionist painting and made the acquaintance of Manet. While a student in Paris, he attended Taine's lectures on art, which were later summarized to form his *Philosophie de l'art,* took copious notes, some of which survive in manuscript, and arrived ultimately at a position strongly opposed to Taine's, which he put forward in his notes on Impressionism and, less directly, in 'L'Art moderne en Allemagne', and in his contributions to the *Gazette des beaux-arts* and its supplement, the *Chronique des arts et de la curiosité.* At moments of creative discouragement he considered the possibility of making his name as an art critic.

The suggestion that a connection can be traced between Laforgue's interest in painting in general, and in Impressionism in particular, and his poetic style and ambitions is not an idea that would have seemed strange to his contemporaries. Baudelaire's views on the relatedness of the art-forms—the visual arts, literature, and music—were by now common currency, and his famous essay *Le Peintre de la vie moderne* was interpreted with poetry as well as the visual arts in mind. Zola freely acknowledged a literary debt to Impressionist painting: 'Je n'ai pas seulement soutenu les Impressionnistes', he wrote, 'je les ai traduits en littérature, par les touches, notes, colorations, par la palette de beaucoup de mes descriptions,' and, significantly stressing the fact that Impressionist painting contributed to literary innovation, he confessed: 'Dans tous mes livres . . . j'ai été en contact et échange avec les peintres.'

Laforgue was convinced of the naturalness of applying the methods of the visual arts to literature. In one passage, the importance of which cannot be overstressed, he contrasted the Impressionists' 'œil naturel' with traditional academic vision, dominated by concepts that he considered artificial, such as line, relief, and perspective. The natural—or Impressionist—eye saw the external world as it really appears, that is, in multiple gradations of prismatic colour:

> où académique ne voit que la lumière blanche, à l'état épandu, l'impressionniste la voit baignant tout non de morte blancheur, mais de mille combats vibrants, de riches décompositions prismatiques. Où l'académique ne voit que le dessin extérieur enfermant le modelé, il voit les réelles lignes vivantes sans forme géométrique mais bâties de mille touches irrégulières qui, de loin, établissent la vie. . . . L'impressionniste voit et rend la nature

telle qu'elle est, c'est-à-dire uniquement en vibrations colorées.

The painting that was Laforgue's favourite in Ephrussi's collection, Monet's 'Baignade à la Grenouillère' (now in the National Gallery), certainly offers a picture of nature—and particularly of the reflective surface of water—'uniquement en vibrations colorées' by means of 'mille touches irrégulières'. These were not achieved with ease, any more than was Laforgue's apparently spontaneous verse. Monet referred to the painting as a 'pochade', though it is in fact somewhere between a rough draft and a finished painting. The use of X-rays has given us a different and much more painstaking image of Impressionist techniques. It has shown how even this painting was much altered during composition, and that it contains surprisingly elaborate combinations of coloured pigments. The Impressionists understood that the human experience of colour is not of single, determinate hues, but of a complex shifting process of interaction. Awareness of this fact led to the emphasis they placed on relationships rather than on objects, a perception that was also central to Laforgue's view of his artistic material. Interestingly, Seurat referred to the technique that he invented not primarily as 'pointillisme', but as 'divisionisme', a term that also highlights relationships rather than objects.

Laforgue drew a parallel between the Impressionist sensitivity to the variety and complexity of visual experience and the 'symphonic' ambitions of Wagner, linking both to the Hartmannian unconscious law governing the universe: 'Plus de mélodie isolée, le tout est une symphonie qui est la vie vivante et variante, comme "les voix de la forêt" des théories de Wagner en concurrence vitale pour la grande voix de la forêt, comme l'Inconscient, loi du monde, est la grande voix mélodique, résultante de la symphonie des consciences de races et d'individus.' Finally, he stated that the central principle behind the Impressionist school had been adopted by writers: 'Ce principe a été, non systématiquement, mais par génie appliqué en poésie et dans le roman chez nous.' No doubt he had Zola and Huysmans in mind for the novel.

As in the case of Baudelaire's essay *Le Peintre de la vie moderne,* much that Laforgue says about the visual arts in his notes on Impressionism can be applied to literature, and it may well be that his study of painting helped him to develop and refine his general aesthetic principles. As Patrick Heron has said [in "Late Picasso," *Modern Painters,* 1, 1988], 'painting is the greatest externaliser of feeling; it renders perceptions actual.' Laforgue's admiration for the Impressionists' fidelity to their perceptions, and for their translation of them into the medium of paint ('something stated out there in the daylight'), no doubt encouraged his similar translation of perceptions into language. When he writes in his art criticism: 'l'objet et le sujet sont donc irrémédiablement mouvants, insaisissables et insaisissants', one feels it is the poet as much as the art critic speaking, and the same could be said of the following highly significant fragment, also from his art criticism: 'Chaque homme est selon son moment dans le temps, son milieu de race et de condition sociale, son moment d'évolution individuelle, un certain clavier sur lequel le monde extérieur joue d'une certaine façon. Mon clavier est perpétuellement changeant et il n'y en a pas un autre identique au mien. Tous les claviers sont légitimes.' Moral criteria are therefore clearly rejected in the evaluation of art. ('La morale n'a rien à voir avec l'art pur, pas plus qu'avec l'amour pur.') The mistake of Taine and his followers was to seek 'par des voies morales, littéraires, spiritualistes, l'idéal plastique'. Like Baudelaire, Laforgue insisted on modernity: 'Il s'agit de n'être pas médiocre. Il faut être un nouveau.' Only in this way could art be interesting, which was of primary importance. He rejected mimetic art; not only was it impossible ('l'œuvre ne sera jamais l'équivalent de la réalité fugitive'), but also it denied the relative nature of 'la vie incessament ondulatoire' and of the human being, that 'créature incomplète et éphémère'. So Laforgue appreciated Impressionism, seeing in it, as Proust was later to do, the 'varied landscape of the hours'. 'There is no better writing on Impressionism that Laforgue's: his excess seems bound up with his powers of description,' writes T. J. Clark [in *The Painting of Modern Life,* 1985], responding to Laforgue's insight, to his receptivity to the new, as well as to his enthusiasm. Of course, what Laforgue brought to his appreciation of Impressionism—taste and sensitivity apart— was the understanding provided by a parallel endeavour, while what he learnt most importantly from Impressionism was to trust the complex and shifting impressions of life that constituted his subjective 'perceptions', and to consider them as natural and valid—indeed, the only legitimate—material for his art.

The 'modern', the ephemeral, the fragmentary, the inconsequential were the realms of the Impressionist painter, as they were also of Laforgue the poet. Impressionist paintings offered glimpses into human existences. Manet, for example, was accused of painting pictures that simply could not be decoded. Had the duel in *Le Déjeuner* taken place or not? What was the relationship of the two women in *Le Balcon*? Was the waitress in *Un bar aux Folies Bergère* a prostitute or a respectable employee—or something in between? Integration was refused both at the narrative and at the pictorial level. A contingent world was presented that was indecipherable, while it was simultaneously recognizable and highly suggestive. The topics selected, echoing the rootlessness and anonymity of life in the modern city, appeared arbitrary, having no known before or after. They were, in Laforgue's words, 'sans nécessité'.

In a significant passage Laforgue explained why these, rather than classical subjects, attracted the modern sensibility:

> Littérairement, avec des goûts d'historien, d'antiquaire, nous pouvons être amoureux sincèrement d'un type de femme du passé, Diane chasseresse, l'Antiope, la Joconde, Marie la Sanguinaire, la Muse de Cortone, la Junon de la villa Ludovici ou Mademoiselle de Lespinasse, Mademoiselle Aïssé, ou Poppée, femme de Néron;—mais telle grisette de Paris, telle jeune fille de salon, telle tête de Burne Jones, telle parisienne de Nittis, etc. . . . —nous fera seule sangloter, nous remuera jusqu'au tréfond de nos entrailles, parce qu'elles sont les sœurs immédiates de notre éphémère, et cela avec son allure d'aujourd'hui, sa coiffure, sa toilette, son regard moderne.

It was a question of the flash of recognition, identification, and, therefore, sympathy. Manet, like Laforgue, captured moments—frequently moments of non-communication between people, as in Laforgue's imagined dialogues, or moments when figures withdrew from the surface world and lost themselves in private meditation. The next minute they would return to the ordinary business of living, but the pause captured by the painting parallels the interior monologues of Laforgue's narrators, and similarly represents the inner level of reverie in an essentially 'modern' and psychological manner.

If the 'modern' interest of Laforgue's subjects in the **Derniers Vers** matched those of the Impressionists, so did his treatment of them, for these paintings were initially criticized for their refusal to take seriously the traditional demands of form, for the haphazard placing of figures in space, and for the unco-ordinated gazes of these figures. In *Le Siècle* of 11 June 1869 Jules Castagnary claimed that: 'Rien d'arbitraire et rien de superflu, telle est la loi de toute composition artistique'; 'comme les personnages dans une comédie, il faut que dans un tableau chaque figure soit à son plan, remplisse son rôle et concoure ainsi à l'expression de l'idée générale.' This was precisely what he did not find in Manet's paintings. In a parallel way, Maurice Grammont, in his *Petit Traité de versification francaise* (1908), refused to entertain the idea that free verse could be considered seriously as poetry, and this also was to be expected. It fulfilled no expectations of regularity, since neither rhyme nor syllabic length could be anticipated: it similarly attacked hallowed traditions. Its harmonies, like those of Impressionist painting, were variable, irrational, and obscure.

The Impressionists' aim of achieving a carefully contrived irregularity was, like Laforgue's, often reached only at a late stage in composition. The most original elements in Manet's paintings have been shown frequently to be late additions; the cat or the choker in the *Olympia* painting, for example, which was originally much closer to Titian's *Venus of Urbino* than it is in its final form, as was *Le Déjeuner sur l'herbe* to the Giorgione-Titian *Concert champêtre*. And, like Laforgue, Manet gloried in originality and 'modernity': 'ils n'ont cessé de me dire que j'étais inégal'; 'ils ne pourraient rien dire de plus élogieux', he insisted. 'Cela a toujours été mon ambition de ne pas demeurer égal à moi-même, de ne pas refaire, le lendemain, ce que j'avais fait la veille, de m'inspirer constamment d'un aspect nouveau, de chercher à faire entendre une note nouvelle.'

If the links between the visual arts and poetry are most clearly seen in the case of Impressionism, Laforgue's poetry nevertheless reflects his many artistic enthusiasms: for Watteau and Gustave Moreau, for the Pre-Raphaelites, and also his more recent German admirations, for Adolf Menzel, like Laforgue—and Huysmans—a 'poet' of factory chimneys, and for Arnold Böcklin, whose bizarre and anachronistic mythological figures influenced not only Laforgue's verse, but also, and more obviously, his *Moralités légendaires*. His aim in art criticism was to convey the sensation of the 'world' created by a particular painter, to write 'une série d'études où, par une accumulation de mots (*sens et sonorités*) choisis, de faits, de sentiments dans la gamme d'un peintre, je *donnerai* la *sensation* du monde créé par ce peintre.' He belongs quite clearly to that group of poets, of which Gautier and Baudelaire are the most prominent, who see their task as analogous to, and intimately connected with, that of the painter, in that both create a world from their imaginative and subjective transformation of a changing reality. It is hardly surprising that Laforgue's poetic aims and methods should match in particular those of the Impressionists, who similarly discovered what might be termed a rhetoric of immediacy.

Laforgue's completion of five short stories, later to be published with one addition as the *Moralités légendaires,* no doubt also had an influence on his poetic manner, since it must have established him in his own eyes as a writer capable of sustained narrative exposition. His earlier excursions into prose had been either brief and unremarkable or had remained in fragmentary form. A connection can be traced between the successful writing of these *Moralités* and Laforgue's move to the longer poem. The *Derniers Vers* are all significantly longer than any of the *Fleurs*. They breathe a greater poetic confidence and expansiveness, which in turn lend the poems greater substance and, ultimately, greater subtlety.

Laforgue's explicit aim in the *Moralités* was to write short stories that were radically different from those of either Maupassant or Villiers de l'Isle-Adam. Given his constant desire for originality, this was hardly surprising. By Pound's time the short story had, in his opinion,

'become vapid, because sixty thousand story writers [had] all set themselves to imitating De Maupassant'. The finely wrought parodic element in the *Moralités,* however, implied 'definitely that certain things in prose were at an end'. Pound draws a parallel between Laforgue's satire in the *Moralités* and Flaubert's in *Bouvard et Pécuchet,* 'if one may compare the flight of a butterfly with the progress of an ox'. What Laforgue also did in the *Moralités,* ironically, was to bring the short story closer to poetry. He speaks of his stories as if they were a volume of poems: 'Je veux . . . faire de mon volume de nouvelles quelque chose de plus qu'un médiocre bouquet de fleurs disparates. Ce sera de l'Art.' Laforgue can scarcely have used the word 'fleur', a recognized metaphor for poem, without intending the parallel to be drawn. It is therefore legitimate to examine the characteristics that the short stories share with Laforgue's verse, and the light they shed on it.

If we consider first their narrative mode and their presentation of character, we see that Laforgue's narrator clearly directs his observations to his reader, keeping himself well in view, so that his sensibility remains the final impression of the stories, as it is of the poems. He establishes an early familiarity with the reader, and the style of his stories, as of his verse, frequently has the intimate character of speech and a deceptive appearance of spontaneity. The narrative voice comments, enumerates, questions, and is both unfailingly courteous and at the same time elusively flippant. The techniques vary, as can be seen from the following examples from **'Persée et Andromède'**, the *moralité* that has been most often linked with the *Derniers Vers,* partly because Leah Lee [Laforgue's wife] seems to be the inspiration behind both works:

Elle a poussé ainsi, vous dis-je . . .

Mais où va-t-elle ainsi, ô puberté, puberté! . . .

Pauvre Andromède, on voit qu'elle ne sait pas où prendre son être pour l'exorciser . . .

Ah! elle s'étirera et gémira jusques à quand?

These brief examples illustrate as many narrative modes: direct intervention, exclamation, interpretative comment, interrogation. Narrative intrusions can frequently, as in Laforgue's verse, consist of a single word. For example, Andromède is described as *'irréprochablement* nue'. But the possibility of reproach has its existence in a mind external to the characters, since there is no indication that Andromède is aware of her nudity, and certainly none that either she or the dragon considered it a matter for self-reproach. It belongs to a world that the narrator and reader share.

The short stories offer, therefore, a self-conscious dialogue with the reader, the interior monologue of two or more voices of the self (here the narrator and the dragon, since the dragon is clearly a persona of the poet, as, of course, are Hamlet and Lohengrin), and the interior monologue of the other main character (here Andromède, and always a girl)—that is, precisely the elements that we have already found in many of the *Fleurs* poems, and those which will be given more expanded poetic treatment in the *Derniers Vers*. As Alain-Fournier remarked [in a 1926 letter to Jacques Rivière]: 'Il [Laforgue] est à la fois l'auteur et le personnage et le lecteur de son livre . . . *Ca n'est plus du roman,* c'est autre chose.'

If the narrator had already been developed with subtlety and complexity in the *Fleurs,* the 'jeune fille' had been given more summary treatment. The various heroines of the *Moralités* are much more detailed and sympathetic creations, and it is arguable that the 'fiancée' of the *Derniers Vers,* with her strong emotional appeal, owes a great deal to these carefully worked portrayals of femininity. Andromède has been linked by all critics with Leah Lee, and the change in Laforgue's writing doubtless reflects his love. We have a heroine intellligent enough to see through the fake hero, Persée, and to bring about her own salvation by her love for the dragon, so that the story of Perseus and Andromeda becomes that of Beauty and Beast, and offers us Laforgue's only happy ending. Andromède, bored, restless, lonely on her island with only the dragon for company, awaiting a transformation in her destiny that is slow in coming, is the epitome of the feminine situation, as well as being the representation of the 'âme du jour'. Not only is she convincingly human; she is portrayed with a comprehension and a tenderness that are an elaboration on anything we have seen in the *Fleurs,* and which remind us of these qualities in the *Derniers Vers,* in a poem such as '**Dimanches IV**', for example.

The *Moralités* consist of two contrasting elements, as must any retelling of myth: a modern and 'realistic' element, and a legendary and imaginary element. Laforgue called the stories 'de vieux canevas brodés d'âmes à la mode'. The later poems offer a parallel contrast between the immediate and modern—conveyed by the main narrative of the poem—and the literary and mythical—conveyed by metaphor and intertextuality. The roles may be reversed, but the essential components are the same, and it is therefore not surprising that some of the techniques of the *Moralités* should find themselves reflected in the *Derniers Vers*. There are many analogies between the 'poetic' passages in the *Moralités* and aspects of the writing of the *Derniers Vers*.

If we continue to take as our main examples '**Persée et Andromède**' and '**L'Hiver qui vient**', we see that, like the poem, the short story evokes an atmosphere from the start. A poetic mood is immediately set by

the imprecise but suggestive details given of the island where Andromède and the dragon live: 'O Patrie monotone et imméritée! . . . L'île seule, en jaunes grises dunes; sous des ciels migrateurs; et puis partout la mer bornant la vue, les cris et l'espérance et la mélancolie.' The interaction between physical and emotional, concrete and abstract, is present in the first sentences of the story. Images support the poetic mood, and frequently have both the delicate precision and the humorous unexpectedness of those in Laforgue's verse; for example, the following description of a brief rainbow: 'et c'est sur le dos des vagues la caresse d'un arc-en-ciel comme une riche dorade qui a monté un instant et aussitôt replonge, stupidement méfiante'. The technical devices of poetry abound: the rhetorical question, the theatrical aside, apostrophe, parenthesis, enumeration, and that particular use of repetition that consists of the recapitulation of a word as a basis for its further development, which Laforgue used so frequently in the *Moralités* that his first publishers, perhaps considering the repetition an oversight, frequently cut it out: 'Andromède reste là . . . hébétée devant *l'horizon, l'horizon* magique dont elle n'a pas voulu . . .' 'Mais sa [the sea's] plainte ne couvre pas *les petits gémissements, les petits gémissements* aigus et rauques d'Andromède, qui . . . scrute sans y penser le mécanisme *des flots, des flots* naissant et mourant à perte de vue.'

This technique appears in more complex guises in '**L'Hiver qui vient**': the similarity can be seen, however, in two simple examples:

> Sur une litière *de jaunes genêts*
> *De jaunes genêts* d'automne.
> Les sous-bois ne sont plus qu'un fumier de
>   *feuilles* mortes;
> *Feuilles,* folioles, qu'un bon vent vous
>   emporte . . .

The fact that, as Laforgue wrote the more poetic passages in '**Persée et Andromède**', he was moving towards the rhythms and sonorities that he would employ in his free verse is most clear if we transpose two short passages into free verse:

> sa chère falaise où la nuit descend,
> la nuit sérieuse,
> oh! sérieuse pour la vie!
> si sérieuse et insaisissable . . .
>
> Où va-t-elle ainsi, ô puberté, puberté!
> par le vent et les dunes,
> avec ces abois de blessée?

In the second example we can observe even the deceptively casual 'rhyming' of free verse. In both we sense the rhythmical phrasing that is central to this form. 'There are highly wrought passages of prose in the

Moralités which, given a nudge . . . break into *vers libre,'* writes David Arkell, and by that, ironically, one means that they naturally tend to divide into the balanced binary and ternary subdivisions of regular verse, so that the prose reader experiences the sensation of inhabiting a poetic world. In his first *moralité* Laforgue had found the writing of prose a painful process: 'Qu'il est plus facile de tailler des strophes que d'établir de la prose!', he confessed to Charles Henry. But it was a craft he learned as he composed his increasingly 'poetic' stories. In **'L'Hiver qui vient'** he moved into free verse with a simultaneous sense of release from the tyrannies of rhyme and the syllabic count, and with the ease and assurance gained in part from the careful shaping of prose sentences into rhythmically balanced units.

THE CREATION OF THE FIRST FREE-VERSE POEM

This was, then, in brief outline, the climate—both external and personal—in which Laforgue moved towards a new conception of what poetry might be. For we cannot doubt that this was a dramatic turning-point in the history of French poetry, which, after the introduction of free verse, could never be remotely the same again. If a later poet, such as Valéry, selected a regular metre for his poem, this now implied a rejection of free verse. If a poet chose to write in free verse, he could do so using a range of subtle alliances with regular metre that his reader was intended to recognize. A free-verse poet who included an alexandrine couplet or an octosyllabic quatrain in his poem now meant something by this inclusion, over and above what was conveyed by the metre itself. Insertions in regular metre took on the status of signs; they had become quotations from another world, and had thus acquired overtones of traditionalism, archaism, or parody. And when a free-verse poet devised novel rhythmical variations or harmonies, these also were enjoyed as deviations from a known norm. No such choices were innocent, and every choice was an implicit statement of intent. Regular metre, with its long and intricate history, stood firmly behind free verse, and it would be very far from the truth to see free verse merely in terms of liberation.

In the early twentieth century young avant-garde poets such as Apollinaire and Max Jacob criticized Laforgue. He was thought not to have been bold enough. Among other things, he was accused of having gone only some of the way towards the liberation of verse: he used so many rhymes, so many octosyllables and alexandrines. The reverse of this accusation would have been more accurate. Laforgue recognized from the start, like Éluard later, that free verse existed in relation to regular verse, that this was unavoidable, and that it was a possible source of richness.

If the move to free verse, especially among younger poets, became something of a stampede, the revolution that had taken place was not quickly understood. Mallarmé, as we have seen, so accurate in his description of what free verse actually was, nevertheless termed it 'une heureuse trouvaille', a phrase that might be applied to something as particularized as the 'impair'. (Gérard Genette, with the advantage of hindsight, more correctly calls it 'une mutation . . . profonde'.) Mallarmé's compliment to Laforgue, that he 'nous initia au charme certain du vers faux', also gives the innovation less than its due, while limiting it severely, and it is clear that he really considered traditional verse and prose poetry—the forms he himself used, with the remarkable exception of 'Un coup de dés . . .'—to be the main alternative choices facing the poet. He, of course, considered the 'liberated' alexandrine to be a major innovation, writing of 'L'Après-midi d'un faune': 'J'y essayais, en effet, de mettre, à côté de l'alexandrin dans toute sa tenue, une sorte de jeu courant pianoté autour, comme qui dirait d'un accompagnement musical fait par le poète lui-même et ne permettant au vers officiel de sortir que dans les grandes occasions.' Laforgue thought quite differently. He chose free verse as opposed to regular metre, writing to Kahn emphatically: 'Je ne ferai jamais plus de vers qu'ainsi', and 'j'aurai un volume ainsi en arrivant à Paris. Je ne fais que ça.' And there is no evidence that he wrote again in any other form. Debauve makes the interesting, but in my view not entirely convincing, suggestion that he might have relented to some extent with regard to his poems in *vers libéré* had he lived longer. Clearly, the twelve poems in free verse were too few to make up a volume. It is possible, he suggests, that, after his marriage, when he was already seriously ill, he considered making more use of the *Fleurs,* and, of course, had he added some poems in *vers libéré* to the *Derniers Vers,* he would have ended up with a hybrid volume like Kahn's *Les Palais nomades,* published in 1887. We are not in a position to judge with certainty, since Laforgue's literary correspondence ceased entirely once he was in Paris. My view is that, being more wholeheartedly committed to free verse at this point than Kahn was, he would not have departed from this form. He might have expanded and reshaped poems from the *Fleurs* (as in III, IV, V, VII, VIII, IX, and X), or written new ones (as in XI and XII).

The evolution of his first free-verse poem, **'L'Hiver qui vient',** can be traced with confidence, since three significantly different versions of it survive. They are the early text published by Kahn in *La Vogue* in September 1886, a later undated and undatable manuscript on which some changes have been made in a neat and careful hand, and the text published by Édouard Dujardin after Laforgue's death, containing his latest alterations. The major changes are between the *La Vogue* text and the manuscript, and they are mainly augmentative in character. The poem becomes considerably enriched by two kinds of addition. The first is unexpected, because it consists of the details of the external world, and provides the concrete frame, as it were, of the poem. But if one remembers that the poem is essentially the re-creation of a stream of consciousness, it is perhaps not so surprising that what apparently causes it, but is in reality the background to it, should be developed in its later versions. The 'cheminées d'usines' (which certainly *appear* intrinsic to the poem), the 'journaux', the 'statistiques sanitaires', the 'spectacles agricoles', and even the pianos are not in the *La Vogue* text, and appear in the poem only in the manuscript version. The inclusion of such banal elements alters (as Barbara Johnson argues of Baudelaire's famous 'batterie de cuisine') not so much our view of the objects themselves, as our perception of the nature of the 'poetic'.

The other kind of addition, a more predictable one, links the poem with art and myth, and so widens its horizons. The monologue acquires richness and depth by these allusions, typically brief, which invite a smile while they offer a spark of illumination. So the 'ornières' (with their Rimbaldian echoes) rise 'en don quichottesques rails', evoking momentarily a delightful world of naïve idealisms, or the picnic baskets conjure up the delicate and elegant idylls painted by Watteau ('Tous les paniers Watteau sous les marronniers'), or the mention of Red Riding Hood transports us to a world of fable. All these references enter the poem only in the manuscript text. (The only reference of this kind present in the *La Vogue* text is a more conventionally classical one, to the river Pactolus, which, like the sun, turns everything to gold.) They help to convey the multilayered quality of the mind, for, as outer landscapes inform the inner 'état d'âme', so the inner landscape surfaces in the images offered by art. They are all more deceiving than they appear. Don Quixote is a tragic as well as a delightfully comic figure; Watteau's idylls do not celebrate anything more elevated than sensual pleasure; and Red Riding Hood was eaten by the wolf. The poem gains complexity by their inclusion, becoming wittier and more poignant simultaneously.

Laforgue also made diminutive changes, chiefly removing anaphora of too simple a kind. The most interesting of these changes is the play with the poem's ending. In the first line of the *La Vogue* text quoted below he used irony to undercut his wish to portray the season of death:

> Nul n'en rendra raison,
> Tous les ans, tous les ans,
> J'essaierai en chœur d'en chanter la note.

In the manuscript version he moved this irony to the end of the poem.

> Tous les ans, tous les ans,
> J'essaierai en chœur d'en donner la note,

> Pour mes compatriotes,
> Mais qu'on ne me demande pas la raison! . . .

But the last two lines are crossed out, and they are not present in the final text. He was clearly still tempted at this late stage to adopt such self-mocking rhetoric—an echo of his former self, recalling the manuscript dedication of the first poem of the **Fleurs** 'aux français de demain'. The removal of these lines allows the poem to end more affirmatively, with the poet's intention to evoke every autumn the season that he had always found particularly compelling, and which he described in **'Persée et Andromède'** as 'esthétique par excellence'.

Of course, we also find substitutive changes, and these reflect a movement towards greater refinement of expression. The following two examples show subtly heightened emotion. In the first, the inclusion of 'loin' in the manuscript version of the description of the soldiers ('Ou les sommiers des ambulances / Pour les soldats *loin* de la France') adds a sense of exile to the existing awareness of their wounds. In the second example intentionality is replaced by anxious enquiry, as 'Vous serez mes seules amours' becomes, after the manuscript stage, 'Serez-vous pas mes seules amours?' Cliché and sentimentality are removed: thus 'perles d'eau' become 'gouttes d'eau', and the gardens that were first 'pauvres' (*La Vogue*), then 'souffreteux' (manuscript), settle for the understated 'modestes'.

More interesting, from the angle of free verse, is the division of the long Whitmanesque line, retained at the manuscript stage, but divided later. Two examples will illustrate the point (in each case, the manuscript version precedes the final version):

> Sur une litière de jaunes genêts d'automne

> Sur une litière de jaunes genêts
> De jaunes genêts d'automne.

> Oh! dans les bruines, toutes mes cheminées
>   d'usines . . .

> Oh! dans les bruines, toutes mes cheminées! . . .
> D'usines . . .

The first introduces musicality; the second gives 'usines' prominence. The bathos of the unexpectedly short line in this second example is a feature of Laforgue's free verse. The most striking incidence of it in this poem is the addition of the words 'Des spectacles agricoles' to the splendidly bombastic line that precedes it:

> Soleils plénipotentiaires des travaux en blonds
>   Pactoles
> Des spectacles agricoles.

Laforgue chiefly divides lines, however, for more obviously lyrical effects. The poems after **'L'Hiver qui vient'** were, on average, composed of shorter lines of more even lengths, as Laforgue gave increasing importance to the creation of rhythm.

The textual changes to **'L'Hiver qui vient'** frequently provide new rhymes, internal rhymes and assonances. When Laforgue introduces the delightful Don Quixote allusion, he is at the same time creating a 'rime alternée' with 'bercails'. The Watteau reference results in a 'rime plate' with the preceding line. When he introduces the image of the ocean of roofs—'Devant l'océan de toitures des faubourgs'—he is creating a rhyme for 'Serez-vous pas mes seules amours?' When he changes:

> Que l'autan, que l'autan
> Effiloche les savates du temps

to the witty:

> Que l'autan, que l'autan
> Effiloche les savates que le temps se tricote!

he is not only creating a rhyme for 'la planète falote'; he is also, by means of alliteration and assonance, heightening the sound patterning of the two lines. And this is generally the case. Laforgue's free verse would seem to illustrate Whitman's belief [articulated in the Preface to *Leaves of Grass*] that 'free growth' progresses inevitably to form: 'The rhyme and uniformity of perfect poems show the free growth of metrical laws, and bud from them as unerringly and loosely as lilacs and roses on a bush, and take shapes as compact as the shapes of chestnuts and oranges, and melons and pears, and shed the perfume impalpable to form.'

As one examines this increasingly delicate phonetic and rhythmical progression, it is difficult to accept Kahn's analysis [in "Préface sur le vers libre"] of Laforgue's reasons for moving to free verse as the whole truth: 'Dans un affranchissement du vers, je cherchais une musique plus complexe, et Laforgue s'inquiétait d'un mode de donner la sensation même, la vérité plus stricte, plus lacée, sans chevilles aucunes, avec le plus d'acuité possible et le plus d'accent personnel, comme parlé.' This is a very good description of Laforgue's psychological quest, which is not in doubt, and Kahn defines accurately the two main areas of innovation—the psychological and the musical— but what, one may ask, can the psychological be without the musical, or the musical without the psychological? Kahn is talking about emphases, but, even so, Laforgue's many references to rhythm and musicality in his letters to him make this a puzzling statement. No doubt, in the early 1880s Kahn did awaken or develop Laforgue's interest in the incantatory quality of poetry, and in the spring of 1882 Laforgue wrote to Charles

Henry: 'je deviens (comme forme) kahnesque et mallarméen'. In the same letter, however, he made the centrally important, and by now thoroughly familiar, statement that illustrates beyond all doubt his interest in the musicality of verse, and in which we find musicality and psychology combined, as they surely must always be: 'Je songe à une poésie qui serait de la psychologie dans une forme de rêve, avec des fleurs, du vent, des senteurs. D'inextricables symphonies avec une phrase (un sujet) mélodique, dont le dessin reparaît de temps en temps.' Reflecting Laforgue's poetic aspirations at a time when he still wrote in regular metre, this description seems particularly applicable to free verse as he developed it.

FURTHER READING

Arkell, David. *Looking for Laforgue: An Informal Biography*. Manchester: Carcanet Press, 1979, 248 p.

> A major biography of Laforgue in English. Imparts biographical detail in casual tone and reprints many letters and other documents concerning Laforgue's life.

Collie, Michael. "An Evaluation." In *Jules Laforgue*, pp. 90-112. London: Athlone Press, 1977.

> Attempts to define Laforgue's worldview, emphasizing in particular the poet's notions of the body, desire, and women.

Cowley, Malcolm. "Laforgue in America: A Testimony." In his *And I Worked at the Writer's Trade: Chapters of Literary History, 1918-1978*, pp. 69-81. New York: Viking Press, 1978.

> Explores, largely through personal memory, Laforgue's influence on early twentieth-century American writers.

Eliot, T. S. "The Nineteenth Century: Summary and Comparison" and "Laforgue and Corbière in Our Time." In his *The Varieties of Metaphysical Poetry*, pp. 207-28 and 281-98. New York: Harcourt Brace and Co., 1993.

> Originally delivered as lectures in 1926 and 1933, the essays define Laforgue as a modern receptacle of seventeenth-century metaphysical poetry, placing him between that tradition and Eliot's own age.

Erkkila, Betsy. "Walt Whitman and Jules Laforgue." *Walt Whitman Review* 24, No. 1 (March 1978): 71-77.

> Argues that Whitman was a primary influence on Laforgue, especially regarding his experiments with free verse.

Hannoosh, Michele. "The Early Laforgue: *Tessa*." *French Forum* 8, No. 1 (January 1983): 20-32.

> Offers a rare discussion of Laforgue's unpublished play, *Tessa*, which he wrote almost a year before his

first poem. Hannoosh demonstrates connections between *Tessa* and Laforgue's later work.

————. "Metaphysicality and Belief: Eliot on Laforgue." *Comparative Literature* 39, No. 4 (Fall 1987): 340-51.

Examines Laforgue's influence on Eliot beyond poetic similarities, with specific attention to the lectures, collected in *The Varieties of Metaphysical Poetry*, in which Eliot offers his evaluation of Laforgue's metaphysical qualities.

————. *Parody and Decadence: Laforgue's "Moralités légendaires."* Columbus, OH: Ohio State University Press, 1989, 241 p.

Studies Laforgue's collection of short stories in-depth, considering them in the context of late-nineteenth-century French aesthetics.

————. "The Poet as Art Critic: Laforgue's Aesthetic Theory." *Modern Language Review* 79, No. 3 (July 1984): 553-69.

Gathers information from disparate sources—Laforgue's notebooks, published and unpublished articles—in order to suggest Laforgue's guiding aesthetic principles and to demonstrate his aptitude as a critic of the visual arts.

Holmes, Anne. "Jules Laforgue's 1883 'Agenda': Love and Art." *French Studies* XLVII, No. 4 (October 1993): 422-34.

Reconstructs Laforgue's theories of aesthetics and desire from passages in his notes for the year 1883.

Newman, Francis. An introduction to *Six Moral Tales from Jules Laforgue*, by Jules Laforgue, edited and translated by Francis Newman, pp. 9-26. New York: Horace Liveright, 1928.

A general discussion of *Moral Tales* that includes a brief overview of Laforgue's life.

Peyre, Henri. "Jules Laforgue: 1860-1887." In *The Poem Itself*, edited by Stanley Burnshaw, pp. 60-3. New York: Holt, Rinehart and Winston, 1960.

Brief, focused comments on four of Laforgue's major poems. Peyre provides the original French text, his English translation, and a short textual analysis of each poem.

Ramsey, Warren, ed. *Jules Laforgue: Essays on a Poet's Life and Work.* Carbondale, IL: Southern Illinois University Press; London, Amsterdam: Feffer & Simons, 1969, 194 p.

A collection of essays by such critics as Ramsey, Henri Peyre, Peter Brooks, and William Jay Smith. Includes comparisons of Laforgue's work with that of other writers, as well as discussions of Laforgue's style, symbolism, and dramatic presentation.

Scofield, Martin. "'Your Only Jig-Maker': Jules Laforgue." In his *The Ghosts of Hamlet*, pp. 34-44. Cambridge: Cambridge University Press, 1980.

Investigates Laforgue's literary preoccupation with Hamlet.

Smith, William Jay. An Introduction to *Moral Tales* by Jules Laforgue, translated by William Jay Smith, pp. xi-xxvi. New York: New Directions Books, 1985.

Biographical, thematic, and cultural overview of *Moral Tales*.

Sonnenfeld, Albert. "Hamlet and the German Jules Laforgue." *Yale French Studies* No. 33 (December 1964): 92-100.

With Helen Phelps Bailey and Scofield (see above), one of the primary studies of Laforgue's use of the Hamlet figure throughout his work.

Unger, Leonard. "Laforgue, Conrad, and T. S. Eliot." In his *The Man in the Name: Essays on the Experience of Poetry*, pp. 190-242. Minneapolis: University of Minnesota Press, 1956.

Cites examples of Laforgue's influence on the poetry of T. S. Eliot.

Additional coverage of Laforgue's life and career is contained in the following sources published by Gale Research: *Nineteenth-Century Literature Criticism,* **Vol. 5; and** *Short Story Criticism,* **Vol. 20.**

Elias Lönnrot

1802-1884

Finnish folklorist, linguist, and physician.

INTRODUCTION

Best known for his compilation of traditional Finnish poetry in the epic *Kalevala,* Lönnrot published numerous other collections of traditional Finnish poetry, proverbs, riddles, and incantations, as well as original works on medicine and linguistics. As a folklorist and linguist, he is credited with promoting the recognition of Finnish as a national language and with laying the groundwork for the development of a Finnish national literature.

Biographical Information

Fourth of seven children of a tailor and a peasant's daughter, Elias Lönnrot was born in Sammatti, Finland (then part of Sweden). Despite his family's poverty he managed to attend high school and the University of Turku, working first as a pharmacist's assistant, then as a tutor, to support himself during his studies. He became interested in folklore while studying at the University of Turku under the noted philologist and folklorist Reinhold von Becker. He was also inspired by the ideas of German philosopher and critic Johann Gottfried von Herder (1744-1803), one of the first scholars to recognize the importance of folklore to world literature, and Finnish historian Henrik Gabriel Porthan (1739-1804), who had begun collecting Finnish folklore in 1766. After receiving his medical degree in 1832, Lönnrot was assigned as a circuit physician. While travelling around the Finnish countryside and serving the local inhabitants, he also expanded his knowledge of Finnish folklore and folk practices. He eventually took several leaves of absence from his medical practice to collect traditional poetry and proverbs and to work on various other literary projects, including the preparation of a Finnish dictionary. In the 1830s and 1840s, Lönnrot undertook numerous journeys to various parts of Finland, Estonia, Ingria, and eastern Karelia (the area of the Russo-Finnish border from the Gulf of Finland to the Arctic Circle). Dressed as a common laborer, he sought out folksingers and transcribed their songs, elements of which are believed to date back as far as 500 B.C. He would later arrange them, noting, "I followed what I observed the best singers paid attention to in matters of arrangement, and . . . when no help was forthcoming from that quarter, I sought basis for arrangement in the songs

themselves." In the late 1840s, Lönnrot became increasingly interested in linguistics; from 1853 to 1862, he taught Finnish language and literature at the University of Helsinki. He died in Sammatti in 1884.

Major Works

Believing he was recreating a coherent epic poem from the surviving fragments of traditional poetry he and others had recorded, Lönnrot presented his first attempt at epic reconstruction in 1835. This was the *Kalevala taikka Vanhoja Karjalan Runoja Suomen kansan muinoisista ajoista* ("The Kalevala, or Old Karelian Songs from the Ancient Times of the Finnish People"), which consists of thirty-two "runes," or songs. This 12,978-line work was superseded in 1849 by the enlarged second edition, the *New Kalevala,* whose 22,795 lines are divided into fifty runes. From that time, the 1835 edition has been known as the *Old Kalevala.* When modern critics cite the *Kalevala,* they are referring to the *New Kalevala.* The *Kalevala* consists of unrhymed, non-strophic trochaic tetrameter lines, now referred to as the *Kalevala* meter. Most familiar to English readers from Longfellow's *Hiawatha,* where at times it sounds monotonous and forced, the *Kalevala* meter is far more melodious in the original Finnish. Critics distinguish in the *Kalevala* four intertwined story cycles, all of which concern the interactions of the heroes of Kalevala ("land of heroes") with the people of Pohjola ("north land"). Drawing on poetry gathered by himself and others, Lönnrot published several other folklore collections besides the *Kalevala: Kantele* (1829-31; "The Harp"), the *Kanteletar* (1840; "The Spirit of the Harp"), the *Sananlaskut* (1842; "Proverbs"), the *Arvoitukset* (1844; "Riddles"), and *Suomen kansan muinaisia loitsorunoja* (1880; "Old Metrical Charms of the Finnish People"). His notes also became the basis for the thirty-three volume *Suomen kansan vanhat runot* (1908-48; "Ancient Poems of the Finnish People").

Critical Reception

Most critical evaluations of Lönnrot's work focus on the *Kalevala.* Translations of the *Old Kalevala* into Swedish in 1841 and into French in 1845 made the Finnish tales known to a wide readership and garnered immediate acclaim. The first English translation appeared in 1888. Most early criticism focused on the nature of the work and the circumstances of its composition. Lönnrot's contemporaries believed that he had restored a long-lost epic to its original form, although later research revealed that supposition to be incorrect. Several nineteenth-century experts, including the noted German scholars Max Müller and Jacob Grimm, hailed the *Kalevala* as a complete national epic on the level of the *Iliad* or the *Nibelungenlied.* In the late nineteenth century, scholars began to realize that Lönnrot had intervened substantially in the original material he had collected, piecing together lines from numerous variants of individual songs, standardizing the language, changing character names to fit his concept of the story line, and creating prefatory, final, and linking verses (totalling less than five per cent of the overall poem). As a result, modern commentators tend to treat the *Kalevala* as a creative work in its own right and to agree with Lönnrot's own view of himself as belonging to a long line of rune-singers. Opinions of the meaning of the work also vary: Lönnrot himself saw the *Kalevala* as primarily historical, illustrating early conflicts between Finns and Lapps, while modern critics prefer a symbolic or mythological interpretation. Another focus of recent critical interest has been the role of the *Kalevala* in the development of Finnish national identity in the late nineteenth through the early twentieth centuries. Although very little commentary exists in English on Lönnrot's other works, a recent English translation of the *Kanteletar,* a collection of folksongs composed and sung by women, promises to attract critical attention, particularly by virtue of its

sometimes humorous, sometimes bitter perspectives on the lives and status of women in traditional Finnish society.

PRINCIPAL WORKS

Kantele [editor] (poetry) 1829-31
Kalevala taikka Vanhoja Karjalan Runoja Suomen kansan muinoisista ajoista [editor] (poetry) 1835, enlarged edition, 1849
Kanteletar [editor] (poetry) 1840
Sananlaskut [editor] (proverbs) 1842
Arvoitukset [editor] (riddles) 1844
Finsk-Svenski Lexikon ("Finnish-Swedish Dictionary") 2 vols. (dictionary) 1874-80
Suomen kansan muinaisia loitsorunoja [editor] (poetry) 1880
The Kalevala [editor] 2 vols. (translated by John Martin Crawford) (poetry) 1888
Kalevala, The Land of Heroes [editor] (translated by W. F. Kirby) (poetry) 1907
Suomen kansan vanhat runot [compiler] 33 vols. (poetry) 1908-48
The Kalevala, or Poems of the Kalevala District [editor] (translated by Francis Peabody Magoun, Jr.) (poetry) 1963
The Kalevala: An Epic Poem after Oral Tradition [editor] (translated by Keith Bosley) (poetry) 1989
The Kanteletar: Lyrics and Ballads after Oral Tradition [editor] (selected and translated by Keith Bosley) (poetry) 1992

* Assembled from his notes.

CRITICISM

Elias Lönnrot (essay date 1835)

SOURCE: "Preface to the 'Old Kalevala'," in *The Kalevala; or, Poems of the Kaleva District,* edited by Elias Lönnrot, translated by Francis Peabody Magoun, Jr., Cambridge, Mass.: Harvard University Press, 1963, pp. 365-74.

[In the following excerpt from his preface to the first edition of the Kalevala, *later known as the* Old Kalevala, *Lönnrot discusses the nature of the poems and the way in which he compiled and organized them.]*

I have tried to put these songs into some sort of order, a task of which I should give some account. Since to my knowledge no one has previously tried to order them or so much as mentioned doing so, I will first report on how I came upon this idea. Already while reading the songs previously collected, particularly those collected by Ganander, I at least wondered whether one might not possibly find songs about Väinämöinen, Ilmarinen, and Lemminkäinen and other memorable forebears of ours until from these had been got longer accounts, too, just as we see that the Greeks [in the Homeric poems] and the Icelanders [in the *Poetic* or *Elder Edda*] and others got songs of their forebears. This idea was just getting a firm place in my mind when in 1826 with the help of Reinhold von Beckner, associate professor of history at Turku (Swedish Abo), I got to writing a B.A. thesis on Väinämöinen, and while preparing it I saw that there was no lack of tales about him. I also wondered why Ganander had not already done this, but I soon came to understand that he did not have the songs necessary for the task. He published the best passages in the songs he collected in his *Mythologia Fennica* (Turku, 1798), but he had scarcely any of these in very ample form. An early death had taken off Zachris Topelius, Sr.; otherwise he would in the course of time have been able to devote himself to this work.

If I knew now that the order in which these songs have been planned here would be pleasing to others, I would stop and say no more about it, but the matter is such that what one person thinks suitable another views as inappropriate. In my opinion the songs run along fairly well in the order in which they are arranged, but they might perhaps go better in some other. While organizing them I paid attention to two things: first, I followed what I observed the best singers paid attention to in matters of arrangement; and second, when no help was forthcoming from that quarter, I sought a basis for arrangement in the songs themselves and arranged them accordingly.

The reader may ask whether our ancestors sang these songs in any sequence or sang them singly. It seems to me that these songs, as it happens, turn up singly. The various songs about Väinämöinen, Ilmarinen, and Lemminkäinen must be the compositions not of one person but of several. One singer memorized one thing, another another, what each individual had observed or heard. But nowadays I scarcely find a single song which seems to have been preserved down to our time in just its original words. Everybody will see how easily poetic composition eludes many of the peasants if he undertakes to sing completely about any familiar subject whatever, and discovers of course that the very best memory cannot preserve word for word what is heard in long songs sung by another. But he will more easily remember the subject matter, and from passage to passage, if remembering most of them he relates it in verse to someone else, forgetting some passages, improving others. One can gradually distort the basic plot of a song from its original character so that it is told quite differently. This has already happened partly

at least in the case of proper names. What formerly may have been told of memorable men and women with their right names might, as Christianity spread in the country [from ca. A.D. 1150], be changed so that in place of the men one often put Jesus Christ, St. Peter, Herod, Judas, and others, in place of the women the Virgin Mother Mary.

That the subjects sung about in the songs were not all without some foundation in fact anybody will easily understand, but what the real truth is—what things may be described in some other way in a song, what ones may be completely invented—is now quite difficult to distinguish. Certain matters, even when one hears especially odd things or somewhat incredible ones, should on careful investigation somehow clear up. None of us should view Väinämöinen's and Ilmarinen's troubles as deriving from the disappearance of the sun and the moon, and how would the dame of North Farm (*Pohja*) have hidden them in the hill? But when one remembers what is said of our forefathers' coming here, that they got here to the far north from very southerly lands, and what we know about the disappearance of the sun in winter in high latitudes, we will realize that had they gone clear up north, this phenomenon could, as something strange to them, even arouse a great fear that the sun had gone forever. If also they had wars with the Lapps who formerly lived in Finnish territory, Lapps from whom there was reason to fear everything bad and who were regarded as superior wizards, then the mistress of North Farm soon got the blame for it. And what in the first instance could come to be told about the disappearance of the sun could later also get to be told of the moon and stars. . . .

In these poems one meets the Finnish language and Finnish poetics in perhaps a purer form than in any other book. Many words and phrases appear here and there in their original form or in the same form as one hears them in the mouth of the peasantry. Persons learned in other languages, even though they of course command Finnish, often find it hard not to change the basic nature of the language to conform with other languages. For the peasant population, however, which understands nothing but its mother tongue, this danger is nonexistent . . .

Concerning Finnish songs it has probably already been stated that they are certainly of two different kinds: narrative songs and magic songs. It may also have been mentioned that the charms were from the beginning nothing but narrative songs which later, according to the material, began to be changed into something else. The poems in the present book are mostly narrative. What I judged to be the main version among these is not on that account more valuable for the investigation of ancient matters than what one hears told some other way. Both have been got from the same places and are equally old. A few individual songs I got from so many singers and in so many different forms that it is certainly an open question which is the best variant. In other songs the difficulty for me was to get them in a very full form from one singer or another. There are both those persons who hold our old songs indeed in great esteem and those who esteem them very little. I would not want the songs to be disparaged nor to be biasedly regarded on the other hand as very great. These are not by any means on a par with those of the Greeks and Romans, but it is quite all right if they at least show that our forebears were not unenlightened in their intellectual efforts—and the songs at least show that. . . .

Lauri Honko (essay date 1960)

SOURCE: "The *Kalevala* and Finnish Culture," in *The Finns in North America: A Social Symposium,* edited by Ralph J. Jalkanen, Michigan State University Press, 1969, pp. 46-52.

[*In the following excerpt, originally published in 1960, Honko discusses the cultural milieu in which the* Kalevala *was compiled and reviews the course of its subsequent study.*]

Few works have had so pervasive an effect upon a nation's life as the epic **Kalevala**. Its influence upon Finnish music, art, and poetry is recent enough to be remembered by everyone; its unique place in Finnish literature is recognized by all.

Two characteristics of the age, romanticism and the awakening of the Finnish national consciousness, prepared the way for an enthusiastic reception of the **Kalevala**. Admiration for the undefiled "folk," a basic trait of romanticism, led to attempts to preserve folk literature. The publication of folk poetry and literature by Thomas Percy in England and Johann Gottfried von Herder in Germany, and the songs of Ossian, composed in Scotland by James Macpherson, are representative of such attempts. In time, these products of the late eighteenth century became known in Finland among the "pre-romantics," a group which included Henrik Gabriel Porthan, a professor of rhetoric; Frans Mikael Franzen, a poet; and Kristfrid Ganander, a pastor at Rantsila. However, these foreign works did not initiate Finnish romanticism; rather they stimulated a movement which had already begun. For example, Porthan was uninfluenced by Herderian romanticism when he began his broad researches into the poetry of the people with his Depoesi fennica 1766-1778. If anything, Porthan should be regarded as a predecessor rather than an imitator. When Finland was joined to Russia, the inheritors of the Porthan tradition, the so-called romanticists of Turku, strove to produce an awakening of the national consciousness and

collected materials necessary to the study of the Finnish language and poetry.

The ties with the Swedish romanticists were particularly strong at this time. One of the many Finnophiles studying in Sweden was K. A. Gottlund. While a university student at Upsala in 1817, Gottlund wrote: "If we wished to gather together the ancient folksongs and compile and order them into a systematic whole; whatever may become of them, an epic drama or what have you, it may bring to life a new *Homer, Ossiad,* or *Nibelungenlied;* and in its singular creative brilliance and glory, awakened to its sense of independence, the Finnish nation would receive both the admiration of its contemporaries as well as that of the generations to come." But considerable time elapsed before his dream became a reality.

After the University of Turku was destroyed by fire, it was moved to Helsinki, where the Saturday Society was soon organized. A cultural and political discussion group, the Society had about thirty members, the majority of whom achieved a significant place in science, art, or politics. In 1831, some of the Society's members organized the Finnish Literature Society, an original and effective supporter of Elias Lönnrot's efforts to collect and publish folk poems and songs.

In 1834, Lönnrot wrote to a friend:

> As I compared these (the results of my collections on my fourth journey) to what I had seen before, I was seized by a desire to organize them into a single whole in order to make of the Finnish legends of the gods something similar to that of the *Edda*, the saga of the Icelanders. So I threw myself into the labors before me immediately and continued working for a number of weeks, actually months, at least until Christmas, when I had quite a volume of poems about Väinämöinen in exactly the order in which I desired them. I gave attention especially to the time sequences of the feats accomplished by the heroes of the poems.

Thus, the concept of a Finnish epic was born, with prototypes from the ancient Scandinavian epics uppermost in Lönnrot's mind. However, recognizing the magnitude and importance of the task, he doubted his ability to carry out such a work:

> I am not certain whether the task or compilation or concatenation of the sagas of the gods should be accomplished by a single individual, or preferably by a number of persons working together, since our posterity will probably place this compilation on a par with the *Edda* by the Gothenborgains or at least those of Hesiod, if not Homer, by the Greeks and Romans.

Lönnrot's fifth trip, on which he discovered the most knowledgeable of the singers of ancient runes, Arhippa

Perttunen, was so fruitful that it was February 28, 1835, before Lönnrot was able to write the preface to his work, *The Kalevala, or Old Karelian Songs from the Ancient Times of the Finnish People* (Kalevala Taikka Wanhoja Karjalan Runoja Suomen Kansan muinaisista Aijoista).

At the 1835 annual meeting of the Finnish Literature Society, J. G. Linsén announced:

> In collecting a vast number of runes in the Archangel district, Lönnrot, in fitting them together into a whole, has made the remarkable discovery that there exists, in fact, a great and complete mythological national epic which has now been compiled by its collector into thirty-two runes in which the principal songs tell of Väinämöinen's deeds of a heroic nature and also of his destiny. Painstakingly and with almost superhuman application to his task, the discerning discoverer and compiler achieved a marvelous result in the success of his endeavors in that he has fitted together the scattered pieces of these ancient Finnish runes and thus preserved them from certain disappearance; or more rightfully, he has brought to the light of day that which already existed only as fragments and were indeed hidden and forgotten. The poems were published under the name *Kalevala*—an invaluable gift not only to Finnish but also to European literature, which must add these precious memorials to Finnish poetry and the songs of the Ionians as well as those of the Caledonians.

This concept of Lönnrot's contribution is in complete harmony with the romantic view of the nature and creation of folk songs and epic poems. The *Kalevala* was seen as a complete epic saved by Lönnrot from fragmentation. Now restored to its pristine form, it could tell the tale of the ancient Finns, the phases of their history, and their customs and religion. No single individual, neither Lönnrot nor the rune-singers, played a critical part in the *Kalevala's* creation; its creator was "the people," the collective creative genius active in the earliest language and poetry of all cultures. If someone questioned this collective creative process, the explanation was that folk runes and epics were born gradually: in being communicated from mouth to mouth, they occasionally received an addition here and another there until "the people's creative spirit" modified its creation into completeness. In fact, few questioned this process. The basic romantic viewpoint was so strong that the nature of Lönnrot's labors was never actually recognized, although he spoke about it quite openly. The *Kalevala* was—or so it was acknowledged—from its inception, a pristine and complete epic poem, born in antiquity. Lönnrot was simply the successful reconstructor of this ancient masterpiece.

The flaws in this hypothesis are revealed by Lönnrot's letter to Fabian Collan: "I suppose you are amazed that in all this I have nothing to do but to follow the runes.

Therefore, I must explain to you that from the runes collected to date I could get at least seven volumes of *Kalevalas,* each unlike the other." This letter, dated 25-5-1848, was written a year before the manuscript for the new *Kalevala* was completed. Lönnrot had in his possession the results of four trips made by himself as well as the collections of A. J. Sjögen, M. A. Castrén, D. E. D. Europaus, H. A. Reinholm, August Ahlqvist, Fr. Polén, and Z. Sirelius. The sheer magnitude of the materials forced Lönnrot to choose among alternatives, even to the extent of modifying the theme and structure of the old *Kalevala*. He wrote of this problem: "The poems, especially those at the beginning will be in a different order from the previous ones, to bring about a more cohesive and natural entity. The many repetitions afford so vast a selection in form and verbiage that one could often wish for fewer riches from which to make a choice." However, when the researchers began to argue about the place and time of the *Kalevala's* birth, they forgot completely that the epic as they knew it was born at the desk of Elias Lönnrot.

The publication of the old *Kalevala* awakened a powerful national consciousness. J. G. Linsén said in 1836, that if Porthan still lived, he would bless this unexpected victory for the land of his birth. Declaring that Finnish literature could now claim a significant place in European literature, Linsén added: "In making these oral runes her very own, Finland can thus, encouraged and self-informed, learn to know its antiquity and also the future potential of its intellectual development. Finland can now say to itself: 'I, too, have a history' (Suomi voi sanoa insellensa minullakin on historia!)." M. A. Castrén, a young scholar from the North, conjectured: "If I wished to prophesy a future for Finland, when its young men enlivened by true patriotism and willing to lay aside foreign cultures and confessing only that to be true, which had developed from their very own intellectual life and effort; I could well seek the foundation for these hopes in the very *Kalevala* itself."

The powerful need for a national political self-consciousness was the greatest single factor in the *Kalevala's* success. Interest was first aroused by the fact that the Finnish "hoi polloi," of whose language little was understood, had now been proved to be the protector of a great treasure. In addition to the influence of the romantic milieu, Ruenberg threw the weight of his prestige in defense of the work. Comparing it favorably with the greatest artistic accomplishments of the Greeks, he thus helped the *Kalevala* to achieve recognition. Ironically, each of these inspired pronouncements was delivered in Swedish; the Swedish-speaking intelligentsia were especially interested in the *Kalevala* although their acquaintance with it was rather superficial because of the difficulties of language. Even such a Finnophile as Volmar Schildt-Kilpinen acknowledged ten years after its publication that "I feel like a blind man with regard to the runes, in many instances playing a guessing game at what may have been in the mind of the creator, for I cannot grasp it completely."

On the other hand, the Finnish-speaking people knew very little about the *Kalevala*. The only Finnish-language newspaper in the country, *Sanan-saattaja Viipurista,* did publish a brief but dry article in which both the name of the epic and its author were misspelled. The first edition of the *Kalevala,* consisting of five hundred volumes, was sold out twelve years after the date of publication. Nevertheless, this apparent lack of interest is in no way indicative of the *Kalevala's* importance. It was, as Martti Haavio has since expressed it, not only "the symbol of Finnish nationalism; but it was actually its crown jewel. It formed a kind of capital, which could hardly as yet be fully drawn upon. It was a cultural goal toward which the oppressed spirit of the Finnish nationalism groped."

Before long, the discussion concerning the *Kalevala* was joined more closely to the program of awakening the national consciousness and was a factor in the struggle over the language question. In 1845, the new editor of the *Mehilainen,* J. V. Snellman, began directing his readers to become acquainted with the *Kalevala:* "Young men, each Swedish word which you utter from this moment onward shall be, relatively speaking, lost from this literature, from the name of Finland, and from your own dignity. Only your mother tongue will afford your works and name a place in the world." When the decree of censorship in 1850 threatened to put an end to the strengthening cause of Finnish patriotism, scores of university students, helped by gifts from their home districts, journeyed to the backwoods and towns with the *Kalevala* in their knapsacks to continue Lönnrot's work.

The peacefully begun national awakening was seriously impeded when the country was torn asunder by political factions and the language struggle. The Swedish movement challenged the originality and true nature of the *Kalevala;* C. G. Estlander contended that the epic was nothing more than a counterfeit based upon runes of the Ossian-type. As Lönnrot's original notations of the runes had been lost (they were later discovered by chance among some discarded papers), the task of quickly gathering "replications of the *Kalevala*" was begun. This task was doubly beneficial, for it not only refuted Estlander's contentions but also helped to renew the lagging interest in rune collection. The *Kalevala* is original in the same sense that the Homeric epics, the *Edda* legends and the *Niebelungenlied* are original. It is based upon original, although separately sung, runes and upon smaller folk epics (the Sampo-epic, the Lemminkainen-epic and the Kullervo-epic). Both Homer and Lönnrot compiled the runes

of the rhapsodists and runesingers into a broader and systematic whole. On the other hand, the *Kalevala* cannot be compared either to Macpherson's *Ossiad,* which contains only a sprinkling of original folk songs, or to the two literary epics inspired by the *Kalevala,* the *Kalevipoeg* by the Estonian Kreutzwald and *Hiawatha* by the American Longfellow.

About 1860, numerous *Kalevala*-inspired works began to appear: Aleksis Kivi's Kullervo-tragedy, Sjöstrand's sculptures, Ekman's paintings, von Schantzin's Kullervo overture, and Topelius' *Princess of Cypress*. The 1890's were the golden age of folk romanticism. Artists journeyed to the wilds of Kauko-Karjala in search of the milieu from which the runes had come. Four names are pre-eminent among the multitude of artists in this period: Jean Sibelius, Akseli Gallen-Kallela, Juhani Aho, and Eino Leino.

About the same time that realism began to be a factor in literature, the maturation of research in folk poetry caused a re-evaluation. Julius Krohn in his lectures on the *Kalevala* in 1875 reported that he had concluded "that the published *Kalevala,* although it is so carefully compiled, or, better, especially because it is so carefully concatenated, does not lend itself at all to scientific research." In other words, it had become quite clear to the researcher that the problem of "replication of variant readings of the *Kalevala*" indicated that one could solve the problem of the variant forms and rich folk-runes only by attaching the original runes themselves as basic sources. Examination should be focused primarily upon the developmental history of the separate poems, their structure and age, and not upon the synthesis created by Lönnrot which did not contain all of the runes and therefore could not reveal the richness of the variant readings and the nature of folk poetry. The researcher must also investigate the prose forms contained in the descriptive runes, legends, proverbs, and riddles. A similar impulse to extend Finnish literary culture can be observed in the other works of Elias Lönnrot, who had published works on incantations, proverbs, and riddles (arvotuksia), and was presently at work on a monumental Finnish dictionary. At this time, *Kalevala* research became separated from research on Finnish folk runes. The latter utilized geographic-historical methodology to uncover a cultural basis for the creation of runes. The former devoted itself to delineating the problems related to the compilation of the *Kalevala* and to critically examining the epic as literature. Today, nearly one hundred years after this work was published, it is possible to mark the excellent achievements of both schools. The "Finnish method" used in the investigation of sagas achieved prominence in its day, even in foreign countries; later, when the methodology used in folk research became multifaceted, it served to illumine the history and nature of folk poems and lyrics. *Kalevala* research, in its investigation of the individual runes, has clarified the sources of the verses and has revealed the creativity of Elias Lönnrot. Contemporary scholars assign the modern *Kalevala* research to literary science; the special artistic creative process which resulted in Elias Lönnrot's *Kalevala* is best explained through the methodology of literary criticism.

The foregoing has attempted to trace the meaning of the *Kalevala* in terms of the cultural-historical situation into which it came. Neither the *Kalevala* nor the folk-songs which comprised it were understood in any profound sense for a long time. A considerable interval elapsed before it was possible to interpret the strange words and obscure language of the runes, and to recognize the poetic values in the text. In spite of these obstacles, the effect of the *Kalevala* is immeasurable. It has been said that the greater part of Finland's history during the past generation is a direct or indirect result of the publication of this folk epic. Simply in the area of political history it has been crucial. In almost all the fields of artistic endeavor the *Kalevala's* influence has been pervasive: it gave birth to new branches of learning; it fructified the Finnish language, thus laying a corner-stone for Finnish literature; and it brought the name of Finland to the attention of the world. Only an epic and only a folk epic at that could have accomplished so much.

William A. Wilson (essay date 1975)

SOURCE: "The *Kalevala* and Finnish Politics," in *Journal of the Folklore Institute,* Vol. XII, No. 2-3, 1975, pp. 131-55.

[*In the following excerpt, Wilson takes a critical look at the historical relationship between Finnish nationalist politics and the study of the* Kalevala.]

Folklore studies in Finland have from the beginning been intimately connected with the struggle of Finnish nationalists to achieve first cultural and then political independence. Probably in no other country has the marriage of folklore research and national aspirations produced such dramatic results. At the beginning of the nineteenth century, the Finns, fragmented into several dialect groups and lacking the binding ties of a common literature and a written record of their national past, were ill-prepared to face the century of Russian rule and attempted Russification of their culture that lay ahead. Then in 1835 Elias Lönnrot published the *Kalevala,* the national epic based on the old heroic songs that Lönnrot and his compatriots had collected from the Finnish hinterlands and that Lönnrot had welded into a unified whole. In the following decades, a small band of scholar-patriots dipped deeply into this folklore as they forged a literary language, created a national literature and sought to reconstruct the prehistoric period when Finns had walked on Finnish soil as

free men. The *Kalevala* and the cultural works based on it gave the Finns a newfound pride in their past, courage to face an uncertain future, and, above all, a feeling of self-esteem they had never known before. That their beleaguered little nation on the fringe of Western civilization had produced an epic comparable, in their own minds at least, to the great Homeric epics was to be a never-ending source of pride to the Finns. The *Kalevala* had become their book of independence, their passport into the family of civilized nations. A nation that had created the *Kalevala,* they repeatedly told themselves, was not destined to die. In 1907 the great lyric poet Eino Leino summed up the feeling of the times in these words:

> The national spirit which appears in it is the spirit of a free nation. . . . In reading it we feel ourselves to be free and independent. . . . From it there steps before us a nation which enjoys its existence. . . . It is no slave nation . . . nor is it an upstart nation, but rather a nation which has its own customs, traditions, gods and concepts of life. It is *old Finland.* . . . The Finnish tongue in the *Kalevala* sounds freely, brightly and victoriously. It gives a picture of a nation which is sovereign.

That a decade later Finland was able to take advantage of unsettled world conditions and in actuality to become sovereign was due in no small part to the feelings of cultural identity and national unity engendered by the *Kalevala*.

But in the years following independence both Finnish political ideology and the folklore research that underpinned it in many instances tended toward extremism. This development was due largely to two points of view which had by then gained widespread acceptance and to shifting national aspirations and commensurate adjustments in folklore theory. Both points of view had deep roots in the past but in the volatile years between the world wars had emerged with renewed force.

The first of these was the firm conviction that the ancient *Kalevala* poems provided an untarnished reflector of the pristine national soul—the conviction that one ought to look to these poems, or to the *Kalevala* itself (which in the popular fancy was synonymous with authentic folklore) to discover what it really meant to be a Finn and to find historical models on which to build the society of contemporary Finland.

The belief that folklore was the abode of the mystical national soul was, of course, nothing new. It had been developed by Herder and the German Romantics at the end of the eighteenth century and, at the beginning of the nineteenth, had been responsible for turning Finnish folklorists to nationalism and Finnish nationalists to folklore. Weakened momentarily in the 1870s and

Folk singers with an accompanist.

1880s by the spread of empiricism and positivism, it had received new life at the turn of the century from the neo-romantic movement, which stressed feeling and intuition, and from the anti-positivism and loss of faith in reason that grew out of World War I. By the time independence had been won in 1917, every schoolchild had been taught again and again that Finnish folk poetry was a mirror for all that was one hundred percent Finnish. In the following years, if anything, the belief grew still stronger and continued as a means of influencing cultural-political thought. In 1921, for example, E. A. Saarimaa, a prominent educator, instructed his fellow teachers: "The national significance of our folklore . . . entitles it to a prominent position in the national literature studied in our secondary schools. But particularly the fact that our nation's individuality is best revealed in this poetry makes learning it important. The nation's soul is nowhere reflected so clearly as in its almost collectively created poetry. And one of the most important tasks of the secondary school is to acquaint the students with their own nation."

The second point of view that made possible the political exploitation of folklore was the belief that folklore was to be handmaiden to the state—that the end of folklore research was service of the fatherland. Once again this belief found support in the teachings of Herder, who had argued that an individual could receive his fullest development only as an integral part of his particular nation and that service to that nation was the highest endeavor of man. Through the years preceding Finnish independence, this service had been expressed primarily in attempts to advance Finnish culture, to create a national literature, to elevate the vernacular tongue, and to draw nearer the common folk. But following independence, nationalistic endeavors took on a harsher tone. The milder spirit of Herder gave way to that of Hegel, and individuality yielded to national or racial loyalty. The following oath read to initiates at the swearing-in ceremony of the Academic Karelian Society, the

university's most influential and politically active student organization, reflects something of the changed spirit: "From this moment on you no longer belong to yourselves but to the Fatherland. You stand before an open door; on this side is everything which a weak human will consider worthwhile and desirable: *I, myself.* On the other side is self-denial: *The Fatherland.* You step through the door and shut it behind you with an unopenable bolt: *your manly oaths.*"

Sentiments such as this one soon began to echo in the statements of folklorists. For example, in a youth publication Valdemar Rantoja wrote: "Folklore research is with us in Finland a national branch of science whose task is to reveal the earliest development of the Finnish spirit and to create an ideological-historical foundation for our nation's independent life and for its historical duty." And in a doctoral ceremony, in the militaristic tones typical of the time, Martti Haavio, one of the country's most brilliant young folklorists and during the 1920s, a leading figure in the Academic Karelian Society, declared: "Only a free man can carry a sword, not a slave nor the servile minded. . . . In this land we have been chosen to fight on behalf of that culture which we received as an inheritance; indeed, to conquer new areas for it. Only so long as science in this land is free will there be a sword in our hands; only so long as there is a sword in our hands will science be free. And without free science that fatherland to whose service we have consecrated ourselves can never flourish."

The trouble with this argument is that when a scholar has consecrated himself above all else to the service of his fatherland, the demands of his scholarship all too easily yield to the needs of that fatherland. He becomes a patriot first and a scholar second. In such instances, folklore continues to serve as a mirror for culture, but the image reflected depends on the political predisposition of the man holding the mirror. Such was frequently the case in Finland in the years following independence, as folklore study at times became not just a means of understanding culture, but also a tool for manipulating minds. Intellectual leaders and propagandists from both sides of the political spectrum interpreted Finnish epic poetry to fit their own views and then, in the name of loyalty to one's heritage, used this poetry to advocate diametrically opposed courses of political action—the political right to generate in the citizenry a militaristic posture and to argue for an expansionist foreign policy; the political left to counter the ideology of the right and to argue for a classless, communistic society.

FOLKLORE AND THE POLITICAL RIGHT

Folklore and Militarism

In preparation for "***Kalevala*** Day" in 1917 (the annual commemoration of the publication of the epic) Eino Leino wrote in the popular press:

To honor the *Kalevala* is to us Finns the same as honoring one's own deepest being; to come to know the *Kalevala* is the same as knowing the wellsprings of one's own spirit; to rejoice over the *Kalevala* is the same as rejoicing over the swelling, streaming sunshine of one's own breast, over faith in life and over fulfillment. If a Finn does not care to read the *Kalevala,* then that testifies that he does not care to glance at the pages of his own book of destiny; if a Finn does not like the *Kalevala,* then that testifies that he does not like anything nor anybody, for only one who loves his own primeval self can radiate love around him. But if a Finn ridicules the *Kalevala,* then that is a sin against the Holy Ghost.

Though the *Kalevala* was never widely read, except in school assignments, Leino's words suggest the symbolical force the epic had achieved in the minds of the people. It was important simply because it was there, a spiritual monument to the greatness of ancient Finland. Thus ten months later, with independence now achieved, cultural leaders quite naturally looked to the *Kalevala* and to the more genuine old heroic poems from which it had been formed to seek guidance in determining what kind of nation independent Finland should become. The answer was clear: a strong militaristic nation, a great northern power.

This answer was based in part on the Finns' swelling pride, on their understandable desire, after centuries of foreign rule, to become masters of their own fate and to recapture that lost age of glory and heroism revealed to them by the *Kalevala.* But, perhaps more important, it was based on the national will to survive, on the firm conviction that only by becoming militarily strong could Finland hope to resist the malevolent powers emanating from the East. Following a divisive civil war in 1918, which many Finns blamed on Russia, and following the Peace of Tartu in 1920, which the political right, as we shall see, considered a betrayal of Finland's legitimate territorial interests in the East, there developed in the land a militant anti-communism and an unrelenting hate of the Soviet Union. Russians were no longer Russians; they were "our hereditary foe" or, more often and more disparagingly, simply "Ruskis" ("Ryssät"). And they were denounced from all quarters in the most inflammatory terms. On "*Kalevala* Day" in 1923, for instance, Elias Simojoki, a theology student and later a Lutheran pastor, declared to Helsinki University students that to love their fatherland they would have to hate Russia:

> Hate of the Ruski was the power which made Finland free. Hate of the Ruski . . . is the Finnish Spirit. . . . Do you know how to hate as one hates in blood wrath, as your forefathers hated? . . . Death to the Ruskis, whatever be their color. In the name of the blood spilled by our forefathers, death to the destroyers and spoilers of our homes, our kinsmen, and our fatherland. Death to the dividers of Kaleva's race, to the polluter of the Finnish nation. In the name of Finland's lost honor and her coming greatness, death to the Ruskis. On this "*Kalevala* Day," in the name of our fatherland's rising greatness and the awakening of our people, let a rousing cry of holy love and hate travel through the tribe of Kullervo and through our beloved birthland.

Simojoki's intemperate blast was more extreme than most but still not atypical. Three days earlier Martti Haavio had told a university audience that "nothing good can come from Moscow—against Moscow we *must wage battle*." And Haavio's friend, E. E. Kaila, wrote: "By the power of a strong national feeling and an active patriotism—hate of the Ruski—every individual and the entire society are to sacrifice themselves to this work, so that when the hour strikes we will not be caught napping but will be ready for battle on behalf of our national freedom, our state independence, and humane culture, ready for the battle and for victory."

To stir up this martial spirit, to glorify fighting and reckless courage, and to convince their countrymen that they were capable of greatness, Finnish nationalists turned to the ideal world revealed in native folk poetry, and particularly to the militaristic world which the dean of Finnish folklorists, Kaarle Krohn, had recently discovered in the *Kalevala* poems.

At the turn of the century there had been little in Krohn's folklore theory and in his study of the *Kalevala* heroes that would lift the Finns' flagging self-esteem and spur them on to heroic actions of their own. Nurtured by the evolutionary and positivistic spirit of his youth and following, in part, lines laid down by his father Julius, Kaarle Krohn had argued in his great work *Kalevalan runojen historia* (*The History of the Kalevala Poems,* 1903-1910) that though a few of the *Kalevala* poems had mythological origins—the famous heroes Väinämöinen and Ilmarinen he considered to be gods of the water and air—the majority of them had clearly derived from medieval Catholic saints' legends which had arrived in Finland from the West. Beginning life in southwest Finland as small poetic "germ cells," the poems had migrated slowly across the land to the remote province of northeast (Viena) Karelia, sloughing off in the process original Christian names, which were replaced by those of the old pagan gods, and evolving all the time into the longer poems and clusters of poems which Lönnrot had eventually collected and shaped into the *Kalevala.* In none of this then—the lack of a solid historical or mythological foundation for the epic poetry, the lack of an heroic age, the development of the poetry from borrowed rather than from indigenous materials, and the late blossoming of the poetry—was there much grist for the nationalists' mill. But as Finland began to struggle toward independence, Krohn began to change his theory. Indeed, few scholars have opposed the theories of other men with the vigor that Kaarle Krohn was in the ensuing years to oppose those that had once been his own.

From the end of the nineteenth century a spirit of resistance to Russian oppression had been developing in the land. Its first manifestation had been the 523,000 signatures (half the adult population) sent to the czar in 1899 to protest violation of Finland's constitutional guarantees. This petition was soon followed in 1902 by the refusal of three-fifths of the youths of conscription age to report for the draft, by the refusal of Finns in general to obey edicts they considered illegal, by the assassination of Governor General Bobrikov in 1904, and by the general strike in 1905, which in its beginning stages, at least, had been an act of unified resistance against the Russians. At the beginning of World War I, a number of young Finnish activists, having come to believe in the force of arms as the proper means to achieve political ends, sought military training in Germany while others of their number, for the first time seriously considering the possibility of political independence, had sought German assurances that in the event of Russia's defeat Germany would support Finland's bid for freedom. These political activities and aspirations had been further augmented by neo-romanticism in art, music, and literature, which had once again focused attention on the *Kalevala* and the golden age of the past. The folklore-inspired productions of Eino Leino, Jean Sibelius, and Akseli Gallén-Kallela, the fervent patriotic sermons given in 1902 on the one-hundreth anniversary of Elias Lönnrot's birth, and the *Kalevala* celebrations held across the land in 1910 on the seventy-fifth anniversary of the publication of the epic all contributed to the Finns' sense of national self-esteem. And it was in the midst of this political climate in 1914 that Kaarle Krohn, in two short essays ("The Heroes" and "Kalevala and His Kin") dramatically suggested that he had been wrong in his earlier *Kalevala* interpretations and that the ancient Finns really had had a famous past.

These essays were only preliminary steps to the major works to come, and in the intervening years the public waited somewhat anxiously to see what direction Krohn would take. Shortly before the March Revolution that would thrust Finland down the road to independence, J. R. Danielson-Kalmari, a leading historian and politician, declared in a speech at Helsinki university: "[Krohn] has presented the view that in the *Kalevala* we have before us much more historical material based on actual happenings . . . than we have ordinarily been accustomed to see. With great interest the Finnish people expect now, and have the right to expect, that *Kalevala* research will clarify this matter and show to what extent this new view is accurate."

The Finnish people had not long to wait. The following year Krohn published *Kalevalankysymyksiä* (Kal-

evala Questions, 1918), which turned his former theories upside down and provided ample material from which the disciples of militarism could seek sustenance. Krohn now argued that the heroic poems had not begun life as insignificant poetic germ cells but as individually created artistic wholes which had often fragmented as they migrated from southwest Finland to Viena Karelia; that the original poems had not been composed in the Middle Ages but in the Late Iron Age (700-1100), during the warlike period corresponding to the Scandinavian Viking Age; and, most important, that the events described in the poems had derived neither from mythology nor from saints' legends, but from actual historical events. This meant that the principal heroes of the poems—Väinämöinen, Ilmarinen, Lemminkäinen—were real men, Finnish Viking chieftains who had once walked as free men on free Finnish soil and had with the sword won honor and fame for the fatherland.

To the end of his life, Krohn continued to write about his country's epic poetry, producing among other works his monumental *Kalevalastudien* (1924-1928) and remaining throughout unshakably committed to his new faith: once restored to their original forms through comparative textual analysis, the old poems would prove to be purely native poetry recounting the gallant exploits of fearsome Finnish heroes. A year before his death, Krohn wrote of old Väinämöinen, the greatest of these heroes, that he had been "a great man of good lineage," and "had been a battle-tested sea warrior, more skilled than his fellows in the use of the sword."

To the academic community Krohn explained that his changed view had resulted simply from an honest assessment of "observed facts." But that the change was also politically motivated and that Krohn, like so many others, was overwhelmed by the martial spirit of the times seems clear from even a cursory glance at his statements in popular publications.

In April, 1919, for example, in the leading nationalist paper *Uusi Suomi*, Krohn boldly defended his new historical view, gave a stirring account of the epic heroes—their consuming love of battle, their daring pillaging expeditions—and then, by quoting with obvious approval a statement by the Danish scholar F. Ohrt, suggested in conclusion that Finland's changed political situation had required a corresponding change in folklore interpretation:

> The formerly peaceful Finland has become militaristic, which during these unsettled times is good. *Kalevala* scholarship has followed the same road. Before the great war the notion prevailed that the *Kalevala* primarily depicted the thoughts and cares of a people living in peaceful circumstances, that the power of the word rather than of the sword was its ideal. Now from the *Kalevala* the clamor of warlike sea adventurers reverberates [and] golden

hilts and dragon-crested ship prows gleam. The young people grown up in a Finland that has achieved its independence can in their imaginations return, project themselves back, to the folklore heroes and from them can gain inspiration for a common struggle.

In 1923, in an essay prepared for the schools and the general public, he wrote: "After a century of scholarship . . . that daring supposition (the idea of the poems' historical validity) has changed to a scientific conviction at the very time when the Finnish nation has attained its external independence and has shown itself capable of both understanding and creating history." To what extent he manipulated his data, either consciously or unconsciously, to inspire those creating Finland's new history is a question that lies beyond easy answer. It is perhaps best to take him at his own word. Shortly before his death he wrote: "At the time we were fighting for our independence there arose before my eyes an age following but similar to the Scandinavian Viking Age, when Finns, still independent, embarked on sea expeditions, appearing in turn on the shores of Sweden." And for Kaarle Krohn that splendid Viking vision seems, to borrow a phrase from Robert Frost, to have "made all the difference."

Krohn died in 1933, but not until the end of World War II was his vision of a glorious past to fade from the minds of the Finns. Of the many scholars who helped keep it alive, two of the most influential were Jalmari Jaakkola and Martti Haavio. Though each departed somewhat from Krohn in their historical reconstructions, each, following him, believed epic poetry to be the key to the distant past, and each found revealed in that poetry a dazzling, heroic world.

Jaakkola, the first to hold the prestigious chair in Finnish history established at the University of Helsinki in 1932, was also one of the first professional historians to make the study of ancient history the study of folklore and thus lend further credence to Krohn's point of view. Just as the Aurorea Borealis shimmered in the distant northern sky, so too, argued Jaakkola, did folk poetry provide a brilliant road back to the ancient Finns: "And that poetic flash, in spite of all its gilding, reveals a great reality which the tools of research can never penetrate as deeply as . . . the ancient Finnish heroic song." In his major work, *Suomen varhaishistoria* (*Early Finnish History,* 1935) he stated in the preface that he intended to depict "the life of ancient Finland as it was reflected in the mirror of the period, the *Kalevala* heroic poetry." In the following pages, he brought vividly to life the different Finnish tribes who had lived and fought in Finland in those glorious years between 800 and 1100.

Easily the most brilliant and productive of Krohn's students was Martti Haavio, whose eloquent pen car-

ried the message of folklore to a large portion of the populace. In a number of short articles and in two long studies meant for both scholarly and popular audiences—*Suomalainen muinaisrunous* (*Ancient Finnish Poetry,* 1933) and *Suomalaisen muinaisrunouden maailma* (*The World of Ancient Finnish Poetry,* 1935)—Haavio defended folklore as a mirror for culture in an eminently reasonable manner. Yet when he moved from general principles to specific descriptions of the Viking culture reflected in the heroic layer of poetry, he was carried away by the same enthusiasm for scenes of battle and conquest that had overcome his predecessors. "Our old poetry," he said, "relays to us information from the *Kalevala* culture, from the Finnish heroic age about which history is silent." This heroic age "was restless and warlike, a Finnish society in which a spirit of battle held sway." Of its heroes, Haavio declared: "Their carefree warrior-mentality is reflected in many passages in the poems; their yearning for fighting expeditions is sincere and often overwhelming." After describing in considerable detail this warrior society, he exclaimed with a burst of pride: "Rich bounty, beautiful women, the honor of men, wilderness expeditions, pillaging expeditions, sea voyages, battles, blood revenge—there are some catchwords that capitally characterize the Finnish Viking Age."

It is surprising that in a man like Haavio, essentially a scholar, scenes of conquest should evoke feelings of admiration, and that both he and his readers should find great cause for pride in having had ancestral heroes whose principal virtue seemed to be an overwhelming desire to wage fierce battle against their neighbors. Few can deny, however, that Haavio's eloquent rhetoric did tend to lend a rather pleasing prospect to the battle, pleasing enough, at least, to inculcate in young men ardent for glory what Wilfred Owen has called "that old lie, *dulce et decorum est pro patria mori.*"

Had Finnish folklorists simply been ivory tower academicians writing for other folklorists, their ideas would probably have had little impact on the general public. But they were not. Most of them were also political activists and folklore popularizers. They spoke at patriotic ceremonies; they helped prepare readers and folklore teaching guides for the public schools; and they wrote constantly for popular publications, including official and semi-official military journals.

One of the earliest of these articles and one that set the tone for many to follow was written by Väinö Salminen (a docent and later professor of Finnish folklore) and published in *Suomen Sotilas* (*The Finnish Soldier*) on "*Kalevala* Day" 1921. "One often hears the claim," stated Salminen, "that our forefathers did not admire heroic acts and warlike exploits, since these supposedly are not sung about in the ancient *Kalevala* poetry. That claim does not hold true. In the old poetry both the warrior's bearing and fighting capability are depicted with rapture." To prove this point and to provide Finland's modern young warriors with an inspiring model for action, Salminen described, in carefully selected detail, the feats of the hero Kullervo. A capital hero, Kullervo lusted after battle, proclaiming:

> Soma on sotahan kuolla
> kaunis miekan kalskehesen.

> [It is sweet to die in war,
> Beautiful to die in the
>   clashing of swords.]

And when the call to battle sounded, he left for the fight with a gay, rejoicing heart. Such heroism, however, was not without its rewards, for Finnish warriors, Salminen melodramatically informed his readers, had always been much admired by the people, and particularly by Finnish maidens, who would gaze from their windows at passing young heroes and sigh:

> Voi kun tuo minun olisi,
> Suven syömättä olisin,
> aastajankin einehettä.

> [Oh, if he were only mine,
> I would go a summer without eating,
> A year without food.]

"From the Kullervo poems alone," concluded Salminen, "we see that war heroes and battle were not alien to the ancient Finns."

The comments with which the editors of the journal introduced Salminen's article are as instructive as the article itself and clearly reveal the purpose for which it was published: "The most magnificent spiritual creation of our forefathers, the *Kalevala,* must not remain a stranger to a single Finnish youth. On this day, eighty-five years after the publication of our national poems, there is reason to recall in the columns of *The Finnish Soldier* what the *Kalevala* has to say particularly to the Finnish soldier." In the following years Finnish folklorists would continue to argue that the *Kalevala* did indeed have much to say to the youth of the nation, and to its soldiers. Fourteen years later, for instance, Martti Haavio was still developing the same themes. In a "*Kalevala* Day" article in *Hakkapeliitta* (a publication of the Civil Defense Corps), he declared that "the heart of the *Kalevala* poetry is simply war poetry." Through this poetry, he argued, "we arrive in the midst of that age when Scandinavian Vikings in swift-sailing ships plowed the seas of the world, destroying, burning and plundering. Finnish society—our heroic poetry makes this perfectly clear—is a war society." In another militaristic essay, this one published in *Laivas-tolehti (The Navy Journal)*, Haavio discussed ancient Finnish heroes of the sea. Väinämöinen, for instance, was a great sea warrior and the society that had sung about him was a "Finnish war society in which the sea, war, and sea warfare were extremely popular, in which heroism was a virtue, in which a sea warrior merited the highest praise." The poems describing young Ahti, another bold and battle-hungry sea hero, were, exulted Haavio, "the clearest, the most human, and in my opinion the most beautiful of our heroic poetry."

If the warlike spirit of the epic poems, then, was the true Finnish spirit, and if the epic heroes, the prototypes of Finnish character, were men of the sword, eager to take up arms to achieve their just ends, the lesson to patriotic Finnish youth was clear, "go and do likewise."

Folklore and Greater Finland

For most Finns, achieving their just ends meant simply becoming strong enough to defend their borders and to maintain their independence. But among some members of the political right, it meant not just defending borders but expanding them eastward.

When Finland became independent, East Karelia and Ingria, where most of the *Kalevala* poetry had been collected, remained in Russian hands. For years these regions had comprised a sort of Finnish holy land where artists, musicians, and literary men, not to mention troops of folklorists, had made pilgrimages to seek creative inspiration and to imbue themselves with the spirit of the *Kalevala*. In 1920, at the Peace of Tartu, which the political right considered a cowardly betrayal of Finland's national interests, Finland and Russia agreed to keep existing borders, Russia's one concession being to grant East Karelia local autonomy. When the Bolsheviks failed to keep even this promise, Finland appealed to the Hague Court of International Justice and to the League of Nations, but to no avail.

The door had thus been nailed shut. A hue and cry of anger spread across the land, talk of holy war filled the air, and men swore sacred oaths never to sheathe their swords until their tribal brethren had been freed. The goal was to wrest Ingria and particularly East Karelia from Russia—by peaceful means if possible but by force if necessary—and to combine them with Finland proper into a Greater Finland (*Suur Suomi*), held together by the bonds of blood and culture.

The Greater Finland issue is far too complex for detailed discussion here. It deserves at least brief attention, however, because some of the same folklorists who admired their heroic ancestors' reliance on the sword were also among those militantly raising their voices in defense of an enlarged fatherland. For example, in 1919 Väinö Salminen wrote: "The Finnish race does not wish to seize foreign land. But from centuries of hard experience it has certainly learned enough that at long last it has categorically determined to take control in that area which has belonged to it from times immemorial." In 1923, in a speech before the Estonian-Finnish University Club, Martti Haavio proclaimed: "[The Finnish race] must for all time knock down that pillar on which is inscribed *The Kingdom of the Ruskis*—and must erect one a thousand times higher on which is [written] IMPERIUM FENNICUM." In 1935, in a harsh essay entitled "What Has the *Kalevala* To Say to Contemporary Youth?" Matti Kuusi, inspired by the heroic vision of Jalmari Jaakkola, declared: "It is understood that Finnish destiny is contingent upon this alternative, 'national destruction—national greatness. Either—or!' . . . only a desire for Finnish greatness can withstand the pressure of the Slavic desire for greatness. Thus an organic part of the youth's national ideology is belief in the coming liberation of the Finnish tribes beyond the border, Viena, Aunus, Ingria."

From our perspective today, the Finns' desire to appropriate these areas, which bordered Leningrad and contained the Murmansk Railway, seems foolhardy. But one should recall that in its first years, at least, the Soviet Union was torn by civil war and by a struggle for survival. The Finns, sharing the prevalent belief that the Bolsheviks would soon be toppled from power, felt that in the subsequent realignment of Russia's borders Finland would have a more reasonable claim than others to East Karelia. Further, if the dream of a Greater Finland sounded like misty eyed idealism, so too had the dream of an independent Finland a century earlier. With that first dream now realized, the young men of the new republic set out with firm resolve to bring to pass the second. And in the propaganda campaign that developed, they once again found in folklore a most effective weapon.

The advocates of a Greater Finland based their argument on two major premises. The first was the belief that Finland, Karelia, and Ingria were ethnically one people and ought therefore to be one nation. There was much talk of achieving Finland's "natural borders," those which, as Väinö Salminen pointed out, God had intended for her. The belief in nation-states as living organisms having gained considerable ground, it was generally felt that the divided Finnish tribes could never fulfill their destiny until they had become one nation. "The incorporation of all Karelia into Finland," explained Salminen, "is, frankly speaking, a condition of survival for the Finnish race and, at the same time, a condition of survival for the East Karelian nation." This belief in ethnic unity was based on a common ancestry, on a common language, and, most important for our purposes, on a shared body of folk poetry.

Some Finns felt this poetry to be an ancestral inheritance from the misty past, from the period of Balto-Finnic unity when the Finns, Karelians, and Ingrians had lived together as one people and before they had migrated to their present homelands, taking with them their language and folk poetry. Others like Kaarle Krohn believed the poems had originated much later in Western Finland and then, through automigration, had moved slowly to the east and northeast where they had been preserved and reshaped by the Ingrians and Karelians. But whether viewed as a racial inheritance from primordial times or as collective creations resulting from their automigration, the poems came to represent for political activists the "binding tie" holding together the members of the Finnish race.

The symbolical significance that political activists found in this binding tie is illustrated well in an essay published by the Academic Karelian Society, the organization most devoted to the Greater Finland dream. "The *Kalevala*," stated the essay, "is the strongest witness of that affinity which holds sway between Karelia and the rest of Finland. It above all testifies that the Karelian nation and the Finnish nation are *one* nation. . . . The Finnish nation is not yet what it should be. Finnish nationality does not yet shape the Finnish state. . . . The duty of our present generation of Finns is . . . to work for the accomplishment of that goal which the *Kalevala* has initiated." As the activists worked toward that goal, they turned also to narratives in the epic itself, and particularly to the story of "Lemminkäinen's Mother" to symbolize the hoped for establishment of Greater Finland. Lemminkäinen, killed by a treacherous enemy, cut to pieces and then thrown into the river Tuonela, was raked up from the river by his mother, put back together, and resuscitated. In like manner, Finnish patriots, supposedly stirred by the same kind of love that had moved Lemminkäinen's mother, were attempting to join together the divided parts of the "natural" Finnish body and bring it once again to life.

The second premise on which the advocates of a Greater Finland based their demand for territorial aggrandizement was the belief that the publication of the *Kalevala* had prepared the way for Finnish independence and that the Finns, therefore, were now honor bound to bring independence to the Karelians and Ingrians, who had kept the old poems alive after they had faded in Finland proper. The following "*Kalevala* Day" editorial published in the influential newspaper, *Aamulehti,* is typical of the statements that echoed throughout the 1920s and 1930s:

> Without the *Kalevala,* Finnish national spirit and culture scarcely would have been able to rise to that strength, richness, and significance necessary for the birth of an independent Finland. . . . The Finnish nation must therefore remember the great debt of gratitude to Karelia and its singing folk who, through the *Kalevala* songs, have in a forceful manner indirectly influenced both the development of a Finnish national spirit and culture and, by the same token, the birth of a free and independent Finland.

... On both sides of the state border the same tribe is still living, and on the Russian side it is still without that rightful political, national, linguistic, and cultural independence which it has prepared for Finland through the poems of the *Kalevala*. ... The Kalevala obligates the Finnish people and state seriously to turn their attention to the plight of these border lands, to whom we owe a debt of gratitude for preserving the ancient spiritual treasure of our nation. ... The badly oppressed Ingria, which has likewise been instrumental in preserving both the *Kalevala* poems and other folklore . . . , also deserves our attention.

Proclamations like this one often deplored the deprivations suffered by the surviving folksingers at the hands of the Bolsheviks. "The homes of these men," wrote Martti Haavio, "are presently being pillaged by oppressors; their boys and girls are presently slaves: there where the kantele and the Sampo anciently rang out, there sounds now a sorrowful lament. During these very days Ingria's singing villages are being emptied of their occupants; the sons of the double-headed eagle are raging frightfully in the dwelling places of the Finns, places where our wonderful folk poems once took refuge." In like manner, E. N. Setälä, a professor of Finnish language and literature, and a prominent politician and statesman, declared in a stirring "*Kalevala* Day" address: "Listen, listen to the lament of Karelia from those everlasting backwoods, from the shores of wilderness lakes where the *Kalevala* songs once echoed. ... The voice of that lament sounds over the Finnish land; it wrings our hearts."

In this same address, Setälä referred to the Karelians as "the last border guard of Western civilization." Some years earlier Kustavi Grotenfelt had similarly argued that Finland could fill its mission as Western civiliza-

tion's vanguard "against the chaos of the East and against Bolshevism" only when it had attained its natural border. Between the wars this position became entrenched in the thinking of the political right. Finland, it was believed, was destined valiantly to serve as the West's last outpost against Eastern barbarism, as "the steel wall," as Haavio put it, "protecting [the West] from Moscow." This historical calling could be fulfilled, however, only if Finland were to become Greater Finland. The advocates of territorial expansion could thus appeal not only to narrow national interests but also to an unselfish concern for the welfare of Western culture.

In a public school reader published in 1930, Setälä complained to students that a "strict prohibition" stopped the Finns from crossing the border into the *Kalevala* song country of East Karelia and that only in their imaginations could they envision "that land of broad backwoods, of great lakes, and of the poems." But in a little over a decade the Finns had actually crossed that border, not just in imagination but in fact. On November 30, 1939, Russia, having failed to win from Finland territorial concessions claimed necessary to protect the approaches to Leningrad, had attacked. In the short and vicious Winter War that followed, the Finns paid a terrible price in lost land and lost lives, but at the war's end (March 12, 1940) had managed to keep their independence intact. Fifteen months later, allied now with Germany, the country entered the conflict again, moving quickly into territory lost during the Winter War, and into East Karelia.

The Finns have always claimed officially that they moved across the border not to annex new territory but simply to establish a better line of defense. Whatever the case may be, there is no question that for many who lived this moment in history, the beginning of the war signaled the long-awaited realization of the Greater Finland dream, the restoration to Finland proper of the land that had preserved the *Kalevala*. An editorial in the Academic Karelian Society's principal publication proclaimed: "The moral justification for Greater Finland is irrefutable: it is based on the salvation of the Finnish race and culture from destruction by the East." And Vilho Helanen, a long-time Society leader, declared: "Now is the day of the fulfillment of our great visions."

The tone of statements such as these was set by none other than Marshal Mannerheim, commander-in-chief of Finland's armies and one of the country's most powerful men. Three days after the war began he "summoned" his troops and fellow citizens to follow him in a "holy war against the enemy of our nation." And two weeks later, as the army prepared for a major thrust eastward, he declared, in an emotional order of the day:

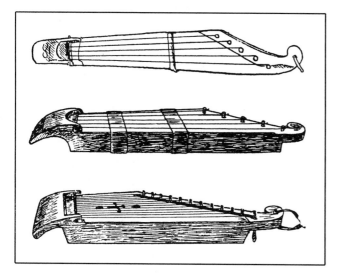

Top and middle: top and side views of five-string Kantele. *Bottom: a twelve-string* Kantele.

In the War of Liberation in 1918, I swore to the Finnish and Viena Karelians that I would not sheathe my sword until Finland and East Karelia were free. . . .

For twenty-three years [the Karelian provinces of] Viena and Aunus have awaited the fulfillment of this promise. . . .

Fighters in the war of liberation, famous men of the Winter War, my gallant soldiers! A new day has dawned. . . . Karelian freedom and a great Finland glimmer before us in the powerful avalanche of world historical events.

Whether Mannerheim, in spite of these words, was really committed to the Greater Finland dream is highly debatable. What he was committed to was the destruction of Bolshevism, which he despised. That he chose to allude to the dream, however, in order to rally the army and nation behind him in his struggle against the forces of the Kremlin demonstrates how firmly he believed that dream had seized the public imagination.

It was a dream, as we have seen, based solidly in folklore. And through these days of trouble and triumph, folklore continued to play an important political role, as the old arguments about ethnic unity and debts of honor were repeated with renewed fervor. As the Finnish armies moved intoxicatingly forward, Jalmari Jaakkola published a pontifical defense of the creation of a Greater Finland in the New Europe then taking shape and declared: "More clearly than any war or battle the *Kalevala* heroic poems show to both Finland and Europe that East Karelia belongs by spirit and nature to Finland." In November, 1941, a Finno-Ugric Conference sponsored by the Finnish League and attended by numerous officials, including the President of the Republic, was held in Helsinki. In one of the several politically volatile speeches given at the conference, the well-known poet V. A. Koskenniemi, referring to the old folk poems, praised the heroic Finnish army for pushing the Finnish border eastward: "A great poetry created by a united race once found its way through the wilderness, from house to house, from home to home, across an artificial border; now the Finnish army of liberation has arrived at these same roads and paths and has opened new ones, in order to pay its debt of honor to Karelia, to the song country of our tribe." Three months later, in the "liberated" village of Vuokkiniemi, where a century earlier Lönnrot had collected some of his best poems, a Finnish army officer, speaking at a "*Kalevala* Day" celebration, made the same point:

> Above all, of the great friends of East Karelia, we must mention Elias Lönnrot, who again and again crossed over the border into the parishes of Vuokkiniemi and Uhtua, collected from these backwoods areas ancient Finnish poems, and from them formed the *Kalevala,* the national epic of the Finnish people. We men of the Finnish army of liberation who last summer crossed the border to drive the Bolshevik oppressor from Viena Karelia and to return these areas to the Finnish race, crossed the border under the power of a sacred emotion. We remembered that we were nearing the villages from which the *Kalevala* poems were once collected. The Finnish troops, who have heroically driven the Russian enemy from Finland's old border, have walked the same paths that the collector of the *Kalevala,* Elias Lönnrot, once walked. . . . We Finns from beyond the former border wanted today, as we moved near the graves of the old Viena singers, to show them and the entire Viena lineage our delayed gratitude.

> To the singers of songs asleep in the grave, the Finnish soldiers want now to say: "We are here!" The rest of Finland owes a great debt of gratitude to this tribe. For Viena Karelia's part in the development of the Finnish nation toward an independent and virile society has been overwhelming. . . . The final result of this holy war is certain. . . . The Finnish land from the Gulf of Bothnia to the White Sea and from Lake Onega to the Gulf of Finland will rise to a new life.

But the glory was short lived. Germany fell, and with it Finland. In the harsh peace terms that followed, the Finns' dreams of a Greater Finland faded forever.

FOLKLORE AND THE POLITICAL LEFT

During the first years of Finnish independence, the extreme left was less able to exploit folklore for political purposes than was the right. First of all, academic folklore study had always been in the hands of the nationalists, and it remained there after 1917; second, the Finnish government sharply curtailed the open publication of Communist propaganda; and third, following the Civil War in 1918, the most effective cultural and political ideologists had been forced to go underground or to seek exile across the border. Thus when the propaganda counterattack began in earnest in the 1930s, it took place not in Finland itself but among Finnish expatriates living in the land to which the political right looked with longing eyes—East Karelia.

Those who have attempted to play down the impact of the Greater Finland movement have generally argued that while its advocates made a lot of noise, they exercised little influence on the actual policies of the Finnish government. This assessment seems reasonably accurate, but it leaves out the crucial fact, as Wolf H. Halsti has pointed out, that they exercised considerable influence on the Soviet government. The Soviets, of course, did not fear a Finnish invasion, but they did fear that one of the greater powers bent on destroying Russia would launch an attack on Leningrad under the pretext of aiding Finland. A totalitarian state allowing no public deviation from official policy, Russia could not believe that the advocates of Greater Finland, considering the intensity of their propaganda, were speaking without government approval, and that Finland would not use the first available opportunity to move against Russia. Indeed, the Soviet Commissar for Foreign Affairs, Maxim Litvinov, once told a Western journalist that Finland had concluded a secret treaty with Germany and Poland to bring to pass the annexation of East Karelia.

That the Communist leaders took Finnish folklore propaganda seriously is clear from the propaganda campaign launched in their own press during the *Kalevala* Jubilee Celebration in 1935, the commemoration in Finland of the centennial anniversary of the publication of the *Kalevala*. Few folklore celebrations, and certainly none in Finland, have ever matched the intensity of this event. *Kalevala* athletic events, *Kalevala* dramatic presentations, *Kalevala* radio programs, *Kalevala* concerts, *Kalevala* art shows, *Kalevala* festivals, and an endless array of fervent *Kalevala* speeches were held throughout Finland, all for the greater glory of the fatherland. At the gala festival held in Helsinki's new exhibition hall, the President spoke, the Minister of Education spoke, and the Speaker of Parliament, Kyösti Kallio, warmed the hearts of Finnish scholars by declaring: "In order to promote research aimed at throwing light on the past of the Finnish race, the Parliament, in session today determined to establish a two-million-mark fund for this research. On behalf of the Parliament it is my honor to wish success to this research."

The Communists, of course, took quite a different view of this research. Press titles such as "Folklore and the Imperialistic Aims of the Finnish Bourgeoisie," "The Attempts of the Finnish Bourgeoisie to Force the *Kalevala* into the Service of Nationalism and Chauvinism," and "To What End has the Finnish Bourgeoisie Used and is Now Using the *Kalevala?*" make their attitude clear. "Thousands of Fascist students," cried one Communist publication, "have been sent throughout the land to arrange *Kalevala* celebrations, that is, to whip up anti-Soviet feeling. . . . The Finnish bourgeoisie have come to the egocentric conclusion that they can without hindrance soil and desecrate the best products of the people's creative ability and force them into the service of their plundering and national oppression." Another wrote: "The Fascists in many ways demonstrate that from a cultural-historical perspective they haven't much to learn from the *Kalevala*. They are not organizing the *Kalevala*'s centennial celebration because of the *Kalevala*'s cultural-historical significance. Warlike impassioned speeches . . . and provocative agitation against our Soviet land are a witness of that." And a Leningrad paper published an intrigu-

ing cartoon which showed the old *Kalevala* hero Väinämöinen sitting with a bewildered look on his face while two uniformed Nazis pinned a swastika arm band on him. A third Nazi, arm raised in a *sieg heil* gesture, was handing him an automatic pistol. The caption read: "One or two more strokes and the old boy will be ours."

To the Communists, the Finns' talk of freeing their racial brethren from Bolshevik oppression was simply a smoke screen behind which members of the Finnish bourgeoisie were masking their true intents of adding Karelian land and natural resources to Finland and thus further lining their own capitalistic pockets. On the basis of Finnish folklore, declared one Red newspaper, "Finland's timber capitalists and industrial magnates" claim that they have the right to appropriate the Karelians' land and to turn the Karelians themselves into "the slaves of the Finnish bourgeoisie." Another wrote: "The nationalistic and chauvinistic wave which has in recent days become particularly strong is a definite preparation by the Fascistic bourgeoisie for the organization of a . . . plundering expedition. The *Kalevala* Centennial Celebration will be used to intensify this struggle." And still another exclaimed: "[The Finnish bourgeoisie is using the *Kalevala*] in the service of their Fascist dictatorship. With its aid Finnish Fascists attempt to fan the flame of nationalism and to seek sympathy, support, and justification for their plans to seize Soviet-Karelia."

These statements show that the Communists had become fully aware of the symbolic importance of folklore in political propaganda and now realized that to counter this propaganda they would have to work out new interpretations of the old poetry. To emphasize this fact and to make the Soviet Karelians aware of "their cultural heritage," the Communists organized their own Jubilee Celebrations throughout East Karelia. On the same day that the cream of Finnish society met in Helsinki to commemorate the *Kalevala,* East Karelia's principal political leaders, many of them Finnish exiles, gathered in the regional capital Petroskoi to pay homage to the same epic. In his opening address Edward Gylling, Chairman of the People's Commissariat, decreed: "We have before us the especially important task of exposing the use of the *Kalevala* poems as the ideological foundation of the Finnish bourgeoisie's imperialistic ambitions, in the service of their Karelian-conquest enterprises and their daydreams of a Greater Finland."

The man to whom this task of exposition fell was the prominent leftist ideologist Yrjö Sirola, one of the leading Social Democrats in Finland's pre-Civil War Parliament and, following his exile, an important politico and educator in East Karelia. In his youth, Sirola had studied folklore, and now in the *Kalevala* song country he took up the pursuit once again, studying the epic this time from a Marxist point of view. During the Jubilee Celebration in 1935, he gave an important "*Kalevala* Day" speech, which was distributed widely through East Karelia, and wrote, with Ivar Lassy, the introduction to a Communist edition of the *Kalevala*. These pieces formed the basis of a new ideological approach.

With intriguing duplicity, Sirola admitted from the outset that his purpose was political—he intended to use folklore to help advance the cause of communism; but at the same time he roundly criticized the Finnish nationalists for their own political interpretations, suggesting that only the progressive Communists were capable of properly understanding the old poems. "In the present circumstances of capitalism's period of decay," he moralized, "bourgeois science is not capable of moving ahead but prompts researchers artifically to reach conclusions which fit the dirty purposes of capitalistic imperialism." The most unacceptable of these conclusions, claimed Sirola, were the notions that the folk poems had originated in Western Finland and had arisen from historical accounts of ancient aristocratic heroes.

Well aware that the theory of the origin of the poems in the West and their migration to the East had provided a convenient symbol in the struggle to unite these areas into a Greater Finland, Sirola claimed that the theory had been concocted by reactionary counter-revolutionists like Kaarle Krohn to justify the seizure of foreign land. Nobody denied, said Sirola, that the poems contained a few Western Finnish words, but these were a result not of migration, but of the Karelian singers' having visited Finland and having brought back to Karelia words they had learned on their trips. The poems themselves, however, were Karelian. They had been collected in Karelia; they had been collected from Karelians; and "without doubt" they had been created by Karelians. They did not link East and West. Thus "the Finnish bourgeoisie who so haughtily celebrate the *Kalevala* and make material and political capital from it, have [had] no part in the original poems from which the *Kalevala* was shaped."

Nor had the supposed ancestors of these Finnish bourgeoisie, the warlike heroes of Viking Finland, had a hand in the creation of the poems. The poems quite obviously could not reflect the feudalistic society of Western Finland, as Krohn claimed they did, because they had not originated there. They reflected instead the social and economic life of ancient Karelia, and it was to this life, not the fantasies of bourgeois scholars, that Karelians ought to look for guidance.

Like his counterparts in Finland proper, Sirola believed that folklore mirrored the spirit of the past, if not the actual events, and that it provided models for future action. As W. Edson Richmond has pointed out [in *Southern Folklore Quarterly,* 1961], romantic nationalism can masquerade as proletarian realism. Certainly this was the case in Sirola's work. Finnish nationalists looked to folklore for a reflection of the national or racial soul; Sirola sought in folklore the soul of the proletariat, of the working class. But in each instance the notion prevailed that folklore surviving from the past revealed a world worthy of study and emulation.

And the golden world of the past that this study brought to the attention of the Karelians was not a society of gallant warriors but of peaceful workers, depicted in their daily round of activities, workers who tilled the soil, cultivated their crops, and built their homesteads "in groups," working always for the greater good of the community. This society, said Sirola, structured around the family, was actually a primitive, or prefeudalistic form of communism. And it was this society that the workers of modern Karelia were building once again:

> The Karelian people today, as they honor their folk poetry, stand amidst a tremendous socialistic construction work, which is changing the forests and lands into a new Sampo mill [the magic mill in the *Kalevala* that ground out good fortune to its owners] and is creating a new socialistic generation.

> The laments of slaves no longer echo through the lands of Karelia, but the victorious songs of a new socialistic construction work. Its Sampo is now the miraculous machinery of hundreds of factories and power plants, saw mills and stone quarries, railroads and canals, tractors and steamships.

Having thus distorted the image, Sirola and his compatriots were now ready to ask their own youth, as right-wing ideologists had asked theirs, to capture the spirit of the *Kalevala* and to study the way of life reflected in it as they set out to build a better tomorrow.

Since the war, Communist leaders in East Karelia have on occasion continued to use folklore to serve their political ends, but in Finland itself the drama seems to have been played out. Folklore studies still prosper, but in a changed political climate and within new theoretical perspectives. In recent years there has been a renewed interest in Karelian studies but without the dreams of grandeur that once accompanied such endeavors. The voices raised in defense of Greater Finland have long fallen silent.

But the issues originally raised by those voices are still very much with us. Should the folklorist be content simply to study the folk and their lore, or should he use his research to bring about social, political, economic or religious change? Should he use the lore he collects and studies only to increase our understanding of and sympathy for the human condition, or should he attempt to use that lore to improve the lives of the people? Should he study folklore to understand his heritage, or should he attempt to shape the destiny of his ethnic group? Should he use folklore to study man or to control man?

With both nationalism and communism still major forces in world politics, with ethnic, sexist, and social movements gaining momentum in our own country, and with folklorists seeking increased state support of folklore study, these are not idle questions. Nor are they meant to be purely rhetorical questions. They have no easy answers.

My own view is that the folklorist's best course lies in always being a scholar first and a patriot or special pleader second—not because the cause one pleads is not worthy, but because his devotion to it too easily clouds his vision and allows him to see only that which serves his ideological ends. In any event, one hopes that those seriously seeking solutions to these questions will begin by examining the fruit that unions of folklore research and political ideology have borne in the past.

Kalevala can of course be read without reference to its anthropological connections. Considered as a piece of imaginative literature it invites comparison with other great epics of world literature as a means of gaining deeper insight into the creation of epic. Some critics have even been tempted to see in *Kalevala* an example of how other great epics could have been composed in a more distant past. Similarly the characters, events, poetic imagery and prosody of *Kalevala* provide a rich field for literary criticism and aesthetic appreciation. Yet our detailed knowledge of why and how Lönnrot compiled his epic brings a further dimension to the assessment of the work's significance linking the analysis of *Kalevala* to the phenomenology of the emerging nation state: *Kalevala* represents an unique attempt in Lönnrot's time to transform the poems of the 'little tradition' of ordinary folk into national literature in the 'great tradition' of education and civilisation.

Michael Branch, in "Kalevala: *From Myth to Symbol,*" *in* Books from Finland, *1985.*

Matti Kuusi, Keith Bosley, and Michael Branch (essay date 1977)

SOURCE: An Introduction to *Finnish Folk Poetry—Epic: An Anthology in Finnish and English,* edited and translated by Matti Kussi, Keith Bosley, and Michael Branch, Finnish Literature Society, 1977, pp. 21-77.

[*In the following excerpt, the authors discuss the historical context of Lönnrot's compilation of the* Kalevala *and review its popular and critical reception.*]

The ideas that inspired Bishop Thomas Percy's *Reliques of Ancient English Poetry* (1765) and Johann Herder's *Stimmen der Völker in Liedern* (1st ed. 1778) found a response in Finland when in 1766 a young academic, Henrik Gabriel Porthan (1739-1804), roundly condemned those of his contemporaries who did not share his admiration for Finnish folk poetry. Porthan, who was to become the most distinguished Finnish scholar and teacher of his day, personally inspired several of his contemporaries and his students to undertake a serious study of folk poetry. He himself wrote about prosody and in 1789 his close friend, Christfrid Ganander (1741-1790), published *Mythologia Fennica*, an encyclopaedia of phenomena associated with folk beliefs and poetry.

Interest in folk poetry grew stronger in the early years of the 19th century, especially after the annexation of Finland by Russia in 1808-1809 and the granting of the status of an autonomous Grand Duchy. By this time, a sense of national consciousness had taken root among students and scholars at the university in Turku and there was a growing desire to discover more about the country's ancient history as a step towards defining the 'national identity'. The study of the related languages and folk poetry made up the principal means by which young men attempted to reconstruct their country's past. By the 1820s young scholars were already undertaking long journeys beyond the eastern frontiers of Finland into Russia to gather the information they needed.

One of those whose attention focused primarily on folk poetry was a doctor of medicine, Elias Lönnrot (1802-1884). After publishing several short studies and collections of folk poetry, he brought out in 1835 the work which finally established the importance of Finnish folk poetry (and with which it has generally been associated ever since) *Kalevala, or old poems of Karelia from the ancient times of the Finnish people*. The first edition contained 32 epic poems (12,078 lines) and was followed by the enlarged and definitive edition of 50 poems (22,795 lines) in 1849. In 1840 Lönnrot published as a companion volume the *Kanteletar,* a collection of 652 lyrical poems and ballads.

Lönnrot had collected the greater part of the material for these works while practising medicine in the Kajaani district of Eastern Finland. In this capacity he had to travel long distances and frequently crossed the frontier into Archangel Karelia where he met singers of folk poetry and noted down their poems. Lönnrot undertook eleven such expeditions and, travelling much of the time on foot, he covered some 13,000 miles and collected 65,000 lines of Kalevala-type poetry. It was from the heroic epic he had found in Archangel Kare-lia and from sources that had been collected earlier that he constructed the 1835 *Kalevala*. The idea of putting the material together to form a long, coherent epic sprang from the practice of the singers he had met and from contemporary literary thinking. He was fa-miliar with F. A. Wolf's theory of the origin of the *Iliad* and *Odyssey* which seemed to him to be sus-tained by the tendency he had observed among singers in Archangel Karelia to combine several epic poems into long, thematically linked sequences.

Lönnrot's contemporaries believed that he had discov-ered a long-lost epic in the backwoods of Karelia and that he had done little more than put it on paper. In fact, Lönnrot had introduced considerable changes into the poems he had used in order to bring them into a narrative sequence and to achieve thematic coherence. He had removed many Christian and other relatively recent features and had changed the names of persons and places. The adventures attributed to Lemminkäin-en, for example, combine in one character the feats of several heroes. According to one calculation, one-third of the total number of lines in the 1835 Kalevala was modified or revised by Lönnrot; more than 600 lines appear to have been composed by Lönnrot himself, for no corresponding variants have ever been discovered. While in terms of its basic components the *Kalevala* has its origin in folk poetry, its overall shape and struc-ture are the work of Elias Lönnrot.

The Romantic View

The appearance of the *Kalevala* was a turning-point in Finnish cultural history. It marked the establishment of a movement that finally saw Finnish acquire equal status with Swedish as a national language. For many de-cades after Finland's union with Russia, Swedish had remained the language of culture, administration and commerce. While the question of russification was considered, no serious moves were made towards this until the end of the 19th century. On the contrary, the Russian authorities did not discourage anything that served to weaken traditional ties with Sweden and the decades following the publication of the *Kalevala* saw a protracted struggle between those Finns who wished to promote Finnish as a national language and those who wished to retain Swedish. The leadership of the former was assumed by J. V. Snellman (1806-1881), a student of Hegel, who gave the necessary impetus to the campaign to achieve equal language rights for the majority of the inhabitants of Finland. In this struggle they pointed to the *Kalevala* as proof that Finnish could be developed into a language of civilisation and cul-ture, and the epic became the cornerstone of the ensu-ing Finnish cultural movement. Schoolchildren had to spend four years studying it; many people could recite from it by heart. It was set to music and became a popular subject for the visual arts. Ice-breakers, res-

taurants, even commercial firms took their names from the *Kalevala* or places and characters mentioned in it. Writers, artists, scholars, students, and philosophers went off to Karelia to follow in Lönnrot's footsteps and to see for themselves the primitive scenery and the people they imagined the *Kalevala* to depict. Many of Finland's greatest talents—including the writers Aleksis Kivi, Eino Leino, the composer Jean Sibelius, the paint-er Akseli Gallen-Kallela, and the sculptor Wäinö Aal-tonen—drew inspiration from the *Kalevala* and the cult that grew up around it.

For many decades the *Kalevala* was seen as a primary source of information about the ancient Finns' history, mythology, way of life, and their understanding of the world around them. Like the tales of Homer and the Scandinavian *Edda,* the *Kalevala* continues to be the subject of scholarly and quasi-scholarly works that attempt to analyse its historical significance. Numer-ous theories have been advanced to explain who Väinämöinen really was and where Pohjola was situ-ated. Although Julius Krohn showed convincingly, as early as 1885, that 'the printed *Kalevala,* skilfully compiled though it is, cannot serve as the basis of scholarly research', amateurs have not been deterred from using it as the starting-point for fantastic flights of imagination into Finnish antiquity. While in Finland serious folklorists and historians abandoned this ap-proach long ago, scholars outside Finland, especially if they do not read Finnish, may still look to Lönnrot's epic as a source of information about ancient Finnish poetry. The results are as reliable as if Liszt were used as a primary source for research into Hungarian folk music.

Despite the warnings of scholars and even the sugges-tion that genuine folk poetry might be of far greater interest and aesthetic quality, the prevailing attitude remained for many years one of unqualified admira-tion. Typical of the unquestioning attitudes were state-ments such as 'For me the *Kalevala* poems have been so sacred that listening to them is like resting one's weary head against some ancient, immovable support' (Gallen-Kallela, 1899) and 'The most remarkable po-etic achievements of the North should not be sought in the works of Bellman, Stagnelius or Runeberg. No, they are to be found in the *Kalevala* and the *Kantele-tar*. These are the miraculous creations of the intelli-gence of the heart' (from the unpublished papers of the Swedish poet Vilhelm Ekelund, 1880-1949). But such attitudes on the part of intelligent and educated people need to be seen in the light of the political situation.

The years 1890-1917, which saw increasing interven-tion by the Tsarist authorities in Finnish affairs, lead-ing at times to the suspension of traditional rights and privileges, was a time of powerful growth of interest in the *Kalevala* and in Karelia: the oppressed people sought hope for the future from a glorious past. When faced with the reality of independence in 1918, how-ever, economic, social and military matters took prece-dence and interest in the *Kalevala* began to fade. More recently, thanks to a growing disenchantment with modern urban life, interest in the *Kalevala,* in Karelian romanticism, and in folklore has begun to revive.

In the Shadow of the Kalevala

Despite the uncritical acclaim of most Finns, there was nevertheless a small group of Finnish scholars, con-temporaries of Lönnrot, who realised that the *Kalevala* was not wholly representative of genuine folk epic. D. E. D. Europaeus (1820-1884), one of the young men who helped to assemble and arrange the material for the 1849 edition of the *Kalevala,* expressed his regret in 1855 that it was 'crammed too full of all kinds of variants and unimportant details,' and, he continued, 'it contains many features that have been made up by the compiler himself . . . In their original form the poems are unified, lively, and full of imagination.' Europaeus complained that the original poems had been spoiled by Lönnrot's attempts to reshape them, to fill gaps with lines taken from other poems, and by the compiler's elaboration of some themes at the expense of others; Europaeus was especially critical of the ten-dency to diminish the part played by the supernatural.

While scholars such as Europaeus appreciated the re-lationship between the *Kalevala* and genuine folk po-etry, the sheer size of Lönnrot's epic overshadowed their reservations. To what could they point to justify their criticisms apart from their own personal experi-ence as collectors? There was very little that could be set against the *Kalevala* as evidence of how the poems were performed by contemporary singers and even less from earlier times. Neither rune-stones nor ancient manuscripts survived to show how Finnish folk poems were performed in pre-Christian times. The earliest surviving documentary source, a 13th century Karelian lightning spell recorded on a piece of birchbark, was discovered in 1957 in the vicinity of Novgorod. Bish-op Agricola's Prayer Book (1544) contains the earliest version of a Finnish proverb, a weather prophecy, and a chant that lists the gestation periods of various ani-mals, while the earliest example of a poem is a spell against the plague, a couplet in the accounts book of the Korsholm Crown Estate, noted down in 1564.

About 1615, the exiled Swedish poet Johannes Mess-enius (1579-1636) copied from the papers of Sigfrid Aronus Forsius (ca 1550-1624) a Latin version of the legend of Bishop Henry and Lalli that was known in the Köyliö district of South-West Finland; a correspond-ing Finnish verse legend was recorded by not later than 1682 (cf. Poems 66, 67). The first Finnish gram-mar, Eskil Petraeus' *Linguae fennicae brevis institutio* (1649) includes eight popular Finnish riddles as illus-trative material. The earliest examples of Kalevala-type

lyric poems are found in a collection compiled in the 1660s by Henrik Florinus (1633-1705) and published in 1702; two poems used in bear rites were published by Petrus Bång (1633-1696) in 1679. Daniel Juslenius (1676-1752) was the first to publish a version of a Finnish ballad, *Death of the Bride,* in his fanciful ac-count of the history of Turku (1700). The earliest manuscript of the historical poem *Duke Charles* dates from 1699.

The first example of old Kalevala epic to catch the attention of Finnish scholars appears to have been variants of the poems about Väinämöinen's voyage and the playing of the *kantele.* Versions of these poems had begun to find their way into poetry and disserta-tions in the 18th century. But many of these had been forgotten, or were not readily available, and in any case their fragmentary information was eclipsed by Lönnrot's epic.

On the Cultural Periphery

A further difficulty faced by Europaeus and those who shared his views was that the efforts of the Lutheran clergy to stamp out folk poetry, together with the grad-ual spread of West European culture from Sweden, had largely eliminated the old tradition from Finland proper, where it existed only in fragments and in a few isolated districts. The areas where it survived were those that represented the cultural periphery in the 19th cen-tury, areas to the east of the boundary of the Grand Duchy which were still isolated either geographically or linguistically, or for both these reasons, from the unifying cultural influences that had spread over most of Europe—the periphery of the Swedish and Russian spheres of influence in the far north: the region east of the frontier of the Grand Duchy of Finland, in the western districts of Archangel Karelia, midway between Oulujärvi in the west and the southern shores of the White Sea in the east. It is a region of lakes, marshes and forests where communications were arduous. In the 19th century its inhabitants still supported them-selves by hunting, fishing, rudimentary—often burn-beat—agriculture and, like their forefathers, eked out a meagre livelihood as pedlars of small wares, travelling long distances on foot in Finland undeterred by offi-cials who tried with little success to stop this illegal trade. It was an area into which the Lutheran Church had not penetrated. The Christianity of these Karelians was that of the Russian Orthodox Church, which tol-erated folk poetry and did not frown so severely on surviving pagan practices. A second area which was similarly isolated from Western influences and whose inhabitants also belonged to the Russian Church, was Olonets and Ladoga Karelia, the region around the northern shores of Lake Ladoga extending north into Olonets and north-west to the Finnish-Russian fron-tier. It was mainly in these areas, Archangel Karelia in the north and Ladoga and Olonets Karelia further south,

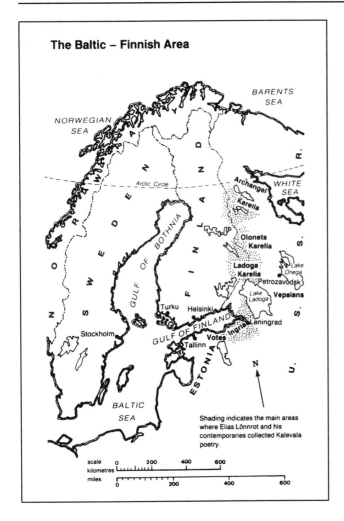

The Baltic – Finnish Area

Shading indicates the main areas where Elias Lönnrot and his contemporaries collected Kalevala poetry.

that the heroic epic was still being sung by men, and occasionally by women, in the 19th century. It is interesting to note that the areas where the Novgorod *bylina* tradition survived most strongly, among the Russian settlers on the shores of Lake Onega and the White Sea, were not far away.

A third area in which Kalevala-type poetry continued to flourish into the 19th century was the Karelian Isthmus and Ingria. While the tradition of male singing died out along the south-east shore of the Gulf of Finland, the singing tradition survived among the womenfolk of three areas in particular: Narvusi, Soikkola, and Hevaa, each of which is isolated at the tip of a cape. These women did not retain the practice of singing relatively long narrative epic sequences, but used fragments of epic in an allusive style to express personal sentiments. It was linguistic rather than geographical isolation that sheltered the Ingrian Finns and those on the Karelian Isthmus from the penetration of new ideas. The oldest group, the Izhors, clung to their old ways in a virtually unchanged form, although nominally they belonged to the Russian Orthodox Church. Of particular interest are the large numbers of Lutheran

Finns who migrated from areas in Eastern Finland to Ingria with the expansion of Sweden in the 17th century. They brought with them their poems, customs and other traditions which, because of the religious difference, generally survived in their old form largely untouched by the traditions of their linguistically related Russian Orthodox neighbours and escaped the excesses of the movement that stamped out most folk poetry in mainland Finland.

Lönnrot was not the first person to realize that a wealth of folk poetry survived across the frontier in Russia. This fact had been well publicized by an Ostrobothnian doctor of medicine, Zachris Topelius (1781-1831). Paralysed by a stroke and unable to move beyond the confines of his home in Uusikaarlepyy on the coast of the Gulf of Bothnia, he used to invite the Karelian pedlars to sing their poems to him and published a selection of them in five slim volumes: *Suomen Kansan Wanhoja Runoja ynnä myös Nykyisempiä Lauluja* (Old poems and more modern songs of the Finns', 1822-1831). In the preface to the last volume Topelius described where collectors should look for poems: 'The only area where the old customs and the old tales of the menfolk survive untouched by outside influences and are sung as part of the daily round is beyond the frontiers of Finland, in a few parishes of the Province of Archangel—especially in the parish of Vuokkiniemi. There the Väinämöinen songs can still be heard, there the *kantele* and the *sampo* [!] still echo and it is from there that I have with great care obtained my best songs.'

It was this that led Lönnrot and others to Archangel Karelia and gave birth to the 1835 ***Kalevala***. In the following years Lönnrot and his disciples, including Europaeus, explored the two other regions described above, the fruits of which are embodied in the second edition of the epic. It was to all three regions that Europaeus, and before long others, urged that collectors should return and undertake a more thorough and exhaustive collection of folk poetry materials. It is uncertain whether Europaeus' motives were those of the modern folklorist, who treats every piece of material as worthy of attention and study, or whether he thought that by assembling and publishing oral literature in a different way from that adopted by Lönnrot, the national cause (of which Europaeus was a prominent exponent) would be better served. Whatever his motives, his ideas gradually found support. Towards the end of the 19th century the collection of folk poetry assumed the proportions of a national movement and literally thousands of scholars have since taken part in it. Perhaps the most important were the great collectors at the turn of the century, whose work provided the foundations and demonstrated the techniques of subsequent collection—men such as J. Länkelä (1833-1916), V. Porkka (1854-1889) and V. Alava (1870-1935), who saved the poetry of Ingria from extinction, and A. A. Borenius-Lähteenkorva (1846-1931), the first scholar to prove that many of the poems in Archangel Karelia had been transmitted from areas further south or west.

John B. Alphonso-Karkala (essay date 1979)

SOURCE: "Transmission of Knowledge by Antero Vipunen to Väinämöinen in *Kalevala* and by Sukra to Kacha in *Mahabharata*," in *Proceedings of the 7th Congress of the International Comparative Literature Association, Volume 2, Comparative Literature Today: Theory and Practice,* edited by Eva Kushner and Roman Struc, Kunst und Wissen, Erich Bieber, 1979, pp. 619-23.

[*In the following excerpt, Alphonso-Karkala examines the symbolic implications of Väinämöinen's quest to obtain three magic words from the giant Antero Vipunen in the* Kalevala.]

In the oral tradition, when natural phenomena were not readily comprehended, people simplified their perception of the existential situation by explaining the then unexplainable through the imagistic logic of the myth. That was a highly skilled science of that time. Such myths invariably made clear in a dramatic shorthand the symbolic meaning of the natural process. One can easily discern the mythification of the natural phenomenon of the gathering of the rain clouds and the accompanying thunder and lightning as the struggle of beings of another order, and the terrifying light and sound are the result of wielding a supreme weapon of destruction, whether the wielder of that dreadful weapon is Siva or Indra, Jehovah or Zeus, Odin or Ukko Jumala. In this manner the incomprehensible phenomenon becomes meaningful within the cultural experience structured by the myth. Similarly, there have been myths to explain human mortality, and human suffering, or even human resurrection—though symbolically—or failure of such resurrection.

This paper is an attempt to present two identical myths relating to the problem of the transmission of knowledge by the possessor of knowledge, to another who seeks to know. The two episodes are taken from the heroic poetry of two different cultures, namely the Finnish epic *Kalevala* and the Sanscrit epic *Mahabharata.* The paper will examine these two myths with a view to determining the cultural attitudes and values behind them, and to gaining some understanding of the purpose and meaning of the myths.

In Lönnröt's *Uusi Kalevala,* the episode relating to the search for knowledge by Väinämöinen and its transmission by Antero Vipunen is contained in Runos XVI-XVII. While building a boat with the power of his songs, Väinämöinen finds himself unable to complete it for want of three magic words, and therefore goes in search of them. First, he seeks to obtain the required knowledge from the brains of animals that float, such as swans, geese, swallows, reindeers. But unable to find any knowledge there, he goes to Tuonela, the region of the dead, hoping to get the knowledge from the wise and the old who have already departed. Upon entering Tuonela, Väinämöinen finds himself in mortal danger and quickly escapes by changing his shape (Runo XVI).

After he returns home, Väinämöinen meditates for a long time as to how to get the needed magic words, until one day a common shepherd tells him that he might get "a hundred phrases and a thousand words" from ancient Antero Vipunen, the wisest, full of craft and famous for his songs. Väinämöinen decides to seek Vipunen, and the smith Ilmarinen forges for him from iron a pair of shoes, a gauntlet, a shirt, and a mighty sword lined with the strongest of steel. However, Ilmarinen warns him that Vipunen has long since perished and he cannot hope to get words or even half a word from him. Disregarding this warning, Väinämöinen goes on his long quest and when he finally arrives, he finds Antero Vipunen lying outstretched on the ground having become one with nature. Trees have grown all over him. Drawing his steel sword, Väinämöinen forces Vipunen's mouth to open wide with a view to awakening him to sing his songs. Instead, Väinämöinen slips, falls into Vipunen's mouth, and he is swallowed by the sleeping giant. Once inside Vipunen's stomach, Väinämöinen forges a smithy with his equipment, causing Vipunen tremendous pain and headache.

The awakened giant, finding some unfriendly intruder in his stomach, threatens in a long monologue to get rid of him. But on hearing no response, Vipunen finally threatens to kill himself to be rid of his sufferings. Then Väinämöinen announces himself from within the Giant's belly, and declares his purpose, namely that he will not stop torturing Vipunen until he teaches him all the charms and songs, and he, Väinämöinen, learns them in full. Vipunen agrees and recites all his store of knowledge and Väinämöinen learns everything gradually. When he has listened enough he jumps out of Vipunen's stomach, and the two bid goodbye to each other in good humour, Vipunen saying:

> Good indeed has been your coming
> Better it is when you depart.

Väinämöinen then goes away with all the new learning and completes his boat. (Runo XVII).

The questions that are posed by this episode are (a) who is Antero Vipunen, the wise old man, and is he dead or alive? (b) Where does Väinämöinen really go to get the knowledge, and how does he obtain it? In order to gain some understanding of the myth, it is necessary to enquire beyond the literal story and grasp, if possible, some of the symbolic meaning since these poems, we are told, were so regarded when they were sung with faith in their potency.

The Kalevala episode no doubt makes Antero Vipunen an enormous Gulliver-like figure lying down in deep sleep, or a kind of Kumbhakarna, the seasonal man who keeps awake for six months and sleeps for six months. The smith, Ilmarinen, points out to Väinämöinen that Vipunen has long since perished, and the source of the knowledge he is seeking is not in the living world. There are instances of heroes journeying to the land of the dead to get special knowledge, like Odysseus going to Hades to consult the spirit of Teiresias, or Aeneas going to the Infernal region to find out directions. Väinämöinen has already made such a journey to Tuonela and escaped from there without acquiring any knowledge. Yet the place where Antero Vipunen is lying on earth, almost dissolved in nature, and the kind of trees that are growing over him, suggest a typical burial place in the tradition of the Finno-Ugric people. Apparently, Antero Vipunen has ceased to exist, yet he is not dead, nor is he completely out of existence. Väinämöinen is able to revive a seemingly dead man on whose body trees have grown, and make him recite songs and charms from his living memory. The myth fails to explain this resurrection of Vipunen—or partial resurrection, if we stretch the literal interpretation. It appears we have to look for some other source of meaning, considering its symbolic and spiritual nature.

In the Finnish folk songs recorded in *Suomen Kansan Vanhat Runot,* among the various names used for this unusual being of immense learning are Ankerus (Unkari or Hungary) and Vironi (Viro or Estonia), these being the names of two other regions where people related to the Finns branched off in their pre-historic migration. What the poet seems to suggest in the personification of the primeval character of Vipunen is that Väinämöinen, perhaps, goes to the cumulative fund of ancestral knowledge of the Finno-Ugric people, and in fact, searches deep in the collective unconscious of the race in the Jungian sense. This includes not only the living, but also those people who have ceased to exist, but whose experience, knowledge, visions, and wisdom continue to live among the surviving members of the race. This is also supported by the view that Antero Vipunen is "a primeval giant or Titan whom some commentators suppose to be the same as Kaleva," the ancestor of the heroes of **Kalevala,** though Kaleva does not appear in person anywhere in the epic, except insofar as the heroes are sometimes referred to as Kaleva poika or Kaleva poijat, sons of Kaleva. As the collective unconscious of Kaleva and Kaleva poijat, Antero Vipunen is conceived partly as having ceased to exist since long ago, as Ilmarinen says, and yet partly as continuing to exist, capable of communicating the store of cumulative knowledge embedded therein.

If Antero Vipunen is a personification of the idea of collective unconscious, or a symbolic person, where does Väinämöinen really go to get the knowledge and how does he get it? The story suggests Väinämöinen undertaking a journey like Dante. Dante goes through the infinite possibility of action over a vertical scale of values in the human mind, oscillating from extreme evil to the highest state of grace; and in that symbolic journey in the interior landscape of the mind, he passes through Inferno, Purgatorio and Paradiso to be enlightened in the end in the Empireo Mobile. Väinämöinen is not shackled by such a theology, or organized hierarchy. Directed by a simple shepherd, he simply leaps over the points of women's needles, over the points of heroes' sword-blades, and comes to apprehend like a shaman in a state of trance, or like a yogi in a state of samadhi, that life is a continuing extension in Time and Space, from womb to womb, and seed to seed; that in such a continuing presence, Vipunen is neither dead nor undead, though over his physical body natural trees have grown; that the essence of life continues to express itself in changing forms. Whether Väinämöinen is entombed in the graveyard of Antero Vipunen or in the mental graveyard of his cultural experience, he listens to the voice of the wisest and most ancient one, and, like Jonah entombed in the belly of a fish by the chastising Jehovah, is enlightened. In such a burial or shrouding, the individual is not dead, but is temporarily suspended from life to scoop up ineffable experience, and is resurrected. In such a psychic hibernation, or state of pregnancy by the mothering entity, knowledge becomes transmitted, and the seeker gradually awakening to self-knowledge is reborn. This descent into the unknown and resurrection therefrom helps the hero to fulfil his task: so Jonah declares his message to Ninevah, Jesus delivers his New Jerusalem, Aeneas reaches his Promised Land, resourceful Odysseus, getting into a new boat, goes home to his wife, and vakaa vanha Väinämöinen goes home and completes his boat. . . .

[W]hat is common in these two myths is the secretive nature of the special knowledge and the unwillingness of the possessor of the knowledge to part with it. The only way to get this classified information is to get into the inner being of the person possessing the knowledge, and while thus entombed in the mothering person, the transfusion of knowledge takes place when the two minds are attentive to a single purpose; in other words, the myth seems to suggest that the knowledge becomes transmitted when two minds understand the same thing, at the same time, and in the same sense. Though there are few situations in which two minds totally understand each other, outside the art of telepathy (such as Michel de Montaigne and his friend

Etienne de La Boétie, or Jalaluddin Rumi and Sha-mas), those myths suggest that the ideal condition for the natural transmission of secret knowledge is a state of pregnancy by the preceptor, when the seeker becomes conceived, and is twice born. In our days of Gutenberg culture and computer knowledge, one needs a vivid imagination to grasp the imagistic logic of the myth in which a seeker of knowledge enters the body of his preceptor and comes out enlightened or illumined!

Robert Harbison (essay date 1980)

SOURCE: "Romantic Localism," in *Deliberate Regression,* Alfred A. Knopf, 1980, pp. 115-47.

[*In the following excerpt, Harbison comments on the absence of a clear scholarly, idealistic, or artistic focus in the* Kalevala.]

[Elias] Lönnrot was a doctor who began to collect fragments of Finnish oral poetry on vacations and tours of medical inspection in rural Finland, without at first the idea of forming them into a whole. After his first publication, *The Harp* (1829-31), two skilled singers in an eastern district gave him a new conception of the songs' homogeneity, though the possibility of putting together a Finnish Ossian had been broached much earlier in an ethnic newspaper.

As he went on Lönnrot not only collected but embodied the folk tradition, becoming a singer who like peasant ones could recite from memory and improvise links and elaborations as he sang. He differed from peasant singers in using transcription to learn the songs, which helped him build a larger repertoire than any of them, while his knowledge of literary models like Homer undoubtedly influenced the way he exercised the singer's right to arrange his material, to reassign actions to different of the stock characters who recur through the poems. But if he is a more radical social type than the Grimms, a case of deep mimicry, he feels correspondingly less ideological commitment to folk literature, casualness in his relation which makes him less important than they in the history of ideas.

Like Runge whose transcription of *The Fisherman's Wife* in the language of fisherfolk fired the Grimms at an early stage in their research, Lönnrot cultivated unscientific closeness to his sources, entering a two-way relation with the informants from which the Grimms kept aloof. His doctoral dissertation had been about magic medicine and he became a popular instructor through medical and agricultural manuals for simple readers, giving them something in return for what he got and even contracting their diseases like typhus. As he lacks, in spite of various linguistic compilations including a Finnish grammar and dictionary, the Grimms' scholarly rigor, so he does the crusading ideology of immersion in a lower class one might expect of a Russian, though he cultivated simplicity and retirement—peasant clothes, a pipe, work at an ingenious desk he had invented, exercise, singing.

The Grimms' materials remain detectably on the scale they naturally occur, though massed differently. Lönnrot while scrupulous in preserving the specificity of his fragments—charms for catching bears hold up the narrative for four hundred lines—imposes on them a principle of coherence borrowed from another culture. Trying to make an epic from these desultory pieces he forges an unachieved Ossian, flat and centerless because he refuses to falsify the indigenous attitude toward his actors into heroism, and preserves even the genre of the components, including recognizable bits from south Finland which are more balladic because in that region singers are women. After the addition of an equal amount of new material in 1849 the *Kalevala* became even more a treasure trove or national display case which contained every single bit of information about the life of the early Finns Lönnrot could turn up. He was at pains to safeguard it from obsolescence with the claim that no new material was likely to appear because he and his assistants had scoured Finland and the songs were dying anyway from exposure to the air of national publicity. He is also concerned to show that odd usages in the poems like impossible tasks set for a suitor, a familiar motif in fairy tales, correspond to customs among the early Finns. He finds ingenious rationalizations of mythic beliefs, like that churches in Finland were built by giants and wrecked at night by demons, rationalizations which depend on the Finns taking their history from the downtrodden Lapps and then overlaying it with bits of their own contrary perspective. Thus giants are Finns as seen by Lapps, and demons Lapps seen by Finns.

A certain lack of the grandeur which the imported notion of epic demands prompted bizarre mythic interpretations Lönnrot confutes by noting prosaic inconsistencies—the character who represents the spirit of fire is afraid of it and gets burned, the spirit of the air is as much at the mercy of contrary winds as others. To imagine a slanging match early in the poem as a contest between water and snow, a pivot between winter and summer, or the voyage to steal back a prized grain mill, simply because the geography is uncertain, as occurring in the blue seas of heaven with the lynchpin of the universe as its goal, are efforts to enlarge the poems to match the scale of one's own biggest feelings. The characters are so obviously petty in themselves that somewhat on the model of Ossian one turns to the circumambient environment for intimations of something larger.

Lönnrot was immune to this need for transcendence which converted the poem's evident responsiveness to nature into an embracing nature cult. He argued instead that early beliefs were close to his own, founded on a single unspecific god. And he was content to lack a transforming vision, to collect pieces of shattered pots and to form them into a pattern but not to see it as the world-tree when he had finished.

The metric form of the original materials is also relaxed and uncomplex, consisting of paired lines, the second of which varies the language but repeats closely the matter of the first. Although the singing depicted in the poem does not take this form, as collected by Lönnrot it was usually sung by two, a lead and a support, one of whom directed its course, leaving the alternate line to be completed by his partner while he prepared the one to follow. They sang clasping each other's hands and rocking back and forth. As it comes through translation the motion of the verse is powerfully physical, and the particular proportions of sound and thought would probably feel much the same in any language, like heaving and then resting on the oars, except that the repeat is not dead calm but an effortless exertion.

Thus the larger motion of the poem no matter how long it dwells on a simple action never becomes involute or intricate but a continuous grooming or polishing. Even the eyes sift the page like shaking a basket of stones, motion which acts as a filter keeping back some of the sense. In formal procedure it is an extreme example, but perhaps typical of anonymous products seeking out the kind of action which is rolled up then comes unrolled, and thus largely performs itself, like the house that Jack built or the hiding of successive kernels in each other and then in successive fish which are then chased and successively cut open to find fire at the end again. Admittedly Wolfram von Eschenbach's *Parzival,* though rude in its way and peculiar for its author's claims of illiteracy, is an extreme example of an authored poem, of a certain intricacy going with inexperience like a literary equivalent of Scandinavian or Celtic interlaced ornament. The professions of ignorance may be ironic adoptions of local coloration from the naïve hero, or licenses for eccentricity, for it is a poem which allows language to become contorted in following grotesque actions, but perhaps it only proves that any action is susceptible of gnarling as each one in Lönnrot is of smoothing. The comparison with Wolfram shows that there are certain kinds of wit and obscurity deeply individual and literary, however much he may pretend to be an oral poet, which could not be passed on by a group product like *Kalevala,* though the thought may feel animistic or mythical, so Wolfram conceives a battle as the struggle between the heraldic emblems on knights' shields instead of the knights themselves, between griffins and ostriches, on whose side a troop of anchors intervenes just as the conceit has begun to feel comfortable. Once he even splits one of these tribal totems between two groups,

The *Kalevala* has a plot or, rather, an assemblage of plots. These stories seize the reader's attention, tease his imagination, and hold him, sometimes more and at other times less captivated, bound to the progress of the narrative. A mere glance at the first twenty-five lines of the *Alku-Kalevala* conjures up a series of associations: a wide array of real and imaginary place names is combined with the description of a bullock so huge that its dimensions can be fathomed only in terms of running-time and flying-time. These images are painted with powerful strokes of the brush, abruptly, at the very beginning of the canto. They are followed by others, some equally dramatic, some more subdued, some subtle and some picturesque, all in epic metre and interspersed with quoted speech.

Robert Austerlitz, in The Poetics of the Kalevala, *in* Books from Finland, *1985.*

an army marked with the front halves of griffins joining a detachment identified by the rear halves.

Surprises on such a scale, of which Wolfram prepares large quantities, are impossible in an orally transmitted work like *Kalevala* with its liking for self-perpetuating chains such as the progress of Vainamoinen's tears in thirteen stages over various parts of his body, clothes, and possessions, running on to reach the lake and settle at its bottom from which they must be retrieved. Even a less automated example like the inquiry into the origin of iron touched off by Vainamoinen's wounding himself with an ax and needing to know how iron came to be, and especially how it came to be "bitter," or able to hurt its maker, in order to staunch the flow of blood—even this historical investigation is self-completing, burgeoning irresponsibly at the expense of the narrative which is always losing its way because it is a purposefulness largely imposed by Lönnrot. Nothing reveals better the difference between the efficiency of the fairy tales and the exiguous spinning-out of the songs than the idle quality of magic in the *Kalevala,* which has become a reflex to be elaborated, whereas in the tale it escapes conscious inspection.

Home feeling not magic runs deepest in the *Kalevala,* local sentiment tied not to geography but to certain usages, mostly connected with the husbanding of things or with cleanliness. This unadventurous meaning of local is well expressed in Gallen-Kallela's peasant interiors of dark wood painted in the 1890s, and more abstractly by his *Kalevala* illustrations which look hewn from wood, a moderate heroism of work. Some of the most poignant moments of the poem are the most obviously interpolated and substitutable, general instructions to brides on how to clean stoves, spoons not forgetting the handles, tables not forgetting the legs, with none of the Homeric feeling that a ritual significance still graces the act.

A nearer example than Homer of a naïvely materialistic world, the *Nibelungenlied,* lays over bare possession and maintenance a powerful mythology of waste. Expenditure is heroism there, sign of a craving within the limited confines for largeness. The *Kalevala* is remarkable for its sober contentment with cleanliness as a measure of civilization and for concentrating on its dark corner without pretending to prefer it to sitting by the window. Though an example of the higher Romantic valuation of custom and usage as concrete history, the sort of thing the eighteenth century had tried to call prejudice, the *Kalevala* is truly extraordinary in how little it presses the claim of its own uniqueness.

Senni Timonen (essay date 1985)

SOURCE: "Lönnrot and His Singers," translated by Satu Salo and Keith Bosley, in *Books from Finland,* Vol. XIX, No. 1, 1985, pp. 24-29.

[*In the following excerpt, Timonen examines the contributions made to Lönnrot's conception of the* Kalevala *by some of the principal singers of Finnish folk poems from whom he collected his material.*]

In the winter of 1834, when the *Kalevala* was taking shape, on Elias Lönnrot's desk there were 27,900 lines of folk poetry, as yet unpublished, each of which had been taken down from private citizens. Most of these singers and wise men (*tietäjät,* literally 'knowers', possessors of magical powers) were still alive and breathing the frosty air of the same winter in their villages far away across the eastern border of the Grand Duchy of Finland. Lönnrot was drawn to these singers, not only because they were his contemporaries, but also because he had direct contact with them. On his five collecting trips of 1828-34, he had personally sought out most of them after journeys of hundreds of miles on foot, on skis, by rowing-boat, on horseback and by sledge, and he had noted down in his own hand most of the material which would form the *Kalevala.* On his journeys, in addition to the texts, he had received other essential building material for the *Kalevala:* firsthand experience of the hunting culture which had kept the old poems alive, and of the people to whose daily life and worldview these songs had belonged.

Earlier collectors seldom mentioned singers. It was poems they were after; the singers were felt to be mere vehicles. The few singers we know of must clearly have been impressive personalities or outstanding performers. Even Lönnrot, who was one of the first Finn-ish travel writers to portray ordinary people, speaks about only a few singers, and then for the most part only in passing. This is why, of the singers who left their mark on the first edition (1835) of the *Kalevala,* only about twenty can be identified. As far as the formation of the *Kalevala* is concerned, these early singers are interesting; they can be truly called the singers of the *Kalevala.* They played an active part in Lönnrot's creative process. In what follows we shall look at those who, as well as adding to the text, can be seen as representing, even initiating, the various, sometimes contradictory dimensions of the final edition (1849) of the *Kalevala.*

1. *The magical: Juhana.* On 28 June 1828 Lönnrot arrived in the parish of Kesälahti in Finnish Karelia (about 30 miles east of Savonlinna). It was a Sunday. He walked six miles from the church in pouring rain and at dusk reached the Kainulainen house, whose master had been praised as a singer to him. Juhana was away floating logs, and Lönnrot had to wait two days. But the time did not drag. 'On the contrary, I took an inexplicable delight in walking in the forest where Kainulainen's father had so often said his prayers to the forest gods and goddesses, and where in former times the "maids of Forestland" had appeared to their favourites. It should be remembered that old Kainulainen had in his day been one of the best hunters in the area and that his good luck in hunting, according to the superstitious belief of the time, depended in large measure on the favour of the forest gods, whom he, better than others, could persuade with his songs.'

On Tuesday the 40-year-old Juhana arrived home, and in the evening Lönnrot heard him sing; he had inherited his father's songs and spells. But Juhana decided that on Wednesday he must go tree-felling with his brothers. On Thursday Lönnrot paid the brothers to hire a replacement for Juhana, who sang all day from morning till evening and declared that his songs had never before come in so handy. Next day the brothers were working indoors, and Juhana was able to continue singing while he worked. The result was 49 poems in all, including spells.

Juhana Kainulainen was the first great wise man, healer and hunter Lönnrot met. Although he also sang good epic poems, the spells he performed were quite clearly more important for the development of the *Kalevala,* as can be seen particularly in the spell scenes of the final edition, for example when Lemminkäinen sets out to subdue the Demon's elk with spells (canto 14). Here, as in many other spell and prayer sequences, many individual lines derive from Juhana. But more important than these is the message that Juhana and singers like him transmitted to Lönnrot, an increasing certainty about the essential function of spells in the epic as a whole. As the *Kalevala* developed, Lönnrot wove more and more spells in among the epic poems.

With them he strove to create a picture of a way of life in which contact with the Beyond is continuous, living, sensitive.

2. The heroic: Ontrei and Arhippa. On 17 June 1833 Lönnrot was for the second time across the border in Archangel Karelia, in the remote village of Vuonninen (100 miles north-east of Kajaani). He writes: 'In the morning Ontrei sang for me. I would have liked him to stay with me for the afternoon too, but he was indispensable for fishing, so he could not stay. I wished him a good catch after making a deal with him that, if they caught a certain amount of fish, he would undertake to sing all the following day; he agreed.' Although the catch was not large, the next day Ontrei Malinen sang a few more poems. Lönnrot took down from him nine long narrative poems complete. The most important was one of 366 lines about the forging and plundering of the mysterious Sampo, the future central theme of the ***Kalevala,*** which Lönnrot now heard for the first time. He had now come within reach of heroic epic.

Next spring, in 1834, in the village of Latvajärvi in Archangel Karelia (about 25 miles south-west of Vuonninen) he found the best of the heroic epic singers, old Arhippa Perttunen. For Lönnrot Arhippa performed about sixty mostly narrative poems, amounting to over 4000 lines. Many of the subjects were already familiar to Lönnrot, but he had nowhere heard or read poems so full and clear. Poems apart, Arhippa was himself a powerful experience for Lönnrot, who gives an exceptionally long description of him in his travel journal and at the same time provides information about the life of epic poetry in Karelia. He speaks, for instance, about the singing-matches which often arose at festivals. The criterion was sheer abundance; it was the custom to bet on one's own 'hero': 'Arhippa said that his village used to put him forward, and he did not remember ever being beaten.'

Arhippa's account of the occasions in his childhood when poems were performed and taught on the shore of Lake Lapukka nearby is a precious document:

> In those days, taking a rest by the camp fire on the shore of Lake Lapukka during fishing trips, that's where you should have been. We had a helper, a man from Lapukka, a fine singer, but not up to my old father. They often sang all night hand in hand by the fire, and the same poem was never sung twice. I was a little lad then, and I listened to them, so bit by bit I learnt the best songs. But I've already forgotten a lot. Not one of my sons will be a singer after I'm gone, as I was after my father. People don't like the old songs any more, as they did in my childhood, when they had pride of place, whether we were working or gathering in the village in our spare time.

Two folk singers and a harp accompanist, 1799.

As he spoke thus of his father, Lönnrot adds, Arhippa was on the point of tears. (In fact, Arhippa's son 'Blind' Miihkali was to become a great singer.)

In the poems of Ontrei and Arhippa, Lönnrot met the highest achievement of popular Finnish-Karelian heroic epic that was to be found at the time. The folk poetry scholar Martti Haavio's characterisation of Ontrei's poems is equally applicable to Arhippa: 'Their pace is steady, thorough, even slow; they tell almost sullenly of great and shocking events . . . In them are battles and displays of wisdom. They are poems whose every line seems to await a Homer, a weaver of epic.' (Finnish scholars traditionally regard Homer as a compiler, like Lönnrot.)

3. The elegiac: Martiska and Matro. On 17 April 1834, in the village of Lonkka in northern Archangel Karelia (about 30 miles north of Latvajärvi) Lönnrot found the well-known reindeer breeder Martiska Karjalainen. Martiska drank rum as he sang, and to Lönnrot's disappointment he got poems mixed up, but on the other hand he composed poems himself. His autobiographical poem about reindeer-rustling and his consequent imprisonment is a compilation in which passages borrowed from traditional lyric alternate with clumsy do-it-yourself efforts. The poem is at its most touching when it describes Martiska's homesickness in prison:

I know well where I was born every place where I grew up but I do not know the place where death faces me here at these strange doors on these unknown ways . . .

We know that Martiska died in prison in 1839.

From these years Lönnrot does not mention many women singers by name, with the exception of one he met soon after leaving Martiska. He came to the large village of Uhtua (now renamed Kalevala by the Soviet authorities, some 45 miles east of Lonkka), where he says he took down a wealth of songs which both men and women could sing. He continues: 'A certain widow, Matro by name, distinguished herself above the others. After she had sung for a day and a half while knitting socks, others took her place . . .'

It has not been possible to establish Matro's identity. It is thought that she was a beggar. She performed lyrical wedding poetry and above all what is called 'women's epic', narrative poetry of a lyrical nature, usually about women and family relationships. The most important of Matro's songs, as regards the *Kalevala,* was 'The Hanged Maid', which Lönnrot had not heard before. The song tells how an unknown man approaches a girl called Anni in the forest. Anni runs weeping home, where her mother tells her to go to the shed and put on her best clothes. In the shed Anni hangs herself with her bridal belts. The mourning mother's tears produce rapids, on their banks trees grow, on the treetops cuckoos settle and sing.

Lönnrot seized as one inspired on this extraordinary song, and fitted it into his heroic epic scheme: Anni became Aino, pledged against her will to the aged wise man Väinämöinen; he changed the gruesome hanging into a dreamlike gliding into water. Thus the great Aino poem of the *Kalevala* was born. Lönnrot's evident bias towards elegy and a classical grace can be seen by comparing his raw material with the *Kalevala* text. Matro concludes her poem with what the cuckoos are saying:

> The third called 'love, love'
> to the nameless child
> the first called 'joy, joy'
> to the joyless child
> the second 'love, love'
> to the loveless child
> the third called 'joy, joy'
> to the child with no father.
> (*Finnish Folk Poetry: Epic,* 104: 111-118)

The lack of sequence, typical of oral poetry, is adjusted in the *Kalevala,* and the whole is amplified:

> The first called 'love, love!'
> the second 'bridegroom, bridegroom!'
> the third called 'joy, joy!'

> That which called 'love, love'!
> called out for three months
> to the loveless girl
> lying in the sea.
> That which called 'bridegroom, bridegroom!'
> called out for six months
> to the sweetheartless bridegroom
> sitting and pining.

> That which called 'joy, joy!'
> called for her lifetime
> to the mother without joy
> weeping all her days.
> (*Kalevala* 4: 490-504)

The *Kalevala* version adds a moving epilogue spoken by the mother, who recalls that the song of the cuckoo announces the renewal of life to everyone but her: 'Let no poor mother/listen long to the cuckoo!'

Martiska and Matro were not great epic singers, but they and singers like them broadened Lönnrot's horizon and hence the scope of the epic. Lönnrot was clearly fascinated by Martiska's lyricism, individuality and detachment. As far as the *Kalevala* is concerned, Martiska's way of incorporating a snatch of lyric elegy into a living epic whole is indicative: by skilfully developing this very technique Lönnrot finally produced an epic that is exceptionally tender and lyrical. He received the material for the lyrical episodes in the *Kalevala* from innumerable singers who have remained anonymous, most of them women: let them be represented here by the old beggar-woman Matro who knitted socks.

4. The illusion of unity: Vaassila. On the evening of 17 September 1833, after Ontrei Malinen had gone fishing, Lönnrot crossed the strait to meet Vaassila Kieleväinen. The poems Ontrei had sung about Väinämöinen were fresh in his mind; everything connected with Väinämöinen excited him, for he was working out a sequence around this wise man who is one of the principal figures in the epic. By now he had a great number of separate poems about Väinämöinen: his problem was how to fuse them together.

Vaassila was very old and he suffered lapses of memory: he could no longer keep whole poems in his head. But Lönnrot was not disappointed: 'Nevertheless, about Väinämöinen and various other mythological characters he told me many things I had not known before. And when it turned out that he had forgotten something I knew about, I questioned him more closely. Then he remembered, and *thus I learned all Väinämöinen's exploits one after another . . .*'

Scholars have made clear that, although the beginning of Lönnrot's Väinämöinen sequence is in fact based on Vaassila, the final *Kalevala* has departed from him to the extent that Vaassila's influence can no longer be substantiated. Something important, however, has remained from Vaassila's ideas. For example, Vaassila's remark in prose 'Then the wedding was held', to which other singers have not referred, made Lönnrot realise that after an epic wooing poem an extensive account of a wedding could be put together out of lyrical wedding poems, such as cantos 20-25 of the *Kalevala*. Of particular interest is the fact that Vaassila suggests ways of combining poems more freely than Lönnrot had until then dared envisage: Vaassila cheerfully combined Väinämöinen poems with poems that did not mention him at all.

Since old Vaassila now viewed the poems from a greater distance than before, he saw that nothing was separate, that all belonged together—Creations, wooings, weddings, Kullervos, Väinämöinens, Golden Brides. . . . It did not matter to Lönnrot that Vaassila's vision might be but an illusion of unity, a momentary structure. The point of that evening was that whoever seeks a new order must be capable of departing from tradition, must be able to forget.

The closer Lönnrot got to the final version of the *Kalevala,* the more he distanced himself from the performances or variants of individual singers. For example, the conclusion of the Lemminkäinen sequence, his resurrection, was based in Lönnrot's early attempt at compilation (1833) on Juhana Kainulainen's performance of 52 lines, that is, almost entirely; but in the final version (1849) Kainulainen's contribution to this passage consists of only 15 lines. Similarly in the final scene of the Sampo story Lönnrot used 42 lines by Ontrei Malinen in 1833, but only 13 lines in 1849. These figures outline the process whereby Lönnrot, in his own oft-quoted words, gradually 'became a soothsayer/and turned into a singer' that is, he freely took it upon himself to 'arrange' the material in his own way. Meanwhile the further Lönnrot distanced himself from the texts of his singers, the more clearly he was able to combine into a whole the dimensions represented by the various types of singer, of which some of the most important have been characterised above.

Already in the late 1830s, but above all in the 1840s, Lönnrot and his successors found many new singers and new singing regions. Beside Orthodox Archangel Karelia, both Lutheran and Orthodox Finnish Karelia, as well as Ingria on the southern side of the Gulf of Finland, proved just as fruitful in their way. The women's contribution grew, and enough lyric poetry accumulated to constitute a new work: the *Kanteletar* appeared in 1840. The most notable lyric virtuoso, who brought to fullness the dimension foreshadowed by Matro, was Mateli Kuivalatar, who lived in the parish of Ilomantsi in Finnish Karelia (35 miles east of Joensuu). The epic dimension was expanded by many Finnish Karelian male singers, most notably by Simana

Sissonen of the same parish. By the end of the century, singers had come to be regarded with a piety that was not far from worship: they became the object of pilgrimages, they were idealistically portrayed in travel writings, literature and art, they were seen as the last noble representatives of a vanished golden age.

Kai Laitinen (essay date 1985)

SOURCE: "The Kalevala and Finnish Literature," translated by Hildi Hawkins, in *Books from Finland,* Vol. XIX, No. 1, 1985, pp. 61-64.

[*In the following excerpt, Laitinen examines the influence of the* Kalevala *on the development of Finnish literature and of a Finnish national identity.*]

I

Finnish literature began with the *Kalevala*.

That statement is at the same time more and less than the truth. A fair amount of literature had been published in Finland before the *Kalevala* appeared in 1835. Bishop Mikael Agricola, who brought Lutheranism to Finland in the sixteenth century, gave a start to Finnish-language literature when he translated the Bible into Finnish, and Swedish-language literature had had a number of distinguished representatives, such as Frans Michael Franzén (1772-1847) and the poet Johan Ludvig Runeberg, who made his debut five years before the *Kalevala* appeared. All the same, it is true to say that it was the publication of the *Kalevala* that gave Finnish-language literature its basis and its sense of importance. It is also arguable, with only a little exaggeration, that within only a few years the *Kalevala* had brought about yet more: the creation of a Finnish national identity.

As we now know, the extraordinarily direct influence of the *Kalevala* was in large part based on two misconceptions. The first of these was put forward by Elias Lönnrot; it was the notion that the folk poetry of which the *Kalevala* is made up actually gave an account of the *history* of the Finnish people. This belief was echoed by many others. And a nation with its own history, so the argument went, had the right to its place among the independent nations.

The other misconception was the belief that the *Kalevala* was part of a huge, fragmented national epic. Lönnrot was supposed to have reconstructed a portion of it from the fragments he collected from ballad singers. Lönnrot himself abandoned this idea fairly early, but it was still current until long after the Second World War. Studies of the way in which the *Kalevala* was put together—especially the work of Professor Väinö Kaukonen—have demonstrated that there is no truth in the notion of a great, lost national epic: it is now clear that Lönnrot constructed the *Kalevala* we know today piece by piece from a number of widely differing sources. But at the time when the *Kalevala* first appeared, the idea of a national epic served its purpose. It reinforced the national identity by demonstrating that Finland was capable of creating a work as impressive as the *Kalevala*. It had not only its own history, but its own ancient culture.

For literature and all the other arts, too, the *Kalevala* formed an important foundation stone: it created a national mythology. The importance of this was recognised in learned circles in Mikael Agricola's time: the foreword to his 1551 translation of the Psaltar acknowledges that 'Väinämöinen hammered hymns.' In his *Mythologia Fennica* of 1789, Christfrid Ganander characterised Väinämöinen as 'Finland's Apollo,' its 'excellent Orpheus', and identified Ilmarinen with Aeolus. The records of folk poetry that survive from before Lönnrot's time mention many other demigods or heroes; it is clear that Finnish mythology was not unknown even then. But it was forced to compete on the one hand with Christian ideology and on the other with Classical mythology. The former was represented by the church, which was quick to condemn folk poetry as 'pagan'; the latter was dominant in the circles of the learned devotees of secular poetry.

Towards the end of the eighteenth century Danish influence brought a new subject into Nordic poetry: Nordic mythology. It replaced Classical subject-matter and the symbolic language that went with it; or at least, it won an honourable place alongside the Classics. In Finland the same phenomenon was more clearly marked than elsewhere, thanks to the *Kalevala*. Finnish mythology had certainly already been studied and presented (Agricola, H. G. Porthan, Christfrid Ganander) and used in poetry (Jaakko Juteini), but it was only with the appearance of Lönnrot's *Kalevala* that it received a unified, organised form.

In the old folk poems there was little continuity in the characters from one poem to the next; often the protagonists could be interchanged at will. Their names, too, appeared in many variants. With the compilation of the *Kalevala*, however, the characters became clearly delineated. Väinämöinen, Ilmarinen, Lemminkäinen, Kullervo, Louhi and the rest became clear, definite literary figures with their own individual histories and destinies. Finnish mythology, in the popular and artistic meaning of the word, was well-established. The heroes of the *Kalevala* and their deeds could now be used as universally recognisable symbols. They could become the bearers of all kinds of nationalistic, ideological and social values. Lönnrot himself had hinted at this possibility in the final verses of the *Kalevala*, in which it is possible to read a demanding programme of national and cultural advancement.

Before the *Kalevala* there was only one universally known work to which it was possible to allude in the certainty that one would be understood. This was the Bible. The appearance of the *Kalevala* changed all this. It offered the young literature of Finland inspiration on two counts: on the one hand subject matter, situations, dramatic confrontations and, above all, powerful characters, and on the other stylistic stimuli in the form of an original and essentially Finnish poetic metre, together with similes, proverbs and metaphors. But the indirect possibilities it offered were equally important. Even today, in works that have nothing whatsoever in common, in subject-matter or form, with the *Kalevala,* one still encounters references to it. A single name, an almost imperceptible allusion, is enough: everyone knows at once what is being referred to.

II

The literature of different periods has used the *Kalevala* and its subject-matter or stylistic devices in different ways. The ways in which writers have treated its heroes and stories reflect the changes that have taken place in Finland's cultural and political climate.

The earliest significant works with subjects taken from the *Kalevala* appeared in the 1860s, when Finnish-language literature was developing rapidly. The subject of Aleksis Kivi's *Kullervo* is taken straight from the *Kalevala* (verses 31-36), but Kivi adds his own characterisation of the hero and an explanation and discussion of the motives for his actions. Like the *Kalevala* hero, Kivi's Kullervo is an implacable avenger who destroys the supposed killer of his parents, and his victim's family. At the same time it is made clear that the cause of Kullervo's rage is oppression and his subjugated position—the 'mark of the slave' is often cited as the origin of his violence. The cause of his destiny and his tragedy lie in himself as well as in his external circumstances. His character is deeper, more complex and more unpredictable than that of his original in the *Kalevala*.

Kullervo has attracted the attention of more than one writer. In a play written in 1895, the poet J. H. Erkko presented the same figure as a social rebel, even a revolutionary. As Raoul Palmgren has pointed out, 'by opposing the landowners and the landless, free men and slaves, the writer has turned the Kullervo story into a *social tragedy*'. The Väinämöinen character makes no secret of the play's political nature. 'In the strong working class/are the original people of the *Kalevala*.' His later play *Pohjolan häät* ('The Northland wedding')—it, too, based on a story from the Kalevala—also touches on the politics of the day, this time the conflict and internal contradictions caused by the period of Russian oppression that began at the end of the nineteenth century.

It has generally been Finnish-language authors who have been drawn to the *Kalevala,* but there are exceptions. Zacharias Topelius, who wrote the first Finnish historical novel and gained the status of a classic children's story writer, was fascinated by the *Kalevala,* and drew the character of the Don Juan figure of his *Prinsessan av Cypern* ('The princess of Cyprus', 1860) from the *Kalevala's* Lemminkäinen. In this fairy-story play Topelius links north and south, Finland and Greece, in a surprising way: the island on which the events take place becomes Cyprus, where Lemminkäinen arrives to seize a bride for himself. Topelius also reserved space for the *Kalevala* in his later, hugely popular, book *Boken om vårt land* ('The book of our land', 1875), in which he gives a knowledgeable account of the contents of the *Kalevala* and stresses the work's quality and significance.

III

J. H. Erkko's *Kalevala*-inspired plays belong to a new period of Finnish literary history, known as national neo-Romanticism. One could equally well call it national symbolism, for in it love of the *Kalevala* and the Karelian landscape in which the poems were collected combines with enthusiasm for the motifs with which Karelian houses, textiles and household objects were decorated, and European symbolism and Art Nouveau. It reached its high point in the last five years of the nineteenth century and the beginning of the twentieth, when many writers and artists made the journey to Karelia (the phenomenon is, indeed, sometimes known as Karelianism). It took with it writers who had begun as realists and social critics, like Juhani Aho, whose historical novel *Panu* (1897) describes the struggle between Christianity and paganism in a remote part of eastern Finland and makes free use of 'national' Kalevala material and sometimes also of its characteristic modes of expression.

The most significant representative of the new school, and at the same time and interesting writer in terms of the direct influence of the *Kalevala,* was the poet Eino Leino. The lyrical poem-drama *Tuonelan jousten* ('Swan of Tuonela'), a youthful work, takes its subject from the *Kalevala* and its timbre from the world of European symbolism. Verlaine's direction 'De la musique avant tout chose!' was clearly very much in Leino's mind, and the *Kalevala,* with its alliteration, vowel harmony and parallelism, lends itself to such treatment. Leino drew from the same material again in his play *Sota volosta* ('War for light', 1902), whose theme is political, the defence of a national culture against an external threat.

Later, however, Leino came to the conclusion that using the *Kalevala* as a direct source was not very fruitful: its characters 'are already, just as they are, complete, crystallised works of art, and as such they do not need extension or polishing at the hands of literature'. All the same, the *Kalevala* remained close to him in many ways: he adapted it for the theatre in 1911—the quotation is from his foreword—but above all, he used its stimuli in a new way. The result was Leino's most powerful work, the collection of poetry entitled *Helkavirsiä,* published in 1903. A second volume appeared as late as 1916. (A selection of the poems appeared in English in 1978 in a translation by Keith Bosley, with a foreword by Michael Branch, under the title *Whitsongs.*)

Helkavirsiä uses the stylistic apparatus of the *Kalevala*—its metre, the way in which the characters express themselves, metaphors in the *Kalevala* style—but not its subject matter. Leino creates his own myth in the spirit of the *Kalevala.* For his heroes are mythical, growing to a poetic stature; most often they are defiant figures, whose destinies show the qualities of Nietzche's *Übermensch* or a kind of tragic optimism. They defy their enemies, society, convention, even death—and die unbowed, open-eyed, unafraid of their fates. The poems of *Helkavirsiä* contain the most memorable of Leino's characters. In the second series of ballads, defiance has softened to resignation, the tone has become more melancholy and the scope widened to include cosmic visions and myths.

Eino Leino's work shows how an artist of genius can best make use of the *Kalevala*: not by copying it, or following it closely, but by developing the stimuli it gives in the artist's own direction. Leino modified the style of expression, reducing the number of repeated verses, varying the rhythm and using more concise and immediate language. His poems are, in their origin and inspiration, close to the *Kalevala;* but they are not overshadowed by it—their strength gives them an independent life.

IV

Since Eino Leino, many writers have used subjects from the *Kalevala* or tried to adapt its style for themselves, but few of them have achieved such impressive results. In the end the enthusiasm for the *Kalevala* resulted in a retreat from it. In newly independent Finland more writers avoided it than followed its inspiration. There are very few subjects taken from the *Kalevala,* for instance, and no *Kalevala* style or metre whatsoever, in the work of V. A. Koskenniemi, the leading poet of the time. This reaction is also apparent in prose. Joel Lehtonen's novel *Kerran kesällä* ('Once in summer', 1917) has a character named Bongman who quotes the *Kalevala* at all times and in all places, worships all things nationalistic with such enthusiasm that the description of him inevitably turns to parody.

Nevertheless, the *Kalevala* was not entirely abandoned. It had earlier been used in the aims of realism and social criticism (J. H. Erkko) and in the spirit of Karelianism and symbolism (Eino Leino), so it is hardly surprising that it should also become involved with the new current of expressionism. This happened in Lauri Haarla's play *Lemmin poika* ('Lemmi's son', 1922), in which the *Kalevala*'s carefree youth develops into a tragic hero. Later, too, Haarla used subjects connected with the *Kalevala* or attempted an imagined 'ancient Finnish', pathetic style; but he was almost alone in his time. Only a very few poets succeeded in combining patriotic fervour and the *Kalevala*. In ceremonial speeches and newspaper articles between the two World Wars, of course, this combination did appear, and often; but in literature it proved difficult to achieve.

The *Kalevala* made its reappearance in Finnish literature much later, and from an unexpected quarter, in the work of Paavo Haavikko, the leading poet of the lyrical modernism of the 1950s. Some of the same subject matter is to be found in the work of contemporary prose writers (Anu Kaipainen, Erkki Mäkinen), but Haavikko was the writer who really brought the *Kalevala* back as a living inspiration for literature. His early works show a keen interest in motifs from Russian history and Byzantium. The subject of his extended poem *Kaksikymmentä ja yksi* ("Twenty and one', 1974) is nothing more nor less than the *Kalevala* story of the stealing of the Sampo. The Sampo is a mysterious object of power which dozens, perhaps hundreds, of theories have attempted to explain. In Haavikko's hands it receives a new interpretation with an economic slant: the Sampo is a Byzantine coin-minting machine that the men of the north steal in the belief that it will bring them prosperity and happiness.

Later Haavikko returned to the *Kalevala* in his work *Rauta-aika* ('Age of Iron', 1982), which also formed the script for a television series that attracted a great deal of attention in Finland. It began with this exhortation: 'Forget! Forget the *Kalevala,* its heroes, words, phrases, forget what you have heard about them, the pictures you have seen.' But at the same time out of the work grows a new, suggestive variation, a picture of the characters and events that we know from the *Kalevala* stressed and coloured in a new way. At the end of the work the characters are tired and resigned; they have had enough of life. Ilmari says, 'It wasn't a bad life. . . . It's certainly taken back everything it's given. We're quite. . . . Let death do its work now. I want to sleep, well and long.' The powerful heroes of the *Kalevala,* shamans who know the secret forces of existence, have become people again; weak, uncertain, tired—people like ourselves.

v

The *Kalevala* at first provided the belief in the right of the Finnish people to their independent existence, cre-

ated for it a rich history and the illusion of a splendid cultural past. Later it became a fruitful source of material for other artists. Each of them found in it something different: Kivi his Kullervo, Erkko his social problems and differences, Leino his myth-creating fantasies, Haavikko his demythified anti-heroes. The *Kalevala* has been a mirror in which each time has seen, in the light of its own interests, that which it has found most interesting and absorbing: itself.

Without the visions to which the *Kalevala,* directly or indirectly, gave birth, Finnish-language literature would be very different from what it is today. It's even worth asking whether it would exist at all?

Keith Bosley (essay date 1985)

SOURCE: "Translating the Kalevala: Midway Reflections," in *Books from Finland,* Vol. XIX, No. 1, 1985, pp. 30-33.

[*In the following essay, written while he was in the process of translating the* Kalevala *into English, Bosley reflects on the special challenges and responsibilities inherent in that task.*]

> Ilmarinen the smith, eternal craftsman,
> forges a fiery eagle, a wivern
> of flame: the feet he hammered out of iron,
> of steel the talons, wings of a boat's sides.
> Up on the wings he clambered, on its back,
> the eagle's wingbone tips, there he sat down,
> there he commanded: 'Eagle, pretty bird,
> fly where I bid you—to the sluggish river
> of Death's dark lord, into the fateful gully!
> Pounce on the Pike, the scaly monster, smite
> the fish that, though well fed, can dart and
>   dodge!' . . .

Nel mezzo del cammin: the half-way point of any long journey is critical. Can we continue as we began? Knowing now what we did not know at the outset, and having invested so much time and effort already, are we still sure of our way? Or must we start all over again? Even God had second thoughts and sent the Flood. In such august company, the translator is a humble clerk. He has his text, at least: he is not creating, he is interpreting—though this lesser endeavour demands its measure of creativity. He is devoting precious years (it may be) to bringing a foreign text to life in his own tongue: is his author still with him as an inspiring presence? If so, are author and translator still worthy of each other? If not, who has slipped from grace?

Such agonisings are inevitable and even appropriate half way. Half way through translating the *Kalevala,* I find myself no less committed to it and no less confident (or, to put it more accurately, no more unconfident) in what I am doing. But can I do it better?

This question prompted the lines above. Ilmarinen the smith must perform three tasks to win the hand of the Maid of the North. He has ploughed the Viper-Field, he has tamed the bear and the wolf of Tuoni, the lord of the dead: now he must catch the pike of Tuoni without a net. This is indeed the stuff of epic; but what is the sound of epic, in English?

> Him the Almighty Power
> Hurld headlong flaming from th'Ethereal Skie
> With hideous ruine and combustion down
> To bottomless perdition, there to dwell
> In Adamantine Chains and penal Fire,
> Who durst defie th'Omnipotent to Arms.

Before the Virgilian thunder of Milton there was the Renaissance grace of Spenser, sounding like his Italian models; there was Chapman, making Homer sound like a ballad—to the delight of Keats:

> This said, he reacht to take his sonne,
>   who (of his armes afraid,
> And then the horse-hair plume, with which
>   he was so overlaid,
> Nodded so horribly) he clingd
>   back to his nurse and cride . . .

A century later, Pope lent the same passage a more 'Classical' elegance:

> Thus having spoke, the illustrious chief of
>   Troy
> Stretch'd his fond arms to clasp the lovely
>   boy.
> The babe clung crying to his nurse's breast,
> Scared at the dazzling helm, and nodding
>   crest.

In English, then, epic has many sounds—the various music of the Renaissance, the homespun, the urbane talk of the Enlightenment, to say nothing of the tub-thump of Anglo-Saxon, the earnest rhapsody of latter days . . .

To an English translator of most Finnish poetry and prose, such considerations are irrelevant. But the translator of the *Kalevala* takes on a tradition that goes back beyond the beginnings of Finnish literature proper and lays the foundations of a whole culture, which he (we have all been men so far) can approach either as an anthropologist or as a humanist. The anthropologist will study resemblances to and differences from the productions of other Noble Savages; the humanist will look for artistic achievement to compare with that nearer home. The present translator is a humanist: that is why he wondered whether the *Kalevala*

Väinämöinen playing the first Kantele; *illustration from Parker Fillmore's 1923 edition of the* Kalevala.

might not be more fittingly rendered into English blank verse.

There is nothing more dignified than the speech of Shakespeare's kings, or of a great poet who finds he has been plagiarised:

> As a three-pronged arrow craftsman-carbed in
>   horn
> flies above the smooth star-glittering ice
> my song had slipped away down the spreading
>   river.

The river is the Ob; the lines are from a folk poem which Peter Sherwood and I translated from Vogul, a Siberian language related to Finnish. The translation of folk poetry from the Finno-Ugrian languages for the forthcoming anthology *The Great Bear* (Finnish Literature Society) reminded me that poetry is universal: the work of an illiterate peasant not only comes from the same organ as that of Baudelaire but can also be usefully compared with it—though, of course, not all illiterate peasants need apply. This is why some of the

Great Bear translations sound surprisingly Western, like these lines from a poem in Ostyak, another Siberian language:

> My children have grown up: my son's a
> hunter
>   catching all he can—
> foxes and squirrels as he roams the forest.
>   I don't need a man.

Folk poetry presents the same variety of register as 'literary' poetry, but the variety is less apparent: in a phonetic text whose layout was largely the whim of the collector, we find here the swing of lyric, there the towering syntactic structure of epic, the song of origins and mysteries. This is where the *Kalevala* has its roots; but for the translator there is another consideration.

The further west Finno-Ugrians migrated, the more concerned they were with what we would call poetic form. Language maintained throughout a more or less uniform complexity, but the structure of their poetry acquired an increasing sense of a music not dependent on grammar. For the Voguls and their neighbours the Ostyaks, poetry was little more than speech heightened by occasion and intensified by parallelism; something similar has been said of the earliest Hebrew poetry. But for the Zyryans, on this side of the Urals, something else was beginning to happen. Here are the opening lines of a lament:

> Of your days you are lying the last day
> of your hours you are lying the last hour . . .

In English these lines are exactly parallel, but in the original the words 'day' and 'hour' are of different length, and the lines differ in a way that grammar does not require. This can only be a metrical requirement: the tune to which the lament was sung (for metre always derives ultimately from song) was making its own demands. Poetry was taking off from rhetoric: in the Baltic area—amoung the Finns, the Ingrians, the Estonians and the rest—metre became a formal principle, with the added device of alliteration. Sound was evolving its own laws, independent of sense: poetry was coming, as Mallarmé told Degas, to be made of words rather than of ideas.

This is why the tradition behind the *Kalevala* is such a challenge to the translator. He does not need to dignify it with blank verse or make it swing with a folk song metre: it has its own sophisticated music. So has Homer, of course; but his translator works within a tradition of his own—that of his distinguished predecessors—and no one thinks less of Homer if his latest translator makes a mockery of him. On the other hand the translator of Finnish folk poetry, and especially of

the *Kalevala,* has a responsibility. Because he is taking his readers into largely—or even totally—unfamiliar territory, they have to trust him; they are going to make their judgement in the light of his performance, rather like a concert audience hearing a new work. If he makes a mess of it, they will conclude at best that the *Kalevala* is a curiosity, at worst that the nation is wretched indeed which accords such a work pride of place in its heritage. If the epic has suffered at the hands of its English translators, it is in no small part because they have failed to appreciate its music. The plain prose of Francis Peabody Magoun Jr (1963) makes no pretensions, but before him both John Martin Crawford (1889) and William Forsell Kirby (1907) were seduced by the crude parody of Kalevala metre which Longfellow used for *Hiawatha;* he in turn was seduced by Schiefner's German translation, which was doubtless influenced by Goethe's attempt at reproducing the original metre in his 1810 version of a Finnish folk lyric (*Kam der liebe Wohlbekannte*). The great heresy in the art of verse translation is the urge to reproduce the original metre; it is like trying to wear someone else's shoes. This heresy flourishes most when a translator is working from an 'exotic' language, like Finnish, for which a common culture does not suggest equivalents—the Italian hendecasyllable, the French alexandrine, the English iambic pentamer. The 'exotic' metre, like any other, has its irregularities, and here the heretic takes a tumble: with his uncertain footing, he must play safe and stick to his 'rules'. Meanwhile, of the millions of lines of Finnish folk poetry collected, it has been estimated that about half are 'irregular', and the tension thus created is an essential ingredient. To translate it therefore into *Hiawatha* metre is to reduce it to light verse, and its mythology to fairy tale.

The *Kalevala* has many voices, from a cosmic scorn that recalls the Book of Job:

> Neither were you seen
> neither seen nor heard
> when this earth was made
> when the air was formed
> when the air's pillar was fixed
> when the sky's arch was fastened
> when the moon was steered
> when the sun was helped
> when the Great Bear was stretched out
> when the sky was filled with stars.
>   (3:245-254)

—all the way down to advice to a bride:

> Begin sweeping the floor-joints
> take a broom to the floorboards:
> throw water upon the floor—
> don't throw it over a child!
> If you see a child upon the floor
> even if 'tis sister-in-law's child

lift the child on to a bench
wash its eyes and smooth its hair
put some bread into its hand
spread some butter on the house
put a wood-chip in its hand!

                                    (23:181-192)

There is the alternation of narrative and spell, when the action stops and the language bursts into flower, rather as in classical opera a recitative leads into an aria:

> Hold, blood, your leaking
> and gore, your rippling
> on my head slopping
> spraying on my breasts!
> Blood, stand like a wall
> stay, gore, like a fence
> like an iris in the sea
> stand, sedge among moss
> a boulder at a field edge
> a rock amid steep rapids!

                                    (9:343-352)

These quotations demonstrate one translator's working solution—it can be no more than that—to the main problem in translating the **Kalevala** into English: there is no cultural equivalent. Oral tradition, in which the **Kalevala** is rooted, is central to Finnish culture but peripheral to English. The greatest figures in Finnish literature—men like Arhippa Perttunen and his son Miihkali, women like Larin Paraske—could not read or write, and yet they commanded a repertoire running to thousands of lines: the English translator needs to invent a style to convey that richness without sounding 'literary'. I have had to unlearn the vocabulary of my education and remember the earthier speech of my relatives, who always 'answered' but never 'replied', yet relished a vivid turn of phrase that would be lost on my friends: in Hampstead Garden Suburb no one is 'on short commons'. I have also, unexpectedly, found Scottish terminology useful, though on reflection this is not so remarkable: in many ways the Finns have more in common with the Scots than with the English. So the troublesome *linna* (in modern Finnish 'castle', in oral tradition a fortified settlement) becomes 'burgh' rather than the larger 'town' or even 'borough'; *penkerelle, pänkerelle* becomes 'to its banks and braes', and *kana* as a term of endearment is literally rendered 'hen' because that is how the Glaswegian addresses his lassie—Magoun's equally demotic 'chick' is simply not affectionate enough. Unlike many of my immediate countrymen, I am aware that the language we call English has boasted two literary dialects since the Renaissance, when Gavin Douglas produced the first translation of Virgil into our 'rurall vulgar gros'.

The English translator of the **Kalevala** needs also to invent a metre. Which is absurd; but *Hiawatha* just won't do. It trots; the **Kalevala** dances. The metre I arrived at by trial and error for *Finnish Folk Poetry: Epic* over ten years ago seems to work for the **Kalevala,** which is reassuring. It is a line of seven, sometimes of five, occasionally of nine, syllables, thus cutting across the English grain of an even number of syllables divided into 'feet', so that the rhythm is always shifting; French, Welsh and Japanese poets would recognise it. Any attempt at imitating the original alliteration would lead me too far from a text full of concrete particulars; I discovered that long ago too. So I shall continue as before, translating line for line; the more cavalier blank verse with which I began these reflections is for the next translator, who will have me to build on.

An excerpt from *Kanteletar,* translated by Keith Bosley:

Grinding song

Mouth draws wolf into the trap
tongue draws stoat into the snare
will a maid into marriage
  wish into another house.
  Grind, grind, young maiden
  grind, young maiden's will
  grind, hand and grind, foot
grind, mitten and grind, stocking
grind, grindstone and grind
a maid to a husband's house:
she has a mind for a man
smoulders for the village boys.
A boat's will is for waters
a ship's will for waves
a maid's will is for marriage
her wish into another house;
for a maid even at birth
a daughter is lulled
from papa's to husband's house
from husband's house to Death's house.

                    In Books from Finland, *1989.*

Senni Timonen (essay date 1989)

SOURCE: An introduction to "Kanteletar: Women's Voices," in *Books from Finland,* Vol. XXIII, No. 3, 1989, pp. 159-61.

[*In the following excerpt, Timonen briefly reviews the content and organization of the* Kanteletar *and describes Lönnrot's role in compiling the collection.*]

Kanteletar's core is the individual's relationship with others and with the environment: the village, small,

crowded, besieged by poverty, shackled by its prejudices. At the same time it reflects the world: the presence of the encircling forest and the cycle of nature;
and the human condition: joy, sorrow and longing.
Kanteletar complements *Kalevala,* and equals it in its
own genre.

Elias Lönnrot had gathered the basic material for the
book—around 17,000 verses of lyrical folk songs—
himself on numerous, wide-ranging field trips in eastern Finland and Karelia from 1828 onwards. For *Kanteletar,* just as for the *Kalevala,* Lönnrot used not only
his own material but also verses collected and published by earlier travellers. The final result contains
652 poems, made up of 222,201 lines. *Kanteletar,* in
other words, is almost as long as the *Kalevala.*

Lönnrot derived the collection's name from the *kantele,* an ancient Finnish five-stringed musical instrument. By adding the feminine ending, *-tar,* however he
used the folk tradition to create a concept foreign to
that tradition: the idea of a muse of the *kantele,* who
for him meant the symbol of lyric song.

Kanteletar is divided into three sections. Into the first
Lönnrot put the songs that he regarded as being sung
by everyone—men and women, young and old. He
grouped the poems according to the situations in which
they were sung: lamentation, slavery, weddings, shepherd songs, and so on. For instance, **'A plank of flesh'**
belongs to a group of songs about orphans and slaves,
and **'Don't propose on a Sunday'** to a sequence of
folk wisdom, while **'The dance'** is one of a series of
dance songs.

The songs of the second section are grouped according
to the gender, age and social standing of the singer.
There is a large number of girls' songs, about love and
guessing the identity of their husbands to be (**'The
irresistible'**, **'Daydreams'** and **'Grinding song'**).
There are women's songs, with thematic focuses in the
comparison between married and unmarried life, children's futures (**'Lullabies'**) and the characters of husbands (**'The cripple's wife'**). There are men's and
boys' songs which also deal with love and marriage
(**'Deceived'**, **'Against widows'**, **'Marrying in haste'**);
but, in reflection of men's social role, the songs also
open up the world outside the home, with subject matter
including hunting, war, and so on.

Lönnrot devoted the third section to narrative poems
and ballads—most of them belonging to the sphere of
women's life—whose subjects approach the general
themes of poetry (sexual roles, moral problems, examination of human relationships, expressions of wom-
en's viewpoints; compare **'The thoughtful dragon'**).

Scholars have confirmed that in compiling *Kanteletar,*
Lönnrot underwent an artistic liberation, in which a
more aesthetic perception of folk poetry opened up to
him. One of the contributing factors to this new freedom was the nature of the lyrical folk poetry itself,
another came from European influences: the period also
saw the publication of a number of corresponding
collections of the folk poetry of different nations. The
collection of Serbian folk songs published by Vuk
Karadžić as early as 1814-15, which made its way to
Finland in a German translation in the 1830s, appears
to have been particularly inspirational; it is known that
Lönnrot thought highly of it.

Lönnrot's vision of folk poetry is clearly expressed in
his extensive introduction to *Kanteletar.* It is considered one of the most important texts of the Romantic
movement in Finland. In it, Lönnrot contrasts art poetry and folk poetry, particularly lyric folk poetry, and
forcefully champions the latter. Learned poems are
made through thinking, whereas folk poetry 'creates
itself from itself,' says Lönnrot. 'Playing and singing
are like another, more sacred human language, which
to itself or others communicates its desires and thoughts;
which, better than this ordinary, everyday language,
declares its joys and exultations, its sorrows and worries, its happiness and its contentment, its rest, its peace
and the other aspects of its existence.'

Thus it is clear that Lönnrot sees folk song—which he
believes to be of ancient origin—as a better and more
accurate vehicle for the innermost thoughts of the individual than any other form of verbal expression. He
emphasises the communal nature of folk poetry; even
the concept of a named author is, for him, foreign to
the nature of the genre. This idea, together with the
quotations from Herder's famous folk song collection,
demonstrates that the native land of the ideas Lönnrot
adopted was Romantic Germany. As a result of his
profound first-hand knowledge of folk poetry and the
conditions in which it was born, he was able to make
an unusually concrete and original synthesis of Romantic ideas and both his own work and Finnish folk
poetry.

In many of its basic characteristics, *Kanteletar* really
is a genuinely faithful reflection of folk poetry. It follows the same four-foot trochaic rhythm; it is pervaded
by the same organic connection with nature, the same
concrete, realist and melancholy qualities. Lönnrot kept
individual poems separate, and roughly at the same
length as they were recorded; here, unlike in the Kalevala, in other words, he did not try to knit them
together into a coherent narrative.

Nevertheless, his creative editorship is also discernible
in *Kanteletar.* He handled the great majority of the
poems with such force that they can no longer be regarded as genuine examples of folk poetry. According
to Professor Väinö Kaukonen, five different levels of
intervention can be discerned in Lönnrot's work: 1)

simple technical, linguistic editing, with some standardisation; 2) complementing a text with lines from variants of the same poem; 3) collation of a text from two or three completely different, but thematically related, poems; 4) collation of a text from line material from between 10 and 15 different poems; and 5) creation of a new poem in the folk style.

The majority of the **Kanteletar** poems fall into the second and third groups, in which Lönnrot, to a greater or lesser degree, freed himself of the structures of folk poetry in order to create new poems of his own. To simplify, **Kanteletar** was born as follows: the original lyrical folk poetry fragmented in Lönnrot's mind into elements which he then incorporated as parts of a completely new whole; gaps, unevennesses and illogicalities were filled in and corrected in the style of folk poetry. He himself was not conscious of creating anything new, only of improving his material. The technique is almost the same as in the **Kalevala,** but the length—most of the poems are very short—and discrete nature of the **Kanteletar** poems, together with their faithfulness to the dimensions of the original folk songs, make them at least apparently closer to the original material.

In collating the poems, Lönnrot attempted to give as lively and many-sided picture of the world they describe as possible. This portrait is, nevertheless, drawn entirely from his own vision of the poems' world.

Although **Kanteletar,** therefore, is not 'genuine' folk poetry, it does represent an interpretation by the best available expert of what the genuine Finnish folk tradition was like. Because this expert did not write reports but poetry, **Kanteletar** is, in the last analysis, guaranteed by the conception of poetry and the world of its author, the writer and poet Elias Lönnrot.

FURTHER READING

Bixby, James T. Review of the *Kalevala. Unitarian Review* XXXI, No. 4 (April, 1889): 309-27.

    Examines various mythological aspects of the *Kalevala.*

Branch, M. A. Introduction to *Kalevala: The Land of Heroes,* translated by W. F. Kirby, pp. xi-xxxiv. London: Athlone, 1985.

    Identifies four layers of style characteristic of the *Kalevala* and other Finnish folk poetry of its type.

Comparetti, Domenico. "Conclusions." *The Traditional Poetry of the Finns,* translated by Isabella M. Anderton, pp. 327-59. London and New York: Longmans, Green, and Co., 1898.

    Analysis of various aspects of the *Kalevala* which

concludes that it is not comparable to ancient national epics like the *Iliad.*

Crawford, John Martin, editor and translator. Preface to *The Kalevala: The Epic Poem of Finland, Vol. 1,* pp. v-xlix. New York: John B. Alden, Publisher, 1888.

    Views the *Kalevala* as "a contest between Light and Darkness, Good and Evil," and describes it as "one of the most precious contributions to the literature of the world."

Honko, Lauri. "The 'Kalevala' Process." *Folklife Annual* (1986): 66-79.

    Examines the poetic evolution that produced the oral poetry collected by Lönnrot and other scholars and the codification of that poetry in the *Kalevala.*

Kerényi, C. "The Primordial Child in Primordial Times." *Essays on a Science of Mythology: The Myth of the Divine Child and the Mysteries of Eleusis,* by C. G. Jung and C. Kerényi, translated by R. F. C. Hull, Bollingen Series XXII, revised edition, pp. 25-69. Princeton, NJ: Princeton University Press, 1969.

    Examines the tragic figure of Kullervo from the *Kalevala* in terms of the mythological "divine child," a child deity comparable to Dionysus or Hermes in Greek mythology.

Krohn, Julius. Letter to F. Max Muller. *The Athenaeum* 2, No. 3182 (October 20, 1888): 519-20.

    Discusses the evolution of the *Kalevala* and the process used by Lönnrot in assembling the poem.

Lang, Andrew. "The 'Kalevala'." *Homer and the Epic,* pp. 413-19. London and New York: Longmans, Green, and Co., 1893.

    Argues that the *Kalevala* cannot be considered an epic, particularly because of its lack of unity.

Lönnrot, Elias, ed. *The Kalevala; or Poems of the Kalevala District,* translated by Francis Peabody Magoun, Jr. Cambridge, MA: Harvard University Press, 1963, 410 p.

    One of the best modern translations, its introduction and appendixes provide background information about Lönnrot's life, Finnish poetry, and the compilation of the *Kalevala.*

Nyland, Waino. "'Kalevala' as a Reputed Source of Longfellow's 'Song of Hiawatha.'" *American Literature* 22, No. 1 (March, 1950): 1-20.

    Examines the contention that the *Kalevala* is a direct source of Longfellow's *Song of Hiawatha* (1855).

Oinas, Felix J. "The Balto-Finnic Epic." *Heroic Epic and Saga: An Introduction to the World's Great Folk Epics,* edited by Felix J. Oinas, pp. 286-309. Bloomington, IN: Indiana University Press, 1978.

    Briefly explores the composition, form, and influence of the *Kalevala.*

Rexroth, Kenneth. "The Kalevala." *Classics Revisited,* pp. 24-28. New York: New Directions, 1968.

> Finds that the *Kalevala* "succeeds and endures because it expresses a national consciousness, but the consciousness of the kinship of a race of men with all living creatures about them."

Schoolfield, George C. *The Kalevala: Epic of the Finnish People,* translated by Eino Friberg. Helsinki: Otava Publishing Company, 1988.

> Includes an English translation of the *Kalevala* as well as critical materials analyzing the structure of the compilation and its significance for the development of Finnish language, national identity, and culture.

Sealey, Raphaël. "Appendix: The Structure of the 'Kalevala'." *Revue des Etudes Greques* LXX, Nos. 331-33 (July-December, 1957): 352-55.

Finds in the *Kalevala* a unity of structure evidenced through the interweaving of themes, the variation of mood, and the arrangement of the narrative.

Setälä, E. N. "The Centenary of the 'Kalevala': The National Epic of the Finns." *The Slavonic and East European Review* 14, No. 40 (July, 1935): 36-43.

> Compares initial critical reactions to the *Kalevala* with conceptions of it on the poem's centenary, and notes its importance to Finnish nationalism.

Stephens, Anna Cox. "The Kalevala." *Music* II, No. 2 (June, 1892): 133-43.

> Praises the *Kalevala*'s rich use of fantasy and magic and its delicate portrayal of sentiments.

Turunen, Aimo. "Folk Epic to National Epic: Kalevala and Kalevipoeg." *Folklorica: Festschrift for Felix J. Oinas,* edited by Egle Victoria Žygas and Peter Voorheis, pp. 277-89. Bloomington, IN: Research Institute for Inner Asian Studies, 1982.

> Discusses the influence the *Kalevala* has had on subsequent Finnish music, literature, and art.

Additional coverage of the *Kalevala* is contained in the following source published by Gale Research: *Classical and Medieval Literature Criticism*, Vol. 6.

Joseph Smith, Jr.

1805-1844

American religious leader.

INTRODUCTION

Smith's publication of the *Book of Mormon* on April 6, 1830, marked the founding of the Church of Jesus Christ of Latter-Day Saints, or Mormon Church. The Church's Prophet and First Elder, Smith became the most revered yet most reviled Mormon leader among Mormons and non-Mormons alike. Disagreement among Mormon followers over Smith's proclamations and practices led to the Church's splintering into several reorganized sects. Nonetheless, the Mormon Church today has over one million members worldwide.

Biographical Information

The fourth of nine children, Smith was born in 1805 to Joseph Smith, Sr. and Lucy Mack Smith in Sharon, Vermont. In 1816, the family moved to Palmyra, New York, and eventually settled in nearby Manchester. His family's poverty required Smith to work on the farm instead of going to school, so he received little formal education. As a young man, he developed a fascination with occultism and began using special devices and sacrificing small animals for "supernatural" assistance in attempts to discover buried treasure. This led to various accusations of fraud. In 1820, Smith claimed to have received the first of a series of visitations from a divine apparition, Moroni, who appointed him a Prophet of a new religion. Over the next several years he reported a number of similar visits. In 1827, Smith married Emma Hale, the first of his alleged forty-nine wives. In the same year he claimed to have unearthed a set of golden plates from Hill Cumorah (now called "Mormon Hill") near Manchester, a site supposedly disclosed to him by Moroni. With the help of a scribe, Oliver Cowdry, Smith began translating the plates' hieroglyphic inscriptions using two "seer" stones called the *Urim* and *Thummim*. They published their work as the *Book of Mormon* in 1830, officially establishing the Church of Jesus Christ. In 1831, the Church expanded westward to establish the "Land of Zion" in Jackson County, Missouri, garnering support from Ohio residents along the way and establishing a Church in Kirtland. The Mormon Church was thus divided into two main bodies, in Ohio and Missouri. Smith remained in Kirtland until 1838, when he and his followers fled to western Missouri after a number of Church members accused him of fraud and attempted murder. Soon thereafter, however, tensions between Mormons and

non-Mormons in western Missouri culminated in violent clashes between the two groups, and Governor Lilburn Boggs issued an order to expel the Mormons. Smith responded by organizing his own militia, an act for which he was arrested and imprisoned. He escaped in 1839 and met his followers in Commerce, Illinois. In 1840, they obtained a charter from Governor Thomas Carlin, and, renaming Commerce, founded the city of Nauvoo, the largest city in the state. Smith became sole trustee of the Mormon Church and was given unlimited power. In 1841 he formed the Nauvoo Legion, appointing himself lieutenant-general. Elected Nauvoo's first mayor in 1842, he prophesied later that year that the Church would eventually move to the far West. In the same year he was arrested and charged with conspiracy to assassinate Governor Boggs, but was exonerated by the Nauvoo Municipal Court, an act that outraged the non-Mormon populace. Further controversy ensued with his promulgation the next year of a revelation legitimating polygamy. In 1844, Smith formally announced his candidacy for the United States presidency. On June 7 of that year, several Mormon dissidents published the first and only issue of the *Nauvoo Expositor*, a newspaper denouncing Smith's personal behavior and political aspirations. Smith and the Nauvoo City Council responded by declaring martial law in the city and ordering the Legion to destroy the *Expositor*'s press. The state militia arrested Smith and his brother, Hyrum, who were charged with treason and imprisoned in Carthage. There, on the evening of June 27, 1844, they were murdered by a mob of more than 100 men who attacked the jail.

Major Works

During the decade between 1820 and 1830, Joseph Smith made minimal efforts to document his visions and revelations. An 1830 revelation, however, prompted him to chronicle his life's events in order to promote the rise and progress of the Church. According to Smith, the *Book of Mormon*, his first publication, was a translation of a divine proclamation. In fact, most of Smith's writings recount revelations and proclamations that he claimed had been dictated to him. He also commissioned two of his closest associates, Willard Richards and Wilford Woodruff, to document his sermons, discourses, and revelations. In 1839, he dictated the first manuscript for his voluminous *History of the Church of Jesus Christ of Latter-Day Saints* (1902-12) to his clerk, James Mulholland. In conjunction with the *Book of Mormon*, a publication containing Smith's revelations entitled *A Book of Commandments* (1833) and the *Doctrine and Covenants of the Church of the Latter-Day Saints* (1835) provide the foundational doctrine for the Mormon organization.

Critical Reception

Mormons and non-Mormons alike recognized Smith's talent for public speaking. Charles Smith, an eyewitness to one of the Mormon leader's sermons, claimed that when the Prophet spoke, he "drew your soul out in love towards him." Those who met Smith noted his persuasive charm and compelling enthusiasm. His writings, however, were not as well received. Before its first publication by the Wayne *Sentinal*, the *Book of Mormon* was refused publication in the Rochester *Anti-Masonic Inquirer* as "a jumble of unintelligent absurdities." Upon its publication, many commentators judged Smith to be delusional. The book's publication drew bitter opposition from non-Mormon religious groups who considered themselves the true followers of Jesus Christ. Many of Smith's detractors charged that he had plagiarized the text and characterized him as a clever leader of misguided followers and a political menace rather than a Prophet. Beginning in the early twentieth century, some scholars began to approach the *Book of Mormon* as a valuable historical document reflecting the ideals of nineteenth-century American frontier settlers. Modern critics have also regarded the work as an informative biographical source

that provides insight into the psychology of the Mormon leader. While the nature of the *Book of Mormon* continues to be hotly debated, it nonetheless stands as one of the most influential American religious books of the nineteenth century. It became a cornerstone of a large and powerful religious movement that played a major role in the settlement of much of the American West and that continues to be an influential force in the American cultural landscape.

PRINCIPAL WORKS

*The Book of Mormon (theology) 1830
A Book of Commandments (theology) 1833
Doctrine and Covenants of the Church of the Latter-Day Saints (theology) 1835
The Pearl of Great Price, being a choice selection from the revelations, translations, and narrations of Joseph Smith (theology) 1851
†*History of the Church of Jesus Christ of Latter-Day Saints. Period I. History of Joseph Smith, the Prophet, by Himself.* [6 vols.] (theology) 1902-12

*Smith claimed to have translated this work from golden plates between 1827 and 1829.
†The first manuscript for this work is dated June 11, 1839.

CRITICISM

Joseph Smith, Jr. (essay date 1838)

SOURCE: "Extracts from the History of Joseph Smith, the Prophet," in *The Pearl of Great Price,* The Church of Jesus Christ of Latter-Day Saints, 1958, pp. 46-58.

[*In the following excerpt, written in 1838, Smith recounts the circumstances surrounding the transcription and publication of the* Book of Mormon.]

1. Owing to the many reports which have been put in circulation by evil-disposed and designing persons, in relation to the rise and progress of the Church of Jesus Christ of Latter-day Saints, all of which have been designed by the authors thereof to militate against its character as a Church and its progress in the world—I have been induced to write this history, to disabuse the public mind, and put all inquirers after truth in possession of the facts, as they have transpired, in relation both to myself and the Church, so far as I have such facts in my possession

2. In this history I shall present the various events in relation to this Church, in truth and righteousness, as

they have transpired, or as they at present exist being now the eighth year since the organization of the said Church.

3. I was born in the year of our Lord one thousand eight hundred and five, on the twenty-third day of December, in the town of Sharon, Windsor county, State of Vermont. . . . My father, Joseph Smith, Sen., left the State of Vermont, and moved to Palmyra, Ontario (now Wayne) county, in the State of New York, when I was in my tenth year, or thereabouts. In about four years after my father's arrival in Palmyra, he moved with his family into Manchester in the same county of Ontario—. . . .

5. Some time in the second year after our removal to Manchester, there was in the place where we lived an unusual excitement on the subject of religion. It commenced with the Methodists, but soon became general among all the sects in that region of country. Indeed, the whole district of country seemed affected by it, and great multitudes united themselves to the different religious parties, which created no small stir and division amongst the people, some crying, "Lo, here!" and others, "Lo there!" Some were contending for the Methodist faith, some for the Presbyterian, and some for the Baptist.

6. For, notwithstanding the great love which the converts to these different faiths expressed at the time of their conversion, and the great zeal manifested by the respective clergy, who were active in getting up and promoting this extraordinary scene of religious feeling, in order to have everybody converted as they were pleased to call it, let them join what sect they pleased; yet when the converts began to file off, some to one party and some to another, it was seen that the seemingly good feelings of both the priests and the converts were more pretended than real; for a scene of great confusion and bad feeling ensued—priest contending against priest, and convert against convert; so that all their good feelings one for another, if they ever had any, were entirely lost in a strife of words and a contest about opinions. . . .

8. During this time of great excitement my mind was called up to serious reflection and great uneasiness; but though my feelings were deep and often poignant, still I kept myself aloof from all these parties, though I attended their several meetings as often as occasion would permit. In process of time my mind became somewhat partial to the Methodist sect, and I felt some desire to be united with them; but so great were the confusion and strife among the different denominations, that it was impossible for a person young as I was, and so unacquainted with men and things, to come to any certain conclusion who was right and who was wrong.

9. My mind at times was greatly excited, the cry and tumult were so great and incessant. The Presbyterians were most decided against the Baptists and Methodists, and used all the powers of both reason and sophistry to prove their errors, or, at least, to make the people think they were in error. On the other hand, the Baptists and Methodists in their turn were equally zealous in endeavoring to establish their own tenets and disprove all others.

10. In the midst of this war of words and tumult of opinions, I often said to myself: What is to be done? Who of all these parties are right; or, are they all wrong together? If any one of them be right, which is it, and how shall I know it?

11. While I was laboring under the extreme difficulties caused by the contests of these parties of religionists, I was one day reading the Epistle of James, first chapter and fifth verse, which reads: *If any of you lack wisdom, let him ask of God, that giveth to all men liberally, and upbraideth not, and it shall be given him.*

12. Never did any passage of scripture come with more power to the heart of man than this did at this time to mine. It seemed to enter with great force into every feeling of my heart. I reflected on it again and again, knowing that if any person needed wisdom from God, I did; for how to act I did not know, and unless I could get more wisdom than I then had, I would never know; for the teachers of religion of the different sects understood the same passages of scripture so differently as to destroy all confidence in settling the question by an appeal to the Bible.

13. At length I came to the conclusion that I must either remain in darkness and confusion, or else I must do as James directs, that is, ask of God. I at length came to the determination to "ask of God," concluding that if he gave wisdom to them that lacked wisdom, and would give liberally, and not upbraid, I might venture.

14. So, in accordance with this, my determination to ask of God, I retired to the woods to make the attempt. It was on the morning of a beautiful, clear day, early in the spring of eighteen hundred and twenty. It was the first time in my life that I had made such an attempt, for amidst all my anxieties I had never as yet made the attempt to pray vocally.

15. After I had retired to the place where I had previously designed to go, having looked around me, and finding myself alone, I kneeled down and began to offer up the desire of my heart to God. I had scarcely done so, when immediately I was seized upon by some power which entirely overcame me and had such an astonishing influence over me as to bind my tongue so

that I could not speak. Thick darkness gathered around me, and it seemed to me for a time as if I were doomed to sudden destruction.

16. But, exerting all my powers to call upon God to deliver me out of the power of this enemy which had seized upon me, and at the very moment when I was ready to sink into despair and abandon myself to destruction—not to an imaginary ruin, but to the power of some actual being from the unseen world, who had such marvelous power as I had never before felt in any being—just at this moment of great alarm, I saw a pillar of light exactly over my head, above the brightness of the sun, which descended gradually until it fell upon me.

17. It no sooner appeared than I found myself delivered from the enemy which held me bound. When the light rested upon me I saw two Personages, whose brightness and glory defy all description, standing above me in the air. One of them spake unto me, calling me by name and said pointing to the other—*This is My Beloved Son. Hear Him!*

18. My object in going to inquire of the Lord was to know which of all the sects was right that I might know which to join. No sooner, therefore, did I get possession of myself, so as to be able to speak, than I asked the Personages who stood above me in the light, which of all the sects was right—and which I should join.

19. I was answered that I must join none of them, for they were all wrong; and the Personage who addressed me said that all their creeds were an abomination in his sight; that those professors were all corrupt; that: "they draw near to me with their lips but their hearts are far from me, they teach for doctrines the commandments of men, having a form of godliness, but they deny the power thereof."

20. He again forbade me to join with any of them; and many other things did he say unto me which I cannot write at this time. When I came to myself again, I found myself lying on my back, looking up into heaven. When the light had departed, I had no strength; but soon recovering in some degree, I went home. And as I leaned up to the fireplace, mother inquired what the matter was. I replied, "Never mind, all is well—I am well enough off." I then said to my mother, "I have learned for myself that Presbyterianism is not true." It seems as though the adversary was aware, at a very early period of my life, that I was destined to prove a disturber and an annoyer of his kingdom; else why should the powers of darkness combine against me? Why the opposition and persecution that arose against me, almost in my infancy?

21. Some few days after I had this vision, I happened to be in company with one of the Methodist preachers, who was very active in the before mentioned religious excitement; and, conversing with him on the subject of religion, I took occasion to give him an account of the vision which I had had. I was greatly surprised at his behavior; he treated my communication not only lightly, but with great contempt, saying it was all of the devil, that there were no such things as visions or revelations in these days; that all such things had ceased with the apostles, and that there would never be any more of them.

22. I soon found, however, that my telling the story had excited a great deal of prejudice against me among professors of religion, and was the cause of great persecution, which continued to increase; and though I was an obscure boy, only between fourteen and fifteen years of age, and my circumstances in life such as to make a boy of no consequence in the world, yet men of high standing would take notice sufficient to excite the public mind against me, and create a bitter persecution; and this was common among all the sects—all united to persecute me.

23. It caused me serious reflection then, and often has since, how very strange it was that an obscure boy, of a little over fourteen years of age, and one, too, who was doomed to the necessity of obtaining a scanty maintenance by his daily labor, should be thought a character of sufficient importance to attract the attention of the great ones of the most popular sects of the day, and in a manner to create in them a spirit of the most bitter persecution and reviling. But strange or not, so it was, and it was often the cause of great sorrow to myself.

24. However, it was nevertheless a fact that I had beheld a vision. I have thought since, that I felt much like Paul, when he made his defense before King Agrippa, and related the account of the vision he had when he saw a light and heard a voice; but still there were but few who believed him; some said he was dishonest, others said he was mad; and he was ridiculed and reviled. But all this did not destroy the reality of his vision. He had seen a vision, he knew he had, and all the persecution under heaven could not make it otherwise; and though they should persecute him unto death, yet he knew, and would know to his latest breath, that he had both seen a light and heard a voice speaking unto him, and all the world could not make him think or believe otherwise.

25. So it was with me. I had actually seen a light, and in the midst of that light I saw two Personages, and they did in reality speak to me; and though I was hated and persecuted for saying that I had seen a vision, yet it was true; and while they were persecuting me, reviling me, and speaking all manner of evil against me falsely for so saying, I was led to say in my heart: Why persecute me for telling the truth? I have actually

seen a vision; and who am I that I can withstand God, or why does the world think to make me deny what I have actually seen? For I had seen a vision; I knew it, and I knew that God knew it, and I could not deny it, neither dared I do it; at least I knew that by so doing I would offend God, and come under condemnation.

26. I had now got my mind satisfied so far as the sectarian world was concerned—that it was not my duty to join with any of them, but to continue as I was until further directed. I had found the testimony of James to be true—that a man who lacked wisdom might ask of God, and obtain and not be upbraided.

27. I continued to pursue my common vocations in life until the twenty-first of September, one thousand eight hundred and twenty-three, all the time suffering severe persecution at the hands of all classes of men, both religious and irreligious, because I continued to affirm that I had seen a vision.

28. During the space of time which intervened between the time I had the vision and the year eighteen hundred and twenty-three—having been forbidden to join any of the religious sects of the day, and being of very tender years, and persecuted by those who ought to have been my friends and to have treated me kindly, and if they supposed me to be deluded to have endeavored in a proper and affectionate manner to have reclaimed me—I was left to all kinds of temptations; and, mingling with all kinds of society, I frequently fell into many foolish errors, and displayed the weakness of youth, and the foibles of human nature; which, I am sorry to say, led me into divers temptations, offensive in the sight of God. In making this confession, no one need suppose me guilty of any great or malignant sins. A disposition to commit such was never in my nature. But I was guilty of levity, and sometimes associated with jovial company, etc., not consistent with that character which ought to be maintained by one who was called of God as I had been. But this will not seem very strange to any one who recollects my youth, and is acquainted with my native cheery temperament.

29. In consequence of these things, I often felt condemned for my weakness and imperfections; when, on the evening of the above-mentioned twenty-first of September, after I had retired to my bed for the night, I betook myself to prayer and supplication to Almighty God for forgiveness of all my sins and follies, and also for a manifestation to me, that I might know of my state and standing before him; for I had full confidence in obtaining a divine manifestation, as I previously had one.

30. While I was thus in the act of calling upon God, I discovered a light appearing in my room, which continued to increase until the room was lighter than at noonday, when immediately a personage appeared at my bedside standing in the air, for his feet did not touch the floor.

31. He had on a loose robe of most exquisite whiteness. It was a whiteness beyond anything earthly I had ever seen; nor do I believe that any earthly thing could be made to appear so exceedingly white and brilliant. His hands were naked, and his arms also a little above the wrist; so, also, were his feet naked, as were his legs, a little above the ankles. His head and neck were also bare. I could discover that he had no other clothing on but this robe, as it was open, so that I could see into his bosom.

32. Not only was his robe exceedingly white, but his whole person was glorious beyond description, and his countenance truly like lightning. The room was exceedingly light, but not so very bright as immediately around his person. When I first looked upon him, I was afraid; but the fear soon left me.

33. He called me by name, and said unto me that he was a messenger sent from the presence of God to me, and that his name was Moroni; that God had a work for me to do, and that my name should be had for good and evil among all nations, kindreds, and tongues, or that it should be both good and evil spoken of among all people.

34. He said there was a book deposited, written upon gold plates, giving an account of the former inhabitants of this continent, and the source from whence they sprang. He also said that the fulness of the everlasting Gospel was contained in it, as delivered by the Savior to the ancient inhabitants;

35. Also, that there were two stones in silver bows—and these stones, fastened to a breastplate, constituted what is called the Urim and Thummim—deposited with the plates; and the possession and use of these stones were what constituted "seers" in ancient or former times; and that God had prepared them for the purpose of translating the book. . . .

42. Again, he told me, that when I got those plates of which he had spoken—for the time that they should be obtained was not yet fulfilled—I should not show them to any person; neither the breastplate with the Urim and Thummim; only to those to whom I should be commanded to show them; if I did I should be destroyed. While he was conversing with me about the plates, the vision was opened to my mind that I could see the place where the plates were deposited, and that so clearly and distinctly that I knew the place again when I visited it.

43. After this communication, I saw the light in the room begin to gather immediately around the person of him who had been speaking to me, and it continued

to do so until the room was again left dark, except just around him, when, instantly I saw, as it were, a conduit open right up into heaven, and he ascended till he entirely disappeared, and the room was left as it had been before this heavenly light had made its appearance.

44. I lay musing on the singularity of the scene, and marveling greatly at what had been told to me by this extraordinary messenger; when, in the midst of my meditation, I suddenly discovered that my room was again beginning to get lighted, and in an instant, as it were, the same heavenly messenger was again by my bedside.

45. He commenced, and again related the very same things which he had done at his first visit, without the least variation; which having done, he informed me of great judgments which were coming upon the earth, with great desolations by famine, sword, and pestilence; and that these grievous judgments would come on the earth in this generation. Having related these things he again ascended as he had done before.

46. By this time, so deep were the impressions made on my mind, that sleep had fled from my eyes, and I lay overwhelmed in astonishment at what I had both seen and heard. But what was my surprise when again I beheld the same messenger at my bedside, and heard him rehearse or repeat over again to me the same things as before; and added a caution to me, telling me that Satan would try to tempt me (in consequence of the indigent circumstances of my father's family), to get the plates for the purpose of getting rich. This he forbade me, saying that I must have no other object in view in getting the plates but to glorify God, and must not be influenced by any other motive than that of building his kingdom; otherwise I could not get them.

47. After this third visit, he again ascended into heaven as before, and I was again left to ponder on the strangeness of what I had just experienced, when almost immediately after the heavenly messenger had ascended from me for the third time, the cock crowed, and I found that day was approaching, so that our interviews must have occupied the whole of that night.

48. I shortly after arose from my bed, and, as usual, went to the necessary labors of the day; but, in attempting to work as at other times, I found my strength so exhausted as to render me entirely unable. My father, who was laboring along with me, discovered something to be wrong with me, and told me to go home. I started with the intention of going to the house; but, in attempting to cross the fence out of the field where we were, my strength entirely failed me, and I fell helpless on the ground, and for a time was quite unconscious of anything.

49. The first thing that I can recollect was a voice speaking unto me, calling me by name. I looked up, and beheld the same messenger standing over my head, surrounded by light as before. He then again related unto me all that he had related to me the previous night, and commanded me to go to my father and tell him of the vision and commandments which I had received.

50. I obeyed; I returned to my father in the field, and rehearsed the whole matter to him. He replied to me that it was of God, and told me to go and do as commanded by the messenger. I left the field, and went to the place where the messenger had told me the plates were deposited; and owing to the distinctness of the vision which I had had concerning it, I knew the place the instant that I arrived there.

51. Convenient to the village of Manchester, Ontario county, New York, stands a hill of considerable size, and the most elevated of any in the neighborhood. On the west side of this hill, not far from the top, under a stone of considerable size, lay the plates, deposited in a stone box. This stone was thick and rounding in the middle on the upper side, and thinner towards the edges, so that the middle part of it was visible above the ground, but the edge all around was covered with earth.

52. Having removed the earth, I obtained a lever, which I got fixed under the edge of the stone, and with a little exertion raised it up. I looked in, and there indeed did I behold the plates, the Urim and Thummim, and the breastplate, as stated by the messenger. The box in which they lay was formed by laying stones together in some kind of cement. In the bottom of the box were laid two stones crossways of the box, and on these stones lay the plates and the other things with them.

53. I made an attempt to take them out, but was forbidden by the messenger, and was again informed that the time for bringing them forth had not yet arrived, neither would it, until four years from that time; but he told me that I should come to that place precisely in one year from that time and that he would there meet with me, and that I should continue to do so until the time should come for obtaining the plates.

54. Accordingly, as I had been commanded, I went at the end of each year, and at each time I found the same messenger there, and received instruction and intelligence from him at each of our interviews, respecting what the Lord was going to do, and how and in what manner his kingdom was to be conducted in the last days. . . .

59. At length the time arrived for obtaining the plates, the Urim and Thummim, and the breastplate. On the twenty-second day of September, one thousand eight hundred and twenty-seven, having gone as usual at the

end of another year to the place where they were deposited, the same heavenly messenger delivered them up to me with this charge: that I should be responsible for them; that if I should let them go carelessly, or through any neglect of mine, I should be cut off, but that if I would use all my endeavors to preserve them, until he, the messenger, should call for them, they should be protected.

60. I soon found out the reason why I had received such strict charges to keep them safe, and why it was that the messenger had said that when I had done what was required at my hand, he would call for them. For no sooner was it known that I had them, than the most strenuous exertions were used to get them from me. Every stratagem that could be invented was resorted to for that purpose. The persecution became more bitter and severe than before, and multitudes were on the alert continually to get them from me if possible. But by the wisdom of God, they remained safe in my hands, until I had accomplished by them what was required at my hand. When, according to arrangements, the messenger called for them, I delivered them up to him; and he has them in his charge until this day, being the second day of May, one thousand eight hundred and thirty-eight.

61. The excitement, however, still continued, and rumor with her thousand tongues was all the time employed in circulating falsehoods about my father's family, and about myself. If I were to relate a thousandth part of them, it would fill up volumes. The persecution, however, became so intolerable that I was under the necessity of leaving Manchester, and going with my wife to Susquehanna county, in the State of Pennsylvania. While preparing to start—being very poor, and the persecution so heavy upon us that there was no probability that we would ever be otherwise—in the midst of our afflictions we found a friend in a gentleman by the name of Martin Harris, who came to us and gave me fifty dollars to assist us on our journey. Mr. Harris was a resident of Palmyra township, Wayne county, in the State of New York, and a farmer of respectability.

62. By this timely aid was I enabled to reach the place of my destination in Pennsylvania; and immediately after my arrival there I commenced copying the characters off the plates. I copied a considerable number of them, and by means of the Urim and Thummim I translated some of them, which I did between the time I arrived at the house of my wife's father, in the month of December, and the February following.

63. Sometime in this month of February, the aforementioned Mr. Martin Harris came to our place, got the characters which I had drawn off the plates, and started with them to the city of New York. For what took place relative to him and the characters, I refer to his own account of the circumstances, as he related them to me after his return, which was as follows:

64. "I went to the city of New York, and presented the characters which had been translated, with the translation thereof, to Professor Charles Anthon, a gentleman celebrated for his literary attainments. Professor Anthon stated that the translation was correct, more so than any he had before seen translated from the Egyptian. I then showed him those which were not yet translated, and he said that they were Egyptian, Chaldaic, Assyriac, and Arabic; and he said they were true characters. He gave me a certificate, certifying to the people of Palmyra that they were true characters, and that the translation of such of them as had been translated was also correct. I took the certificate and put it into my pocket, and was just leaving the house, when Mr. Anthon called me back, and asked me how the young man found out that there were gold plates in the place where he found them. I answered that an angel of God had revealed it unto him.

65. "He then said to me, 'Let me see that certificate.' I accordingly took it out of my pocket and gave it to him, when he took it and tore it to pieces, saying that there was no such thing now as ministering of angels, and that if I would bring the plates to him he would translate them. I informed him that part of the plates were sealed, and that I was forbidden to bring them. He replied, 'I cannot read a sealed book.' I left him and went to Dr. Mitchell, who sanctioned what Professor Anthon had said respecting both the characters and the translation."

. . . . .

66. On the 5th day of April, 1829, Oliver Cowdery came to my house, until which time I had never seen him. He stated to me that having been teaching school in the neighborhood where my father resided, and my father being one of those who sent to the school, he went to board for a season at his house, and while there the family related to him the circumstance of my having received the plates, and accordingly he had come to make inquiries of me.

67. Two days after the arrival of Mr. Cowdery (being the 7th of April) I commenced to translate the *Book of Mormon*, and he began to write for me.

68. We still continued the work of translation, when, in the ensuing month (May, 1829), we on a certain day went into the woods to pray and inquire of the Lord respecting baptism for the remission of sins, that we found mentioned in the translation of the plates. While we were thus employed, praying and calling upon the Lord, a messenger from heaven descended in a cloud of light, and having laid his hands upon us, he ordained us, saying:

69. *Upon you my fellow servants, in the name of Messiah, I confer the Priesthood of Aaron, which holds the keys of the ministering of angels, and of the gospel of repentance, and of baptism by immersion for the remission of sins; and this shall never be taken again from the earth until the sons of Levi do offer again an offering unto the Lord in righteousness.*

70. He said this Aaronic Priesthood had not the power of laying on hands for the gift of the Holy Ghost, but that this should be conferred on us hereafter; and he commanded us to go and be baptized, and gave us directions that I should baptize Oliver Cowdery, and that afterwards he should baptize me.

71. Accordingly we went and were baptized. I baptized him first, and afterwards he baptized me—after which I laid my hands upon his head and ordained him to the Aaronic Priesthood, and afterwards he laid his hands on me and ordained me to the same Priesthood—for so we were commanded.

72. The messenger who visited us on this occasion and conferred this Priesthood upon us, said that his name was John, the same that is called John the Baptist in the New Testament, and that he acted under the direction of Peter, James and John, who held the keys of the Priesthood of Melchizedek, which Priesthood, he said would in due time be conferred on us, and that I should be called the first Elder of the Church, and he (Oliver Cowdery) the second. It was on the fifteenth day of May, 1829, that we were ordained under the hand of this messenger, and baptized.

73. Immediately on our coming up out of the water after we had been baptized, we experienced great and glorious blessings from our Heavenly Father. No sooner had I baptized Oliver Cowdery, than the Holy Ghost fell upon him, and he stood up and prophesied many things which should shortly come to pass. And again, so soon as I had been baptized by him, I also had the spirit of prophecy, when, standing up, I prophesied concerning the rise of this Church, and many other things connected with the Church, and this generation of the children of men. We were filled with the Holy Ghost, and rejoiced in the God of our salvation.

74. Our minds being now enlightened, we began to have the scriptures laid open to our understandings, and the true meaning and intention of their more mysterious passages revealed unto us in a manner which we never could attain to previously, nor ever before had thought of. In the meantime we were forced to keep secret the circumstances of having received the Priesthood and our having been baptized, owing to a spirit of persecution which had already manifested itself in the neighborhood.

75. We had been threatened with being mobbed, from time to time, and this, too, by professors of religion. And their intentions of mobbing us were only counteracted by the influence of my wife's father's family (under Divine providence), who had become very friendly to me, and who were opposed to mobs, and were willing that I should be allowed to continue the work of translation without interruption; and therefore offered and promised us protection from all unlawful proceedings, as far as in them lay.

The Nauvoo Expositor (essay date 1844)

SOURCE: An untitled article in *The Nauvoo Expositor,* Vol. 1, No. 1, June 7, 1844.

[*The following excerpt is taken from the first and only issue of the* Nauvoo Expositor, *a paper published by Mormon opponents of Joseph Smith's leadership. In response to the* Expositor's *attacks on himself and Mormonism, on the evening of June 10, Smith and the Nauvoo city council ordered his Nauvoo Legion to destroy the newspaper. Smith's action against the* Expositor *spawned the series of events which led to the murder of Smith and his brother Hyrum on June 27. In the following excerpt, seceders from the Mormon Church at Nauvoo explain the reasons for their dissension.*]

Preamble.

It is with the greatest solicitude for the salvation of the Human Family, and of our own souls, that we have this day assembled. Feign would we have slumbered, and "like the Dove that covers and conceals the arrow that is preying upon its vitals," for the sake of avoiding the furious and turbulent storm of persecution which will gather, soon to burst upon our heads, have covered and concealed that which, for a season, has been brooding among the ruins of our peace: but we rely upon the arm of Jehovah, the Supreme Arbiter of the world, to whom we this day, and upon this occasion, appeal for the rectitude of our intentions.

If that God who gave bounds to the mighty deep, and bade the ocean cease—if that God who organized the physical world, and gave infinity to space, be our front guard and our rear ward, it is futile and vain for man to raise his puny arm against us. God will inspire his ministers with courage and with understanding to consummate his purposes; and if it is necessary, he can snatch them from the fiery furnace, or the Lion's den as he did anciently the three Hebrews from the former, and Daniel from the latter.

As for our acquaintance with the Church of Jesus Christ of Latter Day Saints, we know, no man or set of men can be more thoroughly acquainted with its rise, its organization, and its history, than we have every reason to believe we are. We all verily believe, and many of us know of a surety, that the religion of the Latter Day Saints, as originally taught by Joseph Smith, which is contained in the Old and New Testaments, Book of Covenants, and Book of Mormon, is verily true; and that the pure principles set forth in those books, are the immutable and eternal principles of Heaven, and speaks a language which, when spoken in truth and virtue, sinks deep into the heart of every honest man—Its precepts are invigorating, and in every sense of the word, tend to dignify and ennoble man's conceptions of God and his attributes. It speaks a language which is heard amidst the roar of Artillery, as well as in the silence of midnight: it speaks a language understood by [the] incarcerated spirit, as well as he who is unfettered and free; yet to those who will not see, it is dark, mysterious and secret as the grave.

We believe that all men, professing to be the ministers of God, should keep steadily in view, the honor and glory of God, the salvation of souls, and the amelioration of man's condition: and among their cardinal virtues ought to be found those of faith, hope, virtue and charity; but with Joseph Smith, and many other official characters in the Church, they are words without any meanings attached—worn as ornaments; exotics nurtured for display; virtues which, throwing aside the existence of a God, the peace, happiness, welfare, and good order of society, require that they should be preserved pure, immaculate and uncorroded.

We most solemnly and sincerely declare, God this day being witness of the truth and sincerity of our designs and statements, that happy will it be with those who examine and scan Joseph Smith's pretensions to righteousness; and take counsel of human affairs, and of the experience of times gone by. Do not yield up tranquilly a superiority to that man which the reasonableness of past events, and the laws of our country declare to be pernicious and diabolical. We hope many items of doctrine, as now taught, some of which, however, are taught secretly, and denied openly, (which we know positively is the case,) and others publicly, considerate men will treat with contempt; for we declare them heretical and damnable in their influence, though they find many devotees. How shall he, who has drank of the poisonous draft, teach virtue? In the stead thereof, when the criminal ought to plead *guilty* to the court, the court is obliged to plead guilty to the criminal. We appeal to humanity and ask, what shall we do? Shall we lie supinely and suffer ourselves to be metamorphosed into beasts by the Syren tongue? We answer that our country and our God require that we should rectify the tree. We have called upon him to repent, and as soon as he shewed fruits meet for repentance, we stood ready to seize him by the hand of fellowship, and throw around him the mantle of pro-

tection; for it is the salvation of souls we desire, and not our own aggrandizement.

We are earnestly seeking to explode the vicious principles of Joseph Smith, and those who practice the same abominations and whoredoms; which we verily know are not accordant and consonant with the principles of Jesus Christ and the Apostles; and for that purpose, and with that end in view, with an eye single to the glory of God, we have dared to gird on the armor, and with God at our head, we most solemnly and sincerely declare that the sword of *truth* shall not depart from the thigh, nor the buckler from the arm, until we can enjoy those glorious privileges which nature's God and our country's laws have guaranteed to us—freedom of speech, the liberty of the press, and the right to worship God as seemeth us good.—We are aware, however, that we are hazarding every earthly blessing, particularly property, and probably life itself, in striking this blow at tyranny and oppression: yet notwithstanding, we most solemnly declare that no man, or set of men combined, shall, with impunity, violate obligations as sacred as many which have been violated, unless reason, justice and virtue have become ashamed and sought the haunts of the grave, though our lives be the forfeiture.

Many of us have sought a reformation in the church, without a public exposition of the enormities of crimes practiced by its leaders, thinking that if they would hearken to counsel, and shew fruit meet for repentance, it would be as acceptable with God, as though they were exposed to public gaze,

> For the private path, the secret acts of
>   men,
> If noble, far the noblest of their lives.

but our petitions were treated with contempt; and in many cases the petitioner spurned from their presence, and particularly by Joseph, who would state that if he had sinned, and was guilty of the charges we would charge him with, he would not make acknowledgement, but would rather be damned; for it would detract from his dignity, and would consequently ruin and prove the overthrow of the Church. We would ask him on the other hand, if the overthrow of the Church was not inevitable, to which he often responded, that we would all go to Hell together, and convert it into a heaven, by casting the Devil out; and says he, Hell is by no means the place this world of fools suppose it to be, but on the contrary, it is quite an agreeable place: to which we would now reply, he can enjoy it if he is determined not to desist from his evil ways; but as for us, and ours, we *will* serve the Lord our God!

It is absurd for men to assert that all is well, while wicked and corrupt men are seeking our destruction, by a perversion of sacred things; for all is *not* well, while whoredoms and all manner of abominations are practiced under the cloak of religion. Lo! the wolf is in the fold, arrayed in sheep's clothing, and is spreading death and devastation among the saints: and we say to the watchmen standing upon the walls, cry aloud and spare not, for the day of the Lord is at hand—a day cruel both with wrath and fierce anger, to lay the land desolate.

It is a notorious fact, that many females in foreign climes, and in countries to us unknown, even in the most distant regions of the Eastern hemisphere, have been induced, by the sound of the gospel, to forsake friends, and embark upon a voyage across waters that lie stretched over the greater portion of the globe, as they supposed, to glorify God, that they might thereby stand acquitted in the great day of God Almighty. But what is taught them on their arrival at this place?— They are visited by some of the Strikers, for we know not what else to call them, and are requested to hold on and be faithful, for there are great blessings awaiting the righteous; and that God has great mysteries in store for those who love the Lord, and cling to brother Joseph. They are also notified that brother Joseph will see them soon, and reveal the mysteries of Heaven to their full understanding, which seldom fails to inspire them with new confidence in the Prophet, as well as a great anxiety to know what God has laid up in store for them, in return for the great sacrifice of father and mother, of gold and silver, which they gladly left far behind, that they might be gathered into the fold, and numbered among the chosen of God.—They are visited again, and what is the result? They are requested to meet brother Joseph, or some of the Twelve, at some insulated point, or at some particularly described place on the bank of the Mississippi, or at some room, which wears upon its front—*Positively NO admittance.* The harmless, inoffensive, and unsuspecting creatures, are so devoted to the Prophet, and the cause of Jesus Christ, that they do not dream of the deeplaid and fatal scheme which prostrates happiness, and renders death itself desirable, but they meet him, expecting to receive through him a blessing, and learn the will of the Lord concerning them, and what awaits the faithful follower of Joseph, the Apostle and Prophet of God, when in the stead thereof, they are told, after having been sworn in one of the most solemn manners, to never divulge what is revealed to them, with a penalty of death attached, that God Almighty has revealed it to him, that she should be his (Joseph's) Spiritual wife; for it was right anciently, and God will tolerate it again: but we must keep those pleasures and blessings from the world, for until there is a change in the government, we will endanger ourselves by practicing it—but we can enjoy the blessings of Jacob, David, and others, as well as to be deprived of them, if we do not expose ourselves to the law of the land. She is thunder-struck, faints, recovers, and refuses. The Prophet damns her if she rejects. She thinks of the great sacrifice, and of the many

thousand miles she has traveled over sea and land, that she might save her soul from pending ruin, and replies, God's will be done, and not mine. The Prophet and his devotees in this way are gratified. The next step to avoid public exposition from the common course of things, they are sent away for a time, until all is well; after which they return, as from a long visit. Those whom no power or influence could seduce, except that which is wielded by some individual feigning to be a God, must realize the remarks of an able writer, when he says, "If woman's feelings are turned to ministers of sorrow, where shall she look for consolation?" Her lot is to be wooed and won; her heart is like some fortress that has been captured, sacked abandoned, and left desolate. . . .

The next important item which presents itself for our consideration, is the attempt at Political power and influence, which we verily believe to be preposterous and absurd. We believe it is inconsistent, and not in accordance with the christian religion. We do not believe that God ever raised up a Prophet to christianize a world by political schemes and intrigue. It is not the way God captivates the heart of the unbeliever; but on the contrary, by preaching truth in its own native simplicity, and in its own original purity, unadorned with anything except its own indigenous beauties. Joseph may plead he has been injured, abused, and his petitions treated with contempt by the general government, and that he only desires an influence of a political character that will warrant him redress of grievances; but we care not—the faithful followers of Jesus must bear in this age as well as Christ and the Apostles did anciently; although a frowning world may have crushed him to the dust; although unpitying friends may have passed him by; although hope, the great comforter in affliction, may have burst forth and fled from his troubled bosom; yet, in Jesus there is a balsom for every wound, and a cordial to assuage an agonized mind.

Among the many items of false doctrine that are taught the Church, is the doctrine of *many Gods,* one of the most direful in its effects that has characterized the world for many centuries. We know not what to call it other than blasphemy, for it is most unquestionably, speaking of God in an impious and irreverent manner.—It is contended that there are innumerable Gods as much above the God that presides over this universe, as he is above us; and if he varies from the law unto which he is subjected, he, with all his creatures, will be cast down as was Lucifer; thus holding forth a doctrine which is effectually calculated to sap the very foundation of our faith: and now, O Lord! shall we set still and be silent, while thy name is thus blasphemed, and thine honor, power and glory, brought into disrepute? See Isaiah c 43, v 10: 44, 6-8; 45, 5, 6, 21, 22; and book of Covenants, page 26 and 39.

In the dark ages of Popery, when bigotry, superstition, and tyranny held universal sway over the empire of reason, there was some semblance of justice in the inquisitorial deliberations, which, however, might have been dictated by prudence, or the fear of consequences: but we are no longer forced to appeal to those states that are now situated under the influence of Popery for examples of injustice, cruelty and oppression—we can appeal to the acts of the inquisitorial department organized in *Nauvoo*, by Joseph and his accomplices, for specimens of injustice of the most pernicious and diabolical character that ever stained the pages of the historian.

It was in Rome, and about the twelfth century, when Pope Innocent III, ordered father Dominic to excite the Catholic princes and people to extirpate heretics. But it is in this enlightened and intelligent nineteenth century, and in Nauvoo—a place professing to be the nucleus of the world, that Joseph Smith has established an inquisition, which, if it is suffered to exist, will prove more formidable and terrible to those who are found opposing the iniquities of Joseph and his associates, than even the Spanish inquisition did to heretics as they termed them.

On Thursday evening, the 18th of April, there was a council called, unknown to the Church, which tried, condemned, and cut off brothers Wm. Law, Wilson Law, and sister Law, (Wm's. wife,) brother R. D. Foster, and one brother Smith, with whom we are unacquainted; which we contend is contrary to the book of Doctrine and Covenants, for our law condemnest no man until he is heard. We abhor and protest against any council or tribunal in this Church, which will not suffer the accused to stand in its midst and plead their own cause. If an Agrippa would suffer a Paul, whose eloquence surpassed, as it were, the eloquence of men, to stand before him, and plead his own cause, why should Joseph, with others, refuse to hear individuals in their own defence?—We answer, it is because the court fears the atrocity of its crimes will be exposed to public gaze. We wish the public to thoroughly understand the nature of this court, and judge of the legality of its acts as seemeth them good.

On Monday, the 15th of April, brother R. D. Foster had a notice served on him to appear before the High Council on Saturday following, the 20th, and answer to charges preferred against him by Joseph Smith. On Saturday, while Mr. Foster was preparing to take his witnesses, 41 in number, to the council-room, that he might make good his charges against Joseph, president Marks notified him that the trial had been on Thursday evening, before the 15th, and that he was cut off from the Church; and that same council cut off the brother Laws', sister Law, and brother Smith, and all without their knowledge. They were not notified, neither did

they dream of any such thing being done, for William Law had sent Joseph and some of the Twelve, special word that he desired an investigation before the Church in General Conference, on the 6th of Ap'l. The court, however, was a tribunal possessing no power to try Wm. Law, who was called by special Revelation, to stand as counsellor to the President of the Church, (Joseph,) which was twice ratified by General Conferences, assembled at Nauvoo, for Brigham Young, one of the Twelve, presided, whose duty it was not, but the President of the High Council. . . .

RESOLUTIONS.

Resolved 1st, That we will not encourage the acts of any court in this church, for the trial of any of its members, which will not suffer the accused to be present and plead their own cause; we therefore declare our decided disapprobation to the course pursued last Thursday evening, (the 18th inst,) in the case of William and Wilson Law, and Mrs. William Law, and R. D. Foster, as being unjust and unauthorized by the laws of the Church, and consequently null and void; for our law judgeth no man unless he be heard; and to all those who approbate a course so unwarranted, unprecedented and so unjust, we would say beware lest the unjust measure you meet to your brethren, be again meeted out to you.

Resolved 2nd, Inasmuch as we have for years borne with the individual follies and iniquities of Joseph Smith, Hyrum Smith, and many other official characters in the Church of Jesus Christ, (conceiving it a duty incumbent upon us so to bear,) and having labored with them repeatedly with all Christian love, meekness and humility, yet to no effect, feel as if forbearance has ceased to be a virtue, and hope of reformation vain; and inasmuch as they have introduced false and damnable doctrines into the Church, such as a plurality of Gods above the God of this universe, and his liability to fall with all his creations; the plurality of wives, for time and eternity: the doctrine of unconditional sealing up to eternal life, against all crimes except that of shedding innocent blood, by a perversion of their priestly authority, and thereby forfeiting the holy priesthood, according to the word of Jesus: "If a man abide not in me, he is cast forth as a branch and is withered, and men gather them and cast them into the fire, and they are burned," St. John, xv. 6. "Whosoever transgresseth and abideth not in the doctrine of Christ, hath not God, he that abideth in the doctrine of Christ, hath both the Father and the Son; if there come any unto you and bring not this doctrine, receive him not into your house, neither bid him God speed, for he that bideth him God speed is a partaker of his evil deeds," we therefore are constrained to denounce them as apostates from the pure and holy doctrines of Jesus Christ.

Resolved 3rd, That we disapprobate and discountenance every attempt to unite church and state; and that we further believe the effort now being made by Joseph Smith for political power and influence, is not commendable in the sight of God.

Resolved 4th, That the hostile *spirit* and conduct manifested by Joseph Smith, and many of his associates towards Missouri, and others inimical to his purposes, are decidedly at variance with the true spirit of Christianity, and should not be encouraged by any people, much less by those professing to be the ministers of the gospel of peace.

Resolved 5th, That while we disapprobate malicious persecutions and prosecutions, we hold that all church members are alike amenable to the laws of the land; and that we further discountenance any chicanery to screen them from the just demands of the same.

Resolved 6th, That we consider the religious influence exercised in financial concerns by Joseph Smith, as unjust as it is unwarranted, for the Book of Doctrine and Covenants makes it the duty of the Bishop to take charge of the financial affairs of the Church, and of all temporal matters pertaining to the same.

Resolved 7th, That we discountenance and disapprobate the attendance at houses of revelling and dancing; dram-shops and theatres; verily believing they have a tendency to lead from paths of virtue and holiness, to those of vice and debauchery.

Resolved 8th, That we look upon the pure and holy doctrines set forth in the Scriptures of Divine truth, as being the immutable doctrines of salvation; and he who abideth in them shall be saved, and he who abideth not in them can not inherit the Kingdom of Heaven.

Resolved 9th, That we consider the gathering in haste, and by sacrifice, to be contrary to the will of God; and that it has been taught by Joseph Smith and others for the purpose of enabling them to sell property at most exhorbitant prices, not regarding the welfare of the Church, but through their covetousness reducing those who had the means to give employment to the poor, to the necessity of seeking labor for themselves; and thus the wealth which is brought into the place is swallowed up by the one great throat, from whence there is no return, which if it had been economically disbursed amongst the whole would have rendered all comfortable.

Resolved 10th, That, notwithstanding our extensive acquaintance with the financial affairs of the Church, we do not know of any property which in reality belongs to the Church (except the Temple) and we therefore consider the injunction laid upon the saints compelling them to purchase property of the Trustee in trust for the Church, is a deception practiced upon them:

and that we look upon the ending of special agents abroad to collect funds for the Temple and other purposes as a humbug practiced upon the saints by Joseph and others, to aggrandize themselves, as we do not believe that the monies and property so collected, have been applied as the donors expected, but have been used for speculative purposes, by Joseph, to gull the saints the better on their arrival at Nauvoo, by buying the lands in the vicinity and selling again to them at tenfold advance; and further that we verily believe the appropriations said to have been subscribed by shares for the building of the Nauvoo House to have been used by J. Smith and Lyman Wight, for other purposes, as out of the mass of stock already taken, the building is far from being finished even to the base.

Resolved 11th, That we consider all secret societies, and combinations under penal oaths and obligations, (professing to be organized for religious purposes,) to be anti-Christian, hypocritical and corrupt.

Resolved 12th, That we will *not* acknowledge any man as king or law-giver to the church; for Christ is our only king and law-giver.

Resolved 13th, That we call upon the honest in heart, in the Church, and throughout the world, to vindicate the pure doctrines of Jesus Christ, whether set forth in the Bible, Book of Mormon, or Book of Covenants; and we hereby withdraw the hand of fellowship, from all those who practice or teach doctrines contrary to the above, until they cease so to do, and show works meet for repentance.

Resolved 14th, That we hereby notify all those holding licences to preach the gospel, who know they are guilty of teaching the doctrine of other Gods above the God of this creation; the plurality of wives: the unconditional sealing up against all crimes, save that of shedding innocent blood: the spoiling of the gentiles, and all other doctrines, (so called) which are contrary to the laws of God, or to the laws of our country, to cease preaching, and to come and make satisfaction, and have their licences renewed.

Resolved 15th, That in all our controversies in defence of truth and righteousness, the weapons of our warfare are not carnal but mighty through God, to the pulling down of the strong holds of Satan; that our strifes are not against flesh, blood, nor bones; but against principalities and power against spiritual wickedness in high places and therefore we will not use carnal weapons save in our own defence.

Francis M. Higbee (essay date 1844)

SOURCE: "Citizens of Hancock County," in *The Nauvoo Expositor,* Vol. 1, No. 1, June 7, 1844.

[In the following excerpt, dated June 5, 1844, the author attempts to dissuade the citizens of Hancock County from voting for Joseph Smith's brother Hyrum in an upcoming election by portraying Joseph Smith as an enemy of the U.S. government.]

CITIZENS OF HANCOCK COUNTY.

It is well known to all of you that the August election is fast approaching, and with it comes the great and terrible conflict. It is destined to be a day pregnant with big events; for it will be the index to the future.— Should we be defeated upon that occasion, our die is cast, and our fate is sealed; but if successful, alike may Joseph Smith, Hyrum Smith, and their devoted followers, as well as their enemies, expect that justice will be meted out. The present is portentous of the great effort that is to be made upon that occasion, by Joseph for power; Hiram Smith is already in the field as a candidate for the legislature, but will *you* support *him,* that same *Hyrum Smith* the devoted follower and brother of Joe, who feigned a revelation from God, directing the citizens of Hancock County to vote for J. P. Hoge, in preference to Cyrus Walker, and by so doing blaspheming the name of God? Will *you,* gentlemen of Hancock County, support a man like that, who claims to move in a different sphere, a sphere entirely above you; one who will trifle with the things of God, and feign converse with the Divinity, for the sake of carrying an election? I will unhesitatingly assume to myself the responsibility of answering in the negative. I flatter myself you are not so depraved, and so blinded to your own interests, as to support a man totally ignorant of the laws of your country, and in every respect alienated from you and your interests.

In supporting *Hyrum Smith,* you, *Citizens of Hancock County,* are supporting Joseph Smith, for whom he (Hyrum) goes teeth and toe nails, for President of the United States. The question may arise here, in voting for Joseph Smith, for whom am I voting? You are voting for a man who contends all governments are to be put down and the *one* established upon its ruins. You are voting for an *enemy* to your government, hear Phelps to Joe in his affidavit before Judge King of Missouri:—"Have you come to the point to resist all law?" "I have," says Joe. You are voting for a sycophant, whose attempt for power find no parallel in history. You are voting for a man who refuses to suffer criminals to be brought to justice, but in the stead thereof, rescues them from the just demands of the law, by *Habeas Corpus.* You are voting for a man who stands indicted, and who is now held to bail, for the crimes of adultery and perjury; two of the gravest crimes known to our laws. Query not then for whom you are voting; it is for one of the blackest and basest scoundrels that has appeared upon the stage of human existence since the days of Nero, and Caligula.

In supporting Hyrum Smith, then, are you not supporting Joseph Smith most assuredly; pause then my *countrymen,* and consider coolly, calmly and deliberately, what you do? Support not that man who is spreading death, devastation and ruin throughout your happy country like a tornado. Infinite are the gradations which mark this man's attempts for power, which if not checked soon, must not only shed a deleterious influence on the face of this county, but on the face of the adjoining counties. He is already proudly boasting that he is beyond your reach; and I regret to think I am under the painful necessity of admitting the fact. Is it not a shame and a disgrace, to think we have a man in our midst, who will defy the laws of our country; the *laws* which shed so gentle and nourishing an influence upon our fathers, which fostered and protected them in their old age from insult and aggression; shall we their sons, lie still and suffer *Joseph Smith* to light up the lamp of tyranny and oppression in our midst? God forbid, lest the departed spirits of our *fathers,* cry from the ground against us. Let us arise in the majesty of our strength and sweep the influence of tyrants and miscreants from the face of the land, as with the breath of heaven. The eagle that is now proudly borne to earth's remotest regions by every gale, will perch himself in the solitude of mid-night if we do not arouse from our lethargy.

It is the worst of absurdities for any individual to say there is a man in our midst who is above the reach of violated law, and not lend a helping hand; all talk and nothing more will not accomplish *that* for your country and your God, which the acts of Washington did. Then gentlemen organize *your selves* and prepare for the dreadful conflict in August; we go with you heart and hand, in the attempt to suppress this contaminating influence which is prostrating our fairest prospects, and spreading desolation throughout our vale. Call into the field your best men under the solemn pledge to go for the unconditional repeal of the Nauvoo Charter, and you have our support; whether they be Whig or Democrat we care not; when a friend presents us with a draught of cool water, we do not stop to inquire whether it is contained in a silver vase, a golden urn or a long handled gourd. We want no base seducer, liar and perjured representative, to represent us in *Springfield,* but while Murrill represents Tennessee in Nashville, Munroe Edwards, New York, in Sing Sing, Br. Joseph may have the extreme goodness to represent Illinois in Alton, if his lawyers do not succeed in quashing the indictments found against him by the Grand Jurors of Hancock County, at the May term 1844.

I. Woodbridge Riley (essay date 1902)

SOURCE: "The Author's Mentality," in *The Founder of Mormonism: A Psychological Study of Joseph Smith, Jr.,* Dodd, Mead & Company, 1902, pp. 141-73.

[In the following excerpt, Riley presents a psychological sketch of Joseph Smith based on his writings in the Book of Mormon, *a work Riley suggests is more useful when regarded as biographical rather than historical or literary.]*

Without further quotation or digression, it remains to get at a psychological estimate of the ***Book of Mormon.*** As literature it is not worth reading,—the educated Mormons fight shy of it; as history it merely casts a side light on a frontier settlement in the twenties; but as biography it has value, it gives, as it were, a cross section of the author's brain. The subject may be most inclusively studied from the standpoint of the constructive imagination, its materials and range, its phases aesthetic and intellective, its aspects emotional and possibly moral. So first, as in the case of the progenitors and their dreams, the objects and scenes and incidents of experience furnished the stuff for the growth of Joseph's mental inwards. In sticking to the plenary inspiration of the ***Book of Mormon,*** the Saints make Smith greater than a genius, for whom there is no such thing as a perfectly new creation, or freedom from the bounds and checks of his situation. But to go on: like the events already cited, this entire 'Sacred History of America' is woven out of those ideas which interested the people of Western New York about 1830. Despite such limitation, the range of Joseph's fancy was extensive; his imagination was not trammeled by his understanding; his information came orally, and there were few books to check him: hence his anachronisms. From the same lack of knowledge, his precognitions of the future are naught. Joseph's prophecies are pseudographs,—events that had happened put as if they were yet to happen. And the aesthetic was as lacking as the prophetic. The 'poems of Joseph' are not half bad, but they are not his; while the picture of his favorite Lamanites is not poetic but prosaic; Cooper idealized the Indian, Smith made him repulsive.

Of the intellective phase of his imagination, something more favorable can be said, yet with strength there was weakness. The ***Book of Mormon,*** as a storehouse of sectarianism, implies a retentive memory and, at the same time, a lack of discriminative judgment. Granted that the style was inflated, because that was the style of the day, and that the thoughts were diffuse, because dictated, yet the feebleness of the critical faculty is shown in various ways. In the midst of the ancient story, modern inventions are grotesquely inserted; the language is biblical, but the ideas are local. The lost tribes of the Jews emigrate to America in vessels which are a cross between Noah's ark and an Erie canal boat. This occasional mixture of sense and nonsense may be matched among his co-religionists, for other readers took the Scriptures literally and interpreted fancifully; nevertheless Joseph's imagination appears to have been seldom controlled by the judicial spirit. In the recension of the first edition he evinced no capacity to se-

lect and reject; to this day there remain strange puerilities. After the natural outburst against free masonry, there occurs the following curiosity of literature:—

> And now I, Moroni, proceed with my record. Therefore behold, it came to pass that because of the secret combinations of Akish and his friends, behold they did overthrow the Kingdom of Omer. And the Lord warned Omer in a dream that he should depart out of the land, wherefore Omer passed by the hill of Shim, and came to a place which was called Ablom; and after that he had anointed Emer to be king the house of Emer did prosper exceedingly and they had horses, and asses, and there were elephants and cureloms and cumoms; all of which were useful unto man, and more especially the elephants and cureloms and cumoms.

Joseph must have been thinking of these his prehistoric Jabberwoks, when he told his followers to beware of 'a fanciful, flowery and heated imagination.' But seriously, whatever the sources of these humors and conceits, they are characteristic of the whole tribe of Smith. Joseph's hypertrophy of imagination was inherited: his aunt composed a vivid poem on death and the grave; his mother could almost see the flutter of demons' wings; his father had a panorama of visions; his grandfather Mack complained of his mind being 'imagining but agitated.' Environment likewise had an influence. Brought up in the area swept by revivals—the 'burnt-over district' as it was called—his imagination was fired by his feelings. Thereby he escaped the cold logic of the schools; he also went beyond the limits of probability. All this had an effect on his character. Ignorant of the subconscious force of unchecked reverie, he considered his every whimsy to be inspired. How far his imagination fostered his credulity, how far he became conscious that his 'translating' was mainly automatic, whether as a dramatically imagined 'seer and revelator,' he was deceived or deceiving,—these are questions for the moralist to decide, after the results are in. The problem, now, is one of letters rather than of ethics,—to see how the characteristics of the book fit the character of the man.

The four chief marks of the ***Book of Mormon*** are a redundant style, fragmentary information, a fanciful archaeology, and an unsystematic theology. The redundancy of style fits the description given by a lawyer [P. H. Burnett], who defended the prophet in his Missouri troubles in 1839. He says [in 'Recollections of a Pioneer', 1880], 'In conversation he was slow, and used too many words to express his ideas and would not generally go directly to a point.' It was this verbosity that made Joseph magnify his microscopic facts many diameters. The inherent paucity of his information accords with the observation of Josiah Quincy, that the prophet 'talked as from a strong mind utterly unenlightened by the teachings of history.' The same thing explains Joseph's lifelong delight in pseudo-archaeology, from his own fireside tales to the citing of Central American discoveries as 'more proofs of the **Book of Mormon,** as a historical and religious record, written in ancient times by a branch of the house of Israel, who peopled America and from whom the Indians are descended.' Now these very flights of fancy were part and parcel of Smith's strange being. If they are not to be connected with the roving habits of his progenitors, they were at least nurtured by the free life of the forest. The boy who withdrew at will into a past world of his own, was the youth who scoured the country for hidden treasure, and the young man who oscillated across the width of the state in search of the elusive gold plates.

Finally his bodily movements are matched by his mental restlessness,—the fourth mark of the man. In his logic he skips the middle term; in his theology he darts from creed to creed; as defender of the faith against Romanism or Infidelity, he is impatient, intolerant. In fine, it may be said that Joseph Smith, in all respects, although in exaggerated form, showed himself the type of Western pioneer, as he was contrasted with the Eastener. Of that type a foreign traveler observed, 'their business is conducted with an almost feverish excitement, . . . their passions are more intense, their religious morality less authoritative, and their convictions less firm.'

To adjust one's ideas of the mental ability of the imaginative, emotional, young American, a comparison may be made with a similar case in English literature. Going back to the reign of George III the origin of the **Book of Mormon** has an instructive likeness to that of the Rowley myth. Thomas Chatterton, 'the marvelous boy' of Bristol, was born in 1752. He was the son of a drunken schoolmaster and a descendant of a line of sextons a century and a half long. Brought up in the shadow of the Church of St. Mary Redcliffe, a dreamy, secretive lad, delighting in heraldry, blackletter manuscripts and local antiquities, at the age of sixteen he brought forth a series of pseudo-antique poems, which, at first, deceived the very elect. Although taught but little and with straitened means, there rose up before the eye of his fancy the mediaeval walls and towers of his native town. To obtain evidence for his imaginings, a monkish pseudonym was adopted. The document, which he sent to Horace Walpole, bore the title, 'The Ryse of Peyncteynge in Englande, Wroten by T. Rowleie, 1469, for Master Canynge.' Walpole was interested but not taken in; the dubious authorship of the Ossianic poems was still in his mind. Meanwhile the critical authorities showed up the skilful forgery, but others were gullible; the Bristol historian accepted Chatterton's fiction for fact, and there sprung up a group of clerical admirers who dabbled in the antique. As to the literary value of the works 'wroten by T. Rowleie' and of the 'account written by the hand of Mormon,' comparisons are odious; yet the coming forth of both arose under somewhat like conditions. In the

days of each young pseudologist, the literature of disguise was rife. Chatterton was preceded by Walpole's pseudonymus *Castle of Otranto,* by the *Reliques* called Percy's, by McPherson's *Fingal,* and other poems attributed to ancient Scottish bards.

And such, in relative measure were the surroundings of the translator of the 'Plates of Nephi.' What happened in Britain was happening here. By his *Knickerbocker History of New York,* Washington Irving was showing to Anglo-Americans of culture how honey could be brought forth out of the dead lion. The Philistines also had their riddles. The puritanic who eschewed novels, were yet devouring romances. In Massachusetts a parchment inscribed with Hebrew characters, being dug up on an 'Indian hill' was accepted as an 'Indian Bible,' although scoffers pronounced it the phylactery of some wandering Jew of a peddlar. In New York state Priest's *American Antiquities* went through three editions in one year, while rumors of a 'Canada Gold Bible' flew over the border. Finally in Ohio the Reverend Solomon Spaulding's romance of ancient America, entitled a 'Manuscript Found,' was creating some stir.

How far did Joseph Smith fasten on this literary driftwood, as it floated on the current of the times? It is here unnecessary to follow the ebb and flow of the tide of speculation. In spite of a continuous stream of conjectural literature, it is as yet impossible to pick out any special document as an original source of the **Book of Mormon**. In particular, the commonly accepted Spaulding theory is insoluble from external evidence and disproved by internal evidence. Joseph Smith's 'Record of the Indians' is a product indigenous to the New York 'Wilderness,' and the authentic work of its 'author and proprietor.' Outwardly, it reflects the local color of Palmyra and Manchester, inwardly, its complex of thought is a replica of Smith's muddled brain. This monument of misplaced energy was possible to the impressionable youth constituted and circumstanced as he was. The acts of Nephi are indeed the acts of Joseph:—'and upon the plates which I made, I did engraven the record of my father, and also of our journeyings in the wilderness, and the prophecies of my father; and also many of my own prophecies have I engraven upon them.'. . .

Fawn M. Brodie (essay date 1945)

SOURCE: "Witnesses for God," in *No Man Knows My History: The Life of Joseph Smith, the Mormon Prophet,* second edition, Alfred A. Knopf, Inc., 1971, pp. 67-82.

[*Brodie, a distinguished biographer and historian and Senior Lecturer in the Department of History at UCLA, is considered a leading authority on Mormon history. In the following excerpt from her biography of Joseph*

Smith, originally published in 1945, Brodie discusses the content and style of the Book of Mormon *and the events surrounding its publication.*]

The **Book of Mormon** was a mutation in the evolution of American literature, a curious sport, at once sterile and potent. Although it bred no imitators outside Mormonism and was ignored by literary critics, it brought several hundred thousand immigrants to America in the nineteenth century. The twentieth century sees the distribution of thousands of copies each year. For more than a hundred years missionaries have heralded it throughout the world as religious history second only to the Bible.

Scholars of American literary history have remained persistently uninterested in the **Book of Mormon**. Their indifference is the more surprising since the book is one of the earliest examples of frontier fiction, the first long Yankee narrative that owes nothing to English literary fashions. Except for the borrowings from the King James Bible, its sources are absolutely American. No sociologist has troubled to draw parallels between the **Book of Mormon** and other sacred books, like the Koran and *Science and Health,* though all are ostensibly divinely inspired and all are an obscure compound of folklore, moral platitude, mysticism, and millennialism.

Every creed perhaps must have its sacred books. And among such books the Mormon Bible is one of the most remarkable for sheer pretension. It is easy enough to deride its style, and painstaking research can uncover the sources of all its ideas. But nothing can detract from the fact that many people have found it convincing history. Henry A. Wallace recognized this when he said in 1937 [in his address before the *New York Times* National Book Fair]: "Of all the American religious books of the nineteenth century, it seems probable that the **Book of Mormon** was the most powerful. It reached perhaps only one per cent of the people of the United States, but it affected this one per cent so powerfully and lastingly that all the people of the United States have been affected, especially by its contribution to opening up one of our great frontiers."

Unwilling to credit Joseph Smith with either learning or talent, detractors of the Mormons within a few years declared that the **Book of Mormon** must have been written by someone else, and eventually laid the mantle of authorship upon one of Joseph's converts, Sidney Rigdon, a Campbellite preacher from Ohio. The theory ran as follows: The **Book of Mormon** was a plagiarism of an old manuscript by one Solomon Spaulding, which Sidney Rigdon had somehow secured from a printing house in Pittsburgh. After adding much religious matter to the story, Rigdon determined to publish it as a newly discovered history of the American Indian. Hearing of the young necromancer Joseph

Smith, three hundred miles away in New York State, he visited him secretly and persuaded him to enact a fraudulent representation of its discovery. Then nine months after the book's publication Smith's missionaries went to Ohio and the pastor pretended to be converted to the new church.

An apostate, Philastus Hurlbut, claimed to have uncovered this deceit in 1833 when he heard old neighbors of Spaulding say that parts of the **Book of Mormon** were the same as the manuscript they had heard read to them twenty years before. But the only Spaulding manuscript Hurlbut could find was a fabulous Indian romance, stuffed with florid sentiment a world away from the simple, monotonous prose and forthright narrative of the Mormon Bible.

Through the years the "Spaulding theory" collected supporting affidavits as a ship does barnacles, until it became so laden with evidence that the casual reader was overwhelmed by the sheer magnitude of the accumulation. The theory requires a careful analysis because it has been so widely accepted. . . .

Recent critics who insist that Joseph Smith suffered from delusions have ignored in the **Book of Mormon** contrary evidence difficult to override. Its very coherence belies their claims. Bernard DeVoto called the book "a yeasty fermentation, formless, aimless, and inconceivably absurd—at once a parody of all American religious thought and something more than a parody, a disintegration. The œstrus of a paranoiac projected it into a new Bible."

Far from being the fruit of an obsession, the **Book of Mormon** is a useful key to Joseph's complex and frequently baffling character. For it clearly reveals in him what both orthodox Mormon histories and unfriendly testimony deny him: a measure of learning and a fecund imagination. The Mormon Church has exaggerated the ignorance of its prophet, since the more meager his learning, the more divine must be his book. Non-Mormons attempting psychiatric analyses have been content to pin a label upon the youth and have ignored his greatest creative achievement because they found it dull. Dull it is, in truth, but not formless, aimless, or absurd. Its structure shows elaborate design, its narrative is spun coherently, and it demonstrates throughout a unity of purpose. Its matter is drawn directly from the American frontier, from the impassioned revivalist sermons, the popular fallacies about Indian origin, and the current political crusades.

Any theory of the origin of the **Book of Mormon** that spotlights the prophet and blacks out the stage on which he performed is certain to be a distortion. For the book can best be explained, not by Joseph's ignorance nor by his delusions, but by his responsiveness to the provincial opinions of his time. He had neither the dili-

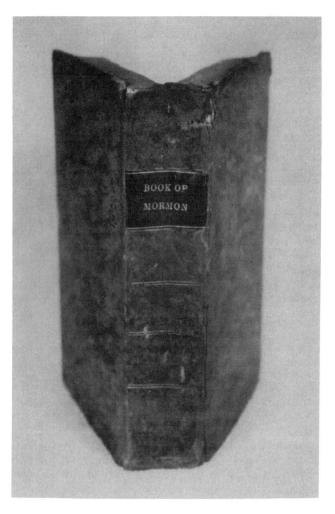

A first edition of The Book of Mormon.

the general resurrection, eternal punishment, who may baptize, and even the question of free masonry, republican government and the rights of man. . . . But he is better skilled in the controversies in New York than in the geography or history of Judea. He makes John baptize in the village of Bethabara and says Jesus was born in Jerusalem."

If one has the curiosity to read through the sermons in the book, one will be impressed with Joseph Smith's ability to argue with equal facility on both sides of a theological debate. Calvinism and Arminianism had equal status, depending upon which prophet was espousing the cause, and even universalism received a hearing. The great atheist Korihor was struck dumb for his blasphemy, yet he stated his case with more eloquence than the prophet who called down upon him the wrath of heaven.

The facility with which profound theological arguments were handled is evidence of the unusual plasticity of Joseph's mind. But this facility was entirely verbal. The essence of the great spiritual and moral truths with which he dealt so agilely did not penetrate into his consciousness. Had it done so, there would have been no book. He knew these truths as intimately as a bright child knows his catechism, but his use of them was utterly opportunistic. The theology of the *Book of Mormon,* like its anthropology, was only a potpourri.

As his history drew near its close and he began seriously to think of publication, Joseph became more and more dissatisfied with the Indian narrative as it stood. He had written a record of a thousand years—600 B.C. to A.D. 400. But apparently he was troubled by rather widespread speculation that the Indians had been in America almost since the days of the Flood. Many thought they had emigrated at the time of the building of the tower of Babel and the great dispersion of tongues, and Joseph seems to have realized that if this theory were to gain in popularity the claims of his book might be scorned.

Writers argued variously that the emigrants had sailed in boats, or crossed Bering Strait on the ice, or traversed the sunken continent that was said to have joined the Old World with the New. Caleb Atwater, when examining the Ohio ruins in 1820, wrote that the mounds marked "the progress of population in the first ages after the dispersion, rising wherever the posterity of Noah came."

Joseph may have received a sketchy introduction to the literature supporting this theory in Ethan Smith's *View of the Hebrews,* which quoted several Indian legends vaguely similar to the story of the great Flood. At any rate he was impressed with the probability of the "dispersionist" thesis, for in the last weeks of writing he dictated a terse little history of a people called

gence nor the constancy to master reality, but his mind was open to all intellectual influences, from whatever province they might blow. If his book is monotonous today, it is because the frontier fires are long since dead and the burning questions that the book answered are ashes.

This is particularly true of the religious matter. In the speeches of the Nephite prophets one may find the religious conflicts that were splitting the churches in the 1820's. Alexander Campbell, founder of the Disciples of Christ, wrote in the first able review of the *Book of Mormon* [which appeared in the *Millennial Harbinger,* Vol. II (February 1831)]: "This prophet Smith, through his stone spectacles, wrote on the plates of Nephi, in his *Book of Mormon,* every error and almost every truth discussed in New York for the last ten years. He decided all the great controversies:— infant baptism, ordination, the trinity, regeneration, repentance, justification, the fall of man, the atonement, transubstantiation, fasting, penance, church government, religious experience, the call to the ministry, the Jaredites, which he appended to the Nephite record. This history, he said, had been recorded on a separate set of twenty-four gold plates. It told the story of Jared, who with some followers had fled the tower of Babel and sailed to America about 2500 B.C. They crossed the sea in eight watertight barges, so constructed that they would sail any side up, with windows placed in both the top and the bottom.

Joseph's preoccupation with magic stones crept into the narrative here as elsewhere. The Jaredites had sixteen stones for lighting their barges; God had touched each one with His finger and made it forever luminous. He had given the Nephites, on the other hand, two crystals with spindles inside which directed the sailing of their ships.

Like Noah's ark, the Jaredite barges contained everything which the settlers might need on the new continent: "their flocks which they had gathered together, male and female of every kind . . . fowls of the air . . . fish of the waters . . . swarms of bees . . . seed of every kind." This little detail regarding cargo, flung casually into the story, partly settled the question of how animals had come to America, a problem men had puzzled over for three centuries. Some believed that angels had carried them, others that God had created two Adams and two Edens. One historian, in speculating on whether or not the animals had been brought in boats, was mystified by the presence of cougars and wolves in the New World. "If we suppose those first peoples so foolish as to carry such pernicious animals to new countries to hunt them, we cannot still think them to have been so mad as to take also many species of serpents for the pleasure of killing them afterward."

Joseph did not trouble to explain the presence of wild animals in America, and he was careless in his choice of domestic beasts. He had the Jaredites bring horses, swine, sheep, cattle, and asses, when it was known even in his own day that Columbus had found the land devoid of these species. He blundered similarly in having the Nephites produce wheat and barley rather than the indigenous maize and potatoes.

Always an eclectic, Joseph never exhausted any theory he had appropriated. He seized a fragment here and another there and of the odd assortment built his history. As we have seen, he left unused the one hypothesis that might have helped to save the book from being made so grotesque by twentieth-century archæological and anthropological research. This neglect was probably a result of his reading *View of the Hebrews,* which had scorned the theory expounding the Asiatic origin of the Indian.

Since the ancient Hebrew was far more real than the contemporary Mongolian to the rural folk of western New York, where the Old Testament was meat and drink and the gathering of Israel marvelously imminent, Joseph's instinct in ignoring the Asiatic theory was sound. Cathay was a barren field for religious enterprise. The old Northwest Territory desired its antiquities to prove the validity of Biblical history. It was not ripe for the archæology and ethnology of another century, which would reconstruct the varied civilizations of pre-Columbian America with infinite labor and painstaking care.

The lengths to which Joseph went to make his book historically plausible showed considerable ingenuity. He took pains to make the narrative chronologically accurate and filled it with predictions of events that had already taken place, stated as if they were yet to happen. He even inserted a prophecy of his own coming, calling himself "a choice seer" and predicting that his name would be called Joseph, "after the name of his·father."

Of the 350 names in the book he took more than a hundred directly from the Bible. Over a hundred others were Biblical names with slight changes in spelling or additions of syllables. But since in the Old Testament no names began with the letters F, Q, W, X, or Y, he was careful not to include any in his manuscript.

Despite these artifices he was conscious that the book had many obvious defects. To explain them away he put an excuse in the mouth of Moroni: "And if our plates had been sufficiently large we should have written in Hebrew; but the Hebrew hath been altered by us also, and if we could have written in Hebrew, ye would have had none imperfection in our record." Even this did not satisfy him, for he felt compelled to apologize on the title-page: "Now if there be fault, it be the mistake of men." This he repeated near the end of the book with a guarded warning: " . . . and if there be faults, they be the faults of a man. But behold, we know no fault. Nevertheless, God knoweth all things; therefore he that condemneth, let him be aware lest he shall be in danger of hell fire."

A careful scrutiny of the ***Book of Mormon*** and the legendary paraphernalia obscuring its origin discloses not only Joseph's inventive and eclectic nature but also his magnetic influence over his friends. Secretaries usually have no illusions about the men from whom they take dictation, but Oliver Cowdery and Martin Harris were caught in the spell of one of the most enigmatic characters of the century.

Since the first-hand accounts describing Joseph are either scurrilous or blindly adoring, it is difficult to call back the essence of what Cowdery in later years described [in his *Defense in a Rehearsal of My Grounds for Separating Myself from the Latter-Day Saints,* 1839] as Joseph's "mysterious power, which even now I fail to fathom." His natural talent as a leader included first of all an intuitive understanding of his followers, which led them to believe he was genuinely clairvoyant. Soon after his coming to Harmony, Cowdery had written back to David Whitmer that Joseph told him "his secret thoughts, and all he had meditated about going to see him, which no man on earth knew, as he supposed, but himself."

But Joseph had more than "second sight," which is common-place among professional magicians. At an early age he had what only the most gifted revivalist preachers could boast of—the talent for making men see visions. This was an aptitude unsuspected in himself until the spring of 1829, when the **Book of Mormon** was nearly complete.

For some time Joseph had been anxious to organize a church. This was the logical outgrowth of the planning of the **Book of Mormon** and stemmed from the same obscure hunger for power and deference that had stimulated his earliest fantasies. And since Joseph was an organizer as well as a dreamer, the building of a church was inevitable. Cowdery, however, who had none of Joseph's audacity, was disturbed because his leader was not even an ordained preacher. They argued the matter of authority and ordination at length, and finally decided to fast for many hours and then go to the woods and pray.

No one can walk in the woods in May without an exaltation of spirit, and when the two men knelt in prayer Cowdery was overcome with a vision of heaven. "The voice of the Redeemer spake peace to us," he said, "while the veil was parted and the angel of God came down clothed with glory, and delivered the anxiously looked for message, and the keys of the Gospel of repentance . . . as we heard we rejoiced, while his love enkindled our souls, and we were rapt in the vision of the Almighty! Where was room for doubt? Nowhere; uncertainty had fled, doubt had sunk, no more to rise, while fiction and deception had fled forever."

Joseph also described this vision, but without hyperbole. He wrote simply that the angel was John the Baptist, who had conferred upon them the true Hebraic priesthood of Aaron and had ordered them to baptize each other. Ten years later Cowdery left Joseph Smith in disillusionment, yet he wrote of this season as hallowed and said of the vision [in his *Defense*]: " . . . the angel was John the Baptist, which I doubt not and deny not."

Thus began the era of miracles among the followers of Joseph Smith. Supernatural phenomena followed hard upon one another as the contagion spread. A rivalry sprang up among Joseph's patrons. Joseph Knight brought a wagonload of provisions thirty miles to aid

in the Lord's work and returned with a revelation in his pocket. David Whitmer's father, not to be outdone, promised free board and lodging if Joseph would finish the translation of the plates back in Fayette, New York.

When David brought his wagon to Harmony to move the couple north to his father's home, he had a minor miracle to tell. Seven acres of his twenty-acre field had been miraculously plowed during the night. Lucy Smith later wrote that three mysterious strangers further hastened his journey by spreading one of his fields with fertilizer. David was eager to see that the plates were carefully packed, but Joseph soberly informed him that they were to be carried by a special messenger. And when along the road they saw a bearded man with a bulging knapsack on his back, he told David that it was the angel messenger in disguise.

Mrs. Whitmer, already burdened with many children, was the only person who resented Joseph's coming. As the days went by she grew more weary and more bewildered. Then one morning she came in from the milking trembling with excitement. On her way to the barn in the mist of the early dawn she had been confronted by an old man with a white beard. "You have been faithful and diligent in your labors," he had said, "but you are tired because of the increase in your toil; it is proper therefore that you should receive a witness that your faith might be strengthened." Whereupon he had showed her the golden plates.

It is probable that no one was more surprised at this than Joseph Smith. The tractable Cowdery had seen a vision after long fasting and intense prayer, but Mother Whitmer had had a vision on his behalf quite by herself, and Joseph doubtless pondered this miracle in his heart with wonder. Moved by the hospitality showered upon him, he repaid it with the only wealth he had, personal revelations carrying the blessings of heaven.

Martin Harris hung about the Whitmer home like a begging spaniel, continually reminding Joseph of his promise that three men were to see the plates. Finally the witnesses were chosen: Harris, Cowdery, and David Whitmer. Joseph instructed them carefully in the Lord's name: "Behold, I say unto you, that you must rely upon my word, which if you do with full purpose of heart, you shall have a view of the plates, and also the breast-plate, the sword of Laban, the Urim and Thummim. . . . And it is by your faith that you shall obtain a view of them. . . . And ye shall testify that you have seen them. . . . And if you do these last commandments of mine, which I have given you, the gates of hell shall not prevail against you."

The four men walked into the woods and knelt in prayer. Joseph led the entreaty, and the others followed in solemn succession. Then they waited silently for a miracle. The summer breeze stirred the leaves above them, and a bird chirped loudly, but nothing happened. The ensuing stillness became oppressive. Then Harris, whose heart was stabbed with doubt, rose shame-faced and wretched. Blaming their failure upon his presence, he asked to go and pray alone.

"He accordingly withdrew from us," Joseph said, "and we knelt down again, and had not been many minutes engaged in prayer, when presently we beheld a light above us in the air, of exceeding brightness; and behold, an angel stood before us. In his hands he held the plates which we had been praying for these to have a view of. He turned over the leaves one by one, so that we could see them, and discern the engravings thereon distinctly. He then addressed himself to David Whitmer, and said, 'David, blessed is the Lord, and he that keeps His commandments;' when, immediately afterwards, we heard a voice from out of the bright light above us, saying, 'These plates have been revealed by the power of God, and they have been translated by the power of God. The translation of them which you have seen is correct, and I command you to bear record of what you now see and hear.'"

Joseph now went in pursuit of Harris, whom he found on his knees near by. Together they prayed, and the prophet said that the same vision came again. Harris sprang to his feet shouting: "'Tis enough; 'tis enough; mine eyes have beheld; mine eyes have beheld; Hosanna, Hosanna, blessed be the Lord."

Following the command of the revelation, the three men signed a statement drawn up by Joseph which was printed at the end of the **Book of Mormon:**

THE TESTIMONY OF THREE WITNESSES

Be it known unto all nations, kindreds, tongues, and people, unto whom this work shall come, that we, through the grace of God the Father, and our Lord Jesus Christ, have seen the plates which contain this record, which is a record of the people of Nephi, and also of the Lamanites, his brethren, and also of the people of Jared, which came from the tower of which hath been spoken; and we also know that they have been translated by the gift and power of God, for his voice hath declared it unto us; wherefore we know of a surety, that the work is true. And we also testify that we have seen the engravings which are upon the plates; and they have been shewn unto us by the power of God, and not of man. And we declare with words of soberness, that an Angel of God came down from heaven, and he brought and laid before our eyes, that we beheld and saw the plates, and the engravings thereon; and we know that it is by the grace of God the Father, and our Lord Jesus Christ, that we beheld and bear record that these things are true. And it is marvellous in

our eyes: Nevertheless, the voice of the Lord commanded us that we should bear record of it; wherefore, to be obedient unto the commandments of God, we bear testimony of these things.—And we know that if we are faithful in Christ, we shall rid our garments of the blood of all men, and be found spotless before the judgement seat of Christ, and shall dwell with him eternally in the heavens. And the honor be to the Father, and to the Son, and to the Holy Ghost, which is one God. Amen.

OLIVER COWDERY

DAVID WHITMER

MARTIN HARRIS

According to the local press of the time, the three witnesses all told different versions of their experience, a fact that makes it all the more likely that the men were not conspirators but victims of Joseph's unconscious but positive talent at hypnosis. Martin Harris was questioned by a Palmyra lawyer, who asked him pointedly: "Did you see the plates and the engravings upon them with your bodily eyes?" To which he replied: "I did not see them as I do that pencil-case, yet I saw them with the eye of faith; I saw them just as distinctly as I see anything around me—though at the time they were covered with a cloth." However, when Harris was a very old man he told one interviewer that he "saw the angel turn the golden leaves over and over" and heard him say: "The book translated from those plates is true and translated correctly."

David Whitmer told the editor of the *Reflector* that Joseph had led him to an open field, where they found the plates lying on the ground. But in later years Whitmer's story too was richly embellished. "We saw not only the plates of the **Book of Mormon**," he said, "but also the brass plates, the plates of the book of Ether, the plates containing the records of the wickedness and secret combinations of the people of the world. . . . there appeared as it were a table with many records or plates upon it, besides the plates of the **Book of Mormon**, also the Sword of Laban, the directors—i.e., the ball which Lehi had, and the Interpreters."

All three witnesses eventually quarreled with Joseph and left his church. At their going he heaped abuse upon them, but none ever denied the reality of his vision, and Cowdery and Harris eventually were rebaptized. Joseph had no fear in vilifying them; he neither expected nor received reprisals. For he had conjured up a vision they would never forget.

Not content with the testimony of the three witnesses, Joseph drew up a second statement:

AND ALSO THE TESTIMONY OF EIGHT WITNESSES

Be it known unto all nations, kindreds, tongues, and people, unto whom this work shall come, that Joseph Smith, Jr. the Author and Proprietor of this work, has shewn unto us the plates of which hath been spoken, which have the appearance of gold; and as many of the leaves as the said Smith has translated, we did handle with our hands; and we also saw the engravings thereon, all of which has the appearance of ancient work, and of curious workmanship. And this we bear record, with words of soberness, that the said Smith has shewn unto us, for we have seen and hefted, and know of a surety, that the said Smith has got the plates of which we have spoken. And we give our names unto the world, to witness unto the world that which we have seen: and we lie not, God bearing witness of it.

CHRISTIAN WHITMER   HIRAM PAGE

JACOB WHITMER   JOSEPH SMITH, SEN.

PETER WHITMER, JR.   HYRUM SMITH

JOHN WHITMER   SAMUEL H. SMITH

It will be seen that four witnesses were Whitmers and three were members of Joseph's own family. The eighth witness, Hiram Page, had married a Whitmer daughter. Mark Twain was later to observe: "I could not feel more satisfied and at rest if the entire Whitmer family had testified."

In later editions the words "Author and Proprietor," which may merely have followed the copyright form, were changed to "translator." The same change was made on the book's title-page, which in the first edition was signed "Joseph Smith, Author and Proprietor."

One of the most plausible descriptions of the manner in which Joseph Smith obtained these eight signatures was written by Thomas Ford [in the *History of Illinois,* 1854], Governor of Illinois, who knew intimately several of Joseph's key men after they became disaffected and left the church. They told Ford that the witnesses were "set to continual prayer, and other spiritual exercises." Then at last "he assembled them in a room, and produced a box, which he said contained the precious treasure. The lid was opened; the witnesses peeped into it, but making no discovery, for the box was empty, they said, 'Brother Joseph, we do not see the plates.' The prophet answered them, 'O ye of little faith! how long will God bear with this wicked and perverse generation? Down on your knees, brethren, every one of you, and pray God for the forgiveness of your sins, and for a holy and living faith which cometh down from heaven.' The disciples dropped to their knees, and began to pray in the fervency of their spirit, sup-

plicating God for more than two hours with fanatical earnestness; at the end of which time, looking again into the box, they were now persuaded that they saw the plates."

Yet it is difficult to reconcile this explanation with the fact that these witnesses, and later Emma and William Smith, emphasized the size, weight, and metallic texture of the plates. Perhaps Joseph built some kind of makeshift deception. If so, it disappeared with his announcement that the same angel that had revealed to him the sacred record had now carried it back into heaven.

Exactly how Joseph Smith persuaded so many of the reality of the golden plates is neither so important nor so baffling as the effect of this success on Joseph himself. It could have made of him a precocious and hard-boiled cynic, as a little experimentation with the new art of "mesmerism" made of the famous preacher LaRoy Sunderland some years later. But there is no evidence of cynicism even in Joseph's most intimate diary entries. The miracles and visions among his followers apparently served only to heighten his growing consciousness of supernatural power. He had a sublime faith in his star, plus the enthusiasm of a man constantly preoccupied with a single subject, and he was rapidly acquiring the language and even the accent of sincere faith.

The ***Book of Mormon*** was printed by Egbert B. Grandin, printer of the local *Wayne Sentinel,* after Joseph had failed to secure a contract from Thurlow Weed, editor of the Rochester *Anti-Masonic Inquirer.* Martin Harris guaranteed $3,000 for the printing of 5,000 copies, agreeing to mortgage his farm if necessary in order to make up the sum. By this time he had left his wife, having satisfied her with a settlement of eighty acres and a house.

Before the printing was finished, however, the professionally righteous citizens of Palmyra formed a citizens' committee and organized a boycott of the ***Book of Mormon.*** When they presented a long list of names to the printer he took fright, stopped the printing, and refused to resume it until he had been paid in full.

Harris had not yet mortgaged his farm and there was no money available. Hyrum Smith, who disliked Harris and suspected that he wanted all the profits from the book sales, suggested that they try to sell the copyright for enough money to ensure publication. Joseph then looked into the Urim and Thummim and received a revelation directing Cowdery and Hiram Page to go to Toronto, where they would find a man anxious to buy it.

"We did not find him," Cowdery later wrote [in his *Defense*], "and had to return surprised and disappointed. . . . I well remember how hard I strove to drive away the foreboding which seized me, that the First Elder had made tools of us, where we thought in the simplicity of our hearts that we were divinely commanded."

This was the first time that a revelation had gone awry. With disarming candor Joseph explained: "Some revelations are of God: some revelations are of man: and some revelations are of the devil. . . . When a man enquires of the Lord concerning a matter, if he is deceived by his own carnal desires, and is in error, he will receive an answer according to his erring heart, but it will not be a revelation from the Lord."

Joseph now had only one resource. Martin Harris had been an embarrassingly zealous proselyter who advertised his own visionary experiences as freely as those of Joseph. He had seen Jesus in the shape of a deer, he said, and had walked with Him two or three miles, talking with Him as familiarly as one man talks with another. The devil, he said, resembled a jackass, with very short, smooth hair similar to that of a mouse. He prophesied that Palmyra would be destroyed by 1836, and that by 1838 Joseph's church would be so large that there would be no need for a president of the United States. Publicly Harris met with amused tolerance and only occasional bitter scorn. Privately Palmyra gossiped about his scandalous conduct with his neighbor Haggard's wife.

In desperation Joseph lashed at Harris with the Lord's word:

> I command you to repent—repent, lest I smite you by the rod of my mouth, and by my wrath, and by mine anger, and your sufferings be sore.

> How sore you know not!

> How exquisite you know not!

> Yea, how hard to bear you know not!!

> . . . And I command you that you preach nought but repentance, and show not these things unto the world until it is wisdom in me. . . .

> And again, I command thee that thou shalt not covet thy neighbor's wife; nor seek thy neighbor's life.

> And again, I command thee that thou shalt not covet thine own property, but impart it freely to the printing of the *Book of Mormon*. . . .

> And misery thou shalt receive if thou wilt slight these counsels; yea, even the destruction of thyself and property. . . .

> Pay the printer's debt! Release thyself from bondage.

Thoroughly scared, Harris hastily sold his farm. Grandin was paid in full, and by March 26, 1830 the *Book of Mormon* was put on sale in the Palmyra bookstore. On April 2 the Rochester *Daily Advertiser* published the first review:

> BLASPHEMY—BOOK OF MORMON, ALIAS THE GOLDEN BIBLE

> The *Book of Mormon* has been placed in our hands. A viler imposition was never practiced. It is an evidence of fraud, blasphemy, and credulity, shocking both to Christians and moralists. The author and proprietor is Joseph Smith, Jr., a fellow who by some hocus pocus acquired such influence over a wealthy farmer of Wayne county that the latter mortgaged his farm for $3,000, which he paid for printing and binding five thousand copies of the blasphemous work.

The Spaulding-Rigdon theory of the authorship of the *Book of Mormon*:

The Spaulding-Rigdon theory of the authorship of the *Book of Mormon* is based on a heterogeneous assortment of letters and affidavits collected between 1833 and 1900. When heaped together without regard to chronology, as in Charles A. Shook's *True Origin of the Book of Mormon,* and without any consideration of the character of either Joseph Smith or Sidney Rigdon, they seem impressive. But the theory is based first of all on the untenable assumption that Joseph Smith had neither the wit nor the learning to write the *Book of Mormon,* and it disregards the fact that the style of the *Book of Mormon* is identical with that of the Mormon prophet's later writings, such as the *Doctrine and Covenants* and *Pearl of Great Price,* but is completely alien to the turgid rhetoric of Rigdon's sermons.

Protagonists of the theory do not explain why, if Rigdon wrote the *Book of Mormon,* he was content to let Joseph Smith found the Mormon Church and hold absolute dominion over it throughout the years, so secure in his position that he several times threatened Rigdon with excommunication when Rigdon opposed his policies. But most important, there is no good evidence to show that Rigdon and Smith ever met before Rigdon's conversion late in 1830. There is, on the contrary, abundant proof that between September 1827 and June 1829, when the *Book of Mormon* was being written, Rigdon was a successful Campbellite preacher in northern Ohio, who if conniving secretly with Joseph Smith, three hundred miles east, was so accomplished a deceiver that none of his intimate friends ever entertained the slightest suspicion of it.

Fawn M. Brodie, in No Man Knows My History, *Knopf, 1945.*

Whitney R. Cross (essay date 1950)

SOURCE: "The Prophet," in *The Burned-over District: The Social and Intellectual History of Enthusiastic Religion in Western New York, 1800-1850,* Cornell, 1950, pp. 138-50.

[*In the following excerpt, Cross suggests that the doctrines and organization of Mormonism were products not of the American frontier but of "that Yankee, rural, emotionalized, and rapidly maturing culture which characterized western New York so markedly in the second quarter of the nineteenth century."*]

The Mormon Church, having survived and grown in the last hundred years as did none of its companion novelties, interests the present generation far more than any other aspect of Burned-over District history. Yet its impact upon the region and period from which it sprang was extremely limited. The Saints made their first westward removal immediately upon founding the religion, when they numbered not more than a hundred persons. The obscurity and scarcity of local material on the subject reinforces the logical conclusion that few western New Yorkers could have been seriously aware of the episode. In this respect it contrasts strongly with the other omens of the day. In another way, however, Mormonism comes closer to being the true oracle than other developments in the inaugural years just before 1831. It was the first original product of the common circumstances which would breed a train of successors within the quarter century. It predicted what was to come, whereas the larger simultaneous excitements merely heated the cauldron from which future experiments would boil.

The Smith family arrived in western New York in 1816 when Joseph was ten years old. Fate had been rough on them in Vermont, where each of several different ventures and consequent removes left them poorer than the one before. The war years had been hard enough in the home state, but peace canceled the business of supplying the armed forces, or indulging in trade with the enemy across the border, which had helped sustain the local economy. The postwar slump which gradually spread over the nation was punctuated in the north country by the frigid summer of 1816. Vermont farmers started west in droves. The Smith family poverty doubtless reached the extreme among the emigrants, since for several generations both the Smith and Mack lines had been running to the visionary rather than to the acquisitive Yankee type. Even so, the Smiths could in no way be considered uncommon in the westering horde. Like the bulk of their fellows, they sought a new start in the acres of New York just about to be enriched by the projected Erie Canal. Unwisely perhaps, again like many others, they shunned the rugged pioneering life demanded by the more primitive regions in Ohio or west of the Genesee in New York, in favor of a community of some age, respectability, and commercial prospects, where they would have a greater struggle to pay for their land.

Northward from Canandaigua, the rolling hills of the Finger Lakes section gradually descend to meet the drumlin-studded Ontario plain. Twelve miles takes one across the line between Ontario and Wayne counties to Palmyra, situated on the lower level among the glacial hills. Halfway between the two towns, nearly in the dead center of the richest soil area in western New York, lies the village of Manchester. All three villages and their immediate vicinities had been early settled and by 1820 had attained populations approximating sixty persons per square mile. From Palmyra north to the lake, habitations appeared less frequently, while a journey of thirty miles west or south would reach towns where little land had been cleared more than ten years.

Canandaigua, the oldest town of the three and in fact one of the two oldest in western New York, had until the twenties enjoyed a dominant position in the region's economy. Here the stage route to Albany crossed the main route to the south, which from the days of the Iroquois had connected Irondequoit Bay, Canandaigua Lake, and the southward-facing valleys of the upper Susquehanna. Up to 1824 Rochester millers had to use pony express to reach the banks at this center. As a seat of culture, the Finger Lakes village retained its leadership even later. For years the country seat of great landlords and their agents, it was for this section a sophisticated, aristocratic community with a strong Episcopal church. Even Presbyterians there maintained a conservative tone throughout the period. Its newspapers and schools had attained establishment and reputation. But with the approach of the canal the economic orientation of the three villages rapidly changed.

Palmyra for a time became the chief local mart. Limited use of the waterway began in 1822, and the same summer brought daily stage and mail service connecting several canal towns with each other and with Canandaigua. By the following autumn the canal had opened to Rochester. Palmyra and Manchester, unlike their southern neighbor, very nearly typified the region. Their folk came chiefly from Connecticut and Vermont. Younger and less culturally sophisticated, they had nevertheless enjoyed the services of evangelistic churches from their earliest days, as well as the schools and journals which always followed in rapid succession. Palmyra particularly would have a considerable bonanza in the early twenties and evince the social restlessness accompanying such rapid expansion. But before the end of that decade the village was destined to come quite suddenly to stability, with even a touch of the doldrums, after the canal had reached Buffalo and Rochester had seized local commercial leadership.

Thus the Smiths came to no frontier or cultural back-wash. Though the society they entered was more youthful, it was less isolated and provincial, more vigorous and cosmopolitan, than Vermont. It was reaching economic stability but remained on the upgrade, whereas rural Vermont had already started into decline.

Nor yet in religion was the younger area less experienced than the homeland. The Great Revival had come here at the turn of the century, just as to western New England. Seven of twelve primary centers of enthusiasm ranged from Palmyra southward. The crest of fervor following the War of 1812 noticeably affected towns sprinkled about the same neighborhood, and the pattern repeated, though less intensively, during the early twenties. So the area had been thoroughly indoctrinated in revivalistic religion throughout thirty years of its youth. And Palmyra at least was old enough by the mid-twenties to exhibit the increased interest in community morals and spirituality which characteristically grew upon villages and countrysides of Yankee stamp as the problems of maturity replaced the struggle to live.

In this richer clime the Smiths and their fellow Vermonters fared better than before. A shop in Palmyra and the labor at hire of father and sons swelled the family funds in two years sufficiently to permit initial payment on a hundred-acre farm practically astride the Palmyra-Manchester town line. It must have been a relatively inferior piece of land, else it would long since have been cleared. It seems to have been contracted for at the height of a speculative boomlet which a decade's time would demonstrate to have been based on false expectations. Evidence exists, in any case, to show that the family exerted considerable diligence and enterprise in hope of completing payment. Nevertheless, the farm had been foreclosed by 1830.

Many companion emigrants, managing more wisely, made good in the Genesee country, some having brought with them at least enough money for the first deposit on a farm. A sizable minority found land values here inflated beyond their earning ability and were making for Michigan or Illinois about the time the Smiths were losing out. In April, 1829, a Manchester clergyman noted: "Many families are floating about . . . because in two or three months they expect to remove." Every circumstance seems to invalidate the obviously prejudiced testimonials of unsympathetic neighbors (collected by one hostile individual whose style of composition stereotypes the language of numerous witnesses) that the Smiths were either squatters or shiftless "frontier drifters." Many an honest and industrious farmer followed their identical experience, pursued by bad luck or poor judgment, and sought a new fling at fortune farther west. No doubt the Smiths, like many of their fellows, wasted valuable time hunting gold at the proper turn of the moon. One of the potent sources of Joseph's local ill repute may well have been the jealousy of other persons who failed to discover golden plates in the glacial sands of the drumlins.

The entire family was at least barely literate. Hyrum had attended a Vermont seminary, and Joseph had some part of a few years' schooling in Palmyra, possibly increased by brief attendance at Bainbridge in 1826. He had belonged to the young men's debating society in Palmyra. Though he read easily, his writing was at best halting and he attained only the rudiments of arithmetic. Probably the family budget had required his labor a good deal of the time when he might have been in school. But this was rather the average than an unusual experience among the poorer Yankee migrants to western New York. Despite testimonials to the contrary, it must be concluded that neither Joseph nor any of his family was especially ignorant according to the standards of the place and time. Interest in things marvelous and supernatural they certainly had abundantly, but even this made them differ only in degree from their neighbors. After all, Joseph's peeping stone attracted loyal followers. The rest of the family, though perhaps not the prophet himself, behaved like others in attending services in revival seasons. Perhaps, as not infrequently happened, they shifted sectarian affiliation considerably as different denominations happened to lead the awakenings from time to time. Joseph, Senior, was by profession Methodist; and Lucy, the mother, and Hyrum, the elder brother, had most recently been Presbyterian when Joseph's thoughts began to turn toward religion.

The whole Smith family seems to have been quite thoroughly typical of the westering Yankees in the Burned-over District. It seems entirely plausible, as his most recent biographer [Fawn Brodie] claims, that Joseph became a prophet in quite accidental fashion. Having risen above his own early experiments in necromancy, his imagination wandered into new realms. When he found others taking his new hobby seriously, he had to live up to expectations and spend the remainder of his short life learning to assume the consequent responsibilities. In so doing he improved and demonstrated his naturally dynamic character. This was nothing more than happens to any man who enjoys the great responsibilities which fate thrusts upon him, though religious leadership demands somewhat rare personal qualities. It might have happened to almost anyone of Joseph's fellow Yankee migrants. The fundamental condition leading to the new faith was the credulity and spiritual yearning which made people anxious to follow a prophet, whoever he might be. In order to explain why Joseph developed into this role one must either utilize faith, traffic in a psychoanalysis which at such a distance from the event becomes highly imaginative, or descend to coincidence. Historical analysis profits little by any of these alternatives.

It should be added, however, that interest in Mormonism was no necessary indication either of extraordinary ignorance or of unusually febrile imaginings. Converts like Brigham Young, Heber Kimball, J. J. Strang, William Phelps, Sidney Rigdon, Orson Pratt, and Lorenzo Snow, to name only a few, had on the whole superior education for their times, and most of them proved to be as vigorously realistic pillars of the church as anyone might desire. The man who exercised primacy over these individuals approached some kind of genius, however it may have been inspired.

What was it, then, about Joseph Smith which satisfied the spiritual needs of his converts? Clearly it was no case of deliberate imposture, no consciously calculated set of devices to attain power over others. Joseph may have gathered some inklings from an imperfect knowledge of the Shakers or of the New Jerusalem on Keuka Lake, just as he did from Owenite communism by way of Sidney Rigdon at Kirtland, Ohio, but he did not premeditate a system for self-advancement patterned upon the observed success of Jemima Wilkinson or anyone else. This kind of hypothesis, like the one which claims that the **Book of Mormon** was copied from Solomon Spaulding's novel on the early Indian wars, is too transparently simple to explain the broad appeal of the new church. Such myths not only distort Joseph's character but also breed serious misconceptions of how any religious novelty is likely to arise. All the spiritual experiments of western New York were alike genuine growths, rooted in a heritage of moral intensity and blossoming in the heat of evangelistic fervor.

The question is better put this way. How did the Church of Latter-day Saints select and emphasize from its Burned-over District milieu those principles of religion and society which would patently attract persons bred in the same environment? First of all, it crystallized and provided an apparently authoritative formulation for what had perhaps been from the beginning the most prominent legend in the region's folklore. The story of a gigantic battle on the hill Cumorah, in which the superior pre-Indian civilization was exterminated, seems today both fantastic and remote from the realm of religion. It was not fantastic to a generation bred in the belief of such a civilization's existence; and neither American society generally nor that of western New York in particular had passed the stage wherein common myth might reinforce Biblical sanction of doctrine.

The **Book of Mormon** also incorporated contemporary interests of the locality, supplementing the sense of familiarity to be gained from its historical approach. Walter F. Prince [in "Psychological Tests for the Authorship of the **Book of Mormon**," *American Journal of Psychology,* XXVII, 1917, and "A Footnote; Authorship of the *Book of Mormon,*" *American Journal of Psychology,* XXX, 1919] proved beyond dispute

thirty years ago, by a rigorous examination of the proper names and other language in the volume, that even if no other evidence existed, it could have been composed only in western New York between 1826 and 1834, so markedly did it reflect Antimasonry and other issues of the day. Unfortunately, his work has been so neglected that the most recent historian of the movement [Brodie] had to demonstrate the proposition all over again, independently.

The prophet, moreover, for all his imagination, was, like the Yankees he led, in many respects an eminently practical man. He combined appeals to reason and self-interest with emotional attractions. The logic of his mythology and theology, specious though it seem to the Gentile of today, satisfied the inbred desire of Yorkers to achieve an orderly, intellectual formulation of their beliefs. Again, he expected all laymen to participate in the priesthood of the church. This democratic and flattering conception paralleled chronologically the developing controversies over clerical influence in most of the sects of western New York; and its reasonableness, like the Mormon approach to doctrine by argument rather than excitement, contrasted pleasantly with the flamboyant oratory of orthodoxy's revivals. And whereas the evangelists emphasized salvation from personal sins in preparation for the life to come, Joseph's ideas about earthly and heavenly society alike judged happiness more largely in terms of physical comfort and earthly abundance. His degree of communism resurrected the strong sense of social obligation that all should have for each and each for all, which had been long declining in the Puritan tradition of old New England. Born Yankees troubled by the problems of security in a more individualistic society found this doctrine pleasing.

In theology, again, this practical emphasis appeared. Alexander Campbell [in his *Delusions: An Analysis of the Book of Mormon,* 1832] very quickly discerned how accurately the **Book of Mormon** reflected "every error and almost every truth discussed in N. York for the last ten years." It presented a definitive answer indeed to every issue of orthodox evangelical religion:

> infant baptism, ordination, the trinity, regeneration, repentance, justification, the fall of man, the atonement, transubstantiation, fasting, penance, church government, religious experience, the call to the ministry, the general resurrection, eternal punishment, who may baptize, and even the question of freemasonary, republican government, and the rights of man.

Especially did the Saints lay emphatic stress upon, and offer concrete instead of vague conceptions of, the very doctrines which thirty years of revivalism had made most intensely interesting to the folk of western New York. They incorporated literal interpretations of the

Bible, made expectation of the millennium coincident with the prophet's career on earth, and provided a mode for fresh revelation direct from God. Above all, in the person of Joseph Smith they found living, intimately available embodiment of their entire faith. How much more effectively than the orthodox evangelists could they hammer home the consciousness of sin and the hope of regeneration which had been preached here since the first settlement of the region!

Mormonism has usually been described as a frontier religion. But study of the circumstances of its origin and its continuing appeal in the area which bred it suggests a different view. The church did not rise during the pioneering era of western New York. Its early recruits came from many sects, but invariably from the longest-settled neighborhoods of the region. Joseph's peregrinations during the period when he was pregnant with the new religion were always eastward, not westward, from his Manchester home. The first congregations of the church formed at Manchester, Fayette in Seneca County, and Colesville in Broome County. These facts, together with the realization of Mormonism's dependence on current excitements and upon myths and doctrines built by the passage of time into the locality's very fabric, demonstrate that the Church of the Saints was not a frontier phenomenon in origin.

Nor did it expand through an appeal to frontiersmen. The far greater gathering of converts from this area came during the region's riper maturity, after Zion itself had removed to the West. And the recruits enlisted here and elsewhere in the East by returning missionaries far outnumbered those gained in areas of the Middle West where Mormon headquarters chanced from time to time to be located. These propositions could best be supported by the church's publication of missionary journals, if they exist in the official archives. Even without that evidence, however, they can be adequately documented from scattered references of orthodox sources to Mormon proselytizing, and from an analysis of the nativity figures in the Utah Territorial Census of 1860.

Whether particularly successful missionary tours are indicated by the concentration in certain years of occasional remarks by others on the Mormon conversions, or whether coincidence is responsible, the notices discovered focus upon 1832 and 1841. During earlier years Mormons had "made considerable inroads in the southern part" of the town of Borodino, whose people, according to the Presbyterian minister, had been "wafted and bemused with *every wind of doctrine,* till they neither know nor care what is truth, or what is error." In northern Allegany County, "A Mormon Preacher came along" carrying "a solemn visage and nearly persuaded some over to his delusion." In the same year Alexander Campbell's strictures on the new faith were republished by Joshua Himes at Boston,

because two Mormons already had fifteen converts from that city. Early the following summer missionaries in the middle Genesee Valley were reported to have collected fifty recruits by making use of the northern lights to scare the superstitious. A few Mormons helped to turn West Otto, in Cattaraugus County, against Presbyterian doctrine in 1835. The *Baptist Register* of Utica began publishing occasional exposures of Mormonism in 1839, intensifying its interest during the following two years. Explanation came forth in February of '41. "Mormon emissaries are now circulating in various directions through the State . . . and in some instances [are] surprisingly successful." The Methodist *Zion's Watchman* in the same year commenced to present anti-Mormon material in some quantity. Occasional press notices emanated from Rochester throughout the forties. One of John Humphrey Noyes's supporters recommended that he visit Utica, where the correspondent and forty-four others had supported a Mormon Church in 1841. The same year a returned missionary visiting friends in Low Hampton requested permission to attend William Miller's preaching.

But what degree of success did this proselytizing achieve, and how did it compare with similar efforts farther west? In 1860, when many original New York converts who had been adults in 1830 must have died, the natives of this state in Utah Territory numbered fewer only than those from Illinois. Iowa, Ohio, Pennsylvania, and Missouri followed in order. The manuscript of the census shows that the numbers from Iowa, Illinois, and Missouri were of such an age range that they must have been mainly the children of the fertile members transplanted from the East. While it is thus clear that few adults joined in the Middle West, many whose nativity was in New England or Pennsylvania had removed once and resided in New York at the time of their conversion. No exact analysis is possible, but it is clear that many more adherents came from the East than from the West, and probably more of them from New York than from any other state. It may not be improper to imagine that the bulk of these hailed from the same Burned-over District which in these very years provided so extensive a personnel for a host of other religious experiments.

To discover when the conversions in the region occurred is again difficult, but basis for an estimate is found by analyzing age groups among the New York-born in Utah in 1860. Of 923 persons so counted, 221 were over 45 and might have been original members, though many presumably emigrated and joined later farther west or came under the influence of the Mormon itinerants who combed this region after 1831. The remainder under 45 could have been children of original members. But since only a hundred persons in all removed to Kirtland, Ohio, in the first hegira, the greater number must have been later converts or their children. Persons under 25, and families with a member in this age group born in this state, could scarcely have emigrated before 1835. The number in this category totals 446 out of the 923 counted, or more than 50 per cent.

It seems conservative to estimate that of Mormons brought into the church from the Burned-over District at least three-fourths must have been gathered by returning itinerants between 1831 and the early fifties. Yankee groups in Ohio, Pennsylvania, and New England itself responded similarly, but less intensively, and after 1850 a substantial portion of new members came from England and Scandinavia. Obviously, then, Mormonism should not be called a frontier religion in terms of the persons it appealed to, any more than it should in terms of its origin.

To be sure the church existed generally on the frontier and kept moving westward with the tide of settlement. It also carried into the West a number of ideas characteristic of the Burned-over District. Its location was determined by the fact that the evangelistic-mindedness from which it developed in the beginning, and which constantly fed it with members, had little tolerance for such an unorthodox offspring, and drove the Saints by its persecution along their westering course. But neither the organization of the church, nor its personnel, nor its doctrines were frontier products. All belonged rather to that Yankee, rural, emotionalized, and rapidly maturing culture which characterized western New York so markedly in the second quarter of the nineteenth century.

Francis W. Kirkham (essay date 1951)

SOURCE: "Final Words, Summary, and Conclusion," in *A New Witness for Christ in America:* The Book of Mormon, Brigham Young University, 1959, pp. 315-26.

[*In the following excerpt, originally published in 1951, Kirkham outlines five different investigations into the origin and teachings of the* Book of Mormon.]

This strange book, the ***Book of Mormon,*** has been before the world for one hundred and twenty years. The person who dictated its contents and secured the copyright declared, "It is not a modern composition by any man in this generation." It came forth and was translated "by the gift and power of God, to convince all men that Jesus is the Christ, manifesting himself to all nations."

Through the one hundred and twenty years since its publication, it has been a challenge to all men to investigate its origin and its teachings. It contains a promise, that the earnest seeker for the evidence of the truth of its claim, namely, that it contains the fulness of the

Gospel as revealed by Jesus Christ, may know if he desires by the power of the Holy Ghost that it is in truth a new witness for Christ in America. . . .

Many books have been written to help the truthseeker in his search to know all the facts about the coming forth of the ***Book of Mormon,*** its translation, and the witnesses to its divine origin. . . .

This present study . . . has been written by invitation to present in the sequence of publication, all the explanations of the ***Book of Mormon,*** including Joseph Smith's. Five comprehensive explanations have been described and illustrated in this study by quotations from newspapers, publications, and books. These are:

(1) The explanation by the Prophet Joseph Smith. It is taken from Joseph Smith's own writings.

(2) The explanation by the residents of Palmyra, New York, where the book was printed and by others who were aware of the announcement of the book, and who had seen or had knowledge of the manuscript and who knew the time, place, and circumstances at its writing and publication.

The evidence of this explanation of the origin of the ***Book of Mormon*** by the people who lived at the place where it was printed comes from three principal sources.

First, from the newspapers published before the book was printed and shortly afterwards. . . .

Second, the explanation given by Obediah Dogberry, the editor of the local paper, who was challenged to give his personal knowledge of its origin. He answered in six letters published within eight months of the printing of the ***Book of Mormon.*** . . .

Third, Reverend Alexander Campbell, founder of the Church of Christ, with whom Sydney Rigdon and Parley P. Pratt were fellow pastors, gave his explanation of the origin of the ***Book of Mormon*** less than one year after the book appeared. One entire edition of the *Evangelical Enquirer* published at Dayton, Ohio, 1830-1831, by the followers of Alexander Campbell, is used to tell the Sydney Rigdon conversion to the divine origin of the ***Book of Mormon,*** and the editor's own information and opinion of its origin and contents.

It is important to emphasize that both believers and non-believers in the divine origin of the book who were acquainted with all the facts, incidents, and conditions resulting in the writing and printing of the book declared that Joseph Smith dictated its contents. They also knew that he did not have the capacity or the ability or the help of others to write the ancient divine record of prophecy, including even the teachings of the Christ, which he describes.

The people of Palmyra who knew the Joseph Smith family, where and how they worked and lived, their daily activities, were also sure Joseph Smith, Jr. had no ability to write such a book with its marvelous claims.

These publications at the time and place of the printing definitely prove that the ***Book of Mormon*** was considered by those who rejected its divine origin as a vile imposition, a book of no consequence to anyone. It would soon pass into oblivion and would be read only by a few ignorant and fanatical believers.

(3) The very different explanation which was made necessary by the rapid increase of the believers in the divine origin of the book.

One year after the ***Book of Mormon*** was printed, Joseph Smith with his family and a few believers at Palmyra, at Fayette, New York, and another small group at Coleville, Susquehanna County, New York, moved to Kirtland, Ohio.

At first, little attention was given by the local people to the followers of this strange new religion except to criticize and denounce their claims. Settlers on new land, builders of homes, roads, schoolhouses, were always welcome on the frontier. The followers of the Prophet increased rapidly. Local conflicts resulted especially as the new settlers began to take part in the political control of the community in which they lived. It was also apparent that the followers of the Prophet were sincere believers, men and women of Christian faith and intelligence.

Opposition and persecution against the Prophet and his followers quickly followed the rapid increase in Church membership. The climax came in the failure of the Kirtland Savings Bank in 1837, the year of the great panic in Western America. The blame for the inability of the bank to pay its depositors was laid upon Joseph Smith and his associates. Others claimed Joseph Smith had failed in his efforts to establish his followers in Jackson County, Missouri. The Prophet organized Zion's Camp in 1834. Over two hundred volunteers marched from Ohio to Missouri to assist their brethren who had already been forced out of their homes into an adjoining county. They were obliged to return to Kirtland disappointed in their undertaking.

The rapid growth of the Church followed by a misunderstanding of the purposes of the migration to Ohio and Missouri brought a new attitude toward Joseph Smith and his followers, and a new emphasis concerning the ***Book of Mormon***. It was now declared that the book had been written by the cunning of some "designing knave" to mislead innocent followers. Joseph Smith, they knew, did not have the ability to write the book. He was the appointed leader of a few false and wicked men who had conceived a fraud and were seeking power.

The people near Kirtland definitely disagreed with the residents at Palmyra who had declared Joseph Smith a poor, ignorant, deluded fanatic. . . . They now proposed a new explanation namely, that persons with greater ability than Joseph Smith had written the ***Book of Mormon*** or copied it from available sources.

Only four years after the Church was organized, Joseph Smith was now called a deceiver, a public nuisance, and "unworthy to live." His followers obeyed his commands which he blasphemously declared were revelations from God. Thus arose the third explanation for the ***Book of Mormon,*** which seemed more satisfactory to the unbeliever. It provided a logical excuse for opposition and persecution of followers of the Prophet who were industrious and who cultivated and subdued the new land on which they settled. These Mormons promoted education and culture; in fact, they prospered more rapidly than their neighbors. They united in a great cause—a religious ideal. They believed and accepted the teachings of their prophet. A revealed counsel given by him directed them to discontinue the use of tobacco, alcoholic beverages and all forms of narcotics. Thus, they were a peculiar people. Moreover, they were Yankees from New England, and Northerners were not welcome in the slave state of Missouri. It now seemed logical to call their prophet a deceiver.

This third explanation of the ***Book of Mormon,*** has been copied into this study from important anti-Mormon books, beginning with *Mormonism Unvailed* (as originally spelled), 1834. The affidavits first printed in this book by the residents of Palmyra and Salem, Ohio, including one by Isaac Hale, father-in-law of the Prophet, have been copied by all anti-Mormon writers for one hundred years. These declarations testify first of the ignorance, delusion and superstition of Joseph Smith; second, that the religious parts of the *Book of Mormon* were written by Sydney Rigdon, and the historical parts were taken from the writings of Solomon Spaulding.

Joseph Smith did not write the book; they knew it could not be explained by assuming he was its author. He was not a mystic; he was just a clever leader of deluded followers.

(4) The imperative explanation that came from the finding (in 1884) of a manuscript written by Solomon Spaulding.

The fourth explanation identified in this study became imperative when a manuscript written by Solomon

Spaulding was found at Honolulu. For fifty years, from 1834 to 1884, in many books and publications, Solomon Spaulding had been given credit for writing a manuscript which had furnished the historical parts of the *Book of Mormon*.

The manuscript found at Honolulu, when printed, definitely proved no relationship. In addition, it was apparent that the writer of the Spaulding manuscript, because of his character, religious beliefs, ability, and knowledge, would have been unable to write the historial and religious contents of the *Book of Mormon*. An effort was made to prove Sydney Rigdon had taken the Spaulding Manuscript from the printing establishment of Patterson and Lambdin at Pittsburg and that it had not been returned to the Spaulding family. The widow and daughter of Solomon Spaulding had already stated the manuscript had been returned and that it was in an "old hair trunk," which Pilastrus Hulburt had searched when he obtained the manuscript later discovered at Honolulu, Hawaii. Thus it was claimed that the manuscript found at Honolulu, was not the one used by Sydney Rigdon, rather a longer one written at a later time which had been lost or destroyed.

(5) The present confusion and lack of unity by modern critics who try to explain the *Book of Mormon* from psychological sources.

The psychological approach is now presented. Joseph Smith did write the *Book of Mormon* after all. The Rigdon-Spaulding theory cannot be proved. Dr. I. W. Riley declares, Joseph Smith was an epileptic; Harry Beardsley calls him a paranoid. Reverend Black says he possessed a "disassociated personality," and Fawn M. Brodie first declares Joseph Smith was a ne'r-do-well, careless youth, next a superstitious religious believer, and then a "myth maker of prodigous talents" who was able to write a fable he called the *Book of Mormon*. He was able to deceive the witnesses and his followers.

Some modern writers hesitate to deny the validity of the documents advanced to prove that the *Book of Mormon* is a joint product of Sydney Rigdon and Solomon Spaulding. They realize how inconsistent it is to refuse to accept the findings and conclusions of writers for one hundred years.

More and more the Rigdon Spaulding theory is abandoned, and Joseph Smith is accepted as the author of the book; its contents can be explained by the environment in which he lived.

Joseph Smith was given no rest or peace by his enemies after he announced his first heavenly vision. Yet, in a brief space of time, acting for our Eternal Father, he revealed to mankind by divine revelation, the Gospel plan of life which today brings joy and happiness, progress and satisfaction to more than one million believers. Finally, with his brother, Hyrum, he sealed his testimony with his blood.

He once said, "No man knows my history." How could a mere man know, or comprehend, or realize the power of God who sustained, guided, and directed him in the organization and development of the Restored Gospel. No man knows the life of Jesus the Christ. It was written best by His disciples who experienced the gift and power of the Holy Ghost, a divine source of intelligence and power that is known only to those who in humility obey his teachings.

It does not now seem logical to call Joseph Smith a deceiver. The results of his teachings are manifest in the lives of the members of one of America's most rapidly growing churches. Definitely, he was not an ignorant, fanatical leader of deluded followers. Was he a rare, mystic leader with ability to write the book and deceive the witnesses and thousands of followers who lived with him? Or is it possible he spoke the truth? Was he, in reality, a prophet of God?

There is a constantly growing interest in the book he gave to the world. Is its "coming forth" evidence of divine power manifested to man? Can it be objectively true that a man, once alive upon this earth, now a resurrected immortal being, gave to Joseph Smith a metallic record engraved in ancient hieroglyphics to be translated by divine power to convince all men that Jesus is the Christ, or in simple words, a revealed knowledge from God of who we are, why we are here, and our life after death, the answer to the enigma of life—the most important question of human existence? If true, what a glorious blessing for the peace, happiness, and eternal progress of man.

Those who testify they know, are grateful beyond expression to their Heavenly Father that in His mercy He has made it possible for man to be a partaker of the blessings and privileges of His gospel; his plan of life which as he lives and obeys His commandments brings to him joy, peace, and love.

They willingly give their time and talents that others, too, may share these gifts and blessings. The greatest gift in human life is the companionship of the Holy Ghost which follows faith, repentence, baptism, and membership in His Church together with humble, earnest obedience to His laws. Jesus the Christ revealed himself to man two thousand years ago, and in His mercy, He has again revealed in plainness, the knowledge of man's existence and the Gospel plan of living for his happiness and eternal progress.

David E. Miller and Della S. Miller (essay date 1974)

SOURCE: An introduction to *Nauvoo: The City of Joseph,* Peregrine Smith, Inc., 1974, pp. 5-10.

[*In the following excerpt, the authors describe the historical significance of the Mormon experiences in Nauvoo, Illinois, and suggest that Joseph Smith's religious and political activity there facilitated the Mormon migration to Utah.*]

During the spring and summer of 1839 thousands of Mormon refugees (recently expelled from the hostile state of Missouri under a harsh gubernatorial "extermination" order accompanied by military force) swarmed into a partially swampy, somewhat fever-infested Mississippi River peninsula in Hancock County, Illinois, to take over the small hamlet of Commerce and establish in its place the City of Nauvoo—soon to become the largest city in the state. The history of the brief Mormon occupation there (1839-46) is one of the outstanding success stories of the mid-West, mid-century American frontier, even though the saints were finally expelled from their beautiful city after only seven years. When the Mormons first arrived there in the spring of 1839, approximately 100 persons occupied the whole peninsula. By 1845 the official Illinois census showed that the city had grown to nearly 12,000, although most contemporary accounts (both Mormon and non-Mormon) regularly over-estimated the population, sometimes stretching the figure up to more than 20,000. By 1846 hundreds of homes of various sizes and materials crowded the region; scores of shops and stores of all kinds were to be found there.

The citizens of Nauvoo developed as rich a social and cultural life as any frontier community of that time. In addition to various church functions, the saints enjoyed musical and theatrical productions as well as debating and public speaking contests. An occasional traveling circus performed in the city. Most able-bodied men were members of the Nauvoo Legion; many were active in the Masonic Lodge—both of which furnished social as well as other enrichment. Celebration of national and other holidays afforded opportunity for parades and private parties, all of which were enjoyed by the expanding populace. Adequate opportunities for education were supplied by elementary and grammar schools as well as a university.

Operating under a very liberal charter granted by the Illinois State Legislature, the Mormons of Nauvoo were able to establish a theocratic city government, the like of which was unknown elsewhere in the American frontier. Although the Nauvoo Charter was patterned primarily after similar charters granted earlier to other Illinois cities, the Mormon city was unique in that most of its citizens were members of the same church. This led quite naturally to a very close correlation between civil and ecclesiastical government; high-ranking church officials held most of the important civic positions as well.

The history of Nauvoo is very closely linked with the activities of Joseph Smith who (before his untimely death) had a hand in most of the city's developments. It was his decision, while still incarcerated in Missouri's Liberty jail—long before he had actually set foot upon Illinois soil—to negotiate with Isaac Galland for land purchases on and near the Commerce peninsula. It was his decree that designated the new location as a "gathering" place for his flock—a place for a new city of Zion. During the cruel expulsion of the Mormons from Missouri some church leaders, then assembling at Quincy, Illinois, had favored a program of scattering the saints throughout the land. Their reasoning seemed quite sound; they well remembered the church's unhappy experiences at Kirtland, Ohio, and the more recent bitter contest that had resulted in their forcible banishment from Missouri. Would it not be better to avoid such troubles in the future by not concentrating in any given area? Joseph Smith vetoed that notion and countered with a call for a mass-movement to the site of Commerce, which he soon renamed Nauvoo. His determination to "gather" rather than "scatter" almost certainly saved the church from fragmentation and very possibly from extinction. The prophet had made a most important decision for the future history of Mormonism.

After moving to the new site the prophet was, by any standard of measurement, Nauvoo's leading citizen. As founder and president of the church, he enjoyed the high esteem and loyalty of his followers, most of whom would eagerly bear testimony that Joseph, as a young man, had talked with God and other heavenly messengers and had, since that time, been in more or less constant communication with the Almighty. Most instructions to private individuals as well as directives to the church as a whole were proclaimed and accepted as direct revelations from God.

Joseph's activities and offices were not limited to religious matters; he was Nauvoo's leading civic and social leader as well as its prophet. In the first election authorized by Nauvoo's city charter he gained a seat on the city council where he assumed the leading role in framing major legislation. When Mayor John C. Bennett "defected" and resigned in 1842, Joseph was elevated to the mayor's chair—a position he held the rest of his life. In addition to being mayor he was also chief justice of the municipal court which was given extensive power by the city council over which he presided. With the founding of the Nauvoo university he took his place as a member of its board of regents. When the city council created the Nauvoo Legion (as an arm of the state's militia), Joseph became its top officer—Lieutenant General—and was duly commissioned by the governor of Illinois. When the Nauvoo Lodge of the Masonic Order was founded, Joseph was honored by an "on sight" elevation to the degree of Master Mason. As trustee-in-trust for the church, President Smith was custodian of all its land and other physical property. In this capacity the prophet became Nauvoo's leading real estate broker. His general retail store became the city's foremost business of its kind; there a person could purchase almost anything: food, clothing, a city lot or a subscription to a local newspaper. Persons considered good credit risks could also borrow money from the proprietor. On the upper floor of the store was the prophet's office where he often met with various church and civic councils. The room also served at times as a Masonic Hall, a theater and a school. The store and its owner were indeed the hub of Nauvoo's civic activity.

In view of all this, it is not surprising that, after the prophet's murder, Brigham Young renamed the Mormon city in honor of its founder and leading citizen: The City of Joseph.

Yet in spite of his popularity and numerous offices, the prophet's life was often a tortured one. Financial obligations were a constant worry. His enemies periodically sought (and sometimes succeeded) to arrest him on one charge or another. He found it necessary to spend many weeks in hiding as a hunted man evading posses sent to apprehend him. By 1844 some of his once-closest friends had become his bitterest enemies. Finally, with an expressed premonition of an imminent violent death at the hands of his enemies, the prophet voluntarily submitted to arrest for his participation in a city council action that had led to the destruction of the Nauvoo *Expositor*. A few days later his body, riddled by gunfire from a mob at Carthage, was brought back to Nauvoo for a secret burial.

The Nauvoo years constitute a major chapter in Mormon church history and provided an immediate background for the great migration of the saints to the Salt Lake Valley. It was in Nauvoo that many of the major doctrines of the church were first proclaimed and/or put into practice. It was at Nauvoo that Joseph Smith first committed to writing his own account of the "first vision" and other incidents associated with the restoration of the gospel and the founding of the Church of Jesus Christ of Latter-day Saints. It was there that he formulated thirteen statements of religious belief, later to become known as the church's Articles of Faith. It was in Nauvoo where the "Book of Abraham" was first published, later to be cannonized as part of the ***Pearl of Great Price***—one of the church's sacred scriptures. It was there that Joseph began to dictate his own ***History of the Church*** which contains many teachings and activities of the prophet not found elsewhere in print.

Among the important doctrines of the church which were destined to become most significant in later church history was the initiation of various sacred temple ordinances for the living and for the dead. The construction of the magnificent Nauvoo Temple where these rites could be performed foreshadowed the extensive temple-building and genealogical research which became very important aspects of the church program after the Mormon migration to the Great Basin. Of special importance for the Nauvoo period and later decades was the initiation of a new Mormon concept of marriage for time and all eternity. Closely related was the accompanying practice of plural marriages, commonly called polygamy. Some leading Mormons may have been involved in this practice prior to the Nauvoo era, but it was in Nauvoo where the revelation authorizing the doctrine was first committed to writing and where the practice gained considerable notoriety, eventually becoming a major factor leading to a significant schism within church ranks.

Gentile opposition to Mormonism became as bitter in Illinois as it had been in Missouri. Non-Mormons generally considered Mormonism the most radical religion of its time and denounced some of the church's teachings, such as the prophet's claims of visitations from heavenly beings, plural marriage and the plurality of Gods. Yet gentile opposition on strictly "religious" grounds did not go far beyond verbal attacks and tirades during the early part of the Nauvoo era. Much more disturbing was the apparent political unity of the saints. Equally alarming to non-Mormons (and also to some members of the church hierarchy) was the doctrine of the political Kingdom of God, a doctrine that gained considerable credence during the spring of 1844 with the prophet's candidacy for the presidency of the United States and the accompanying formation of the secret Council of Fifty to direct this campaign. At that time Mormons held the balance of power in Hancock County; if they were permitted to remain and expand, might they not soon gain control of the whole state? Was there danger that *General* Smith might employ the expertly drilled Nauvoo Legion to help achieve his objectives? Those were expressed fears of some non-Mormon editors and other leaders living in western Illinois. But in spite of growing opposition from without, it is very doubtful that anti-Mormon sentiment would have precipitated a major physical attack on Mormondom or its leaders had not a schism within the church itself opened the door for such action.

During the spring of 1844 a significant cleavage within the church precipitated a chain of events that led directly to the prophet's death. Earlier rumblings of dissatisfaction with the prophet and some of his teachings mushroomed into a full-fledged opposition movement led by several high-ranking church officials. As has already been suggested, major opposition centered around the doctrine and practice of polygamy and the

The Carthage jail, scene of Joseph and Hyrum Smith's murders.

political activities of their once revered prophet-leader. The defectors now denounced Joseph as a "fallen prophet" and attempted a reorganization of the church, naming members from their own ranks as its top officers. After failing to gain a substantial following in this endeavor, some of the disgruntled apostates hit upon the idea of establishing an opposition newspaper in Nauvoo for the avowed purpose of exposing the "misdeeds" and "evil teachings" of the church. Thus, the *Nauvoo Expositor* was born. Its first and only issue came off the press on June 7, 1844.

Outraged at the "infamous" sheet and fearful of the influence it might have if allowed to continue, *Mayor* Smith and the city council declared the *Expositor* to be a public nuisance and ordered the chief of police to destroy the press and pi the type. The order was carried out at once; the date was June 10, 1844. Owners of the destroyed press now joined with anti-Mormon groups inside and outside of Nauvoo, denounced the whole affair as a ruthless violation of the freedom of the press and called for the immediate arrest of the prophet-mayor as the chief instigator of the action. Within a few days Joseph Smith submitted to arrest

and was escorted to Carthage for trial. Upon arrival at the county seat the prophet was also charged with treason against the state for having declared martial law in Nauvoo. Meanwhile Hyrum Smith had been similarly charged. It was the treason charge that led to the incarceration of the Smith brothers in Carthage jail to await trial. That was late in the evening of June 25. Two days later, shortly after 5 o'clock in the afternoon an emotionally charged mob bent on assassination took the law into its own hands, stormed the weakly guarded prison and murdered both men in cold blood.

Anti-Mormon feeling did not die with the murder of the church's two top leaders. Rather, demands for the complete Mormon explusion from the state gained momentum during the following year. Under continuous pressure, Brigham Young (who as president of the quorum of apostles had won out over Sidney Rigdon in a power struggle for church leadership) agreed in September 1845 that the Mormons would evacuate Nauvoo and leave the state during the following year.

Mormon leaders had learned from bitter practical experience that protection of property and personal liberties could not be expected from the federal government which (under the American constitutional system) could not intercede inside state boundaries. (Not until the 1868 adoption of the 14th Amendment to the United States Constitution did the government gain that right.) In Nauvoo, Mormon leaders came to realize that their only hope for security lay in a *state* of their own making, a state in which they would have a commanding majority of votes, where they could draft a constitution and enact laws for their own protection. With this in mind, Joseph Smith had petitioned Congress in December 1843 to have the Nauvoo area separated from the state of Illinois to become a Mormon-controlled territory. This petition was rejected, as it rightfully should have been; the Nauvoo area was much too small for territorial status. Meanwhile church leaders turned their attention to other possible locations.

Fragmentary plans for a major migration to the far West had been in the making since 1842. Numerous council meetings had devoted a great deal of time to discussions of various sites—Texas, the Oregon Country, Vancouver Island. There was much talk of sending out exploring parties to find proper locations; volunteers were called for, and many leading Mormons eagerly stepped forward for that service. But no exploring parties were sent.

During the fall of 1845, after church leaders had obtained all available information about the far West, the valley of the Great Salt Lake in the Great Basin was positively named as the future Mormon mecca. There the saints would not likely be overrun by a gentile population; there they could establish a state which would insure their own protection and hopefully be admitted into the union of American states; there they could continue to build up the Kingdom of God.

Thus the Mormon migration to Utah grew directly out of the Nauvoo experiences and planning. The church simply transplanted itself *en masse* to the new site, taking people, records, doctrine, practices and leadership to the new Zion where the desert would be made to blossom as the rose. But the Zion they left behind, Mormon Nauvoo, retains its importance as a proving ground for examining the limitations of American freedom and for exploring the growth of Mormonism under its founder, Joseph Smith.

Donna Hill (essay date 1977)

SOURCE: "The Book of Mormon," in *Joseph Smith: The First Mormon,* Doubleday & Company, Inc., 1977, pp. 98-105.

[*Hill, herself a Mormon, is an Assistant Professor and head of Teachers' Central Laboratory at Hunter College Library in New York. In the following excerpt,* Hill briefly describes the content of the Book of Mormon *and the responses of contemporary and subsequent readers.*]

The Book of Mormon, nearly six hundred pages of small print in the first edition, contains the chronicles of three groups of immigrants to the New World, most of it concerning a period from about 600 B.C. to A.D. 421. It is in fifteen main divisions, or books, each named after its principal author, and is based upon three sets of plates, or engraved records, the Plates of Nephi (which are of two kinds, larger plates of secular history and smaller sacred records), the Plates of Mormon, an abridgment of the Plates of Nephi made by Mormon with his comments and a continuation by his son, Moroni (who became the angel Moroni), and the Plates of Ether, abridged by Moroni, a history of the Jaredites, who came to the new land when the people were dispersed after the destruction of the Tower of Babel. Other records to which frequent reference is made in *The Book of Mormon* are the Brass Plates of Laban, which contain the ancient Hebrew Scriptures.

Most of *The Book of Mormon* is about the descendants of Lehi, who left Jerusalem with his family in 600 B.C., following God's warning about His pending scourge of the wicked. Lehi and his family built a ship and came to Central or South America, bringing with them the Plates of Laban. Their posterity were soon divided into the righteous light-skinned Nephites and the rebellious dark-skinned Lamanites. Interspersed with accounts of their wars and contentions are the admonitions and teachings of various prophets on numerous subjects such as the nature of man, the fall and the atonement.

The Book of Mormon confirmed that the new land was a land of promise for the descendants of the tribes of Israel (2 Nephi 1:5): "We have obtained a land of promise, a land which is above all other lands; a land which the Lord God hath covenanted with me should be a land for the inheritance of my seed . . . forever and also all those who should be led out of other countries by the hand of the Lord."

But the people must keep the Lord's commandments, Nephi warns, or they would be smitten and scattered. A nation dwinding in faith is told that the time for repentance is brief.

A prophecy of 1 Nephi 22:23 denounces sectarianism and the corruption of churches, "for the time speedily shall come, that all churches which are built up to get gain, and all those who are built up to get power over the flesh, and those who are built up to become popular in the eyes of the world . . . are they who need fear, and tremble, and quake; they are those who must be brought low in the dust . . ."

A warning is given in 2 Nephi 27:20 against the Gentiles who in their pride build many churches in which they "put down the power and the miracles of God, and preach up unto themselves their own wisdom and their own learning . . . and there are many churches built up which cause envyings, and strifes, and malice."

The Book of Mormon was to reconcile religious controversy and settle all disputes over biblical interpretation. As the prophet Lehi said to his son Joseph (2 Nephi 3:12), referring to *The Book of Mormon* and the Bible, "the fruit of thy loins shall write; and the fruit of the loins of Judah shall write; and [these works] . . . shall grow together, unto the confounding of false doctrines and laying down of contentions, and establishing peace among the fruit of thy loins, and bringing them to the knowledge of their fathers in the latter days, and also the knowledge of my covenants, saith the Lord."

In addition, *The Book of Mormon* is another witness for Christ, as in 1 Nephi 13:40: "These last records, which thou has seen among the Gentiles, shall establish the truth of the first . . . and shall make known the plain and precious things which have been taken away from them; and shall make known to all kindreds, tongues, and people, that the Lamb of God is the Son of the Eternal Father, and the Savior of the world; and that all men must come unto him, or they cannot be saved."

About five hundred years after Lehi and his family immigrated to the new land, King Mosiah recommends to his people (29 Mosiah 25-26) that they relinquish the monarchy and choose judges to lead them according to the law and the voice of the majority. The people elect their high priest Alma to be their first chief judge as well, in this way establishing religious and political leadership in one person.

Some 130 years later, the resurrected Christ appears to the Nephites, inhabitants of the new land, His "other sheep," and ministers to them and gives them His message, which includes a reiteration of the Sermon on the Mount (3 Nephi 12).

Jesus warns the wicked of God's vengeance, but adds (3 Nephi 21:22-25), "if they will repent, and hearken unto my words, and harden not their hearts, I will establish my church among them, and they shall come in unto the covenant and be numbered among this the remnant of Jacob, unto whom I have given this land for their inheritance; And they shall assist my people . . . that they may build a city, which shall be called the New Jerusalem. And then shall they assist my people that they may be gathered in . . . And then shall the power of heaven come down among them; and I also will be in the midst."

The ideal society is set forth as existing among the people for some two hundred years after Christ's visit. It is a theocracy, in which all, Nephites and Lamanites alike, are members of the one true church. Peace and harmony prevail, all things are held in common so that no poor, no bondsmen, no thieves or murderers exist among them, strife and religious contention are unknown, "and surely there could not be a happier people among all the people who had been created by the hand of God" (4 Nephi 16).

But they are unable to maintain this level of righteousness. A war between the Nephites and the Lamanites eventually leaves a single Nephite survivor, Moroni, who buries the records of his people with their message for a later generation in the Hill Cumorah.

The Book of Mormon is not easy to read, and from its unpopular reception in some areas, it did not seem likely at first to reach a large audience. However, when ardent young missionaries began to carry the book about the countryside and to urge its prayerful consideration it soon aroused interest.

Alexander Campbell, founder of the Campbellite Church, who was annoyed when some of his followers deserted him for the Mormon faith, considered the book a fraud, and said it had anachronistic ideas on democratic government and the rights of man derived from the United States. As has been suggested, Campbell overlooked the fact that the form of government extolled in the book was more theocratic than republican. Campbell was correct, however, when he said that the book was concerned with the very issues in religion which were then being intensely debated. He said that the author reproduced:

> every error and almost every truth discussed in New York for the last ten years. He decides all the great controversies—infant baptism, ordination, the trinity, regeneration, repentance, justification, the fall of man, the atonement, transubstantiation, fasting, penance, church government, religious experience, the call of the ministry, the general resurrection, eternal punishment, who may baptize, and even the question of free masonry, republican government; and the rights of man.

It seemed to Campbell that Joseph Smith "infallibly decides by his authority every question."

This authority was exactly the basis for much of the appeal of *The Book of Mormon*. That the church founded on that book answered the urgent need of many who like the members of Joseph's family were distressed by sectarian conflict and were looking for an authoritarian revival of the primitive Christian church is demonstrated by the frequency with which converts spoke of the disruption to their faith caused by numerous and contending sects. Notable among these were men who later became vigorous leaders in Joseph's church, among whom were Oliver Cowdery, Brigham Young, Wilford Woodruff, Amasa Lyman and Lorenzo Snow. Hosea Stout, a convert to Mormonism who had been a Methodist, wrote [in his autiobiography published in the *Utah Historical Quarterly*, 1962] that he discovered a hostile spirit between the Methodists and the Cumberlands, and that "It threw me much in the back Grounds to hear preachers slander each other because of small differences of opinion in 'non-essentials' so called."

Joseph Smith's uncle John, in moving from New York State to live near his nephew and others who believed in *The Book of Mormon,* wrote that he was glad to leave that land of confusion. John's son George Albert had been troubled even as a boy by the numbers of different religions and had asked his father for an explanation of their origin. Some of the earliest Mormon converts had not previously joined any religious group, but had remained "seekers" awaiting restoration of the primitive church of Christ, which would offer the gifts of healing and prophecy. Many converts wrote that they had accepted the admonition to read *The Book of Mormon* prayerfully, asking the Lord to manifest to them whether or not it was true, and this was what led them into the Mormon Church.

Jared Carter, from Chenango, Broome County, New York, was traveling on business when he heard of *The Book of Mormon* from a man who opposed it so violently that Jared became fascinated. He got a copy, read it prayerfully and was so moved that he could not keep his mind on his business. He was baptized soon afterward, in February 1831, by Hyrum Smith and that summer he too became a missionary. Among those he met on his mission was Zerah Pulsipher, who stated that if the true church existed on earth he had not yet found it. Zerah read *The Book of Mormon* twice, heard Jared's testimony about the plates and the founding of the church and became convinced.

Parley P. Pratt, who was later to become an apostle of the church, read *The Book of Mormon* with intense excitement, forgetting to eat and sleep, and declared, "As I read, the spirit of the Lord was upon me, and I knew and comprehended that the book was true, as plainly and manifestly as a man comprehends and knows that he exists."

Newel Knight's studies of the Bible had convinced him that a great falling away from the true church had occurred. He read *The Book of Mormon* avidly, and listened to the young prophet, whom he felt spoke plainly and honestly. Newel became convinced that *The Book of Mormon* was a completion of the word of God, a restoration and a fulfillment of the gospel.

Anson Call heard Mormon elders in Ohio in 1833, and though he disliked what they said, he found himself unable to dispute it. He decided that before he met them again, his knowledge of the Bible and *The Book of Mormon* would equal theirs. He spent six months in prayer and study, and became convinced that what the young elders had told him was true.

Many early Mormons were from rural areas, but when missionaries began to labor in the large cities, they made converts there as well. Whether urban or rural, however, most converts had a history of social mobility, economic insecurity, dissatisfaction with contending sects and hope for a millennium in which discord and hardship would be eliminated and status in the Lord's kingdom would depend upon spiritual rather than material values.

Although Alexander Campbell was antagonistic toward *The Book of Mormon,* he came close to understanding the reason for its impact, whereas others who reviewed it usually failed to grasp its religious and sociological significance. Critics most frequently busied themselves with speculations about its origin or with searching for flaws. *The Unitarian* of January 1, 1834, said, "Coming, as Lehi and his family are represented to have done, from Jerusalem, there would be some traces of Jewish manners and customs among the people. But . . . we see no account of sacrifices and of national festivals . . . The exhortations are strongly tinctured with the doctrines of modern Orthodoxy."

In a rather lengthy review of some ten pages, the author [Jason Whitman] made much of grammatical errors and of the number of paragraphs beginning with "and it came to pass," and added that if *The Book of Mormon* were read critically, it would be seen that unlike the Bible, the geographical references in it could not be identified and the customs and controversies of the people were presented as nearly the same before and after the appearance of the Savior. He did, however, make a limited attempt to understand the spread of the Mormon faith, and allowed that there was "some degree of plausibility, both in the course pursued by the preachers, and in the contents of the book itself." He expounded his belief, with examples, that the book was "adapted to the known prejudices of a portion of the community."

Somewhat later, February 13, 1841, a generally sympathetic article with a fair grasp of Mormon uniqueness appeared "From the New Yorker" on page one of the *Iowa Territorial Gazette and Advertiser*. Taking a distinctly opposite view from that of *The Unitarian,* the article said that the work:

> is remarkly [*sic*] free from any allusions that might betray a knowledge of the present practical or social

state of the world . . . It is difficult to imagine a more difficult literary task than to write what may be termed a continuation of the Scriptures, that should . . . fill up many chasms that now seem to exist, and thus receive and lend confirmation . . . To establish a plausibly-sustained theory, that the aborigines of our Continent are descendents of Israel without committing himself by any assertion or description that could be contradicted, shows a degree of talent and research that in an uneducated youth of twenty is almost a miracle of itself.

The writer, while professing astonishment and calling the work "almost a miracle," apparently believed that Joseph Smith was its author. Others who could neither accept Joseph as author nor his statement that the work was a translation from ancient records unearthed under the direction of the angel Moroni tried to advance various theories about the origin of the book.

Some three years after the book was published, Philastus Hurlbut (variously spelled Hurlburt, Hulbert, Hurlbert, etc.), a disgruntled Mormon convert excommunicated from the church in June 1833 for "unChristian conduct with women," heard that one John Spaulding said that *The Book of Mormon* resembled a novel written in 1812 by his brother Solomon, a minister and amateur archaeologist who had died in 1816. Intrigued, Hurlbut went to interview John, his wife and their neighbors, who maintained that, although it had been twenty years since they had heard Solomon read his novel aloud, they remembered it well enough to say that it had remarkable similarities to *The Book of Mormon*. Hurlbut got permission from Solomon's widow to examine her husband's papers, and found the manuscript, but to his disappointment, it was similar to *The Book of Mormon* in only superficial ways. Calling itself a translation of ancient scrolls found in a cave, it was a slim adventure story about pre-Christian immigrants to America. In florid eighteenth-century prose, full of romantic clichés, it was entirely different in style from *The Book of Mormon,* and it had no religious import. It could not be set forth as the original.

Despite the widow Spaulding's statement that her husband had written only one such story, Hurlbut insisted that there must be another manuscript. He tried to prove that Sidney Rigdon, who had known the publisher to whom Spaulding offered his novel, had somehow used the manuscript as a basis for *The Book of Mormon*. The allegation was accepted by a surprising number of people in the nineteenth century including Alexander Campbell, who had believed that Joseph Smith was the author of the book until Sidney Rigdon, his cofounder of the Campbellite Church, joined the Mormons.

Scholars have since concluded that the similarities between the books were mere coincidence and that the accusation of plagiarism was motivated by animosity. Rigdon himself, an intelligent and accomplished man who never showed an inclination to relinquish his due, vigorously maintained throughout his life that he had no part in the production of *The Book of Mormon* and never saw it until it was published.

Other theories were also put forth. In 1904, one writer, Charles W. Brown, quoted a statement that those who knew the family best put no credence in the Spaulding theory, but believed that *The Book of Mormon* was "a production of" the Smiths, aided by Oliver Cowdery. That Cowdery had a part in it is not tenable, however, because he had met the prophet after the work was well advanced. Only part of the manuscript is in his hand, as Joseph's scribe. Cowdery himself said that although he tried, he was unable to produce a single sentence under inspiration.

In the early twentieth century, one scholar [Walter Franklin Prince, in the *American Journal of Phychology,* 1917] offered internal evidence that the book must have been written by a man of Joseph's generation in that region of New York soon after 1826, which seemed to him sufficient proof that the book was by Joseph Smith.

A more recent historian [Fawn M. Brodie, in her *No Man Knows My History,* 1945, rev. 1971] has suggested that Joseph took his theme from Ethan Smith, a Congregationalist minister from Vermont (no relation to the prophet's family so far as is known) whose *View of the Hebrews,* first published in 1823, proposed that the American Indians were descendants of the lost tribes of Israel. In 1842 Joseph Smith mentioned Ethan Smith's work in *Times and Seasons* in the context of a corroboration of *The Book of Mormon,* but there is no evidence that he had an earlier acquaintance with it. It may be, however, that Joseph was previously aware of the idea of the Jewish origin of the Indians, since there was a great deal of popular speculation on that subject well before his time.

Joseph himself [in The *Messenger and Advocate,* 1835] described *The Book of Mormon* as "coming forth out of the treasure of the heart . . . bringing forth out of the heart, things new and old." His attitude toward it was manifested in what he told the Twelve Apostles, that "The *Book of Mormon* was the most correct of any book on earth, and the keystone of our religion, and a man would get nearer to God by abiding by its precepts than by any other book."

The Mormons were not disturbed by controversies over the origins of *The Book of Mormon*. An article in the *Gospel Reflector* of 1841 said, "we are not astonished that the *Book of Mormon* has become a stumbling-block to so many; and the fact that the learned, the wise of this world, and the professors of religion, are our vilest persecutors, and most inveterate enemies, does not discourage us, when we consider that Christ himself was a rock of offence to the Jews."

To the converts, Joseph's church was not only based upon *The Book of Mormon* but the book was its reason for having come into existence. One early writer [Charles W. Brown, cited in the *Shartsville Enterprise Press,* 1904], a non-Mormon, said that at church meetings held in the home of Joseph Smith, Sr., there was no preaching, singing or praying, but the time was spent in reading *The Book of Mormon*. That *The Book of Mormon* was read at meetings is likely true, but it may be doubted that there was no praying, and sermons and hymns were soon well established in the church services. However, Joseph's followers were identified with the book from the outset, and it was not long before they became known by the nickname of "Mormons," or "Mormonites."

The Book of Mormon confirmed what converts already believed, that American society with its religious conflicts and materialistic orientation was doomed unless it could be reformed. To the gratification of those who were so weary of controversy, the teachings of the new church, as based upon the Bible, *The Book of Mormon* and the revelations of the prophet Joseph Smith, provided [an] authoritative, clear and certain outline for salvation.

Richard L. Bushman (essay date 1984)

SOURCE: An introduction to *Joseph Smith and the Beginnings of Mormonism,* University of Illinois Press, 1984, pp. 3-8.

[*In the excerpt below, Bushman describes the religious milieu from which Joseph Smith emerged, arguing that Smith can be "best understood as a person who outgrew his culture."*]

Mormonism, it must be remembered, began with one family, the family of Joseph Smith, Sr., and Lucy Mack Smith of Vermont and New York. Joseph Smith, Jr., the fourth child among nine, became the Prophet and First Elder of the Church of Christ when it was organized on April 6, 1830, but three of the six original organizers were Smiths, just as previously three of the eight witnesses to the golden plates were family members.

Young Joseph Smith's culture was predominantly family culture. So far as the record shows, he had little schooling until he was past twenty. The necessity of work on the family farm kept him at home where someone, probably his father, at one time a school teacher, taught the children. Nor is there a record of church attendance until religious excitement stirred the neigh-

borhood in his early teen years. As a boy and youth, Joseph was almost entirely under the influence of his family and a small circle of acquaintances in the villages of Palmyra and Manchester, New York.

On both the mother's and father's sides, family culture had borne the strains of migration for two generations. Joseph Smith's grandparents were among the large number of migrant pioneers who left the fringe of settlements along the New England coast after the middle of the eighteenth century to clear farms in the heavily forested interior. After a century of relative stability in New England's population a combination of crowding and better opportunities propelled many young men west and north in search of new land. In the 1760s Solomon Mack, Lucy Smith's father, left Lyme, at the mouth of the Connecticut River, for New Hampshire and northern Massachusetts. In the 1770s Asael Smith, Joseph Smith Jr.'s paternal grandfather, moved from Topsfield, Massachusetts, just north of Salem, to New Hampshire, and later to Vermont. Joseph Smith's parents, Joseph Smith, Sr., and Lucy Mack, met and married in Tunbridge, Vermont.

When the Smiths moved to Palmyra, New York, in 1816, they chose an area settled for twenty-five years but still heavily forested. Young Joseph spent his teenage years cutting trees, burning brush, and plowing virgin soil. In a newspaper interview in 1843, Joseph said that when he became confused about the churches as a boy, he chose a place in the woods where his father had a clearing and "went to the stump where I had stuck my axe when I had quit work, and I kneeled down, and prayed. . . ."

The removal from old settlements to new ones separated the Smiths and the Macks from the religion of their fathers. Most eighteenth-century New England towns had one dominant church, the Congregational, still deeply inbued with Calvinist theology and committed to strict church discipline. As new parishes grew on the town periphery, they modeled themselves after the parent church. Only a sprinkling of Baptists, Quakers, and Anglicans here and there interrupted the basic uniformity of belief and practice.

Migration, war, and economic adversity detached Joseph Smith's ancestors from Congregationalism. Solomon Mack, an indentured servant from age four to twenty-one, learned no religion from his master, and lived without religion until age seventy-five, when he was at last converted. His wife, the daughter of a deacon in the Congregational church, taught her children to worship but apparently without formal church connections. Her daughter Lucy was not baptized as a child and joined no church until she finally became a Presbyterian in Palmyra around 1820. On Joseph Smith Sr.'s side, Asael Smith became a Universalist, a believer in salvation for all, and, though associated with the Congregational church from time to time, always dissented from its theology. His son, Joseph Smith, Sr., though privately religious, attended church only sporadically.

The Smiths were religious without being church people. Lucy Smith solemnly promised to serve God with all her heart when an illness brought her close to death in 1803, and then was unable to find a pastor to suit her. She at last persuaded a minister to baptize her without requiring church membership. For seventeen years she read the Bible and prayed with her family before becoming a Presbyterian. Although averse to ministers and churches, Joseph Smith, Sr., had seven inspirational dreams over a span of years, all exhibiting a desire for belief, healing, and direction, all showing dissatisfaction with religion as it existed.

The multiplication of denominations complicated the problem. There were five churches vying for members in Palmyra in 1820 in contrast to the traditional uniformity in New England towns. To Smith eyes, the religious world was in turmoil, marred by hypocrisy and corruption, far removed from the purity and simplicity of the Bible.

In its precarious descent to Joseph Smith, Jr., the Calvinism of his forefathers lost its strength. Asael Smith's Universalism was explicitly heterodox, and all along the line Calvinist belief was diluted. By Joseph Smith's generation, the family could scarcely connect with mainstream Protestantism, which in the nineteenth century was absorbed with evangelical revivalism. Revivalism depended on a Calvinist sense of alienation from God and the belief that grace alone could redeem people. Without the theological foundation the Smiths could not respond, and were destined to live along the margins of evangelical religion.

On the strength of revival conversions, the Baptists and the Methodists grew from tiny minorities in 1780 to the most populous Protestant churches in 1850. Congregationalists and Presbyterians were not far behind. Every major city and almost every rural town saw not just one revival but a succession of them in the decades after 1800. No Smiths of Joseph Sr.'s family were converted. Solomon Mack underwent a classic spiritual rebirth in Vermont in 1811, and for a time Lucy and Joseph attended meetings, but Joseph, Sr., soon withdrew and Lucy did not persist. Lucy and three of the children were sufficiently caught up in the revival in 1820 to join the Presbyterians, but none mentioned conversion in the usual sense. Joseph Smith, Jr., complained that "he wanted to get Religion too, wanted to feel and shout like the rest but could feel nothing."

Aspects of the first vision resembled a conversion experience—the forgiveness of sins and the joy and elation afterward—and Joseph may have first interpreted the experience as conversion. But in later accounts the conversionist elements faded in the telling, and the opening of a new dispensation overshadowed all else. After the church was organized in 1830, evangelical revivalism had no place in Mormon worship. Mormon theology, as it developed in the revelations and in discourses, showed few signs of having wrestled free of Calvinism. A common biblicism united Mormonism and Calvinism, but Calvinism did not establish the framework for Joseph Smith's thought.

The Smiths were more directly affected by Enlightenment skepticism than by Calvinist evangelism. Skepticism had influence within the family itself and figured still more largely in the village through newspaper editors and other local intellectuals. As a percentage of the population, free-thinkers and deists were rare in America, but skeptical attitudes cast a long shadow. In 1828 Robert Owen, the atheistic founder of the unsuccessful utopian community at New Harmony, Indiana, offered to debate anyone on the proposition that religion was founded on ignorance and was the chief source of human misery. Alexander Campbell, the leading spirit in the incipient Disciples of Christ movement, agreed to meet Owen in a Methodist meetinghouse in Cincinnati. For eight days in April they debated. Campbell's concluding speech took twelve hours. Through all fifteen sessions the meetinghouse, with seating for a thousand, was filled to capacity. On the last day Campbell called for a standing vote of those favorable and those opposed to Christianity. Only three listeners stood against Christianity.

The vote probably represented the distribution of sentiment in the country. Few Americans were infidels, but the full house day after day spoke for their fascination with skepticism. Moreover, both contenders made their arguments on the basis of reason. Campbell attempted to prove that hard evidence—well-attested miracles—supported Christian belief. His mode of defense illustrated how faith as well as doubt had embraced the Enlightenment by the beginning of the nineteenth century. Christianity claimed to be as reasonable by Enlightenment standards as science or philosophy.

All of this affected Joseph Smith when he told his family and friends about Moroni and the gold plates. The reaction was quite confused. The price Christianity had paid for assimilating the Enlightenment was to forgo belief in all supernatural happenings except the well-attested events of the Bible. Witchcraft, dreams, revelations, even healings were thrown indiscriminately on the scrapheap of superstition. While in 1692 Cotton Mather, the leading intellectual of his day, could discourse learnedly on the manifestation of witchcraft, no leading divine fifty years later would countenance such talk. The Enlightenment drained Christianity of its belief in the miraculous, except for Bible miracles. Everything else was attributed to ignorant credulity. Joseph Smith's story when it became known was immediately identified as one more example.

A movement among the intellectual elite, of course, could not entirely suppress popular belief in divine and satanic forces affecting everyday life. Common people, surreptitiously to some extent, still entertained traditional beliefs in water-witching and in spells to locate hidden treasure. Many more yearned for a return of the miraculous powers of the original Christian church. A group of practitioners of traditional magic in Palmyra thus reacted quite differently from the newspaper editors to Joseph's story of the golden plates and a protecting angel. They saw Joseph Smith as one of them, tried to absorb him into their company, and grew angry when he drew back.

Joseph was assaulted from two sides in this struggle between modern rationalism and traditional supernaturalism. He had to answer to demands for proof from the newspaper editors and ministers, on the one hand, and extricate himself from the schemes of the Palmyra magicians and money diggers, on the other. At times his closest followers and his own family were confused. One of Joseph Smith's tasks in the years before 1830 was to define his calling and mission so as not to be misunderstood, and to set his own course, apart from rationalism or superstition.

Joseph Smith is best understood as a person who outgrew his culture. The usual purpose of historical analysis is to depict persons and ideas as the sum total of the historical forces acting on them. Mormonism has customarily been seen as the product of the culture emanating from upstate New York and Puritan-Yankee New England. The shortcoming of this form of analysis is that it exaggerates similarities and suppresses differences. Everything in Mormonism that resembles the local culture assumes importance, and everything unusual fades into insignificance. The original and innovative, a great deal of what is most interesting, are obscured. . . .

[P]arts of early Mormonism did resemble aspects of the environment; other parts were alien and peculiar. In some passages the **Book of Mormon** and the **Book of Moses** appear to come from another world entirely. Single-minded attribution of these works to upstate New York culture blinds us to many of their most interesting qualities. We can understand Mormonism better if it is seen as an independent creation, drawing from its environment but also struggling against American culture in an effort to realize itself.

Joseph Smith astounded and offended the people of Palmyra. His achievements, even before he left New York, were hardly what they expected from the son of Lucy and Joseph Smith, Sr. When he was just twenty-four, he organized a church, published a large and complex book of sacred writings, and began to teach a Christian gospel familiar yet strange. All this is more than could be attributed to their own small-town rural culture. Mormonism appeared to be, as the scripture said, a stone cut out of the mountains without hands. . . .

Jan Shipps (essay date 1985)

SOURCE: A prologue to *Mormonism: The Story of a New Religious Tradition,* University of Illinois Press, 1985, pp. 1-23.

[*In the excerpt below, Shipps provides a comprehensive, chronological background of Joseph Smith's life prior to the publication of the* Book of Mormon. *Shipps maintains that examining the religious, psychic, social, and economical impact of the "Burnt-Over District" on the Smith family best contextualizes Mormonism's foundational claims and elucidates the integral relationship between magic and religious seership in Smith's early life.*]

Historical chronologies of Mormonism ordinarily open by identifying Joseph Smith as the Mormon prophet and describing the three foundational events that get the LDS story under way. Such accounts first cite Smith's reports of visions of heavenly beings manifested to him in the 1820s when he still lived with his parents on a farm in Palmyra, New York. Then they go on to tell about the coming forth of the **Book of Mormon,** a document said to have been miraculously translated from hieroglyphics engraved on golden plates whose location had been revealed to Smith by an angel. And they describe the formation, in 1830, of the religious institution that was the forerunner of both the Church of Jesus Christ of Latter-day Saints and the Reorganized Church of Jesus Christ of Latter Day Saints, plus a variety of sectarian forms of Mormonism. That this is no ordinary story is made clear, however, by the extraordinary (supernatural) character of two of these three occurrences that are said to have set it in motion.

That Mormon history is not ordinary history either is demonstrated in the multitude of historical accounts of the LDS movement that have been written across the last 150 years, accounts in which these foundational phenomena take on meanings that differ dramatically according to the context into which they are introduced. When the narrative backdrop describes a world wherein apostasy has reigned supreme for nearly 2,000 years, for example, Smith's visions, the appearance of the **Book of Mormon,** and the organization of the church present themselves as light breaking into darkness, light "poured upon the earth in a stream of effulgent glory." Yet these reported visions, the prophet's explanation of the origin of the **Book of Mormon,** and even the organization of the church appear as agents of darkness if they are placed in a post-Enlightenment setting in which humanity had been ushered into a new age, one that had renounced "superstition" and started to glorify self-evident "truth" based on observation and logic.

To be more precise, in the LDS histories adopted as authoritative by the Church of Jesus Christ of Latter-day Saints, the ancient Judeo-Christian past is set forth as the background of Mormonism. Brigham H. Roberts and Joseph Fielding Smith, who wrote the most important official accounts of the Mormon past, both begin the LDS story with the foundation of the world. Their timelines move forward through a series of "dispensations" from Adam to Noah, Noah to Abraham, Abraham to Moses, and Moses to John the Baptist. Then they describe a "dispensation of the meridian of time" marked by the ministry of Jesus of Nazareth. According to the writers of these priestly narratives— Roberts and Smith were both General Authorities of the LDS Church—this "meridian of time" dispensation turned the world into a new path, only to have that path blocked by a "Great Apostasy" which caused the removal of the ancient priesthoods and the true Church of Jesus Christ from the earth. They picture the world being plunged into darkness as a result, a darkness lasting for roughly 1,500 years. In their histories of the Latter-day Saints, this darkness sets the stage for the appearance of Mormonism. A new "dispensation of the fulness of times" opened with the coming forth of the **Book of Mormon** (which meant the reopening of the Judeo-Christian canon), the reintroduction of prophetic leadership for the people of God, the re-formation of the Church of Jesus Christ, the restoration of the priesthoods of Aaron and Melchizedek, and the gathering of the Saints.

This "light breaking into darkness" motif appears, in addition, in LDS histories, official and unofficial, that open with Joseph Smith's 1838 account of his early visions. In his report of the first of these—the one canonized as the First Vision—Smith said that while he was praying in a wood near his home on a spring morning in 1820, he felt himself surrounded with darkness so thick that "sudden destruction" seemed imminent. As the powers of darkness intensified, however, he "saw a pillar of light . . . above the brightness of the sun" which, when it rested on the fourteen-year-old lad, allowed him to see two "personages" who revealed themselves as "the Father and the Son." In this vision, Smith was told not to join any of the existing "sects, for they were all wrong." Consequently, said Smith, he refused to become a church member, explaining that in a vision he had been so commanded. This caused the future prophet to be enmeshed in enmity (darkness), "suffering severe persecution at the hands of all classes of men." Smith's report (as published in the **Pearl**

of Great Price, a work the Saints regard as scripture) continues with the description of a light illuminating his darkened bedroom on the night of 21/22 September 1823. Into this light, said Smith, came a personage whose name was Moroni and who, in three sequential visits, revealed that God had a work for the young man, now aged seventeen, to do. This work was the translation of the **Book of Mormon,** which, the LDS histories say, brought light to those who had been sitting in darkness for a very long time.

Early histories of Mormonism written by non-Mormons often worked out the opposing motif. Placing this same extraordinary story in the context of a world enlightened by science, the Protestant Reformation, and America's "lively experiment" with religion, the authors of such works described Smith's visions and his explanation of the **Book of Mormon's** source as the products of a diseased imagination, if not the elements of a gigantic fraud. Consequently Mormonism was pictured in such accounts as a mixture of superstition and subterfuge that conceals the light of truth. As such works of this sort said, it pandered to the superstitious, the gullible, and the fearful, at least in the beginning. The development of the Mormon movement was therefore described as a menace that would, if unopposed, reverse humanity's forward progress, turning the world backward to the "dark ages."

Books and articles about the Saints that were written in the nineteenth century by antagonistic Gentiles (i.e., persons who were not part of the Mormon community) rarely failed, at some point, to accuse Mormonism of "blinding" its adherents so effectively that when they heard Smith's report of his visions and his explanation of the origins of the **Book of Mormon,** they could not distinguish truth from falsehood. Furthermore, such works nearly always placed the organization of the church against a backdrop picturing the accelerating development of democracy in Jacksonian America. This setting makes the rigid ecclesiastical rankings that came to be a part of Mormonism appear to be the basis of a hierarchical social system, a system typically interpreted as a dark cloud threatening to put out the splendid light illuminating the American scene during the early republic's halcyon days.

This demonstration of what happens when identical accounts of the foundational events of Mormonism are set down within different contexts is presented here at the outset because the fact of the matter is that the "facts" of LDS history do not necessarily speak for themselves. It is as important to remember that the very same descriptions of the very same events can take on radically different meanings when they are placed in different settings as it is to keep in mind that "inside" and "outside" perceptions of what was happening differed at practically every point in LDS history.

While the occurrences here identified as foundational events were indeed the effective beginning of Mormonism, a proper prologue to a study of Mormonism does not open with the visions of the Mormon prophet, the coming forth of the *Book of Mormon,* and the organization of the church, but with the story of the life and hard times of Joseph Smith's family. Although he was the third son, rather than the eldest, the prophet was the namesake of Joseph Smith of Topsfield, who was born in 1771 in Essex County, Massachusetts. A New England farmer and sometime entrepreneur, Joseph Smith, Sr., came from a family whose members had resided in Essex County for four generations. In 1796 he married nineteen-year-old Lucy Mack, the daughter of Lydia and Solomon Mack of Cheshire County, New Hampshire, a family whose members had likewise resided in New England for several generations.

If this marriage did not unite two leading New England households, it nevertheless brought together two venerable families of the region. The groom's grandfather, Samuel Smith, had held responsible positions in Topsfield, serving multiple terms in the state legislature and as selectman and town clerk, in addition to serving as a militia captain in the American Revolution. His son Asael, Joseph's father, moved from Topsfield to Derryfield, New Hampshire, where he served several terms as town clerk. He, too, fought in the Revolution, settling afterward in Tunbridge, Vermont, where, at the time of his son's nuptial, he was a substantial landowner and respected community leader. The bride's paternal grandfather, Ebenezer Mack, had held "a large property and lived in good style" in Lyme, Connecticut, until he met financial problems severe enough to force him to apprentice his son Solomon to a neighboring farmer. This meant that Lucy's father had little or no schooling. Yet at one time or another in his adulthood Solomon held significant properties also, including farms in Lyme and Marlow, New Hampshire, and a schooner large enough to accommodate thirty passengers. While these were all lost by her father through accident or ill fortune, Lucy's brother Stephen succeeded at both farming and business, and at the time of his sister's wedding was a prominent citizen of Tunbridge.

During the first two decades of their marriage, nine children were born to the parents of the lad who would become the Mormon prophet. They were fortunate that only one of the nine, a son named Ephraim, failed to survive infancy. But they were not so fortunate in other ways. In those same twenty years the life of the family was so marked with wretched luck, bad health, and economic disaster that the Smiths were forced to move from place to place in Vermont and New Hampshire at least eight different times. Finally, in 1816, when Joseph Smith, Jr., was ten years old, the family joined the grand out-migration from New England across the Adirondacks to western New York that had started at the close of the American Revolution and continued as the construction of the Erie Canal acted as a magnet for settlement in that area.

Seeking a better means than they had yet found to secure a livelihood, Joseph Smith, Sr., his wife, Lucy, and their children stopped about twenty miles east of Rochester and rented a house in the village of Palmyra. They lived two years in town, working at whatever came to hand in order to survive and get together enough cash to make a down payment on a farm. Then, when they had accumulated enough capital, they arranged to buy a farm in nearby Manchester. As had happened to the family several times before, however, once again the members of the family made a valiant effort to move back into the ranks of property holders, only to be deceived by their creditors. They were never dispossessed from the holding which they had improved and on which they built a comfortable home, but neither were they ever able to obtain a title to the farm in Manchester that they believed was rightfully theirs.

Thus it was that the Mormon prophet grew up in a family that had lost status, one that, as the saying goes, had seen better days. His parents apparently worked very hard and they were persons of considerable learning (as is revealed by surviving holograph letters written by his mother and by the fact that his father knew enough to have been hired to teach school in Sharon, Vermont). But Joseph and Lucy were unable to prevent the drift that carried the Smith family away from the solid center of respectability toward the fringes of polite society. This was particularly the case after they left New England, since the family connections that had helped to preserve the respectability of their branch of the family were effectively abandoned when the prophet's parents decided to emigrate to western New York. There, as landless settlers, they were easily relegated to marginal status.

Although a different approach to religion might have helped the Smith family maintain its status in New England, the family was never a part of respectable, mainline Protestantism of the Presbyterian, Congregational, Baptist, or Methodist variety. Instead, the Smiths were a part of a heterogeneous assemblage of Christian "seekers" who were believers of a very special kind. Often intensely religious, in the sense of being pious and devout, the persons who fit securely in this category seem either to have had a history of having moved into and then back out of various evangelical denominations and groups organized on the basis of "no creed but the Bible," or else to have gone to the other extreme, refusing to affiliate with ecclesiastical organizations of either type. Although Christianity's apostolic period was the main source of their inspiration, many of these people were heirs to the early

American religious heritage of magical noninstitutionalized religious practices, practices that were described by Jon Butler in 1979 in an article in the *American Historical Review* and to which Marvin Hill referred in asserting that necromancy and religious faith were not incompatible in nineteenth-century America. As did the religious lives of many of their forebears, the religious lives of people like the Smith family held in suspension both a reliance on magic and the occult arts and a thoroughgoing acceptance of the truth of the claims set out in the Judeo-Christian scriptures. This made them receptive to ideas that existing churches would have defined as unorthodox; it made them seekers after truth wherever it might be found.

By crossing the Adirondacks, the Smith family entered into what, in the early nineteenth century, was an unrestricted arena as far as religion was concerned. In western New York the various Christian denominations contended openly for members. Revivals swept across the land with such regularity that it became known as the "burnt" district because the fires of religion had burned over it so many different times. The resulting emphasis on religion encouraged the development of a pattern of Bible study that made Christian primitivism flourish; it favored the creation of new religious movements that did not fit into the denominational framework; and it allowed Masonry (complete with mythological, doctrinal, ritual, and social dimensions that made it a proto-religious movement) to grow and prosper to such an extent that it generated an important anti-Masonry movement. Furthermore, conditions in this region produced an atmosphere of experimentation that made it likely that novel religious ideas—which would have been dismissed out of hand in more settled situations—would here receive serious consideration.

For many years now, serious students of Mormonism have recognized the importance to the story of Mormon beginnings of the situation in western New York during the future prophet's childhood and adolescence. In recounting what happened, however, scholars typically describe the Burned-over District primarily in terms of its impact on Joseph Smith, Jr. In so doing, they fail to represent fully the religious and psychic as well as social and economic impact that living in the district had on the Smith family, and how living in a family that was searching for truth wherever it might be found intensified the impact that the region's religious environment had on the future prophet.

During much of the decade of the 1820s, the Smith family was virtually a microcosm of the religious macrocosm in which it was immersed. The senior Joseph was a curious combination of deist and seeker. His father had given him a copy of Thomas Paine's *Age of Reason* that he seems to have read with great interest. Yet he was also influenced by dreams which—

according to his wife's history of the family—were filled with transparent symbols of an impending restoration of truth to the earth and which started him on a search for true religion outside the pathways of orthodoxy. Smith *père* held himself aloof from organized religion, as did his eldest son, Alvin, but Lucy Mack Smith and three of her children (the family's second and fourth sons, Hyrum and Samuel, and eldest daughter, Sophronia) joined the Presbyterian Church in Palmyra. This brought an intense biblicism directly into the family circle, and it made the family members aware of the various theological arguments concerning the degree of congenital depravity human beings are heir to, as well as introducing them to the struggle between enthusiasm and conservatism that marked the early nineteenth-century experience of this denomination. Hyrum joined the Masons, too, adding that element to the multiplicity of religious ideas presenting themselves for discussion within the Smith ménage. Moreover, magic and the occult were so fascinating to the prophet's father—and perhaps also to Alvin and other members of the family—that the more esoteric components of the western New York religio-cultural situation were additional ingredients in the immediate familial milieu in which Joseph Smith, Jr., grew to manhood.

If chronological accounts of Mormonism proceed directly from descriptions of the family's move from New England and characterizations of the region in which the Smiths settled to the young prophet's story, focus is not kept on the family unit long enough to describe young Joseph's experiences in the context of the religious ambience within the Smith family circle. Although the world, as represented in Joseph Smith's own history by a clergyman of a popular Christian denomination, scoffed, Joseph's family thought that unbelief closes the way to knowledge, and the teenager's accounts of his visions were, for that reason, apparently accepted without question. The Smiths welcomed Joseph's announcement that he had obtained a treasure trove that "contained the fulness of the everlasting Gospel"; they believed in him when he said that "a great and marvelous work [was] about to come forth unto the children of men"; and they strongly supported his efforts to make this work available to humanity in the latter days. Their immediately positive reactions to the surprising information imparted to them by one of their own number makes the Smith family's response to the prophet so critical to the LDS story that accounts of Mormon beginnings are incomplete when so much emphasis is placed on Joseph Smith, Jr., that his family recedes into the background.

Although he remembered having reported it at the time it occurred only to members of his own family and to one member of the clergy in Palmyra, fourteen-year-old Joseph Smith's "First Vision" is now widely regarded as the initial episode in Mormon history. Fixed in time and place in Smith's canonized account as having been manifested in a grove of trees on the family farm on the morning of a beautiful clear day in the spring of 1820, this theophany answered the lad's question about which of the "sects" were right and which were wrong. When the two personages appeared to him in that "pillar of light," they told him that he must not join any of the existing denominations for they were all wrong, an injunction that kept him from becoming a Presbyterian and, as it turned out, moved him closer to the position on religion taken by his father.

When he wrote his history for posterity the Mormon prophet summarized the events of his life during the decade of the 1820s. He pursued his "common vocations in life," he said, even though he was "persecuted" because he insisted that a vision had been manifested to him in what is now called the "sacred grove." Yet Smith said he beheld a second vision during the night of 21/22 September 1823. This time it was a vision of an angel who identified himself as Moroni, "a messenger sent from the presence of God" to tell of records written on gold plates which, along with two special stones called the Urim and Thummim, were buried in a hill not far from the Smith family farm. From Moroni the young man learned that "the possession and use of these stones were what constituted 'seers' in ancient or former times, and that God had prepared them for the purpose of translating the book" that was engraved in "Reformed Egyptian" characters on the gold plates.

As often as the stories of Joseph Smith's visions are repeated, it is surprising that very little emphasis is placed on Smith's description of how he was affected by these two experiences in which he received his divine calling. At the conclusion of his description of the 1820 experience, Joseph said, "When I came to myself again, I found myself lying on my back looking up to heaven . . . I had no strength." Then, recalling the aftermath of the night of 21/22 September 1823 in which his interviews with the angel Moroni "must have occupied the whole of that night," Joseph said his strength was so exhausted that when he tried to work alongside his father as usual he found he could not. Leaving his father's side, he started back to the house, only to fall "helpless to the ground, and for a time [to be] quite unconscious of anything." It stands to reason that it was the phenomenon of visionary trance to which Smith referred, and if this is, in fact, correct, then these trances, coming in response to divine calling, parallel a similar trance in which Saul became Paul on the road to Damascus. Possibly they also parallel instances of "possession trance" that legitimated prophetic figures in pre-exilic Israel.

When he was told of the existence of the gold plates and the Urim and Thummim in the 1823 vision, Joseph Smith was also told by the angel Moroni that he

had been called to the task of translating the engravings on the plates with the aid of the "ancient seers." This was an unusual assignment, but it does not appear quite so strange when it is placed in historical context. Smith's "First Vision" caused him to stay away from the orthodox Christianity of his day. As he worked alongside his elder brothers and his father—who was particularly predisposed toward the miraculous and willing to search for truth in unorthodox places—the lad came into contact with the folk magic that was very much present in his region of the country. Prior to his having reported the vision in which he learned about the existence of a record graven on plates of gold, Joseph had found a "seerstone," a smooth stone "the size but not the shape of a hen's egg," whose magical properties reputedly made possible the location of lost objects and metals hidden beneath the surface of the earth. His possession of this occult article, which he found while helping his brother Alvin dig a well for one Willard Chase, allowed the Smith family to take up what was known in those days as "money-digging."

Because Smith's efforts to find ordinary buried treasure were gradually transformed into a search for treasure of infinitely greater value, he later dismissed his youthful treasure-hunting activities as trivial and unimportant, but they were recalled in later years by neighbors of the Smith family, who connected them to Joseph's claim of having found plates of gold. In one of the many affidavits about the Smith family during the 1820s that Philastus Hurlbut collected in 1833 for publication in *Mormonism Unvailed [sic]*, Willard Chase claimed that the prophet told him "that if it had not been for that [seer]stone . . . he would not have found the book." Lucy Harris, the daughter of one of the prophet's very first followers, suggested that Martin Harris also believed that Smith's gold treasure had been located with the stone, in which Joseph could see "anything he wished." This same belief was later held by some of Smith's followers, for Hosea Stout wrote in his diary in 1856 that Brigham Young "exhibited the Seer's stone with which The Prophet Joseph discovered the plates of the ***Book of Mormon***."

If such evidence does not establish a *direct* connection between the prophet's having possessed a seerstone and his having gained possession of a treasure whose secret had to be unlocked with "stones [that] were what constituted 'seers' in ancient or former times," chronology establishes an *implicit* connection. Joseph's 1820 vision was followed in 1822 by his finding a seerstone. In 1823, he reported to his mother and father that he had learned of the existence of a cache of gold plates, but he said he was unable to gain possession of them until 1827. He was, nevertheless, permitted (or required) to make annual visits in September 1824, 1825, and 1826 to see the plates in the place where they were buried and to talk with the angel Moroni.

During those same four years, the Joseph Smiths, father and son, were very much engaged in the hunting of treasure, and in one instance in 1826, their failure to find any led to a trial in Bainbridge, New York, in which the younger of the two was charged with being a disorderly person, a "glass looker," and/or an impostor. Then, in September 1827, Joseph Smith, Jr., said that he had gained possession of the gold plates and the Urim and Thummim, an instrument that apparently functioned in the manner of a seerstone, revealing a longlost story to the young prophet.

According to his mother's reminiscences, Joseph had told his family about the plates and described the importance of their contents to them long before he actually obtained the treasure. Joseph's story may have amazed his parents and siblings, yet any questions they had were obviously answered within the family circle, for the response of the family to the announcement that one of their own had been selected to translate a mysterious record that would be their means of salvation shows a family united in the belief that "a marvelous work and a wonder" was about to come forth. Members of the family who had joined the Palmyra Presbyterians stopped attending the services of that church as their expectations about the impending restoration of the apostolic form of Christianity took hold in their religious imaginations. And all the family members extended such assistance as they could manage to further the work of the one of their number through whom they believed God had started to speak anew to their generation.

In January 1827, some eight months before he reported that the plates were in his possession, Joseph married Emma Hale of Harmony, Pennsylvania, and brought her back to live with him on the Smith family farm in Manchester. Emma was the daughter of Isaac Hale, a man who had formed his opinion of Joseph when the Smiths were engaged in the search for treasure that had led to the Bainbridge court trial. He very much disapproved of Joseph's money-digging activities and he very much disapproved of the match. Yet his daughter seems also to have accepted her new husband's calling without question, and, as did his family of lineage, she seems to have supported him in his efforts to accomplish what he told her he had been called to do. As the story goes, Emma went along when Joseph took a horse and wagon borrowed without permission from Joseph Knight, Sr., to fetch the Urim and Thummim and the gold plates. Moreover, when the news that he possessed the plates had stimulated so many attempts to get them away from Joseph that he decided he would have to leave Manchester and go elsewhere to prepare the translation of the record, Emma braved her father's disapproval by traveling with her husband back to Harmony, Pennsylvania, where his work of translation might proceed without impediment.

The members of Joseph's own family and his wife were not the only persons who were involved with him in preparing the **Book of Mormon** for presentation to the world. Other active participants in the work that went forward between fall 1827, when Joseph said the plates and the ancient seers were entrusted to him, and spring 1830, when the **Book of Mormon** was published, were Martin Harris, a prosperous farmer from the Palmyra region; Joseph Knight, Sr., a friend of the Smith family whose home was in Colesville, New York; Oliver Cowdery, a young schoolteacher who came to board with the Smiths in Manchester after Emma and Joseph left for Pennsylvania; and various members of the family of Peter and Mary Whitmer, who lived in Fayette, in Seneca County, New York. These were all persons who not only came to believe that Joseph had gold plates, but also to accept his claim that the plates were actually a book whose text contained the fulness of the gospel that would lead to salvation. For that reason, it is not surprising that they brought provisions or money, or provided free room and board, so that Joseph could work at translating, rather than at plowing fields and harvesting crops, nor that they were willing to do much more.

Despite extant reminiscences of several of the persons involved, an air of mystery surrounds what went on as the **Book of Mormon** and Mormonism itself came into being. It is clear, however, that Harmony, in the Susquehanna country in northern Pennsylvania, was the central locale of action between December 1827 and June 1829. In the latter summer, Joseph and Emma moved north to Fayette, New York, where they boarded with the Whitmer family until the translation of the book was completed at some point early in 1830. Oliver Cowdery, who served as Smith's chief scribe from 7 April 1829 forward, boarded there as well. Other persons who had started to follow Joseph also made their way to Fayette. In addition, the parents of Joseph Smith and one or another of his siblings occasionally visited from Manchester, keeping the family in close touch with the progress of the translation of the record.

The seer-stone used by Joseph Smith.

A number of references to the gold plates are found in the historical record—Joseph said that they were carried south hidden in a forty-gallon barrel of beans, for example, and Lucy Smith remembered later that they were sometimes kept in a red morocco trunk on Emma's bureau—but, despite a great deal of somewhat naive speculation, the importance of the plates to the process of translation has never been established. The ancient seers and/or Joseph's seerstone seem, rather, to have been the key to the procedure by which the *Book of Mormon* came into existence. "Through the medium of the Urim and Thummim, I translated the record by the gift and power of God," said Joseph Smith in an 1842 statement that is consistent with descriptions of his having dictated the text of the *Book of Mormon* to various scribes as he sat with his face buried in his hat, wherein he had placed a seerstone. Emma Smith and Oliver Cowdery both recalled that this was the way Joseph worked, adding that he could work that way for hours on end. Joseph never indicated when, or if, he had to consult the "Reformed Egyptian" hieroglyphics that were said to have been engraved on the gold plates that he said he had, but invaluable evidence survives to explain exactly how the gift of translation worked.

The exhilaration that Oliver Cowdery felt in the spring of 1829 as he recorded the words that were spoken by Joseph led him to petition for a similar gift of translation. God responded, said Joseph Smith, with a revelation to Cowdery promising that he would "receive a knowledge concerning the engravings of old records" through a manifestation of the Holy Ghost "which shall come upon you and which shall dwell in your heart." Although this revelation made it clear that this manifestation of knowledge "in your mind and in your heart" was to be his gift, Cowdery apparently tried his hand at translating in the manner of Joseph Smith. His lack of success led to a second revelation, also given through Joseph Smith, in which God clarified the translation process:

> Behold you have not understood, you have supposed that I would give it [the gift of translation] unto you when you took no thought, save it was to ask me; but behold I say unto you that you must study it out in your mind; then you must ask me if it be right, and if it is right, I will cause that your bosom shall burn within you: therefore, you shall feel that it is right; but if it be not right, you shall have no such feelings, but you shall have a stupor of thought that shall cause you to forget the thing which is wrong: therefore, you cannot write that which is sacred, save it be given you from me.

Although the hieroglyphics may not have been necessary to the translation procedure, they were very important in an episode involving Martin Harris and two eminent scholars in which the divine origin of the gold plates and the ancient record was verified for Joseph.

Harris was the prosperous yet credulous Palmyra farmer who extended the financial support that allowed Joseph and Emma to leave Manchester in 1827, and he soon followed them to Harmony, where he became Joseph's scribe. In 1828, in response to a vision that he had had, in which he was commanded to show a document containing "characters which [Joseph] had drawn off the plates" to knowledgeable scholars, Harris traveled to the East to show such a document to Professor Samuel L. Mitchill of Rutgers and Professor Charles Anthon of Columbia College. Because the report Harris brought back focused attention on the scholars and not on what they had said, the significance of this episode was overlooked for many years. Mitchill said that he could not read the document, while Anthon—having asked to see the plates themselves rather than the incomplete copy, and having learned that this would be impossible—told Harris that he could not read a "sealed book."

These results no doubt disappointed Harris, but the scholars' inability to read what he said he had copied from the plates did not disappoint Joseph Smith. Quite the reverse. In his thinking, as revealed in a note in his own hand written on the back of the sheet containing the characters, the statements of Mitchill and Anthon were convincing evidence that the record engraved on the plates was, in fact, the sealed book that the learned could not read, the book "delivered to him that is not learned," which preceded "a marvelous work and a wonder" that God would inaugurate, according to prophecy recorded in Isaiah 29, on the day when the book comes forth. Then, the Old Testament prophet had said, the deaf shall "hear the words of the book, and the eyes of the blind shall see out of obscurity, and out of darkness, the meek also shall increase their joy in the Lord, and the poor among men shall rejoice in the Holy One of Israel."

Martin Harris somewhat inadvertently played an even more crucial role in bringing Mormonism into being when he persuaded Joseph to let him take the first 116 pages of the text of the *Book of Mormon* from Pennsylvania back to Palmyra to show his wife and family. Harris had been investing his time and his substance in support of Joseph Smith's work. His motivation in asking for this privilege was probably his desire to prove to his family that the work was "of God." This Joseph Smith no doubt realized. Possibly he even anticipated needing to call on Harris's financial resources so that the *Book of Mormon* could be published. Yet Joseph was exceedingly reluctant to disregard the charge he had received to be personally responsible for the plates (and, by extension, the text of the record) until they should be returned to the heavenly messenger from whom they had been given into his hand. If he let the plates (or the text) go carelessly or through any neglect of his own, Joseph feared being "cut off"; the Urim and Thummim and the plates might be taken from him, and he would be powerless to fulfill his calling.

When Harris continued to importune for permission to show the foolscap pages to his wife, who was suspicious of the Smith family and unsympathetic to the work at hand, Joseph decided, however, that it would be best to "inquire of the Lord through the Urim and Thummim if he might not do so." Joseph first received a negative answer, but Harris was so adamant about needing to convince his wife that the work in which he was engaged was divinely mandated that Joseph kept reiterating his inquiry through the Urim and Thummim until he became convinced that he had permission to let Harris take the writing home. He required the scribe to promise to show the text to members of his immediate family and to no one else, however. This Harris did, solemnly convenanting with Joseph to abide by these conditions, and in early June 1828, he left for Palmyra carrying with him the only existing copy of the first 116 pages of the text of the *Book of Mormon.*

A tragic conclusion to Emma's first pregnancy (in which she had a long and very hard labor, only to give birth to a baby that lived less than a day) initially kept Joseph's mind off the fact that he had allowed the *Book of Mormon* text to leave his hands. For two weeks he thought of little else than the death of the child and the dreadful illness of his wife. But as Emma regained her health, Joseph started to worry about what he had agreed to and the fact that he had not heard from Martin Harris in nearly a month.

Therefore, as soon as he felt it safe to leave Emma in her mother's care, he started for the Palmyra area to retrieve the manuscript. But soon after he reached the Smith farm in Manchester, Joseph learned, to his great dismay, that the 116 pages had disappeared and that Harris, who had broken his covenant, showing the pages to many persons, had absolutely no idea what had happened to them. This knowledge almost drove Joseph to despair, for he believed that all was lost. "He wept and groaned and walked the floor continually," his mother said, and "all the family [was] in the same situation of mind . . . for sobs and groans and the most bitter lamentations filled the house." The expectations of Joseph and his family that had been "so fondly anticipated . . . the source of so much secret gratification had in a moment fled."

A close reading of Joseph Smith's own history, the revelations dated 1828 and early 1829, especially as printed in the Book of Commandments, and Lucy Mack Smith's history of her son reveal how vitally important to the development of Joseph Smith's religious career was the loss of the forepart of the *Book of Mormon* manuscript and Smith's reaction to the loss. Worried beyond all consolation, the future prophet immediately returned to Pennsylvania. The trip gave him plenty of

time for reflection. He must have thought about how he had ignored the negative answers he received when he initially inquired through the Urim and Thummim whether he should let Martin Harris take the manuscript home to show his wife and family, for as soon as he reached home, "he commenced humbling [himself] before the Lord," pouring out his soul in supplication that he might "be forgiven of all that [he] had done contrary to [the Lord's] will."

Joseph later told his mother how contrite he had been, adding that an angel came as he was praying and took both the plates and the Urim and Thummim from him. The angel had informed him, however, that if he would be "humble and penitent" it was possible that these things could be returned to him. "Repent of that which thou has done which is contrary to the commandment which I [the Lord] gave you," Joseph said he was told, for "thou art still chosen and art again called to the work."

The authors of most historical accounts move from a description of the loss of the 116 pages of manuscript directly to what many call the "convenient" revelation, in which Joseph was told not to retranslate the story from the same plates he had used before, but to translate the story as it was recorded on "the plates of Nephi." Then authors go on to describe the subsequent completion of the text of the *Book of Mormon*. In so doing, they fail to recognize the significance of the period between late summer 1828 and early spring 1829 as a time when Joseph Smith seems to have come to terms with his calling.

The connection (or lack thereof) between ordinary magic and the working of the divine hand was not clarified in the earliest days of Mormonism. The *Book of Mormon* and Smith's religious claims were rejected by many of the persons who had known him in the 1820s because they remembered him as a practitioner of the magic arts. Yet if Martin Harris, Oliver Cowdery, and Smith's own father may be taken as typical, some of Joseph's earliest followers accepted his book and his claims for precisely the same reason. The retrospective account of his life that Smith wrote in 1838, from the standpoint of having successfully established himself as a prophet, fails to mention any questions Joseph entertained regarding this issue. Yet it stands to reason that Smith, too, might sometimes have wondered about the nature of the connection between magical practice and manifestations of divinity despite his convictions about the reality of his visions and the assurances his father gave him that they were "of God."

If the episode in the early spring of 1828, when Harris carried the document on which the characters had been copied to show them to the scholars, helped Joseph to see what he was doing in the context of Isaiah 29, as the notation on the back of the document indicates that it did, the loss of the manuscript pages that summer and the period of deep reflection that followed allowed Joseph to resolve any remaining doubts as he came to a full comprehension of the nature of his gift. While he said that the plates and the ancient seers were returned to him on 22 September 1828 (exactly one year from the day on which he had first reported that they were in his possession), Joseph did not immediately begin translating, even though he had received the revelation in July that had solved the worrisome problem that might have arisen if a second translation had been compared with the one that had been lost. He could have set to work immediately with his wife serving as scribe, but he went, rather, "to laboring with his hands upon a small farm" that summer, an occupation that encouraged contemplative thought and led him to a clearer understanding of what lay ahead.

From the standpoint of theology, comparison of this period of bucolic introspection in Joseph Smith's life and the forty days that Jesus spent in the wilderness would be improper. From a structural perspective, however, when the goal is determining developmental patterns in religious leadership, these two periods of retrospection are reasonably parallel. Forward progress on the translation stopped to allow Smith this period of spiritual preparation. As did the wilderness period in the life of Jesus, this period immediately preceded the inauguration of Smith's public ministry.

By February 1829, when Joseph Smith, Sr., and Lucy arrived to visit Joseph and Emma and, incidentally, to learn what was going on, Joseph had become fully aware of what he had to do. This is clear because he started translating again, and because a revelation to his father, probably given through the Urim and Thummim, announced triumphantly that "a marvelous work [was] about to come forth among the children of men." This revelation called the senior Joseph into the service of God. "For behold the field is white already to harvest: and lo, he that thrusteth in his sickle with his might, the same layeth up in store that he perisheth not, but bringeth salvation to the soul."

While the time for the work to begin had clearly come, the plan of procedure was not spelled out until a revelation a month later directed Joseph to finish translating the record before taking on other tasks. ("For I [God] will grant unto you no other gift until my purpose is fulfilled in this, for I will grant unto you no other gift until it is finished.") Thereafter, the revelation said, Joseph would be ordained and would go forth to deliver God's words "unto the children of men," for "this generation shall have [God's] word through you." That is, upon completion of the record, Joseph would be called upon to carry out the prophet's task, meaning that he would—as prophets have done down through the ages—speak for God. In addition, three witnesses would be called and ordained, unto whom God would

"show these things and they shall go forth" with God's word as given through Joseph Smith. "And behold, whosoever believeth in [God's] word will [he] visit with the manifestations of [his] spirit, and they shall be born of [God] and their testimony shall go forth. And thus if the people . . . harden not their hearts," God promised to work a reformation among them and establish his church among them, "like unto the church which was taught by [his] disciples in the days of old." But if hearts were hardened against the word, as spoken by Joseph and the witnesses, if people failed to repent and believe, "they would be delivered up unto satan," or, as a later edition of the revelation stated, "consumed away and utterly destroyed by the brightness" of the Lord's return to the earth.

Interspersed among the various parts of the programme in this extraordinarily important revelation (section 5 in the Doctrine and Covenants of both the LDS and RLDS churches) are warnings to Joseph "to repent and walk more uprightly before [the Lord] and to yield to the persuasions of men no more." Perhaps of greater moment, the revelation included warnings about what Joseph must say to Martin Harris. This man had been impressed by Joseph's supernatural abilities as early as 1824 and, for all practical purposes, had been Joseph's patron even before he gained possession of the plates. Yet he had to be told, the revelation said, that Joseph had entered into a covenant with God not to show the things he had been given to any person save those to whom God commanded that they be shown. Harris, who wished to be one of the witnesses, would not be allowed to view the plates unless he humbled himself and agreed that he would say, "Behold I have seen the things and I know of a surety that they are true, for I have seen them, and they have been shown unto me by the power of God and not of man." The revelation continued, "And I [the Lord] command him that he shall say no more unto [people] concerning these things, except he shall say, I have seen them and they have been shown unto me by the power of God. And these are the words which he shall say. But if he deny this . . . behold he is condemned."

Coming as it did, at the end of his period of reflection, this revelation cleared away what might be described as the debris from the Mormon prophet's early career. It dealt with a problem (i.e., Martin Harris) that, in the words of the revelation, was "lying in wait to destroy [Joseph]" even as it reminded him of the significance to his generation of the contents of the record he was translating. This revelation also allowed Joseph to look forward to fulfilling a calling as a prophet who would speak for God, to anticipate the church being established as in apostolic days, and to expect, in the end, "the brightness of the Lord."

During the eighteen months between the end of September 1827 and the end of March 1829, the nature of his calling was clarified and the character of the record that he said he had found was verified for Joseph Smith. Yet other than the section that was lost, not much appears to have actually been done on the translation of the ***Book of Mormon***. After 7 April 1829, however, the work progressed with amazing rapidity. The change in the pace of activity was not entirely due to the fact that Smith's time of seclusion and reflection were at an end, for Oliver Cowdery's assumption of the scribal task seems to have been the catalyst that inaugurated such an astonishing acceleration in the work that the entire book, which would run to nearly 600 pages, was ready to go to the printer early in 1830.

Cowdery, who may have been a distant relative of Joseph Smith through Joseph's grandfather, Solomon Mack, had heard about the plates and the ancient seers from Joseph, Sr., and Lucy Mack Smith. He found the story fascinating enough to go to Pennsylvania to investigate, possibly because he had had some success using a divining rod and was, thus, interested in the folk magic that was so popular in that time and place. Since he arrived on 5 April and started to act as Smith's scribe two days later, it is obvious that he was quickly convinced of the worth of what Joseph was doing and, incidentally, that 6 April was an important day for the LDS movement in 1829, as well as in 1830.

As their dating gives only the month (April 1829) in which three revelations were manifested to Cowdery through Joseph Smith, no determination can be made of the relative importance in Cowdery's decision to join in the work of translation, on the one hand, and Smith's own account of the significance of the project, on the other. Perhaps it was somewhat difficult for Cowdery to distinguish between Joseph as revelator and Joseph as persuasive rhetorician. Yet the revelations surely carry great weight in explaining the intensity of Cowdery's labors across the twelve months between 7 April 1829 and 6 April 1830, the period between the beginning of his assumption of the scribal task and the formal organization of the Church of Jesus Christ. Although one of these communications from the divine was disappointing in its directions to Cowdery to simply serve as Smith's amanuensis rather than translate from the record himself, the others assured Cowdery that he was called to assist in bringing forth a great and marvelous work; that the words he was writing were true; that he and Joseph Smith together held the keys to the ancient scriptures that had been hidden away for nearly 2,000 years; and, in the earliest printings, the revelations also told Cowdery that his work with the divining rod was "of God," a gift that was not unrelated to the work he was currently carrying out.

But while these revelations set what Cowdery and Smith were doing apart from the ordinary business of life, revelation was not required to alert the two men to the momentous nature of their activity. The excitement of discovering a "new witness of Christ" in the words of the story that fell from Smith's lips made the two willing to work at a feverish pace for long hours every day. In addition, as the translation proceeded, exhilarating vistas were opened to them: the announcement of the coming forth of a prophet, whose name, like that of his father, would be Joseph, may have been more or less routine, given the role of Joseph Smith, Jr., in the translation process, but the prospect of the restoration of the priesthoods of Aaron and Melchizedek and the forming again of the church of the lamb of God, as it had existed in apostolic times, raised the expectations of Smith and Cowdery to dizzying heights. In the long run, it is significant that a revelation came to Smith and Cowdery to settle the issue of whether John, the beloved disciple, had "tarried in the flesh or had died," for it foreshadowed revelation's future function in articulating doctrine and settling doctrinal issues. Yet such revelation was not needed in the spring of 1829 to signify to Smith and Cowdery the impending opening of a new dispensation of the fulness of times.

As often happens when the spirit makes itself known to one portion of humanity, the excitement that infected the lives of Joseph and Oliver Cowdery soon became epidemic, and in the remainder of Smith's "little flock" revelation was very much a part of the story. Expectations mounted as revelation was manifested, either through the Urim and Thummim or simply through Joseph Smith himself, informing the various members of the Smith and Whitmer families that a marvelous work and a wonder was about to come forth, that the field was white to the harvest, and that humanity was called to repentance as a necessary prelude to accepting the religious and secular implications of the story contained in Smith's "golden bible."

Several persons, including Joseph Smith's brother Hyrum, were called to preach repentance to their generation. But for the nonce that was all that could be preached, since the church was not yet organized and doctrinal questions were not settled. Before that would happen, the text of the ***Book of Mormon*** had to be completed; its legitimacy as a translation of the engravings on golden plates had to be established through the testimony of witnesses; and the theological ground had to be prepared for the organization of the church.

All three requirements were fulfilled virtually simultaneously. During the summer of 1829, as Emma and Joseph Smith and Oliver Cowdery boarded at the home of Peter and Mary Whitmer, Smith and Cowdery worked tirelessly at the translation. That summer, also, two sets of witnesses were called to see the plates. A trio composed of Cowdery, Martin Harris, and David Whitmer testified in the words of a formula specified in a revelation to Joseph Smith that they had been shown the plates by the power of God and not of man. And a second set of witnesses—eight in number, including five members of the Whitmer family plus Joseph Smith's father and his brothers Hyrum and Samuel—declared in a more prosaic, but no less sincere, fashion that they had "seen and hefted" the plates.

On 15 May 1829 a revelation was manifested to Smith and Cowdery in which the priesthood of Aaron (the Levitical priesthood) was restored to the earth, making baptism under a new and everlasting covenant possible. That was the same month in which Hyrum Smith was called to preach. And soon thereafter Oliver Cowdery and David Whitmer were called into the ministry and assigned to search out and identify potential apostles.

All this made possible the organization of the church. But that formal action did not take place until the publication of the book containing "all those parts of [God's] gospel which [his] disciples desired in their prayers should come forth" had been announced. . . . Then the Mormon movement could begin.

Richard S. Van Wagoner (essay date 1986)

SOURCE: "The *Restoration of all Things*," in his *Mormon Polygamy: A History,* second edition, Signature Books, 1989, pp. 1-16.

[*In the following excerpt, first published in 1986, Van Wagoner describes the philosophical and theological influences on Joseph Smith's attempt at creating a Mormon utopia in the United States.*]

Joseph Smith, Jr., the charismatic founder of Mormonism, emerged from the ferment of Jacksonian America during a time when religion was regaining its hold over American life, when abolitionist groups, temperance movements, and benevolent societies were thriving. Utopian experiments testified to the exuberance of a nation advancing from infancy to childhood. Innocent vitality, limitless resources, a booming economy, and westward expansion nurtured a profound belief in America as a land of new hope, a light to the world.

Into this light came Joseph Smith, the twenty-four-year-old New York farmer who founded a religion based on his translation of a set of gold plates delivered by an angel. The *Book of Mormon,* a record of God's dealings with the pre-Columbian ancestors of the American Indian, not only explained the Hebrew origins of the Indian but established America as a chosen land destined to receive the fullness of the everlasting gospel. Written in King James English, Smith's translation sounded biblical, but its location and conceptual framework were American. The *Book of Mormon* gave American a sacred past and a millen-

nial future. It became the keystone of a new American religion.

God could not have chosen a better place, a better time, or a better people than early nineteenth-century Americans for the "restoration of all things." After a decade of religious revivalism, the blossoming economy of the 1830s had ripened millennial expectations. Word of angelic visitations was greeted enthusiastically. The heavens were being rolled back. Old men were dreaming dreams and young men prophesying. Women were speaking in tongues and children conversing with angels. New faiths mushroomed.

Western New York, where Joseph Smith grew up, was so frequently swept by the fires of religious enthusiasm that it came to be known as the "burned-over district." It was in this milieu that Smith organized the Church of Christ on 6 April 1830, later renamed the Church of Jesus Christ of Latter-day Saints. Like other dynamic movements of the day, the foundling church was influenced not only by restoration Protestant sectarianism but by flourishing contemporary social experiments. Smith's ability to blend current ideas with his own visionary experiences is evident in the growth of his communal vision. His earliest exposure to utopian thought and practices may have stemmed from a religious sect called the Believers in Christ's Second Appearing. Popularly known as Shakers, the group established a community a few miles from Smith's birthplace in Vermont. Mother Ann Lee's celibate society was one of the first communitarian organizations of this kind in the United States.

Joseph Smith was probably also familiar with the Harmonists, who claimed that George Rapp, a Lutheran minister and social reformer, was responding to a vision from the angel Gabriel when in 1804 he brought his followers from Germany to Harmony, Pennsylvania, twenty-five miles north of Pittsburg. The Harmonists, who migrated to Indiana to found New Harmony in 1815 before returning to Ambridge, Pennsylvania, in 1825, experimented, like the Shakers, with shared property and celibacy.

Robert Owen, a wealthy Scottish reformer and industrialist, may have also indirectly shaped Joseph Smith's utopian ideas through one of his most influential American followers. Arriving in the United States in the mid-1820s, Owen promised a "new Eden in the far west" and began establishing communities based on common ownership and equality of work and profit. After purchasing New Harmony from the Harmonists in 1825, he established several other communitarian societies in Ohio, at Kendal and Yellow Springs. Sidney Rigdon, a prominent Protestant minister in the Western Reserve area of Ohio and a follower of Alexander Campbell's Disciples of Christ, attended a debate between Owen and Campbell in 1829. Taken with

Owen's system of "family commonwealths," he tried to implement such a communal order within the Disciples of Christ. Campbell's objections caused Rigdon to leave the Disciples and, with other dissenters, to set up "common-stock" societies at Mentor and Kirtland, Ohio. By the fall of 1830 Rigdon and more than one hundred members of "the family," as they were known, had converted to Mormonism, which, by then, numbered nearly one thousand.

After arriving in Ohio from New York in February 1831, Joseph Smith convinced Rigdon's communal group to abandon the common-stock principle in favor of the "more perfect law of the Lord." On 9 February 1831 Smith announced God's "Law of Consecration and Stewardship." Members were advised that "all things belong to the Lord" and were directed to deed all personal property to the bishop of the church. The bishop then returned a "stewardship" to each head of a household, who was expected to turn over any accrued surplus to the church. Known as the "Order of Enoch," "the Lord's Law," and the "United Order," the Mormon principle of stewardship was intended as a pattern of social and economic reorganization for all mankind. The dream was to unify "a people fragmented by their individualistic search for economic well-being." The Saints, as a group, divested of personal selfishness and greed, were to be prepared by this communal discipline to usher in the millennial reign of Jesus Christ.

Smith's ideas derived much from the New Testament Christian Primitivism of the day. But the deeper roots of his theology lay in his interpretation of the Old Testament. His concept of the Kingdom of God paralleled Israelite theocracy. The idea of a temple, as well as accompanying ordinances of washings, anointings, and covenants, was central to Hebrew worship. Smith's theology of marriage and family too may have drawn on ancient Israelite traditions. Like the biblical patriarchs of old, Mormon males empowered with priesthood were entitled to receive divine guidance in family matters. Women, on the other hand, were denied both priesthood and hierarchic position. This Old Testament focus evidently also drew Smith to the idea of biblical polygamy as part of the "restitution of all things." According to a close friend, Joseph B. Noble, Smith became convinced of the theological necessity of polygamy "while he was engaged in the work of translation of the Scriptures", evidently a reference to Smith's and Rigdon's early 1830 revision of the Bible published later as *The Inspired Version.*

Though polygamy is strongly denounced in several Book of Mormon passages (Jac. 1:15; 2:23-27; 3:5; Mos. 11:2-4, 14; Eth. 10:5), a reading of the Old Testament provides ample evidence that it was acceptable in ancient Israel. Abraham was not the only husband of multiple wives. Jacob had two wives and two concubines (Gen. 29-30); Elkanah had two wives (1 Sam. 1:2); Rehoboam had eighteen wives and sixty concubines (2 Chron. 11:21); Abijah married fourteen women (2 Chron. 13:21); David had a large harem (1 Chron. 14:3); and Solomon managed seven hundred wives and more than three hundred concubines (1 Kings 11:3).

It is difficult to determine exactly when Joseph Smith first felt compelled to practice polygamy. W. W. Phelps recollected three decades after the fact in an 1861 letter to Brigham Young that on 17 July 1831, when he and five others had gathered in Jackson County, Missouri, Smith stated: "It is my will, that in time, ye should take unto you wives of the Lamanites and Nephites [Indians], that their posterity may become white, delightsome and just." Phelps added in a postscript that "about three years after this was given, I asked brother Joseph, privately, how 'we,' that were mentioned in the revelation could take wives of the 'natives' as we were all married men?" He claimed that Smith replied, "In the same manner that Abraham took Hagar and Keturah; and Jacob took Rachel, Bilhah and Zilpha, by *Revelation.*"

In 1869 Mormon apostle Orson Pratt added another perspective, remembering that in early 1832 "Joseph told individuals, then in the Church, that he had inquired of the Lord concerning the principle of plurality of wives, and he received for answer that the principle of taking more wives than one is a true principle, but the time had not yet come for it to be practiced". Polygamy would not be a public practice of Mormonism until 1852, eight years after Smith's death. Smith never publicly advocated polygamy. New Testament monogamy, the official church position throughout his lifetime, was clearly outlined in Smith's 1831 revelations: "Thou shalt love thy wife with all thy heart, and shall cleave unto her and none else"; "It is lawful that [a man] should have one wife, and they twain shall be one flesh".

But from the early days of the church rumors hinted that Smith maintained a private position different from his public posture. His abrupt 1830 departure with his wife, Emma, from Harmony, Pennsylvania, may have been precipitated in part by Levi and Hiel Lewis's accusations that Smith had acted improperly towards a local girl. Five years later Levi Lewis, Emma's cousin, repeated stories that Smith attempted to "seduce Eliza Winters &c.," and that both Smith and his friend Martin Harris had claimed "adultery was no crime" (*Susquehanna Register,* 1 May 1834, reprinted in Howe 1834, 268; see also Newell and Avery 1984, 64). Similar allegations in Hiram, Ohio, reportedly caused problems for Smith in 1832. One account related that on 24 March a mob of men pulled Smith from his bed, beat him, and then covered him with a coat of tar and feathers. Eli Johnson, who allegedly participated in the attack "because he suspected Joseph of being intimate with his sister, Nancy Marinda Johnson, . . . was screaming for Joseph's castration".

Rumors about Smith multiplied. Benjamin F. Winchester, Smith's close friend and leader of Philadelphia Mormons in the early 1840s, later recalled Kirtland accusations of scandal and "licentious conduct" hurled against Smith, "this more especially among the women. Joseph's name was connected with scandalous relations with two or three families".

One of the women whose name was linked to Smith in Kirtland was Vienna Jacques. A second-hand story remembered many years after the event by a "Mrs. Alexander" contended that Polly Beswick, a colorful two-hundred-pound Smith domestic, told her friends that "Jo Smith said he had a revelation to lie with Vienna Jacques, who lived in his family" and that Emma Smith told her "Joseph would get up in the night and go to Vienna's bed." Furthermore, she added, "Emma would get out of humor, fret and scold and flounce in the harness," then Smith would "shut himself up in a room and pray for a revelation . . . state it to her, and bring her around all right."

During an 1873 interview Martin Harris, Book of Mormon benefactor and close friend of Smith, recalled another such incident from the early Kirtland period. "In or about the year 1833," Harris remembered, Joseph Smith's "servant girl" claimed that the prophet had made "improper proposals to her, which created quite a talk amongst the people." When Smith came to him for advice, Harris, supposing that there was nothing to the story, told him to "take no notice of the girl, that she was full of the devil, and wanted to destroy the prophet of god." But according to Harris, Smith "acknowledged that there was more truth than poetry in what the girl said." Harris then said he would have nothing to do with the matter; Smith could get out of the trouble "the best way he knew how".

William E. McLellin, a Mormon apostle who was excommunicated in 1838, further detailed this situation with the unnamed "servant girl" in an 1872 letter to the Smith's eldest son, Joseph III: "I visited your Mother and family in 1847, and held a lengthy conversation with her, retired in the Mansion house in Nauvoo. I did not ask her to tell, but I told her some stories I had heard. And she told me whether I was properly informed. Dr. F[rederick] G. Williams practiced with me in Clay Co. Mo. during the latter part of 1838. And he told me that at your birth [6 November 1832] your father committed an act with a Miss Hill—a hired girl. Emma saw him, and spoke to him. He desisted, but Mrs. Smith refused to be satisfied. He called in Dr. Williams, O. Cowdery, and S. Rigdon to reconcile Emma. But she told them just as the circumstances took place. He found he was caught. He confessed humbly, and begged forgiveness. Emma and all forgave him. She told me this story was true!!"

Accounts such as these have led some historians to conclude that Joseph Smith was licentious. But others have countered that these stories merely indicate his involvement in a heaven-sanctioned system of polygamy, influenced by Old Testament models.

If Smith did take a plural wife in Kirtland during the early 1830s under such a system, the woman was likely Fanny Alger. McLellin's 1872 letter described Alger's relationship with Smith. "Again I told [your mother]," the former apostle wrote, that "I heard that one night she missed Joseph and Fanny Alger. She went to the barn and saw him and Fanny in the barn together alone. She looked through a crack and saw the transaction!!! She told me this story too was verily true." McLellin also detailed the Alger incident to a newspaper reporter for the 6 October 1875 *Salt Lake Tribune*. The reporter stated that McLellin informed him of the exact place "where the first well authenticated case of polygamy took place." According to the article, the marriage occurred "in a barn on the hay mow, and was witnessed by Mrs. Smith through a crack in the door!"

Fanny Ward Alger, one of ten children born to Mormons Samuel Alger and Clarissa Hancock, was nineteen years old when she became a maidservant in the Smith home in 1835. Benjamin F. Johnson, a longtime friend of Smith, described Fanny as "a varry nice & Comly young woman . . . it was whispered eaven then that Joseph *Loved her*." Warren Parrish, Smith's personal secretary, told Johnson that he and Oliver Cowdery both knew that "Joseph had Fanny Alger as a wife for They were Spied upon & found together".

Rumors of Smith's relationship with Alger, whispered about Kirtland during the summer of 1835, may have been the catalyst for the church's announcement of its official position on marriage as well as motivation for Smith's frequent addresses on marital relationships that fall. While Smith was in Michigan his secretary, W. W. Phelps, presented to the church's 17 August 1835 General Assembly a "Chapter of Rules for Marriage among the Saints." This declaration stipulated in part: "Inasmuch as this church of Christ has been reproached with the crime of fornication, and polygamy; we declare that we believe, that one man should have one wife; and one woman, but one husband, except in the case of death, when either is at liberty to marry again." The assembled Saints voted to accept the statement as part of "the faith and principle of this society as a body" by canonizing it in the official Doctrine and Covenants of the church.

This important document, probably introduced by Phelps at Joseph Smith's own request, includes a marriage ceremony and what may be the first scriptural reference to the concept of eternal marriage. Evidently alluding to this, Phelps wrote to his wife Sally on 9 September 1835: "I have it in my heart to give you a little instruction, so that you may know your place, and stand in it, believed, admired, and rewarded, in time and in eternity." One week later he noted that "Br[other] Joseph has preached some of the greatest sermons on the duty of wives to their husbands and the role of all Women, I ever heard." Phelps then expounded on his newly gained understanding of eternal marriage, "Sally . . . you closed your 4th letter to me . . . after the manner of the Gentiles: says Sally *'I remain yours till death.'*" But, Phelps explained, "you will be mine, in this world and in the world to come . . . you may as well as use the word *'forever,'* as *'till death.'*" Phelps's letters make clear that "eternal marriage" was distinct from polygamy, at least in his mind: "I have no right to any other woman in this world nor in the world to come according to the law of the celestial Kingdom."

Despite these 1835 indications of an understanding of the principle of eternal marriage, which would subsequently become synonymous with plural marriage, a distinctly polygamous marriage ceremony was apparently not performed until Joseph Smith was "sealed" to plural wife Louisa Beaman on 5 or 6 April 1841. Smith evidently viewed all marriages prior to this time, including his own to Emma, as valid for "time" only. As late as 1840 he occasionally signed letters to Emma with the benediction "your husband till death." It was not until a 28 May 1843 meeting of the Endowment Council in Nauvoo, Illinois, that the Joseph and Emma Smith were finally sealed for time and eternity in the "new and everlasting covenant of marriage".

But as early as 1835 Smith wanted Mormon couples married by Mormon elders rather than by civil authorities or leaders of other religions. Ohio law refused to recognize Mormon elders as ministers. In a bold display of civil disobedience on 14 November 1835, Smith married Lydia Goldthwait Bailey to Newel Knight. Initially Seymour Brunson, who held a valid minister's license, was to perform the marriage. But as Hyrum Smith began the introductory comments, Joseph Smith stepped forward, stopped his brother, and declared his intent to officiate. The bride later recalled his saying, "Our Elders have been wronged and prosecuted for marrying without a license. The Lord God of Israel has given me authority to unite the people in the holy bonds of matrimony. And from this time forth I shall use that privilege and marry whomsoever I see fit".

Smith's performance of this marriage was one of his earliest efforts to apply heavenly guidelines on earth despite legal technicalities. Not only was Smith not a lawfully recognized minister, but Lydia Bailey, whose non-Mormon husband had deserted her, was never formally divorced. Obviously, Smith saw marriage not as a secular contract but as a sacramental covenant to be sealed by priesthood rather than by civil authority. He commented at the conclusion of the Knight ceremony "that marriage was an institution of heaven, instituted in the garden of Eden; that it was necessary it should be solemnized by the authority of the everlasting Priesthood".

During the next few weeks Smith officiated at numerous other weddings. At the January 1836 wedding of Mormon apostle John F. Boynton and Susan Lowell, he read aloud a license granting any "Minister of the gospel the privilege of solemnizing the rights of matrimony." He then alluded to an "ancient order of marriage" and pronounced upon the bride and groom "the blessings of Abraham, Isaac and Jacob." The next day he signed a certificate of marriage for William F. Calhoon and Nancy M. Gibbs affirming that the ceremony had been performed "agreeable to the rules and regulations of the Church of Jesus Christ of Latter-day Saints on Matrimony".

Smith's plans for Mormon utopia in Ohio and Missouri failed. A national recession devastated his economic plans in Kirtland. And non-Mormons in both places became increasingly nervous about the growing political clout of Mormons. Ohio and Missouri natives were suspicious of the close-knit Mormon lifestyle so contrary to mainstream American life. Disaffected Mormons vied with non-Mormons in hurling accusations against the church. Speculations that the Saints were practicing polygamy compounded such problems.

Within such an environment of suspicion, detractors suspected that the Mormon "Law of Consecration" included a "community of wives." If churchmen could share their property, why not their wives, too? Similar communitarian groups advocating a "community of wives" and other marital variations may have become confused with Smith's followers in the public mind. Parallels were compelling. In the early 1830s another group of "Saints" emerged from the social upheaval in New York. Disciples of revivalist preachers Erasmus Stone, Hiram Sheldon, and Jarvis Rider claimed they were perfect and could no longer sin. They became known as "Perfectionists." As a part of their doctrine, adherents advocated "spiritual wifery," a concept nearly identical to Mormon eternal marriage, wherein "all arrangements for a life in heaven may be made on earth . . . spiritual friendships may be formed, and spiritual bonds contracted, valid for eternity". In 1832 Mormon missionary Orson Hyde, a former member of Sidney Rigdon's "family," visited a group he called "Cochranites" and disdainfully described in his 11 October 1832 journal the group's "Wonderful lustful spirit, because they believe in a 'plurality of wives' which they call spiritual wives, knowing them not after the flesh but after the spirit, but by the *appearance they know one another after the flesh.*"

Another practitioner of spiritual wifery was Robert Matthews, alias "Matthias the Prophet." Matthews announced that "all marriages not made by himself, and according to his doctrine, were of the devil, and that he had come to establish a community of property, and of wives". In 1833 Matthews convinced two of his followers that, as sinners, they were not properly united in wedlock. He claimed power to dissolve the marriage, married the woman himself, prophesied that she was to "become the mother of a spiritual generation," and promised to father her first "spiritual child" himself. After a brief prison sentence, Matthews turned up on Joseph Smith's doorstep in Kirtland as "Joshua, the Jewish Minister". Smith's account of the two-day meeting is sketchy, but apparently Matthews was sent on his way after a disagreement on the "transmigration of the soul."

Linked in the public mind with such colorful religionists as Matthias, Shakers, Harmonists, Perfectionists, Rappites, and Cochranites, Joseph Smith was viewed skeptically by many outsiders. But the real problems in Ohio were caused by insiders. The instability created by disastrous financial decisions involving Smith's Kirtland Safety Anti-Banking Society was compounded by stories about Smith's 1835 relationship with Fanny Alger. Benjamin Johnson years later noted that the Alger incident was "one of the Causes of Apostacy & disruption at Kirtland altho at the time there was little Said publickly upon the subject". At least one account indicated that Fanny became pregnant. Chauncy G. Webb, Smith's grammer teacher, later reported that when the pregnancy became evident, Emma Smith drove Fanny from her home. Webb's daughter, Ann Eliza Webb Young, a divorced wife of Brigham Young, remembered that Fanny was taken into the Webb home on a temporary basis. In fact Joseph Smith's journal entry for 17 October 1835 may contain a cryptic reference to this event: "Called my family together arranged my domestick concerns and dismissed my boarders."

Fanny left Kirtland in September 1836 with her family. Though she married non-Mormon Solomon Custer on 16 November 1836 and was living in Dublin City, Indiana, far from Kirtland, her name still raised eyebrows. Fanny Brewer, a Mormon visitor to Kirtland in 1837, observed "much excitement against the Prophet . . . [involving] an unlawful intercourse between himself and a young orphan girl residing in his family and under his protection".

Much of the excitement was evidently caused by the strong reaction of Smith's close counselor and friend Oliver Cowdery to Smith's presumed liaison with Alger. Apostle David W. Patten, visiting from Missouri in the summer of 1837, went to Cowdery in Kirtland to "enquire of him if a certain story was true respecting J[oseph] Smith's committing adultery with a certain girl." Patten later said that Cowdery "turned on his heel and insinuated as though [Smith] was guilty, he then went on and gave a history of some circumstances respecting the adultery scrape stating that no doubt it was true. Also said that Joseph had told him, he had confessed to Emma".

Church leaders in Missouri questioned Cowdery regarding the Alger incident when he arrived in Far West in the fall of 1837. Thomas B. Marsh, president of the Quorum of Twelve Apostles, stated that when Cowdery was asked "if Joseph Smith jr had confessed to his wife that he was guilty of adultery with a certain girl," Cowdery "cocked up his eye very knowingly and hesitated to answer the question saying he did not know as he was bound to answer the question, yet conveyed the idea that it was true."

Later that fall, during a discussion at the Far West home of George W. Harris, Marsh reported a conversation "between Joseph Smith and Oliver Cowdery when J. Smith asked him if he had ever confessed to him that he was guilty of adultery, when after a considerable winking &c, he said *No*." Smith then gave an apologetic history of the "girl business," adding that "Oliver Cowdery had been his bosom friend, therefore he intrusted him with many things".

After Smith returned to Ohio from Missouri in late 1837 rumors circulated that Cowdery had spread scandalous lies about the prophet and had been chastened by him. The "Second Elder" was furious. He dashed off a 21 January 1838 letter to Smith complaining, "I hear from Kirtland, by the last letters, that you have publickly said, that when you were here I confessed to you that I had willfully lied about you—this compels me to ask you to correct that statement, and give me an explanation—until then you and myself are two." Apparently the word from Kirtland had come from Warren Cowdery, Oliver's brother, because Oliver included a copy of the letter to Smith in a separate letter to Warren. "I can assure you and bro. Lyman [Cowdery]," Oliver angrily wrote to his brother, "I never confessed insinuated or admitted that I ever willfully lied about him. When he was there we had some conversation in which in every instance, I did not fail to affirm that what I had said was strictly true" in the matter of "a dirty, nasty, filthy affair of his and Fanny Algers."

Smith did not respond to Cowdery's letter. He was embroiled in trying to hold the church together in Kirtland. Prominent church leaders Luke Johnson, John Boynton, Warren Parrish, and others had united to denounce Smith as a heretic and "fallen prophet." They urged church members to rally around them in re-establishing the "old standards." After a clamor of accusations from both sides, leaders of the Johnson faction were excommunicated. But then one of the dissidents obtained a warrant for Smith's arrest on a charge of fraud. Under cover of darkness on 12 January 1838 he and first counselor Sidney Rigdon decided to "escape mob violence, which was about to burst upon us under the color of legal process". They fled to Far West, Missouri.

While Smith was en route to Missouri, charges against Oliver Cowdery's church membership were initiated in Far West. Prominent on the list of nine charges was "seeking to destroy the character of President Joseph Smith jr by falsly insinuating that he was guilty of adultry &c." Though Smith arrived at Far West on 14 March 1838, he evidently would not grant Cowdery a requested interview. The Second Elder was excommunicated 12 April 1838, effectively disarming his accusations against the prophet.

Confusion over the exact nature and extent of Joseph Smith's involvement with Fanny Alger has remained to this day. That there was a sexual relationship seems probable. But was Smith's association with his house servant adulterous, as Cowdery charged? Or was she Smith's first plural wife? Apostle Heber C. Kimball, many years later, introduced Fanny's brother John Alger in the Saint George Temple as "brother of the Prophet Josephs first Plural Wife". And in 1899 church leaders performed a proxy marriage for the couple. "The sealings of those named," a temple recorder noted of Alger and the ten other women listed, "were performed during the life of the Prophet Joseph but there is no record thereof. President Lorenzo Snow decided that they be repeated in order that a record might exist; and that this explanation be made".

If Smith and Alger were sealed in a plural marriage as 1899 church leaders were persuaded, who stood as witness for the ordinance? Who performed the ceremony? In the absence of an officiator or witness, did God himself seal the couple, or did Smith, as God's only legitimate earthly agent, marry himself to Alger? Smith did not claim publicly the power to "bind on earth and seal eternally in the heavens" until 3 April 1836, perhaps one year after the Alger incident. Could he have viewed her as his common-law wife, married by connubial relationship rather than by wedding ceremony?

Unfortunately, Smith himself provided no help in clarifying his relationship with Alger. His public denouncements of polygamy during this period compounded the confusion. Only three weeks after Cowdery's excommunication, Smith published a statement in the July 1838 *Elder's Journal* answering several questions about Mormonism. To the question, "Do the Mormons believe in having more wives than one?" he responded emphatically, "No, not at the same time." Several months later, in mid-December, while incarcerated in Liberty, Missouri, he wrote a "Letter to the Church"

which reflected his personal difficulties. Perhaps alluding to the Alger rumors, he asked, "Was it for committing adultery that we were assailed?" He then denied the charge as the "false slander" of "renegade 'Mormon dissenters' . . . running through the world and spreading various foul and libelous reports against us." He dismissed the persistent allegation that the Mormons had "not only dedicated our property, but our families also to the Lord; and Satan, taking advantage of this, has perverted it into licentiousness, such as a community of wives, which is an abomination in the sight of God".

The difficulties between Smith and Cowdery could probably have been resolved if Smith had admitted, at least to Cowdery, that he was introducing plural marriage into the church. But Cowdery, who left viewing Smith's behavior as adulterous, never became reconciled to Mormon polygamy. Church leaders much later unfairly accused Cowdery of taking a plural wife himself. Brigham Young is recorded in 1872 as having said that "while Joseph and Oliver were translating the Book of Mormon, they had a revelation that the order of Patriarchal Marriag and the Sealing was right." Cowdery, according to Young, proposed to Smith, "Why dont we go into the Order of Polygamy, and practice it as the ancients did? We know it is true, then why delay?" Smith warned that "the time has not yet come." Ignoring the prophet's counsel, "Oliver Cowdery took to wife Miss Annie Lyman, cousin to Geo A. Smith. From that time he went into darknes and lost the spirit. Annie Lyman is still alive, a witness to these things".

This second-hand statement of Young, who may not have even been a Mormon at the time of the purported incident, lacks credibility. The Book of Mormon not only consistently denounces polygamy, but it would have been impossible for Cowdery to have been living polygamously during the period charged by Young (1827-30). Cowdery's marriage to his only wife, Elizabeth Ann Whitmer, occurred in 1832, three years after the translation of the Book of Mormon. Furthermore no charges of sexual misconduct were made against Cowdery during his 1838 excommunication trial when there would have been ample opportunity and strong incentive for such retaliation.

Cowdery returned to Mormonism for a short time before his death in 1850 and was shocked when his sister and her husband, Daniel and Phebe Jackson, wrote to him from Illinois in 1846 confirming that polygamy was being practiced by church leaders. "I can hardly think it possible," he wrote, "that though there may be individuals who are guilty of the iniquities spoken of— yet no such practice can be preached or adhered to as a public doctrine." Cowdery viewed polygamy as morally and culturally unthinkable: "Such may do for the followers of Mohamet, it may have done some thousands of years ago, but no people professing to be governed by the pure and holy principles of the Lord Jesus, can hold up their heads before the world at this distance of time, and be guilty of such folly—such wrong—such abomination."

Neither Oliver Cowdery's dim view of polygamy nor the difficulties the Fanny Alger situation caused seriously hampered Joseph Smith's apparent enthusiasm for plural marriage. But shortly after Cowdery's excommunication, events in Far West reached such crisis proportions that the church was again forced to uproot and move.

FURTHER READING

Biography

Barrett, Ivan J. *Joseph Smith and the Restoration.* Second edition. Provo: Young House, 1973, 674 p.

> Outlines the history of Joseph Smith and the Mormon Church to 1846.

Kirkham, Francis W. *A New Witness For Christ in America: The Book of Mormon.* Salt Lake City: Utah Printing Co., 1967, 503 p.

> Traces the history of the *Book of Mormon* from its origins to its printing.

Stenhouse, T.B.H. *The Rocky Mountain Saints.* New York: D. Appleton and Company, 1878, 781 p.

> A comprehensive history of the Mormon Church "from the first vision of Joseph Smith to the last courtship of Brigham Young."

Criticism

Crawley, Peter. "A Comment on Joseph Smith's Account of His First Vision and the 1820 Revival." *Dialogue: A Journal of Mormon Thought* VI, No. 1 (Spring 1971): 106-7.

> Considers the possible effects of the revivalistic atmosphere characteristic of western New York between 1819-21 on Joseph Smith and one of his contemporaries.

Ehat, Andrew F., and Lyndon W. Cook, authors of introduction to *The Words of Joseph Smith,* edited by Andrew F. Ehat and Lyndon W. Cook, pp. xv-xx. Provo: Religious Studies Center, Brigham Young University, 1980.

> Examines the credibility of the persons commissioned by Smith to document his public sermons during the Nauvoo period of Mormon history.

Jessee, C. Dean. "The Early Accounts of Joseph Smith's First Vision." *Brigham Young University Studies* IX, No. 3 (Spring 1969): 275-94.

> A detailed examination of the documentation of Joseph Smith's account of his First Vision.

Kidder, Daniel P. *Mormonism and the Mormons: A Historical View of the Rise and Progress of the Sect Self-Styled Latter-Day Saints.* New York: G. Lane & P. P. Sandford, 1842, 338 p.

> A hostile critique of Mormon doctrine and tenets, often depicting them as religious imposture.

Nineteenth-Century
Literature Criticism

Cumulative Indexes
Volumes 1-53

How to Use This Index

The main references

list all author entries in the following Gale Literary Criticism series:

BLC = *Black Literature Criticism*
CLC = *Contemporary Literary Criticism*
CLR = *Children's Literature Review*
CMLC = *Classical and Medieval Literature Criticism*
DA = *DISCovering Authors*
DC = *Drama Criticism*
HLC = *Hispanic Literature Criticism*
LC = *Literature Criticism from 1400 to 1800*
NCLC = *Nineteenth-Century Literature Criticism*
PC = *Poetry Criticism*
SSC = *Short Story Criticism*
TCLC = *Twentieth-Century Literary Criticism*
WLC = *World Literature Criticism, 1500 to the Present*

The cross-references

list all author entries in the following Gale biographical and literary sources:

AAYA = *Authors & Artists for Young Adults*
AITN = *Authors in the News*
BEST = *Bestsellers*
BW = *Black Writers*
CA = *Contemporary Authors*
CAAS = *Contemporary Authors Autobiography Series*
CABS = *Contemporary Authors Bibliographical Series*
CANR = *Contemporary Authors New Revision Series*
CAP = *Contemporary Authors Permanent Series*
CDALB = *Concise Dictionary of American Literary Biography*
CDBLB = *Concise Dictionary of British Literary Biography*
DLB = *Dictionary of Literary Biography*
DLBD = *Dictionary of Literary Biography Documentary Series*
DLBY = *Dictionary of Literary Biography Yearbook*
HW = *Hispanic Writers*
JRDA = *Junior DISCovering Authors*
MAICYA = *Major Authors and Illustrators for Children and Young Adults*
MTCW = *Major 20th-Century Writers*
NNAL = *Native North American Literature*
SAAS = *Something about the Author Autobiography Series*
SATA = *Something about the Author*
YABC = *Yesterday's Authors of Books for Children*

Literary Criticism Series
Cumulative Author Index

A. E. . . . . TCLC 3, 10
See also Russell, George William

Abasiyanik, Sait Faik 1906-1954
See Sait Faik
See also CA 123

Abbey, Edward 1927-1989 . . . . . . CLC 36, 59
See also CA 45-48; 128; CANR 2, 41

Abbott, Lee K(ittredge) 1947- . . . . . . CLC 48
See also CA 124; DLB 130

Abe, Kobo 1924-1993 . . . . . CLC 8, 22, 53, 81
See also CA 65-68; 140; CANR 24;
DAM NOV; MTCW

Abelard, Peter c. 1079-c. 1142 . . . CMLC 11
See also DLB 115

Abell, Kjeld 1901-1961 . . . . CLC 15
See also CA 111

Abish, Walter 1931- . . . . CLC 22
See also CA 101; CANR 37; DLB 130

Abrahams, Peter (Henry) 1919- . . . . . CLC 4
See also BW 1; CA 57-60; CANR 26;
DLB 117; MTCW

Abrams, M(eyer) H(oward) 1912- . . . CLC 24
See also CA 57-60; CANR 13, 33; DLB 67

Abse, Dannie 1923- . . . . . . CLC 7, 29; DAB
See also CA 53-56; CAAS 1; CANR 4, 46;
DAM POET; DLB 27

Achebe, (Albert) Chinua(lumogu)
1930- . . . . . CLC 1, 3, 5, 7, 11, 26, 51, 75;
BLC; DA; DAB; DAC; WLC
See also AAYA 15; BW 2; CA 1-4R;
CANR 6, 26, 47; CLR 20; DAM MST,
MULT, NOV; DLB 117; MAICYA;
MTCW; SATA 40; SATA-Brief 38

Acker, Kathy 1948- . . . . CLC 45
See also CA 117; 122

Ackroyd, Peter 1949- . . . . CLC 34, 52
See also CA 123; 127; DLB 155; INT 127

Acorn, Milton 1923- . . . . CLC 15; DAC
See also CA 103; DLB 53; INT 103

Adamov, Arthur 1908-1970 . . . . . CLC 4, 25
See also CA 17-18; 25-28R; CAP 2;
DAM DRAM; MTCW

Adams, Alice (Boyd) 1926- . . . CLC 6, 13, 46
See also CA 81-84; CANR 26; DLBY 86;
INT CANR-26; MTCW

Adams, Andy 1859-1935 . . . . TCLC 56
See also YABC 1

Adams, Douglas (Noel) 1952- . . CLC 27, 60
See also AAYA 4; BEST 89:3; CA 106;
CANR 34; DAM POP; DLBY 83; JRDA

Adams, Francis 1862-1893 . . . . . . NCLC 33

Adams, Henry (Brooks)
1838-1918 . . . . . . TCLC 4, 52; DA; DAB;
DAC
See also CA 104; 133; DAM MST; DLB 12,
47

Adams, Richard (George)
1920- . . . . CLC 4, 5, 18
See also AAYA 16; AITN 1, 2; CA 49-52;
CANR 3, 35; CLR 20; DAM NOV;
JRDA; MAICYA; MTCW; SATA 7, 69

Adamson, Joy(-Friederike Victoria)
1910-1980 . . . . CLC 17
See also CA 69-72; 93-96; CANR 22;
MTCW; SATA 11; SATA-Obit 22

Adcock, Fleur 1934- . . . . CLC 41
See also CA 25-28R; CAAS 23; CANR 11,
34; DLB 40

Addams, Charles (Samuel)
1912-1988 . . . . CLC 30
See also CA 61-64; 126; CANR 12

Addison, Joseph 1672-1719 . . . . LC 18
See also CDBLB 1660-1789; DLB 101

Adler, Alfred (F.) 1870-1937 . . . . . TCLC 61
See also CA 119

Adler, C(arole) S(chwerdtfeger)
1932- . . . . CLC 35
See also AAYA 4; CA 89-92; CANR 19,
40; JRDA; MAICYA; SAAS 15;
SATA 26, 63

Adler, Renata 1938- . . . . CLC 8, 31
See also CA 49-52; CANR 5, 22; MTCW

Ady, Endre 1877-1919 . . . . TCLC 11
See also CA 107

Aeschylus
525B.C.-456B.C. . . . . CMLC 11; DA;
DAB; DAC
See also DAM DRAM, MST

Afton, Effie
See Harper, Frances Ellen Watkins

Agapida, Fray Antonio
See Irving, Washington

Agee, James (Rufus)
1909-1955 . . . . TCLC 1, 19
See also AITN 1; CA 108; 148;
CDALB 1941-1968; DAM NOV; DLB 2,
26, 152

Aghill, Gordon
See Silverberg, Robert

Agnon, S(hmuel) Y(osef Halevi)
1888-1970 . . . . CLC 4, 8, 14
See also CA 17-18; 25-28R; CAP 2; MTCW

Agrippa von Nettesheim, Henry Cornelius
1486-1535 . . . . LC 27

Aherne, Owen
See Cassill, R(onald) V(erlin)

Ai 1947- . . . . CLC 4, 14, 69
See also CA 85-88; CAAS 13; DLB 120

Aickman, Robert (Fordyce)
1914-1981 . . . . CLC 57
See also CA 5-8R; CANR 3

Aiken, Conrad (Potter)
1889-1973 . . . CLC 1, 3, 5, 10, 52; SSC 9
See also CA 5-8R; 45-48; CANR 4;
CDALB 1929-1941; DAM NOV, POET;
DLB 9, 45, 102; MTCW; SATA 3, 30

Aiken, Joan (Delano) 1924- . . . . CLC 35
See also AAYA 1; CA 9-12R; CANR 4, 23,
34; CLR 1, 19; DLB 161; JRDA;
MAICYA; MTCW; SAAS 1; SATA 2,
30, 73

Ainsworth, William Harrison
1805-1882 . . . . NCLC 13
See also DLB 21; SATA 24

Aitmatov, Chingiz (Torekulovich)
1928- . . . . CLC 71
See also CA 103; CANR 38; MTCW;
SATA 56

Akers, Floyd
See Baum, L(yman) Frank

Akhmadulina, Bella Akhatovna
1937- . . . . CLC 53
See also CA 65-68; DAM POET

Akhmatova, Anna
1888-1966 . . . . CLC 11, 25, 64; PC 2
See also CA 19-20; 25-28R; CANR 35;
CAP 1; DAM POET; MTCW

Aksakov, Sergei Timofeyvich
1791-1859 . . . . NCLC 2

Aksenov, Vassily
See Aksyonov, Vassily (Pavlovich)

Aksyonov, Vassily (Pavlovich)
1932- . . . . CLC 22, 37
See also CA 53-56; CANR 12, 48

Akutagawa Ryunosuke
1892-1927 . . . . TCLC 16
See also CA 117

Alain 1868-1951 . . . . TCLC 41

Alain-Fournier . . . . TCLC 6
See also Fournier, Henri Alban
See also DLB 65

Alarcon, Pedro Antonio de
1833-1891 . . . . NCLC 1

Alas (y Urena), Leopoldo (Enrique Garcia)
1852-1901 . . . . TCLC 29
See also CA 113; 131; HW

Albee, Edward (Franklin III)
1928- . . . . . . CLC 1, 2, 3, 5, 9, 11, 13, 25,
53, 86; DA; DAB; DAC; WLC
See also AITN 1; CA 5-8R; CABS 3;
CANR 8; CDALB 1941-1968;
DAM DRAM, MST; DLB 7;
INT CANR-8; MTCW

Alberti, Rafael 1902- . . . . CLC 7
See also CA 85-88; DLB 108

Albert the Great 1200(?)-1280 . . . . CMLC 16
See also DLB 115

Alcala-Galiano, Juan Valera y
See Valera y Alcala-Galiano, Juan

Andrews, Elton V.
See Pohl, Frederik

Andreyev, Leonid (Nikolaevich)
1871-1919 . . . . **TCLC 3**
See also CA 104

Andric, Ivo 1892-1975 . . . . **CLC 8**
See also CA 81-84; 57-60; CANR 43;
DLB 147; MTCW

Angelique, Pierre
See Bataille, Georges

Angell, Roger 1920- . . . . **CLC 26**
See also CA 57-60; CANR 13, 44

Angelou, Maya
1928- . . . . **CLC 12, 35, 64, 77; BLC; DA;
DAB; DAC**
See also AAYA 7; BW 2; CA 65-68;
CANR 19, 42; DAM MST, MULT,
POET, POP; DLB 38; MTCW; SATA 49

Annensky, Innokenty Fyodorovich
1856-1909 . . . . **TCLC 14**
See also CA 110

Anon, Charles Robert
See Pessoa, Fernando (Antonio Nogueira)

Anouilh, Jean (Marie Lucien Pierre)
1910-1987 . . . . . . **CLC 1, 3, 8, 13, 40, 50**
See also CA 17-20R; 123; CANR 32;
DAM DRAM; MTCW

Anthony, Florence
See Ai

Anthony, John
See Ciardi, John (Anthony)

Anthony, Peter
See Shaffer, Anthony (Joshua); Shaffer,
Peter (Levin)

Anthony, Piers 1934- . . . . **CLC 35**
See also AAYA 11; CA 21-24R; CANR 28;
DAM POP; DLB 8; MTCW; SAAS 22;
SATA 84

Antoine, Marc
See Proust, (Valentin-Louis-George-Eugene-)
Marcel

Antoninus, Brother
See Everson, William (Oliver)

Antonioni, Michelangelo 1912- . . . . . **CLC 20**
See also CA 73-76; CANR 45

Antschel, Paul 1920-1970
See Celan, Paul
See also CA 85-88; CANR 33; MTCW

Anwar, Chairil 1922-1949 . . . . **TCLC 22**
See also CA 121

Apollinaire, Guillaume . . **TCLC 3, 8, 51; PC 7**
See also Kostrowitzki, Wilhelm Apollinaris
de
See also DAM POET

Appelfeld, Aharon 1932- . . . . **CLC 23, 47**
See also CA 112; 133

Apple, Max (Isaac) 1941- . . . . **CLC 9, 33**
See also CA 81-84; CANR 19; DLB 130

Appleman, Philip (Dean) 1926- . . . . . **CLC 51**
See also CA 13-16R; CAAS 18; CANR 6,
29

Appleton, Lawrence
See Lovecraft, H(oward) P(hillips)

Apteryx
See Eliot, T(homas) S(tearns)

Apuleius, (Lucius Madaurensis)
125(?)-175(?) . . . . **CMLC 1**

Aquin, Hubert 1929-1977 . . . . **CLC 15**
See also CA 105; DLB 53

Aragon, Louis 1897-1982 . . . . **CLC 3, 22**
See also CA 69-72; 108; CANR 28;
DAM NOV, POET; DLB 72; MTCW

Arany, Janos 1817-1882 . . . . **NCLC 34**

Arbuthnot, John 1667-1735 . . . . **LC 1**
See also DLB 101

Archer, Herbert Winslow
See Mencken, H(enry) L(ouis)

Archer, Jeffrey (Howard) 1940- . . . . **CLC 28**
See also AAYA 16; BEST 89:3; CA 77-80;
CANR 22; DAM POP; INT CANR-22

Archer, Jules 1915- . . . . **CLC 12**
See also CA 9-12R; CANR 6; SAAS 5;
SATA 4, 85

Archer, Lee
See Ellison, Harlan (Jay)

Arden, John 1930- . . . . **CLC 6, 13, 15**
See also CA 13-16R; CAAS 4; CANR 31;
DAM DRAM; DLB 13; MTCW

Arenas, Reinaldo
1943-1990 . . . . **CLC 41; HLC**
See also CA 124; 128; 133; DAM MULT;
DLB 145; HW

Arendt, Hannah 1906-1975 . . . . **CLC 66**
See also CA 17-20R; 61-64; CANR 26;
MTCW

Aretino, Pietro 1492-1556 . . . . **LC 12**

Arghezi, Tudor . . . . **CLC 80**
See also Theodorescu, Ion N.

Arguedas, Jose Maria
1911-1969 . . . . **CLC 10, 18**
See also CA 89-92; DLB 113; HW

Argueta, Manlio 1936- . . . . **CLC 31**
See also CA 131; DLB 145; HW

Ariosto, Ludovico 1474-1533 . . . . **LC 6**

Aristides
See Epstein, Joseph

Aristophanes
450B.C.-385B.C. . . . . **CMLC 4; DA;
DAB; DAC; DC 2**
See also DAM DRAM, MST

Arlt, Roberto (Godofredo Christophersen)
1900-1942 . . . . **TCLC 29; HLC**
See also CA 123; 131; DAM MULT; HW

Armah, Ayi Kwei 1939- . . . . **CLC 5, 33; BLC**
See also BW 1; CA 61-64; CANR 21;
DAM MULT, POET; DLB 117; MTCW

Armatrading, Joan 1950- . . . . **CLC 17**
See also CA 114

Arnette, Robert
See Silverberg, Robert

**Arnim, Achim von (Ludwig Joachim von
Arnim)** 1781-1831 . . . . **NCLC 5**
See also DLB 90

Arnim, Bettina von 1785-1859 . . . . **NCLC 38**
See also DLB 90

Arnold, Matthew
1822-1888 . . . . . **NCLC 6, 29; DA; DAB;
DAC; PC 5; WLC**
See also CDBLB 1832-1890; DAM MST,
POET; DLB 32, 57

Arnold, Thomas 1795-1842 . . . . . . **NCLC 18**
See also DLB 55

Arnow, Harriette (Louisa) Simpson
1908-1986 . . . . **CLC 2, 7, 18**
See also CA 9-12R; 118; CANR 14; DLB 6;
MTCW; SATA 42; SATA-Obit 47

Arp, Hans
See Arp, Jean

Arp, Jean 1887-1966 . . . . **CLC 5**
See also CA 81-84; 25-28R; CANR 42

Arrabal
See Arrabal, Fernando

Arrabal, Fernando 1932- . . . **CLC 2, 9, 18, 58**
See also CA 9-12R; CANR 15

Arrick, Fran . . . . **CLC 30**
See also Gaberman, Judie Angell

Artaud, Antonin (Marie Joseph)
1896-1948 . . . . **TCLC 3, 36**
See also CA 104; 149; DAM DRAM

Arthur, Ruth M(abel) 1905-1979 . . . . **CLC 12**
See also CA 9-12R; 85-88; CANR 4;
SATA 7, 26

Artsybashev, Mikhail (Petrovich)
1878-1927 . . . . **TCLC 31**

Arundel, Honor (Morfydd)
1919-1973 . . . . **CLC 17**
See also CA 21-22; 41-44R; CAP 2;
CLR 35; SATA 4; SATA-Obit 24

Asch, Sholem 1880-1957 . . . . **TCLC 3**
See also CA 105

Ash, Shalom
See Asch, Sholem

Ashbery, John (Lawrence)
1927- . . . . . . **CLC 2, 3, 4, 6, 9, 13, 15, 25,
41, 77**
See also CA 5-8R; CANR 9, 37;
DAM POET; DLB 5; DLBY 81;
INT CANR-9; MTCW

Ashdown, Clifford
See Freeman, R(ichard) Austin

Ashe, Gordon
See Creasey, John

Ashton-Warner, Sylvia (Constance)
1908-1984 . . . . **CLC 19**
See also CA 69-72; 112; CANR 29; MTCW

Asimov, Isaac
1920-1992 . . . . . . **CLC 1, 3, 9, 19, 26, 76**
See also AAYA 13; BEST 90:2; CA 1-4R;
137; CANR 2, 19, 36; CLR 12;
DAM POP; DLB 8; DLBY 92;
INT CANR-19; JRDA; MAICYA;
MTCW; SATA 1, 26, 74

Astley, Thea (Beatrice May)
1925- . . . . **CLC 41**
See also CA 65-68; CANR 11, 43

Aston, James
See White, T(erence) H(anbury)

Asturias, Miguel Angel
1899-1974 . . . . **CLC 3, 8, 13; HLC**
See also CA 25-28; 49-52; CANR 32;
CAP 2; DAM MULT, NOV; DLB 113;
HW; MTCW

Atares, Carlos Saura
See Saura (Atares), Carlos

Atheling, William
See Pound, Ezra (Weston Loomis)

Atheling, William, Jr.
See Blish, James (Benjamin)

Atherton, Gertrude (Franklin Horn)
1857-1948 . . . . **TCLC 2**
See also CA 104; DLB 9, 78

Atherton, Lucius
See Masters, Edgar Lee

Atkins, Jack
See Harris, Mark

Atticus
See Fleming, Ian (Lancaster)

Atwood, Margaret (Eleanor)
1939- . . . . . **CLC 2, 3, 4, 8, 13, 15, 25, 44,
84; DA; DAB; DAC; PC 8; SSC 2; WLC**
See also AAYA 12; BEST 89:2; CA 49-52;
CANR 3, 24, 33; DAM MST, NOV,
POET; DLB 53; INT CANR-24; MTCW;
SATA 50

Aubigny, Pierre d'
See Mencken, H(enry) L(ouis)

Aubin, Penelope 1685-1731(?) . . . . **LC 9**
See also DLB 39

Auchincloss, Louis (Stanton)
1917- . . . . **CLC 4, 6, 9, 18, 45**
See also CA 1-4R; CANR 6, 29;
DAM NOV; DLB 2; DLBY 80;
INT CANR-29; MTCW

Auden, W(ystan) H(ugh)
1907-1973 . . . . . . **CLC 1, 2, 3, 4, 6, 9, 11,
14, 43; DA; DAB; DAC; PC 1; WLC**
See also CA 9-12R; 45-48; CANR 5;
CDBLB 1914-1945; DAM DRAM, MST,
POET; DLB 10, 20; MTCW

Audiberti, Jacques 1900-1965 . . . . . . **CLC 38**
See also CA 25-28R; DAM DRAM

Audubon, John James
1785-1851 . . . . **NCLC 47**

Auel, Jean M(arie) 1936- . . . . **CLC 31**
See also AAYA 7; BEST 90:4; CA 103;
CANR 21; DAM POP; INT CANR-21

Auerbach, Erich 1892-1957 . . . . **TCLC 43**
See also CA 118

Augier, Emile 1820-1889 . . . . **NCLC 31**

August, John
See De Voto, Bernard (Augustine)

Augustine, St. 354-430 . . . . . . **CMLC 6; DAB**

Aurelius
See Bourne, Randolph S(illiman)

Austen, Jane
1775-1817 . . . . . **NCLC 1, 13, 19, 33, 51;
DA; DAB; DAC; WLC**
See also CDBLB 1789-1832; DAM MST,
NOV; DLB 116

Auster, Paul 1947- . . . . **CLC 47**
See also CA 69-72; CANR 23

Austin, Frank
See Faust, Frederick (Schiller)

Austin, Mary (Hunter)
1868-1934 . . . . **TCLC 25**
See also CA 109; DLB 9, 78

Autran Dourado, Waldomiro
See Dourado, (Waldomiro Freitas) Autran

Averroes 1126-1198 . . . . **CMLC 7**
See also DLB 115

Avicenna 980-1037 . . . . **CMLC 16**
See also DLB 115

Avison, Margaret 1918- . . . . . **CLC 2, 4; DAC**
See also CA 17-20R; DAM POET; DLB 53;
MTCW

Axton, David
See Koontz, Dean R(ay)

Ayckbourn, Alan
1939- . . . . **CLC 5, 8, 18, 33, 74; DAB**
See also CA 21-24R; CANR 31;
DAM DRAM; DLB 13; MTCW

Aydy, Catherine
See Tennant, Emma (Christina)

Ayme, Marcel (Andre) 1902-1967 . . . **CLC 11**
See also CA 89-92; CLR 25; DLB 72

Ayrton, Michael 1921-1975 . . . . **CLC 7**
See also CA 5-8R; 61-64; CANR 9, 21

Azorin . . . . **CLC 11**
See also Martinez Ruiz, Jose

Azuela, Mariano
1873-1952 . . . . **TCLC 3; HLC**
See also CA 104; 131; DAM MULT; HW;
MTCW

Baastad, Babbis Friis
See Friis-Baastad, Babbis Ellinor

Bab
See Gilbert, W(illiam) S(chwenck)

Babbis, Eleanor
See Friis-Baastad, Babbis Ellinor

Babel, Isaak (Emmanuilovich)
1894-1941(?) . . . . . . **TCLC 2, 13; SSC 16**
See also CA 104

Babits, Mihaly 1883-1941 . . . . **TCLC 14**
See also CA 114

Babur 1483-1530 . . . . **LC 18**

Bacchelli, Riccardo 1891-1985 . . . . . **CLC 19**
See also CA 29-32R; 117

Bach, Richard (David) 1936- . . . . **CLC 14**
See also AITN 1; BEST 89:2; CA 9-12R;
CANR 18; DAM NOV, POP; MTCW;
SATA 13

Bachman, Richard
See King, Stephen (Edwin)

Bachmann, Ingeborg 1926-1973 . . . . . **CLC 69**
See also CA 93-96; 45-48; DLB 85

Bacon, Francis 1561-1626 . . . . **LC 18, 32**
See also CDBLB Before 1660; DLB 151

Bacon, Roger 1214(?)-1292 . . . . . . **CMLC 14**
See also DLB 115

Bacovia, George . . . . **TCLC 24**
See also Vasiliu, Gheorghe

Badanes, Jerome 1937- . . . . **CLC 59**

Bagehot, Walter 1826-1877 . . . . . . **NCLC 10**
See also DLB 55

Bagnold, Enid 1889-1981 . . . . **CLC 25**
See also CA 5-8R; 103; CANR 5, 40;
DAM DRAM; DLB 13, 160; MAICYA;
SATA 1, 25

Bagritsky, Eduard 1895-1934 . . . . . **TCLC 60**

Bagrjana, Elisaveta
See Belcheva, Elisaveta

Bagryana, Elisaveta . . . . **CLC 10**
See also Belcheva, Elisaveta
See also DLB 147

Bailey, Paul 1937- . . . . **CLC 45**
See also CA 21-24R; CANR 16; DLB 14

Baillie, Joanna 1762-1851 . . . . **NCLC 2**
See also DLB 93

Bainbridge, Beryl (Margaret)
1933- . . . . **CLC 4, 5, 8, 10, 14, 18, 22, 62**
See also CA 21-24R; CANR 24;
DAM NOV; DLB 14; MTCW

Baker, Elliott 1922- . . . . **CLC 8**
See also CA 45-48; CANR 2

Baker, Nicholson 1957- . . . . **CLC 61**
See also CA 135; DAM POP

Baker, Ray Stannard 1870-1946 . . . **TCLC 47**
See also CA 118

Baker, Russell (Wayne) 1925- . . . . . . **CLC 31**
See also BEST 89:4; CA 57-60; CANR 11,
41; MTCW

Bakhtin, M.
See Bakhtin, Mikhail Mikhailovich

Bakhtin, M. M.
See Bakhtin, Mikhail Mikhailovich

Bakhtin, Mikhail
See Bakhtin, Mikhail Mikhailovich

Bakhtin, Mikhail Mikhailovich
1895-1975 . . . . **CLC 83**
See also CA 128; 113

Bakshi, Ralph 1938(?)- . . . . **CLC 26**
See also CA 112; 138

Bakunin, Mikhail (Alexandrovich)
1814-1876 . . . . **NCLC 25**

Baldwin, James (Arthur)
1924-1987 . . . . . . **CLC 1, 2, 3, 4, 5, 8, 13,
15, 17, 42, 50, 67, 90; BLC; DA; DAB;
DAC; DC 1; SSC 10; WLC**
See also AAYA 4; BW 1; CA 1-4R; 124;
CABS 1; CANR 3, 24;
CDALB 1941-1968; DAM MST, MULT,
NOV, POP; DLB 2, 7, 33; DLBY 87;
MTCW; SATA 9; SATA-Obit 54

Ballard, J(ames) G(raham)
1930- . . . . **CLC 3, 6, 14, 36; SSC 1**
See also AAYA 3; CA 5-8R; CANR 15, 39;
DAM NOV, POP; DLB 14; MTCW

Balmont, Konstantin (Dmitriyevich)
1867-1943 . . . . **TCLC 11**
See also CA 109

Balzac, Honore de
1799-1850 . . . . **NCLC 5, 35, 53; DA;
DAB; DAC; SSC 5; WLC**
See also DAM MST, NOV; DLB 119

Bambara, Toni Cade
1939- . . . . . **CLC 19, 88; BLC; DA; DAC**
See also AAYA 5; BW 2; CA 29-32R;
CANR 24, 49; DAM MST, MULT;
DLB 38; MTCW

Bamdad, A.
See Shamlu, Ahmad

Banat, D. R.
See Bradbury, Ray (Douglas)

Bancroft, Laura
See Baum, L(yman) Frank

Banim, John 1798-1842 . . . . **NCLC 13**
See also DLB 116, 158, 159

Banim, Michael 1796-1874 . . . . . . **NCLC 13**
See also DLB 158, 159

Banks, Iain
See Banks, Iain M(enzies)

Banks, Iain M(enzies) 1954- . . . . **CLC 34**
See also CA 123; 128; INT 128

Banks, Lynne Reid . . . . **CLC 23**
See also Reid Banks, Lynne
See also AAYA 6

Banks, Russell 1940- . . . . **CLC 37, 72**
See also CA 65-68; CAAS 15; CANR 19;
DLB 130

Banville, John 1945-. . . . . **CLC 46**
See also CA 117; 128; DLB 14; INT 128

Banville, Theodore (Faullain) de
1832-1891 . . . . **NCLC 9**

Baraka, Amiri
1934- . . . . **CLC 1, 2, 3, 5, 10, 14, 33;**
BLC; DA; DAC; DC 6; PC 4
See also Jones, LeRoi
See also BW 2; CA 21-24R; CABS 3;
CANR 27, 38; CDALB 1941-1968;
DAM MST, MULT, POET, POP;
DLB 5, 7, 16, 38; DLBD 8; MTCW

Barbauld, Anna Laetitia
1743-1825 . . . . **NCLC 50**
See also DLB 107, 109, 142, 158

Barbellion, W. N. P. . . . . **TCLC 24**
See also Cummings, Bruce F(rederick)

Barbera, Jack (Vincent) 1945-. . . . . . **CLC 44**
See also CA 110; CANR 45

Barbey d'Aurevilly, Jules Amedee
1808-1889 . . . . **NCLC 1; SSC 17**
See also DLB 119

Barbusse, Henri 1873-1935 . . . . **TCLC 5**
See also CA 105; DLB 65

Barclay, Bill
See Moorcock, Michael (John)

Barclay, William Ewert
See Moorcock, Michael (John)

Barea, Arturo 1897-1957 . . . . **TCLC 14**
See also CA 111

Barfoot, Joan 1946- . . . . **CLC 18**
See also CA 105

Baring, Maurice 1874-1945 . . . . **TCLC 8**
See also CA 105; DLB 34

Barker, Clive 1952- . . . . **CLC 52**
See also AAYA 10; BEST 90:3; CA 121;
129; DAM POP; INT 129; MTCW

Barker, George Granville
1913-1991 . . . . **CLC 8, 48**
See also CA 9-12R; 135; CANR 7, 38;
DAM POET; DLB 20; MTCW

Barker, Harley Granville
See Granville-Barker, Harley
See also DLB 10

Barker, Howard 1946- . . . . **CLC 37**
See also CA 102; DLB 13

Barker, Pat(ricia) 1943-. . . . . . . **CLC 32, 91**
See also CA 117; 122; CANR 50; INT 122

Barlow, Joel 1754-1812 . . . . **NCLC 23**
See also DLB 37

Barnard, Mary (Ethel) 1909-. . . . . . **CLC 48**
See also CA 21-22; CAP 2

Barnes, Djuna
1892-1982 . . . **CLC 3, 4, 8, 11, 29; SSC 3**
See also CA 9-12R; 107; CANR 16; DLB 4,
9, 45; MTCW

Barnes, Julian 1946-. . . . . **CLC 42; DAB**
See also CA 102; CANR 19; DLBY 93

Barnes, Peter 1931- . . . . **CLC 5, 56**
See also CA 65-68; CAAS 12; CANR 33,
34; DLB 13; MTCW

Baroja (y Nessi), Pio
1872-1956 . . . . **TCLC 8; HLC**
See also CA 104

Baron, David
See Pinter, Harold

Baron Corvo
See Rolfe, Frederick (William Serafino
Austin Lewis Mary)

Barondess, Sue K(aufman)
1926-1977 . . . . **CLC 8**
See also Kaufman, Sue
See also CA 1-4R; 69-72; CANR 1

Baron de Teive
See Pessoa, Fernando (Antonio Nogueira)

Barres, Maurice 1862-1923 . . . . **TCLC 47**
See also DLB 123

Barreto, Afonso Henrique de Lima
See Lima Barreto, Afonso Henrique de

Barrett, (Roger) Syd 1946- . . . . **CLC 35**

Barrett, William (Christopher)
1913-1992 . . . . **CLC 27**
See also CA 13-16R; 139; CANR 11;
INT CANR-11

Barrie, J(ames) M(atthew)
1860-1937 . . . . **TCLC 2; DAB**
See also CA 104; 136; CDBLB 1890-1914;
CLR 16; DAM DRAM; DLB 10, 141,
156; MAICYA; YABC 1

Barrington, Michael
See Moorcock, Michael (John)

Barrol, Grady
See Bograd, Larry

Barry, Mike
See Malzberg, Barry N(athaniel)

Barry, Philip 1896-1949 . . . . **TCLC 11**
See also CA 109; DLB 7

Bart, Andre Schwarz
See Schwarz-Bart, Andre

Barth, John (Simmons)
1930- . . . . . . **CLC 1, 2, 3, 5, 7, 9, 10, 14,**
27, 51, 89; SSC 10
See also AITN 1, 2; CA 1-4R; CABS 1;
CANR 5, 23, 49; DAM NOV; DLB 2;
MTCW

Barthelme, Donald
1931-1989 . . . . . . **CLC 1, 2, 3, 5, 6, 8, 13,**
23, 46, 59; SSC 2
See also CA 21-24R; 129; CANR 20;
DAM NOV; DLB 2; DLBY 80, 89;
MTCW; SATA 7; SATA-Obit 62

Barthelme, Frederick 1943-. . . . . **CLC 36**
See also CA 114; 122; DLBY 85; INT 122

Barthes, Roland (Gerard)
1915-1980 . . . . **CLC 24, 83**
See also CA 130; 97-100; MTCW

Barzun, Jacques (Martin) 1907- . . . . **CLC 51**
See also CA 61-64; CANR 22

Bashevis, Isaac
See Singer, Isaac Bashevis

Bashkirtseff, Marie 1859-1884 . . . **NCLC 27**

Basho
See Matsuo Basho

Bass, Kingsley B., Jr.
See Bullins, Ed

Bass, Rick 1958-. . . . . **CLC 79**
See also CA 126

Bassani, Giorgio 1916-. . . . . **CLC 9**
See also CA 65-68; CANR 33; DLB 128;
MTCW

Bastos, Augusto (Antonio) Roa
See Roa Bastos, Augusto (Antonio)

Bataille, Georges 1897-1962 . . . . **CLC 29**
See also CA 101; 89-92

Bates, H(erbert) E(rnest)
1905-1974 . . . . **CLC 46; DAB; SSC 10**
See also CA 93-96; 45-48; CANR 34;
DAM POP; DLB 162; MTCW

Bauchart
See Camus, Albert

Baudelaire, Charles
1821-1867 . . . . . **NCLC 6, 29; DA; DAB;**
DAC; PC 1; SSC 18; WLC
See also DAM MST, POET

Baudrillard, Jean 1929-. . . . . **CLC 60**

Baum, L(yman) Frank 1856-1919 . . . **TCLC 7**
See also CA 108; 133; CLR 15; DLB 22;
JRDA; MAICYA; MTCW; SATA 18

Baum, Louis F.
See Baum, L(yman) Frank

Baumbach, Jonathan 1933- . . . . . . **CLC 6, 23**
See also CA 13-16R; CAAS 5; CANR 12;
DLBY 80; INT CANR-12; MTCW

Bausch, Richard (Carl) 1945- . . . . . . **CLC 51**
See also CA 101; CAAS 14; CANR 43;
DLB 130

Baxter, Charles 1947-. . . . . **CLC 45, 78**
See also CA 57-60; CANR 40; DAM POP;
DLB 130

Baxter, George Owen
See Faust, Frederick (Schiller)

Baxter, James K(eir) 1926-1972 . . . . **CLC 14**
See also CA 77-80

Baxter, John
See Hunt, E(verette) Howard, (Jr.)

Bayer, Sylvia
See Glassco, John

Baynton, Barbara 1857-1929 . . . . . . **TCLC 57**

Bennett, George Harold 1930-
See Bennett, Hal
See also BW 1; CA 97-100

Bennett, Hal .... **CLC 5**
See also Bennett, George Harold
See also DLB 33

Bennett, Jay 1912- .... **CLC 35**
See also AAYA 10; CA 69-72; CANR 11,
42; JRDA; SAAS 4; SATA 41;
SATA-Brief 27

Bennett, Louise (Simone)
1919- .... **CLC 28; BLC**
See also BW 2; DAM MULT; DLB 117

Benson, E(dward) F(rederic)
1867-1940 .... **TCLC 27**
See also CA 114; DLB 135, 153

Benson, Jackson J. 1930- .... **CLC 34**
See also CA 25-28R; DLB 111

Benson, Sally 1900-1972 .... **CLC 17**
See also CA 19-20; 37-40R; CAP 1;
SATA 1, 35; SATA-Obit 27

Benson, Stella 1892-1933 .... **TCLC 17**
See also CA 117; DLB 36, 162

Bentham, Jeremy 1748-1832 ..... **NCLC 38**
See also DLB 107, 158

Bentley, E(dmund) C(lerihew)
1875-1956 .... **TCLC 12**
See also CA 108; DLB 70

Bentley, Eric (Russell) 1916- ...... **CLC 24**
See also CA 5-8R; CANR 6; INT CANR-6

Beranger, Pierre Jean de
1780-1857 .... **NCLC 34**

Berendt, John (Lawrence) 1939- .... **CLC 86**
See also CA 146

Berger, Colonel
See Malraux, (Georges-)Andre

Berger, John (Peter) 1926- ...... **CLC 2, 19**
See also CA 81-84; DLB 14

Berger, Melvin H. 1927- .... **CLC 12**
See also CA 5-8R; CANR 4; CLR 32;
SAAS 2; SATA 5

Berger, Thomas (Louis)
1924- .... **CLC 3, 5, 8, 11, 18, 38**
See also CA 1-4R; CANR 5, 28;
DAM NOV; DLB 2; DLBY 80;
INT CANR-28; MTCW

Bergman, (Ernst) Ingmar
1918- .... **CLC 16, 72**
See also CA 81-84; CANR 33

Bergson, Henri 1859-1941 .... **TCLC 32**

Bergstein, Eleanor 1938- .... **CLC 4**
See also CA 53-56; CANR 5

Berkoff, Steven 1937- .... **CLC 56**
See also CA 104

Bermant, Chaim (Icyk) 1929- ...... **CLC 40**
See also CA 57-60; CANR 6, 31

Bern, Victoria
See Fisher, M(ary) F(rances) K(ennedy)

Bernanos, (Paul Louis) Georges
1888-1948 .... **TCLC 3**
See also CA 104; 130; DLB 72

Bernard, April 1956- .... **CLC 59**
See also CA 131

Berne, Victoria
See Fisher, M(ary) F(rances) K(ennedy)

Bernhard, Thomas
1931-1989 .... **CLC 3, 32, 61**
See also CA 85-88; 127; CANR 32;
DLB 85, 124; MTCW

Berriault, Gina 1926- .... **CLC 54**
See also CA 116; 129; DLB 130

Berrigan, Daniel 1921- .... **CLC 4**
See also CA 33-36R; CAAS 1; CANR 11,
43; DLB 5

Berrigan, Edmund Joseph Michael, Jr.
1934-1983
See Berrigan, Ted
See also CA 61-64; 110; CANR 14

Berrigan, Ted .... **CLC 37**
See also Berrigan, Edmund Joseph Michael,
Jr.
See also DLB 5

Berry, Charles Edward Anderson 1931-
See Berry, Chuck
See also CA 115

Berry, Chuck .... **CLC 17**
See also Berry, Charles Edward Anderson

Berry, Jonas
See Ashbery, John (Lawrence)

Berry, Wendell (Erdman)
1934- .... **CLC 4, 6, 8, 27, 46**
See also AITN 1; CA 73-76; CANR 50;
DAM POET; DLB 5, 6

Berryman, John
1914-1972 ...... **CLC 1, 2, 3, 4, 6, 8, 10,
13, 25, 62**
See also CA 13-16; 33-36R; CABS 2;
CANR 35; CAP 1; CDALB 1941-1968;
DAM POET; DLB 48; MTCW

Bertolucci, Bernardo 1940- .... **CLC 16**
See also CA 106

Bertrand, Aloysius 1807-1841 .... **NCLC 31**

Bertran de Born c. 1140-1215 ..... **CMLC 5**

Besant, Annie (Wood) 1847-1933 ... **TCLC 9**
See also CA 105

Bessie, Alvah 1904-1985 .... **CLC 23**
See also CA 5-8R; 116; CANR 2; DLB 26

Bethlen, T. D.
See Silverberg, Robert

Beti, Mongo .... **CLC 27; BLC**
See also Biyidi, Alexandre
See also DAM MULT

Betjeman, John
1906-1984 ... **CLC 2, 6, 10, 34, 43; DAB**
See also CA 9-12R; 112; CANR 33;
CDBLB 1945-1960; DAM MST, POET;
DLB 20; DLBY 84; MTCW

Bettelheim, Bruno 1903-1990 ...... **CLC 79**
See also CA 81-84; 131; CANR 23; MTCW

Betti, Ugo 1892-1953 .... **TCLC 5**
See also CA 104

Betts, Doris (Waugh) 1932- .... **CLC 3, 6, 28**
See also CA 13-16R; CANR 9; DLBY 82;
INT CANR-9

Bevan, Alistair
See Roberts, Keith (John Kingston)

Bialik, Chaim Nachman
1873-1934 .... **TCLC 25**

Bickerstaff, Isaac
See Swift, Jonathan

Bidart, Frank 1939- .... **CLC 33**
See also CA 140

Bienek, Horst 1930- .... **CLC 7, 11**
See also CA 73-76; DLB 75

Bierce, Ambrose (Gwinett)
1842-1914(?) .... **TCLC 1, 7, 44; DA;
DAC; SSC 9; WLC**
See also CA 104; 139; CDALB 1865-1917;
DAM MST; DLB 11, 12, 23, 71, 74

Billings, Josh
See Shaw, Henry Wheeler

Billington, (Lady) Rachel (Mary)
1942- .... **CLC 43**
See also AITN 2; CA 33-36R; CANR 44

Binyon, T(imothy) J(ohn) 1936- .... **CLC 34**
See also CA 111; CANR 28

Bioy Casares, Adolfo
1914- ... **CLC 4, 8, 13, 88; HLC; SSC 17**
See also CA 29-32R; CANR 19, 43;
DAM MULT; DLB 113; HW; MTCW

Bird, Cordwainer
See Ellison, Harlan (Jay)

Bird, Robert Montgomery
1806-1854 .... **NCLC 1**

Birney, (Alfred) Earle
1904- .... **CLC 1, 4, 6, 11; DAC**
See also CA 1-4R; CANR 5, 20;
DAM MST, POET; DLB 88; MTCW

Bishop, Elizabeth
1911-1979 ...... **CLC 1, 4, 9, 13, 15, 32;
DA; DAC; PC 3**
See also CA 5-8R; 89-92; CABS 2;
CANR 26; CDALB 1968-1988;
DAM MST, POET; DLB 5; MTCW;
SATA-Obit 24

Bishop, John 1935- .... **CLC 10**
See also CA 105

Bissett, Bill 1939- .... **CLC 18; PC 14**
See also CA 69-72; CAAS 19; CANR 15;
DLB 53; MTCW

Bitov, Andrei (Georgievich) 1937-... **CLC 57**
See also CA 142

Biyidi, Alexandre 1932-
See Beti, Mongo
See also BW 1; CA 114; 124; MTCW

Bjarme, Brynjolf
See Ibsen, Henrik (Johan)

Bjornson, Bjornstjerne (Martinius)
1832-1910 .... **TCLC 7, 37**
See also CA 104

Black, Robert
See Holdstock, Robert P.

Blackburn, Paul 1926-1971 ...... **CLC 9, 43**
See also CA 81-84; 33-36R; CANR 34;
DLB 16; DLBY 81

Black Elk 1863-1950 .... **TCLC 33**
See also CA 144; DAM MULT; NNAL

Black Hobart
See Sanders, (James) Ed(ward)

Blacklin, Malcolm
See Chambers, Aidan

Bourget, Paul (Charles Joseph)
1852-1935 .... **TCLC 12**
See also CA 107; DLB 123

Bourjaily, Vance (Nye) 1922- .... **CLC 8, 62**
See also CA 1-4R; CAAS 1; CANR 2;
DLB 2, 143

Bourne, Randolph S(illiman)
1886-1918 .... **TCLC 16**
See also CA 117; DLB 63

Bova, Ben(jamin William) 1932-.... **CLC 45**
See also AAYA 16; CA 5-8R; CAAS 18;
CANR 11; CLR 3; DLBY 81;
INT CANR-11; MAICYA; MTCW;
SATA 6, 68

Bowen, Elizabeth (Dorothea Cole)
1899-1973 ...... **CLC 1, 3, 6, 11, 15, 22;**
SSC 3
See also CA 17-18; 41-44R; CANR 35;
CAP 2; CDBLB 1945-1960; DAM NOV;
DLB 15, 162; MTCW

Bowering, George 1935-........ **CLC 15, 47**
See also CA 21-24R; CAAS 16; CANR 10;
DLB 53

Bowering, Marilyn R(uthe) 1949-... **CLC 32**
See also CA 101; CANR 49

Bowers, Edgar 1924- .... **CLC 9**
See also CA 5-8R; CANR 24; DLB 5

Bowie, David .... **CLC 17**
See also Jones, David Robert

Bowles, Jane (Sydney)
1917-1973 .... **CLC 3, 68**
See also CA 19-20; 41-44R; CAP 2

Bowles, Paul (Frederick)
1910- .... **CLC 1, 2, 19, 53; SSC 3**
See also CA 1-4R; CAAS 1; CANR 1, 19,
50; DLB 5, 6; MTCW

Box, Edgar
See Vidal, Gore

Boyd, Nancy
See Millay, Edna St. Vincent

Boyd, William 1952-........ **CLC 28, 53, 70**
See also CA 114; 120

Boyle, Kay
1902-1992 ..... **CLC 1, 5, 19, 58; SSC 5**
See also CA 13-16R; 140; CAAS 1;
CANR 29; DLB 4, 9, 48, 86; DLBY 93;
MTCW

Boyle, Mark
See Kienzle, William X(avier)

Boyle, Patrick 1905-1982......... **CLC 19**
See also CA 127

Boyle, T. C. 1948-
See Boyle, T(homas) Coraghessan

Boyle, T(homas) Coraghessan
1948- .... **CLC 36, 55, 90; SSC 16**
See also BEST 90:4; CA 120; CANR 44;
DAM POP; DLBY 86

Boz
See Dickens, Charles (John Huffam)

Brackenridge, Hugh Henry
1748-1816 .... **NCLC 7**
See also DLB 11, 37

Bradbury, Edward P.
See Moorcock, Michael (John)

Bradbury, Malcolm (Stanley)
1932- .... **CLC 32, 61**
See also CA 1-4R; CANR 1, 33;
DAM NOV; DLB 14; MTCW

Bradbury, Ray (Douglas)
1920- .... **CLC 1, 3, 10, 15, 42; DA;**
DAB; DAC; WLC
See also AAYA 15; AITN 1, 2; CA 1-4R;
CANR 2, 30; CDALB 1968-1988;
DAM MST, NOV, POP; DLB 2, 8;
INT CANR-30; MTCW; SATA 11, 64

Bradford, Gamaliel 1863-1932..... **TCLC 36**
See also DLB 17

Bradley, David (Henry, Jr.)
1950- .... **CLC 23; BLC**
See also BW 1; CA 104; CANR 26;
DAM MULT; DLB 33

Bradley, John Ed(mund, Jr.)
1958- .... **CLC 55**
See also CA 139

Bradley, Marion Zimmer 1930-..... **CLC 30**
See also AAYA 9; CA 57-60; CAAS 10;
CANR 7, 31; DAM POP; DLB 8;
MTCW

Bradstreet, Anne
1612(?)-1672 ...... **LC 4, 30; DA; DAC;**
PC 10
See also CDALB 1640-1865; DAM MST,
POET; DLB 24

Brady, Joan 1939- .... **CLC 86**
See also CA 141

Bragg, Melvyn 1939- .... **CLC 10**
See also BEST 89:3; CA 57-60; CANR 10,
48; DLB 14

Braine, John (Gerard)
1922-1986 .... **CLC 1, 3, 41**
See also CA 1-4R; 120; CANR 1, 33;
CDBLB 1945-1960; DLB 15; DLBY 86;
MTCW

Brammer, William 1930(?)-1978 .... **CLC 31**
See also CA 77-80

Brancati, Vitaliano 1907-1954..... **TCLC 12**
See also CA 109

Brancato, Robin F(idler) 1936-.... **CLC 35**
See also AAYA 9; CA 69-72; CANR 11,
45; CLR 32; JRDA; SAAS 9; SATA 23

Brand, Max
See Faust, Frederick (Schiller)

Brand, Millen 1906-1980.......... **CLC 7**
See also CA 21-24R; 97-100

Branden, Barbara .... **CLC 44**
See also CA 148

Brandes, Georg (Morris Cohen)
1842-1927 .... **TCLC 10**
See also CA 105

Brandys, Kazimierz 1916-......... **CLC 62**

Branley, Franklyn M(ansfield)
1915- .... **CLC 21**
See also CA 33-36R; CANR 14, 39;
CLR 13; MAICYA; SAAS 16; SATA 4,
68

Brathwaite, Edward Kamau 1930-... **CLC 11**
See also BW 2; CA 25-28R; CANR 11, 26,
47; DAM POET; DLB 125

Brautigan, Richard (Gary)
1935-1984 .... **CLC 1, 3, 5, 9, 12, 34, 42**
See also CA 53-56; 113; CANR 34;
DAM NOV; DLB 2, 5; DLBY 80, 84;
MTCW; SATA 56

Braverman, Kate 1950- .... **CLC 67**
See also CA 89-92

Brecht, Bertolt
1898-1956 ...... **TCLC 1, 6, 13, 35; DA;**
DAB; DAC; DC 3; WLC
See also CA 104; 133; DAM DRAM, MST;
DLB 56, 124; MTCW

Brecht, Eugen Berthold Friedrich
See Brecht, Bertolt

Bremer, Fredrika 1801-1865 ..... **NCLC 11**

Brennan, Christopher John
1870-1932 .... **TCLC 17**
See also CA 117

Brennan, Maeve 1917-............ **CLC 5**
See also CA 81-84

Brentano, Clemens (Maria)
1778-1842 .... **NCLC 1**
See also DLB 90

Brent of Bin Bin
See Franklin, (Stella Maraia Sarah) Miles

Brenton, Howard 1942-........... **CLC 31**
See also CA 69-72; CANR 33; DLB 13;
MTCW

Breslin, James 1930-
See Breslin, Jimmy
See also CA 73-76; CANR 31; DAM NOV;
MTCW

Breslin, Jimmy .... **CLC 4, 43**
See also Breslin, James
See also AITN 1

Bresson, Robert 1901-............ **CLC 16**
See also CA 110; CANR 49

Breton, Andre
1896-1966 ..... **CLC 2, 9, 15, 54; PC 15**
See also CA 19-20; 25-28R; CANR 40;
CAP 2; DLB 65; MTCW

Breytenbach, Breyten 1939(?)- .. **CLC 23, 37**
See also CA 113; 129; DAM POET

Bridgers, Sue Ellen 1942- .... **CLC 26**
See also AAYA 8; CA 65-68; CANR 11,
36; CLR 18; DLB 52; JRDA; MAICYA;
SAAS 1; SATA 22

Bridges, Robert (Seymour)
1844-1930 .... **TCLC 1**
See also CA 104; CDBLB 1890-1914;
DAM POET; DLB 19, 98

Bridie, James.................... **TCLC 3**
See also Mavor, Osborne Henry
See also DLB 10

Brin, David 1950-................ **CLC 34**
See also CA 102; CANR 24;
INT CANR-24; SATA 65

Brink, Andre (Philippus)
1935-.................... **CLC 18, 36**
See also CA 104; CANR 39; INT 103;
MTCW

Brinsmead, H(esba) F(ay) 1922-.... **CLC 21**
See also CA 21-24R; CANR 10; MAICYA;
SAAS 5; SATA 18, 78

Brittain, Vera (Mary)
1893(?)-1970 .... **CLC 23**
See also CA 13-16; 25-28R; CAP 1; MTCW

Broch, Hermann 1886-1951 ...... **TCLC 20**
See also CA 117; DLB 85, 124

Brock, Rose
See Hansen, Joseph

Brodkey, Harold 1930- .... **CLC 56**
See also CA 111; DLB 130

Brodsky, Iosif Alexandrovich 1940-
See Brodsky, Joseph
See also AITN 1; CA 41-44R; CANR 37;
DAM POET; MTCW

Brodsky, Joseph .. **CLC 4, 6, 13, 36, 50; PC 9**
See also Brodsky, Iosif Alexandrovich

Brodsky, Michael Mark 1948- ..... **CLC 19**
See also CA 102; CANR 18, 41

Bromell, Henry 1947- .... **CLC 5**
See also CA 53-56; CANR 9

Bromfield, Louis (Brucker)
1896-1956 .... **TCLC 11**
See also CA 107; DLB 4, 9, 86

Broner, E(sther) M(asserman)
1930- .... **CLC 19**
See also CA 17-20R; CANR 8, 25; DLB 28

Bronk, William 1918- .... **CLC 10**
See also CA 89-92; CANR 23

Bronstein, Lev Davidovich
See Trotsky, Leon

Bronte, Anne 1820-1849 .... **NCLC 4**
See also DLB 21

Bronte, Charlotte
1816-1855 .... **NCLC 3, 8, 33; DA;
DAB; DAC; WLC**
See also AAYA 17; CDBLB 1832-1890;
DAM MST, NOV; DLB 21, 159

Bronte, Emily (Jane)
1818-1848 .... **NCLC 16, 35; DA; DAB;
DAC; PC 8; WLC**
See also AAYA 17; CDBLB 1832-1890;
DAM MST, NOV, POET; DLB 21, 32

Brooke, Frances 1724-1789 .... **LC 6**
See also DLB 39, 99

Brooke, Henry 1703(?)-1783 .... **LC 1**
See also DLB 39

Brooke, Rupert (Chawner)
1887-1915 .... **TCLC 2, 7; DA; DAB;
DAC; WLC**
See also CA 104; 132; CDBLB 1914-1945;
DAM MST, POET; DLB 19; MTCW

Brooke-Haven, P.
See Wodehouse, P(elham) G(renville)

Brooke-Rose, Christine 1926- ...... **CLC 40**
See also CA 13-16R; DLB 14

Brookner, Anita
1928- .... **CLC 32, 34, 51; DAB**
See also CA 114; 120; CANR 37;
DAM POP; DLBY 87; MTCW

Brooks, Cleanth 1906-1994 ..... **CLC 24, 86**
See also CA 17-20R; 145; CANR 33, 35;
DLB 63; DLBY 94; INT CANR-35;
MTCW

Brooks, George
See Baum, L(yman) Frank

Brooks, Gwendolyn
1917- ...... **CLC 1, 2, 4, 5, 15, 49; BLC;
DA; DAC; PC 7; WLC**
See also AITN 1; BW 2; CA 1-4R;
CANR 1, 27; CDALB 1941-1968;
CLR 27; DAM MST, MULT, POET;
DLB 5, 76; MTCW; SATA 6

Brooks, Mel .... **CLC 12**
See also Kaminsky, Melvin
See also AAYA 13; DLB 26

Brooks, Peter 1938- .... **CLC 34**
See also CA 45-48; CANR 1

Brooks, Van Wyck 1886-1963 ...... **CLC 29**
See also CA 1-4R; CANR 6; DLB 45, 63,
103

Brophy, Brigid (Antonia)
1929-1995 .... **CLC 6, 11, 29**
See also CA 5-8R; 149; CAAS 4; CANR 25;
DLB 14; MTCW

Brosman, Catharine Savage 1934- .... **CLC 9**
See also CA 61-64; CANR 21, 46

Brother Antoninus
See Everson, William (Oliver)

Broughton, T(homas) Alan 1936- ... **CLC 19**
See also CA 45-48; CANR 2, 23, 48

Broumas, Olga 1949- .... **CLC 10, 73**
See also CA 85-88; CANR 20

Brown, Charles Brockden
1771-1810 .... **NCLC 22**
See also CDALB 1640-1865; DLB 37, 59,
73

Brown, Christy 1932-1981 .... **CLC 63**
See also CA 105; 104; DLB 14

Brown, Claude 1937- .... **CLC 30; BLC**
See also AAYA 7; BW 1; CA 73-76;
DAM MULT

Brown, Dee (Alexander) 1908- .. **CLC 18, 47**
See also CA 13-16R; CAAS 6; CANR 11,
45; DAM POP; DLBY 80; MTCW;
SATA 5

Brown, George
See Wertmueller, Lina

Brown, George Douglas
1869-1902 .... **TCLC 28**

Brown, George Mackay 1921- .... **CLC 5, 48**
See also CA 21-24R; CAAS 6; CANR 12,
37; DLB 14, 27, 139; MTCW; SATA 35

Brown, (William) Larry 1951- ...... **CLC 73**
See also CA 130; 134; INT 133

Brown, Moses
See Barrett, William (Christopher)

Brown, Rita Mae 1944- ..... **CLC 18, 43, 79**
See also CA 45-48; CANR 2, 11, 35;
DAM NOV, POP; INT CANR-11;
MTCW

Brown, Roderick (Langmere) Haig-
See Haig-Brown, Roderick (Langmere)

Brown, Rosellen 1939- .... **CLC 32**
See also CA 77-80; CAAS 10; CANR 14, 44

Brown, Sterling Allen
1901-1989 .... **CLC 1, 23, 59; BLC**
See also BW 1; CA 85-88; 127; CANR 26;
DAM MULT, POET; DLB 48, 51, 63;
MTCW

Brown, Will
See Ainsworth, William Harrison

Brown, William Wells
1813-1884 .... **NCLC 2; BLC; DC 1**
See also DAM MULT; DLB 3, 50

Browne, (Clyde) Jackson 1948(?)- ... **CLC 21**
See also CA 120

Browning, Elizabeth Barrett
1806-1861 ..... **NCLC 1, 16; DA; DAB;
DAC; PC 6; WLC**
See also CDBLB 1832-1890; DAM MST,
POET; DLB 32

Browning, Robert
1812-1889 .... **NCLC 19; DA; DAB;
DAC; PC 2**
See also CDBLB 1832-1890; DAM MST,
POET; DLB 32; YABC 1

Browning, Tod 1882-1962 .... **CLC 16**
See also CA 141; 117

Brownson, Orestes (Augustus)
1803-1876 .... **NCLC 50**

Bruccoli, Matthew J(oseph) 1931- .. **CLC 34**
See also CA 9-12R; CANR 7; DLB 103

Bruce, Lenny .... **CLC 21**
See also Schneider, Leonard Alfred

Bruin, John
See Brutus, Dennis

Brulard, Henri
See Stendhal

Brulls, Christian
See Simenon, Georges (Jacques Christian)

Brunner, John (Kilian Houston)
1934-1995 .... **CLC 8, 10**
See also CA 1-4R; 149; CAAS 8; CANR 2,
37; DAM POP; MTCW

Bruno, Giordano 1548-1600 .... **LC 27**

Brutus, Dennis 1924- .... **CLC 43; BLC**
See also BW 2; CA 49-52; CAAS 14;
CANR 2, 27, 42; DAM MULT, POET;
DLB 117

Bryan, C(ourtlandt) D(ixon) B(arnes)
1936- .... **CLC 29**
See also CA 73-76; CANR 13;
INT CANR-13

Bryan, Michael
See Moore, Brian

Bryant, William Cullen
1794-1878 ..... **NCLC 6, 46; DA; DAB;
DAC**
See also CDALB 1640-1865; DAM MST,
POET; DLB 3, 43, 59

Bryusov, Valery Yakovlevich
1873-1924 .... **TCLC 10**
See also CA 107

Buchan, John 1875-1940 ... **TCLC 41; DAB**
See also CA 108; 145; DAM POP; DLB 34,
70, 156; YABC 2

Buchanan, George 1506-1582 .... **LC 4**

Buchheim, Lothar-Guenther 1918- ... **CLC 6**
See also CA 85-88

Buchner, (Karl) Georg
1813-1837 .... **NCLC 26**

Buchwald, Art(hur) 1925- .... **CLC 33**
See also AITN 1; CA 5-8R; CANR 21;
MTCW; SATA 10

Buck, Pearl S(ydenstricker)
1892-1973 .... **CLC 7, 11, 18; DA; DAB;**
DAC
See also AITN 1; CA 1-4R; 41-44R;
CANR 1, 34; DAM MST, NOV; DLB 9,
102; MTCW; SATA 1, 25

Buckler, Ernest 1908-1984.... **CLC 13; DAC**
See also CA 11-12; 114; CAP 1;
DAM MST; DLB 68; SATA 47

Buckley, Vincent (Thomas)
1925-1988 .... **CLC 57**
See also CA 101

Buckley, William F(rank), Jr.
1925- .... **CLC 7, 18, 37**
See also AITN 1; CA 1-4R; CANR 1, 24;
DAM POP; DLB 137; DLBY 80;
INT CANR-24; MTCW

Buechner, (Carl) Frederick
1926- .... **CLC 2, 4, 6, 9**
See also CA 13-16R; CANR 11, 39;
DAM NOV; DLBY 80; INT CANR-11;
MTCW

Buell, John (Edward) 1927-........ **CLC 10**
See also CA 1-4R; DLB 53

Buero Vallejo, Antonio 1916- ... **CLC 15, 46**
See also CA 106; CANR 24, 49; HW;
MTCW

Bufalino, Gesualdo 1920(?)-........ **CLC 74**

Bugayev, Boris Nikolayevich 1880-1934
See Bely, Andrey
See also CA 104

Bukowski, Charles
1920-1994 .... **CLC 2, 5, 9, 41, 82**
See also CA 17-20R; 144; CANR 40;
DAM NOV, POET; DLB 5, 130; MTCW

Bulgakov, Mikhail (Afanas'evich)
1891-1940 .... **TCLC 2, 16; SSC 18**
See also CA 105; DAM DRAM, NOV

Bulgya, Alexander Alexandrovich
1901-1956 .... **TCLC 53**
See also Fadeyev, Alexander
See also CA 117

Bullins, Ed 1935- .. **CLC 1, 5, 7; BLC; DC 6**
See also BW 2; CA 49-52; CAAS 16;
CANR 24, 46; DAM DRAM, MULT;
DLB 7, 38; MTCW

Bulwer-Lytton, Edward (George Earle Lytton)
1803-1873 .... **NCLC 1, 45**
See also DLB 21

Bunin, Ivan Alexeyevich
1870-1953 .... **TCLC 6; SSC 5**
See also CA 104

Bunting, Basil 1900-1985.... **CLC 10, 39, 47**
See also CA 53-56; 115; CANR 7;
DAM POET; DLB 20

Bunuel, Luis 1900-1983 .. **CLC 16, 80; HLC**
See also CA 101; 110; CANR 32;
DAM MULT; HW

Bunyan, John
1628-1688 ...... **LC 4; DA; DAB; DAC;**
WLC
See also CDBLB 1660-1789; DAM MST;
DLB 39

Burckhardt, Jacob (Christoph)
1818-1897 .... **NCLC 49**

Burford, Eleanor
See Hibbert, Eleanor Alice Burford

Burgess, Anthony
. **CLC 1, 2, 4, 5, 8, 10, 13, 15, 22, 40, 62,**
81; DAB
See also Wilson, John (Anthony) Burgess
See also AITN 1; CDBLB 1960 to Present;
DLB 14

Burke, Edmund
1729(?)-1797 .... **LC 7; DA; DAB; DAC;**
WLC
See also DAM MST; DLB 104

Burke, Kenneth (Duva)
1897-1993 .... **CLC 2, 24**
See also CA 5-8R; 143; CANR 39; DLB 45,
63; MTCW

Burke, Leda
See Garnett, David

Burke, Ralph
See Silverberg, Robert

Burney, Fanny 1752-1840 .... **NCLC 12, 54**
See also DLB 39

Burns, Robert 1759-1796............ **PC 6**
See also CDBLB 1789-1832; DA; DAB;
DAC; DAM MST, POET; DLB 109;
WLC

Burns, Tex
See L'Amour, Louis (Dearborn)

Burnshaw, Stanley 1906-..... **CLC 3, 13, 44**
See also CA 9-12R; DLB 48

Burr, Anne 1937- .... **CLC 6**
See also CA 25-28R

Burroughs, Edgar Rice
1875-1950 .... **TCLC 2, 32**
See also AAYA 11; CA 104; 132;
DAM NOV; DLB 8; MTCW; SATA 41

Burroughs, William S(eward)
1914- .... **CLC 1, 2, 5, 15, 22, 42, 75;**
DA; DAB; DAC; WLC
See also AITN 2; CA 9-12R; CANR 20;
DAM MST, NOV, POP; DLB 2, 8, 16,
152; DLBY 81; MTCW

Burton, Richard F. 1821-1890.... **NCLC 42**
See also DLB 55

Busch, Frederick 1941- ... **CLC 7, 10, 18, 47**
See also CA 33-36R; CAAS 1; CANR 45;
DLB 6

Bush, Ronald 1946- .... **CLC 34**
See also CA 136

Bustos, F(rancisco)
See Borges, Jorge Luis

Bustos Domecq, H(onorio)
See Bioy Casares, Adolfo; Borges, Jorge
Luis

Butler, Octavia E(stelle) 1947- ..... **CLC 38**
See also BW 2; CA 73-76; CANR 12, 24,
38; DAM MULT, POP; DLB 33;
MTCW; SATA 84

Butler, Robert Olen (Jr.) 1945-..... **CLC 81**
See also CA 112; DAM POP; INT 112

Butler, Samuel 1612-1680 .... **LC 16**
See also DLB 101, 126

Butler, Samuel
1835-1902 ...... **TCLC 1, 33; DA; DAB;**
DAC; WLC
See also CA 143; CDBLB 1890-1914;
DAM MST, NOV; DLB 18, 57

Butler, Walter C.
See Faust, Frederick (Schiller)

Butor, Michel (Marie Francois)
1926- .... **CLC 1, 3, 8, 11, 15**
See also CA 9-12R; CANR 33; DLB 83;
MTCW

Buzo, Alexander (John) 1944-...... **CLC 61**
See also CA 97-100; CANR 17, 39

Buzzati, Dino 1906-1972 .... **CLC 36**
See also CA 33-36R

Byars, Betsy (Cromer) 1928-...... **CLC 35**
See also CA 33-36R; CANR 18, 36; CLR 1,
16; DLB 52; INT CANR-18; JRDA;
MAICYA; MTCW; SAAS 1; SATA 4,
46, 80

Byatt, A(ntonia) S(usan Drabble)
1936- .... **CLC 19, 65**
See also CA 13-16R; CANR 13, 33, 50;
DAM NOV, POP; DLB 14; MTCW

Byrne, David 1952-............... **CLC 26**
See also CA 127

Byrne, John Keyes 1926-
See Leonard, Hugh
See also CA 102; INT 102

Byron, George Gordon (Noel)
1788-1824 ..... **NCLC 2, 12; DA; DAB;**
DAC; WLC
See also CDBLB 1789-1832; DAM MST,
POET; DLB 96, 110

C. 3. 3.
See Wilde, Oscar (Fingal O'Flahertie Wills)

Caballero, Fernan 1796-1877..... **NCLC 10**

Cabell, James Branch 1879-1958 ... **TCLC 6**
See also CA 105; DLB 9, 78

Cable, George Washington
1844-1925 .... **TCLC 4; SSC 4**
See also CA 104; DLB 12, 74; DLBD 13

Cabral de Melo Neto, Joao 1920-... **CLC 76**
See also DAM MULT

Cabrera Infante, G(uillermo)
1929- .... **CLC 5, 25, 45; HLC**
See also CA 85-88; CANR 29;
DAM MULT; DLB 113; HW; MTCW

Cade, Toni
See Bambara, Toni Cade

Cadmus and Harmonia
See Buchan, John

Caedmon fl. 658-680............. **CMLC 7**
See also DLB 146

Caeiro, Alberto
See Pessoa, Fernando (Antonio Nogueira)

Cage, John (Milton, Jr.) 1912-..... **CLC 41**
See also CA 13-16R; CANR 9;
INT CANR-9

Cain, G.
See Cabrera Infante, G(uillermo)

Cain, Guillermo
See Cabrera Infante, G(uillermo)

Cain, James M(allahan)
1892-1977 . . . . **CLC 3, 11, 28**
See also AITN 1; CA 17-20R; 73-76;
CANR 8, 34; MTCW

Caine, Mark
See Raphael, Frederic (Michael)

Calasso, Roberto 1941- . . . . **CLC 81**
See also CA 143

Calderon de la Barca, Pedro
1600-1681 . . . . **LC 23; DC 3**

Caldwell, Erskine (Preston)
1903-1987 . . . . **CLC 1, 8, 14, 50, 60;**
SSC 19
See also AITN 1; CA 1-4R; 121; CAAS 1;
CANR 2, 33; DAM NOV; DLB 9, 86;
MTCW

Caldwell, (Janet Miriam) Taylor (Holland)
1900-1985 . . . . **CLC 2, 28, 39**
See also CA 5-8R; 116; CANR 5;
DAM NOV, POP

Calhoun, John Caldwell
1782-1850 . . . . **NCLC 15**
See also DLB 3

Calisher, Hortense
1911- . . . . **CLC 2, 4, 8, 38; SSC 15**
See also CA 1-4R; CANR 1, 22;
DAM NOV; DLB 2; INT CANR-22;
MTCW

Callaghan, Morley Edward
1903-1990 . . . . . **CLC 3, 14, 41, 65; DAC**
See also CA 9-12R; 132; CANR 33;
DAM MST; DLB 68; MTCW

Calvino, Italo
1923-1985 . . . . . **CLC 5, 8, 11, 22, 33, 39,**
73; SSC 3
See also CA 85-88; 116; CANR 23;
DAM NOV; MTCW

Cameron, Carey 1952- . . . . **CLC 59**
See also CA 135

Cameron, Peter 1959- . . . . **CLC 44**
See also CA 125; CANR 50

Campana, Dino 1885-1932 . . . . **TCLC 20**
See also CA 117; DLB 114

Campanella, Tommaso 1568-1639 . . . . **LC 32**

Campbell, John W(ood, Jr.)
1910-1971 . . . . **CLC 32**
See also CA 21-22; 29-32R; CANR 34;
CAP 2; DLB 8; MTCW

Campbell, Joseph 1904-1987 . . . . **CLC 69**
See also AAYA 3; BEST 89:2; CA 1-4R;
124; CANR 3, 28; MTCW

Campbell, Maria 1940- . . . . **CLC 85; DAC**
See also CA 102; NNAL

Campbell, (John) Ramsey
1946- . . . . **CLC 42; SSC 19**
See also CA 57-60; CANR 7; INT CANR-7

Campbell, (Ignatius) Roy (Dunnachie)
1901-1957 . . . . **TCLC 5**
See also CA 104; DLB 20

Campbell, Thomas 1777-1844 . . . . **NCLC 19**
See also DLB 93; 144

Campbell, Wilfred . . . . **TCLC 9**
See also Campbell, William

Campbell, William 1858(?)-1918
See Campbell, Wilfred
See also CA 106; DLB 92

Campos, Alvaro de
See Pessoa, Fernando (Antonio Nogueira)

Camus, Albert
1913-1960 . . . . **CLC 1, 2, 4, 9, 11, 14, 32,**
63, 69; DA; DAB; DAC; DC 2; SSC 9;
WLC
See also CA 89-92; DAM DRAM, MST,
NOV; DLB 72; MTCW

Canby, Vincent 1924- . . . . **CLC 13**
See also CA 81-84

Cancale
See Desnos, Robert

Canetti, Elias
1905-1994 . . . . . . **CLC 3, 14, 25, 75, 86**
See also CA 21-24R; 146; CANR 23;
DLB 85, 124; MTCW

Canin, Ethan 1960- . . . . **CLC 55**
See also CA 131; 135

Cannon, Curt
See Hunter, Evan

Cape, Judith
See Page, P(atricia) K(athleen)

Capek, Karel
1890-1938 . . . . . . **TCLC 6, 37; DA; DAB;**
DAC; DC 1; WLC
See also CA 104; 140; DAM DRAM, MST,
NOV

Capote, Truman
1924-1984 . . . . . . **CLC 1, 3, 8, 13, 19, 34,**
38, 58; DA; DAB; DAC; SSC 2; WLC
See also CA 5-8R; 113; CANR 18;
CDALB 1941-1968; DAM MST, NOV,
POP; DLB 2; DLBY 80, 84; MTCW

Capra, Frank 1897-1991 . . . . **CLC 16**
See also CA 61-64; 135

Caputo, Philip 1941- . . . . **CLC 32**
See also CA 73-76; CANR 40

Card, Orson Scott 1951- . . . . **CLC 44, 47, 50**
See also AAYA 11; CA 102; CANR 27, 47;
DAM POP; INT CANR-27; MTCW;
SATA 83

Cardenal (Martinez), Ernesto
1925- . . . . **CLC 31; HLC**
See also CA 49-52; CANR 2, 32;
DAM MULT, POET; HW; MTCW

Carducci, Giosue 1835-1907 . . . . **TCLC 32**

Carew, Thomas 1595(?)-1640 . . . . **LC 13**
See also DLB 126

Carey, Ernestine Gilbreth 1908- . . . . **CLC 17**
See also CA 5-8R; SATA 2

Carey, Peter 1943- . . . . **CLC 40, 55**
See also CA 123; 127; INT 127; MTCW

Carleton, William 1794-1869 . . . . . . **NCLC 3**
See also DLB 159

Carlisle, Henry (Coffin) 1926- . . . . . . **CLC 33**
See also CA 13-16R; CANR 15

Carlsen, Chris
See Holdstock, Robert P.

Carlson, Ron(ald F.) 1947- . . . . **CLC 54**
See also CA 105; CANR 27

Carlyle, Thomas
1795-1881 . . **NCLC 22; DA; DAB; DAC**
See also CDBLB 1789-1832; DAM MST;
DLB 55; 144

Carman, (William) Bliss
1861-1929 . . . . **TCLC 7; DAC**
See also CA 104; DLB 92

Carnegie, Dale 1888-1955 . . . . **TCLC 53**

Carossa, Hans 1878-1956 . . . . **TCLC 48**
See also DLB 66

Carpenter, Don(ald Richard)
1931-1995 . . . . **CLC 41**
See also CA 45-48; 149; CANR 1

Carpentier (y Valmont), Alejo
1904-1980 . . . . **CLC 8, 11, 38; HLC**
See also CA 65-68; 97-100; CANR 11;
DAM MULT; DLB 113; HW

Carr, Caleb 1955(?)- . . . . **CLC 86**
See also CA 147

Carr, Emily 1871-1945 . . . . **TCLC 32**
See also DLB 68

Carr, John Dickson 1906-1977 . . . . . . **CLC 3**
See also CA 49-52; 69-72; CANR 3, 33;
MTCW

Carr, Philippa
See Hibbert, Eleanor Alice Burford

Carr, Virginia Spencer 1929- . . . . **CLC 34**
See also CA 61-64; DLB 111

Carrere, Emmanuel 1957- . . . . **CLC 89**

Carrier, Roch 1937- . . . . . **CLC 13, 78; DAC**
See also CA 130; DAM MST; DLB 53

Carroll, James P. 1943(?)- . . . . **CLC 38**
See also CA 81-84

Carroll, Jim 1951- . . . . **CLC 35**
See also AAYA 17; CA 45-48; CANR 42

Carroll, Lewis . . . . **NCLC 2, 53; WLC**
See also Dodgson, Charles Lutwidge
See also CDBLB 1832-1890; CLR 2, 18;
DLB 18; JRDA

Carroll, Paul Vincent 1900-1968 . . . . **CLC 10**
See also CA 9-12R; 25-28R; DLB 10

Carruth, Hayden
1921- . . . . . . **CLC 4, 7, 10, 18, 84; PC 10**
See also CA 9-12R; CANR 4, 38; DLB 5;
INT CANR-4; MTCW; SATA 47

Carson, Rachel Louise 1907-1964 . . . **CLC 71**
See also CA 77-80; CANR 35; DAM POP;
MTCW; SATA 23

Carter, Angela (Olive)
1940-1992 . . . . . . **CLC 5, 41, 76; SSC 13**
See also CA 53-56; 136; CANR 12, 36;
DLB 14; MTCW; SATA 66;
SATA-Obit 70

Carter, Nick
See Smith, Martin Cruz

Carver, Raymond
1938-1988 . . . **CLC 22, 36, 53, 55; SSC 8**
See also CA 33-36R; 126; CANR 17, 34;
DAM NOV; DLB 130; DLBY 84, 88;
MTCW

Cary, Elizabeth, Lady Falkland
1585-1639 . . . . **LC 30**

Cary, (Arthur) Joyce (Lunel)
    1888-1957 . . . . **TCLC 1, 29**
    See also CA 104; CDBLB 1914-1945;
    DLB 15, 100

Casanova de Seingalt, Giovanni Jacopo
    1725-1798 . . . . **LC 13**

Casares, Adolfo Bioy
    See Bioy Casares, Adolfo

Casely-Hayford, J(oseph) E(phraim)
    1866-1930 . . . . **TCLC 24; BLC**
    See also BW 2; CA 123; DAM MULT

Casey, John (Dudley) 1939- . . . . **CLC 59**
    See also BEST 90:2; CA 69-72; CANR 23

Casey, Michael 1947- . . . . **CLC 2**
    See also CA 65-68; DLB 5

Casey, Patrick
    See Thurman, Wallace (Henry)

Casey, Warren (Peter) 1935-1988 . . . **CLC 12**
    See also CA 101; 127; INT 101

Casona, Alejandro . . . . **CLC 49**
    See also Alvarez, Alejandro Rodriguez

Cassavetes, John 1929-1989 . . . . **CLC 20**
    See also CA 85-88; 127

Cassill, R(onald) V(erlin) 1919- . . . **CLC 4, 23**
    See also CA 9-12R; CAAS 1; CANR 7, 45;
    DLB 6

Cassirer, Ernst 1874-1945 . . . . **TCLC 61**

Cassity, (Allen) Turner 1929- . . . . **CLC 6, 42**
    See also CA 17-20R; CAAS 8; CANR 11;
    DLB 105

Castaneda, Carlos 1931(?)- . . . . **CLC 12**
    See also CA 25-28R; CANR 32; HW;
    MTCW

Castedo, Elena 1937- . . . . **CLC 65**
    See also CA 132

Castedo-Ellerman, Elena
    See Castedo, Elena

Castellanos, Rosario
    1925-1974 . . . . **CLC 66; HLC**
    See also CA 131; 53-56; DAM MULT;
    DLB 113; HW

Castelvetro, Lodovico 1505-1571 . . . . . **LC 12**

Castiglione, Baldassare 1478-1529 . . . **LC 12**

Castle, Robert
    See Hamilton, Edmond

Castro, Guillen de 1569-1631 . . . . **LC 19**

Castro, Rosalia de 1837-1885 . . . . . **NCLC 3**
    See also DAM MULT

Cather, Willa
    See Cather, Willa Sibert

Cather, Willa Sibert
    1873-1947 . . . . **TCLC 1, 11, 31; DA;**
                          DAB; DAC; SSC 2; WLC
    See also CA 104; 128; CDALB 1865-1917;
    DAM MST, NOV; DLB 9, 54, 78;
    DLBD 1; MTCW; SATA 30

Catton, (Charles) Bruce
    1899-1978 . . . . **CLC 35**
    See also AITN 1; CA 5-8R; 81-84;
    CANR 7; DLB 17; SATA 2;
    SATA-Obit 24

Cauldwell, Frank
    See King, Francis (Henry)

Caunitz, William J. 1933- . . . . **CLC 34**
    See also BEST 89:3; CA 125; 130; INT 130

Causley, Charles (Stanley) 1917- . . . . . **CLC 7**
    See also CA 9-12R; CANR 5, 35; CLR 30;
    DLB 27; MTCW; SATA 3, 66

Caute, David 1936- . . . . **CLC 29**
    See also CA 1-4R; CAAS 4; CANR 1, 33;
    DAM NOV; DLB 14

Cavafy, C(onstantine) P(eter)
    1863-1933 . . . . **TCLC 2, 7**
    See also Kavafis, Konstantinos Petrou
    See also CA 148; DAM POET

Cavallo, Evelyn
    See Spark, Muriel (Sarah)

Cavanna, Betty . . . . **CLC 12**
    See also Harrison, Elizabeth Cavanna
    See also JRDA; MAICYA; SAAS 4;
    SATA 1, 30

Cavendish, Margaret Lucas
    1623-1673 . . . . **LC 30**
    See also DLB 131

Caxton, William 1421(?)-1491(?) . . . . . **LC 17**

Cayrol, Jean 1911- . . . . **CLC 11**
    See also CA 89-92; DLB 83

Cela, Camilo Jose
    1916- . . . . **CLC 4, 13, 59; HLC**
    See also BEST 90:2; CA 21-24R; CAAS 10;
    CANR 21, 32; DAM MULT; DLBY 89;
    HW; MTCW

Celan, Paul . . . . . . **CLC 10, 19, 53, 82; PC 10**
    See also Antschel, Paul
    See also DLB 69

Celine, Louis-Ferdinand
    . . . . **CLC 1, 3, 4, 7, 9, 15, 47**
    See also Destouches, Louis-Ferdinand
    See also DLB 72

Cellini, Benvenuto 1500-1571 . . . . **LC 7**

Cendrars, Blaise . . . . **CLC 18**
    See also Sauser-Hall, Frederic

Cernuda (y Bidon), Luis
    1902-1963 . . . . **CLC 54**
    See also CA 131; 89-92; DAM POET;
    DLB 134; HW

Cervantes (Saavedra), Miguel de
    1547-1616 . . . . **LC 6, 23; DA; DAB;**
                          DAC; SSC 12; WLC
    See also DAM MST, NOV

Cesaire, Aime (Fernand)
    1913- . . . . **CLC 19, 32; BLC**
    See also BW 2; CA 65-68; CANR 24, 43;
    DAM MULT, POET; MTCW

Chabon, Michael 1965(?)- . . . . **CLC 55**
    See also CA 139

Chabrol, Claude 1930- . . . . **CLC 16**
    See also CA 110

Challans, Mary 1905-1983
    See Renault, Mary
    See also CA 81-84; 111; SATA 23;
    SATA-Obit 36

Challis, George
    See Faust, Frederick (Schiller)

Chambers, Aidan 1934- . . . . **CLC 35**
    See also CA 25-28R; CANR 12, 31; JRDA;
    MAICYA; SAAS 12; SATA 1, 69

Chambers, James 1948-
    See Cliff, Jimmy
    See also CA 124

Chambers, Jessie
    See Lawrence, D(avid) H(erbert Richards)

Chambers, Robert W. 1865-1933 . . . **TCLC 41**

Chandler, Raymond (Thornton)
    1888-1959 . . . . **TCLC 1, 7**
    See also CA 104; 129; CDALB 1929-1941;
    DLBD 6; MTCW

Chang, Jung 1952- . . . . **CLC 71**
    See also CA 142

Channing, William Ellery
    1780-1842 . . . . **NCLC 17**
    See also DLB 1, 59

Chaplin, Charles Spencer
    1889-1977 . . . . **CLC 16**
    See also Chaplin, Charlie
    See also CA 81-84; 73-76

Chaplin, Charlie
    See Chaplin, Charles Spencer
    See also DLB 44

Chapman, George 1559(?)-1634 . . . . . . **LC 22**
    See also DAM DRAM; DLB 62, 121

Chapman, Graham 1941-1989 . . . . . . **CLC 21**
    See also Monty Python
    See also CA 116; 129; CANR 35

Chapman, John Jay 1862-1933 . . . . . **TCLC 7**
    See also CA 104

Chapman, Walker
    See Silverberg, Robert

Chappell, Fred (Davis) 1936- . . . . **CLC 40, 78**
    See also CA 5-8R; CAAS 4; CANR 8, 33;
    DLB 6, 105

Char, Rene(-Emile)
    1907-1988 . . . . **CLC 9, 11, 14, 55**
    See also CA 13-16R; 124; CANR 32;
    DAM POET; MTCW

Charby, Jay
    See Ellison, Harlan (Jay)

Chardin, Pierre Teilhard de
    See Teilhard de Chardin, (Marie Joseph)
    Pierre

Charles I 1600-1649 . . . . **LC 13**

Charyn, Jerome 1937- . . . . **CLC 5, 8, 18**
    See also CA 5-8R; CAAS 1; CANR 7;
    DLBY 83; MTCW

Chase, Mary (Coyle) 1907-1981 . . . . . . **DC 1**
    See also CA 77-80; 105; SATA 17;
    SATA-Obit 29

Chase, Mary Ellen 1887-1973 . . . . **CLC 2**
    See also CA 13-16; 41-44R; CAP 1;
    SATA 10

Chase, Nicholas
    See Hyde, Anthony

Chateaubriand, Francois Rene de
    1768-1848 . . . . **NCLC 3**
    See also DLB 119

Chatterje, Sarat Chandra 1876-1936(?)
    See Chatterji, Saratchandra
    See also CA 109

Chatterji, Bankim Chandra
    1838-1894 . . . . **NCLC 19**

Clarke, Marcus (Andrew Hislop)
  1846-1881 .... NCLC 19

Clarke, Shirley 1925-............ CLC 16

Clash, The
  See Headon, (Nicky) Topper; Jones, Mick;
  Simonon, Paul; Strummer, Joe

Claudel, Paul (Louis Charles Marie)
  1868-1955 .... TCLC 2, 10
  See also CA 104

Clavell, James (duMaresq)
  1925-1994 .... CLC 6, 25, 87
  See also CA 25-28R; 146; CANR 26, 48;
  DAM NOV, POP; MTCW

Cleaver, (Leroy) Eldridge
  1935- .... CLC 30; BLC
  See also BW 1; CA 21-24R; CANR 16;
  DAM MULT

Cleese, John (Marwood) 1939- ..... CLC 21
  See also Monty Python
  See also CA 112; 116; CANR 35; MTCW

Cleishbotham, Jebediah
  See Scott, Walter

Cleland, John 1710-1789 .... LC 2
  See also DLB 39

Clemens, Samuel Langhorne 1835-1910
  See Twain, Mark
  See also CA 104; 135; CDALB 1865-1917;
  DA; DAB; DAC; DAM MST, NOV;
  DLB 11, 12, 23, 64, 74; JRDA;
  MAICYA; YABC 2

Cleophil
  See Congreve, William

Clerihew, E.
  See Bentley, E(dmund) C(lerihew)

Clerk, N. W.
  See Lewis, C(live) S(taples)

Cliff, Jimmy.................... CLC 21
  See also Chambers, James

Clifton, (Thelma) Lucille
  1936- .... CLC 19, 66; BLC
  See also BW 2; CA 49-52; CANR 2, 24, 42;
  CLR 5; DAM MULT, POET; DLB 5, 41;
  MAICYA; MTCW; SATA 20, 69

Clinton, Dirk
  See Silverberg, Robert

Clough, Arthur Hugh 1819-1861.. NCLC 27
  See also DLB 32

Clutha, Janet Paterson Frame 1924-
  See Frame, Janet
  See also CA 1-4R; CANR 2, 36; MTCW

Clyne, Terence
  See Blatty, William Peter

Cobalt, Martin
  See Mayne, William (James Carter)

Cobbett, William 1763-1835 ..... NCLC 49
  See also DLB 43, 107, 158

Coburn, D(onald) L(ee) 1938- ...... CLC 10
  See also CA 89-92

Cocteau, Jean (Maurice Eugene Clement)
  1889-1963 .... CLC 1, 8, 15, 16, 43; DA;
                                    DAB; DAC; WLC
  See also CA 25-28; CANR 40; CAP 2;
  DAM DRAM, MST, NOV; DLB 65;
  MTCW

Codrescu, Andrei 1946- .... CLC 46
  See also CA 33-36R; CAAS 19; CANR 13,
  34; DAM POET

Coe, Max
  See Bourne, Randolph S(illiman)

Coe, Tucker
  See Westlake, Donald E(dwin)

Coetzee, J(ohn) M(ichael)
  1940- .... CLC 23, 33, 66
  See also CA 77-80; CANR 41; DAM NOV;
  MTCW

Coffey, Brian
  See Koontz, Dean R(ay)

Cohan, George M. 1878-1942 ..... TCLC 60

Cohen, Arthur A(llen)
  1928-1986 .... CLC 7, 31
  See also CA 1-4R; 120; CANR 1, 17, 42;
  DLB 28

Cohen, Leonard (Norman)
  1934- .... CLC 3, 38; DAC
  See also CA 21-24R; CANR 14;
  DAM MST; DLB 53; MTCW

Cohen, Matt 1942- .... CLC 19; DAC
  See also CA 61-64; CAAS 18; CANR 40;
  DLB 53

Cohen-Solal, Annie 19(?)- .... CLC 50

Colegate, Isabel 1931- .... CLC 36
  See also CA 17-20R; CANR 8, 22; DLB 14;
  INT CANR-22; MTCW

Coleman, Emmett
  See Reed, Ishmael

Coleridge, Samuel Taylor
  1772-1834 ..... NCLC 9, 54; DA; DAB;
                              DAC; PC 11; WLC
  See also CDBLB 1789-1832; DAM MST,
  POET; DLB 93, 107

Coleridge, Sara 1802-1852 ...... NCLC 31

Coles, Don 1928- .... CLC 46
  See also CA 115; CANR 38

Colette, (Sidonie-Gabrielle)
  1873-1954 ...... TCLC 1, 5, 16; SSC 10
  See also CA 104; 131; DAM NOV; DLB 65;
  MTCW

Collett, (Jacobine) Camilla (Wergeland)
  1813-1895 .... NCLC 22

Collier, Christopher 1930- .... CLC 30
  See also AAYA 13; CA 33-36R; CANR 13,
  33; JRDA; MAICYA; SATA 16, 70

Collier, James L(incoln) 1928- ..... CLC 30
  See also AAYA 13; CA 9-12R; CANR 4,
  33; CLR 3; DAM POP; JRDA;
  MAICYA; SAAS 21; SATA 8, 70

Collier, Jeremy 1650-1726.......... LC 6

Collier, John 1901-1980.......... SSC 19
  See also CA 65-68; 97-100; CANR 10;
  DLB 77

Collins, Hunt
  See Hunter, Evan

Collins, Linda 1931-.............. CLC 44
  See also CA 125

Collins, (William) Wilkie
  1824-1889 .... NCLC 1, 18
  See also CDBLB 1832-1890; DLB 18, 70,
  159

Collins, William 1721-1759 .... LC 4
  See also DAM POET; DLB 109

Collodi, Carlo 1826-1890 .... NCLC 54
  See also Lorenzini, Carlo
  See also CLR 5

Colman, George
  See Glassco, John

Colt, Winchester Remington
  See Hubbard, L(afayette) Ron(ald)

Colter, Cyrus 1910- .... CLC 58
  See also BW 1; CA 65-68; CANR 10;
  DLB 33

Colton, James
  See Hansen, Joseph

Colum, Padraic 1881-1972......... CLC 28
  See also CA 73-76; 33-36R; CANR 35;
  CLR 36; MAICYA; MTCW; SATA 15

Colvin, James
  See Moorcock, Michael (John)

Colwin, Laurie (E.)
  1944-1992 .... CLC 5, 13, 23, 84
  See also CA 89-92; 139; CANR 20, 46;
  DLBY 80; MTCW

Comfort, Alex(ander) 1920-........ CLC 7
  See also CA 1-4R; CANR 1, 45; DAM POP

Comfort, Montgomery
  See Campbell, (John) Ramsey

Compton-Burnett, I(vy)
  1884(?)-1969 ...... CLC 1, 3, 10, 15, 34
  See also CA 1-4R; 25-28R; CANR 4;
  DAM NOV; DLB 36; MTCW

Comstock, Anthony 1844-1915 .... TCLC 13
  See also CA 110

Comte, Auguste 1798-1857....... NCLC 54

Conan Doyle, Arthur
  See Doyle, Arthur Conan

Conde, Maryse 1937-............. CLC 52
  See also Boucolon, Maryse
  See also BW 2; DAM MULT

Condillac, Etienne Bonnot de
  1714-1780 .... LC 26

Condon, Richard (Thomas)
  1915-............ CLC 4, 6, 8, 10, 45
  See also BEST 90:3; CA 1-4R; CAAS 1;
  CANR 2, 23; DAM NOV;
  INT CANR-23; MTCW

Congreve, William
  1670-1729 .... LC 5, 21; DA; DAB;
                              DAC; DC 2; WLC
  See also CDBLB 1660-1789; DAM DRAM,
  MST, POET; DLB 39, 84

Connell, Evan S(helby), Jr.
  1924- .... CLC 4, 6, 45
  See also AAYA 7; CA 1-4R; CAAS 2;
  CANR 2, 39; DAM NOV; DLB 2;
  DLBY 81; MTCW

Connelly, Marc(us Cook)
  1890-1980 .... CLC 7
  See also CA 85-88; 102; CANR 30; DLB 7;
  DLBY 80; SATA-Obit 25

Connor, Ralph .... TCLC 31
  See also Gordon, Charles William
  See also DLB 92

Crebillon, Claude Prosper Jolyot de (fils)
1707-1777 . . . . **LC 28**

Credo
See Creasey, John

Creeley, Robert (White)
1926- . . . . . **CLC 1, 2, 4, 8, 11, 15, 36, 78**
See also CA 1-4R; CAAS 10; CANR 23, 43;
DAM POET; DLB 5, 16; MTCW

Crews, Harry (Eugene)
1935- . . . . **CLC 6, 23, 49**
See also AITN 1; CA 25-28R; CANR 20;
DLB 6, 143; MTCW

Crichton, (John) Michael
1942- . . . . **CLC 2, 6, 54, 90**
See also AAYA 10; AITN 2; CA 25-28R;
CANR 13, 40; DAM NOV, POP;
DLBY 81; INT CANR-13; JRDA;
MTCW; SATA 9

Crispin, Edmund . . . . **CLC 22**
See also Montgomery, (Robert) Bruce
See also DLB 87

Cristofer, Michael 1945(?)- . . . . **CLC 28**
See also CA 110; DAM DRAM; DLB 7

Croce, Benedetto 1866-1952 . . . . . . **TCLC 37**
See also CA 120

Crockett, David 1786-1836 . . . . **NCLC 8**
See also DLB 3, 11

Crockett, Davy
See Crockett, David

Crofts, Freeman Wills
1879-1957 . . . . **TCLC 55**
See also CA 115; DLB 77

Croker, John Wilson 1780-1857 . . **NCLC 10**
See also DLB 110

Crommelynck, Fernand 1885-1970 . . **CLC 75**
See also CA 89-92

Cronin, A(rchibald) J(oseph)
1896-1981 . . . . **CLC 32**
See also CA 1-4R; 102; CANR 5; SATA 47;
SATA-Obit 25

Cross, Amanda
See Heilbrun, Carolyn G(old)

Crothers, Rachel 1878(?)-1958 . . . . . **TCLC 19**
See also CA 113; DLB 7

Croves, Hal
See Traven, B.

Crowfield, Christopher
See Stowe, Harriet (Elizabeth) Beecher

Crowley, Aleister . . . . **TCLC 7**
See also Crowley, Edward Alexander

Crowley, Edward Alexander 1875-1947
See Crowley, Aleister
See also CA 104

Crowley, John 1942- . . . . **CLC 57**
See also CA 61-64; CANR 43; DLBY 82;
SATA 65

Crud
See Crumb, R(obert)

Crumarums
See Crumb, R(obert)

Crumb, R(obert) 1943- . . . . **CLC 17**
See also CA 106

Crumbum
See Crumb, R(obert)

Crumski
See Crumb, R(obert)

Crum the Bum
See Crumb, R(obert)

Crunk
See Crumb, R(obert)

Crustt
See Crumb, R(obert)

Cryer, Gretchen (Kiger) 1935- . . . . . **CLC 21**
See also CA 114; 123

Csath, Geza 1887-1919 . . . . **TCLC 13**
See also CA 111

Cudlip, David 1933- . . . . **CLC 34**

Cullen, Countee
1903-1946 . . . . . . **TCLC 4, 37; BLC; DA;**
DAC
See also BW 1; CA 108; 124;
CDALB 1917-1929; DAM MST, MULT,
POET; DLB 4, 48, 51; MTCW; SATA 18

Cum, R.
See Crumb, R(obert)

Cummings, Bruce F(rederick) 1889-1919
See Barbellion, W. N. P.
See also CA 123

Cummings, E(dward) E(stlin)
1894-1962 . . . . . . **CLC 1, 3, 8, 12, 15, 68;**
DA; DAB; DAC; PC 5; WLC 2
See also CA 73-76; CANR 31;
CDALB 1929-1941; DAM MST, POET;
DLB 4, 48; MTCW

Cunha, Euclides (Rodrigues Pimenta) da
1866-1909 . . . . **TCLC 24**
See also CA 123

Cunningham, E. V.
See Fast, Howard (Melvin)

Cunningham, J(ames) V(incent)
1911-1985 . . . . **CLC 3, 31**
See also CA 1-4R; 115; CANR 1; DLB 5

Cunningham, Julia (Woolfolk)
1916- . . . . **CLC 12**
See also CA 9-12R; CANR 4, 19, 36;
JRDA; MAICYA; SAAS 2; SATA 1, 26

Cunningham, Michael 1952- . . . . **CLC 34**
See also CA 136

Cunninghame Graham, R(obert) B(ontine)
1852-1936 . . . . **TCLC 19**
See also Graham, R(obert) B(ontine)
Cunninghame
See also CA 119; DLB 98

Currie, Ellen 19(?)- . . . . **CLC 44**

Curtin, Philip
See Lowndes, Marie Adelaide (Belloc)

Curtis, Price
See Ellison, Harlan (Jay)

Cutrate, Joe
See Spiegelman, Art

Czaczkes, Shmuel Yosef
See Agnon, S(hmuel) Y(osef Halevi)

Dabrowska, Maria (Szumska)
1889-1965 . . . . **CLC 15**
See also CA 106

Dabydeen, David 1955- . . . . **CLC 34**
See also BW 1; CA 125

Dacey, Philip 1939- . . . . **CLC 51**
See also CA 37-40R; CAAS 17; CANR 14,
32; DLB 105

Dagerman, Stig (Halvard)
1923-1954 . . . . **TCLC 17**
See also CA 117

Dahl, Roald
1916-1990 . . . . . . **CLC 1, 6, 18, 79; DAB;**
DAC
See also AAYA 15; CA 1-4R; 133;
CANR 6, 32, 37; CLR 1, 7; DAM MST,
NOV, POP; DLB 139; JRDA; MAICYA;
MTCW; SATA 1, 26, 73; SATA-Obit 65

Dahlberg, Edward 1900-1977. . . **CLC 1, 7, 14**
See also CA 9-12R; 69-72; CANR 31;
DLB 48; MTCW

Dale, Colin . . . . **TCLC 18**
See also Lawrence, T(homas) E(dward)

Dale, George E.
See Asimov, Isaac

Daly, Elizabeth 1878-1967. . . . . **CLC 52**
See also CA 23-24; 25-28R; CAP 2

Daly, Maureen 1921- . . . . **CLC 17**
See also AAYA 5; CANR 37; JRDA;
MAICYA; SAAS 1; SATA 2

Damas, Leon-Gontran 1912-1978 . . . **CLC 84**
See also BW 1; CA 125; 73-76

Dana, Richard Henry Sr.
1787-1879 . . . . **NCLC 53**

Daniel, Samuel 1562(?)-1619 . . . . **LC 24**
See also DLB 62

Daniels, Brett
See Adler, Renata

Dannay, Frederic 1905-1982 . . . . **CLC 11**
See also Queen, Ellery
See also CA 1-4R; 107; CANR 1, 39;
DAM POP; DLB 137; MTCW

D'Annunzio, Gabriele
1863-1938 . . . . **TCLC 6, 40**
See also CA 104

d'Antibes, Germain
See Simenon, Georges (Jacques Christian)

Danticat, Edwidge 1969- . . . . **CLC 91**

Danvers, Dennis 1947- . . . . **CLC 70**

Danziger, Paula 1944- . . . . **CLC 21**
See also AAYA 4; CA 112; 115; CANR 37;
CLR 20; JRDA; MAICYA; SATA 36,
63; SATA-Brief 30

Da Ponte, Lorenzo 1749-1838 . . . . **NCLC 50**

Dario, Ruben
1867-1916 . . . . **TCLC 4; HLC; PC 15**
See also CA 131; DAM MULT; HW;
MTCW

Darley, George 1795-1846 . . . . **NCLC 2**
See also DLB 96

Daryush, Elizabeth 1887-1977. . . . **CLC 6, 19**
See also CA 49-52; CANR 3; DLB 20

Dashwood, Edmee Elizabeth Monica de la
Pasture 1890-1943
See Delafield, E. M.
See also CA 119

Daudet, (Louis Marie) Alphonse
1840-1897 . . . . **NCLC 1**
See also DLB 123

Daumal, Rene   1908-1944 . . . . **TCLC 14**
See also CA 114

Davenport, Guy (Mattison, Jr.)
    1927- . . . . **CLC 6, 14, 38; SSC 16**
See also CA 33-36R; CANR 23; DLB 130

Davidson, Avram   1923-
See Queen, Ellery
See also CA 101; CANR 26; DLB 8

Davidson, Donald (Grady)
    1893-1968 . . . . **CLC 2, 13, 19**
See also CA 5-8R; 25-28R; CANR 4;
    DLB 45

Davidson, Hugh
See Hamilton, Edmond

Davidson, John   1857-1909 . . . . **TCLC 24**
See also CA 118; DLB 19

Davidson, Sara   1943- . . . . **CLC 9**
See also CA 81-84; CANR 44

Davie, Donald (Alfred)
    1922-1995 . . . . **CLC 5, 8, 10, 31**
See also CA 1-4R; 149; CAAS 3; CANR 1,
    44; DLB 27; MTCW

Davies, Ray(mond Douglas)   1944- . . **CLC 21**
See also CA 116; 146

Davies, Rhys   1903-1978 . . . . **CLC 23**
See also CA 9-12R; 81-84; CANR 4;
    DLB 139

Davies, (William) Robertson
    1913- . . . . . . **CLC 2, 7, 13, 25, 42, 75, 91;**
                    DA; DAB; DAC; WLC
See also BEST 89:2; CA 33-36R; CANR 17,
    42; DAM MST, NOV, POP; DLB 68;
    INT CANR-17; MTCW

Davies, W(illiam) H(enry)
    1871-1940 . . . . **TCLC 5**
See also CA 104; DLB 19

Davies, Walter C.
See Kornbluth, C(yril) M.

Davis, Angela (Yvonne)   1944- . . . . . . **CLC 77**
See also BW 2; CA 57-60; CANR 10;
    DAM MULT

Davis, B. Lynch
See Bioy Casares, Adolfo; Borges, Jorge
    Luis

Davis, Gordon
See Hunt, E(verette) Howard, (Jr.)

Davis, Harold Lenoir   1896-1960 . . . . **CLC 49**
See also CA 89-92; DLB 9

Davis, Rebecca (Blaine) Harding
    1831-1910 . . . . **TCLC 6**
See also CA 104; DLB 74

Davis, Richard Harding
    1864-1916 . . . . **TCLC 24**
See also CA 114; DLB 12, 23, 78, 79;
    DLBD 13

Davison, Frank Dalby   1893-1970 . . . **CLC 15**
See also CA 116

Davison, Lawrence H.
See Lawrence, D(avid) H(erbert Richards)

Davison, Peter (Hubert)   1928- . . . . . **CLC 28**
See also CA 9-12R; CAAS 4; CANR 3, 43;
    DLB 5

Davys, Mary   1674-1732 . . . . **LC 1**
See also DLB 39

Dawson, Fielding   1930- . . . . **CLC 6**
See also CA 85-88; DLB 130

Dawson, Peter
See Faust, Frederick (Schiller)

Day, Clarence (Shepard, Jr.)
    1874-1935 . . . . **TCLC 25**
See also CA 108; DLB 11

Day, Thomas   1748-1789 . . . . **LC 1**
See also DLB 39; YABC 1

Day Lewis, C(ecil)
    1904-1972 . . . . **CLC 1, 6, 10; PC 11**
See also Blake, Nicholas
See also CA 13-16; 33-36R; CANR 34;
    CAP 1; DAM POET; DLB 15, 20;
    MTCW

Dazai, Osamu . . . . **TCLC 11**
See also Tsushima, Shuji

de Andrade, Carlos Drummond
See Drummond de Andrade, Carlos

Deane, Norman
See Creasey, John

de Beauvoir, Simone (Lucie Ernestine Marie
    Bertrand)
See Beauvoir, Simone (Lucie Ernestine
    Marie Bertrand) de

de Brissac, Malcolm
See Dickinson, Peter (Malcolm)

de Chardin, Pierre Teilhard
See Teilhard de Chardin, (Marie Joseph)
    Pierre

Dee, John   1527-1608 . . . . **LC 20**

Deer, Sandra   1940- . . . . **CLC 45**

De Ferrari, Gabriella   1941- . . . . **CLC 65**
See also CA 146

Defoe, Daniel
    1660(?)-1731 . . . . **LC 1; DA; DAB; DAC;**
                        WLC
See also CDBLB 1660-1789; DAM MST,
    NOV; DLB 39, 95, 101; JRDA;
    MAICYA; SATA 22

de Gourmont, Remy
See Gourmont, Remy de

de Hartog, Jan   1914- . . . . **CLC 19**
See also CA 1-4R; CANR 1

de Hostos, E. M.
See Hostos (y Bonilla), Eugenio Maria de

de Hostos, Eugenio M.
See Hostos (y Bonilla), Eugenio Maria de

Deighton, Len . . . . **CLC 4, 7, 22, 46**
See also Deighton, Leonard Cyril
See also AAYA 6; BEST 89:2;
    CDBLB 1960 to Present; DLB 87

Deighton, Leonard Cyril   1929-
See Deighton, Len
See also CA 9-12R; CANR 19, 33;
    DAM NOV, POP; MTCW

Dekker, Thomas   1572(?)-1632 . . . . . . **LC 22**
See also CDBLB Before 1660;
    DAM DRAM; DLB 62

Delafield, E. M.   1890-1943 . . . . **TCLC 61**
See also Dashwood, Edmee Elizabeth
    Monica de la Pasture
See also DLB 34

de la Mare, Walter (John)
    1873-1956 . . . . **TCLC 4, 53; DAB; DAC;**
                     SSC 14; WLC
See also CDBLB 1914-1945; CLR 23;
    DAM MST, POET; DLB 162; SATA 16

Delaney, Franey
See O'Hara, John (Henry)

Delaney, Shelagh   1939- . . . . **CLC 29**
See also CA 17-20R; CANR 30;
    CDBLB 1960 to Present; DAM DRAM;
    DLB 13; MTCW

Delany, Mary (Granville Pendarves)
    1700-1788 . . . . **LC 12**

Delany, Samuel R(ay, Jr.)
    1942- . . . . **CLC 8, 14, 38; BLC**
See also BW 2; CA 81-84; CANR 27, 43;
    DAM MULT; DLB 8, 33; MTCW

De La Ramee, (Marie) Louise   1839-1908
See Ouida
See also SATA 20

de la Roche, Mazo   1879-1961 . . . . . . **CLC 14**
See also CA 85-88; CANR 30; DLB 68;
    SATA 64

Delbanco, Nicholas (Franklin)
    1942- . . . . **CLC 6, 13**
See also CA 17-20R; CAAS 2; CANR 29;
    DLB 6

del Castillo, Michel   1933- . . . . **CLC 38**
See also CA 109

Deledda, Grazia (Cosima)
    1875(?)-1936 . . . . **TCLC 23**
See also CA 123

Delibes, Miguel . . . . **CLC 8, 18**
See also Delibes Setien, Miguel

Delibes Setien, Miguel   1920-
See Delibes, Miguel
See also CA 45-48; CANR 1, 32; HW;
    MTCW

DeLillo, Don
    1936- . . . . . **CLC 8, 10, 13, 27, 39, 54, 76**
See also BEST 89:1; CA 81-84; CANR 21;
    DAM NOV, POP; DLB 6; MTCW

de Lisser, H. G.
See De Lisser, Herbert George
See also DLB 117

De Lisser, Herbert George
    1878-1944 . . . . **TCLC 12**
See also de Lisser, H. G.
See also BW 2; CA 109

Deloria, Vine (Victor), Jr.   1933- . . . . **CLC 21**
See also CA 53-56; CANR 5, 20, 48;
    DAM MULT; MTCW; NNAL; SATA 21

Del Vecchio, John M(ichael)
    1947- . . . . **CLC 29**
See also CA 110; DLBD 9

de Man, Paul (Adolph Michel)
    1919-1983 . . . . **CLC 55**
See also CA 128; 111; DLB 67; MTCW

De Marinis, Rick   1934- . . . . **CLC 54**
See also CA 57-60; CANR 9, 25, 50

Demby, William   1922- . . . . **CLC 53; BLC**
See also BW 1; CA 81-84; DAM MULT;
    DLB 33

Demijohn, Thom
See Disch, Thomas M(ichael)

de Montherlant, Henry (Milon)
See Montherlant, Henry (Milon) de

Demosthenes 384B.C.-322B.C. . . . **CMLC 13**

de Natale, Francine
See Malzberg, Barry N(athaniel)

Denby, Edwin (Orr) 1903-1983 . . . . . **CLC 48**
See also CA 138; 110

Denis, Julio
See Cortazar, Julio

Denmark, Harrison
See Zelazny, Roger (Joseph)

Dennis, John 1658-1734 . . . . **LC 11**
See also DLB 101

Dennis, Nigel (Forbes) 1912-1989 . . . . **CLC 8**
See also CA 25-28R; 129; DLB 13, 15;
MTCW

De Palma, Brian (Russell) 1940- . . . . **CLC 20**
See also CA 109

De Quincey, Thomas 1785-1859 . . . **NCLC 4**
See also CDBLB 1789-1832; DLB 110; 144

Deren, Eleanora 1908(?)-1961
See Deren, Maya
See also CA 111

Deren, Maya . . . . **CLC 16**
See also Deren, Eleanora

Derleth, August (William)
1909-1971 . . . . **CLC 31**
See also CA 1-4R; 29-32R; CANR 4;
DLB 9; SATA 5

Der Nister 1884-1950 . . . . **TCLC 56**

de Routisie, Albert
See Aragon, Louis

Derrida, Jacques 1930- . . . . **CLC 24, 87**
See also CA 124; 127

Derry Down Derry
See Lear, Edward

Dersonnes, Jacques
See Simenon, Georges (Jacques Christian)

Desai, Anita 1937- . . . . . . **CLC 19, 37; DAB**
See also CA 81-84; CANR 33; DAM NOV;
MTCW; SATA 63

de Saint-Luc, Jean
See Glassco, John

de Saint Roman, Arnaud
See Aragon, Louis

Descartes, Rene 1596-1650 . . . . **LC 20**

De Sica, Vittorio 1901(?)-1974 . . . . . **CLC 20**
See also CA 117

Desnos, Robert 1900-1945 . . . . **TCLC 22**
See also CA 121

Destouches, Louis-Ferdinand
1894-1961 . . . . **CLC 9, 15**
See also Celine, Louis-Ferdinand
See also CA 85-88; CANR 28; MTCW

Deutsch, Babette 1895-1982 . . . . **CLC 18**
See also CA 1-4R; 108; CANR 4; DLB 45;
SATA 1; SATA-Obit 33

Devenant, William 1606-1649 . . . . . . **LC 13**

Devkota, Laxmiprasad
1909-1959 . . . . **TCLC 23**
See also CA 123

De Voto, Bernard (Augustine)
1897-1955 . . . . **TCLC 29**
See also CA 113; DLB 9

De Vries, Peter
1910-1993 . . . . **CLC 1, 2, 3, 7, 10, 28, 46**
See also CA 17-20R; 142; CANR 41;
DAM NOV; DLB 6; DLBY 82; MTCW

Dexter, Martin
See Faust, Frederick (Schiller)

Dexter, Pete 1943- . . . . **CLC 34, 55**
See also BEST 89:2; CA 127; 131;
DAM POP; INT 131; MTCW

Diamano, Silmang
See Senghor, Leopold Sedar

Diamond, Neil 1941- . . . . **CLC 30**
See also CA 108

Diaz del Castillo, Bernal 1496-1584 . . **LC 31**

di Bassetto, Corno
See Shaw, George Bernard

Dick, Philip K(indred)
1928-1982 . . . . **CLC 10, 30, 72**
See also CA 49-52; 106; CANR 2, 16;
DAM NOV, POP; DLB 8; MTCW

Dickens, Charles (John Huffam)
1812-1870 . . . . . . **NCLC 3, 8, 18, 26, 37,**
50; DA; DAB; DAC; SSC 17; WLC
See also CDBLB 1832-1890; DAM MST,
NOV; DLB 21, 55, 70, 159; JRDA;
MAICYA; SATA 15

Dickey, James (Lafayette)
1923- . . . . **CLC 1, 2, 4, 7, 10, 15, 47**
See also AITN 1, 2; CA 9-12R; CABS 2;
CANR 10, 48; CDALB 1968-1988;
DAM NOV, POET, POP; DLB 5;
DLBD 7; DLBY 82, 93; INT CANR-10;
MTCW

Dickey, William 1928-1994 . . . . . **CLC 3, 28**
See also CA 9-12R; 145; CANR 24; DLB 5

Dickinson, Charles 1951- . . . . **CLC 49**
See also CA 128

Dickinson, Emily (Elizabeth)
1830-1886 . . . . . . **NCLC 21; DA; DAB;**
DAC; PC 1; WLC
See also CDALB 1865-1917; DAM MST,
POET; DLB 1; SATA 29

Dickinson, Peter (Malcolm)
1927- . . . . **CLC 12, 35**
See also AAYA 9; CA 41-44R; CANR 31;
CLR 29; DLB 87, 161; JRDA; MAICYA;
SATA 5, 62

Dickson, Carr
See Carr, John Dickson

Dickson, Carter
See Carr, John Dickson

Diderot, Denis 1713-1784 . . . . **LC 26**

Didion, Joan 1934- . . . . . **CLC 1, 3, 8, 14, 32**
See also AITN 1; CA 5-8R; CANR 14;
CDALB 1968-1988; DAM NOV; DLB 2;
DLBY 81, 86; MTCW

Dietrich, Robert
See Hunt, E(verette) Howard, (Jr.)

Dillard, Annie 1945- . . . . **CLC 9, 60**
See also AAYA 6; CA 49-52; CANR 3, 43;
DAM NOV; DLBY 80; MTCW;
SATA 10

Dillard, R(ichard) H(enry) W(ilde)
1937- . . . . **CLC 5**
See also CA 21-24R; CAAS 7; CANR 10;
DLB 5

Dillon, Eilis 1920-1994 . . . . **CLC 17**
See also CA 9-12R; 147; CAAS 3; CANR 4,
38; CLR 26; MAICYA; SATA 2, 74;
SATA-Obit 83

Dimont, Penelope
See Mortimer, Penelope (Ruth)

Dinesen, Isak . . . . **CLC 10, 29; SSC 7**
See also Blixen, Karen (Christentze
Dinesen)

Ding Ling . . . . **CLC 68**
See also Chiang Pin-chin

Disch, Thomas M(ichael) 1940- . . . **CLC 7, 36**
See also AAYA 17; CA 21-24R; CAAS 4;
CANR 17, 36; CLR 18; DLB 8;
MAICYA; MTCW; SAAS 15; SATA 54

Disch, Tom
See Disch, Thomas M(ichael)

d'Isly, Georges
See Simenon, Georges (Jacques Christian)

Disraeli, Benjamin 1804-1881 . . **NCLC 2, 39**
See also DLB 21, 55

Ditcum, Steve
See Crumb, R(obert)

Dixon, Paige
See Corcoran, Barbara

Dixon, Stephen 1936- . . . . . **CLC 52; SSC 16**
See also CA 89-92; CANR 17, 40; DLB 130

Dobell, Sydney Thompson
1824-1874 . . . . **NCLC 43**
See also DLB 32

Doblin, Alfred . . . . **TCLC 13**
See also Doeblin, Alfred

Dobrolyubov, Nikolai Alexandrovich
1836-1861 . . . . **NCLC 5**

Dobyns, Stephen 1941- . . . . **CLC 37**
See also CA 45-48; CANR 2, 18

Doctorow, E(dgar) L(aurence)
1931- . . . . . . **CLC 6, 11, 15, 18, 37, 44, 65**
See also AITN 2; BEST 89:3; CA 45-48;
CANR 2, 33; CDALB 1968-1988;
DAM NOV, POP; DLB 2, 28; DLBY 80;
MTCW

Dodgson, Charles Lutwidge 1832-1898
See Carroll, Lewis
See also CLR 2; DA; DAB; DAC;
DAM MST, NOV, POET; MAICYA;
YABC 2

Dodson, Owen (Vincent)
1914-1983 . . . . **CLC 79; BLC**
See also BW 1; CA 65-68; 110; CANR 24;
DAM MULT; DLB 76

Doeblin, Alfred 1878-1957 . . . . **TCLC 13**
See also Doblin, Alfred
See also CA 110; 141; DLB 66

Doerr, Harriet 1910- . . . . **CLC 34**
See also CA 117; 122; CANR 47; INT 122

Domecq, H(onorio) Bustos
See Bioy Casares, Adolfo; Borges, Jorge
Luis

Domini, Rey
See Lorde, Audre (Geraldine)

Dominique
  See Proust, (Valentin-Louis-George-Eugene-) Marcel

Don, A
  See Stephen, Leslie

Donaldson, Stephen R. 1947- ...... **CLC 46**
  See also CA 89-92; CANR 13; DAM POP; INT CANR-13

Donleavy, J(ames) P(atrick)
  1926- .... **CLC 1, 4, 6, 10, 45**
  See also AITN 2; CA 9-12R; CANR 24, 49; DLB 6; INT CANR-24; MTCW

Donne, John
  1572-1631 ...... **LC 10, 24; DA; DAB; DAC; PC 1**
  See also CDBLB Before 1660; DAM MST, POET; DLB 121, 151

Donnell, David 1939(?)- .... **CLC 34**

Donoghue, P. S.
  See Hunt, E(verette) Howard, (Jr.)

Donoso (Yanez), Jose
  1924- .... **CLC 4, 8, 11, 32; HLC**
  See also CA 81-84; CANR 32; DAM MULT; DLB 113; HW; MTCW

Donovan, John 1928-1992 .... **CLC 35**
  See also CA 97-100; 137; CLR 3; MAICYA; SATA 72; SATA-Brief 29

Don Roberto
  See Cunninghame Graham, R(obert) B(ontine)

Doolittle, Hilda
  1886-1961 ..... **CLC 3, 8, 14, 31, 34, 73; DA; DAC; PC 5; WLC**
  See also H. D.
  See also CA 97-100; CANR 35; DAM MST, POET; DLB 4, 45; MTCW

Dorfman, Ariel 1942- .... **CLC 48, 77; HLC**
  See also CA 124; 130; DAM MULT; HW; INT 130

Dorn, Edward (Merton) 1929- ... **CLC 10, 18**
  See also CA 93-96; CANR 42; DLB 5; INT 93-96

Dorsan, Luc
  See Simenon, Georges (Jacques Christian)

Dorsange, Jean
  See Simenon, Georges (Jacques Christian)

Dos Passos, John (Roderigo)
  1896-1970 ...... **CLC 1, 4, 8, 11, 15, 25, 34, 82; DA; DAB; DAC; WLC**
  See also CA 1-4R; 29-32R; CANR 3; CDALB 1929-1941; DAM MST, NOV; DLB 4, 9; DLBD 1; MTCW

Dossage, Jean
  See Simenon, Georges (Jacques Christian)

Dostoevsky, Fedor Mikhailovich
  1821-1881 ..... **NCLC 2, 7, 21, 33, 43; DA; DAB; DAC; SSC 2; WLC**
  See also DAM MST, NOV

Doughty, Charles M(ontagu)
  1843-1926 .... **TCLC 27**
  See also CA 115; DLB 19, 57

Douglas, Ellen .... **CLC 73**
  See also Haxton, Josephine Ayres; Williamson, Ellen Douglas

Douglas, Gavin 1475(?)-1522 .... **LC 20**

Douglas, Keith 1920-1944 .... **TCLC 40**
  See also DLB 27

Douglas, Leonard
  See Bradbury, Ray (Douglas)

Douglas, Michael
  See Crichton, (John) Michael

Douglass, Frederick
  1817(?)-1895 ...... **NCLC 7; BLC; DA; DAC; WLC**
  See also CDALB 1640-1865; DAM MST, MULT; DLB 1, 43, 50, 79; SATA 29

Dourado, (Waldomiro Freitas) Autran
  1926- .... **CLC 23, 60**
  See also CA 25-28R; CANR 34

Dourado, Waldomiro Autran
  See Dourado, (Waldomiro Freitas) Autran

Dove, Rita (Frances)
  1952- .... **CLC 50, 81; PC 6**
  See also BW 2; CA 109; CAAS 19; CANR 27, 42; DAM MULT, POET; DLB 120

Dowell, Coleman 1925-1985 .... **CLC 60**
  See also CA 25-28R; 117; CANR 10; DLB 130

Dowson, Ernest Christopher
  1867-1900 .... **TCLC 4**
  See also CA 105; DLB 19, 135

Doyle, A. Conan
  See Doyle, Arthur Conan

Doyle, Arthur Conan
  1859-1930 .... **TCLC 7; DA; DAB; DAC; SSC 12; WLC**
  See also AAYA 14; CA 104; 122; CDBLB 1890-1914; DAM MST, NOV; DLB 18, 70, 156; MTCW; SATA 24

Doyle, Conan
  See Doyle, Arthur Conan

Doyle, John
  See Graves, Robert (von Ranke)

Doyle, Roddy 1958(?)- .... **CLC 81**
  See also AAYA 14; CA 143

Doyle, Sir A. Conan
  See Doyle, Arthur Conan

Doyle, Sir Arthur Conan
  See Doyle, Arthur Conan

Dr. A
  See Asimov, Isaac; Silverstein, Alvin

Drabble, Margaret
  1939- .... **CLC 2, 3, 5, 8, 10, 22, 53; DAB; DAC**
  See also CA 13-16R; CANR 18, 35; CDBLB 1960 to Present; DAM MST, NOV, POP; DLB 14, 155; MTCW; SATA 48

Drapier, M. B.
  See Swift, Jonathan

Drayham, James
  See Mencken, H(enry) L(ouis)

Drayton, Michael 1563-1631 .... **LC 8**

Dreadstone, Carl
  See Campbell, (John) Ramsey

Dreiser, Theodore (Herman Albert)
  1871-1945 .... **TCLC 10, 18, 35; DA; DAC; WLC**
  See also CA 106; 132; CDALB 1865-1917; DAM MST, NOV; DLB 9, 12, 102, 137; DLBD 1; MTCW

Drexler, Rosalyn 1926- .... **CLC 2, 6**
  See also CA 81-84

Dreyer, Carl Theodor 1889-1968.... **CLC 16**
  See also CA 116

Drieu la Rochelle, Pierre(-Eugene)
  1893-1945 .... **TCLC 21**
  See also CA 117; DLB 72

Drinkwater, John 1882-1937 ...... **TCLC 57**
  See also CA 109; 149; DLB 10, 19, 149

Drop Shot
  See Cable, George Washington

Droste-Hulshoff, Annette Freiin von
  1797-1848 .... **NCLC 3**
  See also DLB 133

Drummond, Walter
  See Silverberg, Robert

Drummond, William Henry
  1854-1907 .... **TCLC 25**
  See also DLB 92

Drummond de Andrade, Carlos
  1902-1987 .... **CLC 18**
  See also Andrade, Carlos Drummond de
  See also CA 132; 123

Drury, Allen (Stuart) 1918- .... **CLC 37**
  See also CA 57-60; CANR 18; INT CANR-18

Dryden, John
  1631-1700 .... **LC 3, 21; DA; DAB; DAC; DC 3; WLC**
  See also CDBLB 1660-1789; DAM DRAM, MST, POET; DLB 80, 101, 131

Duberman, Martin 1930- .... **CLC 8**
  See also CA 1-4R; CANR 2

Dubie, Norman (Evans) 1945- ...... **CLC 36**
  See also CA 69-72; CANR 12; DLB 120

Du Bois, W(illiam) E(dward) B(urghardt)
  1868-1963 ...... **CLC 1, 2, 13, 64; BLC; DA; DAC; WLC**
  See also BW 1; CA 85-88; CANR 34; CDALB 1865-1917; DAM MST, MULT, NOV; DLB 47, 50, 91; MTCW; SATA 42

Dubus, Andre 1936- ... **CLC 13, 36; SSC 15**
  See also CA 21-24R; CANR 17; DLB 130; INT CANR-17

Duca Minimo
  See D'Annunzio, Gabriele

Ducharme, Rejean 1941- .... **CLC 74**
  See also DLB 60

Duclos, Charles Pinot 1704-1772 ..... **LC 1**

Dudek, Louis 1918- .... **CLC 11, 19**
  See also CA 45-48; CAAS 14; CANR 1; DLB 88

Duerrenmatt, Friedrich
  1921-1990 ...... **CLC 1, 4, 8, 11, 15, 43**
  See also CA 17-20R; CANR 33; DAM DRAM; DLB 69, 124; MTCW

Duffy, Bruce (?)- .... **CLC 50**

Ehrenburg, Ilyo (Grigoryevich)
See Ehrenburg, Ilya (Grigoryevich)

Eich, Guenter 1907-1972 . . . . CLC 15
See also CA 111; 93-96; DLB 69, 124

Eichendorff, Joseph Freiherr von
1788-1857 . . . . NCLC 8
See also DLB 90

Eigner, Larry. CLC 9
See also Eigner, Laurence (Joel)
See also CAAS 23; DLB 5

Eigner, Laurence (Joel) 1927-1996
See Eigner, Larry
See also CA 9-12R; CANR 6

Eiseley, Loren Corey 1907-1977 . . . . . CLC 7
See also AAYA 5; CA 1-4R; 73-76;
CANR 6

Eisenstadt, Jill 1963- . . . . CLC 50
See also CA 140

Eisenstein, Sergei (Mikhailovich)
1898-1948 . . . . TCLC 57
See also CA 114; 149

Eisner, Simon
See Kornbluth, C(yril) M.

Ekeloef, (Bengt) Gunnar
1907-1968 . . . . CLC 27
See also CA 123; 25-28R; DAM POET

Ekelof, (Bengt) Gunnar
See Ekeloef, (Bengt) Gunnar

Ekwensi, C. O. D.
See Ekwensi, Cyprian (Odiatu Duaka)

Ekwensi, Cyprian (Odiatu Duaka)
1921- . . . . CLC 4; BLC
See also BW 2; CA 29-32R; CANR 18, 42;
DAM MULT; DLB 117; MTCW;
SATA 66

Elaine . . . . TCLC 18
See also Leverson, Ada

El Crummo
See Crumb, R(obert)

Elia
See Lamb, Charles

Eliade, Mircea 1907-1986 . . . . CLC 19
See also CA 65-68; 119; CANR 30; MTCW

Eliot, A. D.
See Jewett, (Theodora) Sarah Orne

Eliot, Alice
See Jewett, (Theodora) Sarah Orne

Eliot, Dan
See Silverberg, Robert

Eliot, George
1819-1880 . . . . . NCLC 4, 13, 23, 41, 49;
DA; DAB; DAC; WLC
See also CDBLB 1832-1890; DAM MST,
NOV; DLB 21, 35, 55

Eliot, John 1604-1690 . . . . LC 5
See also DLB 24

Eliot, T(homas) S(tearns)
1888-1965 . . . . . CLC 1, 2, 3, 6, 9, 10, 13,
15, 24, 34, 41, 55, 57; DA; DAB; DAC;
PC 5; WLC 2
See also CA 5-8R; 25-28R; CANR 41;
CDALB 1929-1941; DAM DRAM, MST,
POET; DLB 7, 10, 45, 63; DLBY 88;
MTCW

Elizabeth 1866-1941 . . . . TCLC 41

Elkin, Stanley L(awrence)
1930-1995 . . . . . CLC 4, 6, 9, 14, 27, 51,
91; SSC 12
See also CA 9-12R; 148; CANR 8, 46;
DAM NOV, POP; DLB 2, 28; DLBY 80;
INT CANR-8; MTCW

Elledge, Scott. . . . . CLC 34

Elliott, Don
See Silverberg, Robert

Elliott, George P(aul) 1918-1980. . . . . CLC 2
See also CA 1-4R; 97-100; CANR 2

Elliott, Janice 1931- . . . . CLC 47
See also CA 13-16R; CANR 8, 29; DLB 14

Elliott, Sumner Locke 1917-1991 . . . CLC 38
See also CA 5-8R; 134; CANR 2, 21

Elliott, William
See Bradbury, Ray (Douglas)

Ellis, A. E. . . . . CLC 7

Ellis, Alice Thomas. . . . . CLC 40
See also Haycraft, Anna

Ellis, Bret Easton 1964- . . . . CLC 39, 71
See also AAYA 2; CA 118; 123;
DAM POP; INT 123

Ellis, (Henry) Havelock
1859-1939 . . . . TCLC 14
See also CA 109

Ellis, Landon
See Ellison, Harlan (Jay)

Ellis, Trey 1962- . . . . CLC 55
See also CA 146

Ellison, Harlan (Jay)
1934- . . . . CLC 1, 13, 42; SSC 14
See also CA 5-8R; CANR 5, 46;
DAM POP; DLB 8; INT CANR-5;
MTCW

Ellison, Ralph (Waldo)
1914-1994 . . . . CLC 1, 3, 11, 54, 86;
BLC; DA; DAB; DAC; WLC
See also BW 1; CA 9-12R; 145; CANR 24;
CDALB 1941-1968; DAM MST, MULT,
NOV; DLB 2, 76; DLBY 94; MTCW

Ellmann, Lucy (Elizabeth) 1956- . . . . CLC 61
See also CA 128

Ellmann, Richard (David)
1918-1987 . . . . CLC 50
See also BEST 89:2; CA 1-4R; 122;
CANR 2, 28; DLB 103; DLBY 87;
MTCW

Elman, Richard 1934- . . . . CLC 19
See also CA 17-20R; CAAS 3; CANR 47

Elron
See Hubbard, L(afayette) Ron(ald)

Eluard, Paul. . . . . TCLC 7, 41
See also Grindel, Eugene

Elyot, Sir Thomas 1490(?)-1546 . . . . . LC 11

Elytis, Odysseus 1911- . . . . CLC 15, 49
See also CA 102; DAM POET; MTCW

Emecheta, (Florence Onye) Buchi
1944- . . . . CLC 14, 48; BLC
See also BW 2; CA 81-84; CANR 27;
DAM MULT; DLB 117; MTCW;
SATA 66

Emerson, Ralph Waldo
1803-1882 . . . . . NCLC 1, 38; DA; DAB;
DAC; WLC
See also CDALB 1640-1865; DAM MST,
POET; DLB 1, 59, 73

Eminescu, Mihail 1850-1889 . . . . . NCLC 33

Empson, William
1906-1984 . . . . CLC 3, 8, 19, 33, 34
See also CA 17-20R; 112; CANR 31;
DLB 20; MTCW

Enchi Fumiko (Ueda) 1905-1986. . . . CLC 31
See also CA 129; 121

Ende, Michael (Andreas Helmuth)
1929-1995 . . . . CLC 31
See also CA 118; 124; 149; CANR 36;
CLR 14; DLB 75; MAICYA; SATA 61;
SATA-Brief 42; SATA-Obit 86

Endo, Shusaku 1923- . . . . . CLC 7, 14, 19, 54
See also CA 29-32R; CANR 21;
DAM NOV; MTCW

Engel, Marian 1933-1985. . . . . CLC 36
See also CA 25-28R; CANR 12; DLB 53;
INT CANR-12

Engelhardt, Frederick
See Hubbard, L(afayette) Ron(ald)

Enright, D(ennis) J(oseph)
1920- . . . . CLC 4, 8, 31
See also CA 1-4R; CANR 1, 42; DLB 27;
SATA 25

Enzensberger, Hans Magnus
1929- . . . . CLC 43
See also CA 116; 119

Ephron, Nora 1941- . . . . CLC 17, 31
See also AITN 2; CA 65-68; CANR 12, 39

Epsilon
See Betjeman, John

Epstein, Daniel Mark 1948- . . . . CLC 7
See also CA 49-52; CANR 2

Epstein, Jacob 1956- . . . . CLC 19
See also CA 114

Epstein, Joseph 1937- . . . . CLC 39
See also CA 112; 119; CANR 50

Epstein, Leslie 1938- . . . . CLC 27
See also CA 73-76; CAAS 12; CANR 23

Equiano, Olaudah
1745(?)-1797 . . . . LC 16; BLC
See also DAM MULT; DLB 37, 50

Erasmus, Desiderius 1469(?)-1536. . . . LC 16

Erdman, Paul E(mil) 1932- . . . . CLC 25
See also AITN 1; CA 61-64; CANR 13, 43

Erdrich, Louise 1954- . . . . CLC 39, 54
See also AAYA 10; BEST 89:1; CA 114;
CANR 41; DAM MULT, NOV, POP;
DLB 152; MTCW; NNAL

Erenburg, Ilya (Grigoryevich)
See Ehrenburg, Ilya (Grigoryevich)

Erickson, Stephen Michael 1950-
See Erickson, Steve
See also CA 129

Erickson, Steve . . . . CLC 64
See also Erickson, Stephen Michael

Ericson, Walter
See Fast, Howard (Melvin)

Eriksson, Buntel
 See Bergman, (Ernst) Ingmar

Ernaux, Annie 1940- . . . . **CLC 88**
 See also CA 147

Eschenbach, Wolfram von
 See Wolfram von Eschenbach

Eseki, Bruno
 See Mphahlele, Ezekiel

Esenin, Sergei (Alexandrovich)
 1895-1925 . . . . **TCLC 4**
 See also CA 104

Eshleman, Clayton 1935- . . . . **CLC 7**
 See also CA 33-36R; CAAS 6; DLB 5

Espriella, Don Manuel Alvarez
 See Southey, Robert

Espriu, Salvador 1913-1985 . . . . **CLC 9**
 See also CA 115; DLB 134

Espronceda, Jose de 1808-1842 . . . **NCLC 39**

Esse, James
 See Stephens, James

Esterbrook, Tom
 See Hubbard, L(afayette) Ron(ald)

Estleman, Loren D. 1952- . . . . **CLC 48**
 See also CA 85-88; CANR 27; DAM NOV,
 POP; INT CANR-27; MTCW

Eugenides, Jeffrey 1960(?)- . . . . **CLC 81**
 See also CA 144

Euripides c. 485B.C.-406B.C. . . . . **DC 4**
 See also DA; DAB; DAC; DAM DRAM,
 MST

Evan, Evin
 See Faust, Frederick (Schiller)

Evans, Evan
 See Faust, Frederick (Schiller)

Evans, Marian
 See Eliot, George

Evans, Mary Ann
 See Eliot, George

Evarts, Esther
 See Benson, Sally

Everett, Percival L. 1956- . . . . **CLC 57**
 See also BW 2; CA 129

Everson, R(onald) G(ilmour)
 1903- . . . . **CLC 27**
 See also CA 17-20R; DLB 88

Everson, William (Oliver)
 1912-1994 . . . . **CLC 1, 5, 14**
 See also CA 9-12R; 145; CANR 20; DLB 5,
 16; MTCW

Evtushenko, Evgenii Aleksandrovich
 See Yevtushenko, Yevgeny (Alexandrovich)

Ewart, Gavin (Buchanan)
 1916- . . . . **CLC 13, 46**
 See also CA 89-92; CANR 17, 46; DLB 40;
 MTCW

Ewers, Hanns Heinz 1871-1943 . . . **TCLC 12**
 See also CA 109; 149

Ewing, Frederick R.
 See Sturgeon, Theodore (Hamilton)

Exley, Frederick (Earl)
 1929-1992 . . . . **CLC 6, 11**
 See also AITN 2; CA 81-84; 138; DLB 143;
 DLBY 81

Eynhardt, Guillermo
 See Quiroga, Horacio (Sylvestre)

Ezekiel, Nissim 1924- . . . . **CLC 61**
 See also CA 61-64

Ezekiel, Tish O'Dowd 1943- . . . . **CLC 34**
 See also CA 129

Fadeyev, A.
 See Bulgya, Alexander Alexandrovich

Fadeyev, Alexander . . . . **TCLC 53**
 See also Bulgya, Alexander Alexandrovich

Fagen, Donald 1948- . . . . **CLC 26**

Fainzilberg, Ilya Arnoldovich 1897-1937
 See Ilf, Ilya
 See also CA 120

Fair, Ronald L. 1932- . . . . **CLC 18**
 See also BW 1; CA 69-72; CANR 25;
 DLB 33

Fairbairns, Zoe (Ann) 1948- . . . . **CLC 32**
 See also CA 103; CANR 21

Falco, Gian
 See Papini, Giovanni

Falconer, James
 See Kirkup, James

Falconer, Kenneth
 See Kornbluth, C(yril) M.

Falkland, Samuel
 See Heijermans, Herman

Fallaci, Oriana 1930- . . . . **CLC 11**
 See also CA 77-80; CANR 15; MTCW

Faludy, George 1913- . . . . **CLC 42**
 See also CA 21-24R

Faludy, Gyoergy
 See Faludy, George

Fanon, Frantz 1925-1961 . . . . . **CLC 74; BLC**
 See also BW 1; CA 116; 89-92;
 DAM MULT

Fanshawe, Ann 1625-1680 . . . . **LC 11**

Fante, John (Thomas) 1911-1983 . . . **CLC 60**
 See also CA 69-72; 109; CANR 23;
 DLB 130; DLBY 83

Farah, Nuruddin 1945- . . . . **CLC 53; BLC**
 See also BW 2; CA 106; DAM MULT;
 DLB 125

Fargue, Leon-Paul 1876(?)-1947 . . . **TCLC 11**
 See also CA 109

Farigoule, Louis
 See Romains, Jules

Farina, Richard 1936(?)-1966 . . . . **CLC 9**
 See also CA 81-84; 25-28R

Farley, Walter (Lorimer)
 1915-1989 . . . . **CLC 17**
 See also CA 17-20R; CANR 8, 29; DLB 22;
 JRDA; MAICYA; SATA 2, 43

Farmer, Philip Jose 1918- . . . . **CLC 1, 19**
 See also CA 1-4R; CANR 4, 35; DLB 8;
 MTCW

Farquhar, George 1677-1707 . . . . **LC 21**
 See also DAM DRAM; DLB 84

Farrell, J(ames) G(ordon)
 1935-1979 . . . . **CLC 6**
 See also CA 73-76; 89-92; CANR 36;
 DLB 14; MTCW

Farrell, James T(homas)
 1904-1979 . . . . **CLC 1, 4, 8, 11, 66**
 See also CA 5-8R; 89-92; CANR 9; DLB 4,
 9, 86; DLBD 2; MTCW

Farren, Richard J.
 See Betjeman, John

Farren, Richard M.
 See Betjeman, John

Fassbinder, Rainer Werner
 1946-1982 . . . . **CLC 20**
 See also CA 93-96; 106; CANR 31

Fast, Howard (Melvin) 1914- . . . . . . **CLC 23**
 See also AAYA 16; CA 1-4R; CAAS 18;
 CANR 1, 33; DAM NOV; DLB 9;
 INT CANR-33; SATA 7

Faulcon, Robert
 See Holdstock, Robert P.

Faulkner, William (Cuthbert)
 1897-1962 . . . . . **CLC 1, 3, 6, 8, 9, 11, 14,
 18, 28, 52, 68; DA; DAB; DAC; SSC 1;
 WLC**
 See also AAYA 7; CA 81-84; CANR 33;
 CDALB 1929-1941; DAM MST, NOV;
 DLB 9, 11, 44, 102; DLBD 2; DLBY 86;
 MTCW

Fauset, Jessie Redmon
 1884(?)-1961 . . . . **CLC 19, 54; BLC**
 See also BW 1; CA 109; DAM MULT;
 DLB 51

Faust, Frederick (Schiller)
 1892-1944(?) . . . . **TCLC 49**
 See also CA 108; DAM POP

Faust, Irvin 1924- . . . . **CLC 8**
 See also CA 33-36R; CANR 28; DLB 2, 28;
 DLBY 80

Fawkes, Guy
 See Benchley, Robert (Charles)

Fearing, Kenneth (Flexner)
 1902-1961 . . . . **CLC 51**
 See also CA 93-96; DLB 9

Fecamps, Elise
 See Creasey, John

Federman, Raymond 1928- . . . . . . **CLC 6, 47**
 See also CA 17-20R; CAAS 8; CANR 10,
 43; DLBY 80

Federspiel, J(uerg) F. 1931- . . . . **CLC 42**
 See also CA 146

Feiffer, Jules (Ralph) 1929- . . . . **CLC 2, 8, 64**
 See also AAYA 3; CA 17-20R; CANR 30;
 DAM DRAM; DLB 7, 44;
 INT CANR-30; MTCW; SATA 8, 61

Feige, Hermann Albert Otto Maximilian
 See Traven, B.

Feinberg, David B. 1956-1994 . . . . . . **CLC 59**
 See also CA 135; 147

Feinstein, Elaine 1930- . . . . **CLC 36**
 See also CA 69-72; CAAS 1; CANR 31;
 DLB 14, 40; MTCW

Feldman, Irving (Mordecai) 1928- . . . . **CLC 7**
 See also CA 1-4R; CANR 1

Fellini, Federico 1920-1993 . . . . . **CLC 16, 85**
 See also CA 65-68; 143; CANR 33

Felsen, Henry Gregor 1916- . . . . **CLC 17**
 See also CA 1-4R; CANR 1; SAAS 2;
 SATA 1

Forez
See Mauriac, Francois (Charles)

Forman, James Douglas 1932- . . . . . **CLC 21**
See also AAYA 17; CA 9-12R; CANR 4,
19, 42; JRDA; MAICYA; SATA 8, 70

Fornes, Maria Irene 1930- . . . . . **CLC 39, 61**
See also CA 25-28R; CANR 28; DLB 7;
HW; INT CANR-28; MTCW

Forrest, Leon 1937- . . . . **CLC 4**
See also BW 2; CA 89-92; CAAS 7;
CANR 25; DLB 33

Forster, E(dward) M(organ)
1879-1970 . . . . . **CLC 1, 2, 3, 4, 9, 10, 13,
15, 22, 45, 77; DA; DAB; DAC; WLC**
See also AAYA 2; CA 13-14; 25-28R;
CANR 45; CAP 1; CDBLB 1914-1945;
DAM MST, NOV; DLB 34, 98, 162;
DLBD 10; MTCW; SATA 57

Forster, John 1812-1876 . . . . **NCLC 11**
See also DLB 144

Forsyth, Frederick 1938- . . . . . . **CLC 2, 5, 36**
See also BEST 89:4; CA 85-88; CANR 38;
DAM NOV, POP; DLB 87; MTCW

Forten, Charlotte L. . . . . **TCLC 16; BLC**
See also Grimke, Charlotte L(ottie) Forten
See also DLB 50

Foscolo, Ugo 1778-1827 . . . . **NCLC 8**

Fosse, Bob . . . . **CLC 20**
See also Fosse, Robert Louis

Fosse, Robert Louis 1927-1987
See Fosse, Bob
See also CA 110; 123

Foster, Stephen Collins
1826-1864 . . . . **NCLC 26**

Foucault, Michel
1926-1984 . . . . **CLC 31, 34, 69**
See also CA 105; 113; CANR 34; MTCW

Fouque, Friedrich (Heinrich Karl) de la Motte
1777-1843 . . . . **NCLC 2**
See also DLB 90

Fourier, Charles 1772-1837 . . . . . **NCLC 51**

Fournier, Henri Alban 1886-1914
See Alain-Fournier
See also CA 104

Fournier, Pierre 1916- . . . . **CLC 11**
See also Gascar, Pierre
See also CA 89-92; CANR 16, 40

Fowles, John
1926- . . . . . . **CLC 1, 2, 3, 4, 6, 9, 10, 15,
33, 87; DAB; DAC**
See also CA 5-8R; CANR 25; CDBLB 1960
to Present; DAM MST; DLB 14, 139;
MTCW; SATA 22

Fox, Paula 1923- . . . . **CLC 2, 8**
See also AAYA 3; CA 73-76; CANR 20,
36; CLR 1; DLB 52; JRDA; MAICYA;
MTCW; SATA 17, 60

Fox, William Price (Jr.) 1926- . . . . . **CLC 22**
See also CA 17-20R; CAAS 19; CANR 11;
DLB 2; DLBY 81

Foxe, John 1516(?)-1587 . . . . **LC 14**

Frame, Janet . . . . **CLC 2, 3, 6, 22, 66**
See also Clutha, Janet Paterson Frame

France, Anatole . . . . **TCLC 9**
See also Thibault, Jacques Anatole Francois
See also DLB 123

Francis, Claude 19(?)- . . . . **CLC 50**

Francis, Dick 1920- . . . . **CLC 2, 22, 42**
See also AAYA 5; BEST 89:3; CA 5-8R;
CANR 9, 42; CDBLB 1960 to Present;
DAM POP; DLB 87; INT CANR-9;
MTCW

Francis, Robert (Churchill)
1901-1987 . . . . **CLC 15**
See also CA 1-4R; 123; CANR 1

Frank, Anne(lies Marie)
1929-1945 . . . . **TCLC 17; DA; DAB;
DAC; WLC**
See also AAYA 12; CA 113; 133;
DAM MST; MTCW; SATA-Brief 42

Frank, Elizabeth 1945- . . . . **CLC 39**
See also CA 121; 126; INT 126

Franklin, Benjamin
See Hasek, Jaroslav (Matej Frantisek)

Franklin, Benjamin
1706-1790 . . . . . **LC 25; DA; DAB; DAC**
See also CDALB 1640-1865; DAM MST;
DLB 24, 43, 73

Franklin, (Stella Maraia Sarah) Miles
1879-1954 . . . . **TCLC 7**
See also CA 104

Fraser, (Lady) Antonia (Pakenham)
1932- . . . . **CLC 32**
See also CA 85-88; CANR 44; MTCW;
SATA-Brief 32

Fraser, George MacDonald 1925- . . . **CLC 7**
See also CA 45-48; CANR 2, 48

Fraser, Sylvia 1935- . . . . **CLC 64**
See also CA 45-48; CANR 1, 16

Frayn, Michael 1933- . . . . . . **CLC 3, 7, 31, 47**
See also CA 5-8R; CANR 30;
DAM DRAM, NOV; DLB 13, 14;
MTCW

Fraze, Candida (Merrill) 1945- . . . . . **CLC 50**
See also CA 126

Frazer, J(ames) G(eorge)
1854-1941 . . . . **TCLC 32**
See also CA 118

Frazer, Robert Caine
See Creasey, John

Frazer, Sir James George
See Frazer, J(ames) G(eorge)

Frazier, Ian 1951- . . . . **CLC 46**
See also CA 130

Frederic, Harold 1856-1898 . . . . . . **NCLC 10**
See also DLB 12, 23; DLBD 13

Frederick, John
See Faust, Frederick (Schiller)

Frederick the Great 1712-1786 . . . . . . **LC 14**

Fredro, Aleksander 1793-1876 . . . . . **NCLC 8**

Freeling, Nicolas 1927- . . . . **CLC 38**
See also CA 49-52; CAAS 12; CANR 1, 17,
50; DLB 87

Freeman, Douglas Southall
1886-1953 . . . . **TCLC 11**
See also CA 109; DLB 17

Freeman, Judith 1946- . . . . **CLC 55**
See also CA 148

Freeman, Mary Eleanor Wilkins
1852-1930 . . . . **TCLC 9; SSC 1**
See also CA 106; DLB 12, 78

Freeman, R(ichard) Austin
1862-1943 . . . . **TCLC 21**
See also CA 113; DLB 70

French, Albert 1943- . . . . **CLC 86**

French, Marilyn 1929- . . . . . . **CLC 10, 18, 60**
See also CA 69-72; CANR 3, 31;
DAM DRAM, NOV, POP;
INT CANR-31; MTCW

French, Paul
See Asimov, Isaac

Freneau, Philip Morin 1752-1832 . . **NCLC 1**
See also DLB 37, 43

Freud, Sigmund 1856-1939 . . . . **TCLC 52**
See also CA 115; 133; MTCW

Friedan, Betty (Naomi) 1921- . . . . . . **CLC 74**
See also CA 65-68; CANR 18, 45; MTCW

Friedlaender, Saul 1932- . . . . **CLC 90**
See also CA 117; 130

Friedman, B(ernard) H(arper)
1926- . . . . **CLC 7**
See also CA 1-4R; CANR 3, 48

Friedman, Bruce Jay 1930- . . . . **CLC 3, 5, 56**
See also CA 9-12R; CANR 25; DLB 2, 28;
INT CANR-25

Friel, Brian 1929- . . . . **CLC 5, 42, 59**
See also CA 21-24R; CANR 33; DLB 13;
MTCW

Friis-Baastad, Babbis Ellinor
1921-1970 . . . . **CLC 12**
See also CA 17-20R; 134; SATA 7

Frisch, Max (Rudolf)
1911-1991 . . . . . **CLC 3, 9, 14, 18, 32, 44**
See also CA 85-88; 134; CANR 32;
DAM DRAM, NOV; DLB 69, 124;
MTCW

Fromentin, Eugene (Samuel Auguste)
1820-1876 . . . . **NCLC 10**
See also DLB 123

Frost, Frederick
See Faust, Frederick (Schiller)

Frost, Robert (Lee)
1874-1963 . . . . **CLC 1, 3, 4, 9, 10, 13, 15,
26, 34, 44; DA; DAB; DAC; PC 1; WLC**
See also CA 89-92; CANR 33;
CDALB 1917-1929; DAM MST, POET;
DLB 54; DLBD 7; MTCW; SATA 14

Froude, James Anthony
1818-1894 . . . . **NCLC 43**
See also DLB 18, 57, 144

Froy, Herald
See Waterhouse, Keith (Spencer)

Fry, Christopher 1907- . . . . **CLC 2, 10, 14**
See also CA 17-20R; CAAS 23; CANR 9,
30; DAM DRAM; DLB 13; MTCW;
SATA 66

Frye, (Herman) Northrop
1912-1991 . . . . **CLC 24, 70**
See also CA 5-8R; 133; CANR 8, 37;
DLB 67, 68; MTCW

Gasset, Jose Ortega y
See Ortega y Gasset, Jose

Gates, Henry Louis, Jr. 1950- ...... CLC 65
See also BW 2; CA 109; CANR 25;
DAM MULT; DLB 67

Gautier, Theophile
1811-1872 .... NCLC 1; SSC 20
See also DAM POET; DLB 119

Gawsworth, John
See Bates, H(erbert) E(rnest)

Gaye, Marvin (Penze) 1939-1984 ... CLC 26
See also CA 112

Gebler, Carlo (Ernest) 1954- .... CLC 39
See also CA 119; 133

Gee, Maggie (Mary) 1948-........ CLC 57
See also CA 130

Gee, Maurice (Gough) 1931- ...... CLC 29
See also CA 97-100; SATA 46

Gelbart, Larry (Simon) 1923- ... CLC 21, 61
See also CA 73-76; CANR 45

Gelber, Jack 1932-........ CLC 1, 6, 14, 79
See also CA 1-4R; CANR 2; DLB 7

Gellhorn, Martha (Ellis) 1908- .. CLC 14, 60
See also CA 77-80; CANR 44; DLBY 82

Genet, Jean
1910-1986 ... CLC 1, 2, 5, 10, 14, 44, 46
See also CA 13-16R; CANR 18;
DAM DRAM; DLB 72; DLBY 86;
MTCW

Gent, Peter 1942-................ CLC 29
See also AITN 1; CA 89-92; DLBY 82

Gentlewoman in New England, A
See Bradstreet, Anne

Gentlewoman in Those Parts, A
See Bradstreet, Anne

George, Jean Craighead 1919-...... CLC 35
See also AAYA 8; CA 5-8R; CANR 25;
CLR 1; DLB 52; JRDA; MAICYA;
SATA 2, 68

George, Stefan (Anton)
1868-1933 .... TCLC 2, 14
See also CA 104

Georges, Georges Martin
See Simenon, Georges (Jacques Christian)

Gerhardi, William Alexander
See Gerhardie, William Alexander

Gerhardie, William Alexander
1895-1977 .... CLC 5
See also CA 25-28R; 73-76; CANR 18;
DLB 36

Gerstler, Amy 1956-............. CLC 70
See also CA 146

Gertler, T....................... CLC 34
See also CA 116; 121; INT 121

Ghalib........................ NCLC 39
See also Ghalib, Hsadullah Khan

Ghalib, Hsadullah Khan 1797-1869
See Ghalib
See also DAM POET

Ghelderode, Michel de
1898-1962 .... CLC 6, 11
See also CA 85-88; CANR 40;
DAM DRAM

Ghiselin, Brewster 1903- .... CLC 23
See also CA 13-16R; CAAS 10; CANR 13

Ghose, Zulfikar 1935-............. CLC 42
See also CA 65-68

Ghosh, Amitav 1956- .... CLC 44
See also CA 147

Giacosa, Giuseppe 1847-1906 ...... TCLC 7
See also CA 104

Gibb, Lee
See Waterhouse, Keith (Spencer)

Gibbon, Lewis Grassic .... TCLC 4
See also Mitchell, James Leslie

Gibbons, Kaye 1960- .... CLC 50, 88
See also DAM POP

Gibran, Kahlil
1883-1931 .... TCLC 1, 9; PC 9
See also CA 104; DAM POET, POP

Gibson, William
1914- .... CLC 23; DA; DAB; DAC
See also CA 9-12R; CANR 9, 42;
DAM DRAM, MST; DLB 7; SATA 66

Gibson, William (Ford) 1948- ... CLC 39, 63
See also AAYA 12; CA 126; 133;
DAM POP

Gide, Andre (Paul Guillaume)
1869-1951 .... TCLC 5, 12, 36; DA;
DAB; DAC; SSC 13; WLC
See also CA 104; 124; DAM MST, NOV;
DLB 65; MTCW

Gifford, Barry (Colby) 1946-....... CLC 34
See also CA 65-68; CANR 9, 30, 40

Gilbert, W(illiam) S(chwenck)
1836-1911 .... TCLC 3
See also CA 104; DAM DRAM, POET;
SATA 36

Gilbreth, Frank B., Jr. 1911-....... CLC 17
See also CA 9-12R; SATA 2

Gilchrist, Ellen 1935-.. CLC 34, 48; SSC 14
See also CA 113; 116; CANR 41;
DAM POP; DLB 130; MTCW

Giles, Molly 1942- .... CLC 39
See also CA 126

Gill, Patrick
See Creasey, John

Gilliam, Terry (Vance) 1940-....... CLC 21
See also Monty Python
See also CA 108; 113; CANR 35; INT 113

Gillian, Jerry
See Gilliam, Terry (Vance)

Gilliatt, Penelope (Ann Douglass)
1932-1993 .... CLC 2, 10, 13, 53
See also AITN 2; CA 13-16R; 141;
CANR 49; DLB 14

Gilman, Charlotte (Anna) Perkins (Stetson)
1860-1935 .... TCLC 9, 37; SSC 13
See also CA 106

Gilmour, David 1949-............. CLC 35
See also CA 138, 147

Gilpin, William 1724-1804....... NCLC 30

Gilray, J. D.
See Mencken, H(enry) L(ouis)

Gilroy, Frank D(aniel) 1925-........ CLC 2
See also CA 81-84; CANR 32; DLB 7

Ginsberg, Allen
1926- ...... CLC 1, 2, 3, 4, 6, 13, 36, 69;
DA; DAB; DAC; PC 4; WLC 3
See also AITN 1; CA 1-4R; CANR 2, 41;
CDALB 1941-1968; DAM MST, POET;
DLB 5, 16; MTCW

Ginzburg, Natalia
1916-1991 .... CLC 5, 11, 54, 70
See also CA 85-88; 135; CANR 33; MTCW

Giono, Jean 1895-1970......... CLC 4, 11
See also CA 45-48; 29-32R; CANR 2, 35;
DLB 72; MTCW

Giovanni, Nikki
1943- ...... CLC 2, 4, 19, 64; BLC; DA;
DAB; DAC
See also AITN 1; BW 2; CA 29-32R;
CAAS 6; CANR 18, 41; CLR 6;
DAM MST, MULT, POET; DLB 5, 41;
INT CANR-18; MAICYA; MTCW;
SATA 24

Giovene, Andrea 1904-............. CLC 7
See also CA 85-88

Gippius, Zinaida (Nikolayevna) 1869-1945
See Hippius, Zinaida
See also CA 106

Giraudoux, (Hippolyte) Jean
1882-1944 ....TCLC 2, 7
See also CA 104; DAM DRAM; DLB 65

Gironella, Jose Maria 1917-....... CLC 11
See also CA 101

Gissing, George (Robert)
1857-1903 .... TCLC 3, 24, 47
See also CA 105; DLB 18, 135

Giurlani, Aldo
See Palazzeschi, Aldo

Gladkov, Fyodor (Vasilyevich)
1883-1958 .... TCLC 27

Glanville, Brian (Lester) 1931- ...... CLC 6
See also CA 5-8R; CAAS 9; CANR 3;
DLB 15, 139; SATA 42

Glasgow, Ellen (Anderson Gholson)
1873(?)-1945 .... TCLC 2, 7
See also CA 104; DLB 9, 12

Glaspell, Susan (Keating)
1882(?)-1948 .... TCLC 55
See also CA 110; DLB 7, 9, 78; YABC 2

Glassco, John 1909-1981 .... CLC 9
See also CA 13-16R; 102; CANR 15;
DLB 68

Glasscock, Amnesia
See Steinbeck, John (Ernst)

Glasser, Ronald J. 1940(?)-........ CLC 37

Glassman, Joyce
See Johnson, Joyce

Glendinning, Victoria 1937-........ CLC 50
See also CA 120; 127; DLB 155

Glissant, Edouard 1928-........ CLC 10, 68
See also DAM MULT

Gloag, Julian 1930- .... CLC 40
See also AITN 1; CA 65-68; CANR 10

Glowacki, Aleksander
See Prus, Boleslaw

Grass, Guenter (Wilhelm)
1927- ..... **CLC 1, 2, 4, 6, 11, 15, 22, 32, 49, 88; DA; DAB; DAC; WLC**
See also CA 13-16R; CANR 20;
DAM MST, NOV; DLB 75, 124; MTCW

Gratton, Thomas
See Hulme, T(homas) E(rnest)

Grau, Shirley Ann
1929- .... **CLC 4, 9; SSC 15**
See also CA 89-92; CANR 22; DLB 2;
INT CANR-22; MTCW

Gravel, Fern
See Hall, James Norman

Graver, Elizabeth 1964- .... **CLC 70**
See also CA 135

Graves, Richard Perceval 1945- .... **CLC 44**
See also CA 65-68; CANR 9, 26

Graves, Robert (von Ranke)
1895-1985 ..... **CLC 1, 2, 6, 11, 39, 44, 45; DAB; DAC; PC 6**
See also CA 5-8R; 117; CANR 5, 36;
CDBLB 1914-1945; DAM MST, POET;
DLB 20, 100; DLBY 85; MTCW;
SATA 45

Gray, Alasdair (James) 1934- ...... **CLC 41**
See also CA 126; CANR 47; INT 126;
MTCW

Gray, Amlin 1946- .... **CLC 29**
See also CA 138

Gray, Francine du Plessix 1930-.... **CLC 22**
See also BEST 90:3; CA 61-64; CAAS 2;
CANR 11, 33; DAM NOV;
INT CANR-11; MTCW

Gray, John (Henry) 1866-1934 .... **TCLC 19**
See also CA 119

Gray, Simon (James Holliday)
1936- .... **CLC 9, 14, 36**
See also AITN 1; CA 21-24R; CAAS 3;
CANR 32; DLB 13; MTCW

Gray, Spalding 1941- .... **CLC 49**
See also CA 128; DAM POP

Gray, Thomas
1716-1771 ...... **LC 4; DA; DAB; DAC; PC 2; WLC**
See also CDBLB 1660-1789; DAM MST;
DLB 109

Grayson, David
See Baker, Ray Stannard

Grayson, Richard (A.) 1951- .... **CLC 38**
See also CA 85-88; CANR 14, 31

Greeley, Andrew M(oran) 1928- .... **CLC 28**
See also CA 5-8R; CAAS 7; CANR 7, 43;
DAM POP; MTCW

Green, Brian
See Card, Orson Scott

Green, Hannah
See Greenberg, Joanne (Goldenberg)

Green, Hannah .... **CLC 3**
See also CA 73-76

Green, Henry .... **CLC 2, 13**
See also Yorke, Henry Vincent
See also DLB 15

Green, Julian (Hartridge) 1900-
See Green, Julien
See also CA 21-24R; CANR 33; DLB 4, 72;
MTCW

Green, Julien .... **CLC 3, 11, 77**
See also Green, Julian (Hartridge)

Green, Paul (Eliot) 1894-1981 ...... **CLC 25**
See also AITN 1; CA 5-8R; 103; CANR 3;
DAM DRAM; DLB 7, 9; DLBY 81

Greenberg, Ivan 1908-1973
See Rahv, Philip
See also CA 85-88

Greenberg, Joanne (Goldenberg)
1932- .... **CLC 7, 30**
See also AAYA 12; CA 5-8R; CANR 14,
32; SATA 25

Greenberg, Richard 1959(?)- .... **CLC 57**
See also CA 138

Greene, Bette 1934- .... **CLC 30**
See also AAYA 7; CA 53-56; CANR 4;
CLR 2; JRDA; MAICYA; SAAS 16;
SATA 8

Greene, Gael .... **CLC 8**
See also CA 13-16R; CANR 10

Greene, Graham
1904-1991 .... **CLC 1, 3, 6, 9, 14, 18, 27, 37, 70, 72; DA; DAB; DAC; WLC**
See also AITN 2; CA 13-16R; 133;
CANR 35; CDBLB 1945-1960;
DAM MST, NOV; DLB 13, 15, 77, 100,
162; DLBY 91; MTCW; SATA 20

Greer, Richard
See Silverberg, Robert

Gregor, Arthur 1923- .... **CLC 9**
See also CA 25-28R; CAAS 10; CANR 11;
SATA 36

Gregor, Lee
See Pohl, Frederik

Gregory, Isabella Augusta (Persse)
1852-1932 .... **TCLC 1**
See also CA 104; DLB 10

Gregory, J. Dennis
See Williams, John A(lfred)

Grendon, Stephen
See Derleth, August (William)

Grenville, Kate 1950- .... **CLC 61**
See also CA 118

Grenville, Pelham
See Wodehouse, P(elham) G(renville)

Greve, Felix Paul (Berthold Friedrich)
1879-1948
See Grove, Frederick Philip
See also CA 104; 141; DAC; DAM MST

Grey, Zane 1872-1939 .... **TCLC 6**
See also CA 104; 132; DAM POP; DLB 9;
MTCW

Grieg, (Johan) Nordahl (Brun)
1902-1943 .... **TCLC 10**
See also CA 107

Grieve, C(hristopher) M(urray)
1892-1978 .... **CLC 11, 19**
See also MacDiarmid, Hugh; Pteleon
See also CA 5-8R; 85-88; CANR 33;
DAM POET; MTCW

Griffin, Gerald 1803-1840 .... **NCLC 7**
See also DLB 159

Griffin, John Howard 1920-1980 .... **CLC 68**
See also AITN 1; CA 1-4R; 101; CANR 2

Griffin, Peter 1942- .... **CLC 39**
See also CA 136

Griffiths, Trevor 1935- .... **CLC 13, 52**
See also CA 97-100; CANR 45; DLB 13

Grigson, Geoffrey (Edward Harvey)
1905-1985 .... **CLC 7, 39**
See also CA 25-28R; 118; CANR 20, 33;
DLB 27; MTCW

Grillparzer, Franz 1791-1872 ...... **NCLC 1**
See also DLB 133

Grimble, Reverend Charles James
See Eliot, T(homas) S(tearns)

Grimke, Charlotte L(ottie) Forten
1837(?)-1914
See Forten, Charlotte L.
See also BW 1; CA 117; 124; DAM MULT,
POET

Grimm, Jacob Ludwig Karl
1785-1863 .... **NCLC 3**
See also DLB 90; MAICYA; SATA 22

Grimm, Wilhelm Karl 1786-1859 .. **NCLC 3**
See also DLB 90; MAICYA; SATA 22

Grimmelshausen, Johann Jakob Christoffel
von 1621-1676 .... **LC 6**

Grindel, Eugene 1895-1952
See Eluard, Paul
See also CA 104

Grisham, John 1955- .... **CLC 84**
See also AAYA 14; CA 138; CANR 47;
DAM POP

Grossman, David 1954- .... **CLC 67**
See also CA 138

Grossman, Vasily (Semenovich)
1905-1964 .... **CLC 41**
See also CA 124; 130; MTCW

Grove, Frederick Philip .... **TCLC 4**
See also Greve, Felix Paul (Berthold
Friedrich)
See also DLB 92

Grubb
See Crumb, R(obert)

Grumbach, Doris (Isaac)
1918- .... **CLC 13, 22, 64**
See also CA 5-8R; CAAS 2; CANR 9, 42;
INT CANR-9

Grundtvig, Nicolai Frederik Severin
1783-1872 .... **NCLC 1**

Grunge
See Crumb, R(obert)

Grunwald, Lisa 1959- .... **CLC 44**
See also CA 120

Guare, John 1938- .... **CLC 8, 14, 29, 67**
See also CA 73-76; CANR 21;
DAM DRAM; DLB 7; MTCW

Gudjonsson, Halldor Kiljan 1902-
See Laxness, Halldor
See also CA 103

Guenter, Erich
See Eich, Guenter

Hampton, Christopher (James)
1946- . . . . **CLC 4**
See also CA 25-28R; DLB 13; MTCW

Hamsun, Knut . . . . **TCLC 2, 14, 49**
See also Pedersen, Knut

Handke, Peter 1942- . . **CLC 5, 8, 10, 15, 38**
See also CA 77-80; CANR 33;
DAM DRAM, NOV; DLB 85, 124;
MTCW

Hanley, James 1901-1985 . . . **CLC 3, 5, 8, 13**
See also CA 73-76; 117; CANR 36; MTCW

Hannah, Barry 1942- . . . . **CLC 23, 38, 90**
See also CA 108; 110; CANR 43; DLB 6;
INT 110; MTCW

Hannon, Ezra
See Hunter, Evan

Hansberry, Lorraine (Vivian)
1930-1965 . . . . . . **CLC 17, 62; BLC; DA;
DAB; DAC; DC 2**
See also BW 1; CA 109; 25-28R; CABS 3;
CDALB 1941-1968; DAM DRAM, MST,
MULT; DLB 7, 38; MTCW

Hansen, Joseph 1923- . . . . **CLC 38**
See also CA 29-32R; CAAS 17; CANR 16,
44; INT CANR-16

Hansen, Martin A. 1909-1955 . . . . . **TCLC 32**

Hanson, Kenneth O(stlin) 1922- . . . . **CLC 13**
See also CA 53-56; CANR 7

Hardwick, Elizabeth 1916- . . . . **CLC 13**
See also CA 5-8R; CANR 3, 32;
DAM NOV; DLB 6; MTCW

Hardy, Thomas
1840-1928 . . . . . . **TCLC 4, 10, 18, 32, 48,
53; DA; DAB; DAC; PC 8; SSC 2; WLC**
See also CA 104; 123; CDBLB 1890-1914;
DAM MST, NOV, POET; DLB 18, 19,
135; MTCW

Hare, David 1947- . . . . **CLC 29, 58**
See also CA 97-100; CANR 39; DLB 13;
MTCW

Harford, Henry
See Hudson, W(illiam) H(enry)

Hargrave, Leonie
See Disch, Thomas M(ichael)

Harjo, Joy 1951- . . . . **CLC 83**
See also CA 114; CANR 35; DAM MULT;
DLB 120; NNAL

Harlan, Louis R(udolph) 1922- . . . . . **CLC 34**
See also CA 21-24R; CANR 25

Harling, Robert 1951(?)- . . . . **CLC 53**
See also CA 147

Harmon, William (Ruth) 1938- . . . . . **CLC 38**
See also CA 33-36R; CANR 14, 32, 35;
SATA 65

Harper, F. E. W.
See Harper, Frances Ellen Watkins

Harper, Frances E. W.
See Harper, Frances Ellen Watkins

Harper, Frances E. Watkins
See Harper, Frances Ellen Watkins

Harper, Frances Ellen
See Harper, Frances Ellen Watkins

Harper, Frances Ellen Watkins
1825-1911 . . . . **TCLC 14; BLC**
See also BW 1; CA 111; 125; DAM MULT,
POET; DLB 50

Harper, Michael S(teven) 1938- . . **CLC 7, 22**
See also BW 1; CA 33-36R; CANR 24;
DLB 41

Harper, Mrs. F. E. W.
See Harper, Frances Ellen Watkins

Harris, Christie (Lucy) Irwin
1907- . . . . **CLC 12**
See also CA 5-8R; CANR 6; DLB 88;
JRDA; MAICYA; SAAS 10; SATA 6, 74

Harris, Frank 1856(?)-1931 . . . . **TCLC 24**
See also CA 109; DLB 156

Harris, George Washington
1814-1869 . . . . **NCLC 23**
See also DLB 3, 11

Harris, Joel Chandler
1848-1908 . . . . **TCLC 2; SSC 19**
See also CA 104; 137; DLB 11, 23, 42, 78,
91; MAICYA; YABC 1

**Harris, John (Wyndham Parkes Lucas)
Beynon** 1903-1969
See Wyndham, John
See also CA 102; 89-92

Harris, MacDonald . . . . **CLC 9**
See also Heiney, Donald (William)

Harris, Mark 1922- . . . . **CLC 19**
See also CA 5-8R; CAAS 3; CANR 2;
DLB 2; DLBY 80

Harris, (Theodore) Wilson 1921- . . . . **CLC 25**
See also BW 2; CA 65-68; CAAS 16;
CANR 11, 27; DLB 117; MTCW

Harrison, Elizabeth Cavanna 1909-
See Cavanna, Betty
See also CA 9-12R; CANR 6, 27

Harrison, Harry (Max) 1925- . . . . . . **CLC 42**
See also CA 1-4R; CANR 5, 21; DLB 8;
SATA 4

Harrison, James (Thomas)
1937- . . . . **CLC 6, 14, 33, 66; SSC 19**
See also CA 13-16R; CANR 8; DLBY 82;
INT CANR-8

Harrison, Jim
See Harrison, James (Thomas)

Harrison, Kathryn 1961- . . . . **CLC 70**
See also CA 144

Harrison, Tony 1937- . . . . **CLC 43**
See also CA 65-68; CANR 44; DLB 40;
MTCW

Harriss, Will(ard Irvin) 1922- . . . . . . **CLC 34**
See also CA 111

Harson, Sley
See Ellison, Harlan (Jay)

Hart, Ellis
See Ellison, Harlan (Jay)

Hart, Josephine 1942(?)- . . . . **CLC 70**
See also CA 138; DAM POP

Hart, Moss 1904-1961 . . . . **CLC 66**
See also CA 109; 89-92; DAM DRAM;
DLB 7

Harte, (Francis) Bret(t)
1836(?)-1902 . . . . **TCLC 1, 25; DA; DAC;
SSC 8; WLC**
See also CA 104; 140; CDALB 1865-1917;
DAM MST; DLB 12, 64, 74, 79;
SATA 26

Hartley, L(eslie) P(oles)
1895-1972 . . . . **CLC 2, 22**
See also CA 45-48; 37-40R; CANR 33;
DLB 15, 139; MTCW

Hartman, Geoffrey H. 1929- . . . . **CLC 27**
See also CA 117; 125; DLB 67

Hartmann von Aue
c. 1160-c. 1205 . . . . **CMLC 15**
See also DLB 138

Hartmann von Aue 1170-1210 . . . . **CMLC 15**

Haruf, Kent 1943- . . . . **CLC 34**
See also CA 149

Harwood, Ronald 1934- . . . . **CLC 32**
See also CA 1-4R; CANR 4; DAM DRAM,
MST; DLB 13

Hasek, Jaroslav (Matej Frantisek)
1883-1923 . . . . **TCLC 4**
See also CA 104; 129; MTCW

Hass, Robert 1941- . . . . **CLC 18, 39**
See also CA 111; CANR 30, 50; DLB 105

Hastings, Hudson
See Kuttner, Henry

Hastings, Selina . . . . **CLC 44**

Hatteras, Amelia
See Mencken, H(enry) L(ouis)

Hatteras, Owen . . . . **TCLC 18**
See also Mencken, H(enry) L(ouis); Nathan,
George Jean

Hauptmann, Gerhart (Johann Robert)
1862-1946 . . . . **TCLC 4**
See also CA 104; DAM DRAM; DLB 66,
118

Havel, Vaclav
1936- . . . . **CLC 25, 58, 65; DC 6**
See also CA 104; CANR 36; DAM DRAM;
MTCW

Haviaras, Stratis . . . . **CLC 33**
See also Chaviaras, Strates

Hawes, Stephen 1475(?)-1523(?) . . . . . **LC 17**

Hawkes, John (Clendennin Burne, Jr.)
1925- . . . . . . **CLC 1, 2, 3, 4, 7, 9, 14, 15,
27, 49**
See also CA 1-4R; CANR 2, 47; DLB 2, 7;
DLBY 80; MTCW

Hawking, S. W.
See Hawking, Stephen W(illiam)

Hawking, Stephen W(illiam)
1942- . . . . **CLC 63**
See also AAYA 13; BEST 89:1; CA 126;
129; CANR 48

Hawthorne, Julian 1846-1934 . . . . . **TCLC 25**

Hawthorne, Nathaniel
1804-1864 . . . . **NCLC 39; DA; DAB;
DAC; SSC 3; WLC**
See also CDALB 1640-1865; DAM MST,
NOV; DLB 1, 74; YABC 2

Haxton, Josephine Ayres 1921-
See Douglas, Ellen
See also CA 115; CANR 41

Herrmann, Dorothy 1941- .... **CLC 44**
See also CA 107

Herrmann, Taffy
See Herrmann, Dorothy

Hersey, John (Richard)
1914-1993 ..... **CLC 1, 2, 7, 9, 40, 81**
See also CA 17-20R; 140; CANR 33;
DAM POP; DLB 6; MTCW; SATA 25;
SATA-Obit 76

Herzen, Aleksandr Ivanovich
1812-1870 .... **NCLC 10**

Herzl, Theodor 1860-1904 .... **TCLC 36**

Herzog, Werner 1942- .... **CLC 16**
See also CA 89-92

Hesiod c. 8th cent. B.C.- .... **CMLC 5**

Hesse, Hermann
1877-1962 .... **CLC 1, 2, 3, 6, 11, 17, 25,**
69; DA; DAB; DAC; SSC 9; WLC
See also CA 17-18; CAP 2; DAM MST,
NOV; DLB 66; MTCW; SATA 50

Hewes, Cady
See De Voto, Bernard (Augustine)

Heyen, William 1940- .... **CLC 13, 18**
See also CA 33-36R; CAAS 9; DLB 5

Heyerdahl, Thor 1914- .... **CLC 26**
See also CA 5-8R; CANR 5, 22; MTCW;
SATA 2, 52

Heym, Georg (Theodor Franz Arthur)
1887-1912 .... **TCLC 9**
See also CA 106

Heym, Stefan 1913- .... **CLC 41**
See also CA 9-12R; CANR 4; DLB 69

Heyse, Paul (Johann Ludwig von)
1830-1914 .... **TCLC 8**
See also CA 104; DLB 129

Heyward, (Edwin) DuBose
1885-1940 .... **TCLC 59**
See also CA 108; DLB 7, 9, 45; SATA 21

Hibbert, Eleanor Alice Burford
1906-1993 .... **CLC 7**
See also BEST 90:4; CA 17-20R; 140;
CANR 9, 28; DAM POP; SATA 2;
SATA-Obit 74

Higgins, George V(incent)
1939- .... **CLC 4, 7, 10, 18**
See also CA 77-80; CAAS 5; CANR 17;
DLB 2; DLBY 81; INT CANR-17;
MTCW

Higginson, Thomas Wentworth
1823-1911 .... **TCLC 36**
See also DLB 1, 64

Highet, Helen
See MacInnes, Helen (Clark)

Highsmith, (Mary) Patricia
1921-1995 .... **CLC 2, 4, 14, 42**
See also CA 1-4R; 147; CANR 1, 20, 48;
DAM NOV, POP; MTCW

Highwater, Jamake (Mamake)
1942(?)- .... **CLC 12**
See also AAYA 7; CA 65-68; CAAS 7;
CANR 10, 34; CLR 17; DLB 52;
DLBY 85; JRDA; MAICYA; SATA 32,
69; SATA-Brief 30

Higuchi, Ichiyo 1872-1896 .... **NCLC 49**

Hijuelos, Oscar 1951- ...... **CLC 65; HLC**
See also BEST 90:1; CA 123; CANR 50;
DAM MULT, POP; DLB 145; HW

Hikmet, Nazim 1902(?)-1963 ...... **CLC 40**
See also CA 141; 93-96

Hildesheimer, Wolfgang
1916-1991 .... **CLC 49**
See also CA 101; 135; DLB 69, 124

Hill, Geoffrey (William)
1932- .... **CLC 5, 8, 18, 45**
See also CA 81-84; CANR 21;
CDBLB 1960 to Present; DAM POET;
DLB 40; MTCW

Hill, George Roy 1921- .... **CLC 26**
See also CA 110; 122

Hill, John
See Koontz, Dean R(ay)

Hill, Susan (Elizabeth)
1942- .... **CLC 4; DAB**
See also CA 33-36R; CANR 29;
DAM MST, NOV; DLB 14, 139; MTCW

Hillerman, Tony 1925- .... **CLC 62**
See also AAYA 6; BEST 89:1; CA 29-32R;
CANR 21, 42; DAM POP; SATA 6

Hillesum, Etty 1914-1943 .... **TCLC 49**
See also CA 137

Hilliard, Noel (Harvey) 1929- ...... **CLC 15**
See also CA 9-12R; CANR 7

Hillis, Rick 1956- .... **CLC 66**
See also CA 134

Hilton, James 1900-1954 .... **TCLC 21**
See also CA 108; DLB 34, 77; SATA 34

Himes, Chester (Bomar)
1909-1984 .... **CLC 2, 4, 7, 18, 58; BLC**
See also BW 2; CA 25-28R; 114; CANR 22;
DAM MULT; DLB 2, 76, 143; MTCW

Hinde, Thomas .... **CLC 6, 11**
See also Chitty, Thomas Willes

Hindin, Nathan
See Bloch, Robert (Albert)

Hine, (William) Daryl 1936- .... **CLC 15**
See also CA 1-4R; CAAS 15; CANR 1, 20;
DLB 60

Hinkson, Katharine Tynan
See Tynan, Katharine

Hinton, S(usan) E(loise)
1950- .... **CLC 30; DA; DAB; DAC**
See also AAYA 2; CA 81-84; CANR 32;
CLR 3, 23; DAM MST, NOV; JRDA;
MAICYA; MTCW; SATA 19, 58

Hippius, Zinaida .... **TCLC 9**
See also Gippius, Zinaida (Nikolayevna)

Hiraoka, Kimitake 1925-1970
See Mishima, Yukio
See also CA 97-100; 29-32R; DAM DRAM;
MTCW

Hirsch, E(ric) D(onald), Jr. 1928- ... **CLC 79**
See also CA 25-28R; CANR 27; DLB 67;
INT CANR-27; MTCW

Hirsch, Edward 1950- .... **CLC 31, 50**
See also CA 104; CANR 20, 42; DLB 120

Hitchcock, Alfred (Joseph)
1899-1980 .... **CLC 16**
See also CA 97-100; SATA 27;
SATA-Obit 24

Hitler, Adolf 1889-1945 .... **TCLC 53**
See also CA 117; 147

Hoagland, Edward 1932- .... **CLC 28**
See also CA 1-4R; CANR 2, 31; DLB 6;
SATA 51

Hoban, Russell (Conwell) 1925- ... **CLC 7, 25**
See also CA 5-8R; CANR 23, 37; CLR 3;
DAM NOV; DLB 52; MAICYA;
MTCW; SATA 1, 40, 78

Hobbs, Perry
See Blackmur, R(ichard) P(almer)

Hobson, Laura Z(ametkin)
1900-1986 .... **CLC 7, 25**
See also CA 17-20R; 118; DLB 28;
SATA 52

Hochhuth, Rolf 1931- .... **CLC 4, 11, 18**
See also CA 5-8R; CANR 33;
DAM DRAM; DLB 124; MTCW

Hochman, Sandra 1936- .... **CLC 3, 8**
See also CA 5-8R; DLB 5

Hochwaelder, Fritz 1911-1986 ...... **CLC 36**
See also CA 29-32R; 120; CANR 42;
DAM DRAM; MTCW

Hochwalder, Fritz
See Hochwaelder, Fritz

Hocking, Mary (Eunice) 1921- ..... **CLC 13**
See also CA 101; CANR 18, 40

Hodgins, Jack 1938- .... **CLC 23**
See also CA 93-96; DLB 60

Hodgson, William Hope
1877(?)-1918 .... **TCLC 13**
See also CA 111; DLB 70, 153, 156

Hoffman, Alice 1952- .... **CLC 51**
See also CA 77-80; CANR 34; DAM NOV;
MTCW

Hoffman, Daniel (Gerard)
1923- .... **CLC 6, 13, 23**
See also CA 1-4R; CANR 4; DLB 5

Hoffman, Stanley 1944- .... **CLC 5**
See also CA 77-80

Hoffman, William M(oses) 1939- ... **CLC 40**
See also CA 57-60; CANR 11

Hoffmann, E(rnst) T(heodor) A(madeus)
1776-1822 .... **NCLC 2; SSC 13**
See also DLB 90; SATA 27

Hofmann, Gert 1931- .... **CLC 54**
See also CA 128

Hofmannsthal, Hugo von
1874-1929 .... **TCLC 11; DC 4**
See also CA 106; DAM DRAM; DLB 81,
118

Hogan, Linda 1947- .... **CLC 73**
See also CA 120; CANR 45; DAM MULT;
NNAL

Hogarth, Charles
See Creasey, John

Hogg, James 1770-1835 .... **NCLC 4**
See also DLB 93, 116, 159

Holbach, Paul Henri Thiry Baron
1723-1789 .... **LC 14**

Holberg, Ludvig 1684-1754 .... **LC 6**

Holden, Ursula 1921- .... **CLC 18**
See also CA 101; CAAS 8; CANR 22

Holderlin, (Johann Christian) Friedrich
1770-1843 .... **NCLC 16; PC 4**

Holdstock, Robert
See Holdstock, Robert P.

Holdstock, Robert P. 1948-........ **CLC 39**
See also CA 131

Holland, Isabelle 1920- .... **CLC 21**
See also AAYA 11; CA 21-24R; CANR 10,
25, 47; JRDA; MAICYA; SATA 8, 70

Holland, Marcus
See Caldwell, (Janet Miriam) Taylor
(Holland)

Hollander, John 1929-...... **CLC 2, 5, 8, 14**
See also CA 1-4R; CANR 1; DLB 5;
SATA 13

Hollander, Paul
See Silverberg, Robert

Holleran, Andrew 1943(?)-........ **CLC 38**
See also CA 144

Hollinghurst, Alan 1954-....... **CLC 55, 91**
See also CA 114

Hollis, Jim
See Summers, Hollis (Spurgeon, Jr.)

Holmes, John
See Souster, (Holmes) Raymond

Holmes, John Clellon 1926-1988.... **CLC 56**
See also CA 9-12R; 125; CANR 4; DLB 16

Holmes, Oliver Wendell
1809-1894 .... **NCLC 14**
See also CDALB 1640-1865; DLB 1;
SATA 34

Holmes, Raymond
See Souster, (Holmes) Raymond

Holt, Victoria
See Hibbert, Eleanor Alice Burford

Holub, Miroslav 1923-............. **CLC 4**
See also CA 21-24R; CANR 10

Homer
c. 8th cent. B.C.-..... **CMLC 1, 16; DA;**
DAB; DAC
See also DAM MST, POET

Honig, Edwin 1919-............. **CLC 33**
See also CA 5-8R; CAAS 8; CANR 4, 45;
DLB 5

Hood, Hugh (John Blagdon)
1928- .... **CLC 15, 28**
See also CA 49-52; CAAS 17; CANR 1, 33;
DLB 53

Hood, Thomas 1799-1845........ **NCLC 16**
See also DLB 96

Hooker, (Peter) Jeremy 1941-...... **CLC 43**
See also CA 77-80; CANR 22; DLB 40

Hope, A(lec) D(erwent) 1907-.... **CLC 3, 51**
See also CA 21-24R; CANR 33; MTCW

Hope, Brian
See Creasey, John

Hope, Christopher (David Tully)
1944- .... **CLC 52**
See also CA 106; CANR 47; SATA 62

Hopkins, Gerard Manley
1844-1889 ...... **NCLC 17; DA; DAB;**
DAC; PC 15; WLC
See also CDBLB 1890-1914; DAM MST,
POET; DLB 35, 57

Hopkins, John (Richard) 1931-...... **CLC 4**
See also CA 85-88

Hopkins, Pauline Elizabeth
1859-1930 .... **TCLC 28; BLC**
See also BW 2; CA 141; DAM MULT;
DLB 50

Hopkinson, Francis 1737-1791 ...... **LC 25**
See also DLB 31

Hopley-Woolrich, Cornell George 1903-1968
See Woolrich, Cornell
See also CA 13-14; CAP 1

Horatio
See Proust, (Valentin-Louis-George-Eugene-)
Marcel

Horgan, Paul (George Vincent O'Shaughnessy)
1903-1995 .... **CLC 9, 53**
See also CA 13-16R; 147; CANR 9, 35;
DAM NOV; DLB 102; DLBY 85;
INT CANR-9; MTCW; SATA 13;
SATA-Obit 84

Horn, Peter
See Kuttner, Henry

Hornem, Horace Esq.
See Byron, George Gordon (Noel)

Hornung, E(rnest) W(illiam)
1866-1921 .... **TCLC 59**
See also CA 108; DLB 70

Horovitz, Israel (Arthur) 1939-..... **CLC 56**
See also CA 33-36R; CANR 46;
DAM DRAM; DLB 7

Horvath, Odon von
See Horvath, Oedoen von
See also DLB 85, 124

Horvath, Oedoen von 1901-1938... **TCLC 45**
See also Horvath, Odon von
See also CA 118

Horwitz, Julius 1920-1986........ **CLC 14**
See also CA 9-12R; 119; CANR 12

Hospital, Janette Turner 1942-..... **CLC 42**
See also CA 108; CANR 48

Hostos, E. M. de
See Hostos (y Bonilla), Eugenio Maria de

Hostos, Eugenio M. de
See Hostos (y Bonilla), Eugenio Maria de

Hostos, Eugenio Maria
See Hostos (y Bonilla), Eugenio Maria de

Hostos (y Bonilla), Eugenio Maria de
1839-1903 .... **TCLC 24**
See also CA 123; 131; HW

Houdini
See Lovecraft, H(oward) P(hillips)

Hougan, Carolyn 1943- .... **CLC 34**
See also CA 139

Household, Geoffrey (Edward West)
1900-1988 .... **CLC 11**
See also CA 77-80; 126; DLB 87; SATA 14;
SATA-Obit 59

Housman, A(lfred) E(dward)
1859-1936 ...... **TCLC 1, 10; DA; DAB;**
DAC; PC 2
See also CA 104; 125; DAM MST, POET;
DLB 19; MTCW

Housman, Laurence 1865-1959 ..... **TCLC 7**
See also CA 106; DLB 10; SATA 25

Howard, Elizabeth Jane 1923- ... **CLC 7, 29**
See also CA 5-8R; CANR 8

Howard, Maureen 1930- ..... **CLC 5, 14, 46**
See also CA 53-56; CANR 31; DLBY 83;
INT CANR-31; MTCW

Howard, Richard 1929- ...... **CLC 7, 10, 47**
See also AITN 1; CA 85-88; CANR 25;
DLB 5; INT CANR-25

Howard, Robert Ervin 1906-1936... **TCLC 8**
See also CA 105

Howard, Warren F.
See Pohl, Frederik

Howe, Fanny 1940- .... **CLC 47**
See also CA 117; SATA-Brief 52

Howe, Irving 1920-1993........... **CLC 85**
See also CA 9-12R; 141; CANR 21, 50;
DLB 67; MTCW

Howe, Julia Ward 1819-1910 ..... **TCLC 21**
See also CA 117; DLB 1

Howe, Susan 1937-.............. **CLC 72**
See also DLB 120

Howe, Tina 1937-............... **CLC 48**
See also CA 109

Howell, James 1594(?)-1666 .... **LC 13**
See also DLB 151

Howells, W. D.
See Howells, William Dean

Howells, William D.
See Howells, William Dean

Howells, William Dean
1837-1920 .... **TCLC 7, 17, 41**
See also CA 104; 134; CDALB 1865-1917;
DLB 12, 64, 74, 79

Howes, Barbara 1914-............. **CLC 15**
See also CA 9-12R; CAAS 3; SATA 5

Hrabal, Bohumil 1914-........ **CLC 13, 67**
See also CA 106; CAAS 12

Hsun, Lu
See Lu Hsun

Hubbard, L(afayette) Ron(ald)
1911-1986 .... **CLC 43**
See also CA 77-80; 118; CANR 22;
DAM POP

Huch, Ricarda (Octavia)
1864-1947 .... **TCLC 13**
See also CA 111; DLB 66

Huddle, David 1942- .... **CLC 49**
See also CA 57-60; CAAS 20; DLB 130

Hudson, Jeffrey
See Crichton, (John) Michael

Hudson, W(illiam) H(enry)
1841-1922 .... **TCLC 29**
See also CA 115; DLB 98, 153; SATA 35

Hueffer, Ford Madox
See Ford, Ford Madox

Hughart, Barry 1934-............. **CLC 39**
See also CA 137

Hughes, Colin
See Creasey, John

Hughes, David (John) 1930- .... **CLC 48**
See also CA 116; 129; DLB 14

Hughes, Edward James
See Hughes, Ted
See also DAM MST, POET

Kherdian, David 1931-.......... **CLC 6, 9**
See also CA 21-24R; CAAS 2; CANR 39;
CLR 24; JRDA; MAICYA; SATA 16, 74

Khlebnikov, Velimir .... **TCLC 20**
See also Khlebnikov, Viktor Vladimirovich

Khlebnikov, Viktor Vladimirovich 1885-1922
See Khlebnikov, Velimir
See also CA 117

Khodasevich, Vladislav (Felitsianovich)
1886-1939 .... **TCLC 15**
See also CA 115

Kielland, Alexander Lange
1849-1906 .... **TCLC 5**
See also CA 104

Kiely, Benedict 1919-......... **CLC 23, 43**
See also CA 1-4R; CANR 2; DLB 15

Kienzle, William X(avier) 1928- .... **CLC 25**
See also CA 93-96; CAAS 1; CANR 9, 31;
DAM POP; INT CANR-31; MTCW

Kierkegaard, Soren 1813-1855.... **NCLC 34**

Killens, John Oliver 1916-1987..... **CLC 10**
See also BW 2; CA 77-80; 123; CAAS 2;
CANR 26; DLB 33

Killigrew, Anne 1660-1685.......... **LC 4**
See also DLB 131

Kim
See Simenon, Georges (Jacques Christian)

Kincaid, Jamaica 1949- ... **CLC 43, 68; BLC**
See also AAYA 13; BW 2; CA 125;
CANR 47; DAM MULT, NOV;
DLB 157

King, Francis (Henry) 1923-..... **CLC 8, 53**
See also CA 1-4R; CANR 1, 33;
DAM NOV; DLB 15, 139; MTCW

King, Martin Luther, Jr.
1929-1968 .... **CLC 83; BLC; DA; DAB;**
DAC
See also BW 2; CA 25-28; CANR 27, 44;
CAP 2; DAM MST, MULT; MTCW;
SATA 14

King, Stephen (Edwin)
1947-...... **CLC 12, 26, 37, 61; SSC 17**
See also AAYA 1, 17; BEST 90:1;
CA 61-64; CANR 1, 30; DAM NOV,
POP; DLB 143; DLBY 80; JRDA;
MTCW; SATA 9, 55

King, Steve
See King, Stephen (Edwin)

King, Thomas 1943-........ **CLC 89; DAC**
See also CA 144; DAM MULT; NNAL

Kingman, Lee.................... **CLC 17**
See also Natti, (Mary) Lee
See also SAAS 3; SATA 1, 67

Kingsley, Charles 1819-1875..... **NCLC 35**
See also DLB 21, 32; YABC 2

Kingsley, Sidney 1906-1995....... **CLC 44**
See also CA 85-88; 147; DLB 7

Kingsolver, Barbara 1955-...... **CLC 55, 81**
See also AAYA 15; CA 129; 134;
DAM POP; INT 134

Kingston, Maxine (Ting Ting) Hong
1940-................ **CLC 12, 19, 58**
See also AAYA 8; CA 69-72; CANR 13,
38; DAM MULT, NOV; DLBY 80;
INT CANR-13; MTCW; SATA 53

Kinnell, Galway
1927-.......... **CLC 1, 2, 3, 5, 13, 29**
See also CA 9-12R; CANR 10, 34; DLB 5;
DLBY 87; INT CANR-34; MTCW

Kinsella, Thomas 1928-......... **CLC 4, 19**
See also CA 17-20R; CANR 15; DLB 27;
MTCW

Kinsella, W(illiam) P(atrick)
1935-............... **CLC 27, 43; DAC**
See also AAYA 7; CA 97-100; CAAS 7;
CANR 21, 35; DAM NOV, POP;
INT CANR-21; MTCW

Kipling, (Joseph) Rudyard
1865-1936 ...... **TCLC 8, 17; DA; DAB;**
DAC; PC 3; SSC 5; WLC
See also CA 105; 120; CANR 33;
CDBLB 1890-1914; CLR 39; DAM MST,
POET; DLB 19, 34, 141, 156; MAICYA;
MTCW; YABC 2

Kirkup, James 1918-............. **CLC 1**
See also CA 1-4R; CAAS 4; CANR 2;
DLB 27; SATA 12

Kirkwood, James 1930(?)-1989 ...... **CLC 9**
See also AITN 2; CA 1-4R; 128; CANR 6,
40

Kirshner, Sidney
See Kingsley, Sidney

Kis, Danilo 1935-1989 .... **CLC 57**
See also CA 109; 118; 129; MTCW

Kivi, Aleksis 1834-1872 .... **NCLC 30**

Kizer, Carolyn (Ashley)
1925- .... **CLC 15, 39, 80**
See also CA 65-68; CAAS 5; CANR 24;
DAM POET; DLB 5

Klabund 1890-1928.............. **TCLC 44**
See also DLB 66

Klappert, Peter 1942-............. **CLC 57**
See also CA 33-36R; DLB 5

Klein, A(braham) M(oses)
1909-1972 .... **CLC 19; DAB; DAC**
See also CA 101; 37-40R; DAM MST;
DLB 68

Klein, Norma 1938-1989 .... **CLC 30**
See also AAYA 2; CA 41-44R; 128;
CANR 15, 37; CLR 2, 19;
INT CANR-15; JRDA; MAICYA;
SAAS 1; SATA 7, 57

Klein, T(heodore) E(ibon) D(onald)
1947-...................... **CLC 34**
See also CA 119; CANR 44

Kleist, Heinrich von
1777-1811 .... **NCLC 2, 37**
See also DAM DRAM; DLB 90

Klima, Ivan 1931-................ **CLC 56**
See also CA 25-28R; CANR 17, 50;
DAM NOV

Klimentov, Andrei Platonovich 1899-1951
See Platonov, Andrei
See also CA 108

Klinger, Friedrich Maximilian von
1752-1831 .... **NCLC 1**
See also DLB 94

Klopstock, Friedrich Gottlieb
1724-1803 .... **NCLC 11**
See also DLB 97

Knebel, Fletcher 1911-1993........ **CLC 14**
See also AITN 1; CA 1-4R; 140; CAAS 3;
CANR 1, 36; SATA 36; SATA-Obit 75

Knickerbocker, Diedrich
See Irving, Washington

Knight, Etheridge
1931-1991 .... **CLC 40; BLC; PC 14**
See also BW 1; CA 21-24R; 133; CANR 23;
DAM POET; DLB 41

Knight, Sarah Kemble 1666-1727 ..... **LC 7**
See also DLB 24

Knister, Raymond 1899-1932...... **TCLC 56**
See also DLB 68

Knowles, John
1926-...... **CLC 1, 4, 10, 26; DA; DAC**
See also AAYA 10; CA 17-20R; CANR 40;
CDALB 1968-1988; DAM MST, NOV;
DLB 6; MTCW; SATA 8

Knox, Calvin M.
See Silverberg, Robert

Knye, Cassandra
See Disch, Thomas M(ichael)

Koch, C(hristopher) J(ohn) 1932- ... **CLC 42**
See also CA 127

Koch, Christopher
See Koch, C(hristopher) J(ohn)

Koch, Kenneth 1925-......... **CLC 5, 8, 44**
See also CA 1-4R; CANR 6, 36;
DAM POET; DLB 5; INT CANR-36;
SATA 65

Kochanowski, Jan 1530-1584........ **LC 10**

Kock, Charles Paul de
1794-1871 .... **NCLC 16**

Koda Shigeyuki 1867-1947
See Rohan, Koda
See also CA 121

Koestler, Arthur
1905-1983 .... **CLC 1, 3, 6, 8, 15, 33**
See also CA 1-4R; 109; CANR 1, 33;
CDBLB 1945-1960; DLBY 83; MTCW

Kogawa, Joy Nozomi 1935-... **CLC 78; DAC**
See also CA 101; CANR 19; DAM MST,
MULT

Kohout, Pavel 1928-.............. **CLC 13**
See also CA 45-48; CANR 3

Koizumi, Yakumo
See Hearn, (Patricio) Lafcadio (Tessima
Carlos)

Kolmar, Gertrud 1894-1943....... **TCLC 40**

Komunyakaa, Yusef 1947-......... **CLC 86**
See also CA 147; DLB 120

Konrad, George
See Konrad, Gyoergy

Konrad, Gyoergy 1933- ...... **CLC 4, 10, 73**
See also CA 85-88

Konwicki, Tadeusz 1926-..... **CLC 8, 28, 54**
See also CA 101; CAAS 9; CANR 39;
MTCW

Koontz, Dean R(ay) 1945-........ **CLC 78**
See also AAYA 9; BEST 89:3, 90:2;
CA 108; CANR 19, 36; DAM NOV,
POP; MTCW

Kopit, Arthur (Lee) 1937- .... **CLC 1, 18, 33**
See also AITN 1; CA 81-84; CABS 3;
DAM DRAM; DLB 7; MTCW

Kops, Bernard 1926-.............. **CLC 4**
See also CA 5-8R; DLB 13

Kornbluth, C(yril) M. 1923-1958.... **TCLC 8**
See also CA 105; DLB 8

Korolenko, V. G.
See Korolenko, Vladimir Galaktionovich

Korolenko, Vladimir
See Korolenko, Vladimir Galaktionovich

Korolenko, Vladimir G.
See Korolenko, Vladimir Galaktionovich

Korolenko, Vladimir Galaktionovich
1853-1921 .... **TCLC 22**
See also CA 121

Korzybski, Alfred (Habdank Skarbek)
1879-1950 .... **TCLC 61**
See also CA 123

Kosinski, Jerzy (Nikodem)
1933-1991 .... **CLC 1, 2, 3, 6, 10, 15, 53,
70**
See also CA 17-20R; 134; CANR 9, 46;
DAM NOV; DLB 2; DLBY 82; MTCW

Kostelanetz, Richard (Cory) 1940- .. **CLC 28**
See also CA 13-16R; CAAS 8; CANR 38

Kostrowitzki, Wilhelm Apollinaris de
1880-1918
See Apollinaire, Guillaume
See also CA 104

Kotlowitz, Robert 1924-............ **CLC 4**
See also CA 33-36R; CANR 36

Kotzebue, August (Friedrich Ferdinand) von
1761-1819 .... **NCLC 25**
See also DLB 94

Kotzwinkle, William 1938- ... **CLC 5, 14, 35**
See also CA 45-48; CANR 3, 44; CLR 6;
MAICYA; SATA 24, 70

Kozol, Jonathan 1936-............ **CLC 17**
See also CA 61-64; CANR 16, 45

Kozoll, Michael 1940(?)- .... **CLC 35**

Kramer, Kathryn 19(?)- .... **CLC 34**

Kramer, Larry 1935- .... **CLC 42**
See also CA 124; 126; DAM POP

Krasicki, Ignacy 1735-1801 ...... **NCLC 8**

Krasinski, Zygmunt 1812-1859 .... **NCLC 4**

Kraus, Karl 1874-1936 .... **TCLC 5**
See also CA 104; DLB 118

Kreve (Mickevicius), Vincas
1882-1954 .... **TCLC 27**

Kristeva, Julia 1941- .... **CLC 77**

Kristofferson, Kris 1936-.......... **CLC 26**
See also CA 104

Krizanc, John 1956-............. **CLC 57**

Krleza, Miroslav 1893-1981........ **CLC 8**
See also CA 97-100; 105; CANR 50;
DLB 147

Kroetsch, Robert
1927- .... **CLC 5, 23, 57; DAC**
See also CA 17-20R; CANR 8, 38;
DAM POET; DLB 53; MTCW

Kroetz, Franz
See Kroetz, Franz Xaver

Kroetz, Franz Xaver 1946- .... **CLC 41**
See also CA 130

Kroker, Arthur 1945-............. **CLC 77**

Kropotkin, Peter (Aleksieevich)
1842-1921 .... **TCLC 36**
See also CA 119

Krotkov, Yuri 1917-............. **CLC 19**
See also CA 102

Krumb
See Crumb, R(obert)

Krumgold, Joseph (Quincy)
1908-1980 .... **CLC 12**
See also CA 9-12R; 101; CANR 7;
MAICYA; SATA 1, 48; SATA-Obit 23

Krumwitz
See Crumb, R(obert)

Krutch, Joseph Wood 1893-1970.... **CLC 24**
See also CA 1-4R; 25-28R; CANR 4;
DLB 63

Krutzch, Gus
See Eliot, T(homas) S(tearns)

Krylov, Ivan Andreevich
1768(?)-1844 .... **NCLC 1**
See also DLB 150

Kubin, Alfred (Leopold Isidor)
1877-1959 .... **TCLC 23**
See also CA 112; 149; DLB 81

Kubrick, Stanley 1928-............ **CLC 16**
See also CA 81-84; CANR 33; DLB 26

Kumin, Maxine (Winokur)
1925- .... **CLC 5, 13, 28; PC 15**
See also AITN 2; CA 1-4R; CAAS 8;
CANR 1, 21; DAM POET; DLB 5;
MTCW; SATA 12

Kundera, Milan
1929- .... **CLC 4, 9, 19, 32, 68**
See also AAYA 2; CA 85-88; CANR 19;
DAM NOV; MTCW

Kunene, Mazisi (Raymond) 1930-... **CLC 85**
See also BW 1; CA 125; DLB 117

Kunitz, Stanley (Jasspon)
1905- .... **CLC 6, 11, 14**
See also CA 41-44R; CANR 26; DLB 48;
INT CANR-26; MTCW

Kunze, Reiner 1933-............. **CLC 10**
See also CA 93-96; DLB 75

Kuprin, Aleksandr Ivanovich
1870-1938 .... **TCLC 5**
See also CA 104

Kureishi, Hanif 1954(?)-.......... **CLC 64**
See also CA 139

Kurosawa, Akira 1910-............ **CLC 16**
See also AAYA 11; CA 101; CANR 46;
DAM MULT

Kushner, Tony 1957(?)- .... **CLC 81**
See also CA 144; DAM DRAM

Kuttner, Henry 1915-1958........ **TCLC 10**
See also CA 107; DLB 8

Kuzma, Greg 1944-.............. **CLC 7**
See also CA 33-36R

Kuzmin, Mikhail 1872(?)-1936 .... **TCLC 40**

Kyd, Thomas 1558-1594....... **LC 22; DC 3**
See also DAM DRAM; DLB 62

Kyprianos, Iossif
See Samarakis, Antonis

La Bruyere, Jean de 1645-1696..... **LC 17**

Lacan, Jacques (Marie Emile)
1901-1981 .... **CLC 75**
See also CA 121; 104

Laclos, Pierre Ambroise Francois Choderlos
de 1741-1803 .... **NCLC 4**

Lacolere, Francois
See Aragon, Louis

La Colere, Francois
See Aragon, Louis

La Deshabilleuse
See Simenon, Georges (Jacques Christian)

Lady Gregory
See Gregory, Isabella Augusta (Persse)

Lady of Quality, A
See Bagnold, Enid

La Fayette, Marie (Madelaine Pioche de la
Vergne Comtes 1634-1693....... **LC 2**

Lafayette, Rene
See Hubbard, L(afayette) Ron(ald)

Laforgue, Jules
1860-1887 .... **NCLC 5, 53; PC 14;
SSC 20**

Lagerkvist, Paer (Fabian)
1891-1974 .... **CLC 7, 10, 13, 54**
See also Lagerkvist, Par
See also CA 85-88; 49-52; DAM DRAM,
NOV; MTCW

Lagerkvist, Par .... **SSC 12**
See also Lagerkvist, Paer (Fabian)

Lagerloef, Selma (Ottiliana Lovisa)
1858-1940 .... **TCLC 4, 36**
See also Lagerlof, Selma (Ottiliana Lovisa)
See also CA 108; SATA 15

Lagerlof, Selma (Ottiliana Lovisa)
See Lagerloef, Selma (Ottiliana Lovisa)
See also CLR 7; SATA 15

La Guma, (Justin) Alex(ander)
1925-1985 .... **CLC 19**
See also BW 1; CA 49-52; 118; CANR 25;
DAM NOV; DLB 117; MTCW

Laidlaw, A. K.
See Grieve, C(hristopher) M(urray)

Lainez, Manuel Mujica
See Mujica Lainez, Manuel
See also HW

Lamartine, Alphonse (Marie Louis Prat) de
1790-1869 .... **NCLC 11; PC 15**
See also DAM POET

Lamb, Charles
1775-1834 .... **NCLC 10; DA; DAB;
DAC; WLC**
See also CDBLB 1789-1832; DAM MST;
DLB 93, 107; SATA 17

Lamb, Lady Caroline 1785-1828.. **NCLC 38**
See also DLB 116

Lamming, George (William)
1927- .... **CLC 2, 4, 66; BLC**
See also BW 2; CA 85-88; CANR 26;
DAM MULT; DLB 125; MTCW

L'Amour, Louis (Dearborn)
1908-1988 . . . . **CLC 25, 55**
See also AAYA 16; AITN 2; BEST 89:2;
CA 1-4R; 125; CANR 3, 25, 40;
DAM NOV, POP; DLBY 80; MTCW

Lampedusa, Giuseppe (Tomasi) di . . . TCLC 13
See also Tomasi di Lampedusa, Giuseppe

Lampman, Archibald 1861-1899 . . **NCLC 25**
See also DLB 92

Lancaster, Bruce 1896-1963. . . . . . . **CLC 36**
See also CA 9-10; CAP 1; SATA 9

Landau, Mark Alexandrovich
See Aldanov, Mark (Alexandrovich)

Landau-Aldanov, Mark Alexandrovich
See Aldanov, Mark (Alexandrovich)

Landis, John 1950-. . . . . **CLC 26**
See also CA 112; 122

Landolfi, Tommaso 1908-1979. . . **CLC 11, 49**
See also CA 127; 117

Landon, Letitia Elizabeth
1802-1838 . . . . **NCLC 15**
See also DLB 96

Landor, Walter Savage
1775-1864 . . . . **NCLC 14**
See also DLB 93, 107

Landwirth, Heinz 1927-
See Lind, Jakov
See also CA 9-12R; CANR 7

Lane, Patrick 1939-. . . . . **CLC 25**
See also CA 97-100; DAM POET; DLB 53;
INT 97-100

Lang, Andrew 1844-1912. . . . . **TCLC 16**
See also CA 114; 137; DLB 98, 141;
MAICYA; SATA 16

Lang, Fritz 1890-1976 . . . . **CLC 20**
See also CA 77-80; 69-72; CANR 30

Lange, John
See Crichton, (John) Michael

Langer, Elinor 1939- . . . . **CLC 34**
See also CA 121

Langland, William
1330(?)-1400(?) . . . . . . **LC 19; DA; DAB;
DAC**
See also DAM MST, POET; DLB 146

Langstaff, Launcelot
See Irving, Washington

Lanier, Sidney 1842-1881 . . . . **NCLC 6**
See also DAM POET; DLB 64; DLBD 13;
MAICYA; SATA 18

Lanyer, Aemilia 1569-1645 . . . . . **LC 10, 30**
See also DLB 121

Lao Tzu . . . . **CMLC 7**

Lapine, James (Elliot) 1949-. . . . . . **CLC 39**
See also CA 123; 130; INT 130

Larbaud, Valery (Nicolas)
1881-1957 . . . . **TCLC 9**
See also CA 106

Lardner, Ring
See Lardner, Ring(gold) W(ilmer)

Lardner, Ring W., Jr.
See Lardner, Ring(gold) W(ilmer)

Lardner, Ring(gold) W(ilmer)
1885-1933 . . . . **TCLC 2, 14**
See also CA 104; 131; CDALB 1917-1929;
DLB 11, 25, 86; MTCW

Laredo, Betty
See Codrescu, Andrei

Larkin, Maia
See Wojciechowska, Maia (Teresa)

Larkin, Philip (Arthur)
1922-1985 . . . . **CLC 3, 5, 8, 9, 13, 18, 33,
39, 64; DAB**
See also CA 5-8R; 117; CANR 24;
CDBLB 1960 to Present; DAM MST,
POET; DLB 27; MTCW

Larra (y Sanchez de Castro), Mariano Jose de
1809-1837 . . . . **NCLC 17**

Larsen, Eric 1941- . . . . **CLC 55**
See also CA 132

Larsen, Nella 1891-1964 . . . . . **CLC 37; BLC**
See also BW 1; CA 125; DAM MULT;
DLB 51

Larson, Charles R(aymond) 1938-. . . **CLC 31**
See also CA 53-56; CANR 4

Las Casas, Bartolome de 1474-1566. . **LC 31**

Lasker-Schueler, Else 1869-1945 . . **TCLC 57**
See also DLB 66, 124

Latham, Jean Lee 1902-. . . . . **CLC 12**
See also AITN 1; CA 5-8R; CANR 7;
MAICYA; SATA 2, 68

Latham, Mavis
See Clark, Mavis Thorpe

Lathen, Emma . . . . **CLC 2**
See also Hennissart, Martha; Latsis, Mary
J(ane)

Lathrop, Francis
See Leiber, Fritz (Reuter, Jr.)

Latsis, Mary J(ane)
See Lathen, Emma
See also CA 85-88

Lattimore, Richmond (Alexander)
1906-1984 . . . . **CLC 3**
See also CA 1-4R; 112; CANR 1

Laughlin, James 1914-. . . . . **CLC 49**
See also CA 21-24R; CAAS 22; CANR 9,
47; DLB 48

Laurence, (Jean) Margaret (Wemyss)
1926-1987 . . . . **CLC 3, 6, 13, 50, 62;
DAC; SSC 7**
See also CA 5-8R; 121; CANR 33;
DAM MST; DLB 53; MTCW;
SATA-Obit 50

Laurent, Antoine 1952- . . . . **CLC 50**

Lauscher, Hermann
See Hesse, Hermann

Lautreamont, Comte de
1846-1870 . . . . **NCLC 12; SSC 14**

Laverty, Donald
See Blish, James (Benjamin)

Lavin, Mary 1912-. . . . . . **CLC 4, 18; SSC 4**
See also CA 9-12R; CANR 33; DLB 15;
MTCW

Lavond, Paul Dennis
See Kornbluth, C(yril) M.; Pohl, Frederik

Lawler, Raymond Evenor 1922- . . . . **CLC 58**
See also CA 103

Lawrence, D(avid) H(erbert Richards)
1885-1930 . . . . **TCLC 2, 9, 16, 33, 48, 61;
DA; DAB; DAC; SSC 4, 19; WLC**
See also CA 104; 121; CDBLB 1914-1945;
DAM MST, NOV, POET; DLB 10, 19,
36, 98, 162; MTCW

Lawrence, T(homas) E(dward)
1888-1935 . . . . **TCLC 18**
See also Dale, Colin
See also CA 115

Lawrence of Arabia
See Lawrence, T(homas) E(dward)

Lawson, Henry (Archibald Hertzberg)
1867-1922 . . . . **TCLC 27; SSC 18**
See also CA 120

Lawton, Dennis
See Faust, Frederick (Schiller)

Laxness, Halldor. . . . . **CLC 25**
See also Gudjonsson, Halldor Kiljan

Layamon fl. c. 1200-. . . . . **CMLC 10**
See also DLB 146

Laye, Camara 1928-1980 . . . **CLC 4, 38; BLC**
See also BW 1; CA 85-88; 97-100;
CANR 25; DAM MULT; MTCW

Layton, Irving (Peter)
1912-. . . . . **CLC 2, 15; DAC**
See also CA 1-4R; CANR 2, 33, 43;
DAM MST, POET; DLB 88; MTCW

Lazarus, Emma 1849-1887. . . . . **NCLC 8**

Lazarus, Felix
See Cable, George Washington

Lazarus, Henry
See Slavitt, David R(ytman)

Lea, Joan
See Neufeld, John (Arthur)

Leacock, Stephen (Butler)
1869-1944 . . . . **TCLC 2; DAC**
See also CA 104; 141; DAM MST; DLB 92

Lear, Edward 1812-1888 . . . . **NCLC 3**
See also CLR 1; DLB 32; MAICYA;
SATA 18

Lear, Norman (Milton) 1922- . . . . . . **CLC 12**
See also CA 73-76

Leavis, F(rank) R(aymond)
1895-1978 . . . . **CLC 24**
See also CA 21-24R; 77-80; CANR 44;
MTCW

Leavitt, David 1961-. . . . . **CLC 34**
See also CA 116; 122; CANR 50;
DAM POP; DLB 130; INT 122

Leblanc, Maurice (Marie Emile)
1864-1941 . . . . **TCLC 49**
See also CA 110

Lebowitz, Fran(ces Ann)
1951(?)-. . . . . **CLC 11, 36**
See also CA 81-84; CANR 14;
INT CANR-14; MTCW

Lebrecht, Peter
See Tieck, (Johann) Ludwig

le Carre, John . . . . **CLC 3, 5, 9, 15, 28**
See also Cornwell, David (John Moore)
See also BEST 89:4; CDBLB 1960 to
Present; DLB 87

Le Clezio, J(ean) M(arie) G(ustave)
1940- .... CLC 31
See also CA 116; 128; DLB 83

Leconte de Lisle, Charles-Marie-Rene
1818-1894 .... NCLC 29

Le Coq, Monsieur
See Simenon, Georges (Jacques Christian)

Leduc, Violette 1907-1972 .... CLC 22
See also CA 13-14; 33-36R; CAP 1

Ledwidge, Francis 1887(?)-1917 ... TCLC 23
See also CA 123; DLB 20

Lee, Andrea 1953- .... CLC 36; BLC
See also BW 1; CA 125; DAM MULT

Lee, Andrew
See Auchincloss, Louis (Stanton)

Lee, Chang-rae 1965- .... CLC 91
See also CA 148

Lee, Don L. .... CLC 2
See also Madhubuti, Haki R.

Lee, George W(ashington)
1894-1976 .... CLC 52; BLC
See also BW 1; CA 125; DAM MULT;
DLB 51

Lee, (Nelle) Harper
1926- .... CLC 12, 60; DA; DAB; DAC;
WLC
See also AAYA 13; CA 13-16R;
CDALB 1941-1968; DAM MST, NOV;
DLB 6; MTCW; SATA 11

Lee, Helen Elaine 1959(?)- .... CLC 86
See also CA 148

Lee, Julian
See Latham, Jean Lee

Lee, Larry
See Lee, Lawrence

Lee, Laurie 1914- .... CLC 90; DAB
See also CA 77-80; CANR 33; DAM POP;
DLB 27; MTCW

Lee, Lawrence 1941-1990 .... CLC 34
See also CA 131; CANR 43

Lee, Manfred B(ennington)
1905-1971 .... CLC 11
See also Queen, Ellery
See also CA 1-4R; 29-32R; CANR 2;
DLB 137

Lee, Stan 1922- .... CLC 17
See also AAYA 5; CA 108; 111; INT 111

Lee, Tanith 1947- .... CLC 46
See also AAYA 15; CA 37-40R; SATA 8

Lee, Vernon .... TCLC 5
See also Paget, Violet
See also DLB 57, 153, 156

Lee, William
See Burroughs, William S(eward)

Lee, Willy
See Burroughs, William S(eward)

Lee-Hamilton, Eugene (Jacob)
1845-1907 .... TCLC 22
See also CA 117

Leet, Judith 1935- .... CLC 11

Le Fanu, Joseph Sheridan
1814-1873 .... NCLC 9; SSC 14
See also DAM POP; DLB 21, 70, 159

Leffland, Ella 1931- .... CLC 19
See also CA 29-32R; CANR 35; DLBY 84;
INT CANR-35; SATA 65

Leger, Alexis
See Leger, (Marie-Rene Auguste) Alexis
Saint-Leger

Leger, (Marie-Rene Auguste) Alexis
Saint-Leger 1887-1975 .... CLC 11
See Perse, St.-John
See also CA 13-16R; 61-64; CANR 43;
DAM POET; MTCW

Leger, Saintleger
See Leger, (Marie-Rene Auguste) Alexis
Saint-Leger

Le Guin, Ursula K(roeber)
1929- ...... CLC 8, 13, 22, 45, 71; DAB;
DAC; SSC 12
See also AAYA 9; AITN 1; CA 21-24R;
CANR 9, 32; CDALB 1968-1988; CLR 3,
28; DAM MST, POP; DLB 8, 52;
INT CANR-32; JRDA; MAICYA;
MTCW; SATA 4, 52

Lehmann, Rosamond (Nina)
1901-1990 .... CLC 5
See also CA 77-80; 131; CANR 8; DLB 15

Leiber, Fritz (Reuter, Jr.)
1910-1992 .... CLC 25
See also CA 45-48; 139; CANR 2, 40;
DLB 8; MTCW; SATA 45;
SATA-Obit 73

Leimbach, Martha 1963-
See Leimbach, Marti
See also CA 130

Leimbach, Marti .... CLC 65
See also Leimbach, Martha

Leino, Eino .... TCLC 24
See also Loennbohm, Armas Eino Leopold

Leiris, Michel (Julien) 1901-1990 ... CLC 61
See also CA 119; 128; 132

Leithauser, Brad 1953- .... CLC 27
See also CA 107; CANR 27; DLB 120

Lelchuk, Alan 1938- .... CLC 5
See also CA 45-48; CAAS 20; CANR 1

Lem, Stanislaw 1921- .... CLC 8, 15, 40
See also CA 105; CAAS 1; CANR 32;
MTCW

Lemann, Nancy 1956- .... CLC 39
See also CA 118; 136

Lemonnier, (Antoine Louis) Camille
1844-1913 .... TCLC 22
See also CA 121

Lenau, Nikolaus 1802-1850 ..... NCLC 16

L'Engle, Madeleine (Camp Franklin)
1918- .... CLC 12
See also AAYA 1; AITN 2; CA 1-4R;
CANR 3, 21, 39; CLR 1, 14; DAM POP;
DLB 52; JRDA; MAICYA; MTCW;
SAAS 15; SATA 1, 27, 75

Lengyel, Jozsef 1896-1975 .... CLC 7
See also CA 85-88; 57-60

Lennon, John (Ono)
1940-1980 .... CLC 12, 35
See also CA 102

Lennox, Charlotte Ramsay
1729(?)-1804 .... NCLC 23
See also DLB 39

Lentricchia, Frank (Jr.) 1940- ..... CLC 34
See also CA 25-28R; CANR 19

Lenz, Siegfried 1926- .... CLC 27
See also CA 89-92; DLB 75

Leonard, Elmore (John, Jr.)
1925- .... CLC 28, 34, 71
See also AITN 1; BEST 89:1, 90:4;
CA 81-84; CANR 12, 28; DAM POP;
INT CANR-28; MTCW

Leonard, Hugh .... CLC 19
See also Byrne, John Keyes
See also DLB 13

Leopardi, (Conte) Giacomo
1798-1837 .... NCLC 22

Le Reveler
See Artaud, Antonin (Marie Joseph)

Lerman, Eleanor 1952- .... CLC 9
See also CA 85-88

Lerman, Rhoda 1936- .... CLC 56
See also CA 49-52

Lermontov, Mikhail Yuryevich
1814-1841 .... NCLC 47

Leroux, Gaston 1868-1927 .... TCLC 25
See also CA 108; 136; SATA 65

Lesage, Alain-Rene 1668-1747 .... LC 28

Leskov, Nikolai (Semyonovich)
1831-1895 .... NCLC 25

Lessing, Doris (May)
1919- ..... CLC 1, 2, 3, 6, 10, 15, 22, 40,
91; DA; DAB; DAC; SSC 6
See also CA 9-12R; CAAS 14; CANR 33;
CDBLB 1960 to Present; DAM MST,
NOV; DLB 15, 139; DLBY 85; MTCW

Lessing, Gotthold Ephraim
1729-1781 .... LC 8
See also DLB 97

Lester, Richard 1932- .... CLC 20

Lever, Charles (James)
1806-1872 .... NCLC 23
See also DLB 21

Leverson, Ada 1865(?)-1936(?) .... TCLC 18
See also Elaine
See also CA 117; DLB 153

Levertov, Denise
1923- ...... CLC 1, 2, 3, 5, 8, 15, 28, 66;
PC 11
See also CA 1-4R; CAAS 19; CANR 3, 29,
50; DAM POET; DLB 5; INT CANR-29;
MTCW

Levi, Jonathan .... CLC 76

Levi, Peter (Chad Tigar) 1931- ..... CLC 41
See also CA 5-8R; CANR 34; DLB 40

Levi, Primo
1919-1987 .... CLC 37, 50; SSC 12
See also CA 13-16R; 122; CANR 12, 33;
MTCW

Levin, Ira 1929- .... CLC 3, 6
See also CA 21-24R; CANR 17, 44;
DAM POP; MTCW; SATA 66

Levin, Meyer 1905-1981 .... CLC 7
See also AITN 1; CA 9-12R; 104;
CANR 15; DAM POP; DLB 9, 28;
DLBY 81; SATA 21; SATA-Obit 27

Macdonald, Cynthia 1928-...... **CLC 13, 19**
See also CA 49-52; CANR 4, 44; DLB 105

MacDonald, George 1824-1905..... **TCLC 9**
See also CA 106; 137; DLB 18; MAICYA;
SATA 33

Macdonald, John
See Millar, Kenneth

MacDonald, John D(ann)
1916-1986 .... **CLC 3, 27, 44**
See also CA 1-4R; 121; CANR 1, 19;
DAM NOV, POP; DLB 8; DLBY 86;
MTCW

Macdonald, John Ross
See Millar, Kenneth

Macdonald, Ross..... **CLC 1, 2, 3, 14, 34, 41**
See also Millar, Kenneth
See also DLBD 6

MacDougal, John
See Blish, James (Benjamin)

MacEwen, Gwendolyn (Margaret)
1941-1987 .... **CLC 13, 55**
See also CA 9-12R; 124; CANR 7, 22;
DLB 53; SATA 50; SATA-Obit 55

Macha, Karel Hynek 1810-1846.. **NCLC 46**

Machado (y Ruiz), Antonio
1875-1939 .... **TCLC 3**
See also CA 104; DLB 108

Machado de Assis, Joaquim Maria
1839-1908 .... **TCLC 10; BLC**
See also CA 107

Machen, Arthur.......... **TCLC 4; SSC 20**
See also Jones, Arthur Llewellyn
See also DLB 36, 156

Machiavelli, Niccolo
1469-1527 ...... **LC 8; DA; DAB; DAC**
See also DAM MST

MacInnes, Colin 1914-1976...... **CLC 4, 23**
See also CA 69-72; 65-68; CANR 21;
DLB 14; MTCW

MacInnes, Helen (Clark)
1907-1985 .... **CLC 27, 39**
See also CA 1-4R; 117; CANR 1, 28;
DAM POP; DLB 87; MTCW; SATA 22;
SATA-Obit 44

Mackay, Mary 1855-1924
See Corelli, Marie
See also CA 118

Mackenzie, Compton (Edward Montague)
1883-1972 .... **CLC 18**
See also CA 21-22; 37-40R; CAP 2;
DLB 34, 100

Mackenzie, Henry 1745-1831.... **NCLC 41**
See also DLB 39

Mackintosh, Elizabeth 1896(?)-1952
See Tey, Josephine
See also CA 110

MacLaren, James
See Grieve, C(hristopher) M(urray)

Mac Laverty, Bernard 1942-...... **CLC 31**
See also CA 116; 118; CANR 43; INT 118

MacLean, Alistair (Stuart)
1922-1987 .... **CLC 3, 13, 50, 63**
See also CA 57-60; 121; CANR 28;
DAM POP; MTCW; SATA 23;
SATA-Obit 50

Maclean, Norman (Fitzroy)
1902-1990 .... **CLC 78; SSC 13**
See also CA 102; 132; CANR 49;
DAM POP

MacLeish, Archibald
1892-1982 .... **CLC 3, 8, 14, 68**
See also CA 9-12R; 106; CANR 33;
DAM POET; DLB 4, 7, 45; DLBY 82;
MTCW

MacLennan, (John) Hugh
1907-1990 .... **CLC 2, 14; DAC**
See also CA 5-8R; 142; CANR 33;
DAM MST; DLB 68; MTCW

MacLeod, Alistair 1936-..... **CLC 56; DAC**
See also CA 123; DAM MST; DLB 60

MacNeice, (Frederick) Louis
1907-1963 ...... **CLC 1, 4, 10, 53; DAB**
See also CA 85-88; DAM POET; DLB 10,
20; MTCW

MacNeill, Dand
See Fraser, George MacDonald

Macpherson, James 1736-1796 ...... **LC 29**
See also DLB 109

Macpherson, (Jean) Jay 1931-...... **CLC 14**
See also CA 5-8R; DLB 53

MacShane, Frank 1927-........... **CLC 39**
See also CA 9-12R; CANR 3, 33; DLB 111

Macumber, Mari
See Sandoz, Mari(e Susette)

Madach, Imre 1823-1864........ **NCLC 19**

Madden, (Jerry) David 1933- .... **CLC 5, 15**
See also CA 1-4R; CAAS 3; CANR 4, 45;
DLB 6; MTCW

Maddern, Al(an)
See Ellison, Harlan (Jay)

Madhubuti, Haki R.
1942- .... **CLC 6, 73; BLC; PC 5**
See also Lee, Don L.
See also BW 2; CA 73-76; CANR 24;
DAM MULT, POET; DLB 5, 41;
DLBD 8

Maepenn, Hugh
See Kuttner, Henry

Maepenn, K. H.
See Kuttner, Henry

Maeterlinck, Maurice 1862-1949 ... **TCLC 3**
See also CA 104; 136; DAM DRAM;
SATA 66

Maginn, William 1794-1842....... **NCLC 8**
See also DLB 110, 159

Mahapatra, Jayanta 1928-........ **CLC 33**
See also CA 73-76; CAAS 9; CANR 15, 33;
DAM MULT

Mahfouz, Naguib (Abdel Aziz Al-Sabilgi)
1911(?)-
See Mahfuz, Najib
See also BEST 89:2; CA 128; DAM NOV;
MTCW

Mahfuz, Najib............... **CLC 52, 55**
See also Mahfouz, Naguib (Abdel Aziz
Al-Sabilgi)
See also DLBY 88

Mahon, Derek 1941-............. **CLC 27**
See also CA 113; 128; DLB 40

Mailer, Norman
1923- ...... **CLC 1, 2, 3, 4, 5, 8, 11, 14,
28, 39, 74; DA; DAB; DAC**
See also AITN 2; CA 9-12R; CABS 1;
CANR 28; CDALB 1968-1988;
DAM MST, NOV, POP; DLB 2, 16, 28;
DLBD 3; DLBY 80, 83; MTCW

Maillet, Antonine 1929-...... **CLC 54; DAC**
See also CA 115; 120; CANR 46; DLB 60;
INT 120

Mais, Roger 1905-1955 .... **TCLC 8**
See also BW 1; CA 105; 124; DLB 125;
MTCW

Maistre, Joseph de 1753-1821.... **NCLC 37**

Maitland, Sara (Louise) 1950-...... **CLC 49**
See also CA 69-72; CANR 13

Major, Clarence
1936- .... **CLC 3, 19, 48; BLC**
See also BW 2; CA 21-24R; CAAS 6;
CANR 13, 25; DAM MULT; DLB 33

Major, Kevin (Gerald)
1949- .... **CLC 26; DAC**
See also AAYA 16; CA 97-100; CANR 21,
38; CLR 11; DLB 60; INT CANR-21;
JRDA; MAICYA; SATA 32, 82

Maki, James
See Ozu, Yasujiro

Malabaila, Damiano
See Levi, Primo

Malamud, Bernard
1914-1986 ...... **CLC 1, 2, 3, 5, 8, 9, 11,
18, 27, 44, 78, 85; DA; DAB; DAC;
SSC 15; WLC**
See also AAYA 16; CA 5-8R; 118; CABS 1;
CANR 28; CDALB 1941-1968;
DAM MST, NOV, POP; DLB 2, 28, 152;
DLBY 80, 86; MTCW

Malaparte, Curzio 1898-1957 ..... **TCLC 52**

Malcolm, Dan
See Silverberg, Robert

Malcolm X................. **CLC 82; BLC**
See also Little, Malcolm

Malherbe, Francois de 1555-1628..... **LC 5**

Mallarme, Stephane
1842-1898 .... **NCLC 4, 41; PC 4**
See also DAM POET

Mallet-Joris, Francoise 1930-...... **CLC 11**
See also CA 65-68; CANR 17; DLB 83

Malley, Ern
See McAuley, James Phillip

Mallowan, Agatha Christie
See Christie, Agatha (Mary Clarissa)

Maloff, Saul 1922-............... **CLC 5**
See also CA 33-36R

Malone, Louis
See MacNeice, (Frederick) Louis

Malone, Michael (Christopher)
1942-..................... **CLC 43**
See also CA 77-80; CANR 14, 32

Malory, (Sir) Thomas
1410(?)-1471(?) ...... **LC 11; DA; DAB;
DAC**
See also CDBLB Before 1660; DAM MST;
DLB 146; SATA 59; SATA-Brief 33

Marx, Karl (Heinrich)
    1818-1883 . . . . **NCLC 17**
    See also DLB 129

Masaoka Shiki. . . . . **TCLC 18**
    See also Masaoka Tsunenori

Masaoka Tsunenori   1867-1902
    See Masaoka Shiki
    See also CA 117

Masefield, John (Edward)
    1878-1967 . . . . **CLC 11, 47**
    See also CA 19-20; 25-28R; CANR 33;
    CAP 2; CDBLB 1890-1914; DAM POET;
    DLB 10, 19, 153, 160; MTCW; SATA 19

Maso, Carole   19(?)- . . . . **CLC 44**

Mason, Bobbie Ann
    1940- . . . . **CLC 28, 43, 82; SSC 4**
    See also AAYA 5; CA 53-56; CANR 11,
    31; DLBY 87; INT CANR-31; MTCW

Mason, Ernst
    See Pohl, Frederik

Mason, Lee W.
    See Malzberg, Barry N(athaniel)

Mason, Nick   1945- . . . . **CLC 35**

Mason, Tally
    See Derleth, August (William)

Mass, William
    See Gibson, William

Masters, Edgar Lee
    1868-1950 . . . . . . **TCLC 2, 25; DA; DAC;**
                                          PC 1
    See also CA 104; 133; CDALB 1865-1917;
    DAM MST, POET; DLB 54; MTCW

Masters, Hilary   1928- . . . . **CLC 48**
    See also CA 25-28R; CANR 13, 47

Mastrosimone, William   19(?)- . . . . . . **CLC 36**

Mathe, Albert
    See Camus, Albert

Matheson, Richard Burton   1926- . . . **CLC 37**
    See also CA 97-100; DLB 8, 44; INT 97-100

Mathews, Harry   1930- . . . . **CLC 6, 52**
    See also CA 21-24R; CAAS 6; CANR 18,
    40

Mathews, John Joseph   1894-1979 . . . **CLC 84**
    See also CA 19-20; 142; CANR 45; CAP 2;
    DAM MULT; NNAL

Mathias, Roland (Glyn)   1915- . . . . . . **CLC 45**
    See also CA 97-100; CANR 19, 41; DLB 27

Matsuo Basho   1644-1694 . . . . **PC 3**
    See also DAM POET

Mattheson, Rodney
    See Creasey, John

Matthews, Greg   1949- . . . . **CLC 45**
    See also CA 135

Matthews, William   1942- . . . . **CLC 40**
    See also CA 29-32R; CAAS 18; CANR 12;
    DLB 5

Matthias, John (Edward)   1941- . . . . . . **CLC 9**
    See also CA 33-36R

Matthiessen, Peter
    1927- . . . . **CLC 5, 7, 11, 32, 64**
    See also AAYA 6; BEST 90:4; CA 9-12R;
    CANR 21, 50; DAM NOV; DLB 6;
    MTCW; SATA 27

Maturin, Charles Robert
    1780(?)-1824 . . . . **NCLC 6**

Matute (Ausejo), Ana Maria
    1925- . . . . **CLC 11**
    See also CA 89-92; MTCW

Maugham, W. S.
    See Maugham, W(illiam) Somerset

Maugham, W(illiam) Somerset
    1874-1965 . . . . . **CLC 1, 11, 15, 67; DA;**
                                DAB; DAC; SSC 8; WLC
    See also CA 5-8R; 25-28R; CANR 40;
    CDBLB 1914-1945; DAM DRAM, MST,
    NOV; DLB 10, 36, 77, 100, 162; MTCW;
    SATA 54

Maugham, William Somerset
    See Maugham, W(illiam) Somerset

Maupassant, (Henri Rene Albert) Guy de
    1850-1893 . . . . . **NCLC 1, 42; DA; DAB;**
                                    DAC; SSC 1; WLC
    See also DAM MST; DLB 123

Maurhut, Richard
    See Traven, B.

Mauriac, Claude   1914- . . . . **CLC 9**
    See also CA 89-92; DLB 83

Mauriac, Francois (Charles)
    1885-1970 . . . . **CLC 4, 9, 56**
    See also CA 25-28; CAP 2; DLB 65;
    MTCW

Mavor, Osborne Henry   1888-1951
    See Bridie, James
    See also CA 104

Maxwell, William (Keepers, Jr.)
    1908- . . . . **CLC 19**
    See also CA 93-96; DLBY 80; INT 93-96

May, Elaine   1932- . . . . **CLC 16**
    See also CA 124; 142; DLB 44

Mayakovski, Vladimir (Vladimirovich)
    1893-1930 . . . . **TCLC 4, 18**
    See also CA 104

Mayhew, Henry   1812-1887 . . . . . . **NCLC 31**
    See also DLB 18, 55

Mayle, Peter   1939(?)- . . . . **CLC 89**
    See also CA 139

Maynard, Joyce   1953- . . . . **CLC 23**
    See also CA 111; 129

Mayne, William (James Carter)
    1928- . . . . **CLC 12**
    See also CA 9-12R; CANR 37; CLR 25;
    JRDA; MAICYA; SAAS 11; SATA 6, 68

Mayo, Jim
    See L'Amour, Louis (Dearborn)

Maysles, Albert   1926- . . . . **CLC 16**
    See also CA 29-32R

Maysles, David   1932- . . . . **CLC 16**

Mazer, Norma Fox   1931- . . . . **CLC 26**
    See also AAYA 5; CA 69-72; CANR 12,
    32; CLR 23; JRDA; MAICYA; SAAS 1;
    SATA 24, 67

Mazzini, Guiseppe   1805-1872 . . . . **NCLC 34**

McAuley, James Phillip
    1917-1976 . . . . **CLC 45**
    See also CA 97-100

McBain, Ed
    See Hunter, Evan

McBrien, William Augustine
    1930- . . . . **CLC 44**
    See also CA 107

McCaffrey, Anne (Inez)   1926- . . . . . . **CLC 17**
    See also AAYA 6; AITN 2; BEST 89:2;
    CA 25-28R; CANR 15, 35; DAM NOV,
    POP; DLB 8; JRDA; MAICYA; MTCW;
    SAAS 11; SATA 8, 70

McCall, Nathan   1955(?)- . . . . **CLC 86**
    See also CA 146

McCann, Arthur
    See Campbell, John W(ood, Jr.)

McCann, Edson
    See Pohl, Frederik

McCarthy, Charles, Jr.   1933-
    See McCarthy, Cormac
    See also CANR 42; DAM POP

McCarthy, Cormac   1933- . . . . . **CLC 4, 57, 59**
    See also McCarthy, Charles, Jr.
    See also DLB 6, 143

McCarthy, Mary (Therese)
    1912-1989 . . . **CLC 1, 3, 5, 14, 24, 39, 59**
    See also CA 5-8R; 129; CANR 16, 50;
    DLB 2; DLBY 81; INT CANR-16;
    MTCW

McCartney, (James) Paul
    1942- . . . . **CLC 12, 35**
    See also CA 146

McCauley, Stephen (D.)   1955- . . . . . **CLC 50**
    See also CA 141

McClure, Michael (Thomas)
    1932- . . . . **CLC 6, 10**
    See also CA 21-24R; CANR 17, 46;
    DLB 16

McCorkle, Jill (Collins)   1958- . . . . . . **CLC 51**
    See also CA 121; DLBY 87

McCourt, James   1941- . . . . **CLC 5**
    See also CA 57-60

McCoy, Horace (Stanley)
    1897-1955 . . . . **TCLC 28**
    See also CA 108; DLB 9

McCrae, John   1872-1918 . . . . **TCLC 12**
    See also CA 109; DLB 92

McCreigh, James
    See Pohl, Frederik

McCullers, (Lula) Carson (Smith)
    1917-1967 . . . . **CLC 1, 4, 10, 12, 48; DA;**
                                    DAB; DAC; SSC 9; WLC
    See also CA 5-8R; 25-28R; CABS 1, 3;
    CANR 18; CDALB 1941-1968;
    DAM MST, NOV; DLB 2, 7; MTCW;
    SATA 27

McCulloch, John Tyler
    See Burroughs, Edgar Rice

McCullough, Colleen   1938(?)- . . . . . . **CLC 27**
    See also CA 81-84; CANR 17, 46;
    DAM NOV, POP; MTCW

McDermott, Alice   1953- . . . . **CLC 90**
    See also CA 109; CANR 40

McElroy, Joseph   1930- . . . . **CLC 5, 47**
    See also CA 17-20R

McEwan, Ian (Russell)   1948- . . . **CLC 13, 66**
    See also BEST 90:4; CA 61-64; CANR 14,
    41; DAM NOV; DLB 14; MTCW

Meynell, Alice (Christina Gertrude Thompson)
1847-1922 . . . . TCLC 6
See also CA 104; DLB 19, 98

Meyrink, Gustav . . . . TCLC 21
See also Meyer-Meyrink, Gustav
See also DLB 81

Michaels, Leonard
1933- . . . . CLC 6, 25; SSC 16
See also CA 61-64; CANR 21; DLB 130;
MTCW

Michaux, Henri 1899-1984 . . . . . . CLC 8, 19
See also CA 85-88; 114

Michelangelo 1475-1564 . . . . LC 12

Michelet, Jules 1798-1874 . . . . . . NCLC 31

Michener, James A(lbert)
1907(?)- . . . . CLC 1, 5, 11, 29, 60
See also AITN 1; BEST 90:1; CA 5-8R;
CANR 21, 45; DAM NOV, POP; DLB 6;
MTCW

Mickiewicz, Adam 1798-1855 . . . . . NCLC 3

Middleton, Christopher 1926- . . . . . . CLC 13
See also CA 13-16R; CANR 29; DLB 40

Middleton, Richard (Barham)
1882-1911 . . . . TCLC 56
See also DLB 156

Middleton, Stanley 1919- . . . . CLC 7, 38
See also CA 25-28R; CAAS 23; CANR 21,
46; DLB 14

Middleton, Thomas 1580-1627 . . . . DC 5
See also DAM DRAM, MST; DLB 58

Migueis, Jose Rodrigues 1901- . . . . . CLC 10

Mikszath, Kalman 1847-1910 . . . . . TCLC 31

Miles, Josephine
1911-1985 . . . . CLC 1, 2, 14, 34, 39
See also CA 1-4R; 116; CANR 2;
DAM POET; DLB 48

Militant
See Sandburg, Carl (August)

Mill, John Stuart 1806-1873 . . . . . NCLC 11
See also CDBLB 1832-1890; DLB 55

Millar, Kenneth 1915-1983 . . . . CLC 14
See also Macdonald, Ross
See also CA 9-12R; 110; CANR 16;
DAM POP; DLB 2; DLBD 6; DLBY 83;
MTCW

Millay, E. Vincent
See Millay, Edna St. Vincent

Millay, Edna St. Vincent
1892-1950 . . . . . . TCLC 4, 49; DA; DAB;
DAC; PC 6
See also CA 104; 130; CDALB 1917-1929;
DAM MST, POET; DLB 45; MTCW

Miller, Arthur
1915- . . . . CLC 1, 2, 6, 10, 15, 26, 47, 78;
DA; DAB; DAC; DC 1; WLC
See also AAYA 15; AITN 1; CA 1-4R;
CABS 3; CANR 2, 30;
CDALB 1941-1968; DAM DRAM, MST;
DLB 7; MTCW

Miller, Henry (Valentine)
1891-1980 . . . . CLC 1, 2, 4, 9, 14, 43, 84;
DA; DAB; DAC; WLC
See also CA 9-12R; 97-100; CANR 33;
CDALB 1929-1941; DAM MST, NOV;
DLB 4, 9; DLBY 80; MTCW

Miller, Jason 1939(?)- . . . . CLC 2
See also AITN 1; CA 73-76; DLB 7

Miller, Sue 1943- . . . . CLC 44
See also BEST 90:3; CA 139; DAM POP;
DLB 143

Miller, Walter M(ichael, Jr.)
1923- . . . . CLC 4, 30
See also CA 85-88; DLB 8

Millett, Kate 1934- . . . . CLC 67
See also AITN 1; CA 73-76; CANR 32;
MTCW

Millhauser, Steven 1943- . . . . CLC 21, 54
See also CA 110; 111; DLB 2; INT 111

Millin, Sarah Gertrude 1889-1968 . . CLC 49
See also CA 102; 93-96

Milne, A(lan) A(lexander)
1882-1956 . . . . TCLC 6; DAB; DAC
See also CA 104; 133; CLR 1, 26;
DAM MST; DLB 10, 77, 100, 160;
MAICYA; MTCW; YABC 1

Milner, Ron(ald) 1938- . . . . CLC 56; BLC
See also AITN 1; BW 1; CA 73-76;
CANR 24; DAM MULT; DLB 38;
MTCW

Milosz, Czeslaw
1911- . . . CLC 5, 11, 22, 31, 56, 82; PC 8
See also CA 81-84; CANR 23; DAM MST,
POET; MTCW

Milton, John
1608-1674 . . . . . . LC 9; DA; DAB; DAC;
WLC
See also CDBLB 1660-1789; DAM MST,
POET; DLB 131, 151

Min, Anchee 1957- . . . . CLC 86
See also CA 146

Minehaha, Cornelius
See Wedekind, (Benjamin) Frank(lin)

Miner, Valerie 1947- . . . . CLC 40
See also CA 97-100

Minimo, Duca
See D'Annunzio, Gabriele

Minot, Susan 1956- . . . . CLC 44
See also CA 134

Minus, Ed 1938- . . . . CLC 39

Miranda, Javier
See Bioy Casares, Adolfo

Mirbeau, Octave 1848-1917 . . . . . . TCLC 55
See also DLB 123

Miro (Ferrer), Gabriel (Francisco Victor)
1879-1930 . . . . TCLC 5
See also CA 104

Mishima, Yukio
. . . . . . CLC 2, 4, 6, 9, 27; DC 1; SSC 4
See also Hiraoka, Kimitake

Mistral, Frederic 1830-1914 . . . . . . TCLC 51
See also CA 122

Mistral, Gabriela . . . . TCLC 2; HLC
See also Godoy Alcayaga, Lucila

Mistry, Rohinton 1952- . . . . . . CLC 71; DAC
See also CA 141

Mitchell, Clyde
See Ellison, Harlan (Jay); Silverberg, Robert

Mitchell, James Leslie 1901-1935
See Gibbon, Lewis Grassic
See also CA 104; DLB 15

Mitchell, Joni 1943- . . . . CLC 12
See also CA 112

Mitchell, Margaret (Munnerlyn)
1900-1949 . . . . TCLC 11
See also CA 109; 125; DAM NOV, POP;
DLB 9; MTCW

Mitchell, Peggy
See Mitchell, Margaret (Munnerlyn)

Mitchell, S(ilas) Weir 1829-1914 . . TCLC 36

Mitchell, W(illiam) O(rmond)
1914- . . . . CLC 25; DAC
See also CA 77-80; CANR 15, 43;
DAM MST; DLB 88

Mitford, Mary Russell 1787-1855 . . NCLC 4
See also DLB 110, 116

Mitford, Nancy 1904-1973 . . . . CLC 44
See also CA 9-12R

Miyamoto, Yuriko 1899-1951 . . . . . TCLC 37

Mo, Timothy (Peter) 1950(?)- . . . . . . CLC 46
See also CA 117; MTCW

Modarressi, Taghi (M.) 1931- . . . . . . CLC 44
See also CA 121; 134; INT 134

Modiano, Patrick (Jean) 1945- . . . . . CLC 18
See also CA 85-88; CANR 17, 40; DLB 83

Moerck, Paal
See Roelvaag, O(le) E(dvart)

Mofolo, Thomas (Mokopu)
1875(?)-1948 . . . . TCLC 22; BLC
See also CA 121; DAM MULT

Mohr, Nicholasa 1935- . . . . . . CLC 12; HLC
See also AAYA 8; CA 49-52; CANR 1, 32;
CLR 22; DAM MULT; DLB 145; HW;
JRDA; SAAS 8; SATA 8

Mojtabai, A(nn) G(race)
1938- . . . . CLC 5, 9, 15, 29
See also CA 85-88

Moliere
1622-1673 . . . . . LC 28; DA; DAB; DAC;
WLC
See also DAM DRAM, MST

Molin, Charles
See Mayne, William (James Carter)

Molnar, Ferenc 1878-1952 . . . . TCLC 20
See also CA 109; DAM DRAM

Momaday, N(avarre) Scott
1934- . . . CLC 2, 19, 85; DA; DAB; DAC
See also AAYA 11; CA 25-28R; CANR 14,
34; DAM MST, MULT, NOV, POP;
DLB 143; INT CANR-14; MTCW;
NNAL; SATA 48; SATA-Brief 30

Monette, Paul 1945-1995 . . . . CLC 82
See also CA 139; 147

Monroe, Harriet 1860-1936 . . . . TCLC 12
See also CA 109; DLB 54, 91

Monroe, Lyle
See Heinlein, Robert A(nson)

Montagu, Elizabeth 1917- . . . . NCLC 7
See also CA 9-12R

Montagu, Mary (Pierrepont) Wortley
1689-1762 . . . . LC 9
See also DLB 95, 101

Montagu, W. H.
See Coleridge, Samuel Taylor

Montague, John (Patrick)
1929- . . . . **CLC 13, 46**
See also CA 9-12R; CANR 9; DLB 40;
MTCW

Montaigne, Michel (Eyquem) de
1533-1592 . . . . . . **LC 8; DA; DAB; DAC;
WLC**

See also DAM MST

Montale, Eugenio
1896-1981 . . . . **CLC 7, 9, 18; PC 13**
See also CA 17-20R; 104; CANR 30;
DLB 114; MTCW

Montesquieu, Charles-Louis de Secondat
1689-1755 . . . . **LC 7**

Montgomery, (Robert) Bruce 1921-1978
See Crispin, Edmund
See also CA 104

Montgomery, L(ucy) M(aud)
1874-1942 . . . . **TCLC 51; DAC**
See also AAYA 12; CA 108; 137; CLR 8;
DAM MST; DLB 92; JRDA; MAICYA;
YABC 1

Montgomery, Marion H., Jr. 1925- . . **CLC 7**
See also AITN 1; CA 1-4R; CANR 3, 48;
DLB 6

Montgomery, Max
See Davenport, Guy (Mattison, Jr.)

Montherlant, Henry (Milon) de
1896-1972 . . . . **CLC 8, 19**
See also CA 85-88; 37-40R; DAM DRAM;
DLB 72; MTCW

Monty Python
See Chapman, Graham; Cleese, John
(Marwood); Gilliam, Terry (Vance); Idle,
Eric; Jones, Terence Graham Parry; Palin,
Michael (Edward)
See also AAYA 7

Moodie, Susanna (Strickland)
1803-1885 . . . . **NCLC 14**
See also DLB 99

Mooney, Edward 1951-
See Mooney, Ted
See also CA 130

Mooney, Ted . . . . **CLC 25**
See also Mooney, Edward

Moorcock, Michael (John)
1939- . . . . **CLC 5, 27, 58**
See also CA 45-48; CAAS 5; CANR 2, 17,
38; DLB 14; MTCW

Moore, Brian
1921- . . . . . . **CLC 1, 3, 5, 7, 8, 19, 32, 90;
DAB; DAC**
See also CA 1-4R; CANR 1, 25, 42;
DAM MST; MTCW

Moore, Edward
See Muir, Edwin

Moore, George Augustus
1852-1933 . . . . **TCLC 7; SSC 19**
See also CA 104; DLB 10, 18, 57, 135

Moore, Lorrie . . . . **CLC 39, 45, 68**
See also Moore, Marie Lorena

Moore, Marianne (Craig)
1887-1972 . . . . **CLC 1, 2, 4, 8, 10, 13, 19,
47; DA; DAB; DAC; PC 4**
See also CA 1-4R; 33-36R; CANR 3;
CDALB 1929-1941; DAM MST, POET;
DLB 45; DLBD 7; MTCW; SATA 20

Moore, Marie Lorena 1957-
See Moore, Lorrie
See also CA 116; CANR 39

Moore, Thomas 1779-1852. . . . . . . **NCLC 6**
See also DLB 96, 144

Morand, Paul 1888-1976 . . . . **CLC 41**
See also CA 69-72; DLB 65

Morante, Elsa 1918-1985. . . . . . . **CLC 8, 47**
See also CA 85-88; 117; CANR 35; MTCW

Moravia, Alberto. . . . . . **CLC 2, 7, 11, 27, 46**
See also Pincherle, Alberto

More, Hannah 1745-1833 . . . . **NCLC 27**
See also DLB 107, 109, 116, 158

More, Henry 1614-1687. . . . . **LC 9**
See also DLB 126

More, Sir Thomas 1478-1535 . . . . **LC 10, 32**

Moreas, Jean. . . . . **TCLC 18**
See also Papadiamantopoulos, Johannes

Morgan, Berry 1919- . . . . **CLC 6**
See also CA 49-52; DLB 6

Morgan, Claire
See Highsmith, (Mary) Patricia

Morgan, Edwin (George) 1920-. . . . . **CLC 31**
See also CA 5-8R; CANR 3, 43; DLB 27

Morgan, (George) Frederick
1922- . . . . **CLC 23**
See also CA 17-20R; CANR 21

Morgan, Harriet
See Mencken, H(enry) L(ouis)

Morgan, Jane
See Cooper, James Fenimore

Morgan, Janet 1945- . . . . **CLC 39**
See also CA 65-68

Morgan, Lady 1776(?)-1859. . . . . . **NCLC 29**
See also DLB 116, 158

Morgan, Robin 1941-. . . . . **CLC 2**
See also CA 69-72; CANR 29; MTCW;
SATA 80

Morgan, Scott
See Kuttner, Henry

Morgan, Seth 1949(?)-1990 . . . . **CLC 65**
See also CA 132

Morgenstern, Christian
1871-1914 . . . . **TCLC 8**
See also CA 105

Morgenstern, S.
See Goldman, William (W.)

Moricz, Zsigmond 1879-1942 . . . . . **TCLC 33**

Morike, Eduard (Friedrich)
1804-1875 . . . . **NCLC 10**
See also DLB 133

Mori Ogai . . . . **TCLC 14**
See also Mori Rintaro

Mori Rintaro 1862-1922
See Mori Ogai
See also CA 110

Moritz, Karl Philipp 1756-1793 . . . . . . **LC 2**
See also DLB 94

Morland, Peter Henry
See Faust, Frederick (Schiller)

Morren, Theophil
See Hofmannsthal, Hugo von

Morris, Bill 1952-. . . . . **CLC 76**

Morris, Julian
See West, Morris L(anglo)

Morris, Steveland Judkins 1950(?)-
See Wonder, Stevie
See also CA 111

Morris, William 1834-1896 . . . . **NCLC 4**
See also CDBLB 1832-1890; DLB 18, 35,
57, 156

Morris, Wright 1910-. . . **CLC 1, 3, 7, 18, 37**
See also CA 9-12R; CANR 21; DLB 2;
DLBY 81; MTCW

Morrison, Chloe Anthony Wofford
See Morrison, Toni

Morrison, James Douglas 1943-1971
See Morrison, Jim
See also CA 73-76; CANR 40

Morrison, Jim . . . . **CLC 17**
See also Morrison, James Douglas

Morrison, Toni
1931- . . . . **CLC 4, 10, 22, 55, 81, 87;
BLC; DA; DAB; DAC**
See also AAYA 1; BW 2; CA 29-32R;
CANR 27, 42; CDALB 1968-1988;
DAM MST, MULT, NOV, POP; DLB 6,
33, 143; DLBY 81; MTCW; SATA 57

Morrison, Van 1945- . . . . **CLC 21**
See also CA 116

Mortimer, John (Clifford)
1923- . . . . **CLC 28, 43**
See also CA 13-16R; CANR 21;
CDBLB 1960 to Present; DAM DRAM,
POP; DLB 13; INT CANR-21; MTCW

Mortimer, Penelope (Ruth) 1918-. . . . **CLC 5**
See also CA 57-60; CANR 45

Morton, Anthony
See Creasey, John

Mosher, Howard Frank 1943-. . . . . . **CLC 62**
See also CA 139

Mosley, Nicholas 1923-. . . . . **CLC 43, 70**
See also CA 69-72; CANR 41; DLB 14

Moss, Howard
1922-1987 . . . . **CLC 7, 14, 45, 50**
See also CA 1-4R; 123; CANR 1, 44;
DAM POET; DLB 5

Mossgiel, Rab
See Burns, Robert

Motion, Andrew (Peter) 1952-. . . . . . **CLC 47**
See also CA 146; DLB 40

Motley, Willard (Francis)
1909-1965 . . . . **CLC 18**
See also BW 1; CA 117; 106; DLB 76, 143

Motoori, Norinaga 1730-1801 . . . . **NCLC 45**

Mott, Michael (Charles Alston)
1930- . . . . **CLC 15, 34**
See also CA 5-8R; CAAS 7; CANR 7, 29

Moure, Erin 1955- . . . . **CLC 88**
See also CA 113; DLB 60

Mowat, Farley (McGill)
1921- . . . . CLC 26; DAC
See also AAYA 1; CA 1-4R; CANR 4, 24,
42; CLR 20; DAM MST; DLB 68;
INT CANAR-24; JRDA; MAICYA;
MTCW; SATA 3, 55

Moyers, Bill 1934- . . . . CLC 74
See also AITN 2; CA 61-64; CANR 31

Mphahlele, Es'kia
See Mphahlele, Ezekiel
See also DLB 125

Mphahlele, Ezekiel 1919- . . . . . CLC 25; BLC
See also Mphahlele, Es'kia
See also BW 2; CA 81-84; CANR 26;
DAM MULT

Mqhayi, S(amuel) E(dward) K(rune Loliwe)
1875-1945 . . . . TCLC 25; BLC
See also DAM MULT

Mr. Martin
See Burroughs, William S(eward)

Mrozek, Slawomir 1930- . . . . CLC 3, 13
See also CA 13-16R; CAAS 10; CANR 29;
MTCW

Mrs. Belloc-Lowndes
See Lowndes, Marie Adelaide (Belloc)

Mtwa, Percy (?)- . . . . CLC 47

Mueller, Lisel 1924- . . . . CLC 13, 51
See also CA 93-96; DLB 105

Muir, Edwin 1887-1959 . . . . TCLC 2
See also CA 104; DLB 20, 100

Muir, John 1838-1914 . . . . TCLC 28

Mujica Lainez, Manuel
1910-1984 . . . . CLC 31
See also Lainez, Manuel Mujica
See also CA 81-84; 112; CANR 32; HW

Mukherjee, Bharati 1940- . . . . CLC 53
See also BEST 89:2; CA 107; CANR 45;
DAM NOV; DLB 60; MTCW

Muldoon, Paul 1951- . . . . CLC 32, 72
See also CA 113; 129; DAM POET;
DLB 40; INT 129

Mulisch, Harry 1927- . . . . CLC 42
See also CA 9-12R; CANR 6, 26

Mull, Martin 1943- . . . . CLC 17
See also CA 105

Mulock, Dinah Maria
See Craik, Dinah Maria (Mulock)

Munford, Robert 1737(?)-1783 . . . . LC 5
See also DLB 31

Mungo, Raymond 1946- . . . . CLC 72
See also CA 49-52; CANR 2

Munro, Alice
1931- . . . CLC 6, 10, 19, 50; DAC; SSC 3
See also AITN 2; CA 33-36R; CANR 33;
DAM MST, NOV; DLB 53; MTCW;
SATA 29

Munro, H(ector) H(ugh) 1870-1916
See Saki
See also CA 104; 130; CDBLB 1890-1914;
DA; DAB; DAC; DAM MST, NOV;
DLB 34, 162; MTCW; WLC

Murasaki, Lady . . . . CMLC 1

Murdoch, (Jean) Iris
1919- . . . . . CLC 1, 2, 3, 4, 6, 8, 11, 15,
22, 31, 51; DAB; DAC
See also CA 13-16R; CANR 8, 43;
CDBLB 1960 to Present; DAM MST,
NOV; DLB 14; INT CANR-8; MTCW

Murnau, Friedrich Wilhelm
See Plumpe, Friedrich Wilhelm

Murphy, Richard 1927- . . . . CLC 41
See also CA 29-32R; DLB 40

Murphy, Sylvia 1937- . . . . CLC 34
See also CA 121

Murphy, Thomas (Bernard) 1935- . . . CLC 51
See also CA 101

Murray, Albert L. 1916- . . . . CLC 73
See also BW 2; CA 49-52; CANR 26;
DLB 38

Murray, Les(lie) A(llan) 1938- . . . . . CLC 40
See also CA 21-24R; CANR 11, 27;
DAM POET

Murry, J. Middleton
See Murry, John Middleton

Murry, John Middleton
1889-1957 . . . . TCLC 16
See also CA 118; DLB 149

Musgrave, Susan 1951- . . . . CLC 13, 54
See also CA 69-72; CANR 45

Musil, Robert (Edler von)
1880-1942 . . . . TCLC 12; SSC 18
See also CA 109; DLB 81, 124

Muske, Carol 1945- . . . . CLC 90
See also Muske-Dukes, Carol (Anne)

Muske-Dukes, Carol (Anne) 1945-
See Muske, Carol
See also CA 65-68; CANR 32

Musset, (Louis Charles) Alfred de
1810-1857 . . . . NCLC 7

My Brother's Brother
See Chekhov, Anton (Pavlovich)

Myers, L. H. 1881-1944 . . . . TCLC 59
See also DLB 15

Myers, Walter Dean 1937- . . . CLC 35; BLC
See also AAYA 4; BW 2; CA 33-36R;
CANR 20, 42; CLR 4, 16, 35;
DAM MULT, NOV; DLB 33;
INT CANR-20; JRDA; MAICYA;
SAAS 2; SATA 41, 71; SATA-Brief 27

Myers, Walter M.
See Myers, Walter Dean

Myles, Symon
See Follett, Ken(neth Martin)

Nabokov, Vladimir (Vladimirovich)
1899-1977 . . . . . CLC 1, 2, 3, 6, 8, 11, 15,
23, 44, 46, 64; DA; DAB; DAC; SSC 11;
WLC
See also CA 5-8R; 69-72; CANR 20;
CDALB 1941-1968; DAM MST, NOV;
DLB 2; DLBD 3; DLBY 80, 91; MTCW

Nagai Kafu . . . . TCLC 51
See also Nagai Sokichi

Nagai Sokichi 1879-1959
See Nagai Kafu
See also CA 117

Nagy, Laszlo 1925-1978 . . . . CLC 7
See also CA 129; 112

Naipaul, Shiva(dhar Srinivasa)
1945-1985 . . . . CLC 32, 39
See also CA 110; 112; 116; CANR 33;
DAM NOV; DLB 157; DLBY 85;
MTCW

Naipaul, V(idiadhar) S(urajprasad)
1932- . . . . CLC 4, 7, 9, 13, 18, 37; DAB;
DAC
See also CA 1-4R; CANR 1, 33;
CDBLB 1960 to Present; DAM MST,
NOV; DLB 125; DLBY 85; MTCW

Nakos, Lilika 1899(?)- . . . . CLC 29

Narayan, R(asipuram) K(rishnaswami)
1906- . . . . CLC 7, 28, 47
See also CA 81-84; CANR 33; DAM NOV;
MTCW; SATA 62

Nash, (Frediric) Ogden 1902-1971 . . CLC 23
See also CA 13-14; 29-32R; CANR 34;
CAP 1; DAM POET; DLB 11;
MAICYA; MTCW; SATA 2, 46

Nathan, Daniel
See Dannay, Frederic

Nathan, George Jean 1882-1958 . . . TCLC 18
See also Hatteras, Owen
See also CA 114; DLB 137

Natsume, Kinnosuke 1867-1916
See Natsume, Soseki
See also CA 104

Natsume, Soseki . . . . TCLC 2, 10
See also Natsume, Kinnosuke

Natti, (Mary) Lee 1919-
See Kingman, Lee
See also CA 5-8R; CANR 2

Naylor, Gloria
1950- . . . . . CLC 28, 52; BLC; DA; DAC
See also AAYA 6; BW 2; CA 107;
CANR 27; DAM MST, MULT, NOV,
POP; MTCW

Neihardt, John Gneisenau
1881-1973 . . . . CLC 32
See also CA 13-14; CAP 1; DLB 9, 54

Nekrasov, Nikolai Alekseevich
1821-1878 . . . . NCLC 11

Nelligan, Emile 1879-1941 . . . . TCLC 14
See also CA 114; DLB 92

Nelson, Willie 1933- . . . . CLC 17
See also CA 107

Nemerov, Howard (Stanley)
1920-1991 . . . . CLC 2, 6, 9, 36
See also CA 1-4R; 134; CABS 2; CANR 1,
27; DAM POET; DLB 5, 6; DLBY 83;
INT CANR-27; MTCW

Neruda, Pablo
1904-1973 . . . . . CLC 1, 2, 5, 7, 9, 28, 62;
DA; DAB; DAC; HLC; PC 4; WLC
See also CA 19-20; 45-48; CAP 2;
DAM MST, MULT, POET; HW; MTCW

Nerval, Gerard de
1808-1855 . . . . . NCLC 1; PC 13; SSC 18

Nervo, (Jose) Amado (Ruiz de)
1870-1919 . . . . TCLC 11
See also CA 109; 131; HW

Nessi, Pio Baroja y
See Baroja (y Nessi), Pio

Nestroy, Johann 1801-1862 . . . . . . NCLC 42
See also DLB 133

O'Brien, Flann....... **CLC 1, 4, 5, 7, 10, 47**
See also O Nuallain, Brian

O'Brien, Richard 1942-.......... **CLC 17**
See also CA 124

O'Brien, Tim 1946-......... **CLC 7, 19, 40**
See also AAYA 16; CA 85-88; CANR 40;
DAM POP; DLB 152; DLBD 9;
DLBY 80

Obstfelder, Sigbjoern 1866-1900... **TCLC 23**
See also CA 123

O'Casey, Sean
1880-1964 ...... **CLC 1, 5, 9, 11, 15, 88;**
DAB; DAC
See also CA 89-92; CDBLB 1914-1945;
DAM DRAM, MST; DLB 10; MTCW

O'Cathasaigh, Sean
See O'Casey, Sean

Ochs, Phil 1940-1976............. **CLC 17**
See also CA 65-68

O'Connor, Edwin (Greene)
1918-1968 .... **CLC 14**
See also CA 93-96; 25-28R

O'Connor, (Mary) Flannery
1925-1964 .... **CLC 1, 2, 3, 6, 10, 13, 15,**
21, 66; DA; DAB; DAC; SSC 1; WLC
See also AAYA 7; CA 1-4R; CANR 3, 41;
CDALB 1941-1968; DAM MST, NOV;
DLB 2, 152; DLBD 12; DLBY 80;
MTCW

O'Connor, Frank.......... **CLC 23; SSC 5**
See also O'Donovan, Michael John
See also DLB 162

O'Dell, Scott 1898-1989........... **CLC 30**
See also AAYA 3; CA 61-64; 129;
CANR 12, 30; CLR 1, 16; DLB 52;
JRDA; MAICYA; SATA 12, 60

Odets, Clifford
1906-1963 .... **CLC 2, 28; DC 6**
See also CA 85-88; DAM DRAM; DLB 7,
26; MTCW

O'Doherty, Brian 1934-........... **CLC 76**
See also CA 105

O'Donnell, K. M.
See Malzberg, Barry N(athaniel)

O'Donnell, Lawrence
See Kuttner, Henry

O'Donovan, Michael John
1903-1966 .... **CLC 14**
See also O'Connor, Frank
See also CA 93-96

Oe, Kenzaburo
1935-......... **CLC 10, 36, 86; SSC 20**
See also CA 97-100; CANR 36, 50;
DAM NOV; DLBY 94; MTCW

O'Faolain, Julia 1932-....... **CLC 6, 19, 47**
See also CA 81-84; CAAS 2; CANR 12;
DLB 14; MTCW

O'Faolain, Sean
1900-1991 .... **CLC 1, 7, 14, 32, 70;**
SSC 13
See also CA 61-64; 134; CANR 12;
DLB 15, 162; MTCW

O'Flaherty, Liam
1896-1984 .... **CLC 5, 34; SSC 6**
See also CA 101; 113; CANR 35; DLB 36,
162; DLBY 84; MTCW

Ogilvy, Gavin
See Barrie, J(ames) M(atthew)

O'Grady, Standish James
1846-1928 .... **TCLC 5**
See also CA 104

O'Grady, Timothy 1951-.......... **CLC 59**
See also CA 138

O'Hara, Frank
1926-1966 .... **CLC 2, 5, 13, 78**
See also CA 9-12R; 25-28R; CANR 33;
DAM POET; DLB 5, 16; MTCW

O'Hara, John (Henry)
1905-1970 .... **CLC 1, 2, 3, 6, 11, 42;**
SSC 15
See also CA 5-8R; 25-28R; CANR 31;
CDALB 1929-1941; DAM NOV; DLB 9,
86; DLBD 2; MTCW

O Hehir, Diana 1922-............. **CLC 41**
See also CA 93-96

Okigbo, Christopher (Ifenayichukwu)
1932-1967 ..... **CLC 25, 84; BLC; PC 7**
See also BW 1; CA 77-80; DAM MULT,
POET; DLB 125; MTCW

Okri, Ben 1959-................ **CLC 87**
See also BW 2; CA 130; 138; DLB 157;
INT 138

Olds, Sharon 1942-........ **CLC 32, 39, 85**
See also CA 101; CANR 18, 41;
DAM POET; DLB 120

Oldstyle, Jonathan
See Irving, Washington

Olesha, Yuri (Karlovich)
1899-1960 .... **CLC 8**
See also CA 85-88

Oliphant, Laurence
1829(?)-1888 .... **NCLC 47**
See also DLB 18

Oliphant, Margaret (Oliphant Wilson)
1828-1897 .... **NCLC 11**
See also DLB 18, 159

Oliver, Mary 1935-........... **CLC 19, 34**
See also CA 21-24R; CANR 9, 43; DLB 5

Olivier, Laurence (Kerr)
1907-1989 .... **CLC 20**
See also CA 111; 129

Olsen, Tillie
1913- ..... **CLC 4, 13; DA; DAB; DAC;**
SSC 11
See also CA 1-4R; CANR 1, 43;
DAM MST; DLB 28; DLBY 80; MTCW

Olson, Charles (John)
1910-1970 ..... **CLC 1, 2, 5, 6, 9, 11, 29**
See also CA 13-16; 25-28R; CABS 2;
CANR 35; CAP 1; DAM POET; DLB 5,
16; MTCW

Olson, Toby 1937- .... **CLC 28**
See also CA 65-68; CANR 9, 31

Olyesha, Yuri
See Olesha, Yuri (Karlovich)

Ondaatje, (Philip) Michael
1943-... **CLC 14, 29, 51, 76; DAB; DAC**
See also CA 77-80; CANR 42; DAM MST;
DLB 60

Oneal, Elizabeth 1934-
See Oneal, Zibby
See also CA 106; CANR 28; MAICYA;
SATA 30, 82

Oneal, Zibby .... **CLC 30**
See also Oneal, Elizabeth
See also AAYA 5; CLR 13; JRDA

O'Neill, Eugene (Gladstone)
1888-1953 ...... **TCLC 1, 6, 27, 49; DA;**
DAB; DAC; WLC
See also AITN 1; CA 110; 132;
CDALB 1929-1941; DAM DRAM, MST;
DLB 7; MTCW

Onetti, Juan Carlos 1909-1994 ... **CLC 7, 10**
See also CA 85-88; 145; CANR 32;
DAM MULT, NOV; DLB 113; HW;
MTCW

O Nuallain, Brian 1911-1966
See O'Brien, Flann
See also CA 21-22; 25-28R; CAP 2

Oppen, George 1908-1984 .... **CLC 7, 13, 34**
See also CA 13-16R; 113; CANR 8; DLB 5

Oppenheim, E(dward) Phillips
1866-1946 .... **TCLC 45**
See also CA 111; DLB 70

Orlovitz, Gil 1918-1973 .... **CLC 22**
See also CA 77-80; 45-48; DLB 2, 5

Orris
See Ingelow, Jean

Ortega y Gasset, Jose
1883-1955 .... **TCLC 9; HLC**
See also CA 106; 130; DAM MULT; HW;
MTCW

Ortese, Anna Maria 1914-........ **CLC 89**

Ortiz, Simon J(oseph) 1941-....... **CLC 45**
See also CA 134; DAM MULT, POET;
DLB 120; NNAL

Orton, Joe .... **CLC 4, 13, 43; DC 3**
See also Orton, John Kingsley
See also CDBLB 1960 to Present; DLB 13

Orton, John Kingsley 1933-1967
See Orton, Joe
See also CA 85-88; CANR 35;
DAM DRAM; MTCW

Orwell, George
..... **TCLC 2, 6, 15, 31, 51; DAB; WLC**
See also Blair, Eric (Arthur)
See also CDBLB 1945-1960; DLB 15, 98

Osborne, David
See Silverberg, Robert

Osborne, George
See Silverberg, Robert

Osborne, John (James)
1929-1994 ..... **CLC 1, 2, 5, 11, 45; DA;**
DAB; DAC; WLC
See also CA 13-16R; 147; CANR 21;
CDBLB 1945-1960; DAM DRAM, MST;
DLB 13; MTCW

Osborne, Lawrence 1958- .... **CLC 50**

Oshima, Nagisa 1932-............ **CLC 20**
See also CA 116; 121

Oskison, John Milton
1874-1947 .... **TCLC 35**
See also CA 144; DAM MULT; NNAL

Ossoli, Sarah Margaret (Fuller marchesa d')
1810-1850
See Fuller, Margaret
See also SATA 25

Ostrovsky, Alexander
1823-1886 .... **NCLC 30**

Otero, Blas de 1916-1979......... **CLC 11**
See also CA 89-92; DLB 134

Otto, Whitney 1955-............. **CLC 70**
See also CA 140

Ouida .... **TCLC 43**
See also De La Ramee, (Marie) Louise
See also DLB 18, 156

Ousmane, Sembene 1923- .... **CLC 66; BLC**
See also BW 1; CA 117; 125; MTCW

Ovid 43B.C.-18(?).......... **CMLC 7; PC 2**
See also DAM POET

Owen, Hugh
See Faust, Frederick (Schiller)

Owen, Wilfred (Edward Salter)
1893-1918 ...... **TCLC 5, 27; DA; DAB;**
DAC; WLC
See also CA 104; 141; CDBLB 1914-1945;
DAM MST, POET; DLB 20

Owens, Rochelle 1936-............ **CLC 8**
See also CA 17-20R; CAAS 2; CANR 39

Oz, Amos 1939- ... **CLC 5, 8, 11, 27, 33, 54**
See also CA 53-56; CANR 27, 47;
DAM NOV; MTCW

Ozick, Cynthia
1928- .... **CLC 3, 7, 28, 62; SSC 15**
See also BEST 90:1; CA 17-20R; CANR 23;
DAM NOV, POP; DLB 28, 152;
DLBY 82; INT CANR-23; MTCW

Ozu, Yasujiro 1903-1963......... **CLC 16**
See also CA 112

Pacheco, C.
See Pessoa, Fernando (Antonio Nogueira)

Pa Chin .... **CLC 18**
See also Li Fei-kan

Pack, Robert 1929-.............. **CLC 13**
See also CA 1-4R; CANR 3, 44; DLB 5

Padgett, Lewis
See Kuttner, Henry

Padilla (Lorenzo), Heberto 1932-... **CLC 38**
See also AITN 1; CA 123; 131; HW

Page, Jimmy 1944-.............. **CLC 12**

Page, Louise 1955-............. **CLC 40**
See also CA 140

Page, P(atricia) K(athleen)
1916- .... **CLC 7, 18; DAC; PC 12**
See also CA 53-56; CANR 4, 22;
DAM MST; DLB 68; MTCW

Paget, Violet 1856-1935
See Lee, Vernon
See also CA 104

Paget-Lowe, Henry
See Lovecraft, H(oward) P(hillips)

Paglia, Camille (Anna) 1947-....... **CLC 68**
See also CA 140

Paige, Richard
See Koontz, Dean R(ay)

Pakenham, Antonia
See Fraser, (Lady) Antonia (Pakenham)

Palamas, Kostes 1859-1943 .... **TCLC 5**
See also CA 105

Palazzeschi, Aldo 1885-1974....... **CLC 11**
See also CA 89-92; 53-56; DLB 114

Paley, Grace 1922-.... **CLC 4, 6, 37; SSC 8**
See also CA 25-28R; CANR 13, 46;
DAM POP; DLB 28; INT CANR-13;
MTCW

Palin, Michael (Edward) 1943-..... **CLC 21**
See also Monty Python
See also CA 107; CANR 35; SATA 67

Palliser, Charles 1947-........... **CLC 65**
See also CA 136

Palma, Ricardo 1833-1919....... **TCLC 29**

Pancake, Breece Dexter 1952-1979
See Pancake, Breece D'J
See also CA 123; 109

Pancake, Breece D'J.............. **CLC 29**
See also Pancake, Breece Dexter
See also DLB 130

Panko, Rudy
See Gogol, Nikolai (Vasilyevich)

Papadiamantis, Alexandros
1851-1911 .... **TCLC 29**

Papadiamantopoulos, Johannes 1856-1910
See Moreas, Jean
See also CA 117

Papini, Giovanni 1881-1956....... **TCLC 22**
See also CA 121

Paracelsus 1493-1541............. **LC 14**

Parasol, Peter
See Stevens, Wallace

Parfenie, Maria
See Codrescu, Andrei

Parini, Jay (Lee) 1948- .... **CLC 54**
See also CA 97-100; CAAS 16; CANR 32

Park, Jordan
See Kornbluth, C(yril) M.; Pohl, Frederik

Parker, Bert
See Ellison, Harlan (Jay)

Parker, Dorothy (Rothschild)
1893-1967 .... **CLC 15, 68; SSC 2**
See also CA 19-20; 25-28R; CAP 2;
DAM POET; DLB 11, 45, 86; MTCW

Parker, Robert B(rown) 1932-...... **CLC 27**
See also BEST 89:4; CA 49-52; CANR 1,
26; DAM NOV, POP; INT CANR-26;
MTCW

Parkin, Frank 1940-.............. **CLC 43**
See also CA 147

Parkman, Francis, Jr.
1823-1893 .... **NCLC 12**
See also DLB 1, 30

Parks, Gordon (Alexander Buchanan)
1912- .... **CLC 1, 16; BLC**
See also AITN 2; BW 2; CA 41-44R;
CANR 26; DAM MULT; DLB 33;
SATA 8

Parnell, Thomas 1679-1718 .... **LC 3**
See also DLB 94

Parra, Nicanor 1914- .... **CLC 2; HLC**
See also CA 85-88; CANR 32;
DAM MULT; HW; MTCW

Parrish, Mary Frances
See Fisher, M(ary) F(rances) K(ennedy)

Parson
See Coleridge, Samuel Taylor

Parson Lot
See Kingsley, Charles

Partridge, Anthony
See Oppenheim, E(dward) Phillips

Pascoli, Giovanni 1855-1912 ...... **TCLC 45**

Pasolini, Pier Paolo
1922-1975 .... **CLC 20, 37**
See also CA 93-96; 61-64; DLB 128;
MTCW

Pasquini
See Silone, Ignazio

Pastan, Linda (Olenik) 1932- ...... **CLC 27**
See also CA 61-64; CANR 18, 40;
DAM POET; DLB 5

Pasternak, Boris (Leonidovich)
1890-1960 ...... **CLC 7, 10, 18, 63; DA;**
DAB; DAC; PC 6; WLC
See also CA 127; 116; DAM MST, NOV,
POET; MTCW

Patchen, Kenneth 1911-1972 ... **CLC 1, 2, 18**
See also CA 1-4R; 33-36R; CANR 3, 35;
DAM POET; DLB 16, 48; MTCW

Pater, Walter (Horatio)
1839-1894 .... **NCLC 7**
See also CDBLB 1832-1890; DLB 57, 156

Paterson, A(ndrew) B(arton)
1864-1941 .... **TCLC 32**

Paterson, Katherine (Womeldorf)
1932- .... **CLC 12, 30**
See also AAYA 1; CA 21-24R; CANR 28;
CLR 7; DLB 52; JRDA; MAICYA;
MTCW; SATA 13, 53

Patmore, Coventry Kersey Dighton
1823-1896 .... **NCLC 9**
See also DLB 35, 98

Paton, Alan (Stewart)
1903-1988 ...... **CLC 4, 10, 25, 55; DA;**
DAB; DAC; WLC
See also CA 13-16; 125; CANR 22; CAP 1;
DAM MST, NOV; MTCW; SATA 11;
SATA-Obit 56

Paton Walsh, Gillian 1937-
See Walsh, Jill Paton
See also CANR 38; JRDA; MAICYA;
SAAS 3; SATA 4, 72

Paulding, James Kirke 1778-1860.. **NCLC 2**
See also DLB 3, 59, 74

Paulin, Thomas Neilson 1949-
See Paulin, Tom
See also CA 123; 128

Paulin, Tom.................... **CLC 37**
See also Paulin, Thomas Neilson
See also DLB 40

Paustovsky, Konstantin (Georgievich)
1892-1968 .... **CLC 40**
See also CA 93-96; 25-28R

Pavese, Cesare
1908-1950 ..... **TCLC 3; PC 13; SSC 19**
See also CA 104; DLB 128

Pavic, Milorad 1929-............. **CLC 60**
See also CA 136

Payne, Alan
    See Jakes, John (William)

Paz, Gil
    See Lugones, Leopoldo

Paz, Octavio
    1914- .... **CLC 3, 4, 6, 10, 19, 51, 65;**
        DA; DAB; DAC; HLC; PC 1; WLC
    See also CA 73-76; CANR 32; DAM MST,
        MULT, POET; DLBY 90; HW; MTCW

Peacock, Molly   1947- .... **CLC 60**
    See also CA 103; CAAS 21; DLB 120

Peacock, Thomas Love
    1785-1866 .... **NCLC 22**
    See also DLB 96, 116

Peake, Mervyn   1911-1968 ...... **CLC 7, 54**
    See also CA 5-8R; 25-28R; CANR 3;
        DLB 15, 160; MTCW; SATA 23

Pearce, Philippa .... **CLC 21**
    See also Christie, (Ann) Philippa
    See also CLR 9; DLB 161; MAICYA;
        SATA 1, 67

Pearl, Eric
    See Elman, Richard

Pearson, T(homas) R(eid)   1956- .... **CLC 39**
    See also CA 120; 130; INT 130

Peck, Dale   1967- .... **CLC 81**
    See also CA 146

Peck, John   1941- .... **CLC 3**
    See also CA 49-52; CANR 3

Peck, Richard (Wayne)   1934- ...... **CLC 21**
    See also AAYA 1; CA 85-88; CANR 19,
        38; CLR 15; INT CANR-19; JRDA;
        MAICYA; SAAS 2; SATA 18, 55

Peck, Robert Newton
    1928- .... **CLC 17; DA; DAC**
    See also AAYA 3; CA 81-84; CANR 31;
        DAM MST; JRDA; MAICYA; SAAS 1;
        SATA 21, 62

Peckinpah, (David) Sam(uel)
    1925-1984 .... **CLC 20**
    See also CA 109; 114

Pedersen, Knut   1859-1952
    See Hamsun, Knut
    See also CA 104; 119; MTCW

Peeslake, Gaffer
    See Durrell, Lawrence (George)

Peguy, Charles Pierre
    1873-1914 .... **TCLC 10**
    See also CA 107

Pena, Ramon del Valle y
    See Valle-Inclan, Ramon (Maria) del

Pendennis, Arthur Esquir
    See Thackeray, William Makepeace

Penn, William   1644-1718 .... **LC 25**
    See also DLB 24

Pepys, Samuel
    1633-1703 ..... **LC 11; DA; DAB; DAC;**
        WLC
    See also CDBLB 1660-1789; DAM MST;
        DLB 101

Percy, Walker
    1916-1990 .... **CLC 2, 3, 6, 8, 14, 18, 47,**
        65
    See also CA 1-4R; 131; CANR 1, 23;
        DAM NOV, POP; DLB 2; DLBY 80, 90;
        MTCW

Perec, Georges   1936-1982 .... **CLC 56**
    See also CA 141; DLB 83

Pereda (y Sanchez de Porrua), Jose Maria de
    1833-1906 .... **TCLC 16**
    See also CA 117

Pereda y Porrua, Jose Maria de
    See Pereda (y Sanchez de Porrua), Jose
        Maria de

Peregoy, George Weems
    See Mencken, H(enry) L(ouis)

Perelman, S(idney) J(oseph)
    1904-1979 ... **CLC 3, 5, 9, 15, 23, 44, 49**
    See also AITN 1, 2; CA 73-76; 89-92;
        CANR 18; DAM DRAM; DLB 11, 44;
        MTCW

Peret, Benjamin   1899-1959 .... **TCLC 20**
    See also CA 117

Peretz, Isaac Loeb   1851(?)-1915 ... **TCLC 16**
    See also CA 109

Peretz, Yitzkhok Leibush
    See Peretz, Isaac Loeb

Perez Galdos, Benito   1843-1920 ... **TCLC 27**
    See also CA 125; HW

Perrault, Charles   1628-1703 .... **LC 2**
    See also MAICYA; SATA 25

Perry, Brighton
    See Sherwood, Robert E(mmet)

Perse, St.-John .... **CLC 4, 11, 46**
    See also Leger, (Marie-Rene Auguste) Alexis
        Saint-Leger

Perutz, Leo   1882-1957 .... **TCLC 60**
    See also DLB 81

Peseenz, Tulio F.
    See Lopez y Fuentes, Gregorio

Pesetsky, Bette   1932- .... **CLC 28**
    See also CA 133; DLB 130

Peshkov, Alexei Maximovich   1868-1936
    See Gorky, Maxim
    See also CA 105; 141; DA; DAC;
        DAM DRAM, MST, NOV

Pessoa, Fernando (Antonio Nogueira)
    1888-1935 .... **TCLC 27; HLC**
    See also CA 125

Peterkin, Julia Mood   1880-1961 .... **CLC 31**
    See also CA 102; DLB 9

Peters, Joan K.   1945- .... **CLC 39**

Peters, Robert L(ouis)   1924- .... **CLC 7**
    See also CA 13-16R; CAAS 8; DLB 105

Petofi, Sandor   1823-1849 .... **NCLC 21**

Petrakis, Harry Mark   1923- .... **CLC 3**
    See also CA 9-12R; CANR 4, 30

Petrarch   1304-1374 .... **PC 8**
    See also DAM POET

Petrov, Evgeny .... **TCLC 21**
    See also Kataev, Evgeny Petrovich

Petry, Ann (Lane)   1908- ...... **CLC 1, 7, 18**
    See also BW 1; CA 5-8R; CAAS 6;
        CANR 4, 46; CLR 12; DLB 76; JRDA;
        MAICYA; MTCW; SATA 5

Petursson, Halligrimur   1614-1674 .... **LC 8**

Philips, Katherine   1632-1664 .... **LC 30**
    See also DLB 131

Philipson, Morris H.   1926- .... **CLC 53**
    See also CA 1-4R; CANR 4

Phillips, David Graham
    1867-1911 .... **TCLC 44**
    See also CA 108; DLB 9, 12

Phillips, Jack
    See Sandburg, Carl (August)

Phillips, Jayne Anne
    1952- .... **CLC 15, 33; SSC 16**
    See also CA 101; CANR 24, 50; DLBY 80;
        INT CANR-24; MTCW

Phillips, Richard
    See Dick, Philip K(indred)

Phillips, Robert (Schaeffer)   1938- ... **CLC 28**
    See also CA 17-20R; CAAS 13; CANR 8;
        DLB 105

Phillips, Ward
    See Lovecraft, H(oward) P(hillips)

Piccolo, Lucio   1901-1969 .... **CLC 13**
    See also CA 97-100; DLB 114

Pickthall, Marjorie L(owry) C(hristie)
    1883-1922 .... **TCLC 21**
    See also CA 107; DLB 92

Pico della Mirandola, Giovanni
    1463-1494 .... **LC 15**

Piercy, Marge
    1936- .... **CLC 3, 6, 14, 18, 27, 62**
    See also CA 21-24R; CAAS 1; CANR 13,
        43; DLB 120; MTCW

Piers, Robert
    See Anthony, Piers

Pieyre de Mandiargues, Andre   1909-1991
    See Mandiargues, Andre Pieyre de
    See also CA 103; 136; CANR 22

Pilnyak, Boris .... **TCLC 23**
    See also Vogau, Boris Andreyevich

Pincherle, Alberto   1907-1990 ... **CLC 11, 18**
    See also Moravia, Alberto
    See also CA 25-28R; 132; CANR 33;
        DAM NOV; MTCW

Pinckney, Darryl   1953- .... **CLC 76**
    See also BW 2; CA 143

Pindar   518B.C.-446B.C. .... **CMLC 12**

Pineda, Cecile   1942- .... **CLC 39**
    See also CA 118

Pinero, Arthur Wing   1855-1934 ... **TCLC 32**
    See also CA 110; DAM DRAM; DLB 10

Pinero, Miguel (Antonio Gomez)
    1946-1988 .... **CLC 4, 55**
    See also CA 61-64; 125; CANR 29; HW

Pinget, Robert   1919- ...... **CLC 7, 13, 37**
    See also CA 85-88; DLB 83

Pink Floyd
    See Barrett, (Roger) Syd; Gilmour, David;
        Mason, Nick; Waters, Roger; Wright,
        Rick

Pinkney, Edward   1802-1828 ..... **NCLC 31**

Powers, John J(ames)   1945-
See Powers, John R.
See also CA 69-72

Powers, John R. . . . . **CLC 66**
See also Powers, John J(ames)

Pownall, David   1938-. . . . . **CLC 10**
See also CA 89-92; CAAS 18; CANR 49;
DLB 14

Powys, John Cowper
1872-1963 . . . . **CLC 7, 9, 15, 46**
See also CA 85-88; DLB 15; MTCW

Powys, T(heodore) F(rancis)
1875-1953 . . . . **TCLC 9**
See also CA 106; DLB 36, 162

Prager, Emily   1952-. . . . . **CLC 56**

Pratt, E(dwin) J(ohn)
1883(?)-1964 . . . . **CLC 19; DAC**
See also CA 141; 93-96; DAM POET;
DLB 92

Premchand. . . . . **TCLC 21**
See also Srivastava, Dhanpat Rai

Preussler, Otfried   1923-. . . . . **CLC 17**
See also CA 77-80; SATA 24

Prevert, Jacques (Henri Marie)
1900-1977 . . . . **CLC 15**
See also CA 77-80; 69-72; CANR 29;
MTCW; SATA-Obit 30

Prevost, Abbe (Antoine Francois)
1697-1763 . . . . **LC 1**

Price, (Edward) Reynolds
1933- . . . . **CLC 3, 6, 13, 43, 50, 63**
See also CA 1-4R; CANR 1, 37;
DAM NOV; DLB 2; INT CANR-37

Price, Richard   1949- . . . . **CLC 6, 12**
See also CA 49-52; CANR 3; DLBY 81

Prichard, Katharine Susannah
1883-1969 . . . . **CLC 46**
See also CA 11-12; CANR 33; CAP 1;
MTCW; SATA 66

Priestley, J(ohn) B(oynton)
1894-1984 . . . . **CLC 2, 5, 9, 34**
See also CA 9-12R; 113; CANR 33;
CDBLB 1914-1945; DAM DRAM, NOV;
DLB 10, 34, 77, 100, 139; DLBY 84;
MTCW

Prince   1958(?)- . . . . **CLC 35**

Prince, F(rank) T(empleton)   1912-. . **CLC 22**
See also CA 101; CANR 43; DLB 20

Prince Kropotkin
See Kropotkin, Peter (Aleksieevich)

Prior, Matthew   1664-1721. . . . . **LC 4**
See also DLB 95

Pritchard, William H(arrison)
1932- . . . . **CLC 34**
See also CA 65-68; CANR 23; DLB 111

Pritchett, V(ictor) S(awdon)
1900- . . . . . . **CLC 5, 13, 15, 41; SSC 14**
See also CA 61-64; CANR 31; DAM NOV;
DLB 15, 139; MTCW

Private 19022
See Manning, Frederic

Probst, Mark   1925- . . . . **CLC 59**
See also CA 130

Prokosch, Frederic   1908-1989. . . . **CLC 4, 48**
See also CA 73-76; 128; DLB 48

Prophet, The
See Dreiser, Theodore (Herman Albert)

Prose, Francine   1947-. . . . . **CLC 45**
See also CA 109; 112; CANR 46

Proudhon
See Cunha, Euclides (Rodrigues Pimenta) da

Proulx, E. Annie   1935- . . . . **CLC 81**

Proust, (Valentin-Louis-George-Eugene-)
Marcel
1871-1922 . . . . **TCLC 7, 13, 33; DA;
DAB; DAC; WLC**
See also CA 104; 120; DAM MST, NOV;
DLB 65; MTCW

Prowler, Harley
See Masters, Edgar Lee

Prus, Boleslaw   1845-1912 . . . . **TCLC 48**

Pryor, Richard (Franklin Lenox Thomas)
1940- . . . . **CLC 26**
See also CA 122

Przybyszewski, Stanislaw
1868-1927 . . . . **TCLC 36**
See also DLB 66

Pteleon
See Grieve, C(hristopher) M(urray)
See also DAM POET

Puckett, Lute
See Masters, Edgar Lee

Puig, Manuel
1932-1990 . . . **CLC 3, 5, 10, 28, 65; HLC**
See also CA 45-48; CANR 2, 32;
DAM MULT; DLB 113; HW; MTCW

Purdy, Al(fred Wellington)
1918- . . . . **CLC 3, 6, 14, 50; DAC**
See also CA 81-84; CAAS 17; CANR 42;
DAM MST, POET; DLB 88

Purdy, James (Amos)
1923- . . . . **CLC 2, 4, 10, 28, 52**
See also CA 33-36R; CAAS 1; CANR 19;
DLB 2; INT CANR-19; MTCW

Pure, Simon
See Swinnerton, Frank Arthur

Pushkin, Alexander (Sergeyevich)
1799-1837 . . . . . **NCLC 3, 27; DA; DAB;
DAC; PC 10; WLC**
See also DAM DRAM, MST, POET;
SATA 61

P'u Sung-ling   1640-1715 . . . . **LC 3**

Putnam, Arthur Lee
See Alger, Horatio, Jr.

Puzo, Mario   1920- . . . . **CLC 1, 2, 6, 36**
See also CA 65-68; CANR 4, 42;
DAM NOV, POP; DLB 6; MTCW

Pym, Barbara (Mary Crampton)
1913-1980 . . . . **CLC 13, 19, 37**
See also CA 13-14; 97-100; CANR 13, 34;
CAP 1; DLB 14; DLBY 87; MTCW

Pynchon, Thomas (Ruggles, Jr.)
1937- . . . . . **CLC 2, 3, 6, 9, 11, 18, 33, 62,
72; DA; DAB; DAC; SSC 14; WLC**
See also BEST 90:2; CA 17-20R; CANR 22,
46; DAM MST, NOV, POP; DLB 2;
MTCW

Qian Zhongshu
See Ch'ien Chung-shu

Qroll
See Dagerman, Stig (Halvard)

Quarrington, Paul (Lewis)   1953-. . . . **CLC 65**
See also CA 129

Quasimodo, Salvatore   1901-1968 . . . **CLC 10**
See also CA 13-16; 25-28R; CAP 1;
DLB 114; MTCW

Queen, Ellery. . . . . **CLC 3, 11**
See also Dannay, Frederic; Davidson,
Avram; Lee, Manfred B(ennington);
Sturgeon, Theodore (Hamilton); Vance,
John Holbrook

Queen, Ellery, Jr.
See Dannay, Frederic; Lee, Manfred
B(ennington)

Queneau, Raymond
1903-1976 . . . . **CLC 2, 5, 10, 42**
See also CA 77-80; 69-72; CANR 32;
DLB 72; MTCW

Quevedo, Francisco de   1580-1645. . . . **LC 23**

Quiller-Couch, Arthur Thomas
1863-1944 . . . . **TCLC 53**
See also CA 118; DLB 135, 153

Quin, Ann (Marie)   1936-1973 . . . . **CLC 6**
See also CA 9-12R; 45-48; DLB 14

Quinn, Martin
See Smith, Martin Cruz

Quinn, Peter   1947-. . . . . **CLC 91**

Quinn, Simon
See Smith, Martin Cruz

Quiroga, Horacio (Sylvestre)
1878-1937 . . . . **TCLC 20; HLC**
See also CA 117; 131; DAM MULT; HW;
MTCW

Quoirez, Francoise   1935-. . . . . **CLC 9**
See also Sagan, Francoise
See also CA 49-52; CANR 6, 39; MTCW

Raabe, Wilhelm   1831-1910 . . . . **TCLC 45**
See also DLB 129

Rabe, David (William)   1940-. . . **CLC 4, 8, 33**
See also CA 85-88; CABS 3; DAM DRAM;
DLB 7

Rabelais, Francois
1483-1553 . . . . . . **LC 5; DA; DAB; DAC;
WLC**
See also DAM MST

Rabinovitch, Sholem   1859-1916
See Aleichem, Sholom
See also CA 104

Racine, Jean   1639-1699 . . . . **LC 28; DAB**
See also DAM MST

Radcliffe, Ann (Ward)   1764-1823 . . **NCLC 6**
See also DLB 39

Radiguet, Raymond   1903-1923 . . . . **TCLC 29**
See also DLB 65

Radnoti, Miklos   1909-1944 . . . . **TCLC 16**
See also CA 118

Rado, James   1939-. . . . . **CLC 17**
See also CA 105

Radvanyi, Netty   1900-1983
See Seghers, Anna
See also CA 85-88; 110

Rae, Ben
See Griffiths, Trevor

Rezzori (d'Arezzo), Gregor von
1914- . . . . **CLC 25**
See also CA 122; 136

Rhine, Richard
See Silverstein, Alvin

Rhodes, Eugene Manlove
1869-1934 . . . . **TCLC 53**

R'hoone
See Balzac, Honore de

Rhys, Jean
1890(?)-1979 . . . . **CLC 2, 4, 6, 14, 19, 51;
SSC 21**
See also CA 25-28R; 85-88; CANR 35;
CDBLB 1945-1960; DAM NOV; DLB 36,
117, 162; MTCW

Ribeiro, Darcy 1922- . . . . **CLC 34**
See also CA 33-36R

Ribeiro, Joao Ubaldo (Osorio Pimentel)
1941- . . . . **CLC 10, 67**
See also CA 81-84

Ribman, Ronald (Burt) 1932- . . . . **CLC 7**
See also CA 21-24R; CANR 46

Ricci, Nino 1959- . . . . **CLC 70**
See also CA 137

Rice, Anne 1941- . . . . **CLC 41**
See also AAYA 9; BEST 89:2; CA 65-68;
CANR 12, 36; DAM POP

Rice, Elmer (Leopold)
1892-1967 . . . . **CLC 7, 49**
See also CA 21-22; 25-28R; CAP 2;
DAM DRAM; DLB 4, 7; MTCW

Rice, Tim(othy Miles Bindon)
1944- . . . . **CLC 21**
See also CA 103; CANR 46

Rich, Adrienne (Cecile)
1929- . . . . **CLC 3, 6, 7, 11, 18, 36, 73, 76;
PC 5**
See also CA 9-12R; CANR 20;
DAM POET; DLB 5, 67; MTCW

Rich, Barbara
See Graves, Robert (von Ranke)

Rich, Robert
See Trumbo, Dalton

Richard, Keith . . . . **CLC 17**
See also Richards, Keith

Richards, David Adams
1950- . . . . **CLC 59; DAC**
See also CA 93-96; DLB 53

Richards, I(vor) A(rmstrong)
1893-1979 . . . . **CLC 14, 24**
See also CA 41-44R; 89-92; CANR 34;
DLB 27

Richards, Keith 1943-
See Richard, Keith
See also CA 107

Richardson, Anne
See Roiphe, Anne (Richardson)

Richardson, Dorothy Miller
1873-1957 . . . . **TCLC 3**
See also CA 104; DLB 36

Richardson, Ethel Florence (Lindesay)
1870-1946
See Richardson, Henry Handel
See also CA 105

Richardson, Henry Handel . . . . **TCLC 4**
See also Richardson, Ethel Florence
(Lindesay)

Richardson, Samuel
1689-1761 . . . . . . **LC 1; DA; DAB; DAC;
WLC**
See also CDBLB 1660-1789; DAM MST,
NOV; DLB 39

Richler, Mordecai
1931- . . . . **CLC 3, 5, 9, 13, 18, 46, 70;
DAC**
See also AITN 1; CA 65-68; CANR 31;
CLR 17; DAM MST, NOV; DLB 53;
MAICYA; MTCW; SATA 44;
SATA-Brief 27

Richter, Conrad (Michael)
1890-1968 . . . . **CLC 30**
See also CA 5-8R; 25-28R; CANR 23;
DLB 9; MTCW; SATA 3

Ricostranza, Tom
See Ellis, Trey

Riddell, J. H. 1832-1906 . . . . **TCLC 40**

Riding, Laura . . . . **CLC 3, 7**
See also Jackson, Laura (Riding)

Riefenstahl, Berta Helene Amalia 1902-
See Riefenstahl, Leni
See also CA 108

Riefenstahl, Leni . . . . **CLC 16**
See also Riefenstahl, Berta Helene Amalia

Riffe, Ernest
See Bergman, (Ernst) Ingmar

Riggs, (Rolla) Lynn 1899-1954 . . . . **TCLC 56**
See also CA 144; DAM MULT; NNAL

Riley, James Whitcomb
1849-1916 . . . . **TCLC 51**
See also CA 118; 137; DAM POET;
MAICYA; SATA 17

Riley, Tex
See Creasey, John

Rilke, Rainer Maria
1875-1926 . . . . **TCLC 1, 6, 19; PC 2**
See also CA 104; 132; DAM POET;
DLB 81; MTCW

Rimbaud, (Jean Nicolas) Arthur
1854-1891 . . . . . **NCLC 4, 35; DA; DAB;
DAC; PC 3; WLC**
See also DAM MST, POET

Rinehart, Mary Roberts
1876-1958 . . . . **TCLC 52**
See also CA 108

Ringmaster, The
See Mencken, H(enry) L(ouis)

Ringwood, Gwen(dolyn Margaret) Pharis
1910-1984 . . . . **CLC 48**
See also CA 148; 112; DLB 88

Rio, Michel 19(?)- . . . . **CLC 43**

Ritsos, Giannes
See Ritsos, Yannis

Ritsos, Yannis 1909-1990 . . . . . **CLC 6, 13, 31**
See also CA 77-80; 133; CANR 39; MTCW

Ritter, Erika 1948(?)- . . . . **CLC 52**

Rivera, Jose Eustasio 1889-1928 . . . **TCLC 35**
See also HW

Rivers, Conrad Kent 1933-1968 . . . . . . **CLC 1**
See also BW 1; CA 85-88; DLB 41

Rivers, Elfrida
See Bradley, Marion Zimmer

Riverside, John
See Heinlein, Robert A(nson)

Rizal, Jose 1861-1896 . . . . **NCLC 27**

Roa Bastos, Augusto (Antonio)
1917- . . . . **CLC 45; HLC**
See also CA 131; DAM MULT; DLB 113;
HW

Robbe-Grillet, Alain
1922- . . . . . . **CLC 1, 2, 4, 6, 8, 10, 14, 43**
See also CA 9-12R; CANR 33; DLB 83;
MTCW

Robbins, Harold 1916- . . . . **CLC 5**
See also CA 73-76; CANR 26; DAM NOV;
MTCW

Robbins, Thomas Eugene 1936-
See Robbins, Tom
See also CA 81-84; CANR 29; DAM NOV,
POP; MTCW

Robbins, Tom . . . . **CLC 9, 32, 64**
See also Robbins, Thomas Eugene
See also BEST 90:3; DLBY 80

Robbins, Trina 1938- . . . . **CLC 21**
See also CA 128

Roberts, Charles G(eorge) D(ouglas)
1860-1943 . . . . **TCLC 8**
See also CA 105; CLR 33; DLB 92;
SATA-Brief 29

Roberts, Kate 1891-1985 . . . . **CLC 15**
See also CA 107; 116

Roberts, Keith (John Kingston)
1935- . . . . **CLC 14**
See also CA 25-28R; CANR 46

Roberts, Kenneth (Lewis)
1885-1957 . . . . **TCLC 23**
See also CA 109; DLB 9

Roberts, Michele (B.) 1949- . . . . **CLC 48**
See also CA 115

Robertson, Ellis
See Ellison, Harlan (Jay); Silverberg, Robert

Robertson, Thomas William
1829-1871 . . . . **NCLC 35**
See also DAM DRAM

Robinson, Edwin Arlington
1869-1935 . . . . **TCLC 5; DA; DAC; PC 1**
See also CA 104; 133; CDALB 1865-1917;
DAM MST, POET; DLB 54; MTCW

Robinson, Henry Crabb
1775-1867 . . . . **NCLC 15**
See also DLB 107

Robinson, Jill 1936- . . . . **CLC 10**
See also CA 102; INT 102

Robinson, Kim Stanley 1952- . . . . . . **CLC 34**
See also CA 126

Robinson, Lloyd
See Silverberg, Robert

Robinson, Marilynne 1944- . . . . **CLC 25**
See also CA 116

Robinson, Smokey . . . . **CLC 21**
See also Robinson, William, Jr.

Robinson, William, Jr. 1940-
See Robinson, Smokey
See also CA 116

Santiago, Danny .... **CLC 33**
See also James, Daniel (Lewis)
See also DLB 122

Santmyer, Helen Hoover
1895-1986 .... **CLC 33**
See also CA 1-4R; 118; CANR 15, 33;
DLBY 84; MTCW

Santos, Bienvenido N(uqui) 1911-... **CLC 22**
See also CA 101; CANR 19, 46;
DAM MULT

Sapper .... **TCLC 44**
See also McNeile, Herman Cyril

Sappho fl. 6th cent. B.C.-.... **CMLC 3; PC 5**
See also DAM POET

Sarduy, Severo 1937-1993 .... **CLC 6**
See also CA 89-92; 142; DLB 113; HW

Sargeson, Frank 1903-1982 .... **CLC 31**
See also CA 25-28R; 106; CANR 38

Sarmiento, Felix Ruben Garcia
See Dario, Ruben

Saroyan, William
1908-1981 ..... **CLC 1, 8, 10, 29, 34, 56;**
DA; DAB; DAC; SSC 21; WLC
See also CA 5-8R; 103; CANR 30;
DAM DRAM, MST, NOV; DLB 7, 9, 86;
DLBY 81; MTCW; SATA 23;
SATA-Obit 24

Sarraute, Nathalie
1900- .... **CLC 1, 2, 4, 8, 10, 31, 80**
See also CA 9-12R; CANR 23; DLB 83;
MTCW

Sarton, (Eleanor) May
1912-1995 .... **CLC 4, 14, 49, 91**
See also CA 1-4R; 149; CANR 1, 34;
DAM POET; DLB 48; DLBY 81;
INT CANR-34; MTCW; SATA 36;
SATA-Obit 86

Sartre, Jean-Paul
1905-1980 .... **CLC 1, 4, 7, 9, 13, 18, 24,**
44, 50, 52; DA; DAB; DAC; DC 3; WLC
See also CA 9-12R; 97-100; CANR 21;
DAM DRAM, MST, NOV; DLB 72;
MTCW

Sassoon, Siegfried (Lorraine)
1886-1967 .... **CLC 36; DAB; PC 12**
See also CA 104; 25-28R; CANR 36;
DAM MST, NOV, POET; DLB 20;
MTCW

Satterfield, Charles
See Pohl, Frederik

Saul, John (W. III) 1942- .... **CLC 46**
See also AAYA 10; BEST 90:4; CA 81-84;
CANR 16, 40; DAM NOV, POP

Saunders, Caleb
See Heinlein, Robert A(nson)

Saura (Atares), Carlos 1932-....... **CLC 20**
See also CA 114; 131; HW

Sauser-Hall, Frederic 1887-1961.... **CLC 18**
See also Cendrars, Blaise
See also CA 102; 93-96; CANR 36; MTCW

Saussure, Ferdinand de
1857-1913 .... **TCLC 49**

Savage, Catharine
See Brosman, Catharine Savage

Savage, Thomas 1915- .... **CLC 40**
See also CA 126; 132; CAAS 15; INT 132

Savan, Glenn 19(?)- .... **CLC 50**

Sayers, Dorothy L(eigh)
1893-1957 .... **TCLC 2, 15**
See also CA 104; 119; CDBLB 1914-1945;
DAM POP; DLB 10, 36, 77, 100; MTCW

Sayers, Valerie 1952- .... **CLC 50**
See also CA 134

Sayles, John (Thomas)
1950- .... **CLC 7, 10, 14**
See also CA 57-60; CANR 41; DLB 44

Scammell, Michael .... **CLC 34**

Scannell, Vernon 1922- .... **CLC 49**
See also CA 5-8R; CANR 8, 24; DLB 27;
SATA 59

Scarlett, Susan
See Streatfeild, (Mary) Noel

Schaeffer, Susan Fromberg
1941- .... **CLC 6, 11, 22**
See also CA 49-52; CANR 18; DLB 28;
MTCW; SATA 22

Schary, Jill
See Robinson, Jill

Schell, Jonathan 1943-............ **CLC 35**
See also CA 73-76; CANR 12

Schelling, Friedrich Wilhelm Joseph von
1775-1854 .... **NCLC 30**
See also DLB 90

Schendel, Arthur van 1874-1946... **TCLC 56**

Scherer, Jean-Marie Maurice 1920-
See Rohmer, Eric
See also CA 110

Schevill, James (Erwin) 1920-....... **CLC 7**
See also CA 5-8R; CAAS 12

Schiller, Friedrich 1759-1805 .... **NCLC 39**
See also DAM DRAM; DLB 94

Schisgal, Murray (Joseph) 1926-..... **CLC 6**
See also CA 21-24R; CANR 48

Schlee, Ann 1934-................ **CLC 35**
See also CA 101; CANR 29; SATA 44;
SATA-Brief 36

Schlegel, August Wilhelm von
1767-1845 .... **NCLC 15**
See also DLB 94

Schlegel, Friedrich 1772-1829.... **NCLC 45**
See also DLB 90

Schlegel, Johann Elias (von)
1719(?)-1749 .... **LC 5**

Schlesinger, Arthur M(eier), Jr.
1917- .... **CLC 84**
See also AITN 1; CA 1-4R; CANR 1, 28;
DLB 17; INT CANR-28; MTCW;
SATA 61

Schmidt, Arno (Otto) 1914-1979 .... **CLC 56**
See also CA 128; 109; DLB 69

Schmitz, Aron Hector 1861-1928
See Svevo, Italo
See also CA 104; 122; MTCW

Schnackenberg, Gjertrud 1953-..... **CLC 40**
See also CA 116; DLB 120

Schneider, Leonard Alfred 1925-1966
See Bruce, Lenny
See also CA 89-92

Schnitzler, Arthur
1862-1931 .... **TCLC 4; SSC 15**
See also CA 104; DLB 81, 118

Schopenhauer, Arthur
1788-1860 .... **NCLC 51**
See also DLB 90

Schor, Sandra (M.) 1932(?)-1990 ... **CLC 65**
See also CA 132

Schorer, Mark 1908-1977 .... **CLC 9**
See also CA 5-8R; 73-76; CANR 7;
DLB 103

Schrader, Paul (Joseph) 1946-...... **CLC 26**
See also CA 37-40R; CANR 41; DLB 44

Schreiner, Olive (Emilie Albertina)
1855-1920 .... **TCLC 9**
See also CA 105; DLB 18, 156

Schulberg, Budd (Wilson)
1914- .... **CLC 7, 48**
See also CA 25-28R; CANR 19; DLB 6, 26,
28; DLBY 81

Schulz, Bruno
1892-1942 .... **TCLC 5, 51; SSC 13**
See also CA 115; 123

Schulz, Charles M(onroe) 1922-.... **CLC 12**
See also CA 9-12R; CANR 6;
INT CANR-6; SATA 10

Schumacher, E(rnst) F(riedrich)
1911-1977 .... **CLC 80**
See also CA 81-84; 73-76; CANR 34

Schuyler, James Marcus
1923-1991 .... **CLC 5, 23**
See also CA 101; 134; DAM POET; DLB 5;
INT 101

Schwartz, Delmore (David)
1913-1966 ... **CLC 2, 4, 10, 45, 87; PC 8**
See also CA 17-18; 25-28R; CANR 35;
CAP 2; DLB 28, 48; MTCW

Schwartz, Ernst
See Ozu, Yasujiro

Schwartz, John Burnham 1965- .... **CLC 59**
See also CA 132

Schwartz, Lynne Sharon 1939-..... **CLC 31**
See also CA 103; CANR 44

Schwartz, Muriel A.
See Eliot, T(homas) S(tearns)

Schwarz-Bart, Andre 1928-....... **CLC 2, 4**
See also CA 89-92

Schwarz-Bart, Simone 1938-........ **CLC 7**
See also BW 2; CA 97-100

Schwob, (Mayer Andre) Marcel
1867-1905 .... **TCLC 20**
See also CA 117; DLB 123

Sciascia, Leonardo
1921-1989 .... **CLC 8, 9, 41**
See also CA 85-88; 130; CANR 35; MTCW

Scoppettone, Sandra 1936-........ **CLC 26**
See also AAYA 11; CA 5-8R; CANR 41;
SATA 9

Scorsese, Martin 1942- .... **CLC 20, 89**
See also CA 110; 114; CANR 46

Scotland, Jay
See Jakes, John (William)

Scott, Duncan Campbell
1862-1947 .... **TCLC 6; DAC**
See also CA 104; DLB 92

Scott, Evelyn 1893-1963. . . . . **CLC 43**
  See also CA 104; 112; DLB 9, 48

Scott, F(rancis) R(eginald)
  1899-1985 . . . . **CLC 22**
  See also CA 101; 114; DLB 88; INT 101

Scott, Frank
  See Scott, F(rancis) R(eginald)

Scott, Joanna 1960- . . . . **CLC 50**
  See also CA 126

Scott, Paul (Mark) 1920-1978. . . . **CLC 9, 60**
  See also CA 81-84; 77-80; CANR 33;
  DLB 14; MTCW

Scott, Walter
  1771-1832 . . . . **NCLC 15; DA; DAB;**
                 DAC; PC 13; WLC
  See also CDBLB 1789-1832; DAM MST,
  NOV, POET; DLB 93, 107, 116, 144, 159;
  YABC 2

Scribe, (Augustin) Eugene
  1791-1861 . . . . **NCLC 16; DC 5**
  See also DAM DRAM

Scrum, R.
  See Crumb, R(obert)

Scudery, Madeleine de 1607-1701. . . . . **LC 2**

Scum
  See Crumb, R(obert)

Scumbag, Little Bobby
  See Crumb, R(obert)

Seabrook, John
  See Hubbard, L(afayette) Ron(ald)

Sealy, I. Allan 1951- . . . . **CLC 55**

Search, Alexander
  See Pessoa, Fernando (Antonio Nogueira)

Sebastian, Lee
  See Silverberg, Robert

Sebastian Owl
  See Thompson, Hunter S(tockton)

Sebestyen, Ouida 1924- . . . . **CLC 30**
  See also AAYA 8; CA 107; CANR 40;
  CLR 17; JRDA; MAICYA; SAAS 10;
  SATA 39

Secundus, H. Scriblerus
  See Fielding, Henry

Sedges, John
  See Buck, Pearl S(ydenstricker)

Sedgwick, Catharine Maria
  1789-1867 . . . . **NCLC 19**
  See also DLB 1, 74

Seelye, John 1931- . . . . **CLC 7**

Seferiades, Giorgos Stylianou 1900-1971
  See Seferis, George
  See also CA 5-8R; 33-36R; CANR 5, 36;
  MTCW

Seferis, George . . . . **CLC 5, 11**
  See also Seferiades, Giorgos Stylianou

Segal, Erich (Wolf) 1937- . . . . **CLC 3, 10**
  See also BEST 89:1; CA 25-28R; CANR 20,
  36; DAM POP; DLBY 86;
  INT CANR-20; MTCW

Seger, Bob 1945- . . . . **CLC 35**

Seghers, Anna . . . . **CLC 7**
  See also Radvanyi, Netty
  See also DLB 69

Seidel, Frederick (Lewis) 1936- . . . . . **CLC 18**
  See also CA 13-16R; CANR 8; DLBY 84

Seifert, Jaroslav 1901-1986 . . . . . **CLC 34, 44**
  See also CA 127; MTCW

Sei Shonagon c. 966-1017(?) . . . . . . **CMLC 6**

Selby, Hubert, Jr.
  1928- . . . . **CLC 1, 2, 4, 8; SSC 20**
  See also CA 13-16R; CANR 33; DLB 2

Selzer, Richard 1928- . . . . **CLC 74**
  See also CA 65-68; CANR 14

Sembene, Ousmane
  See Ousmane, Sembene

Senancour, Etienne Pivert de
  1770-1846 . . . . **NCLC 16**
  See also DLB 119

Sender, Ramon (Jose)
  1902-1982 . . . . **CLC 8; HLC**
  See also CA 5-8R; 105; CANR 8;
  DAM MULT; HW; MTCW

Seneca, Lucius Annaeus
  4B.C.-65. . . . . **CMLC 6; DC 5**
  See also DAM DRAM

Senghor, Leopold Sedar
  1906- . . . . **CLC 54; BLC**
  See also BW 2; CA 116; 125; CANR 47;
  DAM MULT, POET; MTCW

Serling, (Edward) Rod(man)
  1924-1975 . . . . **CLC 30**
  See also AAYA 14; AITN 1; CA 65-68;
  57-60; DLB 26

Serna, Ramon Gomez de la
  See Gomez de la Serna, Ramon

Serpieres
  See Guillevic, (Eugene)

Service, Robert
  See Service, Robert W(illiam)
  See also DAB; DLB 92

Service, Robert W(illiam)
  1874(?)-1958 . . . . . . **TCLC 15; DA; DAC;**
                          WLC
  See also Service, Robert
  See also CA 115; 140; DAM MST, POET;
  SATA 20

Seth, Vikram 1952- . . . . **CLC 43, 90**
  See also CA 121; 127; CANR 50;
  DAM MULT; DLB 120; INT 127

Seton, Cynthia Propper
  1926-1982 . . . . **CLC 27**
  See also CA 5-8R; 108; CANR 7

Seton, Ernest (Evan) Thompson
  1860-1946 . . . . **TCLC 31**
  See also CA 109; DLB 92; DLBD 13;
  JRDA; SATA 18

Seton-Thompson, Ernest
  See Seton, Ernest (Evan) Thompson

Settle, Mary Lee 1918- . . . . **CLC 19, 61**
  See also CA 89-92; CAAS 1; CANR 44;
  DLB 6; INT 89-92

Seuphor, Michel
  See Arp, Jean

Sevigne, Marie (de Rabutin-Chantal) Marquise
  de 1626-1696 . . . . **LC 11**

Sexton, Anne (Harvey)
  1928-1974 . . . . **CLC 2, 4, 6, 8, 10, 15, 53;**
             DA; DAB; DAC; PC 2; WLC
  See also CA 1-4R; 53-56; CABS 2;
  CANR 3, 36; CDALB 1941-1968;
  DAM MST, POET; DLB 5; MTCW;
  SATA 10

Shaara, Michael (Joseph, Jr.)
  1929-1988 . . . . **CLC 15**
  See also AITN 1; CA 102; 125; DAM POP;
  DLBY 83

Shackleton, C. C.
  See Aldiss, Brian W(ilson)

Shacochis, Bob . . . . **CLC 39**
  See also Shacochis, Robert G.

Shacochis, Robert G. 1951-
  See Shacochis, Bob
  See also CA 119; 124; INT 124

Shaffer, Anthony (Joshua) 1926- . . . . **CLC 19**
  See also CA 110; 116; DAM DRAM;
  DLB 13

Shaffer, Peter (Levin)
  1926- . . . . . . **CLC 5, 14, 18, 37, 60; DAB**
  See also CA 25-28R; CANR 25, 47;
  CDBLB 1960 to Present; DAM DRAM,
  MST; DLB 13; MTCW

Shakey, Bernard
  See Young, Neil

Shalamov, Varlam (Tikhonovich)
  1907(?)-1982 . . . . **CLC 18**
  See also CA 129; 105

Shamlu, Ahmad 1925- . . . . **CLC 10**

Shammas, Anton 1951- . . . . **CLC 55**

Shange, Ntozake
  1948- . . . . **CLC 8, 25, 38, 74; BLC; DC 3**
  See also AAYA 9; BW 2; CA 85-88;
  CABS 3; CANR 27, 48; DAM DRAM,
  MULT; DLB 38; MTCW

Shanley, John Patrick 1950- . . . . **CLC 75**
  See also CA 128; 133

Shapcott, Thomas W(illiam) 1935- . . **CLC 38**
  See also CA 69-72; CANR 49

Shapiro, Jane . . . . **CLC 76**

Shapiro, Karl (Jay) 1913- . . **CLC 4, 8, 15, 53**
  See also CA 1-4R; CAAS 6; CANR 1, 36;
  DLB 48; MTCW

Sharp, William 1855-1905 . . . . **TCLC 39**
  See also DLB 156

Sharpe, Thomas Ridley 1928-
  See Sharpe, Tom
  See also CA 114; 122; INT 122

Sharpe, Tom . . . . **CLC 36**
  See also Sharpe, Thomas Ridley
  See also DLB 14

Shaw, Bernard . . . . **TCLC 45**
  See also Shaw, George Bernard
  See also BW 1

Shaw, G. Bernard
  See Shaw, George Bernard

Shaw, George Bernard
   1856-1950 ... **TCLC 3, 9, 21; DA; DAB;**
                                        DAC; WLC
   See also Shaw, Bernard
   See also CA 104; 128; CDBLB 1914-1945;
   DAM DRAM, MST; DLB 10, 57;
   MTCW

Shaw, Henry Wheeler
   1818-1885 .... **NCLC 15**
   See also DLB 11

Shaw, Irwin   1913-1984...... **CLC 7, 23, 34**
   See also AITN 1; CA 13-16R; 112;
   CANR 21; CDALB 1941-1968;
   DAM DRAM, POP; DLB 6, 102;
   DLBY 84; MTCW

Shaw, Robert   1927-1978 .... **CLC 5**
   See also AITN 1; CA 1-4R; 81-84;
   CANR 4; DLB 13, 14

Shaw, T. E.
   See Lawrence, T(homas) E(dward)

Shawn, Wallace   1943- .... **CLC 41**
   See also CA 112

Shea, Lisa   1953-................ **CLC 86**
   See also CA 147

Sheed, Wilfrid (John Joseph)
   1930-............... **CLC 2, 4, 10, 53**
   See also CA 65-68; CANR 30; DLB 6;
   MTCW

Sheldon, Alice Hastings Bradley
   1915(?)-1987
   See Tiptree, James, Jr.
   See also CA 108; 122; CANR 34; INT 108;
   MTCW

Sheldon, John
   See Bloch, Robert (Albert)

Shelley, Mary Wollstonecraft (Godwin)
   1797-1851 ...... **NCLC 14; DA; DAB;**
                                        DAC; WLC
   See also CDBLB 1789-1832; DAM MST,
   NOV; DLB 110, 116, 159; SATA 29

Shelley, Percy Bysshe
   1792-1822 ...... **NCLC 18; DA; DAB;**
                                        DAC; PC 14; WLC
   See also CDBLB 1789-1832; DAM MST,
   POET; DLB 96, 110, 158

Shepard, Jim   1956-................ **CLC 36**
   See also CA 137

Shepard, Lucius   1947- .... **CLC 34**
   See also CA 128; 141

Shepard, Sam
   1943- .... **CLC 4, 6, 17, 34, 41, 44; DC 5**
   See also AAYA 1; CA 69-72; CABS 3;
   CANR 22; DAM DRAM; DLB 7;
   MTCW

Shepherd, Michael
   See Ludlum, Robert

Sherburne, Zoa (Morin)   1912-...... **CLC 30**
   See also AAYA 13; CA 1-4R; CANR 3, 37;
   MAICYA; SAAS 18; SATA 3

Sheridan, Frances   1724-1766........ **LC 7**
   See also DLB 39, 84

Sheridan, Richard Brinsley
   1751-1816 .... **NCLC 5; DA; DAB;**
                                        DAC; DC 1; WLC
   See also CDBLB 1660-1789; DAM DRAM,
   MST; DLB 89

Sherman, Jonathan Marc .... **CLC 55**

Sherman, Martin   1941(?)- .... **CLC 19**
   See also CA 116; 123

Sherwin, Judith Johnson   1936-... **CLC 7, 15**
   See also CA 25-28R; CANR 34

Sherwood, Frances   1940-.......... **CLC 81**
   See also CA 146

Sherwood, Robert E(mmet)
   1896-1955 .... **TCLC 3**
   See also CA 104; DAM DRAM; DLB 7, 26

Shestov, Lev   1866-1938 .... **TCLC 56**

Shevchenko, Taras   1814-1861 .... **NCLC 54**

Shiel, M(atthew) P(hipps)
   1865-1947 .... **TCLC 8**
   See also CA 106; DLB 153

Shields, Carol   1935-......... **CLC 91; DAC**
   See also CA 81-84

Shiga, Naoya   1883-1971........... **CLC 33**
   See also CA 101; 33-36R

Shilts, Randy   1951-1994 .... **CLC 85**
   See also CA 115; 127; 144; CANR 45;
   INT 127

Shimazaki Haruki   1872-1943
   See Shimazaki Toson
   See also CA 105; 134

Shimazaki Toson .... **TCLC 5**
   See also Shimazaki Haruki

Sholokhov, Mikhail (Aleksandrovich)
   1905-1984 .... **CLC 7, 15**
   See also CA 101; 112; MTCW;
   SATA-Obit 36

Shone, Patric
   See Hanley, James

Shreve, Susan Richards   1939-...... **CLC 23**
   See also CA 49-52; CAAS 5; CANR 5, 38;
   MAICYA; SATA 46; SATA-Brief 41

Shue, Larry   1946-1985............ **CLC 52**
   See also CA 145; 117; DAM DRAM

Shu-Jen, Chou   1881-1936
   See Lu Hsun
   See also CA 104

Shulman, Alix Kates   1932- ...... **CLC 2, 10**
   See also CA 29-32R; CANR 43; SATA 7

Shuster, Joe   1914- .... **CLC 21**

Shute, Nevil .... **CLC 30**
   See also Norway, Nevil Shute

Shuttle, Penelope (Diane)   1947- ..... **CLC 7**
   See also CA 93-96; CANR 39; DLB 14, 40

Sidney, Mary   1561-1621 .... **LC 19**

Sidney, Sir Philip
   1554-1586 ..... **LC 19; DA; DAB; DAC**
   See also CDBLB Before 1660; DAM MST,
   POET

Siegel, Jerome   1914- .... **CLC 21**
   See also CA 116

Siegel, Jerry
   See Siegel, Jerome

Sienkiewicz, Henryk (Adam Alexander Pius)
   1846-1916 .... **TCLC 3**
   See also CA 104; 134

Sierra, Gregorio Martinez
   See Martinez Sierra, Gregorio

Sierra, Maria (de la O'LeJarraga) Martinez
   See Martinez Sierra, Maria (de la
   O'LeJarraga)

Sigal, Clancy   1926-............... **CLC 7**
   See also CA 1-4R

Sigourney, Lydia Howard (Huntley)
   1791-1865 .... **NCLC 21**
   See also DLB 1, 42, 73

Siguenza y Gongora, Carlos de
   1645-1700 .... **LC 8**

Sigurjonsson, Johann   1880-1919... **TCLC 27**

Sikelianos, Angelos   1884-1951 .... **TCLC 39**

Silkin, Jon   1930- .... **CLC 2, 6, 43**
   See also CA 5-8R; CAAS 5; DLB 27

Silko, Leslie (Marmon)
   1948-.......... **CLC 23, 74; DA; DAC**
   See also AAYA 14; CA 115; 122;
   CANR 45; DAM MST, MULT, POP;
   DLB 143; NNAL

Sillanpaa, Frans Eemil   1888-1964... **CLC 19**
   See also CA 129; 93-96; MTCW

Sillitoe, Alan
   1928- .... **CLC 1, 3, 6, 10, 19, 57**
   See also AITN 1; CA 9-12R; CAAS 2;
   CANR 8, 26; CDBLB 1960 to Present;
   DLB 14, 139; MTCW; SATA 61

Silone, Ignazio   1900-1978 .... **CLC 4**
   See also CA 25-28; 81-84; CANR 34;
   CAP 2; MTCW

Silver, Joan Micklin   1935- .... **CLC 20**
   See also CA 114; 121; INT 121

Silver, Nicholas
   See Faust, Frederick (Schiller)

Silverberg, Robert   1935- .... **CLC 7**
   See also CA 1-4R; CAAS 3; CANR 1, 20,
   36; DAM POP; DLB 8; INT CANR-20;
   MAICYA; MTCW; SATA 13

Silverstein, Alvin   1933- .... **CLC 17**
   See also CA 49-52; CANR 2; CLR 25;
   JRDA; MAICYA; SATA 8, 69

Silverstein, Virginia B(arbara Opshelor)
   1937-...................... **CLC 17**
   See also CA 49-52; CANR 2; CLR 25;
   JRDA; MAICYA; SATA 8, 69

Sim, Georges
   See Simenon, Georges (Jacques Christian)

Simak, Clifford D(onald)
   1904-1988 .... **CLC 1, 55**
   See also CA 1-4R; 125; CANR 1, 35;
   DLB 8; MTCW; SATA-Obit 56

Simenon, Georges (Jacques Christian)
   1903-1989 .... **CLC 1, 2, 3, 8, 18, 47**
   See also CA 85-88; 129; CANR 35;
   DAM POP; DLB 72; DLBY 89; MTCW

Simic, Charles   1938-... **CLC 6, 9, 22, 49, 68**
   See also CA 29-32R; CAAS 4; CANR 12,
   33; DAM POET; DLB 105

Simmons, Charles (Paul)   1924-..... **CLC 57**
   See also CA 89-92; INT 89-92

Simmons, Dan   1948-............. **CLC 44**
   See also AAYA 16; CA 138; DAM POP

Simmons, James (Stewart Alexander)
   1933-...................... **CLC 43**
   See also CA 105; CAAS 21; DLB 40**

Simms, William Gilmore
1806-1870 . . . . **NCLC 3**
See also DLB 3, 30, 59, 73

Simon, Carly 1945- . . . . **CLC 26**
See also CA 105

Simon, Claude 1913- . . . . . . **CLC 4, 9, 15, 39**
See also CA 89-92; CANR 33; DAM NOV;
DLB 83; MTCW

Simon, (Marvin) Neil
1927- . . . . **CLC 6, 11, 31, 39, 70**
See also AITN 1; CA 21-24R; CANR 26;
DAM DRAM; DLB 7; MTCW

Simon, Paul 1942(?)- . . . . **CLC 17**
See also CA 116

Simonon, Paul 1956(?)- . . . . **CLC 30**

Simpson, Harriette
See Arnow, Harriette (Louisa) Simpson

Simpson, Louis (Aston Marantz)
1923- . . . . **CLC 4, 7, 9, 32**
See also CA 1-4R; CAAS 4; CANR 1;
DAM POET; DLB 5; MTCW

Simpson, Mona (Elizabeth) 1957- . . . **CLC 44**
See also CA 122; 135

Simpson, N(orman) F(rederick)
1919- . . . . **CLC 29**
See also CA 13-16R; DLB 13

Sinclair, Andrew (Annandale)
1935- . . . . **CLC 2, 14**
See also CA 9-12R; CAAS 5; CANR 14, 38;
DLB 14; MTCW

Sinclair, Emil
See Hesse, Hermann

Sinclair, Iain 1943- . . . . **CLC 76**
See also CA 132

Sinclair, Iain MacGregor
See Sinclair, Iain

Sinclair, Mary Amelia St. Clair 1865(?)-1946
See Sinclair, May
See also CA 104

Sinclair, May . . . . **TCLC 3, 11**
See also Sinclair, Mary Amelia St. Clair
See also DLB 36, 135

Sinclair, Upton (Beall)
1878-1968 . . . . . . **CLC 1, 11, 15, 63; DA;**
DAB; DAC; WLC
See also CA 5-8R; 25-28R; CANR 7;
CDALB 1929-1941; DAM MST, NOV;
DLB 9; INT CANR-7; MTCW; SATA 9

Singer, Isaac
See Singer, Isaac Bashevis

Singer, Isaac Bashevis
1904-1991 . . . . **CLC 1, 3, 6, 9, 11, 15, 23,**
38, 69; DA; DAB; DAC; SSC 3; WLC
See also AITN 1, 2; CA 1-4R; 134;
CANR 1, 39; CDALB 1941-1968; CLR 1;
DAM MST, NOV; DLB 6, 28, 52;
DLBY 91; JRDA; MAICYA; MTCW;
SATA 3, 27; SATA-Obit 68

Singer, Israel Joshua 1893-1944 . . . **TCLC 33**

Singh, Khushwant 1915- . . . . **CLC 11**
See also CA 9-12R; CAAS 9; CANR 6

Sinjohn, John
See Galsworthy, John

Sinyavsky, Andrei (Donatevich)
1925- . . . . **CLC 8**
See also CA 85-88

Sirin, V.
See Nabokov, Vladimir (Vladimirovich)

Sissman, L(ouis) E(dward)
1928-1976 . . . . **CLC 9, 18**
See also CA 21-24R; 65-68; CANR 13;
DLB 5

Sisson, C(harles) H(ubert) 1914- . . . . . **CLC 8**
See also CA 1-4R; CAAS 3; CANR 3, 48;
DLB 27

Sitwell, Dame Edith
1887-1964 . . . . **CLC 2, 9, 67; PC 3**
See also CA 9-12R; CANR 35;
CDBLB 1945-1960; DAM POET;
DLB 20; MTCW

Sjoewall, Maj 1935- . . . . **CLC 7**
See also CA 65-68

Sjowall, Maj
See Sjoewall, Maj

Skelton, Robin 1925- . . . . **CLC 13**
See also AITN 2; CA 5-8R; CAAS 5;
CANR 28; DLB 27, 53

Skolimowski, Jerzy 1938- . . . . **CLC 20**
See also CA 128

Skram, Amalie (Bertha)
1847-1905 . . . . **TCLC 25**

Skvorecky, Josef (Vaclav)
1924- . . . . **CLC 15, 39, 69; DAC**
See also CA 61-64; CAAS 1; CANR 10, 34;
DAM NOV; MTCW

Slade, Bernard . . . . **CLC 11, 46**
See also Newbound, Bernard Slade
See also CAAS 9; DLB 53

Slaughter, Carolyn 1946- . . . . **CLC 56**
See also CA 85-88

Slaughter, Frank G(ill) 1908- . . . . . . **CLC 29**
See also AITN 2; CA 5-8R; CANR 5;
INT CANR-5

Slavitt, David R(ytman) 1935- . . . **CLC 5, 14**
See also CA 21-24R; CAAS 3; CANR 41;
DLB 5, 6

Slesinger, Tess 1905-1945 . . . . **TCLC 10**
See also CA 107; DLB 102

Slessor, Kenneth 1901-1971 . . . . **CLC 14**
See also CA 102; 89-92

Slowacki, Juliusz 1809-1849 . . . . . **NCLC 15**

Smart, Christopher
1722-1771 . . . . **LC 3; PC 13**
See also DAM POET; DLB 109

Smart, Elizabeth 1913-1986 . . . . **CLC 54**
See also CA 81-84; 118; DLB 88

Smiley, Jane (Graves) 1949- . . . . **CLC 53, 76**
See also CA 104; CANR 30, 50;
DAM POP; INT CANR-30

Smith, A(rthur) J(ames) M(arshall)
1902-1980 . . . . **CLC 15; DAC**
See also CA 1-4R; 102; CANR 4; DLB 88

Smith, Anna Deavere 1950- . . . . **CLC 86**
See also CA 133

Smith, Betty (Wehner) 1896-1972 . . . **CLC 19**
See also CA 5-8R; 33-36R; DLBY 82;
SATA 6

Smith, Charlotte (Turner)
1749-1806 . . . . **NCLC 23**
See also DLB 39, 109

Smith, Clark Ashton 1893-1961 . . . . **CLC 43**
See also CA 143

Smith, Dave . . . . **CLC 22, 42**
See also Smith, David (Jeddie)
See also CAAS 7; DLB 5

Smith, David (Jeddie) 1942-
See Smith, Dave
See also CA 49-52; CANR 1; DAM POET

Smith, Florence Margaret 1902-1971
See Smith, Stevie
See also CA 17-18; 29-32R; CANR 35;
CAP 2; DAM POET; MTCW

Smith, Iain Crichton 1928- . . . . **CLC 64**
See also CA 21-24R; DLB 40, 139

Smith, John 1580(?)-1631 . . . . **LC 9**

Smith, Johnston
See Crane, Stephen (Townley)

Smith, Joseph, Jr. 1805-1844 . . . . **NCLC 53**

Smith, Lee 1944- . . . . **CLC 25, 73**
See also CA 114; 119; CANR 46; DLB 143;
DLBY 83; INT 119

Smith, Martin
See Smith, Martin Cruz

Smith, Martin Cruz 1942- . . . . **CLC 25**
See also BEST 89:4; CA 85-88; CANR 6,
23, 43; DAM MULT, POP;
INT CANR-23; NNAL

Smith, Mary-Ann Tirone 1944- . . . . . **CLC 39**
See also CA 118; 136

Smith, Patti 1946- . . . . **CLC 12**
See also CA 93-96

Smith, Pauline (Urmson)
1882-1959 . . . . **TCLC 25**

Smith, Rosamond
See Oates, Joyce Carol

Smith, Sheila Kaye
See Kaye-Smith, Sheila

Smith, Stevie . . . . **CLC 3, 8, 25, 44; PC 12**
See also Smith, Florence Margaret
See also DLB 20

Smith, Wilbur (Addison) 1933- . . . . . **CLC 33**
See also CA 13-16R; CANR 7, 46; MTCW

Smith, William Jay 1918- . . . . **CLC 6**
See also CA 5-8R; CANR 44; DLB 5;
MAICYA; SAAS 22; SATA 2, 68

Smith, Woodrow Wilson
See Kuttner, Henry

Smolenskin, Peretz 1842-1885 . . . . **NCLC 30**

Smollett, Tobias (George) 1721-1771 . . **LC 2**
See also CDBLB 1660-1789; DLB 39, 104

Snodgrass, W(illiam) D(e Witt)
1926- . . . . **CLC 2, 6, 10, 18, 68**
See also CA 1-4R; CANR 6, 36;
DAM POET; DLB 5; MTCW

Snow, C(harles) P(ercy)
1905-1980 . . . . . . **CLC 1, 4, 6, 9, 13, 19**
See also CA 5-8R; 101; CANR 28;
CDBLB 1945-1960; DAM NOV; DLB 15,
77; MTCW

Snow, Frances Compton
See Adams, Henry (Brooks)

Stannard, Martin 1947- . . . . **CLC 44**
See also CA 142; DLB 155

Stanton, Maura 1946- . . . . **CLC 9**
See also CA 89-92; CANR 15; DLB 120

Stanton, Schuyler
See Baum, L(yman) Frank

Stapledon, (William) Olaf
1886-1950 . . . . **TCLC 22**
See also CA 111; DLB 15

Starbuck, George (Edwin) 1931- . . . . **CLC 53**
See also CA 21-24R; CANR 23;
DAM POET

Stark, Richard
See Westlake, Donald E(dwin)

Staunton, Schuyler
See Baum, L(yman) Frank

Stead, Christina (Ellen)
1902-1983 . . . . **CLC 2, 5, 8, 32, 80**
See also CA 13-16R; 109; CANR 33, 40;
MTCW

Stead, William Thomas
1849-1912 . . . . **TCLC 48**

Steele, Richard 1672-1729 . . . . **LC 18**
See also CDBLB 1660-1789; DLB 84, 101

Steele, Timothy (Reid) 1948- . . . . **CLC 45**
See also CA 93-96; CANR 16, 50; DLB 120

Steffens, (Joseph) Lincoln
1866-1936 . . . . **TCLC 20**
See also CA 117

Stegner, Wallace (Earle)
1909-1993 . . . . **CLC 9, 49, 81**
See also AITN 1; BEST 90:3; CA 1-4R;
141; CAAS 9; CANR 1, 21, 46;
DAM NOV; DLB 9; DLBY 93; MTCW

Stein, Gertrude
1874-1946 . . . . . . **TCLC 1, 6, 28, 48; DA;
DAB; DAC; WLC**
See also CA 104; 132; CDALB 1917-1929;
DAM MST, NOV, POET; DLB 4, 54, 86;
MTCW

Steinbeck, John (Ernst)
1902-1968 . . . . . . **CLC 1, 5, 9, 13, 21, 34,
45, 75; DA; DAB; DAC; SSC 11; WLC**
See also AAYA 12; CA 1-4R; 25-28R;
CANR 1, 35; CDALB 1929-1941;
DAM DRAM, MST, NOV; DLB 7, 9;
DLBD 2; MTCW; SATA 9

Steinem, Gloria 1934- . . . . **CLC 63**
See also CA 53-56; CANR 28; MTCW

Steiner, George 1929- . . . . **CLC 24**
See also CA 73-76; CANR 31; DAM NOV;
DLB 67; MTCW; SATA 62

Steiner, K. Leslie
See Delany, Samuel R(ay, Jr.)

Steiner, Rudolf 1861-1925 . . . . **TCLC 13**
See also CA 107

Stendhal
1783-1842 . . . . **NCLC 23, 46; DA; DAB;
DAC; WLC**
See also DAM MST, NOV; DLB 119

Stephen, Leslie 1832-1904 . . . . **TCLC 23**
See also CA 123; DLB 57, 144

Stephen, Sir Leslie
See Stephen, Leslie

Stephen, Virginia
See Woolf, (Adeline) Virginia

Stephens, James 1882(?)-1950 . . . . . . **TCLC 4**
See also CA 104; DLB 19, 153, 162

Stephens, Reed
See Donaldson, Stephen R.

Steptoe, Lydia
See Barnes, Djuna

Sterchi, Beat 1949- . . . . **CLC 65**

Sterling, Brett
See Bradbury, Ray (Douglas); Hamilton,
Edmond

Sterling, Bruce 1954- . . . . **CLC 72**
See also CA 119; CANR 44

Sterling, George 1869-1926 . . . . **TCLC 20**
See also CA 117; DLB 54

Stern, Gerald 1925- . . . . **CLC 40**
See also CA 81-84; CANR 28; DLB 105

Stern, Richard (Gustave) 1928- . . . **CLC 4, 39**
See also CA 1-4R; CANR 1, 25; DLBY 87;
INT CANR-25

Sternberg, Josef von 1894-1969 . . . . . **CLC 20**
See also CA 81-84

Sterne, Laurence
1713-1768 . . . . . . **LC 2; DA; DAB; DAC;
WLC**
See also CDBLB 1660-1789; DAM MST,
NOV; DLB 39

Sternheim, (William Adolf) Carl
1878-1942 . . . . **TCLC 8**
See also CA 105; DLB 56, 118

Stevens, Mark 1951- . . . . **CLC 34**
See also CA 122

Stevens, Wallace
1879-1955 . . . . **TCLC 3, 12, 45; DA;
DAB; DAC; PC 6; WLC**
See also CA 104; 124; CDALB 1929-1941;
DAM MST, POET; DLB 54; MTCW

Stevenson, Anne (Katharine)
1933- . . . . **CLC 7, 33**
See also CA 17-20R; CAAS 9; CANR 9, 33;
DLB 40; MTCW

Stevenson, Robert Louis (Balfour)
1850-1894 . . . . . **NCLC 5, 14; DA; DAB;
DAC; SSC 11; WLC**
See also CDBLB 1890-1914; CLR 10, 11;
DAM MST, NOV; DLB 18, 57, 141, 156;
DLBD 13; JRDA; MAICYA; YABC 2

Stewart, J(ohn) I(nnes) M(ackintosh)
1906-1994 . . . . **CLC 7, 14, 32**
See also CA 85-88; 147; CAAS 3;
CANR 47; MTCW

Stewart, Mary (Florence Elinor)
1916- . . . . **CLC 7, 35; DAB**
See also CA 1-4R; CANR 1; SATA 12

Stewart, Mary Rainbow
See Stewart, Mary (Florence Elinor)

Stifle, June
See Campbell, Maria

Stifter, Adalbert 1805-1868 . . . . . . **NCLC 41**
See also DLB 133

Still, James 1906- . . . . **CLC 49**
See also CA 65-68; CAAS 17; CANR 10,
26; DLB 9; SATA 29

Sting
See Sumner, Gordon Matthew

Stirling, Arthur
See Sinclair, Upton (Beall)

Stitt, Milan 1941- . . . . **CLC 29**
See also CA 69-72

Stockton, Francis Richard 1834-1902
See Stockton, Frank R.
See also CA 108; 137; MAICYA; SATA 44

Stockton, Frank R. . . . . **TCLC 47**
See also Stockton, Francis Richard
See also DLB 42, 74; DLBD 13;
SATA-Brief 32

Stoddard, Charles
See Kuttner, Henry

Stoker, Abraham 1847-1912
See Stoker, Bram
See also CA 105; DA; DAC; DAM MST,
NOV; SATA 29

Stoker, Bram . . . . **TCLC 8; DAB; WLC**
See also Stoker, Abraham
See also CDBLB 1890-1914; DLB 36, 70

Stolz, Mary (Slattery) 1920- . . . . **CLC 12**
See also AAYA 8; AITN 1; CA 5-8R;
CANR 13, 41; JRDA; MAICYA;
SAAS 3; SATA 10, 71

Stone, Irving 1903-1989 . . . . **CLC 7**
See also AITN 1; CA 1-4R; 129; CAAS 3;
CANR 1, 23; DAM POP;
INT CANR-23; MTCW; SATA 3;
SATA-Obit 64

Stone, Oliver 1946- . . . . **CLC 73**
See also AAYA 15; CA 110

Stone, Robert (Anthony)
1937- . . . . **CLC 5, 23, 42**
See also CA 85-88; CANR 23; DLB 152;
INT CANR-23; MTCW

Stone, Zachary
See Follett, Ken(neth Martin)

Stoppard, Tom
1937- . . . . . . **CLC 1, 3, 4, 5, 8, 15, 29, 34,
63, 91; DA; DAB; DAC; DC 6; WLC**
See also CA 81-84; CANR 39;
CDBLB 1960 to Present; DAM DRAM,
MST; DLB 13; DLBY 85; MTCW

Storey, David (Malcolm)
1933- . . . . **CLC 2, 4, 5, 8**
See also CA 81-84; CANR 36;
DAM DRAM; DLB 13, 14; MTCW

Storm, Hyemeyohsts 1935- . . . . **CLC 3**
See also CA 81-84; CANR 45;
DAM MULT; NNAL

Storm, (Hans) Theodor (Woldsen)
1817-1888 . . . . **NCLC 1**

Storni, Alfonsina
1892-1938 . . . . **TCLC 5; HLC**
See also CA 104; 131; DAM MULT; HW

Stout, Rex (Todhunter) 1886-1975 . . . **CLC 3**
See also AITN 2; CA 61-64

Stow, (Julian) Randolph 1935- . . **CLC 23, 48**
See also CA 13-16R; CANR 33; MTCW

Tallent, Elizabeth (Ann) 1954- ..... **CLC 45**
See also CA 117; DLB 130

Tally, Ted 1952- .... **CLC 42**
See also CA 120; 124; INT 124

Tamayo y Baus, Manuel
1829-1898 .... **NCLC 1**

Tammsaare, A(nton) H(ansen)
1878-1940 .... **TCLC 27**

Tan, Amy 1952- .... **CLC 59**
See also AAYA 9; BEST 89:3; CA 136;
DAM MULT, NOV, POP; SATA 75

Tandem, Felix
See Spitteler, Carl (Friedrich Georg)

Tanizaki, Jun'ichiro
1886-1965 ...... **CLC 8, 14, 28; SSC 21**
See also CA 93-96; 25-28R

Tanner, William
See Amis, Kingsley (William)

Tao Lao
See Storni, Alfonsina

Tarassoff, Lev
See Troyat, Henri

Tarbell, Ida M(inerva)
1857-1944 .... **TCLC 40**
See also CA 122; DLB 47

Tarkington, (Newton) Booth
1869-1946 .... **TCLC 9**
See also CA 110; 143; DLB 9, 102;
SATA 17

Tarkovsky, Andrei (Arsenyevich)
1932-1986 .... **CLC 75**
See also CA 127

Tartt, Donna 1964(?)- .... **CLC 76**
See also CA 142

Tasso, Torquato 1544-1595 .... **LC 5**

Tate, (John Orley) Allen
1899-1979 .... **CLC 2, 4, 6, 9, 11, 14, 24**
See also CA 5-8R; 85-88; CANR 32;
DLB 4, 45, 63; MTCW

Tate, Ellalice
See Hibbert, Eleanor Alice Burford

Tate, James (Vincent) 1943- ... **CLC 2, 6, 25**
See also CA 21-24R; CANR 29; DLB 5

Tavel, Ronald 1940- .... **CLC 6**
See also CA 21-24R; CANR 33

Taylor, C(ecil) P(hilip) 1929-1981 ... **CLC 27**
See also CA 25-28R; 105; CANR 47

Taylor, Edward
1642(?)-1729 ... **LC 11; DA; DAB; DAC**
See also DAM MST, POET; DLB 24

Taylor, Eleanor Ross 1920- .... **CLC 5**
See also CA 81-84

Taylor, Elizabeth 1912-1975 ... **CLC 2, 4, 29**
See also CA 13-16R; CANR 9; DLB 139;
MTCW; SATA 13

Taylor, Henry (Splawn) 1942- ...... **CLC 44**
See also CA 33-36R; CAAS 7; CANR 31;
DLB 5

Taylor, Kamala (Purnaiya) 1924-
See Markandaya, Kamala
See also CA 77-80

Taylor, Mildred D. .... **CLC 21**
See also AAYA 10; BW 1; CA 85-88;
CANR 25; CLR 9; DLB 52; JRDA;
MAICYA; SAAS 5; SATA 15, 70

Taylor, Peter (Hillsman)
1917-1994 ..... **CLC 1, 4, 18, 37, 44, 50,
71; SSC 10**
See also CA 13-16R; 147; CANR 9, 50;
DLBY 81, 94; INT CANR-9; MTCW

Taylor, Robert Lewis 1912- .... **CLC 14**
See also CA 1-4R; CANR 3; SATA 10

Tchekhov, Anton
See Chekhov, Anton (Pavlovich)

Teasdale, Sara 1884-1933 .... **TCLC 4**
See also CA 104; DLB 45; SATA 32

Tegner, Esaias 1782-1846 .... **NCLC 2**

Teilhard de Chardin, (Marie Joseph) Pierre
1881-1955 .... **TCLC 9**
See also CA 105

Temple, Ann
See Mortimer, Penelope (Ruth)

Tennant, Emma (Christina)
1937- .... **CLC 13, 52**
See also CA 65-68; CAAS 9; CANR 10, 38;
DLB 14

Tenneshaw, S. M.
See Silverberg, Robert

Tennyson, Alfred
1809-1892 .... **NCLC 30; DA; DAB;
DAC; PC 6; WLC**
See also CDBLB 1832-1890; DAM MST,
POET; DLB 32

Teran, Lisa St. Aubin de .... **CLC 36**
See also St. Aubin de Teran, Lisa

Terence 195(?)B.C.-159B.C. ...... **CMLC 14**

Teresa de Jesus, St. 1515-1582 ...... **LC 18**

Terkel, Louis 1912-
See Terkel, Studs
See also CA 57-60; CANR 18, 45; MTCW

Terkel, Studs .... **CLC 38**
See also Terkel, Louis
See also AITN 1

Terry, C. V.
See Slaughter, Frank G(ill)

Terry, Megan 1932- .... **CLC 19**
See also CA 77-80; CABS 3; CANR 43;
DLB 7

Tertz, Abram
See Sinyavsky, Andrei (Donatevich)

Tesich, Steve 1943(?)- .... **CLC 40, 69**
See also CA 105; DLBY 83

Teternikov, Fyodor Kuzmich 1863-1927
See Sologub, Fyodor
See also CA 104

Tevis, Walter 1928-1984 .... **CLC 42**
See also CA 113

Tey, Josephine .... **TCLC 14**
See also Mackintosh, Elizabeth
See also DLB 77

Thackeray, William Makepeace
1811-1863 .... **NCLC 5, 14, 22, 43; DA;
DAB; DAC; WLC**
See also CDBLB 1832-1890; DAM MST,
NOV; DLB 21, 55, 159; SATA 23

Thakura, Ravindranatha
See Tagore, Rabindranath

Tharoor, Shashi 1956- .... **CLC 70**
See also CA 141

Thelwell, Michael Miles 1939- ..... **CLC 22**
See also BW 2; CA 101

Theobald, Lewis, Jr.
See Lovecraft, H(oward) P(hillips)

Theodorescu, Ion N. 1880-1967
See Arghezi, Tudor
See also CA 116

Theriault, Yves 1915-1983 .... **CLC 79; DAC**
See also CA 102; DAM MST; DLB 88

Theroux, Alexander (Louis)
1939- .... **CLC 2, 25**
See also CA 85-88; CANR 20

Theroux, Paul (Edward)
1941- .... **CLC 5, 8, 11, 15, 28, 46**
See also BEST 89:4; CA 33-36R; CANR 20,
45; DAM POP; DLB 2; MTCW;
SATA 44

Thesen, Sharon 1946- .... **CLC 56**

Thevenin, Denis
See Duhamel, Georges

Thibault, Jacques Anatole Francois
1844-1924
See France, Anatole
See also CA 106; 127; DAM NOV; MTCW

Thiele, Colin (Milton) 1920- .... **CLC 17**
See also CA 29-32R; CANR 12, 28;
CLR 27; MAICYA; SAAS 2; SATA 14,
72

Thomas, Audrey (Callahan)
1935- .... **CLC 7, 13, 37; SSC 20**
See also AITN 2; CA 21-24R; CAAS 19;
CANR 36; DLB 60; MTCW

Thomas, D(onald) M(ichael)
1935- .... **CLC 13, 22, 31**
See also CA 61-64; CAAS 11; CANR 17,
45; CDBLB 1960 to Present; DLB 40;
INT CANR-17; MTCW

Thomas, Dylan (Marlais)
1914-1953 ... **TCLC 1, 8, 45; DA; DAB;
DAC; PC 2; SSC 3; WLC**
See also CA 104; 120; CDBLB 1945-1960;
DAM DRAM, MST, POET; DLB 13, 20,
139; MTCW; SATA 60

Thomas, (Philip) Edward
1878-1917 .... **TCLC 10**
See also CA 106; DAM POET; DLB 19

Thomas, Joyce Carol 1938- .... **CLC 35**
See also AAYA 12; BW 2; CA 113; 116;
CANR 48; CLR 19; DLB 33; INT 116;
JRDA; MAICYA; MTCW; SAAS 7;
SATA 40, 78

Thomas, Lewis 1913-1993 .... **CLC 35**
See also CA 85-88; 143; CANR 38; MTCW

Thomas, Paul
See Mann, (Paul) Thomas

Thomas, Piri 1928- .... **CLC 17**
See also CA 73-76; HW

Thomas, R(onald) S(tuart)
1913- .... **CLC 6, 13, 48; DAB**
See also CA 89-92; CAAS 4; CANR 30;
CDBLB 1960 to Present; DAM POET;
DLB 27; MTCW

Trogdon, William (Lewis) 1939-
See Heat-Moon, William Least
See also CA 115; 119; CANR 47; INT 119

Trollope, Anthony
1815-1882 . . . . . **NCLC 6, 33; DA; DAB;
DAC; WLC**
See also CDBLB 1832-1890; DAM MST,
NOV; DLB 21, 57, 159; SATA 22

Trollope, Frances 1779-1863 . . . . . **NCLC 30**
See also DLB 21

Trotsky, Leon 1879-1940 . . . . **TCLC 22**
See also CA 118

Trotter (Cockburn), Catharine
1679-1749 . . . . **LC 8**
See also DLB 84

Trout, Kilgore
See Farmer, Philip Jose

Trow, George W. S. 1943- . . . . **CLC 52**
See also CA 126

Troyat, Henri 1911- . . . . **CLC 23**
See also CA 45-48; CANR 2, 33; MTCW

Trudeau, G(arretson) B(eekman) 1948-
See Trudeau, Garry B.
See also CA 81-84; CANR 31; SATA 35

Trudeau, Garry B. . . . . **CLC 12**
See also Trudeau, G(arretson) B(eekman)
See also AAYA 10; AITN 2

Truffaut, Francois 1932-1984 . . . . **CLC 20**
See also CA 81-84; 113; CANR 34

Trumbo, Dalton 1905-1976 . . . . **CLC 19**
See also CA 21-24R; 69-72; CANR 10;
DLB 26

Trumbull, John 1750-1831 . . . . . . **NCLC 30**
See also DLB 31

Trundlett, Helen B.
See Eliot, T(homas) S(tearns)

Tryon, Thomas 1926-1991 . . . . **CLC 3, 11**
See also AITN 1; CA 29-32R; 135;
CANR 32; DAM POP; MTCW

Tryon, Tom
See Tryon, Thomas

Ts'ao Hsueh-ch'in 1715(?)-1763 . . . . **LC 1**

Tsushima, Shuji 1909-1948
See Dazai, Osamu
See also CA 107

Tsvetaeva (Efron), Marina (Ivanovna)
1892-1941 . . . . **TCLC 7, 35; PC 14**
See also CA 104; 128; MTCW

Tuck, Lily 1938- . . . . **CLC 70**
See also CA 139

Tu Fu 712-770 . . . . **PC 9**
See also DAM MULT

Tunis, John R(oberts) 1889-1975 . . . **CLC 12**
See also CA 61-64; DLB 22; JRDA;
MAICYA; SATA 37; SATA-Brief 30

Tuohy, Frank . . . . **CLC 37**
See also Tuohy, John Francis
See also DLB 14, 139

Tuohy, John Francis 1925-
See Tuohy, Frank
See also CA 5-8R; CANR 3, 47

Turco, Lewis (Putnam) 1934- . . . **CLC 11, 63**
See also CA 13-16R; CAAS 22; CANR 24;
DLBY 84

Turgenev, Ivan
1818-1883 . . . . . . **NCLC 21; DA; DAB;
DAC; SSC 7; WLC**
See also DAM MST, NOV

Turgot, Anne-Robert-Jacques
1727-1781 . . . . **LC 26**

Turner, Frederick 1943- . . . . **CLC 48**
See also CA 73-76; CAAS 10; CANR 12,
30; DLB 40

Tutu, Desmond M(pilo)
1931- . . . . **CLC 80; BLC**
See also BW 1; CA 125; DAM MULT

Tutuola, Amos 1920- . . . **CLC 5, 14, 29; BLC**
See also BW 2; CA 9-12R; CANR 27;
DAM MULT; DLB 125; MTCW

Twain, Mark
. . . . . **TCLC 6, 12, 19, 36, 48, 59; SSC 6;
WLC**
See also Clemens, Samuel Langhorne
See also DLB 11, 12, 23, 64, 74

Tyler, Anne
1941- . . . . **CLC 7, 11, 18, 28, 44, 59**
See also BEST 89:1; CA 9-12R; CANR 11,
33; DAM NOV, POP; DLB 6, 143;
DLBY 82; MTCW; SATA 7

Tyler, Royall 1757-1826 . . . . **NCLC 3**
See also DLB 37

Tynan, Katharine 1861-1931 . . . . **TCLC 3**
See also CA 104; DLB 153

Tyutchev, Fyodor 1803-1873 . . . . . **NCLC 34**

Tzara, Tristan . . . . **CLC 47**
See also Rosenfeld, Samuel
See also DAM POET

Uhry, Alfred 1936- . . . . **CLC 55**
See also CA 127; 133; DAM DRAM, POP;
INT 133

Ulf, Haerved
See Strindberg, (Johan) August

Ulf, Harved
See Strindberg, (Johan) August

Ulibarri, Sabine R(eyes) 1919- . . . . . **CLC 83**
See also CA 131; DAM MULT; DLB 82;
HW

Unamuno (y Jugo), Miguel de
1864-1936 . . . . **TCLC 2, 9; HLC; SSC 11**
See also CA 104; 131; DAM MULT, NOV;
DLB 108; HW; MTCW

Undercliffe, Errol
See Campbell, (John) Ramsey

Underwood, Miles
See Glassco, John

Undset, Sigrid
1882-1949 . . . . **TCLC 3; DA; DAB;
DAC; WLC**
See also CA 104; 129; DAM MST, NOV;
MTCW

Ungaretti, Giuseppe
1888-1970 . . . . **CLC 7, 11, 15**
See also CA 19-20; 25-28R; CAP 2;
DLB 114

Unger, Douglas 1952- . . . . **CLC 34**
See also CA 130

Unsworth, Barry (Forster) 1930- . . . . **CLC 76**
See also CA 25-28R; CANR 30

Updike, John (Hoyer)
1932- . . . . . . **CLC 1, 2, 3, 5, 7, 9, 13, 15,
23, 34, 43, 70; DA; DAB; DAC; SSC 13;
WLC**
See also CA 1-4R; CABS 1; CANR 4, 33;
CDALB 1968-1988; DAM MST, NOV,
POET, POP; DLB 2, 5, 143; DLBD 3;
DLBY 80, 82; MTCW

Upshaw, Margaret Mitchell
See Mitchell, Margaret (Munnerlyn)

Upton, Mark
See Sanders, Lawrence

Urdang, Constance (Henriette)
1922- . . . . **CLC 47**
See also CA 21-24R; CANR 9, 24

Uriel, Henry
See Faust, Frederick (Schiller)

Uris, Leon (Marcus) 1924- . . . . **CLC 7, 32**
See also AITN 1, 2; BEST 89:2; CA 1-4R;
CANR 1, 40; DAM NOV, POP; MTCW;
SATA 49

Urmuz
See Codrescu, Andrei

Urquhart, Jane 1949- . . . . **CLC 90; DAC**
See also CA 113; CANR 32

Ustinov, Peter (Alexander) 1921- . . . . **CLC 1**
See also AITN 1; CA 13-16R; CANR 25;
DLB 13

Vaculik, Ludvik 1926- . . . . **CLC 7**
See also CA 53-56

Valdez, Luis (Miguel)
1940- . . . . **CLC 84; HLC**
See also CA 101; CANR 32; DAM MULT;
DLB 122; HW

Valenzuela, Luisa 1938- . . . **CLC 31; SSC 14**
See also CA 101; CANR 32; DAM MULT;
DLB 113; HW

Valera y Alcala-Galiano, Juan
1824-1905 . . . . **TCLC 10**
See also CA 106

Valery, (Ambroise) Paul (Toussaint Jules)
1871-1945 . . . . **TCLC 4, 15; PC 9**
See also CA 104; 122; DAM POET; MTCW

Valle-Inclan, Ramon (Maria) del
1866-1936 . . . . **TCLC 5; HLC**
See also CA 106; DAM MULT; DLB 134

Vallejo, Antonio Buero
See Buero Vallejo, Antonio

Vallejo, Cesar (Abraham)
1892-1938 . . . . **TCLC 3, 56; HLC**
See also CA 105; DAM MULT; HW

Valle Y Pena, Ramon del
See Valle-Inclan, Ramon (Maria) del

Van Ash, Cay 1918- . . . . **CLC 34**

Vanbrugh, Sir John 1664-1726 . . . . . . **LC 21**
See also DAM DRAM; DLB 80

Van Campen, Karl
See Campbell, John W(ood, Jr.)

Vance, Gerald
See Silverberg, Robert

Vance, Jack . . . . **CLC 35**
See also Vance, John Holbrook
See also DLB 8

Von Rachen, Kurt
See Hubbard, L(afayette) Ron(ald)

von Rezzori (d'Arezzo), Gregor
See Rezzori (d'Arezzo), Gregor von

von Sternberg, Josef
See Sternberg, Josef von

Vorster, Gordon 1924- . . . . **CLC 34**
See also CA 133

Vosce, Trudie
See Ozick, Cynthia

Voznesensky, Andrei (Andreievich)
1933- . . . . **CLC 1, 15, 57**
See also CA 89-92; CANR 37;
DAM POET; MTCW

Waddington, Miriam 1917- . . . . **CLC 28**
See also CA 21-24R; CANR 12, 30;
DLB 68

Wagman, Fredrica 1937- . . . . **CLC 7**
See also CA 97-100; INT 97-100

Wagner, Richard 1813-1883 . . . . . . **NCLC 9**
See also DLB 129

Wagner-Martin, Linda 1936- . . . . **CLC 50**

Wagoner, David (Russell)
1926- . . . . **CLC 3, 5, 15**
See also CA 1-4R; CAAS 3; CANR 2;
DLB 5; SATA 14

Wah, Fred(erick James) 1939- . . . . . **CLC 44**
See also CA 107; 141; DLB 60

Wahloo, Per 1926-1975 . . . . **CLC 7**
See also CA 61-64

Wahloo, Peter
See Wahloo, Per

Wain, John (Barrington)
1925-1994 . . . . **CLC 2, 11, 15, 46**
See also CA 5-8R; 145; CAAS 4; CANR 23;
CDBLB 1960 to Present; DLB 15, 27,
139, 155; MTCW

Wajda, Andrzej 1926- . . . . **CLC 16**
See also CA 102

Wakefield, Dan 1932- . . . . **CLC 7**
See also CA 21-24R; CAAS 7

Wakoski, Diane
1937- . . . . . **CLC 2, 4, 7, 9, 11, 40; PC 15**
See also CA 13-16R; CAAS 1; CANR 9;
DAM POET; DLB 5; INT CANR-9

Wakoski-Sherbell, Diane
See Wakoski, Diane

Walcott, Derek (Alton)
1930- . . . . **CLC 2, 4, 9, 14, 25, 42, 67, 76;**
BLC; DAB; DAC
See also BW 2; CA 89-92; CANR 26, 47;
DAM MST, MULT, POET; DLB 117;
DLBY 81; MTCW

Waldman, Anne 1945- . . . . **CLC 7**
See also CA 37-40R; CAAS 17; CANR 34;
DLB 16

Waldo, E. Hunter
See Sturgeon, Theodore (Hamilton)

Waldo, Edward Hamilton
See Sturgeon, Theodore (Hamilton)

Walker, Alice (Malsenior)
1944- . . . . **CLC 5, 6, 9, 19, 27, 46, 58;**
BLC; DA; DAB; DAC; SSC 5
See also AAYA 3; BEST 89:4; BW 2;
CA 37-40R; CANR 9, 27, 49;
CDALB 1968-1988; DAM MST, MULT,
NOV, POET, POP; DLB 6, 33, 143;
INT CANR-27; MTCW; SATA 31

Walker, David Harry 1911-1992 . . . . **CLC 14**
See also CA 1-4R; 137; CANR 1; SATA 8;
SATA-Obit 71

Walker, Edward Joseph 1934-
See Walker, Ted
See also CA 21-24R; CANR 12, 28

Walker, George F.
1947- . . . . **CLC 44, 61; DAB; DAC**
See also CA 103; CANR 21, 43;
DAM MST; DLB 60

Walker, Joseph A. 1935- . . . . **CLC 19**
See also BW 1; CA 89-92; CANR 26;
DAM DRAM, MST; DLB 38

Walker, Margaret (Abigail)
1915- . . . . **CLC 1, 6; BLC**
See also BW 2; CA 73-76; CANR 26;
DAM MULT; DLB 76, 152; MTCW

Walker, Ted . . . . **CLC 13**
See also Walker, Edward Joseph
See also DLB 40

Wallace, David Foster 1962- . . . . **CLC 50**
See also CA 132

Wallace, Dexter
See Masters, Edgar Lee

Wallace, (Richard Horatio) Edgar
1875-1932 . . . . **TCLC 57**
See also CA 115; DLB 70

Wallace, Irving 1916-1990 . . . . . . **CLC 7, 13**
See also AITN 1; CA 1-4R; 132; CAAS 1;
CANR 1, 27; DAM NOV, POP;
INT CANR-27; MTCW

Wallant, Edward Lewis
1926-1962 . . . . **CLC 5, 10**
See also CA 1-4R; CANR 22; DLB 2, 28,
143; MTCW

Walley, Byron
See Card, Orson Scott

Walpole, Horace 1717-1797 . . . . **LC 2**
See also DLB 39, 104

Walpole, Hugh (Seymour)
1884-1941 . . . . **TCLC 5**
See also CA 104; DLB 34

Walser, Martin 1927- . . . . **CLC 27**
See also CA 57-60; CANR 8, 46; DLB 75,
124

Walser, Robert
1878-1956 . . . . **TCLC 18; SSC 20**
See also CA 118; DLB 66

Walsh, Jill Paton . . . . **CLC 35**
See also Paton Walsh, Gillian
See also AAYA 11; CLR 2; DLB 161;
SAAS 3

Walter, Villiam Christian
See Andersen, Hans Christian

Wambaugh, Joseph (Aloysius, Jr.)
1937- . . . . **CLC 3, 18**
See also AITN 1; BEST 89:3; CA 33-36R;
CANR 42; DAM NOV, POP; DLB 6;
DLBY 83; MTCW

Ward, Arthur Henry Sarsfield 1883-1959
See Rohmer, Sax
See also CA 108

Ward, Douglas Turner 1930- . . . . **CLC 19**
See also BW 1; CA 81-84; CANR 27;
DLB 7, 38

Ward, Mary Augusta
See Ward, Mrs. Humphry

Ward, Mrs. Humphry
1851-1920 . . . . **TCLC 55**
See also DLB 18

Ward, Peter
See Faust, Frederick (Schiller)

Warhol, Andy 1928(?)-1987 . . . . **CLC 20**
See also AAYA 12; BEST 89:4; CA 89-92;
121; CANR 34

Warner, Francis (Robert le Plastrier)
1937- . . . . **CLC 14**
See also CA 53-56; CANR 11

Warner, Marina 1946- . . . . **CLC 59**
See also CA 65-68; CANR 21

Warner, Rex (Ernest) 1905-1986 . . . . **CLC 45**
See also CA 89-92; 119; DLB 15

Warner, Susan (Bogert)
1819-1885 . . . . **NCLC 31**
See also DLB 3, 42

Warner, Sylvia (Constance) Ashton
See Ashton-Warner, Sylvia (Constance)

Warner, Sylvia Townsend
1893-1978 . . . . **CLC 7, 19**
See also CA 61-64; 77-80; CANR 16;
DLB 34, 139; MTCW

Warren, Mercy Otis 1728-1814 . . . **NCLC 13**
See also DLB 31

Warren, Robert Penn
1905-1989 . . . . **CLC 1, 4, 6, 8, 10, 13, 18,**
39, 53, 59; DA; DAB; DAC; SSC 4; WLC
See also AITN 1; CA 13-16R; 129;
CANR 10, 47; CDALB 1968-1988;
DAM MST, NOV; DLB 2, 48,
152; DLBY 80, 89; INT CANR-10;
MTCW; SATA 46; SATA-Obit 63

Warshofsky, Isaac
See Singer, Isaac Bashevis

Warton, Thomas 1728-1790 . . . . **LC 15**
See also DAM POET; DLB 104, 109

Waruk, Kona
See Harris, (Theodore) Wilson

Warung, Price 1855-1911 . . . . **TCLC 45**

Warwick, Jarvis
See Garner, Hugh

Washington, Alex
See Harris, Mark

Washington, Booker T(aliaferro)
1856-1915 . . . . **TCLC 10; BLC**
See also BW 1; CA 114; 125; DAM MULT;
SATA 28

Washington, George 1732-1799 . . . . . . **LC 25**
See also DLB 31

Wassermann, (Karl) Jakob
1873-1934 . . . . **TCLC 6**
See also CA 104; DLB 66

Wasserstein, Wendy
1950- . . . . **CLC 32, 59, 90; DC 4**
See also CA 121; 129; CABS 3;
DAM DRAM; INT 129

Waterhouse, Keith (Spencer)
1929- . . . . **CLC 47**
See also CA 5-8R; CANR 38; DLB 13, 15;
MTCW

Waters, Frank (Joseph)
1902-1995 . . . . **CLC 88**
See also CA 5-8R; 149; CAAS 13; CANR 3,
18; DLBY 86

Waters, Roger 1944- . . . . **CLC 35**

Watkins, Frances Ellen
See Harper, Frances Ellen Watkins

Watkins, Gerrold
See Malzberg, Barry N(athaniel)

Watkins, Paul 1964- . . . . **CLC 55**
See also CA 132

Watkins, Vernon Phillips
1906-1967 . . . . **CLC 43**
See also CA 9-10; 25-28R; CAP 1; DLB 20

Watson, Irving S.
See Mencken, H(enry) L(ouis)

Watson, John H.
See Farmer, Philip Jose

Watson, Richard F.
See Silverberg, Robert

Waugh, Auberon (Alexander) 1939- . . **CLC 7**
See also CA 45-48; CANR 6, 22; DLB 14

Waugh, Evelyn (Arthur St. John)
1903-1966 . . . . . . **CLC 1, 3, 8, 13, 19, 27,
44; DA; DAB; DAC; WLC**
See also CA 85-88; 25-28R; CANR 22;
CDBLB 1914-1945; DAM MST, NOV,
POP; DLB 15, 162; MTCW

Waugh, Harriet 1944- . . . . **CLC 6**
See also CA 85-88; CANR 22

Ways, C. R.
See Blount, Roy (Alton), Jr.

Waystaff, Simon
See Swift, Jonathan

Webb, (Martha) Beatrice (Potter)
1858-1943 . . . . **TCLC 22**
See also Potter, Beatrice
See also CA 117

Webb, Charles (Richard) 1939- . . . . . . **CLC 7**
See also CA 25-28R

Webb, James H(enry), Jr. 1946- . . . . **CLC 22**
See also CA 81-84

Webb, Mary (Gladys Meredith)
1881-1927 . . . . **TCLC 24**
See also CA 123; DLB 34

Webb, Mrs. Sidney
See Webb, (Martha) Beatrice (Potter)

Webb, Phyllis 1927- . . . . **CLC 18**
See also CA 104; CANR 23; DLB 53

Webb, Sidney (James)
1859-1947 . . . . **TCLC 22**
See also CA 117

Webber, Andrew Lloyd . . . . **CLC 21**
See also Lloyd Webber, Andrew

Weber, Lenora Mattingly
1895-1971 . . . . **CLC 12**
See also CA 19-20; 29-32R; CAP 1;
SATA 2; SATA-Obit 26

Webster, John 1579(?)-1634(?) . . . . **DC 2**
See also CDBLB Before 1660; DA; DAB;
DAC; DAM DRAM, MST; DLB 58;
WLC

Webster, Noah 1758-1843 . . . . **NCLC 30**

Wedekind, (Benjamin) Frank(lin)
1864-1918 . . . . **TCLC 7**
See also CA 104; DAM DRAM; DLB 118

Weidman, Jerome 1913- . . . . **CLC 7**
See also AITN 2; CA 1-4R; CANR 1;
DLB 28

Weil, Simone (Adolphine)
1909-1943 . . . . **TCLC 23**
See also CA 117

Weinstein, Nathan
See West, Nathanael

Weinstein, Nathan von Wallenstein
See West, Nathanael

Weir, Peter (Lindsay) 1944- . . . . **CLC 20**
See also CA 113; 123

Weiss, Peter (Ulrich)
1916-1982 . . . . **CLC 3, 15, 51**
See also CA 45-48; 106; CANR 3;
DAM DRAM; DLB 69, 124

Weiss, Theodore (Russell)
1916- . . . . **CLC 3, 8, 14**
See also CA 9-12R; CAAS 2; CANR 46;
DLB 5

Welch, (Maurice) Denton
1915-1948 . . . . **TCLC 22**
See also CA 121; 148

Welch, James 1940- . . . . **CLC 6, 14, 52**
See also CA 85-88; CANR 42;
DAM MULT, POP; NNAL

Weldon, Fay
1933- . . . . **CLC 6, 9, 11, 19, 36, 59**
See also CA 21-24R; CANR 16, 46;
CDBLB 1960 to Present; DAM POP;
DLB 14; INT CANR-16; MTCW

Wellek, Rene 1903- . . . . **CLC 28**
See also CA 5-8R; CAAS 7; CANR 8;
DLB 63; INT CANR-8

Weller, Michael 1942- . . . . **CLC 10, 53**
See also CA 85-88

Weller, Paul 1958- . . . . **CLC 26**

Wellershoff, Dieter 1925- . . . . **CLC 46**
See also CA 89-92; CANR 16, 37

Welles, (George) Orson
1915-1985 . . . . **CLC 20, 80**
See also CA 93-96; 117

Wellman, Mac 1945- . . . . **CLC 65**

Wellman, Manly Wade 1903-1986 . . **CLC 49**
See also CA 1-4R; 118; CANR 6, 16, 44;
SATA 6; SATA-Obit 47

Wells, Carolyn 1869(?)-1942 . . . . . . **TCLC 35**
See also CA 113; DLB 11

Wells, H(erbert) G(eorge)
1866-1946 . . . . **TCLC 6, 12, 19; DA;
DAB; DAC; SSC 6; WLC**
See also CA 110; 121; CDBLB 1914-1945;
DAM MST, NOV; DLB 34, 70, 156;
MTCW; SATA 20

Wells, Rosemary 1943- . . . . **CLC 12**
See also AAYA 13; CA 85-88; CANR 48;
CLR 16; MAICYA; SAAS 1; SATA 18,
69

Welty, Eudora
1909- . . . . . . **CLC 1, 2, 5, 14, 22, 33; DA;
DAB; DAC; SSC 1; WLC**
See also CA 9-12R; CABS 1; CANR 32;
CDALB 1941-1968; DAM MST, NOV;
DLB 2, 102, 143; DLBD 12; DLBY 87;
MTCW

Wen I-to 1899-1946 . . . . **TCLC 28**

Wentworth, Robert
See Hamilton, Edmond

Werfel, Franz (V.) 1890-1945 . . . . . . **TCLC 8**
See also CA 104; DLB 81, 124

Wergeland, Henrik Arnold
1808-1845 . . . . **NCLC 5**

Wersba, Barbara 1932- . . . . **CLC 30**
See also AAYA 2; CA 29-32R; CANR 16,
38; CLR 3; DLB 52; JRDA; MAICYA;
SAAS 2; SATA 1, 58

Wertmueller, Lina 1928- . . . . **CLC 16**
See also CA 97-100; CANR 39

Wescott, Glenway 1901-1987 . . . . **CLC 13**
See also CA 13-16R; 121; CANR 23;
DLB 4, 9, 102

Wesker, Arnold 1932- . . **CLC 3, 5, 42; DAB**
See also CA 1-4R; CAAS 7; CANR 1, 33;
CDBLB 1960 to Present; DAM DRAM;
DLB 13; MTCW

Wesley, Richard (Errol) 1945- . . . . **CLC 7**
See also BW 1; CA 57-60; CANR 27;
DLB 38

Wessel, Johan Herman 1742-1785 . . . . **LC 7**

West, Anthony (Panther)
1914-1987 . . . . **CLC 50**
See also CA 45-48; 124; CANR 3, 19;
DLB 15

West, C. P.
See Wodehouse, P(elham) G(renville)

West, (Mary) Jessamyn
1902-1984 . . . . **CLC 7, 17**
See also CA 9-12R; 112; CANR 27; DLB 6;
DLBY 84; MTCW; SATA-Obit 37

West, Morris L(anglo) 1916- . . . . . **CLC 6, 33**
See also CA 5-8R; CANR 24, 49; MTCW

West, Nathanael
1903-1940 . . . . . **TCLC 1, 14, 44; SSC 16**
See also CA 104; 125; CDALB 1929-1941;
DLB 4, 9, 28; MTCW

West, Owen
See Koontz, Dean R(ay)

West, Paul 1930- . . . . **CLC 7, 14**
See also CA 13-16R; CAAS 7; CANR 22;
DLB 14; INT CANR-22

West, Rebecca 1892-1983 . . **CLC 7, 9, 31, 50**
See also CA 5-8R; 109; CANR 19; DLB 36;
DLBY 83; MTCW

Westall, Robert (Atkinson)
1929-1993 .... CLC 17
See also AAYA 12; CA 69-72; 141;
CANR 18; CLR 13; JRDA; MAICYA;
SAAS 2; SATA 23, 69; SATA-Obit 75

Westlake, Donald E(dwin)
1933- .... CLC 7, 33
See also CA 17-20R; CAAS 13; CANR 16,
44; DAM POP; INT CANR-16

Westmacott, Mary
See Christie, Agatha (Mary Clarissa)

Weston, Allen
See Norton, Andre

Wetcheek, J. L.
See Feuchtwanger, Lion

Wetering, Janwillem van de
See van de Wetering, Janwillem

Wetherell, Elizabeth
See Warner, Susan (Bogert)

Whalen, Philip 1923- .... CLC 6, 29
See also CA 9-12R; CANR 5, 39; DLB 16

Wharton, Edith (Newbold Jones)
1862-1937 ...... TCLC 3, 9, 27, 53; DA;
DAB; DAC; SSC 6; WLC
See also CA 104; 132; CDALB 1865-1917;
DAM MST, NOV; DLB 4, 9, 12, 78;
DLBD 13; MTCW

Wharton, James
See Mencken, H(enry) L(ouis)

Wharton, William (a pseudonym)
.... CLC 18, 37
See also CA 93-96; DLBY 80; INT 93-96

Wheatley (Peters), Phillis
1754(?)-1784 .... LC 3; BLC; DA; DAC;
PC 3; WLC
See also CDALB 1640-1865; DAM MST,
MULT, POET; DLB 31, 50

Wheelock, John Hall 1886-1978 .... CLC 14
See also CA 13-16R; 77-80; CANR 14;
DLB 45

White, E(lwyn) B(rooks)
1899-1985 .... CLC 10, 34, 39
See also AITN 2; CA 13-16R; 116;
CANR 16, 37; CLR 1, 21; DAM POP;
DLB 11, 22; MAICYA; MTCW;
SATA 2, 29; SATA-Obit 44

White, Edmund (Valentine III)
1940- .... CLC 27
See also AAYA 7; CA 45-48; CANR 3, 19,
36; DAM POP; MTCW

White, Patrick (Victor Martindale)
1912-1990 .. CLC 3, 4, 5, 7, 9, 18, 65, 69
See also CA 81-84; 132; CANR 43; MTCW

White, Phyllis Dorothy James 1920-
See James, P. D.
See also CA 21-24R; CANR 17, 43;
DAM POP; MTCW

White, T(erence) H(anbury)
1906-1964 .... CLC 30
See also CA 73-76; CANR 37; DLB 160;
JRDA; MAICYA; SATA 12

White, Terence de Vere
1912-1994 .... CLC 49
See also CA 49-52; 145; CANR 3

White, Walter F(rancis)
1893-1955 .... TCLC 15
See also White, Walter
See also BW 1; CA 115; 124; DLB 51

White, William Hale 1831-1913
See Rutherford, Mark
See also CA 121

Whitehead, E(dward) A(nthony)
1933- .... CLC 5
See also CA 65-68

Whitemore, Hugh (John) 1936- ..... CLC 37
See also CA 132; INT 132

Whitman, Sarah Helen (Power)
1803-1878 .... NCLC 19
See also DLB 1

Whitman, Walt(er)
1819-1892 ..... NCLC 4, 31; DA; DAB;
DAC; PC 3; WLC
See also CDALB 1640-1865; DAM MST,
POET; DLB 3, 64; SATA 20

Whitney, Phyllis A(yame) 1903- .... CLC 42
See also AITN 2; BEST 90:3; CA 1-4R;
CANR 3, 25, 38; DAM POP; JRDA;
MAICYA; SATA 1, 30

Whittemore, (Edward) Reed (Jr.)
1919- .... CLC 4
See also CA 9-12R; CAAS 8; CANR 4;
DLB 5

Whittier, John Greenleaf
1807-1892 .... NCLC 8
See also CDALB 1640-1865; DAM POET;
DLB 1

Whittlebot, Hernia
See Coward, Noel (Peirce)

Wicker, Thomas Grey 1926-
See Wicker, Tom
See also CA 65-68; CANR 21, 46

Wicker, Tom .... CLC 7
See also Wicker, Thomas Grey

Wideman, John Edgar
1941- .... CLC 5, 34, 36, 67; BLC
See also BW 2; CA 85-88; CANR 14, 42;
DAM MULT; DLB 33, 143

Wiebe, Rudy (Henry)
1934- .... CLC 6, 11, 14; DAC
See also CA 37-40R; CANR 42;
DAM MST; DLB 60

Wieland, Christoph Martin
1733-1813 .... NCLC 17
See also DLB 97

Wiene, Robert 1881-1938 .... TCLC 56

Wieners, John 1934- .... CLC 7
See also CA 13-16R; DLB 16

Wiesel, Elie(zer)
1928- ...... CLC 3, 5, 11, 37; DA; DAB;
DAC
See also AAYA 7; AITN 1; CA 5-8R;
CAAS 4; CANR 8, 40; DAM MST,
NOV; DLB 83; DLBY 87; INT CANR-8;
MTCW; SATA 56

Wiggins, Marianne 1947- .... CLC 57
See also BEST 89:3; CA 130

Wight, James Alfred 1916-
See Herriot, James
See also CA 77-80; SATA 55;
SATA-Brief 44

Wilbur, Richard (Purdy)
1921- ... CLC 3, 6, 9, 14, 53; DA; DAB;
DAC
See also CA 1-4R; CABS 2; CANR 2, 29;
DAM MST, POET; DLB 5;
INT CANR-29; MTCW; SATA 9

Wild, Peter 1940- .... CLC 14
See also CA 37-40R; DLB 5

Wilde, Oscar (Fingal O'Flahertie Wills)
1854(?)-1900 .... TCLC 1, 8, 23, 41; DA;
DAB; DAC; SSC 11; WLC
See also CA 104; 119; CDBLB 1890-1914;
DAM DRAM, MST, NOV; DLB 10, 19,
34, 57, 141, 156; SATA 24

Wilder, Billy .... CLC 20
See also Wilder, Samuel
See also DLB 26

Wilder, Samuel 1906-
See Wilder, Billy
See also CA 89-92

Wilder, Thornton (Niven)
1897-1975 ...... CLC 1, 5, 6, 10, 15, 35,
82; DA; DAB; DAC; DC 1; WLC
See also AITN 2; CA 13-16R; 61-64;
CANR 40; DAM DRAM, MST, NOV;
DLB 4, 7, 9; MTCW

Wilding, Michael 1942- .... CLC 73
See also CA 104; CANR 24, 49

Wiley, Richard 1944- .... CLC 44
See also CA 121; 129

Wilhelm, Kate .... CLC 7
See also Wilhelm, Katie Gertrude
See also CAAS 5; DLB 8; INT CANR-17

Wilhelm, Katie Gertrude 1928-
See Wilhelm, Kate
See also CA 37-40R; CANR 17, 36; MTCW

Wilkins, Mary
See Freeman, Mary Eleanor Wilkins

Willard, Nancy 1936- .... CLC 7, 37
See also CA 89-92; CANR 10, 39; CLR 5;
DLB 5, 52; MAICYA; MTCW;
SATA 37, 71; SATA-Brief 30

Williams, C(harles) K(enneth)
1936- .... CLC 33, 56
See also CA 37-40R; DAM POET; DLB 5

Williams, Charles
See Collier, James L(incoln)

Williams, Charles (Walter Stansby)
1886-1945 .... TCLC 1, 11
See also CA 104; DLB 100, 153

Williams, (George) Emlyn
1905-1987 .... CLC 15
See also CA 104; 123; CANR 36;
DAM DRAM; DLB 10, 77; MTCW

Williams, Hugo 1942- .... CLC 42
See also CA 17-20R; CANR 45; DLB 40

Williams, J. Walker
See Wodehouse, P(elham) G(renville)

Williams, John A(lfred)
1925- .... CLC 5, 13; BLC
See also BW 2; CA 53-56; CAAS 3;
CANR 6, 26; DAM MULT; DLB 2, 33;
INT CANR-6

Literary Criticism Series
Cumulative Topic Index

This index lists all topic entries in Gale's *Classical and Medieval Literature Criticism, Contemporary Literary Criticism, Literature Criticism from 1400 to 1800, Nineteenth-Century Literature Criticism,* and *Twentieth-Century Literary Criticism.*

Topic Index

NCLC Cumulative Nationality Index

Nationality Index

INDIAN
Chatterji, Bankim Chandra **19**
Dutt, Toru **29**
Ghalib **39**

IRISH
Allingham, William **25**
Banim, John **13**
Banim, Michael **13**
Boucicault, Dion **41**
Carleton, William **3**
Croker, John Wilson **10**
Darley, George **2**
Edgeworth, Maria **1, 51**
Ferguson, Samuel **33**
Griffin, Gerald **7**
Jameson, Anna **43**
Le Fanu, Joseph Sheridan **9**
Lever, Charles (James) **23**
Maginn, William **8**
Mangan, James Clarence **27**
Maturin, Charles Robert **6**
Moore, Thomas **6**
Morgan, Lady **29**
O'Brien, Fitz-James **21**

ITALIAN
Da Ponte, Lorenzo **50**
Foscolo, Ugo **8**
Gozzi, (Conte) Carlo **23**
Leopardi, (Conte) Giacomo **22**
Manzoni, Alessandro **29**
Mazzini, Guiseppe **34**
Nievo, Ippolito **22**

JAPANESE
Higuchi Ichiyo **49**
Motoori, Norinaga **45**

LITHUANIAN
Mapu, Abraham (ben Jekutiel) **18**

MEXICAN
Lizardi, Jose Joaquin Fernandez de **30**

NORWEGIAN
Collett, (Jacobine) Camilla (Wergeland) **22**
Wergeland, Henrik Arnold **5**

POLISH
Fredro, Aleksander **8**
Krasicki, Ignacy **8**
Krasinski, Zygmunt **4**
Mickiewicz, Adam **3**
Norwid, Cyprian Kamil **17**
Slowacki, Juliusz **15**

ROMANIAN
Eminescu, Mihail **33**

RUSSIAN
Aksakov, Sergei Timofeyvich **2**
Bakunin, Mikhail (Alexandrovich) **25**
Bashkirtseff, Marie **27**
Belinski, Vissarion Grigoryevich **5**
Chernyshevsky, Nikolay Gavrilovich **1**
Dobrolyubov, Nikolai Alexandrovich **5**
Dostoevsky, Fedor Mikhailovich **2, 7, 21, 33, 43**
Gogol, Nikolai (Vasilyevich) **5, 15, 31**
Goncharov, Ivan Alexandrovich **1**
Herzen, Aleksandr Ivanovich **10**
Karamzin, Nikolai Mikhailovich **3**
Krylov, Ivan Andreevich **1**
Lermontov, Mikhail Yuryevich **5**
Leskov, Nikolai (Semyonovich) **25**
Nekrasov, Nikolai Alekseevich **11**
Ostrovsky, Alexander **30**
Pisarev, Dmitry Ivanovich **25**
Pushkin, Alexander (Sergeyevich) **3, 27**
Saltykov, Mikhail Evgrafovich **16**
Smolenskin, Peretz **30**
Turgenev, Ivan **21**

Tyutchev, Fyodor **34**
Zhukovsky, Vasily **35**

SCOTTISH
Baillie, Joanna **2**
Beattie, James **25**
Campbell, Thomas **19**
Ferrier, Susan (Edmonstone) **8**
Galt, John **1**
Hogg, James **4**
Jeffrey, Francis **33**
Lockhart, John Gibson **6**
Mackenzie, Henry **41**
Oliphant, Margaret (Oliphant Wilson) **11**
Scott, Walter **15**
Stevenson, Robert Louis (Balfour) **5, 14**
Thomson, James, **18**
Wilson, John **5**

SPANISH
Alarcon, Pedro Antonio de **1**
Caballero, Fernan **10**
Castro, Rosalia de **3**
Espronceda, Jose de **39**
Larra (y Sanchez de Castro), Mariano Jose de **17**
Tamayo y Baus, Manuel **1**
Zorrilla y Moral, Jose **6**

SWEDISH
Almqvist, Carl Jonas Love **42**
Bremer, Fredrika **11**
Tegner, Esaias **2**

SWISS
Amiel, Henri Frederic **4**
Burckhardt, Jacob **49**
Keller, Gottfried **2**
Wyss, Johann David Von **10**

ISBN 0-8103-9299-2

90000

9 780810 392991